PHILIP'S

STREET ATLAS
East Kent

Ashford, Canterbury, Dover, Folkestone, Maidstone, Margate

www.philips-maps.co.uk

First published in 1989 by
Philip's, a division of
Octopus Publishing Group Ltd
www.octopusbooks.co.uk
2–4 Heron Quays, London E14 4JP
An Hachette UK Company
www.hachettelivre.co.uk

Fourth edition 2009
First impression 2009
EKTDA

ISBN 978-1-84907-018-8 (spiral)

© Philip's 2009

Ordnance Survey®

This product includes mapping data licensed
from Ordnance Survey® with the permission
of the Controller of Her Majesty's Stationery
Office. © Crown copyright 2009. All rights
reserved. Licence number 100011710.

Speed camera data provided by
PocketGPSWorld.com Ltd

Post Office is a trade mark of Post Office Ltd in
the UK and other countries.

Printed by Toppan, China

Contents

II	Mobile safety cameras
III	**Key to map symbols**
IV	**Key to map pages**
VI	**Route planning**
VIII	Major administrative and Postcode boundaries
1	**Street maps** at 3½ inches to 1 mile
210	**Index** of towns, villages, streets, hospitals, industrial estates, railway stations, schools, shopping centres, universities and places of interest

Digital Data

The exceptionally high-quality mapping found in this atlas is available as digital data in TIFF format, which is easily convertible to other bitmapped (raster) image formats.

The index is also available in digital form as a standard database table. It contains all the details found in the printed index together with the National Grid reference for the map square in which each entry is named.

For further information and to discuss your requirements, please contact victoria.dawbarn@philips-maps.co.uk

Mobile safety cameras

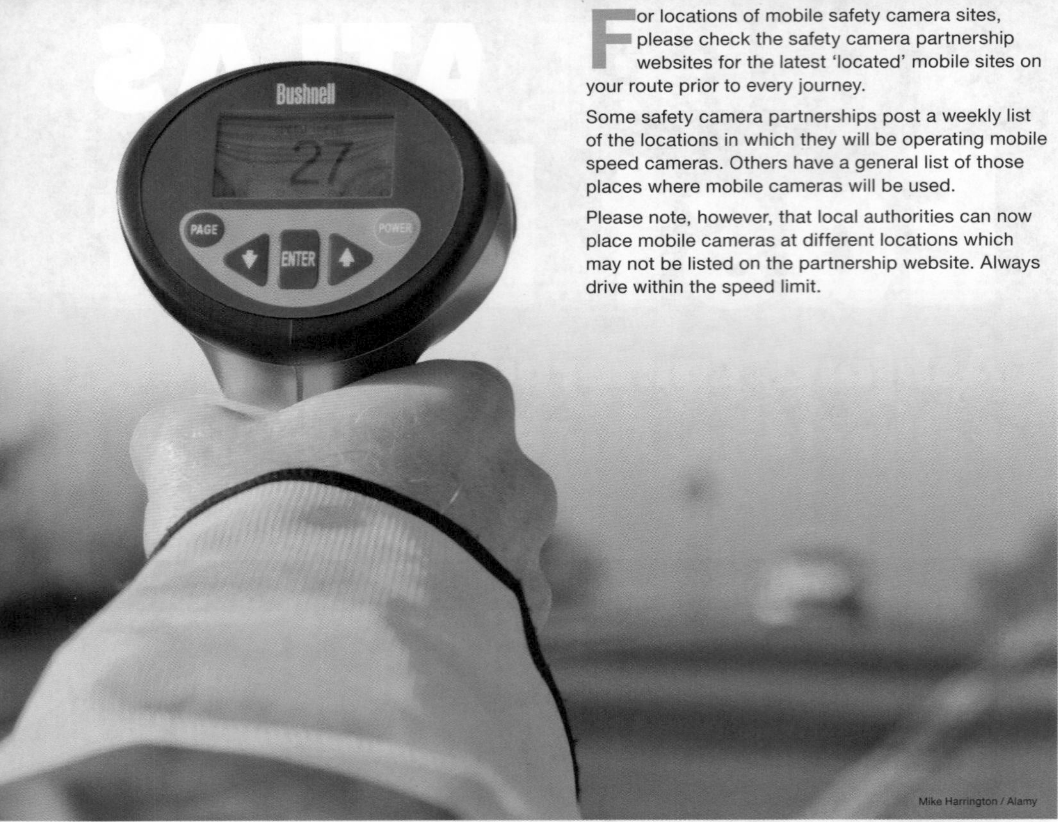

Mike Harrington / Alamy

For locations of mobile safety camera sites, please check the safety camera partnership websites for the latest 'located' mobile sites on your route prior to every journey.

Some safety camera partnerships post a weekly list of the locations in which they will be operating mobile speed cameras. Others have a general list of those places where mobile cameras will be used.

Please note, however, that local authorities can now place mobile cameras at different locations which may not be listed on the partnership website. Always drive within the speed limit.

Useful websites

Kent and Medway Safety Camera Partnership
www.kmscp.org

London Safety Camera Partnership
www.lscp.org.uk

Surrey Safety Camera Partnership
www.surrey-safecam.org

Sussex Safer Roads Partnership
www.sussexsaferroads.gov.uk

Further information
www.dvla.gov.uk
www.thinkroadsafety.gov.uk
www.dft.gov.uk
www.road-safe.org

Key to map symbols

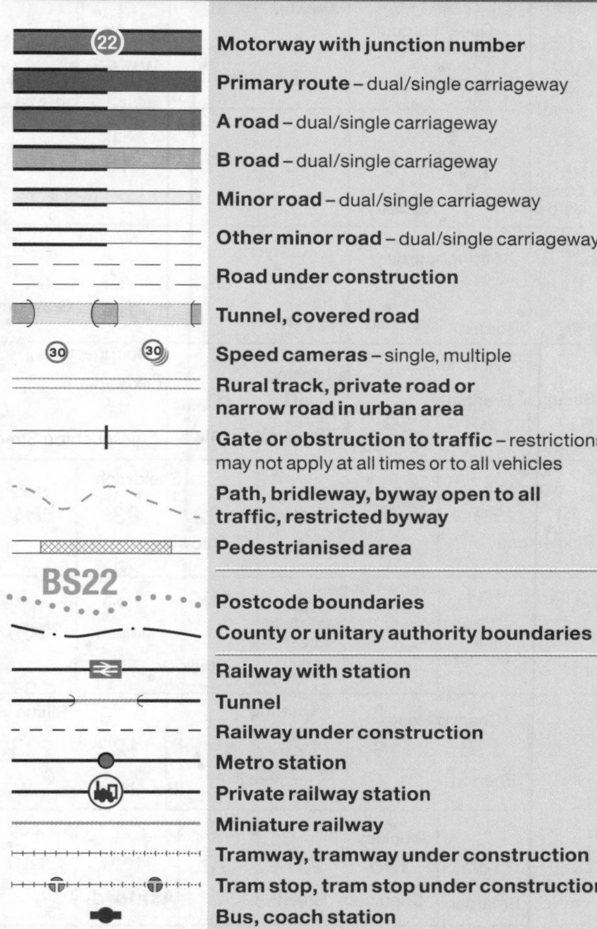

Motorway with junction number (22)

Primary route – dual/single carriageway

A road – dual/single carriageway

B road – dual/single carriageway

Minor road – dual/single carriageway

Other minor road – dual/single carriageway

Road under construction

Tunnel, covered road

Speed cameras – single, multiple

Rural track, private road or narrow road in urban area

Gate or obstruction to traffic – restrictions may not apply at all times or to all vehicles

Path, bridleway, byway open to all traffic, restricted byway

Pedestrianised area

BS22 Postcode boundaries

County or unitary authority boundaries

Railway with station

Tunnel

Railway under construction

Metro station

Private railway station

Miniature railway

Tramway, tramway under construction

Tram stop, tram stop under construction

Bus, coach station

Ambulance station

Coastguard station

Fire station

Police station

Accident and Emergency entrance to hospital

Hospital

Place of worship

Information centre – open all year

Shopping centre, parking

Park and Ride, Post Office

Camping site, caravan site

Golf course, picnic site

Church   ROMAN FORT   Non-Roman antiquity, Roman antiquity

Univ   Important buildings, schools, colleges, universities and hospitals

Woods, built-up area

River Medway   Water name

River, weir

Stream

Canal, lock, tunnel

Water

Tidal water

58   87   246   Adjoining page indicators and overlap bands – the colour of the arrow and band indicates the scale of the adjoining or overlapping page (see scale below)

The dark grey border on the inside edge of some pages indicates that the mapping does not continue onto the adjacent page

The small numbers around the edges of the maps identify the 1-kilometre National Grid lines

Abbreviations

Acad	Academy	Meml	Memorial
Allot Gdns	Allotments	Mon	Monument
Cemy	Cemetery	Mus	Museum
C Ctr	Civic centre	Obsy	Observatory
CH	Club house	Pal	Royal palace
Coll	College	PH	Public house
Crem	Crematorium	Recn Gd	Recreation ground
Ent	Enterprise	Resr	Reservoir
Ex H	Exhibition hall	Ret Pk	Retail park
Ind Est	Industrial Estate	Sch	School
IRB Sta	Inshore rescue boat station	Sh Ctr	Shopping centre
Inst	Institute	TH	Town hall / house
Ct	Law court	Trad Est	Trading estate
L Ctr	Leisure centre	Univ	University
LC	Level crossing	W Twr	Water tower
Liby	Library	Wks	Works
Mkt	Market	YH	Youth hostel

The map scale on the pages numbered in blue is 3½ inches to 1 mile
5.52 cm to 1 km • 1 : 18 103

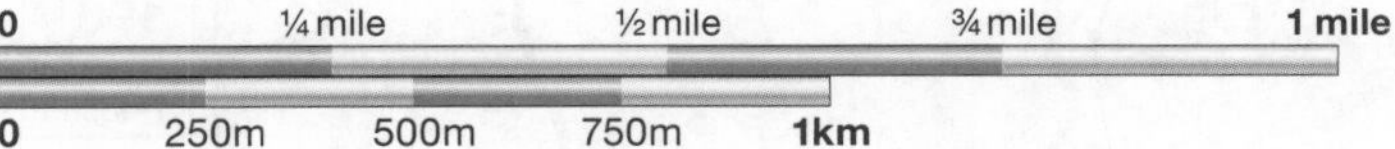

0	¼ mile	½ mile	¾ mile	1 mile
0	250m	500m	750m	1km

Key to map pages

113 Map pages at
3½ inches to 1 mile

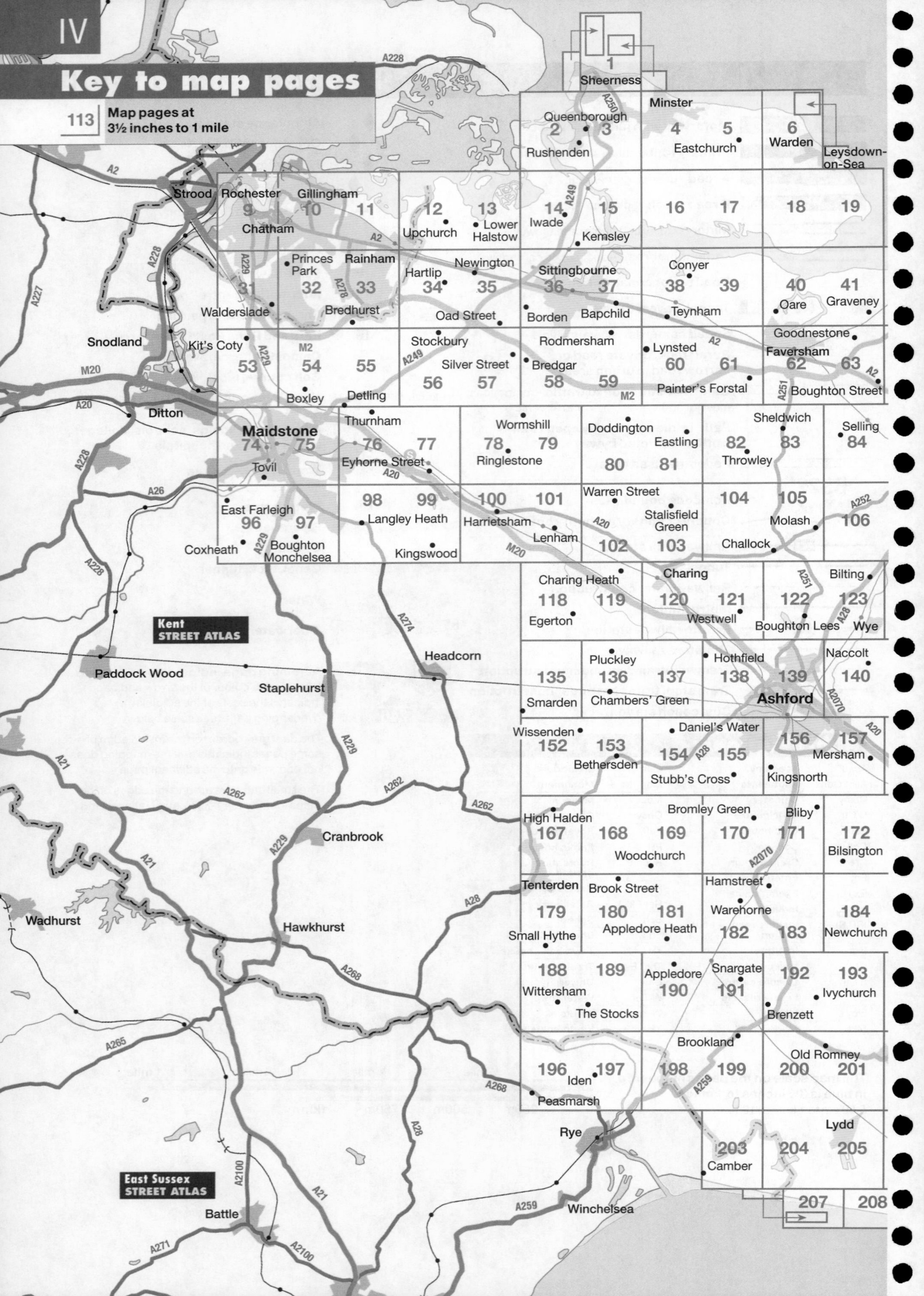

A228

A2

Strood
Rochester **9** Gillingham **11**
10
Chatham
A2

A229

A227
Snodland

A228
M20

Ditton

A26
Tovil

A228

A274

Kent
STREET ATLAS

Paddock Wood

Staplehurst

A262

A262

A21

A229

A262

Cranbrook

A21
Wadhurst

Hawkhurst

A268

A265

East Sussex
STREET ATLAS

Battle

A21

A2100

A271

A2100

Sheerness
1

A250
Queenborough Minster
2 **3** **4** **5** **6**
Rushenden Eastchurch Warden Leysdown-
on-Sea

A249
12 **13** **14** **15** **16** **17** **18** **19**
Upchurch Lower Iwade
Halston Kemsley

Princes Rainham Newington Sittingbourne Conyer
Park Hartlip **34** **35** **36** **37** **38** **39** **40** **41**
31 **32** **33** Oare Graveney
Bredhurst Oad Street Borden Bapchild Teynham
Walderslade Goodnestone
Kit's Coty M2 Stockbury Rodmersham Lynsted A2 Faversham
53 **54** **55** Silver Street **60** **61** **62** **63**
Boxley A249 **56** **57** Bredgar Painter's Forstal A251 Boughton Street
Detling **58** **59** M2

Maidstone Thurnham Wormshill Sheldwich Selling
74 **76** **77** **78** **79** Doddington **82** **83** **84**
75 Eyhorne Street Ringlestone Eastling Throwley
East Farleigh A20 Warren Street **80** **81** **104** **105** A252
96 **98** **99** **100** **101** **102** Stalisfield **106**
97 Langley Heath Harrietsham A20 Green Molash
Coxheath Boughton Lenham **102** **103** Challock
Monchelsea Kingswood M20 Charing

Charing Heath Charing Bilting
118 **119** **120** **121** **122** **123**
Egerton Westwell Boughton Lees Wye
Naccolt
Headcorn Pluckley Hothfield **140**
135 **136** **137** **138** **139**
Smarden Chambers' Green Ashford A2070

Wissenden Daniel's Water **156** **157**
152 **153** **154** **155** Mersham
Bethersden A28 Stubb's Cross Kingsnorth

High Halden Bromley Green Bliby
167 **168** **169** **170** **171** **172**
Woodchurch A2070 Bilsington

Tenterden Brook Street Hamstreet
179 **180** **181** Warehorne **184**
Small Hythe Appledore Heath **182** **183** Newchurch

188 **189** Appledore Snargate **192** **193**
Wittersham **190** **191** Ivychurch
The Stocks Brenzett

Brookland Old Romney
196 **197** **198** **199** **200** **201**
Iden A259
Peasmarsh

Rye Lydd
203 **204** **205**
Camber

A259 Winchelsea **207** **208**

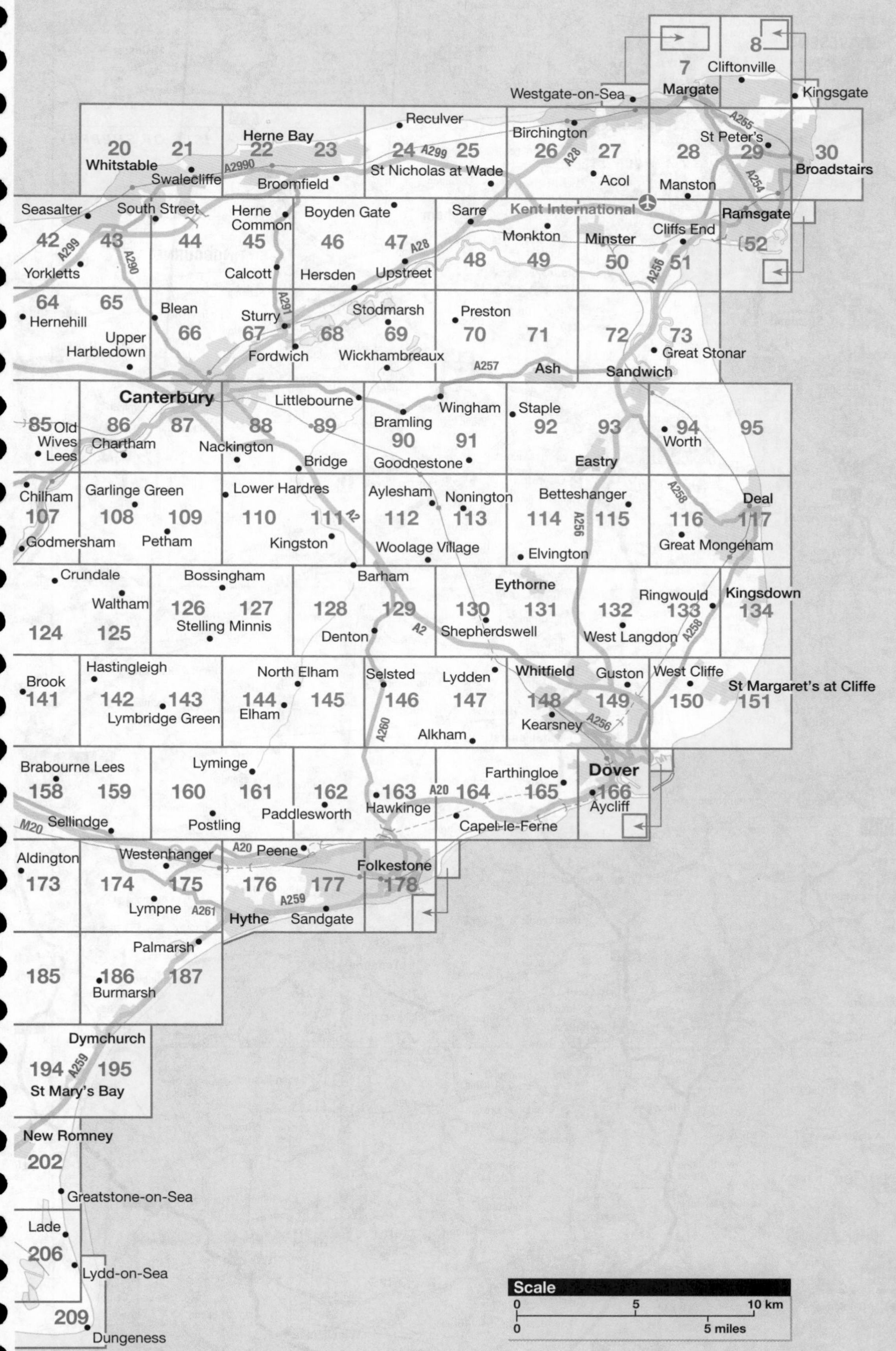

7
8
Cliftonville
Margate
Westgate-on-Sea
Kingsgate
Reculver
Herne Bay
20
21
22
23
24
25
26
27
28
29
30
Whitstable
Swalecliffe
Broomfield
St Nicholas at Wade
Birchington
Acol
St Peter's
Broadstairs
Manston
Kent International
Ramsgate
Seasalter
South Street
Herne Common
Boyden Gate
Sarre
Monkton
Minster
Cliffs End
42
43
44
45
46
47
48
49
50
51
52
Yorkletts
Calcott
Hersden
Upstreet
64
65
66
67
68
69
70
71
72
73
Hernehill
Blean
Sturry
Stodmarsh
Preston
Upper Harbledown
Fordwich
Wickhambreaux
Great Stonar
Ash
Sandwich
Canterbury
Littlebourne
Wingham
Staple
85
86
87
88
89
90
91
92
93
94
95
Old Wives Lees
Chartham
Nackington
Bridge
Bramling
Goodnestone
Eastry
Worth
Chilham
Garlinge Green
Lower Hardres
Aylesham
Nonington
Betteshanger
Deal
107
108
109
110
111
112
113
114
115
116
117
Godmersham
Petham
Kingston
Woolage Village
Elvington
Great Mongeham
Crundale
Bossingham
Barham
Eythorne
Ringwould
Kingsdown
Waltham
124
125
126
127
128
129
130
131
132
133
134
Stelling Minnis
Denton
Shepherdswell
West Langdon
Hastingleigh
North Elham
Selsted
Lydden
Whitfield
Guston
West Cliffe
St Margaret's at Cliffe
Brook
141
142
143
144
145
146
147
148
149
150
151
Lymbridge Green
Elham
Alkham
Kearsney
Dover
Brabourne Lees
Lyminge
Farthingloe
158
159
160
161
162
163
164
165
166
Hawkinge
Paddlesworth
Aycliff
Sellindge
Postling
Capel-le-Ferne
Aldington
Westenhanger
Peene
Folkestone
173
174
175
176
177
178
Lympne
Hythe
Sandgate
Palmarsh
185
186
187
Burmarsh
Dymchurch
194
195
St Mary's Bay
New Romney
202
Greatstone-on-Sea
Lade
206
Lydd-on-Sea
209
Dungeness
A299
A2990
A28
A290
A291
A257
A256
A258
A254
A255
A2
A260
A20
A259
A261
M20
Scale
0
5
10 km
0
5 miles

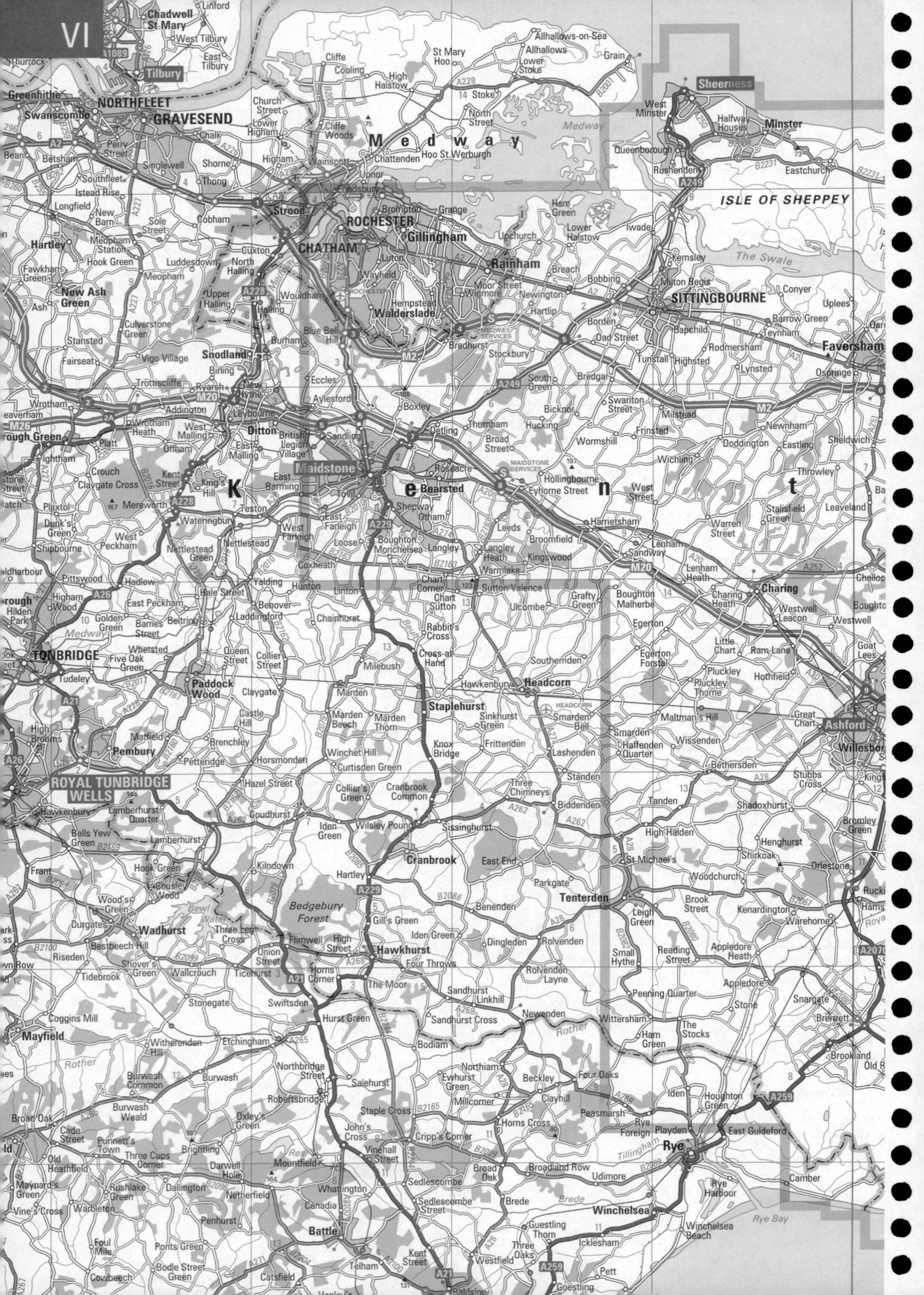
VI
Chadwell St Mary
Linford
West Tilbury
East Tilbury
Tilbury
Thurrock
Greenhithe
NORTHFLEET
GRAVESEND
Swanscombe
Chalk
Cliffe
Cooling
High Halstow
St Mary Hoo
Allhallows-on-Sea
Allhallows
Lower Stoke
Grain
Stoke
North Street
Medway
Church Street
Lower Higham
Cliffe Woods
Higham
Hoo St.Werburgh
Chattenden
Wainscott
Upnor
Frindsbury
Strood
ROCHESTER
Gillingham
Brompton
Grange
CHATHAM
Rainham
Upchurch
Ham Green
Lower Halstow
Iwade
Sheerness
West Minster
Halfway Houses
Minster
Queenborough
Rushenden
Eastchurch
ISLE OF SHEPPEY
The Swale
Kemsley
Milton Regis
SITTINGBOURNE
Conyer
Uplees
Bobbing
Breach
Newington
Hartlip
Borden
Oad Street
Bapchild
Teynham
Barrow Green
Rodmersham
Tunstall
Highsted
Lynsted
Faversham
Ospringe
Stockbury
Bredgar
South Green
Swanton Street
Milstead
Bicknor
Hucking
Frinsted
Wormshill
Newnham
Doddington
Eastling
Sheldwich
Wichling
Throwley
Bearsted
Hollingbourne
Eyhorne Street
West Street
Harrietsham
Lenham
Sandway
Lenham Heath
Charing
Charing Heath
Stalisfield Green
Warren Street
Leaveland
Westwell
Westwell Leacon
Little Chart
Ram Lane
Pluckley
Pluckley Thorne
Hothfield
Great Chart
Ashford
Willesborough
Kent
Medway
Bean
Betsham
Perry Street
Singlewell
Shorne
Thong
Southfleet
Istead Rise
Longfield
New Barn
Sole Street
Cobham
Hartley
Meopham Station
Hook Green
Meopham
Luddesdown
Cuxton
North Halling
Fawkham Green
New Ash Green
Ash
Upper Halling
Halling
Wouldham
Blue Bell Hill
Walderslade
Wayfield
Luton
Hempstead
Wigmore
Moor Street
Bredhurst
Culverstone Green
Stansted
Fairseat
Vigo Village
Snodland
Burham
Birling
Trottiscliffe
Ryarsh
New Hythe
Eccles
Aylesford
Boxley
Wrotham
Addington
Leybourne
Wrotham Heath
West Malling
Ditton
British Legion Village
Sandling
Detling
Thurnham
Broad Street
Platt
Ightham
Offham
East Malling
Maidstone
Roseacre
Crouch
Claygate Cross
Kent Street
King's Hill
East Barming
Tovil
Plaxtol
Mereworth
Teston
Wateringbury
Shepway
Otham
Dunk's Green
West Peckham
East Farleigh
West Farleigh
Loose
Boughton Monchelsea
Langley
Leeds
Broomfield
Shipbourne
Nettlestead
Nettlestead Green
Langley Heath
Kingswood
Coxheath
Warmlake
Pittswood
Hadlow
Yalding
Hunton
Linton
Chart Corner
Chart Sutton
Sutton Valence
Grafty Green
Boughton Malherbe
Ulcombe
Egerton
Egerton Forstal
Higham Wood
East Peckham
Hale Street
Benover
Golden Green
Barnes Street
Beltring
Laddingford
Chainhurst
Rabbit's Cross
Cross-at-Hand
Southernden
TONBRIDGE
Five Oak Green
Whetsted
Queen Street
Collier Street
Milebush
Tudeley
Paddock Wood
Claygate
Marden
Hawkenbury
Headcorn
Staplehurst
Sinkhurst Green
Smarden Bell
Smarden
Maltman's Hill
High Brooms
Castle Hill
Matfield
Marden Beech
Marden Thorn
Frittenden
Haffenden Quarter
Wissenden
Pembury
Brenchley
Winchet Hill
Knox Bridge
Lashenden
Bethersden
Petteridge
Horsmonden
Curtisden Green
Standen
Stubbs Cross
ROYAL TUNBRIDGE WELLS
Hazel Street
Collier's Green
Cranbrook Common
Three Chimneys
Tanden
Lamberhurst Quarter
Goudhurst
Biddenden
Shadoxhurst
Hawkenbury
Iden Green
Wilsley Pound
Sissinghurst
High Halden
Bromley Green
Bells Yew Green
Lamberhurst
Henghurst
Kilndown
Cranbrook
East End
St Michael's
Shirkoak
Frant
Hook Green
Hartley
Woodchurch
Orlestone
Cousley Wood
Parkgate
Tenterden
Brook Street
Kenardington
Wood's Green
Bedgebury Forest
Benenden
Leigh Green
Warehorne
Durgates
Bewl Water
Gill's Green
Wadhurst
Three Leg Cross
Flimwell
High Street
Iden Green
Dingleden
Rolvenden
Small Hythe
Reading Street
Appledore Heath
Bestbeech Hill
Riseden
Union Street
Hawkhurst
Four Throws
Shover's Green
Wallcrouch
Ticehurst
Horns Corner
Rolvenden Layne
Appledore
Tidebrook
The Moor
Sandhurst
Linkhill
Peening Quarter
Snargate
Stonegate
Swiftsden
Stone
Coggins Mill
Hurst Green
Sandhurst Cross
Newenden
Wittersham
The Stocks
Brenzett
Mayfield
Witherenden Hill
Etchingham
Bodiam
Rother
Ham Green
Brookland
Northbridge Street
Northiam
Burwash Common
Burwash
Salehurst
Ewhurst Green
Beckley
Four Oaks
Robertsbridge
Millcorner
Clayhill
Iden
Houghton Green
Broad Oak
Burwash Weald
Staple Cross
Peasmarsh
Oxley's Green
Horns Cross
Rye Foreign
Playden
East Guldeford
Cade Street
Punnett's Town
Brightling
John's Cross
Cripp's Corner
Rye
Three Cups Corner
Vinehall Street
Tillingham
Old Heathfield
Darwell Hole
Mountfield
Broad Oak
Broadland Row
Udimore
Camber
Maynard's Green
Dallington
Sedlescombe
Rushlake Green
Netherfield
Whatlington
Rye Harbour
Vine's Cross
Warbleton
Canadia
Sedlescombe Street
Brede
Winchelsea
Penhurst
Guestling Thorn
Winchelsea Beach
Rye Bay
Battle
Icklesham
Foul Mile
Ponts Green
Three Oaks
Kent Street
Westfield
Bodle Street Green
Cowbeech
Catsfield
Telham
Pett
Baldslow
Guestling

Route planning

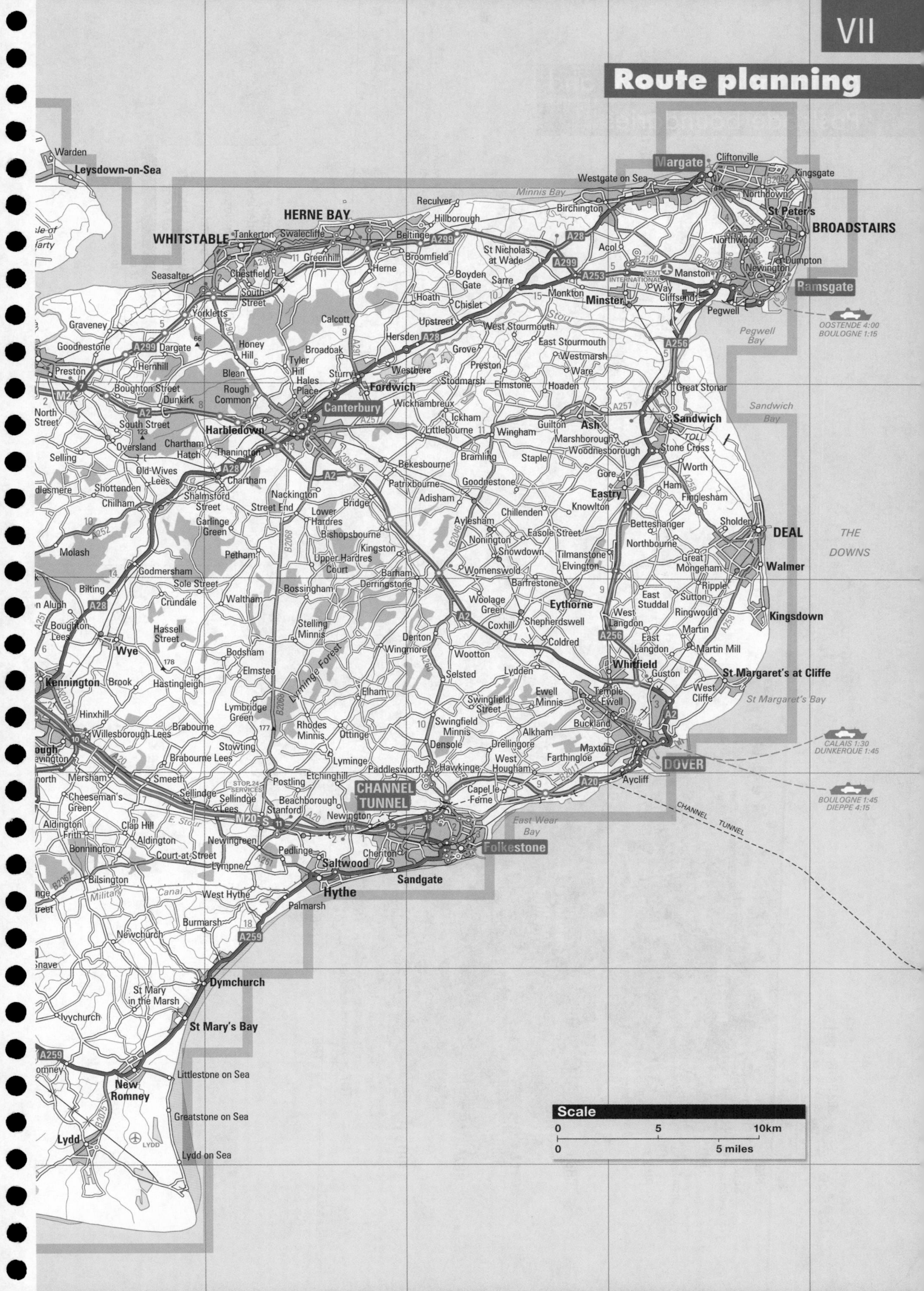
Warden
Leysdown-on-Sea
WHITSTABLE
HERNE BAY
Tankerton
Swalecliffe
Reculver
Hillborough
Beltinge
Minnis Bay
Westgate on Sea
Margate
Cliftonville
Kingsgate
Birchington
Northdown
St Peter's
BROADSTAIRS
Northwood
Dumpton
Newington
Ramsgate
Pegwell
Pegwell Bay
OOSTENDE 4:00
BOULOGNE 1:15
Seasalter
Chestfield
Greenhill
Herne
Broomfield
St Nicholas at Wade
Acol
Manston
KENT INTERNATIONAL
Boyden Gate
Sarre
Monkton
Minster
Cliffsend
South Street
Yorkletts
Hoath
Chislet
Calcott
Upstreet
West Stourmouth
Stour
East Stourmouth
Graveney
Goodnestone
Dargate
Honey Hill
Broadoak
Hersden
Grove
Westmarsh
Ware
Preston
Hernhill
Blean
Tyler Hill
Hales Place
Sturry
Westbere
Stodmarsh
Elmstone
Hoaden
Great Stonar
Boughton Street
Dunkirk
Rough Common
Fordwich
Canterbury
Wickhambreux
Ickham
Sandwich Bay
North Street
South Street
Harbledown
Littlebourne
Wingham
Guilton
Ash
Sandwich
Oversland
Chartham Hatch
Thanington
Bramling
Marshborough
Woodnesborough
Staple
Stone Cross
TOLL
Selling
Old Wives Lees
Bekesbourne
Worth
Chartham
Patrixbourne
Goodnestone
Gore
Ham
Shottenden
Shalmsford Street
Nackington
Adisham
Eastry
Finglesham
Chilham
Street End
Bridge
Knowlton
Lower Hardres
Chillenden
Betteshanger
Sholden
DEAL
THE DOWNS
Garlinge Green
Bishopsbourne
Aylesham
Easole Street
Molash
Nonington
Northbourne
Kingston
Snowdown
Tilmanstone
Petham
Upper Hardres Court
Womenswold
Elvington
Great Mongeham
Walmer
Godmersham
Barham
Derringstone
Barfrestone
Bilting
Sole Street
Ripple
Bossingham
Crundale
Waltham
Eythorne
East Studdal
Sutton
Woolage Green
Ringwould
West Langdon
Kingsdown
Boughton Lees
Hassell Street
Stelling Minnis
Coxhill
Shepherdswell
Martin
Coldred
East Langdon
Martin Mill
Denton
Wye
Wingmore
Wootton
Bodsham
Elmsted
Lyminge Forest
Whitfield
Selsted
Lydden
Guston
St Margaret's at Cliffe
Kennington
Brook
Hastingleigh
Temple Ewell
West Cliffe
Elham
Ewell Minnis
St Margaret's Bay
Swingfield Street
Lymbridge Green
Hinxhill
Rhodes Minnis
Buckland
Braborne
Swingfield Minnis
Willesborough Lees
Ottinge
Alkham
Densole
Drellingore
CALAIS 1:30
DUNKERQUE 1:45
Stowting
Maxton
Brabourne Lees
Lyminge
Hawkinge
West Hougham
Farthingloe
DOVER
Paddlesworth
Mersham
Smeeth
Etchinghill
Postling
Aycliff
Cheeseman's Green
Sellindge
Beachborough
CHANNEL TUNNEL
Capel le Ferne
BOULOGNE 1:45
DIEPPE 4:15
Aldington Frith
Clap Hill
E. Stour
Stanford
Newington
Aldington
CHANNEL TUNNEL
East Wear Bay
Bonnington
Newingreen
Court-at-Street
Pedlinge
Cheriton
Folkestone
Lympne
Saltwood
Sandgate
Bilsington
Hythe
Royal Military Canal
West Hythe
Palmarsh
Burmarsh
Newchurch
Dymchurch
St Mary in the Marsh
Ivychurch
St Mary's Bay
Littlestone on Sea
New Romney
Greatstone on Sea
Lydd
LYDD
Lydd on Sea
Scale
0
5
10km
0
5 miles

Major administrative and Postcode boundaries

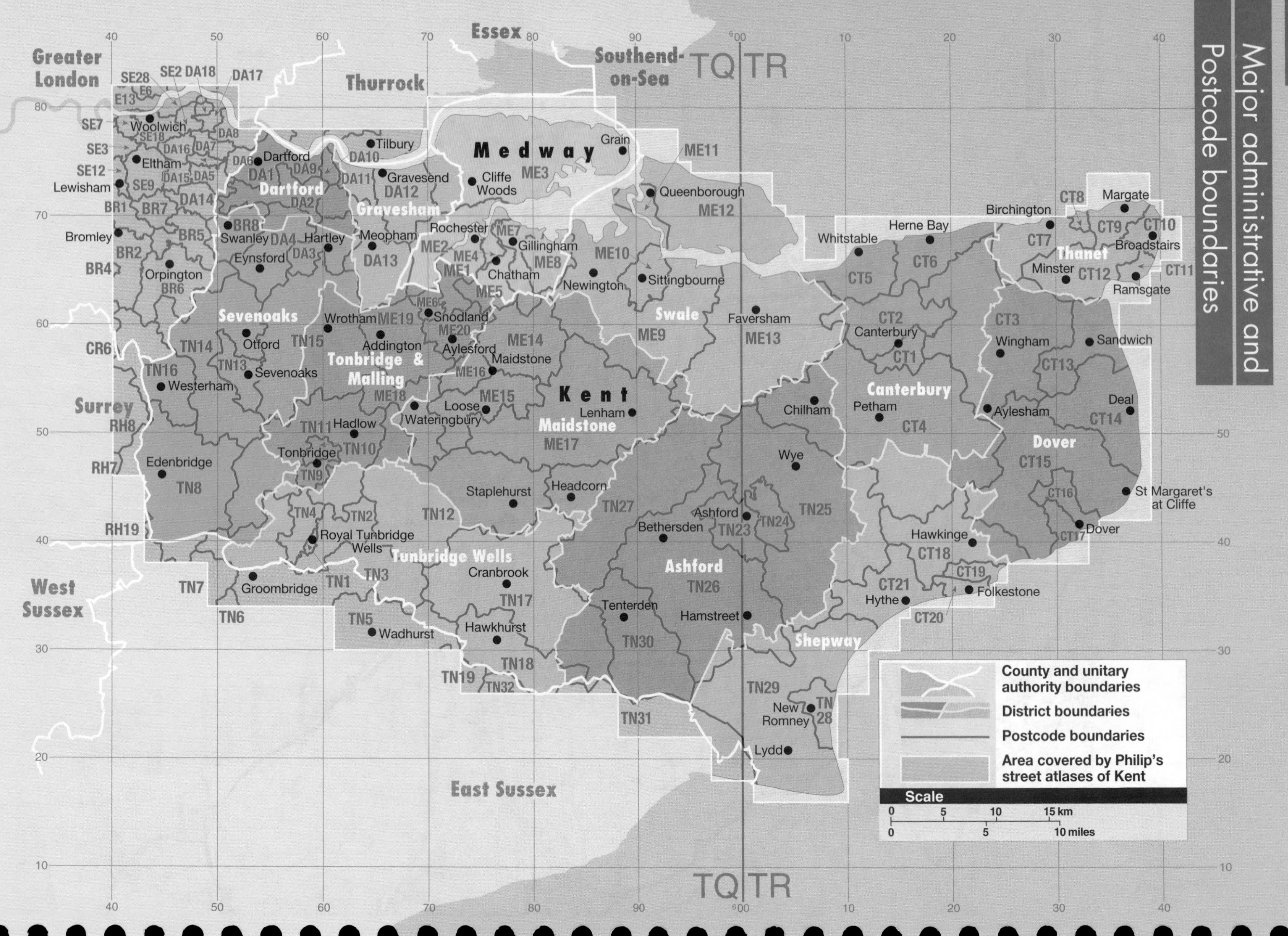

Scale

County and unitary authority boundaries
District boundaries
Postcode boundaries
Area covered by Philip's street atlases of Kent

0 5 10 15 km
0   5   10 miles

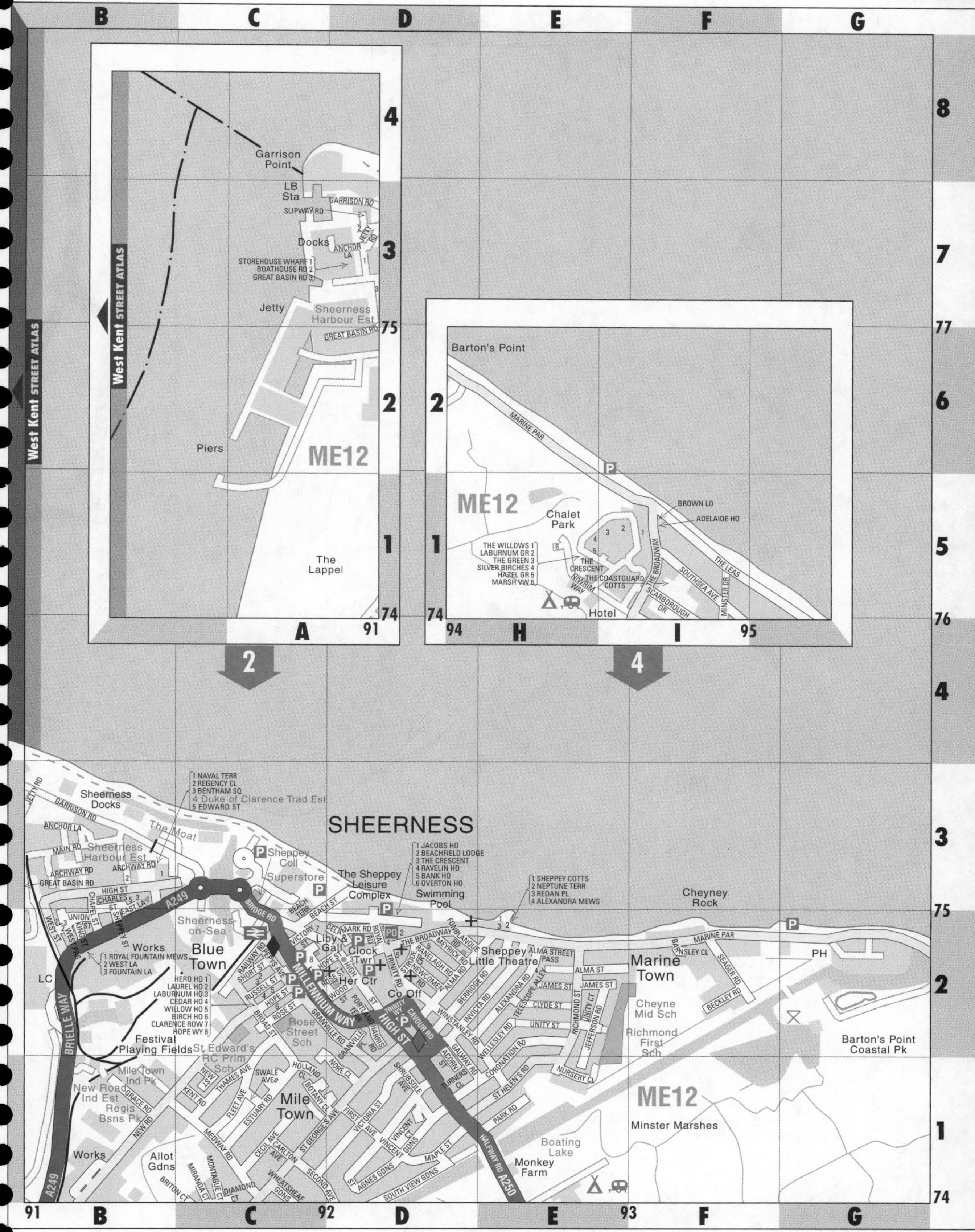

West Kent STREET ATLAS

B   C   D   E   F   G

8

Garrison
Point

LB
Sta
GARRISON RD
SLIPWAY RD

Docks   ANCHOR LA   7

STOREHOUSE WHARF 1
BOATHOUSE RD 2
GREAT BASIN RD 3

Jetty   Sheerness
Harbour Est   75
GREAT BASIN RD

2   6

Piers

ME12

Barton's Point

MARINE PAR

ME12   P

BROWN LO
ADELAIDE HO

Chalet
Park

THE WILLOWS 1
LABURNUM GR 2
THE GREEN 3
SILVER BIRCHES 4
HAZEL GR 5
MARSH VW 6

THE
CRESCENT
THE COASTGUARD
COTTS

THE LEAS

SOUTHSEA AVE.

MINSTER DR

77

5

1   The Lappel

74   91

A   74   94   H   I   95   76

2   4

4

1 NAVAL TERR
2 REGENCY CL
3 BENTHAM SQ
4 Duke of Clarence Trad Est
5 EDWARD ST

Sheerness
Docks

The Moat

SHEERNESS

1 JACOBS HO
2 BEACHFIELD LODGE
3 THE CRESCENT
4 RAVELIN HO
5 BANK HO
6 OVERTON HO

Cheyney
Rock

3

ANCHOR LA
MAIN RD
ARCHWAY RD
GREAT BASIN RD
Sheerness
Harbour Est
ARCHWAY RD

Sheppey
Coll

Sheppey
Superstore

The Sheppey
Leisure
Complex

Swimming
Pool

1 SHEPPEY COTTS
2 NEPTUNE TERR
3 REDAN PL
4 ALEXANDRA MEWS

75

HIGH ST
CHARLES ST
EAST LA
UNION RD

Sheerness-
on-Sea
Blue
Town

Liby &
Gal
Clock
Twr

The Broadway
MEYRICK RD

Sheppey
Little Theatre

Marine
Town

MARINE PAR

P   PH

2

Works

1 ROYAL FOUNTAIN MEWS
2 WEST LA
3 FOUNTAIN LA

HERO HO 1
LAUREL HO 2
LABURNUM HO 3
CEDAR HO 4
WILLOW HO 5
BIRCH HO 6
CLARENCE ROW 7
HOPE WY 8

Her Ctr
Co Off

ALMA ST
JAMES ST

Cheyne
Mid Sch

Richmond
First
Sch

Barton's Point
Coastal Pk

LC

Festival
Playing Fields

St Edward's
RC Prim
Sch

Rose
Street
Sch

HIGH ST

ME12

1

Mile Town
Ind Pk

New Road
Ind Est
Regis
Bsns Pk

Mile
Town

ST HELEN'S RD
PARK RD

NURSERY CL

Minster Marshes

Works

Allot
Gdns

Boating
Lake
Monkey
Farm

A249   A250

74

91   B   C   92   D   E   93   F   G

2

3

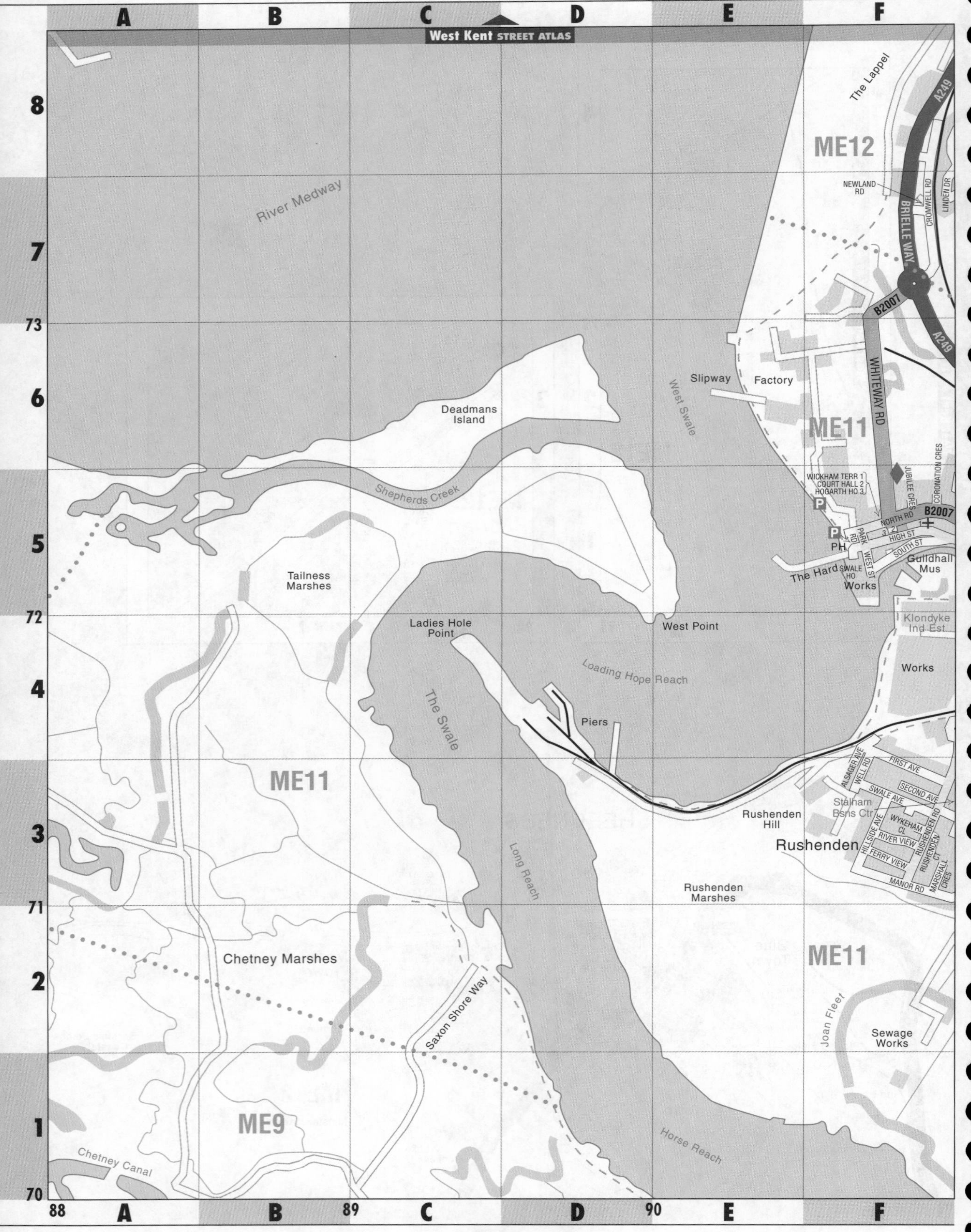

West Kent STREET ATLAS

A   B   C   D   E   F

8

7

73

6

5

72

4

3

71

2

1

70

88   A   B   89   C   D   90   E   F

The Lappel

ME12

NEWLAND RD

A249

CROMWELL RD

LINDEN DR

BRIELLE WAY

B2007

WHITEWAY RD

A249

River Medway

West Swale

Slipway   Factory

ME11

Deadmans Island

Shepherds Creek

WICKHAM TERR 1
COURT HALL 2
HOGARTH HO 3

JUBILEE CRES

CORONATION CRES

P

NORTH RD

PARK RD

B2007

P

PH

HIGH ST

SOUTH ST

WEST ST

The Hard

SWALE HO

Guildhall Mus

Works

Tailness Marshes

West Point

Klondyke Ind Est

Works

Ladies Hole Point

Loading Hope Reach

The Swale

Piers

ME11

FIRST AVE

ALSAGER AVE

WELL RD

SWALE AVE

SECOND AVE

Stainam Bsns Ctr

WYKEHAM CL

RIVER VIEW

HILLSIDE AVE

RUSHENDEN RD

RUSHENDEN CL

MARSHALL CRES

FERRY VIEW

MANOR RD

Rushenden Hill

Rushenden

Long Reach

Rushenden Marshes

71

Chetney Marshes

ME11

Saxon Shore Way

Joan Fleet

Sewage Works

ME9

Horse Reach

Chetney Canal

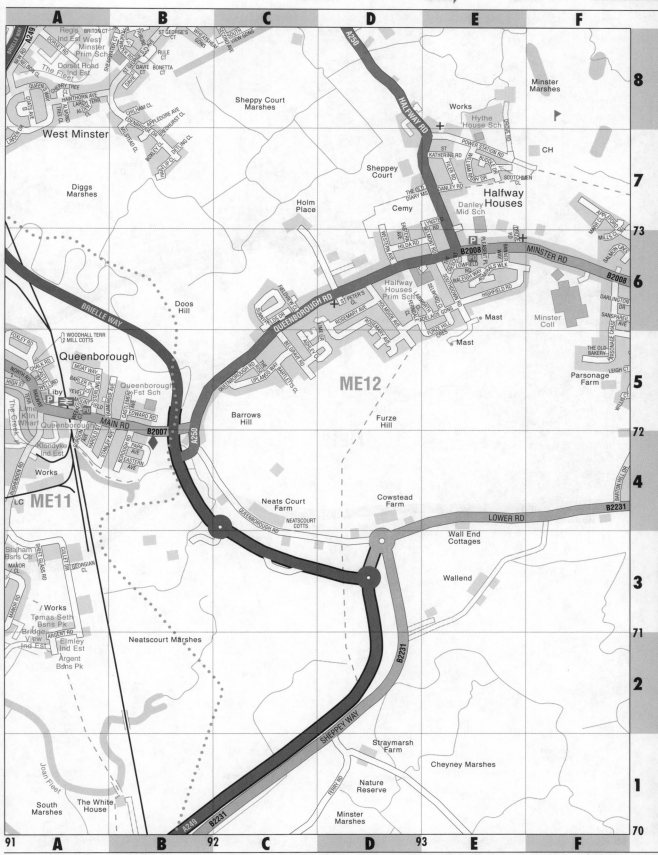

1 4

A B C D E F

Regis Ind Est
West Minster Prim Sch
Dorset Road Ind Est
The Fleet
West Minster
Diggs Marshes
Sheppy Court Marshes
Works
Hythe House Sch
CH
Minster Marshes
Sheppey Court
Halfway Houses
Danley Mid Sch
Cemy
Holm Place
Halfway Houses Prim Sch
Doos Hill
Mast
Minster Coll
Parsonage Farm
Queenborough
Queenborough Fst Sch
Liby
Lime Kiln Wharf
Queenborough
Klondyke Ind Est
Works
ME11
LC
Barrows Hill
ME12
Furze Hill
Neats Court Farm
Cowstead Farm
Wall End Cottages
Wallend
Stalham Bsns Ctr
Works
Tomas Seth Bsns Pk
Bridge View Ind Est
Elmley Ind Est
Argent Bsns Pk
Neatscourt Marshes
Straymarsh Farm
Cheyney Marshes
Nature Reserve
Minster Marshes
South Marshes
The White House
The Creek
Joan Fleet

A249 BRIELLE WAY NEW RD NELSON CL DORSET RD BRITON CT BRIDGEWATER RD SHEARWATER CT TRIBUNE CT ST GEORGE'S CT ST GEORGE'S AVE RULE CT BONETTA CT DAVIE CT WHEATSHEAF GDNS SECOND AVE SOUTH VIEW GDNS QUEEN'S WAY COATS AVE CHERRY TREE CL HAWTHORN AVE LARCH TERR ALDER CL ALMOND TREE CL LINDEN DR CHILHAM CL APPLEDORE AVE EDENBRIDGE DR BREDHURST CL MILSTEAD CL BOXLEY CL DETLING CL HARTLIP CL

A250 HALFWAY RD POWER STATION RD ST KATHERINE RD FILER RD WILLIAM RIGBY DR BUDDLE DR DROVE RD SCOTCHMEN CL THE OLD DIARY MS DANLEY RD LYNSTED RD EASTERN AVE BELMONT RD WESTERN AVE HILDA RD B2008 PLEASENT PL BANNER WAY DROVE RD MINSTER RD THE CRESCENT LOWFIELD RD RALEIGH WAY ADMIRALS WLK HIGHFIELD RD SOUTHDOWN RD SELWOOD CL LADWORTH CL FERNDALE CL ADELAIDE GDNS FURZE HILL CRES HOLMSIDE AVE ROSEMARY AVE ST PETER'S CL QUEENBOROUGH RD FIELDVIEW CL SUMMERFIELDS DR LIME GR ASHLEY CL BELGRAVE RD THE RISE UPLANDS WAY BARTLETTS CL APPLEFORD DR MARR CL MILLS CL SALMON CRES DARLINGTON DR SANSPAREIL AVE PARSONAGE CHASE THE OLD BAKERY LEIGH CT WILLIS CT BARTON HILL DR

FOXLEY RD 1 WOODHALL TERR 2 MILL COTTS CHALK RD NORTH RD HIGH ST CASTLE ST WELL RD RAILWAY TERR MOAT WAY BARLER PL YEVELE CL MOUNT FIELD STERLING RD DUMERGUE AVE CASTLEMERE AVE EDWARD RD WEEKES CT MAIN RD B2007 GORDON AVE HAROLD ST STANLEY AVE BOROUGH RD PARK AVE EASTERN AVE RUSHENDEN RD

QUEENBOROUGH RD NEATSCOURT COTTS LOWER RD B2231 SHEET GLASS RD CULLET DR GEORGIAN CL MANOR CL MANOR RD ARGENT RD SHEPPEY WAY FERRY RD A249

8 7 73 6 5 72 4 3 71 2 1 70

91 92 93

A B C D E F

15 4

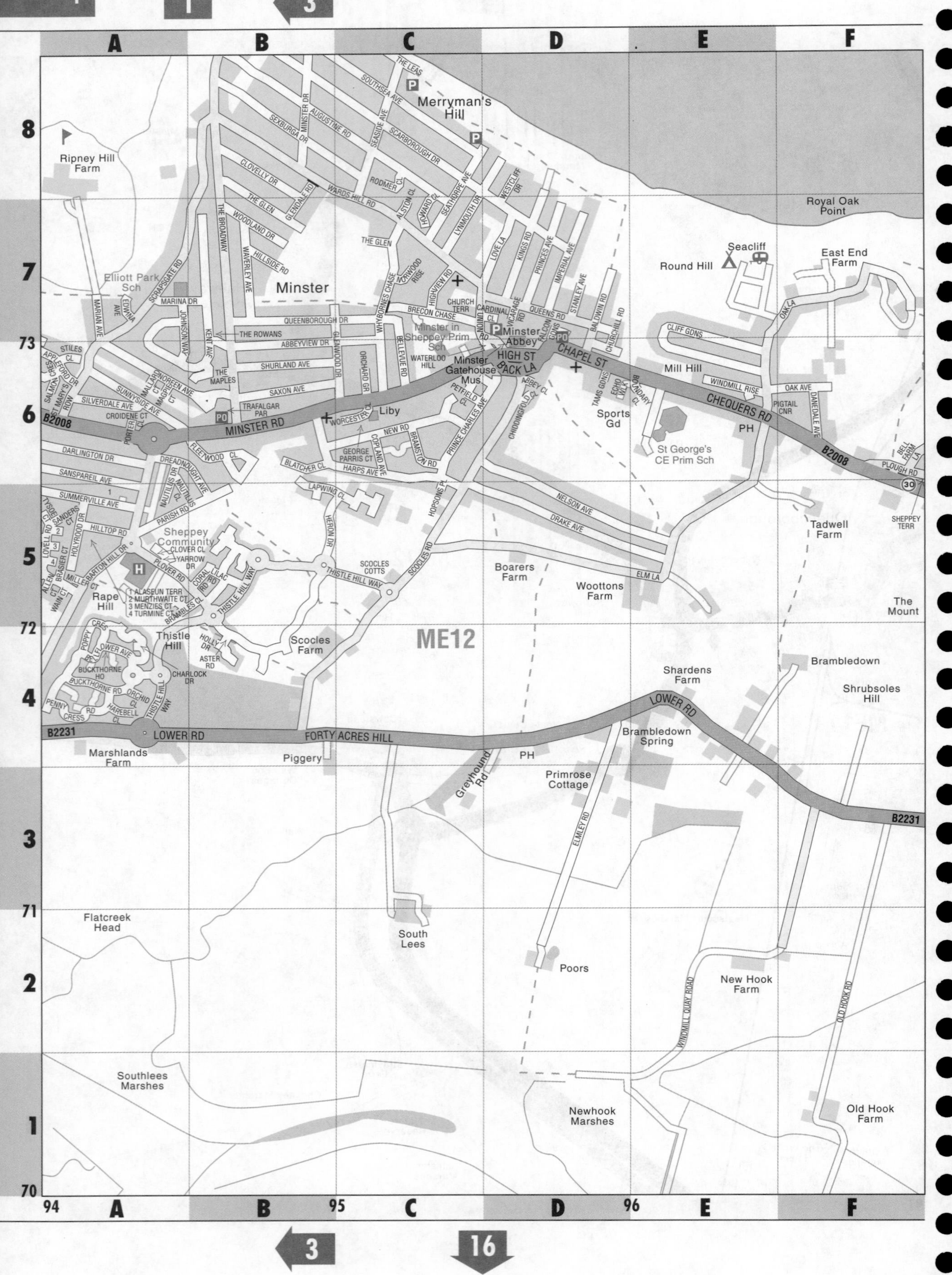
Merryman's Hill
Ripney Hill Farm
Minster
Elliott Park Sch
Minster in Sheppey Prim Sch
Minster Abbey
Minster Gatehouse Mus
HIGH ST
CHAPEL ST
CHEQUERS RD
MINSTER RD
B2008
Liby
Mill Hill
Sports Gd
St George's CE Prim Sch
Royal Oak Point
Seacliff
Round Hill
East End Farm
Tadwell Farm
Sheppey Community
Rape Hill
Thistle Hill
Scocles Farm
Boarers Farm
Woottons Farm
ME12
The Mount
Brambledown
Shardens Farm
Shrubsoles Hill
LOWER RD
B2231
FORTY ACRES HILL
Marshlands Farm
Piggery
PH
Brambledown Spring
Primrose Cottage
Greyhound Rd
ELMLEY RD
Flatcreek Head
South Lees
Poors
New Hook Farm
WINDMILL QUAY ROAD
OLD HOOK RD
Southlees Marshes
Newhook Marshes
Old Hook Farm

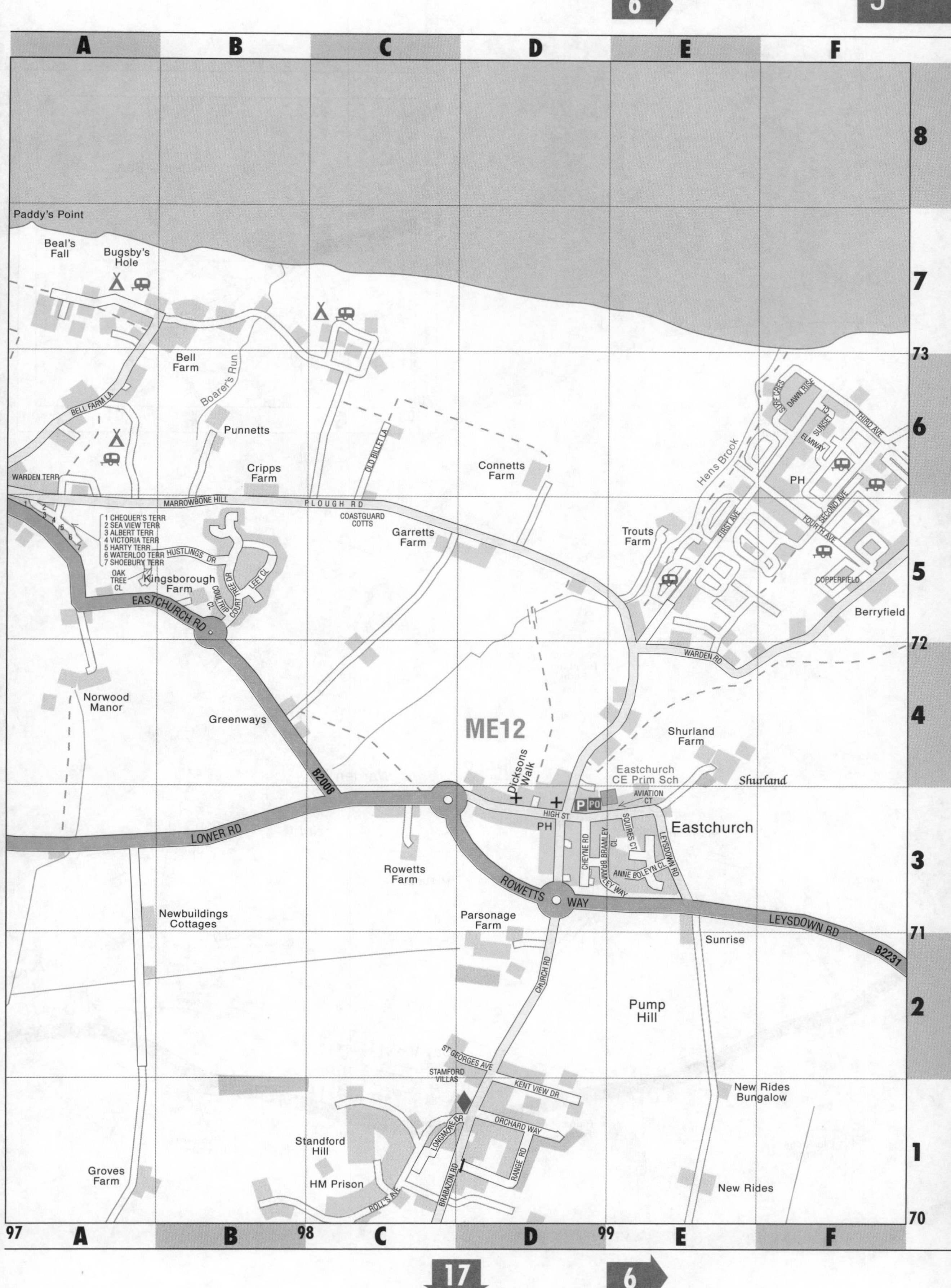

A B C D E F

8

7

73

6

Paddy's Point

Beal's Fall

Bugsby's Hole

Bell Farm

Boarer's Run

Punnetts

Cripps Farm

Connetts Farm

BELL FARM LA

WARDEN TERR

MARROWBONE HILL

PLOUGH RD

OLD BULLEN LA

COASTGUARD COTTS

1 CHEQUER'S TERR
2 SEA VIEW TERR
3 ALBERT TERR
4 VICTORIA TERR
5 HARTY TERR
6 WATERLOO TERR
7 SHOEBURY TERR

OAK TREE CL

Garretts Farm

HUSTLINGS DR

COULTIP CL

COURT TREE CL

LEET CL

Kingsborough Farm

EASTCHURCH RD

Trouts Farm

Hens Brook

FIRST AVE

SECOND AVE

THIRD AVE

FOURTH AVE

SUNSET CRES

DAWN RISE

ELM WAY

PH

Copperfield

Berryfield

72

5

Norwood Manor

Greenways

B2008

ME12

Shurland Farm

Shurland

WARDEN RD

4

LOWER RD

Rowetts Farm

Dicksons Walk

Eastchurch CE Prim Sch

HIGH ST

PH

PO

P

AVIATION CT

CHEYNE RD

BRAMLEY CL

SQUIRES CT

ANNE BOLEYN CL

BRAMLEY WAY

LEYSDOWN RD

Eastchurch

3

Newbuildings Cottages

ROWETTS WAY

Parsonage Farm

Sunrise

LEYSDOWN RD

B2231

71

CHURCH RD

Pump Hill

2

ST GEORGES AVE

STAMFORD VILLAS

KENT VIEW DR

New Rides Bungalow

Standford Hill

LONGMORE DR

BRABAZON RD

ORCHARD WAY

RANGE RD

1

Groves Farm

HM Prison

ROLL'S AV

New Rides

70

A B C D E F

Leysdown-on-Sea

71

2

GROVE AVE
EASTERN RD
SAND CT
NUTTS AVE
B2231 LEYSDOWN RD
THAMES CT
PO
THE PROMENADE
MANOR WAY
B2231
PH
PRIORY CT
PARK AVE
WING RD
WING RD
SHELLNESS RD
P

1

Holiday Village
ME12
SHURLAND AVE
SEAVIEW AVE
WING RD

70

03 G H 04

19

8

7

73

6

Swanley Farm

Barrows Brook

NORMAN RD

MANOR WAY

Cartts Farm

COASTGUARD HOS

Warden Point

5

PH

WARDEN RD
WARDEN WAY

72

Barnland Farm

Thorn Hill

4

ME12

Warden

THORN HILL RD
CLIFF DR
PRESTON HALL GDNS
SEA APP
ST JAMES CL
IMPERIAL DR
SEASALTER CL
KNOLL WAY
BUCKLERS CL
WATERSIDE
VIEW
CLIFF VIEW GDNS
JETTY RD
EMPRESS GDNS
MELOD
EMERALD VIEW
WINDSOR GDNS
CLARENCE GDNS
ST CLEMENTS RD
BEACH APP
LEICESTER GDNS
SEA VIEW GDNS
CONDOR CL
SEA VIEW GDNS

PH

P

3

Rayham

Mustards

WARDEN BAY RD

Holiday Villages

71

2

B2231

Bay View
CORONATION DR
ST CLEMENTS CL
BAY VIEW GDNS
SOUTHVIEW GDNS
MUSTARDS RD
DANES DR
WARDEN VIEW GDNS
CLIFF VIEW GDNS

Mast

B2231

GROVE AVE

+

Cemy

1

Old Rides Farm

HARTY FERRY RD

Rides Farm

LEYSDOWN RD

PH

Paradise Farm

VANITY RD

70

00 A B 01 C D 02 E F

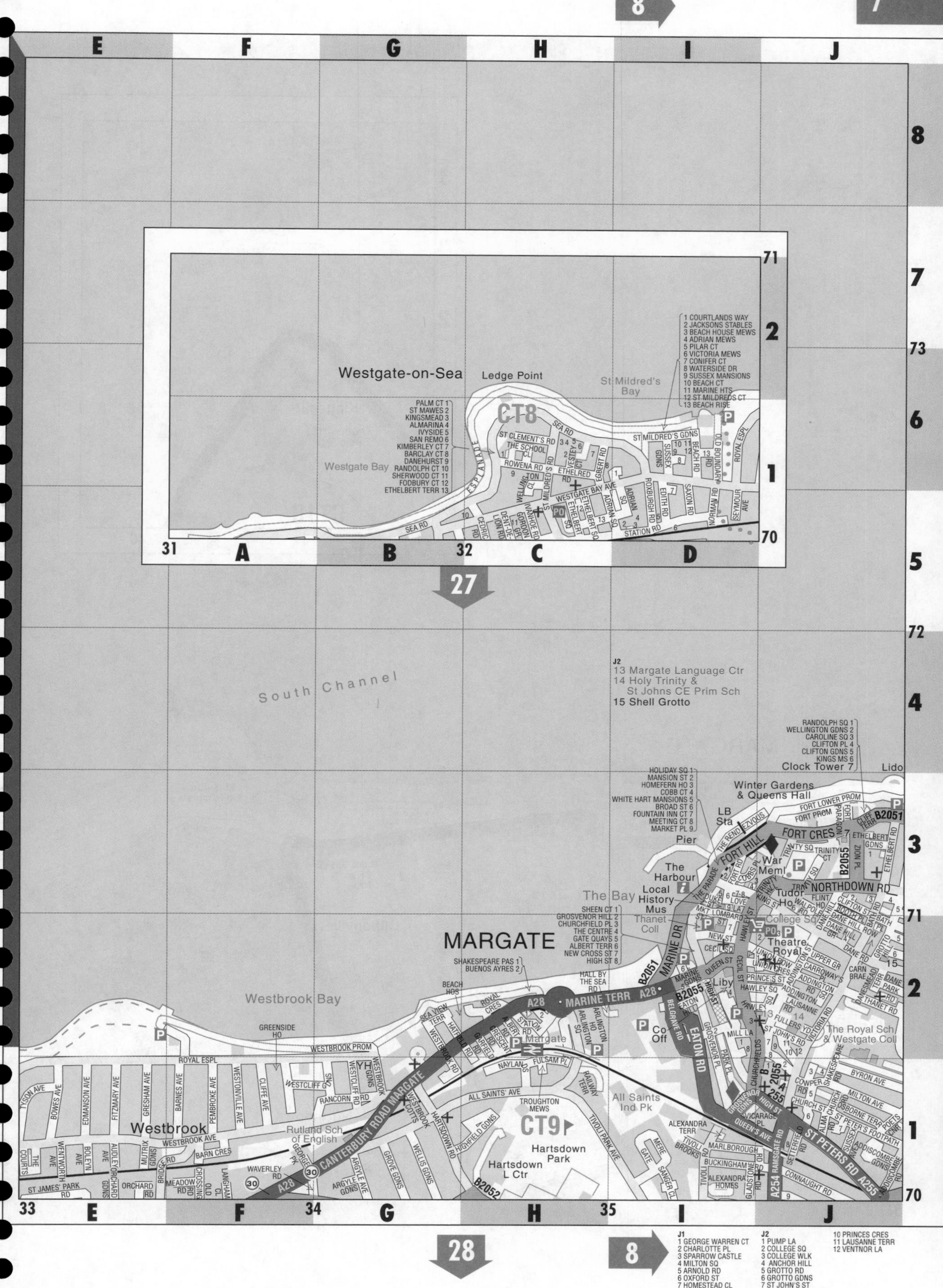

8
E F G H I J
8 7 6 5 4 3 2 1
73 72 71 70
Westgate-on-Sea
Ledge Point
St Mildred's Bay
Westgate Bay
CT8
PALM CT 1
ST MAWES 2
KINGSMEAD 3
ALMARINA 4
IVYSIDE 5
SAN REMO 6
KIMBERLEY CT 7
BARCLAY CT 8
DANEHURST 9
RANDOLPH CT 10
SHERWOOD CT 11
FODBURY CT 12
ETHELBERT TERR 13
1 COURTLANDS WAY
2 JACKSONS STABLES
3 BEACH HOUSE MEWS
4 ADRIAN MEWS
5 PILAR CT
6 VICTORIA MEWS
7 CONIFER CT
8 WATERSIDE DR
9 SUSSEX MANSIONS
10 BEACH CT
11 MARINE HTS
12 ST MILDREDS CT
13 BEACH RISE
SEA RD
ESPLANADE
ST CLEMENT'S RD
THE SCHOOL CL
ROWENA RD
ETHELRED RD
WESTGATE BAY AVE
ST MILDRED'S GDNS
STATION RD
31 A B 32 C D 71 70
27
South Channel
J2
13 Margate Language Ctr
14 Holy Trinity & St Johns CE Prim Sch
15 Shell Grotto
RANDOLPH SQ 1
WELLINGTON GDNS 2
CAROLINE SQ 3
CLIFTON PL 4
CLIFTON GDNS 5
KINGS MS 6
Clock Tower 7
Lido
HOLIDAY SQ 1
MANSION ST 2
HOMEFERN HO 3
COBB CT 4
WHITE HART MANSIONS 5
BROAD ST 6
FOUNTAIN INN CT 7
MEETING CT 8
MARKET PL 9
Winter Gardens & Queens Hall
LB Sta
Pier
The Harbour
Local History Mus
The Bay
Thanet Coll
War Meml
Tudor Ho
College Sq
Theatre Royal
Liby
FORT CRES
FORT HILL
NORTHDOWN RD
B2051
B2055
SHEEN CT 1
GROSVENOR HILL 2
CHURCHFIELD PL 3
THE CENTRE 4
GATE QUAYS 5
ALBERT TERR 6
NEW CROSS ST 7
HIGH ST 8
MARGATE
SHAKESPEARE PAS 1
BUENOS AYRES 2
HALL BY THE SEA RD
MARINE DR
MARINE TERR
A28
Westbrook Bay
BEACH HOS
GREENSIDE HO
WESTBROOK PROM
ROYAL ESPL
YH
Co-Off
EATON RD
The Royal Sch & Westgate Coll
Westbrook
Rutland Sch of English
CANTERBURY ROAD MARGATE
ALL SAINTS' AVE
TROUGHTON MEWS
CT9
Hartsdown Park
Hartsdown L Ctr
All Saints Ind Pk
ST PETERS RD
A254 RAMSGATE RD
A255
B2052
33 E 34 F G H 35 I J 70
28
8
J1
1 GEORGE WARREN CT
2 CHARLOTTE PL
3 SPARROW CASTLE
4 MILTON SQ
5 ARNOLD RD
6 OXFORD ST
7 HOMESTEAD CL
8 VICARAGE CRES
9 CONNAUGHT GDNS
J2
1 PUMP LA
2 COLLEGE SQ
3 COLLEGE WLK
4 ANCHOR HILL
5 GROTTO RD
6 GROTTO GDNS
7 ST JOHN'S ST
8 CHARLOTTE SQ
9 WINDSOR MEWS
10 PRINCES CRES
11 LAUSANNE TERR
12 VENTNOR LA

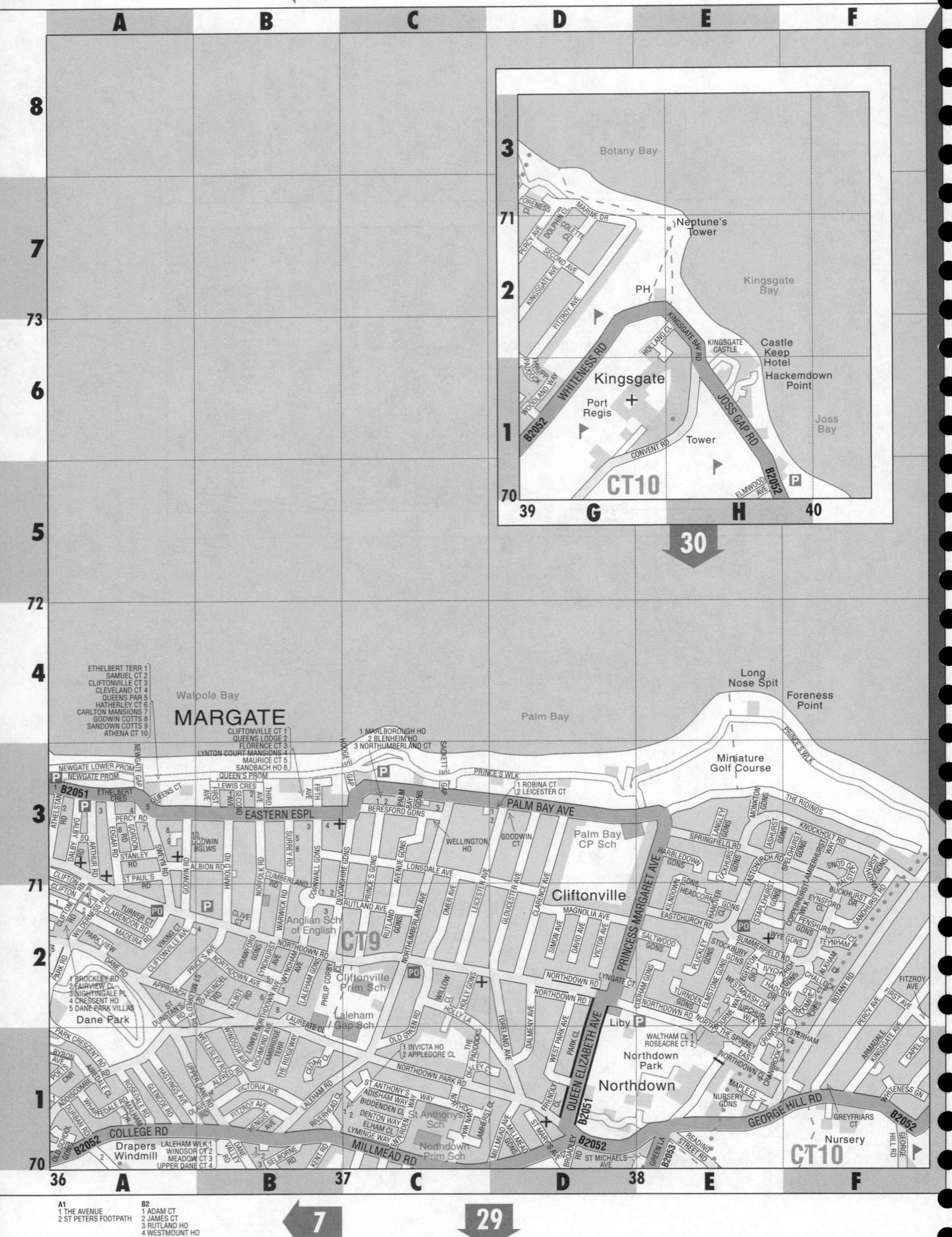

Botany Bay

3

71

2

1

70

Neptune's Tower

PH

Kingsgate Bay

Kingsgate Castle

Castle Keep Hotel

Hackemdown Point

Joss Bay

Kingsgate

Port Regis

Tower

CT10

39   G   H   40

FORENESS CL
PERCY AVE
DOLPHIN CL
COLETTE CT
SECOND AVE
KINGSGATE AVE
FITZROY AVE
WOODLAND WAY
HAWLEY
PADDOCK
B2052
WHITENESS RD
HOLLAND CL
KINGSGATE BAY RD
CONVENT RD
JOSS GAP RD
ELMWOOD AVE
B2052

30

Long Nose Spit

Foreness Point

Walpole Bay

MARGATE

Palm Bay

Miniature Golf Course

Cliftonville

CT9

Northdown

Dane Park

Drapers Windmill

CT10

Nursery

ETHELBERT TERR 1
SAMUEL CT 2
CLIFTONVILLE CT 3
CLEVELAND CT 4
QUEENS PAR 5
HATHERLEY CT 6
CARLTON MANSIONS 7
GODWIN COTTS 8
SANDOWN CTS 9
ATHENA CT 10

CLIFTONVILLE CT 1
QUEENS LODGE 2
FLORENCE CT 3
LYNTON COURT MANSIONS 4
MAURICE CT 5
SANDBACH HO 6

1 MARLBOROUGH HO
2 BLENHEIM HO
3 NORTHUMBERLAND CT

1 ROBINA CT
2 LEICESTER CT

NEWGATE LOWER PROM
NEWGATE PROM
B2051
ETHELBERT CRES
ATHELSTAN RD
DALBY RD
PERCY RD
EDGAR RD
ARTHUR RD
STANLEY RD
ST PAUL'S RD
GORDON RD
SWEYN RD
ALBION RD
HAROLD RD
NORFOLK RD
WARWICK RD
CUMBERLAND RD
CLIVE CT
RUTLAND AVE
CORNWALL GDNS
DEVONSHIRE GDNS
NORTHUMBERLAND RD
PRINCE'S GDNS
PALM BAY AVE
AVENUE GDNS
LONSDALE AVE
SIMON AVE
DAVID AVE
OMER AVE
LEICESTER AVE
GLOUCESTER AVE
VICTOR AVE
CLARENCE AVE
MAGNOLIA AVE
SPRINGFIELD RD
HARBLEDOWN GDNS
KNOCKHOLT RD
THE RIDINGS
LANGLEY GDNS
MONKTON GDNS
SPELDHURST GDNS
ASHURST GDNS
COXHILLS GDNS
EASTCHURCH RD
COPPERHURST WAY
SNOD CT
BUCKHURST DR
SANDHURST CL
EYNSFORD CT
PENSHURST GDNS
WYE GDNS
TEYNHAM GDNS
CHALLOCK
WALMER
FITZROY AVE
FIRST AVE
PERCY AVE
KINGSGATE AVE
CAPEL CL
ARMADALE
WHITENESS GDNS
GEORGE HILL RD
B2052
GREYFRIARS CT
READING STREET RD
GREEN LA
ST MICHAELS AVE
B2052
B2053
BROADLEY RD
QUEEN ELIZABETH AVE
B2051
NORTHDOWN RD
EASTERN ESPL
PALM BAY AVE
PRINCE'S WLK
WELLINGTON HO
GOODWIN CT
Palm Bay CP Sch
Anglian Sch of English
Cliftonville Prim Sch
Laleham Gap Sch
St Anthony's Sch
Northdown Prim Sch
St Michaels Ave
Liby
Northdown Park
QUEENS CT
FIRST AVE
LEWIS CRES
PERCY AVE
OHIL
QUEEN'S PROM
ATHELSTAN
CLIFTON GDNS
CLIFTON RD
TURNER CT
CLARENDON RD
PARK VIEW
DANE RD
MADEIRA RD
VIKING CT
CLIFTONVILLE AVE
PRICE'S AVE
CRAMPTON GDNS
NORTHDOWN RD
LYNCHURST GDNS
WYNDHAM AVE
NORTHDOWN RD
HILLOW CL
MILTON AVE
MILL LA
HOLLY LA
FORELAND AVE
DALMENY AVE
WEST PARK RD
WEST PARK AVE
PRIORY RD
ST MARY'S AVE
AYM
NORTHDOWN WAY
LYNGATE CT
SALTWOOD GDNS
STOCKBURY GDNS
SUMMERFIELD RD
TURDEN GDNS
ELMSTONE GDNS
EBERTON RD
HADLOW
IVYCHURCH
WESTMARSH DR
WYE GDNS
UPCHURCH WLK
THE SPINNEY
EAST
WATERHAM
CRUNDALE
THE DELF
WESTERHAM
BURNE CT
NURSERY GDNS
MAPLE CL
ROSEACRE CT
WALTHAM CL
NORTHDOWN RD
NORTHDOWN RD
PRINCESS MARGARET AVE
KILNDOWN GDNS
HEADCORNER
STAPLEHURST
PLUCKLEY GDNS
BRABOURNE GDNS
BOTANY RD
LEYBOURNE DR
MILLMEAD RD
LALEHAM RD
PHILIP CORBY
LAUREATE CL
OLD GREEN RD
OTLEY CT
THE PADDOCKS
ST ANTHONY'S WAY
DENTON WAY
ELHAM CL
BIDDENDEN CL
ADISHAM WAY
JAMIESON CT
LYMINGE WAY
MILLMEAD WAY
MILLMEAD AVE
RIDGEWAY
WELLESLEY RD
CAMBRIDGE
DUNSTAN
LOWER NORTHDOWN RD
ARUNDEL RD
TALBOT
PRINCE'S AVE
NORTHDOWN AVE
APPROACH RD
PERCY AVE
FITZROY AVE
VICTORIA AVE
KENT RD
SELBORNE RD
VALLEY RD
HENGIST RD
RIDGEWAY CL
ST ANTHONYS RD
SACKETT'S
HODGE'S GAP
BAY GAP
PALM BAY GAP
BERESFORD GDNS
PRINCE'S WLK
HEADS
HODGE'S GAP
SURREY RD
QUEENS GDNS
COLLEGE RD
B2051
MILLMEAD RD
1 INVICTA HO
2 APPLEDORE CL
1 WALTHAM CL
2 ROSEACRE CT
LALEHAM WLK 1
WINDSOR CT 2
MEADOW CT 3
UPPER DANE RD 4
1 BROCKLEY RD
2 FAIRVIEW CL
3 NIGHTINGALE PL
4 CRESCENT HO
5 DANE PARK VILLAS
BYRON
PORTS
ADDISCOMBE RD
DURBAN RD
WHARFEDALE RD
GLENCOE RD
ROSEDALE RD
PARK CRESCENT RD
HASTINGS AVE
ST ANTHONYS
GEORGE HILL RD
FITZROY AVE
FIRST AVE

A1
1 THE AVENUE
2 ST PETERS FOOTPATH

B2
1 ADAM CT
2 JAMES CT
3 RUTLAND HO
4 WESTMOUNT HO
5 HIGHFIELD CT
6 REBECCA CT
7 RICHARD CT
8 LEONA CT

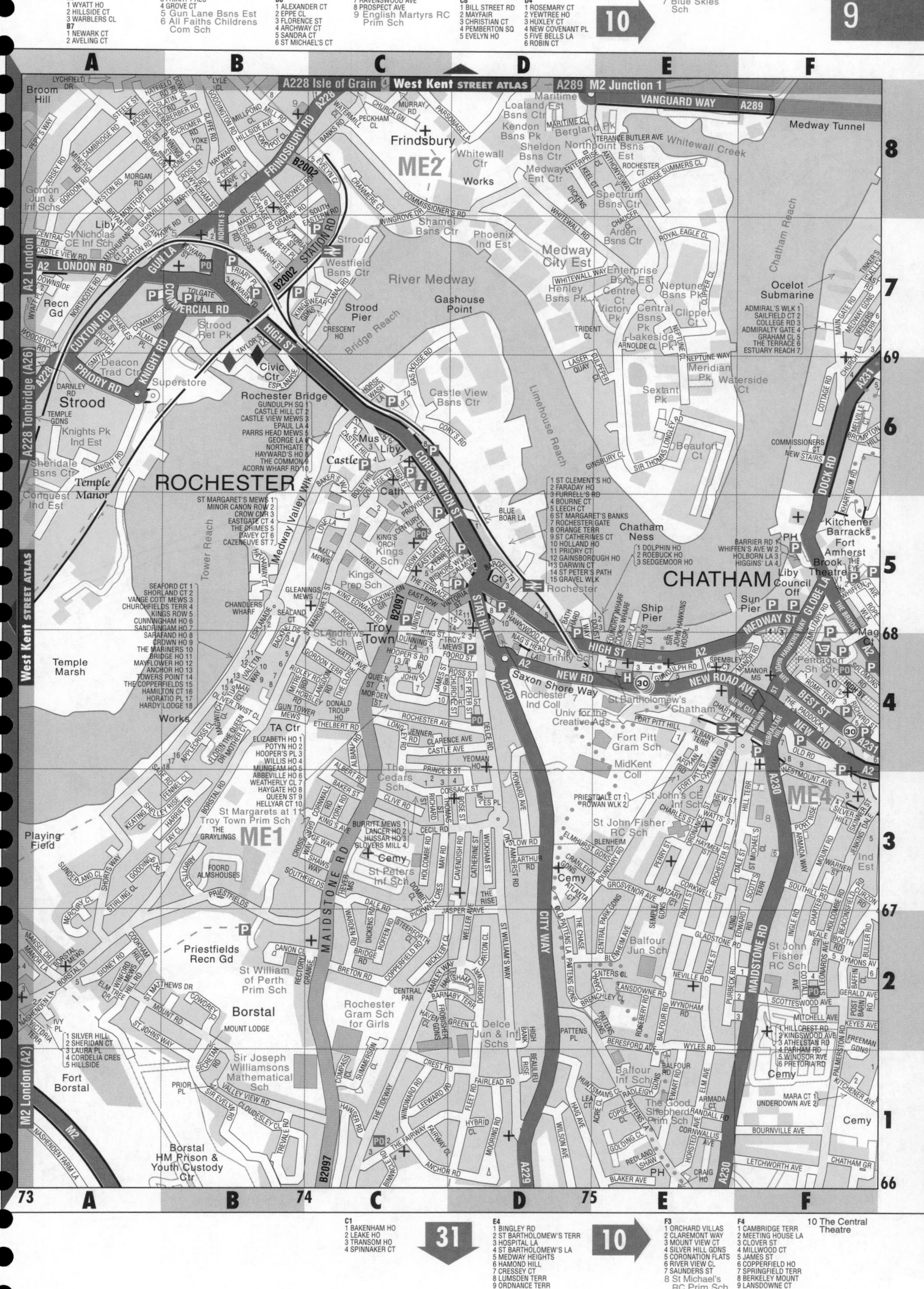

A7
1 WYATT HO
2 HILLSIDE CT
3 WARBLERS CL
B7
1 NEWARK CT
2 AVELING CT
3 FRIARY PREC
4 GROVE CT
5 Gun Lane Bsns Est
6 All Faiths Childrens Com Sch
B8
1 ALEXANDER CT
2 EPPE CL
3 FLORENCE ST
4 ARCHWAY CT
5 SANDRA CT
6 ST MICHAEL'S CT
7 RAVENSWOOD AVE
8 PROSPECT AVE
9 English Martyrs RC Prim Sch
C8
1 BILL STREET RD
2 MAYFAIR
3 CHRISTIAN CT
4 PEMBERTON SQ
5 EVELYN HO
D4
1 ROSEMARY CT
2 YEWTREE HO
3 HUXLEY CT
4 NEW COVENANT PL
5 FIVE BELLS LA
6 ROBIN CT
10
7 Blue Skies Sch
9
A228 Isle of Grain
West Kent STREET ATLAS
A289 M2 Junction 1
VANGUARD WAY
Medway Tunnel
Frindsbury
ME2
River Medway
Medway City Est
ROCHESTER
CHATHAM
Strood
Troy Town
ME1
ME4
Borstal
Chatham Reach
Limehouse Reach
Tower Reach
Temple Marsh
Playing Field
Fort Borstal
Borstal HM Prison & Youth Custody Ctr
Priestfields Recn Gd
Rochester Bridge
A2 London
A228 Tonbridge (A26)
M2 London (A2)
A2 NEW RD
NEW ROAD AVE
HIGH ST
CORPORATION ST
STAR HILL
CITY WAY
MAIDSTONE RD
A229
A230
B2097
A B C D E F
8 7 6 5 4 3 2 1
69 68 67 66
73 74 75
C1
1 BAKENHAM HO
2 LEAKE HO
3 TRANSOM HO
4 SPINNAKER CT
31
E4
1 BINGLEY RD
2 ST BARTHOLOMEW'S TERR
3 HOSPITAL LA
4 ST BARTHOLOMEW'S LA
5 MEDWAY HEIGHTS
6 HAMOND HILL
7 CRESSEY CT
8 LUMSDEN TERR
9 ORDNANCE TERR
10
F3
1 ORCHARD VILLAS
2 CLAREMONT WAY
3 MOUNT VIEW CT
4 SILVER HILL GDNS
5 CORONATION FLATS
6 RIVER VIEW CL
7 SAUNDERS ST
8 St Michael's RC Prim Sch
F4
1 CAMBRIDGE TERR
2 MEETING HOUSE LA
3 CLOVER ST
4 MILLWOOD CT
5 JAMES ST
6 COPPERFIELD HO
7 SPRINGFIELD TERR
8 BERKELEY MOUNT
9 LANSDOWNE CT
10 The Central Theatre

C7
1 AUGUSTA CL
2 ANNVERA HO
3 SUNDERLAND HO
4 LATIMER PL
5 HUNTERS CT
6 KING WILLIAM RD

7 FORSYTH CT

D6
1 Burnt Oak
Prim Sch

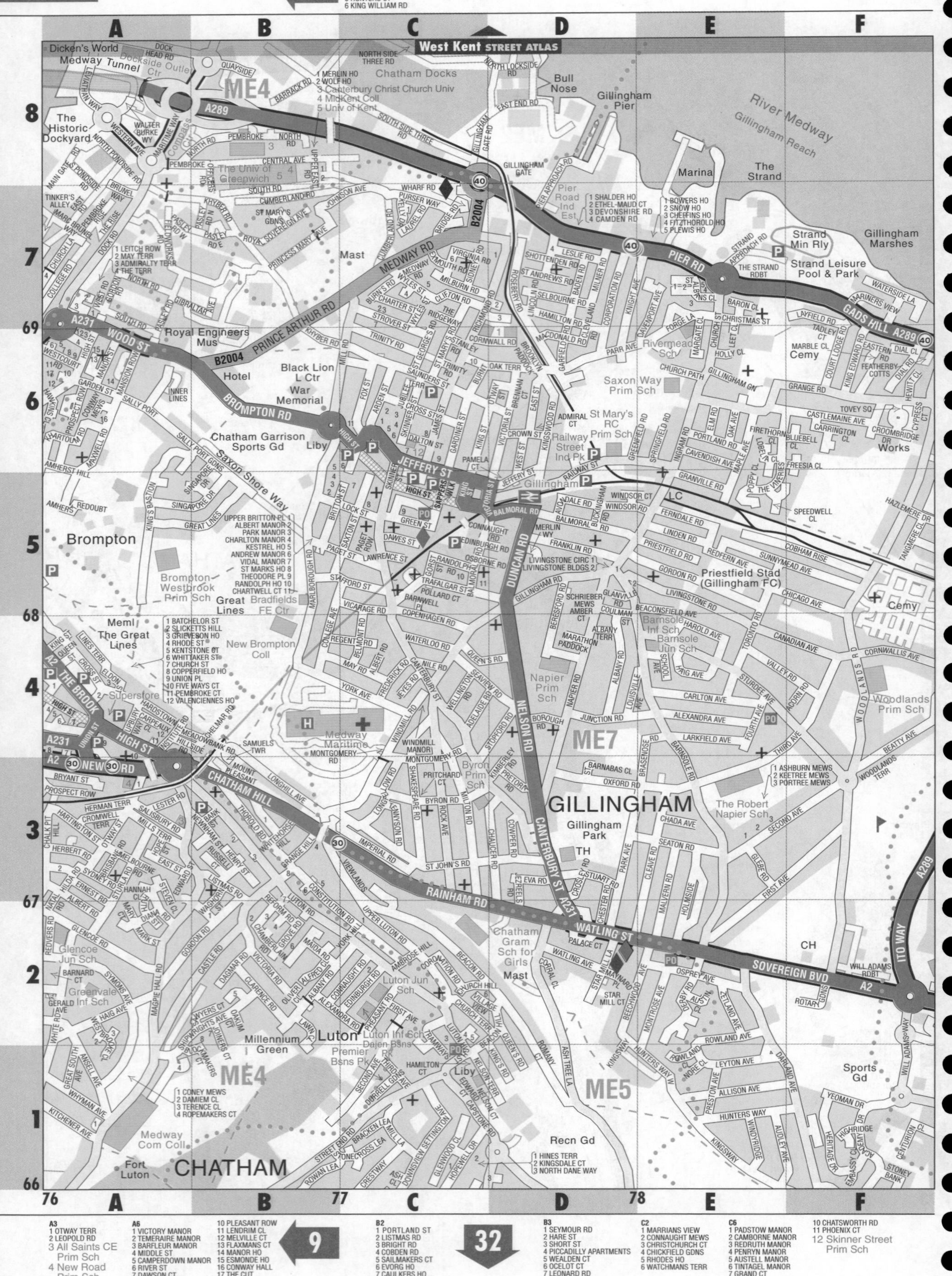

A3
1 OTWAY TERR
2 LEOPOLD RD
3 All Saints CE
Prim Sch
4 New Road
Prim Sch

A6
1 VICTORY MANOR
2 TEMERAIRE MANOR
3 BARFLEUR MANOR
4 MIDDLE ST
5 CAMPERDOWN MANOR
6 RIVER ST
7 DAWSON CT
8 MCCUDDEN ROW
9 PERIE ROW

10 PLEASANT ROW
11 LENDRIM CL
12 MELVILLE CT
13 FLAXMANS CT
14 MANOR HO
15 ESMONDE RD
16 CONWAY HALL
17 THE CUT

B2
1 PORTLAND ST
2 LISTMAS RD
3 BRIGHT RD
4 COBDEN RD
5 SAILMAKERS CT
6 EVORG HO
7 CAULKERS HO
8 THE ENDEAVOUR FOYER

B3
1 SEYMOUR RD
2 HARE ST
3 SHORT ST
4 PICCADILLY APARTMENTS
5 WEALDEN CT
6 OCELOT CT
7 LEONARD RD
8 CONSTITUTION HILL

C2
1 MARRIANS VIEW
2 CONNAUGHT MEWS
3 CHRISTCHURCH CT
4 CHICKFIELD GDNS
5 RHODES HO
6 WATCHMANS TERR

C6
1 PADSTOW MANOR
2 CAMBORNE MANOR
3 REDRUTH MANOR
4 PENRYN MANOR
5 AUSTELL MANOR
6 TINTAGEL MANOR
7 GRAND CT
8 DEANE CT
9 WILL ADAMS CT

10 CHATSWORTH RD
11 PHOENIX CT
12 SKINNER STREET
Prim Sch

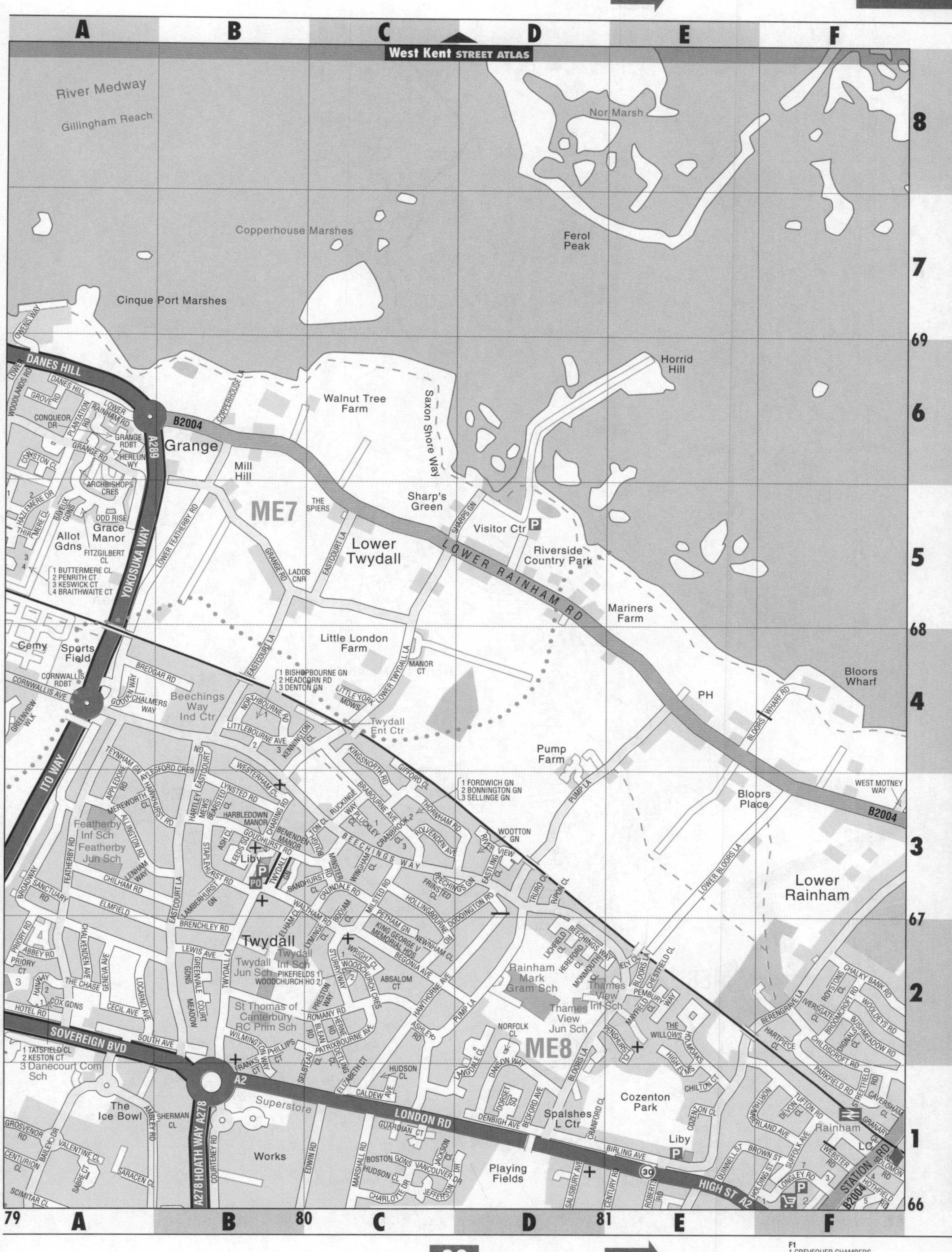

West Kent STREET ATLAS

River Medway

Gillingham Reach

Nor Marsh

Ferol Peak

8

Copperhouse Marshes

7

Cinque Port Marshes

69

Horrid Hill

DANES HILL

B2004

Walnut Tree Farm

Saxon Shore Way

Grange

6

Mill Hill

ME7

Sharp's Green

Visitor Ctr

Riverside Country Park

5

Lower Twydall

LOWER RAINHAM RD

Mariners Farm

68

Little London Farm

Bloors Wharf

4

PH

Beechings Way Ind Ctr

Twydall Ent Ctr

Pump Farm

1 FORDWICH GN
2 BONNINGTON GN
3 SELLINGE GN

WEST MOTNEY WAY

B2004

3

Lower Rainham

Liby

Twydall

67

Rainham Mark Gram Sch

Twydall Inf Sch
Twydall Jun Sch

2

St Thomas of Canterbury RC Prim Sch

Thames View Inf Sch
Thames View Jun Sch

ME8

The Willows

Rainham

SOVEREIGN BVD

A2

Superstore

Cozenton Park

1

The Ice Bowl

Works

London Road

Spalshes L Ctr

Liby

Playing Fields

HIGH ST A2

B2004

66

F1
1 CREVEQUER CHAMBERS
2 Rainham Sh Ctr
3 GRESHAM CL
4 HARRISON CT
5 MAPLINS CL
6 SIGNAL CT
7 SUFFOLK CT

11

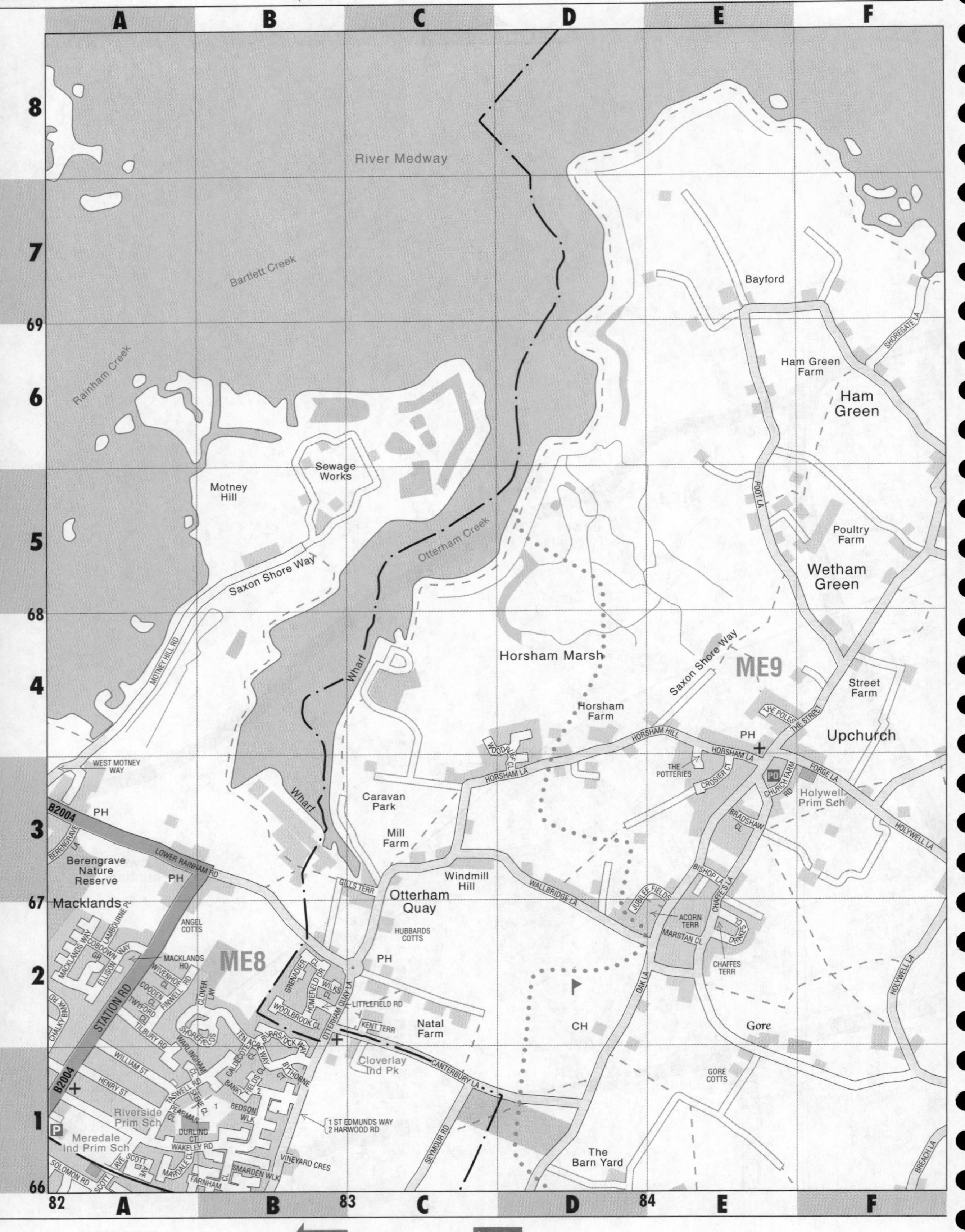

River Medway
Bartlett Creek
Rainham Creek
Otterham Creek
Sewage Works
Motney Hill
Saxon Shore Way
Wharf
Horsham Marsh
Horsham Farm
Caravan Park
Mill Farm
Windmill Hill
Otterham Quay
Bayford
Ham Green Farm
Ham Green
Poultry Farm
Wetham Green
Street Farm
Upchurch
ME9
ME8
PH
Holywell Prim Sch
Berengrave Nature Reserve
Macklands
Natal Farm
Cloverlay Ind Pk
Riverside Prim Sch
Meredale Ind Prim Sch
Gore
GORE COTTS
The Barn Yard
CH
B2004
STATION RD
LOWER RAINHAM RD
MOTNEY HILL RD
WEST MOTNEY WAY
HORSHAM LA
HORSHAM HILL
THE STREET
FORGE LA
HOLYWELL LA
CHURCH FARM RD
BRADSHAW CL
BISHOP LA
CHAFFE'S LA
WALLBRIDGE LA
OAK LA
CANTERBURY LA
SEYMOUR RD
POOT LA
SHOREGATE LA
BREACH LA
THE POLES
THE POTTERIES
CROSIER CT
JUBILEE FIELDS
ACORN TERR
MARSTAN CL
CHAFFES TERR
GILLS TERR
HUBBARDS COTTS
OTTERHAM QUAY LA
LITTLEFIELD RD
KENT TERR
WOOLBROOK CL
ANGEL COTTS
MACKLANDS HO
1 ST EDMUNDS WAY
2 HARWOOD RD
VINEYARD CRES
SMARDEN WLK
FARNHAM CL
SOLOMON RD
SCOTT AVE
WAKELEY RD
DURLING CT
BEDSON WLK
WILLIAM ST
HENRY ST
TILBURY RD
CHALKY BANK RD
BERENGRAVE LA

11
34

14

A · B · C · D · E · F

Millfordhope Creek

Greenborough Marshes

Slaughterhouse Point

The Shade

8

Millfordhope Marsh

Stangate Creek

7

Twinney Creek

69

Barksore Marshes

6

River Medway

Callows House

Halstow Creek

Funton Creek

Twinney Wharf

5

Twinney Acre

68

Frog Farm Cotts

Funton Brick Works

Frog Farm

Saxon Shore Way

Funton

Raspberry Hill La

4

Sewage Works

Great Barksore

Saxon Shore Way

+

Greenways

Stray Farm

Little Barksore

Tiptree Hill

Bell Cotts

CURLEW AVE

HERON

LAPWINS DR

THE GREEN

THE STREET

BURNTWICK DR

THE CRESCENT

CROFT HILL

CROSS LANE DR

VICARAGE LA

BASSER HILL

3

Holywell

Green Farm

PH

WESTMOR

VICARAGE COTTS

Lower Halstow

Tiptree

67

SEA VIEW COTTS

LANDRAIL RD

SCHOOL LA

CUMBERLAND DR

ME9

WESTFIELD COTTS

Elm Farm

Callum Hill

STICKFAST LA

2

The Laurels

Lower Halstow Prim Sch

Boxted Farm

BREACH LA

WADWELL LA

HIGH OAK HILL

Hawes Wood

Great Norwood

BELNOR AVE

1

BOXTED LA

66

85 · A · B · 86 · C · D · 87 · E · F

35
14

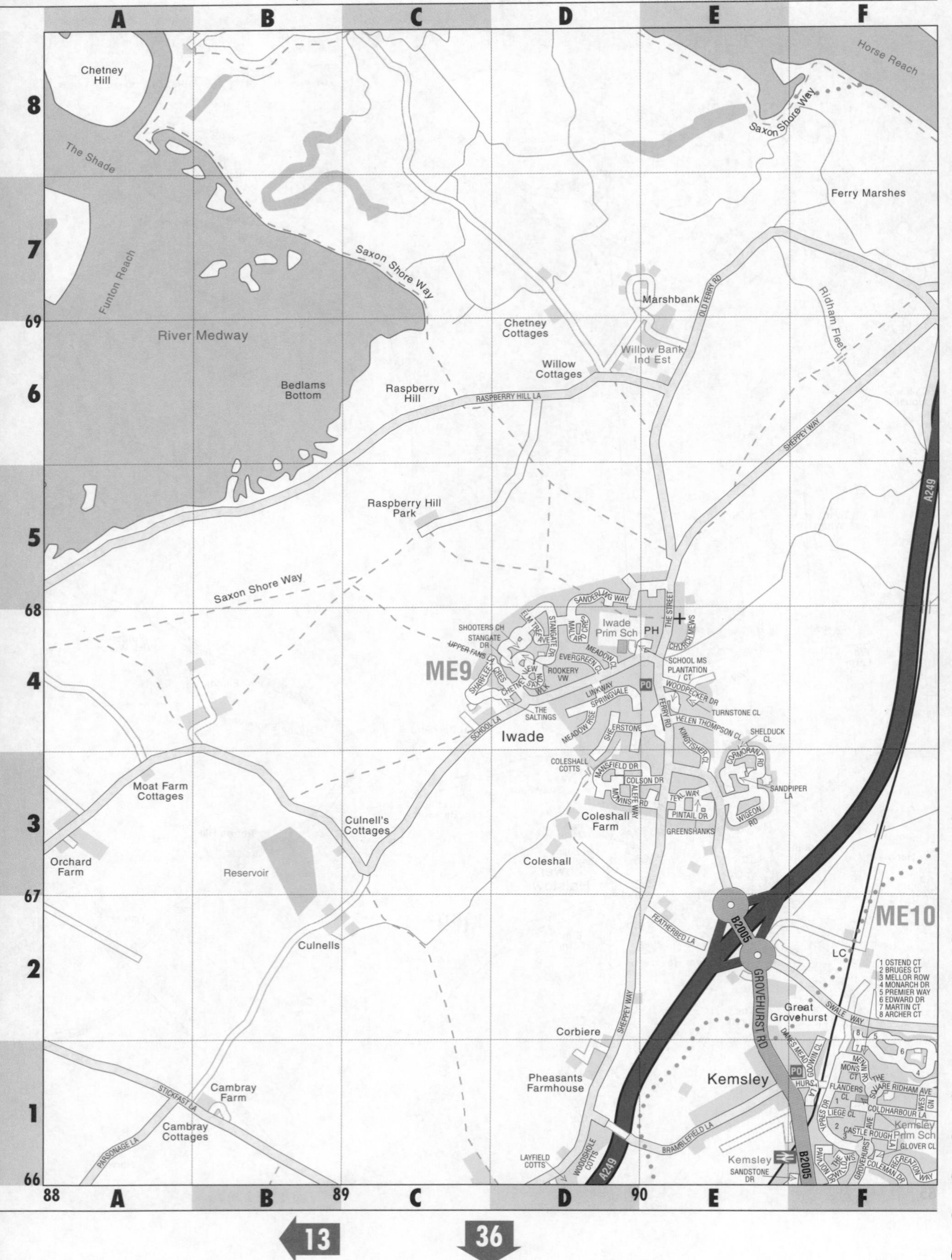
A B C D E F
8
7
69
6
5
68
4
3
67
2
1
66
88 A B 89 C D 90 E F
Chetney Hill
The Shade
Funton Reach
River Medway
Saxon Shore Way
Horse Reach
Ferry Marshes
Marshbank
Chetney Cottages
Willow Bank Ind Est
Willow Cottages
Ridham Fleet
OLD FERRY RD
Bedlams Bottom
Raspberry Hill
RASPBERRY HILL LA
SHEPPEY WAY
Raspberry Hill Park
A249
SANDERLING WAY
THE STREET
Iwade Prim Sch
PH
CHURCH MEWS
SHOOTERS CH
STANGATE DR
UPPER FANS
ME9
ROOKERY VW
EVERGREEN CL
MEADOW CL
SCHOOL MS
PLANTATION CT
WOODPECKER DR
TURNSTONE CL
LINKWAY
SPRINGVALE
THE SALTINGS
SCHOOL LA
MEADOW RISE
Iwade
SHEERSTONE
FERRY RD
HELEN THOMPSON CL
KINGFISHER CL
SHELDUCK CL
CORMORANT RD
COLESHALL COTTS
MANSFIELD DR
COLSON DR
SANDPIPER LA
TEAL WAY
PINTAIL DR
WIGEON RD
GREENSHANKS
Coleshall Farm
Moat Farm Cottages
Orchard Farm
Culnell's Cottages
Reservoir
Coleshall
FEATHERBED LA
B2005
ME10
Culnells
LC
1 OSTEND CT
2 BRUGES CT
3 MELLOR ROW
4 MONARCH DR
5 PREMIER WAY
6 EDWARD DR
7 MARTIN CT
8 ARCHER CT
GROVEHURST RD
SWALE WAY
Great Grovehurst
Corbiere
Kemsley
Pheasants Farmhouse
Cambray Farm
STICKFAST LA
Cambray Cottages
PARSONAGE LA
BRAMBLEFIELD LA
LAYFIELD COTTS
WOODSHOLE COTTS
Kemsley
SANDSTONE DR
RIDHAM AVE
COLDHARBOUR LA
Kemsley Prim Sch
GLOVER CL
COLEMAN DR
THE SQUARE
LIEGE CL
CASTLE ROUGH LA
FLANDERS CL
YPRES DR
PAVILION DR
THE WILLOWS
GROVEHURST AVE
RECREATION WAY

3
16

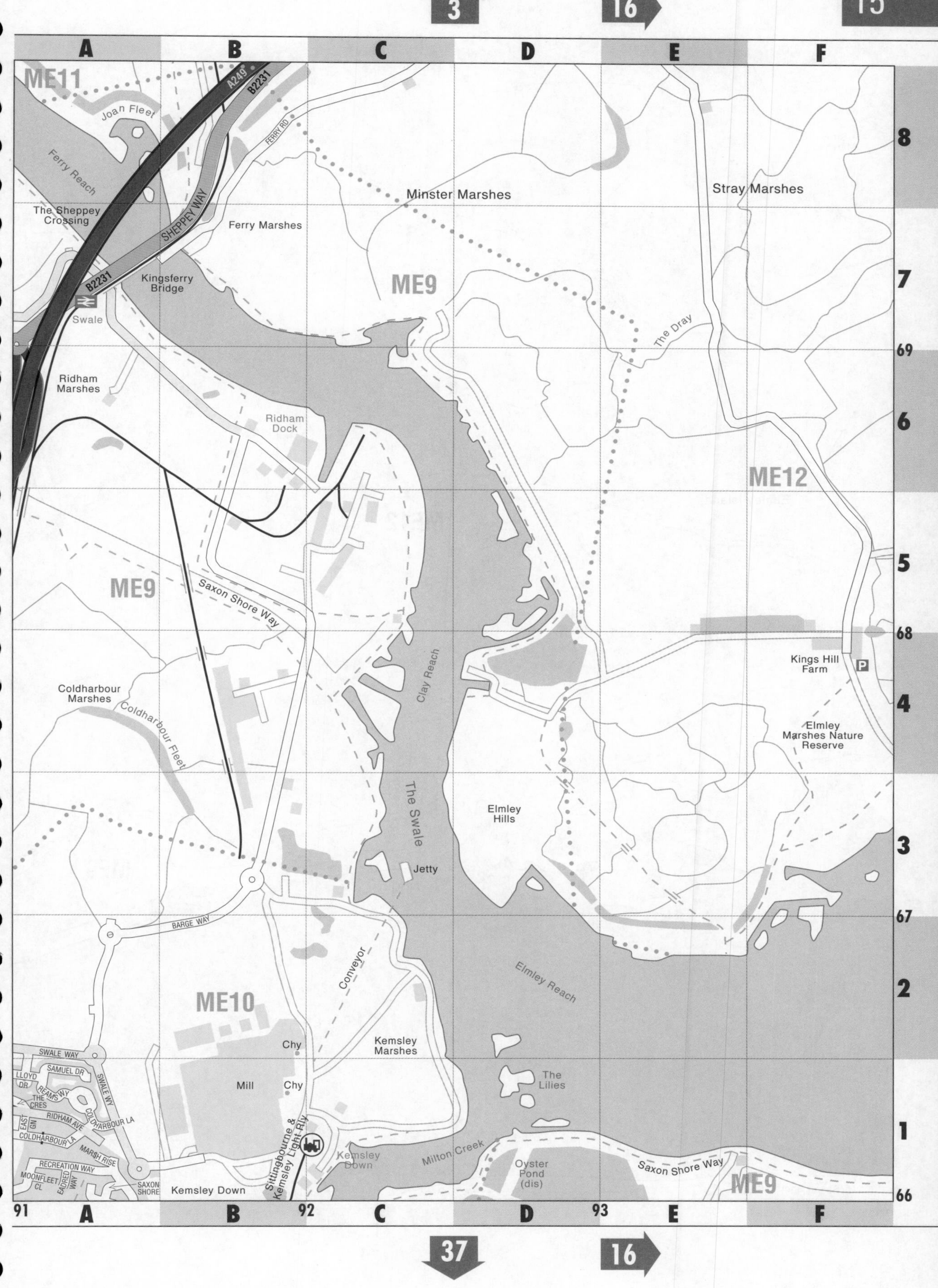
A
B
C
D
E
F
ME11
Joan Fleet
A249
B2231
Ferry Reach
FERRY RD
The Sheppey Crossing
SHEPPEY WAY
Ferry Marshes
Minster Marshes
Stray Marshes
8
B2231
Kingsferry Bridge
ME9
7
Swale
The Dray
69
Ridham Marshes
Ridham Dock
6
ME12
5
ME9
Saxon Shore Way
68
Kings Hill Farm
Clay Reach
Coldharbour Marshes
Coldharbour Fleet
4
Elmley Marshes Nature Reserve
Elmley Hills
The Swale
3
Jetty
BARGE WAY
67
Conveyor
Elmley Reach
2
ME10
Chy
Kemsley Marshes
SWALE WAY
SAMUEL DR
LLOYD DR
SWALE WY
REAMS WY
THE CRES
RIDHAM AVE
COLDHARBOUR LA
EAST GN
COLDHARBOUR LA
MARSH RISE
Mill
Chy
The Lilies
1
RECREATION WAY
MOONFLEET CL
BADRED WAY
SAXON SHORE
Sittingbourne & Kemsley Light Rly
Kemsley Down
Milton Creek
Oyster Pond (dis)
Saxon Shore Way
ME9
Kemsley Down
66
91
92
93

37
16

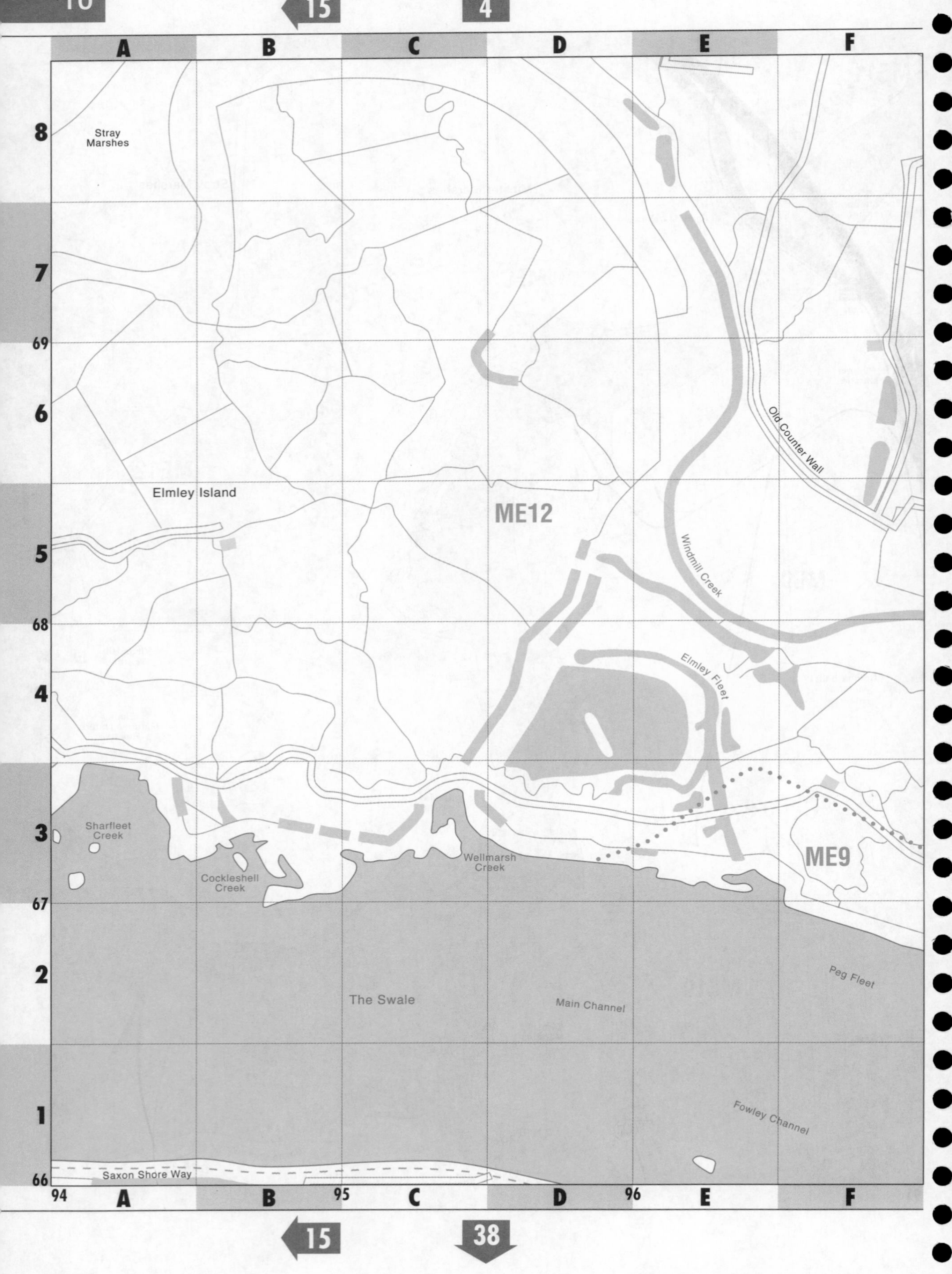

Stray Marshes

Elmley Island

ME12

Old Counter Wall

Windmill Creek

Elmley Fleet

ME9

Sharfleet Creek

Cockleshell Creek

Wellmarsh Creek

The Swale

Main Channel

Peg Fleet

Fowley Channel

Saxon Shore Way

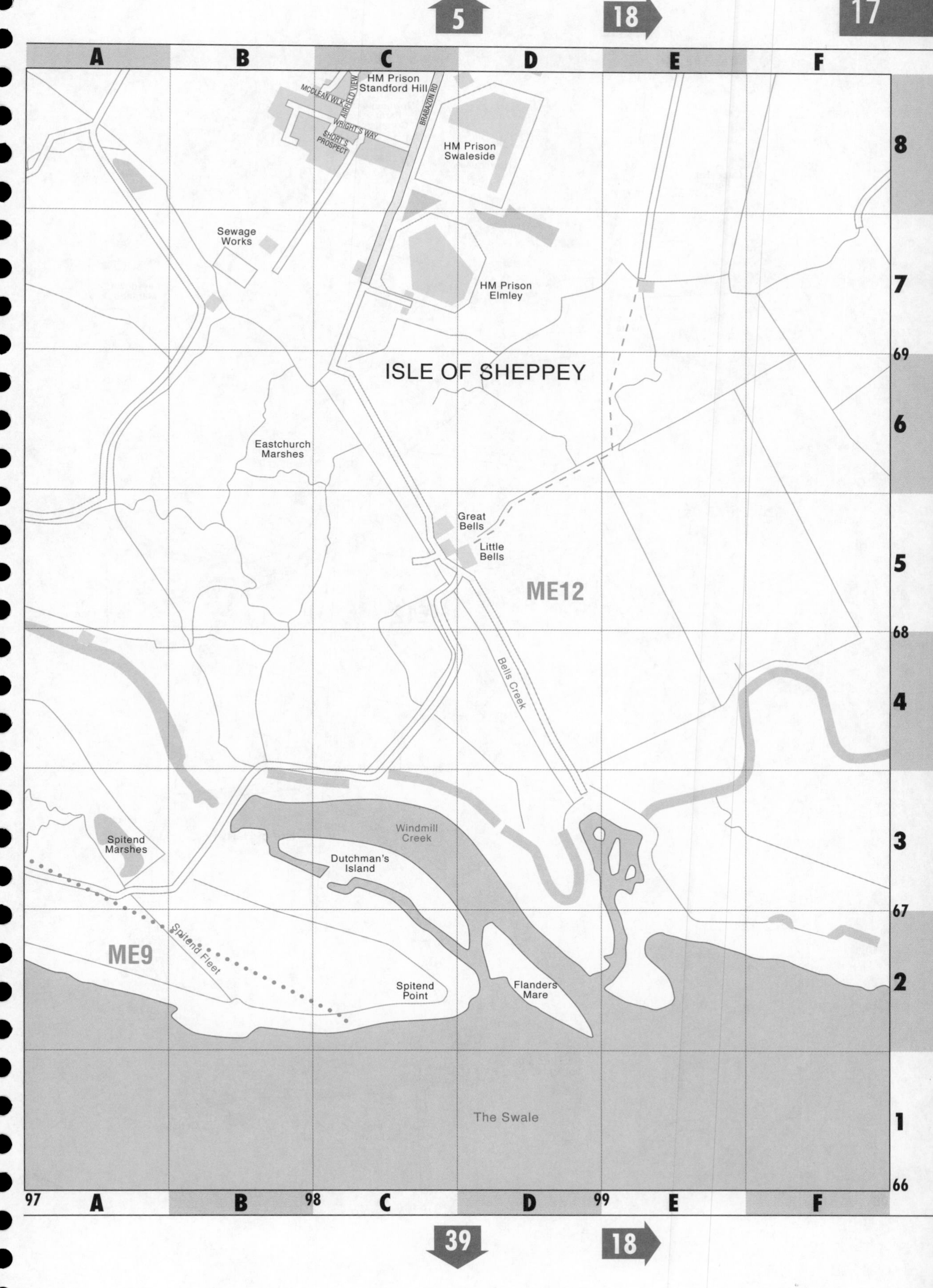

A B C D E F

HM Prison
Standford Hill

MCCLEAN WLK
AIRFIELD VIEW

HM Prison
Swaleside

WRIGHT'S WAY
SHORT'S PROSPECT

BRABAZON RD

8

Sewage
Works

HM Prison
Elmley

7

69

ISLE OF SHEPPEY

6

Eastchurch
Marshes

Great
Bells

Little
Bells

5

ME12

Bells Creek

68

4

Windmill
Creek

Spitend
Marshes

Dutchman's
Island

3

67

Spitend Fleet

ME9

Spitend
Point

Flanders
Mare

2

The Swale

1

66

97 A B 98 C D 99 E F

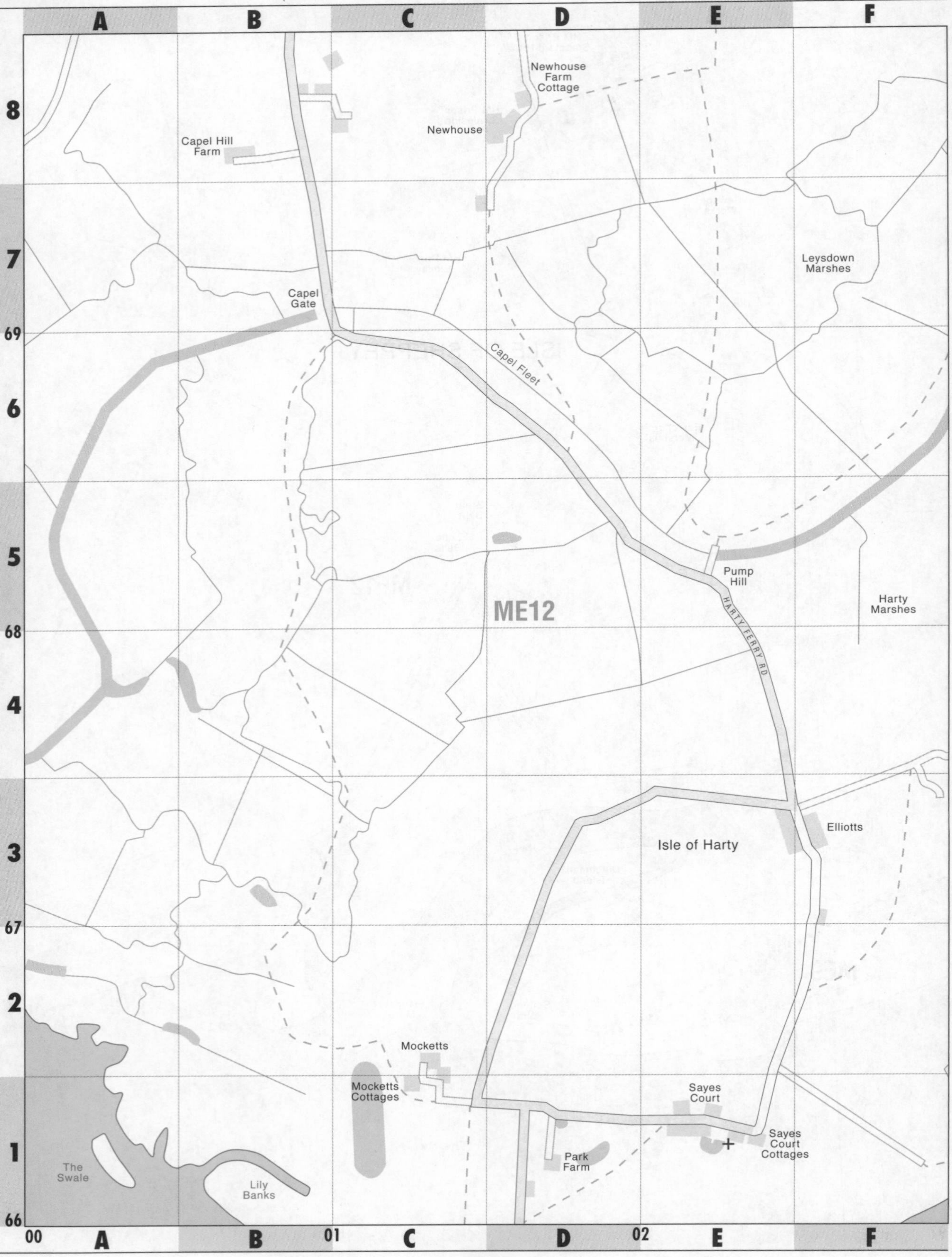

A B C D E F

8

7

69

6

5

68

4

3

67

2

1

66

Capel Hill
Farm

Newhouse
Farm
Cottage

Newhouse

Capel
Gate

Capel Fleet

Leysdown
Marshes

ME12

Pump
Hill

HARTY FERRY RD

Harty
Marshes

Isle of Harty

Elliotts

Mocketts

Mocketts
Cottages

Sayes
Court

Sayes
Court
Cottages

Park
Farm

The
Swale

Lily
Banks

00 A B 01 C D 02 E F

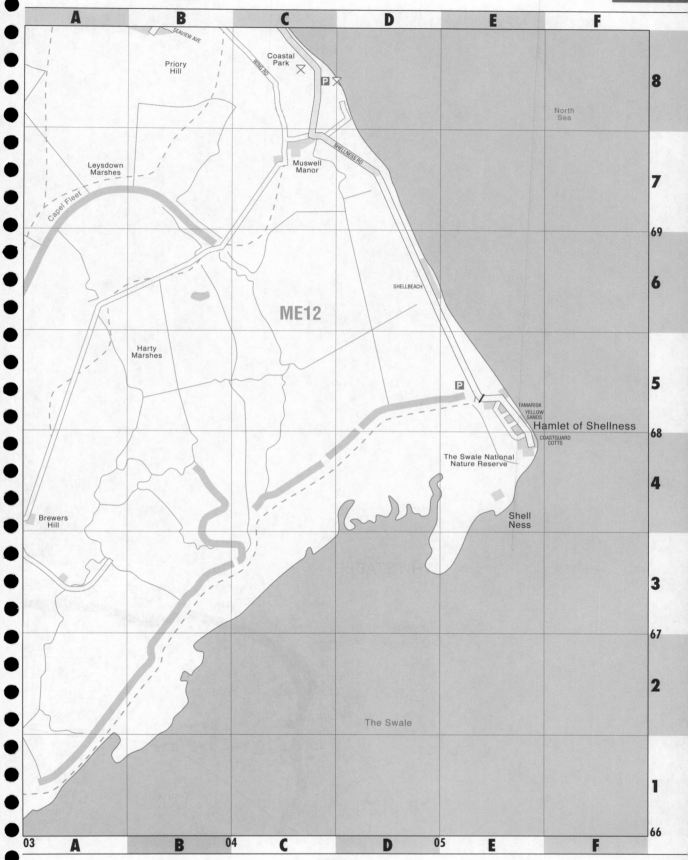

A B C D E F

SEAVIEW AVE

Priory Hill

WING RD

Coastal Park

P

North Sea

8

SHELLNESS RD

Muswell Manor

Leysdown Marshes

7

Capel Fleet

69

SHELLBEACH

6

ME12

Harty Marshes

P

5

TAMARISK

YELLOW SANDS

Hamlet of Shellness

COASTGUARD COTTS

68

The Swale National Nature Reserve

4

Shell Ness

Brewers Hill

3

67

2

The Swale

1

66

03 A B 04 C D 05 E F

41

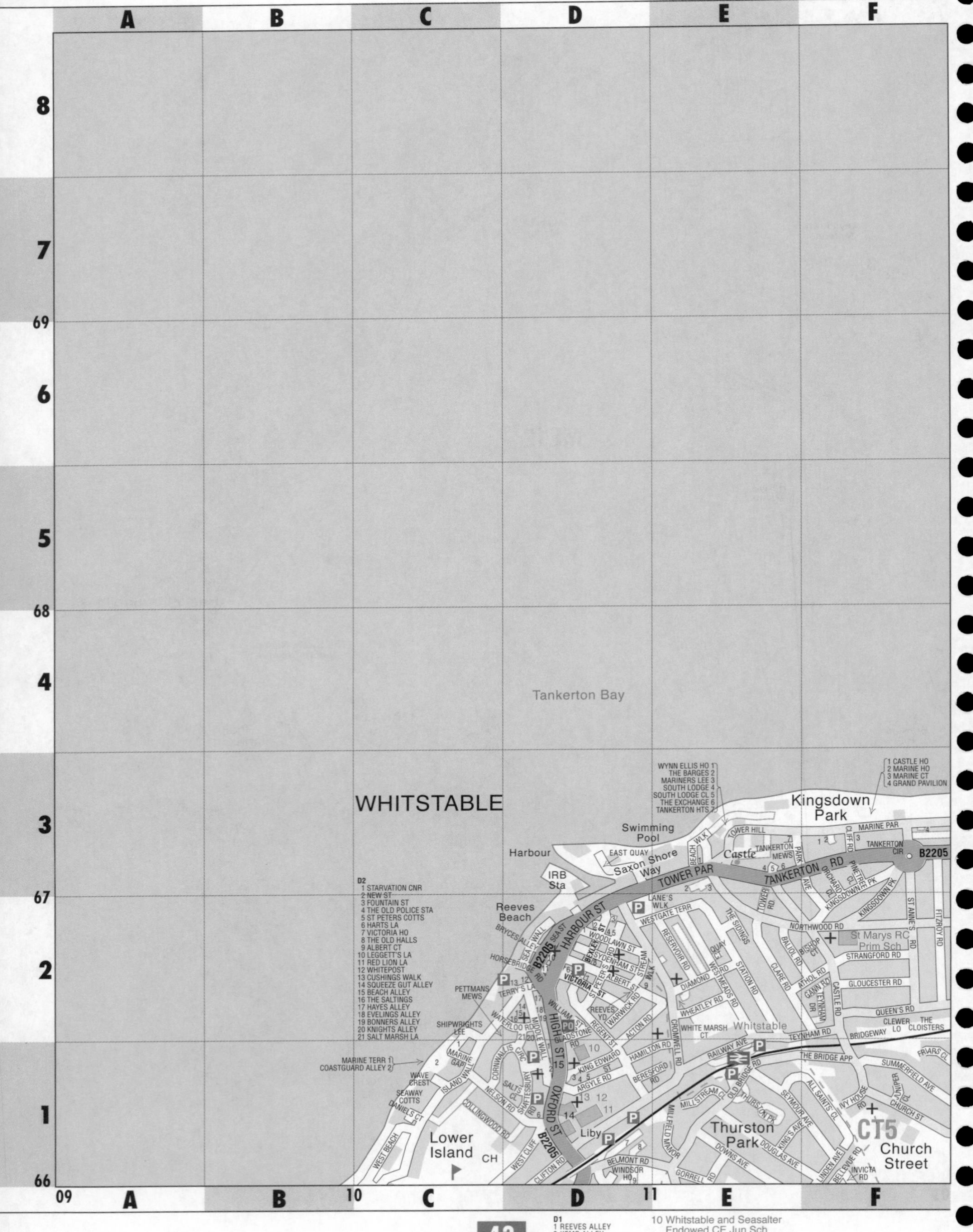

WHITSTABLE

Tankerton Bay

Kingsdown Park

1 CASTLE HO
2 MARINE HO
3 MARINE CT
4 GRAND PAVILION

WYNN ELLIS HO 1
THE BARGES 2
MARINERS LEE 3
SOUTH LODGE 4
SOUTH LODGE CL 5
THE EXCHANGE 6
TANKERTON HTS 7

Swimming Pool

Harbour

Castle

B2205

D2
1 STARVATION CNR
2 NEW ST
3 FOUNTAIN ST
4 THE OLD POLICE STA
5 ST PETERS COTTS
6 HARTS LA
7 VICTORIA HO
8 THE OLD HALLS
9 ALBERT CT
10 LEGGETT'S LA
11 RED LION LA
12 WHITEPOST
13 CUSHINGS WALK
14 SQUEEZE GUT ALLEY
15 BEACH ALLEY
16 THE SALTINGS
17 HAYES ALLEY
18 EVELINGS ALLEY
19 BONNERS ALLEY
20 KNIGHTS ALLEY
21 SALT MARSH LA

Reeves Beach

St Marys RC Prim Sch

White Marsh CT

Whitstable

Lower Island

Thurston Park

CT5
Church Street

MARINE TERR 1
COASTGUARD ALLEY 2

D1
1 REEVES ALLEY
2 KEMP ALLEY
3 SKINNER'S ALLEY
4 OYSTER MEWS
5 OXFORD MANS
6 THE OLD COAL YD
7 BELMONT YD
8 WICKETTS END

10 Whitstable and Seasalter
   Endowed CE Jun Sch
11 Westmeads Com Inf Sch
12 Whitstable Jun Sch
13 St Alphege CE Inf Sch
14 Whitstable Mus & Gallery
15 Playhouse Theatre

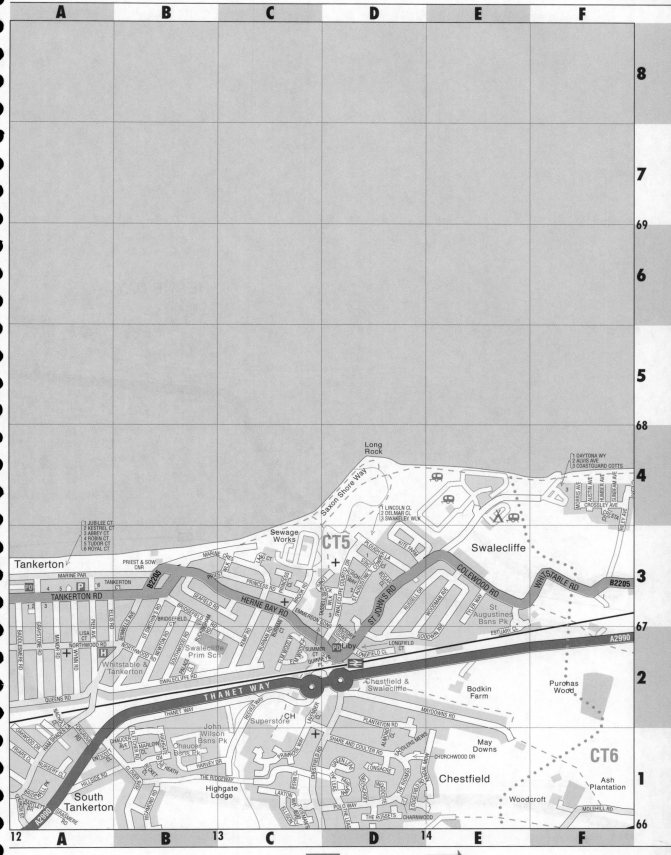

A B C D E F

8
7
69
6
5
68
4

Long Rock

1 DAYTONA WY
2 ALVIS AVE
3 COASTGUARD COTTS

Saxon Shore Way

Sewage Works

CT5

1 LINCOLN CL
2 DELMAR CL
3 SWAKELEY WLK

KITE FARM

Swalecliffe

3 MORRIS AVE
AUSTIN AVE
HUMBER AVE
CROSSLEY AVE
SUNBEAM AVE
CRESTA CL
RILEY AVE

B2205

1 JUBILEE CT
2 KESTREL CT
3 ABBEY CT
4 ROBIN CT
5 TUDOR CT
6 ROYAL CT

Tankerton

MARINE PAR

PRIEST & SOW CNR

MARINE CRES

SIG CT

PLOUGH LA

COPPE LA

COLEWOOD RD

WHITSTABLE RD

B2205

3

PO

P

TANKERTON CT

TANKERTON RD

B2205

PRIEST WLK

PRINCESS RD

PRINCESS CL

BROOK RD

SMIT

ROCK WLK

TASSELL'S

SWALECLIFFE COURT DR

CHURCH WAY

ST AUGUSTINE'S RD

ELIZABETH

ST JOHN'S RD

RUSSELL DR

WOODMAN AVE

TYLER WAY

St Augustines Bsns Pk

ESTUARY CL

67

A2990

GRAYSTONE RD

BADDLESMERE RD

MANOR RD

LISA CT

PIER AVE

ELLIS RD

NORTHWOOD RD

BENNELLS AVE

ST SWITHIN'S RD

SOUTHWOOD RD

NEWTON RD

BRIDGEFIELD RD

BRIDGEFIELD CT

BUCKINGHAM RD

KEMP RD

BURNAN RD

BURANT RD

ELM WOOD W

ELM WOOD CL

SUMMER CT

QUINNEYS PL

PO Lilby

LONGFIELD CL

LONGFIELD CT

GOODWIN AVE

A2990

HERNE BAY RD

SEAFIELD RD

EMMERSON GDNS

RECTORY GDNS

2

H

Whitstable & Tankerton

Swalecliffe Prim Sch

SWALECLIFFE RD

QUEENS RD

THANET WAY

Chestfield & Swalecliffe

Bodkin Farm

Purchas Wood

CT6

OAKWOOD DR

FRIARS CL

NURSERY CL

BRIDEWELL PK

CHURCH ST

HAM SHADES LA

FOXGROVE

ENTICOTT CL

CLOVER RISE

RICHMOND RD

CHAUCER AVE

FLETCHER RD

MARLOW CT

HIGHGATE

THE HEATH

CHAUCER Bsns Pk

John Wilson Bsns Pk

HARVEY DR

THE RIDGEWAY

Highgate Lodge

REEVES WAY

LAVENDER RD

Superstore

CH

Thanet Way

PRIMROSE WAY

CHESTFIELD RD

PLANTATION RD

SHARE AND COULTER RD

ALMOND RD

MAYDOWNS RD

SADDLERS MEWS

CHURCHWOOD DR

May Downs

Woodcroft

Ash Plantation

MOLEHILL RD

1

South Tankerton

HILLSIDE RD

BECKET

LAXTON WAY

TOYMAN'S

ELLISON CL

THE RUSSETS

CHARNWOOD

POLO WAY

THE LEAS

GREEN LEAS

FERN CL

FALCON

BEECHCROFT

LONGACRE

AVOCETTE

LODGE FIELD

KENDAL MDW

THE RIDINGS

Chestfield

66

12 A 13 B C 14 D E F

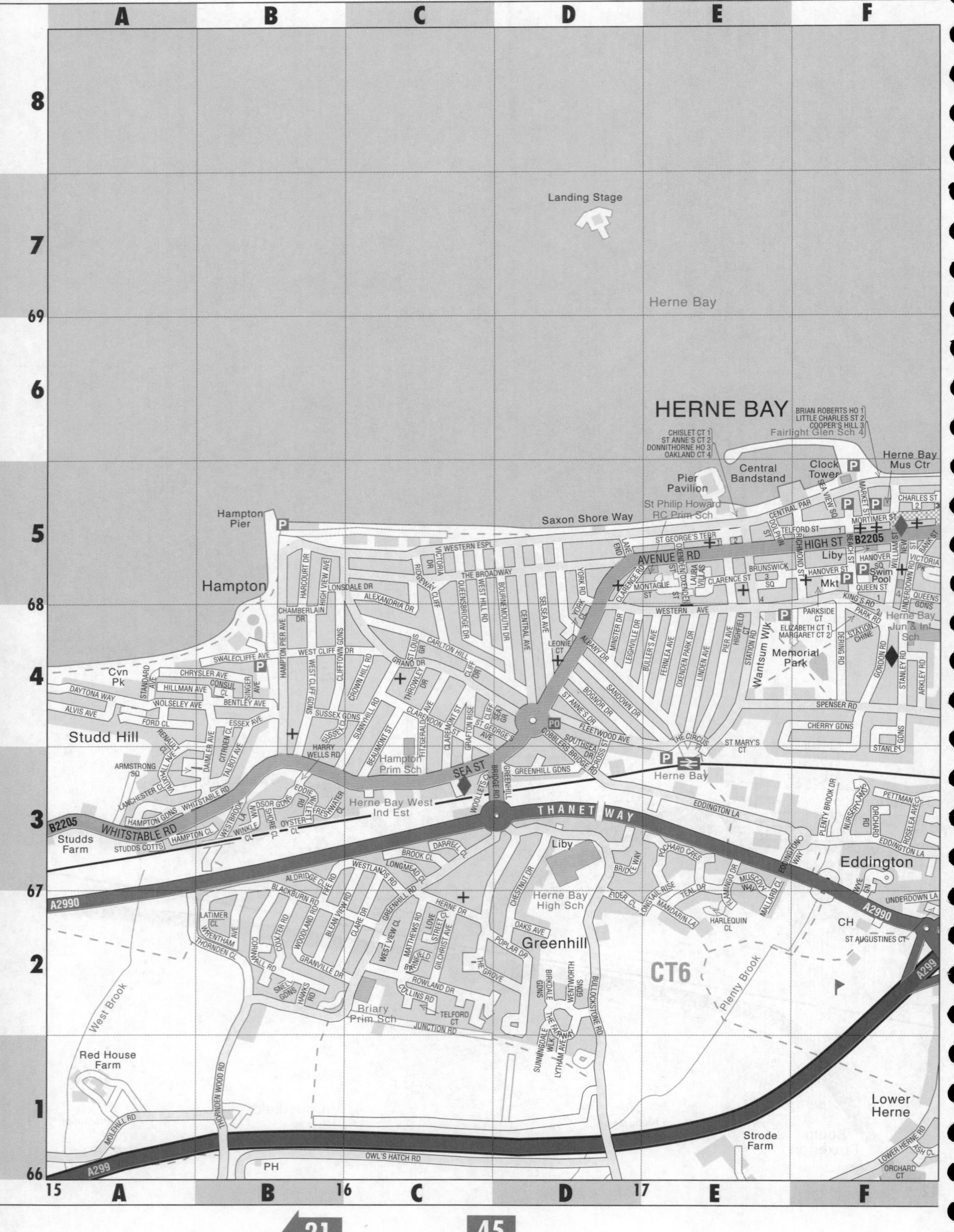

21

HERNE BAY

Herne Bay

Landing Stage

BRIAN ROBERTS HO 1
LITTLE CHARLES ST 2
COOPER'S HILL 3
Fairlight Glen Sch 4

CHISLET CT 1
ST ANNE'S CT 2
DONNITHORNE HO 3
OAKLAND CT 4

Herne Bay Mus Ctr

Pier
Pavilion

Central
Bandstand

Clock
Tower

CHARLES ST

St Philip Howard
RC Prim Sch

Saxon Shore Way

Hampton
Pier

St George's Terr

CENTRAL PAR

HIGH ST
Liby

B2205

Telford St

Hampton

AVENUE RD

Brunswick
SQ

Hanover
SQ

Swim
Pool

QUEENS
GDNS

Clarence St

Montague

Hanover ST
Mkt
QUEEN ST

Western Ave

Parkside
CT

ELIZABETH CT 1
MARGARET CT 2

Herne Bay
Jun & Inf
Sch

Cvn
Pk

STATION
CHINE

Studd Hill

Memorial
Park

CHERRY GDNS

SPENSER RD

Hampton
Prim Sch

SEA ST

THE CIRCUS

ST MARY'S
CT

PO

Herne Bay

GREENHILL GDNS

Herne Bay

Herne Bay West
Ind Est

THANET WAY

EDDINGTON LA

B2205
WHITSTABLE RD

Studds
Farm

STUDDS COTTS

HAMPTON CL

A2990

Eddington

A2990

UNDERDOWN LA

A299

West Brook

Herne Bay
High Sch

Greenhill

CH
ST AUGUSTINES CT

CT6

Plenty Brook

Briary
Prim Sch

Red House
Farm

JUNCTION RD

Lower
Herne

Strode
Farm

A299

PH

OWL'S HATCH RD

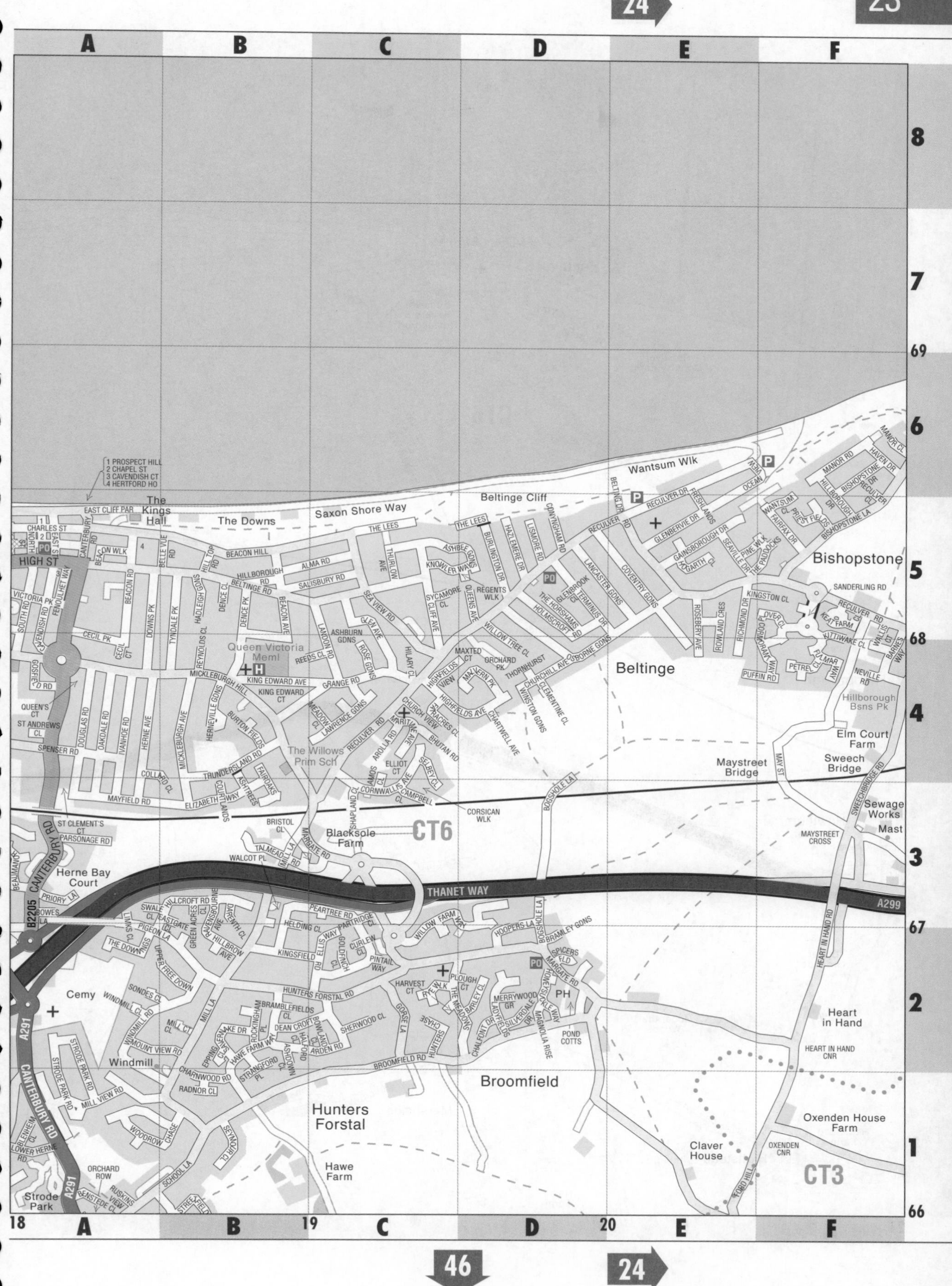
24
A
B
C
D
E
F
8
7
69
6
5
68
4
3
67
2
1
66
18
19
20
46
24
1 PROSPECT HILL
2 CHAPEL ST
3 CAVENDISH CT
4 HERTFORD HO
Wantsum Wlk
Beltinge Cliff
Saxon Shore Way
The Kings Hall
The Downs
EAST CLIFF PAR
CHARLES ST
HIGH ST
BEACON HILL
ALMA RD
SALISBURY RD
HILLBOROUGH RD
BELTINGE RD
THE LEES
RECULVER DR
RECULVER RD
GLENBERVIE DR
GAINSBOROUGH DR
FRESHLANDS
OCEAN
MANOR RD
HAVEN DR
BISHOPSTONE DR
BISHOPSTONE LA
Bishopstone
SANDERLING RD
KINGSTON CL
ROSEBERY AVE
ROWLAND CRES
RICHMOND DR
PUFFIN RD
PETREL CL
NEVILLE RD
Hillborough Bsns Pk
Elm Court Farm
Sweech Bridge
Maystreet Bridge
MAY ST
SWEECHBRIDGE RD
Sewage Works
Mast
MAYSTREET CROSS
Beltinge
LANCASTER GDNS
COVENTRY GDNS
HOLMSCROFT RD
WILLOW TREE CL
THORNHURST
CHURCHILL AVE
WINSTON GDNS
CLEMENTINE CL
CHARTWELL AVE
HIGHFIELDS AVE
BHUTAN RD
CHURCH VIEW
MARITIME AVE
ELLIOT CT
CORNWALLIS AVE
CAMPBELL
CORSICAN WLK
Queen Victoria Meml
KING EDWARD AVE
KING EDWARD CT
MICKLEBURGH HILL
GRANGE RD
LAWRENCE GDNS
RECULVER RD
The Willows Prim Sch
BURTON FIELDS
TRUNDERSLAND RD
ASHTREES
FAIROAKS
ELIZABETH WAY
COURTLANDS
MAYFIELD RD
COLLARD CL
DOUGLAS RD
OAKDALE RD
IVANHOE RD
HERNE AVE
MICKLEBURGH AVE
HERNEVILLE GDNS
SPENSER RD
ST ANDREWS CL
QUEEN'S CT
CECIL PK
VICTORIA PK
SOUTH RD
DOWNS PK
TYNDALE PK
REYNOLDS CL
HADLEIGH GDNS
DENCE PK
BEACON AVE
BOGSHOLE LA
CT6
Blacksole Farm
BRISTOL CL
SHAPLAND CL
MARGATE RD
WALCOT PL
TALMEAD RD
ST CLEMENT'S CT
PARSONAGE RD
Herne Bay Court
CANTERBURY RD
B2205
PRIORY LA
BOWES LA
THANET WAY
A299
HEART IN HAND RD
PEARTREE RD
HELDING CL
KINGSFIELD RD
PINTAIL WAY
WILLOW FARM WAY
HOOPERS LA
BRAMLEY GDNS
SPICERS FLD
HARVEST CT
PLOUGH CT
MERRYWOOD GR
PH
POND COTTS
MAGNOLIA RISE
Heart in Hand
HEART IN HAND CNR
HUNTERS FORSTAL RD
BRAMBLEFIELDS CL
SHERWOOD CL
DEAN CROFT
ARDEN RD
HUNTERS CHASE
BROOMFIELD RD
Broomfield
Hunters Forstal
Hawe Farm
Cemy
Windmill
WINDMILL RD
MOUNT VIEW RD
CHARNWOOD RD
RADNOR CL
MILL VIEW RD
STRODE PARK RD
WOODROW CHASE
SCHOOL LA
SEYMOUR CL
ORCHARD ROW
RUSKINS VIEW
Strode Park
A291
CANTERBURY RD
UPPER FREE DOWN
SONDES CL
THE DOWNINGS
PIGEON LA
HILLBROW AVE
SWALE CL
EASTGATE CL
GREEN ACRES CL
Claver House
Oxenden House Farm
OXENDEN CNR
FORD HILL
CT3

23

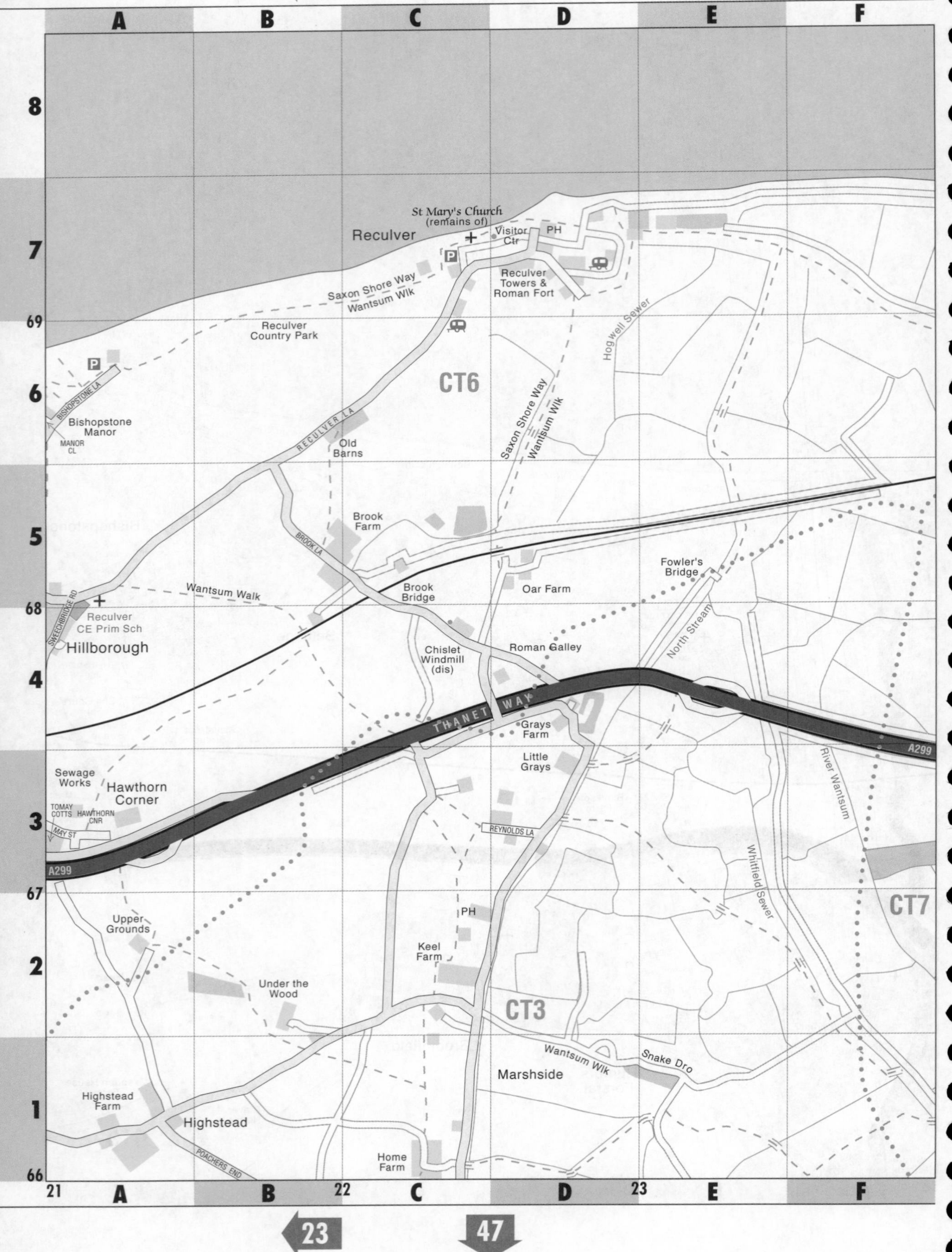
A
B
C
D
E
F
8
7
69
6
5
68
4
3
67
2
1
66
21
22
23
St Mary's Church
(remains of)
Reculver
Visitor
Ctr
PH
Reculver
Towers &
Roman Fort
Saxon Shore Way
Wantsum Wlk
Reculver
Country Park
Hogwell Sewer
CT6
BISHOPSTONE LA
Bishopstone
Manor
MANOR
CL
RECULVER LA
Old
Barns
Saxon Shore Way
Wantsum Wlk
Brook
Farm
BROOK LA
Fowler's
Bridge
SWEECHBRIDGE RD
Wantsum Walk
Brook
Bridge
Oar Farm
Reculver
CE Prim Sch
Hillborough
North Stream
Chislet
Windmill
(dis)
Roman Galley
THANET WAY
Grays
Farm
Little
Grays
A299
Sewage
Works
Hawthorn
Corner
TOMAY
COTTS
HAWTHORN
CNR
MAY ST
REYNOLDS LA
River Wantsum
A299
Whitfield Sewer
CT7
PH
Upper
Grounds
Keel
Farm
Under the
Wood
CT3
Wantsum Wlk
Snake Dro
Marshside
Highstead
Farm
Highstead
POACHERS END
Home
Farm

23
47

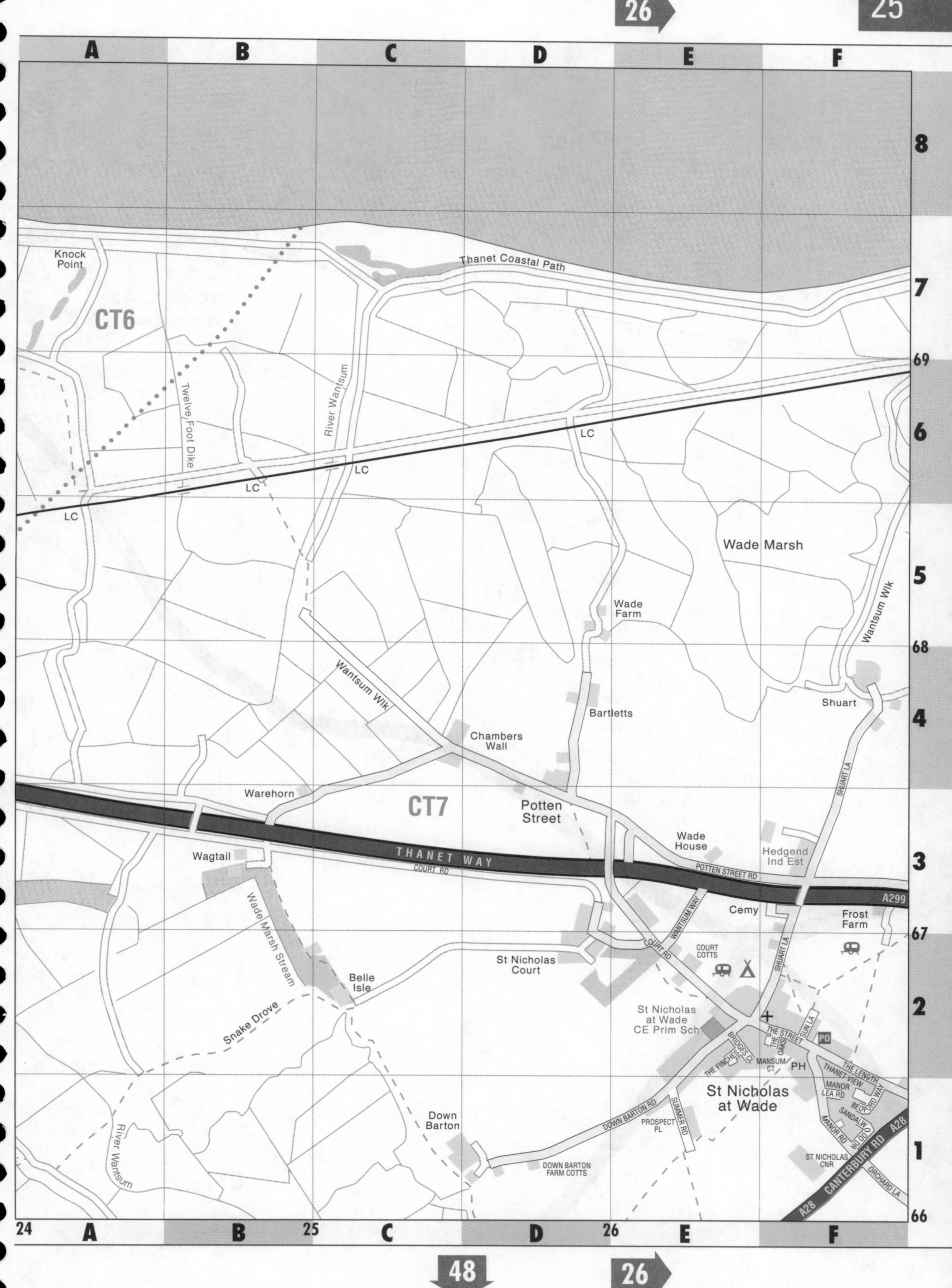

A   B   C   D   E   F

8

7

Knock
Point

CT6

Thanet Coastal Path

69

6

River Wantsum

LC

LC

LC

Twelve Foot Dike

LC

Wade Marsh

Wantsum Wlk

5

Wade
Farm

68

Wantsum Wlk

Shuart

4

Chambers
Wall

Bartletts

Shuart La

Warehorn

CT7

Potten
Street

Wade
House

Hedgend
Ind Est

3

Wagtail

THANET WAY

COURT RD

POTTEN STREET RD

Cemy

A299

Frost
Farm

67

Wade Marsh Stream

WANTSUM WAY

COURT COTTS

COURT RD

Belle
Isle

St Nicholas
Court

Shuart La

Snake Drove

St Nicholas
at Wade
CE Prim Sch

THE OAKS

SUN LA

THE STREET

PO

THE LENGTH

2

THE FINCHES CT

BRIDGES CT

MANSUM
CT

PH

THANET VIEW

MANOR
LEA RD

BERY

THANET WAY

River Wantsum

Down
Barton

DOWN BARTON RD

SUMNER RD

PROSPECT
PL

St Nicholas
at Wade

SANDALW

MANOR RD

ST NICHOLAS
CNR

CANTERBURY RD

A28

A28

ORCHARD LA

Down Barton
Farm Cotts

1

66

24   A   B   25   C   D   26   E   F

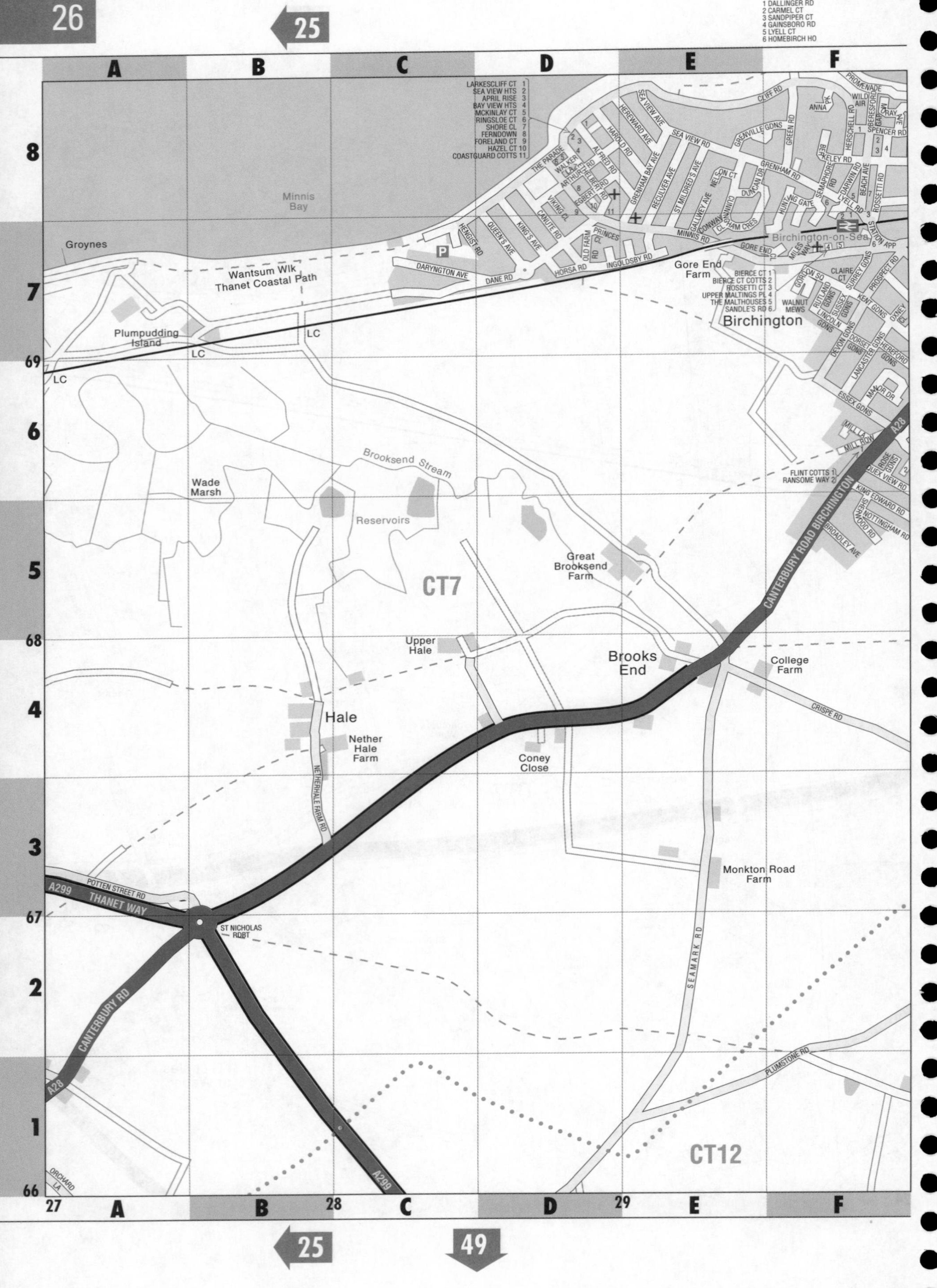
25
F8
1 DALLINGER RD
2 CARMEL CT
3 SANDPIPER CT
4 GAINSBORO RD
5 LYELL CT
6 HOMEBIRCH HO
7 BERESFORD CT
A
B
C
D
E
F
8
7
69
6
5
68
4
3
67
2
1
66
LARKESCLIFF CT 1
SEA VIEW HTS 2
APRIL RISE 3
BAY VIEW HTS 4
MCKINLAY CT 5
RINGSLOE CT 6
SHORE CL 7
FERNDOWN 8
FORELAND CT 9
HAZEL CT 10
COASTGUARD COTTS 11
Minnis Bay
Groynes
Wantsum Wlk
Thanet Coastal Path
Plumpudding Island
LC
THE PARADE
WALKER LA
ARTHUR RD
EGBERT RD
ALFRED RD
ETHELBERT RD
HAROLD RD
HEREWARD AVE
SEA VIEW AVE
SEA VIEW RD
GRENHAM BAY AVE
RECULVER AVE
ST MILDRED'S AVE
GALLWEY AVE
CONWAY CL
CUNNINGHAM CRES
DUNCAN DR
NELSON CT
GRENHAM RD
GRENVILLE GDNS
GREEN RD
CLIFF RD
HUNTING GATE
SEMAPHORE RD
BEACH AVE
DARWIN RD
LYELL RD
ROSSETTI RD
HERSCHELL RD
BERESFORD GAP
SPENCER RD
MURRAY AVE
PROMENADE
WILD AIR
ANNA PK
BERKELEY RD
VIKING CL
CANUTE RD
KING'S AVE
QUEEN'S AVE
HENGIST RD
DARYNGTON AVE
DANE RD
HORSA RD
OLD FARM RD
PRINCES CL
INGOLDSBY RD
MINNIS RD
GORE END CL
MILES WAY
STATION APP
Birchington-on-Sea
Gore End Farm
BIERCE CT 1
BIERCE CT COTTS 2
ROSSETTI CT 3
UPPER MALTINGS PL 4
THE MALTHOUSES 5
SANDLE'S RD 6
WALNUT MEWS
GORDON SQ
RUTLAND GDNS
CLAIRE CT
SURREY GDNS
SUSSEX GDNS
PROSPECT RD
KENT GDNS
LINCOLN GDNS
DEVON GDNS
DORSET GDNS
LANCASTER GDNS
HEREFORD GDNS
ESSEX GDNS
MANOR DR
MILL LA
MILL ROW
Birchington
Wade Marsh
Brooksend Stream
Reservoirs
CT7
Great Brooksend Farm
FLINT COTTS 1
RANSOME WAY 2
ROSE GDNS
QUEX VIEW RD
KING EDWARD RD
SHERWOOD RD
NOTTINGHAM RD
BROADLEY AVE
A28
CANTERBURY ROAD BIRCHINGTON
Upper Hale
Brooks End
College Farm
CRISPE RD
Hale
Nether Hale Farm
NETHERHALE FARM RD
Coney Close
Monkton Road Farm
SEAMARK RD
POTTEN STREET RD
A299
THANET WAY
ST NICHOLAS RDBT
CANTERBURY RD
PLUMSTONE RD
CT12
ORCHARD LA
27
28
29

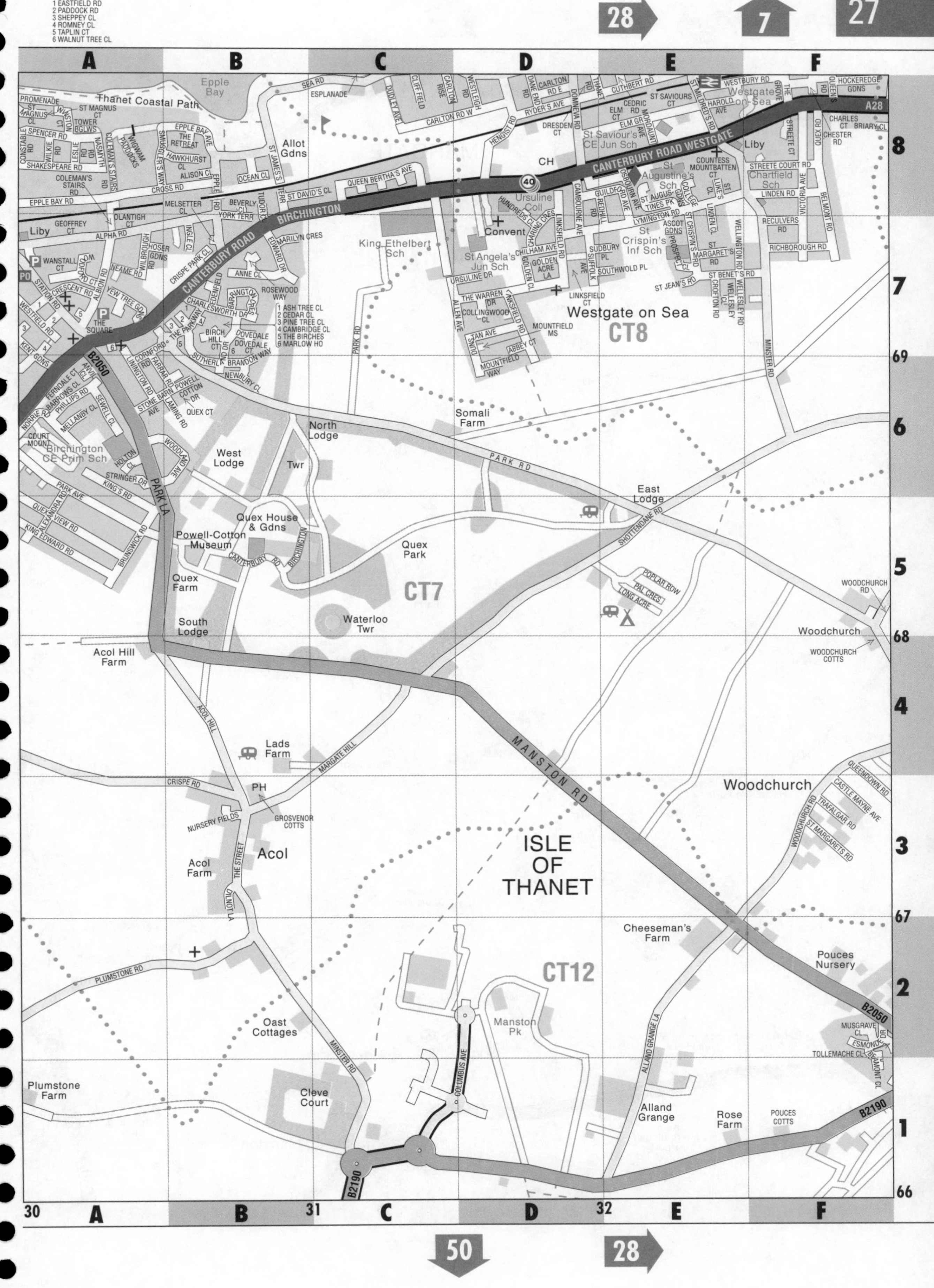

27 | 7

B8
1 OLD CROSSING RD
2 CAMELLIA CL
3 ROSELAWN GDNS
4 BALMORAL RD
5 EDINBURGH WLK
6 GLEBE GDNS

MARGATE

CANTERBURY ROAD

MARGATE

A28

B2052

GEORGE V AVE

B2052

HARTSDOWN RD

A254

COLLEGE RD

B2052

A255

St James'
Park Rd

Mutrix Rd

Garranted

Hartsdown
Tech Coll

Tivoli Rd

Salmestone
Prim Sch

Alexandra
Rd

Ulster
Rd

Oast
Ct

Queen
Elizabeth the
Queen Mother

H

Briary Cl

Michelle
Gdns

Alicia Ave

Noble
Gdns

Oak Tree
Gr

Dent-de-Lion
Ct

Edinburgh
Cres

Maynard Ave

Waverley Rd

Garrard Ave

Westfield Rd

Lavender Cl

Swallow
Cl

Heather

Honeysuckle
Cl

Garlinge Prim Sch

Salmestone
Grange

St Gregorys
RC Prim Sch

Cemy

Crem

Nash La

Nash
Court

Ramsgate Rd

Rowe Cl

Farley Rd

Elmley Way

Chapel
Hill Cl

Garlinge

Dent-de-Lion
Rd

Welsdene
Rd

Lenham
Gdns

Glebe
Rd

Lissle Ave

Ellington
Ave

Brooke Ave

Birds Ave

Fulham Ave

Kingston Ave

Caxton Rd

Chapel Rd

Allot Gdns

Kingfisher
Cl

Stephen's

8

7

69

6

5

68

4

67

3

2

1

66

Dent-de-Lion
Farm

Zeila Farm

California

Twenties

Hill View

Shottendane Rd

Hengrove
Farm

Shottendane Rd

CT9

Chapel Bottom

Chalkhole
Farm

Flete

Piggeries

Norfolk Rd

Victoria
Rd

Wellington Rd

Lydden
Farm

Red House
Farm

Flete Rd

Shottendane
Farm

Knold Pk

Pirbank
Gdns

Jacob Cl

Sycamore Cl

Wks

Halfmile Ride

Nash
Farm

Westwood
Ind Est

Enterprise
Wy

Continental App

Retreat
Farm

Woodchurch Rd

Westgate Ave

CT7

Grove Villas

Manston Rd

Vincent
Farm

Vincent Rd

Flete Farm

Manston Court Rd

Lydden

Caravan
Park

Valley Rd

Coldswood Rd

Coldswood
Farm

Rose
Cotts

Haine

The Nook
Hackthorn Farm

Queendown Rd

The
Bungalow

Nursery

Masts

Fleete
Court Farm

Preston Rd

Haine Rd

Haine
Cottage

B2050

B2190

Bell-Davies
Dr

RAF Manston Spitfire &
Hurricane Meml Mus

Manston Court
Cotts

CT12

Manston
Court

Wood Farm

Caravan
Park

Spratling St

Spratling La

Saddlers
Ms

St Johns

Spratling
Street
Farm

Manston Rd

P

P

P

Kent
International
Airport

Worlds
Wonder

The Green

St Catherine's

Elm Gr

The Leys

Highlands Glade

Greensole La

Manston

B2050

Grove
Farm

PH

Dargor
La

A256

Haine
Ind Est

Leigh Rd

Olietta Rd

33 | A | 34 | B | C | 35 | D | E | F

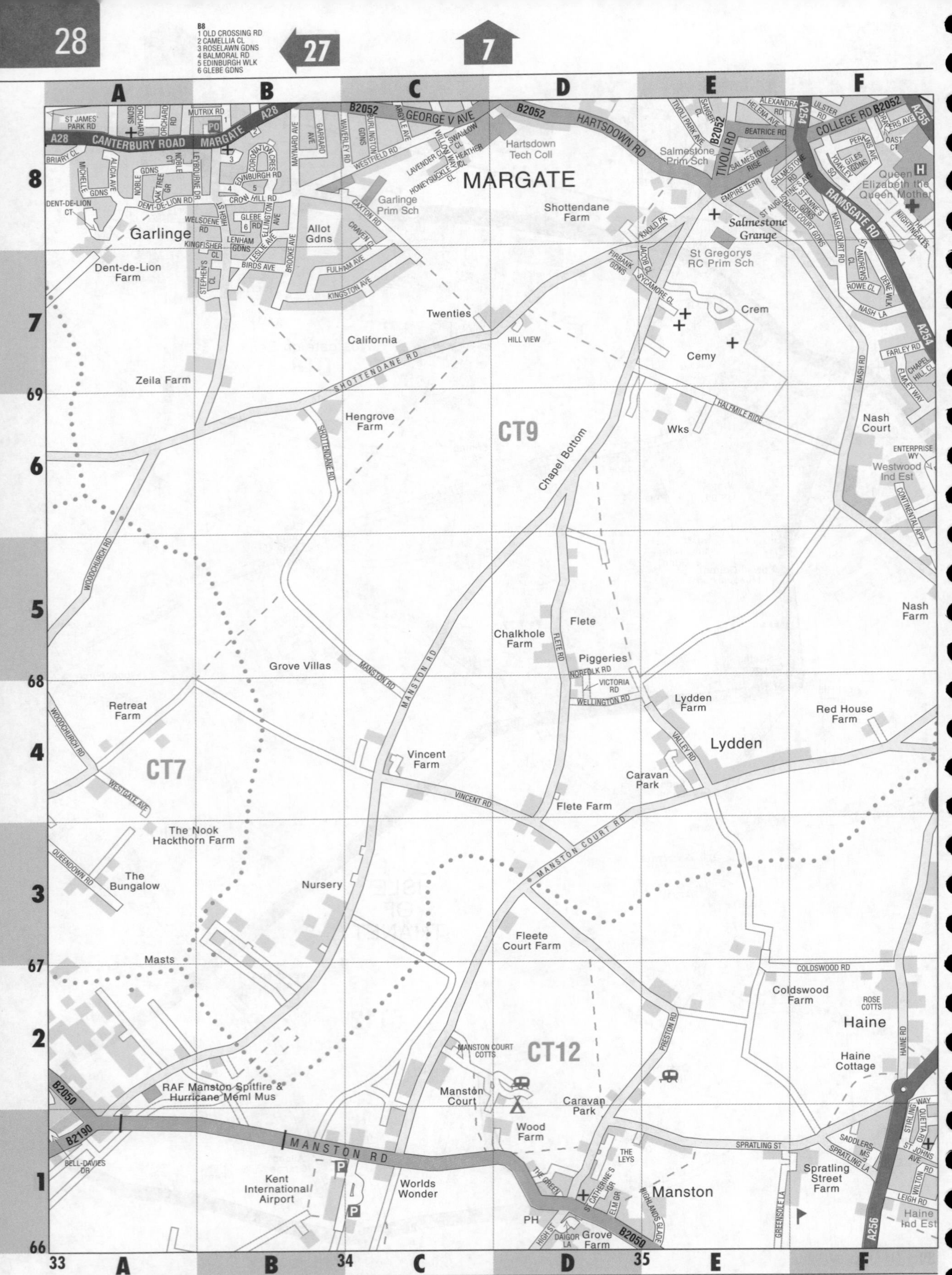

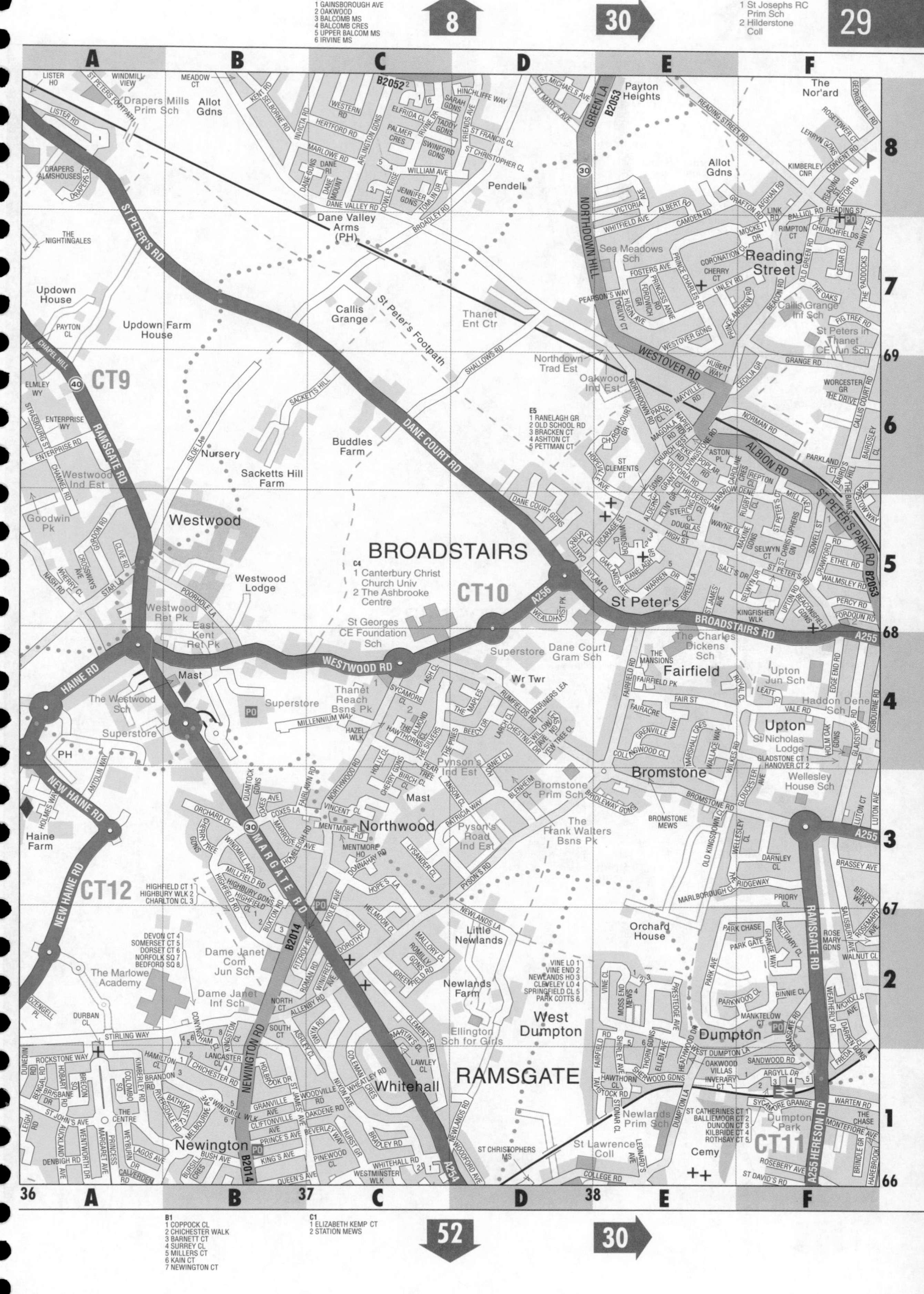

29
8
30
52
C8
1 GAINSBOROUGH AVE
2 OAKWOOD
3 BALCOMB MS
4 BALCOMB CRES
5 UPPER BALCOM MS
6 IRVINE MS
F5
1 St Josephs RC Prim Sch
2 Hilderstone Coll
A
B
C
D
E
F
Drapers Mills Prim Sch
Allot Gdns
Payton Heights
The Nor'ard
Pendell
Dane Valley Arms (PH)
Sea Meadows Sch
Reading Street
Updown House
Callis Grange
St Peter's Footpath
Thanet Ent Ctr
Callis Grange Inf Sch
St Peters in Thanet CE Jun Sch
Updown Farm House
CT9
Northdown Trad Est
Oakwood Ind Est
E5
1 RANELAGH GR
2 OLD SCHOOL RD
3 BRACKEN CT
4 ASHTON CT
5 PETTMAN CT
Buddles Farm
Nursery
Sacketts Hill Farm
Westwood Ind Est
Goodwin Pk
Westwood
BROADSTAIRS
C4
1 Canterbury Christ Church Univ
2 The Ashbrooke Centre
CT10
Westwood Lodge
St Peter's
Westwood Ret Pk
East Kent Ret Pk
St Georges CE Foundation Sch
Superstore
Dane Court Gram Sch
The Charles Dickens Sch
Fairfield
Upton Jun Sch
Mast
The Westwood Sch
Thanet Reach Bsns Pk
Wr Twr
Haddon Dene Sch
Upton
St Nicholas Lodge
Superstore
PH
Pynson's Ind Est
Bromstone
Wellesley House Sch
Bromstone Prim Sch
Mast
Northwood
The Frank Walters Bsns Pk
Pyson's Road Ind Est
Haine Farm
CT12
HIGHFIELD CT 1
HIGHBURY WLK 2
CHARLTON CL 3
Little Newlands
Orchard House
DEVON CT 4
SOMERSET CT 5
DORSET CT 6
NORFOLK SQ 7
BEDFORD SQ 8
Dame Janet Com Jun Sch
The Marlowe Academy
Dame Janet Inf Sch
Newlands Farm
VINE LO 1
VINE END 2
NEWLANDS HO 3
CLEVELEY LO 4
SPRINGFIELD CL 5
PARK COTTS 6
West Dumpton
Dumpton
Ellington Sch for Girls
RAMSGATE
Whitehall
ST CATHERINES CT 1
BALLIEMOOR CT 2
DUNOON CT 3
KILBRIDE CT 4
ROTHSAY CT 5
Dumpton Park
Newlands Prim Sch
Newington
St Lawrence Coll
Cemy
CT11
ST CHRISTOPHERS MS
ST PETER'S RD
DANE COURT RD
RAMSGATE RD
WESTWOOD RD
BROADSTAIRS RD
NORTHDOWN HILL
WESTOVER RD
ALBION RD
ST PETER'S PARK RD
HAINE RD
NEW HAINE RD
MARGATE RD
NEWINGTON RD
RAMSGATE RD
A255 HERESON RD
A255
A256
A254
B2014
B2052
B2053
36
37
38
66
67
68
69
1
2
3
4
5
6
7
8
B1
1 COPPOCK CL
2 CHICHESTER WALK
3 BARNETT CT
4 SURREY CL
5 MILLERS CT
6 KAIN CT
7 NEWINGTON CT
C1
1 ELIZABETH KEMP CT
2 STATION MEWS

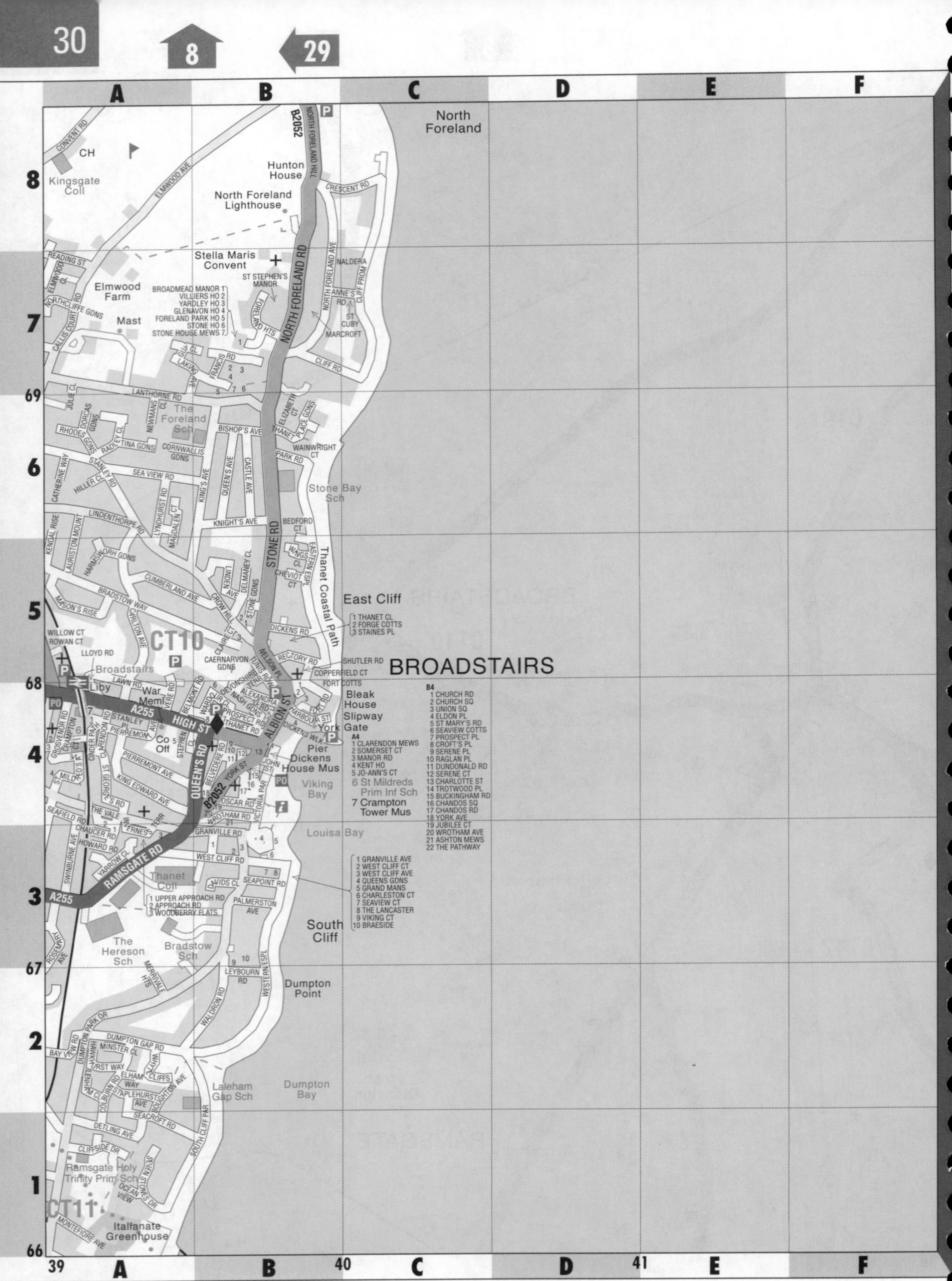

North Foreland

CH
Kingsgate Coll

Hunton House

North Foreland Lighthouse

Stella Maris Convent

St Stephen's Manor

Elmwood Farm

BROADMEAD MANOR 1
VILLIERS HO 2
YARDLEY HO 3
GLENAVON HO 4
FORELAND PARK HO 5
STONE HO 6
STONE HOUSE MEWS 7

Mast

NALDERA

St CUBY
MARCROFT

The Foreland Sch

Stone Bay Sch

East Cliff

1 THANET CL
2 FORGE COTTS
3 STAINES PL

CT10

Broadstairs

War Meml

SHUTLER RD
COPPERFIELD CT
FORT COTTS

BROADSTAIRS

Bleak House
Slipway Gate

Pier
Dickens House Mus

Viking Bay

Louisa Bay

South Cliff

Dumpton Point

Dumpton Bay

Thanet Coll

Laleham Gap Sch

Ramsgate Holy Trinity Prim Sch

CT11

Italianate Greenhouse

A4
1 CLARENDON MEWS
2 SOMERSET CT
3 MANOR RD
4 KENT HO
5 JO-ANN'S CT
6 St Mildreds Prim Inf Sch
7 Crampton Tower Mus

B4
1 CHURCH RD
2 CHURCH SQ
3 UNION SQ
4 ELDON PL
5 ST MARY'S RD
6 SEAVIEW COTTS
7 PROSPECT PL
8 CROFT'S PL
9 SERENE PL
10 RAGLAN PL
11 DUNDONALD RD
12 SERENE CT
13 CHARLOTTE ST
14 TROTWOOD PL
15 BUCKINGHAM RD
16 CHANDOS SQ
17 CHANDOS RD
18 YORK AVE
19 JUBILEE CT
20 WROTHAM AVE
21 ASHTON MEWS
22 THE PATHWAY

1 GRANVILLE AVE
2 WEST CLIFF CT
3 WEST CLIFF AVE
4 QUEENS GDNS
5 GRAND MANS
6 CHARLESTON CT
7 SEAVIEW CT
8 THE LANCASTER
9 VIKING CT
10 BRAESIDE

The Hereson Sch

Bradstow Sch

1 UPPER APPROACH RD
2 APPROACH RD
3 WOODBERRY FLATS

West Kent STREET ATLAS

Grid columns: A B C D E F
Grid rows: 8 7 65 6 5 64 4 3 63 2 1 62
Grid references bottom: 73 A B 74 C D 75 E F 62

ME1 · ROCHESTER · ME4 · CHATHAM · ME5

Nashenden Farm
Nine Acre Wood
Little Monk Wood
Well Wood
Barn Wood
Monk Wood
Gorse Wood
Upper Nashenden Farm
Burham Hill Farm
Burham Common
North Downs Way
COMMON RD
PH
Syle Wood
Middle Hill
Bridge Woods
Middlehill Wood
Buckmore Park International Kart Circuit
Lord Leas
MAIDSTONE RD
ROCHESTER RD 1
ASHLEIGH GDNS 2
Blue Bell Hill
Impton Wood
Crem
Walderslade
Tunbury Prim Sch
Marlow Copse
Hepplewhite Mews
Podkin Wood
Tunbury Ave

M2
MAIDSTONE RD
PILOT RD
B2097
SIR EVELYN RD
HORWOOD CL
TADLEY CT
WAKE RD
HM Prison
SYLEWOOD CL
The Thomas Aveling Liby Sch
Warren Wood Com Prim Sch
FRISTON WAY
BEDGEBURY CL
BEATTY RD
ARETHUSA RD
AJAX RD
LEANDER RD
ORION RD
PENNANT RD
EMERALD CL
ESTRELLA CL
BARKIS CL
APPLEBY CL
CITY WAY
A229
DAY CL
GERRARD AVE
GRAFTON AVE
JACKSON AVE
DOWNER CT
HUNTSMAN'S CNR
Chatham Gram Sch for Boys
Chatham South Sch
THORNDIKE
THORNDIKE HO
MAIDSTONE RD
A230
PARK RD
COLCHESTER AVE
ROOSEVELT AVE
EDEN CL
CHERBOURG CRES
WALLACE RD
DUVAL DR
ST STEPHENS MEWS
WILSON AVE
ARGYLE CL
THE RIDGEWAY
ME4
A230
HORSTED WAY
A229
PRIMROSE CL
Fort Horsted
MidKent Coll
CHATHAM
ALAMEIN AVE
DUNKIRK DR
TOBRUK WAY
ARNHEM DR
WATFIELD RD
BURMA WAY
CHURCHILL AVE
Ridge Meadow Prim Sch
Horsted Farm
LONGDOWN HO
THE HAWTHORNS
AMETHYST AVE
CROSSWAY
GREENWAY
VALE DR
WEST DR
SHIRLEY AVE
Superstore
Horsted Ret Pk
Horsted Jun & Inf Schs
Superstores
Hotel
Factories
Rochester Airport
Rochester Airport Ind Est
LANKESTER PARKER RD
FORWARD WAY
LAKER RD
ROCHESTER RD
MAIDSTONE RD
A229
B2097
Wks
Superstore
BRADFIELDS AVE W
Liby
BECKLEY MEWS
Greenacre Sch
MYRTLE CRES
GORSE AVE
HEATHER
WEEDS WOOD RD
KINGS OAK MEWS
Oaklands Inf & Jun Sch
SPEEDWELL AVE
LARKSPUR RD
CHESTNUT AVE
OAKLAND
PRINCES AVE
WINCHESTER AVE
GLANTON GDNS
MANOR RD
SNOD
ME5
Taddington Wood
Kit Hill
MARSTON WLK
SINDAL SHAW HO
VICTORIA RD
WOODLANDS CT
WALDER BY PASS
VILLAGE BY PASS
HALLSFIELD RD
MAIDSTONE RD
MAIDSTONE RD
TADDINGTON WOODS
WALDERS AVE WOODS
ROBIN HOOD LANE (LOWER)
ROBIN HOOD LANE (UPPER)
GLENEAGLES CT
FORESTERS CL
MERCER CT
LAURIE GRAY AVE
WARREN RD
MILL LA
CHATHAM
M2
A229

E4
1 LAVENDER CL
2 ASPEN WAY
3 HONEYSUCKLE CL
4 GENTIAN CL

F4
1 MALLOW WAY
2 JASMINE CL
3 HAREBELL CL
4 ROSEMARY CL
5 LINDEN HO
6 OAK HO

F5
1 SAFFRON WAY
2 WILLOW HO
3 PINE HO
4 ROWAN HO
5 HAWTHORN HO
6 BLEAKWOOD RD
7 Walderslade Girls Sch

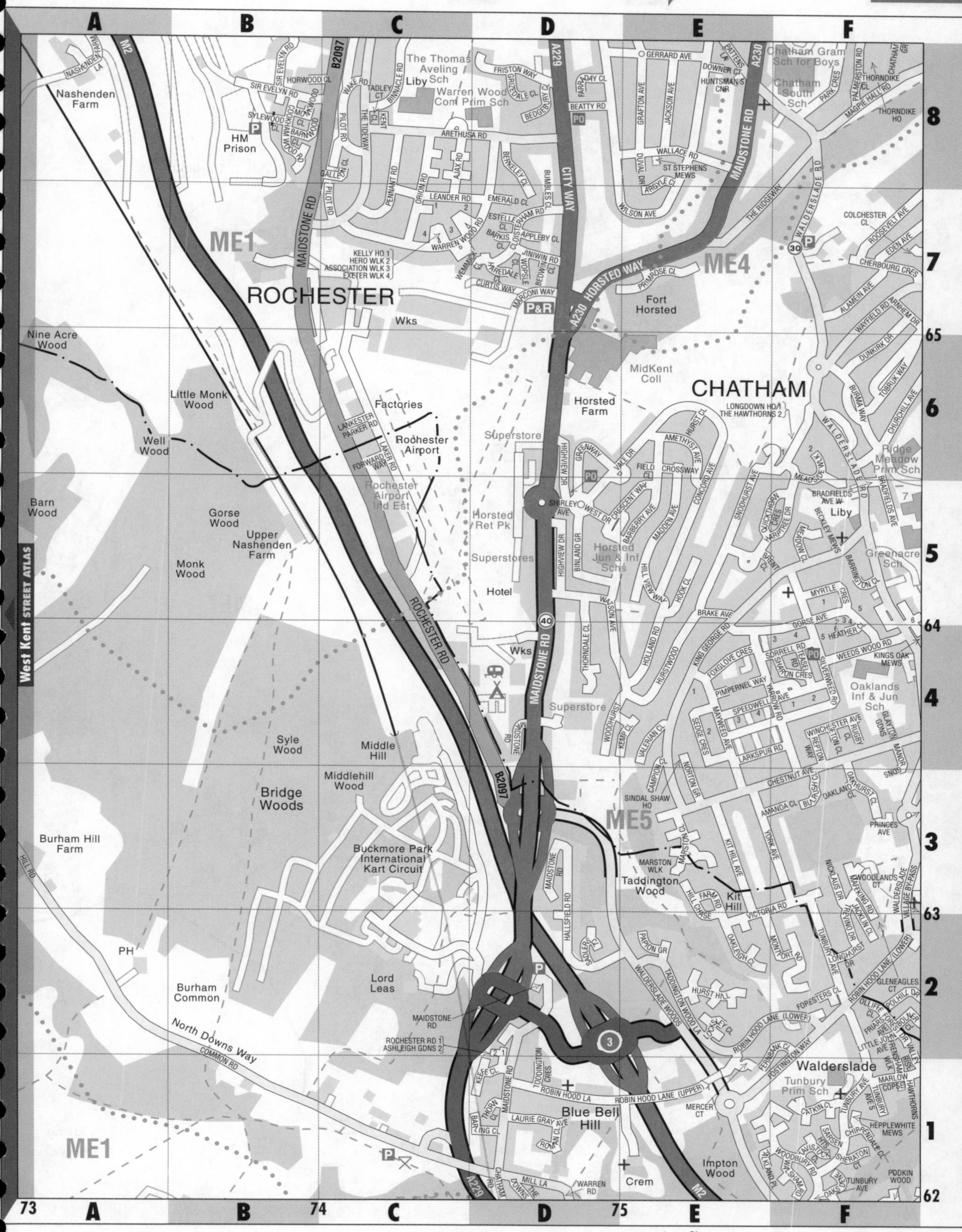

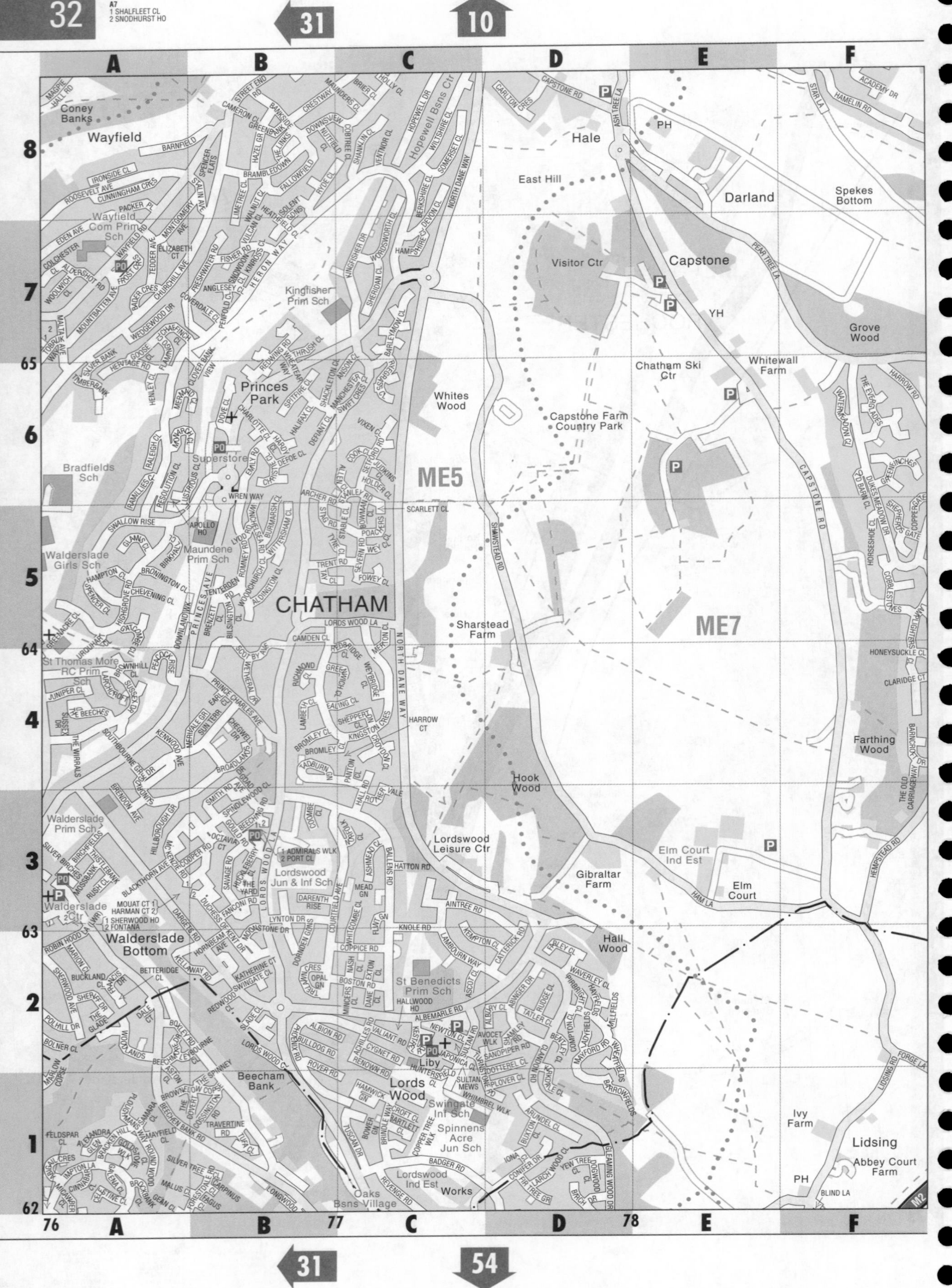
Coney Banks
Wayfield
Hale
East Hill
Darland
Spekes Bottom
Visitor Ctr
Capstone
YH
Grove Wood
Kingfisher Prim Sch
Hopewell Bsns Ctr
Wayfield Com Prim Sch
Chatham Ski Ctr
Whitewall Farm
Princes Park
Whites Wood
Capstone Farm Country Park
Superstore
Bradfields Sch
ME5
Apollo HO
Maundene Prim Sch
Walderslade Girls Sch
CHATHAM
Sharstead Farm
ME7
St Thomas More RC Prim Sch
Farthing Wood
Hook Wood
Walderslade Prim Sch
Lordswood Leisure Ctr
Elm Court Ind Est
Lordswood Jun & Inf Sch
Gibraltar Farm
Elm Court
Walderslade Ctr
Walderslade Bottom
Hall Wood
St Benedicts Prim Sch
Beecham Bank
Lords Wood
Swingate Inf Sch
Spinnens Acre Jun Sch
Ivy Farm
Lidsing
Abbey Court Farm
Lordswood Ind Est
Works
Oaks Bsns Village
CAPSTONE RD
NORTH DANE WAY
LORDS WOOD LA
SHAWSTEAD RD
PRINCES AVE
HAM LA
PEAR TREE LA
ASH TREE LA
LIDSING RD
BADGER RD
76
77
78
62
63
64
65
1
2
3
4
5
6
7
8
A
B
C
D
E
F

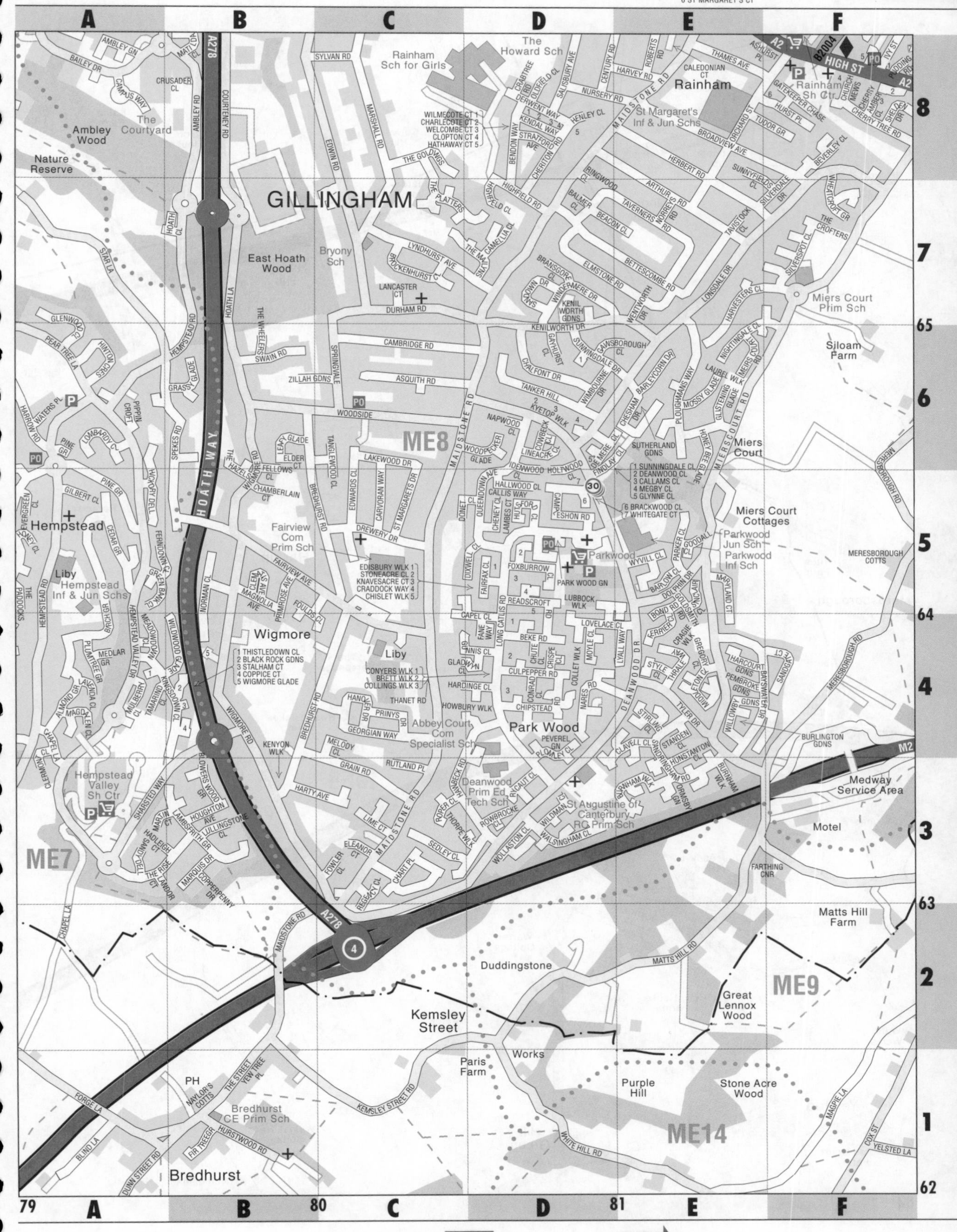

55

34

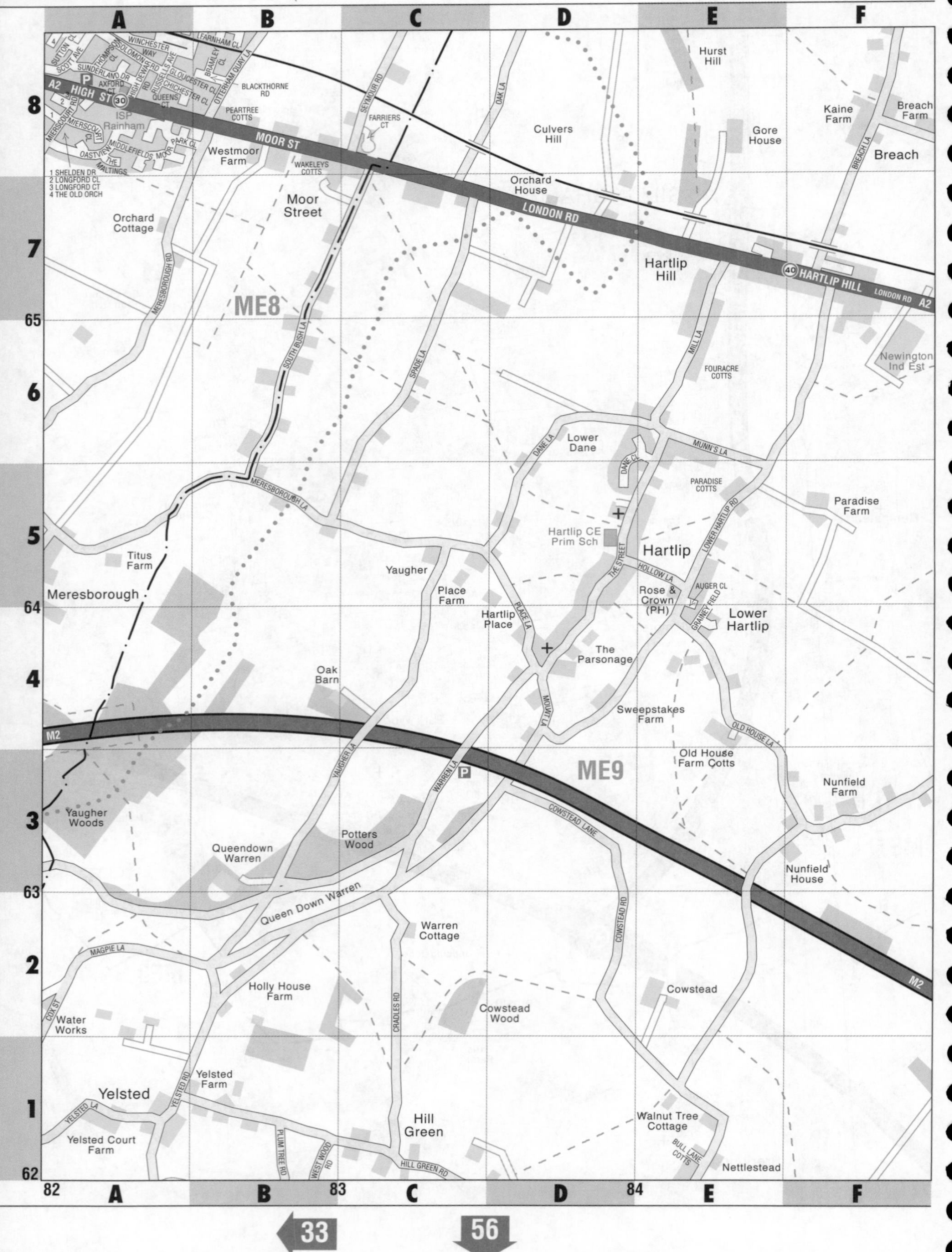
A B C D E F
8
7
65
6
5
64
4
3
63
2
1
62
82 83 84
A2 HIGH ST
MOOR ST
LONDON RD
HARTLIP HILL
LONDON RD A2
M2
ISP Rainham
Westmoor Farm
Moor Street
Orchard Cottage
ME8
ME9
Culvers Hill
Orchard House
Hurst Hill
Gore House
Kaine Farm
Breach Farm
Breach
Hartlip Hill
Newington Ind Est
FOURACRE COTTS
Lower Dane
PARADISE COTTS
Paradise Farm
Hartlip CE Prim Sch
Hartlip
Titus Farm
Meresborough
Yaugher
Place Farm
Hartlip Place
Rose & Crown (PH)
Lower Hartlip
The Parsonage
Oak Barn
Sweepstakes Farm
Old House Farm Cotts
Nunfield Farm
Yaugher Woods
Potters Wood
Queendown Warren
Queen Down Warren
Nunfield House
Warren Cottage
Holly House Farm
Cowstead Wood
Cowstead
Water Works
Yelsted Farm
Yelsted
Hill Green
Walnut Tree Cottage
Yelsted Court Farm
Nettlestead
MERESBOROUGH RD
SOUTH BUSH LA
MERESBOROUGH LA
SPADE LA
OAK LA
SEYMOUR RD
DANE LA
DANE CL
MILL LA
MUNN'S LA
LOWER HARTLIP RD
THE STREET
HOLLOW LA
AUGER CL
GRAINEY FIELD
PLACE LA
MOUNT LA
OLD HOUSE LA
YAUGHER LA
WARREN LA
COWSTEAD LANE
COWSTEAD RD
BREACH LA
MAGPIE LA
COX ST
CRADLES RD
YELSTED RD
YELSTED LA
PLUM TREE RD
WEST WOOD RD
HILL GREEN RD
BULL LANE COTTS
BLACKTHORNE RD
PEARTREE COTTS
FARRIERS CT
WAKELEYS COTTS
WINCHESTER WAY
FARNHAM CL
SUTTON CL
SCOTT AVE
THOMPSON CL
SOLOMON RD
SUNDERLAND DR
AXFORD CT
HIGH DEWAR RD
RUSSELLS AVE
GLOUCESTER CL
CHICHESTER CL
QUEENS CT
BRAMLEY CL
OTTERHAM QUAY LA
MIERSCOURT RD
MIERSCOURT CL
OASTVIEW
MIDDLEFIELDS
MOOR PARK CL
THE MALTINGS
1 SHELDEN DR
2 LONGFORD CL
3 LONGFORD CT
4 THE OLD ORCH

13
36

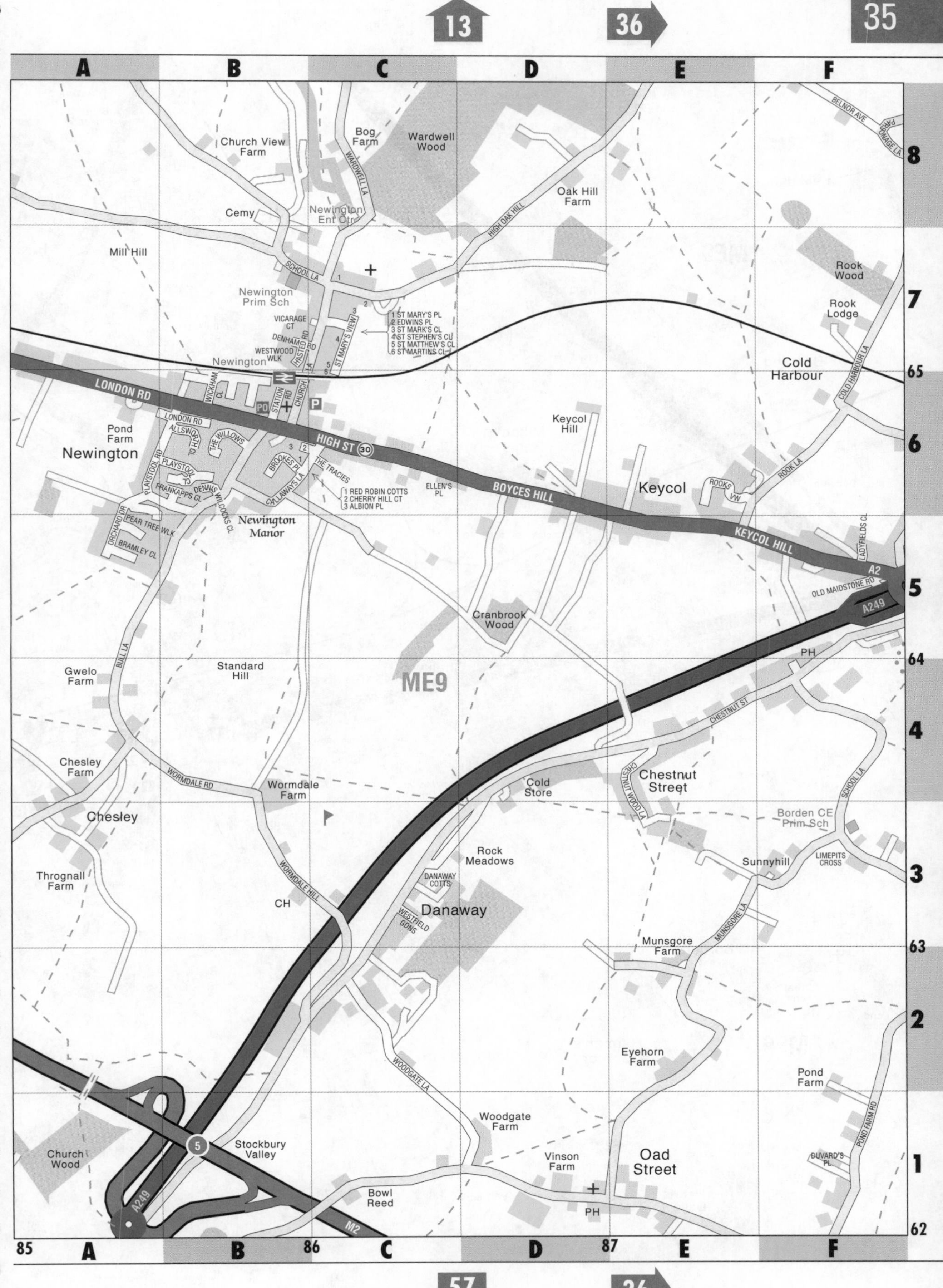
A
B
C
D
E
F
8
7
65
6
5
64
4
3
63
2
1
62
85
86
87
Church View Farm
Bog Farm
Wardwell Wood
WARDWELL LA
Oak Hill Farm
HIGH OAK HILL
BELNOR AVE
Cemy
Newington Ent Ctre
Mill Hill
SCHOOL LA
Newington Prim Sch
Rook Wood
Rook Lodge
VICARAGE CT
DENHAM RD
WESTWOOD WLK
PASTEAD RD
ST MARY'S VIEW
1 ST MARY'S PL
2 EDWINS PL
3 ST MARK'S CL
4 ST STEPHEN'S CL
5 ST MATTHEW'S CL
6 ST MARTINS CL
Newington
Cold Harbour
COLD HARBOUR LA
LONDON RD
WICKHAM CL
STATION RD
CHURCH LA
PO
P
HIGH ST
30
Pond Farm
Newington
ALLSWORTH CL
THE WILLOWS
PLAYSTOOL RD
PLAYSTOOL CL
FRANKAPPS CL
DENNIS
BROOKES PL
CALLAWAYS LA
THE TRACIES
1 RED ROBIN COTTS
2 CHERRY HILL CT
3 ALBION PL
ELLEN'S PL
BOYCES HILL
Keycol Hill
Keycol
ROOKS VW
ROOK LA
KEYCOL HILL
LADYFIELDS CL
A2
OLD MAIDSTONE RD
A249
ORCHARD DR
PEAR TREE WLK
BRAMLEY CL
WILCOCKS CL
Newington Manor
Cranbrook Wood
Gwelo Farm
Standard Hill
ME9
BULL LA
PH
CHESTNUT ST
Chesley Farm
WORMDALE RD
Wormdale Farm
Cold Store
Chestnut Street
CHESTNUT WOOD LA
SCHOOL LA
Chesley
Borden CE Prim Sch
Rock Meadows
Sunnyhill
LIMEPITS CROSS
Thrognall Farm
WORMDALE HILL
CH
DANAWAY COTTS
Danaway
WESTFIELD GDNS
MUNSGORE LA
Munsgore Farm
Eyehorn Farm
Pond Farm
WOODGATE LA
Woodgate Farm
POND FARM RD
Church Wood
5
Stockbury Valley
Vinson Farm
Oad Street
DUVARD'S PL
A249
Bowl Reed
PH
M2

57
36

D6
1 MOONSTONE SQ
2 RUBY CL
3 AMETHYST DR
4 REALGAR CT
5 RAITE GN
6 FIRE OPAL WY
7 TRONA CT
8 PIPPIN CL

Grid columns: A B C D E F
Grid rows: 8 7 65 6 5 64 4 3 63 2 1 62

SITTINGBOURNE

ME9
ME10

Parsonage Farm
Parsonage La
Cold Harbour La
Howt Green
Stickfast Farm
Upper Toes
Nether Toes
Church Farm
Quinton Farm House
Bobbing Prim Sch
Bobbing
Bobbing Court
Bobbing Hill
Grove Dairy Farm
Motel
Grove Park CP Sch
Milton Regis
Key Street
Key St
A2
A249
Cherry Fields
The Westlands Sch
Playing Field
Cryalls
Cryalls Bsns Est
London Rd
Chalkwell
Woodgrove Prim Sch
Borden Hall
Hall
Street Farm
Borden
Pond House
Harman's Corner
Fernleigh
Hearts Delight
Waymarks

Blue Houses
Cricketers Cl
Beauvoir Dr
Grovehurst Rd
Saffron Way
Green Porch Cl
Superstore
Trinity Trad Est
Regis Manor Com Prim Sch
Milton Court Prim Sch
Works
Recn Gd
Saxon Shore Way
Milton Creek
Sittingbourne
Sittingbourne Retail Pk
Crown Quay La
Sittingbourne Ind Pk
Eurolink Way
St Michael's Rd
Dover St
West St
Mag Ct
War Mem
Liby
Swallows Ctr
Superstore
The Avenue
Theatre
Borden Gram Sch
Avenue of Remembrance
Cemys
Spicer Homes
Memorial
Highsted Gram Sch
Fulston Manor Sch
Eden Village

Staplehurst Lodge Ind Est
1 Norwood Wlk E
2 Wentworth Ho
1 Deham Ho
Roentgen Ho 2
Pincus Ho 3
1 Sunstone Dr
2 Sapphire Cl
3 Jade Cl
4 Olivine Cl
Albion Terr 1
Oyster Cl 2
Cross La 3
Brambling Rise 4
1 Allenby Wlk
Nelson Wlk 2
Collingwood Wlk 3
Norwood Wlk W 4
Andrews Wlk 5
Gainsborough Cl 6
King Arthur Ct 1
Knights Ct 2
1 Meadow Ho
2 Lower Bannister Cotts
St Peter's RC Prim Sch
Minterne Jun Sch
The Oaks Inf Sch
Trotts Hall Gdns 1
The Burrs 2
Miefield 3
Chilton Gn 4
Glovers Cres

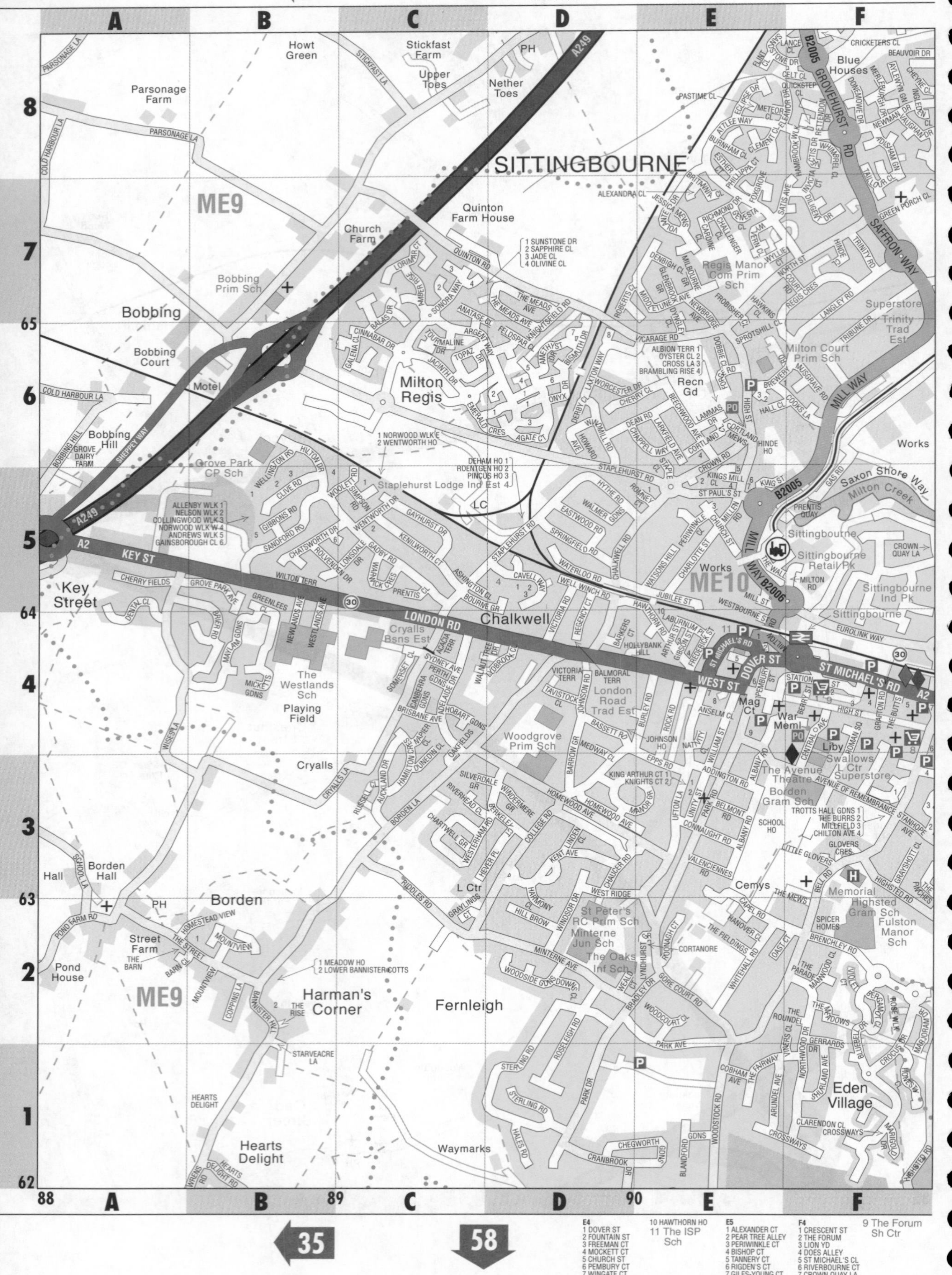

E4
1 DOVER ST
2 FOUNTAIN ST
3 FREEMAN ST
4 MOCKETT CT
5 CHURCH ST
6 PEMBURY CT
7 WINGATE CT
8 THE CLOISTERS
9 MIDDLETON CT

10 HAWTHORN HO
11 THE ISP Sch

E5
1 ALEXANDER CT
2 PEAR TREE ALLEY
3 PERIWINKLE CT
4 BISHOP CT
5 TANNERY CT
6 RIGDEN'S CT
7 GILES-YOUNG CT

F4
1 CRESCENT ST
2 THE FORUM
3 LION YD
4 DOES ALLEY
5 ST MICHAEL'S CL
6 RIVERBOURNE CT
7 CROWN QUAY LA
8 Bell Sh Ctr

9 The Forum Sh Ctr

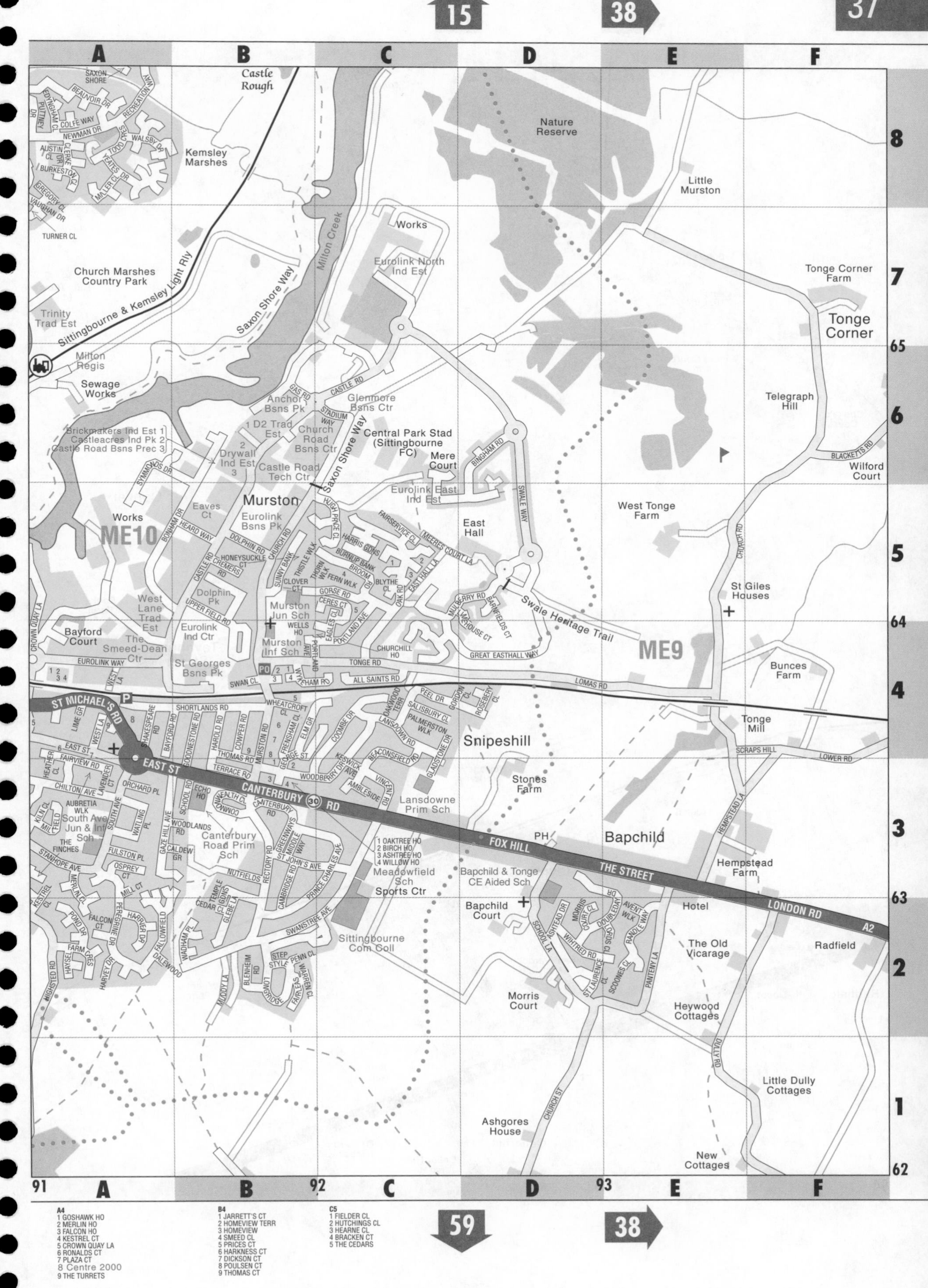
15
38
A
B
C
D
E
F
8
7
65
6
5
64
4
3
63
2
1
62
91
92
93
Castle Rough
Kemsley Marshes
Nature Reserve
Little Murston
SAXON SHORE
BEAUVOIR DR
RECREATION WAY
COLFE WAY
NEWMAN DR
WALSBY DR
TODD CRES
AUSTIN CL
YEATES DR
BURKESTON CL
MILLER CL
GREGORY CL
VAUGHAN DR
TURNER CL
Church Marshes Country Park
Sittingbourne & Kemsley Light Rly
Saxon Shore Way
Milton Creek
Works
Eurolink North Ind Est
Tonge Corner Farm
Tonge Corner
Trinity Trad Est
Milton Regis
Sewage Works
GAS RD
CASTLE RD
Anchor Bsns Pk
Glenmore Bsns Ctr
STADIUM WAY
1 D2 Trad Est
Church Road Bsns Ctr
Central Park Stad (Sittingbourne FC)
Telegraph Hill
Brickmakers Ind Est 1
Castleacres Ind Pk 2
Castle Road Bsns Prec 3
2 Drywall Ind Est 3
Castle Road Tech Ctr
Mere Court
BINGHAM RD
BLACKETTS RD
Wilford Court
SYMMONDS DR
Murston
Eurolink East Ind Est
SWALE WAY
West Tonge Farm
Works
Eaves Ct
Eurolink Bsns Pk
HUGH PRICE CL
FAIRSERVICE CL
East Hall
ME10
BONHAM DR
HEARD WAY
DOLPHIN RD
CHURCH RD
HARRIS GDNS
MEERES COURT LA
HONEYSUCKLE CT
CREMERS RD
SUNNY BANK
THISTLE WLK
BURNUP BANK
BROOM RD
CASTLE RD
CLOVER CT
THORN WLK
FERN WLK
BLYTHE CL
EAST HALL LA
OAK RD
St Giles Houses
West Lane Trad Est
Dolphin Pk
GORSE RD
MULBERRY RD
LIMEHOUSE CT
BARNFIELDS CT
Swale Heritage Trail
CROWN QUAY LA
UPPER FIELD RD
Murston Jun Sch
CERES CT
Bayford Court
Eurolink Ind Ctr
WELLS HO
EAGLES CL
PORTLAND AVE
The Smeed-Dean Ctr
Murston Inf Sch
CHURCHILL HO
GREAT EASTHALL WAY
ME9
Bunces Farm
EUROLINK WAY
St Georges Bsns Pk
TONGE RD
PO
WYKEHAM RD
ALL SAINTS RD
SWAN CL
LOMAS RD
WHEATCROFT CL
ST MICHAEL'S RD
P
SHORTLANDS RD
PEEL DR
GORDON CL
ROSEBERY CL
SALISBURY CL
Tonge Mill
LIME GR
WEST LA
SHAKESPEARE RD
BAYFORD RD
GOODNESTONE RD
HAROLD RD
COWPER RD
MURSTON RD
FRENSHAM CL
ELM GR
OAKWOOD TERR
LANSDOWN RD
PALMERSTON WLK
Snipeshill
SCRAPS HILL
LOWER RD
EAST ST
FAIRVIEW RD
THOMAS RD
GEORGE ST
COOMBE DR
BEACONSFIELD RD
GLADSTONE DR
HEATHER CL
LAVENDER CT
TERRACE RD
WOODBERRY DR
KESWICK AVE
Stones Farm
CHILTON AVE
ORCHARD PL
ECHO HO
CANTERBURY RD
VINCENT RD
AMBLESIDE
Lansdowne Prim Sch
AUBRETIA WLK
SCHOOL RD
HEALTH CL
30
South Ave Jun & Inf Sch
SOUTH AVE
WATLING PL
GAZE HILL AVE
WOODLANDS RD
CANTERBURY RD
FOX HILL
PH
Bapchild
HEMPSTEAD LA
THE FINCHES
Canterbury Road Prim Sch
1 OAKTREE HO
2 BIRCH HO
3 ASHTREE HO
4 WILLOW HO
FULSTON PL
CALDEW GR
GREENWAYS
MIDDLE WAY
STANHOPE AVE
OSPREY CT
NUTFIELDS
RECTORY RD
ST JOHN'S AVE
PRINCE CHARLES AVE
Meadowfield Sch
Sports Ctr
Bapchild & Tonge CE Aided Sch
THE STREET
Hempstead Farm
MERLIN CL
MILL CT
TEMPLE GDNS
CAMBRIDGE RD
KESTREL CL
CEDAR CL
GLEBE LA
Bapchild Court
ASHTEAD DR
MORRIS COURT CL
DOUBLEDAY DR
AVENT WLK
Hotel
LONDON RD
A2
POND DR
FALCON CT
PEREGRINE DR
HARRIER DR
FALLOWFIELD
SWANSTREE AVE
SCHOOL LA
WIHTRED RD
RANDLE WAY
Sittingbourne Com Coll
The Old Vicarage
Radfield
FARM CRES
HAYSEL
HARVEY DR
DALEWOOD
WADHAM PL
BLENHEIM RD
STEP STYLE
PENN CL
WARREN CL
FAIRLEAS
LONGRIDGE
SCOONES CL
PAINTENY LA
HIGHSTED RD
MUDDY LA
ST LAURENCE CL
Morris Court
Heywood Cottages
DULLY RD
Little Dully Cottages
CHURCH ST
Ashgores House
New Cottages
59
38
A4
1 GOSHAWK HO
2 MERLIN HO
3 FALCON HO
4 KESTREL CT
5 CROWN QUAY LA
6 RONALDS CT
7 PLAZA CT
8 Centre 2000
9 THE TURRETS
B4
1 JARRETT'S CT
2 HOMEVIEW TERR
3 HOMEVIEW
4 SMEED CL
5 PRICES CT
6 HARKNESS CT
7 DICKSON CT
8 POULSEN CT
9 THOMAS CT
C5
1 FIELDER CL
2 HUTCHINGS CL
3 HEARNE CL
4 BRACKEN CT
5 THE CEDARS

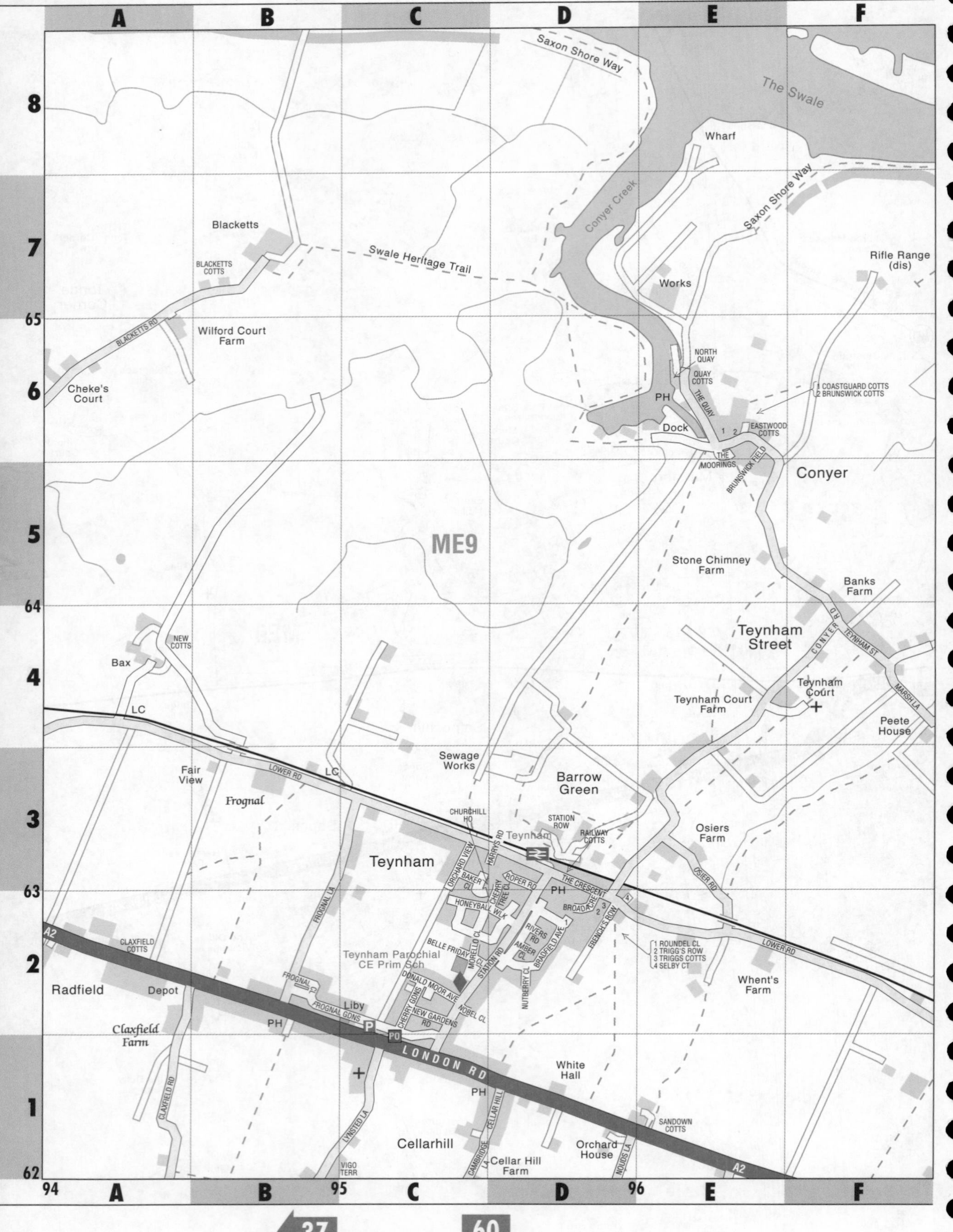

A · B · C · D · E · F

8

7

Blacketts

BLACKETTS
COTTS

65

Wilford Court
Farm

6

Cheke's
Court

BLACKETTS RD

Saxon Shore Way

The Swale

Swale Heritage Trail

Conyer Creek

Saxon Shore Way

Wharf

Works

Rifle Range
(dis)

NORTH
QUAY

QUAY
COTTS

PH

THE QUAY

Dock

1 COASTGUARD COTTS
2 BRUNSWICK COTTS

EASTWOOD
COTTS

THE
MOORINGS

BRUNSWICK FIELD

Conyer

5

ME9

Stone Chimney
Farm

Banks
Farm

64

NEW
COTTS

Bax

Teynham
Street

O.D. TEYNHAM ST

Teynham
Court

MARSH LA

Peete
House

4

LC

Teynham Court
Farm

Fair
View

LOWER RD

LC

Frognal

Sewage
Works

Barrow
Green

Osiers
Farm

OSIER RD

3

CHURCHILL
HO

STATION
ROW

Teynham

RAILWAY
COTTS

Teynham

ORCHARD VIEW

BAKER CL

MABYN'S RD

ROPER RD

CHERRY TREE DR

THE CRESCENT

PH

BROADA...

FRENCH'S ROW

1 ROUNDEL CL
2 TRIGG'S ROW
3 TRIGGS COTTS
4 SELBY CT

LOWER RD

63

FROGNAL LA

HONEYBALL WLK

MORELLO CL

STATION RD

AMBER

RIVERS
RD

BROADFIELD AVE

NUTBERRY CL

A2

CLAXFIELD
COTTS

Radfield

Depot

Teynham Parochial
CE Prim Sch

BELLE FRIDAY

DONALD MOOR AVE

NOBEL CL

Whent's
Farm

2

FROGNAL

Liby

FROGNAL GDNS

PH

CHERRY GDNS

NEW GARDENS
RD

P

PO

Claxfield
Farm

CLAXFIELD RD

LYNSTED LA

LONDON RD

PH

CAMBRIDGE

CELLAR HILL

White
Hall

Sandown
Cotts

NOLDS LA

A2

1

Cellarhill

VIGO
TERR

Cellar Hill
Farm

Orchard
House

62

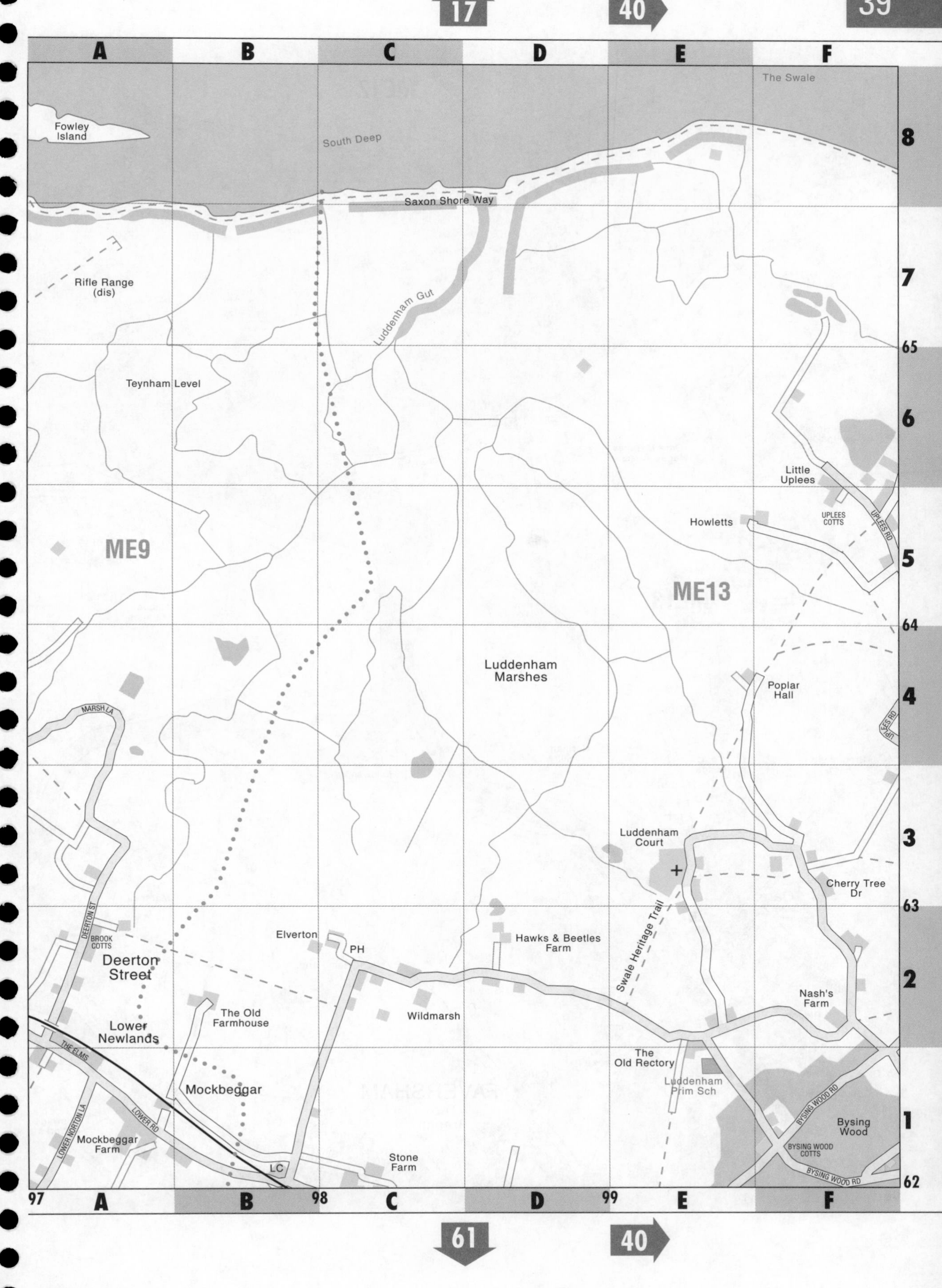

A B C D E F

8

The Swale

Fowley
Island

South Deep

Saxon Shore Way

7

Rifle Range
(dis)

Luddenham Gut

65

6

Teynham Level

Little
Uplees

UPLEES
COTTS

UPLEES RD

Howletts

ME9

ME13

5

64

Luddenham
Marshes

Poplar
Hall

4

UPLEES RD

Luddenham
Court

3

Cherry Tree
Dr

+

63

Swale Heritage Trail

Elverton

PH

Hawks & Beetles
Farm

BROOK
COTTS

DEERTON ST

Deerton
Street

Wildmarsh

Nash's
Farm

2

MARSH LA

The Old
Farmhouse

Lower
Newlands

THE ELMS

The
Old Rectory

Luddenham
Prim Sch

Mockbeggar

BYSING WOOD RD

Bysing
Wood

1

LOWER NORTON LA

LOWER RD

Mockbeggar
Farm

Stone
Farm

LC

BYSING WOOD
COTTS

BYSING WOOD RD

62

97 A B 98 C D 99 E F

A B C D E F

The Ferry Inn (PH)

HARTY FERRY RD

ME12

8

The Swale

7

Uplees Marshes

65

6

Visitor Ctr

P

Saxon Shore Way

Gate House Bungalow

Oare Marshes Nature Reserve

Nagden Marshes

5

ME13

HARTY FERRY COTTS

64

4

Faversham Creek

Broomfield Farm

Court Lodge

Norman's Hill

PH

Hollowshore

Ham Marshes

UPLEES RD

UPLEES RD

3

Oare Creek

CHURCH RD

Pheasant Farm

Wharf

Works

63

Oare

HARRISON TERR

RUSSELL

COLEGATES

PO

PH

COLEGATES CL

MOUNT PLEASANT

THE STREET

Ham Farm

2

COLEGATES RD

B2045

JOHN HALL CL

Works

Gravel Works

Piggery

Windmill (dis)

WINDMILL LA

Ham Rd

1

WESTERN LINK

SEAGER RD

PH

ORE RD

Gate House

FAVERSHAM
The Brents

Brents Ind Est
Shipyard Area

North Quay
South Quay

Saxon Shore Way

Faversham Creek

Sewage Works

Oare Gunpowder Works Country Park

MAYLAND CL

CHURCHILL WAY

WELLS WAY

WRIGHT CT

Works

Davington Prim Sch

CRYSTAL RD

SPRINGHEAD RD

LARKSFIELD RD

BROOK RD

UPPER BRENTS

WATERSIDE CL

Wharf

ABBEY FIELDS

62

BYSING WOOD RD

B2045

WILDISH RD

IVORY CT

BYSING WOOD RD

SHERWOOD DR

JEMISON

PRIORY PL

NCH CL

00 A B 01 C D 02 E F

19
42

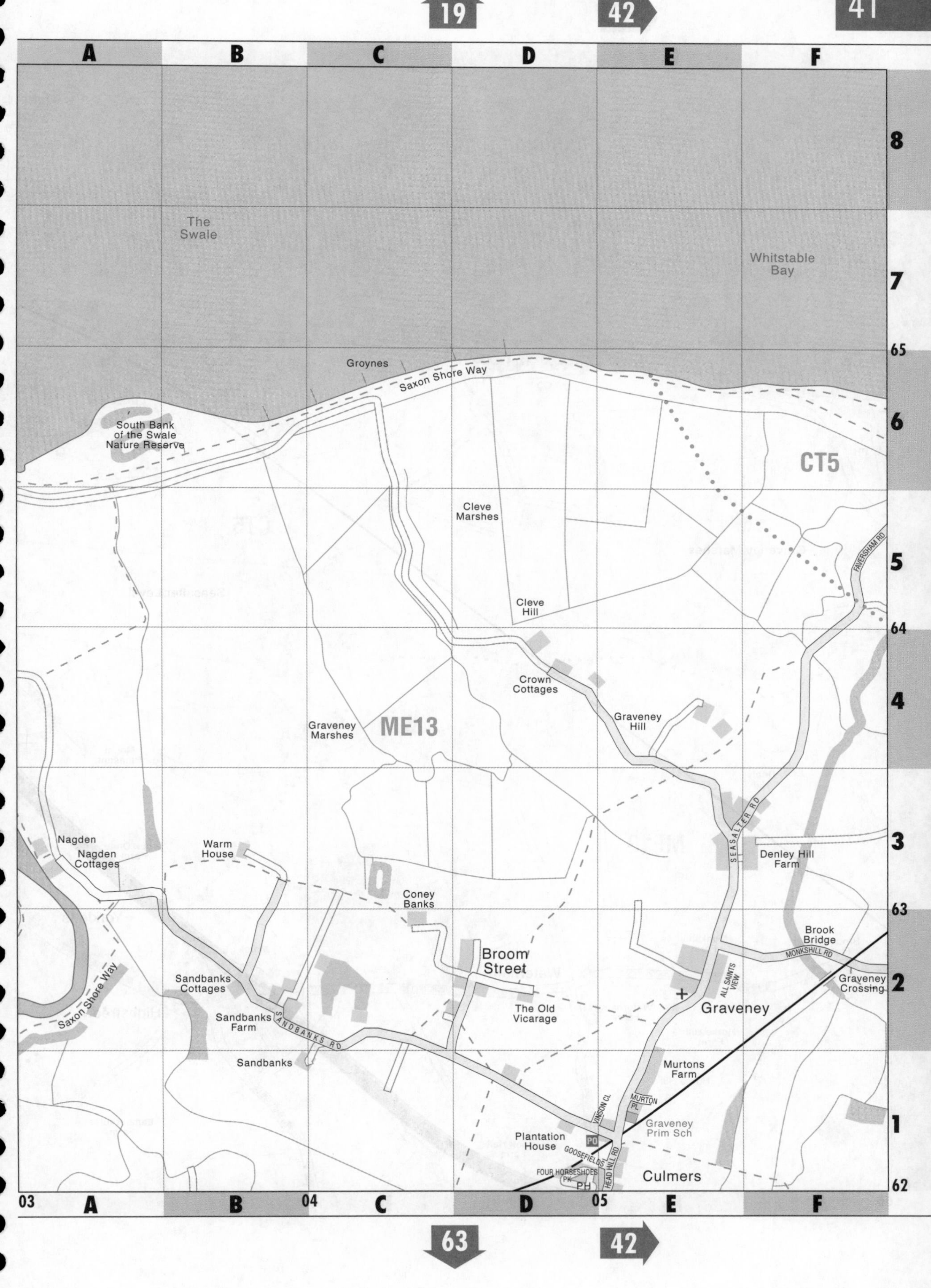
The Swale
Whitstable Bay
Groynes
Saxon Shore Way
South Bank of the Swale Nature Reserve
CT5
Cleve Marshes
Faversham Rd
Cleve Hill
Crown Cottages
Graveney Hill
Graveney Marshes
ME13
Seasalter Rd
Nagden
Nagden Cottages
Warm House
Denley Hill Farm
Coney Banks
Brook Bridge
Monkshill Rd
Broom Street
Sandbanks Cottages
All Saints View
Graveney Crossing
Saxon Shore Way
Sandbanks Farm
The Old Vicarage
Graveney
Sandbanks Rd
Sandbanks
Murtons Farm
Vinson Cl
Murton Pl
Graveney Prim Sch
Plantation House
PO
Goosefields
Head Hill Rd
Four Horseshoes
PK
PH
Culmers
A
B
C
D
E
F
8
7
6
5
4
3
2
1
65
64
63
62
03
04
05

63
42

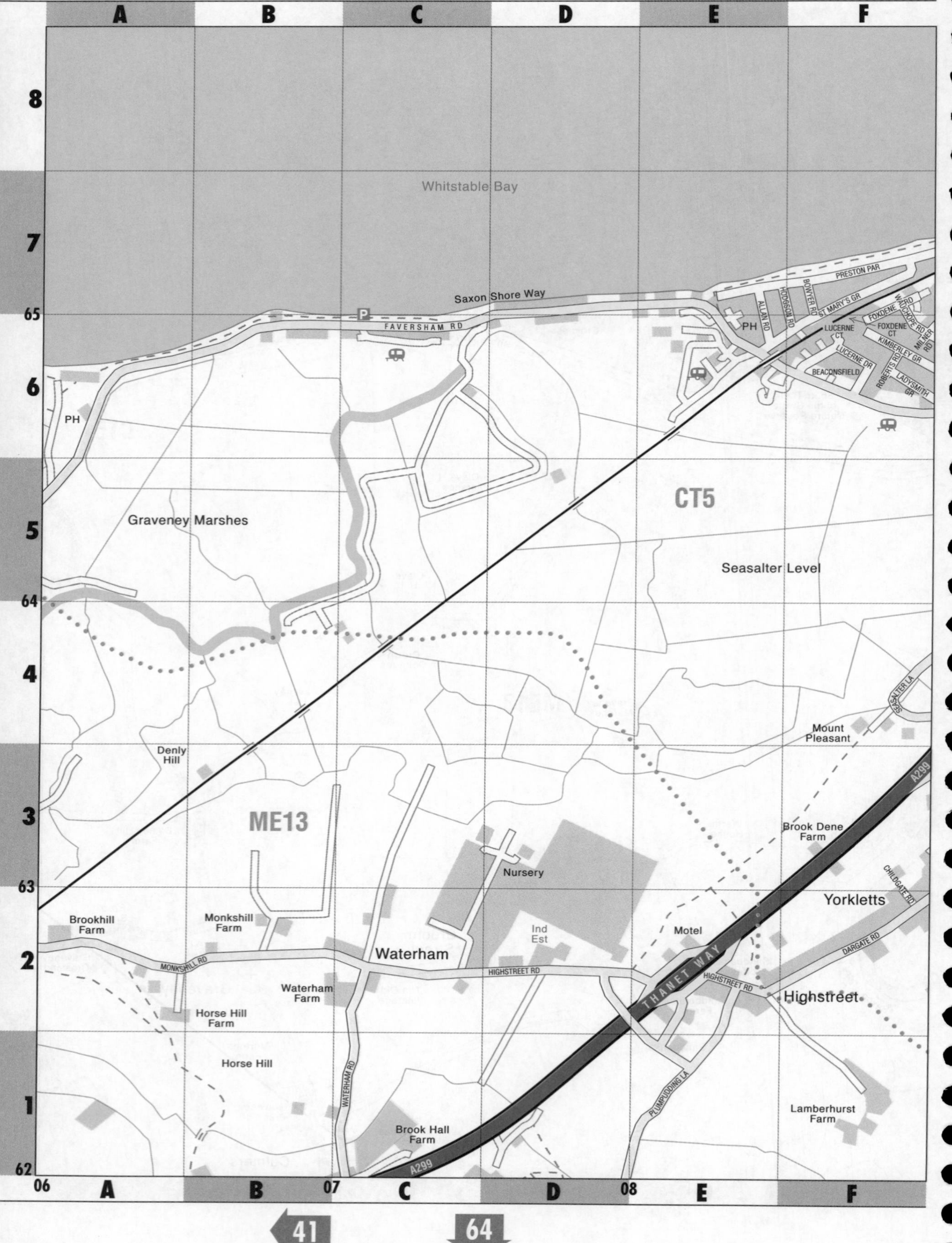

Whitstable Bay

Saxon Shore Way

P

FAVERSHAM RD

PH

PRESTON PAR

BOWYER RD

HOPSON RD

ST MARY'S GR

ALAN RD

LUCERNE CT

FOXDENE WAY

VICTORY RD

FOXDENE RD

MILLER RD

LUCERNE DR

KIMBERLEY GR

PH

ROBERTS RD

LADYSMITH GR

BEACONSFIELD

CT5

Seasalter Level

Graveney Marshes

Mount Pleasant

ASHTERLA

A299

ME13

Denly Hill

Brook Dene Farm

CHILDGATE RD

Yorkletts

Nursery

63

Brookhill Farm

Monkshill Farm

Ind Est

Motel

DARGATE RD

Waterham

MONKSHILL RD

HIGHSTREET RD

THANET WAY

HIGHSTREET RD

Highstreet

Waterham Farm

WATERHAM RD

Horse Hill Farm

PLOMPTON LA

Horse Hill

Brook Hall Farm

Lamberhurst Farm

A299

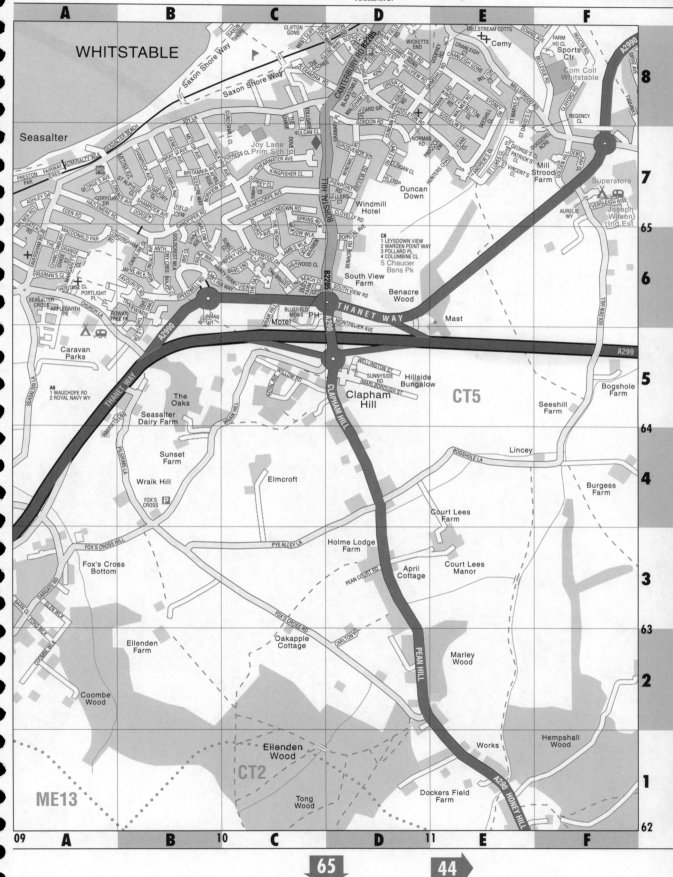

20
44

D8
1 JAFFA CT
2 MARINERS CT
3 NORFOLK ST
4 WHITBOURNE CT
5 OLD PRINTWORKS CL
6 SADDLETON GR

WHITSTABLE

Seasalter

Saxon Shore Way

Saxon Shore Way

CLIFTON GDNS

CANTERBURY RD

MILLSTREAM COTTS

DOWNS AVE

Cemy

FARM HO CL

Sports Ctr

Com Coll Whitstable

A2990

8

Joy Lane Prim Sch

Mill Strood Farm

Superstore

Joseph Wilson rInd Est

7

65

Duncan Down

Windmill Hotel

Aurelie Wy

Eversleigh Rise

C6
1 LEYSDOWN VIEW
2 WARDEN POINT WAY
3 POLLARD PL
4 COLUMBINE CL
5 Chaucer Bsns Pk

South View Farm

Benacre Wood

Golden Hill

6

THANET WAY

Mast

Motel

THANET WAY

A290

A299

Bluefield Mews PH

Montpelier Ave

Wellington St

Sunnyside Rd

Marlborough St

Hillside Bungalow

Seeshill Farm

Bogshole Farm

5

Caravan Parks

A6
1 WAUCHOPE RD
2 ROYAL NAVY WY

THANET WAY

The Oaks

Willow Rd

Royal La

Wraik Hill

Clapham Hill

CT5

Lincey

Bogshole La

64

Seasalter Dairy Farm

Sunset Farm

Wraik Hill

Fox's Cross

Elmcroft

Clapham Hill

Burgess Farm

4

Court Lees Farm

Fox's Cross Hill

Pye Alley La

Holme Lodge Farm

Pean Court Rd

April Cottage

Court Lees Manor

3

Fox's Cross Bottom

Fox's Cross Rd

Carlton Rd

Pean Hill

63

Ellenden Farm

Oakapple Cottage

Marley Wood

Coombe Walk

Ford Wlk

Barn Cl

Dargate Rd

Glen Wlk

Coombe Wood

2

Ellenden Wood

CT2

Works

Hempshall Wood

1

ME13

Tong Wood

Dockers Field Farm

A290 HONEY HILL

62

09

A

B

10

C

D

11

E

F

43
21

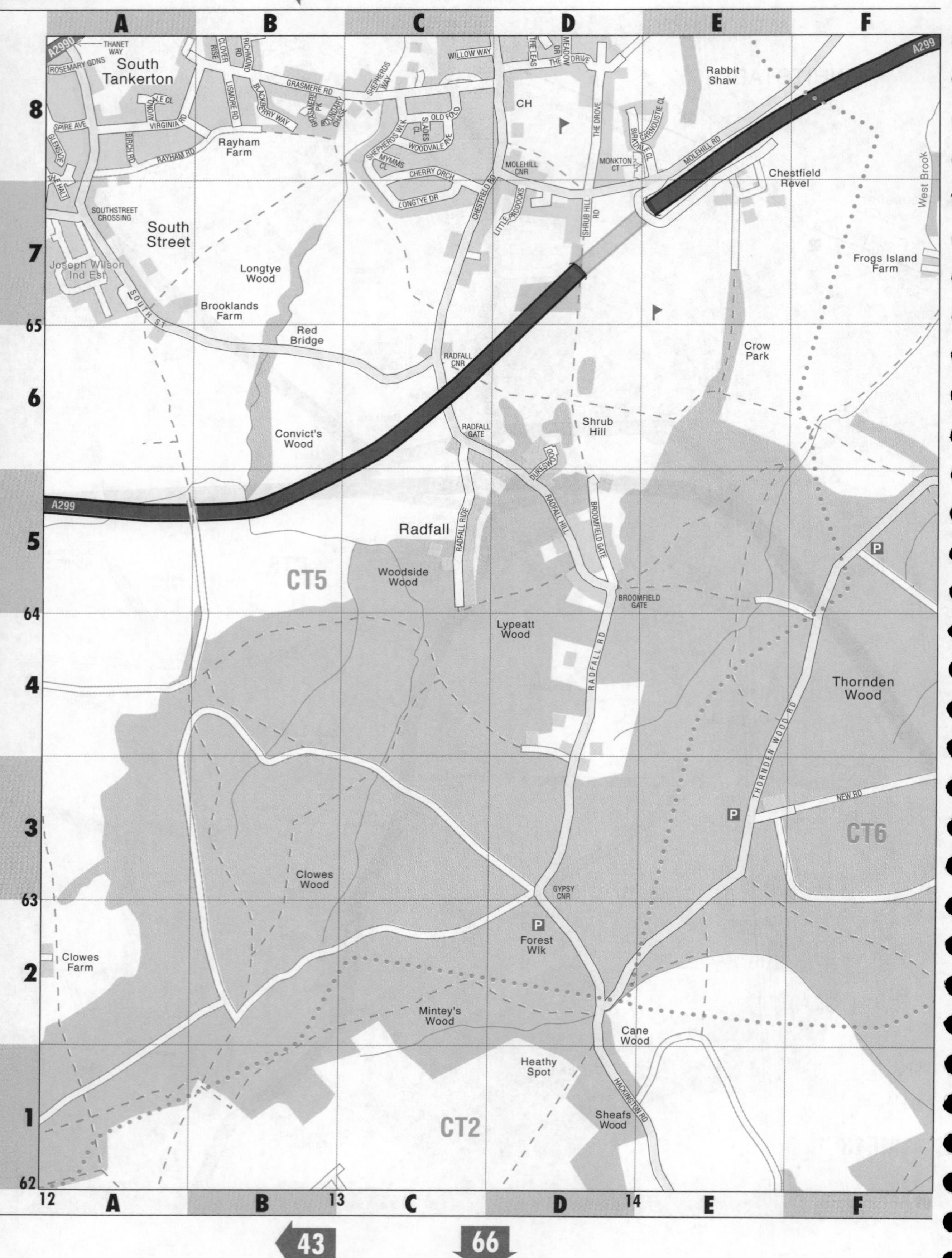
A
B
C
D
E
F
8
7
65
6
5
64
4
3
63
2
1
62
12
13
14
A2990
A299
THANET WAY
ROSEMARY GDNS
South Tankerton
CLOVER RISE
RICHMOND RD
WILLOW WAY
THE LEAS
MEADOW DR
THE DRIVE
GRASMERE RD
SHEPHERDS WAY
AVONDALE CL
SPIRE AVE
VIRGINIA RD
LISMORE RD
BLACKBERRY WAY
GRASMERE PK
BOUNDARY CHASE
OLD FOLD
SLADES CL
WOODVALE AVE
SHEPHERDS WLK
MYMMS CL
CHERRY ORCH
LONGTYE DR
CH
THE DROVE
CARNOUSTIE CL
BIRKDALE CL
MONKTON CT
MOLEHILL RD
MOLEHILL CNR
Rabbit Shaw
Rayham Farm
RAYHAM RD
BIRCH RD
GLENSIDE
THE HALT
SOUTHSTREET CROSSING
South Street
Joseph Wilson Ind Est
SOUTH ST
Longtye Wood
Brooklands Farm
Red Bridge
CHESTFIELD RD
LITTLE PADDOCKS
SHRUB HILL RD
Chestfield Revel
West Brook
Frogs Island Farm
Crow Park
RADFALL CNR
Shrub Hill
Convict's Wood
RADFALL GATE
DUKESWOOD
RADFALL HILL
BROOMFIELD GATE
Radfall
RADFALL RIDE
CT5
Woodside Wood
BROOMFIELD GATE
Lypeatt Wood
RADFALL RD
Thornden Wood
THORNDEN WOOD RD
NEW RD
P
CT6
Clowes Wood
GYPSY CNR
Forest Wlk
Clowes Farm
Mintey's Wood
Cane Wood
Heathy Spot
HACKINGTON RD
Sheafs Wood
CT2

43
66

22
46

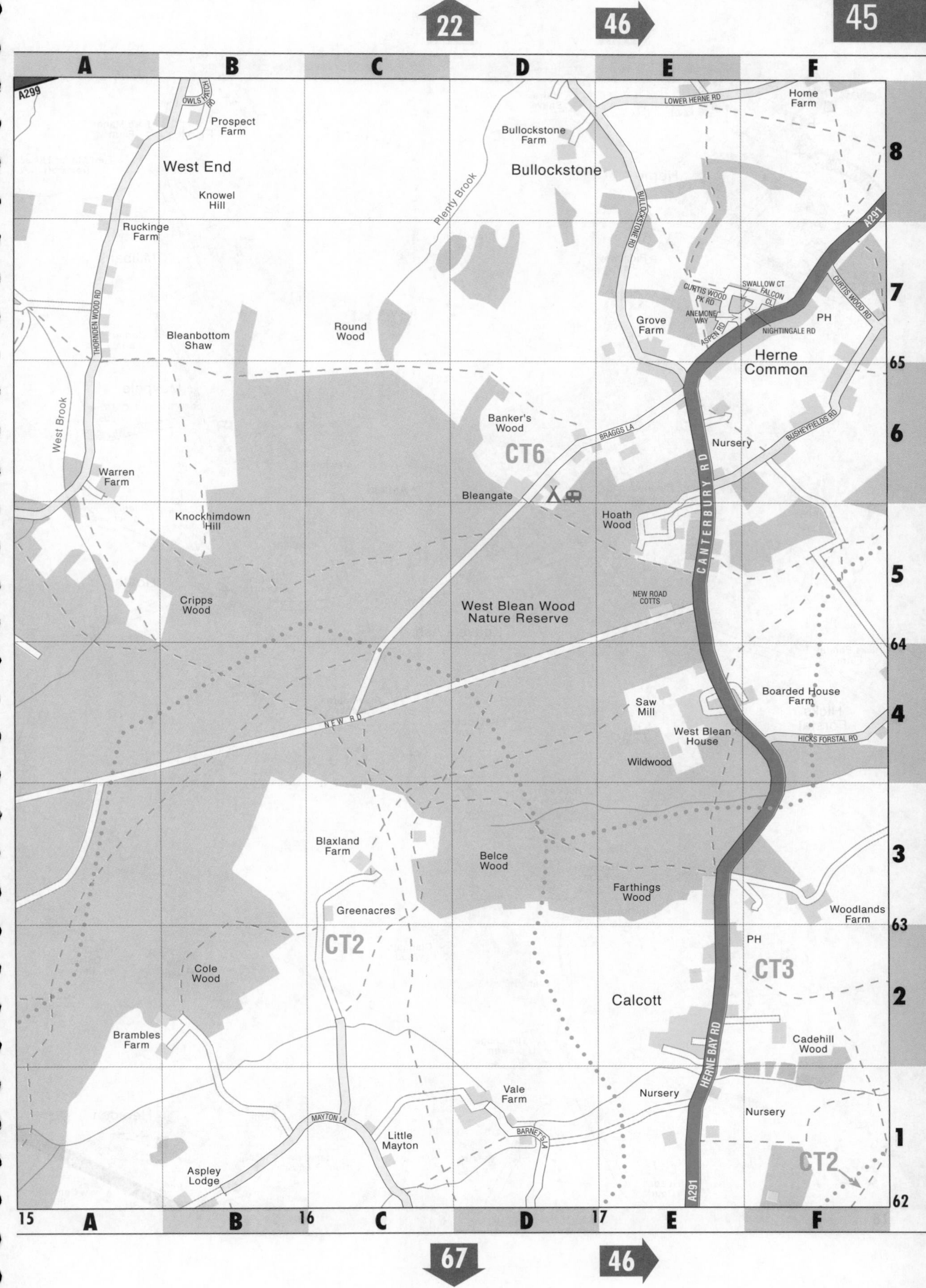
A
B
C
D
E
F
A299
OWLS HATCH RD
Prospect Farm
West End
Knowel Hill
Ruckinge Farm
THORNDEN WOOD RD
Bleanbottom Shaw
West Brook
Warren Farm
Knockhimdown Hill
Cripps Wood
Round Wood
Plenty Brook
Bullockstone Farm
Bullockstone
LOWER HERNE RD
Home Farm
BULLOCKSTONE RD
A291
CURTIS WOOD PK RD
SWALLOW CT
FALCON CL
ANEMONE WAY
ASPEN RD
NIGHTINGALE RD
CURTIS WOOD RD
PH
Grove Farm
Herne Common
Banker's Wood
CT6
BRAGGS LA
BUSHEYFIELDS RD
Nursery
Bleangate
Hoath Wood
CANTERBURY RD
NEW ROAD COTTS
West Blean Wood Nature Reserve
NEW RD
Saw Mill
Boarded House Farm
West Blean House
HICKS FORSTAL RD
Wildwood
Blaxland Farm
Belce Wood
Farthings Wood
Greenacres
Woodlands Farm
CT2
PH
CT3
Cole Wood
Calcott
Brambles Farm
Cadehill Wood
HERNE BAY RD
Vale Farm
Nursery
Nursery
MAYTON LA
Little Mayton
BARNETTS LA
Aspley Lodge
CT2
A291
8
7
65
6
5
64
4
3
63
2
1
62
15
16
17

67
46

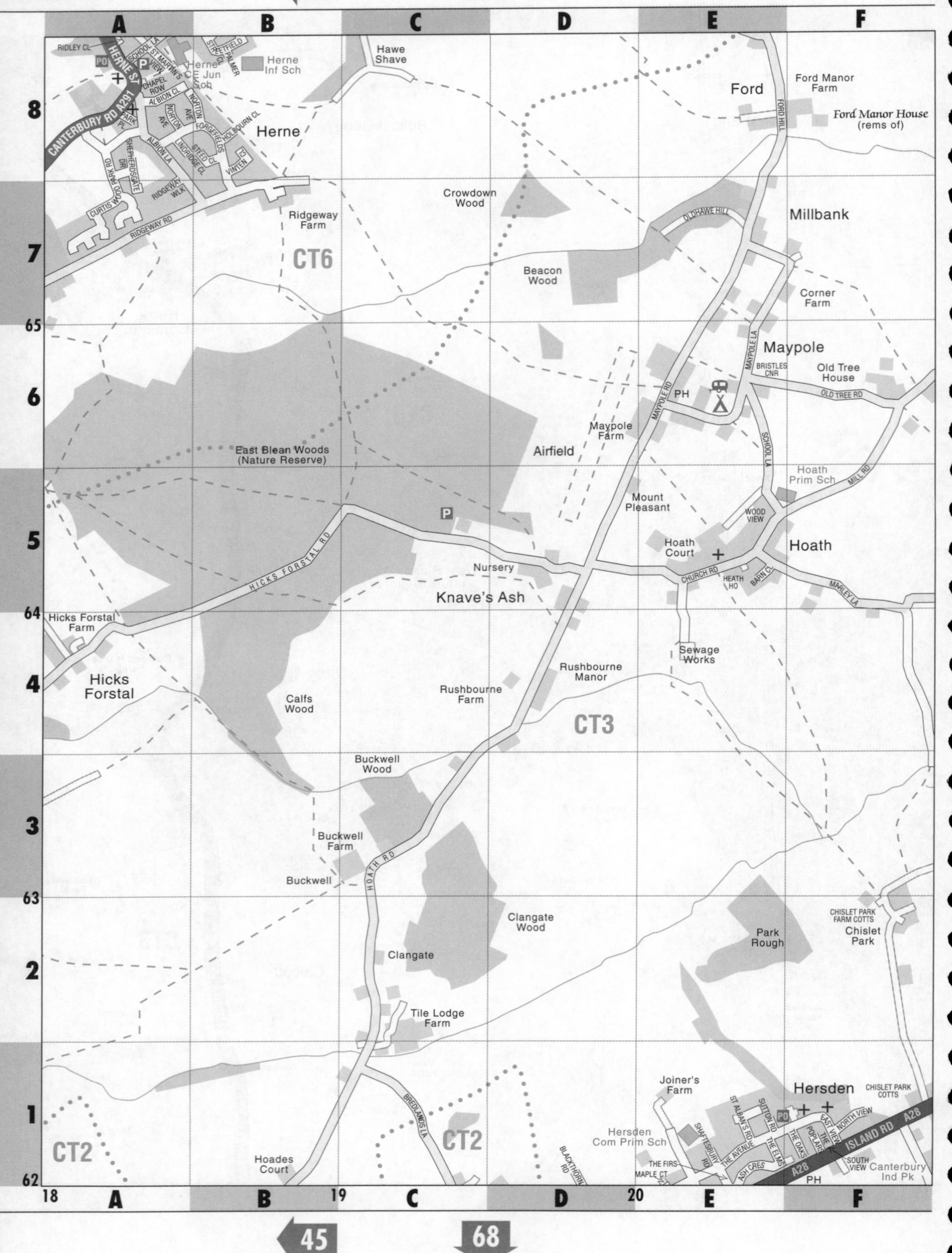

45
23

RIDLEY CL
PO
P
SCHOOL LA
ST MARTIN'S
Herne CE Jun Sch
SKETFIELD
Herne Inf Sch

CANTERBURY RD A291
CHAPEL ROW
ALBION LA
MORTON AVE
FORGEFIELDS
HOLBOURN CL
VINTEN

Herne

CURTIS CL
OLD PARK CLOSE
SHEPHERDSGATE DR
RIDGEWAY WLK
RIDGEWAY RD

Hawe Shave

Ford

Ford Manor Farm

Ford Manor House (rems of)

FORD HILL

Millbank

OLDHAWE HILL

Corner Farm

Ridgeway Farm

CT6

Crowdown Wood

Beacon Wood

MAYPOLE LA

Maypole

BRISTLES CNR

Old Tree House

PH

OLD TREE RD

8

7

65

6

East Blean Woods (Nature Reserve)

Maypole Farm

MAYPOLE RD

Airfield

SCHOOL LA

Hoath Prim Sch

MILL RD

Mount Pleasant

WOOD VIEW

P

Hoath Court

Hoath

HICKS FORSTAL RD

Nursery

Knave's Ash

CHURCH RD

HEATH HO

BARN CL

MARLEY LA

5

64

Hicks Forstal Farm

Sewage Works

Rushbourne Manor

CT3

4

Hicks Forstal

Calfs Wood

Rushbourne Farm

Buckwell Wood

HOATH RD

3

Buckwell Farm

Buckwell

Clangate Wood

Park Rough

CHISLET PARK FARM COTTS

Chislet Park

63

2

Clangate

Tile Lodge Farm

Joiner's Farm

Hersden

CHISLET PARK COTTS

A28

ISLAND RD

1

CT2

BREDLANDS LA

CT2

BLACKTHORN RD

Hersden Com Prim Sch

SHAFTESBURY RD

ST ALBAN'S RD

SUTTON RD

PO

THE AVENUE

THE ELMS

THE OAKS

CASTLE RD

THE POPLARS

NORTH VIEW

A28

SOUTH VIEW

Canterbury Ind Pk

62

Hoades Court

THE FIRS

MAPLE CT

ASH CRES

PH

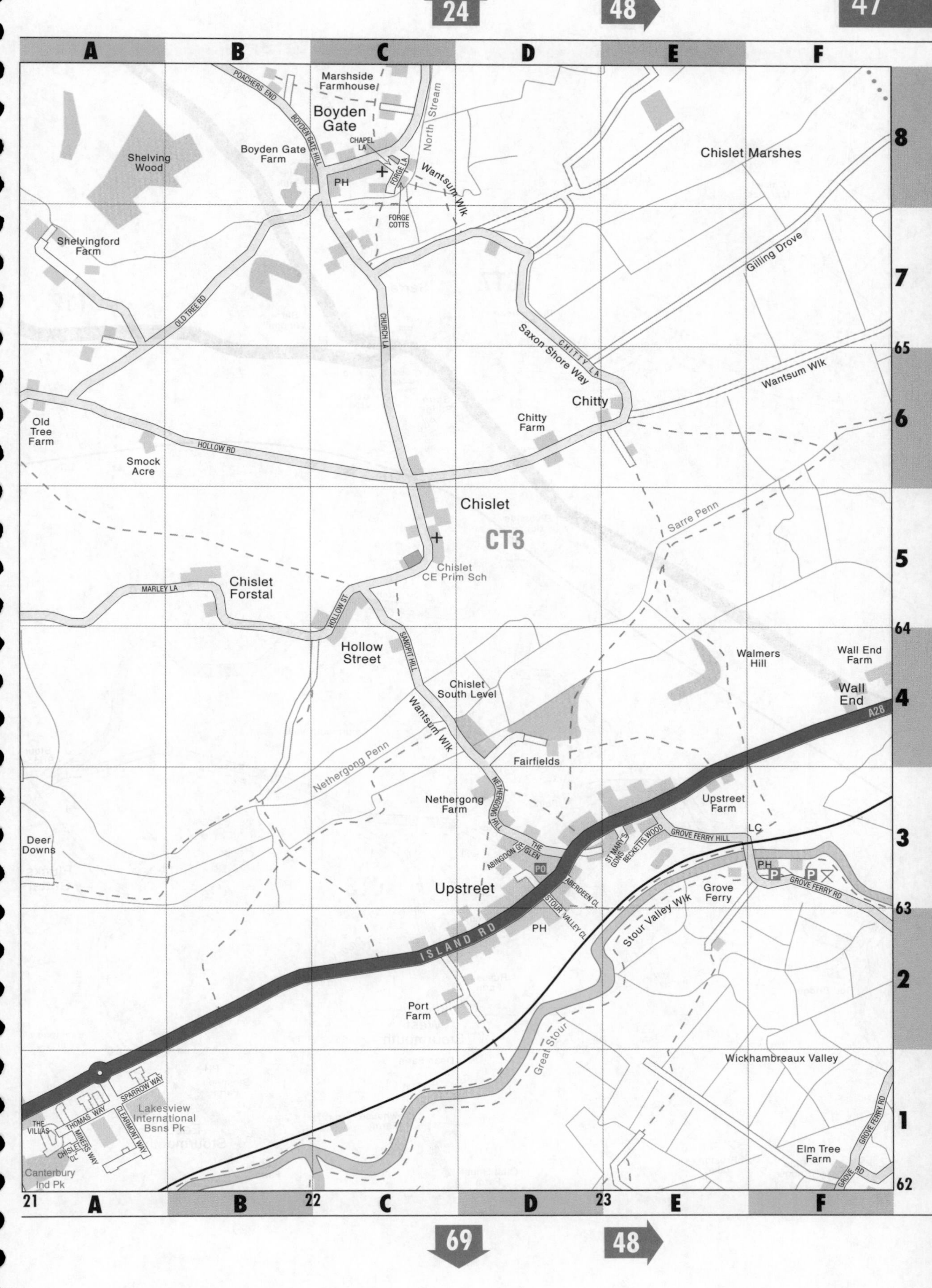

A   B   C   D   E   F

8

Chislet Marshes

Marshside
Farmhouse

Boyden
Gate

POACHERS END

Shelving
Wood

Boyden Gate
Farm

CHAPEL
LA

FORGE LA

PH

FORGE
COTTS

BOYDEN GATE HILL

North Stream

Wantsum Wlk

Gilling Drove

7

Shelvingford
Farm

OLD TREE RD

CHURCH LA

CHITTY LA

Saxon Shore Way

65

Wantsum Wlk

Old
Tree
Farm

HOLLOW RD

Chitty

Chitty
Farm

6

Smock
Acre

Sarre Penn

5

Chislet

CT3

Chislet
CE Prim Sch

MARLEY LA

Chislet
Forstal

HOLLOW ST

Walmers
Hill

Wall End
Farm

64

Hollow
Street

SANDPIT HILL

Chislet
South Level

Wall
End

4

A28

Wantsum Wlk

Nethergong Penn

Fairfields

Upstreet
Farm

LC

Deer
Downs

NETHERGONG HILL

THE GLEN

ABINGDON CL

Nethergong
Farm

Upstreet

PO

ST MARY'S GDNS

BECKETTS WOOD

GROVE FERRY HILL

PH
P   P

GROVE FERRY RD

3

PH

STOUR VALLEY CL

ABERDEEN CL

ISLAND RD

Stour Valley Wlk

Grove
Ferry

63

2

Port
Farm

Great Stour

Wickhambreaux Valley

Lakesview
International
Bsns Pk

SPARROW WAY

THOMAS WAY

CLAREMONT WAY

MINTERS WAY

THE
VILLAS

CHISLET CL

Canterbury
Ind Pk

Elm
Tree
Farm

GROVE FERRY RD

GROVE RD

1

62

47 25

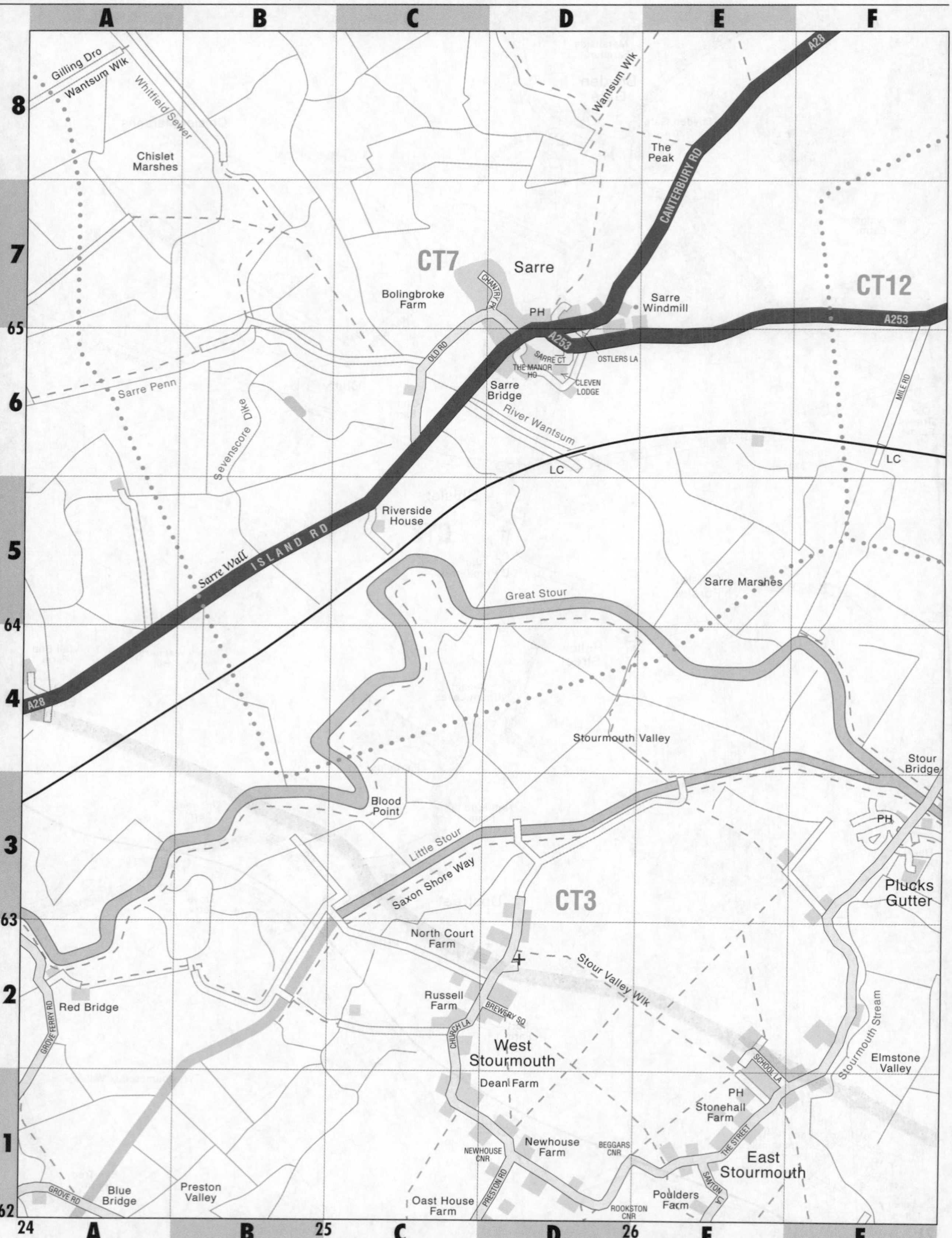

A B C D E F

8

Gilling Dro
Wantsum Wlk
Whitfield Sewer

Chislet
Marshes

7

CT7
Sarre
Bolingbroke
Farm
CHANTRY LA
The Peak
CANTERBURY RD
A28

Sarre Windmill
CT12

65
PH
A253
OLD RD
Sarre Ct
OSTLERS LA
A253
MILE RD

6
Sarre Penn
THE MANOR HO
Sarre
Bridge
CLEVEN
LODGE
LC
Sevenscore Dike
River Wantsum

LC

5
SARRE WALL
ISLAND RD
Riverside
House
Great Stour
Sarre Marshes

64

4
A28
Stourmouth Valley
Stour
Bridge

PH

3
Blood
Point
Little Stour
Saxon Shore Way
CT3
Plucks
Gutter

63
North Court
Farm
Stour Valley Wlk

2
Red Bridge
GROVE FERRY RD
Russell
Farm
CHURCH LA
BREWERY SQ
Stourmouth Stream
Elmstone
Valley

West
Stourmouth
SCHOOL LA

1
Deanl Farm
PH
Stonehall
Farm
THE STREET
Newhouse
Farm
East
Stourmouth
NEWHOUSE CNR
BEGGARS CNR
PRESTON RD
SARTON LA

62
Blue
Bridge
Preston
Valley
Oast House
Farm
ROOKSTON CNR
Poulders
Farm
GROVE RD

24 A B 25 C D 26 E F

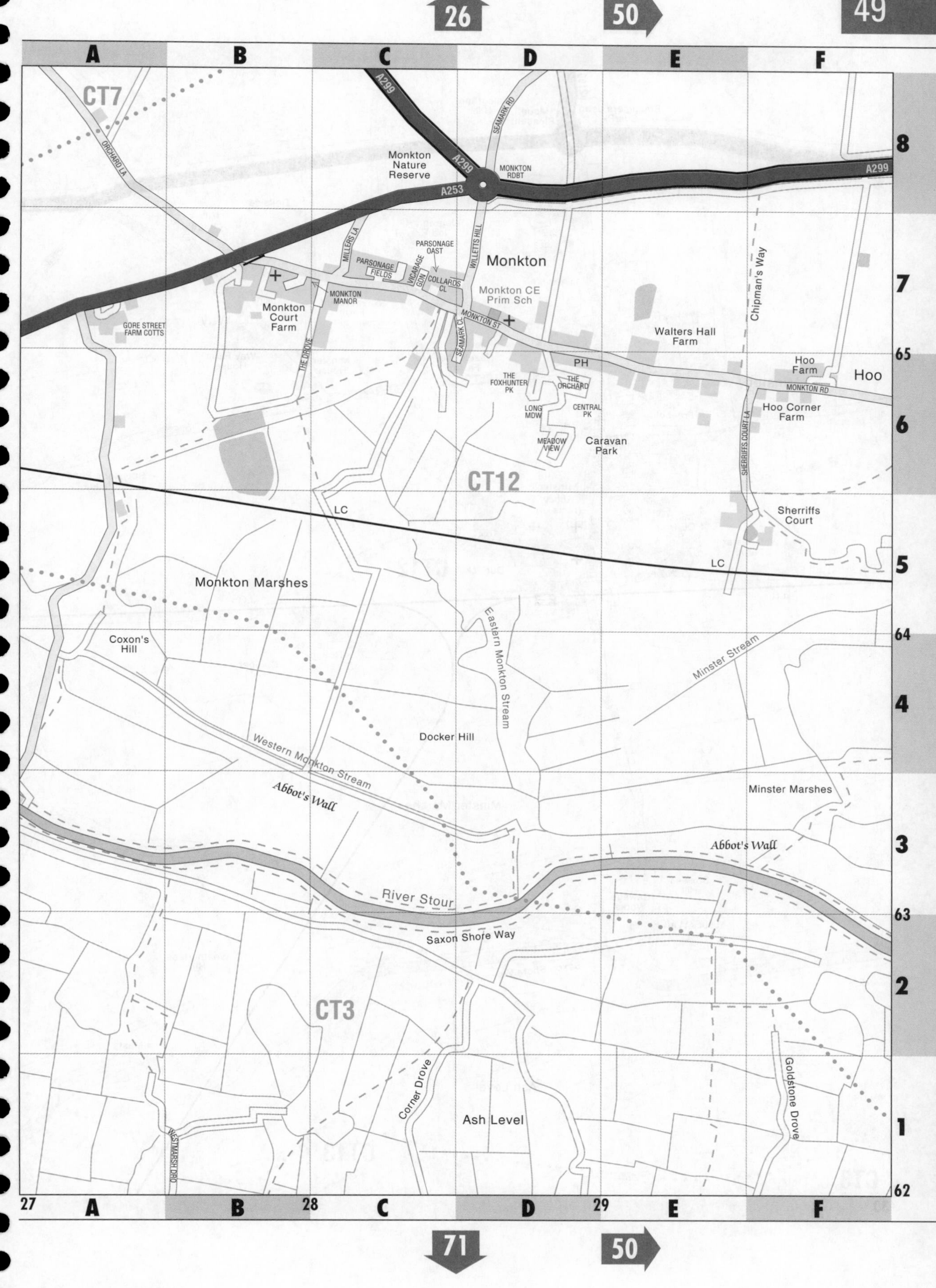
A
B
C
D
E
F
8
7
65
6
5
64
4
3
63
2
1
62
27
28
29
CT7
ORCHARD LA
A299
SEAMARK RD
Monkton
Nature
Reserve
MONKTON
RDBT
A253
A299
PARSONAGE
OAST
MILLERS LA
WILLETTS HILL
Monkton
PARSONAGE
FIELDS
VICARAGE
GDN
COLLARDS
CL
Monkton CE
Prim Sch
Chipman's Way
MONKTON
MANOR
Monkton
Court
Farm
GORE STREET
FARM COTTS
MONKTON ST
SEAMARK CL
Walters Hall
Farm
THE DROVE
PH
THE
FOXHUNTER
PK
THE
ORCHARD
Hoo
Farm
Hoo
MONKTON RD
LONG
MDW
CENTRAL
PK
Hoo Corner
Farm
SHERRIFFS COURT LA
MEADOW
VIEW
Caravan
Park
CT12
LC
Sherriffs
Court
LC
Monkton Marshes
Eastern Monkton Stream
Coxon's
Hill
Minster Stream
Docker Hill
Western Monkton Stream
Abbot's Wall
Minster Marshes
Abbot's Wall
River Stour
Saxon Shore Way
CT3
Goldstone Drove
Corner Drove
Ash Level
W STMARSH DRO
A
B
C
D
E
F

49
27

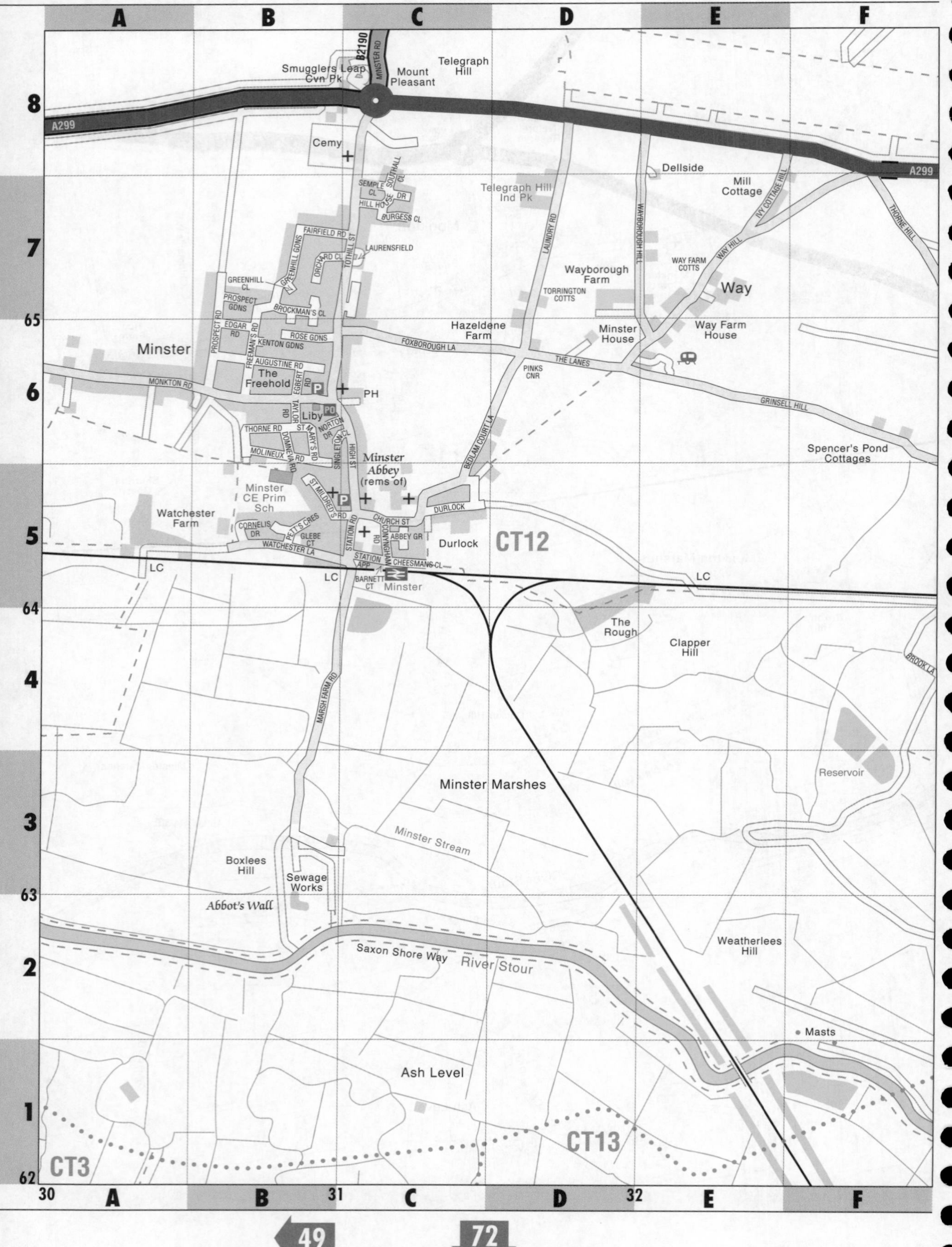
A
B
C
D
E
F
8
7
65
6
5
64
4
3
63
2
1
62
30
31
32
B2190
MINSTER RD
Smugglers Leap
Cvn Pk
Mount
Pleasant
Telegraph
Hill
A299
Cemy
SEMPLE CL
SOUTHALL CL
HILL HO
ROSE DR
BURGESS CL
FAIRFIELD RD
LAURENSFIELD
TOTHILL ST
ORCHARD CL
GREENHILL GDNS
GREENHILL CL
PROSPECT GDNS
BROCKMAN'S CL
EDGAR RD
PROSPECT RD
FREEMAN'S RD
ROSE GDNS
KENTON GDNS
AUGUSTINE RD
Minster
The
Freehold
EGBERT RD
MONKTON RD
PH
Liby
PO
THORNE RD
TAYLOR RD
ST MARY'S RD
NORTON DR
SINGLETON CL
HIGH ST
MOLINEUX RD
DOMNEVA RD
Minster
Abbey
(rems of)
Minster
CE Prim
Sch
Watchester
Farm
ST MILDRED'S RD
CORNELIS DR
PETT'S CRES
GLEBE CT
STATION RD
CHURCH ST
DURLOCK
MONKTON RD
ABBEY GR
WATCHESTER LA
STATION APP
CHEESMANS CL
BARNETT CT
Minster
Durlock
CT12
LC
LC
LC
Telegraph Hill
Ind Pk
LAUNDRY RD
Dellside
Mill
Cottage
IVY COTTAGE HILL
THORNE HILL
WAYBOROUGH HILL
WAY HILL
WAY FARM COTTS
Wayborough
Farm
TORRINGTON COTTS
Way
Hazeldene
Farm
FOXBOROUGH LA
Minster
House
Way Farm
House
PINKS CNR
THE LANES
GRINSELL HILL
BEDLAM COURT LA
Spencer's Pond
Cottages
The
Rough
Clapper
Hill
BROOK LA
MARSH FARM RD
Reservoir
Minster Marshes
Minster Stream
Boxlees
Hill
Sewage
Works
Abbot's Wall
Saxon Shore Way
River Stour
Weatherlees
Hill
Masts
Ash Level
CT13
CT3

49
72

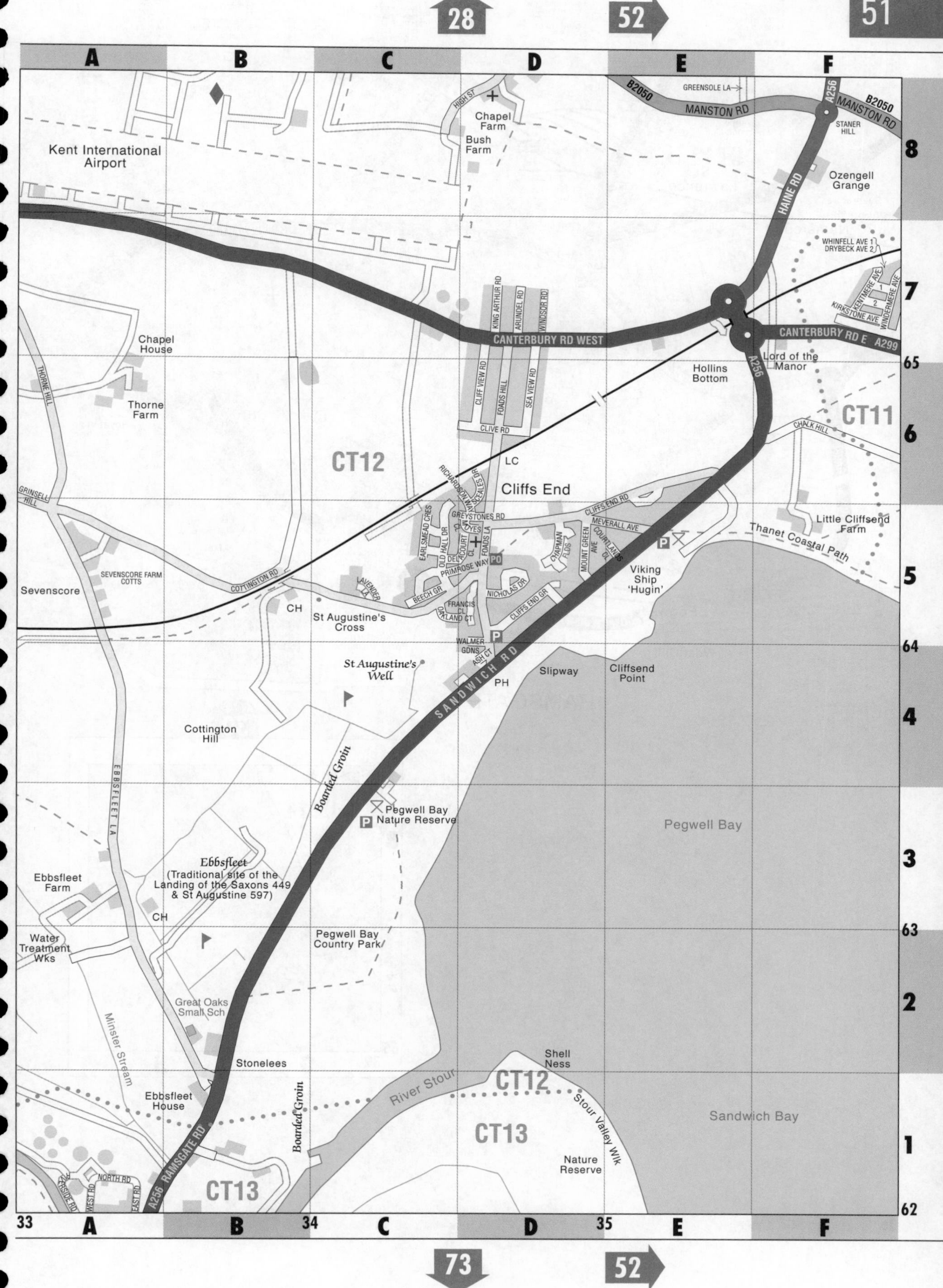

A B C D E F

8
7
65
6
5
64
4
3
63
2
1
62

Kent International
Airport

B2050
GREENSOLE LA→
MANSTON RD
A256
B2050
MANSTON RD
STANER HILL

HAINE RD
Ozengell
Grange

HIGH ST
Chapel
Farm
Bush
Farm

WHINFELL AVE 1
DRYBECK AVE 2
KENTMERE AVE
WINDERMERE AVE
KIRKSTONE AVE

KING ARTHUR RD
ARUNDEL RD
WINDSOR RD

CANTERBURY RD WEST
CANTERBURY RD E A299

Chapel
House

Lord of the
Manor

CT11

Thorne
Farm

CLIFF VIEW RD
FOADS HILL
SEA VIEW RD

Hollins
Bottom

A256

CHALK HILL

THORNE HILL

CLIVE RD

CT12

LC

Cliffs End

Little Cliffsend
Farm

Thanet Coastal Path

GRINSELL HILL

RICHBOROUGH WAY
SCALES RD

GREYSTONES RD

CLIFFS END RD

MEVERALL AVE

COURT CL

MOUNT GREEN AVE

SEVENSCORE FARM COTTS

EARL SMEAD CRES
OLD HALL DR
DELF
HOVES
FOADS LA

CHAPMAN FLDS

Viking Ship
'Hugin'

P

Sevenscore

COTTINGTON RD

LAVENDER
BEECH GR
PRIMROSE WAY
PO
NICHOLAS DR
CLIFFS END GR

P

CH

FRANCIS CL
OAKLAND CT

St Augustine's
Cross

WALMER GDNS
ASH CT

P

PH

Slipway

Cliffsend
Point

St Augustine's
Well

SANDWICH RD

Cottington
Hill

Bounded Groin

Pegwell Bay

EBBSFLEET LA

Pegwell Bay
Nature Reserve
P

Ebbsfleet
Farm

Ebbsfleet
(Traditional site of the
Landing of the Saxons 449
& St Augustine 597)

Pegwell Bay
Country Park

CH

Water
Treatment
Wks

Great Oaks
Small Sch

Stonelees

Shell
Ness

CT12

River Stour

Stour Valley Wlk

Sandwich Bay

Minster Stream

Bounded Groin

CT13

Ebbsfleet
House

RAMSGATE RD
A256

NORTH RD
WEST RD
EAST RD

CT13

Nature
Reserve

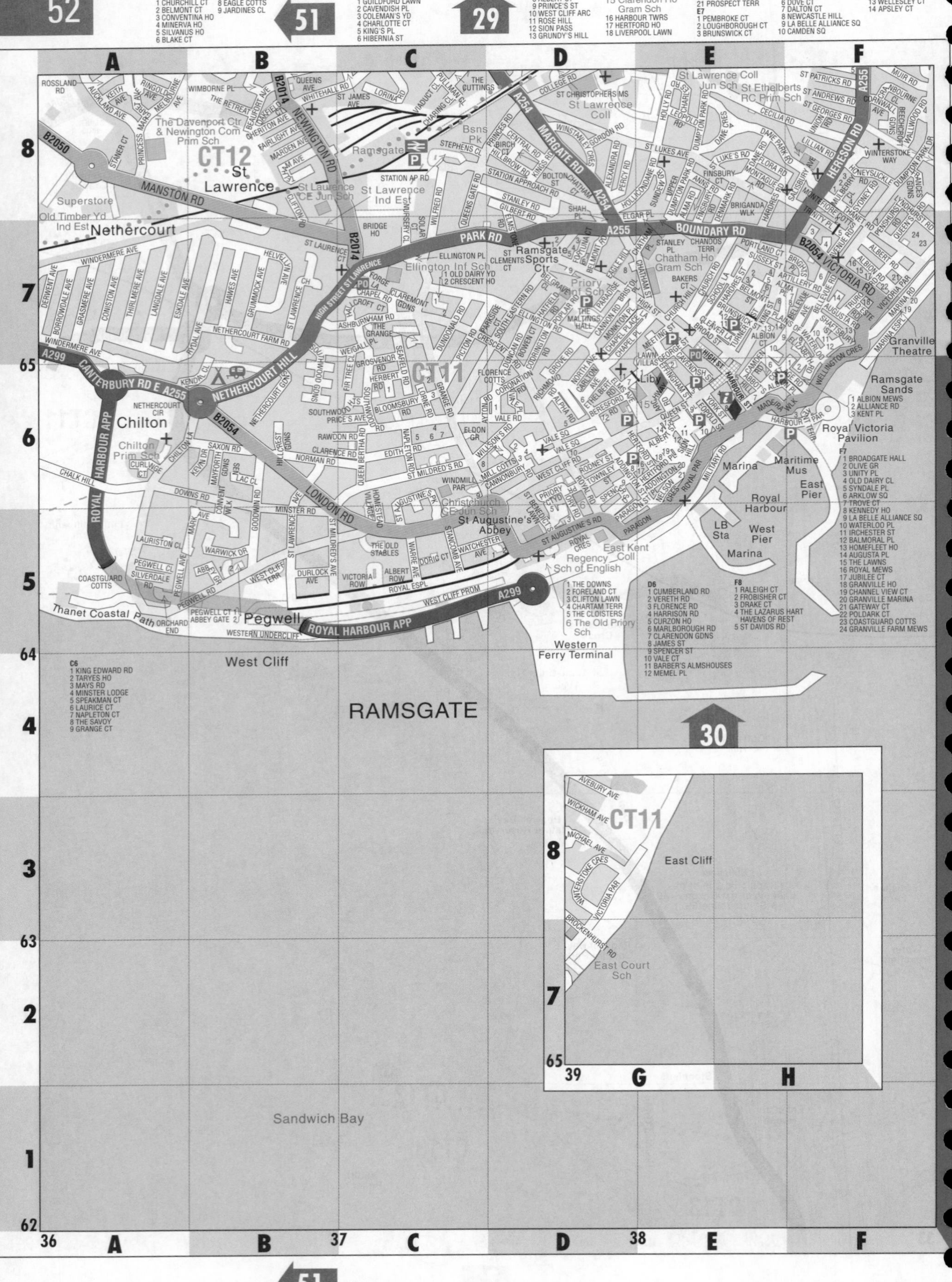
D7
1 CHURCHILL CT
2 BELMONT CT
3 CONVENTINA HO
4 MINERVA HO
5 SILVANUS HO
6 BLAKE CT
7 COLLINGWOOD CT
8 EAGLE COTTS
9 JARDINES CL
51
E6
1 GUILDFORD LAWN
2 CAVENDISH PL
3 COLEMAN'S YD
4 CHARLOTTE CT
5 KING'S PL
6 HIBERNIA ST
29
7 ALBION HILL
8 ALBERT CT
9 PRINCE'S ST
10 WEST CLIFF ARC
11 ROSE HILL
12 SION PASS
13 GRUNDY'S HILL
14 ST MICHAEL'S ALLEY
15 Clarendon Ho Gram Sch
16 HARBOUR TWRS
17 HERTFORD HO
18 LIVERPOOL LAWN
19 ADELAIDE GDNS
20 PROSPECT CT
21 PROSPECT TERR
E7
1 PEMBROKE CT
2 LOUGHBOROUGH CT
3 BRUNSWICK CT
4 BARTON CT
5 PACKER'S LA
6 DOVE CT
7 DALTON CT
8 NEWCASTLE HILL
9 LA BELLE ALLIANCE SQ
10 CAMDEN SQ
11 STAFFORDSHIRE ST
12 UNION ST
13 WELLESLEY CT
14 APSLEY CT
A
B
C
D
E
F
8
7
6
5
4
3
2
1
65
64
63
62
36
37
38
CT12
St Lawrence
Nethercourt
Ramsgate
CT11
Chilton
Pegwell
MANSTON RD
PARK RD
BOUNDARY RD
HIGH STREET ST LAWRENCE
NETHERCOURT HILL
CANTERBURY RD E A255
LONDON RD
ROYAL HARBOUR APP
HERESON RD
VICTORIA RD
MARGATE RD
NEWINGTON RD
St Augustine's Abbey
Ramsgate Sports Ctr
Granville Theatre
Ramsgate Sands
Royal Victoria Pavilion
Maritime Mus
Royal Harbour
East Pier
West Pier
Marina
Western Ferry Terminal
West Cliff
Thanet Coastal Path
RAMSGATE
Sandwich Bay
A1
1 ALBION MEWS
2 ALLIANCE RD
3 KENT PL
F7
1 BROADGATE HALL
2 OLIVE GR
3 UNITY PL
4 OLD DAIRY CL
5 SYNDALE PL
6 ARKLOW SQ
7 TROVE CT
8 KENNEDY HO
9 LA BELLE ALLIANCE SQ
10 WATERLOO PL
11 IRCHESTER ST
12 BALMORAL PL
13 HOMEFLEET HO
14 AUGUSTA PL
15 THE LAWNS
16 ROYAL MEWS
17 JUBILEE CT
18 GRANVILLE HO
19 CHANNEL VIEW CT
20 GRANVILLE MARINA
21 GATEWAY CT
22 POLDARK CT
23 COASTGUARD COTTS
24 GRANVILLE FARM MEWS
1 THE DOWNS
2 FORELAND CT
3 CLIFTON LAWN
4 CHARTAM TERR
5 THE CLOISTERS
6 The Old Priory Sch
D6
1 CUMBERLAND RD
2 VERETH RD
3 FLORENCE RD
4 HARRISON RD
5 CURZON HO
6 MARLBOROUGH RD
7 CLARENDON GDNS
8 JAMES ST
9 SPENCER ST
10 VALE CT
11 BARBER'S ALMSHOUSES
12 MEMEL PL
F8
1 RALEIGH CT
2 FROBISHER CT
3 DRAKE CT
4 THE LAZARUS HART HAVENS OF REST
5 ST DAVIDS RD
C6
1 KING EDWARD RD
2 TARYES HO
3 MAYS RD
4 MINSTER LODGE
5 SPEAKMAN CT
6 LAURICE CT
7 NAPLETON CT
8 THE SAVOY
9 GRANGE CT
30
CT11
East Cliff
East Court Sch
AVEBURY AVE
WICKHAM AVE
MICHAEL AVE
WINTERSTOKE CRES
VICTORIA PAR
BROCKENHURST RD
39
G
H
51

31
54

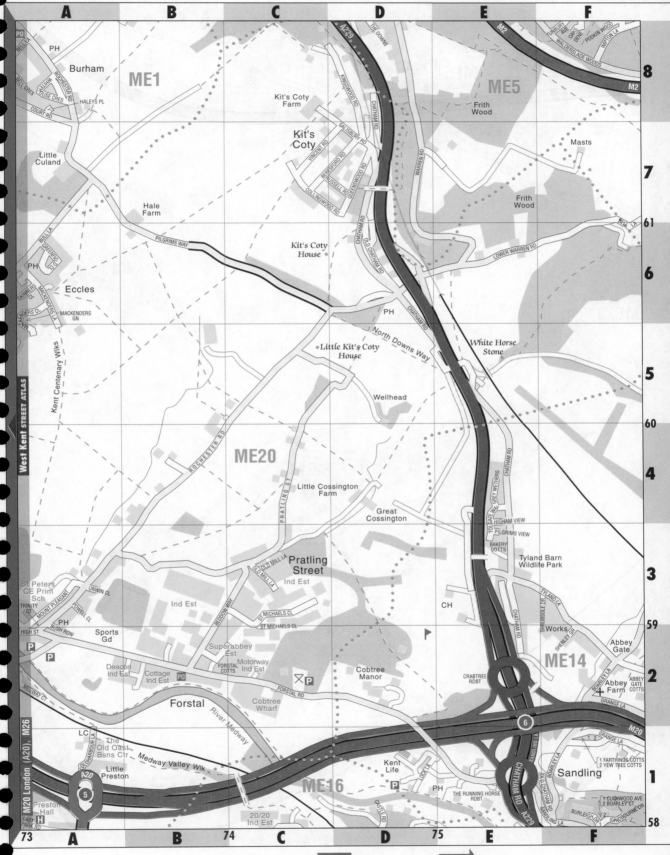
A
B
C
D
E
F
Burham
ME1
Kit's Coty Farm
ME5
Frith Wood
Kit's Coty
Little Culand
Masts
Frith Wood
Hale Farm
PILGRIMS WAY
Kit's Coty House
LOWER WARREN RD
Eccles
MACKENDERS GN
PH
North Downs Way
Little Kit's Coty House
White Horse Stone
Kent Centenary Wlks
Wellhead
ME20
ROCHESTER RD
PRATLING ST
Little Cossington Farm
Great Cossington
Pratling Street
Ind Est
Tyland Barn Wildlife Park
St Peters CE Prim Sch
Ind Est
Sports Gd
CH
Works
Abbey Gate
Superabbey Est
Motorway Ind Est
ME14
Deacon Ind Est
Cottage Ind Est
Cobtree Manor
CRABTREE RDBT
Abbey Farm
Forstal
Cobtree Wharf
FORSTAL RD
River Medway
M20
The Old Oast Bsns Ctr
Medway Valley Wlk
Kent Life
Sandling
Little Preston
ME16
THE RUNNING HORSE RDBT
Preston Hall
20/20 Ind Est
CHATHAM RD
A229
M2
M20 London (A20), M26
West Kent STREET ATLAS
8
7
61
6
5
60
4
3
59
2
1
58
73
74
75

74
54

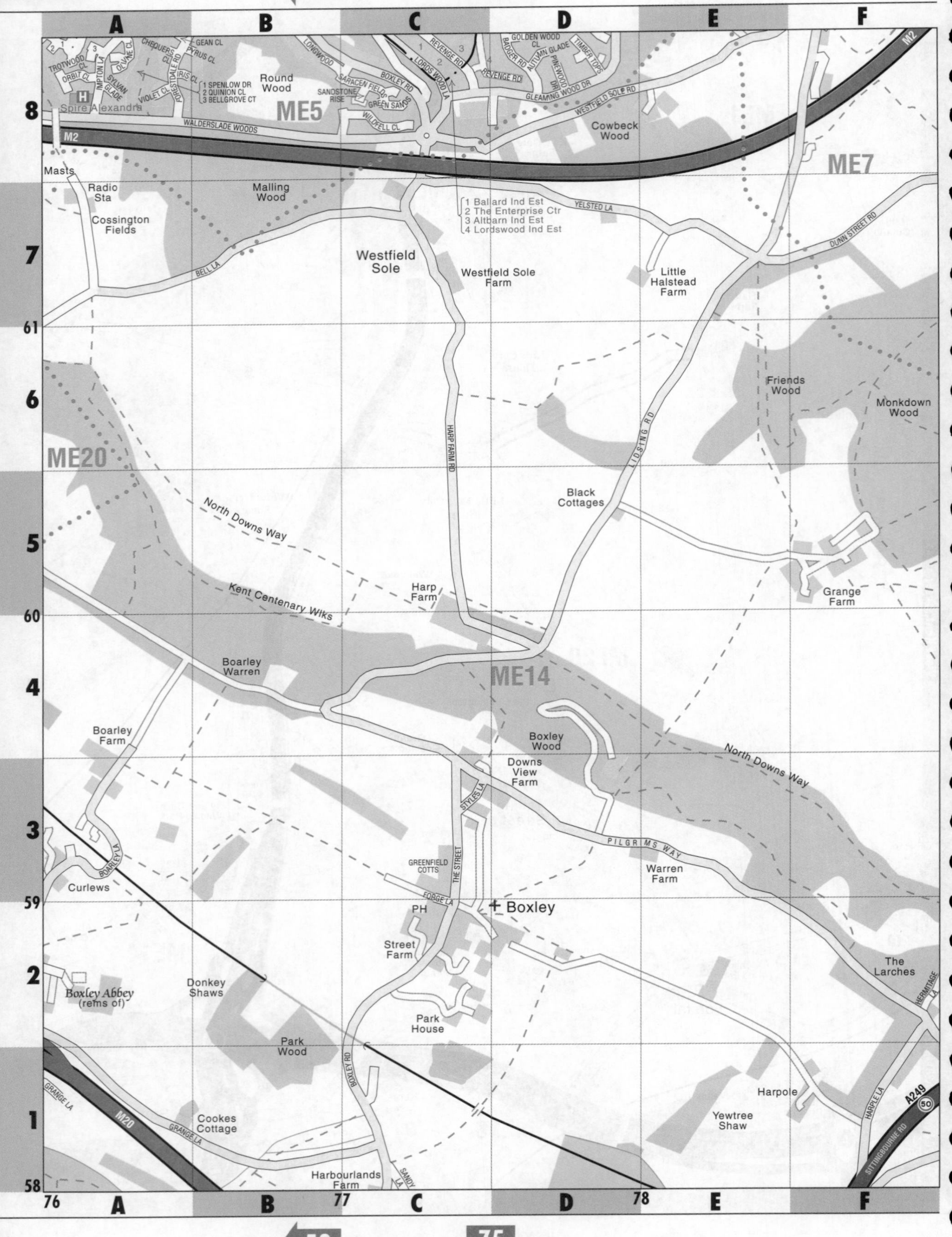

53
32

A **B** **C** **D** **E** **F**

TROTWOOD
ORBIT CL
SYLVAN GLADE
CHEQUERS CL
PRIUS CL
GEAN CL
LONGWOOD
REVENGE RD
GOLDEN WOOD CL
BADGER RD
AUTUMN GLADE
TIMBER TOPS

Spire Alexandra
H

Round Wood

8

1 SPENLOW DR
2 QUINION CL
3 BELLGROVE CT

MARACEN FIELDS
SANDSTONE RISE
GREEN SANDS
WILDFELL CL

ME5

BOXLEY RD
LORDS WOOD LA

REVENGE RD

GLEAMING WOOD DR
WESTFIELD SOLE RD

Cowbeck Wood

WALDERSLADE WOODS

M2

ME7

Masts

Radio Sta

Malling Wood

1 Ballard Ind Est
2 The Enterprise Ctr
3 Altbarn Ind Est
4 Lordswood Ind Est

YELSTED LA

DUNN STREET RD

Cossington Fields

7

Westfield Sole

Westfield Sole Farm

Little Halstead Farm

BELL LA

61

ME20

6

HARP FARM RD

LDSTNG RD

Friends Wood

Monkdown Wood

North Downs Way

Black Cottages

5

Kent Centenary Wlks

Harp Farm

Grange Farm

60

Boarley Warren

ME14

North Downs Way

4

Boarley Farm

Boxley Wood

Downs View Farm

3

Curlews

STYLES LA

PILGRIMS WAY

Warren Farm

59

BOARLEY LA

Greenfield Cotts

THE STREET

+ Boxley

PH

FORGE LA

Street Farm

The Larches

2

Boxley Abbey (rems of)

Donkey Shaws

Park House

HERMITAGE LA

BOXLEY RD

Park Wood

Harpole

A249
50

GRANGE LA

M20

Cookes Cottage

GRANGE LA

SANDY

Yewtree Shaw

HARPLE LA

SITTINGBOURNE RD

1

58

76
A
B
77
C
D
78
E
F

Harbourlands Farm

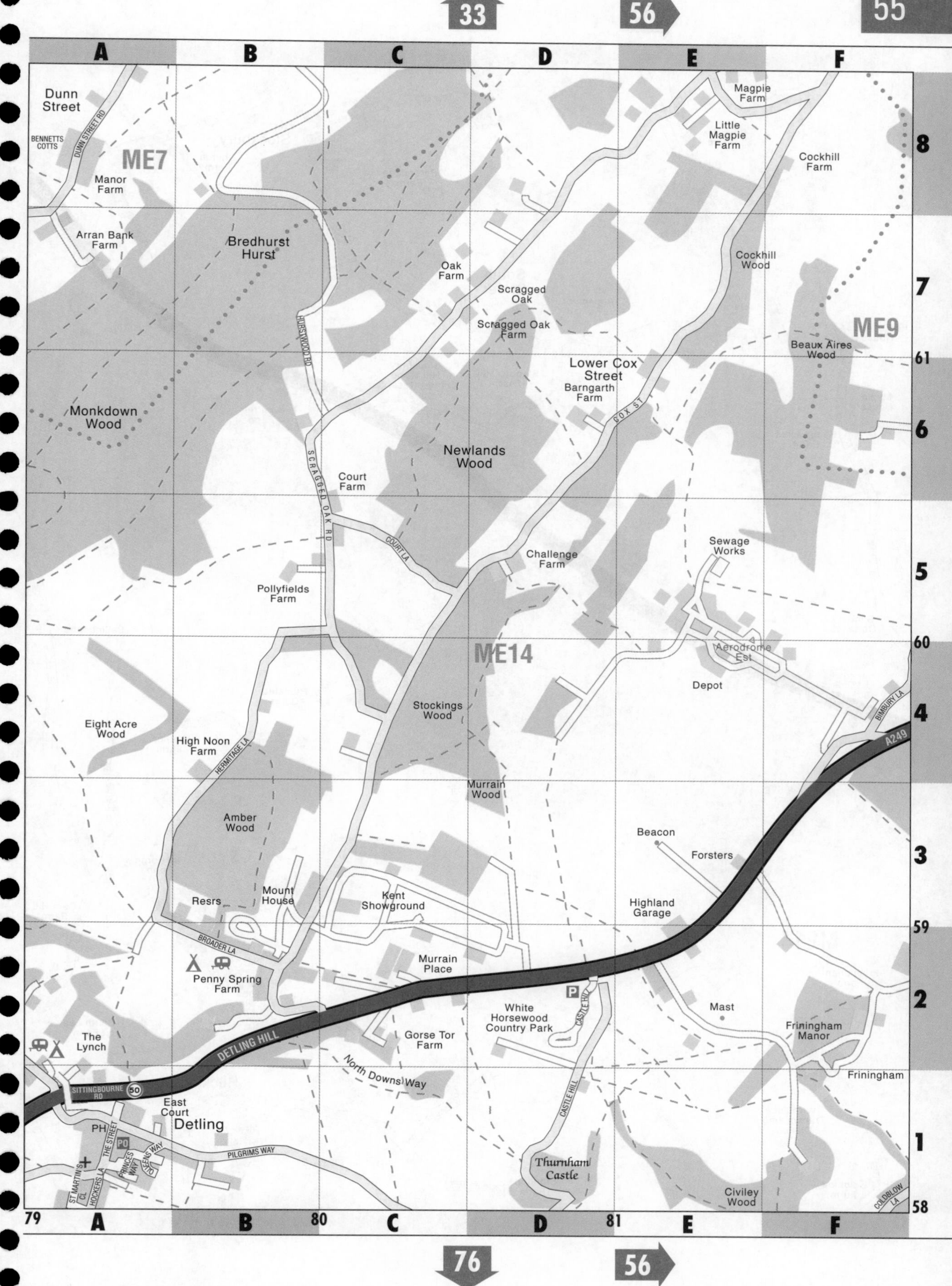
A
B
C
D
E
F
8
7
61
6
5
60
4
3
59
2
1
58
79
80
81
Dunn Street
BENNETTS COTTS
DUNN STREET RD
ME7
Manor Farm
Arran Bank Farm
Bredhurst Hurst
Monkdown Wood
HURSTWOOD RD
Oak Farm
Scragged Oak
Scragged Oak Farm
Magpie Farm
Little Magpie Farm
Cockhill Farm
Cockhill Wood
ME9
Beaux Aires Wood
Lower Cox Street
Barngarth Farm
COX ST
Newlands Wood
SCRAGGED OAK RD
Court Farm
COURT LA
Challenge Farm
Sewage Works
Pollyfields Farm
ME14
Aerodrome Est
Depot
Stockings Wood
Eight Acre Wood
High Noon Farm
HERMITAGE LA
BIMBURY LA
A249
Murrain Wood
Amber Wood
Beacon
Forsters
Resrs
Mount House
Kent Showground
Highland Garage
BROADER LA
Murrain Place
Penny Spring Farm
CASTLE HILL
White Horsewood Country Park
Mast
Gorse Tor Farm
Friningham Manor
The Lynch
DETLING HILL
North Downs Way
Friningham
SITTINGBOURNE RD
50
East Court
Detling
PH
THE STREET
PO
QUEENS WAY
PRINCES WAY
PILGRIMS WAY
ST MARTIN'S CL
HOCKERS LA
Thurnham Castle
Civiley Wood
COLDBLOW LA

55
34

A B C D E F
8
7
61
6
5
60
4
3
59
2
1
58
82
83
84
HILL GREEN RD
NORTHDOWN
THE STREET
BULL LA
CHURCH LA
PH
Stockbury
HARROW CT
CEDAR GDNS
PO
Parsonage Farm
Church Farm
HONEYCROCK HILL
AMELS HILL
CHURCH HILL
A249
Plum Tree Farm
PLUM TREE LA
WEST WOOD RD
West Wood
YELSTED RD
South Street
Four Oaks
Appsmoor Farm
SOUTH STREET RD
Beaux Aires House
Hillside Farm
PH
SOUTH GREEN LA
Maple House
Hove Cottage
Steppes Hill Farm
Stockbury Hill Wood Nature Reserve
CHALKY RD
STEPS HILL RD
Squirrels Farm
Keepers Cottage
Beaux Aires Farm
Hall Wood
HAYES LA
BIMBURY LA
Longreach Wood
ME9
Squirrel Wood
Bimbury Cottages
Ballingdane
Rumsted Court
RUMSTEAD LA
RUMSTEAD RD
Yetnor Farm
A249
Longton Wood
OLD FORGE LA
SOUTHLEES LA
Appsfield
Old Forge Farm
Cam Hill Farm
ME14
Little Budds Farm
Friningham Farm
Long Wood
South Leas Farm
COLDBLOW LA
Pond Farm
POND FARM RD
ME17
Hucking
CHURCH RD
Wireless Transmitting Station
COLDHARBOUR LA
PH
Coldblow Farm
Stanhope Farm
SCRAGGED OAK RD
BROAD STREET HILL
P

55
77

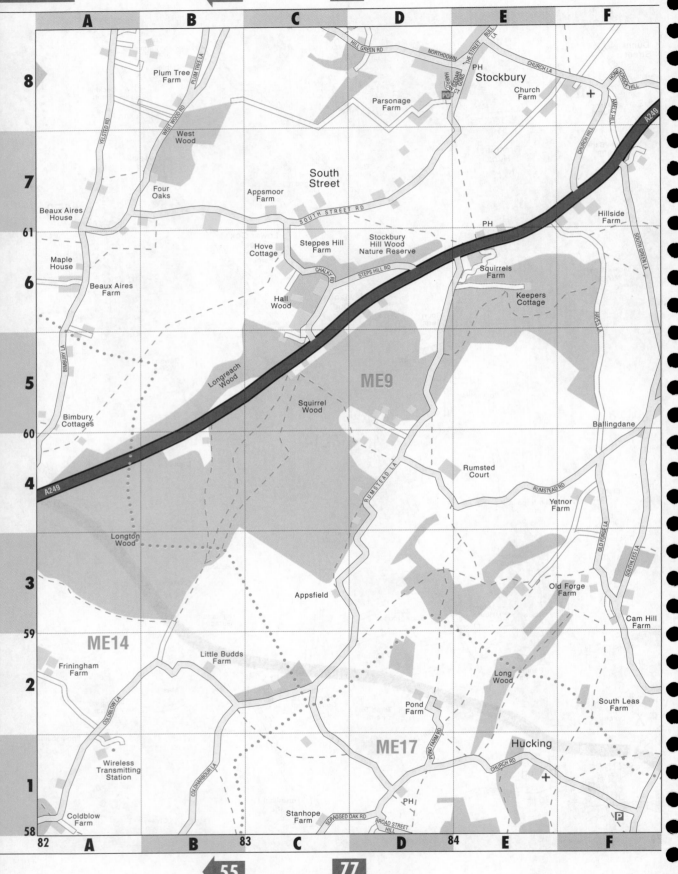

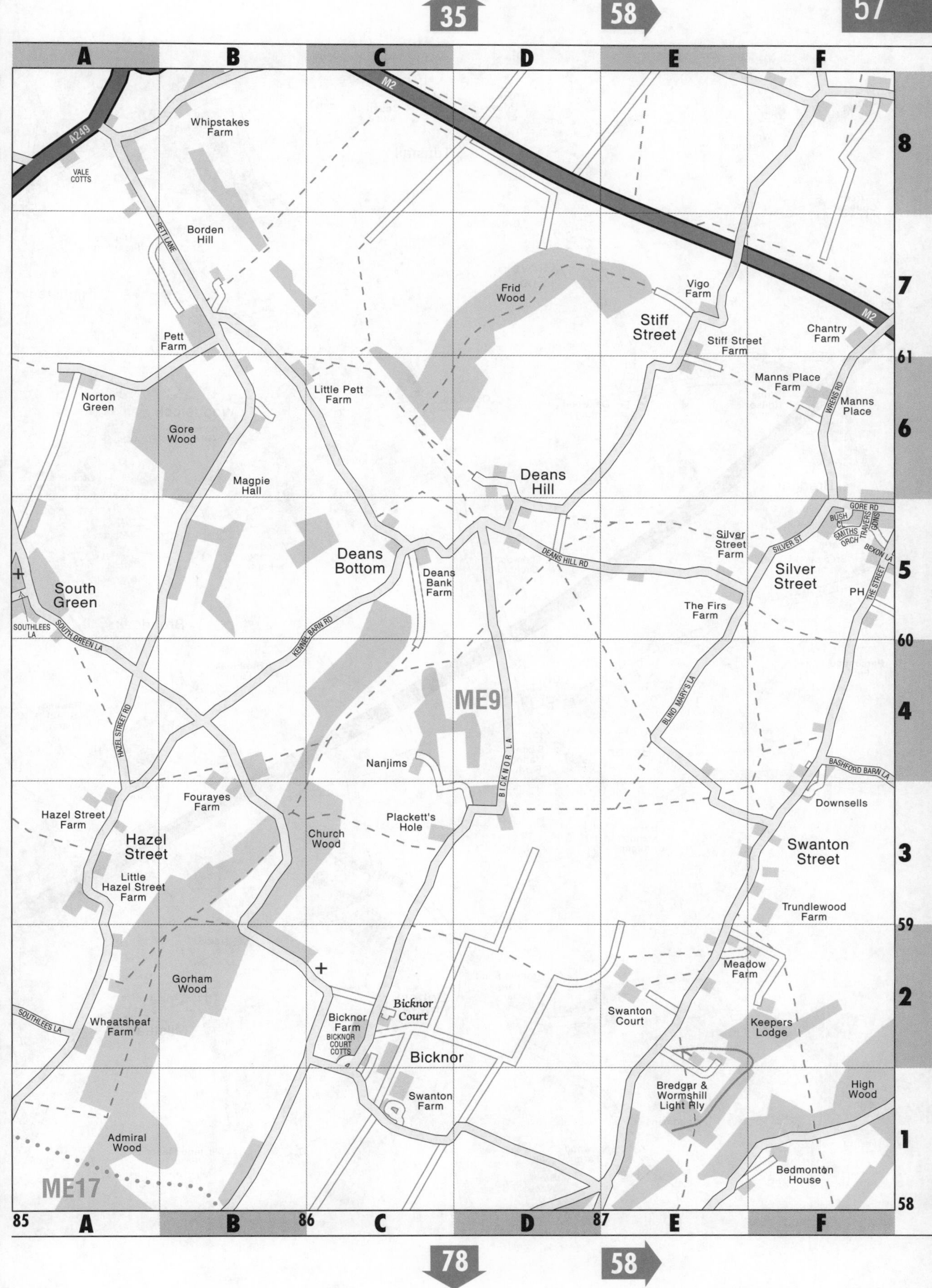

A B C D E F

8
7
61
6
5
60
4
59
3
2
1
58

85 A B 86 C D 87 E F

M2

A249

VALE
COTTS

Whipstakes
Farm

PETT LANE

Borden
Hill

Pett
Farm

Norton
Green

Gore
Wood

Little Pett
Farm

Magpie
Hall

Frid
Wood

Stiff
Street

Vigo
Farm

Stiff Street
Farm

Chantry
Farm

M2

Manns Place
Farm

WRENS RD

Manns
Place

Deans
Hill

Deans
Bottom

Deans
Bank
Farm

DEANS HILL RD

Silver
Street
Farm

SILVER ST

Silver
Street

GORE RD
BUSH
CL
SMITHS
ORCH
TRAVERS
GDNS
BEXON LA
THE STREET

PH

South
Green

SOUTHLEES
LA

SOUTH GREEN LA

KENNIC BARN RD

ME9

The Firs
Farm

BLIND MARY'S LA

60

HAZEL STREET RD

Nanjims

BICKNOR LA

Bashford Barn La

Downsells

Hazel Street
Farm

Fourayes
Farm

Plackett's
Hole

Church
Wood

Swanton
Street

Hazel
Street

Little
Hazel Street
Farm

Trundlewood
Farm

SOUTHLEES LA

Gorham
Wood

Meadow
Farm

Wheatsheaf
Farm

Bicknor
Farm

BICKNOR
COURT
COTTS

Bicknor
Court

Bicknor

Swanton
Court

Keepers
Lodge

Swanton
Farm

Bredgar &
Wormshill
Light Rly

High
Wood

ME17

Admiral
Wood

Bedmonton
House

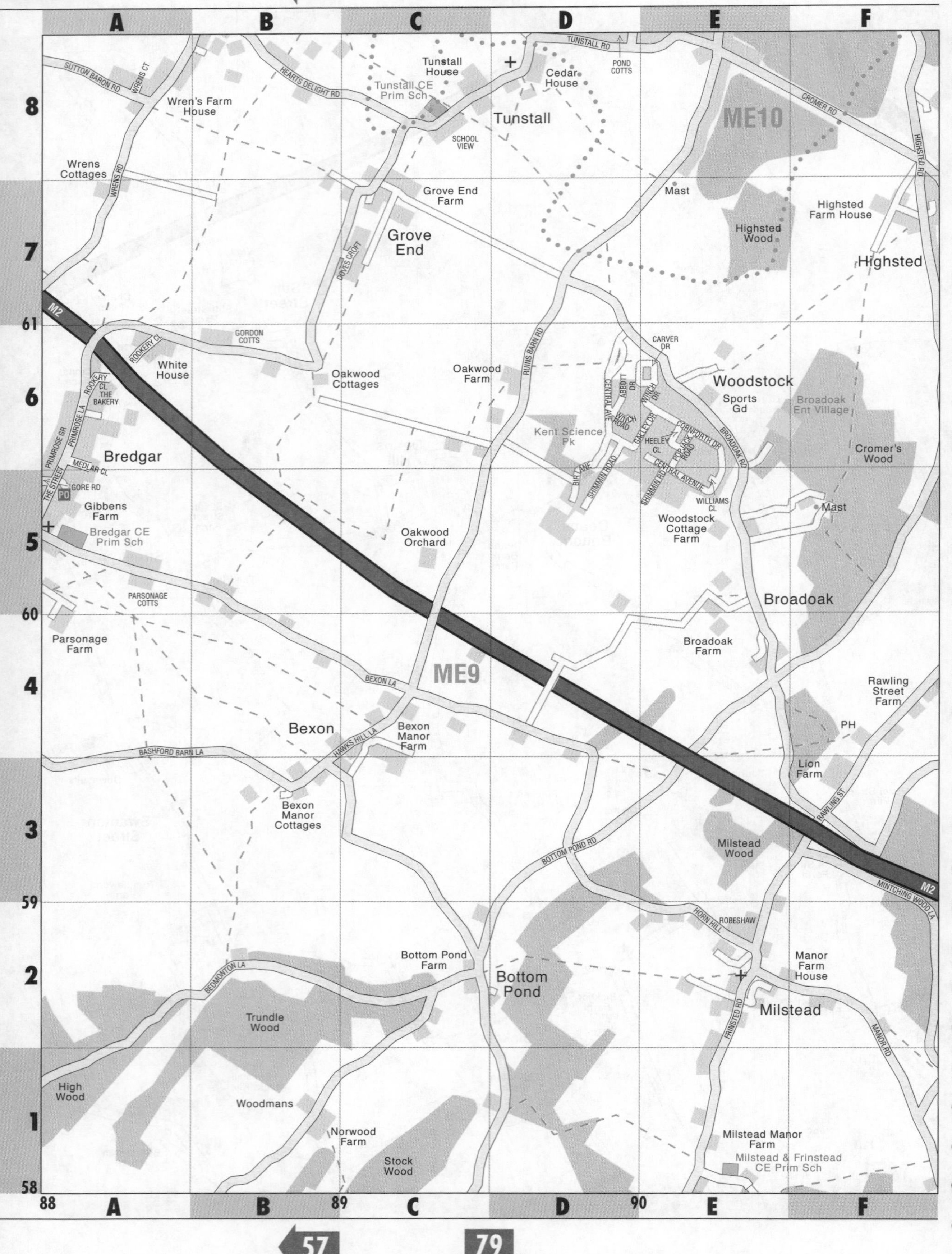
A
B
C
D
E
F
8
7
61
6
5
60
4
3
59
2
1
58
88
89
90
SUTTON BARON RD
WRENS CT
Wren's Farm House
HEARTS DELIGHT RD
Tunstall House
Tunstall CE Prim Sch
Cedar House
TUNSTALL RD
POND COTTS
Tunstall
SCHOOL VIEW
ME10
CROMER RD
HIGHSTED RD
Wrens Cottages
WRENS RD
Grove End Farm
Mast
Highsted Farm House
Highsted Wood
Grove End
DOVES CROFT
Highsted
M2
GORDON COTTS
ROOKERY CL
White House
Oakwood Cottages
Oakwood Farm
RUINS BARN RD
CARVER DR
Woodstock
Sports Gd
Broadoak Ent Village
ROOKERY CL
THE BAKERY
CENTRAL AVE
ABBOTT DR
WINCH DR
WINCH ROAD
GALLEY DR
CORNFORTH DR
HEELEY CL
PODJACK ROAD
BROADOAK RD
Kent Science Pk
Cromer's Wood
PRIMROSE GR
PRIMROSE LA
Bredgar
MEDLAR CL
THE STREET
GORE RD
PO
BIRT LANE
SHIMMIN ROAD
SHIMMIN RD
CENTRAL AVENUE
WILLIAMS CL
Mast
Gibbens Farm
Bredgar CE Prim Sch
Oakwood Orchard
Woodstock Cottage Farm
PARSONAGE COTTS
Broadoak
Parsonage Farm
Broadoak Farm
ME9
BEXON LA
Rawling Street Farm
Bexon
Bexon Manor Farm
HAWKS HILL LA
PH
BASHFORD BARN LA
Lion Farm
RAWLING ST
Bexon Manor Cottages
BOTTOM POND RD
Milstead Wood
MINTCHING WOOD LA
M2
HORN HILL
ROBESHAW
Bottom Pond Farm
Bottom Pond
Manor Farm House
BEDMONTON LA
Milstead
FRINSTED RD
Trundle Wood
MANOR RD
High Wood
Woodmans
Norwood Farm
Milstead Manor Farm
Milstead & Frinstead CE Prim Sch
Stock Wood

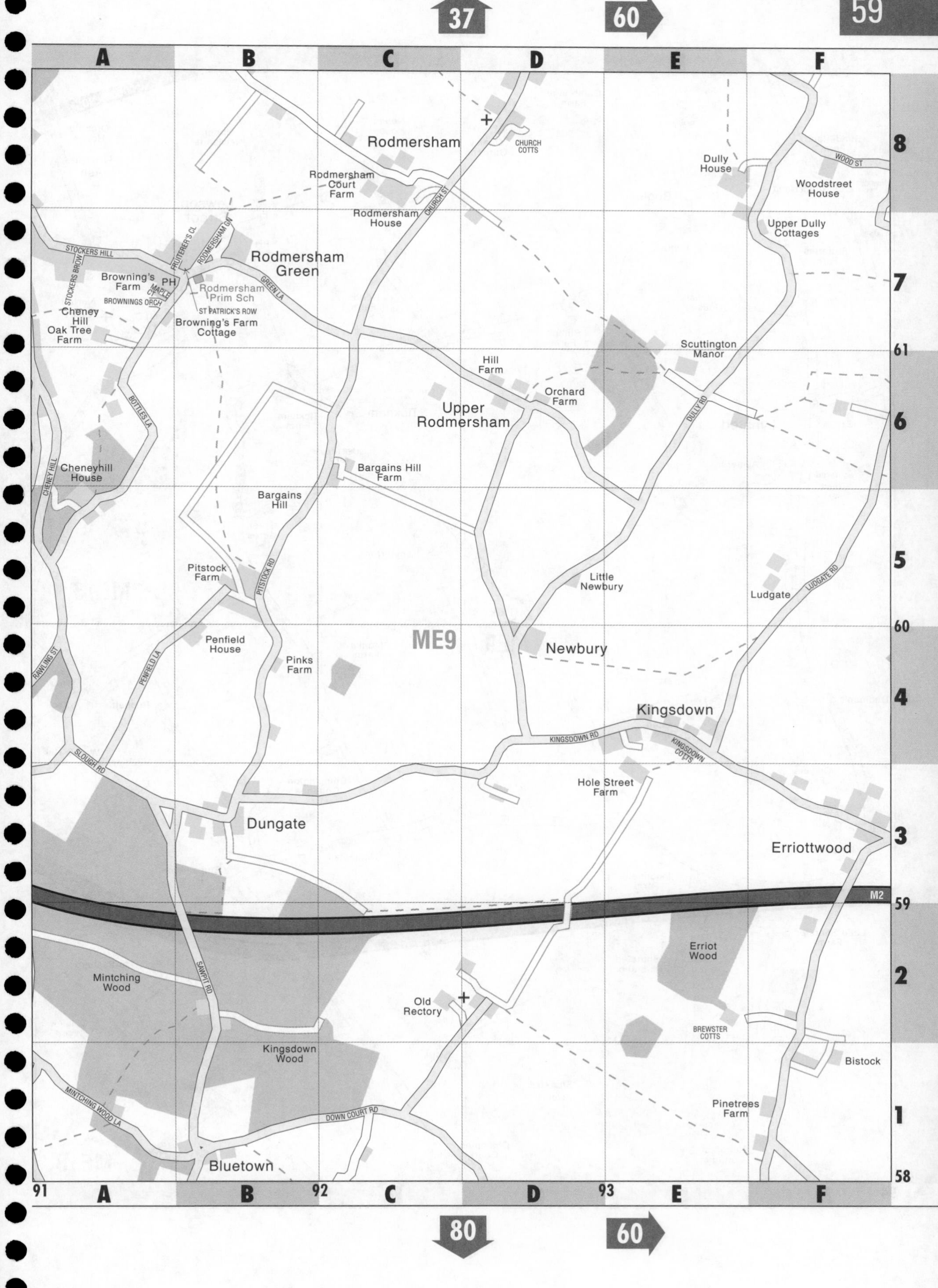
37
60
A
B
C
D
E
F
Rodmersham
CHURCH COTTS
Rodmersham Court Farm
Rodmersham House
CHURCH ST
Dully House
WOOD ST
Woodstreet House
Upper Dully Cottages
STOCKERS HILL
STOCKERS BROW
FRUITERER'S CL
RODMERSHAM GN
Rodmersham Green
Browning's Farm
PH
MAPLE CT
BROWNINGS ORCH
Rodmersham Prim Sch
ST PATRICK'S ROW
GREEN LA
Cheney Hill
Oak Tree Farm
Browning's Farm Cottage
Scuttington Manor
Hill Farm
Orchard Farm
Upper Rodmersham
DULLY RD
BOTTLES LA
Cheneyhill House
CHENEY HILL
Bargains Hill Farm
Bargains Hill
Pitstock Farm
PITSTOCK RD
Little Newbury
Ludgate
LUDGATE RD
Penfield House
ME9
Newbury
Pinks Farm
RAWLING ST
PENFIELD LA
Kingsdown
KINGSDOWN RD
KINGSDOWN COTTS
SLOUGH RD
Hole Street Farm
Dungate
Erriottwood
M2
Erriot Wood
Mintching Wood
SAWPIT RD
Old Rectory
BREWSTER COTTS
Bistock
Kingsdown Wood
MINTCHING WOOD LA
DOWN COURT RD
Pinetrees Farm
Bluetown
8
7
61
6
5
60
4
3
59
2
1
58
91
92
93
80
60

59
38

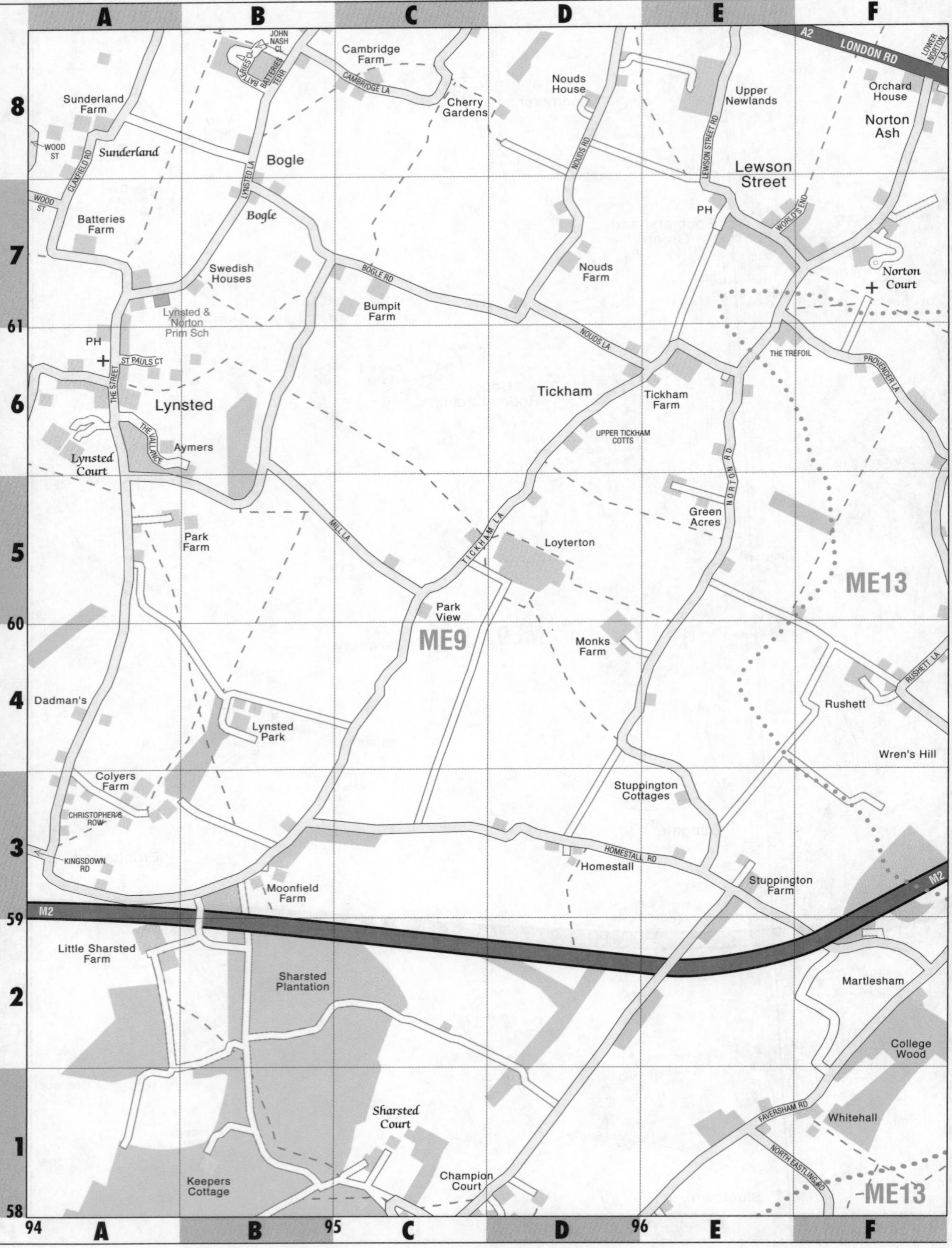

A　B　C　D　E　F

8

Sunderland Farm

WOOD ST

CLAXFIELD RD

Sunderland

WOOD ST

Batteries Farm

JOHN NASH CL

BATT... TERR

Cambridge Farm

CAMBRIDGE LA

Cherry Gardens

Bogle

LYNSTED LA

Nouds House

Upper Newlands

A2 LONDON RD

LOWER NORTON LA

Orchard House

Norton Ash

7

Bogle

Swedish Houses

BOGLE RD

Bumpit Farm

Nouds Farm

NOUDS RD

LEWSON STREET RD

Lewson Street

PH

WORLD'S END

Norton Court

61

Lynsted & Norton Prim Sch

PH

ST PAULS CT

THE STREET

NOUDS LA

THE TREFOIL

PROVENDER LA

6

Lynsted

THE VALLANCE

Aymers

Tickham

Tickham Farm

UPPER TICKHAM COTTS

NORTON RD

Lynsted Court

Park Farm

MILL LA

TICKHAM LA

Loyterton

Green Acres

ME13

5

Park View

ME9

Monks Farm

60

4

Dadman's

Lynsted Park

Rushett

RUSHETT LA

Wren's Hill

3

Colyers Farm

CHRISTOPHER'S ROW

KINGSDOWN RD

Moonfield Farm

HOMESTALL RD

Homestall

Stuppington Cottages

Stuppington Farm

M2

59

M2

Little Sharsted Farm

Sharsted Plantation

Martlesham

2

College Wood

1

Sharsted Court

FAVERSHAM RD

NORTH EASTLING RD

Whitehall

ME13

58

Keepers Cottage

Champion Court

94　A　B　95　C　D　96　E　F

39
62
A
B
C
D
E
F
LOWER NORTON LA
ME9
A2
LOWER RD
FOUR OAKS
BYSING WOOD RD
BENNETTS GDNS
BUCKLAND COTTS
8
Beacon House
Beacon Hill House
Beacon Hill
B2045
WESTERN LINK
Glebelands
LONDON RD
Stone Chapel
SUMPTER WAY
Works
7
Round Wood
61
PROVENDER LA
Telegraph Bank
Syndale Farm
Motel
Provender
Provender Farm
Syndale Farm Cottages
6
Judd's Hill
Dairy Cottage
Winbourne Farm
Judd's Wood
COXETT HILL
Provender Wood
Coxett Wood
Coxett Lodge
5
FAVERSHAM RD
ABBOTS HILL
60
Putt Wood
The Oaks
WATER LA
M2
Water Works
ME13
4
Caravan Park
Parsonage Farm
Tickham Hunt Kennels
Hanslett's House
HANSLETT'S LA
PAINTER'S FORSTAL RD
Lorenden Park
WELL LA
Hanslett's Farm
Scott's Farm
Whitehill
Hillside
3
Lorenden Prep Sch
Painters Farm
CADES ORCH
Painter's Forstal
GREEN LEES
59
PH
Bayfield
BAYFIELD
MUMMERY CT
MEADOW BANK
BAY BANKS
ME9
2
ELVERLAND LA
EASTLING RD
Churchman's Farm
STALISFIELD RD
New Barn Farm
BOX LA
Kennaways
Elverland Farm
THROWLEY RD
1
58
97
98
99
82
62

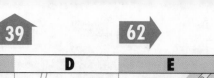

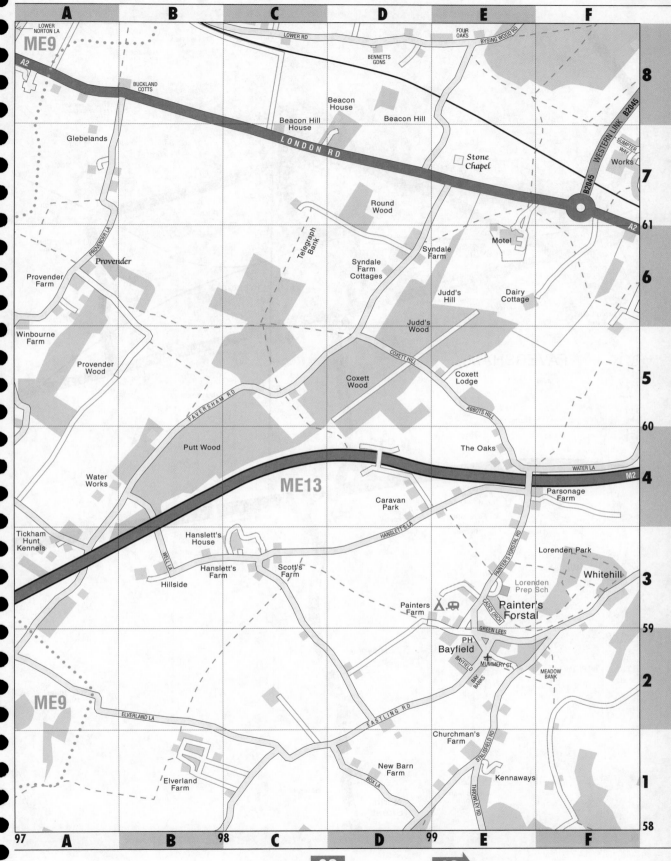

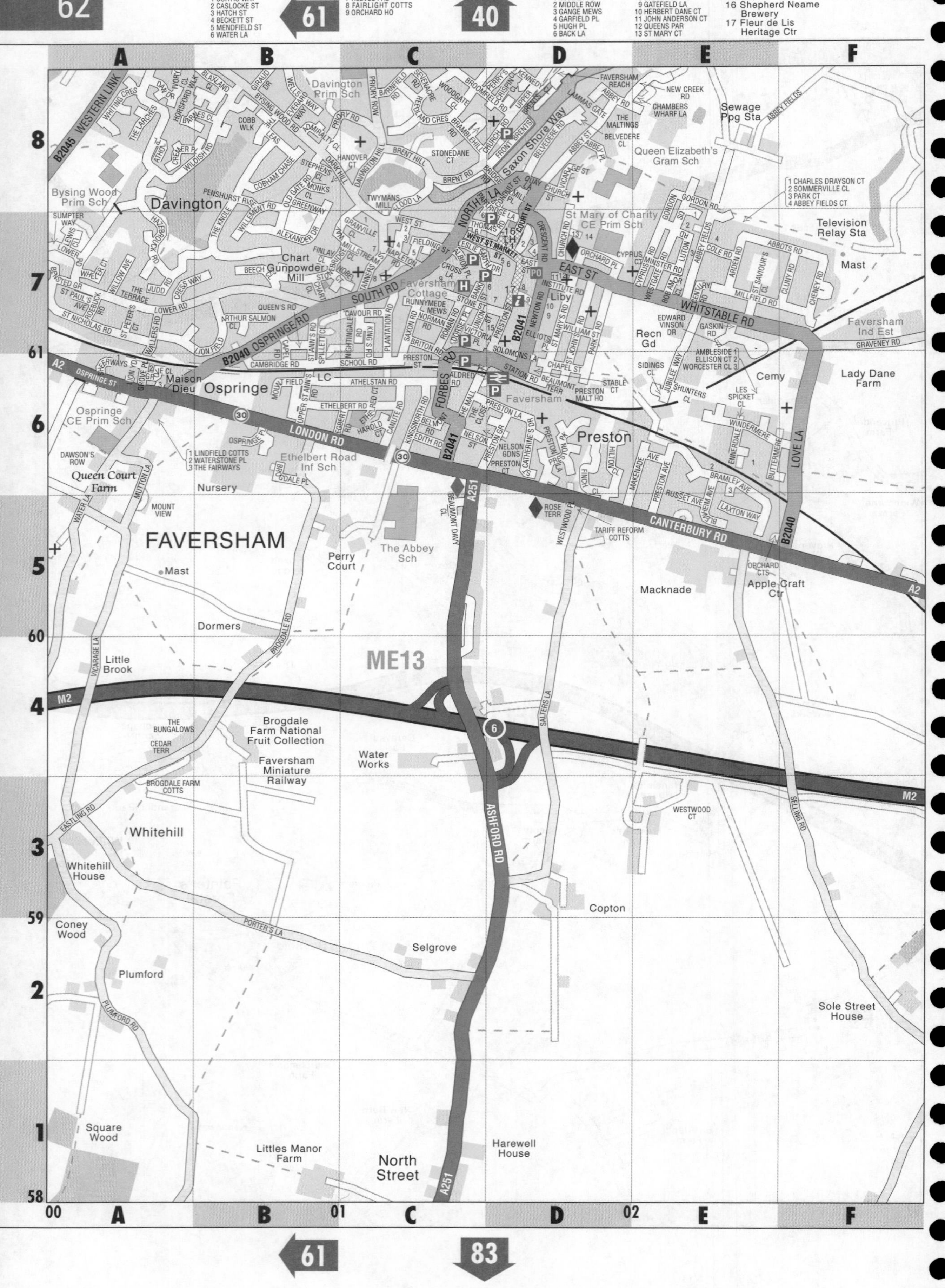

41
64

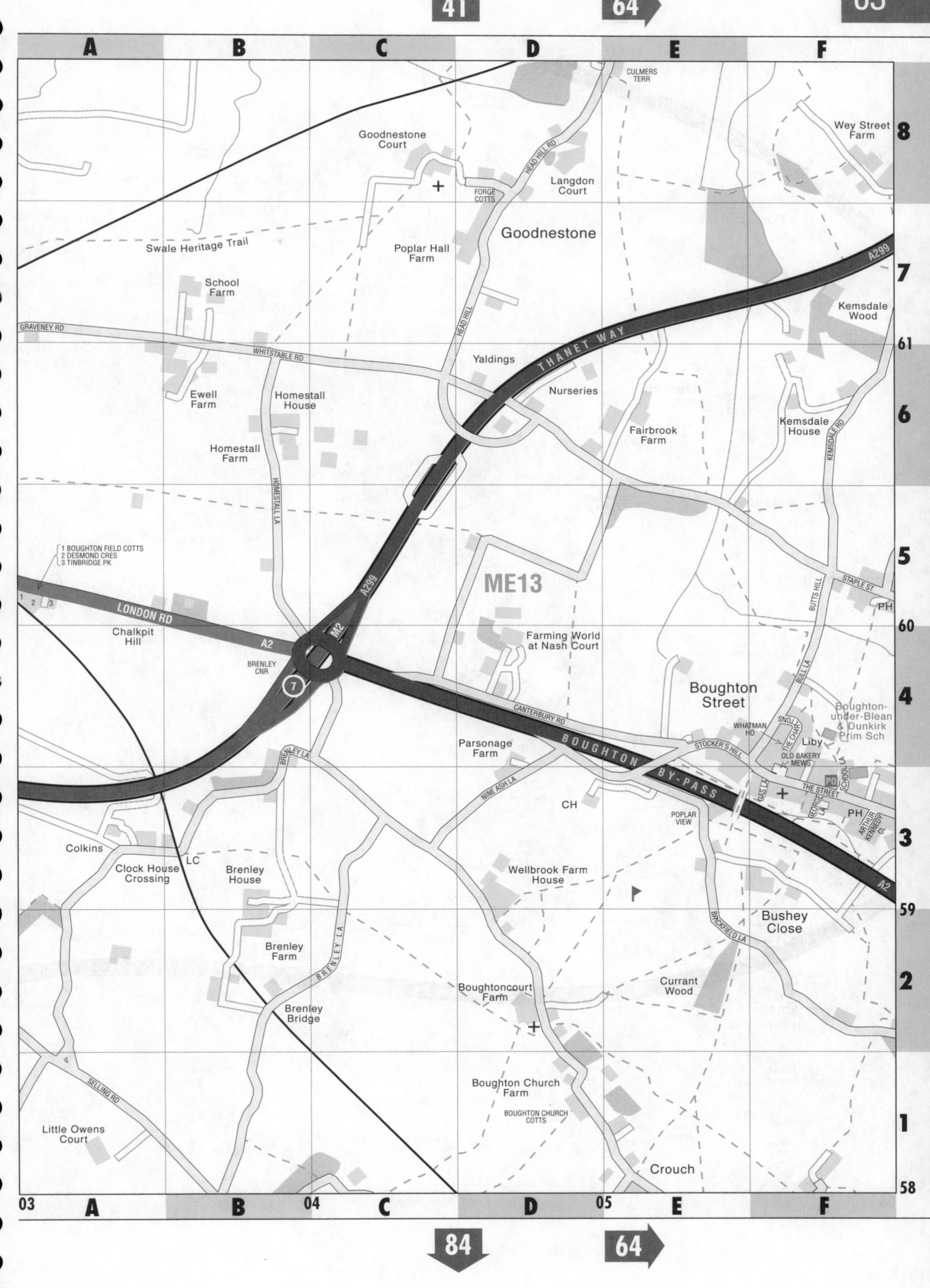

A
B
C
D
E
F
CULMERS TERR
Wey Street Farm
8
Goodnestone Court
HEAD HILL RD
Langdon Court
FORGE COTTS
Goodnestone
Swale Heritage Trail
Poplar Hall Farm
A299
7
School Farm
Kemsdale Wood
GRAVENEY RD
HEAD HILL
WHITSTABLE RD
THANET WAY
61
Yaldings
Nurseries
Ewell Farm
Homestall House
6
Fairbrook Farm
Kemsdale House
KEMSDALE RD
Homestall Farm
HOMESTALL LA
1 BOUGHTON FIELD COTTS
2 DESMOND CRES
3 TINBRIDGE PK
5
A299
ME13
STAPLE ST
BUTTS HILL
PH
LONDON RD
M2
Chalkpit Hill
A2
Farming World at Nash Court
60
BRENLEY CNR
7
Boughton Street
BULL LA
4
CANTERBURY RD
Boughton-under-Blean & Dunkirk Prim Sch
WHATMAN HO
SNOL
THE CHAR
Liby
Parsonage Farm
BOUGHTON BY-PASS
STOCKER'S HILL
OLD BAKERY MEWS
BRENLEY LA
PO
SCHOOL LA
NINE ASH LA
THE STREET
GAS LA
CH
POPLAR VIEW
GEORGE LA
PH
ARTHUR KENNEDY CL
3
Colkins
LC
Clock House Crossing
Brenley House
Wellbrook Farm House
A2
Bushey Close
59
BACKFIELD LA
Brenley Farm
BRENLEY LA
Currant Wood
2
Boughtoncourt Farm
Brenley Bridge
SELLING RD
Boughton Church Farm
BOUGHTON CHURCH COTTS
1
Little Owens Court
Crouch
58
03
04
05

84
64

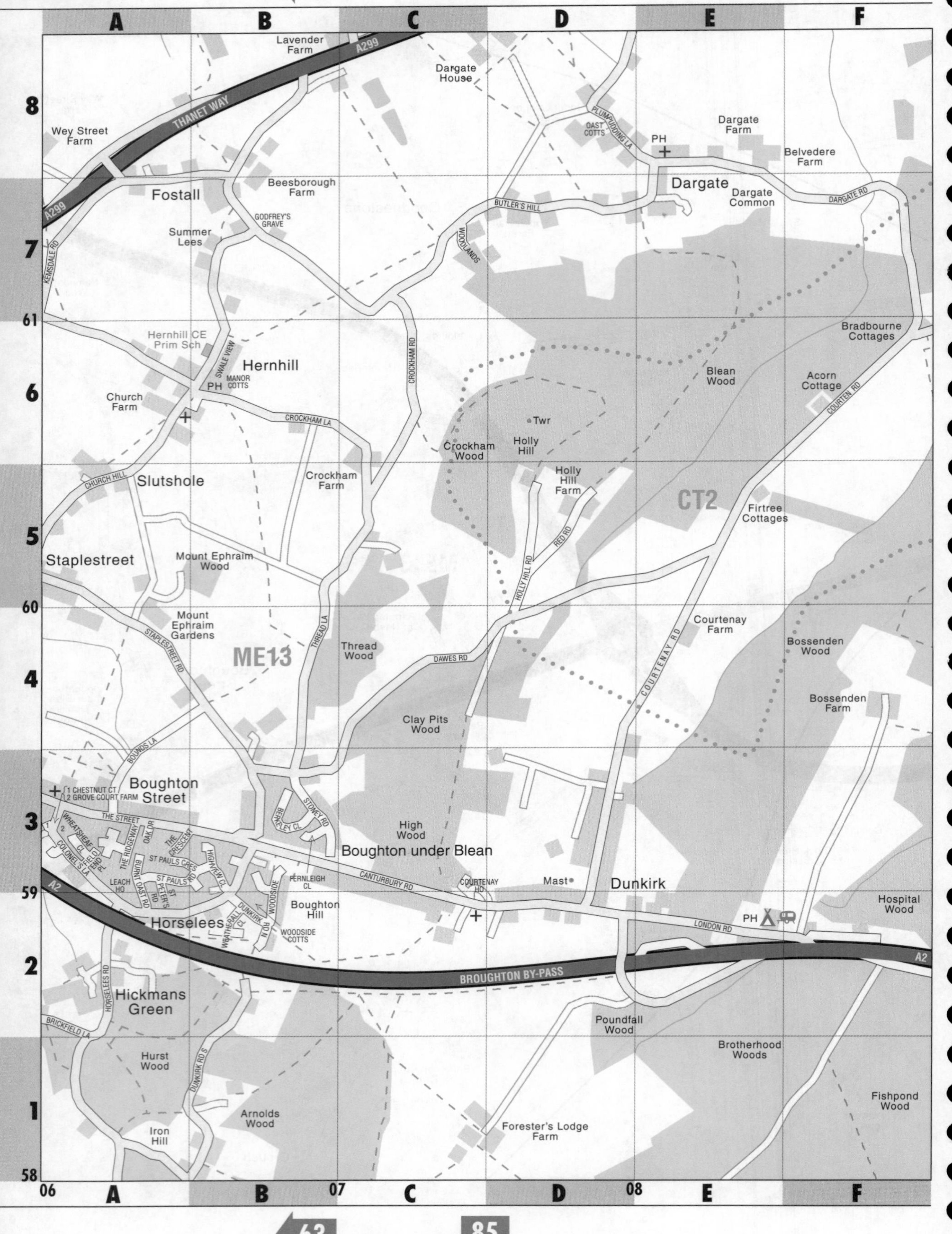
63
42
Lavender Farm
A299
Dargate House
THANET WAY
Wey Street Farm
Dargate Farm
OAST COTTS
PLUMPUDDING LA
PH
Belvedere Farm
Fostall
Beesborough Farm
Dargate
Dargate Common
DARGATE RD
BUTLER'S HILL
GODFREY'S GRAVE
Summer Lees
WOODLANDS
KEMSDALE RD
Bradbourne Cottages
Hernhill CE Prim Sch
SWALE VIEW
Hernhill
Blean Wood
Acorn Cottage
PH
MANOR COTTS
CROCKHAM RD
Church Farm
COURTEN RD
CROCKHAM LA
Twr
Crockham Wood
Holly Hill
Holly Hill Farm
CHURCH HILL
Slutshole
Crockham Farm
CT2
Firtree Cottages
RED RD
Staplestreet
Mount Ephraim Wood
HOLLY HILL RD
Mount Ephraim Gardens
Courtenay Farm
STAPLESTREET RD
THREAD LA
Bossenden Wood
ME13
Thread Wood
DAWES RD
COURTENAY RD
Bossenden Farm
Clay Pits Wood
BOUNDS LA
Boughton Street
1 CHESTNUT CT
2 GROVE COURT FARM
THE STREET
BERKLEY CL
STONEY RD
High Wood
WHEATSHEAF CL
COLONEL'S LA
THE RIDGEWAY
OAK DR
THE CRESCENT
Boughton under Blean
ST PAULS CRES
HIGHVIEW CL
LEACH HO
BURNT OAST RD
ST PAULS RD
ST PETER'S
FERNLEIGH CL
CANTURBURY RD
COURTENAY HO
Mast
Dunkirk
A2
Boughton Hill
Hospital Wood
Horselees
WHEATERALL CL
DUNKIRK RD N
WOODSIDE
WOODSIDE COTTS
PH
LONDON RD
BROUGHTON BY-PASS
Hickmans Green
HORSELEES RD
BRICKFIELD LA
Poundfall Wood
Brotherhood Woods
Hurst Wood
DUNKIRK RD S
Fishpond Wood
Arnolds Wood
Iron Hill
Forester's Lodge Farm
A B C D E F
8 7 6 5 4 3 2 1
61 60 59 58
06 07 08
63
85

43
66

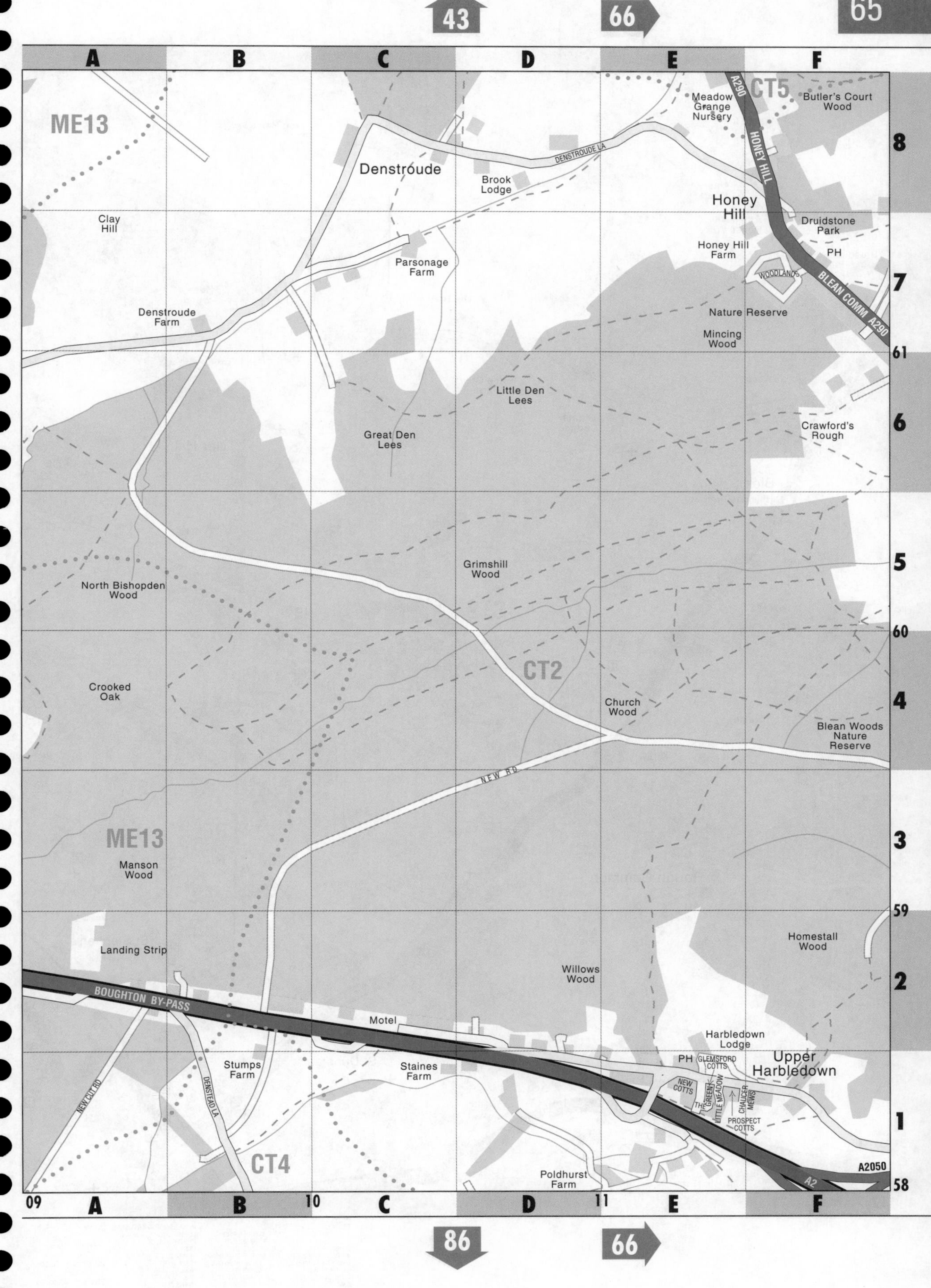
A
B
C
D
E
F
ME13
CT5
A290
HONEY HILL
Meadow Grange Nursery
Butler's Court Wood
8
Denstroude
DENSTROUDE LA
Brook Lodge
Honey Hill
Clay Hill
Druidstone Park
Honey Hill Farm
PH
Parsonage Farm
WOODLANDS
BLEAN COMM A290
7
Denstroude Farm
Nature Reserve
Mincing Wood
61
Little Den Lees
6
Great Den Lees
Crawford's Rough
5
Grimshill Wood
North Bishopden Wood
60
CT2
Crooked Oak
4
Church Wood
Blean Woods Nature Reserve
NEW RD
ME13
3
Manson Wood
59
Homestall Wood
Landing Strip
Willows Wood
2
BOUGHTON BY-PASS
Motel
Harbledown Lodge
PH
GLEMSFORD COTTS
Upper Harbledown
Stumps Farm
Staines Farm
NEW COTTS
GREEN
TH
LITTLE MEADOW
CHAUCER MEWS
PROSPECT COTTS
1
NEW CUT RD
DENSTEAD LA
CT4
Poldhurst Farm
A2
A2050
58
09
10
11

86
66

A B C D E F

8 Walnut Tree Farm · Well Court · Frog Hall

Amery Court · Timber Wood

Arbele House

7 Broadlands Ind Est · Daw's Wood · The Radfall · Honey Wood · Great Hall Wood

The Halt

61 THE GAP · Chestnut Ave · Clocktower Par · Tyler Hill Rd · Hothe Court Farm

6 Church Cottage · Tyler Hill · Little Hall Wood

Blean · Hillside Farm · PH

5 Luckett's Farm · Little Hall Farm

Blean Hill · Tile Kiln Hill · Woolf Coll · Darwin Coll

60 Blean Prim Sch · Park Wood Rd · Brotherhood Wood · Green Dell

CT2 · Park Wood · University of Kent Canterbury · Templeman Liby

4 Masts · Bishopden Ct · Farthings Ct · Rutherford Coll · Downs Rd

Clowes Ct · Homestall Ct · Grimshill Ct · Thornden Ct · Ellenden Ct · Marley Ct · Tudor Ct · Willows Ct · Denstead Ct

Eliot Coll · The Archbishop's Sch · Keynes Coll · Moorfield

3 Moat La · Oaks Pk · Kent College Canterbury · St Edmund's Junior School · Chaucer Coll

New Rd · Ravenscourt Rd · Lovell Rd · St Edmund's Sch · Cranborne Wlk

59 Firtree Cl · Ross Gdns · Rough Common · PH · Wtr Twr · Hilltop Rd · St Stephen's

Stockwood Chase

2 Stock Wood · Neal's Place · Whitstable Rd · Recn Ctr

Garden Cl

1 Hall Place · The Grove Canterbury Christ Church Univ · St Dunstan's · Canterbury West · Reg Off

Chancel Ct · Joseph Conrad Ho · Runcie Pl · Cemy

58 Kent Coll Canterbury Inf & Jun Sch · A2050 · RHEIMS WAY · The Friars

A2050 · Harbledown · Summer Hill

12 A 13 B C 14 D E F

65 87

E1
1 ROSIERS CT
2 CROSS ST
3 LIONARD HO
4 ST DUNSTANS CT
5 WESTERLY MEWS
6 CRANMER HO
7 THE MALTINGS
8 WESTGATE CT

F1
1 ST STEPHENS HO
2 BARTON MILL CT
3 GREAT STOUR PL
4 ST STEPHENS PATHWAY
5 ST STEPHENS FIELDS
6 GAMMONS YD
7 THE MERCHANT STORE
8 KIRBY'S HEIGHTS
9 TEMPLAR CT

10 WESTSIDE APARTMENTS
11 RIVERSIDE CT
12 STERLING CT
13 STOURSIDE STUDIOS
14 WESTGATE HALL RD
15 CHANTRY CT
16 BLACKFRIARS ST
17 ST ALPHEGE LA
18 THE CLOISTERS
19 ST PETER'S ST

20 St Peters Sch of English
21 Kent Music Sch
22 Sidney Cooper Gallery
23 Kent Masonic Liby & Mus

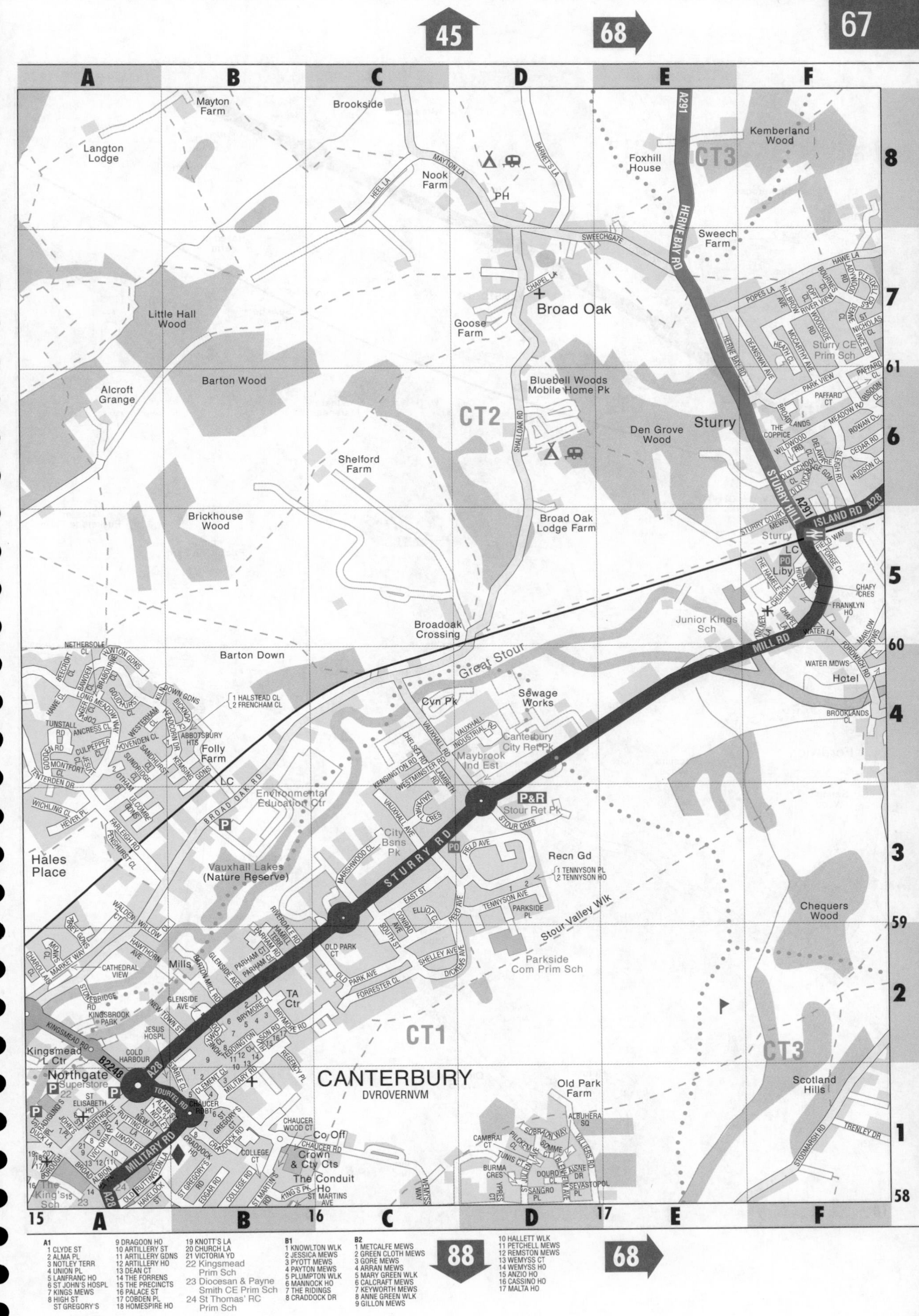

A1
1 CLYDE ST
2 ALMA PL
3 NOTLEY TERR
4 UNION PL
5 LANFRANC HO
6 ST JOHN'S HOSPL
7 KINGS MEWS
8 HIGH ST
　ST GREGORY'S

9 DRAGOON HO
10 ARTILLERY ST
11 ARTILLERY GDNS
12 ARTILLERY HO
13 DEAN CT
14 THE FORRENS
15 THE PRECINCTS
16 PALACE ST
17 COBDEN PL
18 HOMESPIRE HO

19 KNOTT'S LA
20 CHURCH LA
21 VICTORIA YD
22 Kingsmead
　Prim Sch
23 Diocesan & Payne
　Smith CE Prim Sch
24 St Thomas' RC
　Prim Sch

B1
1 KNOWLTON WLK
2 JESSICA MEWS
3 PYOTT MEWS
4 PAYTON MEWS
5 PLUMPTON WLK
6 MANNOCK HO
7 THE RIDINGS
8 CRADDOCK DR

B2
1 METCALFE MEWS
2 GREEN CLOTH MEWS
3 GORE MEWS
4 ARRAN MEWS
5 MARY GREEN WLK
6 CALCRAFT MEWS
7 KEYWORTH MEWS
8 ANNE GREEN WLK
9 GILLON MEWS

10 HALLETT WLK
11 PETCHELL MEWS
12 REMSTON MEWS
13 WEMYSS CT
14 WEMYSS HO
15 ANZIO HO
16 CASSINO HO
17 MALTA HO

67
46

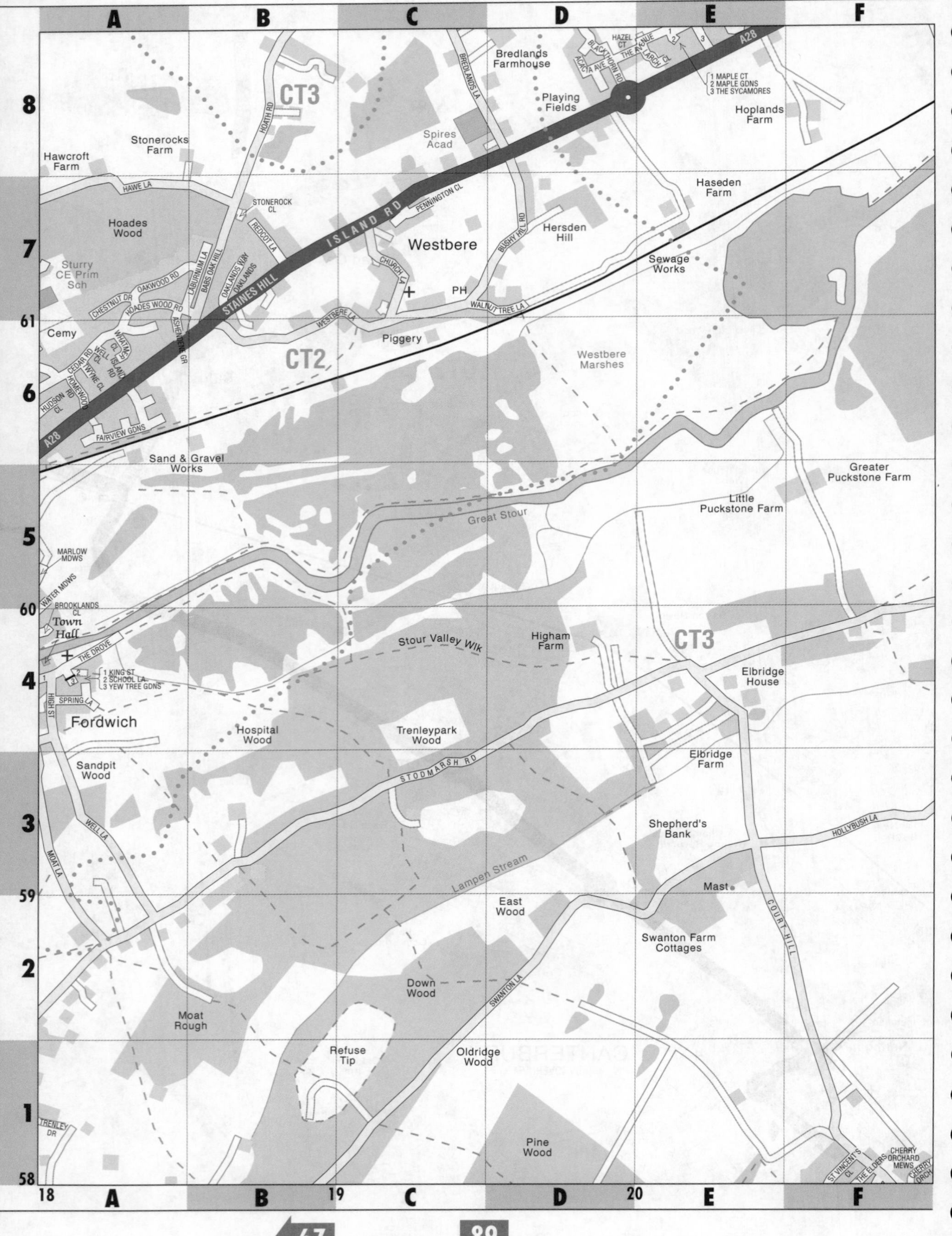
A
B
C
D
E
F
8
7
61
6
5
60
4
3
59
2
1
58
18
19
20
CT3
CT2
Bredlands Farmhouse
Playing Fields
Spires Acad
Stonerocks Farm
Hawcroft Farm
Hoplands Farm
Haseden Farm
Hoades Wood
Sturry CE Prim Sch
Westbere
Hersden Hill
Sewage Works
PH
Cemy
Piggery
Westbere Marshes
Sand & Gravel Works
Great Stour
Little Puckstone Farm
Greater Puckstone Farm
Town Hall
Higham Farm
Stour Valley Wlk
Elbridge House
Fordwich
Hospital Wood
Trenleypark Wood
Elbridge Farm
Sandpit Wood
Shepherd's Bank
Lampen Stream
Mast
East Wood
Swanton Farm Cottages
Down Wood
Moat Rough
Refuse Tip
Oldridge Wood
Pine Wood
A28
ISLAND RD
STAINES HILL
HAWE LA
HOATH RD
BREDLANDS LA
BUSHY HILL RD
WALNUT TREE LA
WESTBERE LA
CHURCH LA
PENNINGTON CL
STONEROCK CL
REDCOT LA
OAKLANDS WAY
OAKLANDS
BABS OAK HILL
LABURNUM LA
OAKWOOD RD
CHESTNUT DR
HOADES WOOD RD
ASHENDEN GR
WHATMER CL
ISLAND RD
WELL CL
CEDAR RD
HOMEWOOD RD
WYNNE CL
HUDSON CL
FAIRVIEW GDNS
HAZEL CT
BLACKTHORN RD
ACACIA AVE
THE AVENUE
LARCH CL
1 MAPLE CT
2 MAPLE GDNS
3 THE SYCAMORES
MARLOW MDWS
WATER MDWS
BROOKLANDS CL
THE DROVE
1 KING ST
2 SCHOOL LA
3 YEW TREE GDNS
HIGH ST
SPRING LA
STODMARSH RD
WELL LA
MOAT LA
SWANTON LA
COURT HILL
HOLLYBUSH LA
TRENLEY DR
ST VINCENT'S CL
THE ELDERS
CHERRY ORCHARD MEWS
CHERRY ORCH

67
89

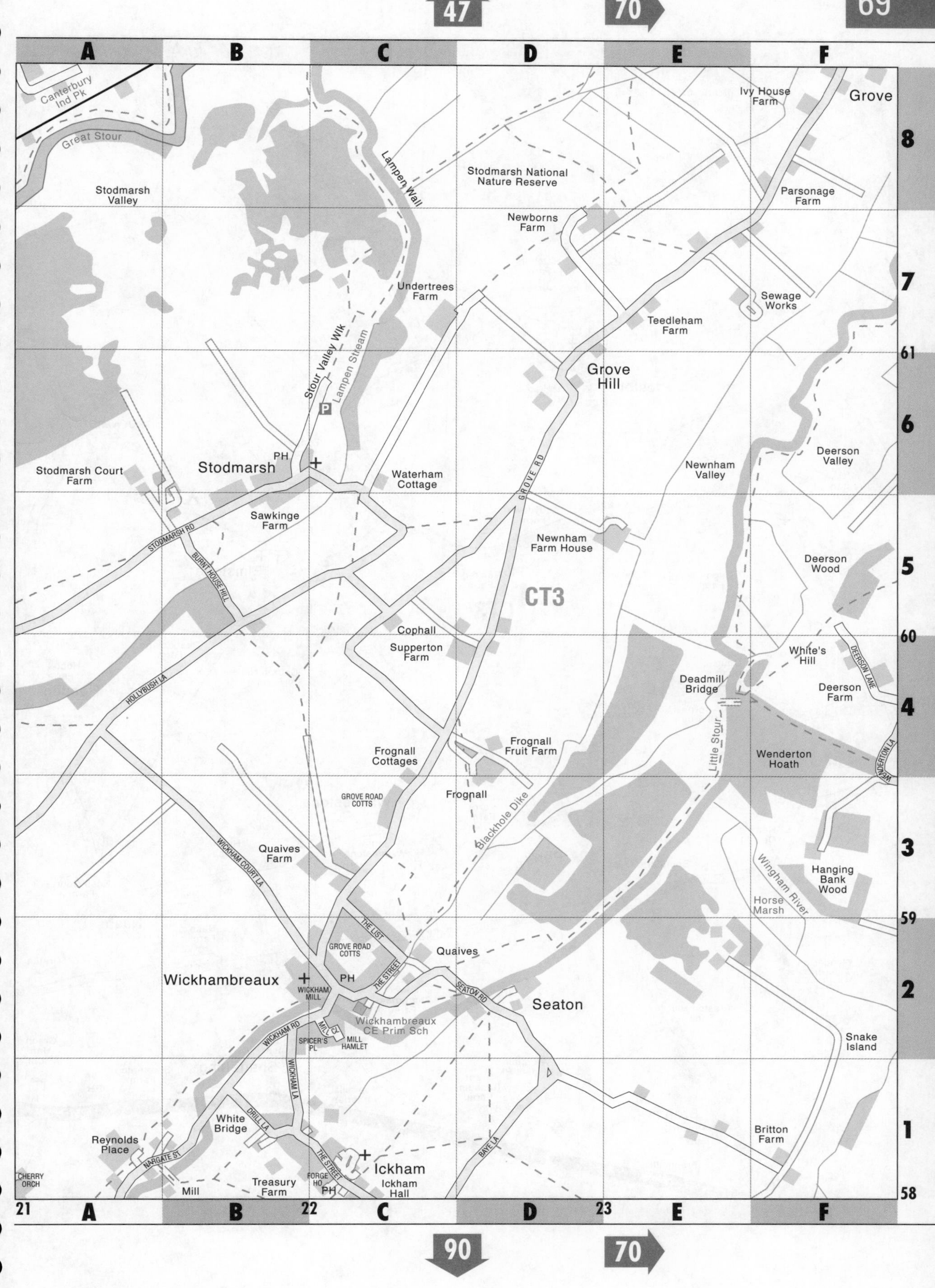
47
70
A
B
C
D
E
F
Canterbury Ind Pk
Great Stour
Stodmarsh Valley
Lampen Wall
Stodmarsh National Nature Reserve
Ivy House Farm
Grove
Parsonage Farm
Newborns Farm
Undertrees Farm
Sewage Works
Teedleham Farm
Grove Hill
Stour Valley Wlk
Lampen Stream
P
PH
Stodmarsh
Stodmarsh Court Farm
Waterham Cottage
Newnham Valley
Deerson Valley
Sawkinge Farm
STODMARSH RD
BURNT HOUSE HILL
GROVE RD
Newnham Farm House
Deerson Wood
CT3
Cophall
Supperton Farm
White's Hill
DEERSON LANE
Deadmill Bridge
Deerson Farm
HOLLYBUSH LA
Frognall Cottages
Frognall Fruit Farm
Little Stour
Wenderton Hoath
WENDERTON LA
GROVE ROAD COTTS
Frognall
Blackhole Dike
Quaives Farm
WICKHAM COURT LA
Wingham River
Hanging Bank Wood
Horse Marsh
THE LIST
GROVE ROAD COTTS
Quaives
Wickhambreaux
PH
WICKHAM MILL
THE STREET
SEATON RD
Seaton
Wickhambreaux CE Prim Sch
WICKHAM RD
MILL CL
SPICER'S PL
MILL HAMLET
WICKHAM LA
Snake Island
White Bridge
DRILL LA
Reynolds Place
NARGATE ST
BAYE LA
Britton Farm
CHERRY ORCH
Mill
Treasury Farm
FORGE HO
THE STREET
PH
Ickham
Ickham Hall
8
7
61
6
5
60
4
3
59
2
1
58
21
22
23
90
70

A B C D E F

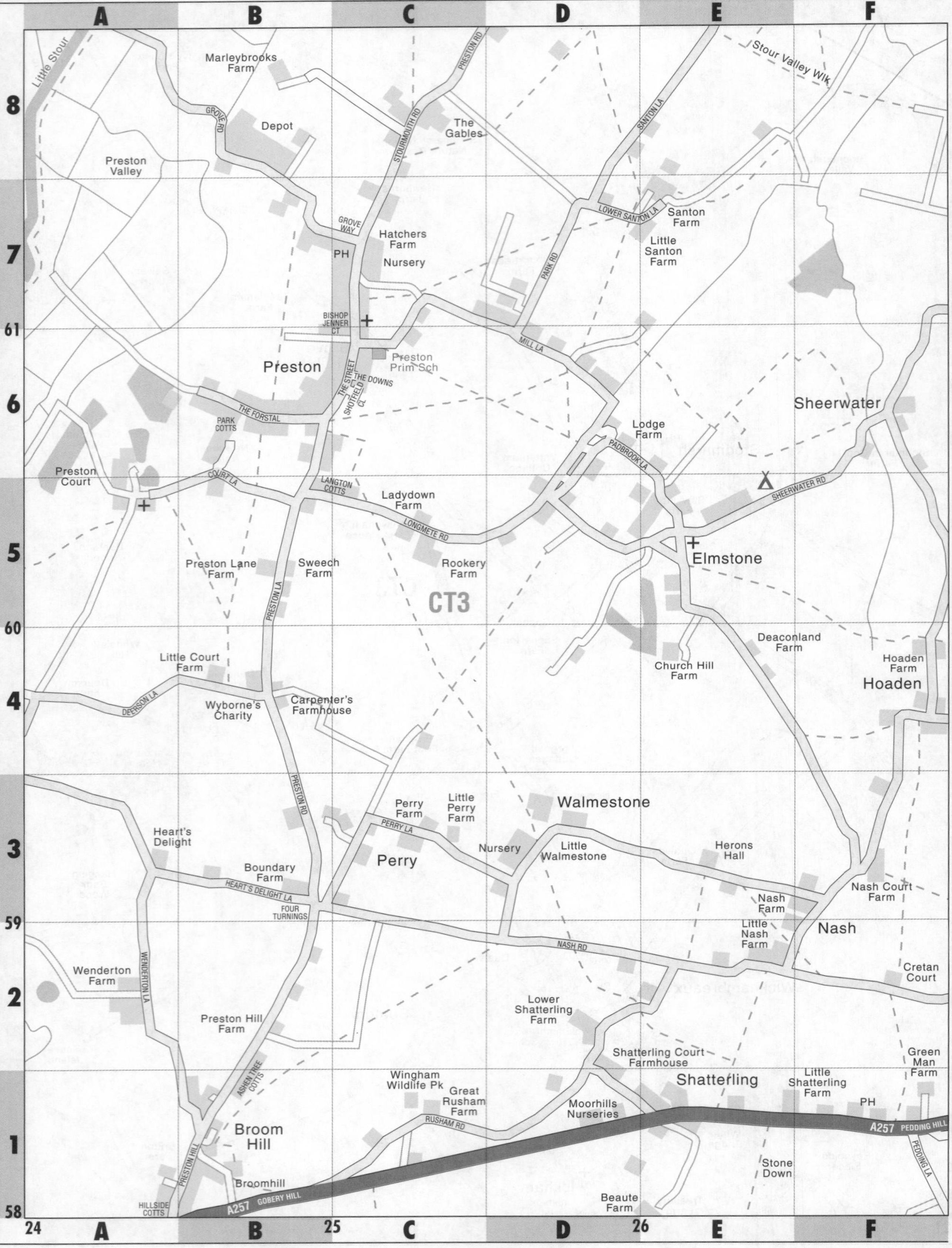

8

Marleybrooks Farm

Little Stour

GROVE RD

Depot

Preston Valley

STOURMOUTH RD

PRESTON RD

The Gables

Stour Valley Wlk

SANTON LA

GROVE WAY

Hatchers Farm

Nursery

LOWER SANTON LA

Santon Farm

PH

7

PARK RD

Little Santon Farm

61

BISHOP JENNER CT

THE STREET

SMITHFIELD CT

Preston Prim Sch

Preston

MILL LA

THE DOWNS

6

THE FORSTAL

PARK COTTS

Preston

PADBROOK LA

Lodge Farm

Sheerwater

COURT LA

LANGTON COTTS

Ladydown Farm

SHEERWATER RD

Preston Court

LONGMETE RD

Elmstone

5

Preston Lane Farm

Sweech Farm

Rookery Farm

CT3

PRESTON LA

60

Little Court Farm

Deaconland Farm

Hoaden Farm

DEERSON LA

Wyborne's Charity

Carpenter's Farmhouse

Church Hill Farm

Hoaden

4

PRESTON RD

Perry Farm

Little Perry Farm

Walmestone

Heart's Delight

PERRY LA

Nursery

Little Walmestone

Herons Hall

Nash Court Farm

3

Boundary Farm

Perry

HEART'S DELIGHT LA

Nash Farm

FOUR TURNINGS

Little Nash Farm

Nash

59

NASH RD

Cretan Court

Wenderton Farm

WENDERTON LA

2

Preston Hill Farm

Lower Shatterling Farm

Shatterling Court Farmhouse

Green Man Farm

ASHEN TREE COTTS

Wingham Wildlife Pk

Great Rusham Farm

Moorhills Nurseries

Shatterling

Little Shatterling Farm

PH

Broom Hill

RUSHAM RD

A257

PEDDING HILL

1

PRESTON HILL

Broomhill

Stone Down

PEDDING LA

HILLSIDE COTTS

A257 GOBERY HILL

Beaute Farm

58

24 A B 25 C D 26 E F

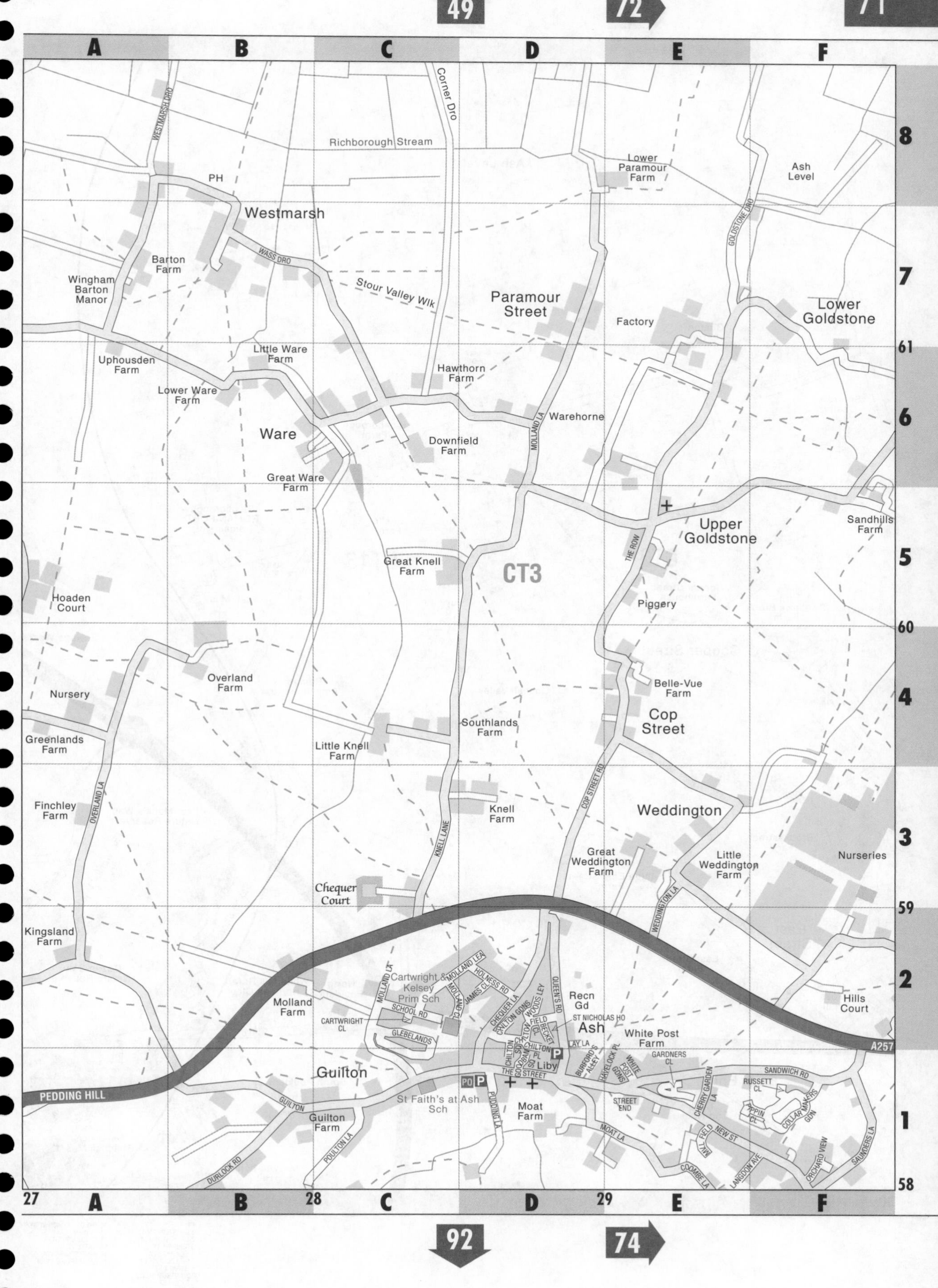
49
72
A B C D E F
8
7
61
6
5
60
4
3
59
2
1
58
27
28
29
Corner Dro
Richborough Stream
WESTMARSH DRO
PH
Westmarsh
WASS DRO
Barton Farm
Wingham Barton Manor
Stour Valley Wlk
Paramour Street
Lower Paramour Farm
Ash Level
GOLDSTONE DRO
Factory
Lower Goldstone
Little Ware Farm
Uphousden Farm
Hawthorn Farm
Lower Ware Farm
Ware
MOLLAND LA
Warehorne
Downfield Farm
Great Ware Farm
Upper Goldstone
Sandhills Farm
THE ROW
Great Knell Farm
CT3
Hoaden Court
Piggery
Overland Farm
Belle-Vue Farm
Nursery
Southlands Farm
Cop Street
Greenlands Farm
Little Knell Farm
COP STREET RD
Knell Farm
Weddington
Finchley Farm
OVERLAND LA
KNELL LANE
Great Weddington Farm
Little Weddington Farm
Nurseries
Chequer Court
WEDDINGTON LA
Kingsland Farm
Cartwright & Kelsey Prim Sch
MOLLAND LEA
HOLNESS RD
JAMES CL
MOLLAND LA
QUEEN'S RD
Recn Gd
Hills Court
Molland Farm
SCHOOL RD
CARTWRIGHT CL
GLEBELANDS
CHEQUER LA
WOODS LEY
ST NICHOLAS HO
Ash
White Post Farm
GARDNERS CL
A257
Guilton
Liby
THE STREET
SANDWICH RD
PEDDING HILL
PO
P
RUSSETT CL
St Faith's at Ash Sch
PUDDING LA
Moat Farm
STREET END
CHERRY GARDEN LA
PIPPIN CL
COLLAR MAKERS GDN
GUILTON
Guilton Farm
POULTON LA
MOAT LA
MILL FIELD
NEW ST
DURLOCK RD
COOMBE LA
LANGDON AVE
ORCHARD VIEW
SAUNDERS LA
92
74

71 50

A B C D E F

8

Ash Level

White House

7

Richborough Stream

WHITEHOUSE DRO

61

Guston Farm

Bride Farm

RUBERY DRO

6

Sparrow Castle

Richborough Farm

Fleet Farm

Castle Farm

Richborough ROMAN FORT (remains of)

5

CT3

CT13

CASTLE COTTS

Cooper Street Farmhouse

Mus

Swallows Brook Farm

60

COOPER STREET DRO

Cooper Street

Sewage Works

Stour Valley Wlk

4

Goshall Valley

Roman Amphitheatre

Goshall Stream

River Stour

RAMSGATE RD A256

3

Brookestreet Farm

Pfizer Monk's Wall Nature Reserve

The Monks' Wall

MONK'S WAY

LC

Little East Street Farm

RICHBOROUGH RD

59

North Poulders Stream

Saxon Shore Way

East Street

Gazen Salts Nature Reserve

2

East Street Farm

North Poulders

White Mill Rural Heritage Ctr

WANTSUME LEES

GOSS HALL LA

Goss Hall

Ind Est

MILL CL

A257 SANDWICH RD

A257 THE CAUSEWAY ASH RD LC

STRAND ST

Sandwich Inf Sch

CRIPPS WY

THE BUTTS

PARADISE

Each End

South Poulders

1

Each End House

Sandwich Guildhall Mus

ST THOMAS'S HOSPL

Each Manor Farm

Mary-le-bone Hill

WOODNESBOROUGH RD

A256

MOAT SOLE

CATTLE MKT

LC

P

58

30 A B 31 C D 32 E F

71 93

F1
1 GUESTLING MILL CT
2 CREIGHTON FLATS
3 CHURCH ST
4 VICARAGE LA
5 GUILDCOUNT LA
6 HARNET ST
7 WANTSUM MEWS
8 STOUR CT
9 LOOP COURT MEWS
10 THE OLD COACHWORKS
11 TANNERY LA
12 ST JOHN'S COTTS
13 WATTS YD
14 WHITEFRIARS WAY
15 WHITEFRIARS MDW

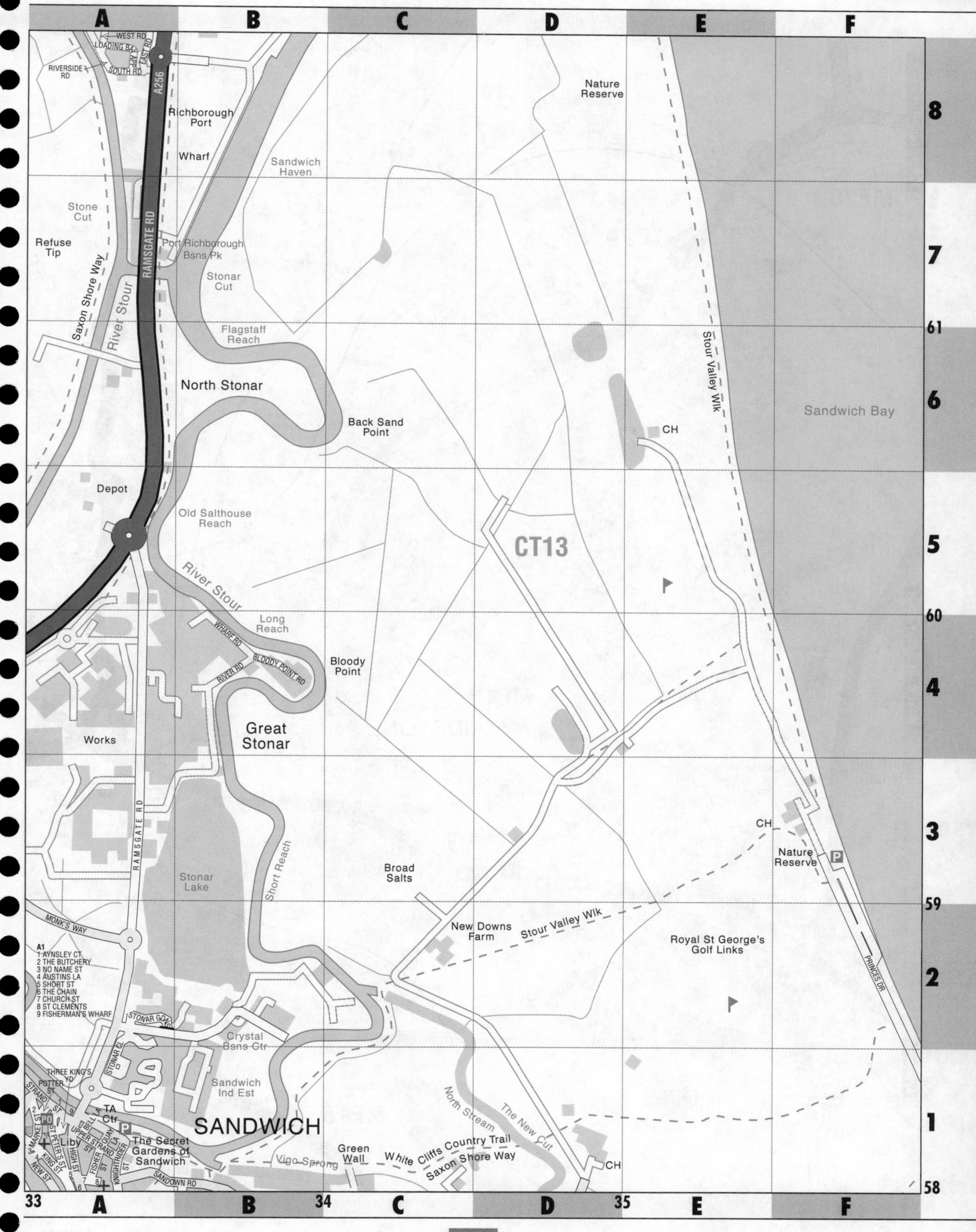

A	B	C	D	E	F

WEST RD
LOADING BAY
RIVERSIDE RD
SOUTH RD
A256
QUAY RD

Richborough Port

Wharf

Stone Cut

Refuse Tip

Saxon Shore Way

River Stour

RAMSGATE RD

Port Richborough Bsns Pk

Stonar Cut

Flagstaff Reach

Sandwich Haven

Nature Reserve

8

7

61

North Stonar

Back Sand Point

6

Stour Valley Wlk

Sandwich Bay

Depot

Old Salthouse Reach

River Stour

CH

CT13

5

Works

WHARF RD

RIVER RD

BLOODY POINT RD

Long Reach

Bloody Point

Great Stonar

60

4

RAMSGATE RD

Stonar Lake

Short Reach

Broad Salts

CH

Nature Reserve

P

CH

3

59

MONK'S WAY

A1
1 AYNSLEY CT.
2 THE BUTCHERY
3 NO NAME ST
4 AUSTINS LA
5 SHORT ST
6 THE CHAIN
7 CHURCH ST
8 ST CLEMENTS
9 FISHERMAN'S WHARF

New Downs Farm

Stour Valley Wlk

Royal St George's Golf Links

PRINCES DR

2

STONAR RD

Crystal Bsns Ctr

Sandwich Ind Est

THREE KING'S YD

POTTER ST

TA Ctr

P

Libry

The Secret Gardens of Sandwich

SANDWICH

Green Wall

Vigo Spring

White Cliffs Country Trail

Saxon Shore Way

North Stream

The New Cut

CH

1

STRAND ST
MARKET ST
KING ST
NEW ST
HIGH ST
UPPER STRAND ST
FISHER ST
KNIGHTRIDER
SANDOWN RD

58

33	A	B	34	C	D	35	E	F

53

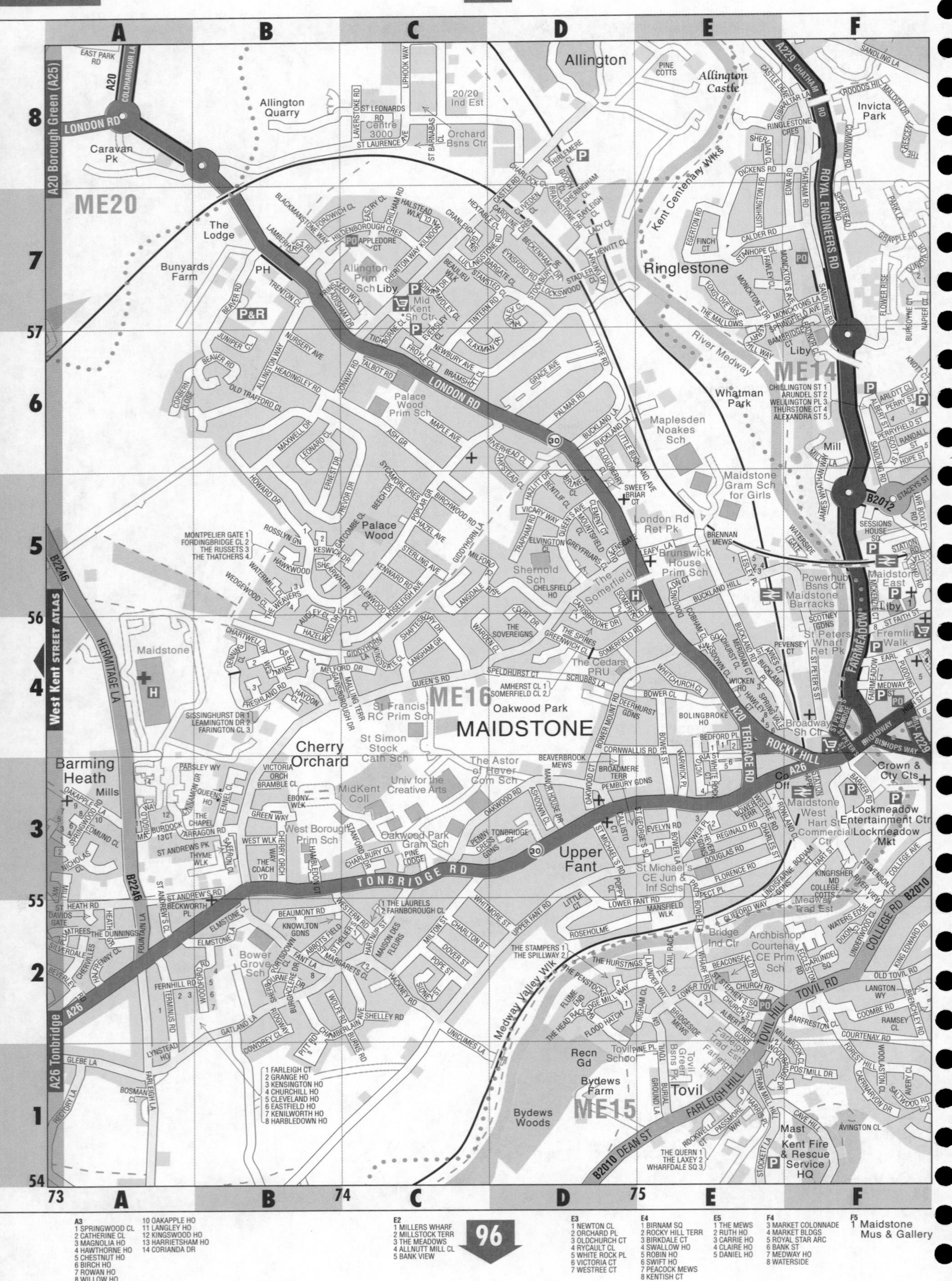

96

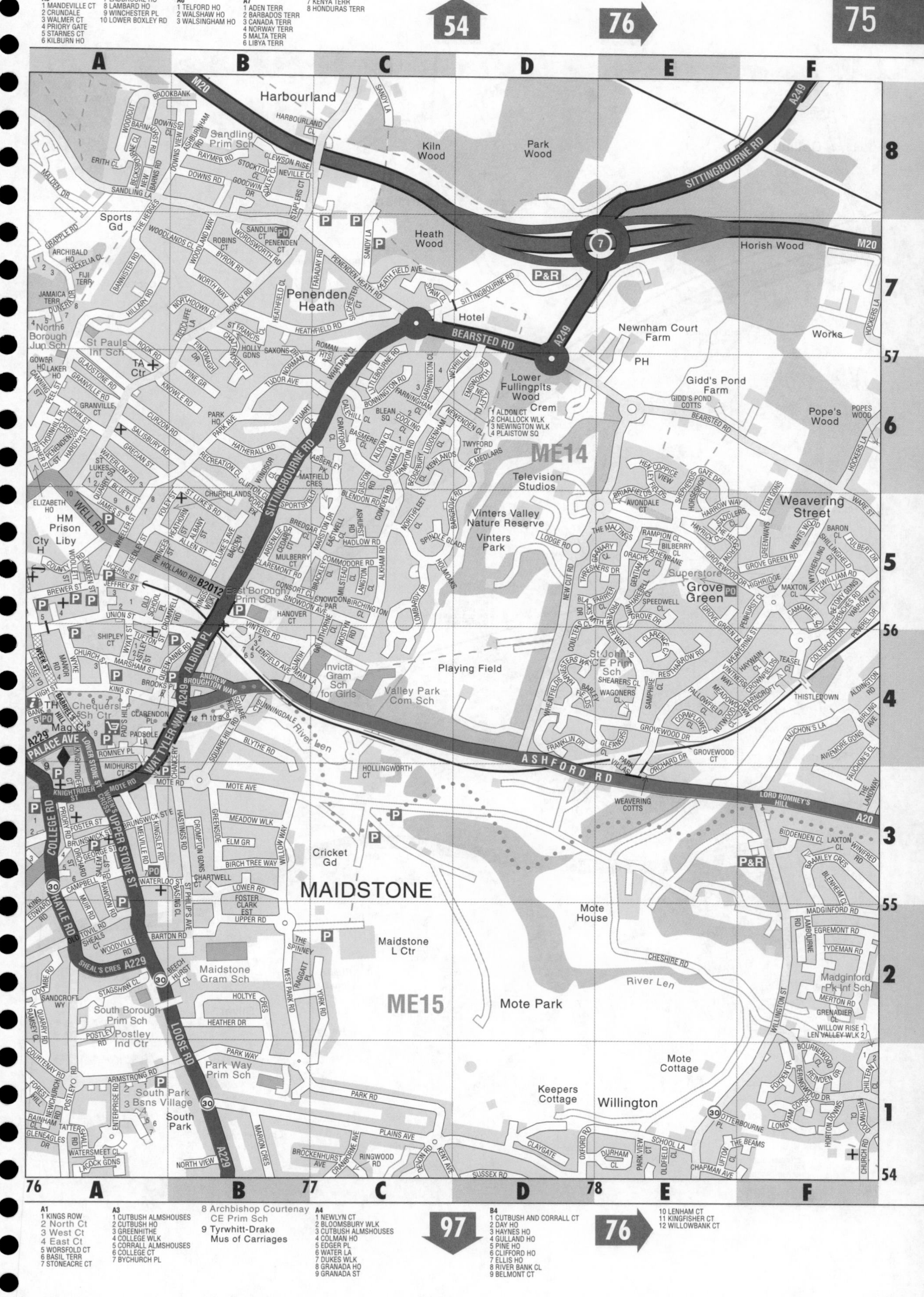
A5
1 MANDEVILLE CT
2 CRUNDALE
3 WALMER CT
4 PRIORY GATE
5 STARNES CT
6 KILBURN HO
7 LADBROOKE HO
8 LAMBARD HO
9 WINCHESTER PL
10 LOWER BOXLEY RD
A6
1 TELFORD HO
2 WALSHAW HO
3 WALSINGHAM HO
A7
1 ADEN TERR
2 BARBADOS TERR
3 CANADA TERR
4 NORWAY TERR
5 MALTA TERR
6 LIBYA TERR
7 KENYA TERR
8 HONDURAS TERR
54
76
A
B
C
D
E
F
8
7
57
6
5
56
4
3
55
2
1
54
Harbourland
Kiln Wood
Park Wood
Sandling Prim Sch
Sports Gd
Heath Wood
Horish Wood
Penenden Heath
Hotel
Newnham Court Farm
Works
North Borough Jun Sch
St Pauls Inf Sch
TA Ctr
Lower Fullingpits Wood
Crem
PH
Gidd's Pond Farm
Pope's Wood
ME14
Television Studios
Weavering Street
HM Prison
Cty H
Liby
Vinters Valley Nature Reserve
Vinters Park
Superstore
Grove Green
East Borough Prim Sch
Playing Field
St John's CE Prim Sch
Invicta Gram Sch for Girls
Valley Park Com Sch
Chequers Sh Ctr
Mag Ct
TH
River Len
Cricket Gd
MAIDSTONE
Mote House
Maidstone L Ctr
Maidstone Gram Sch
ME15
Mote Park
Madginford Pk Inf Sch
South Borough Prim Sch
Postley Ind Ctr
Park Way Prim Sch
Mote Cottage
South Park Bsns Village
South Park
Keepers Cottage
Willington
M20
A249
A20
A229
B2012
SITTINGBOURNE RD
BEARSTED RD
ASHFORD RD
LORD ROMNEY'S HILL
WELL RD
HOLLAND RD
ALBION PL
WAT TYLER WAY
PALACE AVE
COLLEGE RD
UPPER STONE ST
LOWER STONE ST
HAYLE RD
LOOSE RD
SHEAL'S CRES
PARK WAY
PARK RD
PLAINS AVE
WILLINGTON ST
MADGINFORD RD
GROVEWOOD DR
GROVE GREEN RD
HOCKERS LA
NEW CUT RD
MOTE AVE
MOTE RD
KNIGHTRIDER ST
HEATHFIELD RD
PENENDEN HEATH RD
BOXLEY RD
CHESHIRE RD
SANDLING LA
76
A
B
77
C
D
78
E
F
A1
1 KINGS ROW
2 North Ct
3 West Ct
4 East Ct
5 WORSFOLD CT
6 BASIL TERR
7 STONEACRE CT
A3
1 CUTBUSH ALMSHOUSES
2 CUTBUSH HO
3 GREENHITHE
4 COLLEGE WLK
5 CORRALL ALMSHOUSES
6 COLLEGE CT
7 BYCHURCH PL
8 Archbishop Courtenay CE Prim Sch
9 Tyrwhitt-Drake Mus of Carriages
A4
1 NEWLYN CT
2 BLOOMSBURY WLK
3 CUTBUSH ALMSHOUSES
4 COLMAN HO
5 EDGER PL
6 WATER LA
7 DUKES WLK
8 GRANADA HO
9 GRANADA ST
97
B4
1 CUTBUSH AND CORRALL CT
2 DAY HO
3 HAYNES HO
4 GULLAND HO
5 PINE HO
6 CLIFFORD HO
7 ELLIS HO
8 RIVER BANK CL
9 BELMONT CT
76
10 LENHAM CT
11 KINGFISHER CT
12 WILLOWBANK CT

A B C D E F

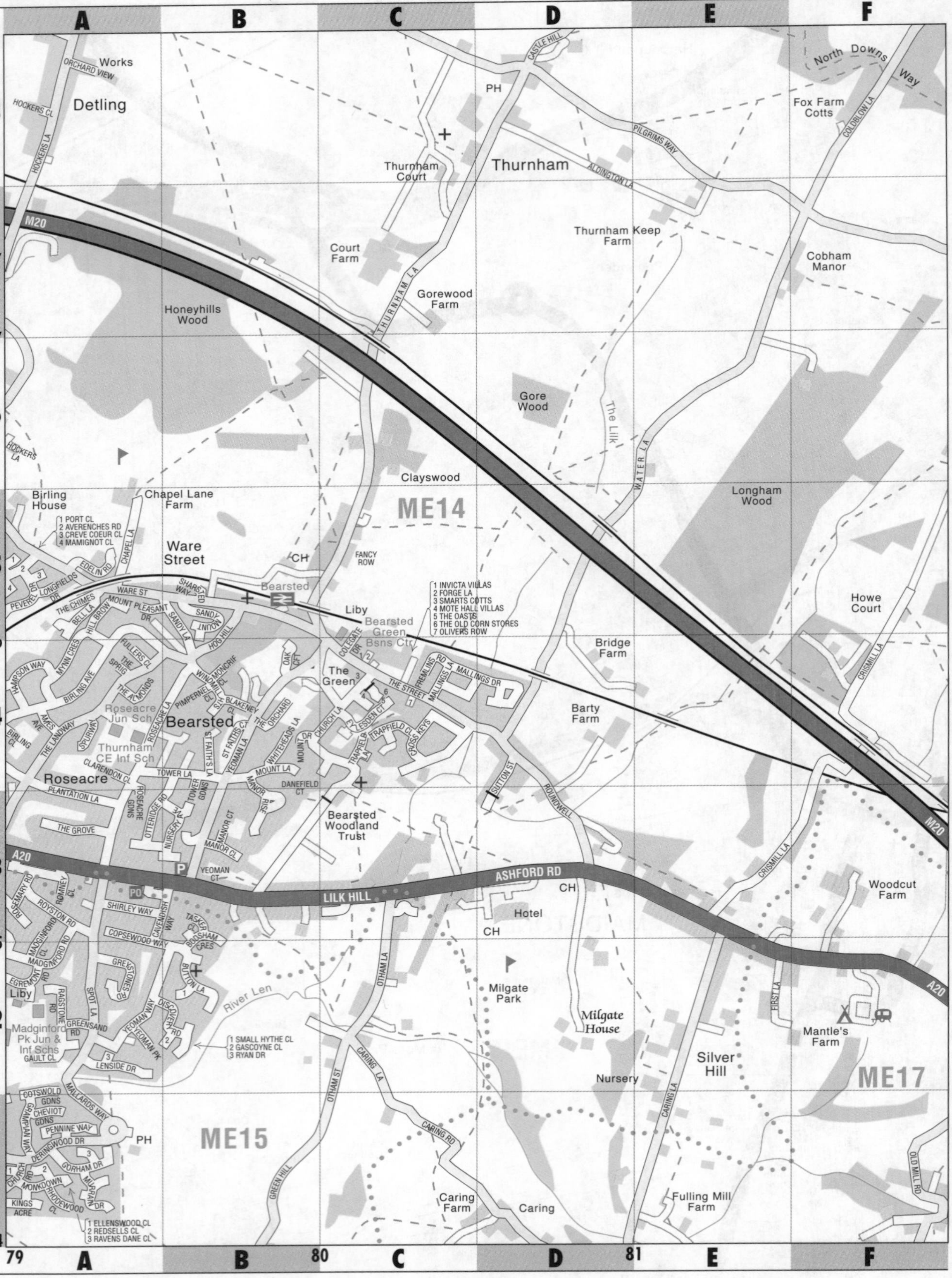

8
Detling
Works
ORCHARD VIEW
HOOKERS CL
HOOKERS LA

Thurnham Court
PH
CASTLE HILL
Thurnham
North Downs Way
Fox Farm Cotts
PILGRIMS WAY
ALDINGTON LA

7
M20
Court Farm
Thurnham LA
Gorewood Farm
Thurnham Keep Farm
Cobham Manor

57
Honeyhills Wood

6
HOOKERS LA
Gore Wood
The Lilk
WATER LA
Longham Wood

Birling House
Chapel Lane Farm
Clayswood
ME14
Howe Court

5
1 PORT CL
2 AVERENCHES RD
3 CREVE COEUR CL
4 MAMIGNOT CL
Ware Street
CHAPEL LA
EDELN RD
CH
FANCY ROW
1 INVICTA VILLAS
2 FORGE LA
3 SMARTS COTTS
4 MOTE HALL VILLAS
5 THE OASIS
6 THE OLD CORN STORES
7 OLIVERS ROW

LONGFIELDS
PEVEREL
THE CHIMES
BELL LA
WARE ST
MOUNT PLEASANT
SHARSTED WAY
SANDY LA
LINTON
Liby
Bearsted Green Bsns Ctr

56
SIMPSON WAY
MYTIN CRES
BIRLING AVE
FULLERS LA
THE SPRIG
THE POPLARS
WINGROVE
PIMPERNEL MEWS
ST BLAKENEY
ORCHARD
OAK CTT
The Green
THE STREET
MALLINGS RD
MALLINGS LA
MALLINGS DR
Bridge Farm

4
BIRLING DR
AVE
THE LANDWAY
OSPREY WAY
Roseacre Jun Sch
ROSEACRE LA
Bearsted
ST FAITHS LA
YEOMAN LA
WHITEHEADS LA
MOUNT LA
CHURCH LA
TRAFFIELD
ESSEX LA
CROSS KEYS
STUTTON ST
ROUNDWELL
Barty Farm

Thurnham CE Inf Sch
CLARENDON CL
TOWER LA
SWOD
MANOR DR
MANOR RISE
DANEFIELD CT
M20

3
Roseacre
PLANTATION LA
THE GROVE
A20
NURSERY LA
LEDBRIDGE
MANOR CL
YEOMAN CT
P
LILK HILL
ASHFORD RD
CH
CRISMILL LA
Woodcut Farm

Bearsted Woodland Trust
PO
SHIRLEY WAY
Hotel
CH

55
ROSEMARY RD
ROYSTON RD
MADGINFORD RD
MADGINFORD
CALEHILL
TASKER WAY
BRISHAM CRES
COPSEWOOD WAY
BUTTON LA
OTHAM LA
CH
FIRST LA

2
Liby
RALSTON RD
EGREMONT RD
GREENSAND RD
GREENSTONE
DISCOVERY RD
YEOMAN PK
YEOMAN WAY
1 SMALL HYTHE CL
2 GASCOYNE CL
3 RYAN DR
River Len
OTHAM ST
CARING LA
Milgate Park
Milgate House
Mantle's Farm
ME17

Madginford Pk Jun & Inf Schs
GAULT CL
LENSIDE DR
Nursery
Silver Hill

1
COTSWOLD GDNS
CHEVIOT GDNS
PENNINE WAY
DEERINGWOOD DR
BRAMPTON WAY
GORHAM DR
PH
MALLARDS WAY
GREEN HILL
ME15
CARING RD
Milgate
Fulling Mill Farm

KINGS ACRE
MOUNDOWN
BRIDGEWOOD DR
1 ELLENSWOOD CL
2 REDSELLS CL
3 RAVENS DANE CL
Caring Farm
Caring
OLD MILL RD

54
79 A B 80 C D 81 E F

56
78

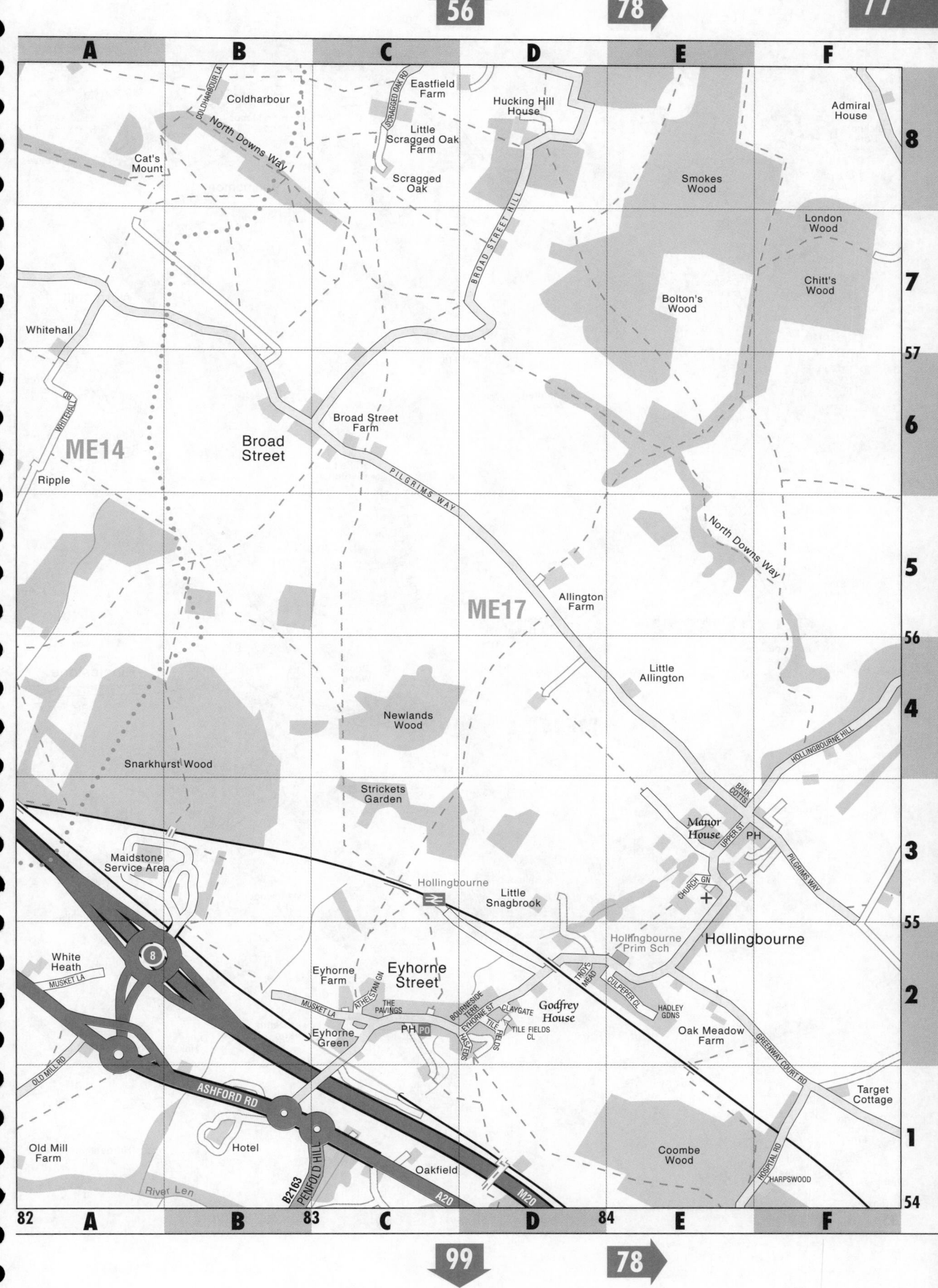
A
B
C
D
E
F
Coldharbour
COLDHARBOUR LA
North Downs Way
Cat's Mount
Eastfield Farm
SCRAGGED OAK RD
Little Scragged Oak Farm
Scragged Oak
Hucking Hill House
BROAD STREET HILL
Smokes Wood
Admiral House
London Wood
Chitt's Wood
Bolton's Wood
Whitehall
WHITEHALL RD
ME14
Ripple
Broad Street
Broad Street Farm
PILGRIMS WAY
North Downs Way
ME17
Allington Farm
Little Allington
Newlands Wood
Snarkhurst Wood
HOLLINGBOURNE HILL
Strickets Garden
BANK COTTS
Manor House
UPPER ST
PH
PILGRIMS WAY
CHURCH GN
Maidstone Service Area
Hollingbourne
Little Snagbrook
Hollingbourne Prim Sch
Hollingbourne
White Heath
MUSKET LA
Eyhorne Farm
Eyhorne Street
ATHELSTAN GN
THE PAVINGS
MUSKET LA
BOURNESIDE TERR
EYHORNE ST
CLAYGATE
TILL
FIELDS
Godfrey House
TILE FIELDS CL
TROYS MEAD
CULPEPER CL
HADLEY GDNS
Oak Meadow Farm
GREENWAY COURT RD
Eyhorne Green
PH
PO
HASTEDS
OLD MILL RD
ASHFORD RD
Target Cottage
Old Mill Farm
Hotel
B2163
PENFOLD HILL
Oakfield
Coombe Wood
HOSPITAL RD
HARPSWOOD
River Len
A20
M20
8
7
57
6
5
56
4
3
55
2
1
54
82
83
84

99
78

77
57

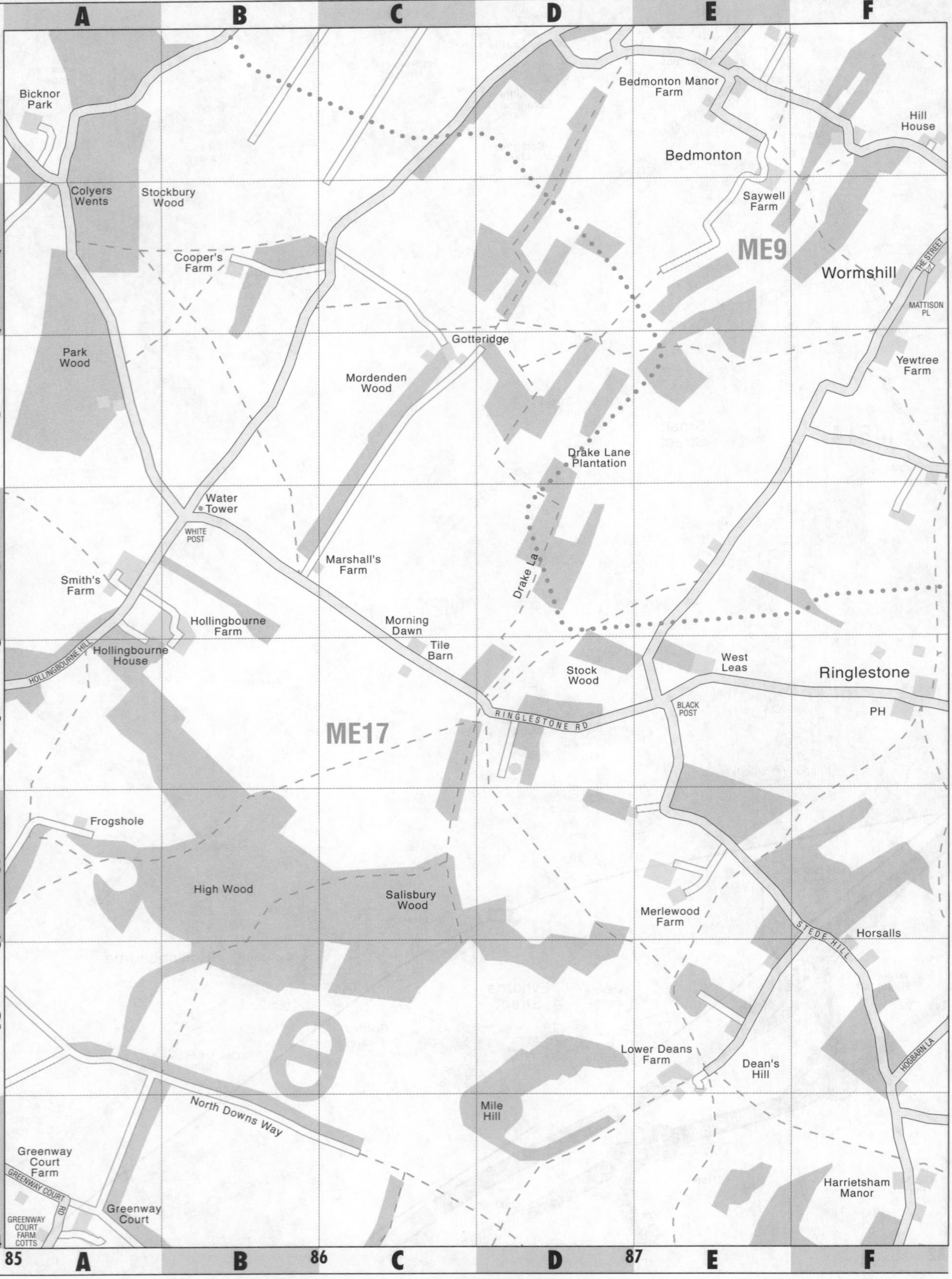

A **B** **C** **D** **E** **F**

8

Bicknor Park

Bedmonton Manor Farm

Hill House

Colyers Wents

Stockbury Wood

Bedmonton

Saywell Farm

7

Cooper's Farm

ME9

Wormshill

THE STREET

57

Gotteridge

MATTISON PL

Park Wood

Mordenden Wood

Yewtree Farm

6

Drake Lane Plantation

Water Tower

WHITE POST

Drake La

5

Marshall's Farm

Smith's Farm

Morning Dawn

56

Hollingbourne Farm

Tile Barn

Stock Wood

West Leas

Ringlestone

HOLLINGBOURNE HILL

Hollingbourne House

4

BLACK POST

PH

ME17

RINGLESTONE RD

3

Frogshole

High Wood

Salisbury Wood

Merlewood Farm

STEDE HILL

Horsalls

55

2

Lower Deans Farm

Dean's Hill

HOGBARN LA

North Downs Way

Mile Hill

1

Greenway Court Farm

GREENWAY COURT RD

Harrietsham Manor

Greenway Court

54

GREENWAY COURT FARM COTTS

85 **A** **B** 86 **C** **D** 87 **E** **F**

77
100

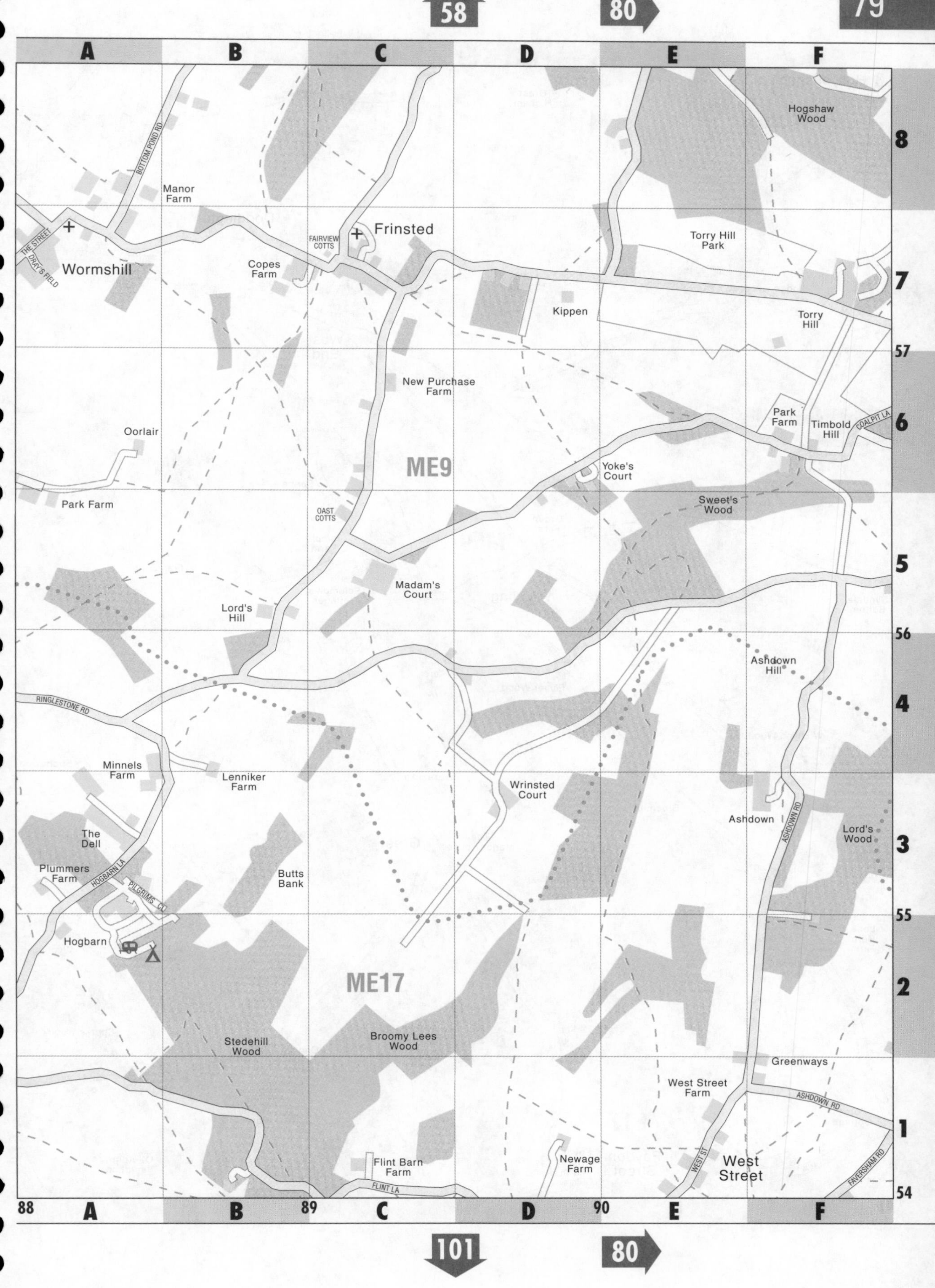
A
B
C
D
E
F
8
7
6
5
4
3
2
1
57
56
55
54
88
89
90
Hogshaw Wood
BOTTOM POND RD
Manor Farm
THE STREET
DRAY'S FIELD
Wormshill
FAIRVIEW COTTS
Frinsted
Copes Farm
Torry Hill Park
Kippen
Torry Hill
New Purchase Farm
Park Farm
Timbold Hill
COALPIT LA
Oorlair
ME9
Yoke's Court
Park Farm
Sweet's Wood
OAST COTTS
Madam's Court
Lord's Hill
Ashdown Hill
RINGLESTONE RD
Minnels Farm
Lenniker Farm
Wrinsted Court
Ashdown
ASHDOWN RD
Lord's Wood
The Dell
Plummers Farm
HOGBARN LA
PILGRIMS CT
Butts Bank
Hogbarn
ME17
Stedehill Wood
Broomy Lees Wood
Greenways
West Street Farm
ASHDOWN RD
Newage Farm
WEST ST
West Street
FAVERSHAM RD
Flint Barn Farm
FLINT LA

79
59

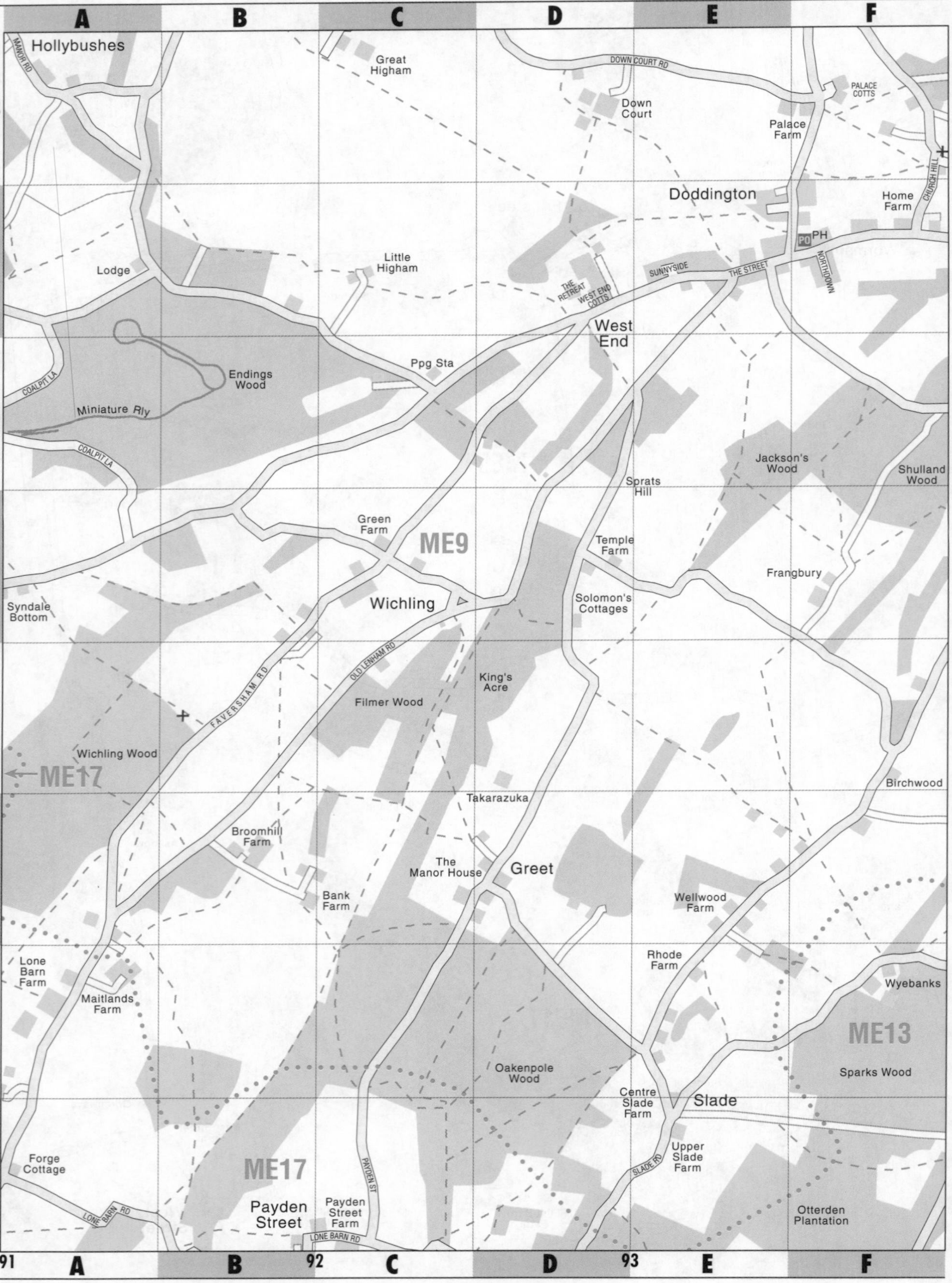

A **B** **C** **D** **E** **F**

Hollybushes

Great Higham

DOWN COURT RD

Down Court

PALACE COTTS

Palace Farm

8

Doddington

Home Farm

Lodge

Little Higham

PO PH

7

THE RETREAT
WEST END COTTS
SUNNYSIDE
THE STREET
NORTHTOWN

West End

57

Ppg Sta

Endings Wood

COALPIT LA

Miniature Rly

6

Jackson's Wood

Shulland Wood

COALPIT LA

Sprats Hill

Green Farm

ME9

Temple Farm

Frangbury

5

Syndale Bottom

Wichling

Solomon's Cottages

56

King's Acre

FAVERSHAM RD

OLD LENHAM RD

Filmer Wood

4

Wichling Wood

Birchwood

ME17

Takarazuka

Broomhill Farm

The Manor House

Greet

Wellwood Farm

3

Bank Farm

55

Rhode Farm

Wyebanks

Lone Barn Farm

ME13

Maitlands Farm

2

Oakenpole Wood

Sparks Wood

Centre Slade Farm

Slade

PAYDEN ST

SLADE RD

Forge Cottage

Upper Slade Farm

1

ME17

LONE BARN RD

Payden Street

Payden Street Farm

Otterden Plantation

54

LONE BARN RD

91 **A** **B** 92 **C** **D** 93 **E** **F**

79
102

60
82

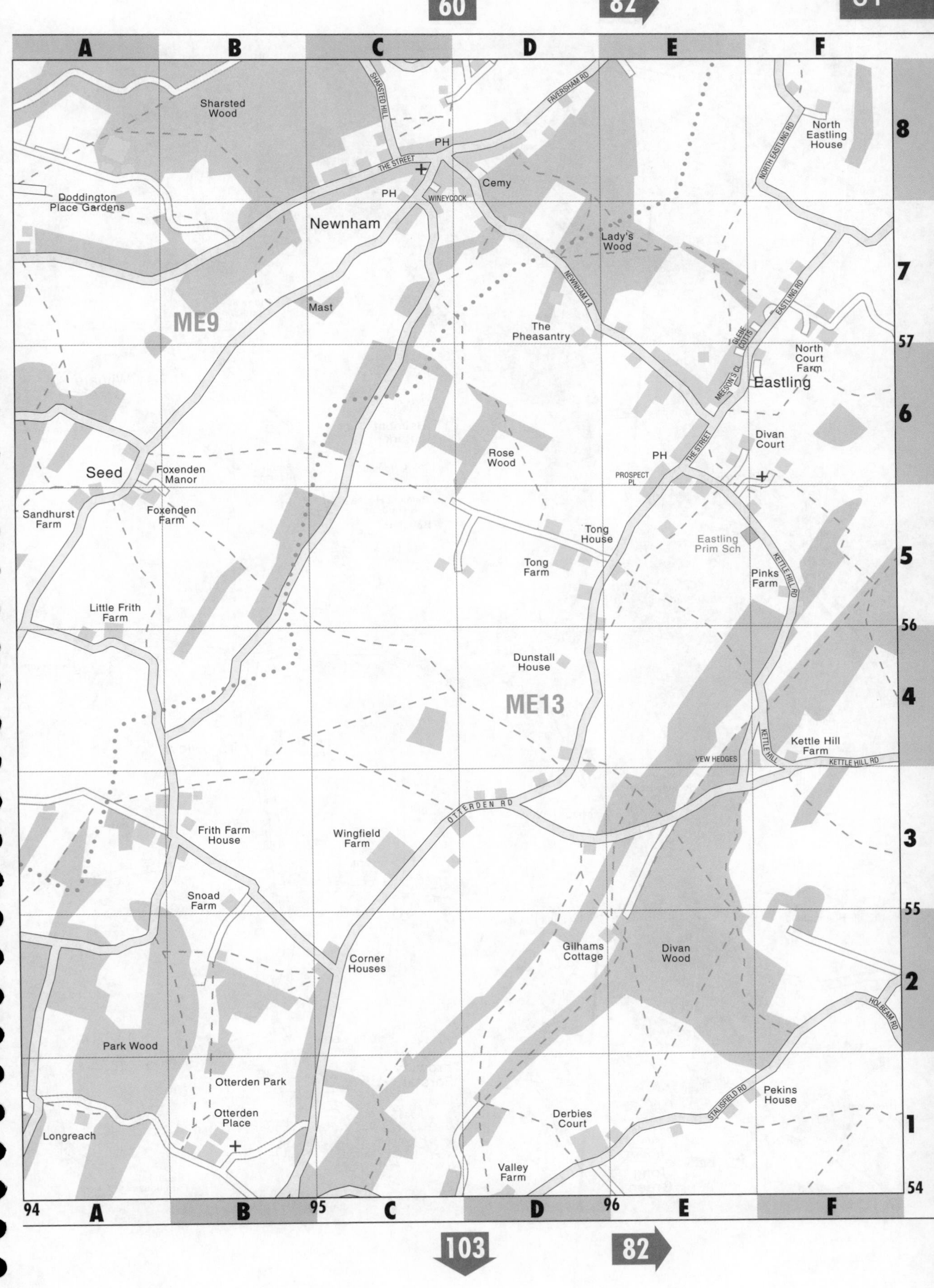
A
B
C
D
E
F
Sharsted Wood
SHARSTED HILL
FAVERSHAM RD
North Eastling House
NORTH EASTLING RD
8
PH
THE STREET
Doddington Place Gardens
PH
WINEYCOCK
Cemy
Newnham
Lady's Wood
7
NEWNHAM LA
EASTLING RD
Mast
ME9
The Pheasantry
GLEBE COTTS
57
North Court Farm
MEESON'S CL
Eastling
6
Divan Court
Rose Wood
PH
THE STREET
Seed
Foxenden Manor
PROSPECT PL
Sandhurst Farm
Foxenden Farm
Tong House
Eastling Prim Sch
Tong Farm
KETTLE HILL RD
5
Pinks Farm
Little Frith Farm
56
Dunstall House
ME13
4
Kettle Hill Farm
YEW HEDGES
KETTLE HILL
KETTLE HILL RD
OTTERDEN RD
Frith Farm House
Wingfield Farm
3
Snoad Farm
55
Gilhams Cottage
Divan Wood
Corner Houses
2
HOLBEAM RD
Park Wood
Otterden Park
Pekins House
STALISFIELD RD
Otterden Place
Derbies Court
1
Longreach
Valley Farm
54
94
95
96

103
82

81
61

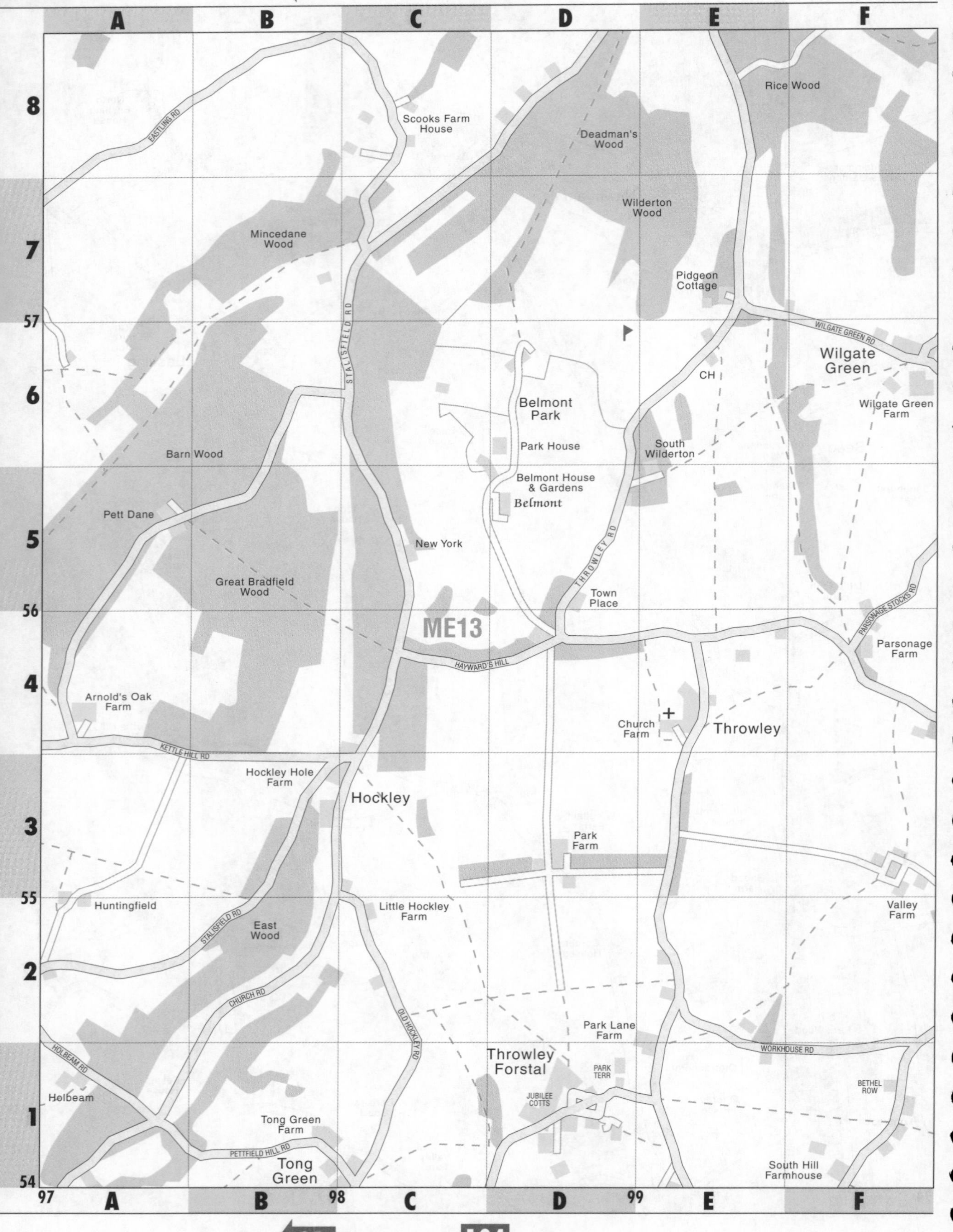
A
B
C
D
E
F
8
7
57
6
5
56
4
3
55
2
1
54
97
98
99
EASTLING RD
Scooks Farm House
Deadman's Wood
Rice Wood
Mincedane Wood
Wilderton Wood
Pidgeon Cottage
STALISFIELD RD
WILGATE GREEN RD
Wilgate Green
CH
Belmont Park
Wilgate Green Farm
Park House
South Wilderton
Barn Wood
Belmont House & Gardens
Belmont
Pett Dane
New York
THROWLEY RD
Great Bradfield Wood
Town Place
PARSONAGE STOCKS RD
ME13
Parsonage Farm
HAYWARD'S HILL
Arnold's Oak Farm
Church Farm
Throwley
KETTLE HILL RD
Hockley Hole Farm
Hockley
Park Farm
Huntingfield
Little Hockley Farm
Valley Farm
STALISFIELD RD
East Wood
CHURCH RD
OLD HOCKLEY RD
Park Lane Farm
HOLBEAM RD
WORKHOUSE RD
Throwley Forstal
PARK TERR
BETHEL ROW
Holbeam
JUBILEE COTTS
Tong Green Farm
PETTFIELD HILL RD
Tong Green
South Hill Farmhouse

81
104

62
84

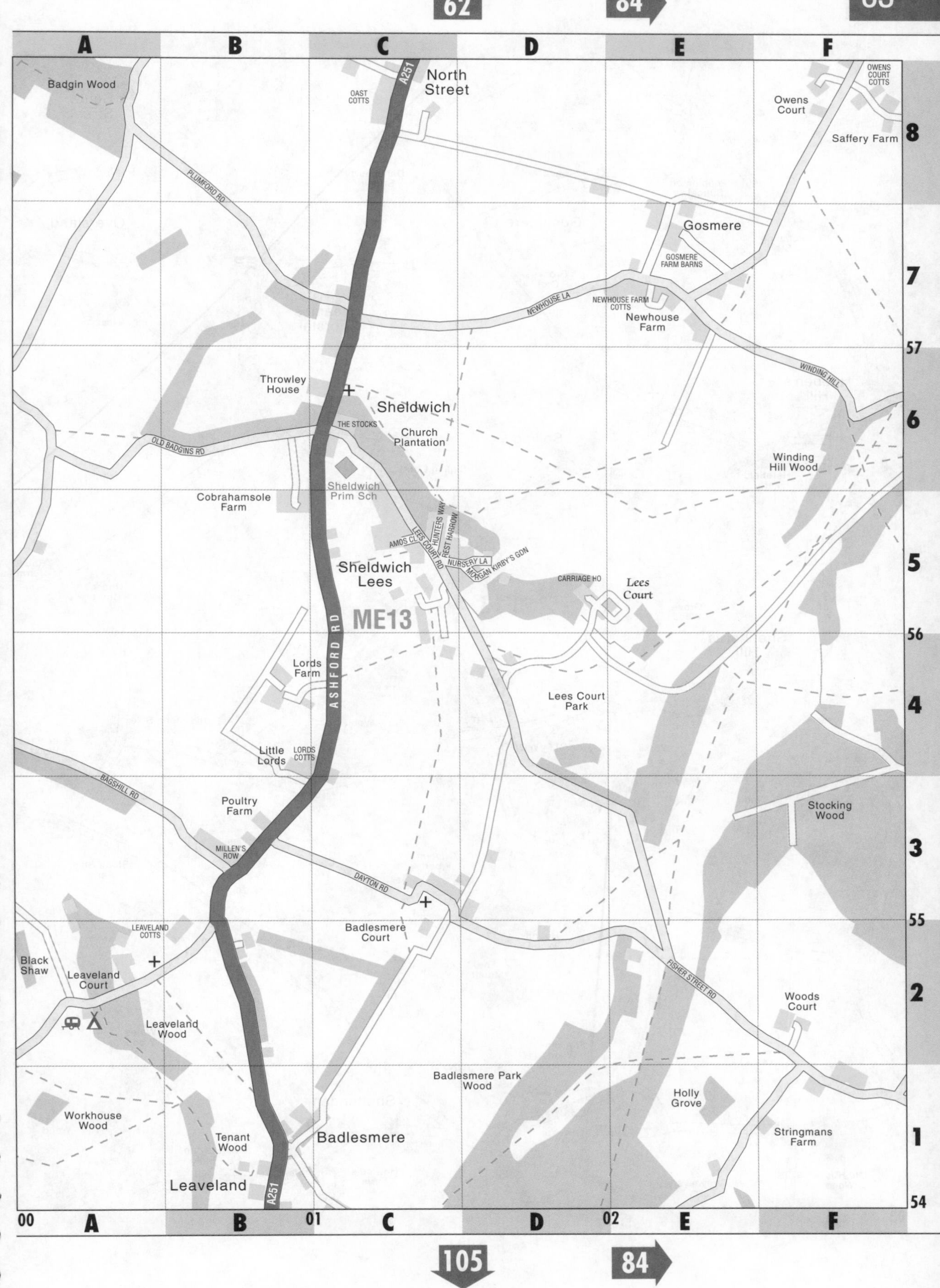
A
B
C
D
E
F
Badgin Wood
OAST COTTS
A251
North Street
OWENS COURT COTTS
Owens Court
Saffery Farm
8
PLUMFORD RD
Gosmere
GOSMERE FARM BARNS
7
NEWHOUSE LA
NEWHOUSE FARM COTTS
Newhouse Farm
57
WINDING HILL
Throwley House
Sheldwich
THE STOCKS
Church Plantation
6
OLD BADGINS RD
Winding Hill Wood
Sheldwich Prim Sch
Cobrahamsole Farm
HUNTERS WAY
REST HARROW
AMOS CL
LEES COURT RD
NURSERY LA
MORGAN KIRBY'S GDN
Sheldwich Lees
5
CARRIAGE HO
Lees Court
ME13
56
ASHFORD RD
Lords Farm
Lees Court Park
4
Little Lords
LORDS COTTS
BAGSHILL RD
Stocking Wood
Poultry Farm
MILLEN'S ROW
3
DAYTON RD
LEAVELAND COTTS
Badlesmere Court
55
Black Shaw
Leaveland Court
FISHER STREET RD
Woods Court
2
Leaveland Wood
Badlesmere Park Wood
Holly Grove
Workhouse Wood
Tenant Wood
Badlesmere
Stringmans Farm
1
Leaveland
A251
54
00
01
02

105
84

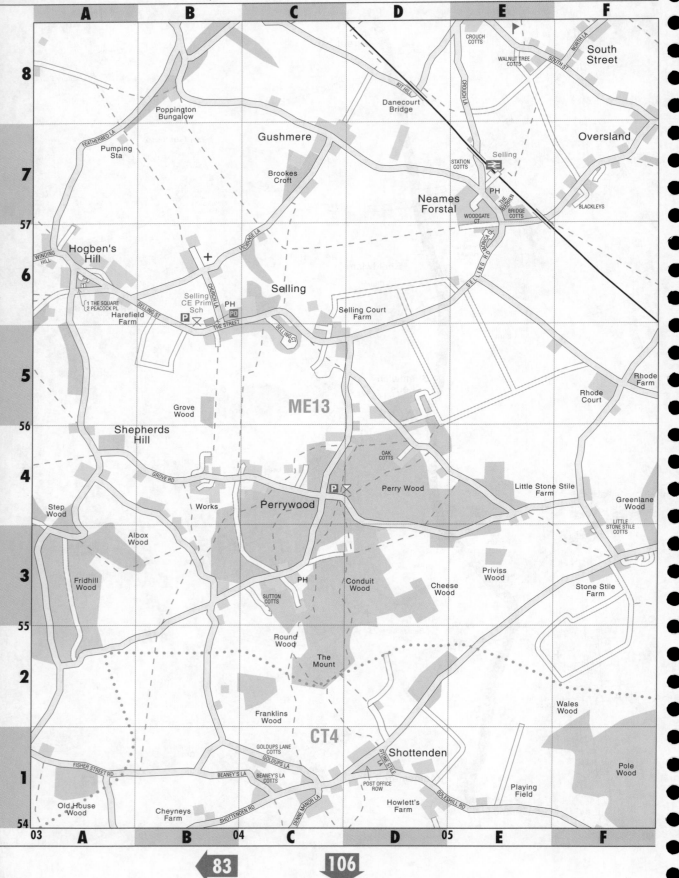

83
63

A   **B**   **C**   **D**   **E**   **F**

8

7

57

6

Hogben's Hill

FEATHERBED LA
WINDING HILL
Pumping Sta
Poppington Bungalow

Gushmere

Brookes Croft

Danecourt Bridge
KIT HILL
CROUCH CTS
CROUCH LA
WALNUT TREE COTTS
NORTH LA
SOUTH ST
South Street

Oversland

STATION COTTS
Selling
PH
THE WARREN
WOODGATE CT
BRIDGE COTTS
BLACKLEYS

Neames Forstal

VICARAGE LA
+
Selling CE Prim Sch
CHURCH LA
PH
PO
Selling
SELLING RD
SELLING RD

1 THE SQUARE
2 PEACOCK PL
Harefield Farm
SELLING ST
P
THE STREET
SELLING CT

Selling Court Farm

Rhode Farm

5

Grove Wood

ME13

Rhode Court

56

Shepherds Hill

4

GROVE RD

OAK COTTS

Perry Wood

Little Stone Stile Farm

Greenlane Wood

Step Wood

Works

Perrywood
P

Albox Wood

LITTLE STONE STILE COTTS

3

Fridhill Wood

PH
SUTTON COTTS

Conduit Wood

Cheese Wood

Priviss Wood

Stone Stile Farm

55

Round Wood

The Mount

2

Wales Wood

Franklins Wood

CT4

FISHER STREET RD

GOLDUPS LANE COTTS
GOLDUPS LA

BEANEY'S LA
BEANEY'S LA COTTS

STONE STILE LA
Shottenden

SOLESHILL RD

Playing Field

Pole Wood

1

Old House Wood

Cheyneys Farm

SHOTTENDEN RD

DENNE MANOR LA

POST OFFICE ROW

Howlett's Farm

54

03   **A**   **B**   04   **C**   **D**   05   **E**   **F**

83
106

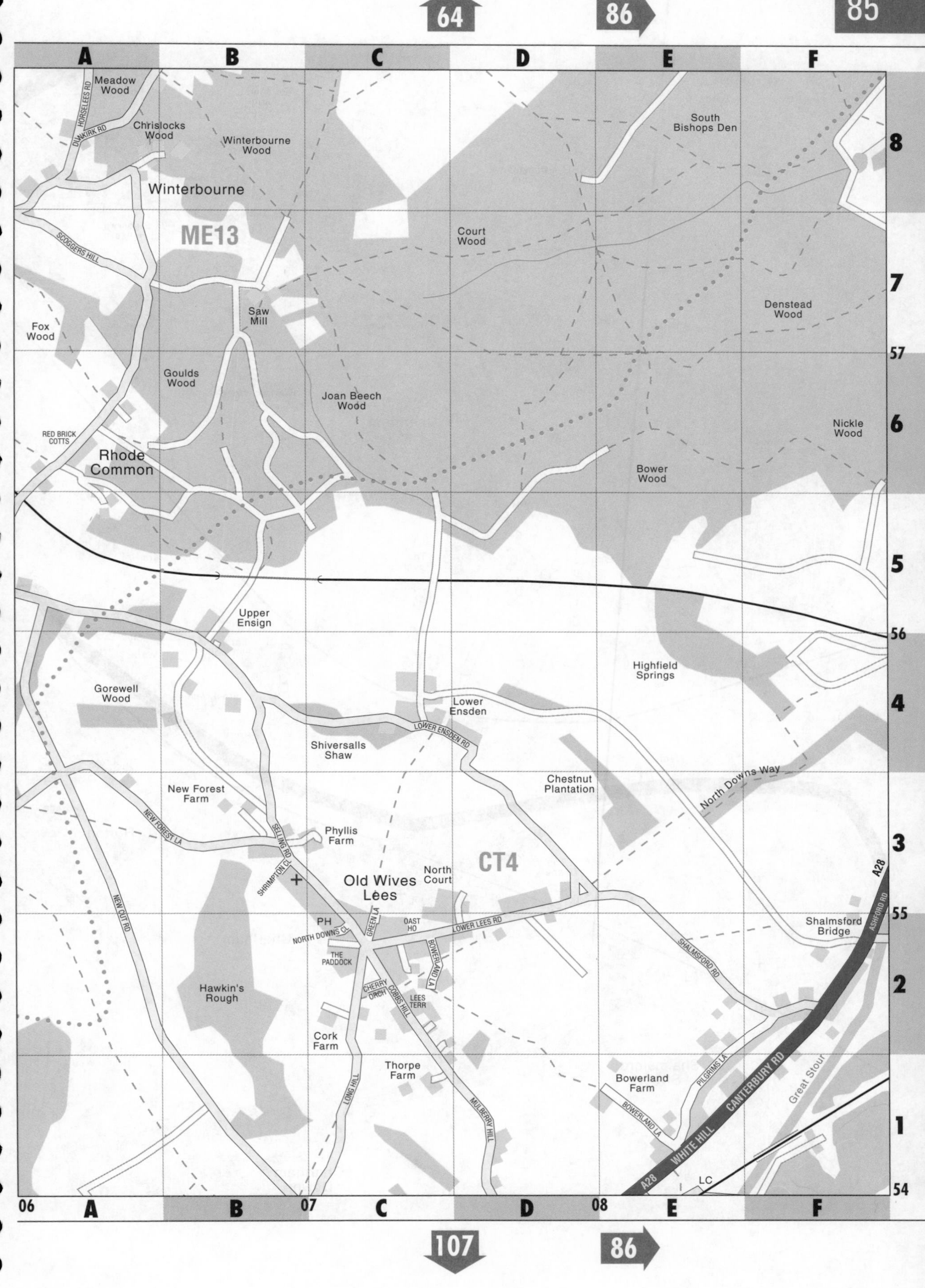

64
86
A
B
C
D
E
F
Meadow Wood
HORSELEES RD
DUNKIRK RD
Chrislocks Wood
Winterbourne Wood
South Bishops Den
Winterbourne
ME13
SCOGGERS HILL
Court Wood
Saw Mill
Fox Wood
Denstead Wood
Goulds Wood
Joan Beech Wood
Nickle Wood
RED BRICK COTTS
Rhode Common
Bower Wood
Upper Ensign
Highfield Springs
Gorewell Wood
Lower Ensden
LOWER ENSDEN RD
Shiversalls Shaw
Chestnut Plantation
New Forest Farm
North Downs Way
NEW FOREST LA
SELLING RD
Phyllis Farm
CT4
SHRIMPTON CL
Old Wives Lees
North Court
NEW CUT RD
PH
GREEN LA
OAST HO
LOWER LEES RD
NORTH DOWNS CL
THE PADDOCK
BOWERLAND LA
SHALMSFORD RD
Shalmsford Bridge
ASHFORD RD
A28
Hawkin's Rough
CHERRY ORCH
COBBS HILL
LEES TERR
Cork Farm
Thorpe Farm
PILGRIMS LA
Great Stour
CANTERBURY RD
Bowerland Farm
LONG HILL
MULBERRY HILL
BOWERLAND LA
WHITE HILL
A28
LC
8
7
57
6
5
56
4
3
55
2
1
54
06
07
08
107
86

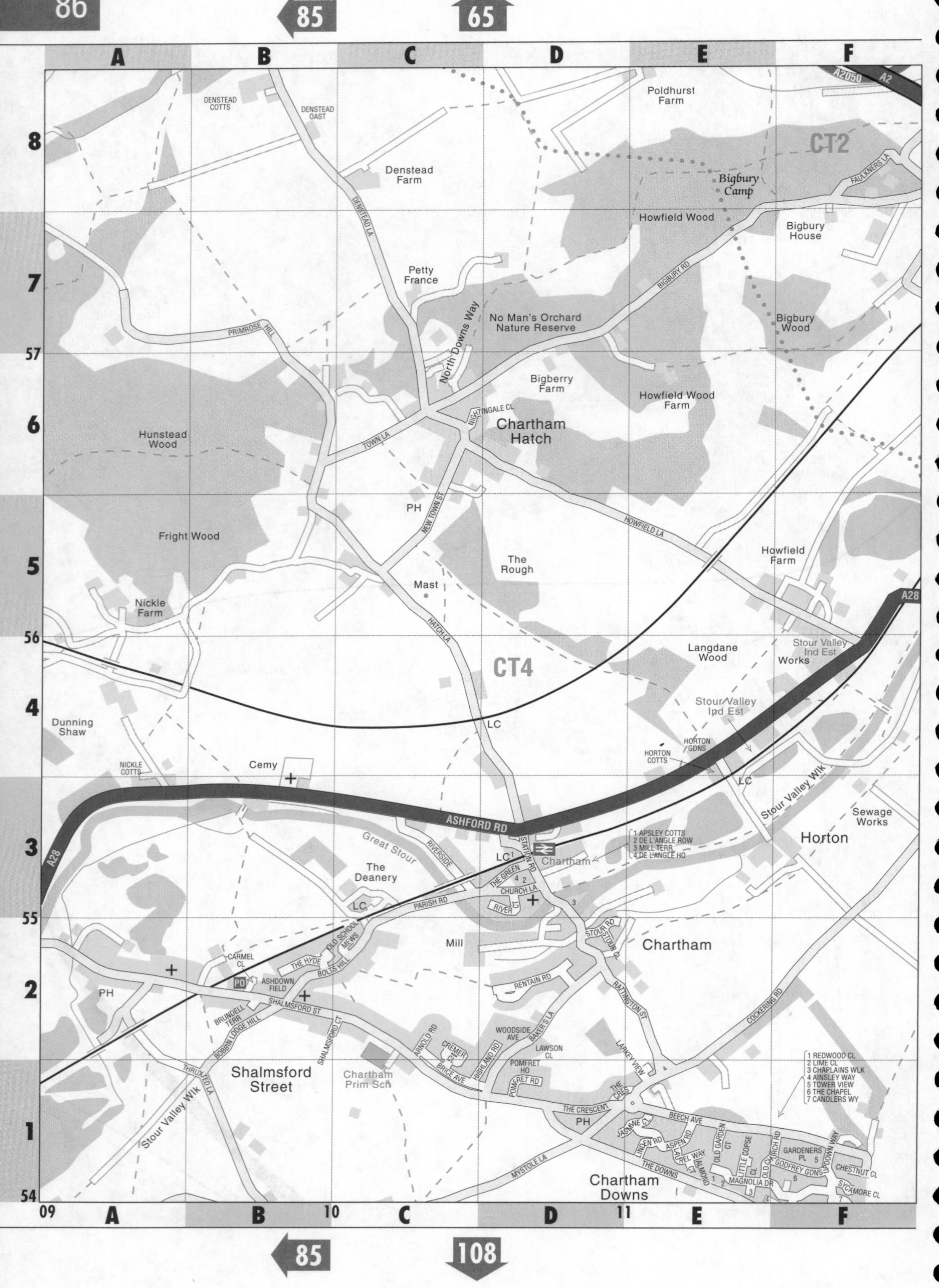

85 65

8
7
57
6
5
56
4
3
55
2
1
54

A B C D E F

85

A2050 A2
CT2

Denstead Cotts
Denstead Oast
Denstead Farm
Poldhurst Farm
Bigbury Camp
Howfield Wood
Bigbury House
FALKNERS LA

Petty France
Primrose Hill
North Downs Way
No Man's Orchard Nature Reserve
Bigbury Rd
Bigbury Wood

Hunstead Wood
Town La
Nightingale Cl
Bigberry Farm
Chartham Hatch
Howfield Wood Farm

Fright Wood
PH
New Town St
Howfield La
Howfield Farm

The Rough
Howfield Farm
A28

Nickle Farm
Mast
Hatch La
CT4
Langdane Wood
Works
Stour Valley Ind Est

Dunning Shaw
LC
Stour Valley Ind Est
Horton Gdns
Horton Cotts
LC
Stour Valley Wlk
Sewage Works
Horton

Nickle Cotts
Cemy
Ashford Rd
LC
1 Apsley Cotts
2 De L'Angle Row
3 Mill Terr
4 De L'Angle Ho
Chartham

A28
Great Stour
Riverside
The Deanery
LC
Station Rd
LC
The Green
Church La
River

Carmel Cl
Old School Mews
The Hyde
Bolts Hill
Parish Rd
Mill
Stour St
Chartham
Cockering Rd

PH
PO
Ashdown Field
Shalmsford St
Brundell Terr
Robin Lodge Hill
Shalmsford Ct
Rentain Rd
Baltington St

Thruxted La
Stour Valley Wlk
Shalmsford Street
Chartham Prim Sch
Barnett Rd
Cremer Cl
Brice Ave
Highland Rd
Woodside Ave
Lawson Cl
Pomfret Ho
Pomfret Rd
Larkey View

1 Redwood Cl
2 Lime Cl
3 Chaplains Wlk
4 Ainsley Way
5 Tower View
6 The Chapel
7 Candlers Wy

The Crescent
PH
Beech Ave
Jasmine Cl
Linden Rd
Aspen Cl
Laurel Way
Almond Cl
The Downs
Old Garden Ct
Little Copse
Birch Rd
Old Garden
Godfrey Gdns
Chestnut Cl
Gardeners Pl
Mystole La
Magnolia Dr
Sycamore Cl

Shalmsford Street
Chartham Downs
Mystole La

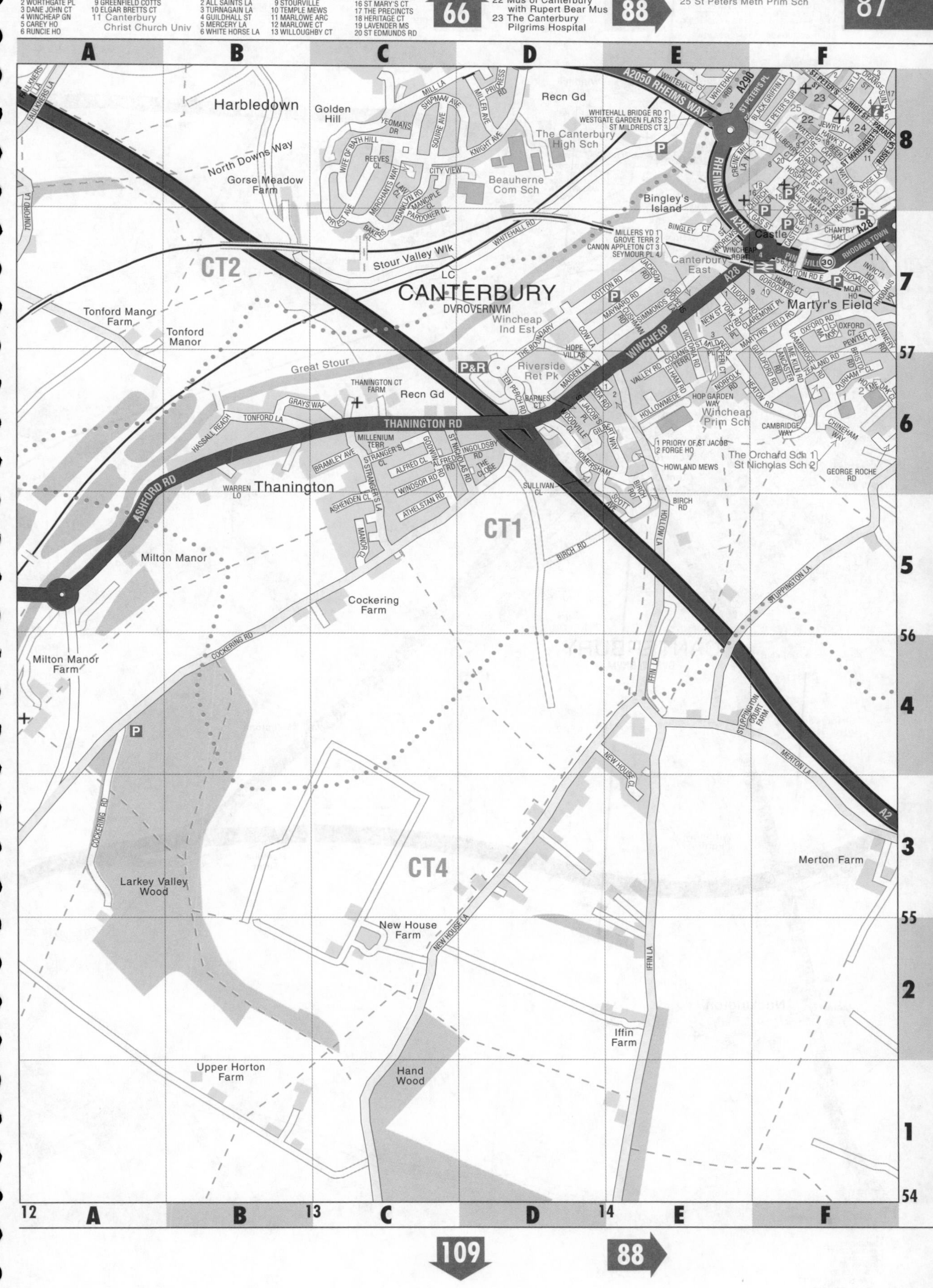

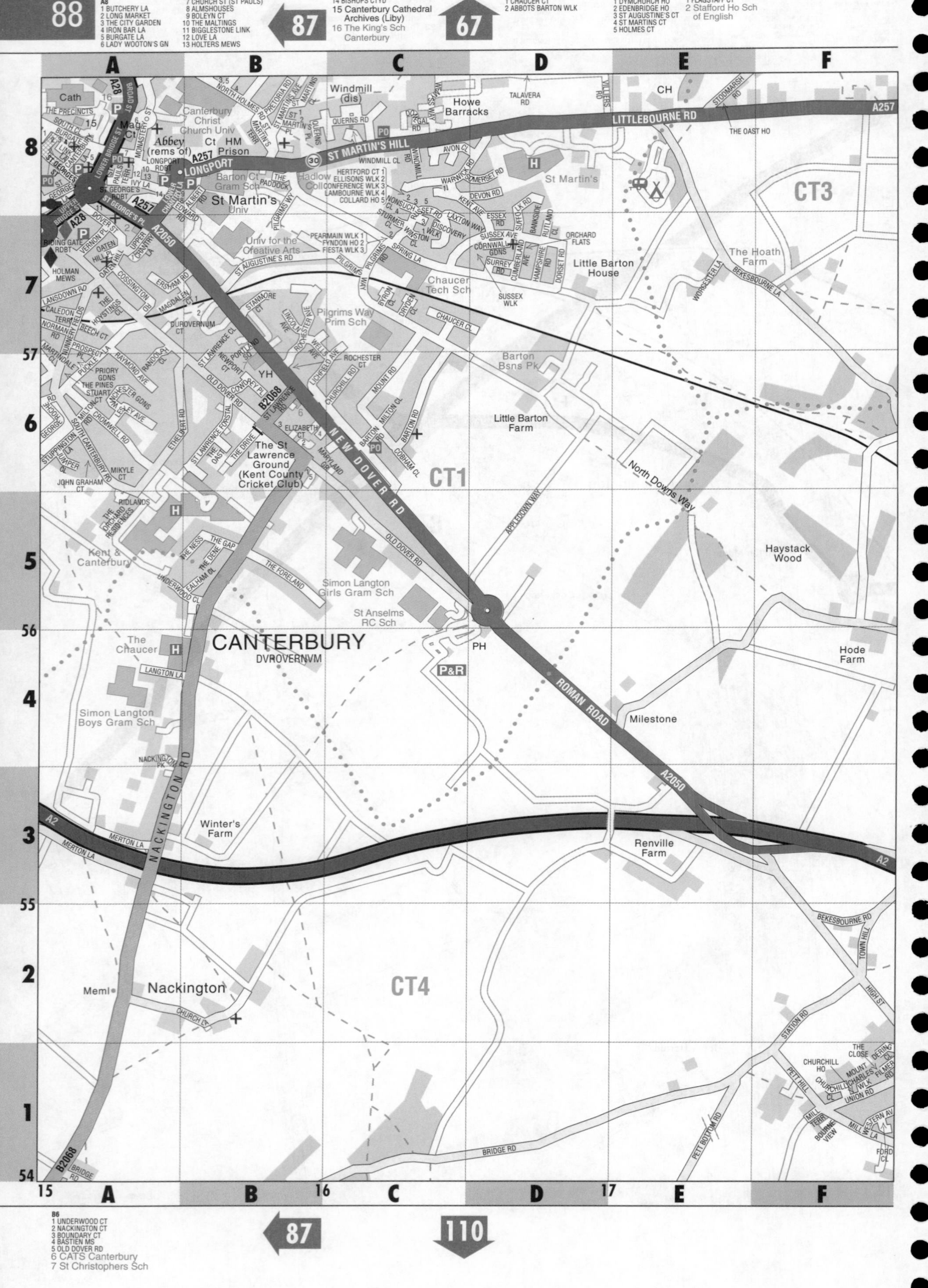

68
90

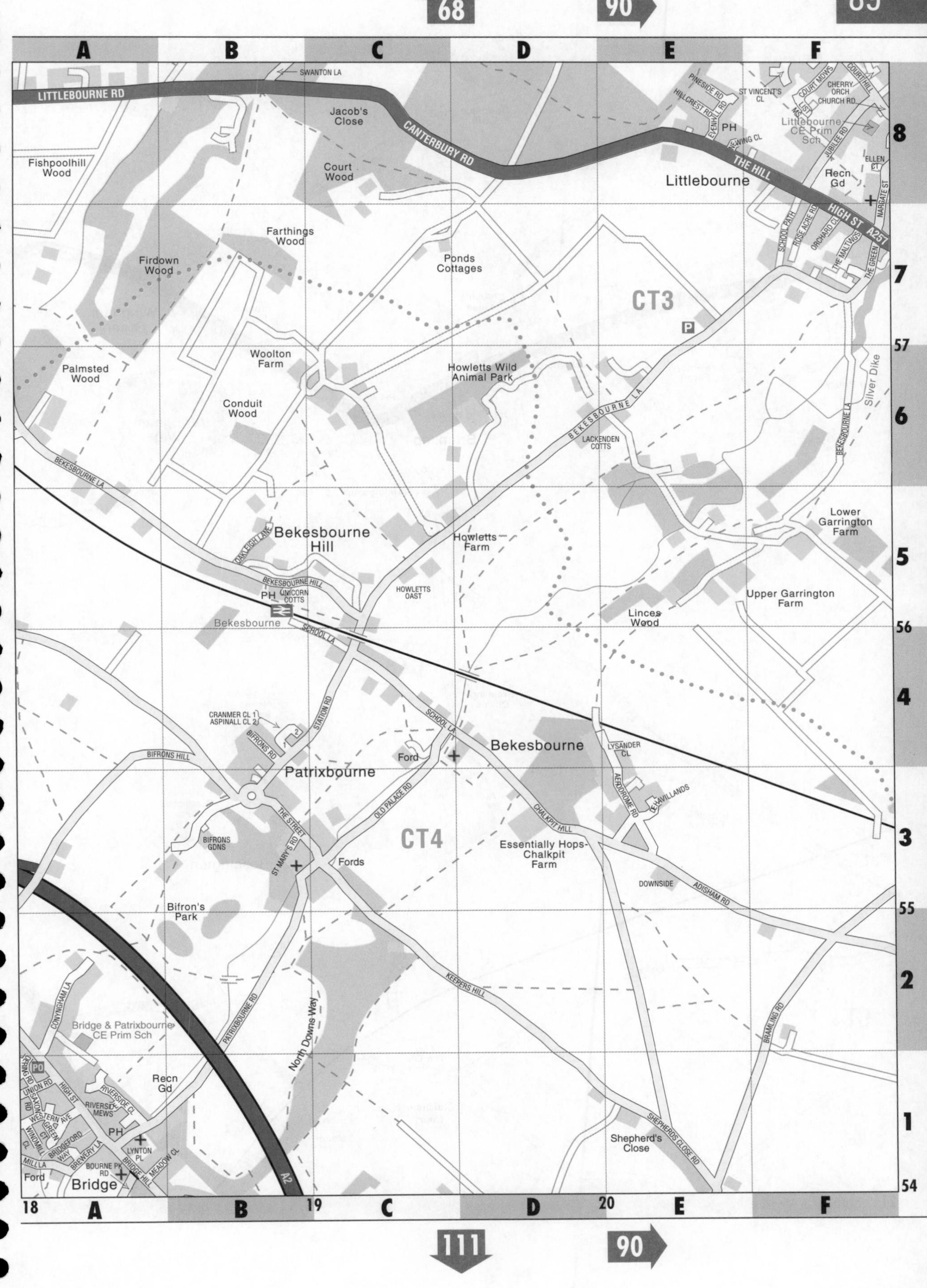
A
B
C
D
E
F
LITTLEBOURNE RD
SWANTON LA
Jacob's Close
CANTERBURY RD
Court Wood
Fishpoolhill Wood
Farthings Wood
Firdown Wood
Ponds Cottages
CT3
Littlebourne
THE HILL
HIGH ST
A257
Littlebourne CE Prim Sch
Recn Gd
PH
Palmsted Wood
Woolton Farm
Conduit Wood
Howletts Wild Animal Park
BEKESBOURNE LA
LACKENDEN COTTS
Silver Dike
Lower Garrington Farm
Bekesbourne Hill
Howletts Farm
HOWLETTS OAST
UNICORN COTTS
Bekesbourne
SCHOOL LA
Upper Garrington Farm
Linces Wood
CRANMER CL 1
ASPINALL CL 2
STATION RD
BIFRONS RD
BIFRONS HILL
Patrixbourne
Ford
Bekesbourne
LYSANDER CL
AERODROME RD
DE HAVILLANDS
CHALKPIT HILL
CT4
BIFRONS GDNS
THE STREET
OLD PALACE RD
Fords
Essentially Hops-Chalkpit Farm
DOWNSIDE
ADISHAM RD
Bifron's Park
KEEPERS HILL
North Downs Way
PATRIXBOURNE RD
Bridge & Patrixbourne CE Prim Sch
BRAMLING RD
Recn Gd
RIVERSIDE MEWS
LYNTON PL
MEADOW CL
BRIDGE HILL
BOURNE PK RD
Bridge
Ford
A2
Shepherd's Close
SHEPHERDS CLOSE RD
8
7
57
6
5
56
4
3
55
2
1
54
18
19
20

111
90

89
69

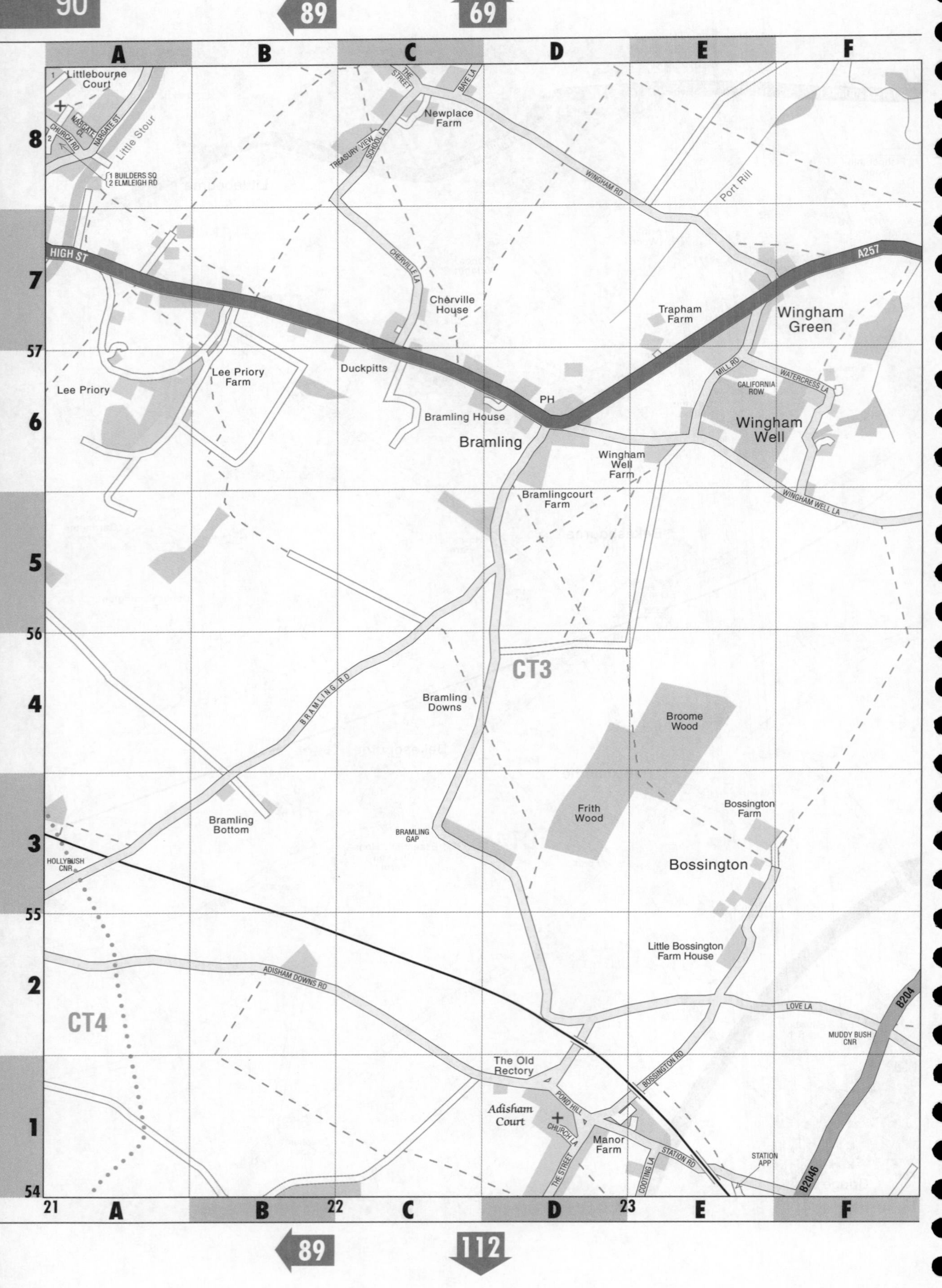
A
B
C
D
E
F
8
7
57
6
5
56
4
3
55
2
1
54
21
22
23
Littlebourne Court
NARGATE CL
NARGATE ST
CHURCH RD
Little Stour
1 BUILDERS SQ
2 ELMLEIGH RD
THE STREET
BAYE LA
Newplace Farm
TREASURY VIEW
SCHOOL LA
WINGHAM RD
Port Rill
HIGH ST
A257
CHERVILLE LA
Cherville House
Trapham Farm
Wingham Green
Lee Priory Farm
Duckpitts
Lee Priory
MILL RD
WATERCRESS LA
CALIFORNIA ROW
PH
Bramling House
Wingham Well
Bramling
Wingham Well Farm
Bramlingcourt Farm
WINGHAM WELL LA
CT3
BRAMLING RD
Bramling Downs
Broome Wood
Frith Wood
Bossington Farm
Bramling Bottom
BRAMLING GAP
Bossington
HOLLYBUSH CNR
Little Bossington Farm House
ADISHAM DOWNS RD
LOVE LA
B2046
B204
CT4
MUDDY BUSH CNR
The Old Rectory
BOSSINGTON RD
POND HILL
Adisham Court
CHURCH LA
Manor Farm
STATION RD
STATION APP
THE STREET
COOTING LA

89
112

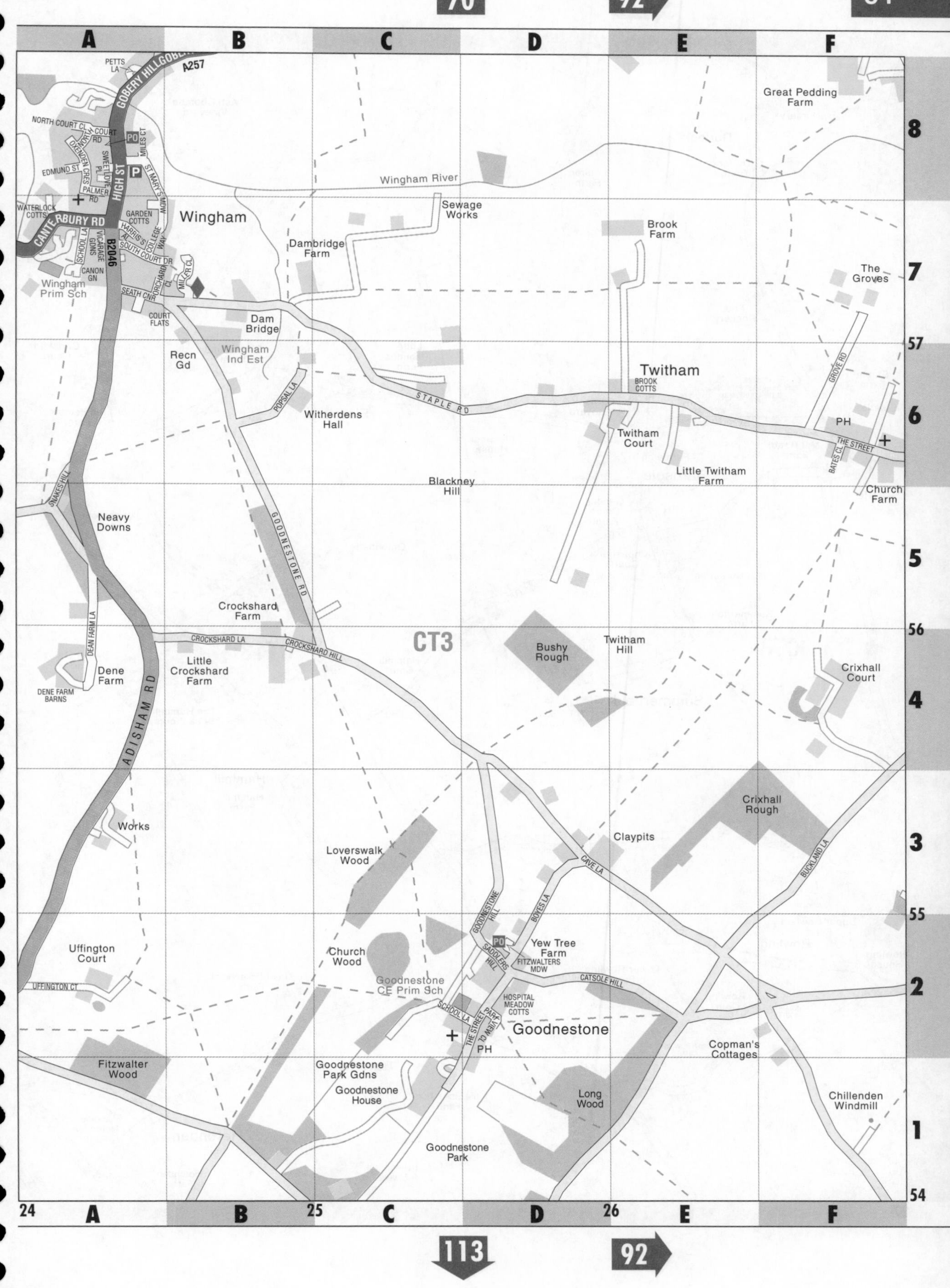
70
92
A
B
C
D
E
F
8
7
57
6
5
56
4
3
55
2
1
54
24
25
26
113
92
GOBERY HILL
A257
PETTS LA
NORTH COURT CL
NORTH COURT RD
OXENDEN CRES
SWEETLOVE PL
MILES CT
PO
P
EDMUND ST
HIGH ST
ST MARY'S MDW
PALMER RD
WATERLOCK COTTS
GARDEN COTTS
CANTERBURY RD
HARRIS'S AL
COLLEGE WAY
SOUTH COURT DR
B2046
SCHOOL LA
VICARAGE GDNS
CANON GN
ORCHARD CL
MILLER CL
SEATH CNR
COURT FLATS
Wingham
Wingham Prim Sch
Wingham River
Sewage Works
Dambridge Farm
Dam Bridge
Recn Gd
Wingham Ind Est
POPSAL LA
Witherdens Hall
STAPLE RD
Brook Farm
Great Pedding Farm
The Groves
Twitham
BROOK COTTS
Twitham Court
Little Twitham Farm
GROVE RD
PH
THE STREET
BATES CL
Church Farm
Blackney Hill
SNAKES HILL
Neavy Downs
GOODNESTONE RD
Crockshard Farm
DEAN FARM LA
CROCKSHARD LA
CROCKSHARD HILL
CT3
Bushy Rough
Twitham Hill
Crixhall Court
Dene Farm
DENE FARM BARNS
Little Crockshard Farm
ADISHAM RD
Crixhall Rough
Works
Claypits
Loverswalk Wood
GAVE LA
BOYES LA
GOODNESTONE HILL
BUCKLAND LA
SADDLERS HILL
PO
Yew Tree Farm
FITZWALTERS MDW
Church Wood
CATSOLE HILL
Uffington Court
Goodnestone CE Prim Sch
UFFINGTON CT
HOSPITAL MEADOW COTTS
SCHOOL LA
PARK VIEW CL
THE STREET
Goodnestone
PH
Copman's Cottages
Fitzwalter Wood
Goodnestone Park Gdns
Goodnestone House
Long Wood
Chillenden Windmill
Goodnestone Park

A   **B**   **C**   **D**   **E**   **F**

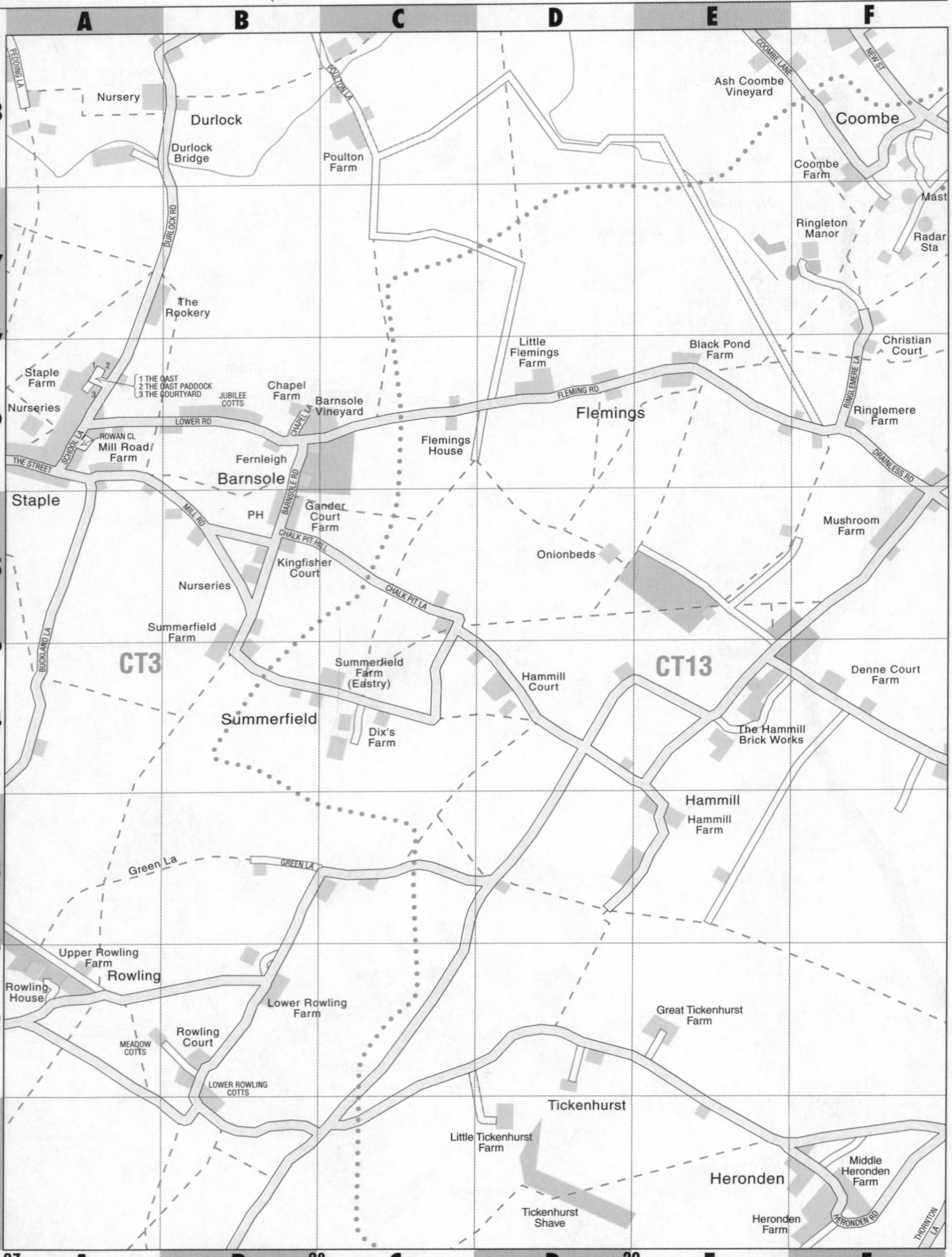

Nursery

Durlock

Durlock Bridge

Poulton Farm

POULTON LA

Ash Coombe Vineyard

Coombe

NEW ST

COOMBE LANE

Coombe Farm

Mast

8

Ringleton Manor

Radar Sta

DURLOCK RD

The Rookery

7

Little Flemings Farm

Black Pond Farm

Christian Court

RINGLEMERE LA

57

Staple Farm

1 THE OAST
2 THE OAST PADDOCK
3 THE COURTYARD

Chapel Farm

Barnsole Vineyard

FLEMING RD

Flemings

Ringlemere Farm

6

Nurseries

JUBILEE COTTS

LOWER RD

CHAPEL LA

Flemings House

DRAINLESS RD

SCHOOL LA

ROWAN CL

Mill Road/ Farm

Fernleigh

Barnsole

BARNSOLE RD

THE STREET

Staple

PH

MILL RD

Gander Court Farm

Mushroom Farm

BUCKLAND LA

Kingfisher Court

CHALK PIT HILL

Onionbeds

CT3

CT13

Denne Court Farm

Nurseries

CHALK PIT LA

5

Summerfield Farm

56

Summerfield Farm (Eastry)

Hammill Court

4

Summerfield

Dix's Farm

The Hammill Brick Works

Hammill

Hammill Farm

Green La

GREEN LA

3

55

Upper Rowling Farm

Rowling

Great Tickenhurst Farm

Rowling House

Lower Rowling Farm

2

MEADOW COTTS

Rowling Court

Tickenhurst

LOWER ROWLING COTTS

Little Tickenhurst Farm

Heronden

Middle Heronden Farm

1

Tickenhurst Shave

Heronden Farm

HERONDEN RD

THORNTON LA

54

72
94

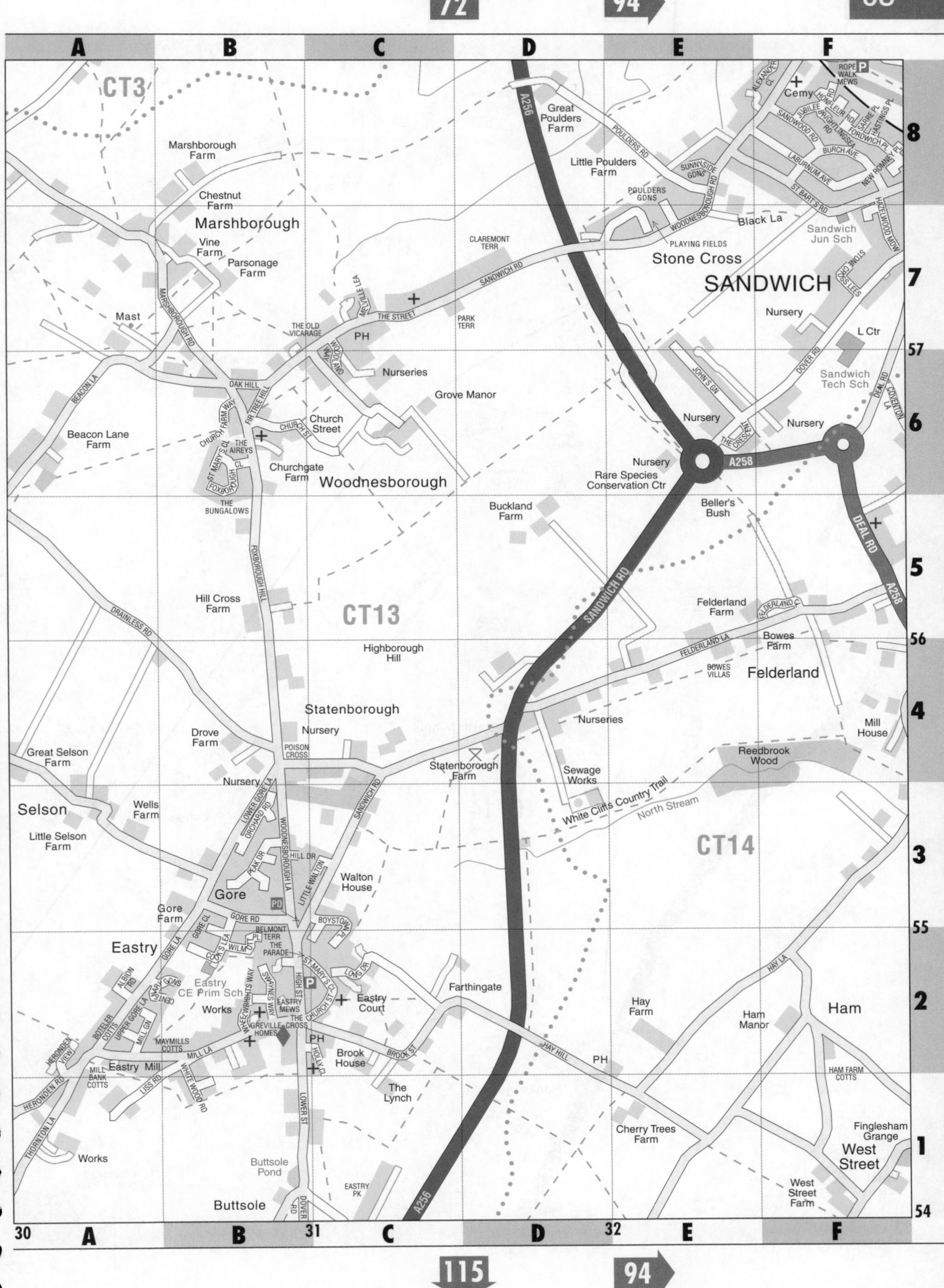
A
B
C
D
E
F
CT3
CT13
CT14
Marshborough Farm
Chestnut Farm
Marshborough
Vine Farm
Parsonage Farm
Mast
MARSHBOROUGH RD
BEACON LA
Beacon Lane Farm
OAK HILL
FIR TREE HILL
CHURCH FARM WAY
ST MARY'S CL
THE AIREYS
FOXBOROUGH CL
THE BUNGALOWS
CHURCH ST
Church Street
Churchgate Farm
Woodnesborough
THE OLD VICARAGE
MELVILLE LEA
THE STREET
PH
WOODLAND WAY
Nurseries
Grove Manor
SANDWICH RD
CLAREMONT TERR
PARK TERR
A256
Great Poulders Farm
Little Poulders Farm
POULDERS RD
POULDERS GDNS
SUNNYSIDE GDNS
WOODNESBOROUGH RD
PLAYING FIELDS
Stone Cross
Black La
SANDWICH
ALEXANDER CL
Cemy
ROPE WALK MEWS
HONFLEUR RD
JUBILEE RD
SANDWOOD RD
BRIGHTLINGSEA RD
SARRE PL
HASTINGS PL
FORDWICH PL
BURCH AVE
LABURNUM AVE
NEW ROMNEY PL
ST BART'S RD
HAZELWOOD MDW
Sandwich Jun Sch
STONE CROSS LEES
Nursery
L Ctr
DOVER RD
Sandwich Tech Sch
DEAL RD
COVENTON LA
JOHN'S GN
THE CRESCENT
A258
Rare Species Conservation Ctr
Beller's Bush
Buckland Farm
DEAL RD
SANDWICH RD
Felderland Farm
FELDERLAND CL
FELDERLAND LA
Bowes Farm
BOWES VILLAS
Felderland
Mill House
Hill Cross Farm
DRAINLESS RD
FOXBOROUGH HILL
Highborough Hill
Statenborough
Drove Farm
Great Selson Farm
POISON CROSS
Statenborough Farm
Nurseries
Reedbrook Wood
Sewage Works
White Cliffs Country Trail
North Stream
Selson
Little Selson Farm
Wells Farm
LOWER GORE LA
ORCHARD RD
WOODNESBOROUGH LA
HILL DR
PEAK DR
SANDWICH RD
Walton House
LITTLE WALTON
Gore
PO
Gore Farm
GORE RD
BOYSTOWN PL
GORE CL
GORE LA
BELMONT TERR
THE PARADE
Eastry
COOKS LEA
WILMOTT PL
ST MARY'S CL
LONG DR
ALBION RD
CENTRAL GDNS
Eastry CE Prim Sch
SWAYNES WAY
HIGH ST
P
Eastry Court
Farthingate
Works
EASTRY MEWS
THE CROSS
CHURCH ST
GREVILLE HOMES
WHEELWRIGHTS WAY
UPPER GORE LA
MILL GN
BOTELER COTTS
MAYMILLS COTTS
MILL LA
HERONDEN VIEW
HERONDEN RD
MILL BANK COTTS
Eastry Mill
LISS RD
WHITE WOOD RD
Brook House
BROOK ST
HOLLY CL
The Lynch
HAY HILL
Hay Farm
HAY LA
Ham Manor
Ham
HAM FARM COTTS
LOWER ST
THORNTON LA
Works
Buttsole Pond
Buttsole
DOVER RD
EASTRY PK
Cherry Trees Farm
Finglesham Grange
West Street
West Street Farm
8
7
57
6
5
56
4
3
55
2
1
54
30
31
32

115
94

93
73

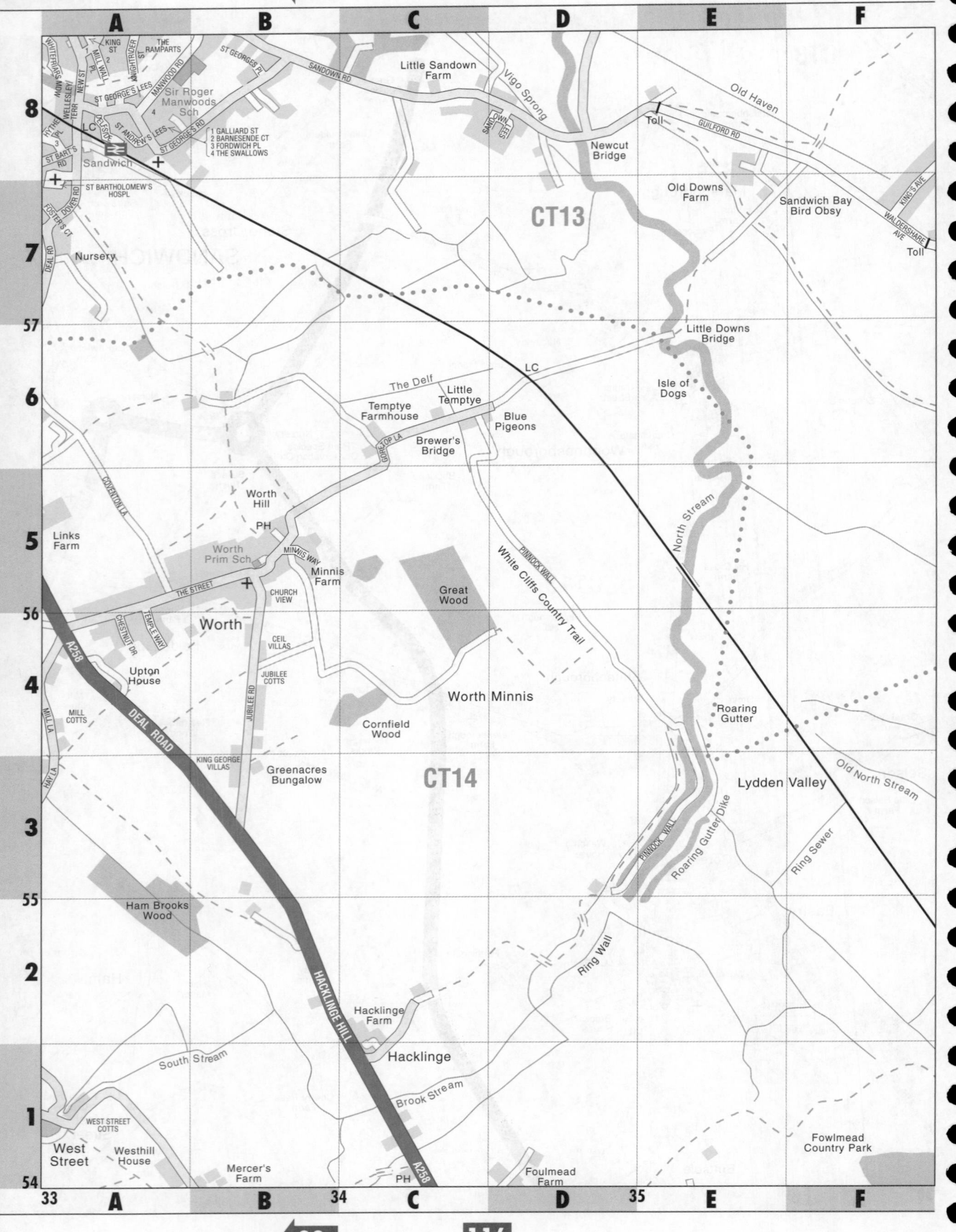

A
B
C
D
E
F
8
7
57
6
5
56
4
3
55
2
1
54
33
34
35
Little Sandown Farm
Vigo Sprong
Old Haven
Toll
Guilford Rd
Newcut Bridge
Sir Roger Manwoods Sch
Sandwich
St Bartholomew's Hospl
Old Downs Farm
Sandwich Bay Bird Obsy
CT13
Waldershare Ave
King's Ave
Nursery
Little Downs Bridge
LC
The Delf
Little Temptye
Temptye Farmhouse
Blue Pigeons
Brewer's Bridge
Isle of Dogs
Worth Hill
PH
Links Farm
Worth Prim Sch
Minnis Farm
Great Wood
White Cliffs Country Trail
North Stream
The Street
Church View
Worth
Ceil Villas
Jubilee Cotts
Upton House
Worth Minnis
Cornfield Wood
Roaring Gutter
Mill Cotts
Deal Road
King George Villas
Greenacres Bungalow
CT14
Lydden Valley
Old North Stream
Roaring Gutter Dike
Pinnock Wall
Ring Sewer
Ham Brooks Wood
Hacklinge Hill
Ring Wall
Hacklinge Farm
Hacklinge
South Stream
Brook Stream
West Street Cotts
West Street
Westhill House
Mercer's Farm
PH
A258
Foulmead Farm
Fowlmead Country Park
1 Galliard St
2 Barnesende Ct
3 Fordwich Pl
4 The Swallows

93
116

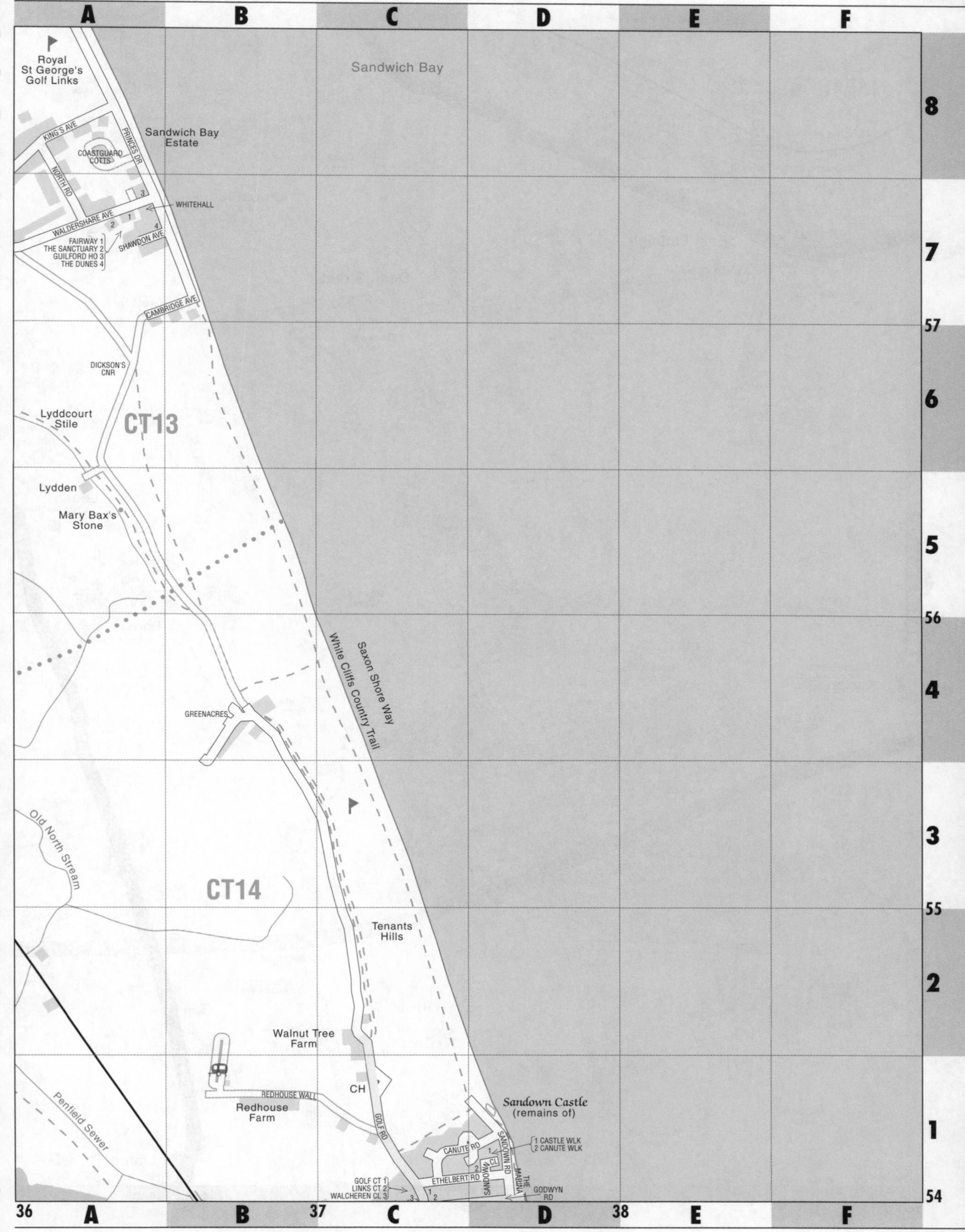

Sandwich Bay

Royal
St George's
Golf Links

Sandwich Bay
Estate

KING'S AVE
COASTGUARD
COTTS

NORTH RD
PRINCES DR

WHITEHALL

WALDERSHARE AVE
FAIRWAY 1
THE SANCTUARY 2
GUILFORD HO 3
THE DUNES 4
SHANDON AVE

CAMBRIDGE AVE

DICKSON'S
CNR

Lyddcourt
Stile

CT13

Lydden

Mary Bax's
Stone

GREENACRES

White Cliffs Country Trail
Saxon Shore Way

Old North Stream

CT14

Tenants
Hills

Walnut Tree
Farm

REDHOUSE WALL

Redhouse
Farm

CH

GOLF RD

Sandown Castle
(remains of)

1 CASTLE WLK
2 CANUTE WLK

CANUTE RD

SANDOWN RD

ETHELBERT RD
SANDOWN
CL

THE MARENA

GODWYN
RD

GOLF CT 1
LINKS CT 2
WALCHEREN CL 3

Penfield Sewer

74

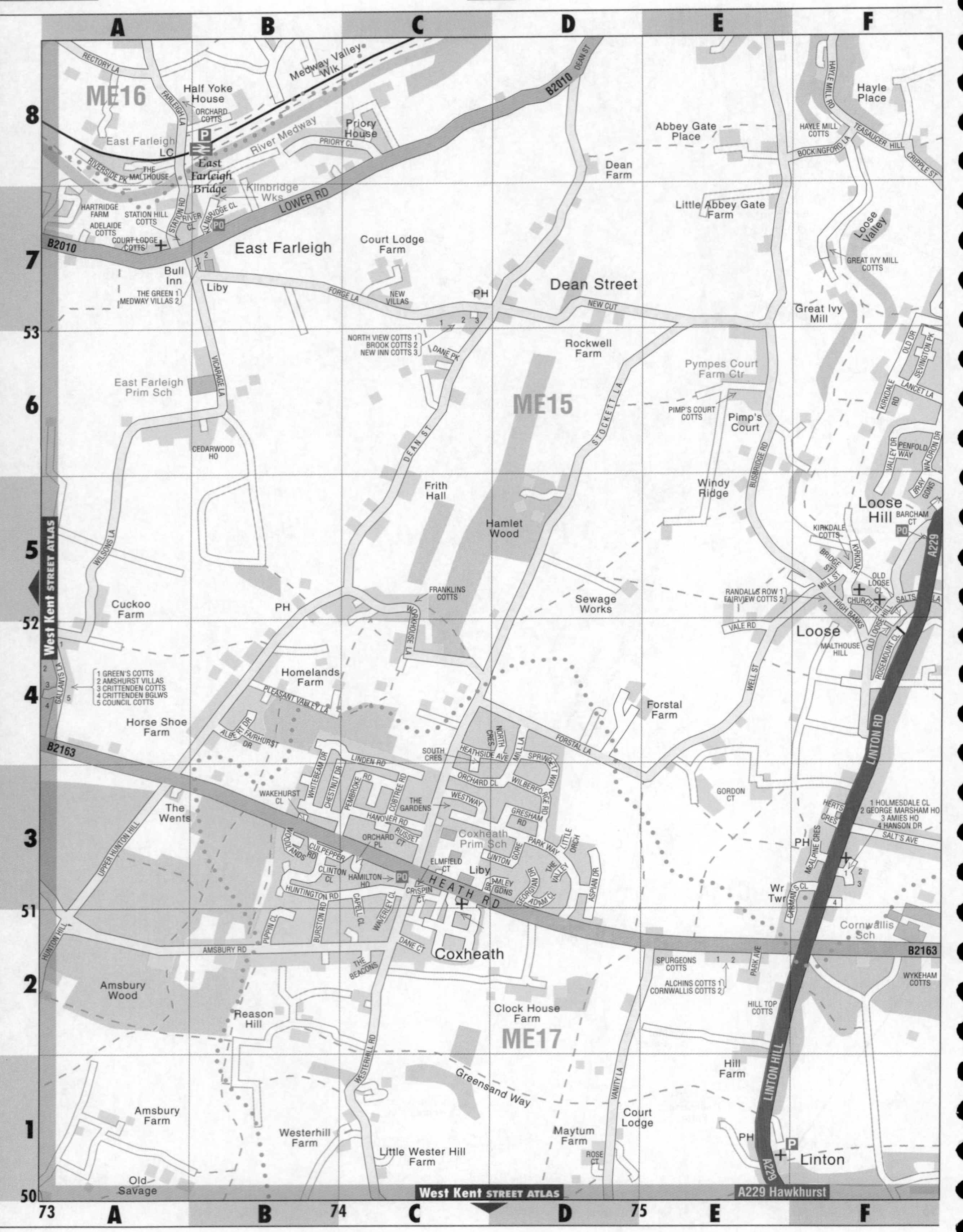

A
B
C
D
E
F
ME16
ME15
ME17
RECTORY LA
Medway Valley Wlk
Half Yoke House
FARLEIGH LA
ORCHARD COTTS
East Farleigh
LC
East Farleigh Bridge
RIVERSIDE PK
THE MALTHOUSE
River Medway
Priory House
PRIORY CL
B2010
DEAN ST
Kilnbridge Wks
LOWER RD
HARTRIDGE FARM
STATION HILL COTTS
ADELAIDE COTTS
COURT LODGE COTTS
STATION RD
RIVER CL
KILNBRIDGE CL
PO
East Farleigh
Court Lodge Farm
Bull Inn
Liby
THE GREEN 1
MEDWAY VILLAS 2
FORGE LA
NEW VILLAS
PH
Dean Street
NEW CUT
Abbey Gate Place
Dean Farm
Little Abbey Gate Farm
Hayle Place
HAYLE MILL RD
HAYLE MILL COTTS
BOCKINGFORD LA
TEASAUCER HILL
CRIPPLE ST
Loose Valley
GREAT IVY MILL COTTS
Great Ivy Mill
NORTH VIEW COTTS 1
BROOK COTTS 2
NEW INN COTTS 3
DANE PK
Rockwell Farm
Pympes Court Farm Ctr
East Farleigh Prim Sch
VICARAGE LA
PIMP'S COURT COTTS
Pimp's Court
STOCKETT LA
OLD DR
SEVINGTON PK
LANCET LA
KIRKDALE RD
VALLEY DR
PENFOLD WAY
WALDRON DR
BRAY GDNS
CEDARWOOD HO
Frith Hall
Windy Ridge
BUSBRIDGE RD
Loose Hill
BARCHAM CT
Hamlet Wood
KIRKDALE COTTS
KIRKDALE
BRIDGE ST
A229
WILSONS LA
FRANKLINS COTTS
Sewage Works
OLD LOOSE CL
CHURCH ST
SALTS
Cuckoo Farm
PH
WORKHOUSE LA
RANDALLS ROW 1
FAIRVIEW COTTS 2
MILL ST
HIGH BANKS
VALE RD
Loose
MALTHOUSE HILL
OLD LOOSE HILL
ROSEMOUNT CL
1 GREEN'S COTTS
2 AMSHURST VILLAS
3 CRITTENDEN COTTS
4 CRITTENDEN BGLWS
5 COUNCIL COTTS
GALLANTS LA
Homelands Farm
PLEASANT VALLEY LA
WELL ST
Forstal Farm
Horse Shoe Farm
ALBERT DR
FAIRHURST DR
NORTH CRES
MILL LA
FORSTAL LA
B2163
LINDEN RD
SOUTH CRES
HEATHSIDE AVE
SPRINGETT WAY
ORCHARD CL
WILBERFORCE RD
LINTON RD
GORDON CT
WAKEHURST CL
WHITEBEAM DR
CHESTNUT DR
PEMBROKE RD
COBTREE RD
THE GARDENS
WESTWAY
GRESHAM RD
The Wents
HANOVER RD
RUSSET CT
Coxheath Prim Sch
PARK WAY
LITTLE ORCH
HERTS CRES
1 HOLMESDALE CL
2 GEORGE MARSHAM HO
3 AMIES HO
4 HANSON DR
SALT'S AVE
PH
MCALPINE CRES
UPPER HUNTON HILL
WOODLANDS
CULPEPPER RD
ORCHARD PL
CLINTON CL
HAMILTON HO
ELMFIELD CT
LINTON GORE
THE VALLEY
ASPIAN DR
Liby
HEATH RD
CRISPIN CT
BRAMLEY GDNS
GEORGIAN DR
ADAM CL
Wr Twr
GARMANS CL
HUNTINGTON RD
CAPELL CL
WAVERLEY CL
PIPPIN CL
BURSTON RD
Cornwallis Sch
HUNTON HILL
AMSBURY RD
DANE CT
Coxheath
THE BEACONS
SPURGEONS COTTS
ALCHINS COTTS 1
CORNWALLIS COTTS 2
PARK AVE
WYKEHAM COTTS
Amsbury Wood
Reason Hill
Clock House Farm
HILL TOP COTTS
WESTERHILL RD
Greensand Way
Hill Farm
LINTON HILL
VANITY LA
Court Lodge
Amsbury Farm
Westerhill Farm
Maytum Farm
Little Wester Hill Farm
ROSE CT
PH
Linton
Old Savage
8
7
53
6
5
52
4
3
51
2
1
50
73
74
75

A229 Hawkhurst

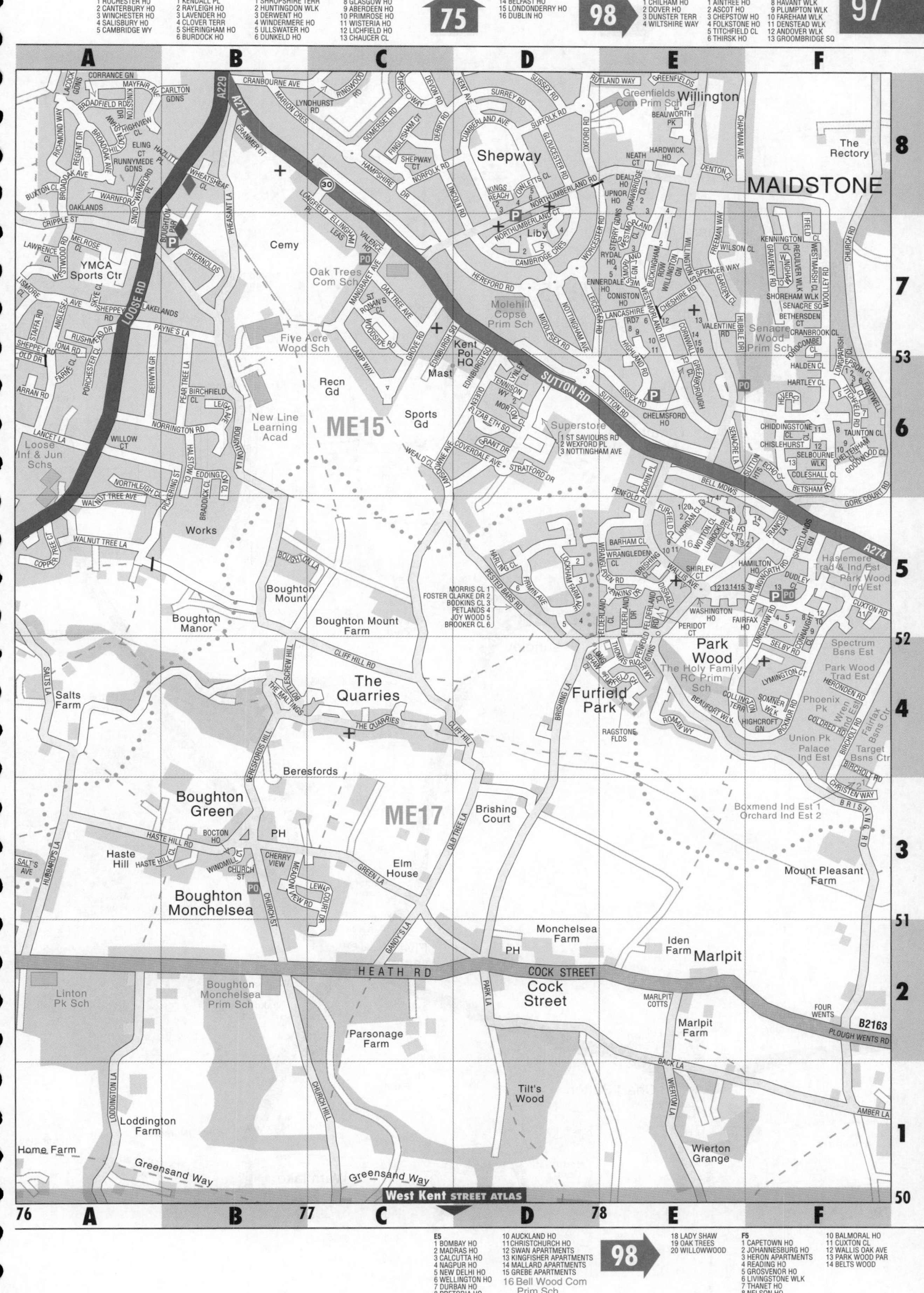

97
76

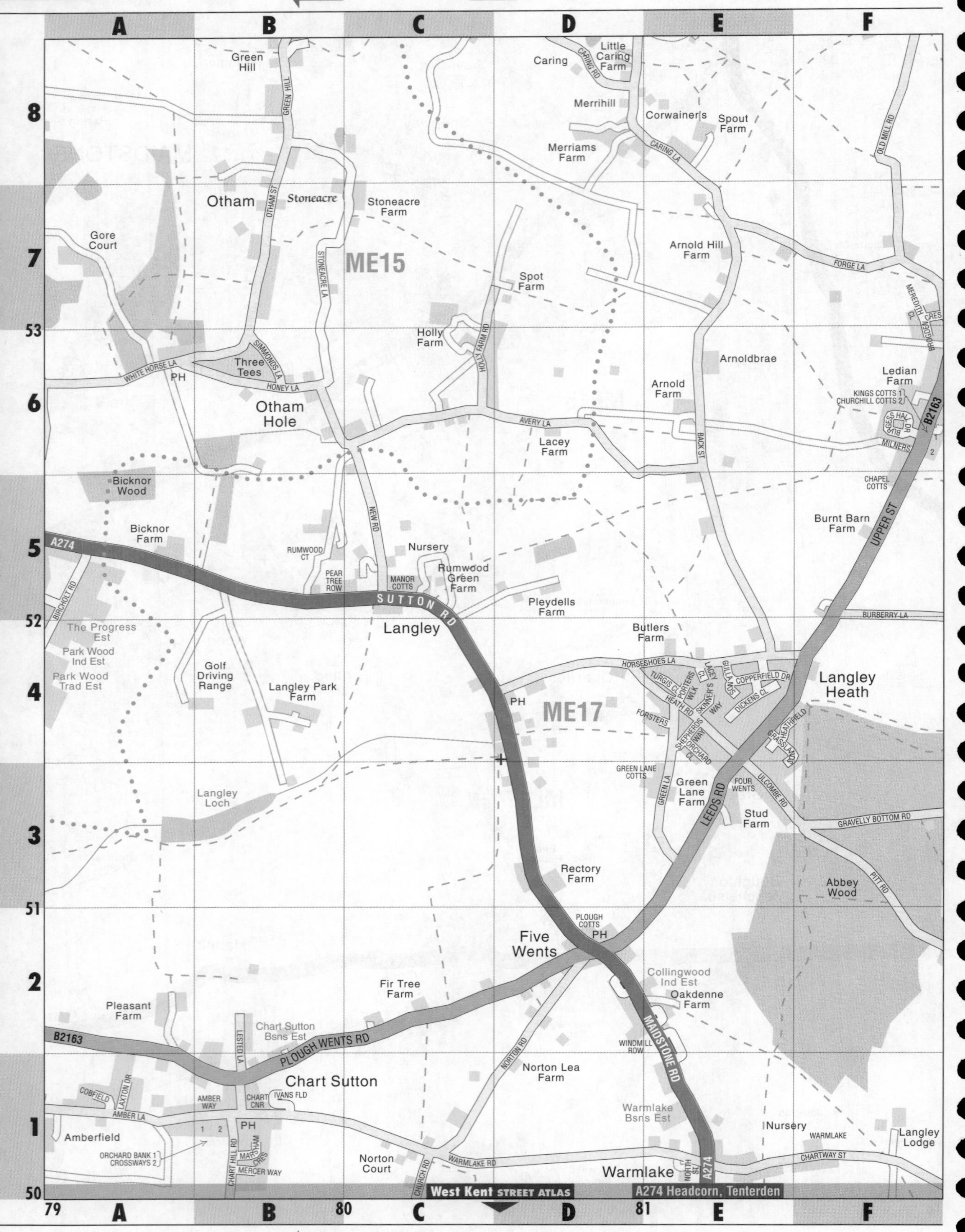
A B C D E F
8 7 53 6 5 52 4 3 51 2 1 50
79 80 81
Green Hill
Caring
Little Caring Farm
CARING RD
Merrihill
Corwainer's
Spout Farm
Merriams Farm
CARING LA
OLD MILL RD
GREEN HILL
Otham
OTHAM ST
Stoneacre
Stoneacre Farm
Gore Court
ME15
STONEACRE LA
Arnold Hill Farm
FORGE LA
Spot Farm
MEREDITH CL
CRES
Holly Farm
HOLLY FARM RD
Arnoldbrae
SIMMONDS LA
Three Tees
WHITE HORSE LA
PH
HONEY LA
Arnold Farm
Ledian Farm
KINGS COTTS 1
CHURCHILL COTTS 2
Otham Hole
AVERY LA
BACK ST
B2163
Lacey Farm
MILNERS
Bicknor Wood
CHAPEL COTTS
NEW RD
Bicknor Farm
Burnt Barn Farm
A274
RUMWOOD CT
Nursery
UPPER ST
PEAR TREE ROW
MANOR COTTS
Rumwood Green Farm
SUTTON RD
Pleydells Farm
BIRCHOLT RD
BURBERRY LA
The Progress Est
Langley
Butlers Farm
Park Wood Ind Est
Park Wood Trad Est
HORSESHOES LA
TURGIS CL
PORTERS WLK
LACEY CL
GULLANDS
COPPERFIELD DR
Golf Driving Range
Langley Park Farm
HEATH RD
SKINNER'S WAY
DICKENS CL
Langley Heath
PH
ME17
FORSTERS
HEATHFIELD
SHEPHERDS WAY
GRASSLANDS
ORCHARD CL
GREEN LANE COTTS
Langley Loch
GREEN LA
Green Lane Farm
FOUR WENTS
LEEDS RD
ULCOMBE RD
Stud Farm
GRAVELLY BOTTOM RD
Rectory Farm
Abbey Wood
PITT RD
PLOUGH COTTS
PH
Five Wents
Collingwood Ind Est
Oakdenne Farm
Fir Tree Farm
Pleasant Farm
Chart Sutton Bsns Est
B2163
LESTED LA
PLOUGH WENTS RD
MAIDSTONE RD
WINDMILL ROW
NORTON RD
Norton Lea Farm
Chart Sutton
COBFIELD
LAKTON DR
AMBER WAY
CHART CNR
IVANS FLD
AMBER LA
Warmlake Bsns Est
PH
Amberfield
Nursery
WARMLAKE
Langley Lodge
ORCHARD BANK 1
CROSSWAYS 2
CHART HILL RD
MARSHAM CRES
MERCER WAY
Norton Court
CHURCH RD
WARMLAKE RD
Warmlake
NORTH ST
A274
CHARTWAY ST
West Kent STREET ATLAS
A274 Headcorn, Tenterden

97

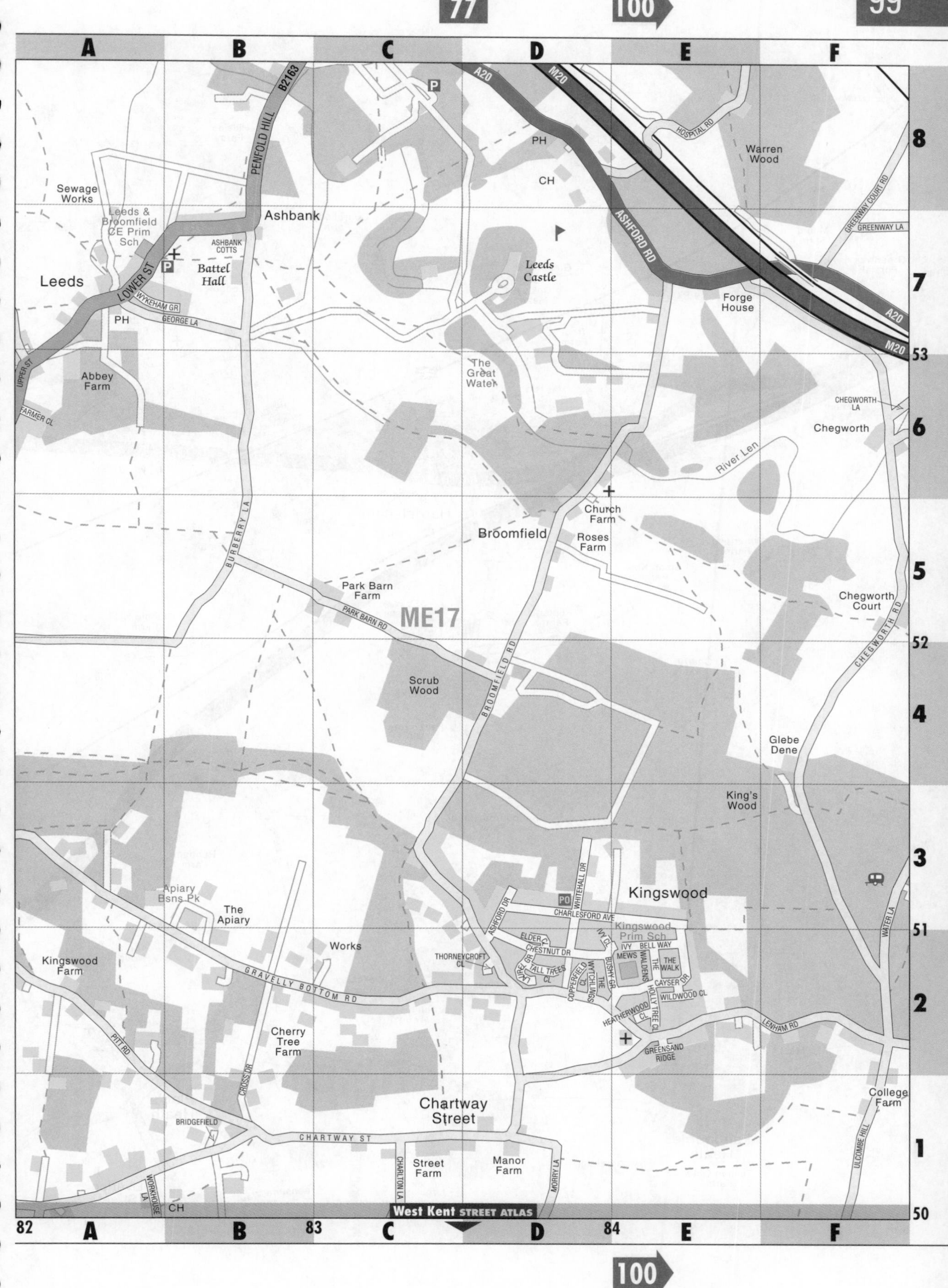
77
100
A
B
C
D
E
F
8
7
53
6
5
52
4
3
51
2
1
50
82
83
84
B2163
PENFOLD HILL
A20
M20
HOSPITAL RD
Warren Wood
PH
CH
Sewage Works
Leeds & Broomfield CE Prim Sch
Ashbank
ASHBANK COTTS
Battel Hall
Leeds
LOWER ST
WYKEHAM GR
GEORGE LA
PH
Leeds Castle
ASHFORD RD
GREENWAY COURT RD
GREENWAY LA
Forge House
UPPER ST
Abbey Farm
FARMER CL
The Great Water
CHEGWORTH LA
Chegworth
River Len
Church Farm
Broomfield
Roses Farm
BURBERRY LA
Park Barn Farm
PARK BARN RD
ME17
Chegworth Court
CHEGWORTH RD
Scrub Wood
BROOMFIELD RD
Glebe Dene
King's Wood
Kingswood
WHITEHALL DR
PO
ASHFORD DR
CHARLESFORD AVE
Kingswood Prim Sch
Apiary Bsns Pk
The Apiary
Works
Kingswood Farm
THORNEYCROFT CL
ELDER CL
CHESTNUT DR
TALL TREES CL
LAUREL GR
COPPERFIELD CL
WYTCHLINGS
THE
BUSHY GR
IVY CL
IVY MEWS
BELL WAY
WALDENS
THE
THE WALK
CAYSER DR
WILDWOOD CL
HOLLY TREE CL
HEATHERWOOD CL
GREENSAND RIDGE
LENHAM RD
WATER LA
GRAVELLY BOTTOM RD
PITT RD
Cherry Tree Farm
CROSS DR
College Farm
Chartway Street
BRIDGEFIELD
CHARTWAY ST
Street Farm
Manor Farm
CHARLTON LA
MORRY LA
ULCOMBE HILL
WORKHOUSE LA
CH
West Kent STREET ATLAS

100

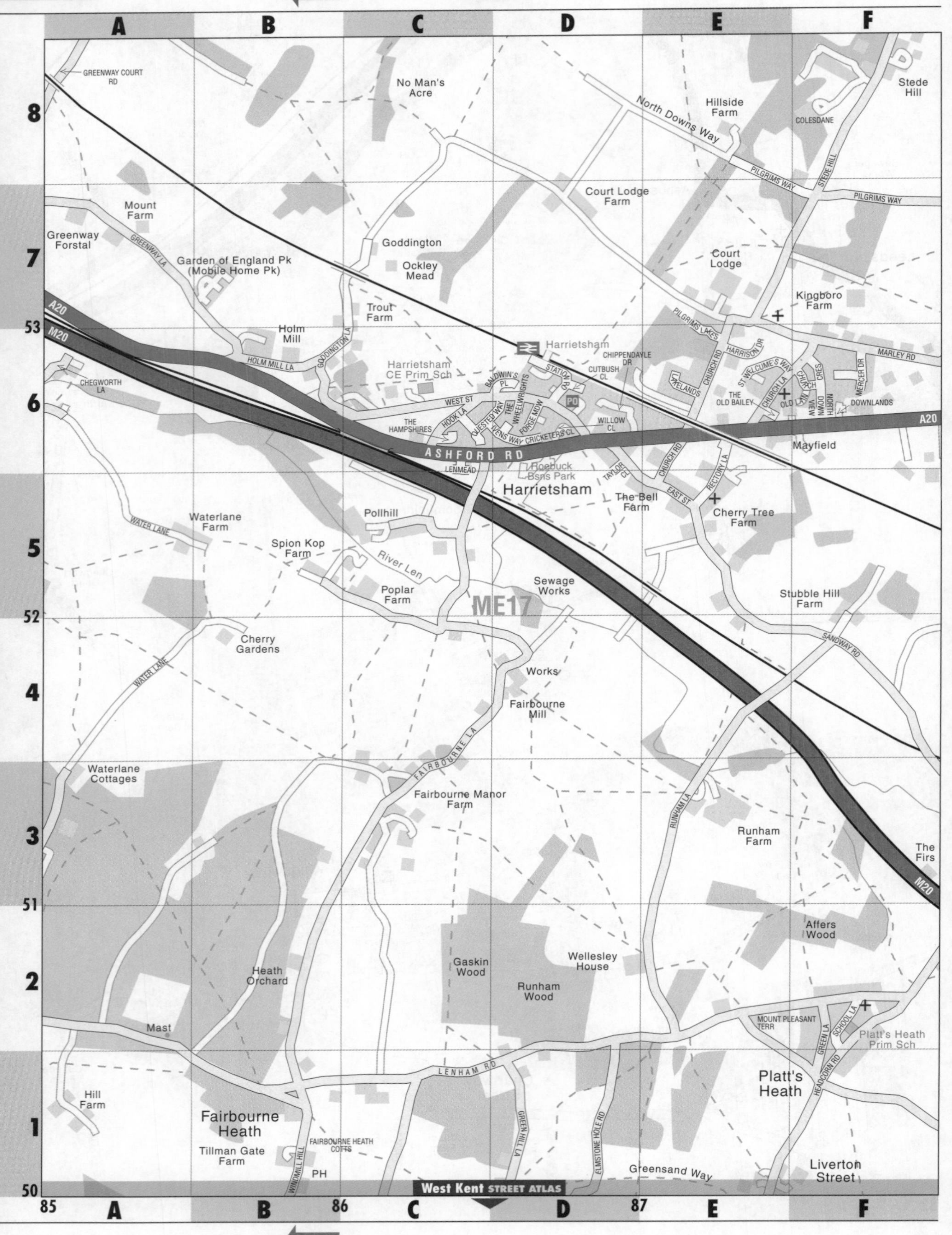
A
B
C
D
E
F
8
7
53
6
5
52
4
3
51
2
1
50
85
86
87
GREENWAY COURT RD
No Man's Acre
North Downs Way
Hillside Farm
Stede Hill
COLESDANE
STEDE HILL
PILGRIMS WAY
PILGRIMS WAY
Mount Farm
Court Lodge Farm
Greenway Forstal
GREENWAY LA
Goddington
Court Lodge
Garden of England Pk (Mobile Home Pk)
Ockley Mead
Kingsboro Farm
A20
M20
Trout Farm
PILGRIMS LAKES
Holm Mill
GODDINGTON LA
Harrietsham
CHIPPENDAYLE DR
HARRISON DR
MARLEY RD
HOLM MILL LA
Harrietsham CE Prim Sch
STATION RD
CUTBUSH CL
ST WELCUME'S WAY
CHEGWORTH LA
BALDWIN'S PL
THE WHEELWRIGHTS
AYELANDS
CHURCH RD
THE OLD BAILEY
CHURCH LA
CHURCH VIEW
DOWN CRES
NORTH DOWN
MERCER DR
DOWNLANDS
WEST ST
PO
OLD
A20
THE HAMPSHIRES
HOOK LA
QUESTED WAY
FORGE MDW
WILLOW CL
STEVENS WAY
CRICKETERS CL
ASHFORD RD
Mayfield
LENMEAD
Roebuck Bsns Park
TAYLOR CL
CHURCH RD
RECTORY LA
Harrietsham
EAST ST
The Bell Farm
Cherry Tree Farm
Pollhill
Waterlane Farm
WATER LANE
Spion Kop Farm
River Len
Sewage Works
Stubble Hill Farm
Poplar Farm
ME17
Cherry Gardens
SANDWAY RD
WATER LANE
Works
Fairbourne Mill
Waterlane Cottages
FAIRBOURNE LA
Fairbourne Manor Farm
RUNHAM LA
Runham Farm
The Firs
M20
Affers Wood
Gaskin Wood
Wellesley House
Heath Orchard
Runham Wood
MOUNT PLEASANT TERR
SCHOOL LA
GREEN LA
Mast
Platt's Heath Prim Sch
LENHAM RD
HEADCORN RD
Platt's Heath
Hill Farm
Fairbourne Heath
GREEN HILL LA
ELMSTONE HOLE RD
Tillman Gate Farm
FAIRBOURNE HEATH COTTS
WINDMILL HILL
PH
Greensand Way
Liverton Street
West Kent STREET ATLAS

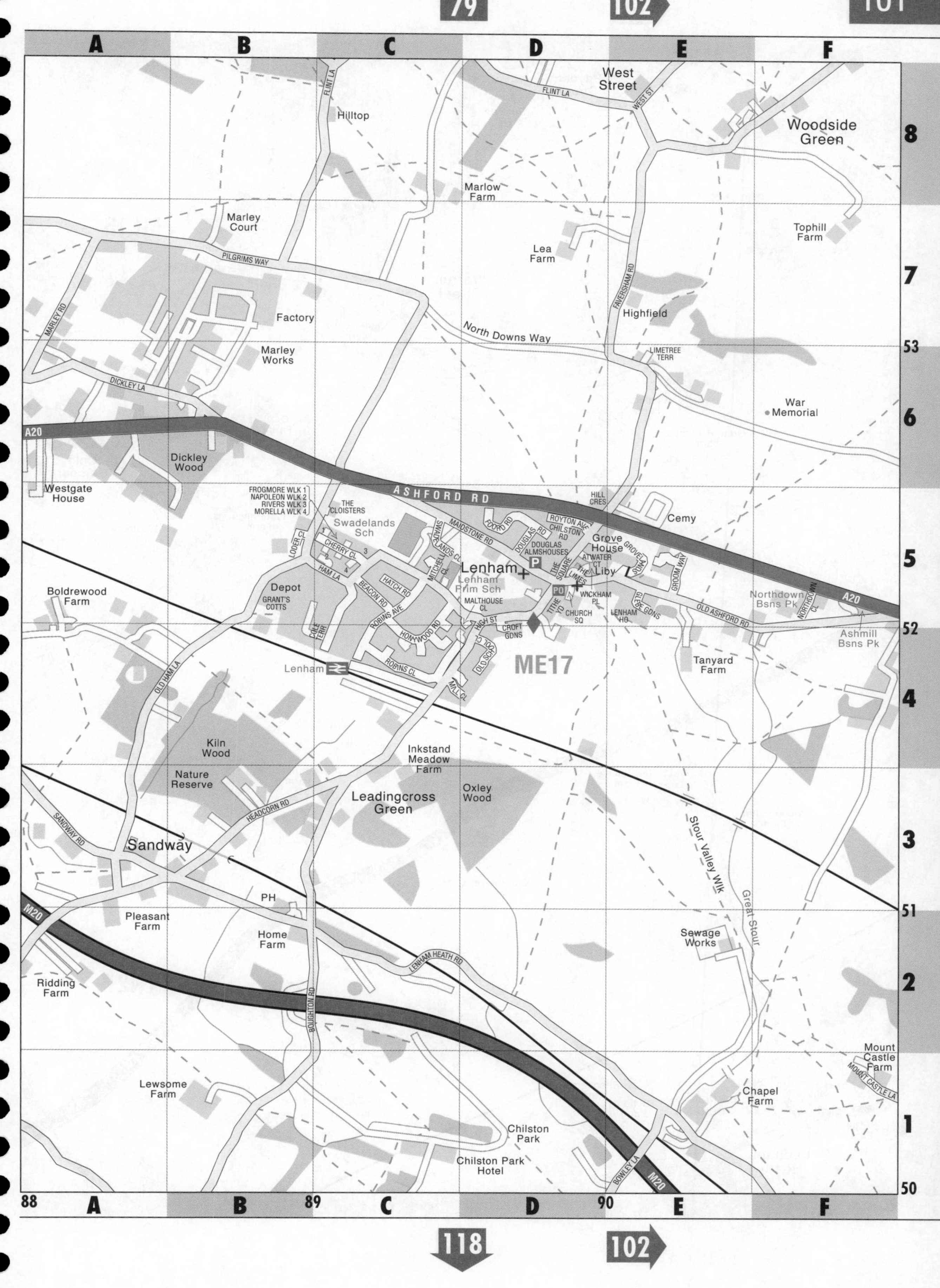

79
102

West Street
West St
Woodside Green

Flint La
Flint La

Hilltop

Marlow Farm

Tophill Farm

Marley Court

Pilgrims Way

Lea Farm

Faversham Rd

Marley Rd

Factory

North Downs Way

Highfield

Marley Works

Limetree Terr

Dickley La

War Memorial

A20

Dickley Wood

Ashford Rd

Hill Cres

Cemy

Westgate House

Frogmore Wlk 1
Napoleon Wlk 2
Rivers Wlk 3
Morella Wlk 4

The Cloisters

Swadelands Sch

Maidstone Rd

Royton Ave
Chilston Rd

Grove House
Liby

Grovefield

Cherry Cl

Ham La

Douglas Almshouses

Lenham

Groom Way

Depot
Grant's Cotts

Beacon Rd

Hatch Rd

Mitchell

Lenham Prim Sch

Atwater Ct
The Limes

PO

Old Ashford Rd

A20

Boldrewood Farm

Homewood Rd

Robins Ave

Malthouse Cl

Wickham Pl
Church Sq

Lenham Hd

Northdown Bsns Pk

Northdown

Lenham Gdns

Ashmill Bsns Pk

Robins Cl

High St

Croft Gdns

ME17

Tanyard Farm

Old Ham La

Kiln Wood

Inkstand Meadow Farm

Oxley Wood

Nature Reserve

Headcorn Rd

Leadingcross Green

Stour Valley Wlk

Sewage Works

Great Stour

Sandway Rd

Sandway

PH

M20

Pleasant Farm

Home Farm

Boughton Rd

Lenham Heath Rd

Ridding Farm

Mount Castle Farm

Lewsome Farm

Chilston Park

M20

Bowley La

Chapel Farm

Mount Castle La

Chilston Park Hotel

101
80

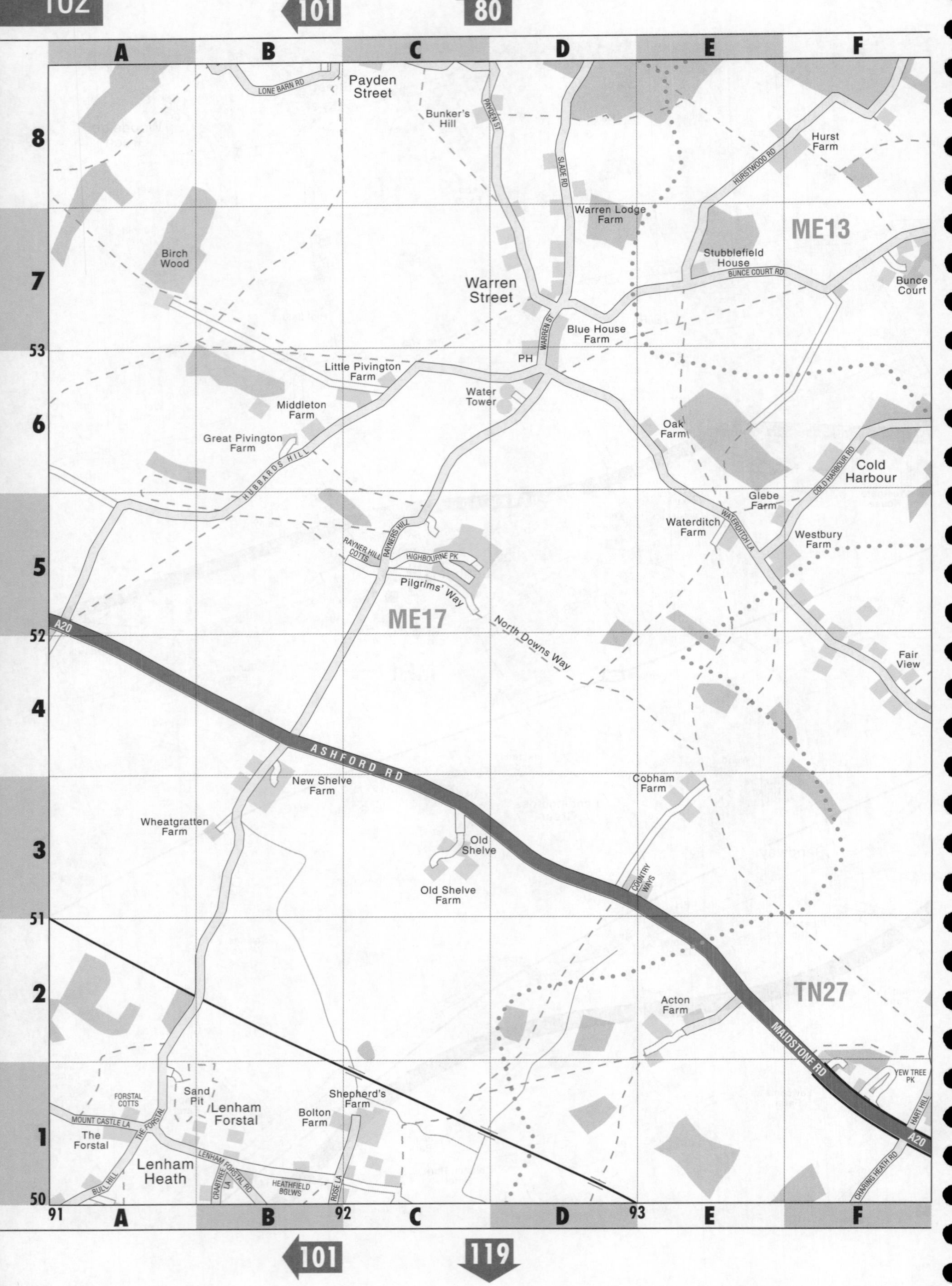
A
B
C
D
E
F
8
7
53
6
5
52
4
3
51
2
1
50
91
92
93
Payden Street
LONE BARN RD
Bunker's Hill
PAYDEN ST
SLADE RD
Hurst Farm
HURSTWOOD RD
Warren Lodge Farm
ME13
Birch Wood
Stubblefield House
BUNCE COURT RD
Bunce Court
Warren Street
WARREN ST
Blue House Farm
PH
Little Pivington Farm
Water Tower
Middleton Farm
Oak Farm
Great Pivington Farm
HUBBARDS HILL
Cold Harbour
COLD HARBOUR RD
Glebe Farm
Waterditch Farm
WATERDITCH LA
Westbury Farm
RAYNERS HILL
RAYNER HILL COTTS
HIGHBOURNE PK
Pilgrims' Way
ME17
North Downs Way
A20
Fair View
ASHFORD RD
New Shelve Farm
Cobham Farm
Wheatgratten Farm
Old Shelve
COUNTRY WAYS
Old Shelve Farm
TN27
Acton Farm
MAIDSTONE RD
YEW TREE PK
HART HILL
Shepherd's Farm
Sand Pit
FORSTAL COTTS
Lenham Forstal
Bolton Farm
MOUNT CASTLE LA
THE FORSTAL
The Forstal
Lenham Heath
LENHAM FORSTAL RD
BULL HILL
CRANTREE LA
HEATHFIELD BGLWS
ROSE LA
CHARING HEATH RD

101
119

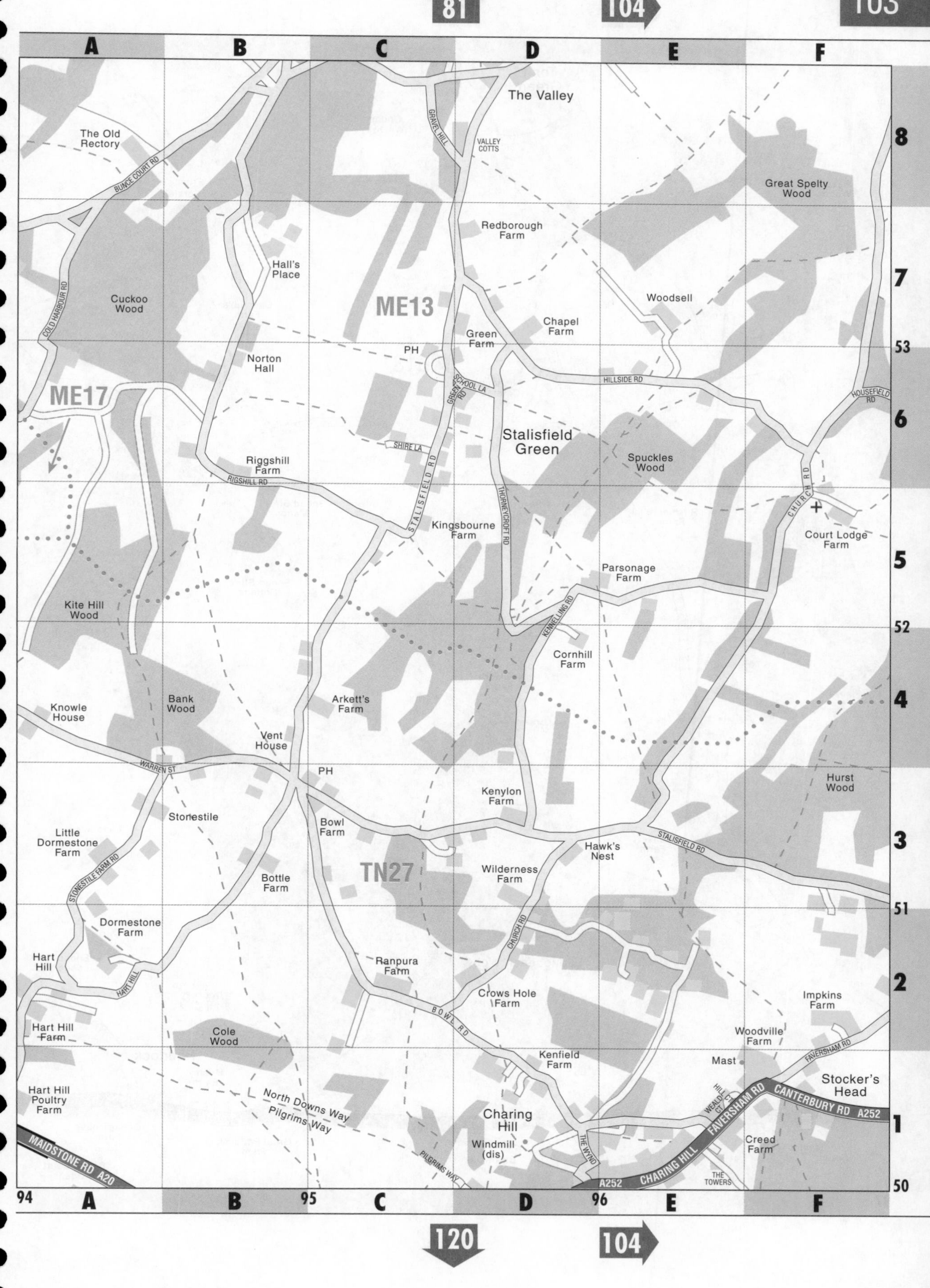

81
104

A B C D E F

8

The Old
Rectory

The Valley

GRAVEL HILL

VALLEY
COTTS

Great Spelty
Wood

BUNCE COURT RD

Cuckoo
Wood

COLD HARBOUR RD

Redborough
Farm

Woodsell

7

Hall's
Place

ME13

Chapel
Farm

Green
Farm

PH

53

SCHOOL LA

HILLSIDE RD

ME17

Norton
Hall

GREEN RD

HOUSEFIELD
RD

Stalisfield
Green

6

Riggshill
Farm

SHIRE LA

Spuckles
Wood

RIGSHILL RD

STALISFIELD RD

THORNEYCROFT RD

CHURCH RD

Kingsbourne
Farm

Court Lodge
Farm

5

Parsonage
Farm

Kite Hill
Wood

52

Bank
Wood

Arkett's
Farm

KENNELLING RD

Cornhill
Farm

4

Knowle
House

Vent
House

Hurst
Wood

WARREN ST

PH

Kenylon
Farm

Stonestile

Bowl
Farm

Hawk's
Nest

STALISFIELD RD

3

Little
Dormestone
Farm

TN27

Wilderness
Farm

STONESTILE FARM RD

Bottle
Farm

51

Hart
Hill

HART HILL

Ranpura
Farm

CHURCH RD

Impkins
Farm

2

Hart Hill
Farm

Cole
Wood

BOWL RD

Crows Hole
Farm

Woodville
Farm

Mast

Kenfield
Farm

FAVERSHAM RD

Hart Hill
Poultry
Farm

Stocker's
Head

WEALD CT

FAVERSHAM RD

CANTERBURY RD A252

North Downs Way
Pilgrims Way

Charing
Hill

Windmill
(dis)

HILL VW

Creed
Farm

1

MAIDSTONE RD A20

PILGRIMS WAY

THE POND

A252

CHARING HILL

THE
TOWERS

50

94 A B 95 C D 96 E F

103
82

A B C D E F

8
7
53
6
52
5
4
51
3
2
1
50

CHURCH RD

Hazel Wood

Tong Green

Dodds Willows

Bell's Forstal

HEEL RD

CROSS LA

ALMSHOUSE RD

LOOSE DOWN RD

Heel Farm

Cadman's Farm

ME13

Almhouse Cottages

OAST LA

HOUSEFIELD RD

Hurst Wood

Rushmere Farm

Snoad Street Manor

Codling Wood

Snoad Street Cottage

Newlands Farm

NEWLANDS FARM COTTS

Tir Beg

Monkery Farm

FAVERSHAM RD

PH

Landew's Farm

STALISFIELD RD

Snoad Lodge

TN27

Longbeech Wood

MONKERY LA

TN25

Paddock

Brisley Farm

GREEN LA

A252

CANTERBURY RD

A252

Woodlands Country Club

Great Paddock Fram

Cedar House Farm

Burnt Oak Farm

Beech Court Gardens

97 A B 98 C D 99 E F 50

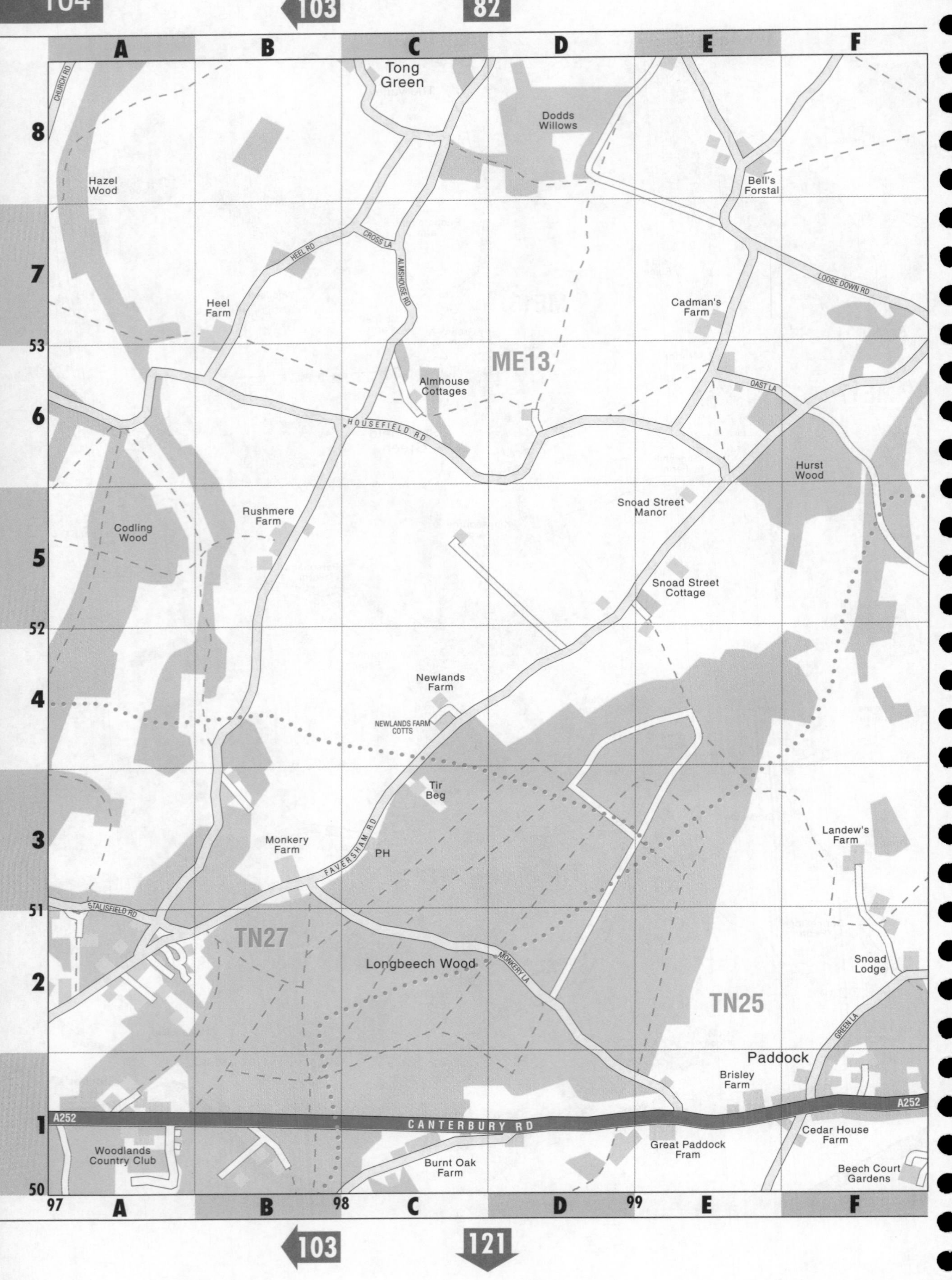

103
121

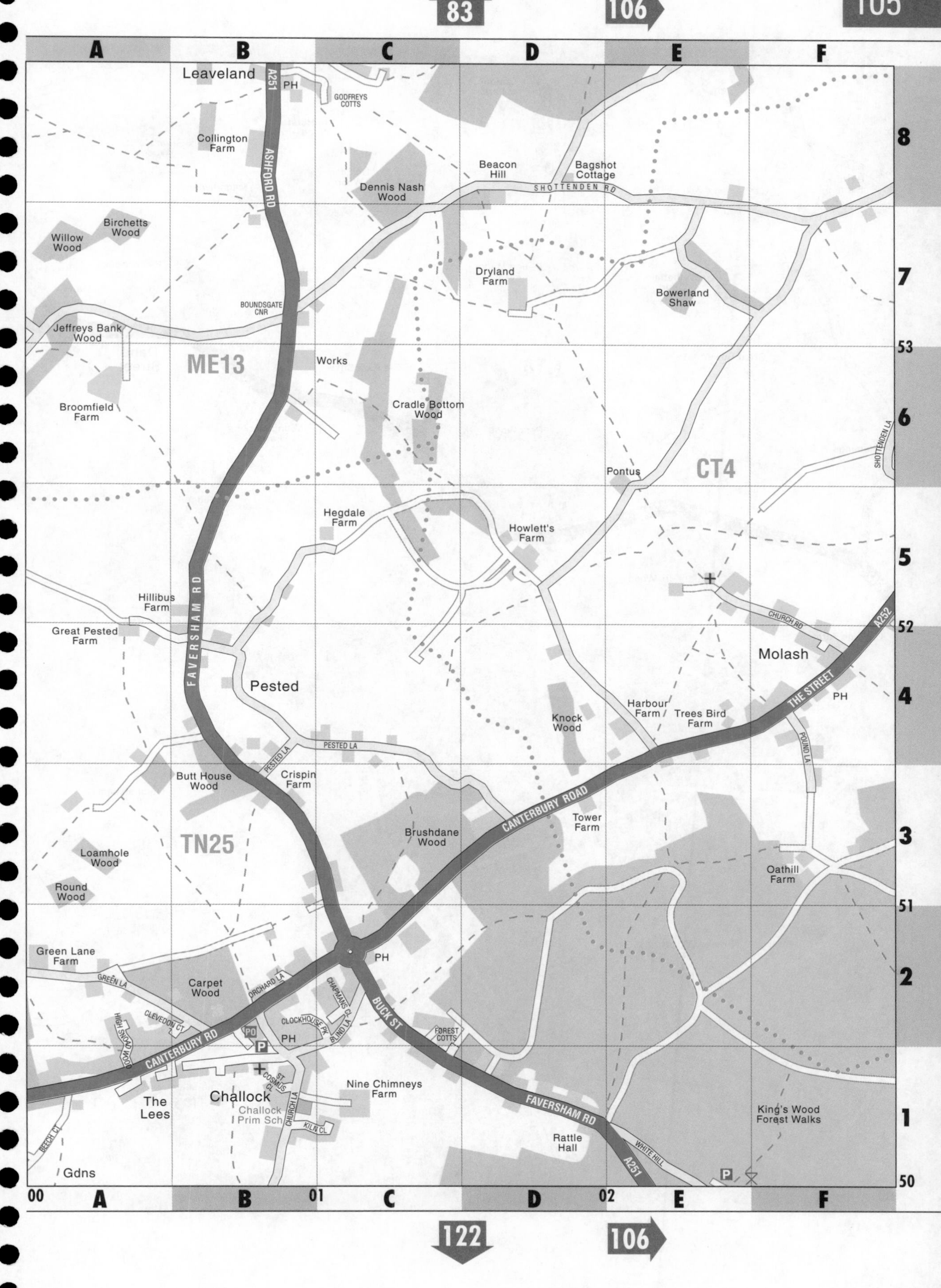

A B C D E F

8
7
53
6
5
52
4
3
51
2
1
50

Leaveland
PH
GODFREYS COTTS
Collington Farm
Dennis Nash Wood
Beacon Hill
Bagshot Cottage
SHOTTENDEN RD
ASHFORD RD
A251

Birchetts Wood
Willow Wood
Dryland Farm
Bowerland Shaw

BOUNDSGATE CNR
Jeffreys Bank Wood
ME13
Works
SHOTTENDEN LA

Broomfield Farm
Cradle Bottom Wood
Pontus
CT4

FAVERSHAM RD

Hegdale Farm
Howlett's Farm

Hillibus Farm
CHURCH RD
A252

Great Pested Farm
Molash

Pested
Harbour Farm
Trees Bird Farm
THE STREET
PH

Knock Wood
POUND LA

Butt House Wood
Crispin Farm
PESTED LA
PESTED LA

Brushdane Wood
Tower Farm
CANTERBURY ROAD
Oathill Farm

TN25
Loamhole Wood

Round Wood

Green Lane Farm
GREEN LA
PH

Carpet Wood
ORCHARD LA
CHAPMANS LA
BUCK ST

CLEVEDON LA
CLOCKHOUSE PK
BLIND LA
FOREST COTTS

HIGH SAND WOOD
CANTERBURY RD
PO
P
PH
FAVERSHAM RD

The Lees
Challock
ST COSMUS CL
Nine Chimneys Farm
King's Wood Forest Walks

Challock Prim Sch
CHURCH LA
KILN CL
Rattle Hall
WHITE HILL
A251

Gdns
BEECH CT
P

105
84

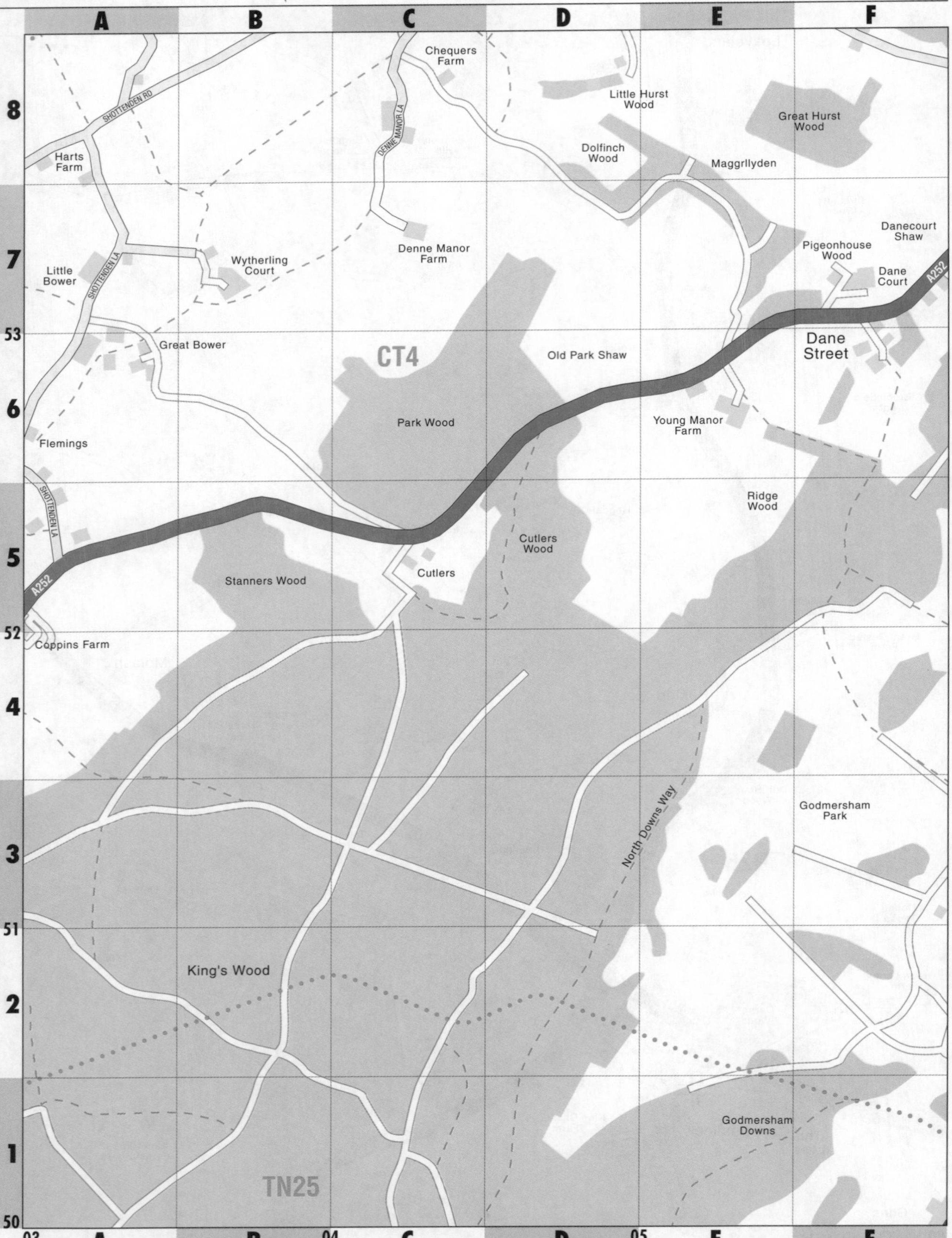

A B C D E F

8

Chequers Farm

Little Hurst Wood

Great Hurst Wood

DENNE MANOR LA

Harts Farm

SHOTTENDEN RD

Dolfinch Wood

Maggrllyden

7

Little Bower

SHOTTENDEN LA

Wytherling Court

Denne Manor Farm

Pigeonhouse Wood

Danecourt Shaw

Dane Court

A252

53

Great Bower

CT4

Old Park Shaw

Dane Street

6

Flemings

Park Wood

Young Manor Farm

Ridge Wood

SHOTTENDEN LA

5

A252

Stanners Wood

Cutlers

Cutlers Wood

52

Coppins Farm

4

North Downs Way

Godmersham Park

3

51

King's Wood

2

Godmersham Downs

1

TN25

50

03 A B 04 C D 05 E F

85 108

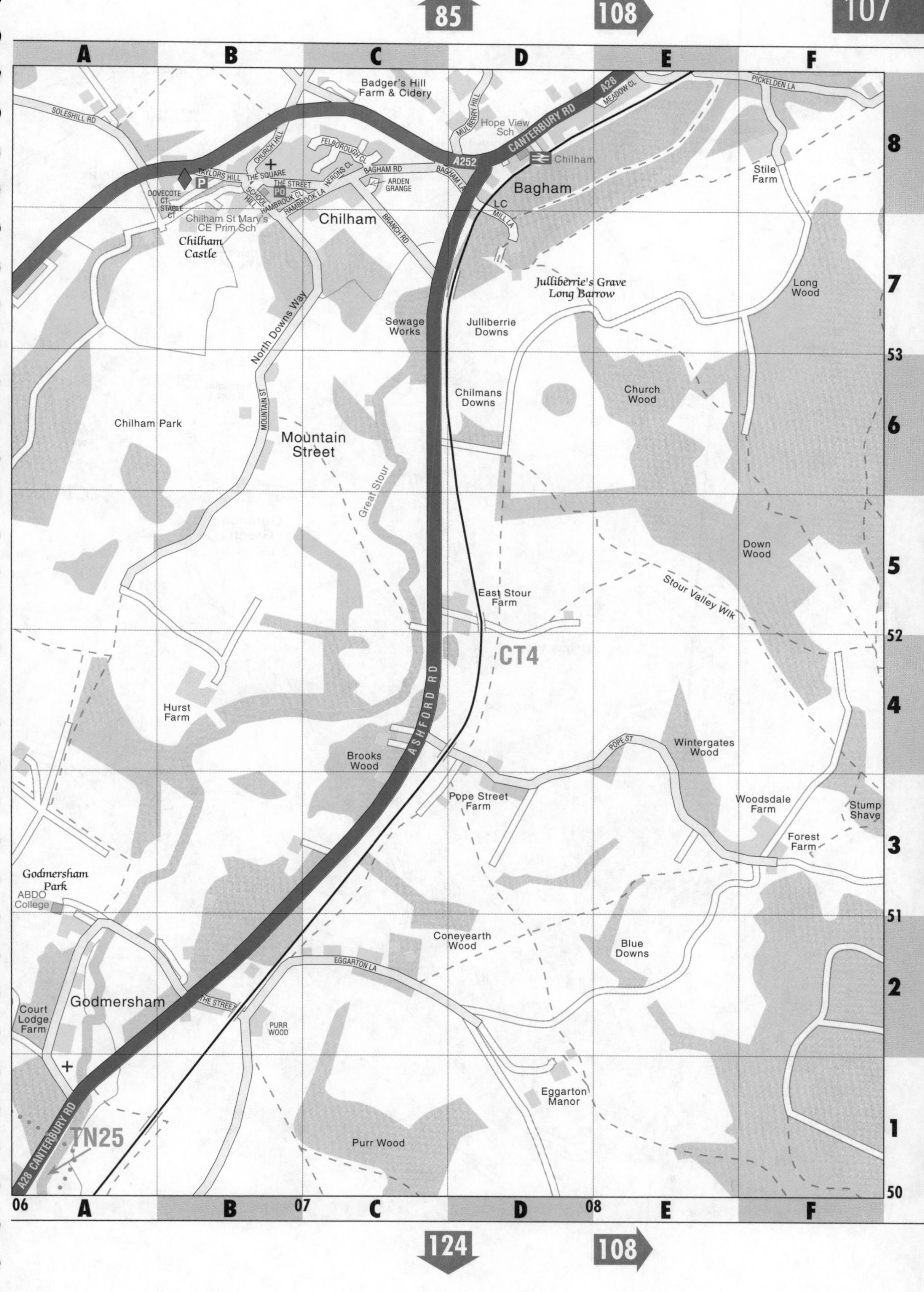
A
B
C
D
E
F
Badger's Hill
Farm & Cidery
SOLESHILL RD
CHURCH HILL
FELBOROUGH CL
MULBERRY HILL
Hope View
Sch
CANTERBURY RD
A28
MEADOW CL
PICKELDEN LA
A252
Chilham
TAYLORS HILL
THE SQUARE
BAGHAM RD
BAGHAM LA
THE STREET
HERONS CL
ARDEN
GRANGE
DOVECOTE
CT
STABLE
CT
SCHOOL
HILL
HAMBROOK CL
HAMBROOK LA
Bagham
LC
MILL LA
Stile
Farm
8
Chilham St Mary's
CE Prim Sch
Chilham
BRANCH RD
Chilham
Castle
Julliberrie's Grave
Long Barrow
Long
Wood
7
North Downs Way
Sewage
Works
Julliberrie
Downs
53
Chilmans
Downs
Church
Wood
MOUNTAIN ST
Chilham Park
Mountain
Street
6
Great Stour
Down
Wood
5
Stour Valley Wlk
East Stour
Farm
52
CT4
ASHFORD RD
Hurst
Farm
4
Wintergates
Wood
POPE ST
Brooks
Wood
Pope Street
Farm
Woodsdale
Farm
Stump
Shave
Forest
Farm
3
Godmersham
Park
ABDO
College
51
Coneyearth
Wood
Blue
Downs
EGGARTON LA
2
Court
Lodge
Farm
Godmersham
THE STREET
PURR
WOOD
Eggarton
Manor
1
A28 CANTERBURY RD
TN25
Purr Wood
50
06
07
08

124 108

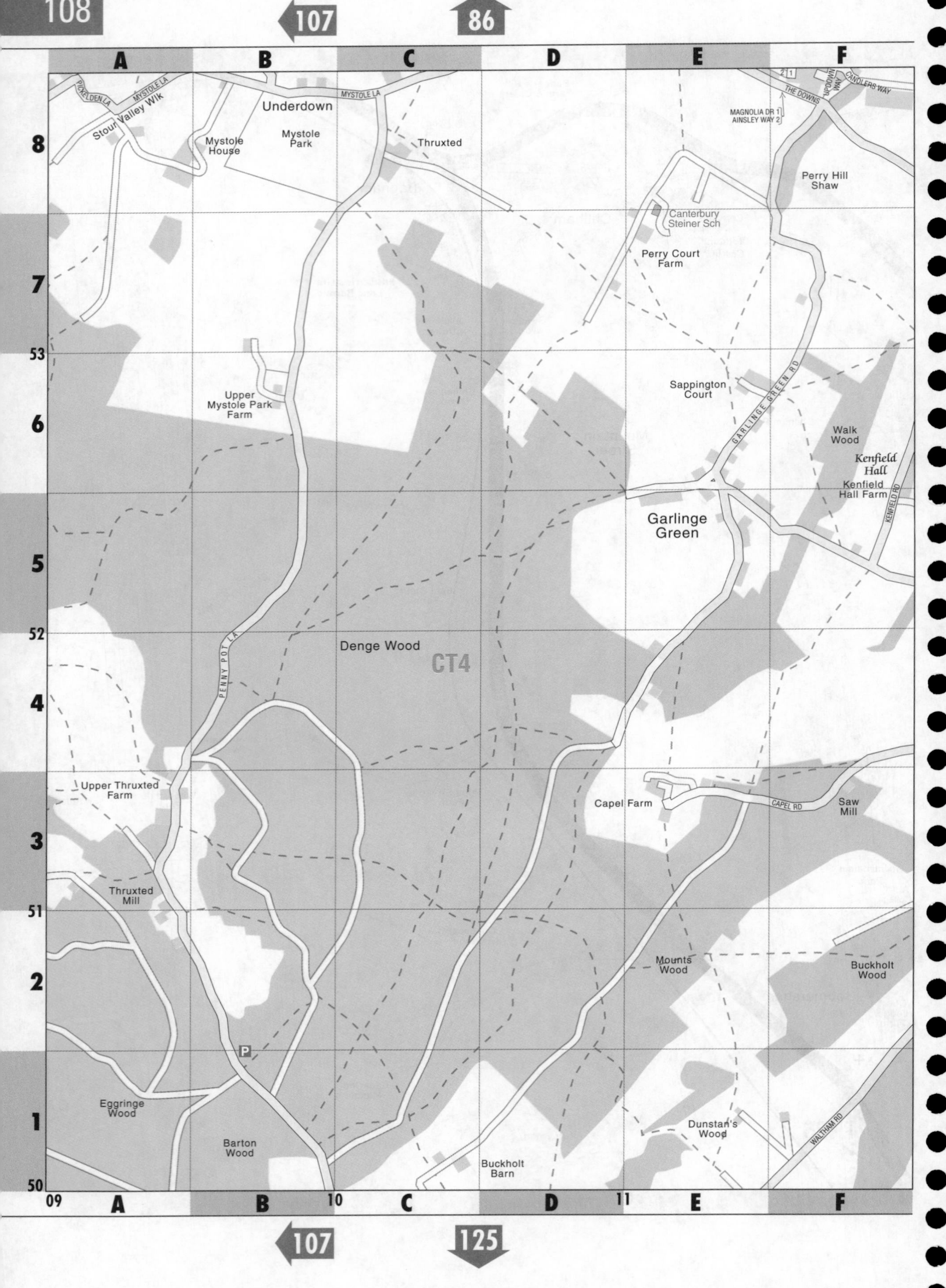

107
86

A   B   C   D   E   F

8

Stour Valley Wlk
PICKELDEN LA
MYSTOLE LA
Underdown
Mystole LA
Mystole House
Mystole Park
Thruxted

THE DOWNS
CANDLERS WAY
MAGNOLIA DR 1
AINSLEY WAY 2
Perry Hill Shaw

7

Canterbury Steiner Sch
Perry Court Farm

53

Upper Mystole Park Farm

Sappington Court

GARLINGE GREEN RD

Walk Wood

6

Kenfield Hall
Kenfield Hall Farm
KENFIELD RD

Garlinge Green

5

PENNY POT LA

52

Denge Wood
CT4

4

Upper Thruxted Farm
Capel Farm
CAPEL RD
Saw Mill

3

Thruxted Mill

51

Mounts Wood
Buckholt Wood

2

P

1

Eggringe Wood
Barton Wood
Dunstan's Wood
WALTHAM RD

Buckholt Barn

50

09   A   B   10   C   D   11   E   F

107
125

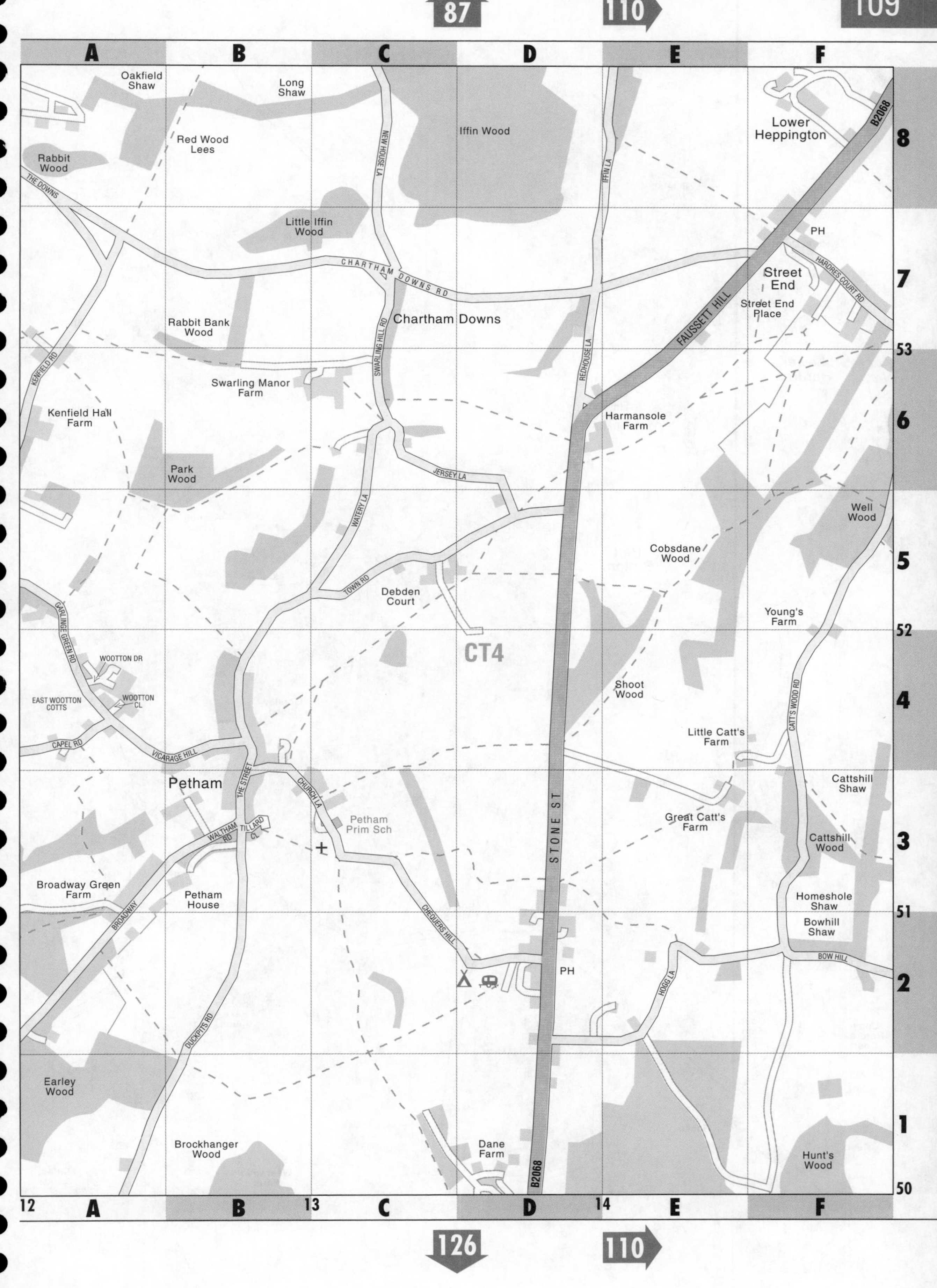

A   B   C   D   E   F

Oakfield Shaw
Long Shaw
Red Wood Lees
Iffin Wood
Lower Heppington
Rabbit Wood
B2068
8
THE DOWNS
NEW HOUSE LA
PH
Little Iffin Wood
CHARTHAM DOWNS RD
Street End
HARDRES COURT RD
7
IFFIN LA
FAUSSETT HILL
Rabbit Bank Wood
Chartham Downs
Street End Place
SWARLING HILL RD
KENFIELD RD
53
Swarling Manor Farm
REDHOUSE LA
6
Kenfield Hall Farm
Harmansole Farm
Park Wood
JERSEY LA
Well Wood
WATERY LA
Cobsdane Wood
5
Young's Farm
GARLING GREEN RD
TOWN RD
Debden Court
52
CATT'S WOOD RD
WOOTTON DR
CT4
Shoot Wood
4
EAST WOOTTON COTTS
WOOTTON CL
Little Catt's Farm
Cattshill Shaw
CAPEL RD
VICARAGE HILL
STONE ST
Great Catt's Farm
Cattshill Wood
3
THE STREET
CHURCH LA
Petham
Petham Prim Sch
Homeshole Shaw
WALTHAM RD
TILLARD CL
Broadway Green Farm
Petham House
51
Bowhill Shaw
BROADWAY
CHEQUERS HILL
PH
HOGG LA
BOW HILL
2
DUCKPITS RD
Earley Wood
1
Brockhanger Wood
Dane Farm
Hunt's Wood
B2068
50

12   A   B   13   C   D   14   E   F

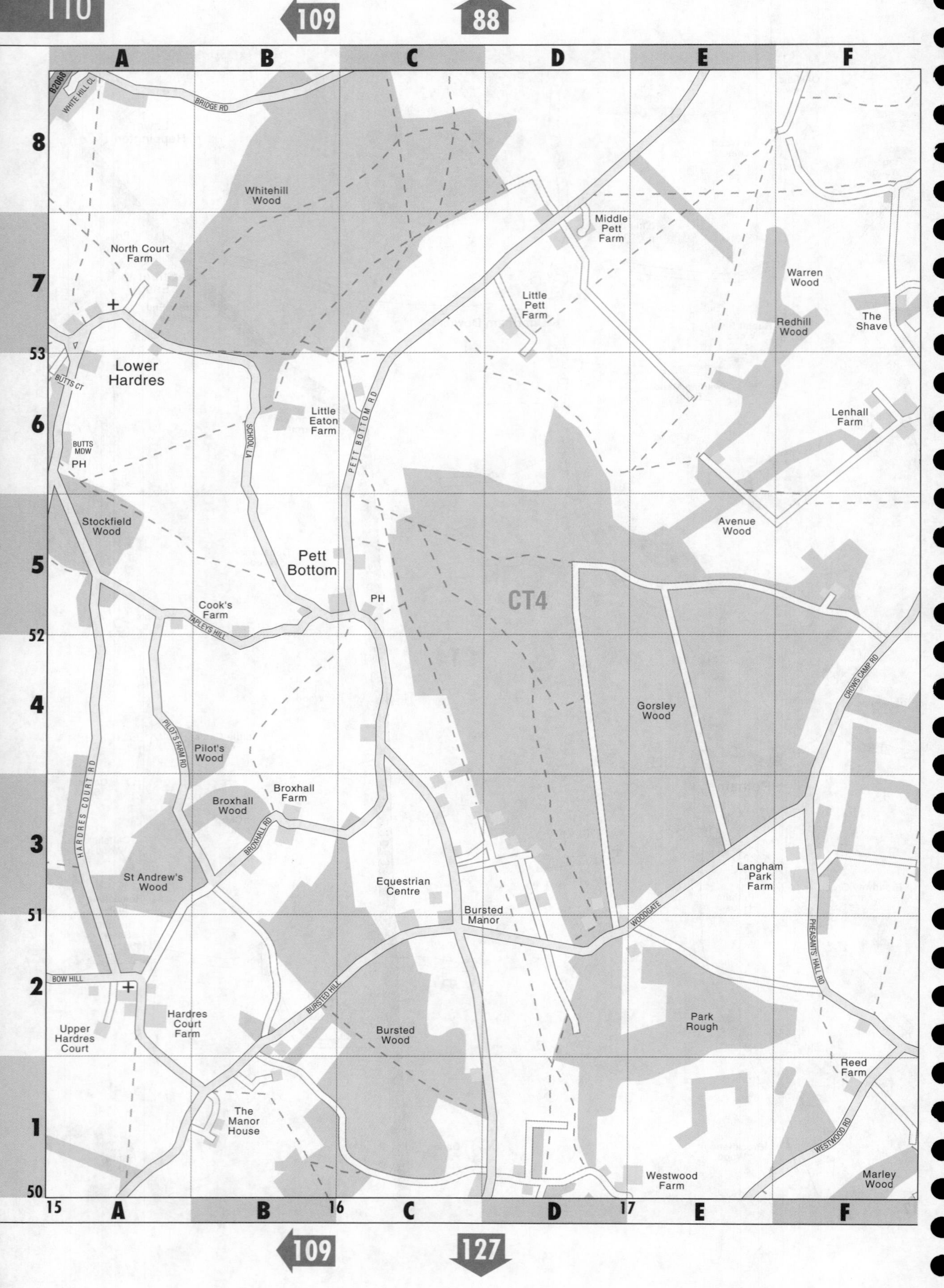

109
88

A   B   C   D   E   F

8

WHITE HILL CL
B2068
BRIDGE RD

Whitehill
Wood

Middle
Pett
Farm

7

North Court
Farm

Little
Pett
Farm

Warren
Wood

Redhill
Wood

The
Shave

53

Lower
Hardres

BUTTS CT

SCHOOL LA

Little
Eaton
Farm

PETT BOTTOM RD

Lenhall
Farm

6

BUTTS
MDW
PH

Stockfield
Wood

Pett
Bottom

PH

Avenue
Wood

5

Cook's
Farm

TAPLEYS HILL

CT4

52

CROWS CAMP RD

4

PILOT'S FARM RD

HARDRES COURT RD

Pilot's
Wood

Gorsley
Wood

Broxhall
Farm

3

Broxhall
Wood

BROXHALL RD

Langham
Park
Farm

St Andrew's
Wood

Equestrian
Centre

51

Bursted
Manor

WOODGATE

PHEASANTS HALL RD

2

BOW HILL

Hardres
Court
Farm

BURSTED HILL

Bursted
Wood

Park
Rough

Reed
Farm

Upper
Hardres
Court

1

The
Manor
House

WESTWOOD RD

50

Westwood
Farm

Marley
Wood

15   A   B   16   C   D   17   E   F

109
127

89
112

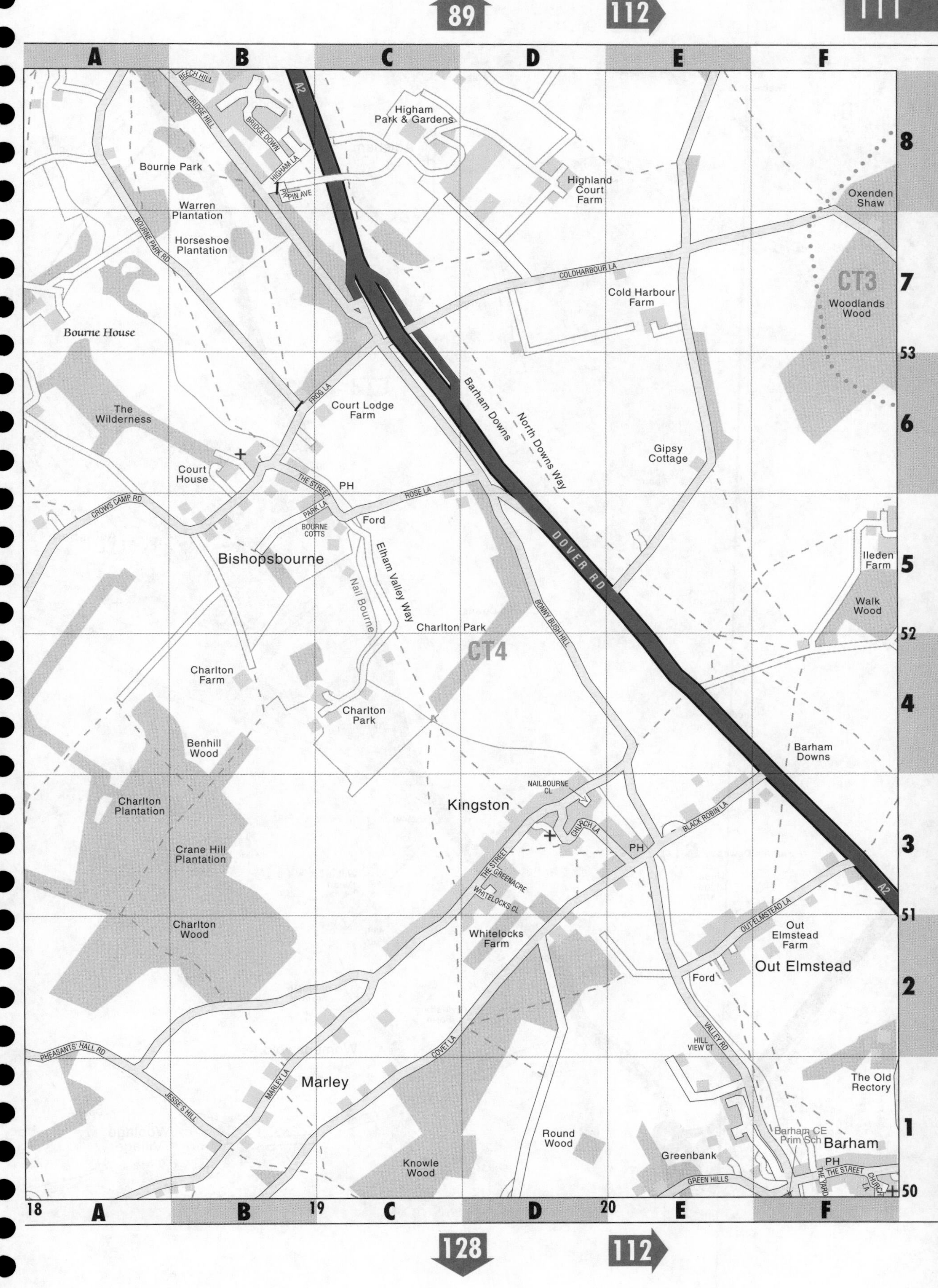
A
B
C
D
E
F
8
7
53
6
5
52
4
3
51
2
1
50
18
19
20
A2
BEECH HILL
BRIDGE HILL
BRIDGE DOWN
HIGHAM LA
PIN AVE
Higham
Park & Gardens
Highland
Court
Farm
Oxenden
Shaw
Bourne Park
Warren
Plantation
Horseshoe
Plantation
BOURNE PARK RD
COLDHARBOUR LA
Cold Harbour
Farm
CT3
Woodlands
Wood
Bourne House
FROG LA
Court Lodge
Farm
Barham Downs
North Downs Way
The
Wilderness
Court
House
Gipsy
Cottage
THE STREET
PH
ROSE LA
CROWS CAMP RD
PARK LA
Ford
BOURNE
COTTS
DOVER RD
Bishopsbourne
Elham Valley Way
Nail Bourne
Ileden
Farm
Walk
Wood
Charlton Park
BONNY BUSH HILL
CT4
Charlton
Farm
Charlton
Park
Benhill
Wood
Barham
Downs
NAILBOURNE
CL
Charlton
Plantation
Kingston
BLACK ROBIN LA
CHURCH LA
Crane Hill
Plantation
PH
THE STREET
GREENACRE
WHITELOCKS CL
Charlton
Wood
Whitelocks
Farm
OUT ELMSTEAD LA
Out
Elmstead
Farm
Out Elmstead
Ford
VALLEY RD
HILL
VIEW CT
PHEASANTS' HALL RD
COVET LA
The Old
Rectory
MARLEY LA
Marley
JESSE'S HILL
Round
Wood
Barham CE
Prim Sch
Barham
Knowle
Wood
Greenbank
PH
THE STREET
GREEN HILLS
THE YARD
CHURCH LA

128
112

111
90

A B C D E F

CT4

Twelve Acre Shaw

Adisham CE Prim Sch

Adisham

Bloodden

Station App

Ratling Court

8

Woodlands Manor

WOODLANDS RD

DONKEY LA

THE STREET

COOTING LA

B2046

RATLING RD

7

Oxenden Wood

Cooting Farm

53

Pitt Wood

CT3

6

Woodlands Wood

1 ULLSWATER GDNS
2 ENNERDALE GDNS

DORMAN AVE N

TENNYSON GDNS
COLERIDGE GDNS
THIRLMERE GDNS
BUTTERMERE GDNS
DERWENT WAY
GRASMERE WAY
WINDERMERE GDNS
WORDSWORTH AVE
CORNWALLIS RD
KINGS RD
BURGESS RD

Aylesham Prim Sch

5

Well Wood

Cooting Downs

WOODLAND AVE
NEWMAN RD
VALE VIEW RD
NETTLE INC
CHIPPS CL
SNOWDOWN CT
MILNER RD
DEANERY CT
BRIAR CL
MARKET PL
Aylesham
QUEENS RD
HYDE PL
BELL GR

52

COX CL
ASH RD
HILL CRES
SYCAMORE
ELM RD
OAKSIDE RD
BEVAN WAY
COOTING RD
BOULEVARD COURTENAYS
EASTRY CT
CRES
HAWTHORN CL
MARKET AVE
DORMAN AVE S
CLARENDON RD
SPINNEY LA

4

Ileden Wood

Aylesham Wood

COVERT RD
SPINNEY LA

Aylesham Ind Est

Ackholt Wood

3

Barham Downs

CT4

Upper Digges Farm

AYLESHAM CNR

Willow Wood

CT15

51

A2

POND LA

Well Wood

Chalk Wood

2

RECTORY LA
DOVER RD
ADISHAM RD
North Downs Way

Cemy

Nethersole Farm

Aylesham Farm

CHURCH LA
THE STREET

Womenswold

1

DOVER RD
OLD DOVER RD
B2046
A260
GRAVEL CASTLE RD

Westmore Cottages

Snow Down

Woolage Village

THE GREEN
NETHERSOLE RD
CORONA RD
THE PLACE
FIRS RD

50

21 A B 22 C D 23 E F

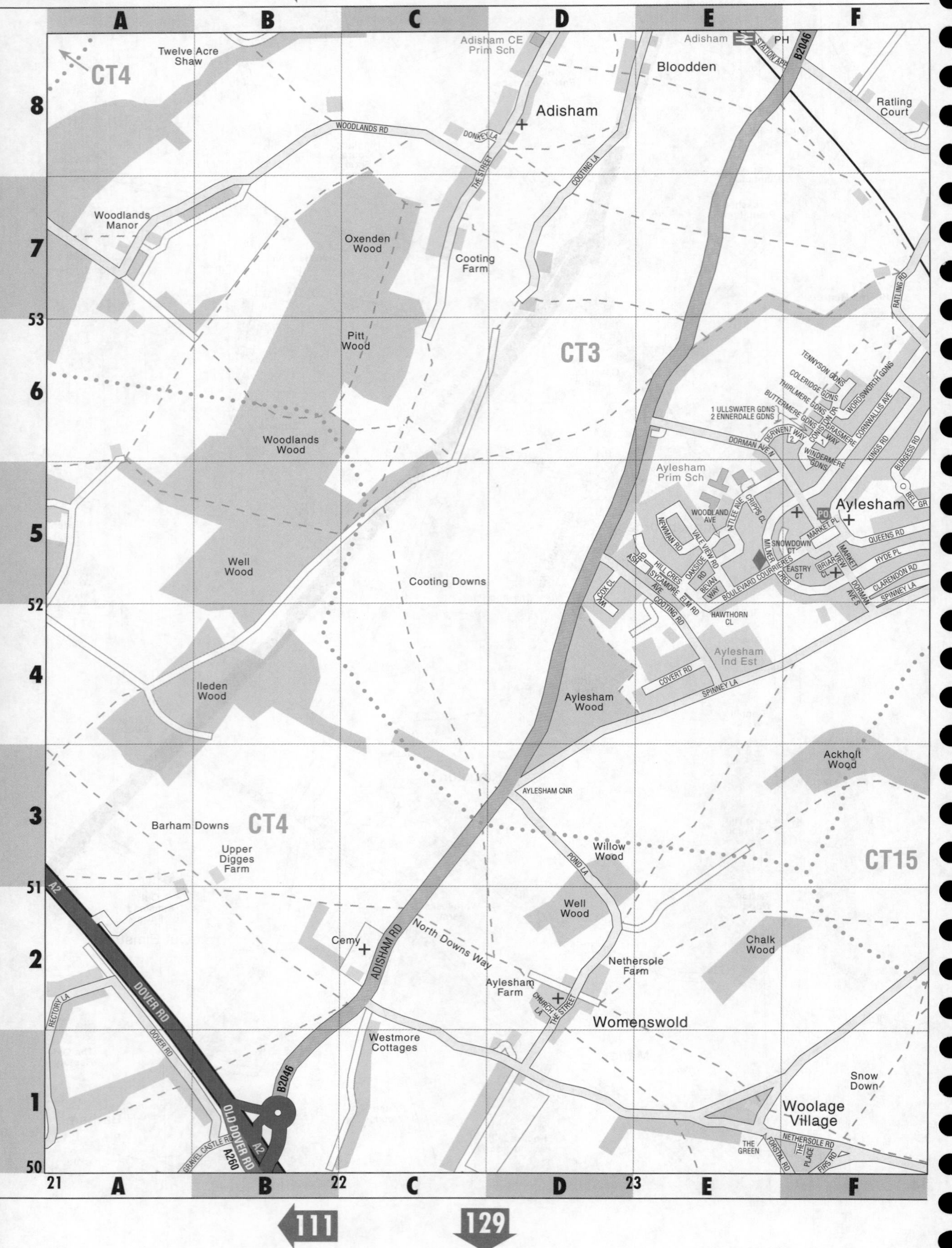

111
129

91
114

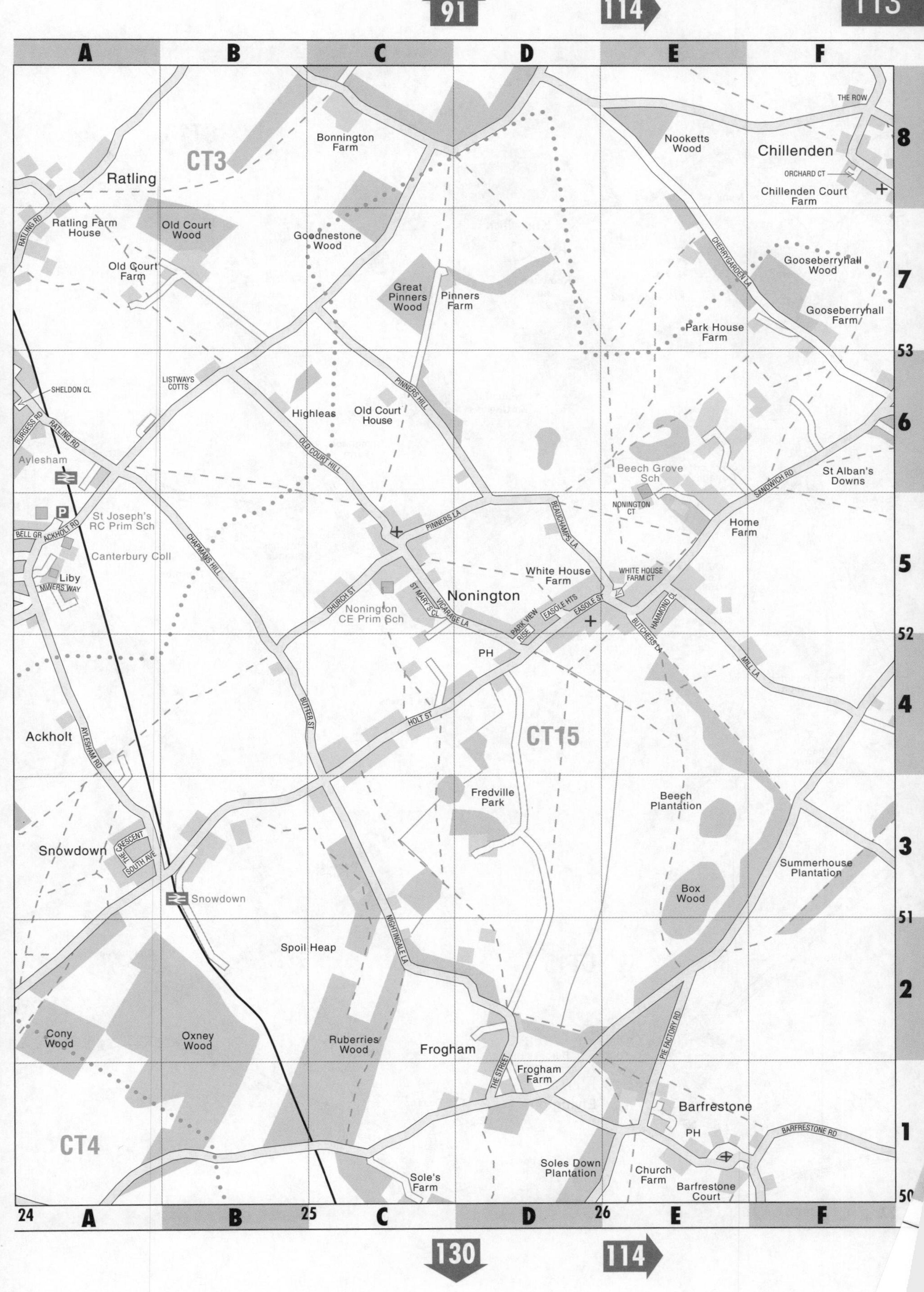
A
B
C
D
E
F
8
7
53
6
5
52
4
3
51
2
1
50
24
25
26
Ratling
CT3
Bonnington Farm
Nooketts Wood
Chillenden
THE ROW
ORCHARD CT
Chillenden Court Farm
Ratling Farm House
Old Court Wood
Goodnestone Wood
Old Court Farm
Great Pinners Wood
Pinners Farm
Gooseberryhall Wood
Gooseberryhall Farm
Park House Farm
RATLING RD
CHERRYGARDEN LA
LISTWAYS COTTS
SHELDON CL
Highleas
Old Court House
PINNERS HILL
BURGESS RD
RATLING RD
Aylesham
OLD COURT HILL
Beech Grove Sch
St Alban's Downs
NONINGTON CT
SANDWICH RD
St Joseph's RC Prim Sch
PINNERS LA
BEAUCHAMPS LA
Home Farm
BELL GR
ACKHOLT RD
Canterbury Coll
CHAPMANS HILL
Liby
MIVERS WAY
White House Farm
WHITE HOUSE FARM CT
CHURCH ST
ST MARY'S CL
Nonington
Nonington CE Prim Sch
VICARAGE LA
PARK VIEW RISE
EASOLE HTS
EASOLE ST
HAMMOND CL
BUTCHERS LA
PH
MILL LA
HOLT ST
Ackholt
AYLESHAM RD
BUTTER ST
CT15
Fredville Park
Beech Plantation
Snowdown
THE CRESCENT
SOUTH AVE
Summerhouse Plantation
Snowdown
Box Wood
Spoil Heap
NIGHTINGALE LA
Cony Wood
Oxney Wood
Ruberries Wood
Frogham
PIE FACTORY RD
THE STREET
Frogham Farm
Barfrestone
PH
BARFRESTONE RD
CT4
Soles Down Plantation
Church Farm
Sole's Farm
Barfrestone Court

130
114

113
92

A | **B** | **C** | **D** | **E** | **F**

CT13

8

YEW TREE FARM

SHORT ST

PH

War Meml

Knowlton

Home Wood

The Warren

CT3

Home Farm

Knowlton Court

Black La

7

CUCKOLDS CNR

Knowlton Park

THORNTON LA

SANDWICH RD

53

The Grove

Manorial Earthworks

Shingleton Wood

Shingleton Farm

Venson Farm

6

Dover Lodge Cottages

Round Wood

Shingleton Cottages

CT14

Thorntonhill Cottages

St Alban's Downs

Thornton Farm

Thornton Wood

5

Kelk Hill

Kittington Cottages

52

Brown Pudding Plantation

Garden Wood

The Downs

PIKE RD

SCHOOL RD

DUKE CT

4

Kittington Farm

Thornton Wood

Beeches Farm

3

51

Craythorne Firs

CT15

Spoil Heap

2

POPLAR DR

CYPRESS GR

BEECH DR

FISH GR

CHERRY GR

SWEETBRIAR LA

OAK GR

Burgess Hill

Works

BARVILLE RD

ROMAN WAY

FAIRVIEW RD

ST JOHNS RD

CHAUCER ST

LARCH RD

MILNER RD

Pike Road Ind Est

1

ADELAIDE RD

TERRACE RD

MILNER ST

PO

Elvington

ELMTON LA

MILLYARD WAY

WIGMORE LA

SANDWICH RD

BARFRESTONE RD

Sports Gd

ADELAIDE RD

50

27 | **A** | **B** | **28** | **C** | **D** | **29** | **E** | **F**

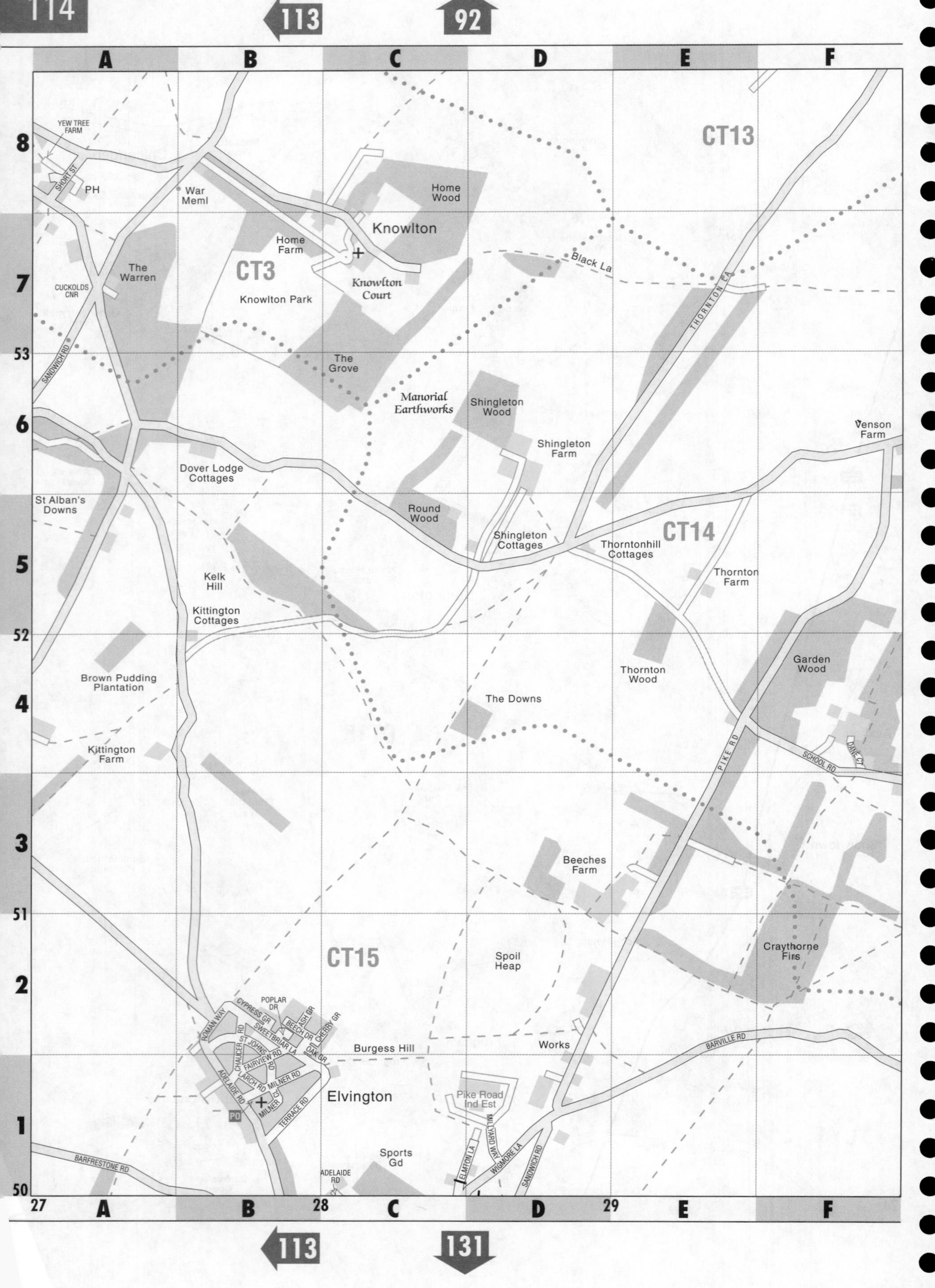

113
131

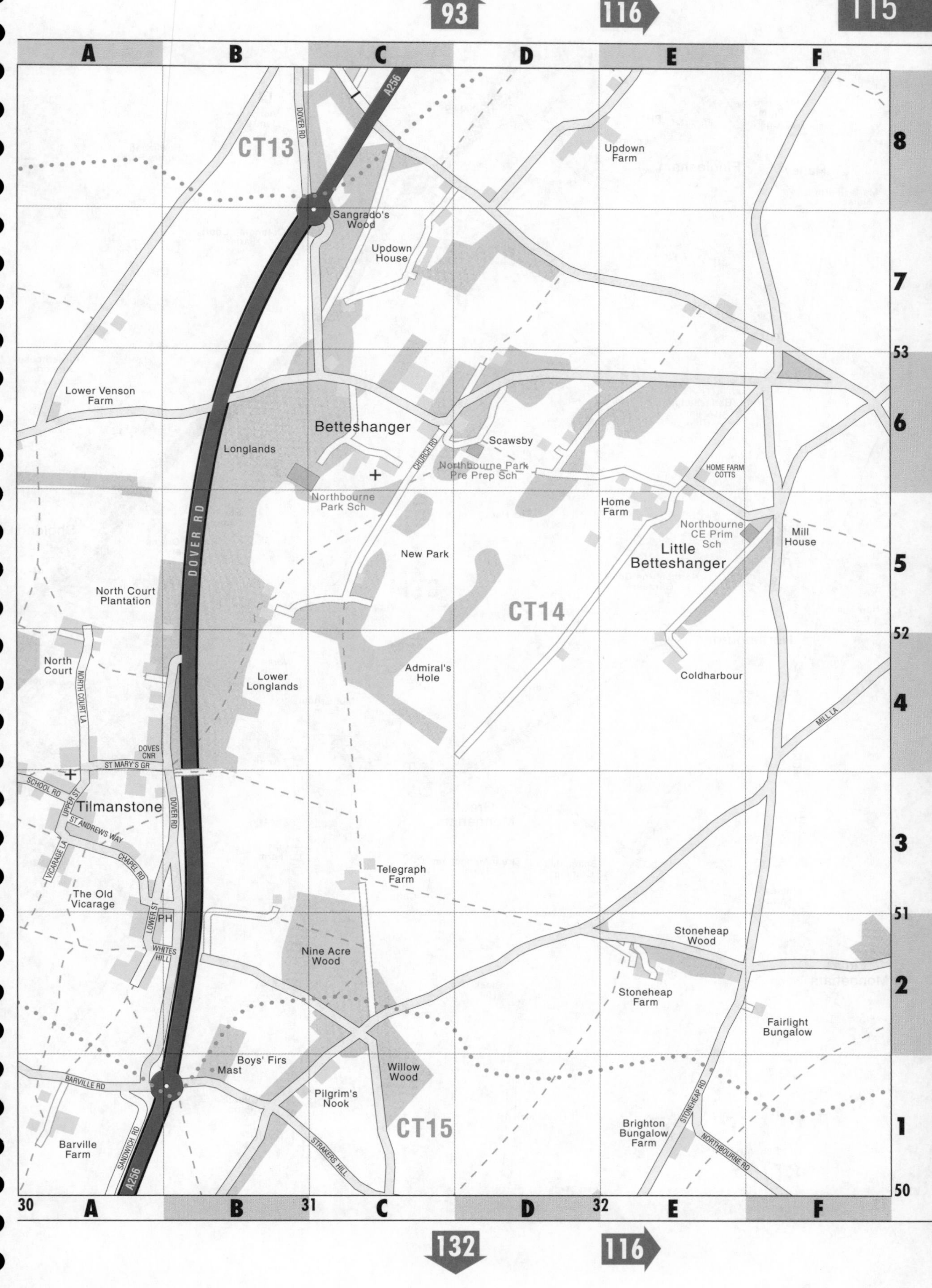
93
116
A
B
C
D
E
F
8
7
53
6
5
52
4
3
51
2
1
50
30
31
32
132
CT13
A256
DOVER RD
Updown
Farm
Sangrado's
Wood
Updown
House
Lower Venson
Farm
Betteshanger
Longlands
Scawsby
CHURCH RD
Northbourne Park
Pre Prep Sch
Northbourne
Park Sch
HOME FARM
COTTS
Home
Farm
Northbourne
CE Prim
Sch
Mill
House
Little
Betteshanger
New Park
North Court
Plantation
CT14
North
Court
NORTH COURT LA
Lower
Longlands
Admiral's
Hole
Coldharbour
MILL LA
DOVES
CNR
ST MARY'S GR
SCHOOL RD
UPPER ST
Tilmanstone
ST ANDREWS WAY
VICARAGE LA
CHAPEL RD
Telegraph
Farm
The Old
Vicarage
LOWER ST
PH
WHITES
HILL
Stoneheap
Wood
Nine Acre
Wood
Stoneheap
Farm
Fairlight
Bungalow
Boys' Firs
Mast
Willow
Wood
BARVILLE RD
Pilgrim's
Nook
STONEHEAP RD
CT15
Brighton
Bungalow
Farm
NORTHBOURNE RD
Barville
Farm
SANDWICH RD
STRAKERS HILL

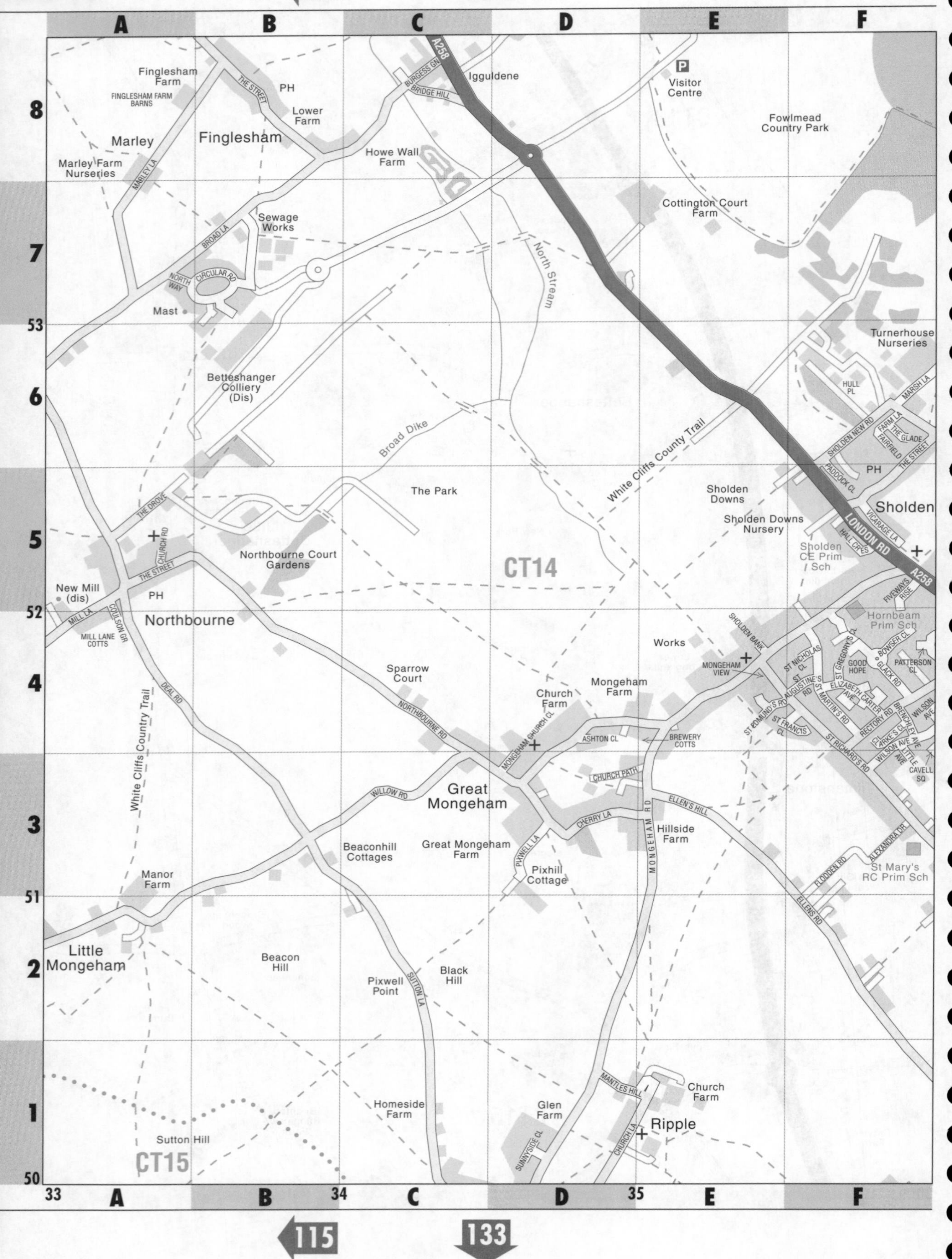
A
B
C
D
E
F
8
7
53
6
5
52
4
3
51
2
1
50
33
34
35
A258
Igguldene
Visitor Centre
Finglesham Farm
FINGLESHAM FARM BARNS
PH
Lower Farm
Fowlmead Country Park
Marley
Finglesham
Marley Farm Nurseries
Howe Wall Farm
Cottington Court Farm
Sewage Works
Mast
North Stream
Turnerhouse Nurseries
Betteshanger Colliery (Dis)
HULL PL
Broad Dike
White Cliffs County Trail
The Park
Sholden Downs
Sholden
Sholden Downs Nursery
Sholden CE Prim Sch
CT14
Northbourne Court Gardens
New Mill (dis)
PH
Northbourne
MILL LANE COTTS
Hornbeam Prim Sch
Works
Sparrow Court
Church Farm
Mongeham Farm
MONGEHAM VIEW
GOOD HOPE
BREWERY COTTS
Great Mongeham
White Cliffs Country Trail
Hillside Farm
Beaconhill Cottages
Great Mongeham Farm
Pixhill Cottage
St Mary's RC Prim Sch
Manor Farm
Little Mongeham
Beacon Hill
Pixwell Point
Black Hill
Church Farm
Homeside Farm
Glen Farm
Ripple
Sutton Hill
CT15

95

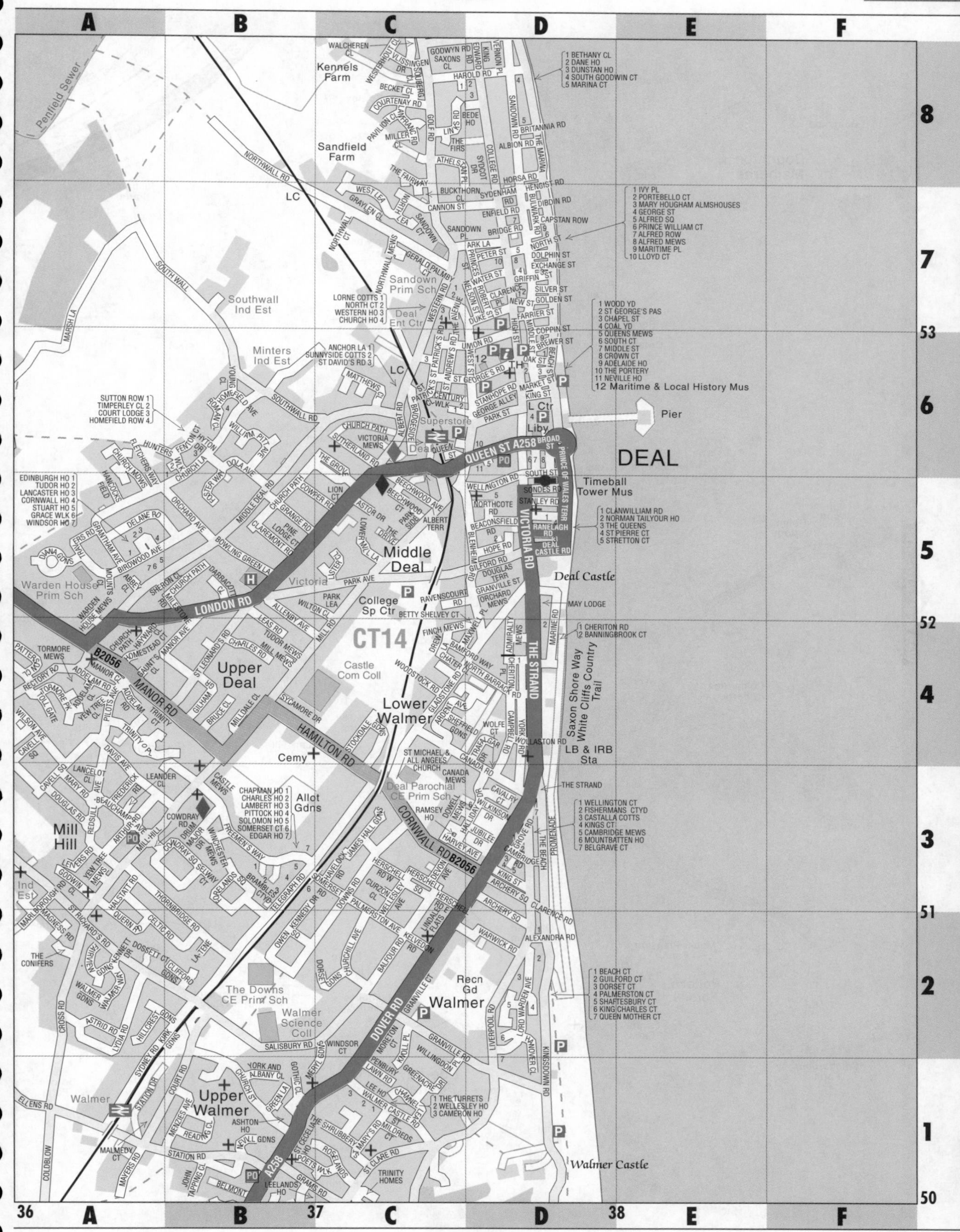
A
B
C
D
E
F
8
7
53
6
5
52
4
3
51
2
1
50
36
37
38
Kennels Farm
Sandfield Farm
Penfield Sewer
NORTHWALL RD
LC
SOUTH WALL
Southwall Ind Est
Minters Ind Est
MARSH LA
Sandown Prim Sch
Deal Ent Ctr
Superstore
Deal
QUEEN ST A258
BROAD ST
PRINCE OF WALES TERR
DEAL
Pier
L Ctr
Liby
TH
Timeball Tower Mus
VICTORIA RD
Middle Deal
Victoria
LONDON RD
Warden House Prim Sch
College Sp Ctr
CT14
Castle Com Coll
Deal Castle
THE STRAND
Upper Deal
MANOR RD
B2056
HAMILTON RD
Lower Walmer
Cemy
Allot Gdns
Deal Parochial CE Prim Sch
CORNWALL RD B2056
Mill Hill
Ind Est
Saxon Shore Way
White Cliffs Country Trail
LB & IRB Sta
The Downs CE Prim Sch
Walmer Science Coll
DOVER RD
Recn Gd
Walmer
Upper Walmer
Walmer
A258
Walmer Castle
1 BETHANY CL
2 DANE HO
3 DUNSTAN HO
4 SOUTH GOODWIN CT
5 MARINA CT
1 IVY PL
2 PORTEBELLO CT
3 MARY HOUGHAM ALMSHOUSES
4 GEORGE ST
5 ALFRED SQ
6 PRINCE WILLIAM CT
7 ALFRED ROW
8 ALFRED MEWS
9 MARITIME PL
10 LLOYD CT
1 WOOD YD
2 ST GEORGE'S PAS
3 CHAPEL ST
4 COAL YD
5 QUEENS MEWS
6 SOUTH CT
7 MIDDLE ST
8 CROWN CT
9 ADELAIDE HO
10 THE PORTERY
11 NEVILLE HO
12 Maritime & Local History Mus
LORNE COTTS 1
NORTH CT 2
WESTERN HO 3
CHURCH HO 4
ANCHOR LA 1
SUNNYSIDE COTTS 2
ST DAVID'S RD 3
SUTTON ROW 1
TIMPERLEY CL 2
COURT LODGE 3
HOMEFIELD ROW 4
EDINBURGH HO 1
TUDOR HO 2
LANCASTER HO 3
CORNWALL HO 4
STUART HO 5
GRACE WLK 6
WINDSOR HO 7
1 CLANWILLIAM RD
2 NORMAN TAILYOUR HO
3 THE QUEENS
4 ST PIERRE CT
5 STRETTON CT
MAY LODGE
1 CHERITON RD
2 BANNINGBROOK CT
CHAPMAN HO 1
CHARLES HO 2
LAMBERT HO 3
PITTOCK HO 4
SOLOMON HO 5
SOMERSET CT 6
EDGAR HO 7
THE STRAND
1 WELLINGTON CT
2 FISHERMANS CTYD
3 CASTALLA COTTS
4 KINGS CT
5 CAMBRIDGE MEWS
6 MOUNTBATTEN HO
7 BELGRAVE CT
1 BEACH CT
2 GUILFORD CT
3 DORSET CT
4 PALMERSTON CT
5 SHAFTESBURY CT
6 KING CHARLES CT
7 QUEEN MOTHER CT
1 THE TURRETS
2 WELLESLEY HO
3 CAMERON HO

134

101

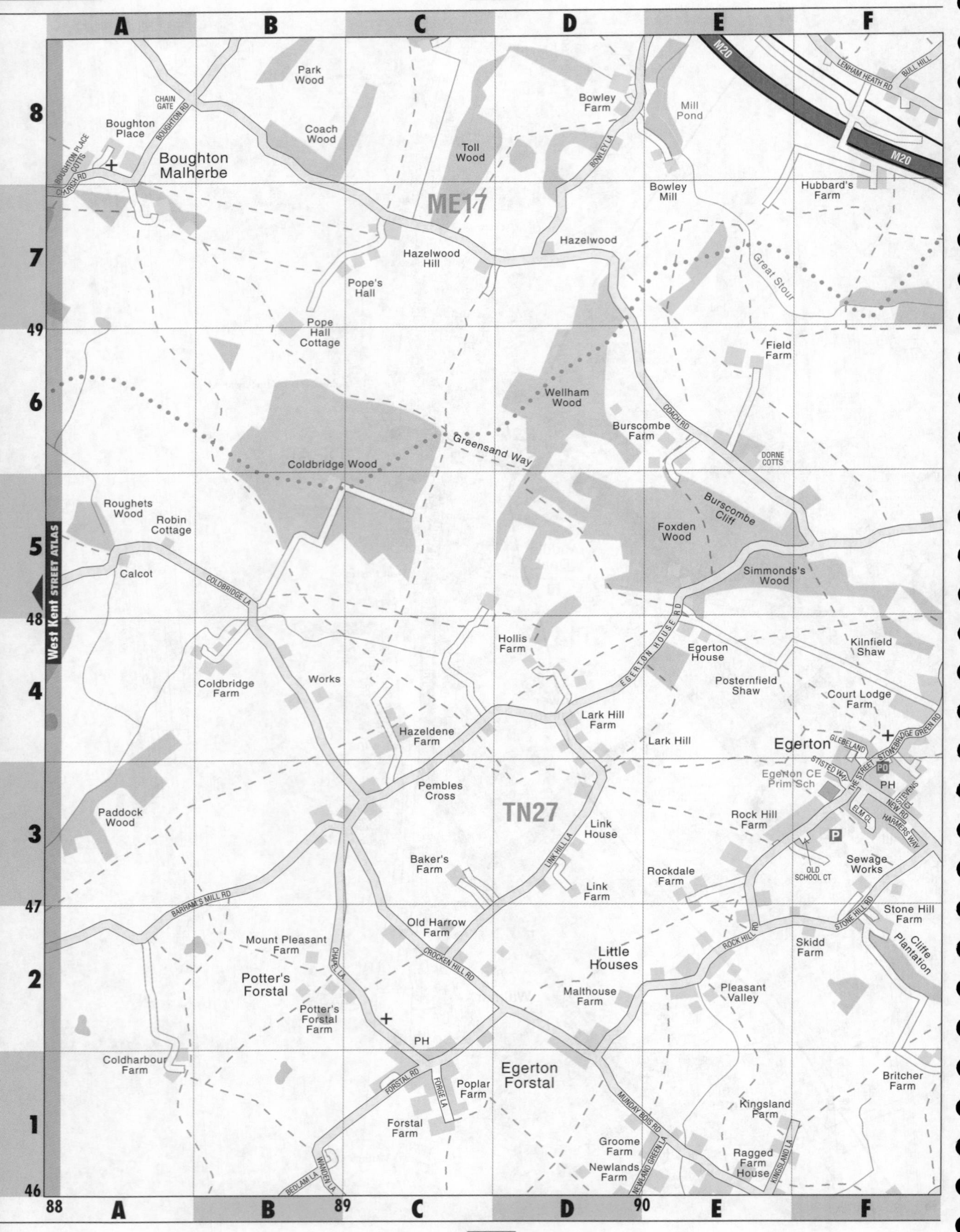
A B C D E F
8 7 49 6 5 48 4 3 47 2 1 46
88 89 90
M20
Park Wood
Coach Wood
Toll Wood
Bowley Farm
Mill Pond
Boughton Place
Boughton Malherbe
CHAIN GATE
BOUGHTON RD
BOUGHTON PLACE COTTS
CHURCH RD
BOWLEY LA
LENHAM HEATH RD
BULL HILL
Bowley Mill
Hubbard's Farm
ME17
Hazelwood
Hazelwood Hill
Pope's Hall
Great Stour
Pope Hall Cottage
Field Farm
Wellham Wood
Burscombe Farm
COACH RD
Greensand Way
Coldbridge Wood
DORNE COTTS
Burscombe Cliff
Roughets Wood
Robin Cottage
Foxden Wood
Calcot
COLDBRIDGE LA
Simmonds's Wood
West Kent STREET ATLAS
Hollis Farm
EGERTON HOUSE RD
Egerton House
Kilnfield Shaw
Works
Coldbridge Farm
Posternfield Shaw
Court Lodge Farm
Lark Hill Farm
Hazeldene Farm
Lark Hill
Egerton
GLEBELAND
STONEBRIDGE GREEN RD
STISTED WAY
THE STREET
PO
Egerton CE Prim Sch
PH
STEVENS CL
NEW RD
ELM CL
HARMERS WAY
Pembles Cross
TN27
Paddock Wood
Link House
Rock Hill Farm
LINK HILL LA
P
Baker's Farm
Sewage Works
OLD SCHOOL CT
Rockdale Farm
Link Farm
BARRAM'S MILL RD
STONE HILL RD
Stone Hill Farm
Old Harrow Farm
Skidd Farm
Cliffe Plantation
Mount Pleasant Farm
ROCK HILL RD
CHAPEL LA
CROCKEN HILL RD
Little Houses
Potter's Forstal
Pleasant Valley
Malthouse Farm
Potter's Forstal Farm
PH
Coldharbour Farm
Egerton Forstal
Britcher Farm
Poplar Farm
FORSTAL RD
FORGE LA
MUNDAY BOIS RD
Kingsland Farm
Forstal Farm
Groome Farm
NEWLAND GREEN LA
Ragged Farm House
KINGSLAND LA
Newlands Farm
BEDLAM LA
WANDEN LA

135

102
120

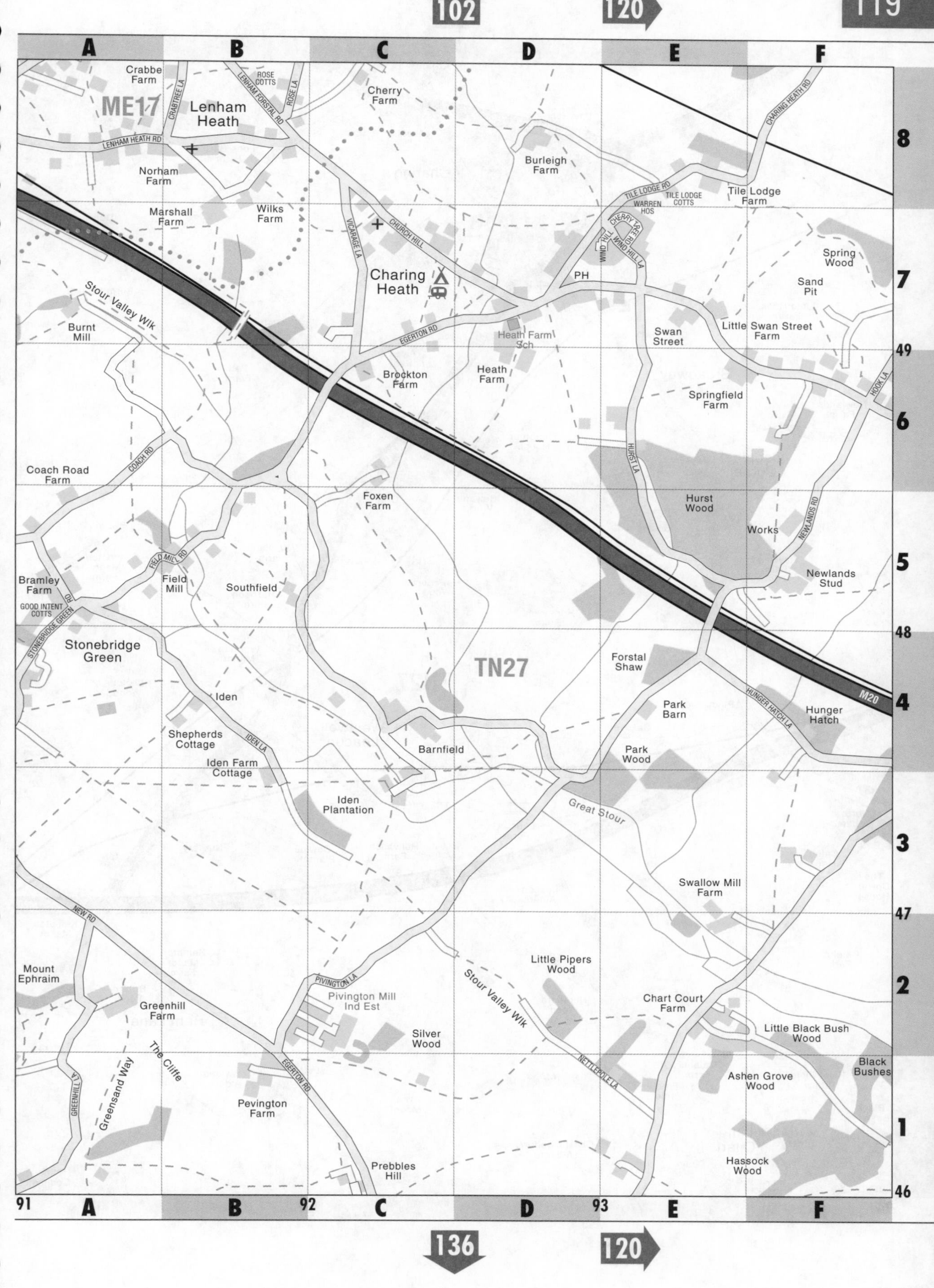
A
B
C
D
E
F
Crabbe Farm
ME17
Lenham Heath
CRABTREE LA
LENHAM FORSTAL RD
ROSE COTTS
ROSE LA
Cherry Farm
LENHAM HEATH RD
Norham Farm
Burleigh Farm
CHARING HEATH RD
8
Marshall Farm
Wilks Farm
VICARAGE LA
CHURCH HILL
TILE LODGE RD
WARREN HOS
TILE LODGE COTTS
Tile Lodge Farm
WIND HILL
CHERRY TREE RD
WIND HILL LA
Spring Wood
Charing Heath
PH
Sand Pit
7
Stour Valley Wlk
Burnt Mill
EGERTON RD
Heath Farm Sch
Swan Street
Little Swan Street Farm
49
Brockton Farm
Heath Farm
Springfield Farm
HOOK LA
6
COACH RD
HURST LA
Coach Road Farm
Foxen Farm
Hurst Wood
Works
NEWLANDS RD
FIELD MILL RD
5
Bramley Farm
Field Mill
Southfield
Newlands Stud
GOOD INTENT COTTS
STONEBRIDGE GREEN RD
48
Stonebridge Green
Forstal Shaw
TN27
M20
Iden
Park Barn
Hunger Hatch
HUNGER HATCH LA
4
Shepherds Cottage
IDEN LA
Barnfield
Park Wood
Iden Farm Cottage
Iden Plantation
Great Stour
3
Swallow Mill Farm
NEW RD
47
Mount Ephraim
Little Pipers Wood
PIVINGTON LA
Stour Valley Wlk
2
Greenhill Farm
Pivington Mill Ind Est
Chart Court Farm
Little Black Bush Wood
Silver Wood
Greensand Way
The Cliffe
NETTLEPOLE LA
Black Bushes
GREENHILL LA
EGERTON RD
Ashen Grove Wood
Pevington Farm
1
Prebbles Hill
Hassock Wood
91
92
93
46

136
120

119 103

A B C D E F

8

Great Hook

Hotel

Charing CE Prim Sch

NORTHERN BY-PASS

PILGRIMS WAY

CHARING HILL A252

A20

A252

Longbeech Wood

Lone Barn Farm

PILGRIMS WAY

Clearmount PK

Charing

SAYER RD

WHEELER RD

CENTENARY

DOWNS WAY

BRINCHLEY MEWS

DOWNS CL

CLEARMOUNT

THE HILL

HAFFENDEN MDW

SCHOOL RD

MOAT CL

HIGH ST

PILGRIMS CT

MARKET PL

ELIZABETHAN

THE GLEBE

PETT LA

WOODBROOK

Liby

PO

P

North Downs Way

Dencher Wood

7

Little Hook Farm

HOOK LA

ELLEN CL

RUGLY'S RD

TATCHELL RD

WAY

HITHER FIELD

BURLEIGH RD

STATION RD

MAIDSTONE RD

THE MOAT

OLD ASHFORD RD

MOAT

PYM HO

ASHFORD RD

TOLL LA

Burnt House Farm

Works

49

Charing

HARDWICKE HO

MOAT PK

Alder Bed

Pett Place

Broadway

Pett Farm

Puncheons

6

Newlands Farm

CHARING HEATH RD

Slaughter House

MAIDSTONE RD

WICKEN LA

WESTWELL LA

Coppins' Corner

Pepper Alley

Sewage Works

Crem

Wicken Farm

Wooton Manor Farm

5

PLUCKLEY RD

Beesmount

GREENSAND WAY

Raywood Farm

Ray Wood

Honeywood Rough

Newcourt Wood

Harrison Farm

Wooton Manor

Lacton Wood

TN25

48

Raywood Office Complex

TN27

Works

Grove Wood

4

M20

The Pincushion

Oakover

Westwell Leacon

THE LEACON COTTS

LEACON COTTS

HUNGER HATCH LA

Calehill Heath

Leacon Farm

Hollybush Farm

Cowlees Plantation

Nursery

LEDA COTTS

3

North Lodge

Calehill House

Leacon Alders

GREENSAND WAY

HURSTFORD LA

Kempton Manor

M20

47

The Dower House

Hotel

2

Calehill Park

Hurstford Wood

TN26

Kempton Manor Farm

Britton Farm

Lake House

A20

PH

Calehill Farm

Ram Lane

COOMBE GR

CHAPEL ROW

CHAPEL RD

River Field Shaw

Freeds Alders

Great Stour

The Mount

Cowlees Alders

LAKESIDE GDNS

1

Black Bushes

Mill Ponds

BANNISTER HOS

Little Chart

Chart Meadow Alders

Hothfield Common

Stour Valley Wlk

THE TERRACE

46

94 A B 95 C D 96 E F

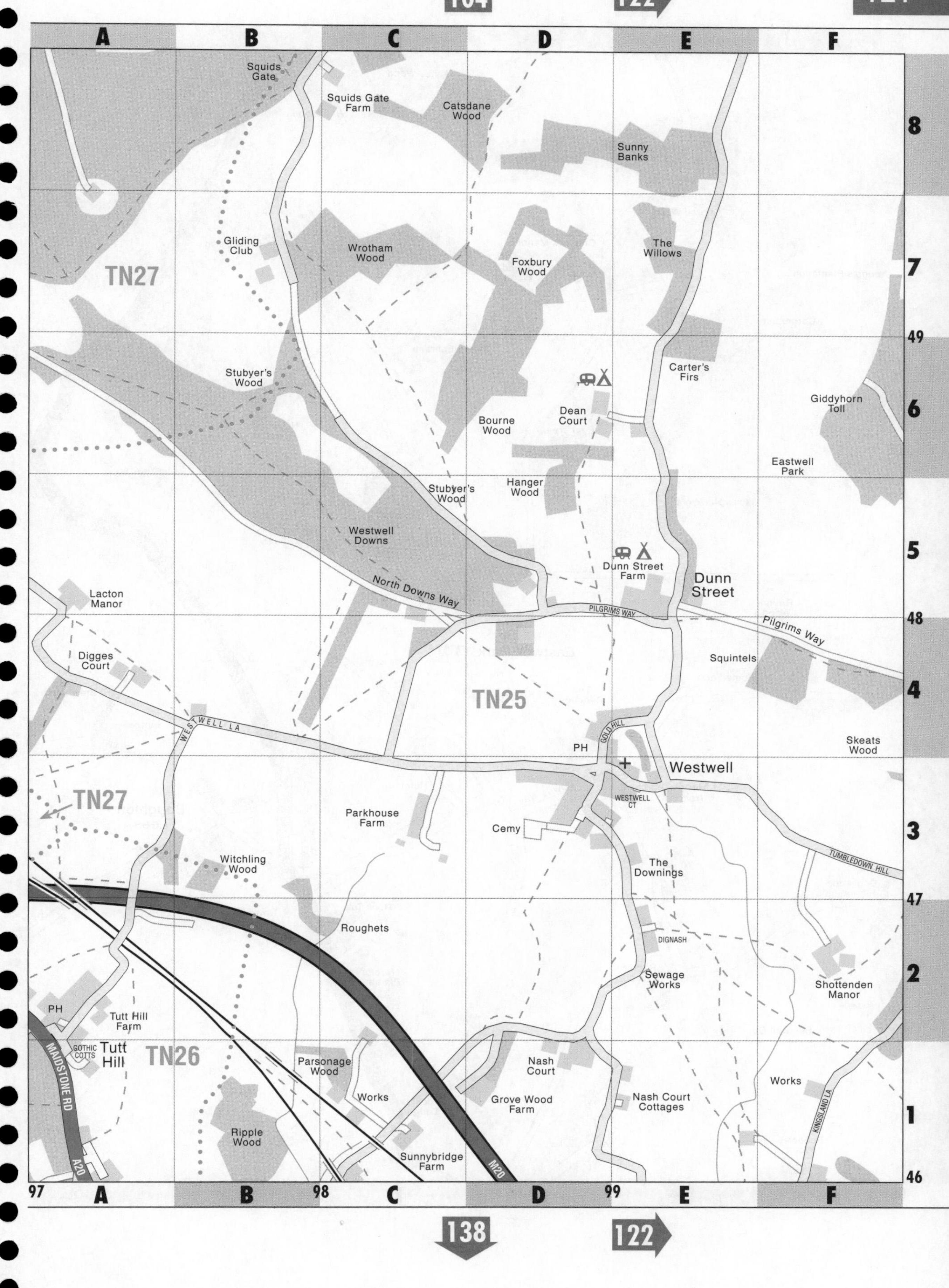
A
B
C
D
E
F
8
7
49
6
5
48
4
3
47
2
1
46
97
98
99
Squids Gate
Squids Gate Farm
Catsdane Wood
Sunny Banks
Gliding Club
Wrotham Wood
Foxbury Wood
The Willows
TN27
Stubyer's Wood
Carter's Firs
Dean Court
Bourne Wood
Giddyhorn Toll
Eastwell Park
Hanger Wood
Stubyer's Wood
Westwell Downs
Dunn Street Farm
Dunn Street
North Downs Way
PILGRIMS WAY
Pilgrims Way
Lacton Manor
Digges Court
Squintels
TN25
WESTWELL LA
GOLD HILL
PH
Westwell
Skeats Wood
TN27
Parkhouse Farm
Cemy
WESTWELL CT
The Downings
TUMBLEDOWN HILL
Witchling Wood
Roughets
DIGNASH
Sewage Works
Shottenden Manor
PH
Tutt Hill Farm
GOTHIC COTTS
Tutt Hill
TN26
MAIDSTONE RD
Parsonage Wood
Nash Court
Works
Grove Wood Farm
Nash Court Cottages
Works
KINGSLAND LA
Ripple Wood
Sunnybridge Farm
A20
M20

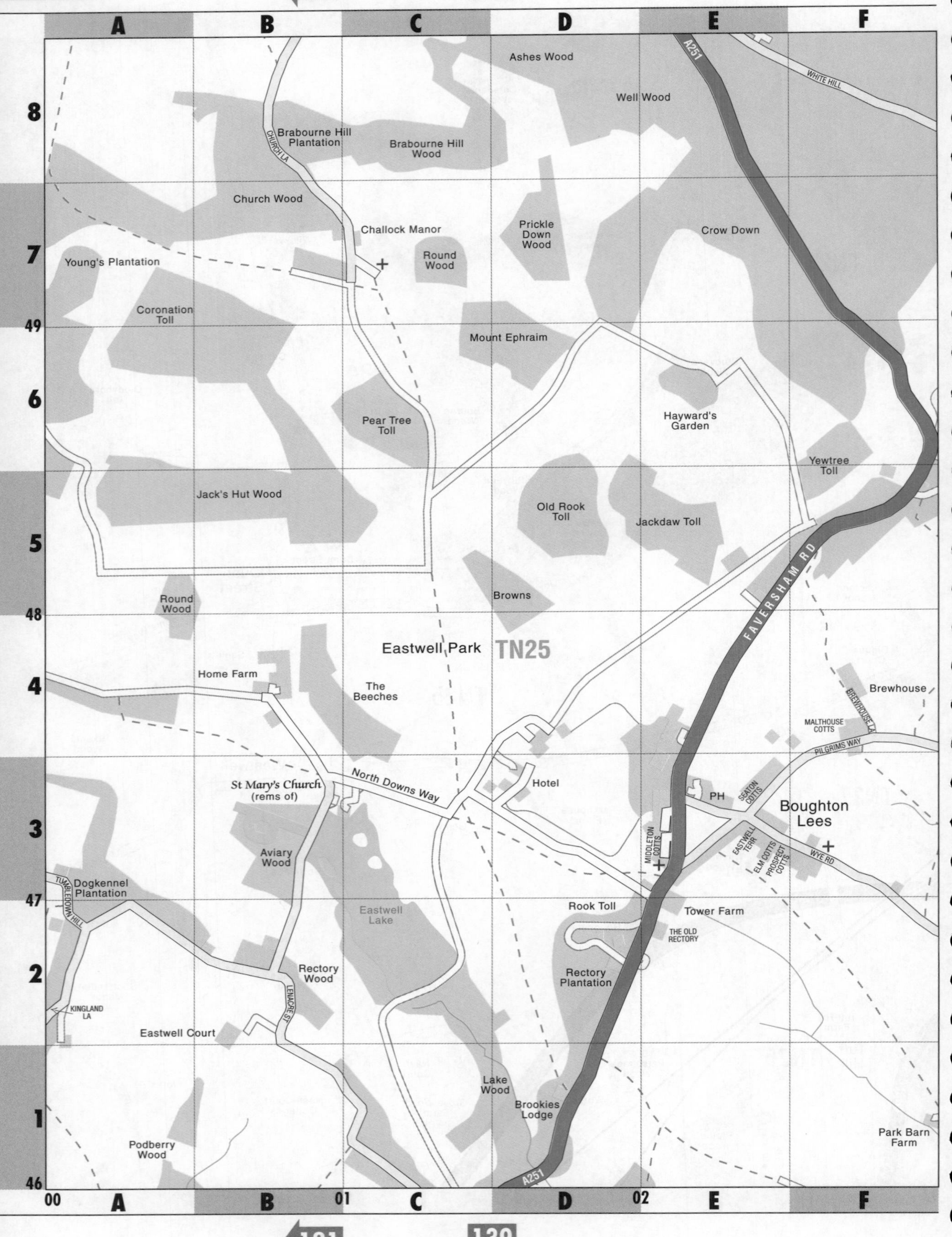
A
B
C
D
E
F
8
7
49
6
5
48
4
3
47
2
1
46
00
01
02
Ashes Wood
Well Wood
WHITE HILL
A251
Brabourne Hill Plantation
Brabourne Hill Wood
CHURCH LA
Church Wood
Challock Manor
Prickle Down Wood
Crow Down
Round Wood
Young's Plantation
Coronation Toll
Mount Ephraim
Pear Tree Toll
Hayward's Garden
Yewtree Toll
Jack's Hut Wood
Old Rook Toll
Jackdaw Toll
Browns
FAVERSHAM RD
Round Wood
Eastwell Park
TN25
Home Farm
The Beeches
Brewhouse
BREWHOUSE LA
MALTHOUSE COTTS
PILGRIMS WAY
St Mary's Church (rems of)
North Downs Way
Hotel
PH
SEATON COTTS
Boughton Lees
MIDDLETON COTTS
EASTWELL TERR
ELM COTTS
PROSPECT COTTS
WYE RD
Aviary Wood
Dogkennel Plantation
TUMBLEDOWN HILL
Eastwell Lake
Rook Toll
Tower Farm
THE OLD RECTORY
Rectory Wood
LENACRE ST
Rectory Plantation
KINGLAND LA
Eastwell Court
Lake Wood
Brookies Lodge
Podberry Wood
Park Barn Farm
A251

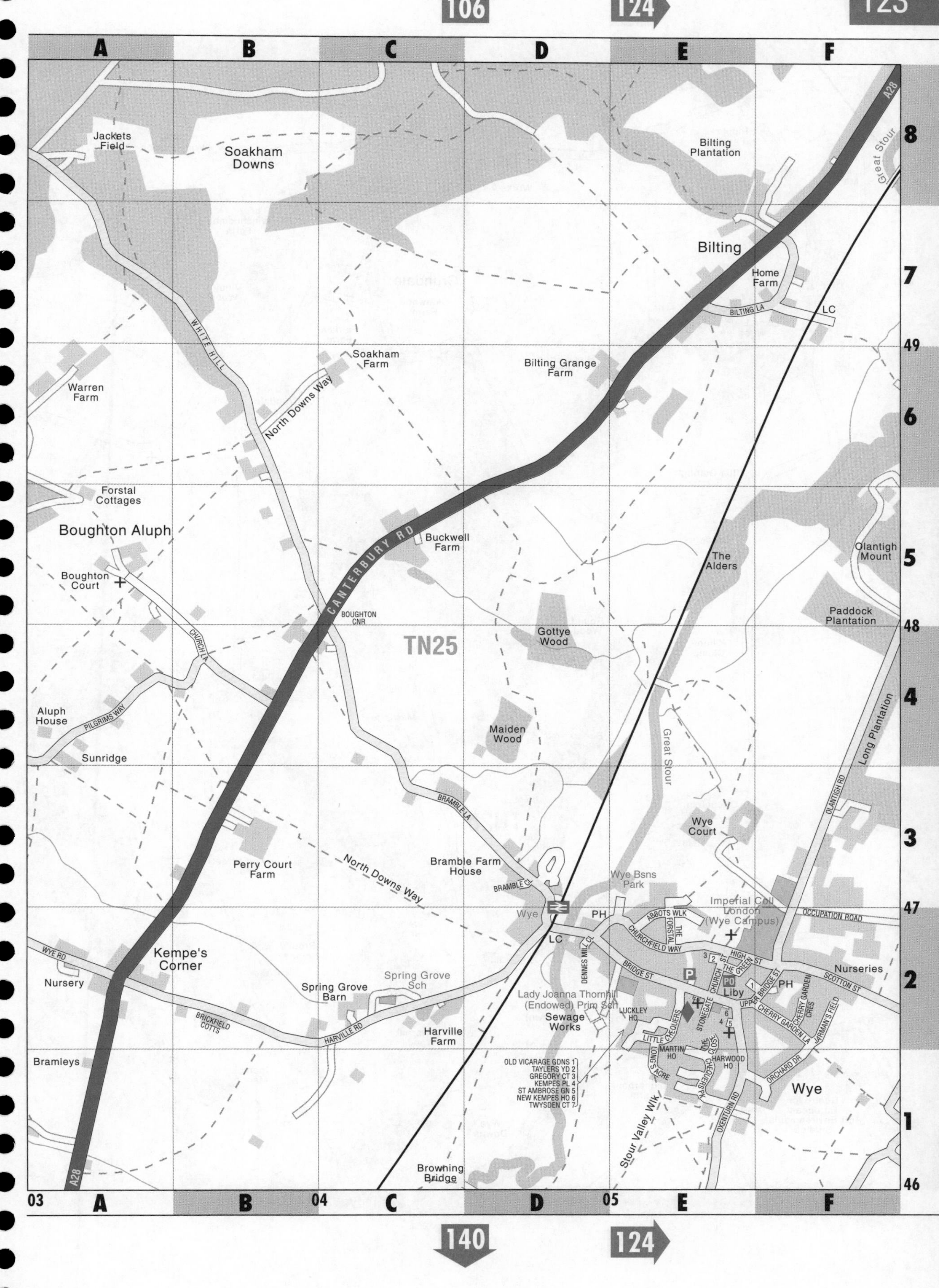
A
B
C
D
E
F
Jackets Field
Soakham Downs
Bilting Plantation
Great Stour
A28
8
Bilting
Home Farm
BILTING LA
LC
7
WHITE HILL
Soakham Farm
Bilting Grange Farm
49
Warren Farm
North Downs Way
6
Forstal Cottages
Boughton Aluph
CANTERBURY RD
Buckwell Farm
The Alders
Olantigh Mount
5
Boughton Court
BOUGHTON CNR
Paddock Plantation
CHURCH LA
TN25
Gottye Wood
48
Aluph House
PILGRIMS WAY
Maiden Wood
Great Stour
Long Plantation
4
Sunridge
BRAMBLE LA
OLANTIGH RD
Wye Court
3
Perry Court Farm
North Downs Way
Bramble Farm House
BRAMBLE CL
Wye Bsns Park
Imperial Coll London (Wye Campus)
Wye
PH
ABBOTS WLK
THE FORSTAL
OCCUPATION ROAD
47
LC
CHURCHFIELD WAY
WYE RD
Kempe's Corner
DENNES MILL CL
HIGH ST
THE GREEN
CHURCH ST
Nurseries
BRIDGE ST
P
PO
Liby
UPPER BRIDGE ST
PH
SCOTTON ST
Nursery
Spring Grove Sch
Spring Grove Barn
Lady Joanna Thornhill (Endowed) Prim Sch
CHERRY GARDEN CRES
JARMAN'S FIELD
2
BRICKFIELD COTTS
HARVILLE RD
Sewage Works
LUCKLEY HO
CHEQUERS
STONEGATE
CHERRY GARDEN LA
Harville Farm
LITTLE CHEQUERS
MARTIN HO
THE CLOSE
HARWOOD HO
Bramleys
ORCHARD DR
LONG'S ACRE
OLD VICARAGE GDNS 1
TAYLERS YD 2
GREGORY CT 3
KEMPES PL 4
ST AMBROSE GN 5
NEW KEMPES HO 6
TWYSDEN CT 7
Wye
Stour Valley Wlk
OXENTURN RD
1
A28
Browning Bridge
46
03
04
05

123
107

A   B   C   D   E   F

A28

Great Stour

8

Ripple Farm

Trimworth Manor

Little Winchcombe

Works

Thornham Lodge

Winchcombe Farm

7

Tye Wood

OLANTIGH ROAD

Crundale

CT4

Glenwood Farm

Viney's Wood

Oxen Lees Wood

Great Stour

49

Black Edge Wood

Fairisle Farm

Church Wood

6

Crundale House

Little Olantigh Farm

Warren Wood

Crundale Downs

Nursery

Marriage Wood

5

Roughets

48

Round Wood

Kidney Clump

Marriage Hill

4

Stour Valley Wlk

Marriage Farm

Beech Wood

TN25

Sheepfold

3

Mast

Pett Street Farm

North Downs Way

HASELL ST

47

Down Farm

Prout's Spinney

2

Meml (Crown)

Hurst Wood

SCOTTON ST

Collyerhill Wood

COLDHARBOUR LA

1 WITHERSDANE COTTS
2 BERNARD SUNLEY HALL
3 THE GARDEN HALL

Coombe Manor

Withersdane Hall

Coldharbour Farm

AMAGE ROAD COTTS

1

Centre for European Agri-Environmental Studies

AMAGE RD

Wye Downs

Little Combe

46

06   A   B   07   C   D   08   E   F

123
141

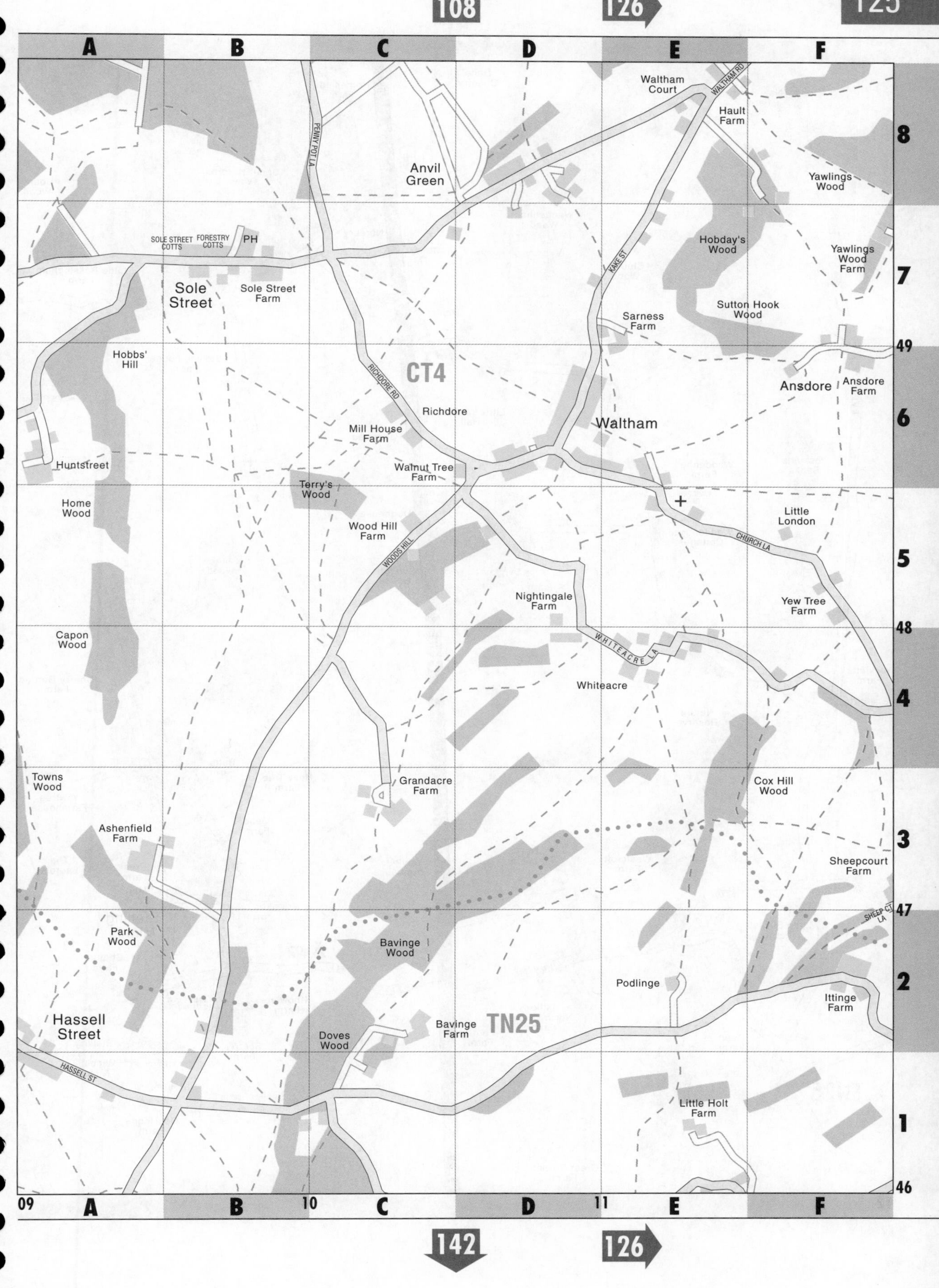

108
126
142
126

A B C D E F

8
7
49
6
5
48
4
3
47
2
1
46

09 10 11

Waltham Court
WALTHAM RD
Hault Farm
Yawlings Wood
Anvil Green
Hobday's Wood
Yawlings Wood Farm
KAKE ST
Sutton Hook Wood
SOLE STREET COTTS
FORESTRY COTTS
PH
Sole Street
Sole Street Farm
Sarness Farm
Ansdore
Ansdore Farm
PENNY POT LA
Hobbs' Hill
CT4
RICHDORE RD
Richdore
Waltham
Mill House Farm
Little London
Walnut Tree Farm
Huntstreet
Terry's Wood
CHURCH LA
Home Wood
Wood Hill Farm
WOODS HILL
Nightingale Farm
Yew Tree Farm
Capon Wood
WHITEACRE LA
Whiteacre
Towns Wood
Cox Hill Wood
Grandacre Farm
Ashenfield Farm
Sheepcourt Farm
SHEEP CT LA
47
Park Wood
Bavinge Wood
Podlinge
Ittinge Farm
Hassell Street
Doves Wood
Bavinge Farm
TN25
HASSELL ST
Little Holt Farm

125
109

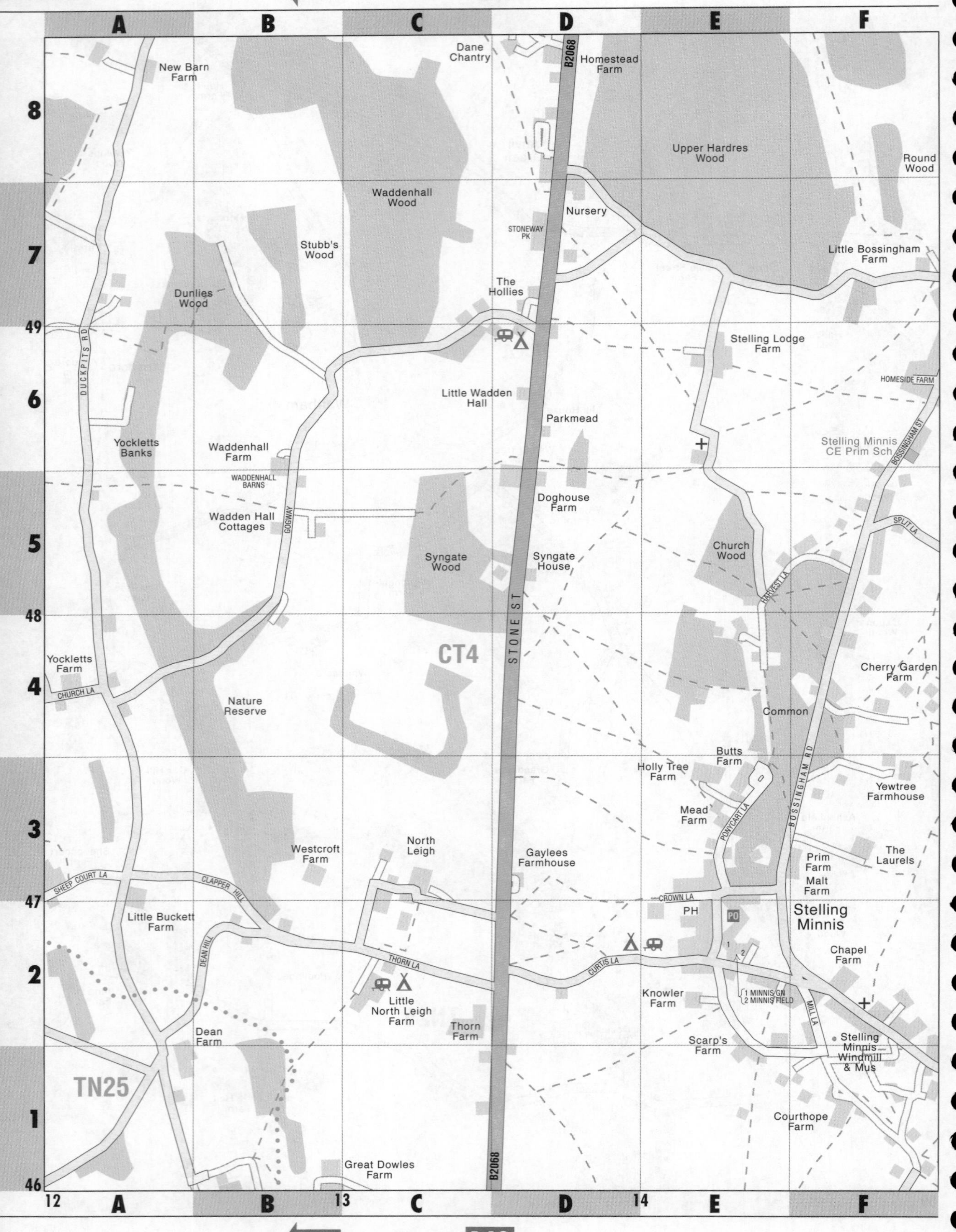
A
B
C
D
E
F
8
7
49
6
5
48
4
3
47
2
1
46
12
13
14
New Barn Farm
Dane Chantry
B2068
Homestead Farm
Upper Hardres Wood
Round Wood
Waddenhall Wood
Nursery
Stubb's Wood
STONEWAY PK
Little Bossingham Farm
Dunlies Wood
The Hollies
Stelling Lodge Farm
DUCKPITS RD
HOMESIDE FARM
Little Wadden Hall
Parkmead
Yockletts Banks
Waddenhall Farm
Stelling Minnis CE Prim Sch
BOSSINGHAM ST
WADDENHALL BARNS
Doghouse Farm
Wadden Hall Cottages
GOGWAY
SPLIT LA
Church Wood
Syngate Wood
Syngate House
HARVEST LA
STONE ST
CT4
Yockletts Farm
Cherry Garden Farm
CHURCH LA
Nature Reserve
Common
Butts Farm
Holly Tree Farm
BOSSINGHAM RD
Yewtree Farmhouse
Mead Farm
PONYCART LA
North Leigh
Westcroft Farm
Gaylees Farmhouse
Prim Farm
The Laurels
Malt Farm
SHEEP COURT LA
CLAPPER HILL
CROWN LA
PH
PO
Stelling Minnis
Little Buckett Farm
DEAN HILL
THORN LA
CURTIS LA
Chapel Farm
Little North Leigh Farm
Knowler Farm
1 MINNIS GN
2 MINNIS FIELD
MILL LA
Dean Farm
Thorn Farm
Scarp's Farm
Stelling Minnis Windmill & Mus
TN25
Courthope Farm
Great Dowles Farm

125
143

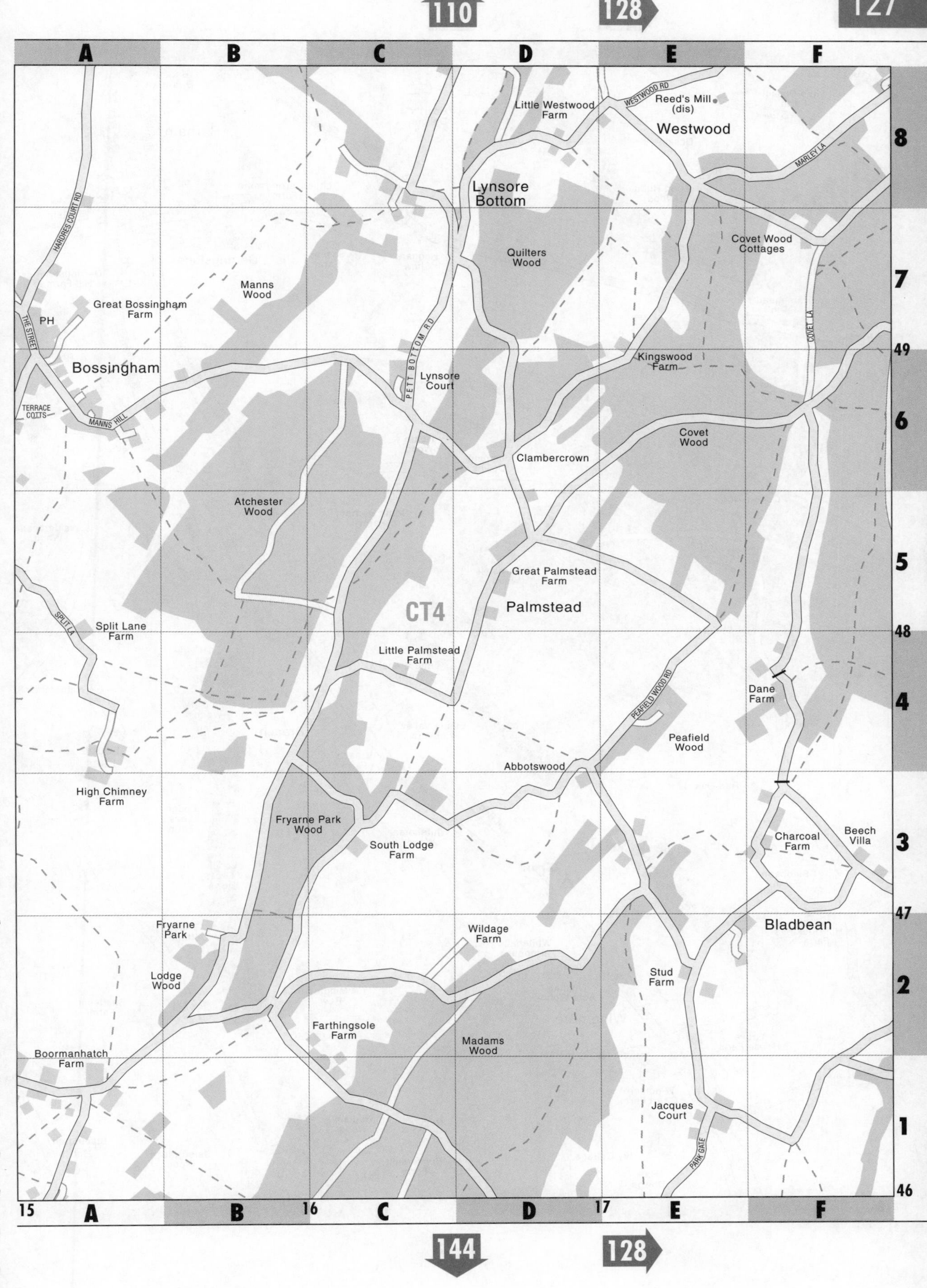

110
128
144
128

A B C D E F

8
7
49
6
5
48
4
3
47
2
1
46

15 16 17

HARDRES COURT RD
THE STREET
PH
Great Bossingham Farm
Manns Wood
Bossingham
TERRACE COTTS
MANNS HILL
SPLIT LA
Split Lane Farm
High Chimney Farm
Boormanhatch Farm

Little Westwood Farm
WESTWOOD RD
Reed's Mill (dis)
Westwood
Lynsore Bottom
Quilters Wood
Covet Wood Cottages
MARLEY LA
COVET LA
PETIT BOTTOM RD
Lynsore Court
Kingswood Farm
Clambercrown
Covet Wood
Atchester Wood
CT4
Great Palmstead Farm
Palmstead
Little Palmstead Farm
PEAFIELD WOOD RD
Peafield Wood
Dane Farm
Abbotswood
Charcoal Farm
Beech Villa
Fryarne Park Wood
South Lodge Farm
Bladbean
Fryarne Park
Lodge Wood
Wildage Farm
Stud Farm
Farthingsole Farm
Madams Wood
Jacques Court
PARK GATE

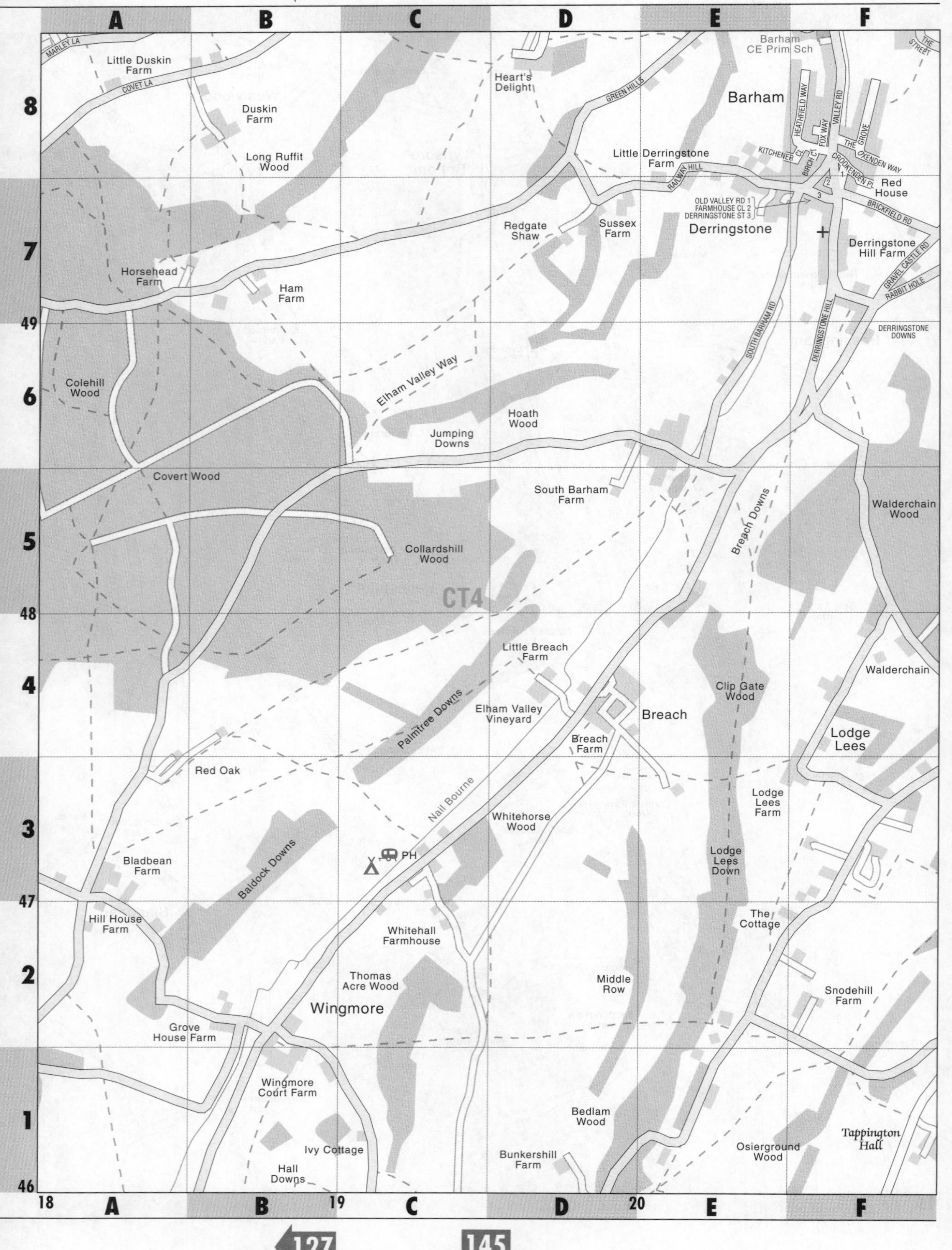

Little Duskin Farm

MARLEY LA

COVET LA

Duskin Farm

Long Ruffit Wood

Heart's Delight

Barham CE Prim Sch

GREEN HILLS

Barham

Little Derringstone Farm

RAILWAY HILL

KITCHENER

HEATHFIELD WAY

BIRCH CL

FOX WAY

VALLEY RD

THE GROVE

THE STREET

OXENDEN WAY

Redgate Shaw

Sussex Farm

OLD VALLEY RD 1
FARMHOUSE CL 2
DERRINGSTONE ST 3

Derringstone

Red House

BRICKFIELD RD

CROOKENDEN PL

DERRINGSTONE HILL

Derringstone Hill Farm

GRAVEL CASTLE RD

RABBIT HOLE

Horsehead Farm

Ham Farm

SOUTH BARHAM RD

DERRINGSTONE DOWNS

Colehill Wood

Elham Valley Way

Hoath Wood

Jumping Downs

Covert Wood

South Barham Farm

Breach Downs

Walderchain Wood

Collardshill Wood

CT4

Little Breach Farm

Walderchain

Palmtree Downs

Elham Valley Vineyard

Breach

Clip Gate Wood

Lodge Lees

Red Oak

Nail Bourne

Whitehorse Wood

Breach Farm

Lodge Lees Farm

Bladbean Farm

Baldock Downs

PH

Lodge Lees Down

Hill House Farm

Whitehall Farmhouse

The Cottage

Thomas Acre Wood

Middle Row

Snodehill Farm

Wingmore

Grove House Farm

Wingmore Court Farm

Ivy Cottage

Hall Downs

Bedlam Wood

Bunkershill Farm

Osierground Wood

Tappington Hall

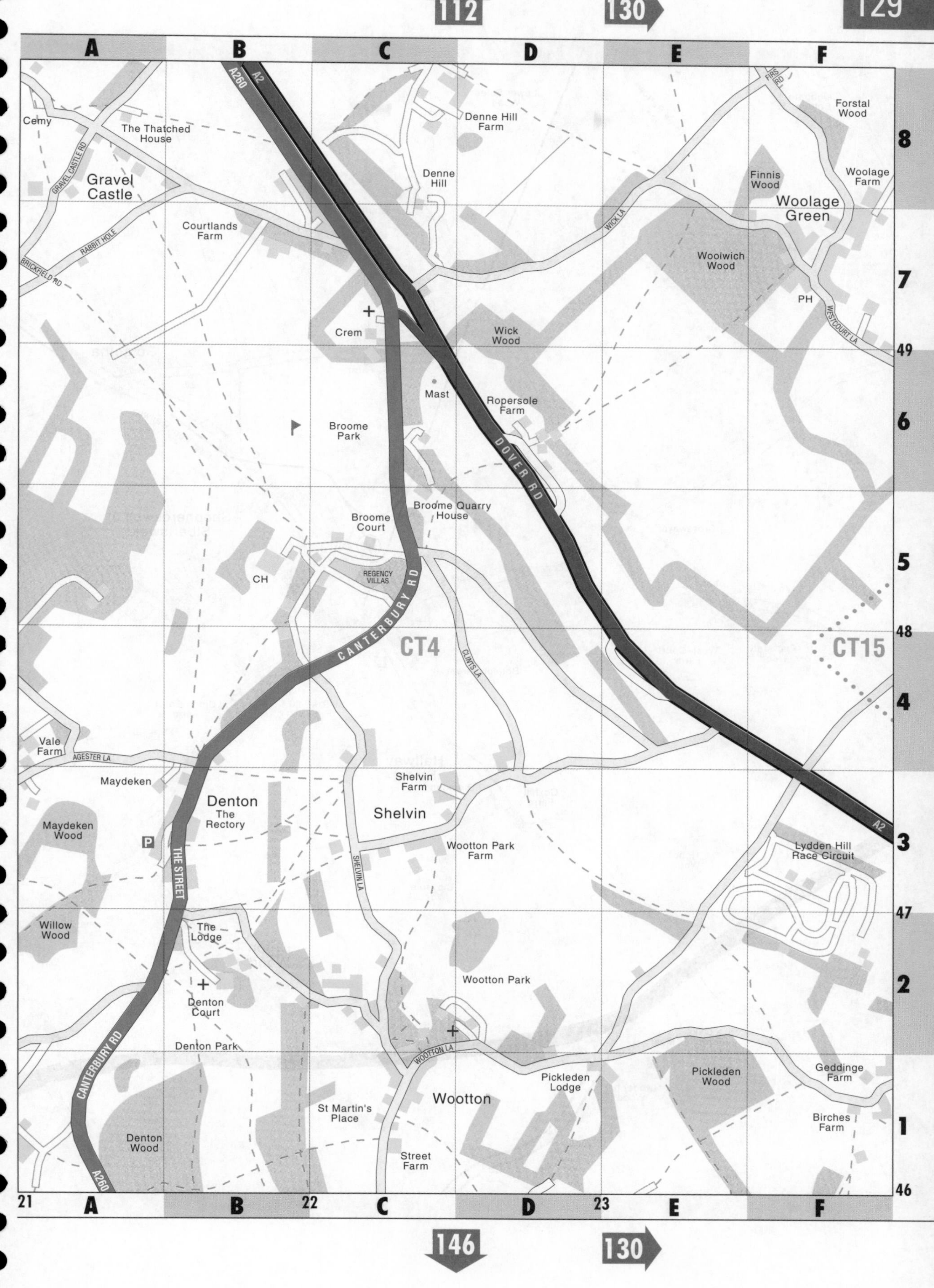

A B C D E F

8
7
49
6
5
48
4
3
47
2
1
46

A B C D E F

Cemy
The Thatched House
Gravel Castle
Courtlands Farm
GRAVEL CASTLE RD
RABBIT HOLE
BRICKFIELD RD

A260
A2

Denne Hill Farm
Denne Hill

WICK LA
FIRS RD
Forstal Wood
Finnis Wood
Woolage Farm
Woolage Green
Woolwich Wood
PH
WEST COURT LA

Crem
Wick Wood
Mast
Broome Park
Ropersole Farm

DOVER RD

Broome Quarry House
Broome Court
CH
REGENCY VILLAS
CANTERBURY RD

CT4
CT15

GUNGE LA

Vale Farm
AGESTER LA
Maydeken
Denton
The Rectory
Shelvin Farm
Shelvin
Wootton Park Farm
Lydden Hill Race Circuit

Maydeken Wood
P
THE STREET
SHELVIN LA

Willow Wood
The Lodge
Denton Court
Denton Park
Wootton Park

St Martin's Place
WOOTTON LA
Wootton
Pickleden Lodge
Pickleden Wood
Geddinge Farm

CANTERBURY RD
A260

Denton Wood
Street Farm
Birches Farm

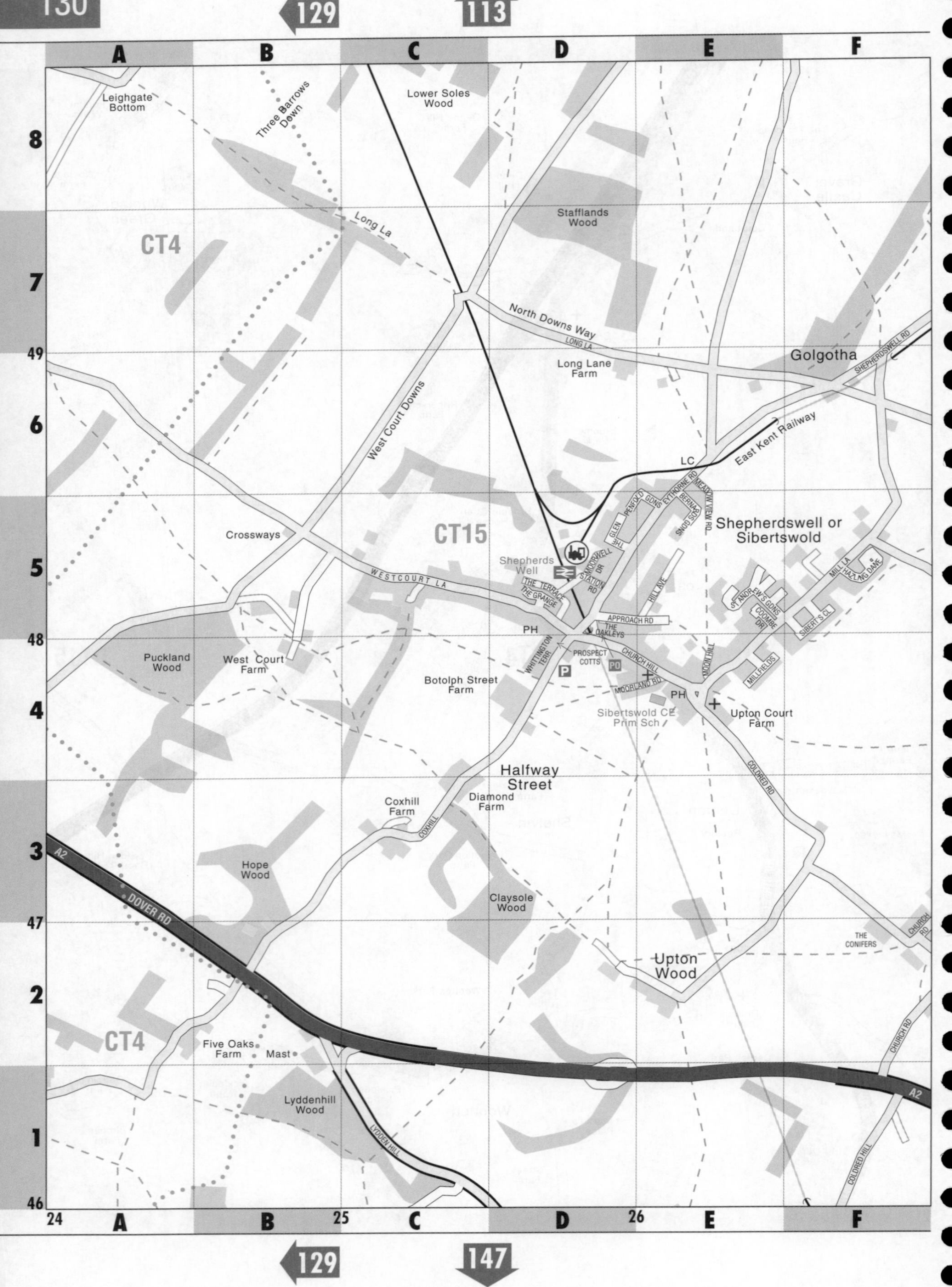

129
113

A   B   C   D   E   F

8

Leighgate
Bottom

Lower Soles
Wood

Three Barrows Down

Stafflands
Wood

Long La

CT4

7

North Downs Way

49

Golgotha

LONG LA

Long Lane
Farm

SHEPHERDSWELL RD

6

East Kent Railway

West Court Downs

LC

5

Crossways

CT15

Shepherdswell or
Sibertswold

Shepherds
Well

GLEN

PENFOLD

GONG

STHORNE RD

BERNAL

MEADOW VIEW RD

CROSS

MILL LA

HAZL AG DARE

WESTCOURT LA

LOVEWELL DR

THE TERRACE

STATION RD

ST ANDREWS GDNS

COOMBE DRI

SIBERT'S CL

THE GRANGE

HILL AVE

48

PH

THE OAKLEYS

APPROACH RD

MOORHILL

MILL FIELDS

WHITTINGTON TERR

PROSPECT
COTTS

PD

CHURCH HILL

Puckland
Wood

West Court
Farm

Botolph Street
Farm

P

4

MOORLAND RD

PH

Sibertswold CE
Prim Sch

Upton Court
Farm

COLDRED RD

Halfway
Street

Coxhill
Farm

Diamond
Farm

COXHILL

3

A2

Hope
Wood

DOVER RD

Claysole
Wood

47

THE
CONIFERS

Upton
Wood

CHURCH RD

2

CT4

Five Oaks
Farm

Mast

A2

Lyddenhill
Wood

LYDDEN HILL

COLDRED HILL

CHURCH RD

1

46

24   A   B   25   C   D   26   E   F

129
147

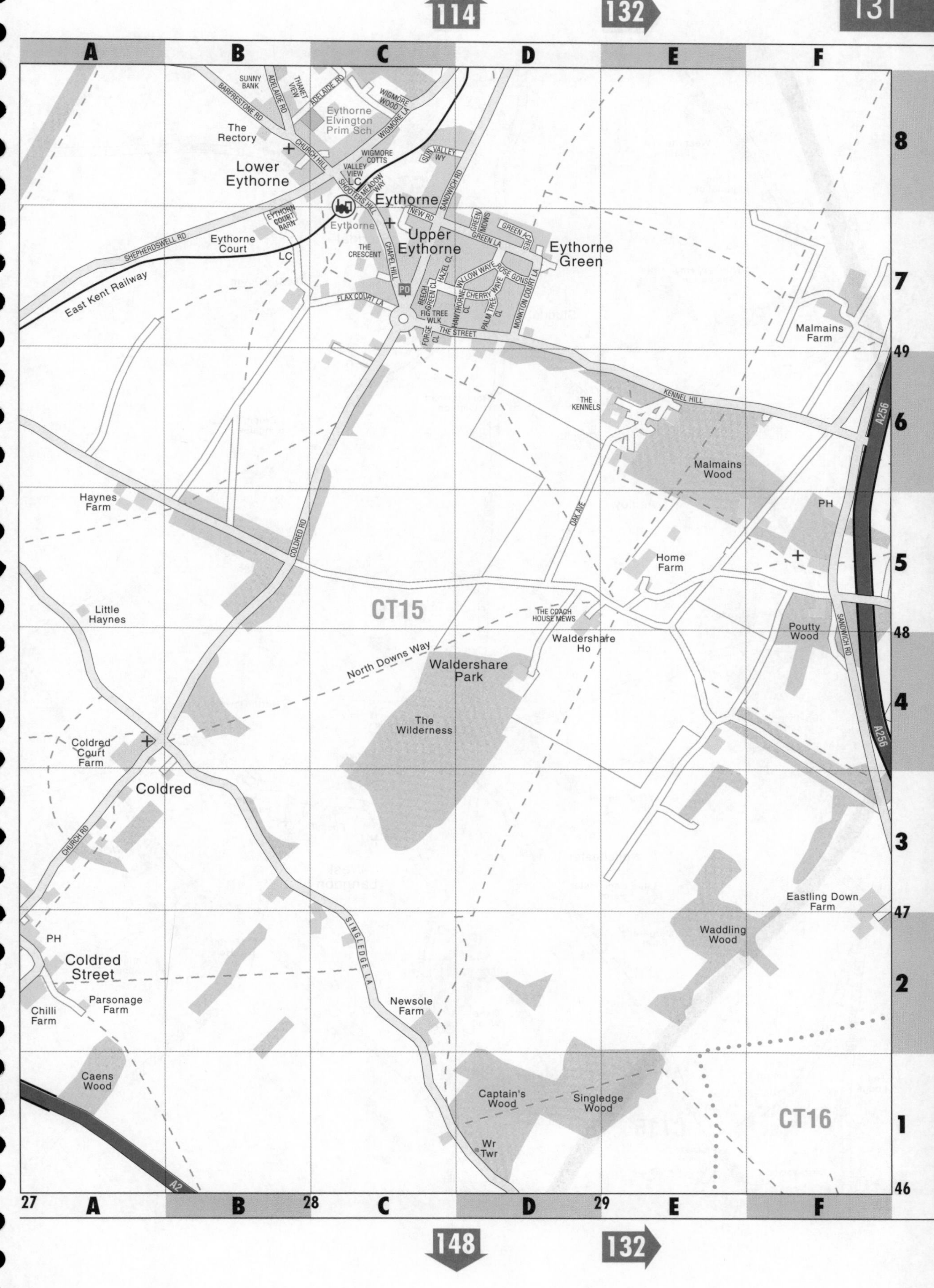

114
132
148
132

A B C D E F

8
7
49
6
5
48
4
3
47
2
1
46

27 28 29

Lower Eythorne
The Rectory
SUNNY BANK
BARFRESTONE RD
ADELAIDE RD
THANET VIEW
CHURCH HILL
Eythorne Elvington Prim Sch
WIGMORE WOOD
WIGMORE LA
WIGMORE COTTS
VALLEY WY
VALLEY VIEW
MEADOW WY
SANDWICH RD
LC
SHEPHERDSWELL RD
Eythorne Court
EYTHORNE COURT BARN
Eythorne
SHOOTERS HILL
LC
THE CRESCENT
CHAPEL HILL
PO
Upper Eythorne
NEW RD
GREEN MEWS
GREEN LA
GREEN CL
Eythorne Green
FORGE CL
BEECH CL
GREEN CL
HAZEL CL
FIG TREE WLK
HAWTHORNE CL
LOW WAYE
CHERRY CL
PALM TREE CL
ROSE GONSRT CL
MONKTON COURT LA
THE STREET
FLAX COURT LA
East Kent Railway

Malmains Farm

CT15

KENNEL HILL
THE KENNELS
COLDRED RD
Haynes Farm

Malmains Wood
PH
A256
A256
SANDWICH RD
OAK AVE
Home Farm
Little Haynes

THE COACH HOUSE MEWS
Waldershare Ho
Poutty Wood

North Downs Way
Waldershare Park

Coldred Court Farm
Coldred
The Wilderness
CHURCH RD

Eastling Down Farm

Waddling Wood

PH
Coldred Street
SINGLEDGE LA
Parsonage Farm
Newsole Farm

Chilli Farm
Caens Wood

Captain's Wood
Singledge Wood
CT16

Wr Twr

A2

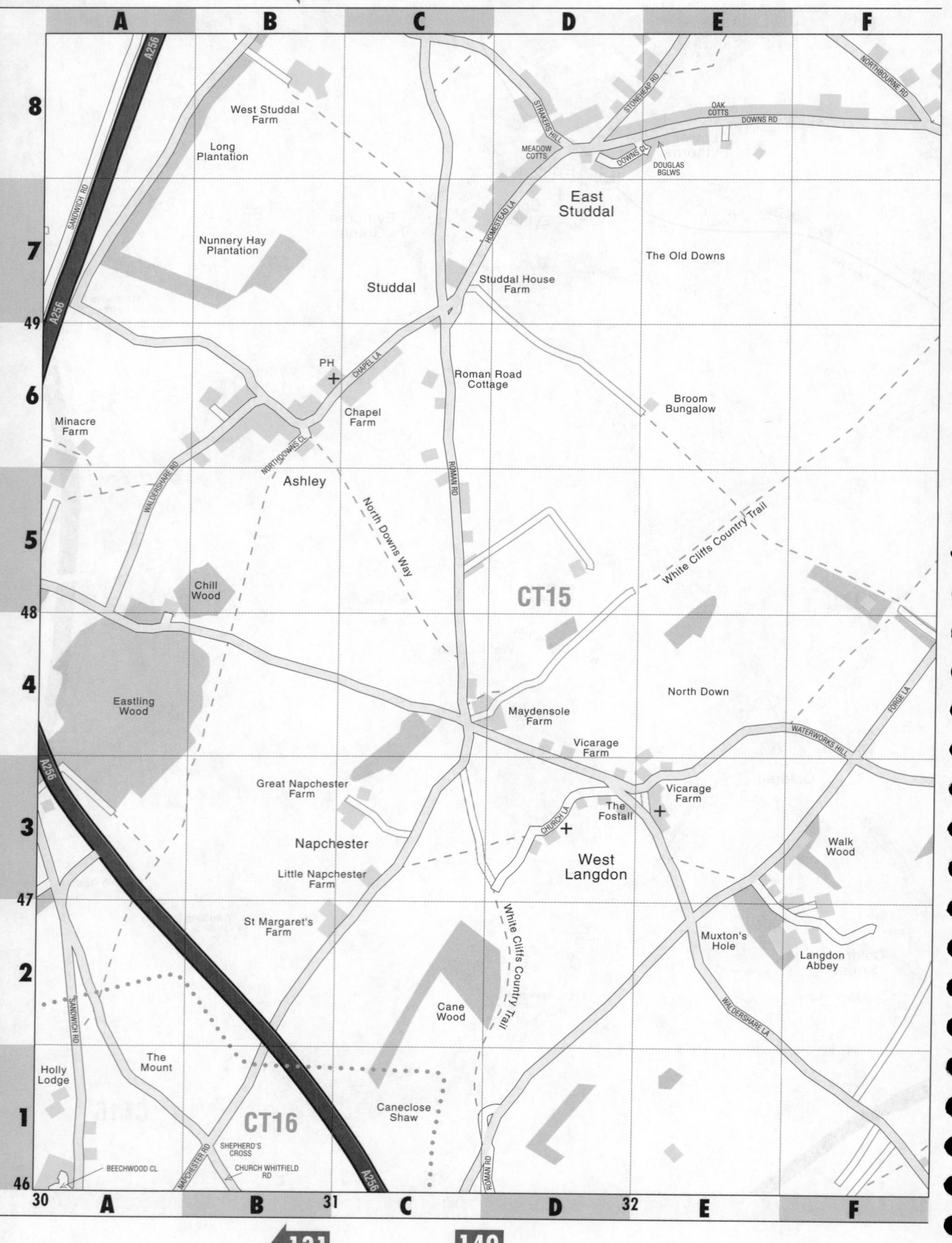

A | B | C | D | E | F

8

West Studdal Farm

Long Plantation

STRAKERS HILL

STONEHEAP RD

MEADOW COTTS

OAK COTTS
DOWNS RD

DOWNS CL
DOUGLAS BGLWS

NORTHBOURNE RD

East Studdal

7

Nunnery Hay Plantation

Studdal

Studdal House Farm

The Old Downs

49

CHAPEL LA

PH
+

Roman Road Cottage

6

Minacre Farm

Chapel Farm

Broom Bungalow

NORTHDOWNS CL

WALDERSHARE RD

Ashley

North Downs Way

ROMAN RD

White Cliffs Country Trail

5

Chill Wood

CT15

48

Eastling Wood

North Down

4

Maydensole Farm

WATERWORKS HILL

FORGE LA

A256

Great Napchester Farm

Vicarage Farm

Vicarage Farm
+

The Fostall

Walk Wood

3

Napchester

CHURCH LA
+

West Langdon

47

Little Napchester Farm

St Margaret's Farm

White Cliffs Country Trail

Muxton's Hole

Langdon Abbey

WALDERSHARE LA

2

SANDWICH RD

The Mount

Cane Wood

Holly Lodge

CT16

Caneclose Shaw

1

ROMAN RD

NAPCHESTER RD

SHEPHERD'S CROSS

A256

46

BEECHWOOD CL

CHURCH WHITFIELD RD

30 | A | B | 31 | C | D | 32 | E | F

116
134

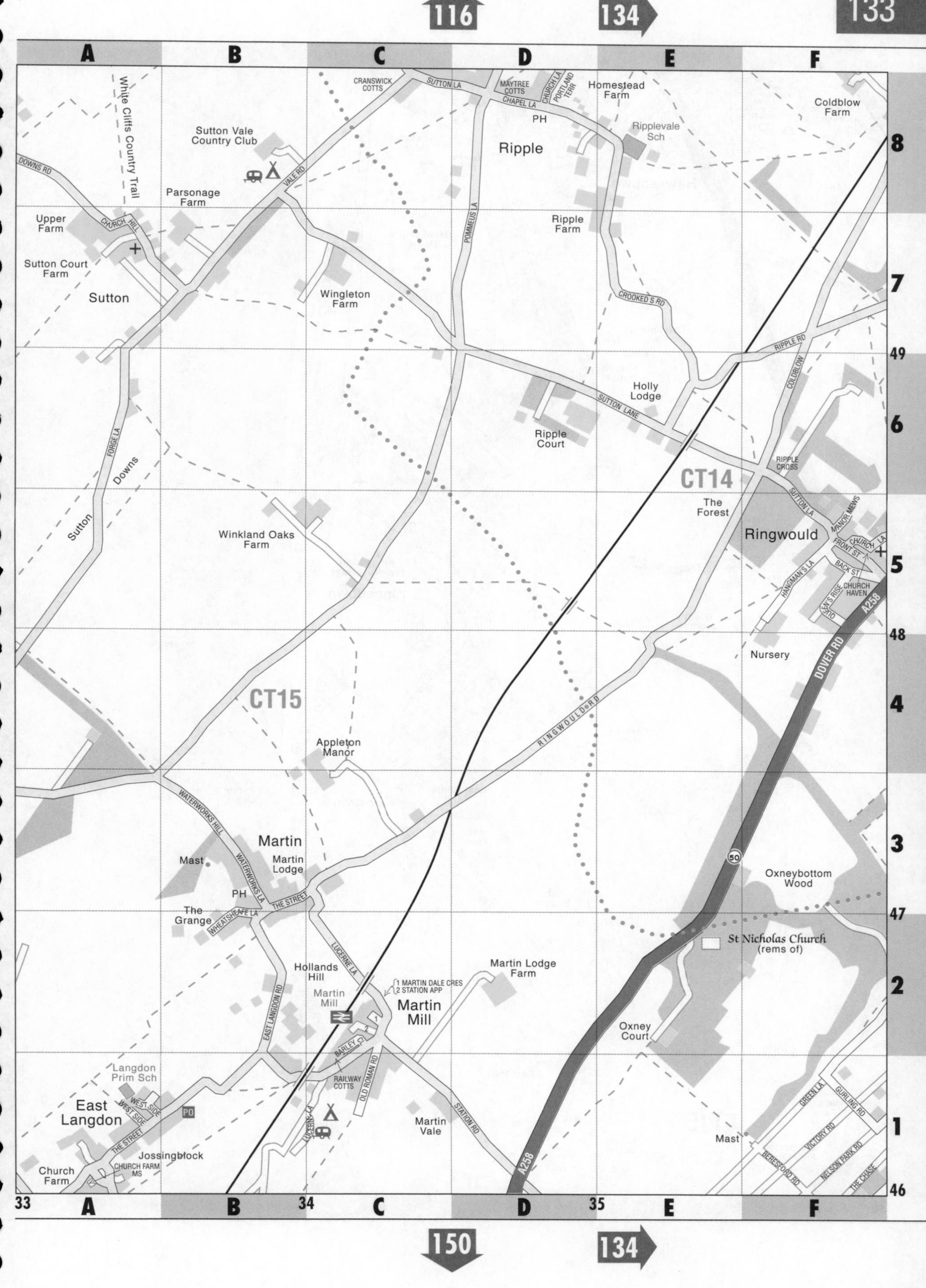
A
B
C
D
E
F
White Cliffs Country Trail
CRANSWICK COTTS
SUTTON LA
MAYTREE COTTS
CHAPEL LA
CHURCH LA
PORTLAND TERR
Homestead Farm
Coldblow Farm
Sutton Vale Country Club
PH
Ripplevale Sch
Ripple
DOWNS RD
VALE RD
Parsonage Farm
Upper Farm
CHURCH HILL
POMMEUS LA
Ripple Farm
Sutton Court Farm
Sutton
Wingleton Farm
CROOKED S RD
RIPPLE RD
COLDBLOW
PH
Holly Lodge
SUTTON LANE
Ripple Court
FORGE LA
Downs
Sutton
RIPPLE CROSS
CT14
The Forest
SUTTON LA
MANOR MEWS
Ringwould
CHURCH LA
FRONT ST
BACK ST
HANGMAN'S LA
QUEEN'S RISE
CHURCH HAVEN
Winkland Oaks Farm
A258
DOVER RD
Nursery
CT15
RINGWOULD RD
Appleton Manor
WATERWORKS HILL
Martin
Mast
Martin Lodge
WATERWORKS LA
PH
THE STREET
Oxneybottom Wood
The Grange
WHEATSHEAF LA
St Nicholas Church (rems of)
LUCERNE LA
Hollands Hill
1 MARTIN DALE CRES
2 STATION APP
Martin Lodge Farm
Martin Mill
Martin Mill
EAST LANGDON RD
BARLEY CL
Oxney Court
Langdon Prim Sch
RAILWAY COTTS
OLD ROMAN RD
East Langdon
WEST SIDE
PO
LUCERNE LA
Martin Vale
STATION RD
GREEN LA
GURLING RD
VICTORY RD
Mast
THE STREET
Jossingblock
CHURCH FARM MS
Church Farm
BERESFORD RD
NELSON PARK RD
THE CHASE
8
7
49
6
5
48
4
3
47
2
1
46
33
34
35

150
134

133
117

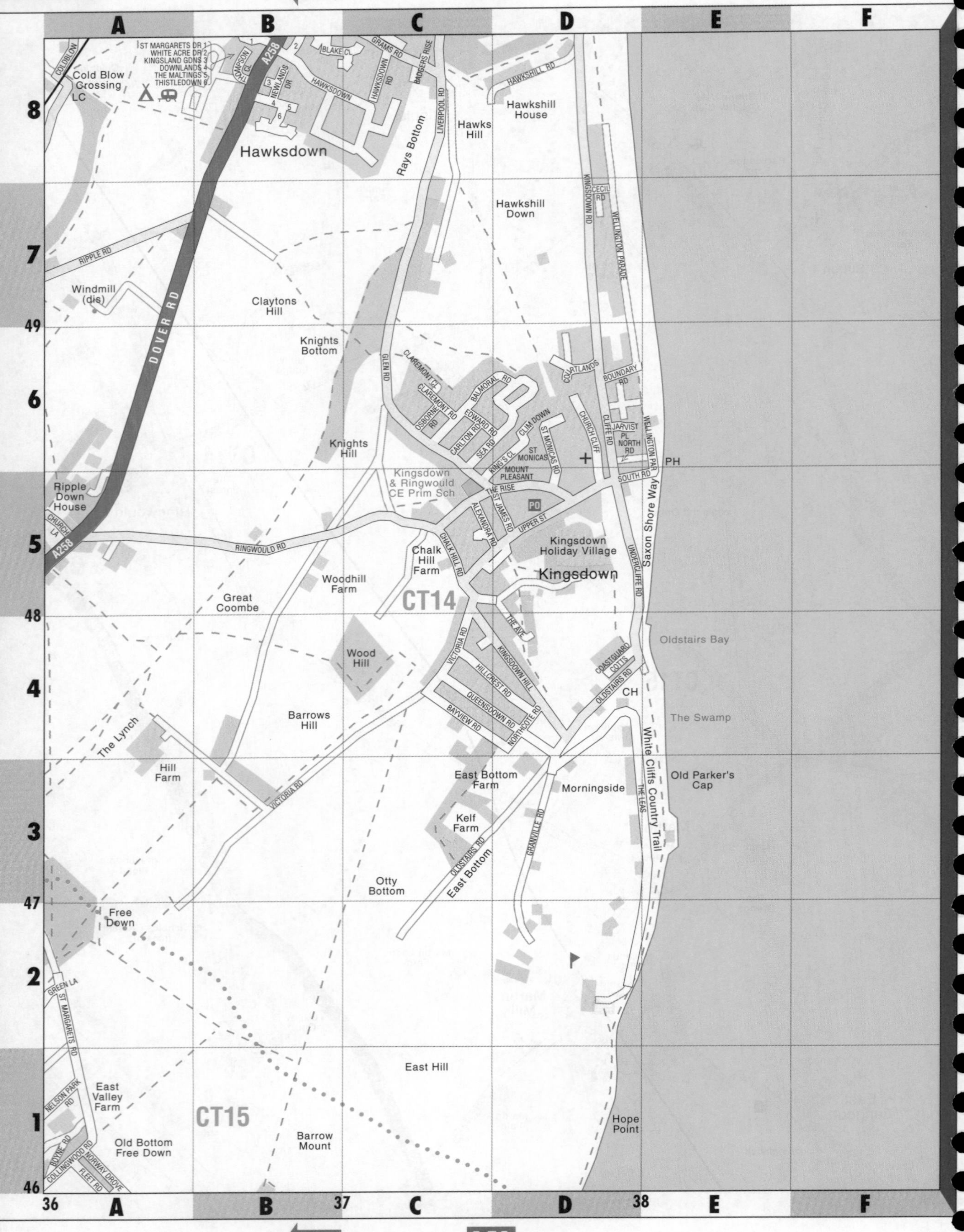
A
B
C
D
E
F
8
7
49
6
5
48
4
3
47
2
1
46
36
37
38
ST MARGARETS DR 1
WHITE ACRE DR 2
KINGSLAND GDNS 3
DOWNLANDS 4
THE MALTINGS 5
THISTLEDOWN 6
Cold Blow Crossing LC
Hawksdown
Rays Bottom
Hawks Hill
Hawkshill House
Hawkshill Down
HAWKSHILL RD
LIVERPOOL RD
BADGERS RISE
GRAMS RD
BLAKE CL
HAWKSDOWN RD
HAWKSDOWN
NEWLANDS DR
A258
DOVER RD
RIPPLE RD
Windmill (dis)
Claytons Hill
Knights Bottom
Knights Hill
Ripple Down House
CHURCH LA
RINGWOULD RD
Kingsdown & Ringwould CE Prim Sch
GLEN RD
CLAREMONT CL
CLAREMONT RD
OSBORNE RD
BALMORAL RD
EDWARD RD
CARLTON RD
SEA RD
KING'S CL
CLIM DOWN
ST MONICAS
ST MONICAS RD
MOUNT PLEASANT
CHURCH CLIFF
COURTLANDS
KINGSDOWN RD
CECIL RD
WELLINGTON PARADE
BOUNDARY RD
CLIFFE RD
JARVIST PL
NORTH RD
WELLINGTON PAR
SOUTH RD
PH
THE RISE
ST JAMES RD
ALEXANDRA RD
UPPER ST
PO
Kingsdown Holiday Village
Kingsdown
Saxon Shore Way
UNDERCLIFFE RD
Chalk Hill Farm
CHALK HILL RD
Woodhill Farm
Great Coombe
CT14
THE AVE
VICTORIA RD
KINGSDOWN HILL
HILLCREST RD
QUEENSDOWN RD
BAYVIEW RD
NORTHCOTE RD
COASTGUARD COTTS
OLDSTAIRS RD
CH
Oldstairs Bay
The Swamp
Wood Hill
Barrows Hill
The Lynch
Hill Farm
East Bottom Farm
Morningside
THE LEAS
White Cliffs Country Trail
Old Parker's Cap
Kelf Farm
GRANVILLE RD
OLDSTAIRS RD
East Bottom
Otty Bottom
Free Down
GREEN LA
ST MARGARETS RD
East Hill
East Valley Farm
NELSON PARK RD
CT15
Old Bottom Free Down
Barrow Mount
Hope Point
BOYNE RD
COLLINGWOOD RD
NORWAY DRIVE
FLEET RD

133
151

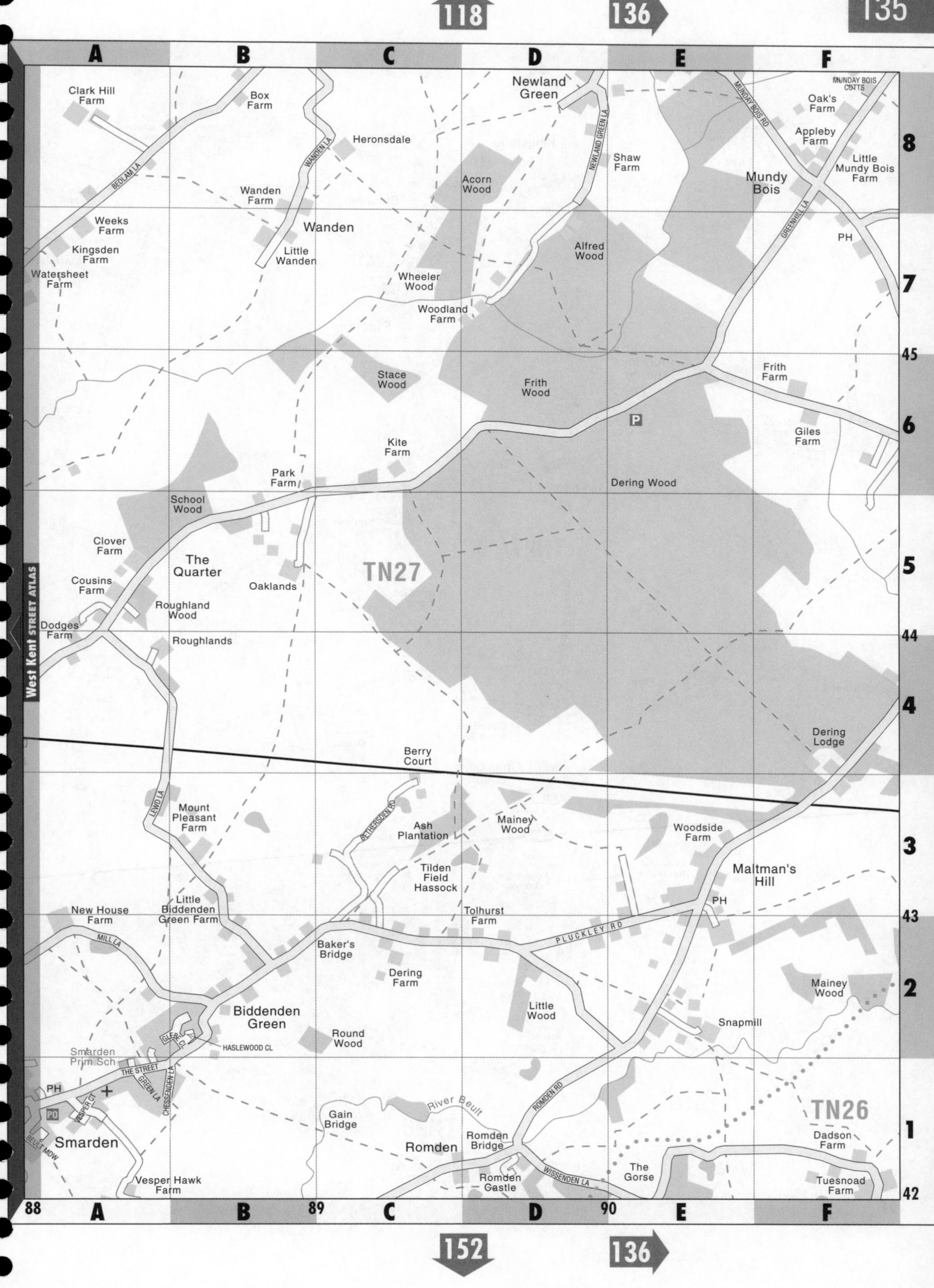

West Kent STREET ATLAS

Clark Hill Farm
Box Farm
Heronsdale
BEDLAM LA
WANDEN LA
Wanden Farm
Wanden
Little Wanden
Weeks Farm
Kingsden Farm
Watersheet Farm
Newland Green
NEWLAND GREEN LA
MUNDAY BOIS RD
MUNDAY BOIS COTTS
Oak's Farm
Appleby Farm
Little Mundy Bois Farm
Shaw Farm
Acorn Wood
Mundy Bois
GREENHILL LA
PH
Alfred Wood
Wheeler Wood
Woodland Farm
Stace Wood
Frith Wood
Frith Farm
Giles Farm
Kite Farm
P
Dering Wood
Park Farm
School Wood
Clover Farm
The Quarter
Oaklands
TN27
Cousins Farm
Roughland Wood
Dodges Farm
Roughlands
Dering Lodge
Berry Court
ERWD LA
Mount Pleasant Farm
RETHERSDEN RD
Ash Plantation
Mainey Wood
Woodside Farm
Maltman's Hill
Tilden Field Hassock
PH
Little Biddenden Green Farm
Tolhurst Farm
PLUCKLEY RD
New House Farm
MILL LA
Baker's Bridge
Dering Farm
Biddenden Green
GLEB...
HASLEWOOD CL
Round Wood
Little Wood
Snapmill
Mainey Wood
Smarden Prim Sch
THE STREET
GREEN LA
CHESSENDEN LA
PESPER CT
PH
PO
River Beult
ROMDEN RD
TN26
Smarden
BEULT MDW
Gain Bridge
Romden
Romden Bridge
WISSENDEN LA
The Gorse
Dadson Farm
Vesper Hawk Farm
Romden Castle
Tuesnoad Farm

88 89 90

A B C D E F

8 7 45 6 5 44 4 3 43 2 1 42

← 135
↑ 119

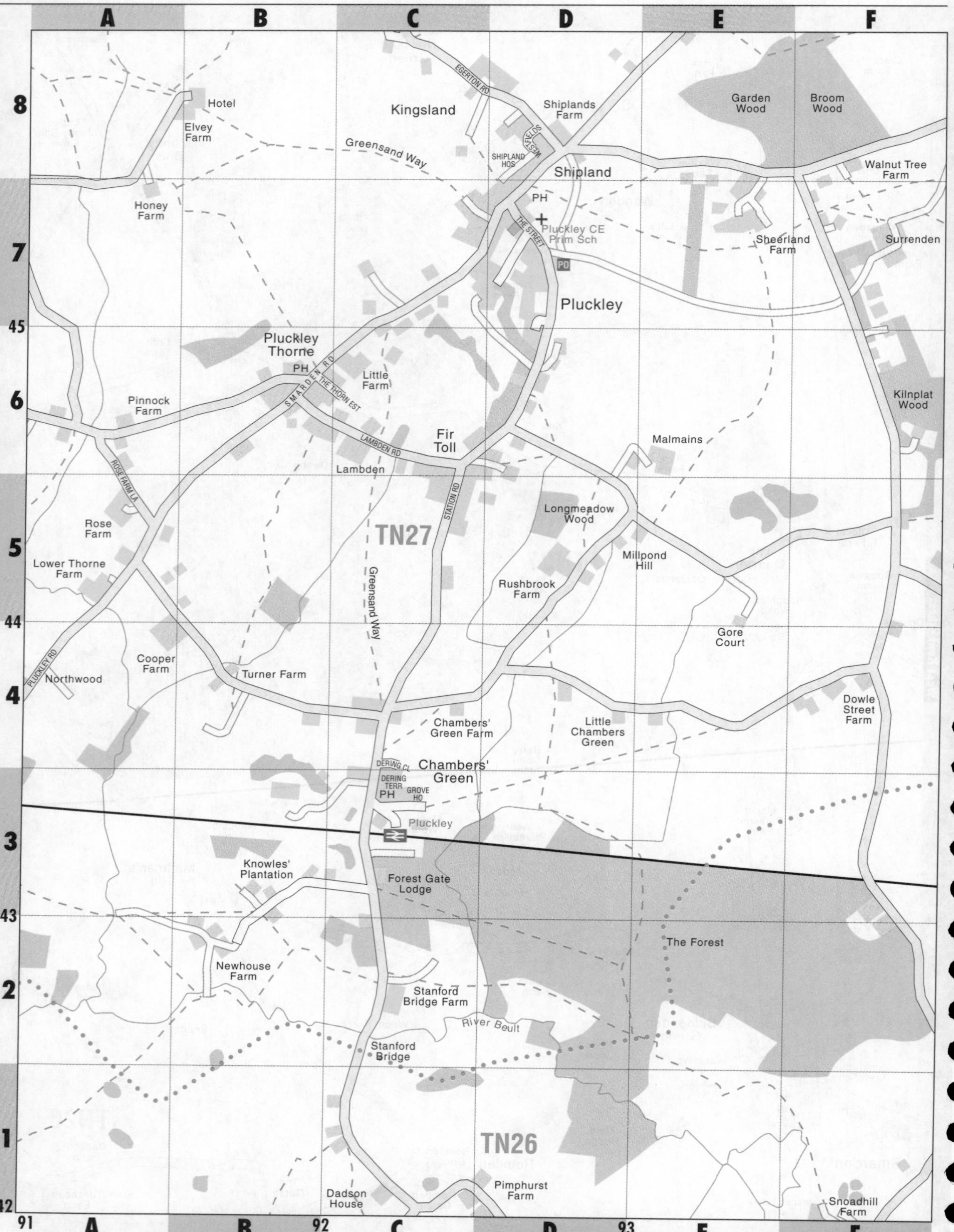

A B C D E F

8

Kingsland

Shiplands
Farm

Garden
Wood

Broom
Wood

Hotel

Elvey
Farm

Greensand Way

EGERTON RD

SHIPLAND
HOS

Shipland

Walnut Tree
Farm

PH

Pluckley CE
Prim Sch

THE STREET

Sheerland
Farm

Surrenden

7

45

Honey
Farm

PO

Pluckley

Pluckley
Thorne

PH

SMARDEN RD

THE THORN EST

Little
Farm

Kilnplat
Wood

6

Pinnock
Farm

LAMBDEN RD

Fir
Toll

Lambden

STATION RD

Malmains

Rose
Farm

ROSE FARM LA

TN27

Longmeadow
Wood

Millpond
Hill

5

44

Lower Thorne
Farm

Greensand Way

Rushbrook
Farm

Gore
Court

PLUCKLEY RD

Cooper
Farm

Turner Farm

Dowle
Street
Farm

4

Northwood

Chambers'
Green Farm

Little
Chambers
Green

DERWG CL

DERING
TERR PH

Chambers'
Green

GROVE
HO

3

Knowles'
Plantation

Pluckley

Forest Gate
Lodge

43

The Forest

Newhouse
Farm

2

Stanford
Bridge Farm

River Beult

Stanford
Bridge

1

TN26

42

Dadson
House

Pimphurst
Farm

Snoadhill
Farm

91   A   B   92   C   D   93   E   F

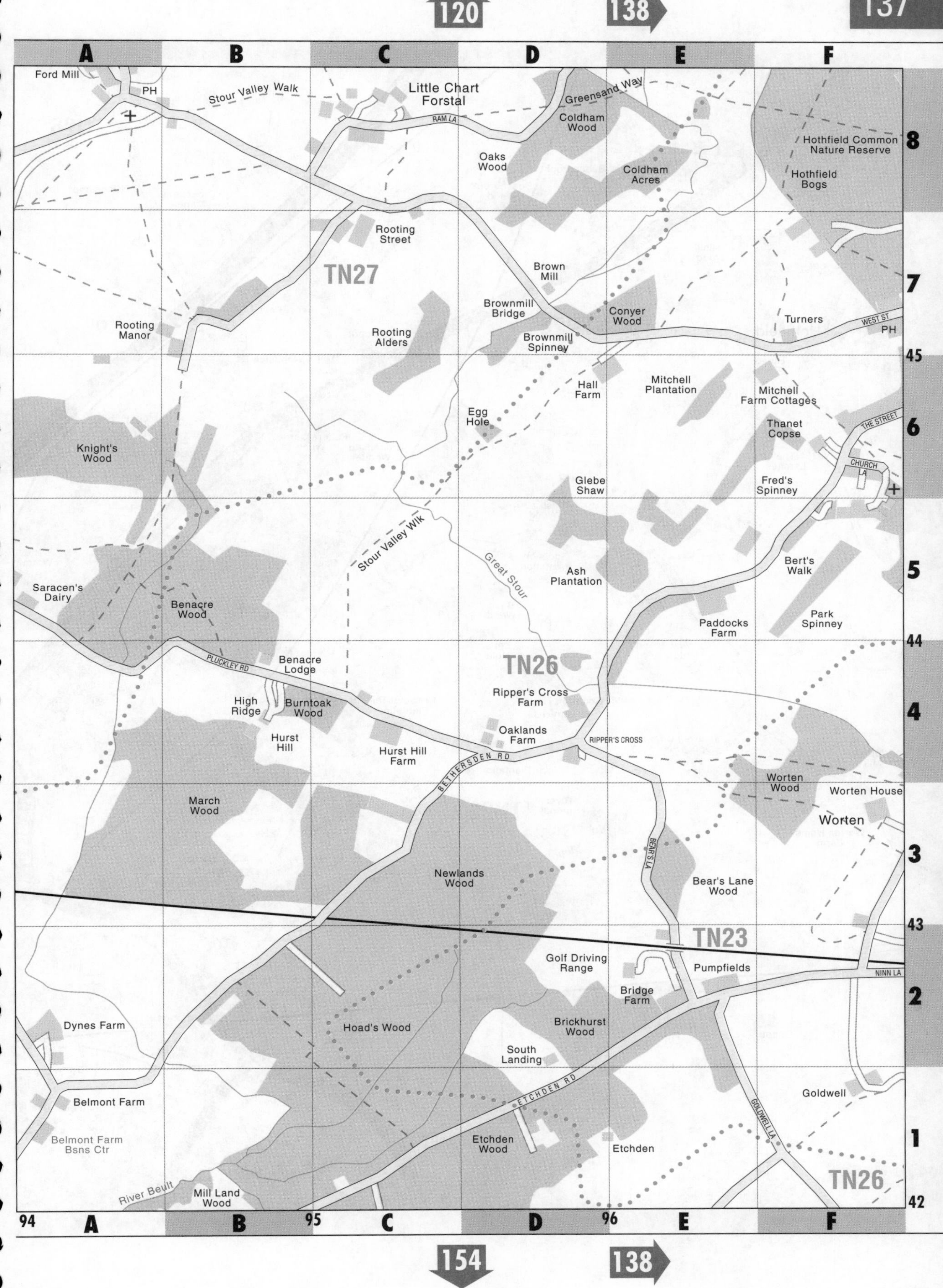

A   B   C   D   E   F

Ford Mill
PH
Stour Valley Walk
Little Chart Forstal
Greensand Way
Coldham Wood
RAM LA
Hothfield Common Nature Reserve
8
Oaks Wood
Coldham Acres
Hothfield Bogs

Rooting Street
TN27
Brown Mill
7
Brownmill Bridge
Conyer Wood
Turners
WEST ST
PH
Rooting Manor
Rooting Alders
Brownmill Spinney
45
Hall Farm
Mitchell Plantation
Mitchell Farm Cottages
Egg Hole
Thanet Copse
THE STREET
6
Knight's Wood
CHURCH LA
Glebe Shaw
Fred's Spinney

Stour Valley Wlk
Great Stour
Ash Plantation
Bert's Walk
5
Saracen's Dairy
Benacre Wood
Paddocks Farm
Park Spinney
PLUCKLEY RD
Benacre Lodge
44
TN26
Ripper's Cross Farm
4
High Ridge
Burntoak Wood
Oaklands Farm
RIPPER'S CROSS
Hurst Hill
Hurst Hill Farm
BETHERSDEN RD
Worten Wood
Worten House
March Wood
Worten
Newlands Wood
BEAR'S LA
Bear's Lane Wood
3
43
TN23
Golf Driving Range
Pumpfields
NINN LA
2
Dynes Farm
Bridge Farm
Hoad's Wood
Brickhurst Wood
Goldwell
GOLDWELL LA
Belmont Farm
South Landing
Belmont Farm Bsns Ctr
ETCHDEN RD
Etchden Wood
Etchden
TN26
1
River Beult
Mill Land Wood
42

137
121

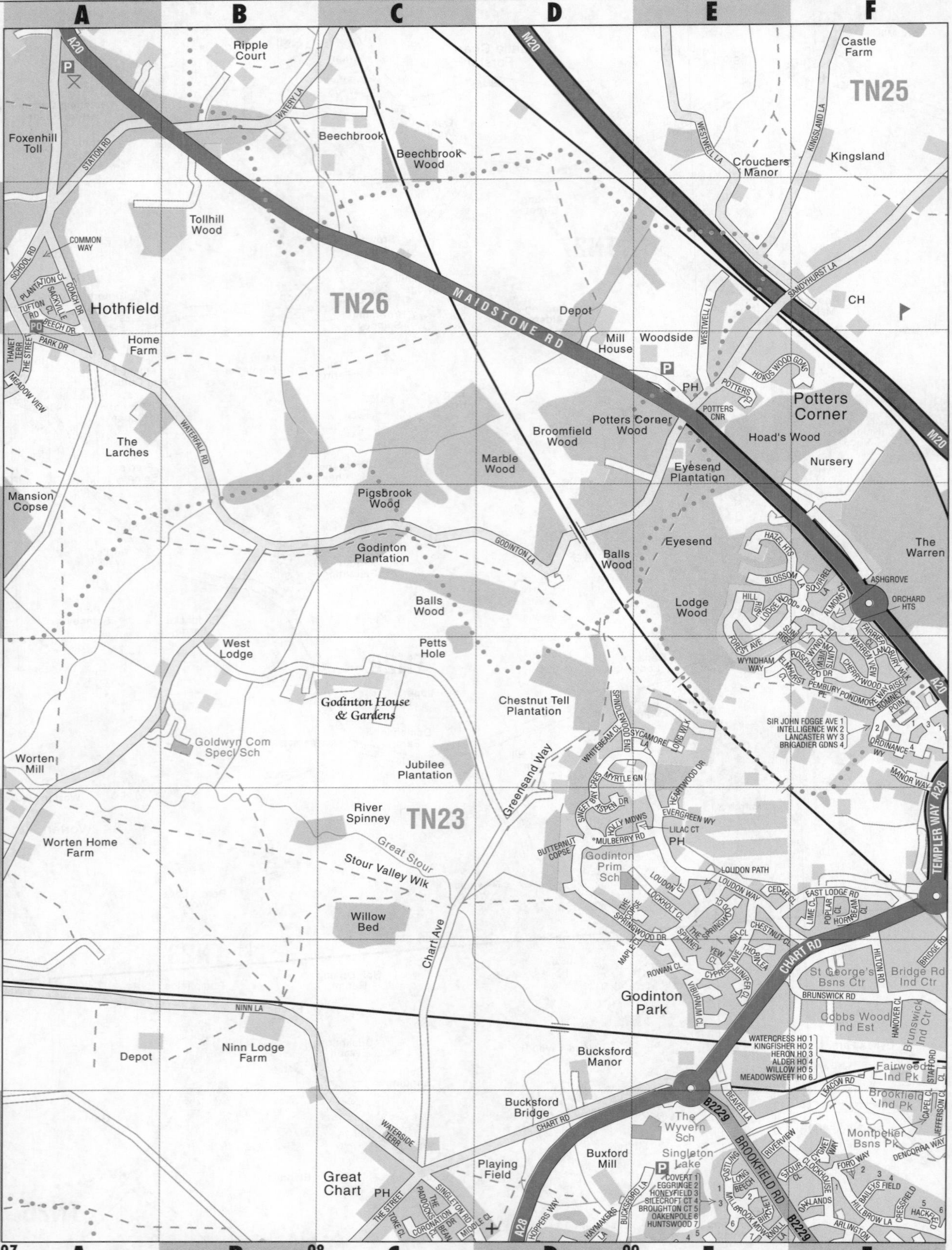

A B C D E F

8

TN25

Ripple Court

Castle Farm

A20

Foxenhill Toll

Beechbrook

Beechbrook Wood

WATERY LA

WESTWELL LA

Crouchers Manor

Kingsland

KINGSLAND LA

7

Tollhill Wood

TN26

MAIDSTONE RD

SANDYHURST LA

CH

STATION RD

Hothfield

COMMON WAY

PLANTATION CL
LUFTON RD
SACKVILLE DR
BEECH DR
COACH DR

PO

THANET TERR
THE STREET
PARK DR

Depot

Mill House

Woodside

45

Home Farm

WATERFALL RD

PH

Potters Corner Wood

Potters Corner

HOAD'S WOOD GDN

POTTERS CNR

HILL RISE

MEADOW VIEW

6

The Larches

Broomfield Wood

Marble Wood

Eyesend Plantation

Hoad's Wood

Nursery

Potters Corner

M20

Mansion Copse

Pigsbrook Wood

Godinton Plantation

GODINTON LA

Balls Wood

Eyesend

The Warren

HAZEL HTS
BLOSSOM LA
SORREL
LAYMOND
ROSEWOOD DR

5

Godinton Plantation

Balls Wood

Lodge Wood

ASHGROVE
ORCHARD HTS

HILL RISE
FOREST AVE
WARREN VIEW
FAIRMEAD
PEMBURY FE
POND MOOR

44

West Lodge

Petts Hole

WYNDHAM WAY

A20

4

Goldwyn Com Spec Sch

Godinton House & Gardens

Chestnut Tell Plantation

LONG WLK

SYCAMORE LA

SIR JOHN FOGGE AVE 1
INTELLIGENCE WK 2
LANCASTER WY 3
BRIGADIER GDNS 4

ORDNANCE WY

MANOR WAY

Worten Mill

Jubilee Plantation

GREENSAND WAY

WHITEBEAM CL
SPRINGWOOD END
ASPEN LA

HEARTWOOD DR

EVERGREEN WY

LILAC CT

TEMPLER WAY A28

3

Worten Home Farm

River Spinney

TN23

Great Stour

Stour Valley Wlk

CHART AVE

SWEET BRIAR CRES
MYRTLE GDN

HOLLY MDWS

MULBERRY RD

PH

BUTTERNUT COPSE

Godinton Prim Sch

LOUDON PATH

LOUDON WAY
LOCKHOLT CL

CEDAR

EAST LODGE RD

LIME CL
POPLAR CL
HORNBEAM CL

BRIDGE RD

43

Willow Bed

THE BIRCHES
SPRINGWOOD DR

MAPLE CL

CHESTNUT CL

YEW CL
THORN CL
ROWAN CL

CYPRESS AVE
JUNIPER CL

LABURNUM AVE

CHART RD

St George's Bsns Ctr

Bridge Rd Ind Ctr

2

NINN LA

Godinton Park

BRUNSWICK RD

Cobbs Wood Ind Est

HANOVER CL

BRUNSWICK IND CTR
STAFFORD CL

Depot

Ninn Lodge Farm

Bucksford Manor

WATERCRESS HO 1
KINGFISHER HO 2
HERON HO 3
ALDER HO 4
WILLOW HO 5
MEADOWSWEET HO 6

Fairwood Ind Pk

Buckford Bridge

WATERSIDE TERR

CHART RD

The Wyvern Sch

Singleton Lake

BEAVER LA

BROOKFIELD RD

B2229

BUYLVERN

Brookfield Ind Pk

Montpelier Bsns Pk

DENCORRA WAY

1

Great Chart

PH

THE STREET

CORONATION DR

SINGLETON RD
MIDDLE CL

Playing Field

HOPPERS WAY

A28

Buxford Mill

P

COVERT 1
EGGRINGE 2
HONEYFIELD 3
BILECROFT CT 4
BROUGHTON CT 5
OAKENPOLE 6
HUNTSWOOD 7

LONG BEECH

PENTLING CL

LEACON RD

FORD WAY

OAKLANDS

HILLBROW LA

B2229

ARLINGTON

42

97 A 98 B C 99 D E F

137
155

Map grid references A–F (columns), 1–8 (rows)

Key place names and labels:

TN25, TN24, TN23, TN25

ASHFORD

Kennington, Kennington Lees, Goat Lees, Bockhanger, Bybrook, Barrow Hill, Golden Ball

Tile Lodge Wood, Lenacre Hall Farm, The Towers Sch, Ulley Farm, Wilmington Farm, Kennington Hall, Alders, Sandyhurst Farm

Downs View Inf Sch, Kennington CE Jun Sch, Kennington CE Prim Sch, Kings Meadow, Osier Field, St Marys Gn

Phoenix Com Prim Sch, Bockhanger Liby, Spearpoint Cnr

Eurogate Bsns Pk, Eureka L Pk, Superstore, Hotel, Warren Ret Pk, Drovers Rdbt

St Teresas RC Prim Sch, Highworth Gram Sch for Girls, Ashford Civil Ceremony Off, Cemy, Hotel, Copperwood

Sewage Works, Water Tower, Factory, Julie Rose Athletics Stadium

James Haney Dr, Great Burton Ho, Penlee Point

Ashford Sch of Art & Design, Highpoint Bsns Village, Heron Bsns Ctr, Kingfisher Bsns Pk, Henwood Bsns Ctr, Javelin Enterprise Pk, Henwood Ind Est, Works, Mace Ind Est

Riverside Bsns Pk, Ashford Sch, East Hill, Stour Valley Wlk, The Norton Knatchbull Sch

Ashford St Mary's CE Prim Sch, Chart Road Ind Est, Ind Est, Fairwood Ind Est

ASHFORD, Cty & Mag Ct Liby, PO, Godinton Way Ind Est, The Stour Ctr, C Ctr

Victoria Park, Victoria Road Prim Sch, Victoria Road Ind Pk, Hillyfields Rise, The Ray Clements Skate Pk, The North Sch, Ashford Int

Major roads: A251, A2042, A28, A20, A292, A2070, A20, M20, A2042

Road/street names: TRINITY RD, FAVERSHAM RD, CANTERBURY RD, WILLESBOROUGH RD, FOUGERES WAY, SIMONE WEIL AVE, MAIDSTONE RD, CHART RD, NEW ST, SOMERSET RD, STATION RD, ELWICK RD, MACE LA, HYTHE RD, HIGH ST, TUFTON ST, LOWER QUEENS RD, QUEENS RD

Street index:

B2
1 ENGINEERS CT
2 PARK MALL
3 ST GEORGE'S SQ
4 GILBERT RD
5 NEW RENTS
6 CASTLE ST
7 KINGS PAR
8 COUNTY SQ
9 TUFTON WLK
10 CHURCH YARD PAS
11 HEMPSTED ST
12 MARKET LA
13 ELWICK LA
14 REGENTS CT
15 Ashford Borough Mus
16 County Square Sh Ctr
17 British MK IV Tank

B3
1 BARROW HILL TERR
2 BARROW HILL PL
3 GRAVEL WLK
4 WOLSELEY PL

C2
1 KNOTTS SQ
2 CHAPEL MEWS
3 MIDDLE ROW
4 CHURCH YD
5 ASHDALE HO
6 COLLEGE CT
7 LESLEY CHALK HO
8 Ashford Sch of Art & Design

139   123

A   B   C   D   E   F

8
7
45
6
5
44
4
43
3
2
42

A28 CANTERBURY RD A28

Wilmington Farm

EAST MOUNTAIN LA

Stour Valley Walk

The Hermitage

Withersdane Green

Withersdane

OSBORN RD

GRIFFIN'S CNR

HERON'S BROOK

Great Stour

Raymond Court Cottages

Naccolt

POTTERY COTTS

Sewage Works

NAT'S LA

Stour Valley Wlk

Bourne Dyke

TN25

Appleby Farm

Sillibourne Farm

Blackwall Farm

Great Bromley Farm

BLACKWALL RD

Chapel Bridge

Sales Wood

Moneytree Farm

Conningbrook Manor

A2070 WILLESBOROUGH RD

Goodcheap Farm

GOODCHEAP LA

Plumpton Farm

Longport Bridge

TN24

Goose Green

Boarfield Wood

BLACKWALL RD N

Lees Farm

KINGS CHASE

WILLOW BANK

BLACKWALL RD S

Flowergarden Wood

Court Lodge Farm

Alders

KENNINGTON RD

LEESWOOD

WILSON CL

Willesborough Lees

Sweetwillow Wood

Hinxhill

WALL HILL CL

ABBEY WAY

FOUNTAINS

SILVER HILL RD

LEES RD

SANDY LA

HINXHILL RD

Ouseley Farm

South Oaks

BOCKHAM LA

Windmill

HYTHE RD

A292

CORALS CL

LEES RD

YEOMAN GDNS

A2070

M20

William Harvey

P

H

1 REDYEAR CT
2 REDYEAR COTTS
3 WILLESBOROUGH IND PK
4 SILVER HILL GDNS
5 WINDMILL CL
6 FIELD END

03   A   B   04   C   D   05   E   F

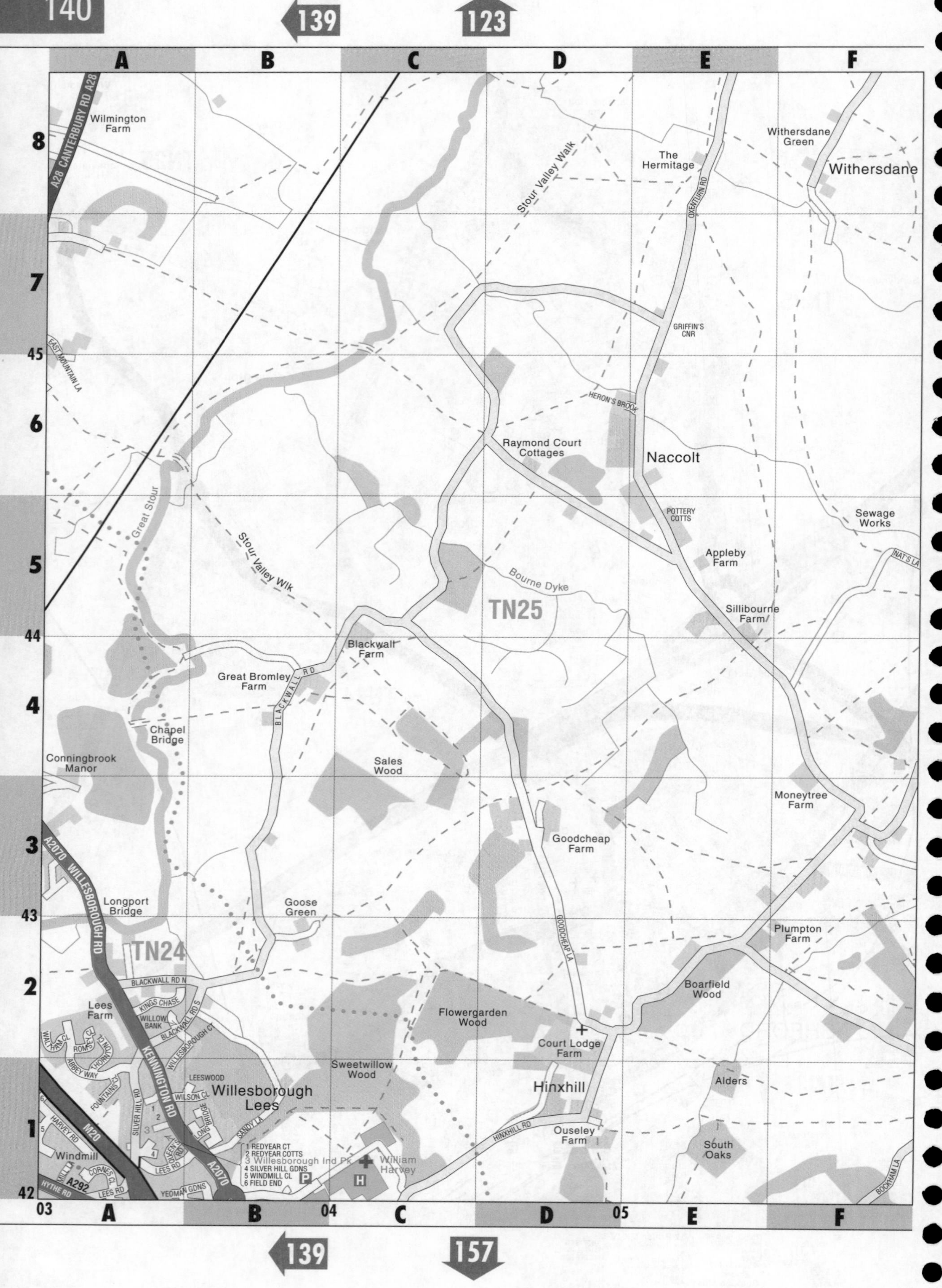

124
142

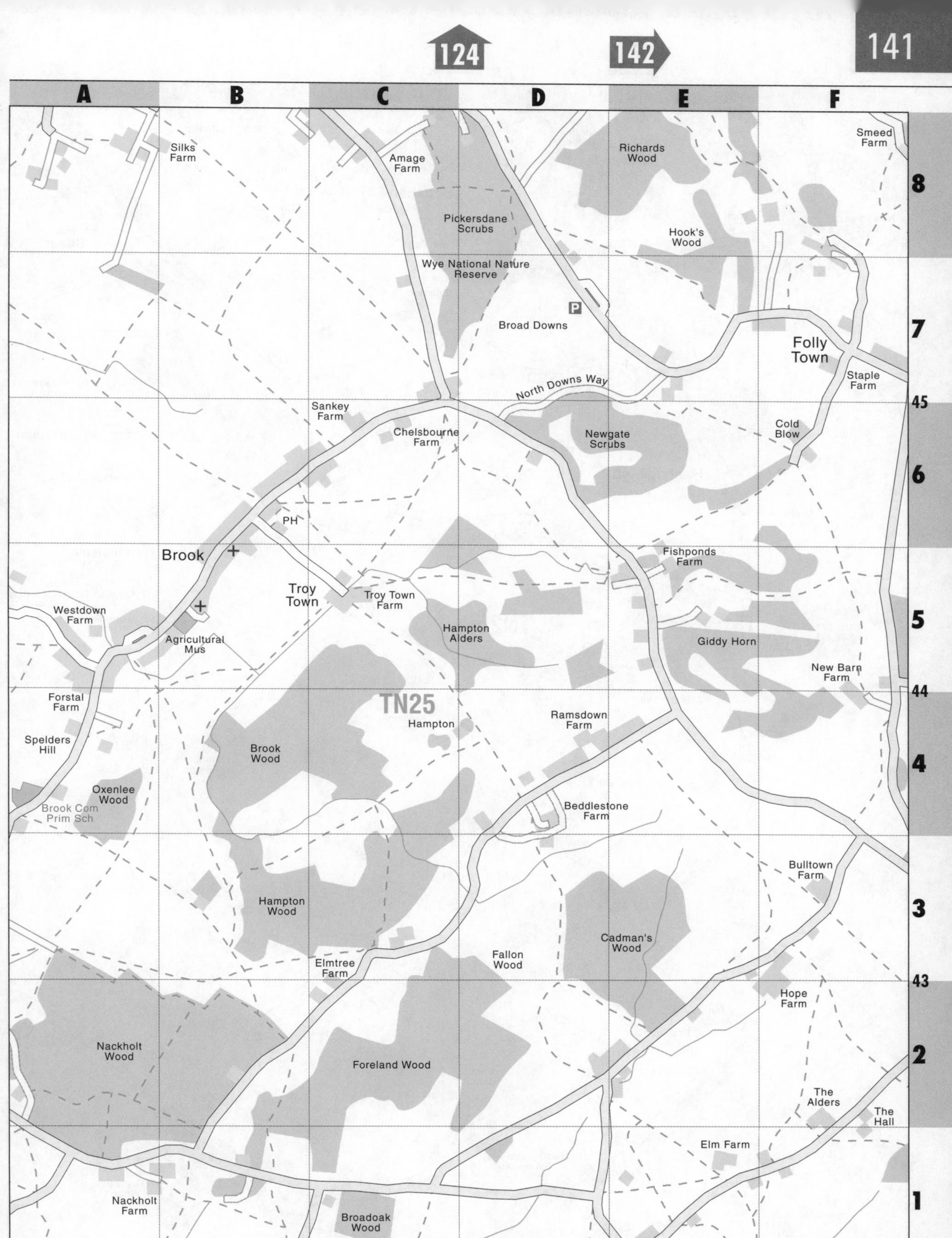
A
B
C
D
E
F
Silks Farm
Amage Farm
Richards Wood
Smeed Farm
8
Pickersdane Scrubs
Hook's Wood
Wye National Nature Reserve
P
Broad Downs
7
Folly Town
Staple Farm
North Downs Way
45
Sankey Farm
Chelsbourne Farm
Newgate Scrubs
Cold Blow
6
PH
Brook
Fishponds Farm
Troy Town
Troy Town Farm
Westdown Farm
Hampton Alders
5
Giddy Horn
Agricultural Mus
New Barn Farm
44
Forstal Farm
TN25
Hampton
Ramsdown Farm
Spelders Hill
Brook Wood
4
Oxenlee Wood
Brook Com Prim Sch
Beddlestone Farm
Bulltown Farm
Hampton Wood
3
Cadman's Wood
Fallon Wood
Elmtree Farm
43
Hope Farm
Nackholt Wood
Foreland Wood
2
The Alders
The Hall
Elm Farm
1
Nackholt Farm
Broadoak Wood
Burch Farmhouse
42
06
07
08

158
142

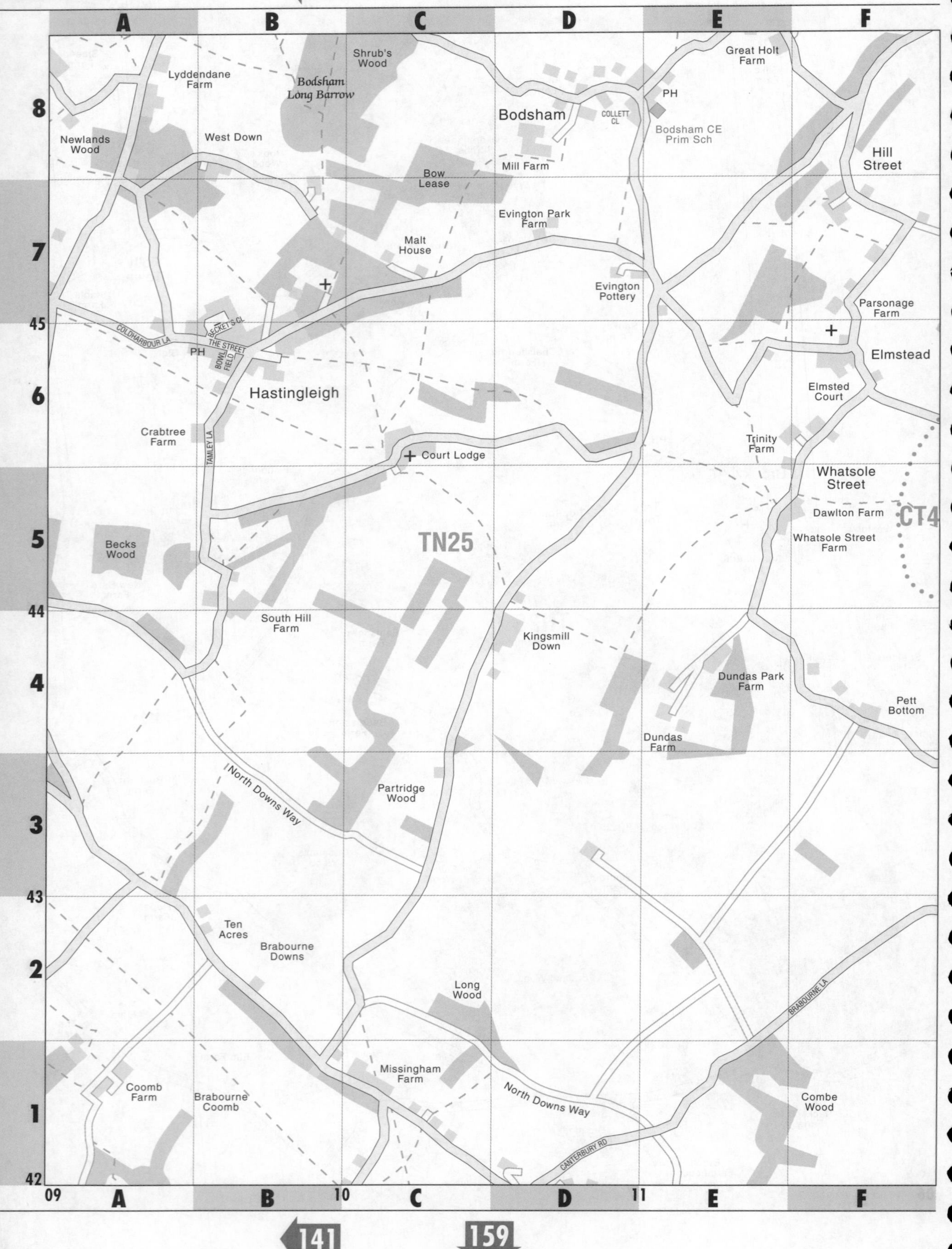

Lyddendane Farm

Shrub's Wood

Bodsham Long Barrow

Great Holt Farm

Bodsham

PH

Collett Cl

Bodsham CE Prim Sch

Hill Street

Newlands Wood

West Down

Bow Lease

Mill Farm

Evington Park Farm

Parsonage Farm

Malt House

Coldharbour La

The Street

Becket's Cl

PH

Bowl Field

Hastingleigh

Evington Pottery

Elmstead

Crabtree Farm

Tamley La

Court Lodge

Elmsted Court

Trinity Farm

Whatsole Street

Dawlton Farm

CT4

TN25

Whatsole Street Farm

Becks Wood

Kingsmill Down

South Hill Farm

Dundas Park Farm

Pett Bottom

Dundas Farm

North Downs Way

Partridge Wood

Ten Acres

Brabourne Downs

Long Wood

Brabourne La

Coomb Farm

Brabourne Coomb

Missingham Farm

North Downs Way

Combe Wood

Canterbury Rd

09 A B 10 C D 11 E F

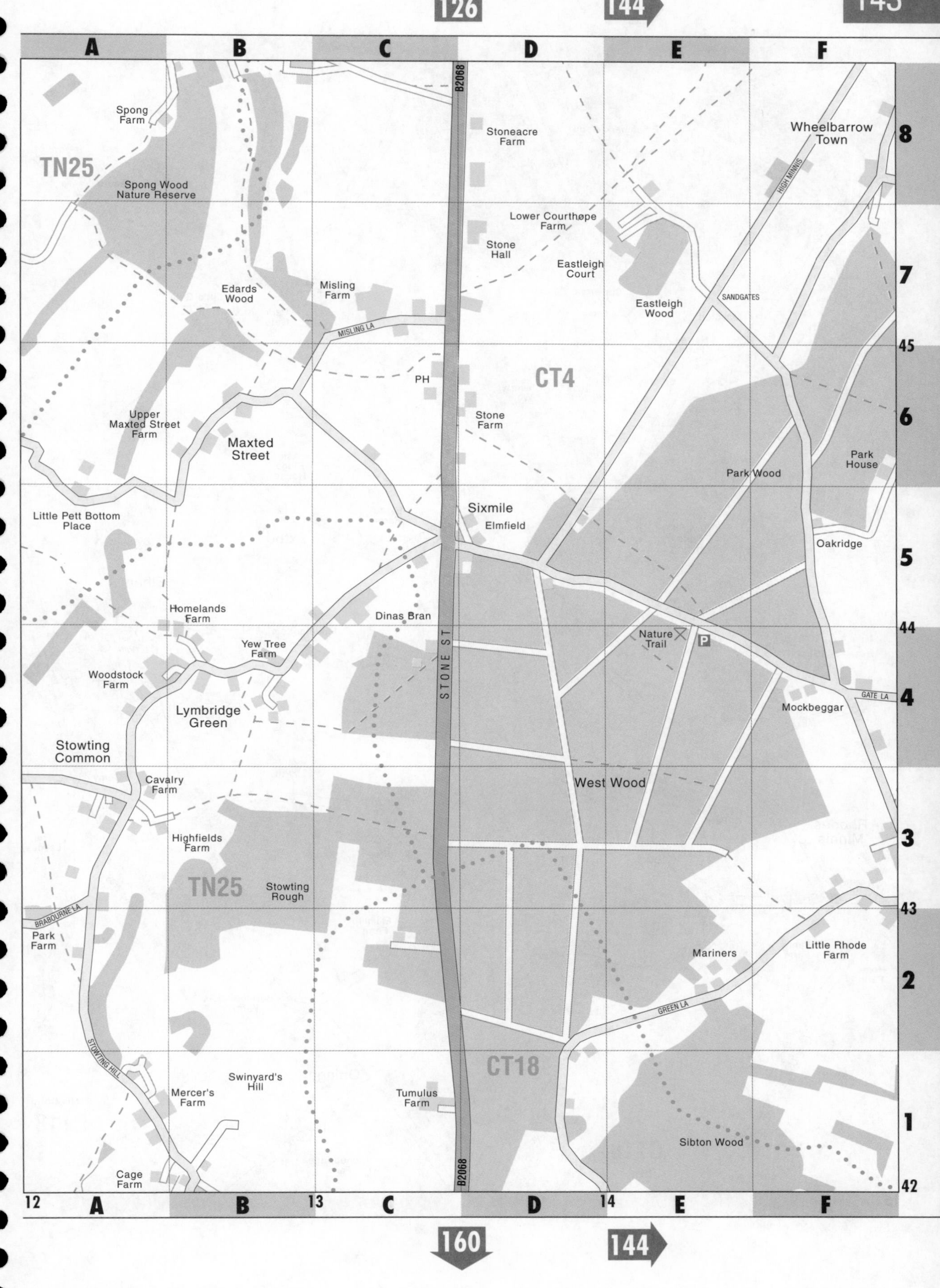
126
144
A
B
C
D
E
F
8
7
45
6
5
44
4
3
43
2
1
42
12
13
14
160
144
Spong Farm
TN25
Spong Wood Nature Reserve
Edards Wood
Misling Farm
MISLING LA
B2068
Stoneacre Farm
Lower Courthope Farm
Stone Hall
Eastleigh Court
Eastleigh Wood
SANDGATES
HIGH MINNIS
Wheelbarrow Town
PH
CT4
Stone Farm
Upper Maxted Street Farm
Maxted Street
Park Wood
Park House
Little Pett Bottom Place
Sixmile
Elmfield
Oakridge
Homelands Farm
Dinas Bran
Nature Trail
P
Yew Tree Farm
Woodstock Farm
STONE ST
GATE LA
Mockbeggar
Lymbridge Green
Stowting Common
Cavalry Farm
West Wood
Highfields Farm
TN25
Stowting Rough
BRABOURNE LA
Park Farm
Mariners
Little Rhode Farm
GREEN LA
STOWTING HILL
CT18
Swinyard's Hill
Mercer's Farm
Tumulus Farm
Sibton Wood
Cage Farm

143
127

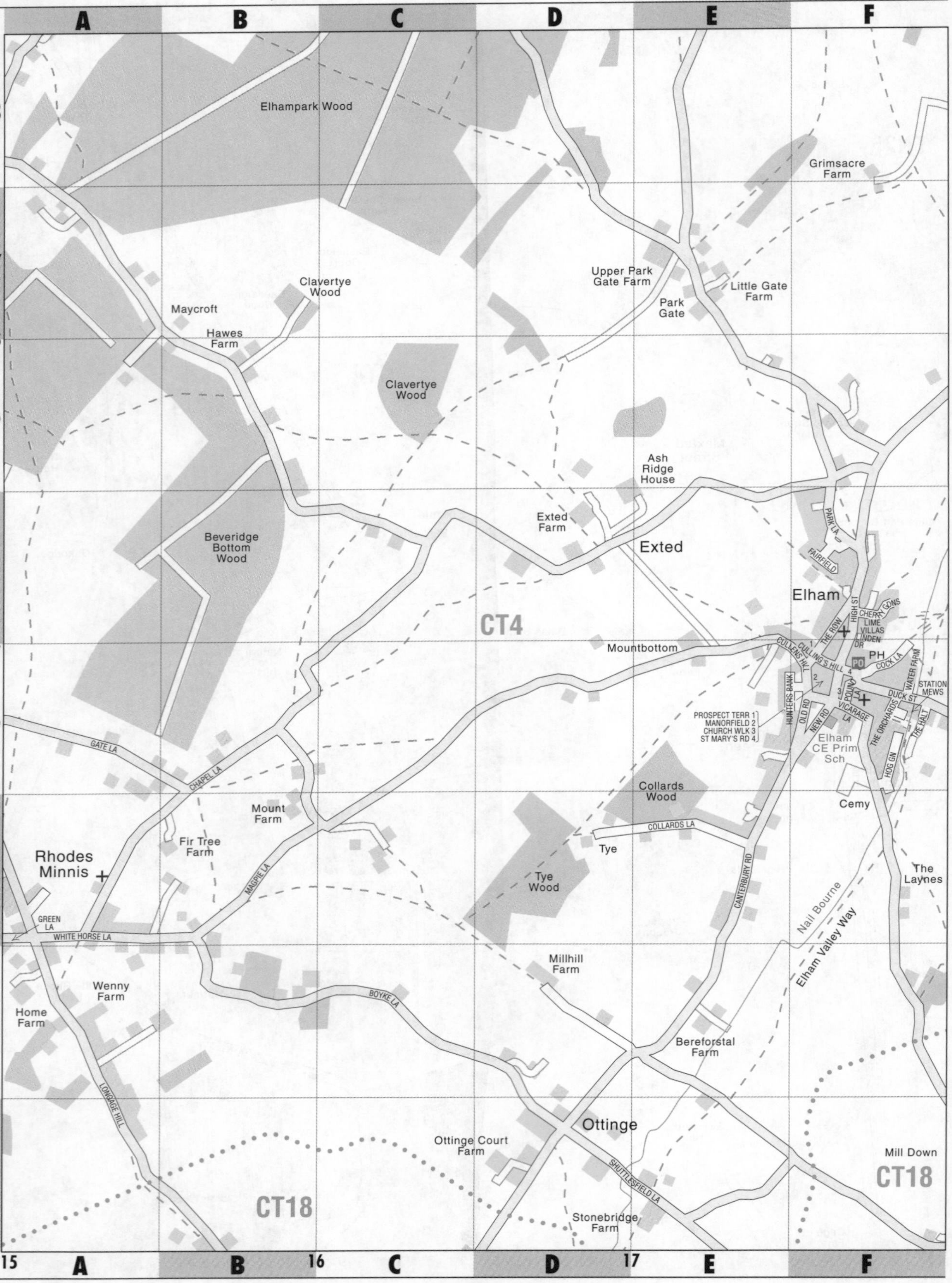

A B C D E F

8

Elhampark Wood

7

Upper Park
Gate Farm

Grimsacre
Farm

Clavertye
Wood

Maycroft

Little Gate
Farm

45

Park
Gate

Hawes
Farm

6

Clavertye
Wood

Ash
Ridge
House

Beveridge
Bottom
Wood

5

Exted
Farm

Exted

Elham

44

CT4

Mountbottom

PH
PO
CHERRY
LIME
VILLAS
LINDEN
THE ROW
HIGH ST
CULLING'S HILL
FAIRFIELD
PARK LA

STATION
MEWS
WATER FARM
DUCK ST
COCK LA

4

GATE LA

CHAPEL LA

Collards
Wood

PROSPECT TERR 1
MANORFIELD 2
CHURCH WLK 3
ST MARY'S RD 4

Elham
CE Prim
Sch

VICARAGE
LA
NEW RD
OLD RD
HUNTERS BANK

THE ORCHARDS
HOG GN
THE CULVERS
DR HALT

Cemy

Mount
Farm

Fir Tree
Farm

COLLARDS LA

Tye

The
Laynes

Rhodes
Minnis

3

MAGPIE LA

Tye
Wood

CANTERBURY RD

Nail Bourne

43

GREEN
LA

WHITE HORSE LA

Millhill
Farm

Elham Valley Way

2

Wenny
Farm

BOYKE LA

Home
Farm

Bereforstal
Farm

LONGAGE HILL

Ottinge

Ottinge Court
Farm

Mill Down
CT18

1

CT18

SHUTTLESFIELD LA

Stonebridge
Farm

42

15 A B 16 C D 17 E F

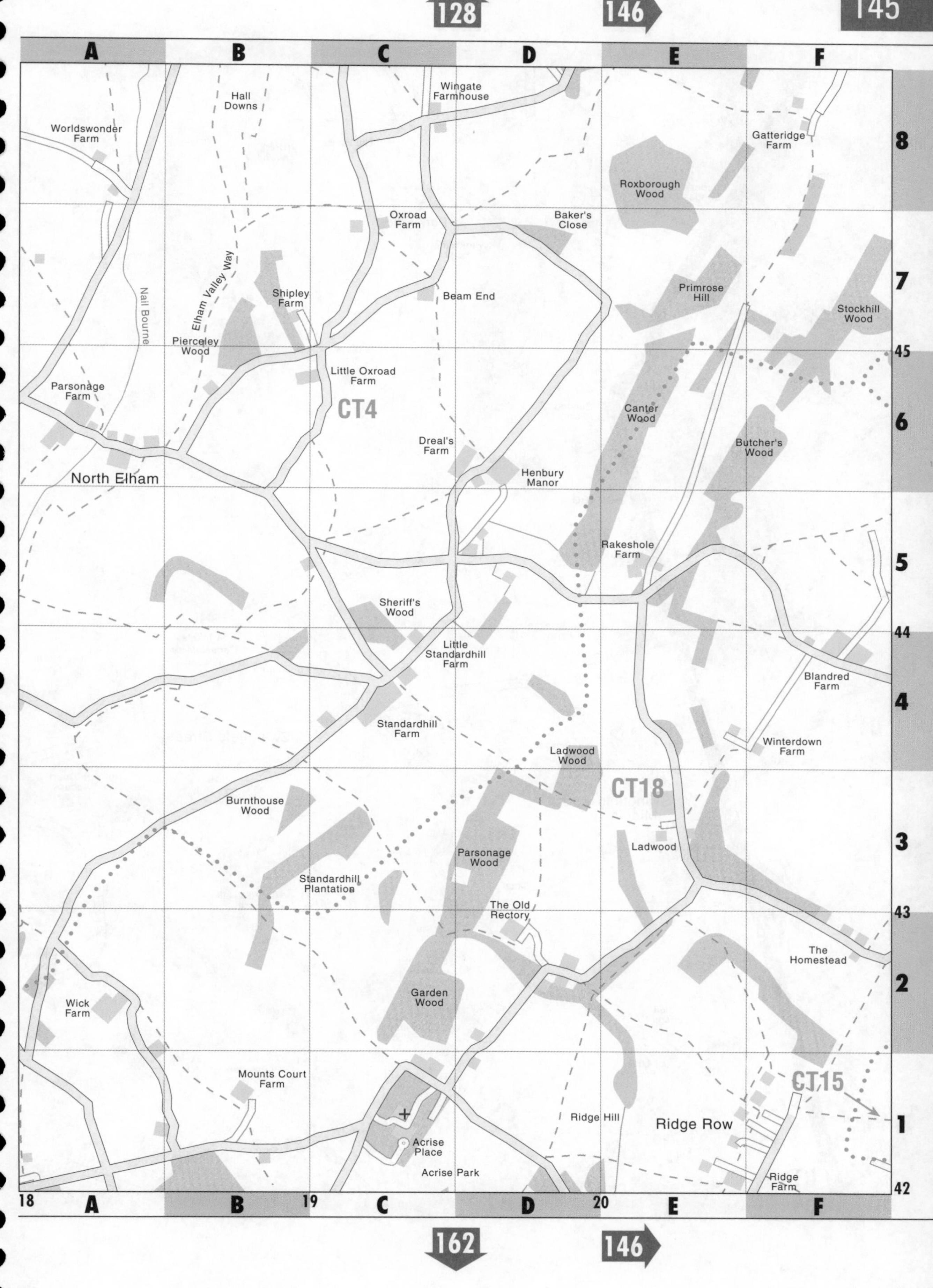

A B C D E F

8 7 45 6 5 44 4 3 43 2 1 42

18 A B 19 C 20 D E F

Worldswonder Farm
Hall Downs
Wingate Farmhouse
Gatteridge Farm
Roxborough Wood
Oxroad Farm
Baker's Close
Nail Bourne
Elham Valley Way
Shipley Farm
Beam End
Primrose Hill
Stockhill Wood
Pierceley Wood
Little Oxroad Farm
CT4
Canter Wood
Butcher's Wood
Parsonage Farm
Dreal's Farm
Henbury Manor
North Elham
Rakeshole Farm
Sheriff's Wood
Little Standardhill Farm
Blandred Farm
Standardhill Farm
Ladwood Wood
CT18
Winterdown Farm
Burnthouse Wood
Ladwood
Standardhill Plantation
Parsonage Wood
The Old Rectory
The Homestead
Wick Farm
Garden Wood
Mounts Court Farm
Acrise Place
Ridge Hill
Ridge Row
CT15
Acrise Park
Ridge Farm

← 145
↑ 129

A   B   C   D   E   F

8

Summer House Wood

Keeper's Lodge

Hill House Farm

Park Wood

CT4

Park Side

Park Side Farm

7

Biggin Wood

WOOTTON LA

Park Wood

Park Wood

West Lees Wood

45

Brenstan

Selsted Farm

6

Selsted CE Prim Sch

Selsted

CANTERBURY RD

Stony Lane Wood

Newland's Farm

Stockham

5

44

Little Smezzel Farm

MANSELL LA

St John's Commandery (rems of)

North Court

4

CT18

REGAL LA

CT15

St Johns Farm

Swingfield Street

North Court Wood

Smezzel

Swingfield Minnis

3

Hoad Farm

The Butterfly Centre

Mast

Beard's Hall Farm

Ellinge House

HOAD RD

43

Boyington Court

2

FOX HOLT RD

Foxholt Cottage

Boyington Wood

Little Foxholt

Everden Cottage

1

Red House Farm

Pound Farm

Great Everden Farm

42

A260

CT18

21   A   B 22 C   D 23 E   F

← 145
↓ 163

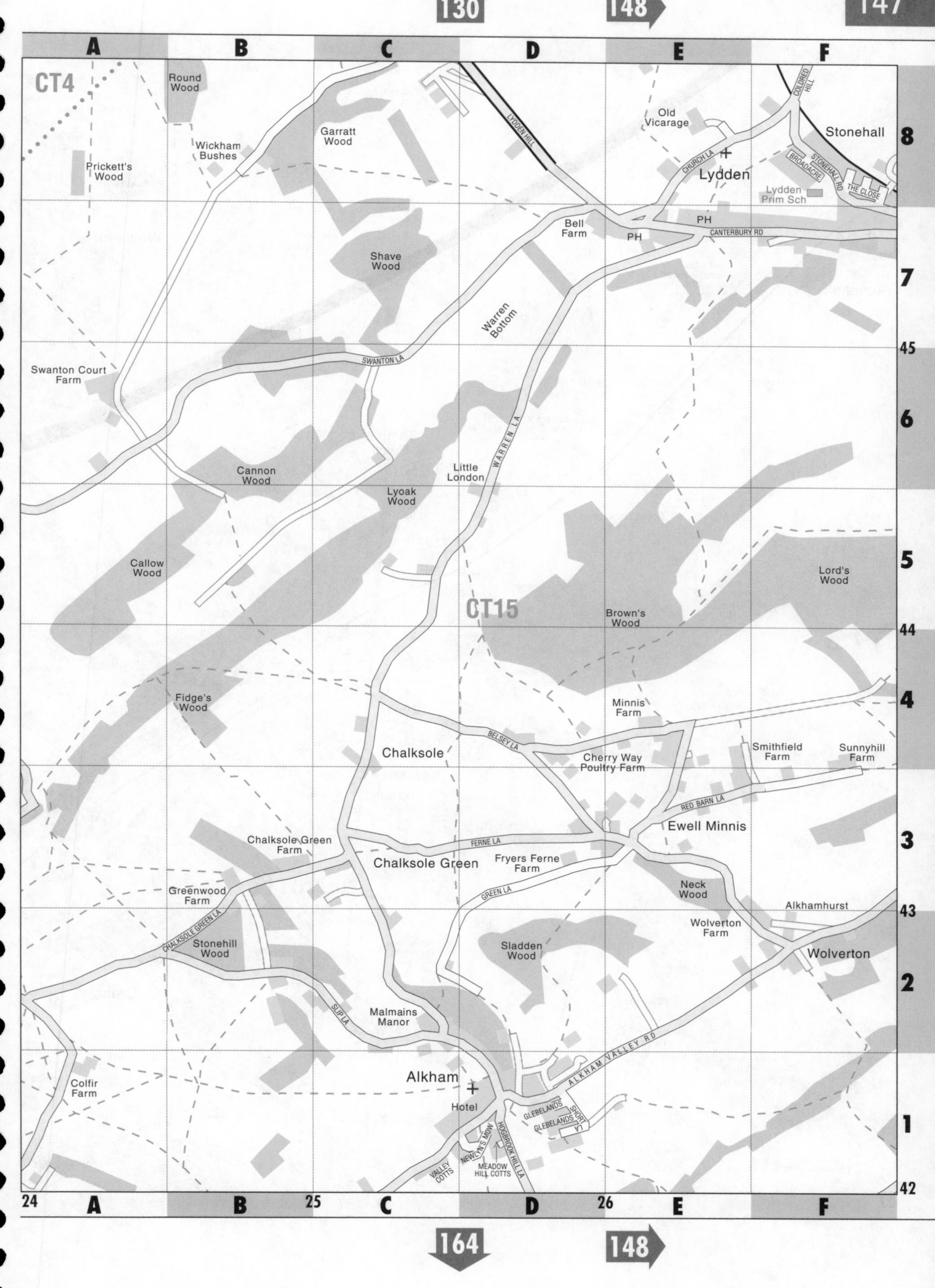

130
148

CT4

A B C D E F

Round Wood

Prickett's Wood

Wickham Bushes

Garratt Wood

LYDDEN HILL

Old Vicarage

CHURCH LA

Lydden

Stonehall

COLDRED HILL

BROADACRE

STONEHALL RD

THE CLOSE

Lydden Prim Sch

8

Bell Farm

PH

PH

CANTERBURY RD

7

Shave Wood

Warren Bottom

45

Swanton Court Farm

SWANTON LA

6

Cannon Wood

Lyoak Wood

Little London

WARREN LA

Callow Wood

Lord's Wood

5

CT15

Brown's Wood

44

Fidge's Wood

Minnis Farm

4

Chalksole

BELSEY LA

Cherry Way Poultry Farm

Smithfield Farm

Sunnyhill Farm

RED BARN LA

Ewell Minnis

3

Chalksole Green Farm

Chalksole Green

FERNE LA

Fryers Ferne Farm

Neck Wood

Alkhamhurst

Greenwood Farm

GREEN LA

Wolverton Farm

43

CHALKSOLE GREEN LA

Stonehill Wood

Sladden Wood

Wolverton

2

SLIP LA

Malmains Manor

ALKHAM VALLEY RD

Colfir Farm

Alkham

Hotel

GLEBELANDS

GLEBELANDS

GLEBELANDS CL

VALLEY COTTS

NEWLYN'S MDW

HOGBROOK HILL LA

MEADOW HILL COTTS

1

24

A B C 25 C D 26 E F

42

147
131

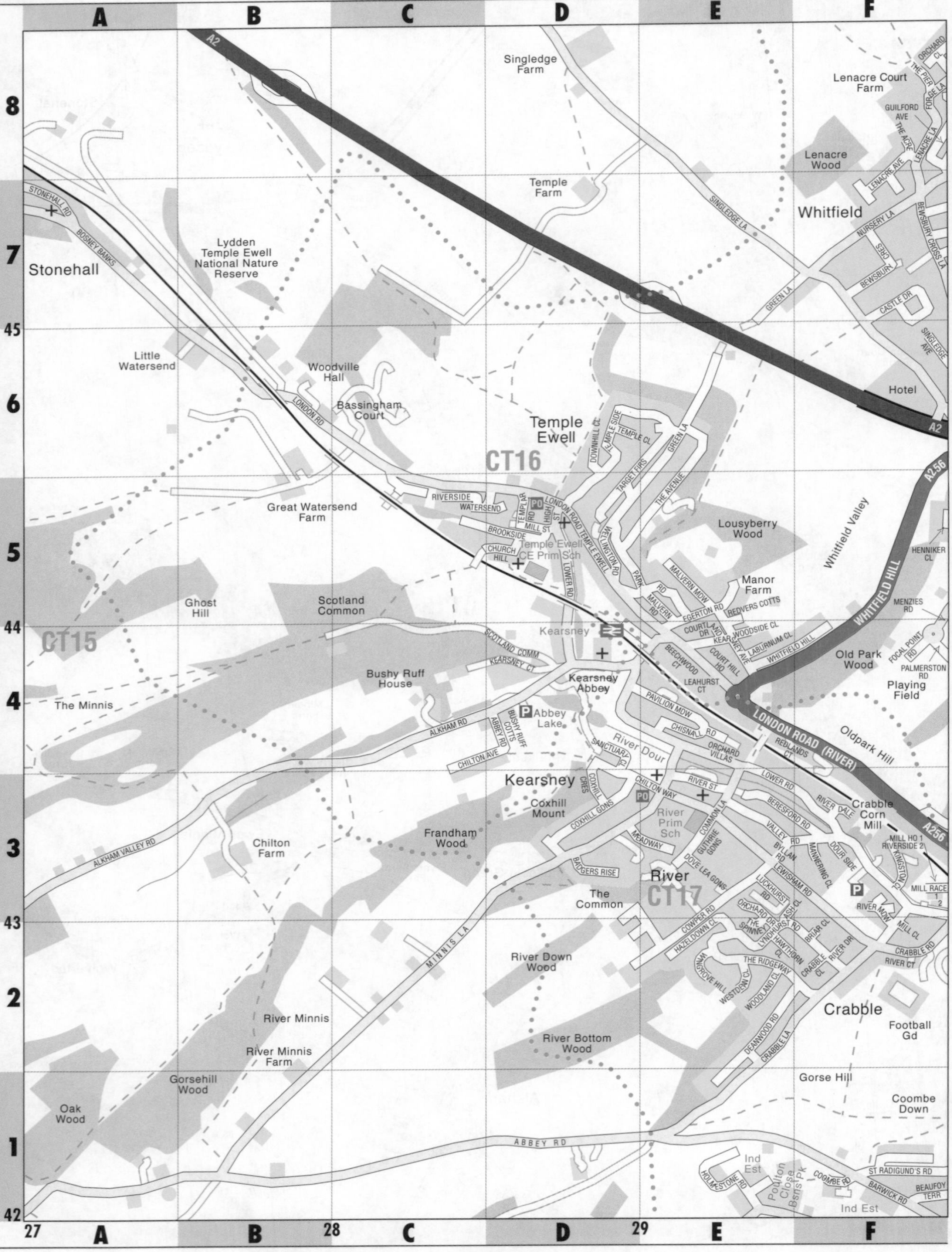

A B C D E F

8

7

45

6

Stonehall

Little
Watersend

Lydden
Temple Ewell
National Nature
Reserve

STONEHALL RD

BOSNEY BANKS

A2

Singledge
Farm

Temple
Farm

Whitfield

Lenacre Court
Farm

Lenacre
Wood

ORCHARD
THE PIER
FORGE LA
GUILFORD
AVE

NURSERY LA

SIBG

BEWSBURY CROSS LA

BEWSBURY

CASTLE DR

SINGLEDGE AVE

Hotel

A2

Woodville
Hall

Bassingham
Court

LONDON RD

Temple
Ewell

CT16

GREEN LA

DOWNHILL CL

APPLE SIDE

TEMPLE CL

TARGE FURS

THE AVENUE

GREEN LA

A256

WHITFIELD HILL

Whitfield
Valley

HENNIKER
CL

Great Watersend
Farm

RIVERSIDE
WATERSEND

BROOKSIDE

TEMPLE EWELL

MILL ST

LONDON ROAD

WELLINGTON PDE

Lousyberry
Wood

MENZIES
RD

5

Ghost
Hill

Scotland
Common

Church
Hill

Temple Ewell
CE Prim Sch

LOWER RD

Kearsney

PARK

MALVERN MOW

MALVERN
RD

EGERTON RD

COURT LA

REDVERS COTTS

Manor
Farm

COURT
DR

WOODSIDE CL

KEAR

Old Park
Wood

FOCAL POINT

PALMERSTON
RD

44

CT15

The Minnis

Bushy Ruff
House

SCOTLAND COMM

KEARSNEY CT

Kearsney
Abbey

BEECHWOOD
CT

WHITFIELD HILL

LABURNUM CL

LEAHURST
CT

Playing
Field

4

P

Abbey
Lake

ALKHAM RD

BUSHY RUFF COTT RD

ABBEY RD

SANCTUARY
CL

CHILTON AVE

PAVILION MOW

River Dour

CHISNALL RD

ORCHARD
VILLAS

LONDON ROAD (RIVER)

Oldpark Hill

REDLANDS
CL

LOWER RD

3

Chilton
Farm

ALKHAM VALLEY RD

Frandham
Wood

COXHILL GDNS

Coxhill
Mount

BADGERS RISE

COXHILL DENS

SANCTUARY
CL

CHILTON WAY

MEADAWAY

PO

River
Prim
Sch

RIVER ST

BERESFORD RD

COMMON LA

DOVE LEA GDNS

GUILFORD GDNS

RIVER DALE

VALLEY
RD

BYLLAN
RD

LEWISHAM RD

MANNERING CL

DOUR SIDE

Crabble
Corn
Mill

MILL HO 1
RIVERSIDE 2

A256

43

River

CT17

The
Common

River Down
Wood

THE SPINNEY

COWPER RD

HAZELDOWN CL

LYNHURST RD

ORCHARD
RD

LICHFIELD
RD

COMMON LA

LICHFIELD RD

P

LYNHURST CL

RIVER DR

CRABBLE
RD

River Mew

MILL CL

MILL RACE

River Ct

2

River Minnis

MINNIS LA

River Bottom
Wood

GROVE HILL

WESTON CL

WOODLAND RD

THE RIDGEWAY

DEANWOOD RD

CRABBLE LA

Crabble

Football
Gd

1

Oak
Wood

Gorsehill
Wood

River Minnis
Farm

ABBEY RD

Gorse Hill

Coombe
Down

42

HOLMESTONE RD

Ind
Est

COOMBE RD

Pavilion
Close

Bens Pk

Ind Est

ST RADIGUND'S RD

BARWICK RD

BEAUFOY
TERR

27 A B 28 C D 29 E F

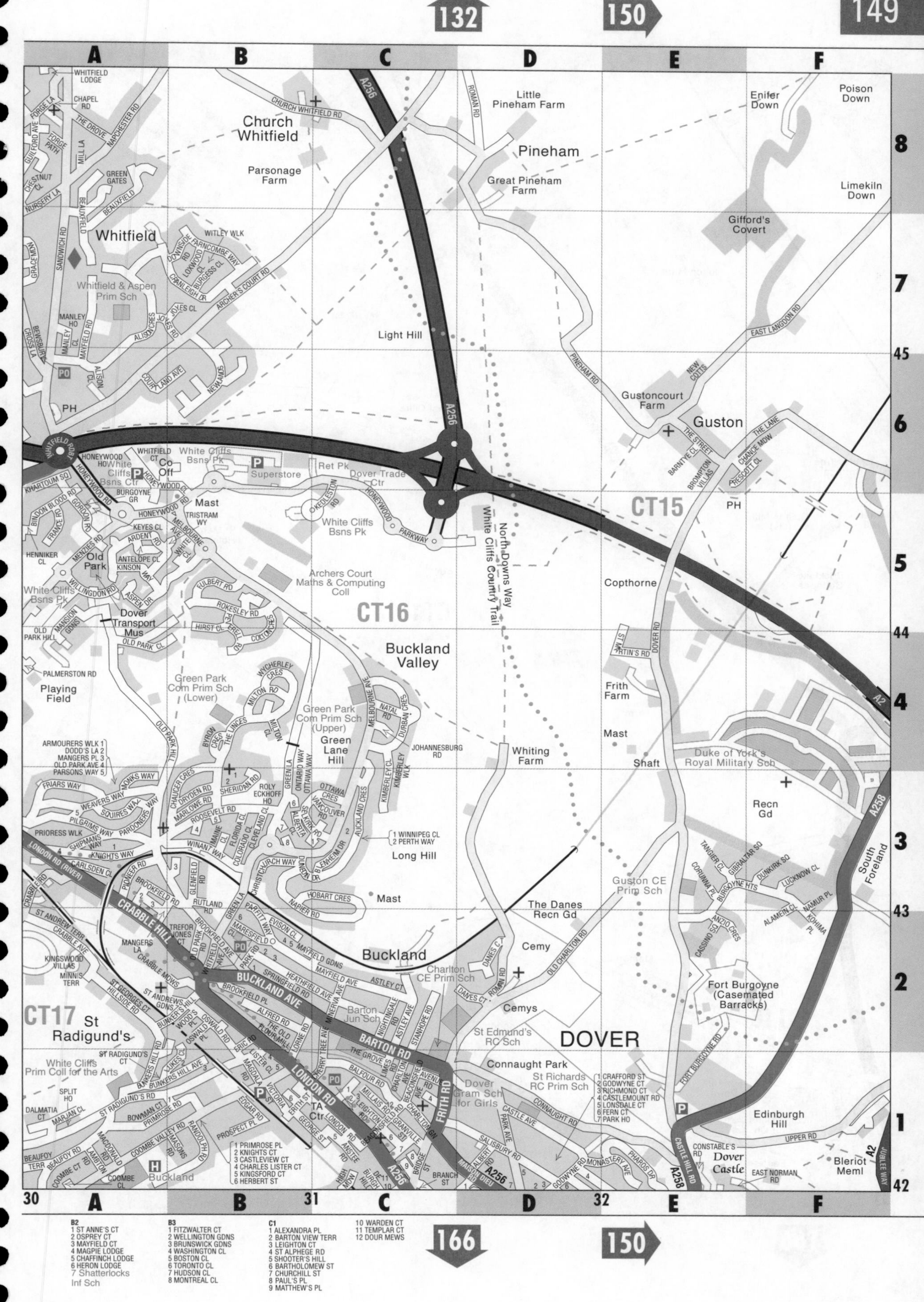
132
150
A
B
C
D
E
F
8
7
45
6
5
44
4
3
43
2
1
42
30
31
32
Church Whitfield
Little Pineham Farm
Pineham
Great Pineham Farm
Parsonage Farm
Enifer Down
Poison Down
Limekiln Down
Gifford's Covert
Whitfield
Whitfield & Aspen Prim Sch
Light Hill
Gustoncourt Farm
Guston
CT15
CT16
White Cliffs Bsns Pk
Superstore
Dover Trade Ctr
Archers Court Maths & Computing Coll
Dover Transport Mus
Old Park
Buckland Valley
North Downs Way
White Cliffs Country Trail
Copthorne
Frith Farm
Playing Field
Green Park Com Prim Sch (Lower)
Green Park Com Prim Sch (Upper)
Green Lane Hill
Whiting Farm
Duke of York's Royal Military Sch
Recn Gd
Long Hill
Guston CE Prim Sch
The Danes Recn Gd
South Foreland
Buckland
Charlton CE Prim Sch
Cemy
Cemys
Fort Burgoyne (Casemated Barracks)
CT17
St Radigund's
Barton Jun Sch
St Edmund's RC Sch
DOVER
Connaught Park
St Richards RC Prim Sch
White Cliffs Prim Coll for the Arts
Dover Gram Sch for Girls
Edinburgh Hill
Dover Castle
Bleriot Meml
A256
A2
A258
1 PRIMROSE PL
2 KNIGHTS CT
3 CASTLEVIEW CT
4 CHARLES LISTER CT
5 KINGSFORD CT
6 HERBERT ST
1 CRAFFORD ST
2 GODWYNE CT
3 RICHMOND CT
4 CASTLEMOUNT RD
5 LONSDALE CT
6 FERN CT
7 PARK HO
ARMOURERS WLK 1
DODD'S LA 2
MANGERS PL 3
OLD PARK AVE 4
PARSONS WAY 5
1 WINNIPEG CL
2 PERTH WAY
B2
1 ST ANNE'S CT
2 OSPREY CT
3 MAYFIELD CT
4 MAGPIE LODGE
5 CHAFFINCH LODGE
6 HERON LODGE
7 Shatterlocks Inf Sch
B3
1 FITZWALTER CT
2 WELLINGTON GDNS
3 BRUNSWICK GDNS
4 WASHINGTON CL
5 BOSTON CL
6 TORONTO CL
7 HUDSON CL
8 MONTREAL CL
C1
1 ALEXANDRA PL
2 BARTON VIEW TERR
3 LEIGHTON CT
4 ST ALPHEGE RD
5 SHOOTER'S HILL
6 BARTHOLOMEW ST
7 CHURCHILL ST
8 PAUL'S PL
9 MATTHEW'S PL
10 WARDEN CT
11 TEMPLAR CT
12 DOUR MEWS
166
150

149
133

A B C D E F

8

White Hill

Solton Close

THE STREET
EAST LANGDON RD
WALDERSHARE RD
GUSTON RD

Mill Hill

GREEN LA
VICTORY RD
STATION RD
NELSON PARK RD
HARDY RD
SEYMOUR RD
COLLINGWOOD RD

Nelson Park

7

Famine Down

Solton Manor Farm

Langdon Cross

The Old Sch
Liby

MILLFIELD
KINGSDOWN RD
THE CHASE
THE AVENUE

45

A258

POND LA

Townsend Farm

TOWNSEND FARM RD
HIGH ST
ASH GR
WELL LA
CRIPPS LA
ST KNOTTS LA

6

Cherry Tree Cottage

West Cliffe Farm

Wallet's Court

West Cliffe

DOVER RD

CLIFFE HO 1
HEATH CT 2
WELL LA
P
VICARAGE
ST GEORGES PL
GLEBE RD
REACH RD
ROYSTON GDNS
REACH CL
CHURCH

5

East Hill

Guston Mill (dis)

THE LANE

50

South Foreland

St Margarets Holiday Park

ROMAN WAY
LANGDON CL

Brickfield Cottages

44

PH

CT15

Reach Court Farm

Bere Wood

4

A2

A258

Bere Farm

LIGHTHOUSE RD
SEA VIEW RD
GOODWIN RD

3

WT Sta

Wanstone Farm

South Foreland Lighthouse

43

JUBILEE WAY

Masts

Memorials

UPPER RD

Bantam Hole

Fan Point

2

CT16

Saxon Shore Way

White Cliffs Country Trail

Fan Bay

Langdon Hole

Crab Bay

Mast

Fox Hill Down

CLIFF RD

Langdon Bay

1

A2

SOUTH FORELAND

White Cliffs Visitor Ctr

P

Langdon Cliffs

NORTH CAMBER WAY

SOUTH CAMBER WAY

EASTERN ARM N

Broadlees Bottom

Eastern Docks

E RAMP
UPPER RD
THE FAN

42

33 A B 34 C D 35 E F

166
149

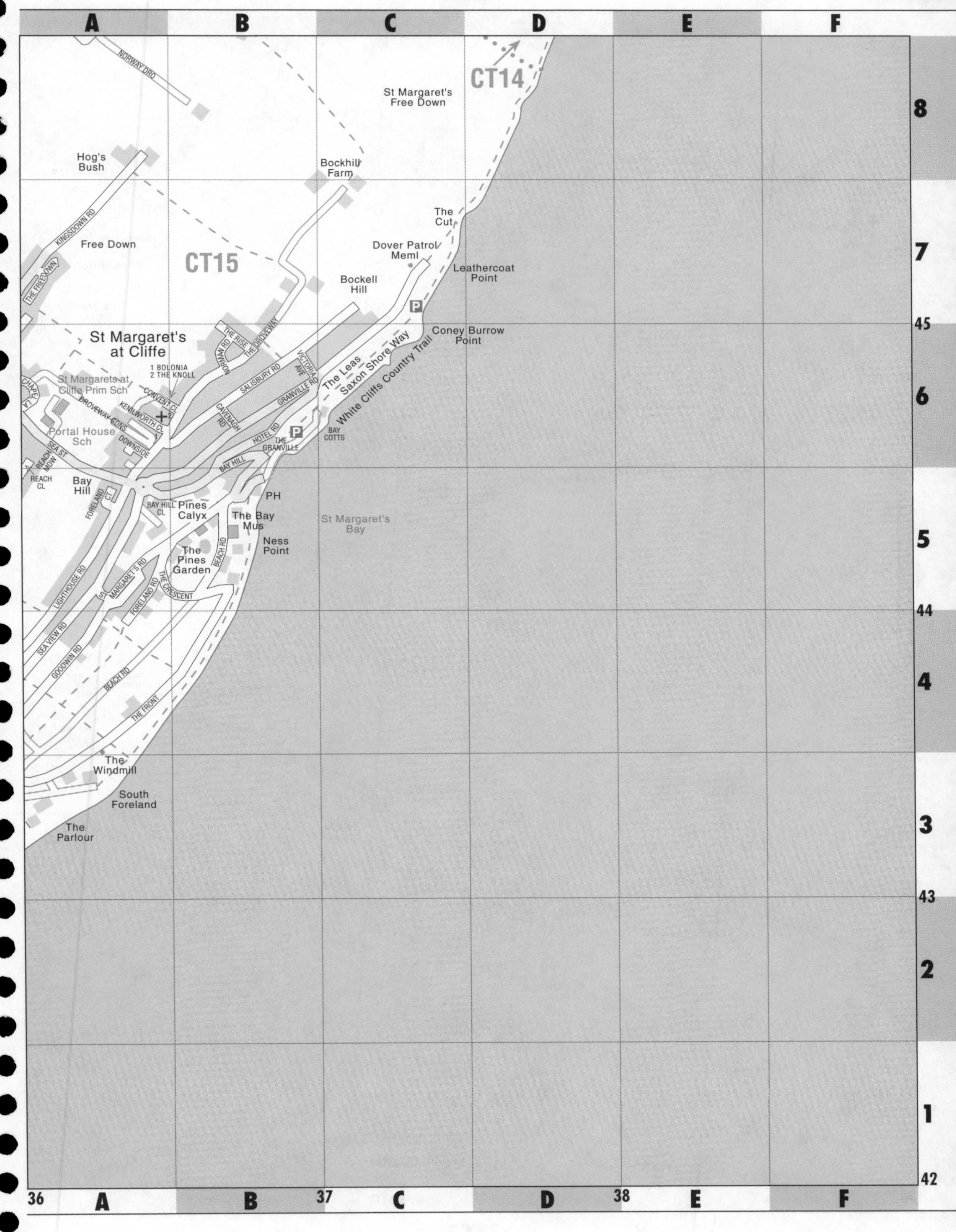

A B C D E F

8

CT14

St Margaret's
Free Down

Hog's
Bush

Bockhill
Farm

NORWAY DRO

The
Cut

7

Free Down

KINGSDOWN RD

CT15

Dover Patrol
Meml

Leathercoat
Point

THE FREEDOWN

Bockell
Hill

P

45

St Margaret's
at Cliffe

THE RISE

THE DROVEWAY

NORMAN RD

Coney Burrow
Point

The Leas

Saxon Shore Way

St Margarets at
Cliffe Prim Sch

1 BOLONIA
2 THE KNOLL

CONVENT CL

SALISBURY RD

VICTORIA AVE

GRANVILLE RD

White Cliffs Country Trail

6

CHAPEL LA

CAVANAGH RD

KEMLWORTH CL

DOWNSIDE

DROVEWAY GDNS

Portal House
Sch

HOTEL RD

P

THE
GRANVILLE

BAY
COTTS

SEA ST

Bay Hill

REACH MDW

BAY HILL

FORELAND

BAY HILL CL

PH

REACH
CL

Pines
Calyx

The Bay
Mus

St Margaret's
Bay

5

SEA VIEW RD

LIGHTHOUSE RD

ST MARGARET'S RD

FORELAND RD

BEACH RD

THE CRESCENT

The
Pines
Garden

Ness
Point

44

GOODWIN RD

REACH RD

THE FRONT

4

The
Windmill

3

South
Foreland

The
Parlour

43

2

1

42

36 A 37 B C 38 D E F

135

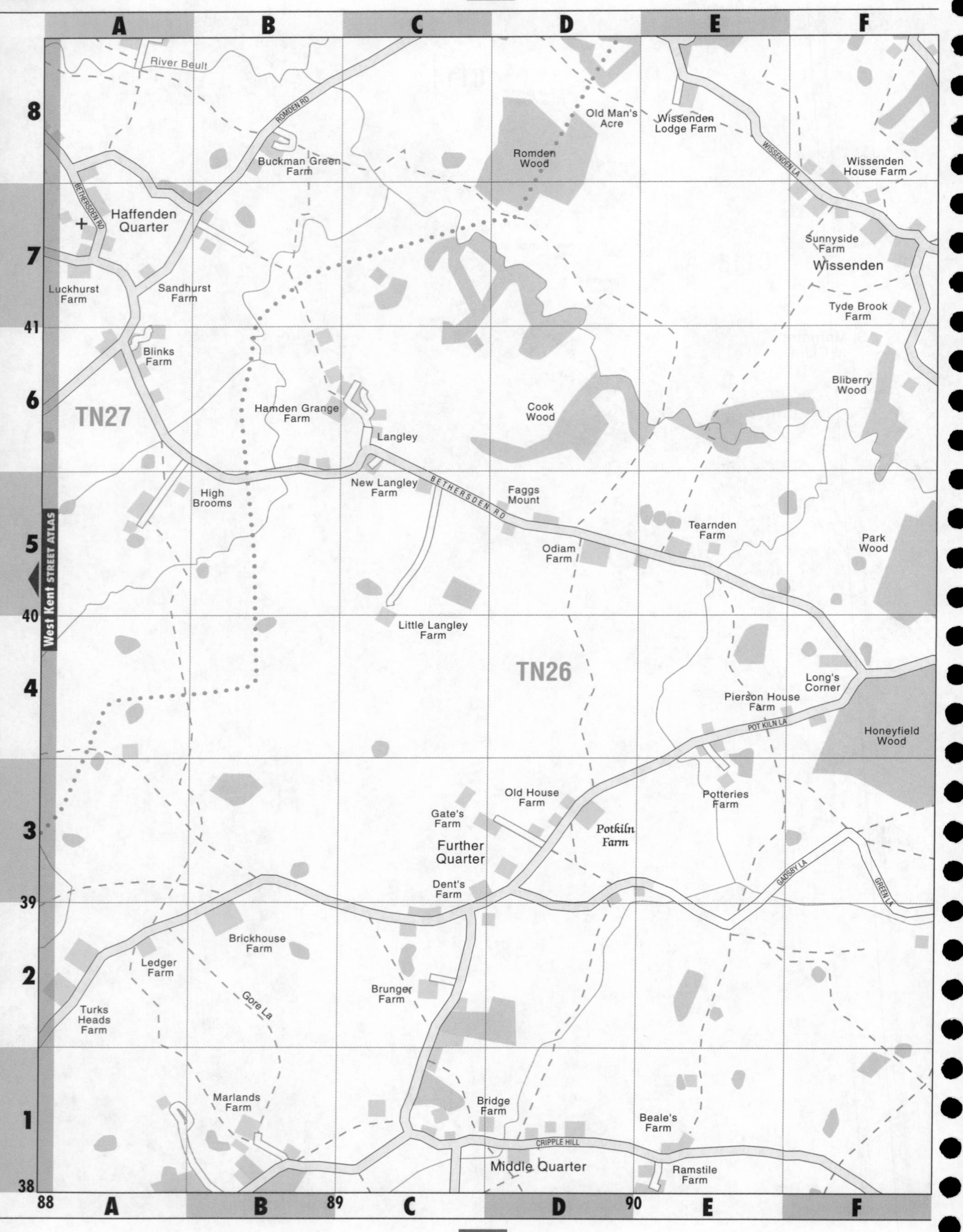

167

West Kent STREET ATLAS

River Beult

ROMDEN RD

Buckman Green Farm

Old Man's Acre

Romden Wood

Wissenden Lodge Farm

WISSENDEN LA

Wissenden House Farm

Haffenden Quarter

BETHERSDEN RD

Sunnyside Farm

Wissenden

Luckhurst Farm

Sandhurst Farm

Tyde Brook Farm

Blinks Farm

TN27

Bliberry Wood

Hamden Grange Farm

Cook Wood

Langley

BETHERSDEN RD

New Langley Farm

Faggs Mount

Tearnden Farm

Park Wood

High Brooms

Odiam Farm

Little Langley Farm

TN26

Long's Corner

Pierson House Farm

POT KILN LA

Honeyfield Wood

Old House Farm

Potteries Farm

Gate's Farm

Further Quarter

Potkiln Farm

Dent's Farm

GAMSEY LA

GREEN LA

Brickhouse Farm

Ledger Farm

Gore La

Brunger Farm

Turks Heads Farm

Marlands Farm

Bridge Farm

Beale's Farm

CRIPPLE HILL

Middle Quarter

Ramstile Farm

136
154

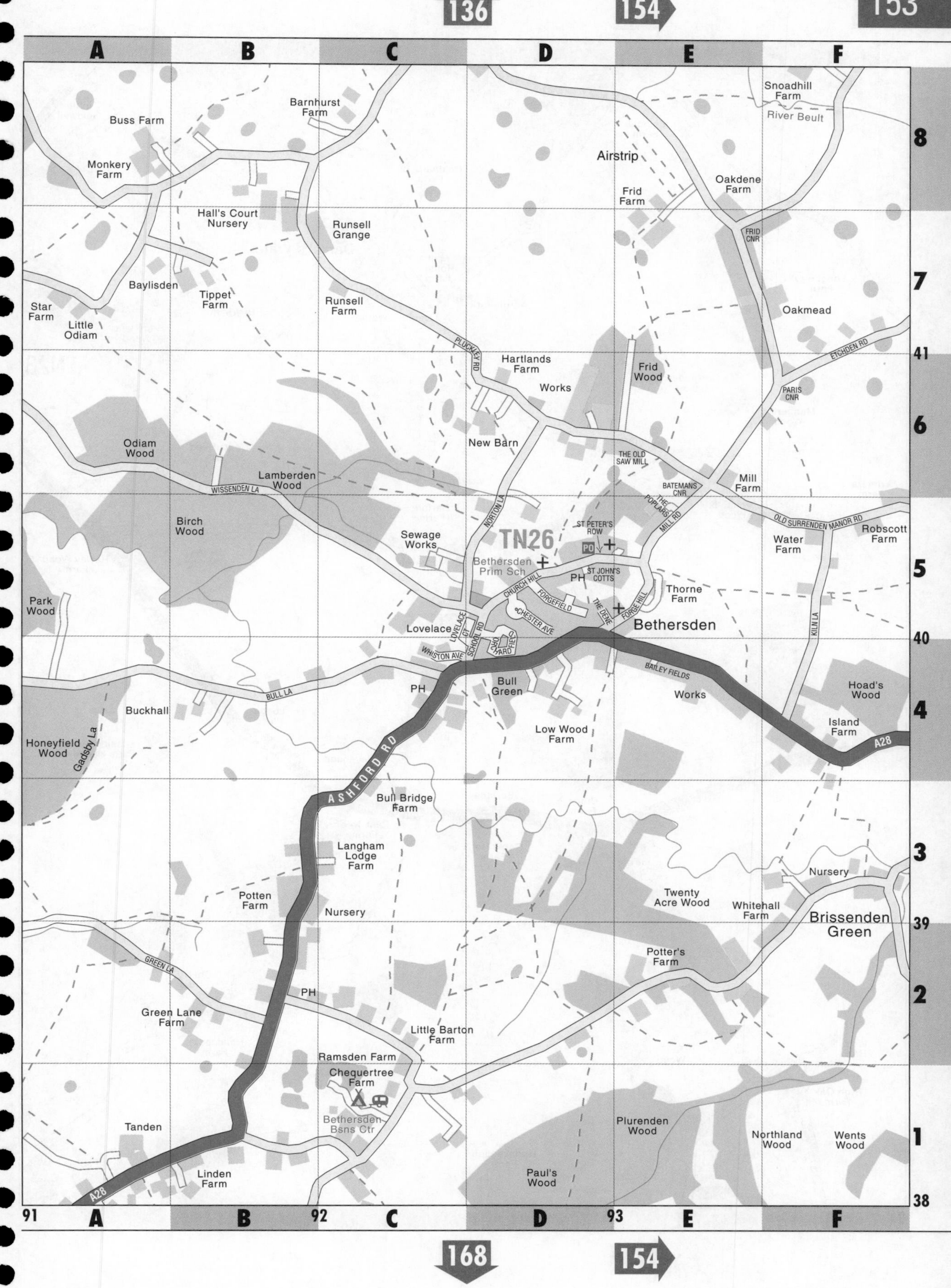
A B C D E F
8
7
41
6
5
40
4
3
39
2
1
38
91 92 93
Buss Farm
Barnhurst Farm
Snoadhill Farm
River Beult
Airstrip
Monkery Farm
Oakdene Farm
Frid Farm
Hall's Court Nursery
Runsell Grange
FRID CNR
Baylisden
Tippet Farm
Runsell Farm
Star Farm
Little Odiam
Oakmead
PLUCKLEY RD
ETCHDEN RD
Hartlands Farm
Frid Wood
Works
PARIS CNR
Odiam Wood
New Barn
THE OLD SAW MILL
Lamberden Wood
WISSENDEN LA
BATEMANS CNR
Mill Farm
THE POPLARS
Birch Wood
NORTON LA
ST PETER'S ROW
MILL RD
OLD SURRENDEN MANOR RD
Robscott Farm
Water Farm
Sewage Works
TN26
PO
Bethersden Prim Sch
PH
ST JOHN'S COTTS
CHURCH HILL
FORGEFIELD
Thorne Farm
Park Wood
CHESTER AVE
THE DENE
FORGE HILL
LOVELACE CT
SCHOOL RD
ORCHARD FIELD
Lovelace
Bethersden
WHISTON AVE
KILN LA
BAILEY FIELDS
BULL LA
PH
Bull Green
Works
Hoad's Wood
Buckhall
Island Farm
Low Wood Farm
Honeyfield Wood
Gadsby La
A28
ASHFORD RD
Bull Bridge Farm
Langham Lodge Farm
Potten Farm
Nursery
Twenty Acre Wood
Whitehall Farm
Nursery
Brissenden Green
Potter's Farm
GREEN LA
PH
Green Lane Farm
Little Barton Farm
Ramsden Farm
Chequertree Farm
Bethersden Bsns Ctr
Plurenden Wood
Northland Wood
Wents Wood
Tanden
Linden Farm
Paul's Wood
A28

168
154

153
137

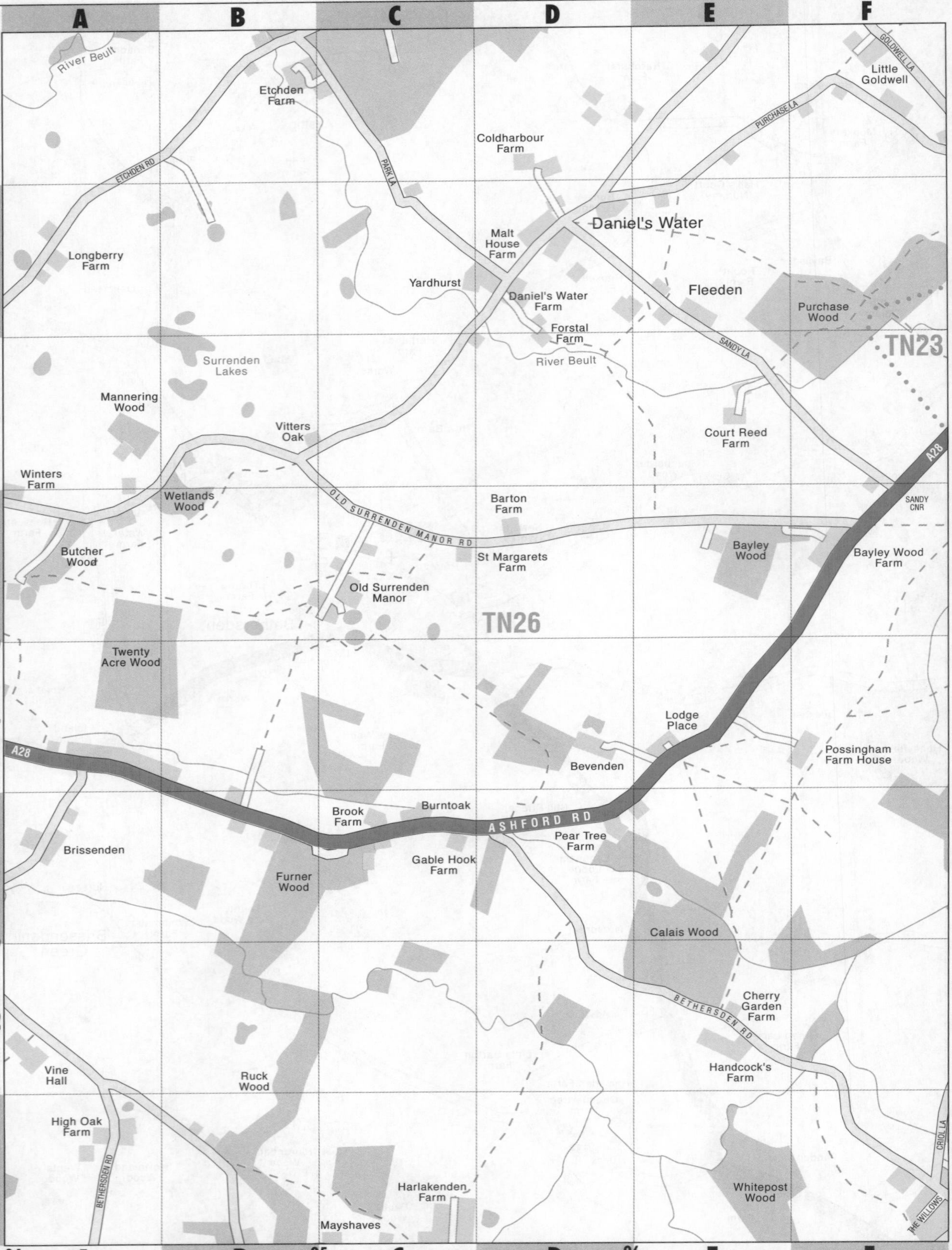

A   **B**   **C**   **D**   **E**   **F**

8

River Beult

GOLDWELL LA

Little
Goldwell

Etchden
Farm

PURCHASE LA

Coldharbour
Farm

ETCHDEN RD

7

Longberry
Farm

Malt
House
Farm

Daniel's Water

PARK LA

Yardhurst

Fleeden

41

Daniel's Water
Farm

Purchase
Wood

Forstal
Farm

SANDY LA

TN23

River Beult

Surrenden
Lakes

6

Mannering
Wood

Court Reed
Farm

Vitters
Oak

A28

Winters
Farm

OLD SURRENDEN MANOR RD

Wetlands
Wood

Barton
Farm

SANDY
CNR

Bayley
Wood

Bayley Wood
Farm

Butcher
Wood

5

St Margarets
Farm

Old Surrenden
Manor

TN26

40

Twenty
Acre Wood

4

Lodge
Place

Possingham
Farm House

A28

Bevenden

Brook
Farm

Burntoak

ASHFORD RD

Brissenden

Pear Tree
Farm

Gable Hook
Farm

3

Furner
Wood

Calais Wood

39

BETHERSDEN RD

2

Cherry
Garden
Farm

Vine
Hall

Ruck
Wood

Handcock's
Farm

High Oak
Farm

BETHERSDEN RD

CRIOL LA

1

Whitepost
Wood

Harlakenden
Farm

Mayshaves

THE WILLOWS

38

94   **A**   **B**   **95**   **C**   **D**   **96**   **E**   **F**

153
169

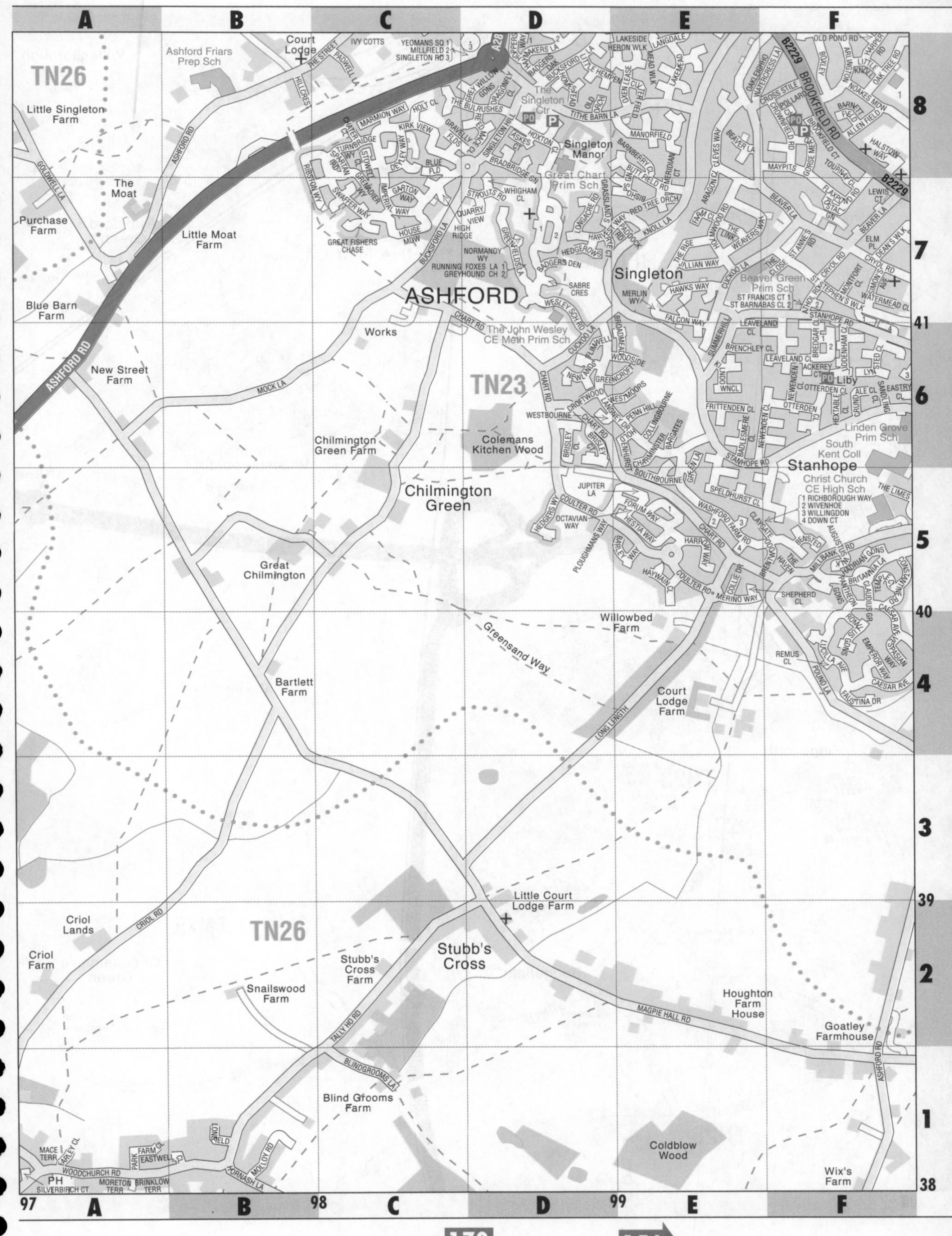
A
B
C
D
E
F
8
7
41
6
5
40
4
3
39
2
1
38
97
98
99
TN26
TN23
TN26
Little Singleton Farm
Ashford Friars Prep Sch
Court Lodge
IVY COTTS
YEOMANS SQ 1
MILLFIELD 2
SINGLETON RD 3
A28
The Moat
Purchase Farm
Little Moat Farm
Blue Barn Farm
New Street Farm
ASHFORD RD
GOLDWELL LA
MOCK LA
Works
ASHFORD
CHART RD
The Singleton Ctr
Singleton Manor
Great Chart Prim Sch
The John Wesley CE Meth Prim Sch
GREAT FISHERS CHASE
NORMANDY WY
RUNNING FOXES LA 1
GREYHOUND CH 2
SABRE CRES
WESLEY SCH RD
Singleton
Beaver Green Prim Sch
ST FRANCIS CT 1
ST BARNABAS CL 2
B2229
BROOKFIELD RD
Liby
Linden Grove Prim Sch
South Kent Coll
Stanhope
Christ Church CE High Sch
1 RICHBOROUGH WAY
2 WIVENHOE
3 WILLINGDON
4 DOWN CT
THE LIMES
Chilmington Green Farm
Colemans Kitchen Wood
Chilmington Green
Great Chilmington
Willowbed Farm
Greensand Way
Bartlett Farm
Court Lodge Farm
LONG LENGTH
Little Court Lodge Farm
Criol Lands
Criol Farm
CRIOL RD
Stubb's Cross
Stubb's Cross Farm
Snailswood Farm
TALLY HO RD
BLINDGROOMS LA
Blind Grooms Farm
MAGPIE HALL RD
Houghton Farm House
Goatley Farmhouse
ASHFORD RD
Coldblow Wood
Wix's Farm
WOODCHURCH RD
HORNASH LA
MOLLOY RD
PH
SILVERBIRCH CT
MORETON TERR
BRINKLOW TERR
MACE TERR
EASTWELL

155
139

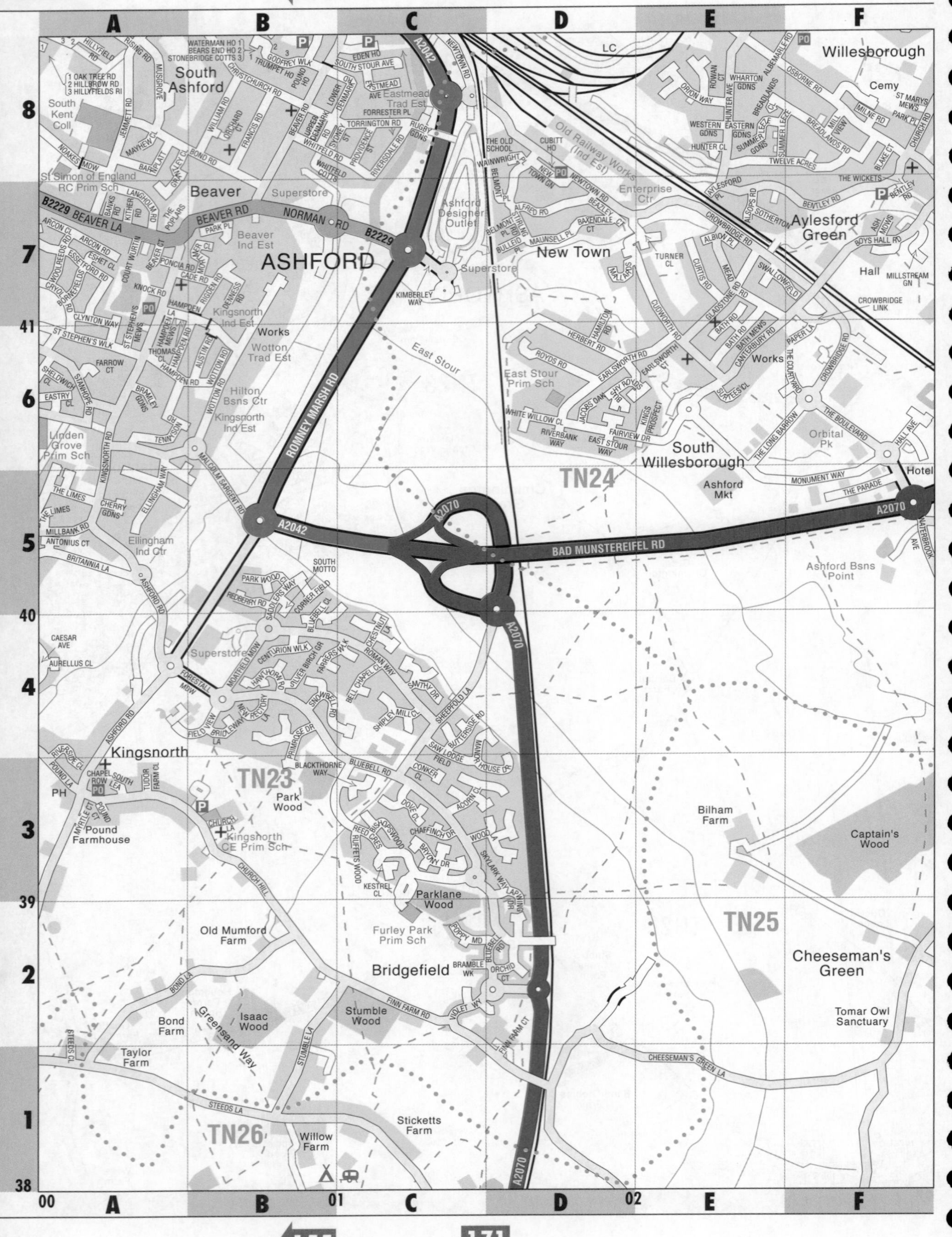
A
B
C
D
E
F
8
7
41
6
5
40
4
3
39
2
1
38
00
01
02
South Ashford
South Kent Coll
ASHFORD
Beaver
B2229 BEAVER LA
BEAVER RD
NORMAN RD
B2229
Beaver Ind Est
Superstore
Kingsnorth Ind Est
Works
Wotton Trad Est
Hilton Bsns Ctr
Kingsnorth Ind Est
Linden Grove Prim Sch
Ellingham Ind Ctr
St Simon of England RC Prim Sch
Eastmead Trad Est
Ashford Designer Outlet
A2042
ROMNEY MARSH RD
A2070
BAD MUNSTEREIFEL RD
East Stour
Old Railway Works (Ind Est)
Enterprise Ctr
New Town
LC
Willesborough
Cemy
Aylesford Green
Hall
East Stour Prim Sch
South Willesborough
TN24
Ashford Mkt
Orbital Pk
Hotel
Ashford Bsns Point
MALCOLM SARGENT RD
SOUTH MOTTO
Superstore
Kingsnorth
TN23
Park Wood
Kingsnorth CE Prim Sch
Pound Farmhouse
PH
Parklane Wood
Furley Park Prim Sch
Bridgefield
Old Mumford Farm
Bond Farm
Isaac Wood
Stumble Wood
Taylor Farm
Greensand Way
FINN FARM RD
STEEDS LA
TN26
Willow Farm
Sticketts Farm
Bilham Farm
TN25
Captain's Wood
Cheeseman's Green
Tomar Owl Sanctuary
CHEESEMAN'S GREEN LA

155
171

140
158

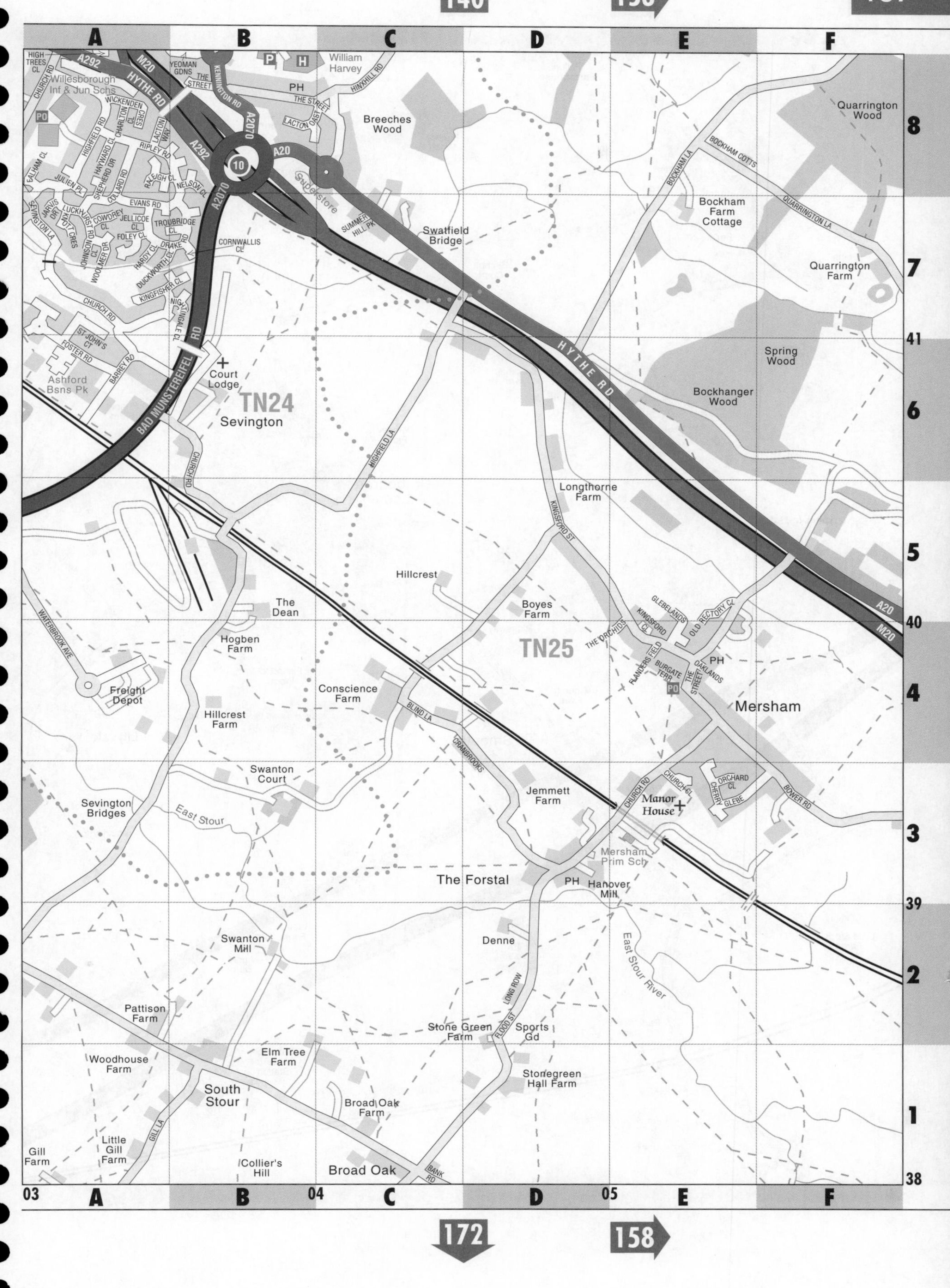
Quarrington Wood
Breeches Wood
William Harvey
Willesborough Inf & Jun Schs
Bockham Farm Cottage
Swatfield Bridge
Quarrington Farm
Spring Wood
Bockhanger Wood
Court Lodge
TN24
Sevington
Ashford Bsns Pk
Longthorne Farm
Hillcrest
The Dean
Boyes Farm
Hogben Farm
TN25
Freight Depot
Conscience Farm
Mersham
Hillcrest Farm
Swanton Court
Jemmett Farm
Manor House
Sevington Bridges
East Stour
Mersham Prim Sch
The Forstal
Hanover Mill
Swanton Mill
Denne
East Stour River
Pattison Farm
Stone Green Farm
Sports Gd
Woodhouse Farm
Elm Tree Farm
Stonegreen Hall Farm
South Stour
Broad Oak Farm
Little Gill Farm
Gill Farm
Collier's Hill
Broad Oak
HYTHE RD
BAD MUNSTEREIFEL RD
A292
M20
A20
A2070
KINGSFORD ST
HIGHFIELD LA
BLIND LA
CHURCH RD
BOCKHAM LA
QUARRINGTON LA
BOWER RD
LONG ROW
FLOOD ST
GILL LA
WATERBROOK AVE

172
158

157
141

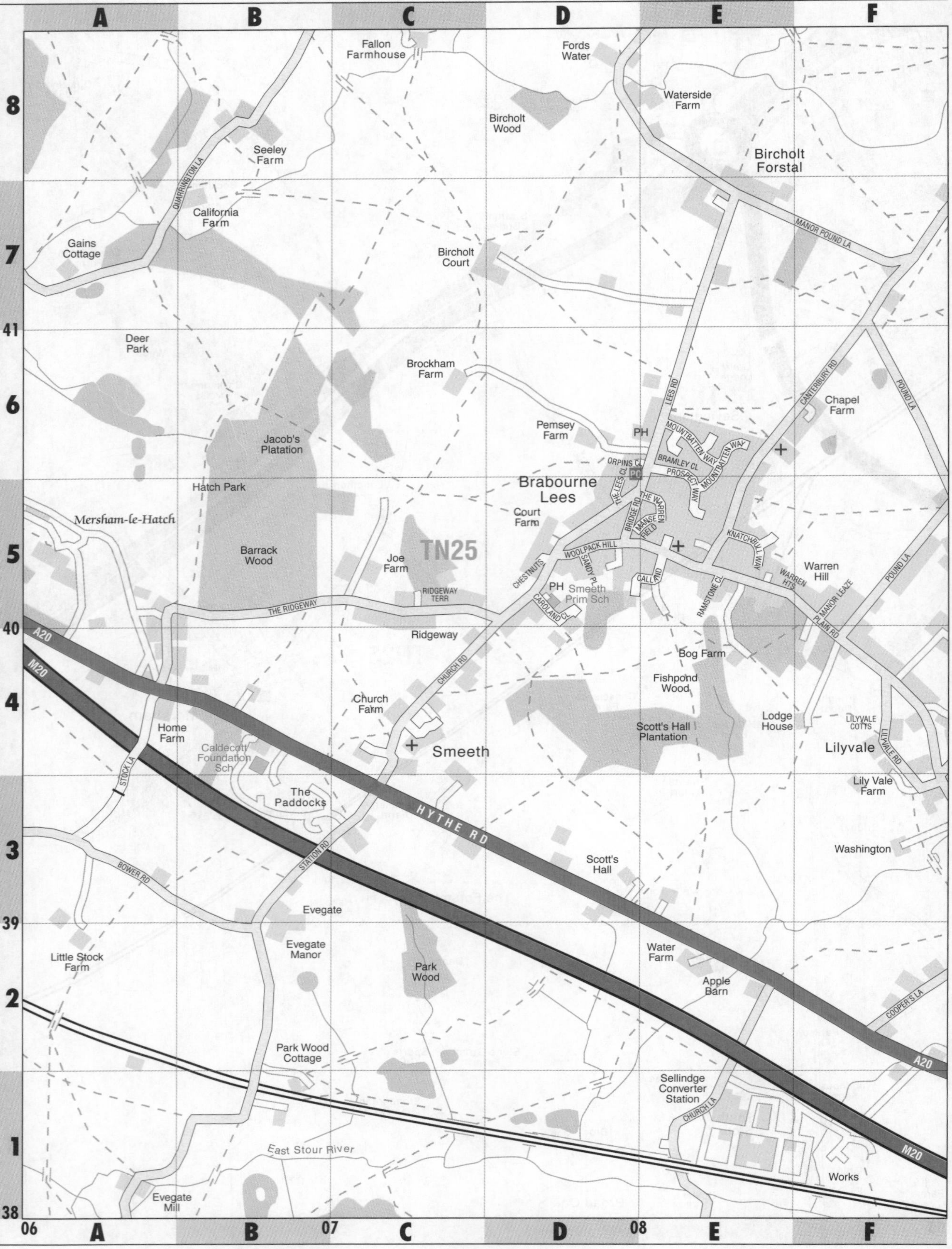

A B C D E F

8

7

41

6

Gains
Cottage

Deer
Park

QUARRINGTON LA

Seeley
Farm

California
Farm

Fallon
Farmhouse

Bircholt
Wood

Fords
Water

Waterside
Farm

Bircholt
Forstal

MANOR POUND LA

Bircholt
Court

Brockham
Farm

Jacob's
Platation

Hatch Park

Mersham-le-Hatch

Barrack
Wood

Pemsey
Farm

PH

Chapel
Farm

CANTERBURY RD

POUND LA

5

Joe
Farm

RIDGEWAY
TERR

TN25

Court
Farm

CHESTNUTS

Woolpack Hill

Smeeth
Prim Sch

PH

SANDY PL

ORPINS CL

BRAMLEY CL

LEES RD

MOUNTBATTEN WAY

PROSPECT WAY

MOUNTBATTEN WAY

THE LEES CL

PO

BRIDGE RD

THE WARREN

MANSE
FIELD

KNATCHBULL WAY

RAMSTONE CL

WARREN
HTS

Brabourne
Lees

Warren
Hill

MANOR LS
LATE

PLAIN RD

40

A20

THE RIDGEWAY

Ridgeway

CHURCH RD

CAROLAND CL

CALL RD

Bog Farm

Fishpond
Wood

Lilyvale

LILYVALE
COTTS

LILYVALE RD

POUND LA

4

M20

Home
Farm

Caldecott
Foundation
Sch

STOCK LA

Church
Farm

Smeeth

Scott's Hall
Plantation

Lodge
House

Lily Vale
Farm

39

Little Stock
Farm

BOWER RD

The
Paddocks

STATION RD

Evegate

Evegate
Manor

Park Wood
Cottage

Park
Wood

HYTHE RD

Scott's
Hall

Water
Farm

Apple
Barn

Washington

COOPER'S LA

A20

3

2

East Stour River

Sellindge
Converter
Station

CHURCH LA

M20

1

Works

38

06 A B 07 C D 08 E F

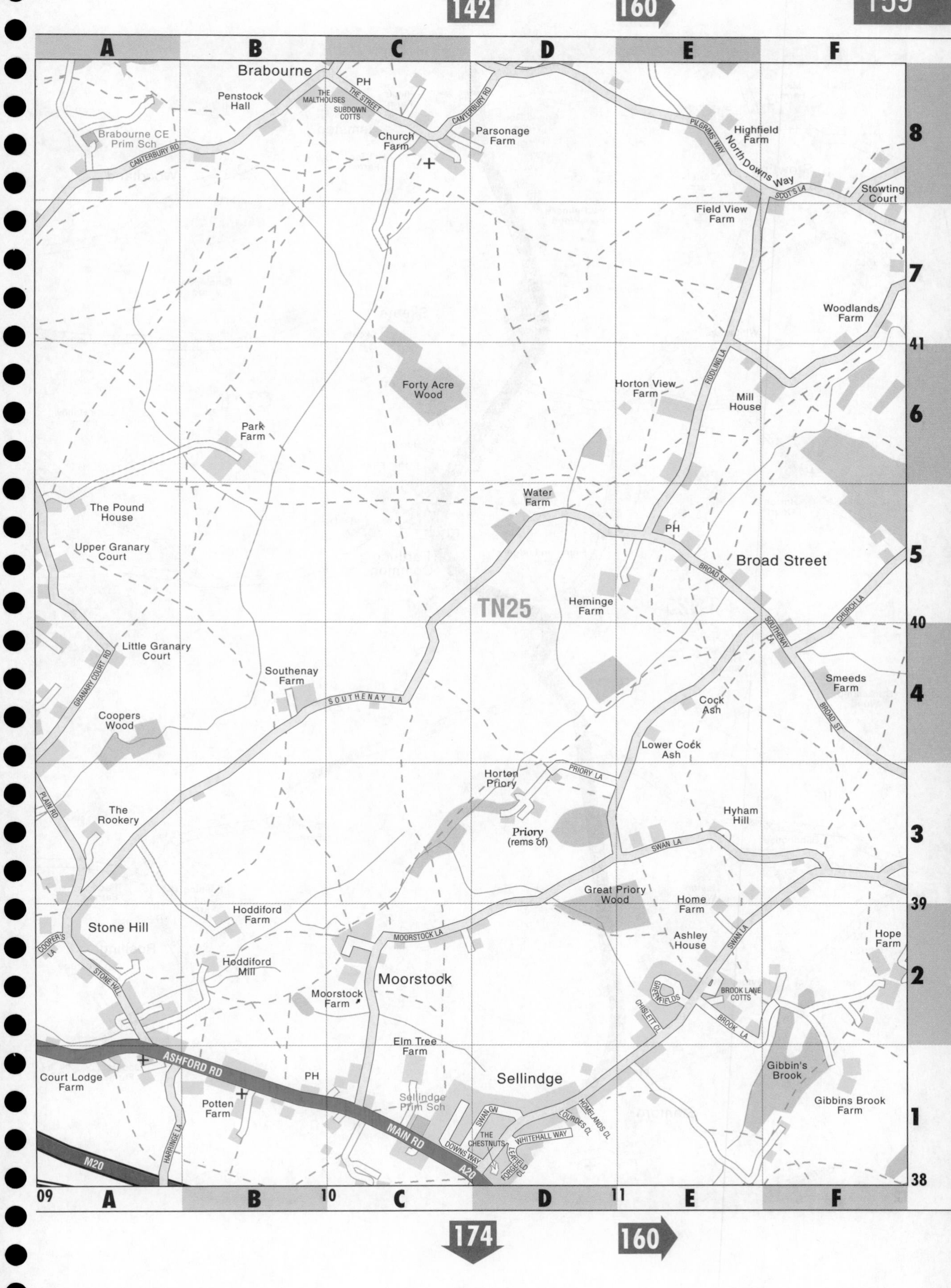
A
B
C
D
E
F
Brabourne
PH
Penstock Hall
THE MALTHOUSES
THE STREET
SUBDOWN COTTS
CANTERBURY RD
Brabourne CE Prim Sch
CANTERBURY RD
Church Farm
Parsonage Farm
PILGRIMS' WAY
Highfield Farm
North Downs Way
SCOT'S LA
Stowting Court
Field View Farm
8
7
Woodlands Farm
41
Forty Acre Wood
FIDDLING LA
Horton View Farm
Mill House
6
Park Farm
The Pound House
Water Farm
PH
Upper Granary Court
Broad Street
BROAD ST
5
TN25
Heminge Farm
CHURCH LA
SOUTHENAY LA
40
Little Granary Court
GRANARY COURT RD
Southenay Farm
SOUTHENAY LA
Smeeds Farm
4
Cock Ash
BROAD ST
Coopers Wood
Lower Cock Ash
PLAIN RD
Horton Priory
PRIORY LA
The Rookery
Hyham Hill
Priory (rems of)
3
SWAN LA
Great Priory Wood
39
Home Farm
Hoddiford Farm
Stone Hill
COOPER'S LA
MOORSTOCK LA
Ashley House
SWAN LA
Hope Farm
Hoddiford Mill
STONE HILL
Moorstock
2
Moorstock Farm
GREENFIELDS
BROOK LANE COTTS
CHISLETT CL
BROOK LA
Elm Tree Farm
ASHFORD RD
Court Lodge Farm
PH
Sellindge
Gibbin's Brook
Potten Farm
Sellindge Prim Sch
SWAN GN
HOMELANDS CL
LOURDES CL
Gibbins Brook Farm
1
THE CHESTNUTS
WHITEHALL WAY
MAIN RD
HARRINGE LA
DOWNS WAY
LEAFIELD
FORGEFIELD
M20
A20
38
09
A
B
10
C
D
11
E
F

159
143

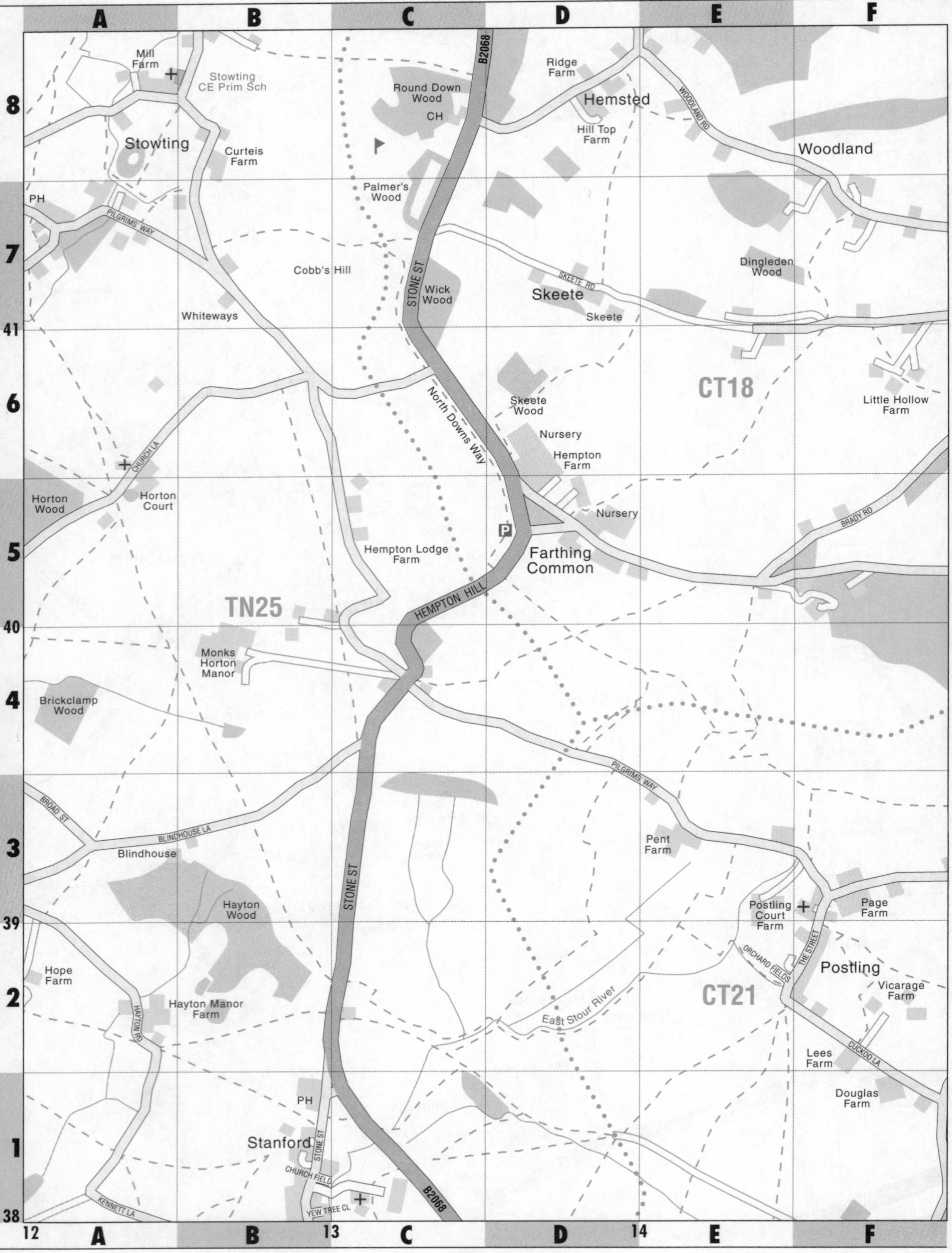

A   B   C   D   E   F

8

Mill Farm
Stowting CE Prim Sch
Round Down Wood
CH
Ridge Farm
Hemsted
Woodland
Stowting
Curteis Farm
Hill Top Farm
WOODLAND RD

7

PH
PILGRIMS WAY
Palmer's Wood
Dingleden Wood
Cobb's Hill
SKEETE RD
Wick Wood
Skeete
Skeete

41

STONE ST
Whiteways
Skeete

6

North Downs Way
Skeete Wood
CT18
Nursery
Hempton Farm
Little Hollow Farm
CHURCH LA

Horton Wood
Horton Court
Nursery
BRADY RD

5

P
Hempton Lodge Farm
Farthing Common

TN25
HEMPTON HILL

40

Monks Horton Manor

4

Brickclamp Wood

PILGRIMS WAY

3

BROAD ST
BLINDHOUSE LA
Blindhouse
Pent Farm
Postling Court Farm
THE STREET
Page Farm

39

Hayton Wood
STONE ST
Postling
ORCHARD FIELDS
CT21
Vicarage Farm

2

Hope Farm
HAYTON RD
Hayton Manor Farm
East Stour River
Lees Farm
CUCKOO LA

1

PH
STONE ST
Stanford
CHURCH FIELD
B2068
Douglas Farm

38

KENNETT LA
YEW TREE CL

12   A   B   13   C   D   14   E   F

159
175

B2068

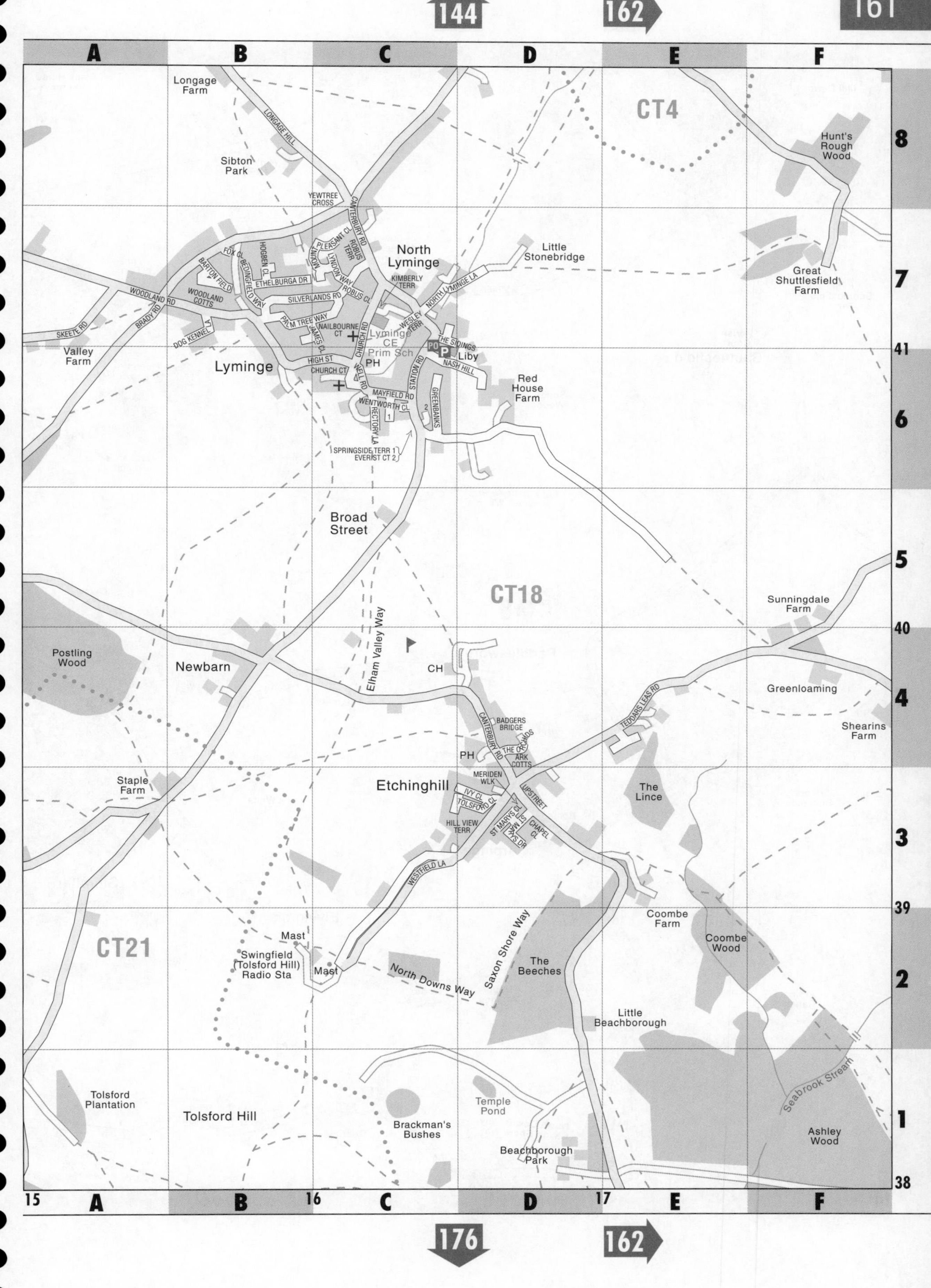

A   B   C   D   E   F

8
7
41
6
5
40
4
3
39
2
1
38

15   A   B   16   C   D   17   E   F

CT4

Longage Farm
Sibton Park
LONGAGE HILL
CANTERBURY RD
YEWTREE CROSS
North Lyminge
Little Stonebridge
Hunt's Rough Wood
Great Shuttlesfield Farm

BARTON FIELD
FOX CL
HEDINGFIELD WAY
WOODLAND RD
WOODLAND COTTS
BRADY RD
SKEETE RD
Valley Farm
DOG KENNEL LA
HOGBEN CL
ETHELBURGA DR
MONIN
PLEASNT CL
JACOBUS CL
HOBUS CL
YNION
PALM TREE WAY
SILVERLANDS RD
JAMES PL
KIMBERLY TERR
NORTH LYMINGE LA
NAILBOURNE CT
Lyminge
HIGH ST
CHURCH CT
WELL RD
HONING RD
WESLEY TERR
Lyminge CE Prim Sch
PH
PO
P
Liby
THE SIDINGS
NASH HILL
Red House Farm
MAYFIELD RD
WENTWORTH CL
RECTORY LA
STATION RD
GREENBANKS
SPRINGSIDE TERR 1
EVERIST CT 2

Broad Street

CT18

Postling Wood
Newbarn
Elham Valley Way
CH
Sunningdale Farm
40
Greenloaming
Shearins Farm

Staple Farm
BADGERS BRIDGE
CANTERBURY RD
THE CROSS
PH
ARK COTTS
MERIDEN WLK
IVY CL
TOLSFORD CL
Etchinghill
ST MARYS CL
UPSTREET
CHAPEL CL
HILL VIEW TERR
FEDARS LEAS RD
The Lince
Coombe Farm
Coombe Wood

CT21

Mast
Swingfield (Tolsford Hill) Radio Sta
Mast
WESTFIELD LA
North Downs Way
Saxon Shore Way
The Beeches
Little Beachborough
Seabrook Stream

Tolsford Plantation
Tolsford Hill
Brackman's Bushes
Temple Pond
Beachborough Park
Ashley Wood

161 ◀ 145 ▲

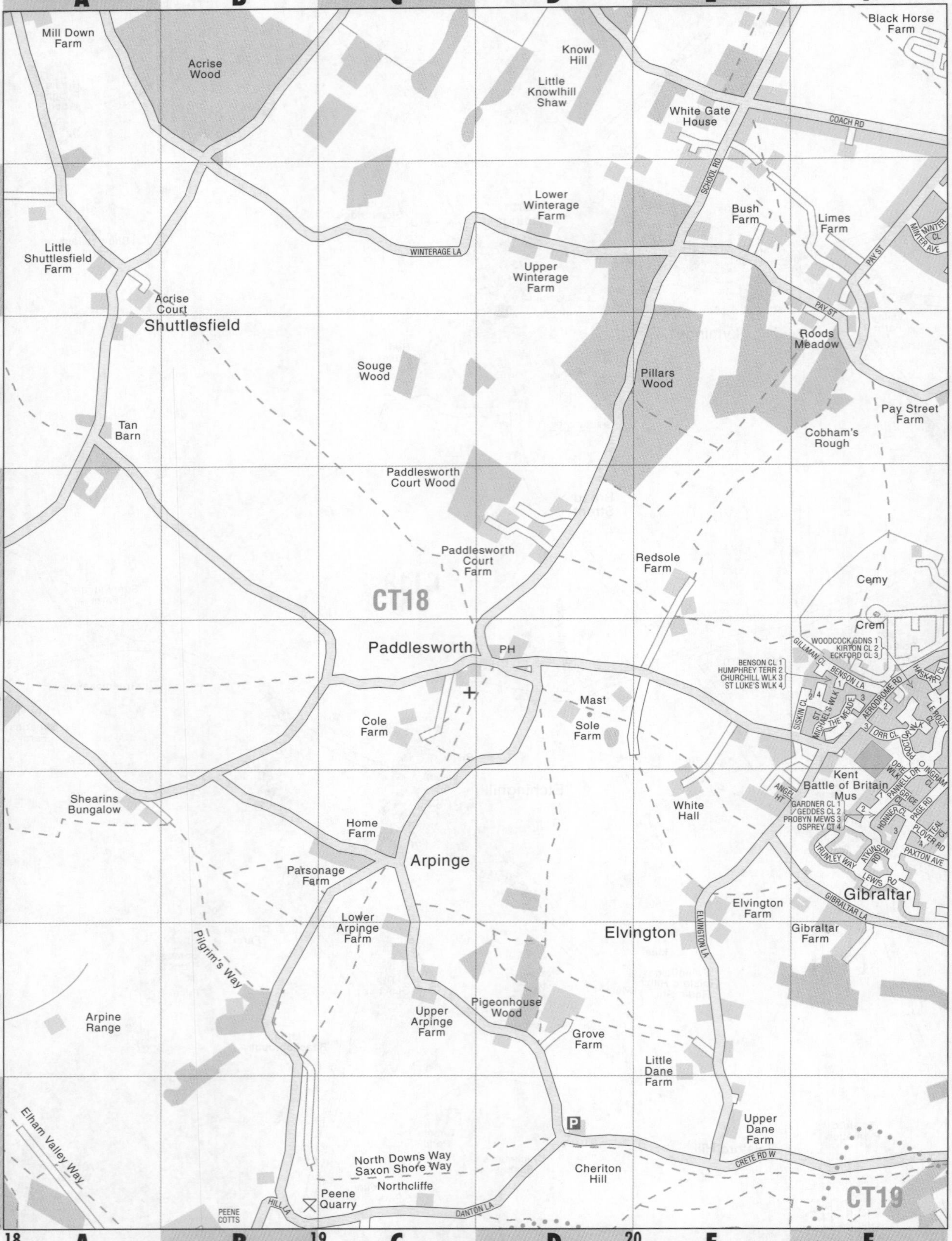

	A	B	C	D	E	F

8
Mill Down Farm
Acrise Wood
Knowl Hill
Little Knowlhill Shaw
White Gate House
COACH RD
Black Horse Farm

7
Little Shuttlesfield Farm
Lower Winterage Farm
WINTERAGE LA
Bush Farm
Upper Winterage Farm
Limes Farm
PAY ST
MINTER CL
MINTER AVE

41
Acrise Court
Shuttlesfield
PAY ST
Roods Meadow

6
Souge Wood
Pillars Wood
Pay Street Farm

Tan Barn
Cobham's Rough

Paddlesworth Court Wood

5
Paddlesworth Court Farm
Redsole Farm
CT18
Cemy

40
Crem
WOODCOCK GDNS 1
KIRTON CL 2
ECKFORD CL 3

Paddlesworth
PH
BENSON CL 1
HUMPHREY TERR 2
CHURCHILL WLK 3
ST LUKE'S WLK 4

4
Cole Farm
Mast
Sole Farm

Shearins Bungalow
White Hall
Kent Battle of Britain Mus
GARDNER CL 1
GEDDES CL 2
PROBYN MEWS 3
OSPREY CT 4

3
Home Farm
Arpinge
Elvington Farm
Gibraltar
GIBRALTAR LA

Parsonage Farm
Pilgrim's Way

39
Lower Arpinge Farm
Elvington
ELVINGTON LA
Gibraltar Farm

2
Arpine Range
Upper Arpinge Farm
Pigeonhouse Wood
Grove Farm
Little Dane Farm

1
Eltham Valley Way
P
North Downs Way
Saxon Shore Way
Northcliffe
Cheriton Hill
CRETE RD W
Upper Dane Farm
CT19

38
HILL LA
Peene Cotts
Peene Quarry
DANTON LA

18	A	B	19	C	D	20	E	F

146
164

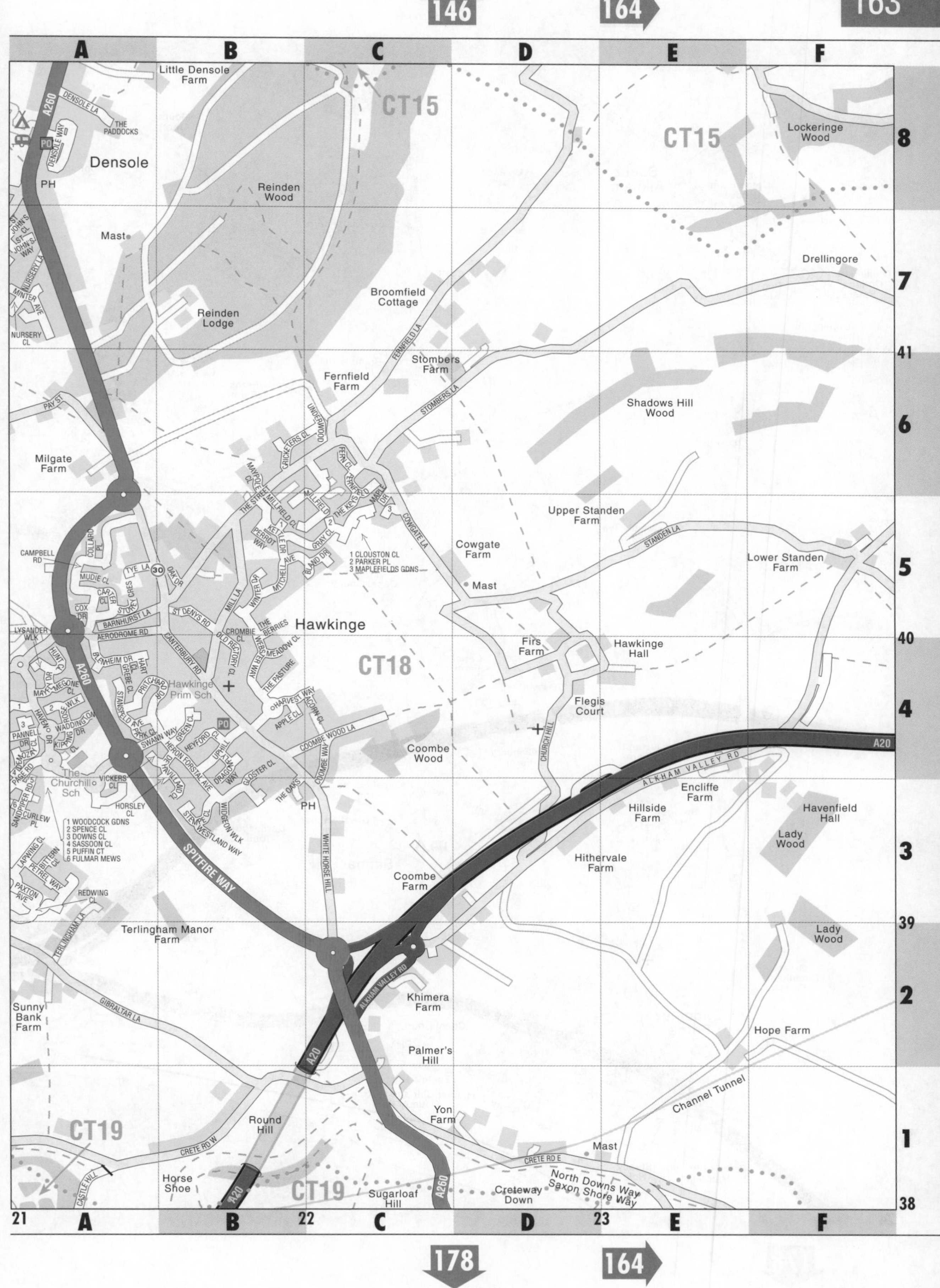
Little Densole Farm
CT15
Densole
Reinden Wood
Lockeringe Wood
Mast
Drellingore
Broomfield Cottage
Reinden Lodge
Stombers Farm
Fernfield Farm
Shadows Hill Wood
Milgate Farm
Upper Standen Farm
Cowgate Farm
Lower Standen Farm
Hawkinge
Mast
Firs Farm
Hawkinge Hall
CT18
Hawkinge Prim Sch
Flegis Court
Coombe Wood
The Churchill Sch
Encliffe Farm
Hillside Farm
Havenfield Hall
Lady Wood
Hithervale Farm
Coombe Farm
Terlingham Manor Farm
Lady Wood
Khimera Farm
Sunny Bank Farm
Hope Farm
Palmer's Hill
Channel Tunnel
Yon Farm
Round Hill
CT19
Mast
Horse Shoe
Sugarloaf Hill
Creteway Down
North Downs Way
Saxon Shore Way
A260
A20
SPITFIRE WAY
ALKHAM VALLEY RD
STANDEN LA
STOMBERS LA
FERNFIELD LA
COWGATE LA
CHURCH HILL
WHITE HORSE HILL
COOMBE WOOD LA
GIBRALTAR LA
CRETE RD W
CRETE RD E
TERLINGHAM LA
1 CLOUSTON CL
2 PARKER PL
3 MAPLEFIELDS GDNS
1 WOODCOCK GDNS
2 SPENCE CL
3 DOWNS CL
4 SASSOON CL
5 PUFFIN CT
6 FULMAR MEWS
A B C D E F
8 7 41 6 5 40 4 3 39 2 1 38
21 22 23

178
164

163
147

A B C D E F

8

Mount Ararat

Moorlands

South Alkham

Upton Farm House

Uplands Farm

Hogbrook Hill La

Lonebarn Farm

Poulton Farm

7

Drellingore Cottage Farm

Ppg Sta

Meggett Farm

Meggett La

Alkham Valley Rd

Drellingore

Copt Hill Farm

41

Bramble Hill Cottage

Ferns Farm

CT15

6

Tumble Tye Farm

5

Capel Church Farm

Broadsole La
Path Field Cot's
Forge Field
Queen's Lea
Lacy Carpe
The Street
Young's Pl
Mill La
Lowslip Hill

West Hougham

Hockley Sole

40

The Old Sch

Capel Farm

Crook's Court La

White Hill

Gravel La

Chalk Pit Wood

4

A20

Hurst Farm

Hollingbury Farm

Satmore La

Satmar La

Swinge Hill

CT18

Hurst La

Channel Tunnel

Capel House Farm

Great Satmar Farm

Dawkinge Wood

3

Cauldham La

Capel St

Capel-le-Ferne Prim Sch

Satmore La

Winehouse La

Satmar

39

Green La

Eliza Dr
Beth Dr
Lancaster Ave

Masts

Abbot's Land Farm

A20

Great Cauldham Farm

Beatrice Rd
Alexandra Rd
Anomale Rd
Helena Rd

NEW DOVER RD

PH

B2011

2

Capel-le-Ferne

Victoria Rd
Clarendon Rd
Albert Rd
Albany Rd

Old Dover Rd

Capel Court Pk

PH

Cauldham Cl
Sea View Cl
Capel St

North Downs Way
Saxon Shore Way

Eagle's Nest

East Cliff and Warren Country Park

1

Reece Adams Ho

Battle of Britain Memorial

Steady Hole

The Warren

B2011

38

24 A B 25 C D 26 E F

178
163

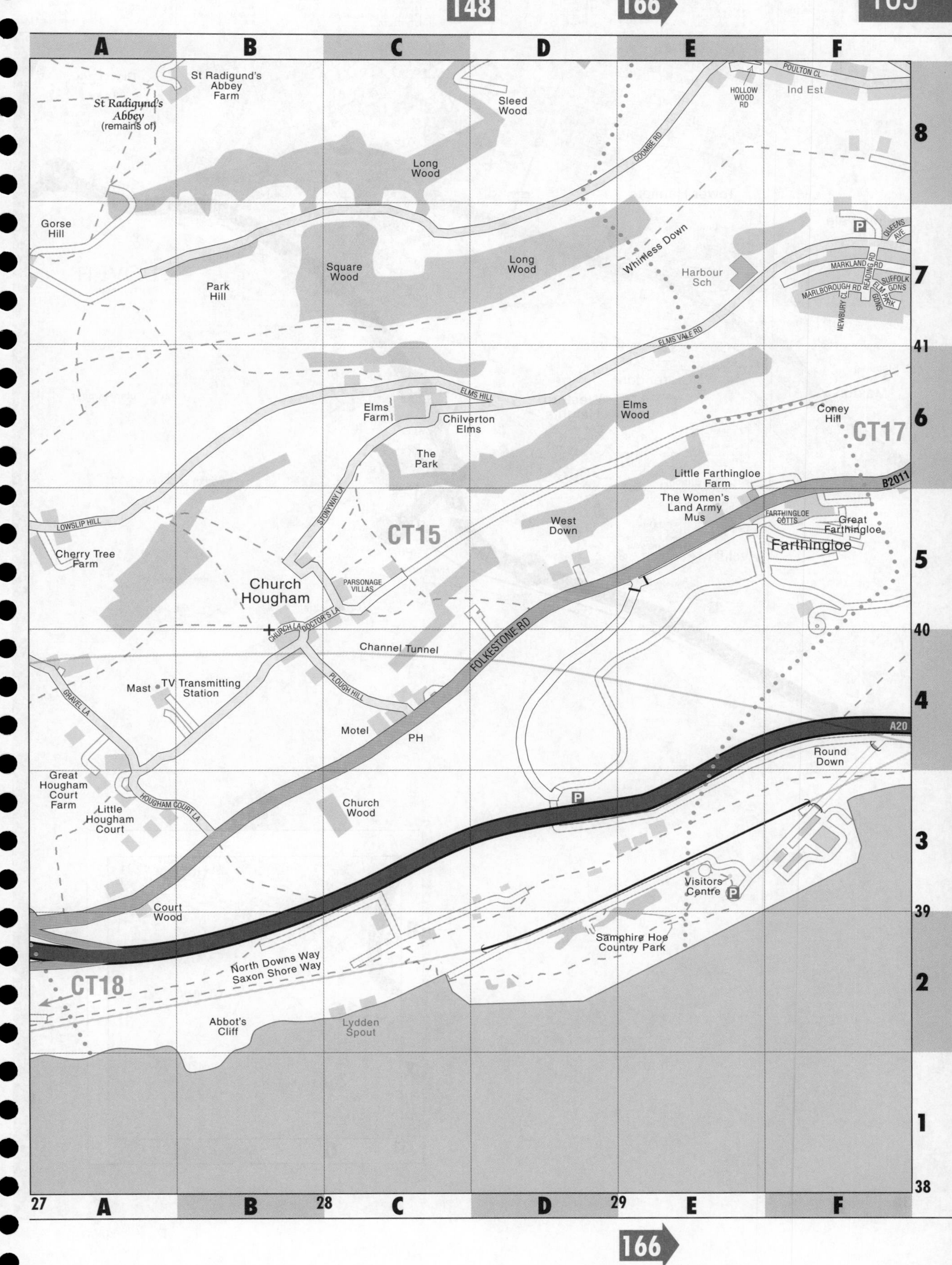
A
B
C
D
E
F
St Radigund's Abbey Farm
St Radigund's Abbey (remains of)
Sleed Wood
POULTON CL
HOLLOW WOOD RD
Ind Est
8
COOMBE RD
Long Wood
Gorse Hill
QUEENS AVE
Whinless Down
Long Wood
Harbour Sch
MARKLAND RD
READING RD
SUFFOLK GDNS
ELM PARK GDNS
MARLBOROUGH RD
NEWBURY CL
7
Square Wood
Park Hill
ELMS VALE RD
41
ELMS HILL
Elms Farm
Chilverton Elms
Elms Wood
Coney Hill
6
CT17
The Park
Little Farthingloe Farm
B2011
The Women's Land Army Mus
LOWSLIP HILL
STONYWAY LA
West Down
FARTHINGLOE COTTS
Great Farthingloe
CT15
Farthingloe
Cherry Tree Farm
5
Church Hougham
PARSONAGE VILLAS
DOCTOR'S LA
CHURCH LA
40
FOLKESTONE RD
Channel Tunnel
GRAVEL LA
Mast
TV Transmitting Station
PLOUGH HILL
4
A20
Motel
PH
Round Down
Great Hougham Court Farm
Little Hougham Court
HOUGHAM COURT LA
Church Wood
3
Visitors Centre
Court Wood
39
Samphire Hoe Country Park
North Downs Way
Saxon Shore Way
CT18
2
Abbot's Cliff
Lydden Spout
1
38
27
28
29

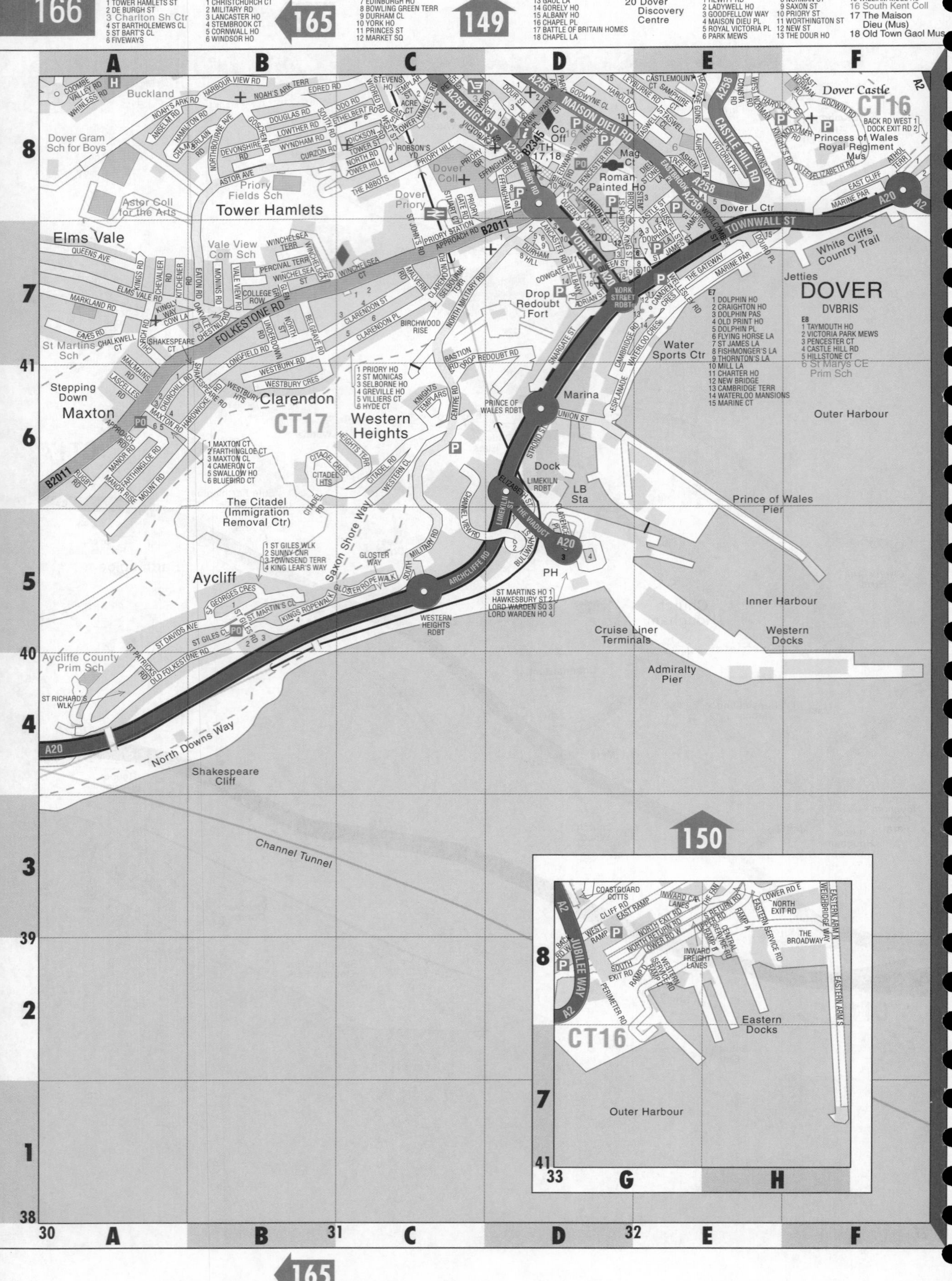

166

C8
1 TOWER HAMLETS ST
2 DE BURGH ST
3 Charlton Sh Ctr
4 ST BARTHOLEMEWS CL
5 ST BART'S CL
6 FIVEWAYS

D7
1 CHRISTCHURCH CT
2 MILITARY RD
3 LANCASTER HO
4 STEMBROOK CT
5 CORNWALL RD
6 WINDSOR HO

165

D7
7 EDINBURGH HO
8 BOWLING GREEN TERR
9 DURHAM CL
10 PRINCES ST
11 YORK HO
12 MARKET SQ

149

D7
13 GAOL LA
14 GORELY HO
15 ALBANY HO
16 CHAPEL PL
17 BATTLE OF BRITAIN HOMES
18 CHAPEL LA

19 BENCH ST
20 Dover
Discovery
Centre

D8
1 HEWITT RD
2 LADYWELL HO
3 GOODFELLOW WAY
4 MAISON DIEU PL
5 ROYAL VICTORIA PL
6 PARK MEWS

7 LADYWELL
8 NORMAN ST
9 SAXON ST
10 PRIORY ST
11 WORTHINGTON ST
12 NEW ST
13 THE DOUR RD

14 SNELGROVE HO
15 WILLIAM MUGE HO
16 South Kent Coll
17 The Maison
    Dieu (Mus)
18 Old Town Gaol Mus

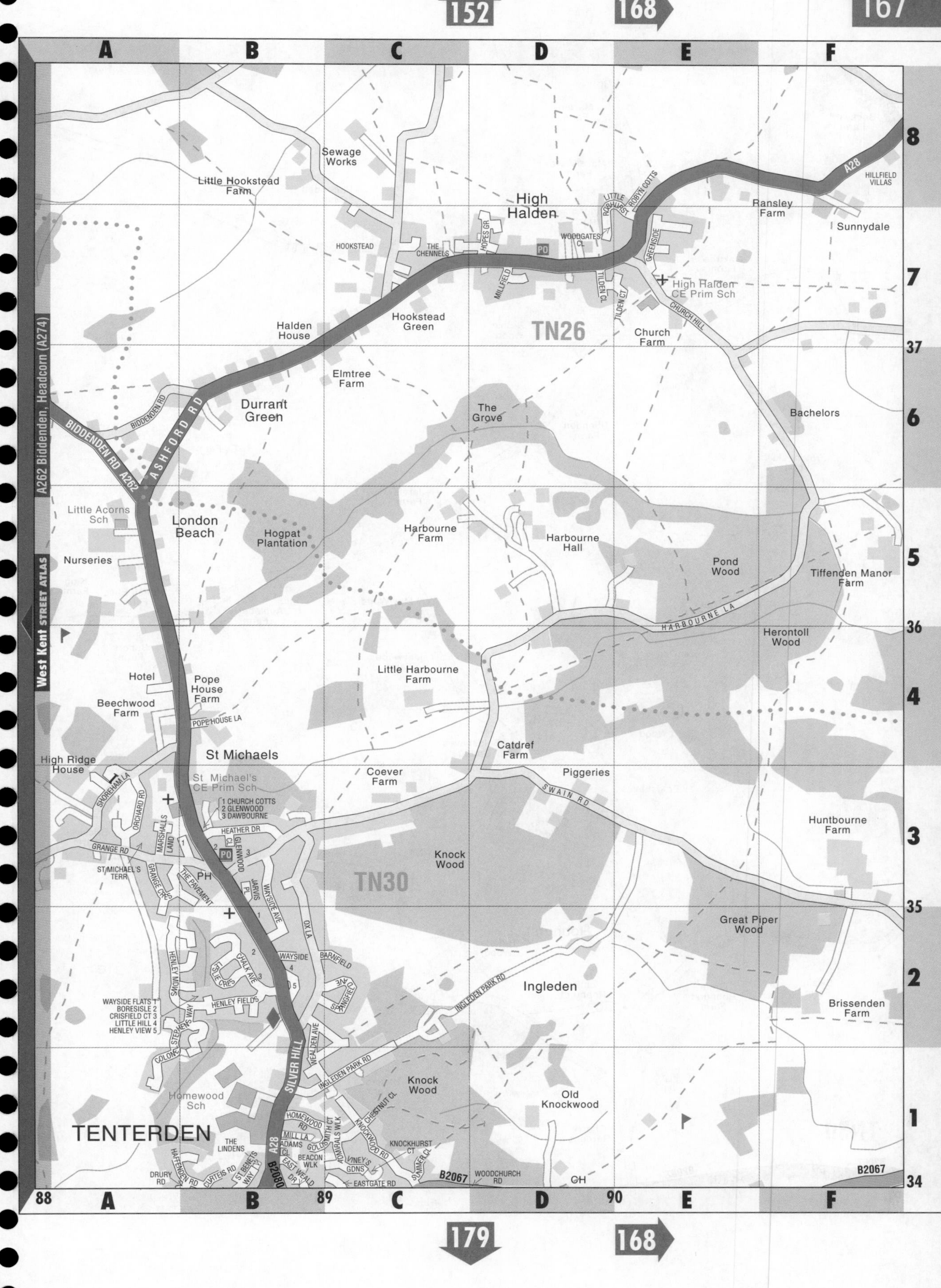

A B C D E F

8 7 37 6 5 36 4 3 35 2 1 34

West Kent STREET ATLAS

A262 Biddenden, Headcorn (A274)

BIDDENDEN RD A262

BIDDENDEN RD

ASHFORD RD

A28

HILLFIELD VILLAS

Ransley Farm

Sunnydale

High Halden

Little Robyns Ley

Robyns Cotts

Greenside

High Halden CE Prim Sch

CHURCH HILL

Church Farm

Bachelors

Sewage Works

Little Hookstead Farm

HOOKSTEAD

THE CHENNELS

HOPES GR

WOODGATES CL

PO

MILLFIELD

TILDEN CL

TILDEN CT

TN26

Hookstead Green

Halden House

Elmtree Farm

Durrant Green

The Grove

Tiffenden Manor Farm

Little Acorns Sch

London Beach

Hogpat Plantation

Harbourne Farm

Harbourne Hall

Pond Wood

HARBOURNE LA

Herontoll Wood

Nurseries

Hotel

Beechwood Farm

Pope House Farm

POPE HOUSE LA

Little Harbourne Farm

Catdref Farm

Piggeries

SWAIN RD

Huntbourne Farm

High Ridge House

St Michaels

St Michael's CE Prim Sch

1 CHURCH COTTS
2 GLENWOOD
3 DAWBOURNE

Coever Farm

Knock Wood

TN30

Great Piper Wood

SHOREHAM LA

ORCHARD RD

GRANGE RD

St MICHAEL'S TERR

MARSHALLS LAND

GRANGE CRES

HEATHER DR

GLENWOOD PL

PO

JARVIS PL

WAYSIDE AVE

OXLA

BARNFIELD

WAYSIDE

PH

THE PAVEMENT

SPRINGFIELD AVE

STILE CRES

CREEK AVE

HENLEY MEWS

HENLEY FIELDS

STEPHENS WAY

COLONE

Ingleden

INGLEDEN PARK RD

Brissenden Farm

WAYSIDE FLATS 1
BORESISLE 2
CRISFIELD CT 3
LITTLE HILL 4
HENLEY VIEW 5

Homewood Sch

TENTERDEN

THE LINDENS

HOMEWOOD RD

SILVER HILL

A28

B2080

MILL LA

ADAMS CL

GOLDS CT

BEACON WLK

VINEY'S GDNS

ST BRITS WAY

EAST WEALD DR

HAFFENDEN RD

DRURY RD

CURTEIS RD

CHESTNUT CL

KNOCKWOOD RD

ADMIRALS WLK

WEALDEN AVE

INGLEDEN PARK RD

EASTGATE RD

WOODCHURCH RD

B2067

CH

KNOCKHURST CT

Knock Wood

Old Knockwood

SILVER CL

B2067

88   89   90

167
153

A B C D E F

8

ASHFORD RD
A28
THE MARTINS
Brickyard
Farm

Marten
Farm

Mace View
Farm

Plurenden
Manor

Lyndhurst
Farm

PLURENDEN
MANOR FARM
COTTS

PLURENDEN RD

7

Oaktree
Farm

CUCKOLD'S
CNR

Brook
Wood

37

Coomb
Wood

6

Little
Tiffenden
Farm

Grove
Farm

Trottingale
Wood

Jarvis
Farm

SHIRKOAK
PK

5

TN26

REDBROOK ST

May Wood

Appleberry
Farm

Church Elms
Farm

King
Farm

36

Great Doney
Wood

Maywood
Farm

Butlers
Farm

4

Barn Wood

Boldshaves
Cottage

Boldshaves

Godfrey
Wood

Ghyll Wood
Farm

BRICKWALL
TERR
WEST
END

Brickwall
Farm

3

SUSAN'S HILL

Susan's Hill
Farm

35

SWAIN RD

Robhurst

Ruffets
Wood

2

Swain
Farm

Great
Robhurst
Farm

Little
Robhurst

Haycross
Wood

Maiden
Wood

Haycross
Farm

1

TN30

Cherry
Gardens

B2067
WOODCHURCH RD

BROOK ST

B2067

34

91 A B 92 C D 93 E F

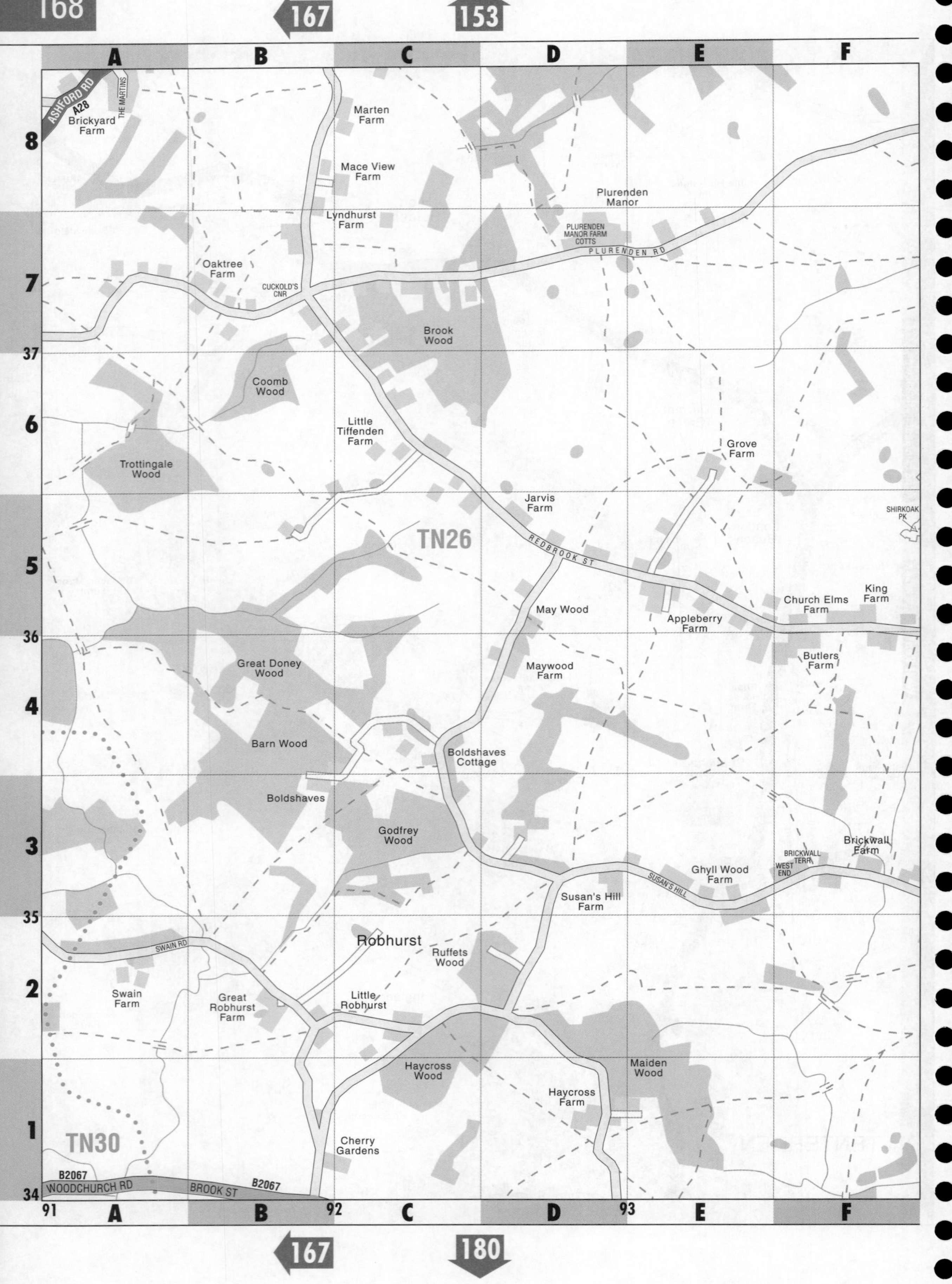

167
180

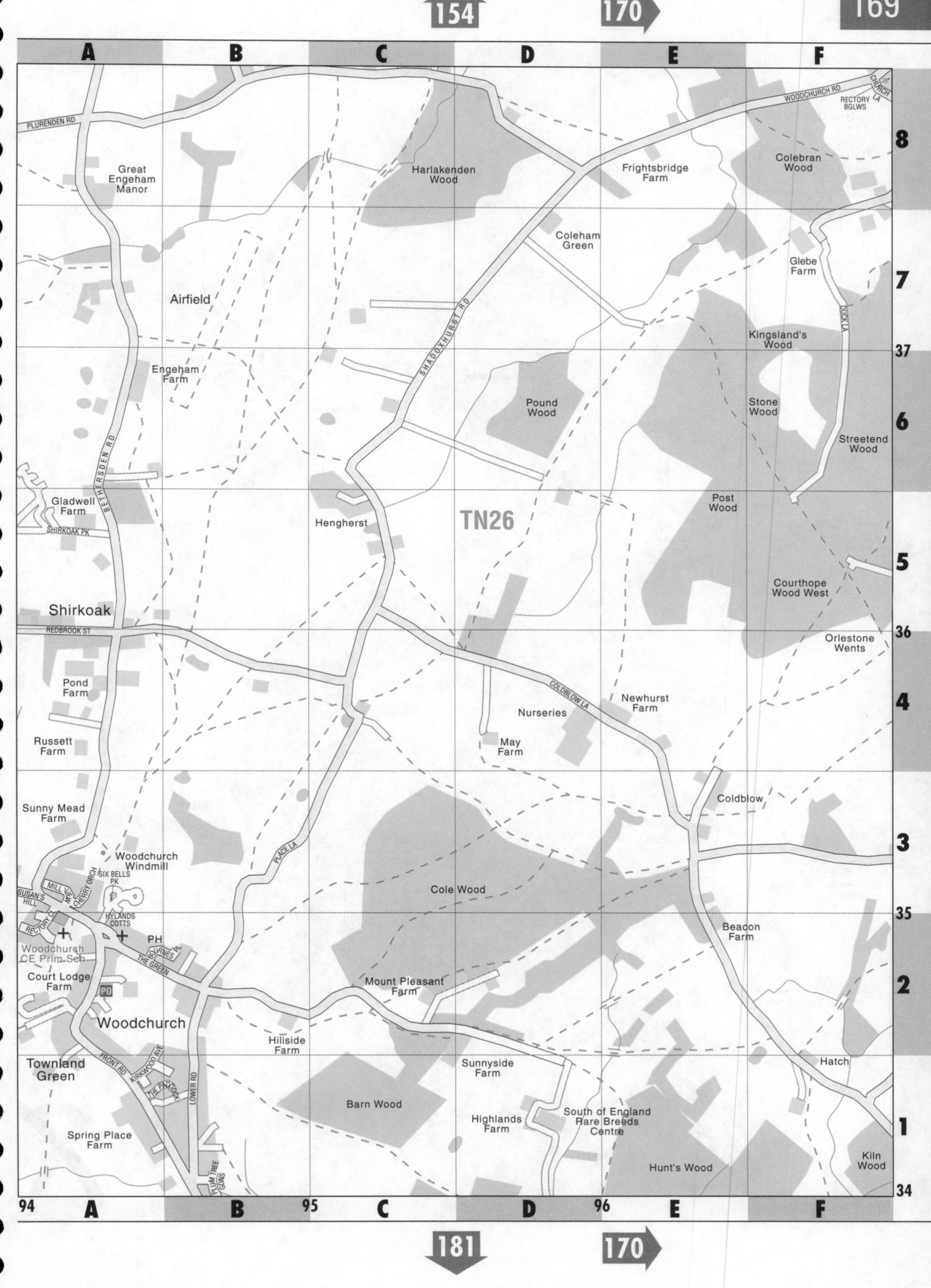
A
B
C
D
E
F
PLURENDEN RD
WOODCHURCH RD
CHURCH LA
RECTORY BGLWS
Great Engeham Manor
Harlakenden Wood
Frightsbridge Farm
Colebran Wood
Coleham Green
Glebe Farm
Airfield
SHADOXHURST RD
DUCK LA
Kingsland's Wood
Engeham Farm
Pound Wood
Stone Wood
Streetend Wood
BETHERSDEN RD
Gladwell Farm
SHIRKOAK PK
Hengherst
TN26
Post Wood
Courthope Wood West
Shirkoak
REDBROOK ST
Orlestone Wents
Pond Farm
COLDBLOW LA
Newhurst Farm
Nurseries
Russett Farm
May Farm
Coldblow
Sunny Mead Farm
Woodchurch Windmill
PLACE LA
SIX BELLS PK
SUSAN'S HILL
MILL VW
CHERRY ORCH
Cole Wood
RECTORY CL
HYLANDS COTTS
PH
BYRNES PL
THE GREEN
Beacon Farm
Woodchurch CE Prim Sch
Court Lodge Farm
PO
Mount Pleasant Farm
Woodchurch
Hillside Farm
Townland Green
FRONT RD
KIRKWOOD AVE
THE PADDOCK
LOWER RD
Sunnyside Farm
Hatch
Barn Wood
Highlands Farm
South of England Rare Breeds Centre
Spring Place Farm
PLUM TREE GDNS
Hunt's Wood
Kiln Wood
8
7
37
6
5
36
4
3
35
2
1
34
94
95
96

A B C D E F

8

St Peter's Way
MARINE CL
Shadoxhurst
THE STREET
DUCK LA
Nursery
Alex
Farm

Coxland
Wood

Works

ASHFORD RD

7

Hillcrest Farm

Upper Toke's
Wood

CHURCH LA

Nursery

Great Turrels
Wood

HORNASH LA

Manor
Farm

Forty Acre
Wood

37

Nickley
Wood

Bambridge Wood

Bromley
Green

6

Moat
Farm

NICKLEY WOOD RD

Dering
Wood

Poplar
Farm

Little
Hurst

Bromley Green
Farm

BROMLEY GREEN RD

5

Courthope
Wood East

Jenkey
Farm

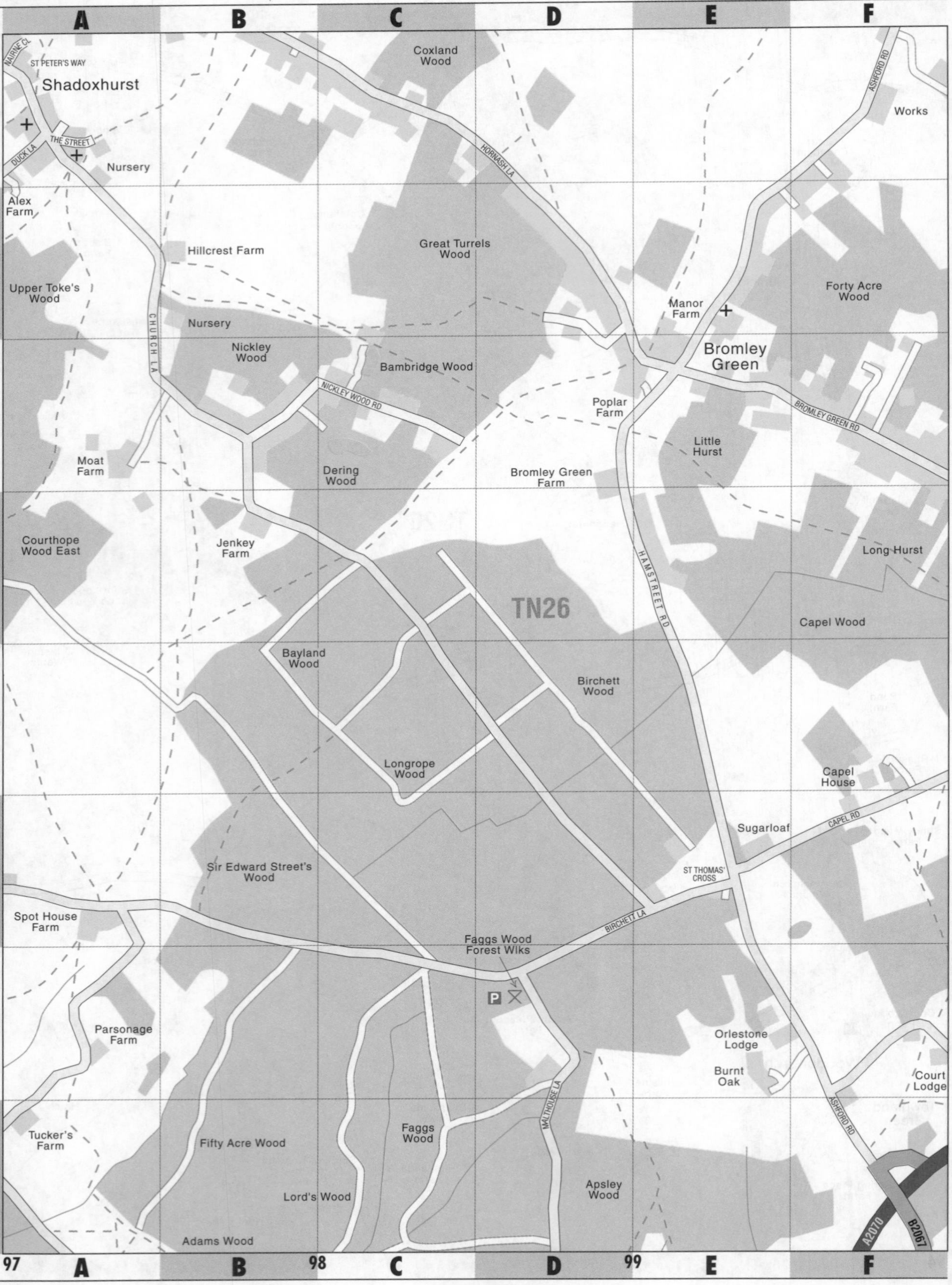

TN26

HAMSTREET RD

Long Hurst

Capel Wood

36

Bayland
Wood

Birchett
Wood

4

Longrope
Wood

Capel
House

Sugarloaf

CAPEL RD

3

Sir Edward Street's
Wood

St Thomas'
Cross

BIRCHETT LA

Spot House
Farm

35

Faggs Wood
Forest Wlks

P

2

Parsonage
Farm

WALTHOUSE LA

Orlestone
Lodge

Burnt
Oak

Court
Lodge

ASHFORD RD

1

Tucker's
Farm

Fifty Acre Wood

Faggs
Wood

Apsley
Wood

A2070

B2067

Lord's Wood

34

Adams Wood

97 A B 98 C D 99 E F

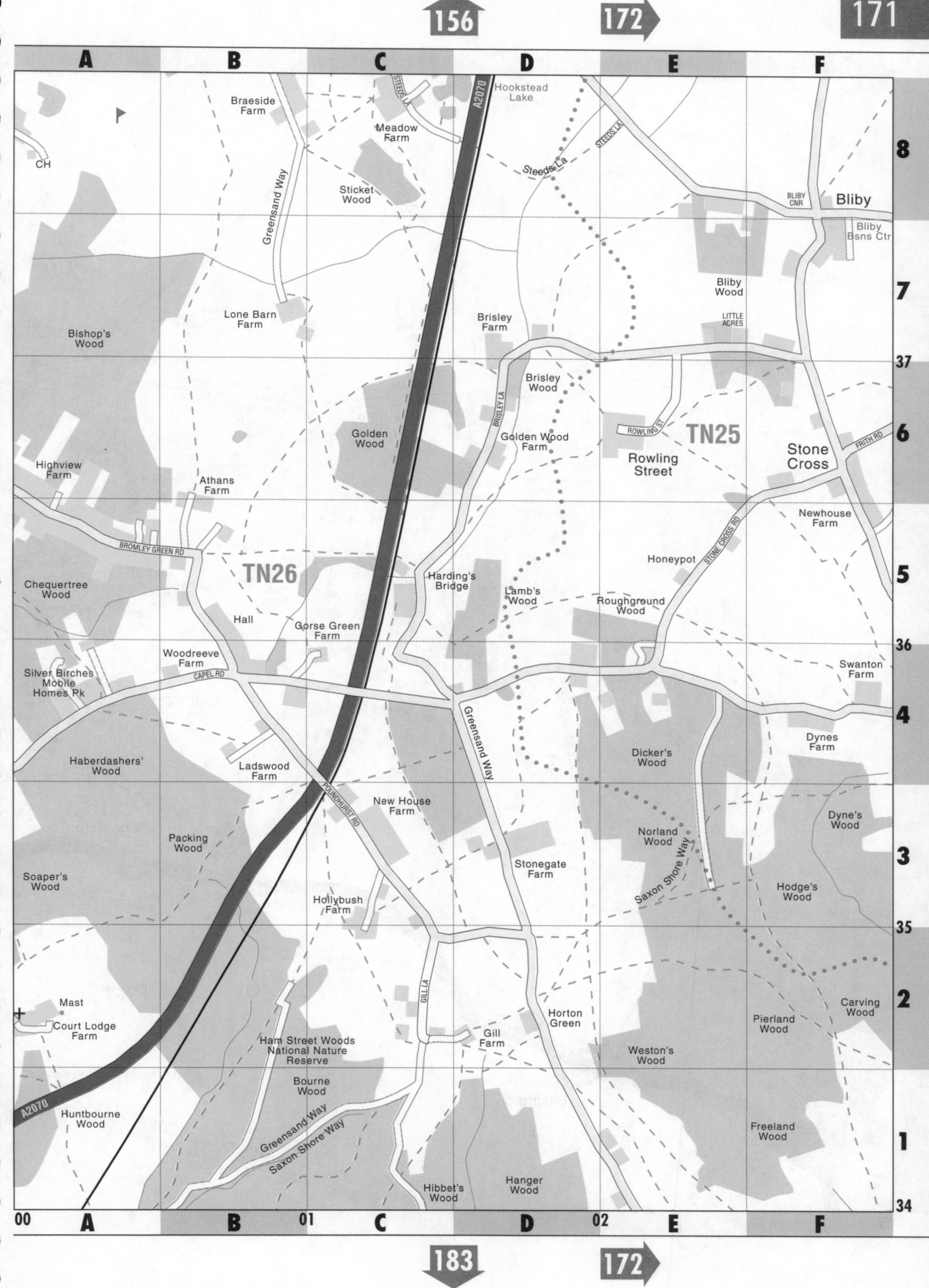
156
172
A
B
C
D
E
F
8
7
37
6
5
36
4
3
35
2
1
34
00
01
02
Braeside Farm
Meadow Farm
Hookstead Lake
A2070
STEEDS LA
Steeds La
CH
Greensand Way
Sticket Wood
BLIBY CNR
Bliby
Bliby Bsns Ctr
Bliby Wood
LITTLE ACRES
Lone Barn Farm
Brisley Farm
Bishop's Wood
Brisley Wood
BRISLEY LA
Golden Wood
Golden Wood Farm
ROWLING ST
TN25
Rowling Street
Stone Cross
FRITH RD
Highview Farm
Athans Farm
Newhouse Farm
BROMLEY GREEN RD
TN26
Harding's Bridge
Honeypot
STONE CROSS RD
Chequertree Wood
Lamb's Wood
Roughground Wood
Hall
Gorse Green Farm
Woodreeve Farm
Swanton Farm
Silver Birches Mobile Homes Pk
CAPEL RD
Greensand Way
Dynes Farm
Haberdashers' Wood
Ladswood Farm
Dicker's Wood
POUNDHURST RD
New House Farm
Dyne's Wood
Norland Wood
Packing Wood
Saxon Shore Way
Stonegate Farm
Soaper's Wood
Hodge's Wood
Hollybush Farm
Mast
GILL LA
Carving Wood
Court Lodge Farm
Horton Green
Pierland Wood
Gill Farm
Ham Street Woods National Nature Reserve
Weston's Wood
Bourne Wood
A2070
Huntbourne Wood
Greensand Way
Saxon Shore Way
Freeland Wood
Hibbet's Wood
Hanger Wood
183
172

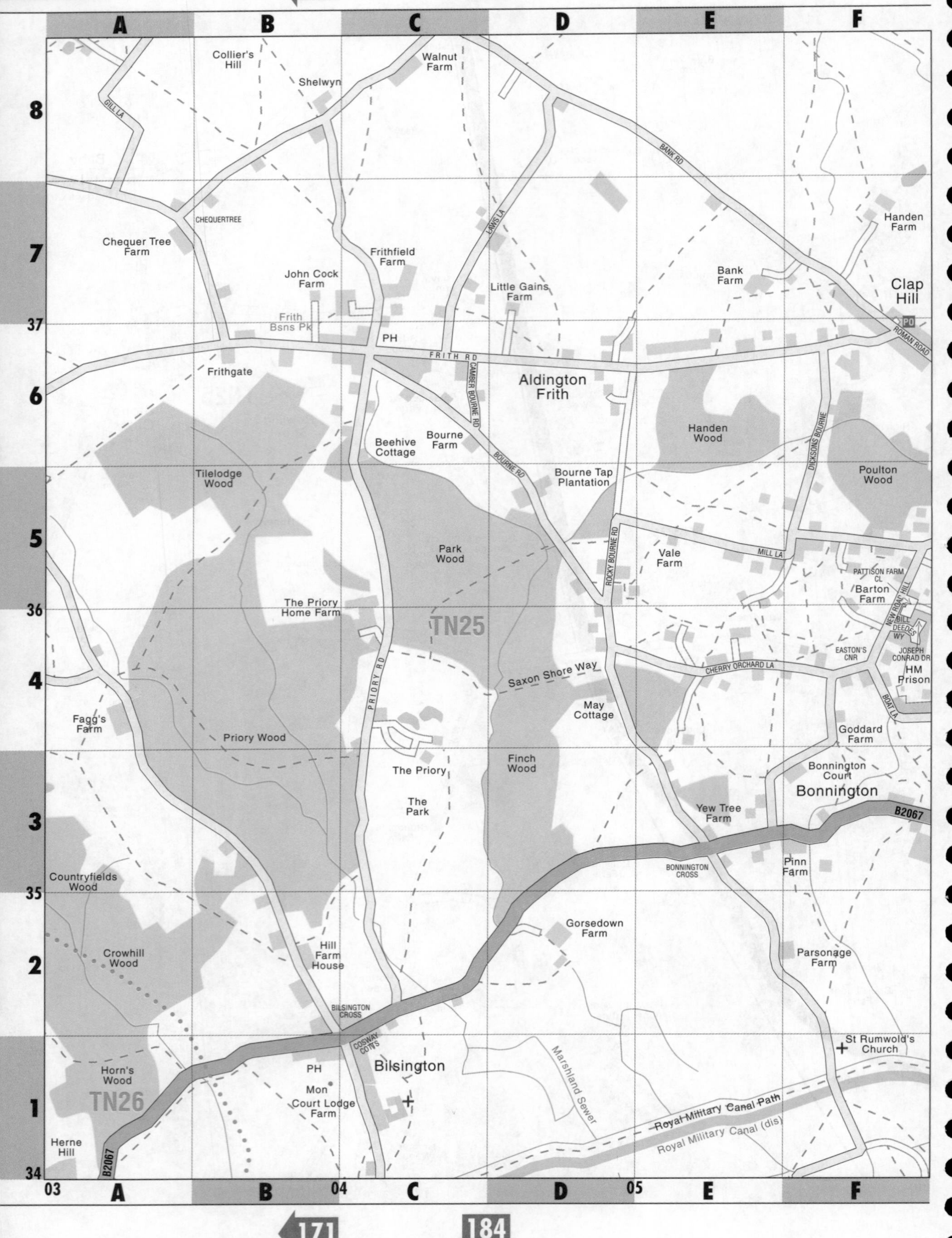

171
157
171
184

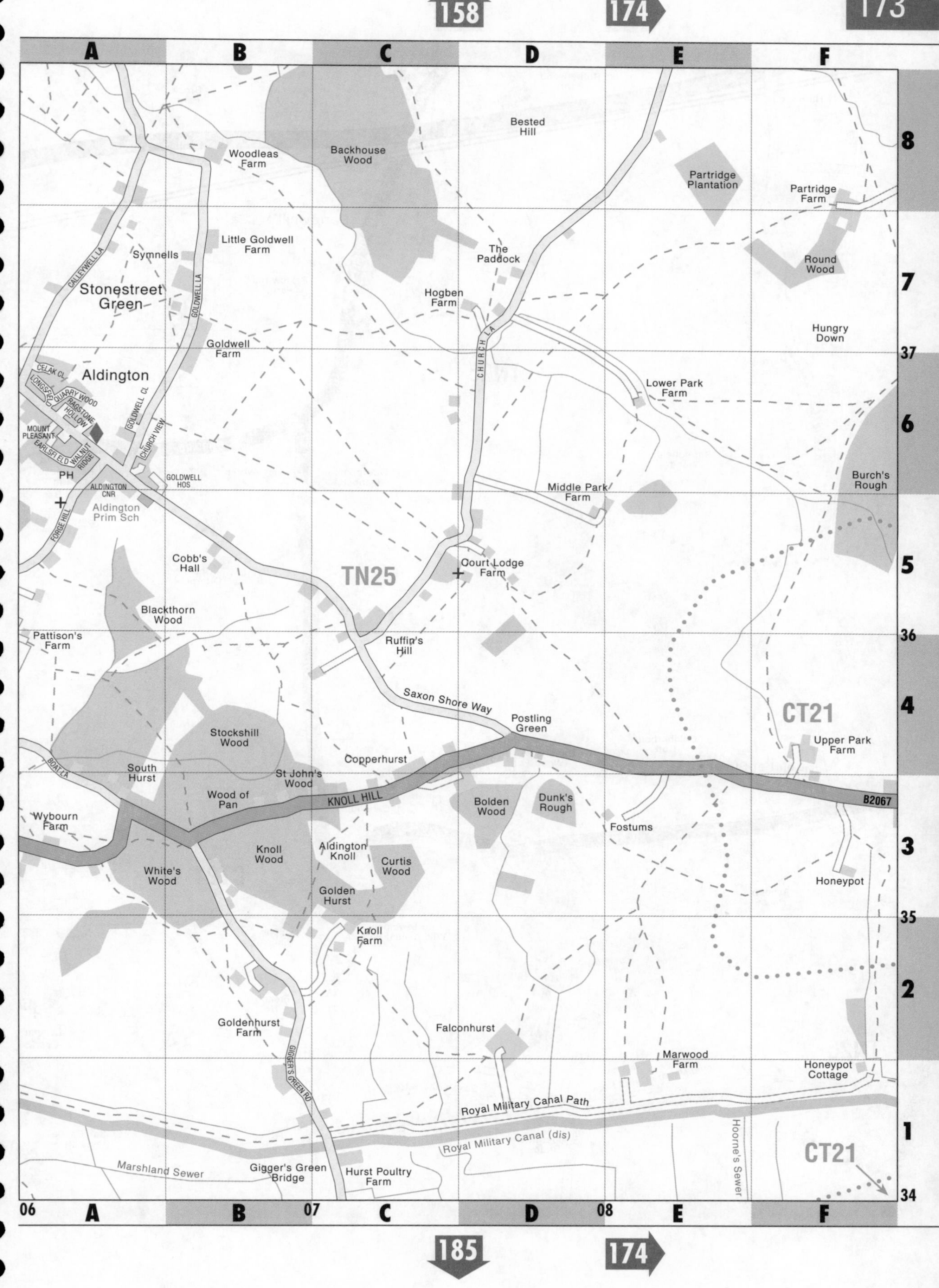

A   B   C   D   E   F

8

Bested Hill

Woodleas Farm

Backhouse Wood

Partridge Plantation

Partridge Farm

Little Goldwell Farm

Symnells

The Paddock

Round Wood

7

Stonestreet Green

Hogben Farm

Goldwell Farm

Hungry Down

CALLEYWELLS LA

GOLDWELL LA

CHURCH LA

37

CELAK CL

Aldington

Lower Park Farm

6

QUARRY WOOD
FLAGSTONE HOLLOW

GOLDWELL CL

MOUNT PLEASANT

EARLSFIELD

LONGFIELD

WALNUT RIDGE

CHURCH VIEW

GOLDWELL HOS

Middle Park Farm

Burch's Rough

PH

ALDINGTON CNR

Aldington Prim Sch

FORGE HILL

Cobb's Hall

TN25

Court Lodge Farm

5

Blackthorn Wood

Pattison's Farm

Ruffin's Hill

36

Saxon Shore Way

Stockshill Wood

Postling Green

CT21

4

BOAT LA

South Hurst

Copperhurst

Upper Park Farm

St John's Wood

Wood of Pan

KNOLL HILL

Bolden Wood

Dunk's Rough

B2067

Wybourn Farm

Fostums

White's Wood

Knoll Wood

Aldington Knoll

Curtis Wood

Honeypot

3

Golden Hurst

35

Knoll Farm

2

GIGGER'S GREEN RD

Goldenhurst Farm

Falconhurst

Marwood Farm

Honeypot Cottage

Royal Military Canal Path

CT21

1

Royal Military Canal (dis)

Hoorne's Sewer

Marshland Sewer

Gigger's Green Bridge

Hurst Poultry Farm

34

173
159

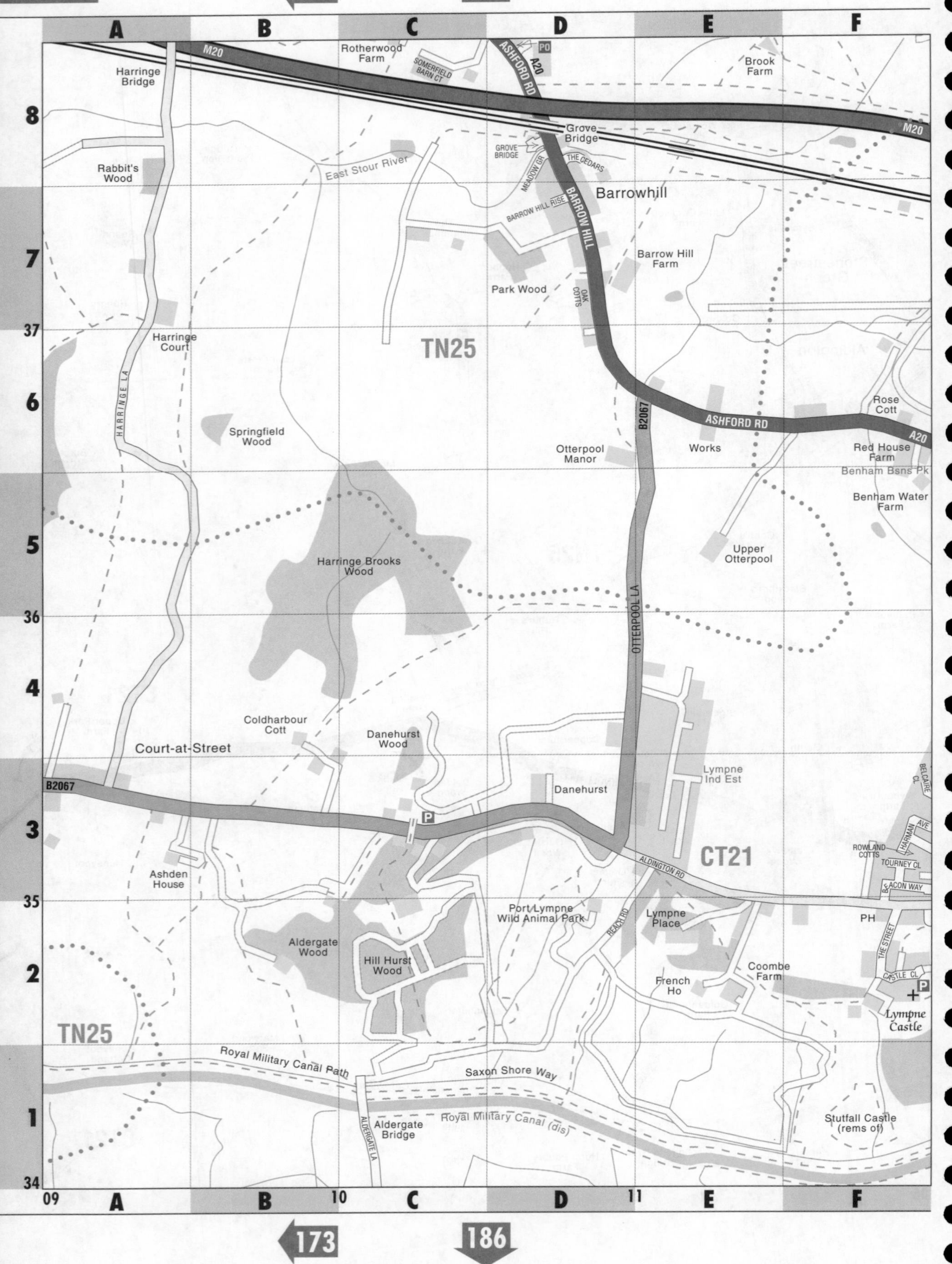
A
B
C
D
E
F
M20
Harringe Bridge
Rotherwood Farm
SOMERFIELD BARN CT
ASHFORD RD
A20
PO
Brook Farm
8
Grove Bridge
GROVE BRIDGE
THE CEDARS
MEADOW GR
M20
Rabbit's Wood
East Stour River
BARROW HILL
Barrowhill
BARROW HILL RISE
7
Barrow Hill Farm
Park Wood
OAK COTTS
37
Harringe Court
TN25
HARRINGE LA
6
Rose Cott
B2067
ASHFORD RD
A20
Springfield Wood
Otterpool Manor
Works
Red House Farm
Benham Bsns Pk
Benham Water Farm
5
Harringe Brooks Wood
Upper Otterpool
36
OTTERPOOL LA
4
Coldharbour Cott
Danehurst Wood
Court-at-Street
Lympne Ind Est
BELCAIRE CL
B2067
Danehurst
3
P
HARMAN AVE
ROWLAND COTTS
TOURNEY CL
ALDINGTON RD
CT21
BEACON WAY
Ashden House
35
Port Lympne Wild Animal Park
REACH RD
Lympne Place
PH
Aldergate Wood
Hill Hurst Wood
THE STREET
2
Coombe Farm
French Ho
CASTLE CL
P
Lympne Castle
TN25
Royal Military Canal Path
Saxon Shore Way
1
Aldergate Bridge
ALDERGATE LA
Royal Military Canal (dis)
Stutfall Castle (rems of)
34
09
10
11

173
186

160
176

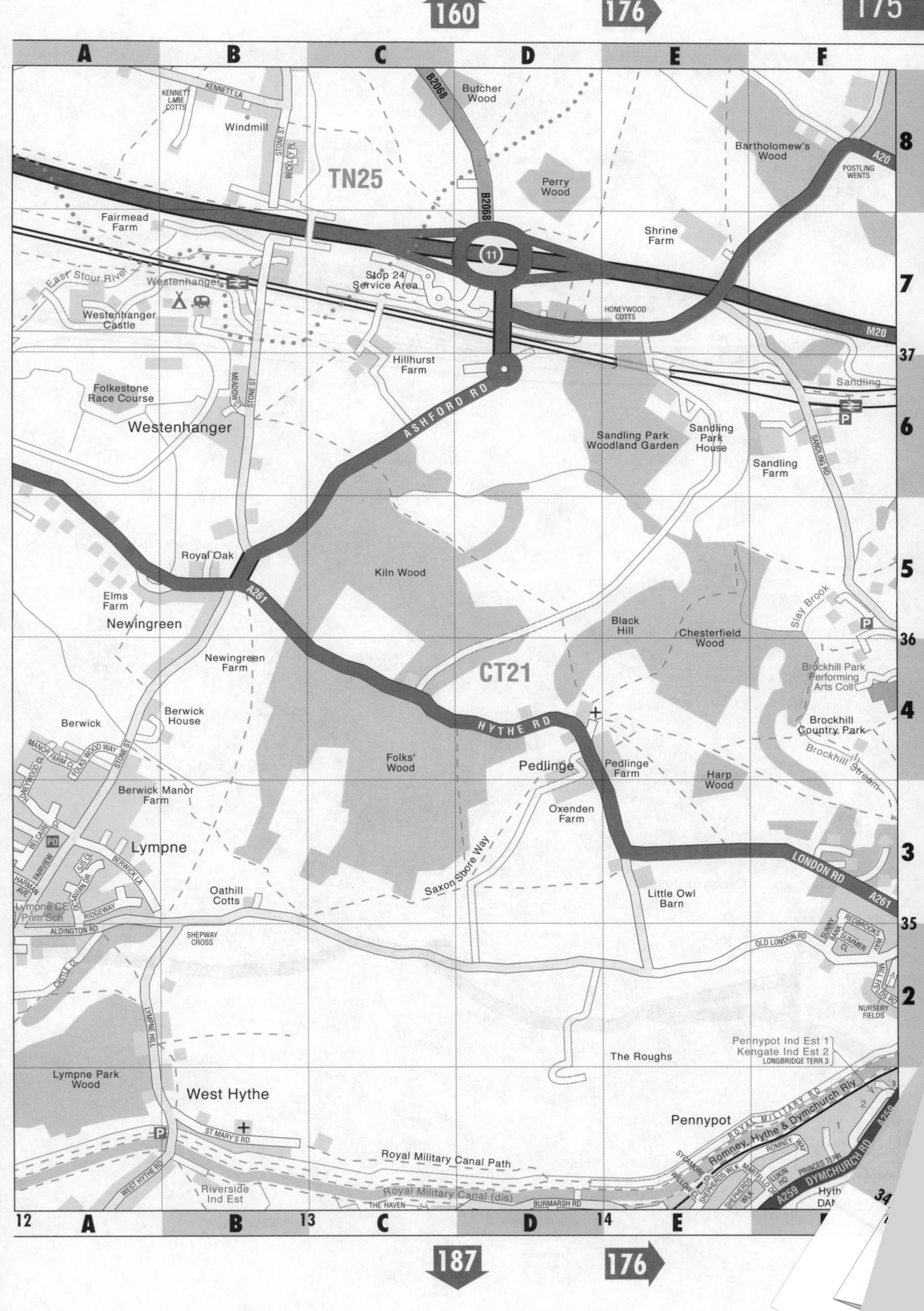
A
B
C
D
E
F
8
7
37
6
5
36
4
3
35
2
34
12
13
14
TN25
CT21
Kennett La
Kennett Lane Cotts
Windmill
Stone St
Beckley Pl
Butcher Wood
B2068
Perry Wood
Bartholomew's Wood
A20
Postling Wents
Fairmead Farm
Shrine Farm
11
East Stour River
Westenhanger
Stop 24 Service Area
Westenhanger Castle
Honeywood Cotts
M20
Hillhurst Farm
Sandling
Folkestone Race Course
Meadow Cl
Westenhanger
Ashford Rd
Sandling Park Woodland Garden
Sandling Park House
Sandling Farm
Sandling Rd
Royal Oak
Kiln Wood
Elms Farm
A261
Newingreen
Slay Brook
Black Hill
Chesterfield Wood
Newingreen Farm
Brockhill Park Performing Arts Coll
Berwick House
Berwick
Hythe Rd
Brockhill Country Park
Manor Farm Cl
Folks Wood Way
Honeywood Cl
Folks' Wood
Pedlinge
Pedlinge Farm
Harp Wood
Brockhill Stream
Berwick Manor Farm
Oxenden Farm
Belcaire Cl
PO
Lympne
Saxon Shore Way
London Rd
Fairview
Harman Ave
Octavian Dr
Berwick La
Oathill Cotts
Little Owl Barn
A261
Lympne CE Prim Sch
Ridgeway
Aldington Rd
Shepway Cross
Old London Rd
Sunny Bank
Summer Cl
Redbrooks Way
Castle Cl
Mill Fields Rd
Nursery Fields
Lympne Hill
Pennypot Ind Est 1
Kengate Ind Est 2
Longbridge Terr 3
The Roughs
Lympne Park Wood
West Hythe
Royal Military Rd
Romney, Hythe & Dymchurch Rly
Pennypot
St Mary's Rd
Romney Way
Royal Military Canal Path
Sycamore Cl
Willow Ct
Shepherds Wlk
Martello Dr
Lukin Ho
Princes Terr
Dymchurch Rd
A259
West Hythe Rd
Riverside Ind Est
Royal Military Canal (dis)
The Haven
Burmarsh Rd

187
176

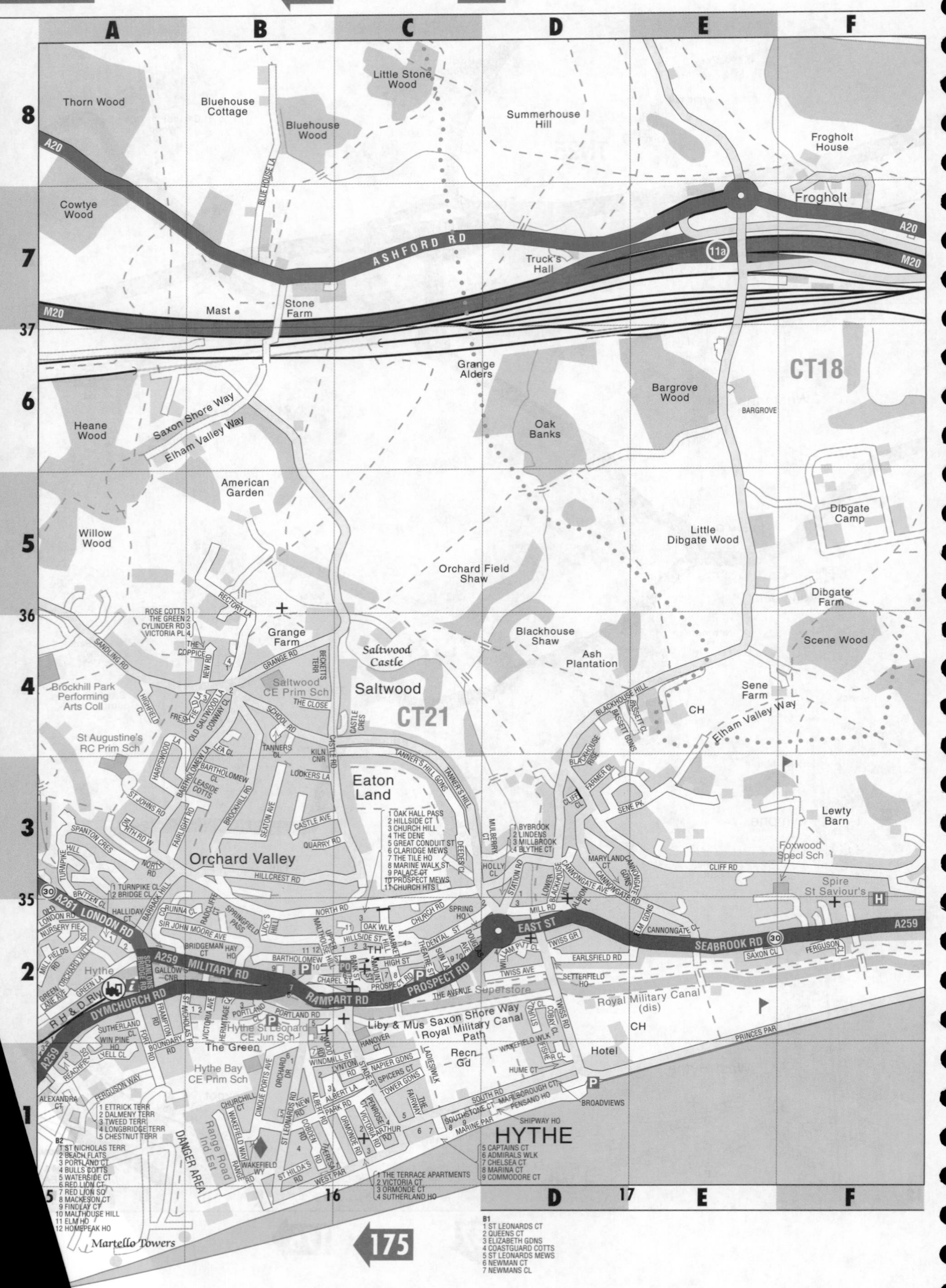

175

161

A B C D E F

8

Thorn Wood

Bluehouse Cottage

Little Stone Wood

Bluehouse Wood

Summerhouse Hill

Frogholt House

A20

7

Cowtye Wood

Frogholt

A20

11a

Truck's Hall

M20

M20

37

Stone Farm

Mast

Grange Alders

Bargrove Wood

BARGROVE

CT18

6

Heane Wood

Saxon Shore Way

Elham Valley Way

Oak Banks

Little Dibgate Wood

Dibgate Camp

5

American Garden

Willow Wood

Orchard Field Shaw

Dibgate Farm

Scene Wood

36

ROSE COTTS 1
THE GREEN 2
CYLINDER RD 3
VICTORIA PL 4

RECTORY LA

Grange Farm

Saltwood Castle

Blackhouse Shaw

Ash Plantation

Sene Farm

4

Brockhill Park Performing Arts Coll

THE COPPICE

Saltwood CE Prim Sch

Saltwood

CT21

CH

Elham Valley Way

St Augustine's RC Prim Sch

THE CLOSE

CASTLE CRES

BASSETT GDNS

3

SPANTON CRES

Orchard Valley

Eaton Land

1 OAK HALL PASS
2 HILLSIDE CT
3 CHURCH HILL
4 THE DENE
5 GREAT CONDUIT ST
6 CLARIDGE MEWS
7 THE TILE HO
8 MARINE WALK ST
9 PALACE GT
10 PROSPECT MEWS
11 CHURCH HTS

1 BYBROOK
2 LINDENS
3 MILLBROOK
4 BLYTHE CT

Lewty Barn

Foxwood Specl Sch

SPIRE St Saviour's

35

A261 LONDON RD

A259

1 TURNPIKE CL
2 BRIDGE CL

HILLCREST RD

NORTH RD

CHURCH RD

CLIFF RD

H

A259

SEABROOK RD

MILITARY RD

2

Hythe

DYMCHURCH RD

RAMPART RD

PROSPECT RD

The Avenue Superstore

EAST ST

Royal Military Canal (dis)

CH

Hotel

R. H. & D. RLY

1

Alexandra Ct

FERGUSON WAY

The Green

Hythe Bay CE Prim Sch

DANGER AREA

Liby & Mus Saxon Shore Way Royal Military Canal Path

Recn Gd

HYTHE

5 CAPTAINS CT
6 ADMIRALS WLK
7 CHELSEA CT
8 MARINA CT
9 COMMODORE CT

1 ETTRICK TERR
2 DALMENY TERR
3 TWEED TERR
4 LONGBRIDGE TERR
5 CHESTNUT TERR

B2
1 ST NICHOLAS TERR
2 BEACH FLATS
3 PORTLAND CT
4 BULLS COTTS
5 WATERSIDE CT
6 RED LION CT
7 RED LION SQ
8 MACKESON CT
9 FINDLAY CT
10 MALTHOUSE HILL
11 ELM HO
12 HOMEPEAK HO

1 THE TERRACE APARTMENTS
2 VICTORIA CT
3 ORMONDE CT
4 SUTHERLAND HO

Martello Towers

175

16

D

17

E

F

B1
1 ST LEONARDS CT
2 QUEENS CT
3 ELIZABETH GDNS
4 COASTGUARD COTTS
5 ST LEONARDS MEWS
6 NEWMAN CT
7 NEWMANS CL

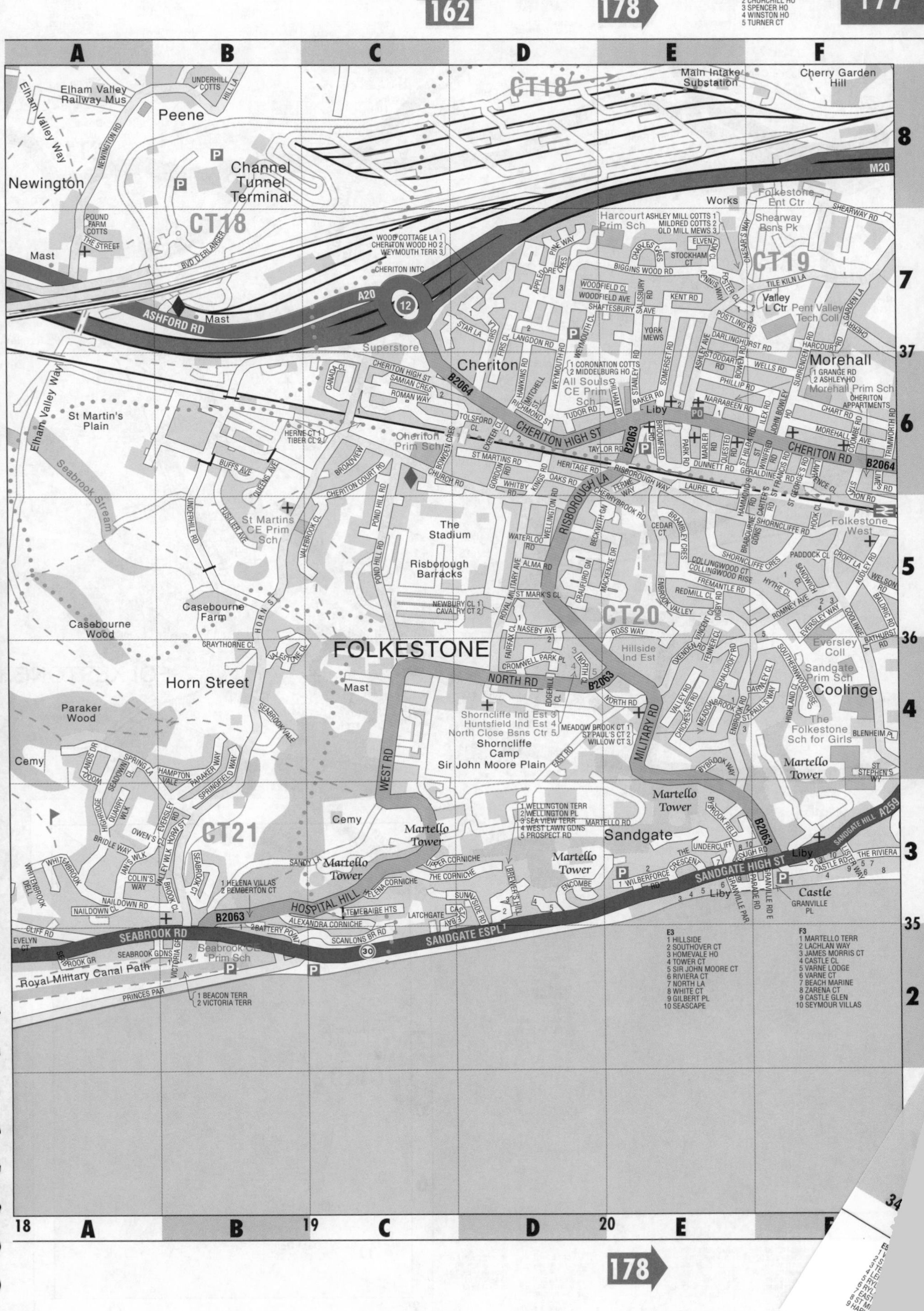

F5
1 WALMER WAY
2 CHURCHILL HO
3 SPENCER HO
4 WINSTON HO
5 TURNER CT

CT18
Main Intake Substation
Cherry Garden Hill
Elham Valley Railway Mus
Peene
UNDERHILL COTTS
M20
8
Newington
Channel Tunnel Terminal
CT18
Works
Folkestone Ent Ctr
Shearway Bsns Pk
POUND FARM COTTS
Mast
Harcourt Prim Sch
ASHLEY MILL COTTS 1
MILDRED COTTS 3
OLD MILL MEWS 2
STOCKHAM CT
CT19
7
Mast
ASHFORD RD
Mast
A20
12
Biggins Wood Rd
WOODFIELD CL
WOODFIELD AVE
SHAFTESBURY AVE
KENT RD
Valley L Ctr
Pent Valley Tech Coll
37
Superstore
Cheriton
WOOD COTTAGE LA 1
CHERITON WOOD HO 2
WEYMOUTH TERR 3
CHERITON INTC
B2064
CHERITON HIGH ST
YORK MEWS
1 CORONATION COTTS
2 MIDDELBURG HO
All Souls CE Prim Sch
Morehall
Morehall Prim Sch
6
St Martin's Plain
CHERITON HIGH ST
SAMIAN CRES
ROMAN WAY
Cheriton Prim Sch
B2063
B2064
CHERITON RD
CHERITON APPARTMENTS
MOREHALL AVE
Folkestone West
5
Casebourne Farm
St Martins CE Prim Sch
The Stadium
Risborough Barracks
WATERLOO CL
ALMA RD
CT20
Hillside Ind Est
36
Casebourne Wood
GRAYTHORNE CL
NEWBURY CL 1
CAVALRY CT 2
NASEBY AVE
ROSS WAY
Eversley Coll
Sandgate Prim Sch
Coolinge
4
Horn Street
Mast
FOLKESTONE
NORTH RD
Shorncliffe Ind Est 3
Huntsfield Ind Est 4
North Close Bsns Ctr 5
MEADOW BROOK CT 1
ST PAUL'S CT 2
WILLOW CT 3
MILITARY RD
The Folkestone Sch for Girls
Paraker Wood
Shorncliffe Camp
Sir John Moore Plain
Martello Tower
Cemy
CT21
Cemy
Martello Tower
1 WELLINGTON TERR
2 WELLINGTON PL
3 SEA VIEW TERR
4 WEST LAWN GDNS
5 PROSPECT RD
Martello Tower
Martello Tower
Sandgate
B2063
SANDGATE HILL
A259
Liby
3
1 HELENA VILLAS
2 PEMBERTON CT
B2063
Martello Tower
UPPER CORNICHE
THE CORNICHE
1 WILBERFORCE RD
ENCOMBE
SANDGATE HIGH ST
Castle
Liby
HOSPITAL HILL
TEMERAIRE HTS
ALEXANDRA CORNICHE
BATTERY POINT
SCANLONS BR RD
30
SANDGATE ESPL
35
CLIFF RD
EVELYN
Royal Military Canal Path
Seabrook CE Prim Sch
SEABROOK RD
PRINCES PAR
1 BEACON TERR
2 VICTORIA TERR
E3
1 HILLSIDE
2 SOUTHOVER CT
3 HOMEVALE HO
4 TOWER CT
5 SIR JOHN MOORE CT
6 RIVIERA CT
7 NORTH LA
8 WHITE CT
9 GILBERT PL
10 SEASCAPE
F3
1 MARTELLO TERR
2 LACHLAN WAY
3 JAMES MORRIS CT
4 CASTLE CL
5 VARNE LODGE
6 VARNE CT
7 BEACH MARINE
8 ZARENA CT
9 CASTLE GLEN
10 SEYMOUR VILLAS
2

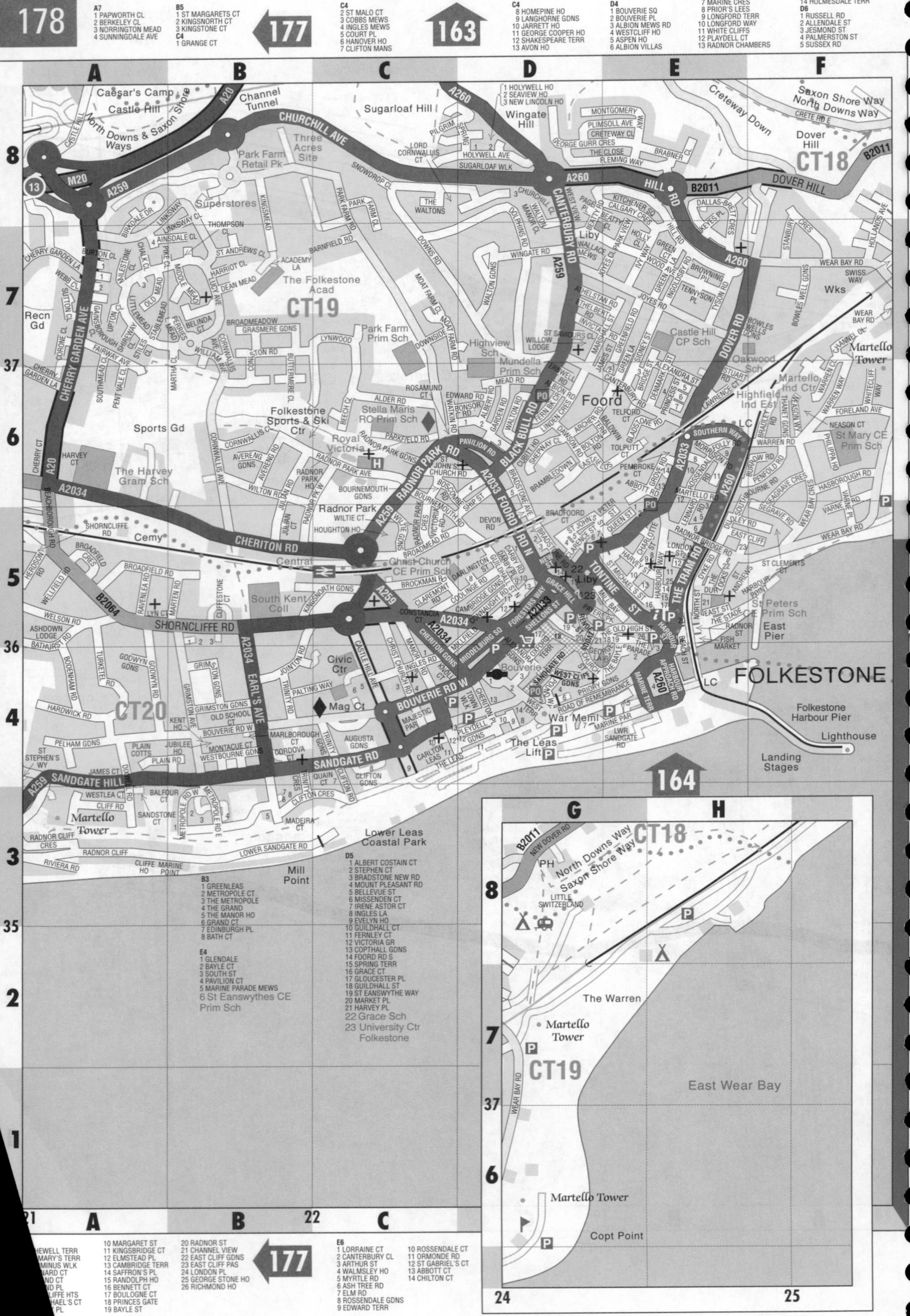
A7
1 PAPWORTH CL
2 BERKELEY CL
3 NORRINGTON MEAD
4 SUNNINGDALE AVE
B5
1 ST MARGARETS CT
2 KINGSNORTH CT
3 KINGSTONE CT
C4
1 GRANGE CT
177
C4
2 ST MALO CT
3 COBBS MEWS
4 INGLES MEWS
5 COURT PL
6 HANOVER HO
7 CLIFTON MANS
163
C4
8 HOMEPINE HO
9 LANGHORNE GDNS
10 JARRETT HO
11 GEORGE COOPER HO
12 SHAKESPEARE TERR
13 AVON HO
D4
1 BOUVERIE SQ
2 BOUVERIE PL
3 ALBION MEWS RD
4 WESTCLIFF HO
5 ASPEN HO
6 ALBION VILLAS
7 MARINE CRES
8 PRIOR'S LEES
9 LONGFORD TERR
10 LONGFORD WAY
11 WHITE CLIFFS
12 PLAYDELL CT
13 RADNOR CHAMBERS
14 HOLMESDALE TERR
D6
1 RUSSELL RD
2 ALLENDALE ST
3 JESMOND ST
4 PALMERSTON ST
5 SUSSEX RD
A B C D E F
Caesar's Camp
Castle Hill
Channel Tunnel
North Downs & Saxon Shore Ways
Sugarloaf Hill
Wingate Hill
Creteway Down
Saxon Shore Way
North Downs Way
Dover Hill
CT18
CHURCHILL AVE
Three Acres Site
Park Farm Retail Pk
Superstores
The Folkestone Acad
CT19
Park Farm Prim Sch
Highview Sch
Mundella Prim Sch
Castle Hill CP Sch
Oakwood Sch
Martello Tower
Martello Ind Ctr
Highfield Ind Est
Foord
Liby
Recn Gd
Sports Gd
Folkestone Sports & Ski Ctr
Stella Maris RC Prim Sch
Royal Victoria
The Harvey Gram Sch
Radnor Park
Cemy
Central
Christ Church CE Prim Sch
South Kent Coll
Civic Ctr
Mag Ct
Bouverie
War Meml
The Leas Lift
St Mary CE Prim Sch
St Peters CE Prim Sch
East Pier
FOLKESTONE
Folkestone Harbour Pier
Lighthouse
Landing Stages
CT20
Martello Tower
Lower Leas Coastal Park
Mill Point
CHERRY GARDEN AVE
CHERITON RD
SHORNCLIFFE RD
SANDGATE RD
SANDGATE HILL
EARL'S AVE
BOUVERIE RD W
RADNOR PARK RD
CANTERBURY RD
BLACK BULL RD
FOORD RD N
TONTINE ST
THE TRAM RD
DOVER RD
DOVER HILL
164
B3
1 GREENLEAS
2 METROPOLE CT
3 THE METROPOLE
4 THE GRAND
5 THE MANOR HO
6 GRAND CT
7 EDINBURGH PL
8 BATH CT
E4
1 GLENDALE
2 BAYLE CT
3 SOUTH ST
4 PAVILION CT
5 MARINE PARADE MEWS
6 St Eanswythes CE Prim Sch
D5
1 ALBERT COSTAIN CT
2 STEPHEN CT
3 BRADSTONE NEW RD
4 MOUNT PLEASANT RD
5 BELLEVUE ST
6 MISSENDEN CT
7 IRENE ASTOR CT
8 INGLES LA
9 EVELYN HO
10 GUILDHALL CT
11 FERNLEY CT
12 VICTORIA GR
13 COPTHALL GDNS
14 FOORD RD S
15 SPRING TERR
16 GRACE CT
17 GLOUCESTER PL
18 GUILDHALL ST
19 ST EANSWYTHE WAY
20 MARKET PL
21 HARVEY PL
22 Grace Sch
23 University Ctr Folkestone
G H
CT18
North Downs Way
Saxon Shore Way
LITTLE SWITZERLAND
The Warren
Martello Tower
CT19
East Wear Bay
Martello Tower
Copt Point
24 25
21 A 22 B C
10 MARGARET ST
11 KINGSBRIDGE CT
12 ELMSTEAD PL
13 CAMBRIDGE TERR
14 SAFFRON'S PL
15 RANDOLPH HO
16 BENNETT CT
17 BOULOGNE CT
18 PRINCES GATE
19 BAYLE ST
20 RADNOR ST
21 CHANNEL VIEW
22 EAST CLIFF GDNS
23 EAST CLIFF PAS
24 LONDON PL
25 GEORGE STONE HO
26 RICHMOND HO
177
E6
1 LORRAINE CT
2 CANTERBURY CL
3 ARTHUR ST
4 WALMSLEY HO
5 MYRTLE RD
6 ASH TREE RD
7 ELM RD
8 ROSSENDALE GDNS
9 EDWARD TERR
10 ROSSENDALE CT
11 ORMONDE RD
12 ST GABRIEL'S CT
13 ABBOTT CT
14 CHILTON CT

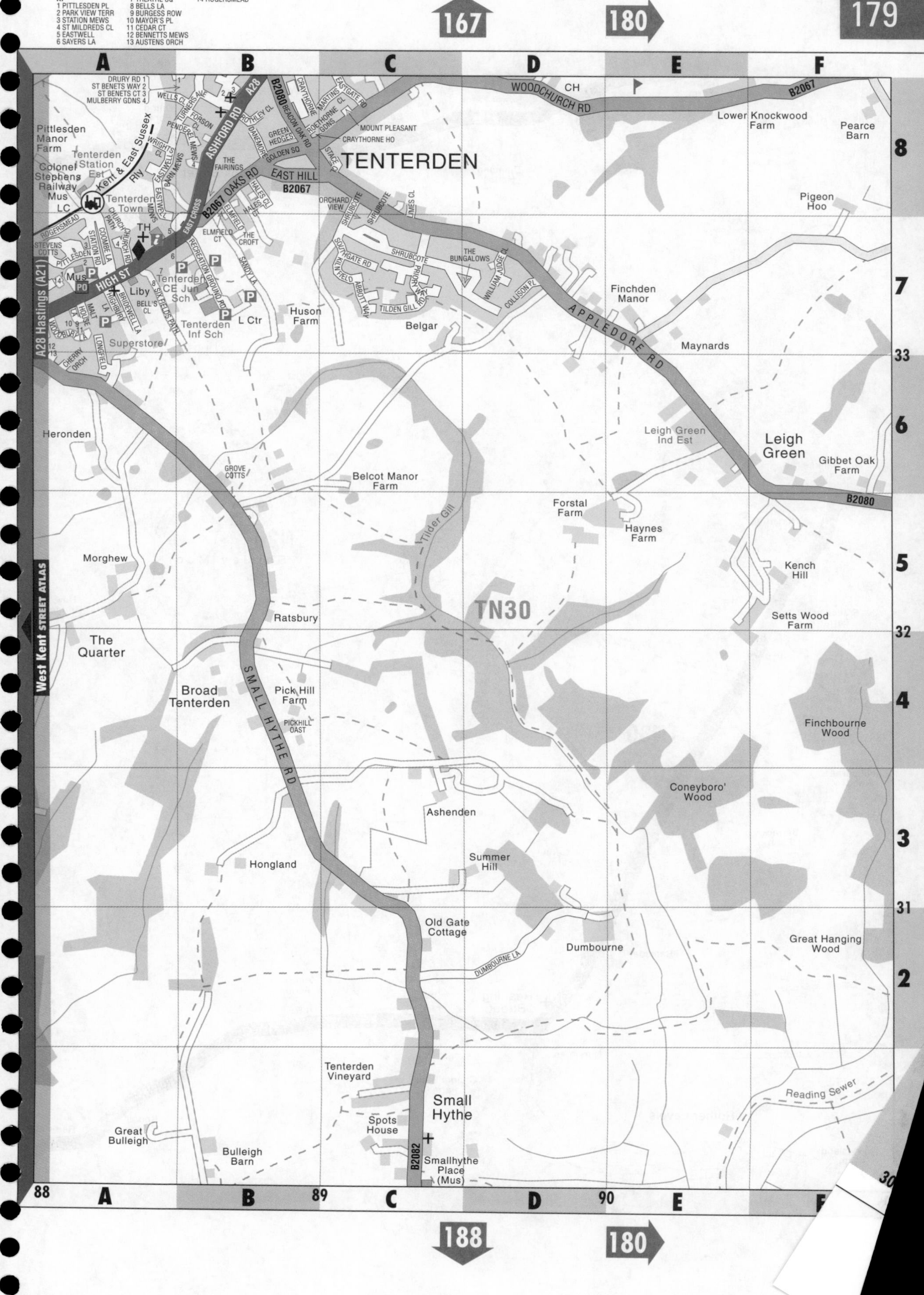

A7
1 PITTLESDEN PL
2 PARK VIEW TERR
3 STATION MEWS
4 ST MILDREDS CL
5 EASTWELL
6 SAYERS LA
7 THEATRE SQ
8 BELLS LA
9 BURGESS ROW
10 MAYOR'S PL
11 CEDAR CT
12 BENNETTS MEWS
13 AUSTENS ORCH
14 ROGERSMEAD
167
180
DRURY RD 1
ST BENETS WAY 2
ST BENETS CT 3
MULBERRY GDNS 4
Pittlesden Manor Farm
Tenterden Station Est
Kent & East Sussex Rly
Colonel Stephens Railway Mus
Tenterden Town
LC
TH
ASHFORD RD
B2067 OAKS RD
HIGH ST
EAST HILL
B2067
B2080
TENTERDEN
WOODCHURCH RD
CH
MOUNT PLEASANT
CRAYTHORNE HO
Lower Knockwood Farm
Pearce Barn
Pigeon Hoo
THE BUNGALOWS
Finchden Manor
APPLEDORE RD
Maynards
Huson Farm
Belgar
Tenterden CE Jun Sch
Tenterden Inf Sch
L Ctr
Liby
Mus
PO
Superstore
A28 Hastings (A21)
Heronden
GROVE COTTS
Belcot Manor Farm
Leigh Green Ind Est
Leigh Green
Gibbet Oak Farm
B2080
Forstal Farm
Haynes Farm
Tilder Gill
Morghew
Kench Hill
TN30
Setts Wood Farm
Ratsbury
The Quarter
Broad Tenterden
Pick Hill Farm
PICKHILL OAST
SMALL HYTHE RD
Finchbourne Wood
Coneyboro' Wood
Ashenden
Hongland
Summer Hill
Old Gate Cottage
Dumbourne
DUMBOURNE LA
Great Hanging Wood
Reading Sewer
Tenterden Vineyard
Small Hythe
Spots House
Great Bulleigh
Bulleigh Barn
B2082
Smallhythe Place (Mus)
West Kent STREET ATLAS
A B C D E F
8 7 6 5 4 3 2
33 32 31 30
88 89 90
188
180

179
168

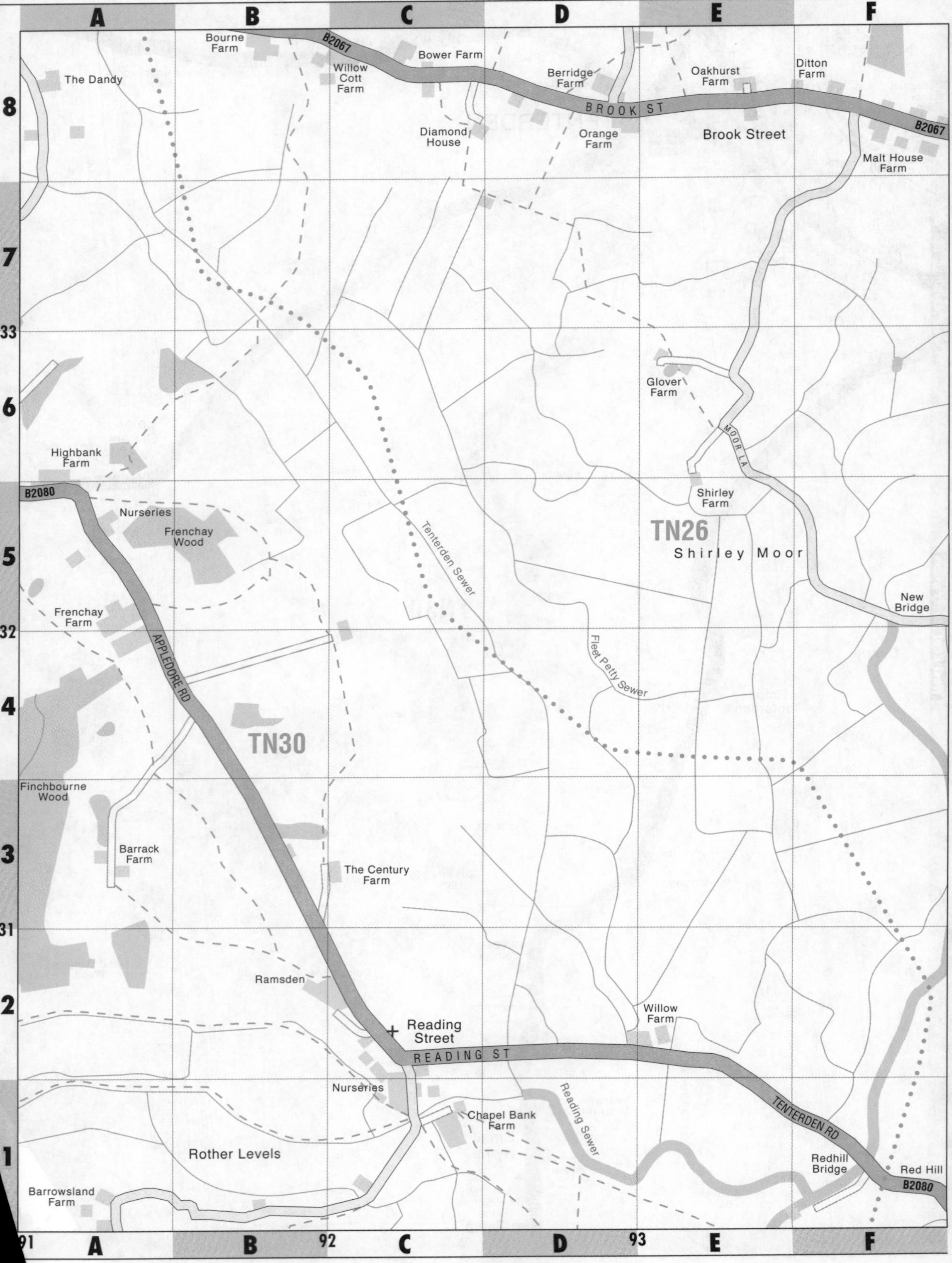

A   B   C   D   E   F

8

7

33

6

5

32

4

3

31

2

1

The Dandy

Bourne Farm

Willow Cott Farm

Bower Farm

B2067

Berridge Farm

Oakhurst Farm

Ditton Farm

BROOK ST

Brook Street

B2067

Diamond House

Orange Farm

Malt House Farm

Glover Farm

MOOR LA

Highbank Farm

B2080

Nurseries

Frenchay Wood

Shirley Farm

TN26

Shirley Moor

New Bridge

Frenchay Farm

Tenterden Sewer

APPLEDORE RD

Fleet Petty Sewer

Finchbourne Wood

TN30

Barrack Farm

The Century Farm

Ramsden

Reading Street

Willow Farm

Nurseries

READING ST

Chapel Bank Farm

Reading Sewer

TENTERDEN RD

Rother Levels

Redhill Bridge

Red Hill

B2080

Barrowsland Farm

91   A   B   92   C   D   93   E   F

179
189

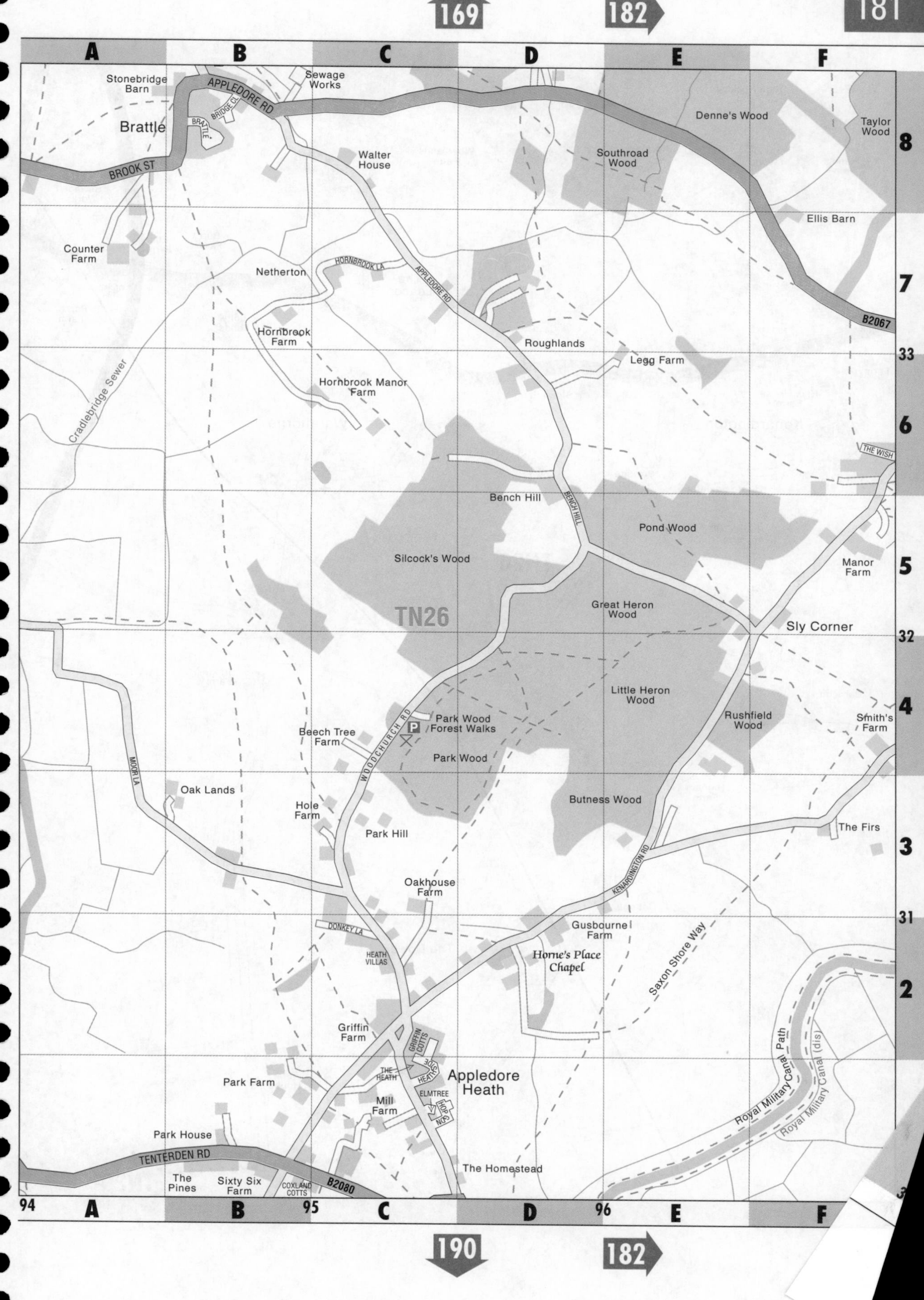

169
182

A   B   C   D   E   F

Stonebridge Barn
APPLEDORE RD
Sewage Works
BRIDGE CL
BRATTLE
Brattle
Walter House
Denne's Wood
Taylor Wood
8
BROOK ST

Counter Farm
Netherton
HORNBROOK LA
APPLEDORE RD
Southroad Wood
Ellis Barn
7

Hornbrook Farm
Roughlands
Legg Farm
B2067
33

Cradlebridge Sewer
Hornbrook Manor Farm
6
THE WISH

Bench Hill
BENCH HILL
Pond Wood
Manor Farm
5

Silcock's Wood
TN26
Great Heron Wood
Sly Corner
32

Little Heron Wood
Rushfield Wood
Smith's Farm
4

Beech Tree Farm
WOODCHURCH RD
P
Park Wood Forest Walks
KENARDINGTON RD
Oak Lands
MOOR LA
Park Wood
Butness Wood
The Firs
3

Hole Farm
Park Hill
Oakhouse Farm
Gusbourne Farm
Saxon Shore Way
31

DONKEY LA
HEATH VILLAS
Horne's Place Chapel
2

Griffin Farm
GRIFFIN COTTS
THE HEATH
HEATH COTTS
Appledore Heath
Royal Military Canal Path
Royal Military Canal (dis)

Park Farm
ELMTREE
HOP GDN
Mill Farm

Park House
TENTERDEN RD
The Pines
Sixty Six Farm
COXLAND COTTS
B2080
The Homestead

94   A   B   95   C   D   96   E   F

A B C D E F

8

High Hockley
Farm

Penfold
Wood

Birch
Wood

Hockley

Woodlands
Farm

Smallman's
Wood

Hamstreet
Prim Sch

A2070

B2067

ASHFORD RD

Sewage
Works

B2067

7

Leacon
Farm

The Leacon

Burr
Farm

Elm
Farm

PROSPECT
PL

WAREHORNE RD

VIADUCT
TERR

Parker
Farm

ORLESTONE
VW

33

B2067

POPLARS

PH

Lofty
Lands

Place
Farm

High House
Farm

Stone Farm

HARDEN'S
VIEW

Warehorne

THE
GREEN

6

Kenardington

PH

CORNER
COTTS

Horsemarsh
Farm

Sewage
Works

Saxon Shore Way

MONKS HILL
COTTS

Battle Hill
Farm

Tinton Manor
Farm

LC

Horsemarsh Sewer

5

TN26

A2070

32

Barncote

Royal Military Canal (dis)

Royal Military Canal Path

Bridge
Farm

4

Bridge
Cottage

Speringbrook Sewer

Higham
Farm

3

Thrift
Cottage

31

LC

The Dowels

Terry
House

2

Blackmen's Arm

1

CHURCH RD

Sedbrook Sewer

0

TN29

171
184

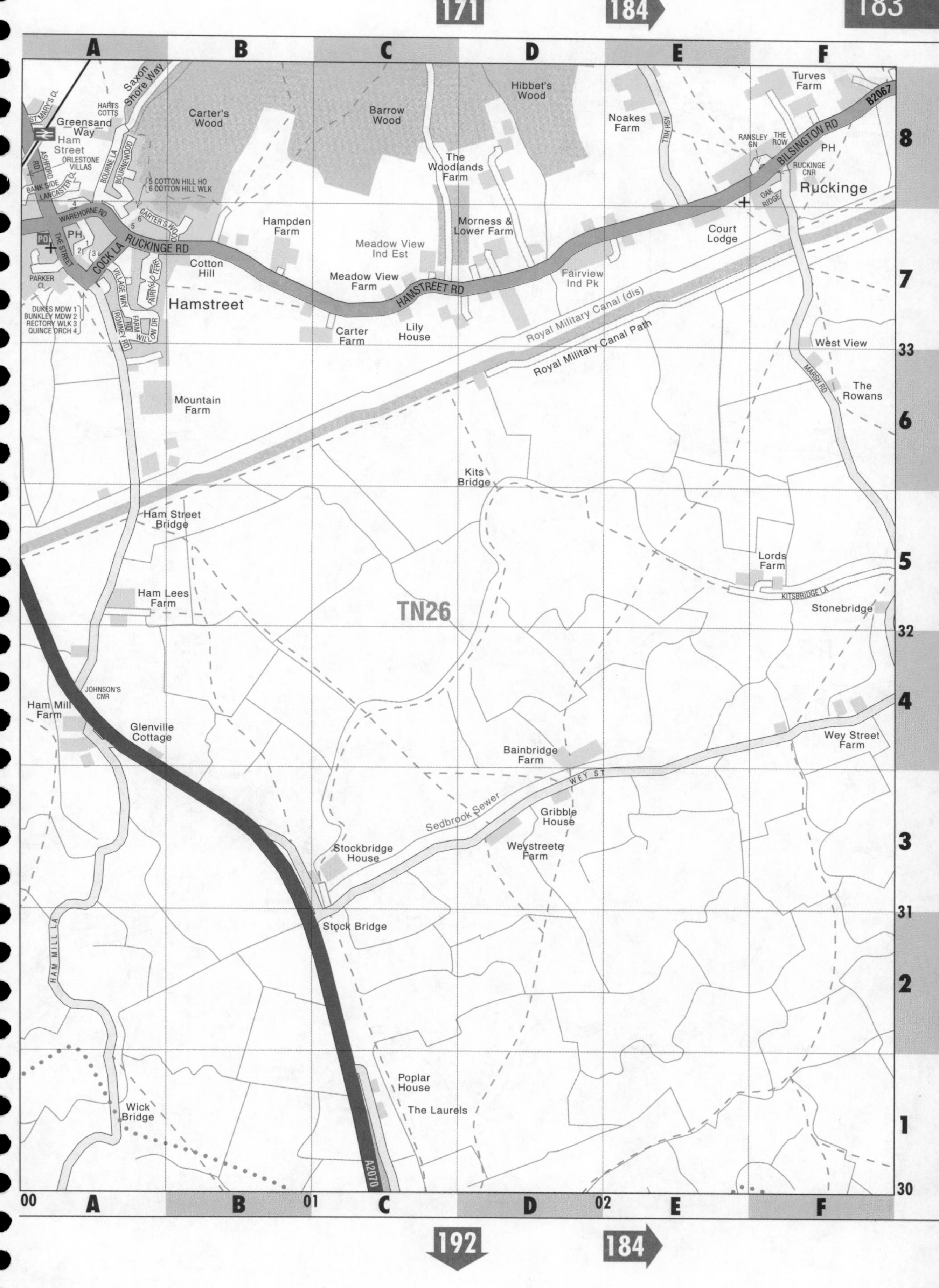
A
B
C
D
E
F
Saxon Shore Way
Carter's Wood
Barrow Wood
Hibbet's Wood
Noakes Farm
Turves Farm
B2067
Greensand Way
Ham Street
HARTS COTTS
ST MARY'S CL
ORLESTONE VILLAS
ASHFORD RD
BANK SIDE
LANCASTER CL
BOURNE LA
BOURNEWOOD
5 COTTON HILL HO
6 COTTON HILL WLK
WAREHORNE RD
CARTER'S WOOD
PH
THE STREET
COCK LA
RUCKINGE RD
PARKER CL
DUKES MDW 1
BUNKLEY MDW 2
RECTORY WLK 3
QUINCE ORCH 4
VILLAGE WAY
ROMNEY RD
FARM RD
WILLOW DR
FAIRVIEW TERR
Hamstreet
Cotton Hill
Hampden Farm
Meadow View Ind Est
Meadow View Farm
The Woodlands Farm
Morness & Lower Farm
Carter Farm
Lily House
HAMSTREET RD
Fairview Ind Pk
ASH HILL
RANSLEY GN
THE ROW
BILSINGTON RD
PH
RUCKINGE CNR
OAK RIDGE
Ruckinge
Court Lodge
Royal Military Canal (dis)
Royal Military Canal Path
West View
MARSH RD
The Rowans
Mountain Farm
Kits Bridge
Ham Street Bridge
Lords Farm
KITSBRIDGE LA
Stonebridge
Ham Lees Farm
TN26
JOHNSON'S CNR
Ham Mill Farm
Glenville Cottage
Bainbridge Farm
Wey Street Farm
WEY ST
Sedbrook Sewer
Gribble House
Weystreete Farm
Stockbridge House
Stock Bridge
HAM MILL LA
Poplar House
The Laurels
Wick Bridge
A2070
8
7
33
6
5
32
4
3
31
2
1
30
00
01
02

192
184

A B C D E F

8

BILSINGTON RD B2067
Herne House
Sewage Works
Royal Military Canal Path
Royal Military Canal (dis)
Marsh Cottage
Quince Cottage
Bridge Farm

7

Sedbrook Sewer
Sedbrook Sewer
Wallstool Sewer
Marshland Sewer

33

Pear Tree Farm
TN25
Honeywood Farm

6

Hans Farm
TAR POT LA
Rock Cottage
Oak Farm
Toll Farm
Bilsington Sewer

5

32

TN26
The Chestnuts
WILLS LA
Wallstool Sewer

4

WEST ST
Will's Farm
Newchurch
MILL LA
Mill House

3

Langdon
PADDIWAYS
CHURCH VIEW
CLARKLANDS
Tower Windmill
Langdon Cottages
TN29
Brooker Farm
Manor House

31

Brenzett Sewer
Brooker Cottage
Four Winds
Stone Bridge

2

Rosedale
NORWOOD LA
New Barn Farm
Sheaty Sewer
Millbank
Hill's Farm

1

NEWCHURCH LA
MELON LA
FROSTLAND LA
Squires Farm
Norwood Farm

30

Lodgeland Bungalow

03 A B 04 C D 05 E F

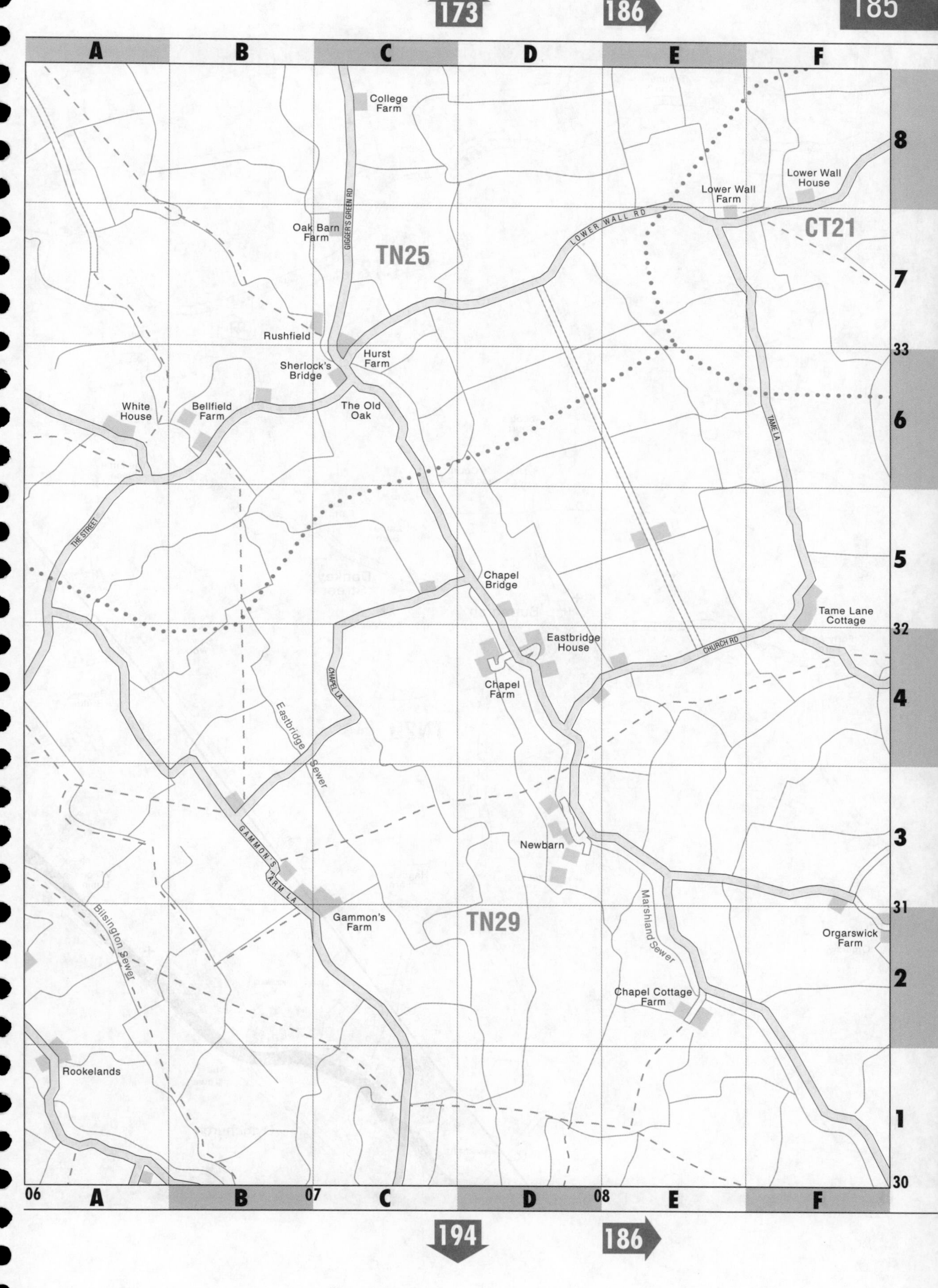

A B C D E F

8

College
Farm

Lower Wall
Farm

Lower Wall
House

GIGGER'S GREEN RD

Oak Barn
Farm

TN25

LOWER WALL RD

CT21

7

33

Rushfield

Hurst
Farm

Sherlock's
Bridge

The Old
Oak

White
House

Bellfield
Farm

TAME LA

6

THE STREET

5

Chapel
Bridge

32

Tame Lane
Cottage

CHURCH RD

CHAPEL LA

Eastbridge
House

Eastbridge Sewer

Chapel
Farm

4

GAMMON'S ARM LA

Newbarn

3

Marshland Sewer

31

Bilsington Sewer

Gammon's
Farm

TN29

Orgarswick
Farm

2

Chapel Cottage
Farm

Rookelands

1

06 A B 07 C D 08 E F 30

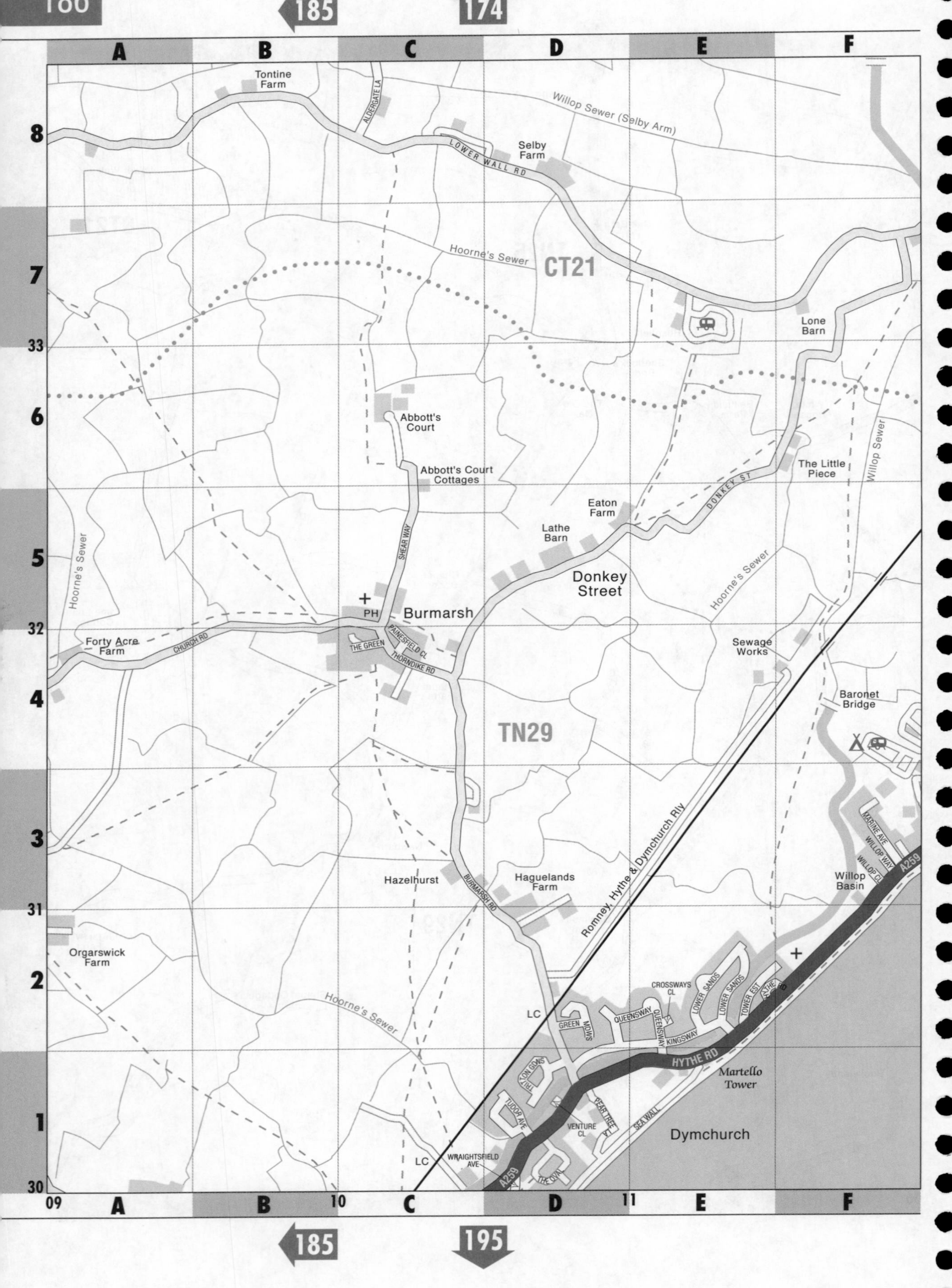

A B C D E F

8

7

33

6

5

32

4

3

31

2

1

30

09 A B 10 C D 11 E F

CT21

Willop Sewer (Selby Arm)

Tontine Farm

ALDERGATE LA

LOWER WALL RD

Selby Farm

Hoorne's Sewer

Lone Barn

Willop Sewer

Abbott's Court

Abbott's Court Cottages

The Little Piece

DONKEY ST

Eaton Farm

Lathe Barn

SHEAR WAY

Donkey Street

Hoorne's Sewer

Hoorne's Sewer

+
PH

Burmarsh

PARK FIELD CL

Sewage Works

Forty Acre Farm

CHURCH RD

THE GREEN

THORNDIKE RD

TN29

Baronet Bridge

Hazelhurst

BURMARSH RD

Haguelands Farm

Romney, Hythe & Dymchurch Rly

Willop Basin

MARINE AVE

WILLOP WAY

WILLOP CL

A259

Orgarswick Farm

Hoorne's Sewer

LC

+

Green Mews

CROSSWAYS CL

Lower Sands

Lower Sands

Tower Est

Tower Est

QUEENSWAY

QUEENSWAY

KINGSWAY

RYTHE RD

HYTHE RD

Martello Tower

TUDOR AVE

LC

WRAIGHTSFIELD AVE

VENTURE CL

PEAR TREE PL

SEA WALL

THE DOWN

A259

Dymchurch

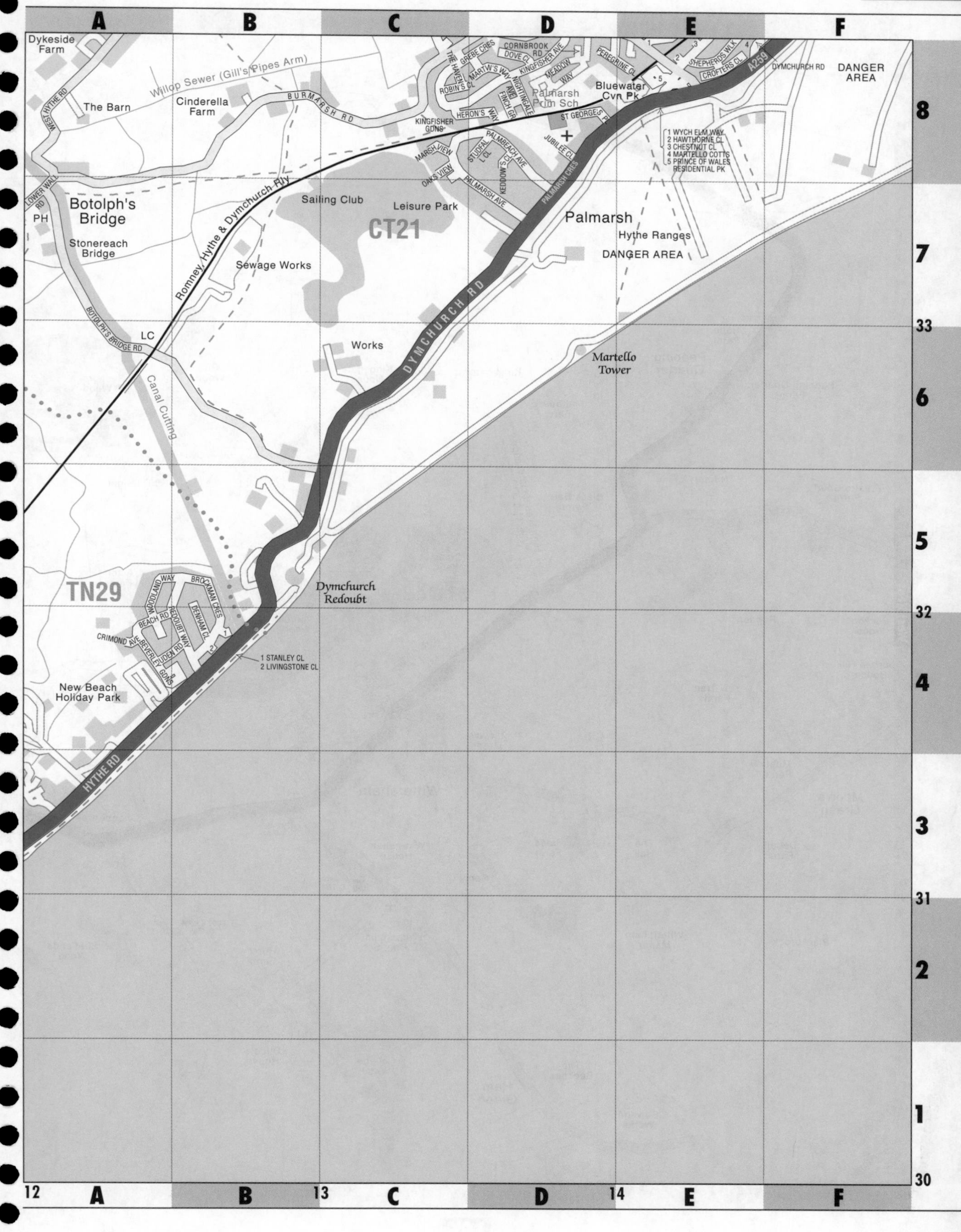
A
B
C
D
E
F
Dykeside Farm
The Barn
Cinderella Farm
Willop Sewer (Gill's Pipes Arm)
WEST HYTHE RD
BURMARSH RD
KINGFISHER GDNS
CORNBROOK RD
DOVE CL
GREBE CRES
THE HAVEN
ROBIN'S CL
MARTIN'S WAY
KINGFISHER AVE
MEADOW WAY
NIGHTINGALE AVE
FINCH GR
HERON'S WAY
Palmarsh Prim Sch
PEREGRINE CL
Bluewater Cvn Pk
ST GEORGE'S PL
JUBILEE CL
SHEPHERDS WLK
CROFTERS CL
A259
DYMCHURCH RD
DANGER AREA
1 WYCH ELM WAY
2 HAWTHORNE CL
3 CHESTNUT CL
4 MARTELLO COTTS
5 PRINCE OF WALES RESIDENTIAL PK
MARSH VIEW
OAKS VIEW
STUDFALL CL
PALMBEACH AVE
KEDDOW'S CL
PALMARSH AVE
PALMARSH CRES
LOWER WALL RD
PH
Botolph's Bridge
Stonereach Bridge
Romney, Hythe & Dymchurch Rly
Sailing Club
Leisure Park
CT21
Palmarsh
Hythe Ranges
DANGER AREA
Sewage Works
BOTOLPH'S BRIDGE RD
LC
Works
DYMCHURCH RD
Canal Cutting
Martello Tower
TN29
WOODLAND WAY
BROCKMAN CRES
BEACH RD
REDOUBT WAY
DENHAM CL
CRIMOND AVE
BEVERLEY GDNS
LUDEN RD
1 STANLEY CL
2 LIVINGSTONE CL
Dymchurch Redoubt
New Beach Holiday Park
HYTHE RD
8
7
33
6
5
32
4
3
31
2
1
30
12
13
14

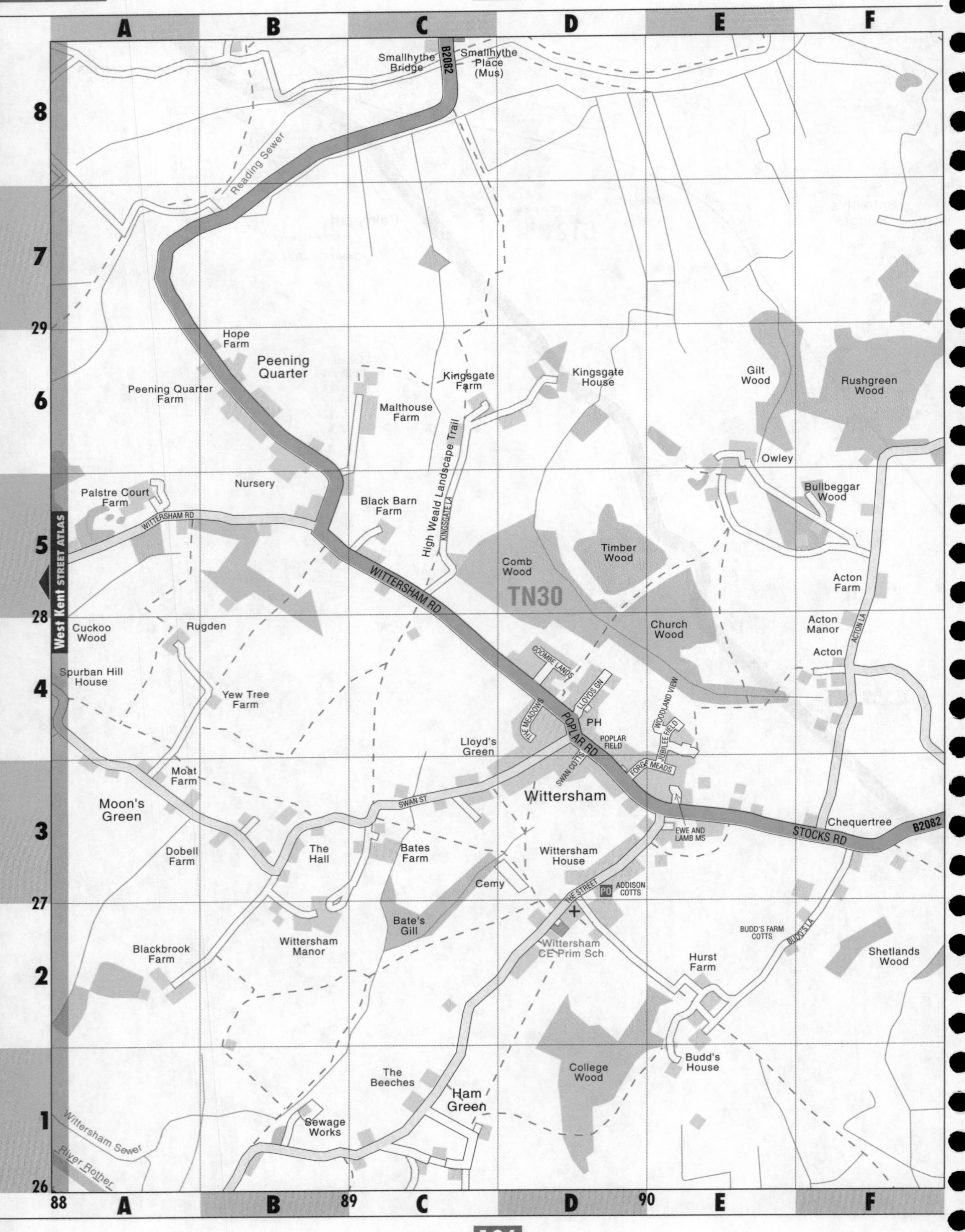

A B C D E F

8

7

29

6

5

28

4

3

27

2

1

26

88 A B 89 C D 90 E F

West Kent STREET ATLAS

Smallhythe Bridge
Smallhythe Place (Mus)
B2082

Reading Sewer

Hope Farm

Peening Quarter

Peening Quarter Farm

Kingsgate Farm

Kingsgate House

Malthouse Farm

Gilt Wood

Rushgreen Wood

Nursery

Palstre Court Farm

WITTERSHAM RD

Black Barn Farm

High Weald Landscape Trail

KINGSGATE LA

Owley

Bullbeggar Wood

Comb Wood

Timber Wood

Acton Farm

TN30

ACTON LA

Church Wood

Acton Manor

Acton

Cuckoo Wood

Rugden

WITTERSHAM RD

Spurban Hill House

Yew Tree Farm

COOMBE LANDS

POPLAR RD

LLOYDS GN

PH

WOODLAND VIEW

JUBILEE FIELD

Moat Farm

Lloyd's Green

SWAN COTTS

POPLAR FIELD

FORGE MEADS

Moon's Green

THE MEADOWS

SWAN ST

Wittersham

EWE AND LAMB MS

Chequertree

STOCKS RD

B2082

Dobell Farm

The Hall

Bates Farm

Wittersham House

Blackbrook Farm

Wittersham Manor

Bate's Gill

Cemy

THE STREET

PO

ADDISON COTTS

BUDD'S FARM COTTS

BUDD'S LA

Shetlands Wood

Wittersham CE Prim Sch

Hurst Farm

The Beeches

Ham Green

Sewage Works

College Wood

Budd's House

Wittersham Sewer

River Rother

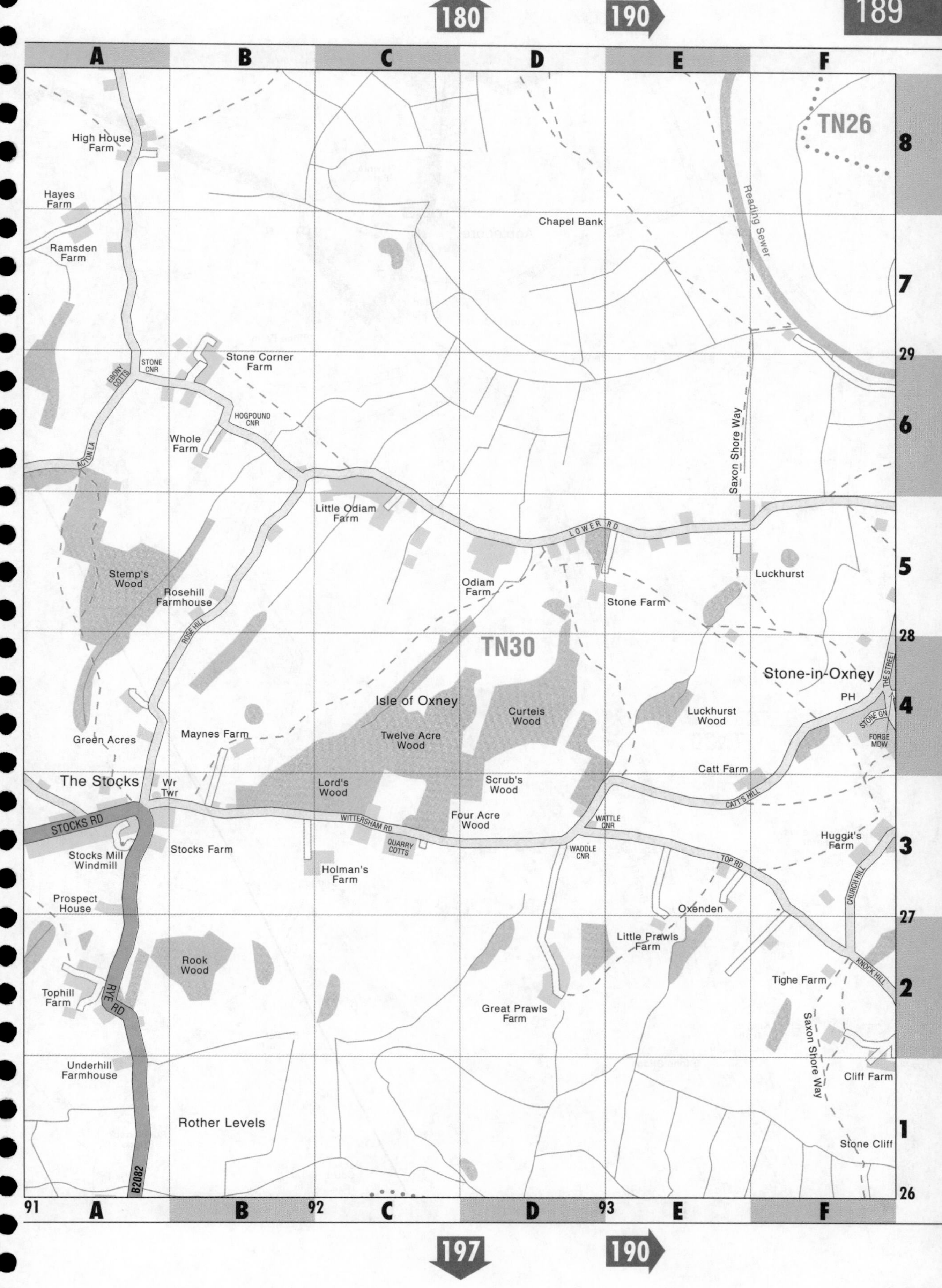
180
190
A
B
C
D
E
F
TN26
8
High House Farm
Hayes Farm
Reading Sewer
Chapel Bank
Ramsden Farm
7
29
Stone Corner Farm
STONE CNR
EBONY COTTS
HOGPOUND CNR
6
Whole Farm
Saxon Shore Way
ACTON LA
Little Odiam Farm
LOWER RD
Stemp's Wood
5
Luckhurst
Odiam Farm
Rosehill Farmhouse
Stone Farm
TN30
28
ROSE HILL
Stone-in-Oxney
THE STREET
PH
Isle of Oxney
Curteis Wood
Luckhurst Wood
4
STONE GN
Green Acres
Maynes Farm
Twelve Acre Wood
FORGE MDW
Catt Farm
The Stocks
Wr Twr
Lord's Wood
Scrub's Wood
CATT'S HILL
Four Acre Wood
WATTLE CNR
STOCKS RD
WITTERSHAM RD
Huggit's Farm
QUARRY COTTS
WADDLE CNR
3
Stocks Mill Windmill
Stocks Farm
TOP RD
Holman's Farm
CHURCH HILL
Prospect House
Oxenden
27
Little Prawls Farm
Rook Wood
KNOCK HILL
Tophill Farm
RYE RD
Tighe Farm
2
Great Prawls Farm
Saxon Shore Way
Underhill Farmhouse
Cliff Farm
1
Rother Levels
Stone Cliff
B2082
26
91
A
B
92
C
D
93
E
F
197
190

189
181

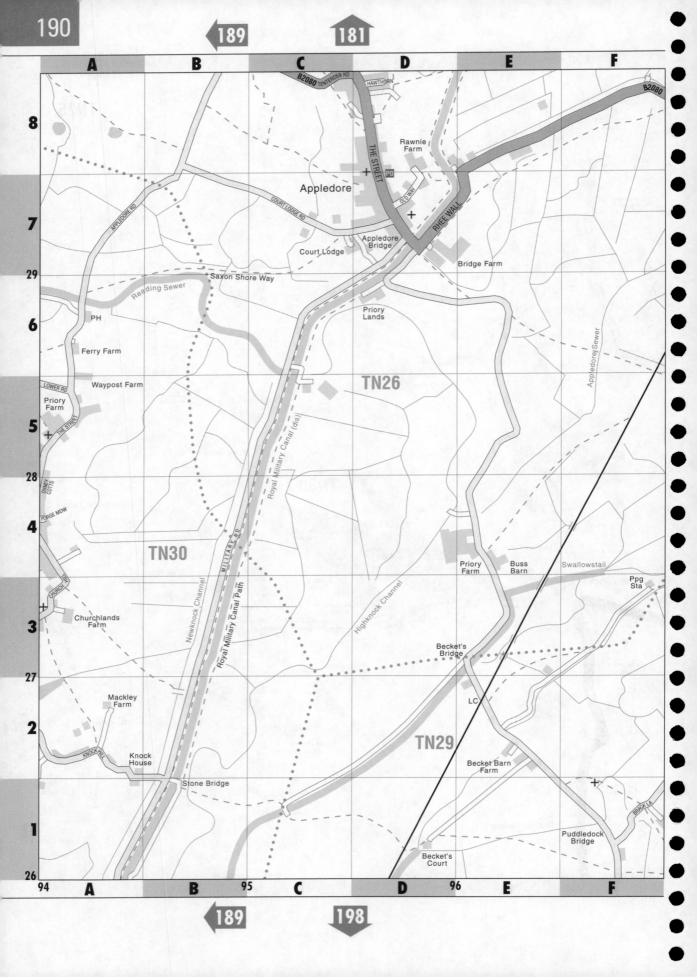

189
198

182
192

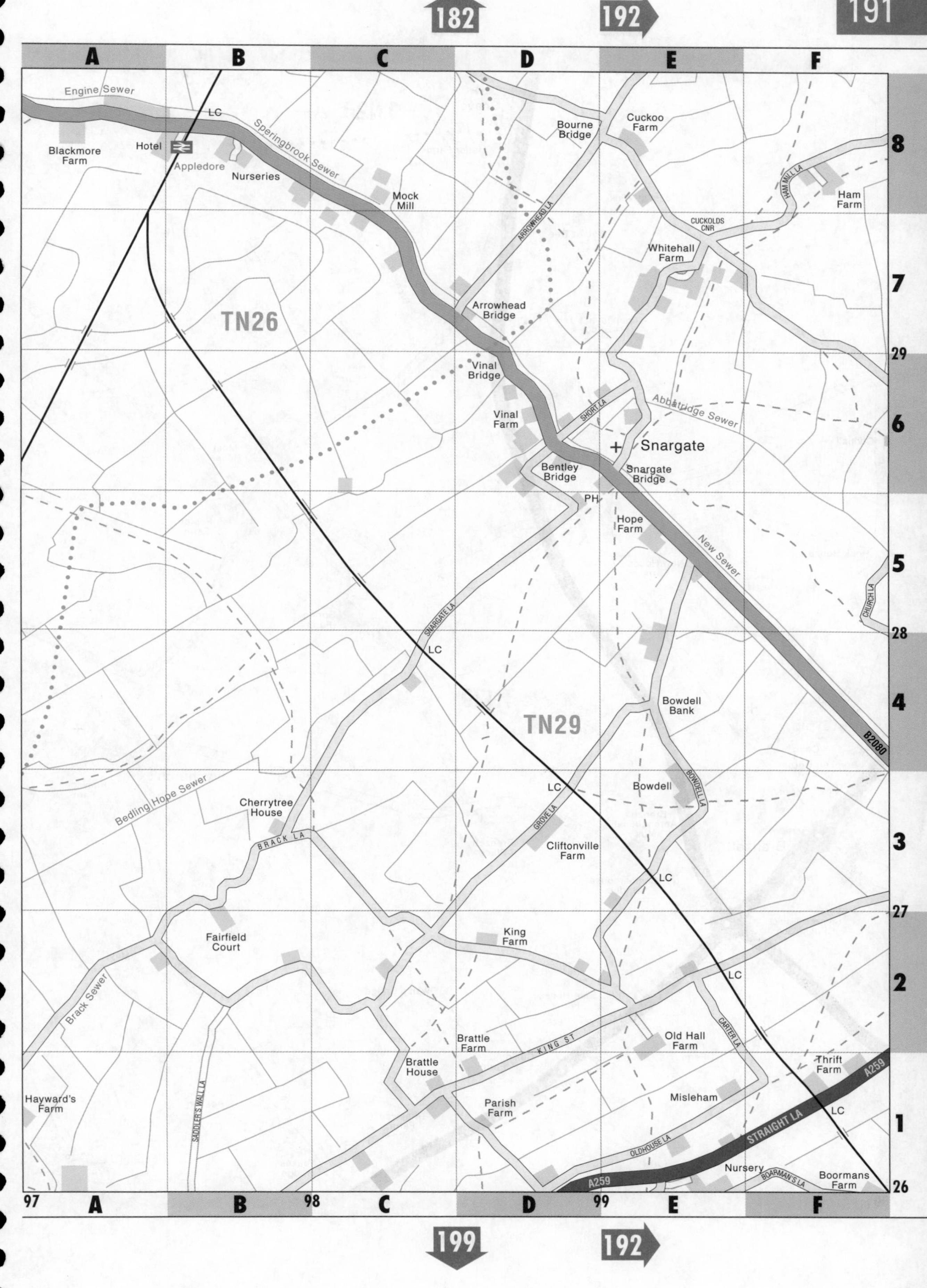
A
B
C
D
E
F
Engine Sewer
LC
Blackmore Farm
Hotel
Appledore
Nurseries
Speringbrook Sewer
Mock Mill
Bourne Bridge
Cuckoo Farm
ARROWHEAD LA
HAM MILL LA
Ham Farm
CUCKOLDS CNR
Whitehall Farm
TN26
Arrowhead Bridge
Vinal Bridge
Vinal Farm
SHORT LA
Abbotsbridge Sewer
Snargate
Bentley Bridge
Snargate Bridge
PH
Hope Farm
New Sewer
CHURCH LA
SNARGATE LA
LC
Bowdell Bank
TN29
B2080
LC
Bowdell
BOWDELL LA
Bedling Hope Sewer
Cherrytree House
GROVE LA
BRACK LA
Cliftonville Farm
LC
Fairfield Court
King Farm
LC
Brack Sewer
CARTER LA
Old Hall Farm
Brattle Farm
KING ST
Brattle House
Thrift Farm
A259
Hayward's Farm
Parish Farm
Misleham
LC
SADDLER'S WALL LA
STRAIGHT LA
OLDHOUSE LA
A259
Nursery
BOARMAN'S LA
Boormans Farm
8
7
29
6
5
28
4
3
27
2
1
26
97
98
99

199
192

A B C D E F

8

Snave
TN26
Manor Farm

Court-at-Wick

Walnut Tree
Farm

7

Abbatridge Sewer
Brenzett Sewer

Hangman's Toll
Bridge

Chapel
Farm

29

Poplar
Farm

6

Codhall
Brenzett
Green

Moat
House

NEWCHURCH LA

Poplar
Farm

CHURCH LA

SPRINGFARM
RD

5

Hook House

New House
Farm

28

Spring
Farm

Abbatridge Sewer

MELON LA

4

TN29

THE
GARDENS

PH

Marsh's
Farm

CHURCH LA

MOOR LA

Cemy

OASTHOUSE
FIELD

B2080

Brenzett Corner
Bridge

Brenzett
Aeronautical
Mus

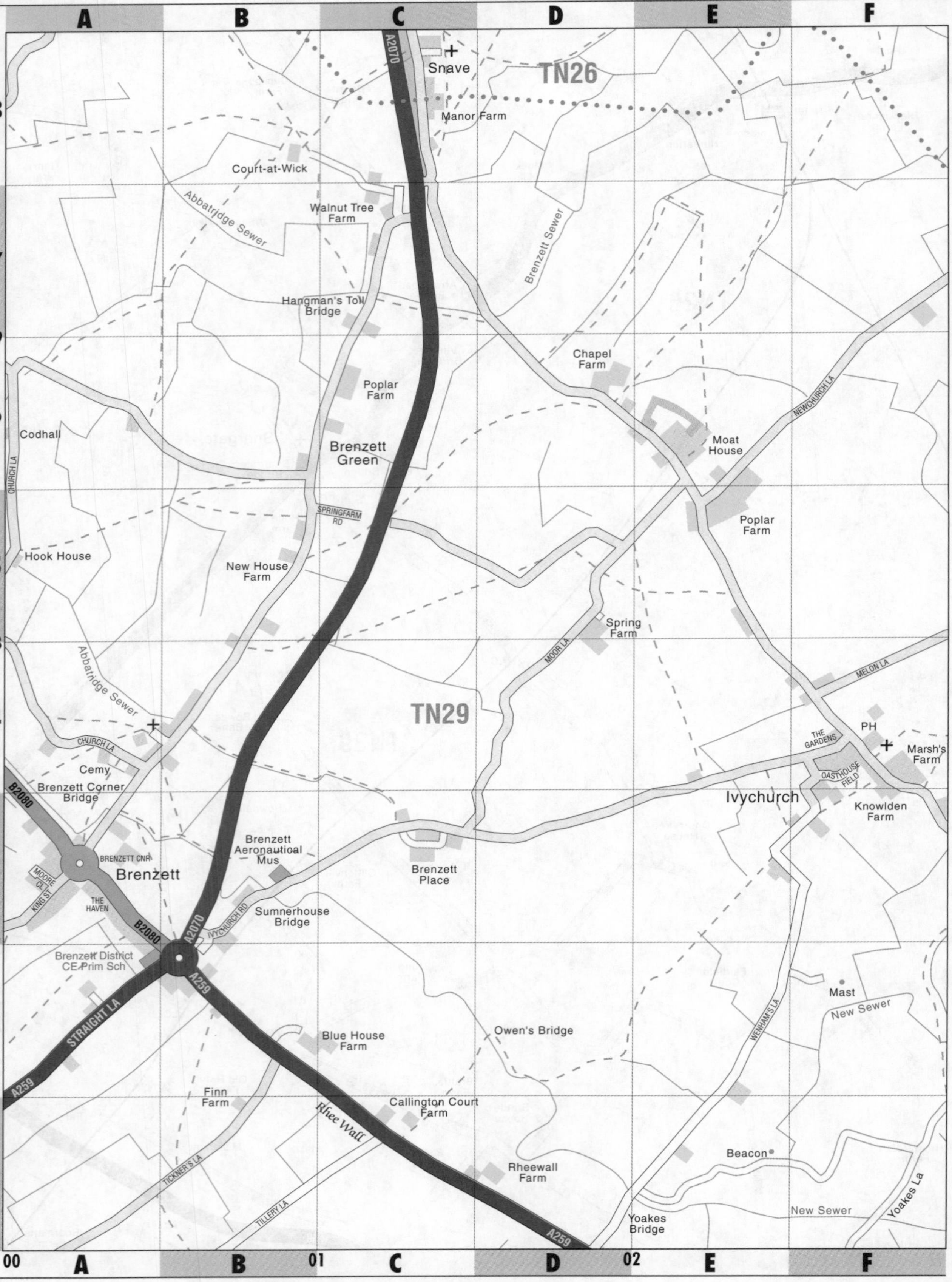

Ivychurch

Knowlden
Farm

3

BRENZETT CNR

Brenzett

Brenzett
Place

MOOR LA
KING ST

THE
HAVEN

B2080

A2070

IVYCHURCH RD

Sumnerhouse
Bridge

27

Brenzett District
CE Prim Sch

A259

WENHAM'S LA

Mast

New Sewer

2

STRAIGHT LA

Blue House
Farm

Owen's Bridge

A259

Finn
Farm

Callington Court
Farm

Beacon

New Sewer

Yoakes La

1

TICKNER'S LA

Rhee Wall

Rheewall
Farm

TILLERY LA

Yoakes
Bridge

A259

26

00 A B 01 C D 02 E F

184
194

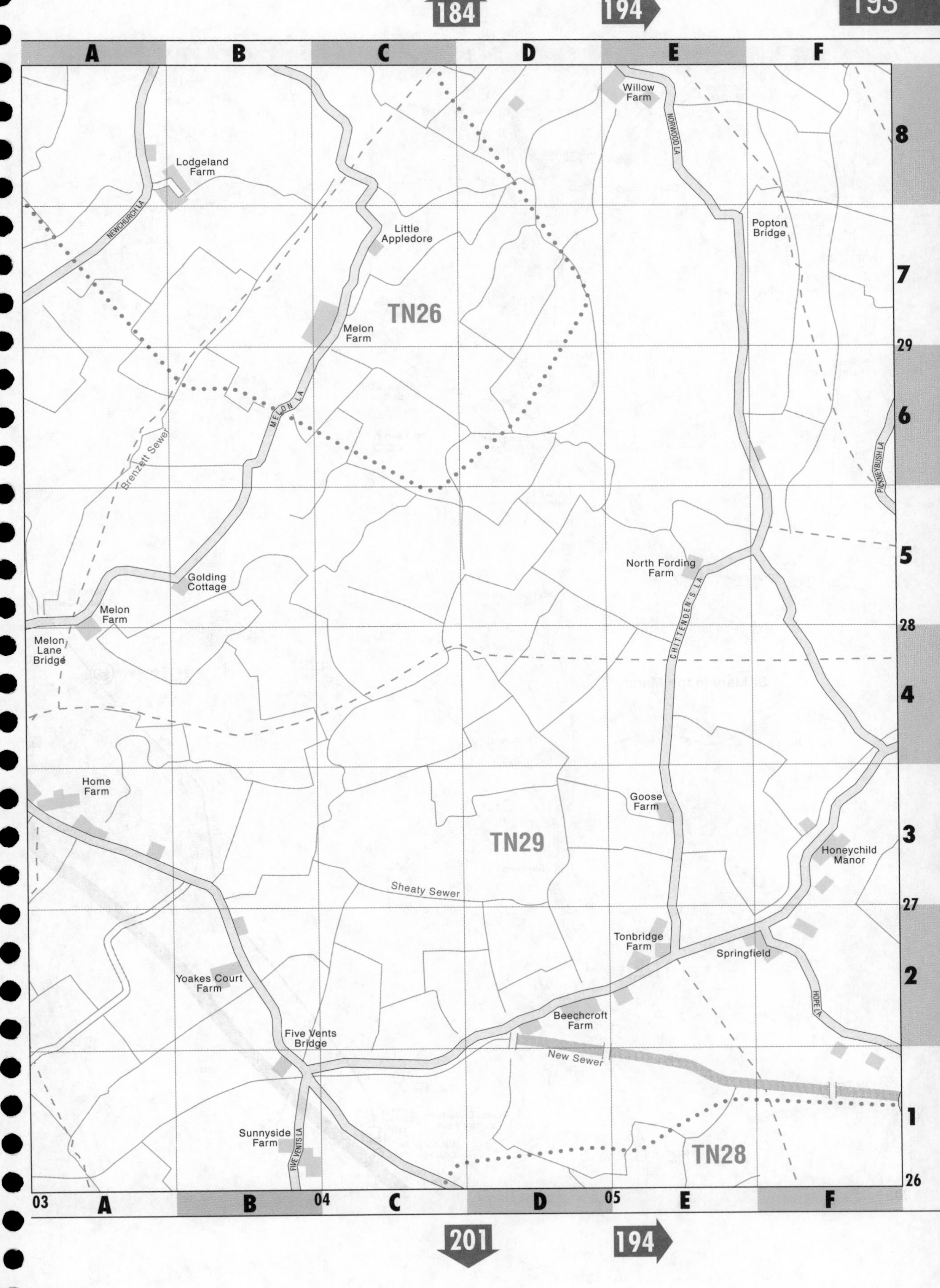
A
B
C
D
E
F
Willow Farm
NORWOOD LA
Lodgeland Farm
NEWCHURCH LA
Little Appledore
Popton Bridge
TN26
Melon Farm
MELON LA
Brenzett Sewer
PICKNEYBUSH LA
North Fording Farm
Golding Cottage
Melon Farm
CHITTENDEN'S LA
Melon Lane Bridge
Home Farm
Goose Farm
TN29
Honeychild Manor
Sheaty Sewer
Tonbridge Farm
Springfield
Yoakes Court Farm
HOPE LA
Beechcroft Farm
Five Vents Bridge
New Sewer
Sunnyside Farm
FIVE VENTS LA
TN28
8
7
29
6
5
28
4
3
27
2
1
26
03
04
05

201
194

193 185

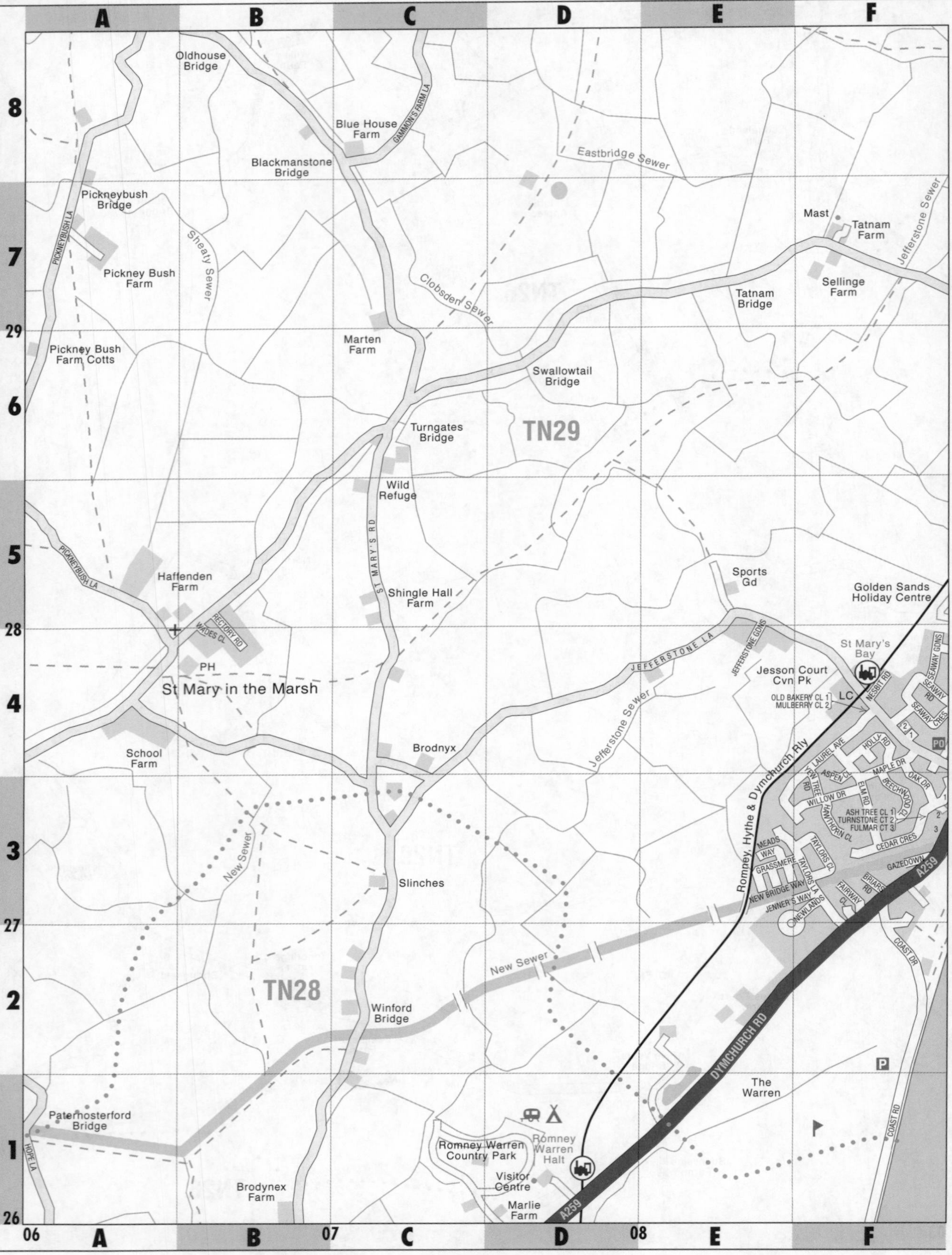

A B C D E F

8

Oldhouse Bridge

Blue House Farm

Blackmanstone Bridge

GAMMON'S FARM LA

Eastbridge Sewer

Pickneybush Bridge

PICKNEYBUSH LA

7

Mast

Tatnam Farm

Pickney Bush Farm

Sheaty Sewer

Clobsden Sewer

Tatnam Bridge

Sellinge Farm

JEFFERSTONE SEWER

29

Pickney Bush Farm Cotts

Marten Farm

Swallowtail Bridge

6

Turngates Bridge

TN29

Wild Refuge

ST MARY'S RD

5

Haffenden Farm

PICKNEY BUSH LA

Shingle Hall Farm

Sports Gd

Golden Sands Holiday Centre

28

RECTORY RD

WADES CL RD

+

St Mary's Bay

JEFFERSTONE LA

JEFFERSTONE GDNS

Jesson Court Cvn Pk

OLD BAKERY CL 1
MULBERRY CL 2

NESBIT RD

SEAWAY RD

SCAWAY CRES

SONS

LC

PO

PH

4

St Mary in the Marsh

Brodnyx

Jefferstone Sewer

LAUREL AVE

HOLLY RD

ASPEN

WILLOW DR

ELM RD

MAPLE DR

OAK DR

BEECHWAY

2

School Farm

New Sewer

ASH TREE CL 1
TURNSTONE CT 2
FULMAR CT 3

HAWTHORN CL

CEDAR CRES

GAZEDOWN

3

Slinches

Romney, Hythe & Dymchurch Rly

MEADS WAY

GRASSMERE

TAYLORS CL

TAYLORS RD

NEW BRIDGE WAY

JENNER'S WAY

ONEWLANDS

BRIARS RD

FAIRWAY CL

A259

COAST DR

27

TN28

New Sewer

2

Winford Bridge

DYMCHURCH RD

The Warren

P

1

Paternosterford Bridge

HOPE LA

Brodynex Farm

Romney Warren Country Park

Romney Warren Halt

Visitor Centre

A259

Marlie Farm

COAST RD

26

06 A B 07 C D 08 E F

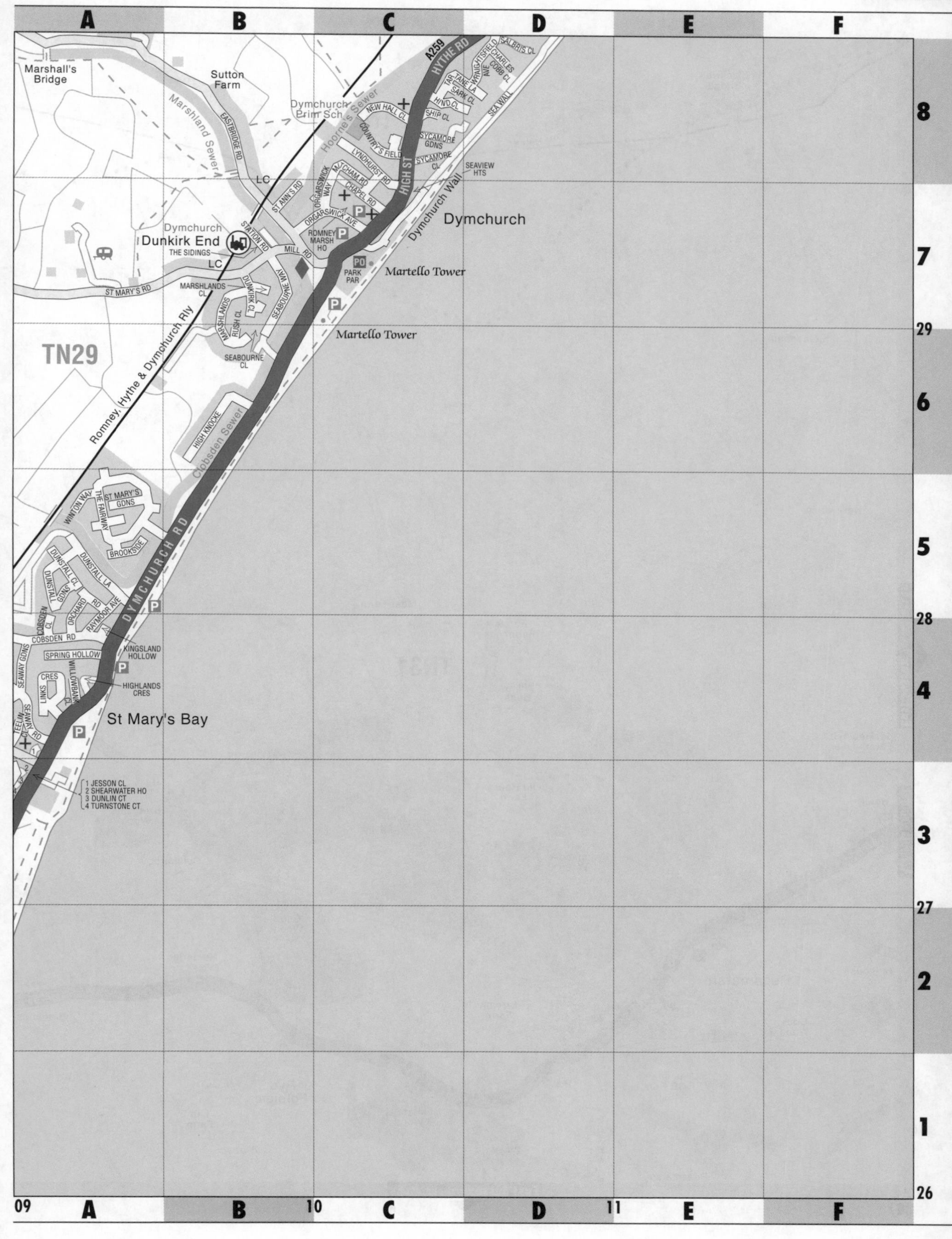

TN29

Marshall's Bridge

Sutton Farm

Marshland Sewer

EASTBRIDGE RD

Dymchurch Prim Sch

Hoorne's Sewer

A259

HYTHE RD

WRIGHTFIELD
SALBRIS CL
FAR LANE LA
HIND CL
SARK CL
CHARLES CL
COBB CL
SEA WALL

NEW HALL CL
COUNTRY'S FIELD

SHIP CL

SYCAMORE GDNS
SYCAMORE CL

SEAVIEW HTS

LC

ST ANN'S RD

ORGARSWICK WAY
MATCHAM RD
LYNDHURST RD

HIGH ST

ORGARSWICK AVE
CHAPEL RD

Dymchurch Wall

Dymchurch

Dymchurch
Dunkirk End
THE SIDINGS

STATION RD

MILL RD

ROMNEY MARSH HO

PO

PARK
PAR

Martello Tower

LC

ST MARY'S RD

MARSHLANDS CL
DUNKIRK CL

MARSHLANDS RUSH CL
SEABOURNE WAY

Romney, Hythe & Dymchurch Rly

SEABOURNE CL

Martello Tower

HIGH KNOCKE

Cobsden Sewer

ST MARY'S GDNS
WINTON WAY
THE FAIRWAY

DYMCHURCH RD

DUNSTALL LA
DUNSTALL CL
DUNSTALL GDNS
DUNSTALL RD
ORCHARD CL
RAYMOOR AVE
BROOKSIDE

COBSDEN CL
COBSDEN RD

SEAWAY GDNS
LINKS CRES
WILLOWBANK
SPRING HOLLOW

KINGSLAND HOLLOW

HIGHLANDS CRES

TEE LANE
ST MARY'S RD

St Mary's Bay

1 JESSON CL
2 SHEARWATER HO
3 DUNLIN CT
4 TURNSTONE CT

09   10   11

8   29   6   5   28   4   3   27   2   1   26

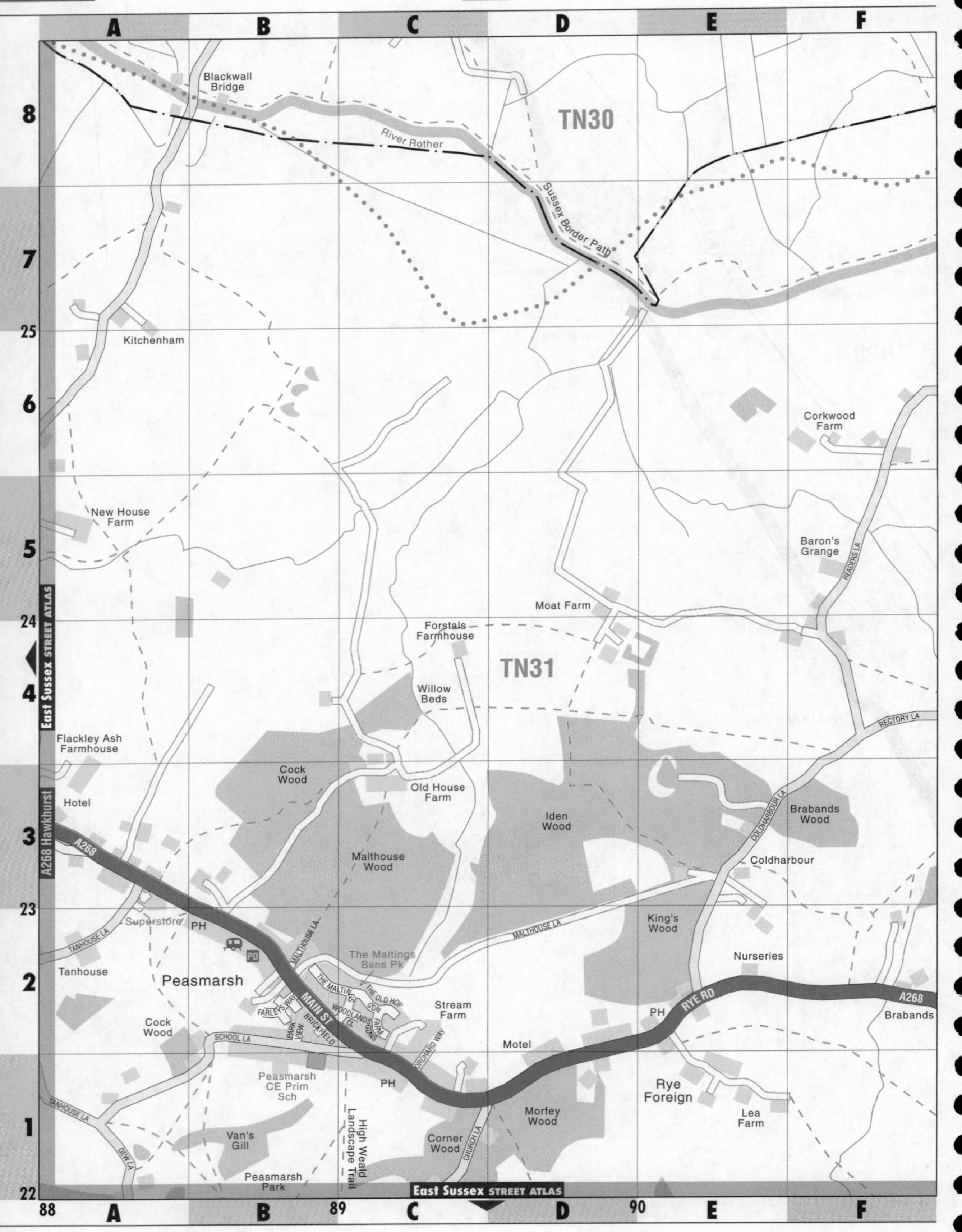

TN30

River Rother

Sussex Border Path

Blackwall
Bridge

Kitchenham

Corkwood
Farm

New House
Farm

Baron's
Grange

READERS LA

Forstals
Farmhouse

Moat Farm

TN31

Willow
Beds

RECTORY LA

Flackley Ash
Farmhouse

Cock
Wood

Old House
Farm

Iden
Wood

COLDHARBOUR LA

Brabands
Wood

Hotel

A268

Coldharbour

Malthouse
Wood

King's
Wood

MALTHOUSE LA.

Nurseries

Superstore

PH

Tanhouse

TANHOUSE LA.

PO

The Maltings
Bsns Pk

Peasmarsh

THE MALTINGS

WOODLANDS GDNS

THE OLD HOP

GUN FARM

Stream
Farm

PH

RYE RD

A268

Brabands

Cock
Wood

MAIN ST

FARLEY

BARN VIEW

BRICKFIELD

SCHOOL LA

ORCHARD WAY

Motel

Rye
Foreign

Lea
Farm

Peasmarsh
CE Prim
Sch

High Weald Landscape Trail

PH

Morfey
Wood

Van's
Gill

TANHOUSE LA.

DEW LA

Corner
Wood

CHURCH LA

Peasmarsh
Park

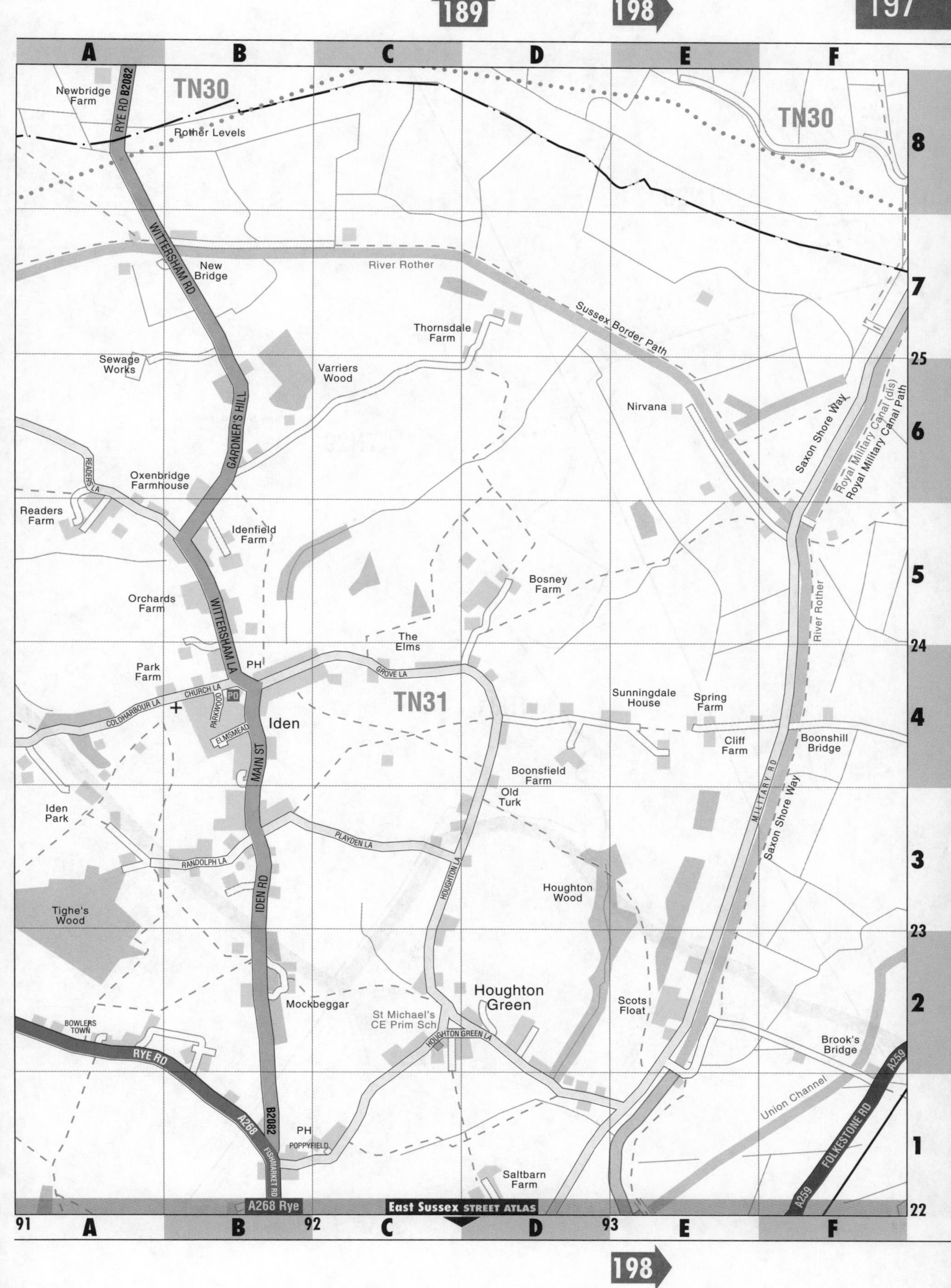

TN30
Newbridge Farm
RYE RD B2082
Rother Levels
TN30

WITTERSHAM RD
New Bridge
River Rother
Sussex Border Path

Sewage Works
Thornsdale Farm
Varriers Wood
Nirvana
Saxon Shore Way
Royal Military Canal (dis)
Royal Military Canal Path

GARDNER'S HILL
Oxenbridge Farmhouse
READERS LA
Readers Farm
Idenfield Farm
Bosney Farm
River Rother

WITTERSHAM LA
Orchards Farm
The Elms
Sunningdale House
Spring Farm
Cliff Farm
Boonshill Bridge

Park Farm
COLDHARBOUR LA
CHURCH LA
PARK RD
PH
PO
ELMSMEAD
GROVE LA
TN31
Iden
Boonsfield Farm
Old Turk
MILITARY RD
Saxon Shore Way

Iden Park
RANDOLPH LA
IDEN RD
PLAYDEN LA
HOUGHTON LA
Houghton Wood

Tighe's Wood
Houghton Green
Scots Float
Brook's Bridge
A259

BOWLERS TOWN
Mockbeggar
St Michael's CE Prim Sch
HOUGHTON GREEN LA
RYE RD
MAIN ST
A268
B2082
FISHMARKET RD
PH POPPYFIELD
Saltbarn Farm
Union Channel
FOLKESTONE RD
A259

8
7
25
6
5
24
4
3
23
2
1

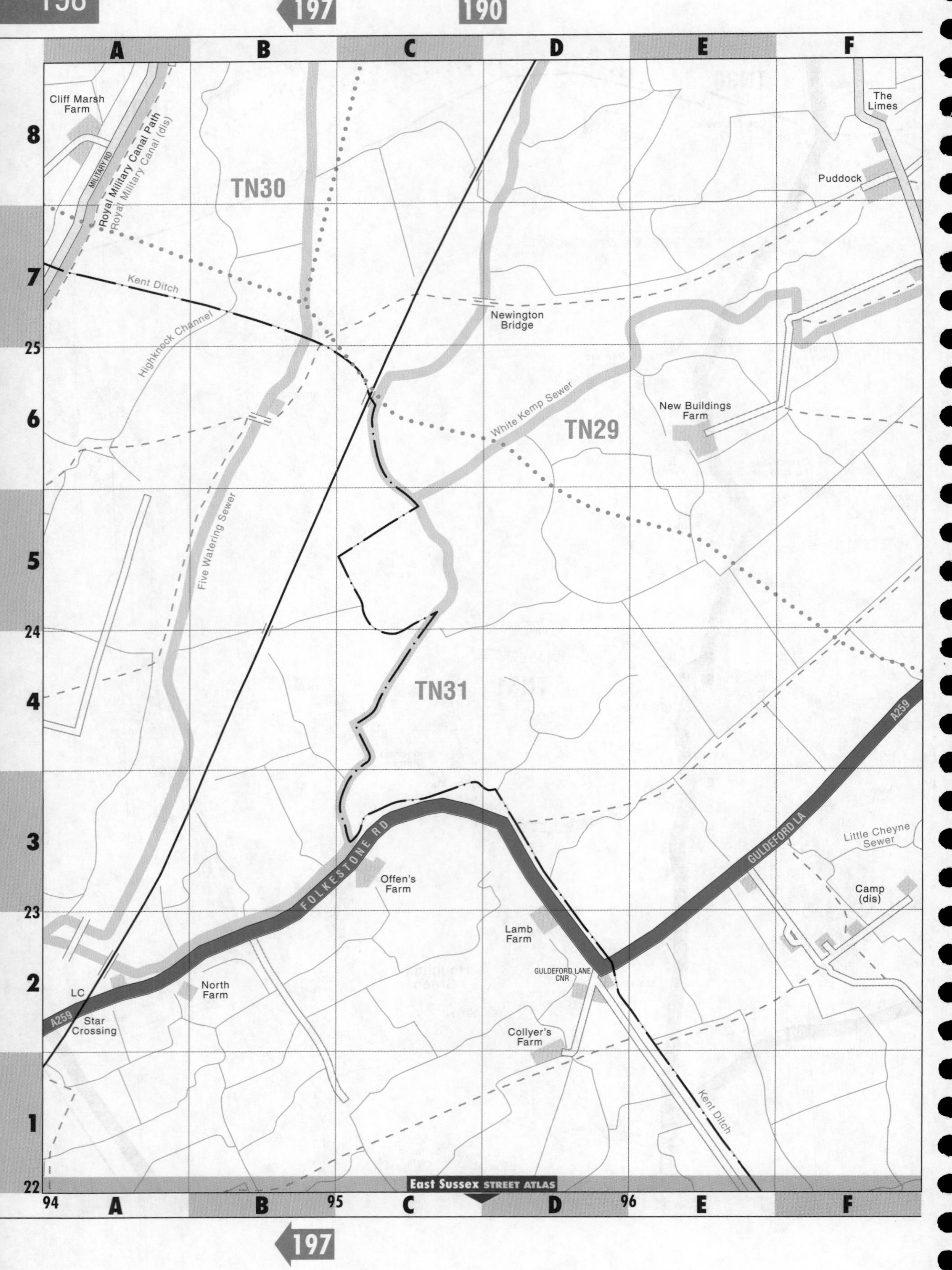

TN30

TN29

TN31

Cliff Marsh
Farm

The
Limes

Puddock

MILITARY RD

Royal Military Canal Path
Royal Military Canal (dis)

Kent Ditch

Highknock Channel

Newington
Bridge

White Kemp Sewer

New Buildings
Farm

Five Watering Sewer

FOLKESTONE RD

Offen's
Farm

Lamb
Farm

GULDEFORD LANE
CNR

North
Farm

Collyer's
Farm

A259

LC

Star
Crossing

GULDEFORD LA

A259

Little Cheyne
Sewer

Camp
(dis)

Kent Ditch

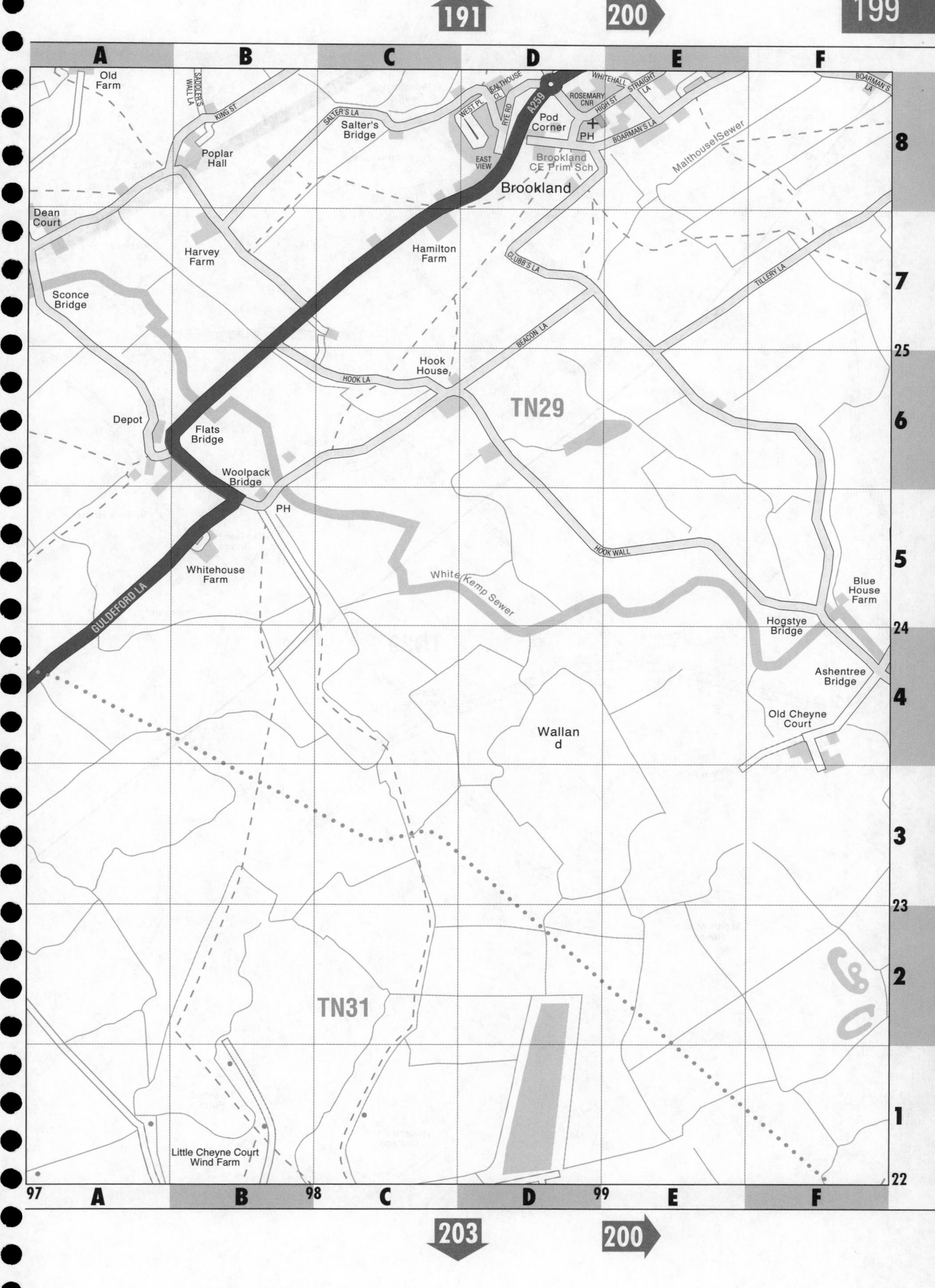

191
200

Old Farm

SADDLER'S WALL LA

KING ST

Poplar Hall

Salter's Bridge

SALTER'S LA

WEST PL

EAST VIEW

EN THOUSE CL

RYE RD

A259

WHITEHALL

HIGH ST

STRAIGHT LA

ROSEMARY CNR

Pod Corner

PH

BOARMAN'S LA

BOARMAN'S LA

Brookland CE Prim Sch

Malthouse Sewer

Brookland

Dean Court

Harvey Farm

Hamilton Farm

CLUBB'S LA

TILLERY LA

Sconce Bridge

BEACON LA

Hook House

HOOK LA

TN29

Depot

Flats Bridge

Woolpack Bridge

PH

Whitehouse Farm

GULDEFORD LA

White Kemp Sewer

HOOK WALL

Blue House Farm

Hogstye Bridge

Ashentree Bridge

Old Cheyne Court

Wallan d

TN31

Little Cheyne Court Wind Farm

8

7

25

6

5

24

4

3

23

2

1

22

97

98

99

A B C D E F

199
192

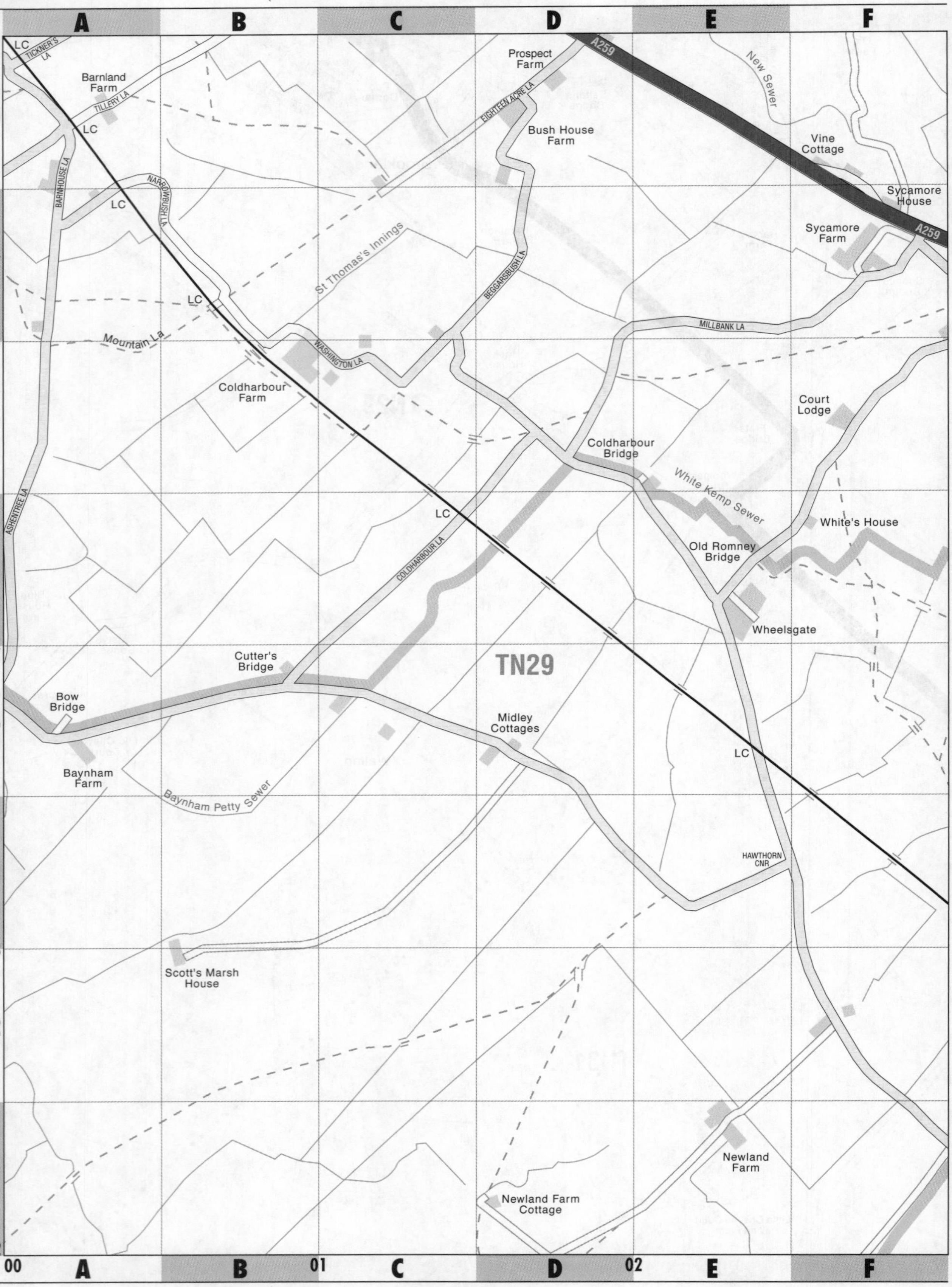

A **B** **C** **D** **E** **F**

LC
TICKNER'S LA

Barnland
Farm

TILLERY LA

8

LC

BARNHOUSE LA

NARROWBUSH LA

LC

Prospect
Farm

A259

EIGHTEEN ACRE LA

Bush House
Farm

New Sewer

Vine
Cottage

Sycamore
House

7

St Thomas's Innings

BEGGARSBUSH LA

A259

Sycamore
Farm

LC

MILLBANK LA

25

Mountain La

ASHENTREE LA

WASHINGTON LA

Coldharbour
Farm

Court
Lodge

6

Coldharbour
Bridge

White Kemp Sewer

LC

COLDHARBOUR LA

White's House

5

Old Romney
Bridge

24

Wheelsgate

Cutter's
Bridge

TN29

Bow
Bridge

4

Midley
Cottages

LC

Baynham
Farm

Baynham Petty Sewer

HAWTHORN
CNR

3

23

Scott's Marsh
House

2

Newland
Farm

1

Newland Farm
Cottage

22

00 **A** **B** 01 **C** **D** 02 **E** **F**

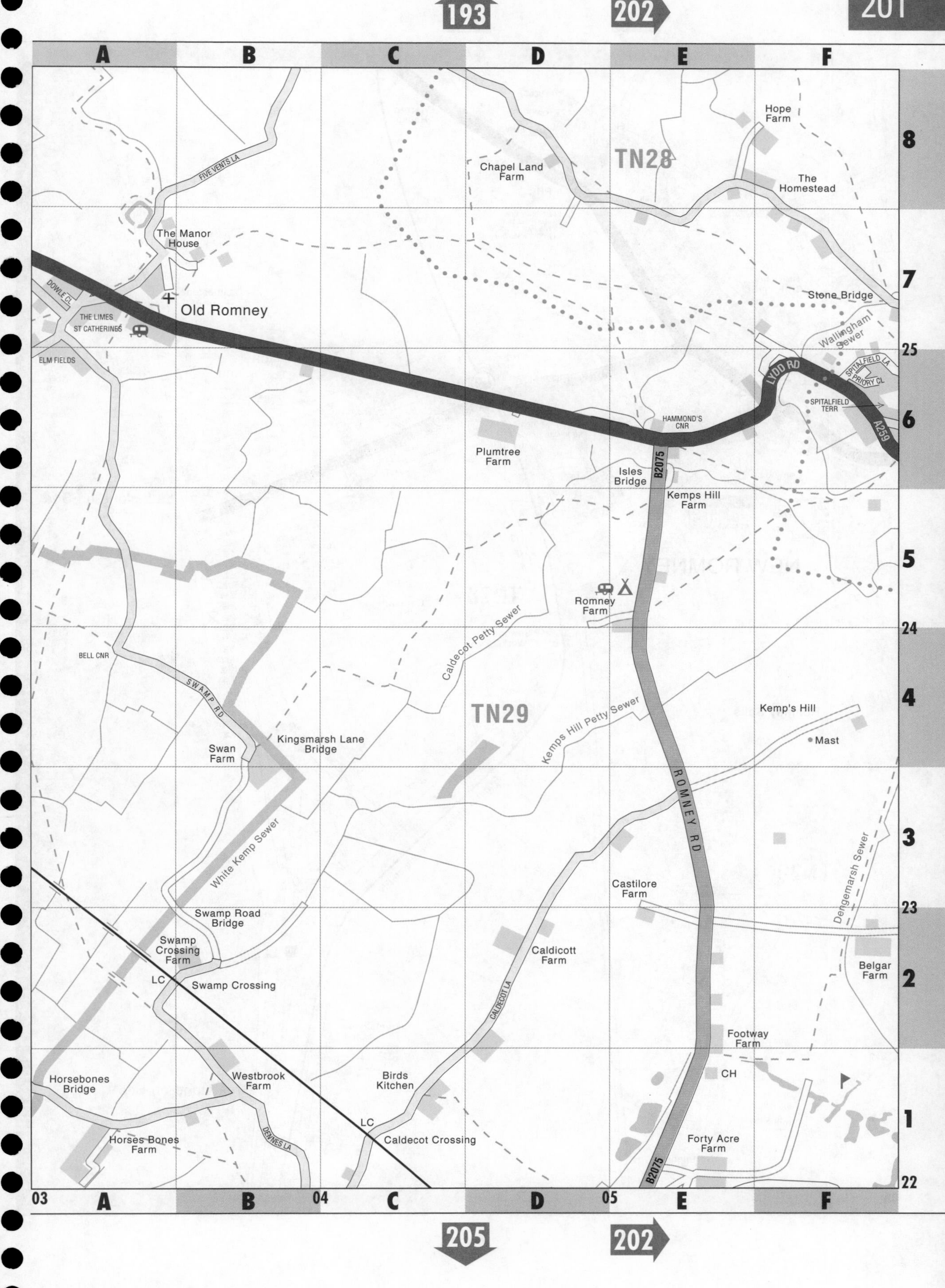

A B C D E F

8

7

25

6

5

24

4

3

23

2

1

22

TN28

Hope Farm

The Homestead

Chapel Land Farm

Stone Bridge

Wallingham Sewer

SPITALFIELD LA

PRIORY CL

LYDD RD

Spitalfield Terr

A259

The Manor House

Old Romney

DOWLE CL

THE LIMES
ST CATHERINES

ELM FIELDS

FIVE VENTS LA

HAMMOND'S CNR

Plumtree Farm

Isles Bridge

Kemps Hill Farm

B2075

Romney Farm

Kemp's Hill

Mast

Caldecot Petty Sewer

Kemps Hill Petty Sewer

TN29

BELL CNR

SWAMP RD

Swan Farm

Kingsmarsh Lane Bridge

White Kemp Sewer

Swamp Road Bridge

Swamp Crossing Farm

LC

Swamp Crossing

Castilore Farm

Caldicott Farm

ROMNEY RD

Dengemarsh Sewer

Belgar Farm

CALDECOT LA

Footway Farm

CH

Horsebones Bridge

Westbrook Farm

Birds Kitchen

LC

Caldecot Crossing

DYNES LA

Horses Bones Farm

Forty Acre Farm

B2075

03

04

05

201 194

A B C D E F

8

GLOUCESTER MEWS
ELLESMERE MEWS
CLARENDON MEWS
Warren House
A259
Warren Farm
ST MARY'S RD
CRAYTHORNE C
RICHMOND DR
ELLIS DR
DYMCHURCH RD
PH
BROADLANDS CRS
BROAD LA
 BOS AVE
WALNER GDNS
BRISSENDEN CL

1 MELBURY MEWS
2 PEMBROKE MEWS
3 WINDSOR MEWS
4 RYSWICK MEWS

Hotel

7

St Nicholas CE Prim Sch
COCKREED
CRAYTHORNE LA
ROLVE LA
WALNER LA
FAIRFIELD RD
CANNON ST
GEORGE LA
OAK LODGE RD
New Romney Main Sewer
LANGPORT RD

Littlestone Tower
COAST RD

25

PRESCOTT HO
FAIRFIELD CT
MAIDEN
B2071
New Romney
BANK HO
MARLBOROUGH
FAIRWAY
CHERRY GDNS
ANNE ROPER CL
ST ANDREW'S RD
ORCHARD RD
MADEIRA RD
CH
SANDCROFT
CH

6

SPITALFIELD LA
SUSSEX RD
WEST ST
NORTH ST
TH
HIGH ST
ASHFORD RD
NEWTON LA
Liby
P
PO
CHURCH RD APP
ON'S RD
A259 LYDD RD
TOOKEY RD
WILES AVE
CHURCH LA
STATION RD
THE CHURCHINGS
THE CHURCHLANDS
ST MARTINS RD
ENGLISH CL
MADGE CRES
HAYWARD'S
GREENLY WAY
AMBERLY WAY
WELLS
THE MEADOWS
MOUNTFIELD RD
STATION APP
WARREN RD
MOUNTFIELD RD
BLENHEIM RD
SUNNYSIDE
LINKS WAY
ST NICHOLAS RD
BLENHEIM RD
LITTLESTONE RD
THE RED HO
FISHERS
THE SALTINGS
CLOVELLY
B2071
Littlestone-on-Sea

SUSSEX RD
ST JOHN'S RD
Cemy

1 GOLDEN SQ
2 MALTHOUSE COTTS
3 ROME HOUSE CNR
4 ROME RD
5 ST LAWRENCE CT
6 VICTORIA ST

SPRINGWOOD CT 1
CHURCHLANDS HO 2
WILES HO 3
DERVILLE HO 4
ASHDOWN CRES 5

NEW ROMNEY

LEAROYD RD
CINQUE PORTS
COLLINS RD

Ind Est

QUEEN'S RD
NETHER RD
PARK RD
MARINE PAR
GS
30
MOUNTFIELD RD

5

TN28

Caravan Pk

VICTORIA RD W
DARCY SQ
THE APARTMENTS 1
LITTLESTONE HO 2
GRAND CT 3
LITTLESTONE CT 4
MULBERRY CT 5
PEMBROKE HO 6
VICTORIA RD
HAMILTON CL
DRAKES LEE
NELSON
MEWS

24

Sewage Works

CLARK RD
CHANNEL WATCH
VARNE MEWS
ARMADA CL
GRAND PDE
COAST DR
P

4

Romney Salts

LB Sta

MEEHAN RD

3

TN29

Romney, Hythe & Dymchurch Rly
DUNES RD
ADIE RD
HARDY RD
ALFRED RD
MEEHAN RD S

23

PH
PO
MERRITT RD
P

2

Greatstone Prim Sch
BALDWIN RD
LC
THE PARADE
ROBERTS RD
BALLARD RD
SEAVIEW RD
LC
Greatstone-on-Sea

1

Dengemarsh Sewer
Mockmill Sewer
Northlade

22

06 A B 07 C D 08 E F

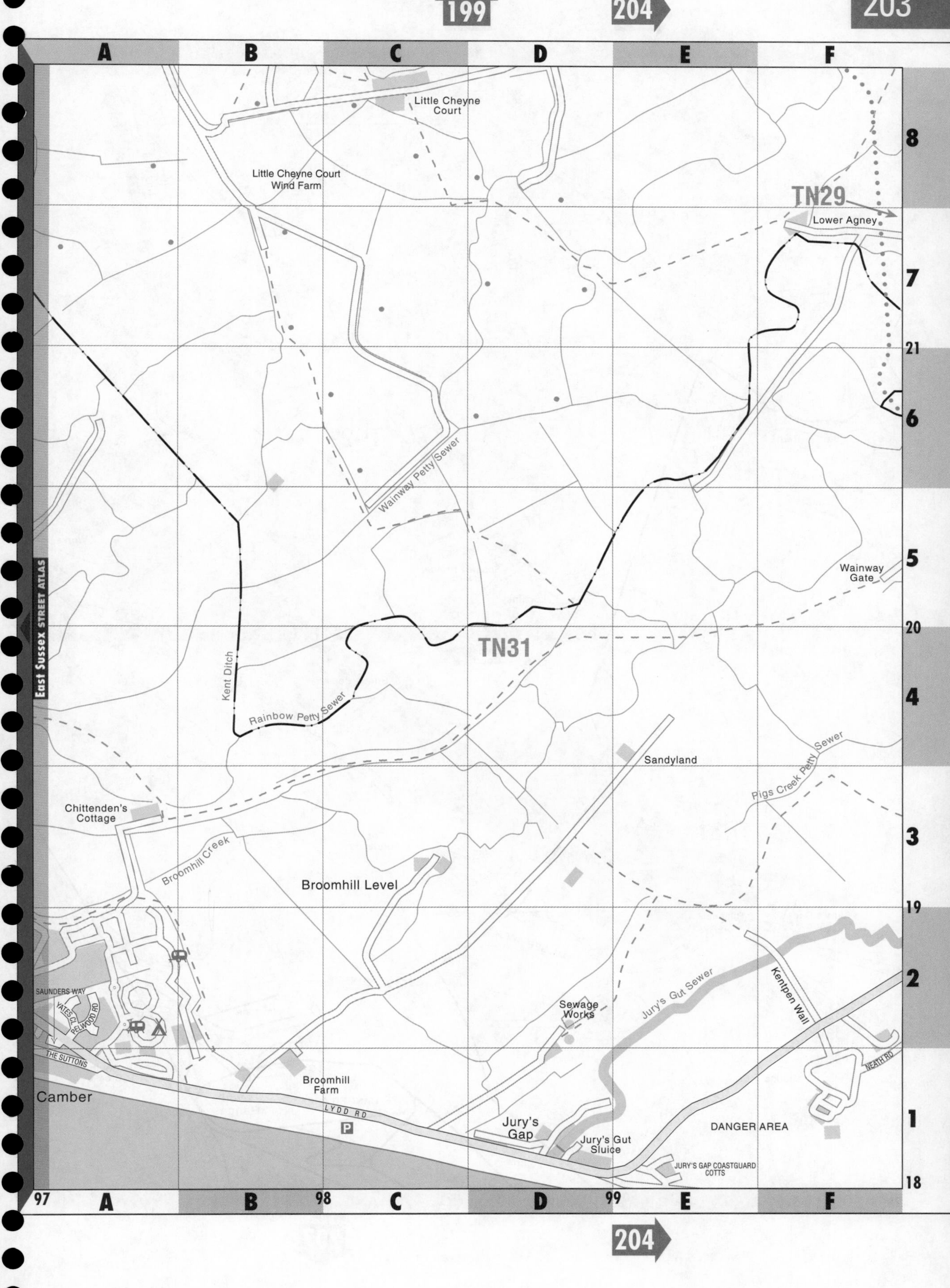

East Sussex STREET ATLAS

Little Cheyne Court

Little Cheyne Court
Wind Farm

TN29
Lower Agney

Wainway Petty Sewer

Wainway
Gate

Kent Ditch

TN31

Rainbow Petty Sewer

Sandyland

Pigs Creek Petty Sewer

Chittenden's
Cottage

Broomhill Creek

Broomhill Level

Jury's Gut Sewer

Kenipen Wall

SAUNDERS WAY

YATES CL
BELWOOD RD

Sewage
Works

THE SUTTONS

NEATH RD

Camber

Broomhill
Farm

LYDD RD

P

Jury's
Gap

Jury's Gut
Sluice

DANGER AREA

JURY'S GAP COASTGUARD
COTTS

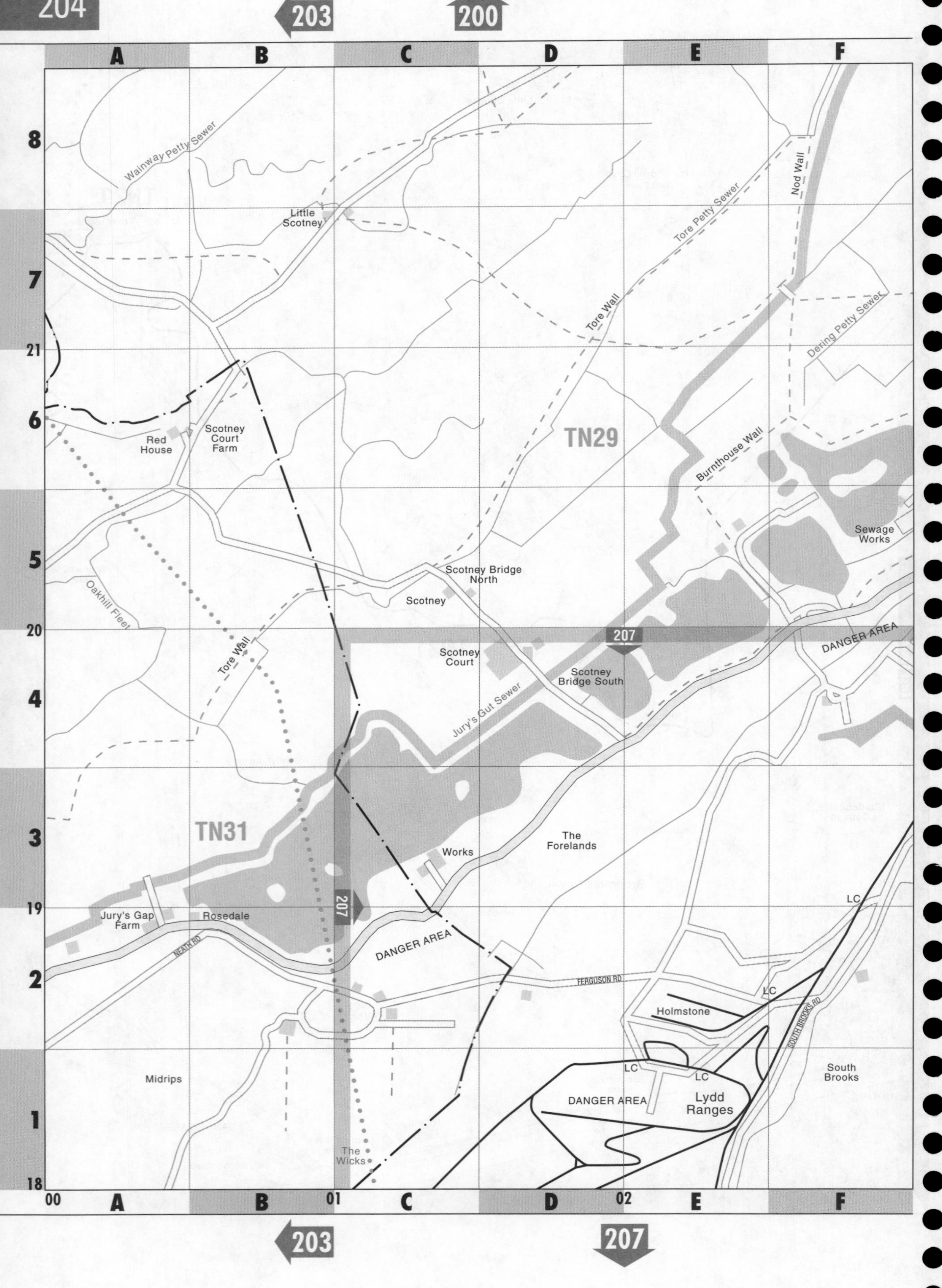

203
200
203
207

A   B   C   D   E   F

8

Wainway Petty Sewer

Little
Scotney

Nod Wall

Tore Petty Sewer

7

Dering Petty Sewer

21

Tore Wall

6

Red
House

Scotney
Court
Farm

TN29

Burnthouse Wall

Sewage
Works

Oakhill Fleet

5

Scotney Bridge
North

Scotney

Tore Wall

DANGER AREA

20

207

4

Scotney
Court

Jury's Gut Sewer

Scotney
Bridge South

TN31

The
Forelands

3

Works

LC

19

Jury's Gap
Farm

Rosedale

207

NEATH RD

DANGER AREA

FERGUSON RD

LC

2

Holmstone

SOUTH BROOKS RD

LC

Midrips

LC

LC

South
Brooks

DANGER AREA

Lydd
Ranges

1

The
Wicks

18

00   A   B   01   C   D   02   E   F

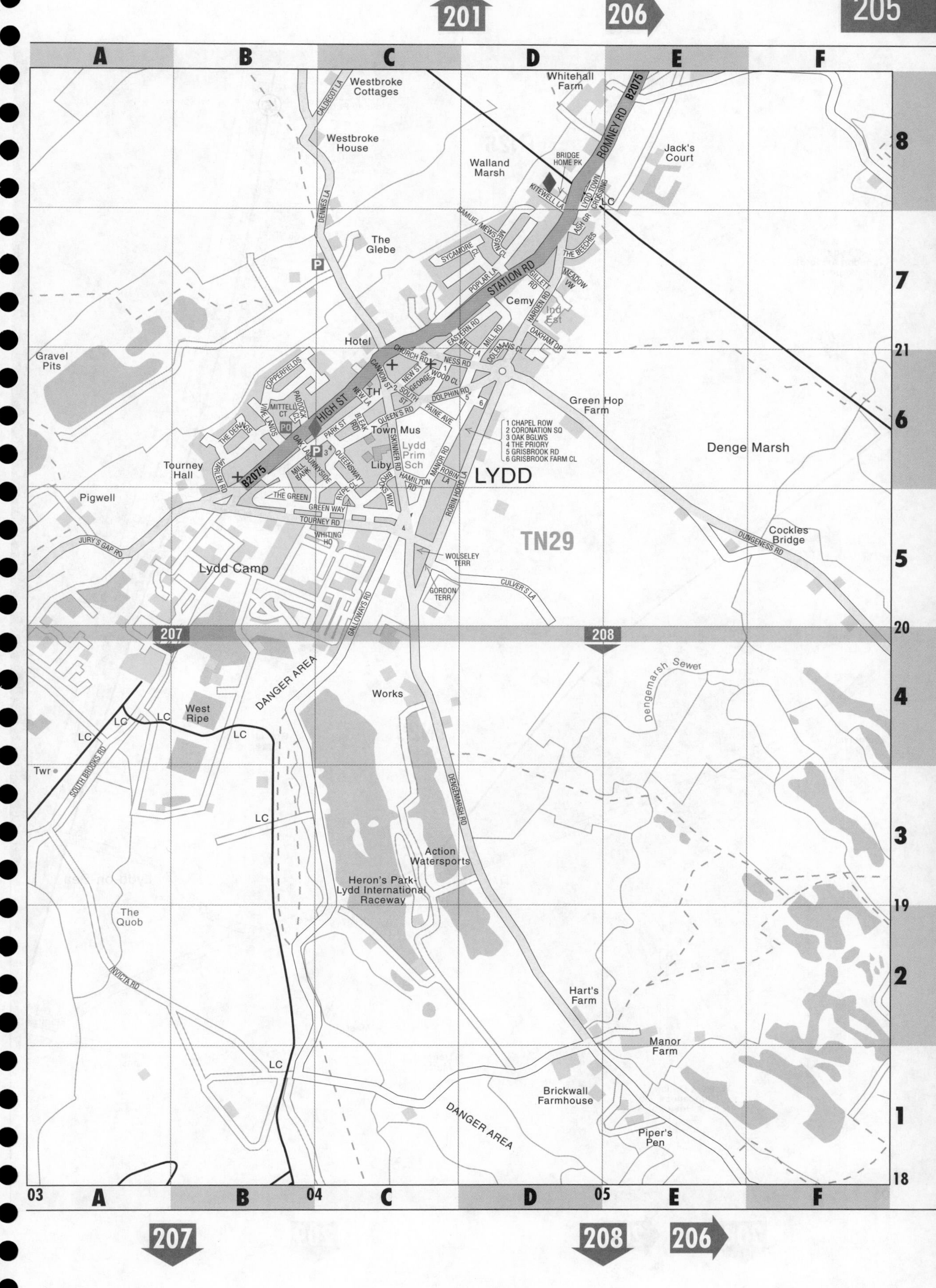
201
206
Westbroke Cottages
Westbroke House
Whitehall Farm
Walland Marsh
Jack's Court
BRIDGE HOME PK
ROMNEY RD
B2075
KITEWELL LA
LYDD TOWN CROSSING
LC
SAMUEL MEWS
ASH GR
THE BEECHES
The Glebe
SYCAMORE CL
MEADOW VW
STATION RD
POPLAR LA
GILLETT RD
HARDEN RD
Cemy
Ind Est
EASTERN RD
MILL LA
MILL RD
COLEMANS CL
OAKHAM DR
Hotel
CHURCH RD
NESS RD
WOOD CL
Gravel Pits
COPPERFIELDS
CANNON ST
NEW ST
SOUTH ST
GEORGE
NEW LA
TH
PADDOCK CL
MITTELL CT
HIGH ST
BLEAK RD
QUEEN'S RD
DOLPHIN RD
PAINE AVE
Green Hop Farm
THE DERINGS
VINELANDS
PO
PARK ST
Town Mus
1 CHAPEL ROW
2 CORONATION SQ
3 OAK BGLWS
4 THE PRIORY
5 GRISBROOK RD
6 GRISBROOK FARM CL
Denge Marsh
Tourney Hall
AMBLEN RD
OAK LA
SUNNYSIDE
QUEENSWAY
SKINNER RD
Lydd Prim Sch
Liby
MANOR RD
ROBIN LA
ROBIN HOOD LA
LYDD
HAMILTON RD
BROOKS WAY
MILL BANK
RYPE CL
THE GREEN
GREEN WAY
TOURNEY RD
Pigwell
WHITING HO
TN29
JURY'S GAP RD
Cockles Bridge
DUNGENESS RD
WOLSELEY TERR
Lydd Camp
GALLOWAYS RD
CULVER'S LA
GORDON TERR
207
208
Dengemarsh Sewer
DANGER AREA
Works
West Ripe
LC
Twr
SOUTH BROOKS RD
DENGEMARSH RD
Action Watersports
Heron's Park-Lydd International Raceway
The Quob
INVICTA RD
Hart's Farm
Manor Farm
Brickwall Farmhouse
Piper's Pen
A
B
C
D
E
F
8
7
21
6
5
20
4
3
19
2
1
18
03
04
05

207
208
206

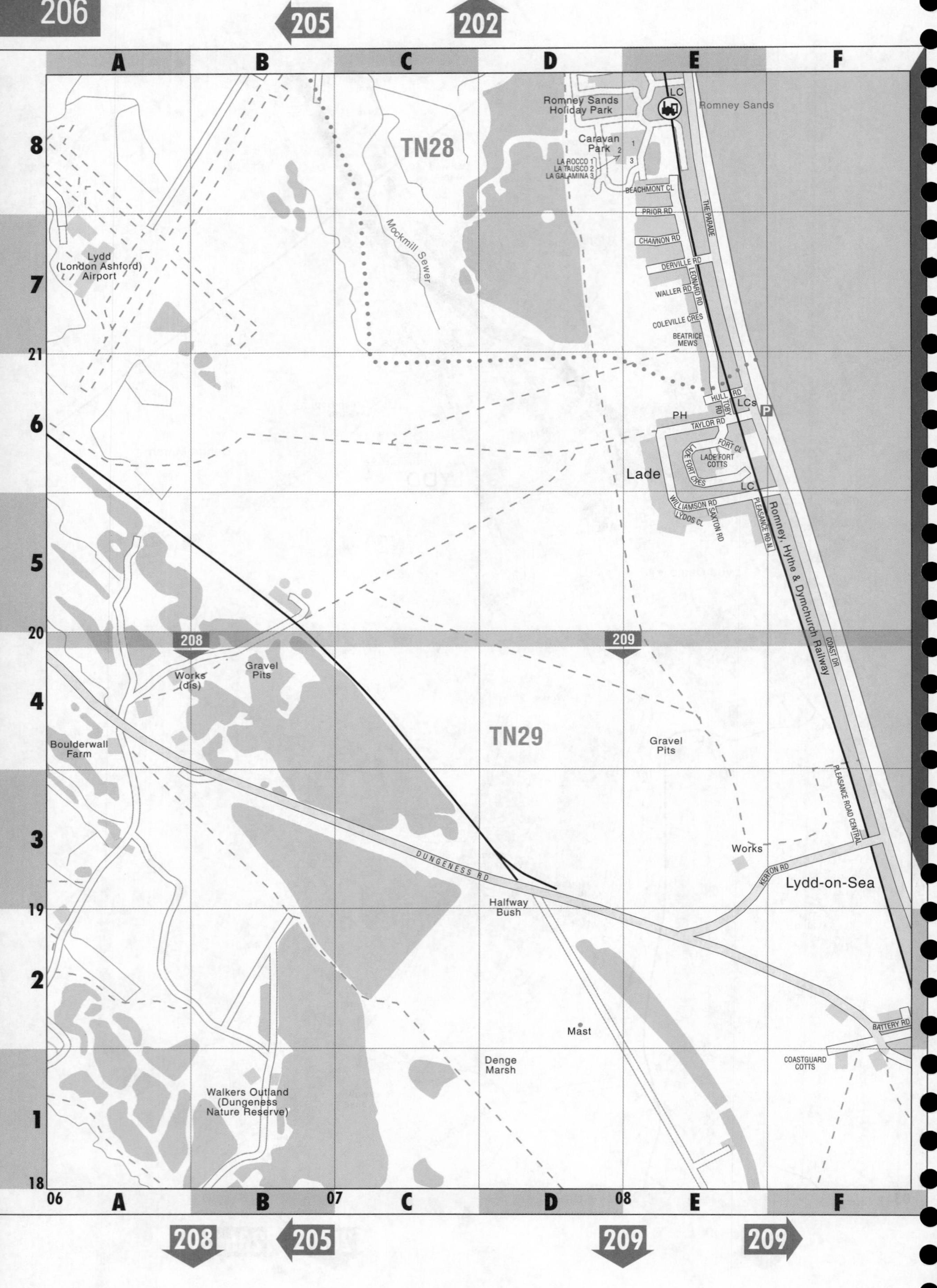

205
202

TN28

Romney Sands
Holiday Park

Romney Sands

LC

Caravan
Park

1
2
3

LA ROCCO 1
LA TAUSCO 2
LA GALAMINA 3

BEACHMONT CL

PRIOR RD

CHANNON RD

DERVILLE RD

WALLER RD

LENNARD RD

THE PARADE

COLEVILLE CRES

BEATRICE
MEWS

Mockmill Sewer

HULL RD

TOBY RD

LCs

PH

TAYLOR RD

P

FORT CL

LADE FORT
COTTS

LADE FORT CRES

Lade

LC

WILLIAMSON RD

LLYDOS CL

SAXTON RD

PLEASANCE RD N

Romney, Hythe & Dymchurch Railway

COAST DR

Lydd
(London Ashford)
Airport

208
209

Works
(dis)

Gravel
Pits

TN29

Gravel
Pits

Boulderwall
Farm

DUNGENESS RD

Works

PLEASANCE ROAD CENTRAL

KERTON RD

Lydd-on-Sea

Halfway
Bush

BATTERY RD

Mast

COASTGUARD
COTTS

Denge
Marsh

Walkers Outland
(Dungeness
Nature Reserve)

208
205
209
209

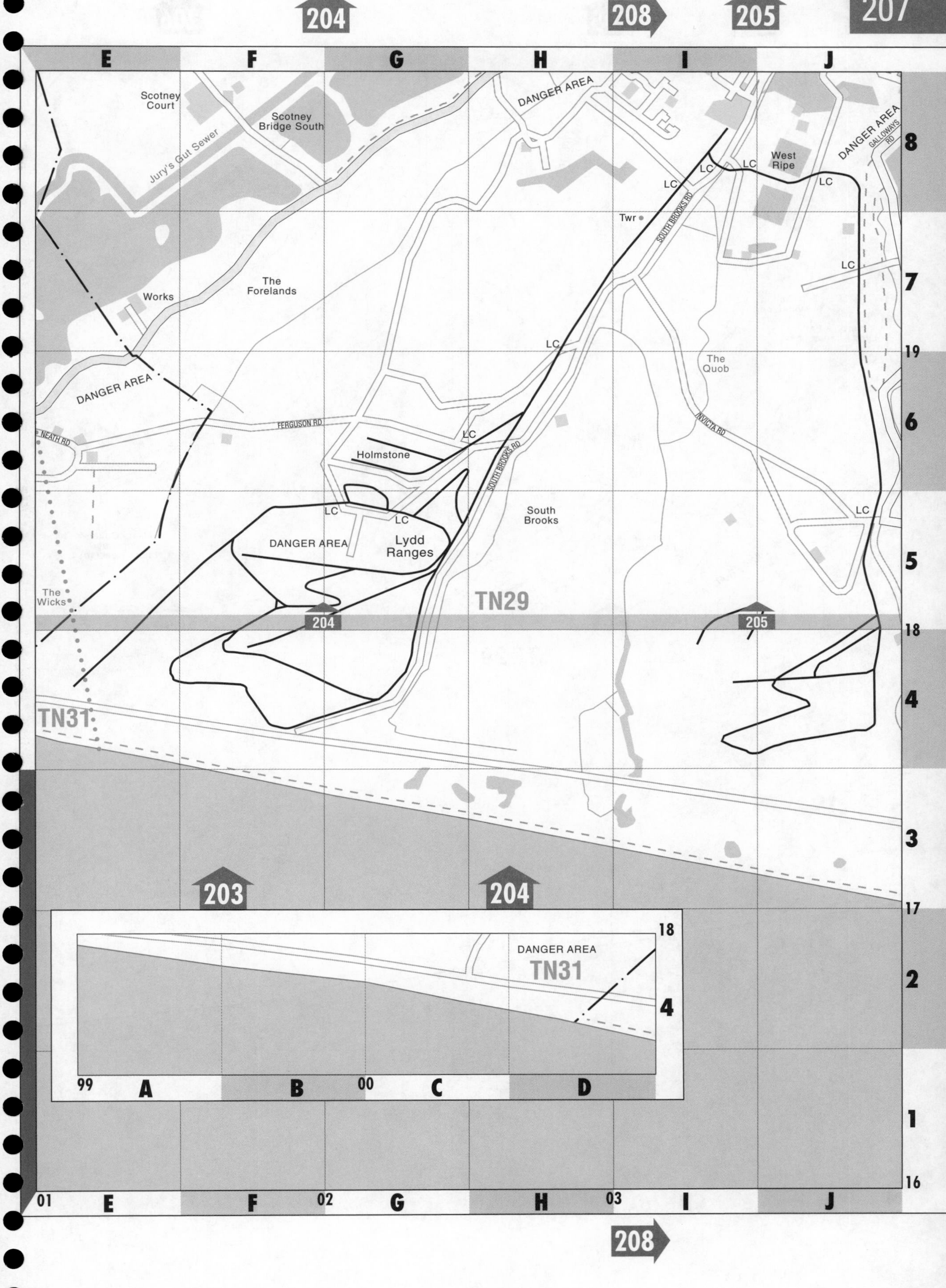

E F G H I J

8
7
19
6
5
18
4
17
2
4
1
16

DANGER AREA

Scotney Court

Scotney
Bridge South

Jury's Gut Sewer

The
Forelands

Works

DANGER AREA

NEATH RD

FERGUSON RD

Holmstone

LC

LC

LC

DANGER AREA

Lydd
Ranges

The
Wicks

LC

South
Brooks

SOUTH BROOKS RD

SOUTH BROOKS RD

LC

Twr

LC

LC

West
Ripe

LC

LC

DANGER AREA

GALLOWAYS RD

The
Quob

INVICTA RD

LC

TN29

TN31

18

DANGER AREA
TN31

4

99 A B 00 C D

01 E F 02 G H 03 I J

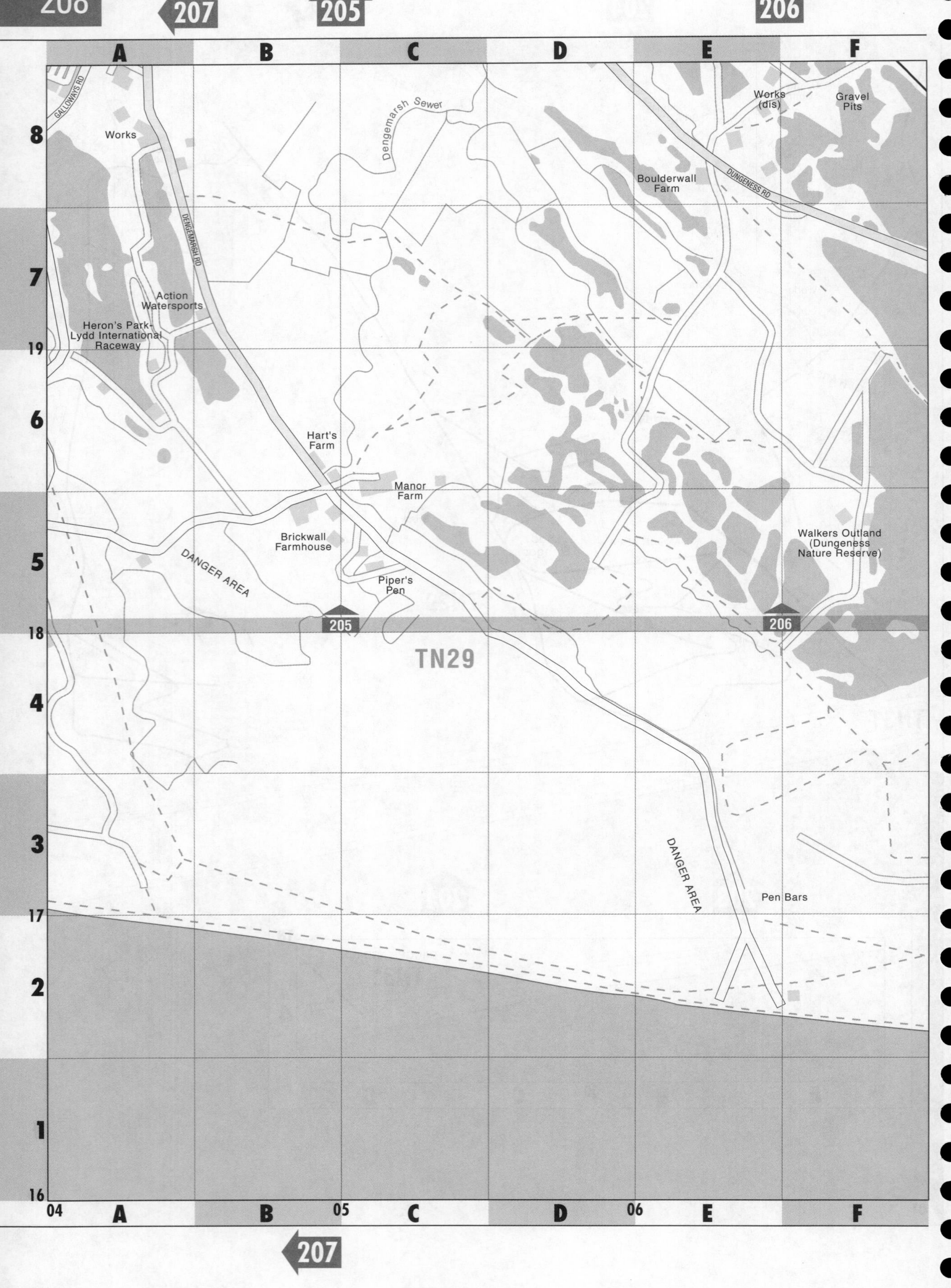

207 205 206

GALLOWAYS RD

Works

DENGEMARSH RD

Dengemarsh Sewer

Works (dis)

Gravel Pits

DUNGENESS RD

Boulderwall Farm

8

Action Watersports

7

Heron's Park-Lydd International Raceway

19

6

Hart's Farm

Manor Farm

Brickwall Farmhouse

Walkers Outland (Dungeness Nature Reserve)

DANGER AREA

5

Piper's Pen

205 206

18

TN29

4

3

DANGER AREA

Pen Bars

17

2

1

16

A B C D E F

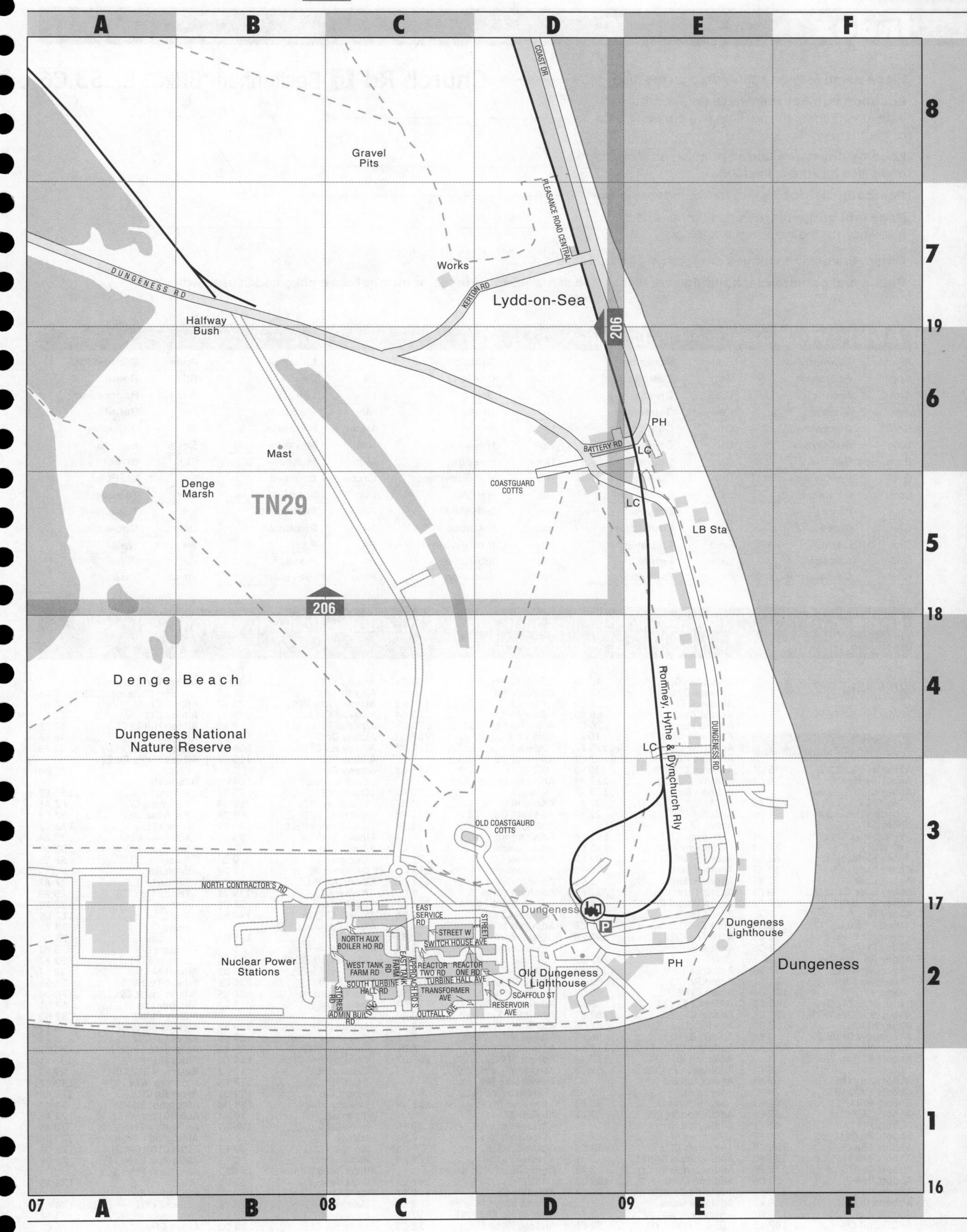

A B C D E F

8

Gravel
Pits

COAST DR

PLEASANCE ROAD CENTRAL

Works

KERTON RD

7

19

Lydd-on-Sea

DUNGENESS RD

Halfway
Bush

206

6

PH

BATTERY RD

LC

Mast

Denge
Marsh

TN29

COASTGUARD
COTTS

LC

LB Sta

5

206

18

Denge Beach

4

Dungeness National
Nature Reserve

Romney, Hythe & Dymchurch Rly

DUNGENESS RD

LC

3

OLD COASTGAURD
COTTS

17

NORTH CONTRACTOR'S RD

EAST
SERVICE
RD

Dungeness

P

Dungeness
Lighthouse

Nuclear Power
Stations

NORTH AUX
BOILER HO RD

STREET W

SWITCH HOUSE AVE

STREET

WEST TANK
FARM RD

EAST TANK
FARM RD

APPROACH RD S

REACTOR
TWO RD

REACTOR
ONE RD

TURBINE HALL AVE

Old Dungeness
Lighthouse

PH

Dungeness

2

SOUTH TURBINE
HALL RD

STORES
RD

TRANSFORMER
AVE

SCAFFOLD ST

ADMIN BUILD
RD

OUTFALL AVE

RESERVOIR
AVE

1

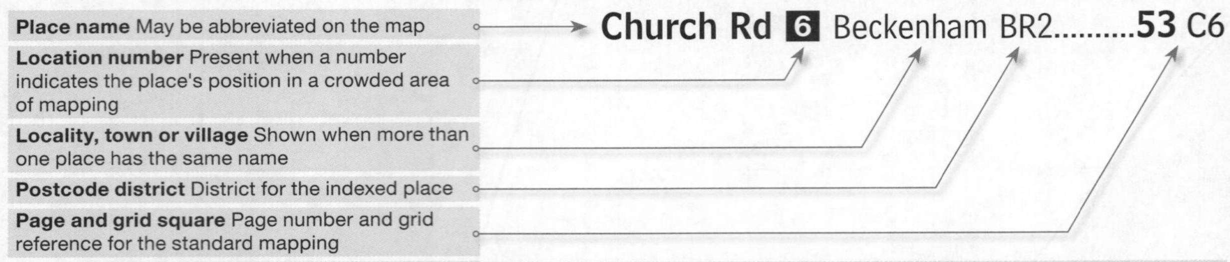

Index

Place name May be abbreviated on the map

Church Rd 6 Beckenham BR2..........**53** C6

Location number Present when a number indicates the place's position in a crowded area of mapping

Locality, town or village Shown when more than one place has the same name

Postcode district District for the indexed place

Page and grid square Page number and grid reference for the standard mapping

Cities, towns and villages are listed in CAPITAL LETTERS

Public and commercial buildings are highlighted in magenta   Places of interest are highlighted in blue with a star★

Abbreviations used in the index

Acad	Academy	Comm	Common	Gd	Ground	L	Leisure	Prom	Promenade
App	Approach	Cott	Cottage	Gdn	Garden	La	Lane	Rd	Road
Arc	Arcade	Cres	Crescent	Gn	Green	Liby	Library	Recn	Recreation
Ave	Avenue	Cswy	Causeway	Gr	Grove	Mdw	Meadow	Ret	Retail
Bglw	Bungalow	Ct	Court	H	Hall	Meml	Memorial	Sh	Shopping
Bldg	Building	Ctr	Centre	Ho	House	Mkt	Market	Sq	Square
Bsns, Bus	Business	Ctry	Country	Hospl	Hospital	Mus	Museum	St	Street
Bvd	Boulevard	Cty	County	HQ	Headquarters	Orch	Orchard	Sta	Station
Cath	Cathedral	Dr	Drive	Hts	Heights	Pal	Palace	Terr	Terrace
Cir	Circus	Dro	Drove	Ind	Industrial	Par	Parade	TH	Town Hall
Cl	Close	Ed	Education	Inst	Institute	Pas	Passage	Univ	University
Cnr	Corner	Emb	Embankment	Int	International	Pk	Park	Wk, Wlk	Walk
Coll	College	Est	Estate	Intc	Interchange	Pl	Place	Wr	Water
Com	Community	Ex	Exhibition	Junc	Junction	Prec	Precinct	Yd	Yard

Index of towns, villages, streets, hospitals, industrial estates, railway stations, schools, shopping centres, universities and places of interest

20/–Ald

20/20 Ind Est ME16...... 74 C8

A

Abberley Pk ME14........ 75 C6
Abbeville Ho ME1........ 9 C4
Abbey Cl
  Deal CT14 ....117 A5
  Minster (Sheppey) ME12.... 4 D6
Abbey Ct
  Westgate on Sea CT8 ....27 D7
  Whitstable CT5 .... 21 A3
Abbey Fields ME13........ 62 E7
Abbey Fields Ct ME13.... 62 E7
Abbey Gate CT11.......... 52 B5
Abbey Gate Cotts ME14... 53 F2
Abbey Gdns CT2 .... 67 A2
Abbey Gr
  Minster (Thanet) CT12.... 50 C5
  Ramsgate CT11 .... 52 B5
Abbey Pl ME13............ 62 D8
Abbey Rd
  Faversham ME13.......... 62 D8
  Gillingham ME8 .... 11 A2
  Kearsney CT16............148 E5
  River CT15, CT16..........148 D1
Abbey Sch The ME13...... 62 C5
Abbey St ME13............ 62 D8
Abbeyview Dr ME12........4 B6
Abbey Way TN24........140 A1
Abbots Barton Wlk 2
  CT1 .... 88 B7
Abbotsbury Hts CT2..... 67 B4
Abbots Field ME16...... 74 B2
Abbots Hill ME13........ 61 E5
Abbot's Hill CT11...... 52 E6
Abbots Pl CT1 .... 66 F1
Abbots Rd ME13.......... 62 F7
Abbots The CT17........166 C8
Abbots Wlk TN25 ...... 123 E2
Abbott Ct 13 CT20......178 D4
Abbott Dr ME9.......... 58 D6
Abbott Rd CT20 ....178 E6
Abbotts Cl CT4 .... 9 B3
Abbott Way TN30........179 C7
ABDO Coll CT4 ....107 A3
Aberdeen Cl CT3........ 47 D3
Aberdeen Ho 9 ME15...... 97 E7
Abigail Cres ME5........ 32 A1

Abingdon Gr CT3 .... 47 D3
Abinger Dr ME5.......... 32 D2
Absalom Ct ME8 .... 11 C2
Acacia Ave CT3 .... 68 D8
Acacia Terr ME10 ...... 36 C4
Academy Dr ME7 ...... 10 F1
Academy La CT19 ......178 B7
Achilles Rd ME5 ...... 32 C2
Ackerey Ct TN23 ......155 F6
ACKHOLT............... 113 A4
Ackholt Rd CT3........113 A5
ACOL 27 B3
Acol Hill CT7 .... 27 B4
Acorn Cl
  Hawkinge CT18.........163 C4
  Kingsnorth TN23 ......156 C3
Acorn Pl ME15.......... 97 E6
Acorn Rd ME7 .... 10 F4
Acorn St ME12.......... 1 D1
Acorn Terr ME9......... 12 E2
Acorn Wharf Rd ME1..... 9 C6
Acre Cl ME1.............9 E1
Acre Ct CT17 ....166 C8
Acre The CT16 ....148 F8
Action Watersports
  TN29..................205 D3
Acton La TN30 ....188 F4
Acton Rd CT5.......... 20 D2
Adam Cl ME17 .... 96 D3
Adam Ct 1 CT19........8 B2
Adams Cl TN30 ....167 B1
Ada Ct ME15............ 87 D6
Adbert Dr ME15........ 96 B4
Addelam Cl CT14........117 A4
Addelam Rd CT14........117 A4
Addington Pl CT11...... 52 E6
Addington Rd
  Margate CT9 ....7 J2
  Sittingbourne ME10...... 36 E3
Addington Sq CT9....... 7 J2
Addington St
  Margate CT9 ....7 J2
  Ramsgate CT11 .... 52 D6
Addiscombe Gdns CT9 .....7 J1
Addiscombe Rd CT9...... 8 A1
Addison Cotts TN30 ....188 D3
Adelaide Dr ME10...... 36 C4
Adelaide Gdns
  Halfway Houses ME12.... 3 E6
  19 Ramsgate CT11...... 52 E6
Adelaide Ho
  Deal CT14 ....117 D6
  Sheerness ME12........1 I1

Adelaide Pl CT1.......... 87 F8
Adelaide Rd
  Elvington CT15..........114 B1
  Gillingham ME7 ...... 10 C4
Aden Terr 1 ME14...... 75 A7
Adie Rd TN28 ....202 D3
ADISHAM.................112 D8
Adisham CE Prim Sch
  CT3 ....112 D8
Adisham Downs Rd CT3,
  CT4 .... 90 B2
Adisham Dr ME16........ 74 B7
Adisham Gdns 1 TN23 ...155 F6
Adisham Gn ME10....... 36 F8
Adisham Rd
  Bekesbourne CT4 ...... 89 E3
  Wingham CT3 .... 91 A4
  Womenswold CT4, CT3 ...112 C2
Adisham Sta CT3 ......112 E8
Adisham Way CT9....... 8 C1
Admin Building Rd TN29 209 C2
Admiral Ct ME7........ 10 D6
Admirals Wlk
  Chatham ME5............ 32 B3
  Halfway Houses ME12.... 3 E6
  Hythe CT21 ....176 C1
  Tenterden TN30 ......167 C1
Admiral's Wlk ME4...... 9 F7
Admiralty Cl ME13 .... 62 B8
Admiralty Mews CT14 ...117 C4
Admiralty Terr ME7 .... 10 A7
Admiralty Wlk CT5 .... 43 A7
Adrian Mews CT8 ...... 7 D1
Adrian Sq CT8 .... 7 D1
Adrian St CT17........166 D7
Aerodrome Est ME14.... 55 E4
Aerodrome Rd
  Bekesbourne CT4 ...... 89 E3
  Hawkinge CT18........163 A4
Afghan Rd
  Broadstairs CT10...... 29 F8
  Chatham ME4.......... 9 E4
Agate Ct ME10.......... 36 D6
Agester La CT4 ....129 A4
Agricultural Mus Brook★
  TN25..................141 B5
Ainsdale Cl CT19........178 B7
Ainsley Way CT4 ...... 108 F8
Aintree Ho 1 ME15...... 97 F6
Aintree Rd ME5........ 32 C3
Airedale Cl CT9........ 8 A1
Aireys The CT13 ...... 93 B6
Airfield View ME12...... 17 C8

Aisne Dr CT1 .... 67 D1
Ajax Rd ME1 .... 31 C8
Alamein Ave ME5 ...... 31 F7
Alamein Cl CT15 ......149 F3
Alaseun Terr ME12...... 4 A5
Albany Dr CT6.......... 22 D4
Albany Ho 15 CT17.....166 D7
Albany Pl CT17........166 D7
Albany Rd
  Capel-le-Ferne CT18 ...164 C1
  Chatham ME4.......... 10 B2
  Gillingham ME7 ...... 10 D4
  Rochester ME1 ...... 9 C4
  Sittingbourne ME10.... 36 E3
Albany St ME14........ 75 B5
Albany Terr
  Chatham ME4.......... 9 E4
  Gillingham ME7 ...... 10 D4
Albemarle Rd
  Ashford TN24..........139 F1
  Chatham ME5.......... 32 C2
Alberta Cl CT16........149 B3
Albert Costain Ct 1
  CT20..................178 D5
Albert Ct
  8 Ramsgate CT12 .... 52 E6
  9 Whitstable CT5.... 20 D2
Albert La CT21 ....176 C1
Albert Manor ME7 .... 10 B5
Albert Pl ME2........9 B7
Albert Rd
  Ashford TN24..........139 B3
  Broadstairs CT10...... 29 E8
  Canterbury CT1 ...... 88 B8
  Capel-le-Ferne CT18 ...164 C2
  Chatham ME4.......... 10 A3
  Deal CT14 ....117 C6
  Dover CT16 ....149 D1
  Folkestone CT19 ......178 D6
  Gillingham ME7 ...... 10 C4
  Margate CT9 ....7 H2
  Ramsgate CT11 ...... 52 F7
  Rochester ME1 ...... 9 C3
Albert Reed Gdns ME15 .. 74 E2
Albert Row CT11........ 52 C5
Albert St
  Maidstone ME14 .... 74 F6
  Ramsgate CT11 ...... 52 E6
  Whitstable CT5........ 20 D2
Albert Terr
  Deal CT14 ....117 C5
  Margate CT9 ....7 I2

Albert Terr continued
  Minster (Sheppey) ME12.... 5 A5
Albion Cl CT6.......... 46 A8
Albion Ct CT11.......... 52 E6
Albion Hill 7 CT11.....52 E6
Albion La CT6.......... 46 A8
Albion Mews CT11...... 52 F6
Albion Mews Rd 3
  CT20..................178 D4
Albion Pl
  Ashford TN24..........156 E7
  Canterbury CT1 ...... 67 A1
  Faversham ME13...... 62 C7
  Hythe CT21 ....176 D2
  Maidstone ME14 .... 75 B4
  Newington ME9 ...... 35 B6
  Ramsgate CT11 ...... 52 E6
Albion Rd
  Birchington CT7........ 27 A7
  Broadstairs CT10...... 29 F6
  Chatham ME5.......... 32 B2
  Deal CT14 ....117 D8
  Eastry CT13 .... 93 A2
  Folkestone CT19 ......178 D6
  Margate CT9 .... 8 B3
  Ramsgate CT11 ...... 52 F7
Albion St CT10........ 30 B4
Albion Terr ME10 ...... 36 E6
Albion Villas 6 CT20...178 D4
Albuhera Sq CT1........ 67 D1
Albury Cl ME5 .... 32 D2
Alchins Cotts ME17 .... 96 E2
Alder Cl ME12 ...... 3 A8
Aldergate La CT21 ....174 C1
Alder Ho TN23 ....138 F1
Alderney Gdns CT10.... 29 E5
Alderney Way TN24 ....139 C7
Alder Rd CT19 ....178 C6
Aldershot Rd ME5...... 32 A7
ALDINGTON............173 A6
Aldington Cl ME5 .... 32 B5
Aldington Cnr TN25 ...173 A6
ALDINGTON FRITH.....172 D6
Aldington La ME14 .... 76 D8
Aldington Prim Sch
  TN25..................173 A5
Aldington Rd
  Lympne CT21 ....174 E3
  Maidstone ME14 .... 75 F4
Aldon Cl ME14.......... 75 C6
Aldon Ct ME14.......... 75 C6
Aldred Rd ME13........ 62 C6
Aldridge Cl CT6........ 22 B3

Alec Pemble Cl TN24 139 E5
Alefe Way ME9 14 D3
Alexander Cl CT13 93 F8
Alexander Ct
1 Rochester ME2 9 B8
1 Sittingbourne ME10 36 E5
Alexander Dr ME13 62 B7
Alexandra Ave ME7 10 E4
Alexandra Cl ME10 36 E7
Alexandra Corniche CT21 177 C3
Alexandra Ct CT21 176 A1
Alexandra Dr CT14 116 F3
Alexandra Gdns CT20 178 D4
Alexandra Glen ME5 32 A1
Alexandra Homes CT9 7 I1
Alexandra Mews ME12 1 E2
Alexandra Pl 1 CT17 149 C1
Alexandra Rd
Birchington CT7 27 A5
Broadstairs CT10 30 B4
Capel-le-Ferne CT18 164 C2
Chatham ME4 10 B2
Deal CT14 117 D2
Kingsdown CT14 134 C5
Margate CT9 28 E8
Ramsgate CT11 52 D8
Sheerness ME12 1 E2
Whitstable CT5 43 C8
Alexandra St
Folkestone CT19 178 E6
Maidstone ME14 74 F6
Alexandra Terr CT9 7 I1
Alexandria Dr CT6 22 C5
Alfred Cl
Canterbury CT1 87 C6
Chatham ME4 10 B2
Alfred Mews CT14 117 D7
Alfred Rd
Ashford TN24 156 D7
Birchington CT7 26 D8
Canterbury CT1 87 C6
Dover CT16 149 B2
Greatstone-on-Sea TN28 202 D3
Margate CT9 8 B1
Alfred Row CT14 117 D7
Alfred Sq CT14 117 D7
Alicia Ave CT9 28 A8
Alison Cl
Birchington CT7 27 B8
Whitfield CT16 149 A6
Alison Cres CT16 149 A7
ALKHAM 147 C1
Alkham Cl CT9 8 F2
Alkham Rd
Maidstone ME14 75 C5
Temple Ewell CT15, CT16 148 C4
Alkham Valley Rd
Alkham CT15 147 E1
Hawkinge CT18, CT15 163 E4
Alland Grange La CT12 27 E2
Allan Rd CT5 42 E6
Allen Ave CT8 27 D7
Allenby Ave CT14 117 B5
Allenby Rd CT12 29 C2
Allenby Wlk ME10 36 B5
Allen Cl ME5 32 C6
Allen Ct ME12 4 A5
Allendale St 2 CT19 178 D6
Allen Field TN23 155 F8
Allen St ME14 75 B5
All Faiths Childrens Com Sch 6 ME2 9 B7
Alliance Rd CT11 52 F6
ALLINGTON 74 D8
Allington Prim Sch ME16 74 C7
Allington Rd ME8 11 A3
Allington Way ME16 74 B6
Allison Ave ME7 10 E1
Allnutt Mill Cl 4 ME15 74 E2
All Saints' Ave CT9 7 H1
All Saints CE Prim Sch 3 ME4 10 A3
All Saints' Cl CT5 20 F1
All Saints Ind Pk CT9 7 I1
All Saints La 2 CT1 87 F8
All Saints Rd ME10 37 C4
All Saints View ME13 41 E2
All Souls CE Prim Sch CT19 177 E6
Allsworth Cl ME9 35 B6
Alma Pl
2 Canterbury CT1 67 A1
Ramsgate CT11 52 E7
Rochester ME2 9 A7
Alma Rd
Folkestone CT20 177 D5
Herne Bay CT6 23 C5
Margate CT9 7 J1
Ramsgate CT11 52 E8
Sheerness ME12 1 D2
Almarina CT8 7 C1
Alma St
Canterbury CT1 67 A1
Sheerness ME12 1 E2
Alma Street Pas ME12 1 E2
Almond Cl
Ashford TN23 138 F5
Broadstairs CT10 29 C4
Whitstable CT5 21 D1
Almond Ct CT4 86 E1
Almond Gr ME7 33 A4
Almond Ho 9 ME16 74 A3
Almonds The ME14 76 A4
Almond Tree Cl ME12 3 A8
Almon Pl ME1 9 D5
Almshouse Rd ME13 104 C7
Almshouses 8 CT1 88 A8
Alpha Rd
Birchington CT7 27 A7
Ramsgate CT11 52 D6
Alsager Ave ME11 2 F3
Alsops Rd TN24 156 E7
Alston Cl ME12 4 C7
Altbarn Ind Est ME5 54 C8
Alvis Ave CT6 22 A4
Amage Rd TN25 141 C8
Amage Road Cotts TN25 124 B1
Amanda Cl ME5 31 F3
Amber Cl ME9 38 D2
Amber Ct ME7 10 D5
Amber La ME17 98 A1
Amber Rise ME10 36 C7
Amber Way ME17 98 B1
Ambleside
Faversham ME13 62 E6
Sittingbourne ME10 37 C3
Ambley Gn ME8 33 A8
Ambley Rd ME8 33 B8
Ambley Wood Nature Reserve* ME7, ME8 33 A8
Ambrose Hill ME5 10 C2
Amels Hill ME9 56 F8
Ames Ave ME14 76 A4
Amethyst Ave ME5 31 E6
Amethyst Dr ME10 36 D6
Amherst Cl
Maidstone ME16 74 D4
Margate CT9 8 C1
Amherst Hill ME7 10 A6
Amherst Rd ME1 9 D3
Amherst Redoubt ME4 10 A5
Amies Ho ME15 96 F3
Amos Cl
Herne Bay CT6 23 C3
Sheldwich ME13 83 C5
Amsbury Rd ME15, ME17 96 B2
Amshurst Villas ME15 96 A4
Anatase Cl ME10 36 C7
Anchor Bsns Pk ME10 37 B6
Anchor Hill 4 CT9 7 J2
Anchor Ho ME1 9 B4
Anchor La
Deal CT14 117 C6
Sheerness ME12 1 B3
Anchor Rd ME1 9 C1
Ancress Cl CT2 67 A4
Andover Wlk 12 ME15 97 F6
Andrew Broughton Way ME14 75 B4
Andrew Manor ME7 10 C6
Andrews Wlk ME10 36 B5
Anemone Way CT6 45 E7
Anerley Cl ME16 74 D7
Angel Cotts ME8 12 A2
Angel Hts CT18 162 E3
Anglesey Ave ME15 97 A7
Anglesey Cl ME5 32 B7
Anglian Sch of English CT9 8 B2
Angus Dr TN24 139 C7
Anna Pk CT7 26 F8
Anne Boleyn Cl ME12 5 E3
Anne Cl CT7 27 B7
Anne Green Wlk 8 CT1 67 B2
Anne Roper Cl TN28 202 E6
Anne's Rd CT10 30 C7
Anns Rd CT11 52 E8
Annvera Ho 2 ME7 10 C7
ANSDORE 125 F6
Ansell Ave ME4 10 A1
Anselm Cl ME10 36 E4
Anselm Rd CT17 166 A8
Anson Cl
Broadstairs CT10 29 D3
Chatham ME5 32 C6
Anstee Rd CT17 149 C1
Antelope Cl CT16 149 A5
Anthony Cres CT5 43 B6
Anthonys Way ME2 9 E8
Antolin Way CT10, CT12 29 A3
Antonius Ct TN23 156 A5
Anvil Cl CT7 27 A6
ANVIL GREEN 125 C8
Anzio Cres CT15 149 E2
Anzio Ho 15 CT1 67 B2
Apartments The TN28 202 E5
Apiary Bsns Pk The ME17 99 B3
Apollo Ho ME5 32 A6
Appleby Cl ME1 31 D7
Appleby Ct TN24 139 D2
Apple Cl CT18 163 B4
Apple Craft Ctr* ME13 62 E5
Applecross Cl ME1 9 B4
APPLEDORE 190 C7
Appledore Ave ME12 3 B8
Appledore Cl CT9 8 C1
Appledore Cres CT19 177 D7
Appledore Ct ME16 74 C7
APPLEDORE HEATH 181 C1
Appledore Rd
Appledore TN26, TN30 190 A7
Brattle TN26 181 C7
Gillingham ME8 11 A3
Tenterden TN30 179 E7
Appledore Sta TN26 191 B8
Appledown Way CT1 88 D5
Appleford Dr ME12 3 F7
Applegarth Pk CT5 43 A6
Appletree Ct 5 ME8 33 F8
Approach Rd
Broadstairs CT10 30 A4
Dover CT17 166 A6
Margate CT9 8 A2
Shepherdswell CT15 130 D5
Approach Road S TN29 209 C2
April Rise
Birchington CT7 26 D8
Whitstable CT5 43 B7
Apsley Cotts CT4 86 D3
Apsley Ct 14 CT11 52 E7
Apsley St TN23 139 B2
Aragon Cl TN23 155 E7
Archbishop Courtenay CE Prim Sch (Tovil Site) ME15 74 E2
Archbishop Courtenay CE Prim Sch (Town Site) 8 ME15 75 A3
Archbishops Cres ME7 11 A5
Archbishop's Sch The CT2 66 E3
Archcliffe Rd CT17 166 C5
Archer Ct ME10 14 F2
Archer Rd
Chatham ME5 32 B6
Folkestone CT19 178 D6
Archers Court Maths & Computing Coll CT16 149 B5
Archer's Court Rd CT15, CT16 149 B7
Archery Sq CT14 117 D3
Archibald Ho ME14 75 A7
Archway Ct 4 ME2 9 B8
Archway Rd
Ramsgate CT11 52 E6
Sheerness ME12 1 B3
Arcon Cl TN23 156 A7
Arcon Rd TN23 156 A7
Arden Bsns Ctr ME2 9 E7
Arden Dr TN24 139 C3
Arden Grange CT4 107 C8
Ardenlee Dr ME14 75 B5
Arden Rd
Faversham ME13 62 E7
Herne Bay CT6 23 C2
Arden St ME7 10 C6
Ardent Ave CT14 117 C4
Ardent Rd CT16 149 A5
Arethusa Rd ME1 31 C8
Argent Bsns Pk ME11 3 A2
Argent Rd ME11 3 A2
Argent Way ME10 36 C6
Argyle Ave CT9 7 G1
Argyle Cl ME1 31 E8
Argyle Gdns CT9 7 G1
Argyle Rd CT5 20 D1
Argyll Dr CT11 29 F1
Ark Cotts CT18 161 D4
Ark La CT14 117 D7
Arkley Rd CT6 22 F4
Arklow Sq 6 CT11 52 F7
Arlington TN23 155 F8
Arlington Gdns CT9 29 C8
Arlington Ho CT9 7 H2
Arlington Sq CT9 7 H2
Arlott Cl ME14 74 F6
Armada Cl TN28 202 E5
Armada Ct ME4 9 E1
Armadale CT10 8 F1
Armada Way ME4 9 F3
Armourers Wlk CT16 149 A3
Armstrong Rd ME15 75 A1
Armstrong Sq CT6 22 A3
Arnhem Dr ME5 31 F7
Arnolde Cl ME2 9 E7
Arnold Rd
Chartham CT4 86 C2
5 Margate CT9 7 J1
Arolla Rd CT6 23 C4
ARPINGE 162 C3
Arran Mews 4 CT1 67 B2
Arran Rd ME15 97 A6
Arrowhead La TN26, TN29 191 D7
Arthur Kennedy Cl ME13 63 F3
Arthur Rd
Birchington CT7 26 D8
Deal CT14 117 A3
Gillingham ME8 33 E7
Hythe CT21 176 C1
Margate CT9 8 A3
Rochester ME1 9 D3
Arthur Salmon Cl ME13 62 B7
Arthur St
3 Folkestone CT19 178 E6
Sittingbourne ME10 36 E4
Artillery Gdns 11 CT1 67 A1
Artillery Ho 12 CT1 67 A1
Artillery Rd CT11 52 F7
Artillery St 10 CT1 67 A1
Arundel Ave ME10 36 E1
Arundel Cl ME5 32 D1
Arundel Rd
Cliffs End CT12 51 D7
Margate CT9 8 B2
Arundel Sq ME15 74 F2
Arundel St ME14 74 F6
Ascot Cl ME5 32 C2
Ascot Gdns CT8 27 E7
Ascot Ho 2 ME15 97 F6
ASH 71 D2
ASHBANK 99 B7
Ashbank Cotts ME17 99 B7
Ashbee Gdns CT6 23 C5
Ashborne Cl TN24 139 D6
Ashbrooke Ctr The 2 CT10 29 C4
Ashburn Gdns CT6 23 C5
Ashburnham Rd
Maidstone ME14 75 B8
Ramsgate CT11 52 C7
Ashburn Mews ME7 10 E3
Ashburton Cl TN24 139 E2
Ash Cl
Ashford TN23 138 E3
Broadstairs CT10 29 C4
Chatham ME5 10 C1
Crabble CT17 148 E3
Gillingham ME8 11 B3
Herne Bay CT6 22 F1
Ash Cres CT3 46 E1
Ash Ct CT12 51 D4
Ashdale Ho 5 TN23 139 C2
Ashdown Cl
Herne Bay CT6 23 B2
Maidstone ME16 74 D3
Ashdown Cres TN28 202 B6
Ashdown Ct TN24 139 C3
Ashdown Field CT4 86 B2
Ashdown Lodge CT20 178 A5
Ashdown Rd ME17, ME9 79 F3
Ashenden Cl CT1 87 C5
Ashendene Gr CT2 68 A6
Ashen Tree Cotts CT3 70 B1
Ashentree La TN29 200 A5
Ashen Tree La CT16 166 E8
ASHFORD 139 A2
Ashford Borough Mus* 15 TN23 139 B2
Ashford Bsns Pk TN24 157 A6
Ashford Bsns Point TN24 156 F5
Ashford Designer Outlet TN24 156 C7
Ashford Dr ME17 99 D3
Ashford Friars Prep Sch TN23 155 B8
Ashford Int Sta TN24 139 C1
Ashford Mkt TN24 156 E5
Ashford Oaks Com Prim Sch 1 TN23 155 F8
Ashford Rd
Ashford TN23 155 B8
Bethersden TN26, TN23 153 C4
Charing TN27 120 C7
Chartham CT4, CT1 86 C3
Folkestone CT18, CT19 177 B7
Godmersham CT4 107 C4
Hamstreet TN26 170 F1
Harrietsham ME17 100 C6
Kingsnorth TN23, TN26 156 A4
Maidstone, Grove Green ME14 75 D4
Maidstone ME14 76 D3
New Romney TN28 202 A6
Sellindge TN25 159 B1
Sheldwich ME13 83 C4
Tenterden, Durrant Green TN26, TN30 167 A6
Tenterden TN30 179 B8
Westenhanger CT21, TN25, CT18 175 C6
Ashford St Mary's CE Prim Sch TN23 139 A3
Ashford Sch of Art & Design 8 TN23 139 C2
Ashford Sch of Art & Design (Henwood Campus) TN25 139 D3
Ashford Sch of Art & Design (Tufton Campus) TN25 139 B2
Ashford Sta TN24 139 C1
Ash Gr
Elvington CT15 114 B2
Lydd TN29 205 D7
Maidstone ME16 74 C6
St Margaret's at Cliffe CT15 150 F6
Ashgrove TN23 138 F5
Ashington Cl ME10 36 C5
Ashleigh Gdns ME5 31 D1
ASHLEY 132 B5
Ashley Ave CT19 177 E6
Ashley Cl
Halfway Houses ME12 3 C5
Ramsgate CT12 29 B2
Ashley Dr CT5 43 A7
Ashley Ho CT19 177 E6
Ashley Mill Cotts CT19 177 E7
Ashley Rd ME8 11 C2
Ash Mdws TN24 156 F7
Ashmead Cl ME5 32 C3
Ashmill Bsns Pk ME17 101 F6
Ash Rd
Aylesham CT3 112 E5
Sandwich CT13 72 E2
Ashtead Dr ME9 37 D2
Ashton Cl CT14 116 D4
Ashton Ct 4 CT10 29 E5
Ashton Ho CT14 117 B1
Ashton Mews 21 CT10 30 B4
Ash Tree Cl
Birchington CT7 27 B7
St Mary's Bay TN29 194 F3
Ashtree Ho ME10 37 B3
Ash Tree La ME5 10 D1
Ash Tree Rd 6 CT19 178 E6
Ashtrees CT6 23 B3
Ashurst Ave CT5 43 C6
Ashurst Gdns CT9 8 E3
Ashurst Pl ME8 33 E8
Ashurst Rd ME14 75 C5
Askes Ct TN23 155 D8
Aspen Cl TN29 194 F3
Aspen Dr
Ashford TN23 138 D3
Dover CT16 149 A5
Aspen Ho 5 CT20 178 D4
Aspen Rd
Chartham CT4 86 E1
Herne CT6 45 E7
Aspen Way 2 ME5 31 E4
Aspian Dr ME17 96 D3
Aspinall Cl CT4 89 A4
Asquith Rd ME8 33 C6
Association Wlk ME1 31 C7
Aster Rd ME12 4 B4
Astley Ave CT16 149 C2
Astley Ct CT16 149 C2
Astley St ME14 75 A4
Aston Cl ME5 32 A2
Aston Pl CT10 29 E6
Astor Ave CT17 166 B8
Astor Coll for the Arts CT17 166 A8
Astor Dr CT14 117 C5
Astor of Hever Com Sch The ME16 74 C3
Astor Rd CT10 29 F8
Astrid Rd CT14 117 A2
Athelstan Gn ME17 77 C2
Athelstan Pl CT14 117 C8
Athelstan Rd
Canterbury CT1 87 C5
Chatham ME4 9 F2
Faversham ME13 62 C6
Folkestone CT19 178 D7
Margate CT9 8 A3
Athena Ct CT9 8 A3
Athol Pl ME13 62 A8
Athol Rd
Ashford TN23 155 F7
Whitstable CT5 20 F2
Athol Terr CT16 166 F8
Atkinson Rd CT18 162 F3
Atkinson Wlk TN24 139 F5
Atlanta Ct ME4 9 D3
Attlee Ave CT3 112 E5
Attlee Way ME10 36 E8
Atwater Ct ME17 101 D5
Aubretia Wlk ME10 37 A3
Auckland Ave CT12 52 A8
Auckland Cres CT16 149 C3
Auckland Dr ME10 36 C3
Auckland Ho 10 ME15 97 E5
Audley Ave
Gillingham ME7 10 E1
Margate CT9 7 E1
Audley Cl ME16 74 B5
Audley Rd CT20 177 F5
Auger Cl ME9 34 E5
Augusta Cl 1 ME7 10 C7
Augusta Gdns CT20 178 C4
Augusta Pl 14 CT11 52 F7
Augusta Rd CT11 52 F7
Augustine Rd
Minster (Sheppey) ME12 4 B8
Minster (Thanet) CT12 50 B6
Augustus Wlk TN23 155 F5
Aurelie Way CT5 43 F7
Aurellus Cl TN23 156 A4
Austell Manor 5 ME7 10 C6
Austens Orch 13 TN30 179 A7
Austin Ave CT6 21 F4
Austin Cl
Gillingham ME5 10 E2
Sittingbourne ME10 37 A8
Austin Rd TN23 156 B6
Austins La 4 CT13 73 A1
Autumn Glade ME5 54 D8
Avebury Ave CT11 52 G8
Aveling Ct 2 ME2 9 B7
Avent Wlk ME9 37 E2
Avenue Gdns CT9 8 C3
Avenue of Remembrance ME10 36 F3
Avenue Rd
Dover CT16 149 C1
Herne Bay CT6 22 E5
Ramsgate CT11 52 F7
Avenue The
Deal CT14 117 C7
Hersden CT3 46 E1
Hythe CT21 176 C2
Kingsdown CT14 134 D4
1 Margate CT9 8 A1
St Margaret's at Cliffe CT15 150 F6
Temple Ewell CT16 148 E5
Avenue Theatre The* ME10 36 F3
Averenches Rd ME14 75 F5
Avereng Gdns CT19 178 B6
Avereng Rd CT19 178 B6
Avery Cl ME15 74 F1
Avery La ME15, ME17 98 D6
Aviation Ct ME12 5 E3
Aviemore Gdns ME14 75 F4
Avington Cl ME15 74 F1
Avocet Wlk ME5 32 D2
Avon Cl CT1 88 C8
Avondale Cl CT5 44 A8
Avondale Ct ME14 75 E5
Avondale Rd
Capel-le-Ferne CT18 164 C2
Gillingham ME7 10 D5
Avon Ho 13 CT20 178 C4
Axford Ct ME8 34 A8
AYCLIFF 166 B5
Aycliffe Cty Prim Sch CT17 166 A4
Aylesbury Rd TN25 139 B7
Aylesford Cres ME8 11 B4
AYLESFORD GREEN 156 F7
Aylesford Pl TN24 156 E7
AYLESHAM 112 F5
Aylesham Cnr CT3 112 D3

Aylesham Ind Est CT3 112 E4
Aylesham Prim Sch CT3 112 E5
Aylesham Rd CT15, CT3 113 A4
Aylesham Sta CT3 113 A6
Aylewyn Gn ME10 36 F8
Aynsley Ct 1 CT13 73 A1
Ayrshire Cl TN24 139 C7
Ayton Rd CT11 52 C6

B

Babs Oak Hill CT2 68 B7
Backfields ME1 9 B4
Back La
6 Faversham ME13 62 D7
Maidstone ME17 97 E1
Minster (Sheppey) ME12 4 D6
Back Road W CT16 166 G8
Back St
Leeds ME17 98 E6
Ringwould CT14 133 F5
Baddlesmere Rd CT5 21 A2
Baden Rd ME7 10 D7
Bader Cres ME5 32 A7
Badger Rd ME5 32 C1
Badgers Bridge CT18 161 D4
Badgers Cl CT2 66 A7
Badgers Den TN23 155 D7
Badger's Hill Farm & Cidery★ CT4 107 C8
Badgers Oak TN23 155 D8
Badgers Rise
Deal CT14 134 C8
Kearsney CT17 148 D3
BADLESMERE 83 C1
Badlesmere Cl TN23 155 E6
Bad Munstereifel Rd TN23, TN24 156 D5
Baffin Cl ME4 9 F2
BAGHAM 107 D8
Bagham La CT4 107 D8
Bagham Rd CT4 107 C8
Bagshill Rd ME13 83 A3
Bailey Dr ME7 11 A1
Bailey Fields TN26 153 E4
Baileys Field TN23 138 F1
Baird's Hill CT10 29 F6
Bairdsley Cl CT10 29 F6
Bakenham Ho 1 ME1 9 C1
Baker Cl ME9 38 C2
Baker Rd CT19 177 E6
Bakers Cl CT2 87 C7
Bakers Ct CT11 52 E7
Baker's La CT4 86 D2
Baker St ME1 9 C3
Baker's Wlk ME1 9 C6
Bakery Cotts ME14 53 E3
Bakery The ME9 58 A6
Balas Dr ME10 36 C7
Balcomb Cres
4 Margate CT9 29 C8
Margate CT9 29 C8
Balcomb Mews 3 CT9 29 C8
Baldric Rd CT20 177 F5
Baldwin Rd
Greatstone-on-Sea TN28 202 D1
Minster (Sheppey) ME12 4 D7
Baldwin's Pl ME17 100 D6
Baldwin Terr CT19 178 D6
Balfour Ct CT20 178 B3
Balfour Inf Sch ME1 9 E1
Balfour Jun Sch ME4 9 E2
Balfour Rd
Chatham ME4 9 E1
Chatham ME4 9 E2
Deal CT14 117 C2
Dover CT16 149 C1
Baliol Rd CT5 20 E2
Ballard Ind Est ME5 54 C8
Ballard Rd TN28 202 D1
Ballens Rd ME5 32 C3
Balliemoor Ct CT11 29 F1
Balliol Rd CT10 29 F8
Ball La TN24 139 F7
Balmer Cl ME8 33 D7
Balmoral Ho 10 ME15 97 F5
Balmoral Pl 12 CT11 52 F7
Balmoral Rd
Gillingham ME7 10 D5
Kingsdown CT14 134 C6
4 Margate CT9 28 B8
Balmoral Terr ME10 36 D4
Bambridge Ct ME14 74 F6
Bamford Way CT14 117 C4
Bank Cotts ME17 77 E3
Bank Ho
New Romney TN28 202 C6
Sheerness ME12 1 D2
Bank Rd TN25 172 E8
Bankside
Canterbury CT1 88 D7
Chatham ME5 32 B8
Bank Side TN26 183 A8
Banks Rd
Ashford TN23 156 A7
Rochester ME2 9 C8
Bank St
Ashford TN23 139 B2
Chatham ME4 10 B3
Faversham ME13 62 C7
Herne Bay CT6 22 F5
Hythe CT21 176 C2
Maidstone ME14 75 A4
Banks The CT10 29 F6
Bank View 5 ME15 74 E2
Banky Fields Cl ME8 12 B1
Banner Way ME12 3 E6
Banningbrook Ct CT14 117 D4
Banning St ME2 9 B8
Bannister Hill ME9 36 B2
Bannister Hos TN26 120 A1
Bannister Rd ME14 75 A7
BAPCHILD 37 E3
Bapchild & Tonge CE Aided Sch ME9 37 D3
Barbados Terr 2 ME14 75 A7
Barberry Ave ME5 31 E5
Barber's Almshouses 11 CT11 52 D6
Barcham Ct ME15 96 F5
Barclay Ct CT8 7 C1
Bardell Terr ME1 9 D5
Barden Ct ME14 75 B5
Barfleur Manor 3 ME7 10 A6
Barfreston Cl ME15 74 F2
BARFRESTONE 113 E1
Barfrestone Rd CT15 114 A1
Bargates TN23 155 E6
Barges The CT5 20 E3
Barge Way ME10 15 B2
Bargrove CT18 176 E6
Bargrove Rd ME14 75 C5
BARHAM
111 F1
128 E8
Barham CE Prim Sch CT4 128 F8
Barham Cl ME15 97 E5
Barham's Mill Rd TN27 118 B3
Barker Rd ME16 74 F3
Barkers Ct ME10 36 D4
Barkis Cl ME1 31 D7
Barler Pl ME11 3 A5
Barley Cl
Herne Bay CT6 23 D2
Martin Mill CT15 133 C2
Barleycorn Dr ME8 33 E6
Barley Fields ME14 75 D4
Barleymow Cl ME5 32 C7
Barley Way TN23 155 E5
Barling Cl ME5 31 D1
Barlow Cl ME8 33 E5
BARMING HEATH 74 A3
Barnaby Terr ME1 9 D2
Barnard Ct ME4 10 A2
Barnberry Cl TN23 155 E8
Barn Cl
Borden ME9 36 A2
Hoath CT3 46 E5
Yorkletts CT5 43 A3
Barn Cres CT9 7 F1
Barncroft Cl ME14 75 F4
Barncroft Dr ME7 32 F4
Barnes Ave CT9 7 F1
Barnes Cl ME13 62 B8
Barnes Ct CT1 87 D6
Barnesende Ct CT13 94 A8
Barnes Way CT6 23 F4
Barnet's La CT2 67 D8
Barnett Ct
Minster (Thanet) CT12 50 C5
3 Ramsgate CT12 29 B1
Barnett Field TN23 155 F8
Barnfield
Chatham ME5 32 A8
Herne Bay CT6 22 C2
Tenterden TN30 167 C2
Barnfield Rd
Faversham ME13 62 C8
Folkestone CT19 178 C7
Barnfields Ct ME10 37 D5
Barnhouse La TN29 200 A8
Barnhurst La CT18 163 A5
Barnhurst Rd ME14 75 A8
Barn Platt TN23 156 A8
Barnsley Cl ME12 1 F2
BARNSOLE 92 B6
Barnsole Inf Sch ME7 10 E4
Barnsole Jun Sch ME7 10 E4
Barnsole Rd
Gillingham ME7 10 E3
Staple CT3 92 B5
Barnsole Vineyard★
Barnsole CT3 92 C6
Sandwich CT3 92 B6
Barn The ME9 36 A2
Barntye Cl CT15 149 E6
Barn Tye Cl CT15 149 E6
Barnwell Pl ME7 10 C5
Barnwood Cl ME1 31 B8
Barn Yard The★ ME9 12 D1
Baron Cl
Gillingham ME7 10 E7
Maidstone ME14 75 F5
Barrack Hill CT21 176 A2
Barrack Rd ME4 10 B8
Barrey Rd TN24 157 A6
Barrier Rd ME4 9 F5
Barrington Cl ME5 31 F5
Barrington Cres CT7 27 B7
Barrowfields ME5 32 D1
Barrow Gr ME10 36 D3
BARROW GREEN 38 D3
BARROWHILL 174 D7
BARROW HILL 139 A3
Barrow Hill
Ashford TN23 139 B2
Barrowhill TN25 174 D7
Barrow Hill Cotts TN23 139 A2
Barrow Hill Pl 2 TN23 139 B3
Barrow Hill Rise TN25 174 D7
Barrow Hill Terr 1 TN23 139 B3
Barrows Cl CT7 27 A6
Bartholomew Cl CT21 176 B3
Bartholomew La CT21 176 B3
Bartholomew St
6 Dover CT16 149 C1
Hythe CT21 176 B2
Bartlett Cl ME5 32 C1
Bartlett Dr CT5 21 A1
Bartletts Cl ME12 3 C5
Barton Bsns Pk CT1 88 D6
Barton Court Gram Sch CT1 88 B8
Barton Ct 4 CT11 52 E7
Barton Field CT18 161 B7
Barton Hill Dr ME12 4 A5
Barton Jun Sch CT16 149 C2
Barton Mill Ct 2 CT2 66 F1
Barton Mill Rd CT1 67 B2
Barton Rd
Canterbury CT1 88 C6
Dover CT16 149 C2
Maidstone ME15 75 A2
Rochester ME2 9 A7
Barton's Point Coastal Pk★ ME12 1 G2
Barton View Terr 2 CT17 149 C1
Barville Rd CT15 114 E2
Barwick Rd CT17 148 F1
Bashford Barn La ME9 58 A4
Basil Terr 6 ME15 75 A1
Basing Cl ME15 75 B3
Baskerville TN24 139 B3
Basmere Cl ME14 75 C6
Basser Hill ME9 13 E3
Bassett Cl CT21 176 E4
Bassett Gdns CT21 176 D4
Bassett Rd ME10 36 D4
Bastien Mews 4 CT1 88 B6
Bastion Rd CT17 166 C6
Batchelor St ME4 10 A4
Bateman Cnr TN26 153 E6
Bates Cl CT3 91 F6
Bath Ct 8 CT20 178 B3
Bath Hard ME1 9 D5
Bath Mews TN24 156 E6
Bath Pl CT9 7 J2
Bath Rd
Ashford TN24 156 E6
Margate CT9 7 J2
Bathurst Cl CT12 29 B1
Bathurst Rd CT20 178 A5
Batteries Cl ME9 60 B8
Batteries Terr ME9 60 B8
Battery Point CT21 177 B2
Battery Rd TN29 209 D6
Battle of Britain Homes 17 CT17 166 D7
Battle of Britain Meml★ CT18 164 A1
Bawden Cl CT2 67 A4
Baxendale Ct TN24 156 D7
Bay Banks ME13 61 E2
Bay Cotts CT15 151 C6
Baye La CT3 69 D1
Bayeux Gdns ME7 11 A5
BAYFIELD 61 E2
Bayfield ME13 61 E2
Bayford Rd ME10 37 A4
Bay Hill CT15 151 B6
Bay Hill Cl CT15 151 A5
Bayle Ct 2 CT20 178 E4
Bayle St 19 CT20 178 E5
Bayle The CT20 178 E4
Bay Mus The★ CT15 151 B5
Bayswater Dr ME8 33 E4
BAY VIEW 6 D2
Bay View Gdns ME12 6 D2
Bay View Hts CT7 26 D8
Bayview Rd
Kingsdown CT14 134 C4
Whitstable CT5 43 D7
Bay View Rd CT10 30 A2
Beach Alley 15 CT5 20 D2
Beach App ME12 6 E3
Beach Ave CT7 26 F8
Beachborough Rd CT19, CT20 178 A5
Beach Ct
Deal CT14 117 D2
Westgate on Sea CT8 7 D1
Beachfield Lodge ME12 1 D2
Beach Flats 2 CT21 176 B2
Beach Hos CT9 7 G2
Beach House Mews CT8 7 D1
Beach Marine 7 CT20 177 F3
Beachmont Cl TN28 206 E8
Beach Rd
Dymchurch TN29 187 A4
St Margaret's at Cliffe CT15 151 B5
Westgate on Sea CT8 7 D1
Beach Rise CT8 7 D1
Beach St
Folkestone CT20 178 E4
Herne Bay CT6 22 F5
Sheerness ME12 1 C2
Beach Terr ME12 1 C2
Beach The CT14 117 D3
Beach Wlk CT5 20 E3
Beacon Ave CT6 23 B5
Beacon Cl ME8 33 D7
Beacon Hill
Gillingham ME5 10 D2
Herne Bay CT6 23 B5
Beacon La
Brookland TN29 199 D7
Woodnesborough CT13 93 A6
Beacon Oak Rd TN30 179 B8
Beacon Rd
Broadstairs CT10 29 F7
Chatham ME5 10 C2
Herne Bay CT6 23 A5
Lenham ME17 101 C5
Beaconsfield CT5 42 F6
Beaconsfield Ave
Dover CT16 149 C1
Gillingham ME7 10 E5
Beaconsfield Gdns CT10 29 F5
Beaconsfield Rd
Canterbury CT2 66 F2
Chatham ME4 9 F3
Deal CT14 117 D5
Dover CT16 149 C1
Maidstone ME15 74 E2
Sittingbourne ME10 37 C4
Beacons The ME17 96 C2
Beacon Terr CT21 177 B2
Beacon Way CT21 174 F3
Beacon Wlk
Herne Bay CT6 23 A5
Tenterden TN30 167 B1
Beamont Cl CT12 27 F2
Beams The ME15 75 F1
Bean Cl TN23 138 C1
Beaney's La CT4 84 C1
Beaney's La Cotts CT4 84 C1
Bears End Ho TN23 156 B8
Bear's La TN23, TN26 137 E3
BEARSTED 76 B4
Bearsted Cl ME8 11 B3
Bearsted Green Bsns Ctr ME14 76 C4
Bearsted Rd ME14 75 E6
Bearsted Sta ME14 76 B5
Beatrice Hills Cl TN24 139 E5
Beatrice Mews TN28 206 E7
Beatrice Rd
Capel-le-Ferne CT18 164 C2
Margate CT9 28 E8
Beatty Ave ME7 10 F4
Beatty Cl CT19 178 E8
Beatty Rd
Folkestone CT19 178 D8
Rochester ME1 31 D8
Beauchamp Ave CT14 117 A3
Beauchamp Cl TN24 139 E5
Beauchamps La CT15 113 D5
Beaufort Ave CT12 52 B8
Beaufort Ct ME2 9 E6
Beaufort Wlk ME15 97 E4
Beaufoy Rd CT17 149 A1
Beaufoy Terr CT17 148 F1
Beauherne Com Sch CT2 87 D8
Beaulieu Rise ME1 9 D1
Beaulieu Wlk ME16 74 C7
Beaumanor CT6 23 A3
Beaumont Davy Cl ME13 62 C5
Beaumont Rd ME16 74 B2
Beaumont St CT6 22 C4
Beaumont Terr ME13 62 D6
Beauvoir Dr ME10 37 A8
Beauworth Pk ME15 97 E8
Beauxfield CT16 149 A7
BEAVER 156 B7
Beaverbrook Mews ME16 74 D3
Beaver Ct TN23 156 A7
Beaver Green Prim Sch TN23 155 E7
Beaver Ind Est TN23 156 B7
Beaver La
Ashford, Beaver TN23 156 A7
Ashford, Singleton TN23 155 F7
Ashford TN23 138 E1
Beaver Rd
Ashford TN23 156 B8
Maidstone ME16 74 B7
Beazley Ct TN24 156 D7
Beckenham Dr ME16 74 D7
Becket Ave CT2 66 D1
Becket Cl
Ash CT3 71 D2
Deal CT14 117 C8
Whitstable CT5 21 B1
Becket Mews CT2 66 F1
Becket's Cl TN25 142 B6
Beckett St 4 ME13 62 C7
Becketts Terr CT21 176 B4
Becketts Wood CT3 47 E3
Beckley Mews ME5 31 F5
Beckley Pl TN25 175 B8
Beckley Rd ME12 1 F2
Becksbourne Cl ME14 75 A8
Beckwith Gn CT20 177 E5
Beckworth Pl ME16 74 B2
Beddow Way ME20 53 B3
Bede Ho CT14 117 D8
Bedford Ave ME8 11 D1
Bedford Ct CT10 30 B6
Bedford Pl ME16 74 E4
Bedford Sq CT12 29 B2
Bedford Way CT7 25 F1
Bedgebury Cl
Maidstone ME14 75 C6
Rochester ME1 31 D8
Bedingfield Way CT18 161 B7
Bedlam Court La CT12 50 C6
BEDMONTON 78 E8
Bedmonton La ME9 58 B2
Bedson Wlk ME8 12 B1
Bedwin Cl ME1 31 D7
Beech Ave CT4 86 E1
Beech Cl
Faversham ME13 62 B7
Folkestone CT19 178 C6
Beech Court Gdns★ TN25 104 F1
Beechcroft CT5 21 D1
Beechcroft Gdns CT11 52 F8
Beech Ct CT1 88 A7
Beech Dr
Broadstairs CT10 29 D4
Elvington CT15 114 B2
Hothfield TN26 138 A7
Maidstone ME16 74 C5
Beechen Bank Rd ME5 32 A1
Beeches The
Chatham ME5 32 A4
Lydd TN29 205 D7
Beech Gr CT12 51 C5
Beech Green Cl CT15 131 C7
Beech Grove Sch CT15 113 E6
Beech Hill CT4 111 B8
Beech Hurst Cl ME15 75 B2
Beeching Rd ME5 32 B3
Beechings Gn ME8 11 C3
Beechings Way ME8 11 C3
Beechings Way Ind Ctr ME8 11 B4
Beechmore Dr ME5 32 A2
Beecholme Dr TN24 139 C5
Beechwood Ave
Deal CT14 117 C5
Gillingham ME5 10 D2
Sittingbourne ME10 36 E6
Beechwood Cl
St Mary's Bay TN29 194 F3
Whitfield CT16 132 A1
Beechwood Ct
Deal CT14 117 C5
Temple Ewell CT16 148 E4
Beecroft Cl CT2 67 A4
Beer Cart La CT1 87 F8
Beggarsbush La TN29 200 D7
Beggars Cnr CT3 48 D1
Begonia Ave ME8 11 C2
Beke Rd ME8 33 D4
BEKESBOURNE 89 D4
BEKESBOURNE HILL 89 B5
Bekesbourne Hill CT4 89 B5
Bekesbourne La
Bekesbourne CT3, CT4 89 E6
Canterbury CT3 88 F7
Littlebourne CT3 89 F6
Bekesbourne Rd CT4 88 F2
Bekesbourne Sta CT4 89 B5
Belcaire Cl CT21 175 A3
Belfast Ho 14 ME15 97 E7
Belgrave Cl CT11 52 D7
Belgrave Ct CT14 117 D3
Belgrave Rd
Dover CT17 166 B7
Halfway Houses ME12 3 C5
Margate CT9 7 I2
Belinda Ct CT19 178 B7
Bell Chapel Cl TN23 156 C4
Bell Cnr TN29 201 A4
Bell Cotts ME9 13 B3
Bell Cres ME1 53 A8
Bell-Davies Dr CT12 28 A1
Belle Friday Cl ME9 38 C2
Bellevue Ave CT11 52 F7
Bellevue Rd
Minster (Sheppey) ME12 4 C6
Ramsgate CT11 52 F7
Whitstable CT5 43 F8
Belle Vue Rd CT6 23 B5
Bellevue St 5 CT20 178 D5
Bell Farm La ME12 5 A6
Bellflower Ave ME12 4 A4
Bell Gr CT3 113 A5
Bellgrove Ct ME5 54 A8
Bell La
Burham ME1 53 A8
Chatham ME14 54 B7
Maidstone ME14 76 A5
Sandwich CT13 73 A1
Bell Mdw ME15 97 E6
Bell Rd
Maidstone ME15 97 E5
Sittingbourne ME10 36 F3
Bell's Cl TN30 179 A7
Bell Shaw 17 ME15 97 E5
Bell Sh Ctr 8 ME10 36 F4
Bells La 8 TN30 179 A7
Bell Way ME17 99 E2
Bell Wood Prim Sch 16 ME15 97 E5
Belmont CT14 117 B1
Belmont Ct
9 Maidstone ME15 75 B4
2 Ramsgate CT11 52 D7
Belmont Farm Bsns Ctr TN26 137 A1
Belmont House & Gdns★ ME13 82 D5
Belmont Pl TN24 156 D7
Belmont Rd
Ashford TN24 139 D6
Broadstairs CT10 30 A4
Faversham ME13 62 C6
Gillingham ME7 10 C4
Halfway Houses ME12 3 E6
Ramsgate CT11 52 D7
Sittingbourne ME10 36 E3
Westgate on Sea CT8 27 F8
Whitstable CT5 20 D1
Belmont St CT11 52 E7
Belmont Terr CT13 93 B3
Belmont Yd 8 CT5 20 D1

Belmore Pk TN24 139 B3
Belnor Ave ME9 13 F1
Belsey La CT15 147 D4
Belting Dr CT6 23 E5
BELTINGE 23 E4
Beltinge Rd CT6 23 B5
Belton Cl CT5 43 E8
Belts Wood 14 ME15 97 F5
Belvedere Cl ME13 62 D8
Belvedere Ho 9 ME15 97 F5
Belvedere Rd
Broadstairs CT10 30 B4
Faversham ME13 62 D8
Benacre Rd CT5 43 D6
Bench Hill TN26 181 D5
Bench St 11 CT16 166 D7
Bendon Way ME8 33 D8
Benenden Manor ME8 11 B3
Bengal Rd CT12 29 A1
Benham Bsns Pk CT21 174 F5
Bennells Ave CT5 21 B3
Bennett Ct 16 CT20 178 E5
Bennetts Cotts ME7 55 A8
Bennetts Gdns ME13 61 D8
Bennetts Mews 12 TN30 179 A7
Benson Cl CT18 162 F4
Benson La CT18 162 F4
Bensted TN23 155 F5
Benstede Cl CT6 23 A1
Bensted Gr ME13 62 A7
Bentham Sq ME12 1 B3
Bentley Ave CT6 22 B4
Bentley Cl ME5 32 D2
Bentley Rd TN24 156 F7
Bentlif Cl ME16 74 D5
Berber Rd ME2 9 B8
Berengrave La ME8 11 F2
Berengrave Nature Reserve★
ME8 12 A3
Beresford Ave ME1 9 E2
Beresford Ct 7 CT7 26 F8
Beresford Gap CT7 26 F8
Beresford Gdns CT9 8 C3
Beresford Rd
Gillingham ME7 10 D4
Kit's Coty ME20 53 D7
Ramsgate CT11 52 D6
River CT17 148 E3
St Margaret's at Cliffe
CT15 133 F1
Whitstable CT5 20 D1
Beresfords Hill ME17 97 B4
Bergamot Cl ME10 36 F2
Bergland Pk ME2 9 D8
Berkeley Cl
Boughton Street ME13 64 B3
2 Folkestone CT19 178 A7
Rochester ME1 31 D8
Berkeley Ct ME10 36 D3
Berkeley Mount 8 ME4 9 F4
Berkeley Rd CT7 26 F8
Berkshire Cl ME5 32 C8
Bernards Gdns CT15 130 E5
Bernard Sunley Hall
TN25 124 A2
Berridge Rd ME12 1 D2
Berries The CT18 163 B5
Berry St ME10 36 F4
Berwick La CT21 175 A3
Berwyn Gr ME15 97 A6
Best La CT1 87 F8
Best St ME4 9 F4
Bethany Cl CT14 117 C8
Bethel Row ME13 82 F1
BETHERSDEN 153 E5
Bethersden Bsns Ctr
TN26 153 C1
Bethersden Ct ME15 97 F7
Bethersden Prim Sch
TN26 153 D5
Bethersden Rd
Hothfield TN26 137 D4
Shadoxhurst TN26 154 E2
Smarden TN27 135 C3
Smarden TN27, TN26 152 C5
Woodchurch TN26 169 A6
Betony Gdns ME14 75 F5
Betsham Rd ME15 97 F6
Betteridge Cl ME5 32 A2
Bettescombe Rd ME8 33 E7
BETTESHANGER 115 C6
Betty Shelvey Ct CT14 117 D4
Beult Mdw TN27 135 A1
Bevan Way CT3 112 E5
Beverley Cl ME8 33 F8
Beverley Gdns TN29 187 A4
Beverley Ho CT2 66 F2
Beverley Rd CT2 66 E2
Beverley Way CT12 29 C1
Beverly Cl CT7 27 B8
Bewsbury Cres CT16 148 F7
Bewsbury Cross La CT16 148 F7
Bexley St CT5 20 D2
BEXON 58 B4
Bexon La ME9 58 C4
Bhutan Rd CT6 23 C4
BICKNOR 57 C2
Bicknor Cl CT2 67 B4
Bicknor Court Cotts ME9 57 C2
Bicknor La ME9 57 D3
Bicknor Rd ME15 97 F4
Biddenden Cl
Maidstone ME15 75 F3
Margate CT9 8 C1
BIDDENDEN GREEN 135 B2
Bierce Court Cotts CT7 26 F7
Bierce Ct CT7 26 F7
Bifrons Gdns CT4 89 B3
Bifrons Hill CT4 89 B4
Bifrons Rd CT4 89 B4
Bigbury Rd CT2, CT4 86 E7
Biggin St CT16 166 D8
Biggins Wood Rd CT19 177 E7
Bigglestone Link 11 CT1 88 A8
Bilberry Cl ME14 75 E5
Bill Deedes Way TN25 172 F4
Billington Gdns TN24 139 E6
Bill Street Rd 1 ME2 9 C8
BILSINGTON 172 C1
Bilsington Cl ME5 32 B5
Bilsington Cross TN25 172 C2
BILTING 123 E7
Bilting La TN25 123 E7
Bimbury La ME14, ME9 56 A5
Bindon Blood Rd CT16 149 A5
Bingham Rd ME10 37 D6
Bingley Ct CT1 87 E7
Bingley Rd 1 ME1 9 E4
Binland Gr ME5 31 D5
Binnacle Rd ME1 31 C8
Binnie Cl CT10 29 F2
Birch Cl
Ashford TN24 139 F2
Broadstairs CT10 29 C3
Birch Ct
Barham CT4 128 F8
Ramsgate CT11 52 D8
Birch Dr ME5 32 D1
Birches The CT7 27 B7
Birchett TN23 138 E1
Birchett La TN26 170 D3
Birchfield Cl ME15 97 B6
Birchfields ME5 32 A3
Birch Gr ME7 33 A4
Birch Hill Ct CT7 27 B7
Birch Ho
6 Maidstone ME16 74 A3
Sheerness ME12 1 C2
Sittingbourne ME10 37 B3
BIRCHINGTON 26 E7
Birchington CE Prim Sch
CT7 27 A6
Birchington Cl ME14 75 C5
Birchington-on-Sea Sta
CT7 26 F7
BIRCHOLT FORSTAL 158 E8
Bircholt Forstal TN25 158 E7
Bircholt Rd ME15 97 F4
Birch Rd
Canterbury CT1 87 E6
Whitstable CT5 44 A8
Birch Tree Way ME15 75 B3
Birchwood Rd ME16 74 C5
Birchwood Rise CT17 166 C7
Birchwood Wlk CT2 66 E2
Birds Ave CT9 28 B7
Birdwood Ave CT14 117 A5
Birkdale Cl CT5 44 D8
Birkdale Ct 3 ME16 74 E4
Birkdale Dr CT19 178 A8
Birkdale Gdns CT6 22 D2
Birkhall Cl ME5 32 A5
Bir La ME9 58 D5
Birling Ave
Gillingham ME8 11 E1
Maidstone ME14 76 A4
Birling Cl ME14 76 A4
Birling Rd TN24 139 D1
Birnam Sq 1 ME16 74 E4
Bishopbourne Gn ME8 11 B4
Bishop Ct
4 Sittingbourne ME10 36 E5
Whitstable CT5 20 F2
Bishopden Ct CT2 66 C4
Bishop Jenner Ct CT3 70 C7
Bishop La ME9 12 E3
Bishop's Ave CT10 30 B6
BISHOPSBOURNE 111 B5
Bishops Ctyd 14 CT1 88 A8
Bishops Gn TN23 155 E7
BISHOPSTONE 23 F5
Bishopstone Dr CT6 23 F6
Bishopstone La CT6 23 F5
Bishops Way
Canterbury CT2 66 D1
Maidstone ME15 74 F4
Bishops Wlk ME1 9 C5
Bishopswood TN23 156 C3
Bismuth Dr ME10 36 D6
Bittern Cl CT18 163 A3
Blackberry Way CT5 44 B8
Black Bull Rd CT19 178 D6
Blackburn Rd CT6 22 B2
Blackdown Dr TN24 139 B4
Blacketts Cotts ME9 38 B7
Blacketts Rd ME9 38 A6
Blackfriars St 16 CT1 66 F1
Black Griffin La CT1 87 F8
Blackhouse Hill CT18,
CT21 176 D4
Blackhouse Rise CT21 176 D3
Blackleys ME13 84 F7
Black Lion L Ctr ME4 10 B6
Blackmanstone Way
ME16 74 B7
Black Post ME17 78 E4
Black Robin La CT4 111 E3
Black Rock Gdns ME7 33 B4
Blacksmith Dr ME14 75 D5
Blackstable Ct CT5 43 D8
Blackthorn Ave ME5 32 A3
Blackthorne Rd ME8 34 B8
Blackthorne Way TN23 156 C3
Blackthorn Rd CT3 68 D8
Blackwall Rd TN24, TN25 140 B4
Blackwall Road N TN24 140 A2
Blackwall Road S TN24 140 A2
BLADBEAN 127 F2
Blake Cl CT14 134 C8
Blake Ct
Ashford TN24 156 F8
6 Ramsgate CT11 52 D7
Blakeney Cl ME14 76 B4
Blaker Ave ME1 9 E1
Bland Dr CT18 163 C5
Blandford Gdns ME10 36 E1
Blatcher Cl ME12 4 B6
Blaxland Cl ME13 62 B8
Bleak Ho★ CT10 30 B4
Bleak House CT10 30 B4
Bleak Rd TN29 205 C6
Bleakwood Rd 6 ME5 31 F5
BLEAN 66 A6
Blean Comm CT2 66 A6
Blean Hill CT2 66 A5
Blean Prim Sch CT2 66 B4
Blean Rd ME8 11 C2
Blean Sq ME14 75 C6
Blean View Rd CT6 22 B2
Blean Woods Nature
Reserve★ CT2 65 F4
Blendon Rd ME14 75 C5
Blenheim Ave
Canterbury CT1 67 D1
Chatham ME4 9 E2
Faversham ME13 62 E5
Blenheim Cl
Broadstairs CT10 29 D3
Herne Bay CT6 23 A1
Maidstone ME15 75 F3
Blenheim Ct ME4 9 E3
Blenheim Dr
Dover CT16 149 C3
Hawkinge CT18 163 A4
Blenheim Ho CT9 8 C3
Blenheim Pl CT20 177 F4
Blenheim Rd
Deal CT14 117 D5
Littlestone-on-Sea TN28 202 D6
Sittingbourne ME10 37 B2
Bleriot Meml★ CT16 149 F1
BLIBY 171 F8
Bliby Bsns Ctr TN25 171 F7
Bliby Cnr TN25 171 F8
Blindgrooms La TN26 155 C1
Blindhouse La TN25 160 B3
Blind La
Bredhurst ME7 33 A1
Challock TN25 105 C2
Gillingham ME7 32 F1
Mersham TN25 157 C4
Blind Mary's La ME9 57 E4
Blockmakers Ct ME4 10 B1
BLOODEN 112 E8
Bloody Point Rd CT13 73 B4
Bloomsbury Rd CT11 52 C6
Bloomsbury Way TN24 139 B7
Bloomsbury Wlk 2 ME15 75 A4
Bloors La ME8 11 D1
Bloors Wharf Rd ME7 11 F4
Blossom La TN25 138 E5
Blowers Wood Gr ME7 33 B3
Bluebell Cl
Gillingham ME7 10 F6
Kingsnorth TN23 156 B4
Bluebell Dr ME10 36 F1
BLUE BELL HILL 31 D1
Bluebell Rd TN23 156 D2
Bluebell Woods Mobile
Home Pk CT2 67 D6
Bluebird Ct CT17 166 A6
Blue Boar La ME1 9 D5
Blue Field TN23 155 C8
Bluefield Mews CT5 43 C6
Blue House La CT21 176 B8
Blue Line La TN24 139 B3
Blue Skies Sch 7 ME1 9 D4
BLUETOWN 59 B1
BLUE TOWN 1 C2
Bluett St ME14 75 A5
Bluewater Cvn Pk CT21 187 E8
Blythe Cl ME10 37 C5
Blythe Ct CT21 176 D2
Blythe Rd ME15 75 B4
Boarley Ct ME14 53 F1
Boarley La ME14 53 F2
Boarman's La TN29 199 E8
Boathouse Rd ME12 1 A3
Boat La TN25 173 A4
Bob Amor Cl ME13 62 E7
BOBBING 36 A7
Bobbing Hill ME9 36 A6
Bobbing Prim Sch ME9 36 B7
Bobbin Lodge Hill CT4 86 B2
Bockham Cotts TN25 157 E8
Bockham La
Ashford TN25 141 A1
Mersham TN25 157 E8
BOCKHANGER 139 C6
Bockhanger Ct TN24 139 D5
Bockhanger La TN24 139 C6
Bockingford La ME15 96 F8
Bocton Ho ME17 97 B3
Bodenham Rd CT20 178 A4
Bodiam Cl ME8 11 C3
Bodiam Ct ME16 74 F3
Bodkins Cl ME17 97 D5
BODSHAM 142 D8
Bodsham CE Prim Sch
TN25 142 E8
Bodsham Cres ME15 76 B3
BOGLE 60 B8
Bogle Rd ME9 60 C7
Bognor Dr CT6 22 D4
Bogshole La
Herne Bay CT6 23 D3
Whitstable CT5 43 E4
Boley Hill ME1 9 C6
Boleyn Ave CT9 7 E1
Boleyn Ct 9 CT1 88 A8
Bolingbroke Ho ME16 74 E3
Bolner Cl ME5 31 F2
Bolonia CT15 151 A6
Bolton Rd CT19 178 D6
Bolton St CT11 52 D8
Bolts Hill CT4 86 C2
Bombay Ho 1 ME15 97 E5
Bond La TN23 156 A2
Bond Rd
Ashford TN23 156 B8
Gillingham ME8 33 E5
Bonetta Ct ME12 3 B8
Bonham Dr ME10 37 B5
Bonners Alley 19 CT5 20 D2
BONNINGTON 172 F3
Bonnington Cross TN25 172 E3
Bonnington Gn ME8 11 C3
Bonnington Rd ME14 75 C6
Bonny Bush Hill CT4 111 D5
Bonsor Rd CT19 178 D6
Boorman Way CT5 43 B6
Booth Pl CT9 7 J3
Booth Rd ME4 9 F2
BORDEN 36 B2
Borden CE Prim Sch ME9 35 F3
Borden Gram Sch ME10 36 F3
Borden La ME10, ME9 36 C3
Boresisle TN30 167 B2
Bornefields TN23 156 A7
Borough CT1 67 A1
Borough Rd
Gillingham ME7 10 D4
Queenborough ME11 3 B4
Borrowdale Ave CT11 52 A7
BORSTAL 9 B2
Borstal Ave CT5 43 D6
Borstal Hill CT5 43 D7
Borstal Mews ME1 9 A2
Borstal Rd ME1 9 B3
Borstal St ME1 9 A2
Boscombe Rd CT19 178 C6
Bosman Cl ME16 74 A1
Bosney Banks CT15 148 A7
BOSSINGHAM 127 A6
Bossingham Rd CT4 126 F3
Bossingham St CT4 126 F6
BOSSINGTON 90 E3
Bossington Rd CT3 90 E1
Boston Cl 5 CT16 149 B3
Boston Gdns ME8 11 C1
Boston Rd ME5 32 C2
Botany Cl ME12 1 C1
Botany Rd CT10 8 F2
Boteler Cotts CT13 93 A2
BOTOLPH'S BRIDGE 187 A7
Botolph's Bridge Rd
CT21 187 A6
Bottlescrew Hill ME17 97 B4
Bottles La ME9 59 A6
BOTTOM POND 58 D2
Bottom Pond Rd ME9 58 D3
BOUGHTON ALUPH 123 A5
Boughton Ave CT10 30 A2
Boughton Church Cotts
ME13 63 D1
Boughton Cl ME8 11 B3
Boughton Cnr TN25 123 C5
Boughton Field Cotts
ME13 63 A5
BOUGHTON GREEN 97 B3
Boughton Hill ME13 64 C3
Boughton La ME15 97 B6
BOUGHTON LEES 122 E3
BOUGHTON MALHERBE 118 A8
BOUGHTON
MONCHELSEA 97 B3
Boughton Monchelsea Prim
Sch ME17 97 B2
Boughton Par ME15 97 A7
Boughton Place Cotts
ME17 118 A8
Boughton Rd ME17 101 B2
BOUGHTON STREET 64 A3
BOUGHTON UNDER
BLEAN 64 C3
Boughton-under-Blean &
Dunkirk Prim Sch ME13 63 F3
Boulevard Courrieres
CT3 112 E5
Boulevard d'Erlanger
CT18 177 B7
Boulevard The TN24 156 F6
Boulogne Ct 17 CT20 178 E5
Boundary Chase CT5 44 B8
Boundary Cl ME12 4 E6
Boundary Ct 3 CT1 88 B6
Boundary Rd
Chatham ME4 9 E3
Deal CT14 134 D6
Hythe CT21 176 A2
Ramsgate CT11 52 E7
Boundary The CT1 87 D7
Boundsgate Cnr ME13 105 B7
Bounds La ME13 64 A3
Bourne Cotts CT4 111 C5
Bourne Ct ME1 9 D5
Bourne Gr ME10 36 C5
Bourne La TN26 183 A8
Bourne Lodge Cl CT2 66 A7
Bournemouth Dr CT6 22 D4
Bournemouth Gdns
CT19 178 C6
Bournemouth Rd CT19 178 C5
Bourne Park Rd CT4 111 A7
Bourne Pk Rd CT4 89 A1
Bourne Rd TN25 172 D5
Bournes Cl CT2 67 F7
Bourneside Terr ME17 77 D2
Bournes Pl TN26 169 A2
Bourne View CT4 88 F1
Bournewood TN26 183 A8
Bournewood Cl ME15 75 F1
Bournville Ave ME4 9 F1
Bouverie Pl 2 CT20 178 D4
Bouverie Road W CT20 178 C4
Bouverie Sh Ctr CT19 178 D4
Bouverie Sq 1 CT20 178 D4
Bowdell La TN29 191 E3
Bowden Cres CT20 177 C6
Bowen Ct CT11 52 D7
Bowen Rd CT19 177 E6
Bowens Field TN23 139 B1
Bower Cl ME16 74 E4
Bower Gn ME5 32 C1
Bower Grove Sch ME16 74 B2
Bower La ME16 74 E3
Bowerland La
Chilham CT4 85 E1
Old Wives Lees CT4 85 C2
Bower Mount Rd ME16 74 D4
Bower Pl ME16 74 E3
Bower Rd TN25 158 A3
Bowers Ho ME7 10 E7
Bower St ME16 74 E4
Bower Terr ME16 74 E3
Bowes Ave CT9 7 E1
Bowes La CT6 23 A3
Bowes Rd ME2 9 B8
Bowes Villas CT14 93 E4
Bow Hill CT4 109 F2
Bowland Cl CT6 23 C2
Bowlers Town TN31 197 A2
Bowles Well Gdns CT19 178 F7
Bowley La ME17 118 D8
Bowl Field TN25 142 B6
Bowling Green La CT14 117 B5
Bowling Green Terr 8
CT17 166 D7
Bowling St CT13 72 F1
Bowl Rd TN27 103 D2
Bowman Cl ME5 32 C5
Bowman Ct CT17 149 A1
Bowser Cl CT14 116 F4
Bowyer Rd CT5 42 F7
Box La ME13 61 D1
BOXLEY 54 D2
Boxley TN23 155 F8
Boxley Cl
Maidstone ME14 75 B8
West Minst ME12 3 B7
Boxley Rd
Chatham ME5 32 B2
Maidstone ME14 75 B7
Boxmend Ind Est ME15 97 F3
Boxted La ME9 13 A1
Boyces Hill ME9 35 D6
BOYDEN GATE 47 C8
Boyden Gate Hill CT3 47 B8
Boyes La CT3 91 D3
Boyke La CT4 144 C2
Boyne Rd CT15 134 A1
Boys Hall Rd TN24 156 F7
Boystown Pl CT13 93 C3
Brabazon Rd ME12 5 C1
Brabner Cl CT19 178 E8
BRABOURNE 159 B8
Brabourne Ave ME8 11 C3
Brabourne CE Prim Sch
TN25 159 A8
Brabourne Cl CT2 67 A4
Brabourne Gdns CT20 177 E5
Brabourne La TN25 142 F2
BRABOURNE LEES 158 D5
Brabourne Rd TN25 141 D6
Bracken Cl TN24 139 C6
Bracken Ct
3 Broadstairs CT10 29 E5
4 Sittingbourne ME10 37 C5
Bracken Hill ME5 32 A1
Bracken Lea ME5 10 C1
Brack La TN29 191 B3
Brackley Cl ME14 75 C5
Brackwood Cl ME8 33 D5
Bradbridge Gn TN23 155 D8
Braddick Cl ME15 97 B6
Bradfield Ave ME9 38 D2
Bradfield Rd TN24 139 B5
Bradfields Ave ME5 31 F5
Bradfields Avenue W ME5 31 F5
Bradfields Further Education
Ctr ME7 10 B5
Bradfields Sch ME5 32 A6
Bradfoord Ct CT20 178 D5
Bradley Dr ME10 36 E2
Bradley Rd
Folkestone CT19 178 F6
Ramsgate CT12 29 C1
Bradshaw Cl ME9 12 E3
Bradstone Ave CT19 178 D6
Bradstone New Rd 3
CT20 178 D5
Bradstone Rd CT20 178 D5
Bradstow Sch CT10 30 A3
Bradstow Way CT10 30 A5
Brady Rd CT18 161 A7
Braeside CT10 30 B3
Braggs La CT6 45 E6

Braithwaite Ct ME7 . . . . **11** A5
Brake Ave ME5 . . . . **31** A5
Bramble Cl
 Maidstone ME16 . . . . **74** B3
 Wye TN25 . . . . **123** D3
Brambledown
 Chatham ME5 . . . . **32** B8
 Folkestone CT19 . . . . **178** D6
Bramblefield La ME10,
 ME9 . . . . **14** E1
Bramblefields Cl CT6 . . . **23** B2
Bramblehill Rd ME13 . . . . **62** C8
Bramble La TN25 . . . . . . **123** C3
Brambles Cl ME12 . . . . **4** A5
Brambles Ctyd CT14 . . . . **117** B3
Bramble Wlk TN23 . . . . . **156** C2
Brambley Cres CT20 . . . . **177** E5
Brambling Rise ME10 . . . . **36** E6
Bramley Ave
 Canterbury CT1 . . . . **87** C6
 Faversham ME13 . . . . **62** E6
Bramley Cl
 Brabourne Lees TN25 . . . . **158** E6
 Eastchurch ME12 . . . . **5** D3
 Gillingham ME8 . . . . **34** B8
 Newington ME9 . . . . **35** A5
Bramley Cres ME15 . . . . . **75** F3
Bramley Gdns
 Ashford TN23 . . . . **156** A6
 Coxheath ME17 . . . . **96** C3
 Herne Bay CT6 . . . . **23** D2
Bramley Way ME12 . . . . . . **5** D3
BRAMLING **90** C6
Bramling Gap CT3 . . . . . . **90** C3
Bramling Rd CT3, CT4 . . . **90** B4
Bramshaw Rd CT2 . . . . . . **66** E2
Bramshott Cl ME16 . . . . . **74** C6
Bramston Rd ME12 . . . . . . **4** C6
Branchley Mews TN27 . . **120** C8
Branch Rd CT4 . . . . **107** C7
Branch St CT16 . . . . **149** C1
Brandon Rd CT12 . . . . **29** A1
Brandon Way CT7 . . . . **27** B6
Bransgore Cl ME8 . . . . . . **33** D7
Brasenose Rd ME7 . . . . . . **10** E4
Brasier Ct ME12 . . . . **4** A5
Brassey Ave CT10 . . . . . . **29** F3
BRATTLE **181** A8
Brattle TN26 . . . . **181** B8
Braunstone Dr ME16 . . . . **74** D7
Bray Gdns ME15 . . . . **96** F5
BREACH
 Derringstone **128** E4
 Newington **34** F8
Breach La ME9 . . . . **13** A2
Breadlands Cl TN24 . . . . **156** E8
Breadlands Rd TN24 . . . . **156** F8
Brecon Chase ME12 . . . . . **4** C7
Brecon Rise TN24 . . . . . . **139** B4
Brecon Sq CT12 . . . . **29** A1
BREDGAR **58** A6
Bredgar CE Prim Sch
 ME9 . . . . **58** A5
Bredgar Cl
 Ashford TN23 . . . . **155** F6
 Maidstone ME14 . . . . **75** C5
Bredgar Rd ME8 . . . . **11** B4
Bredgar & Wormshill Light
 Rly ME9 . . . . **57** E1
BREDHURST **33** B1
Bredhurst CE Prim Sch
 ME7 . . . . **33** B1
Bredhurst Cl ME12 . . . . . . **3** B7
Bredhurst Rd ME8 . . . . . . **33** B4
Bredlands La CT3, CT2 . . . **46** C1
Brenchley Ave CT14 . . . . **116** F4
Brenchley Cl
 Ashford TN23 . . . . **155** E6
 Rochester ME1 . . . . **9** D2
Brenchley Rd
 Gillingham ME8 . . . . **11** B2
 Maidstone ME15 . . . . **74** F2
 Sittingbourne ME10 . . . . . **36** F2
Brendon Ave ME5 . . . . **32** A3
Brendon Dr TN24 . . . . . . **139** B3
Brenley Cnr ME13 . . . . . . **63** B4
Brenley La ME13 . . . . **63** C2
Brennan Ct ME7 . . . . **10** D6
Brennan Mews ME16 . . . . **74** E5
Brent Cl ME5 . . . . **31** E5
Brent Hill ME13 . . . . **62** C8
Brent Rd ME13 . . . . **62** C8
Brents Ind Est ME13 . . . . **40** D1
Brentwood TN23 . . . . **155** F5
BRENZETT **192** A3
Brenzett Aeronautical Mus★
 TN29 . . . . **192** B3
Brenzett Cl ME5 . . . . **32** B5
Brenzett Cnr TN29 . . . . . **192** A3
Brenzett District CE Prim
 Sch TN29 . . . . **192** A2
BRENZETT GREEN **192** C2
Breton Rd ME1 . . . . **9** C2
Brett Wlk ME8 . . . . **33** D4
Brewer St
 Deal CT14 . . . . **117** D6
 Maidstone ME14 . . . . **75** A5
Brewery Cotts CT14 . . . . **116** E4
Brewery La CT4 . . . . **89** A1
Brewery Rd ME10 . . . . **36** C5
Brewery Sq CT3 . . . . **48** D2
Brewhouse La TN25 . . . . **122** F4
Brewster Cotts ME9 . . . . **59** E2
Brian Roberts Ho CT6 . . . **22** F5

Briar Cl
 Ashford TN24 . . . . **139** C6
 Aylesham CT3 . . . . **112** F5
 Crabble CT17 . . . . **148** F2
Briar Fields ME14 . . . . . . **75** E5
Briars Rd TN29 . . . . **194** F3
Briars The CT5 . . . . **43** C6
Briars Wlk CT10 . . . . **29** F3
Briary Cl CT9 . . . . **28** A8
Briary Prim Sch CT6 . . . . . **22** C2
Brice Ave CT4 . . . . **86** C1
Brickfield TN31 . . . . **196** B2
Brickfield Cotts TN25 . . **123** B2
Brickfield La ME13 . . . . . . **63** E2
Brickfield Rd CT4 . . . . . . **128** F7
Brickmakers Ind Est
 ME10 . . . . **37** B6
Brickwall Terr TN26 . . . . **168** F3
Bridewell La TN30 . . . . . **179** A7
Bridewell Pk CT5 . . . . **21** A1
BRIDGE **89** A1
Bridge App The CT5 . . . . . . **20** F1
Bridge Cl
 Hythe CT21 . . . . **176** A2
 Woodchurch TN26 . . . . . . **181** B8
Bridge Cotts ME13 . . . . . **84** E7
Bridge Down CT4 . . . . . . **111** B8
BRIDGEFIELD **156** C2
Bridgefield Cl CT5 . . . . . . **21** B3
Bridgefield Rd CT5 . . . . . . **21** B3
Bridgeford Way CT4 . . . . . **89** A1
Bridge Hill
 Bridge CT4 . . . . **111** B8
 Finglesham CT14 . . . . **116** C8
Bridge Ho
 Ramsgate CT11 . . . . **52** C7
 Rochester ME1 . . . . **9** B4
Bridge Home Pk TN29 . . . **205** D8
Bridge Ind Ctr ME15 . . . . . **74** E2
Bridgeman Ct CT21 . . . . . **176** B2
Bridge Mill Way ME15 . . . **74** D2
Bridge Rd Ind Ctr TN23 . . **138** F2
Bridge Rd
 Ashford TN23 . . . . **138** F2
 Brabourne Lees TN25 . . . . **158** D5
 Bridge CT4 . . . . **88** D1
 Deal CT14 . . . . **117** D6
 Faversham ME13 . . . . **62** D8
 Gillingham ME7 . . . . **10** C7
 Margate CT9 . . . . **7** E1
 Rochester ME1 . . . . **9** C2
 Sheerness ME12 . . . . **1** C2
Bridges Cl CT7 . . . . **25** E2
Bridgeside CT14 . . . . **117** C6
Bridgeside Mews ME15 . . . **74** E2
Bridge St
 Dover CT16 . . . . **149** C1
 Folkestone CT19 . . . . **178** E6
 Maidstone ME15 . . . . **96** F5
 Wye TN25 . . . . **123** C2
Bridge View Ind Est ME11 . . **3** A2
Bridgewater Rd ME12 . . . . **3** B4
Bridgeway CT5 . . . . **20** F2
Bridle Way
 Herne Bay CT6 . . . . **22** D3
 Hythe CT21 . . . . **177** A3
Bridleway Gdns CT10 . . . . **29** E3
Bridleway La TN23 . . . . . **156** B4
Brielle Way
 Queenborough ME11, ME12 . **3** A6
 Sheerness ME12 . . . . **1** B2
Brier Cl ME5 . . . . **32** C8
Brier Rd ME10 . . . . **36** B4
Brigadier Gdns TN23 . . . **138** F4
Briganda Wlk CT11 . . . . . **52** E8
Brightlingsea Rd CT13 . . . **93** F8
Bright Rd 3 ME4 . . . . **10** B2
Brights Pl CT11 . . . . **52** F7
Brindle Gr CT11 . . . . **52** F7
Brindle Way ME5 . . . . **32** C1
Brinklow Terr TN26 . . . . **155** A1
Brisbane Ave ME10 . . . . . **36** C4
Brisbane Dr CT12 . . . . **29** A1
Brisbane Rd ME4 . . . . **10** A3
Brishing Cl ME15 . . . . **97** E5
Brishing La ME17 . . . . **97** D4
Brishing Rd ME15, ME17 . . **97** F3
Brisley Cl TN23 . . . . **155** D6
Brisley Ct TN23 . . . . **155** D6
Brisley La TN26 . . . . **171** D6
Brissenden Cl TN28 . . . . **202** B8
BRISSENDEN GREEN **153** F3
Bristles Cnr CT3 . . . . **46** E6
Bristol Cl CT6 . . . . **23** B3
Bristol Pl CT11 . . . . **52** D7
Bristol Rd CT1 . . . . **87** F6
Britannia Ave CT5 . . . . . . **43** B7
Britannia Cl ME10 . . . . . . **36** E7
Britannia La TN23 . . . . . **155** F5
Britannia Rd CT14 . . . . . **117** D8
British MK IV Tank★ 15
 TN23 . . . . **139** B2
Briton Ct ME12 . . . . **3** B8
Briton Rd ME13 . . . . **62** C7
Britten Cl CT21 . . . . **176** A3
Britton St ME7 . . . . **10** B5
Broadacre
 Lydden CT15 . . . . **147** F8
 Teynham ME9 . . . . **38** D2
Broader La ME15 . . . . **97** A8
Broadfield Cres CT20 . . . **178** A5
Broadfield Rd
 Folkestone CT20 . . . . **178** A5
 Loose ME15 . . . . **97** A8
Broadgate Hall 1 CT11 . . . **52** F7

Broadhurst Dr TN24 . . . . **139** D7
Broad La CT14 . . . . **116** B7
Broadlands CT2 . . . . **67** F6
Broadlands Ave TN28 . . . **202** B8
Broadlands Cres TN28 . . **202** B8
Broadlands Dr ME5 . . . . . . **32** B4
Broadlands Ind Est CT2 . . . **66** A7
Broadley Rd CT10, CT9 . . . **29** C7
Broadmead TN23 . . . . **155** E6
Broadmead Manor CT10 . . **30** B7
Broadmeadow CT19 . . . . . **178** B7
Broadmead Rd CT19 . . . . **178** C5
Broadmere Terr ME16 . . . . **74** D3
BROADOAK **58** E5
BROAD OAK
 Ashford **157** C1
 Sturry **67** D7
Broadoak Ave ME15 . . . . . **97** A8
Broadoak Ent Village ME9 **58** F6
Broadoak Rd ME9 . . . . **58** E6
Broad Oak Rd CT2 . . . . . . **67** B3
Broadsole La CT15 . . . . . **164** E5
Broad St
 Canterbury CT1 . . . . **67** A1
 Deal CT14 . . . . **117** D6
 Margate CT9 . . . . **7** I3
 Ramsgate CT11 . . . . **52** E7
 Sellindge TN25 . . . . **159** D5
 Sheerness ME12 . . . . **1** C2
BROADSTAIRS **30** C5
Broadstairs Rd CT10 . . . . **29** E5
Broadstairs Sta CT10 . . . . **30** A4
BROAD STREET
 Lyminge **161** C1
 Maidstone **77** B6
 Sellindge **159** F5
Broad Street Hill ME17 . . . **77** D7
BROAD TENTERDEN **179** B4
Broadview CT20 . . . . **177** C6
Broadview Ave ME8 . . . . . **33** E8
Broadviews CT21 . . . . **176** D1
BROADWAY **120** B6
Broadway
 Gillingham ME8 . . . . **11** A3
 Maidstone ME14 . . . . **74** F4
 Petham CT4 . . . . **109** A2
Broadway Sh Ctr ME16 . . . . **74** F4
Broadway The
 Broadstairs CT10 . . . . **30** A4
 Dover CT16 . . . . **166** H8
 Herne Bay CT6 . . . . **22** C5
 Minster (Sheppey) ME12 . . . **4** B7
 Sheerness ME12 . . . . **1** D2
Brockbank ME5 . . . . **32** A1
Brockenhurst Ave ME15 . . **75** C1
Brockenhurst Cl
 Canterbury CT2 . . . . **66** E2
 Gillingham ME8 . . . . **33** C7
Brockenhurst Rd CT11 . . . **52** G8
Brockhill Ctry Pk★ CT21 . . **175** F4
Brockhill Park Performing
 Arts Coll CT21 . . . . **175** F4
Brockhill Rd CT21 . . . . . **176** B3
Brockley Rd CT9 . . . . **8** A2
Brockman Cres TN29 . . . **187** B4
Brockman Rd CT20 . . . . . **178** C5
Brockman's Cl CT12 . . . . . **50** B7
Brockman's CI CT12 . . . . . . **50** B7
Brogdale Farm Cotts
 ME13 . . . . **62** A3
Brogdale Farm National Fruit
 Collection★ ME13 . . . . . . **62** B4
Brogdale Pl ME13 . . . . **62** B6
Brogdale Rd ME13 . . . . . . **62** B5
Brogden Cres ME17 . . . . . **98** F7
Bromley Cl ME5 . . . . **32** B4
BROMLEY GREEN **170** E6
Bromley Green Rd TN26 . **171** A5
BROMPTON **10** A5
Brompton Hill ME4 . . . . . . **9** F6
Brompton La ME7 . . . . **9** A8
Brompton Rd ME7 . . . . **10** B6
Brompton Villas CT15 . . . **149** E6
Brompton Westbrook Prim
 Sch ME7 . . . . **10** A5
BROMSTONE **29** E3
Bromstone Mews CT10 . . . **29** E3
Bromstone Prim Sch
 CT10 . . . . **29** D3
Bromstone Rd CT10 . . . . . **29** E3
Bronington Cl ME5 . . . . . . **32** A5
BROOK **141** B5
Brookbank
 Brook TN25 . . . . **141** A5
 Maidstone ME14 . . . . **75** A8
Brook Cl
 Herne Bay CT6 . . . . **22** C3
 Hythe CT21 . . . . **177** B3
Brook Com Prim Sch
 TN25 . . . . **141** A4
Brook Cotts
 East Farleigh ME15 . . . . . . **96** C7
 Staple CT3 . . . . **91** E6
 Teynham ME9 . . . . **39** A2
Brooke Ave CT9 . . . . **28** B7
Brooker Cl ME17 . . . . **97** D5
Brooke Rd TN24 . . . . **139** B3
Brookes Pl ME9 . . . . **35** B6
Brookfield Ave CT16 . . . . **149** B2
Brookfield Ct TN23 . . . . . **155** F8
Brookfield Ind Pk TN23 . . **138** F1
Brookfield Pl CT16 . . . . . **149** B2
Brookfield Rd
 Ashford TN23 . . . . **155** F8
 Dover CT16 . . . . **149** A3
Brook La
 Cliffs End CT12 . . . . **50** F4
 Reculver CT6 . . . . **24** B5

Brook La *continued*
 Sellindge TN25 . . . . **159** E2
BROOKLAND **199** D8
Brookland CE Prim Sch
 TN29 . . . . **199** D8
Brooklands Cl CT2 . . . . . . **67** F4
Brook Lane Cotts TN25 . . **159** E2
Brooklyn Paddock ME7 . . . **10** D6
Brook Rd
 Faversham ME13 . . . . **40** D1
 Whitstable CT5 . . . . **21** C3
BROOKS END **26** E4
Brookside
 St Mary's Bay TN29 . . . . . **195** A5
 Temple Ewell CT16 . . . . . **148** D5
Brooks Pl ME14 . . . . **75** A4
Brook St
 Eastry CT13 . . . . **93** C2
 Woodchurch TN26 . . . . . . **180** D8
Brooks Way TN29 . . . . . . **205** C5
Brook The ME4 . . . . **10** A4
Brook Theatre★ ME4 . . . . . . **9** F5
Broomcroft Rd ME8 . . . . . **11** F2
BROOMFIELD
 Herne Bay **23** D1
 Kingswood **99** D5
Broomfield Cres CT9 . . . . . **8** F2
Broomfield Gate CT5 . . . . **44** D5
Broomfield Rd
 Faversham ME13 . . . . **62** C8
 Folkestone CT19 . . . . **177** E6
 Herne Bay CT6 . . . . **23** C2
 Kingswood ME17 . . . . **99** D4
BROOM HILL **70** B1
Broom Rd ME10 . . . . **37** C5
BROOM STREET **41** D2
Brotherhood Cl CT2 . . . . . **66** D4
Broughton By-Pass ME13 **64** C2
Broughton Ct TN23 . . . . . **138** F1
Brownelow Copse ME5 . . . **32** B1
Brownhill Rd CT2 . . . . **67** B3
Browning Pl CT19 . . . . . . **178** E7
Brownings Orch ME9 . . . . **59** A7
Brown Lo ME7 . . . . **1** I1
Brown St ME8 . . . . **11** F1
Broxhall Rd CT4 . . . . **110** B3
Bruce Cl CT14 . . . . **117** B4
Bruges Ct ME10 . . . . **14** F1
Brundell Terr CT4 . . . . . . **86** B2
Brunell Rd ME16 . . . . **74** D5
Brunel Way ME4 . . . . **10** A7
Brunswick Cotts ME9 . . . . **38** E6
Brunswick Ct 3 CT11 . . . . **52** E7
Brunswick Field ME5 . . . . . **38** E6
Brunswick Gdns 3 CT16 **149** B3
Brunswick House Prim Sch
 ME16 . . . . **74** D5
Brunswick Ind Ctr TN23 . . **138** F2
Brunswick Rd
 Ashford TN23 . . . . **138** F2
 Birchington CT7 . . . . **27** A5
Brunswick Sq CT6 . . . . . . **22** E5
Brunswick St
 Maidstone ME15 . . . . **75** A3
 Ramsgate CT11 . . . . **52** E7
Brunswick Street E ME15 . **75** A3
Bryant Rd ME2 . . . . **9** A7
Bryant St ME4 . . . . **10** A3
Bryces Alley CT5 . . . . **20** D2
Brymore Cl CT1 . . . . **67** B2
Brymore Rd CT1 . . . . **67** B2
Bryony Dr TN23 . . . . **156** C3
Bryony Sch ME8 . . . . **33** C7
Buckhurst Dr CT9 . . . . **8** F2
Buckingham Rd
 15 Broadstairs CT10 . . . . . **30** B4
 Gillingham ME7 . . . . **10** D5
 Margate CT9 . . . . **7** I1
 Whitstable CT5 . . . . **21** B2
Buckingham Row ME15 . . . **97** E7
BUCKLAND **149** C2
Buckland Ave CT16 . . . . . **149** B1
Buckland Cl ME5 . . . . **32** A2
Buckland Cotts ME13 . . . . **61** B8
Buckland Hill ME16 . . . . . **74** E5
Buckland Hospl CT17 . . . **149** A1
Buckland La
 Maidstone ME16 . . . . **74** D6
 Staple CT3 . . . . **92** A4
Buckland Rd ME16 . . . . . . **74** E4
Buckland Rd ME16 . . . . . . **74** E4
BUCKLAND VALLEY **149** C4
Bucklers Cl ME12 . . . . **6** E4
Buckmore Pk-International
 Kart Circuit ME5 . . . . **31** C3
Bucksford La TN23 . . . . . **155** C7
Buck St TN25 . . . . **105** C2
Buckthorn Cl CT14 . . . . . **117** C7
Buckthorne Rd ME12 . . . . . **4** A4
Buddle Dr ME12 . . . . **3** E7
Budd's Farm Cotts TN30 . **188** E3
Budd's La TN30 . . . . **188** F2
Buenos Ayres CT9 . . . . **7** H2
Buffs Ave CT20 . . . . **177** B6
Builders Sq CT3 . . . . **90** A8
Bulldog Rd ME5 . . . . **32** B2
Bulleid Pl ME4 . . . . **156** D7
Buller Rd ME4 . . . . **9** F2
Buller's Ave CT6 . . . . **22** E4
Bull Hill
 Lenham Heath ME17 . . . . **102** A1
 Lenham ME17 . . . . **118** F8
Bull La
 Bethersden TN26 . . . . **153** B4
 Boughton Street ME13 . . . . **63** F4
 Eccles ME20 . . . . **53** A6

Bull La *continued*
 Yelsted ME9 . . . . **34** E2
Bull Lane Cotts ME9 . . . . . **34** E1
BULLOCKSTONE **45** D8
Bullockstone Rd CT6 . . . . **45** E7
Bulls Cotts 4 CT21 . . . . . **176** B2
Bulltown Cnr TN25 . . . . . **141** F3
Bullwark St CT17 . . . . . . **166** D5
Bulrush Cl ME5 . . . . **31** F3
Bulrushes The TN23 . . . . **155** D8
Bulwark Rd CT14 . . . . . . **117** D7
Bumbles Cl ME1 . . . . **31** D7
Bunce Court Rd ME13,
 ME17 . . . . **102** E7
Bungalows The
 Faversham ME13 . . . . **62** A4
 Tenterden TN30 . . . . **179** D7
 Woodnesborough CT13 . . . **93** B5
Bunker's Hill CT17 . . . . . **149** B2
Bunkers Hill Ave CT17 . . **149** B1
Bunkers Hill Rd CT17 . . . **149** A1
Bunkley Mdw TN26 . . . . . **183** A7
Burberry La ME17 . . . . **99** B5
Burch Ave CT13 . . . . **93** F8
Burdock Ct ME16 . . . . **74** A3
Burdock Ho 6 ME8 . . . . . . **97** D8
Burford's Alley CT3 . . . . . **71** D1
Burgate CT1 . . . . **88** A8
Burgate La 5 CT1 . . . . **88** A8
Burgate Terr TN25 . . . . . **157** E4
Burgess Cl
 Minster (Thanet) CT12 . . . . **50** C7
 Whitfield CT16 . . . . **149** B7
Burgess Gn CT14 . . . . **116** C8
Burgess Hall Dr ME17 . . . . **98** F6
Burgess Rd
 Aylesham CT3 . . . . **112** F6
 Rochester ME2 . . . . **9** B7
Burgess Row 9 TN30 . . . . **179** A7
Burghclere Dr ME16 . . . . . **74** B2
Burgoyne Ct ME14 . . . . . . **74** F7
Burgoyne Gr CT16 . . . . . . **149** A5
Burgoyne Hts CT15 . . . . . **149** E3
BURHAM **53** A8
Burial Ground La ME15 . . . **74** E1
Burkeston Cl ME16 . . . . . . **37** A8
Burleigh Dr ME14 . . . . **53** F1
Burleigh Rd TN27 . . . . . . **120** C2
Burley Rd ME10 . . . . **36** E4
Burlington Dr CT6 . . . . . . **23** D5
Burlington Gdns
 Gillingham ME8 . . . . **33** E4
 Margate CT9 . . . . **28** C8
Burma Cres CT1 . . . . **67** D1
BURMARSH **186** C5
Burmarsh Cl ME5 . . . . **32** B5
Burmarsh Rd
 Burmarsh TN29 . . . . **186** C3
 Hythe CT21 . . . . **187** C8
Burma Way ME5 . . . . **31** F6
Burnan Ct CT5 . . . . **21** C2
Burnan Rd CT5 . . . . **21** C2
Burnham Cl ME10 . . . . **36** E8
Burnham Wlk ME8 . . . . . . **33** E3
Burns Rd ME16 . . . . **74** C2
Burn's Rd ME7 . . . . **10** C6
Burnt House Hill CT3 . . . . **69** B5
Burnt Oak Prim Sch 1
 ME7 . . . . **10** D6
Burnt Oak Terr ME7 . . . . . **10** D6
Burnt Oast Rd ME13 . . . . . **64** A3
Burntwick Dr ME9 . . . . . . **13** B3
Burnup Bank ME10 . . . . . . **37** C5
Burritt Mews ME1 . . . . **9** C3
Burrow Rd CT19 . . . . **178** F6
Burrs The ME10 . . . . **36** F3
Burrstock Way ME8 . . . . . **12** B2
Bursill Cres CT12 . . . . **29** B1
Bursted Hill CT4 . . . . **110** B2
Burston Rd ME17 . . . . **96** B2
Burton Cl CT19 . . . . **178** A7
Burton Fields CT6 . . . . . . **23** B4
Burton Rd TN24 . . . . **139** E6
Bus Bridge Rd ME15 . . . . . **96** E6
Bush Ave CT12 . . . . **29** B1
Bush Cl ME9 . . . . **57** F5
Bushey Cl ME13 . . . . **63** F3
Busheyfields Rd CT6 . . . . . **45** F6
Bushmeadow Rd ME8 . . . . **11** F2
Bush Row ME20 . . . . **53** A3
Bushy Gr ME17 . . . . **99** D2
Bushy Hill Rd CT2 . . . . . . **68** D7
Bushy Royds TN24 . . . . . **156** D6
Bushy Ruff Cotts TN25 . . **148** D4
Butchers La CT15 . . . . . . **113** E5
Butchery La 1 CT1 . . . . . . **88** A8
Butchery The 2 CT13 . . . . **73** A1
Butler's Hill CT4 . . . . **64** D7
Butterfly Centre The★
 CT15 . . . . **146** B3
Buttermere ME13 . . . . **62** E6
Buttermere Cl CT19 . . . . . **178** B6
Buttermere Gdns CT3 . . . **112** C6
Butternut Copse TN23 . . . **138** D3
Butterside Rd TN23 . . . . . **156** C4
Butter St CT15 . . . . **113** C4
Butt Field Rd TN23 . . . . . **155** E7
Button La ME15 . . . . **76** B2
Butts Ct CT4 . . . . **110** A6
Butts Hill ME13 . . . . **63** F5
Butts Mdw CT4 . . . . **110** A6
BUTTSOLE **93** B1
Butts The
 Sandwich CT13 . . . . **72** F1
 Sittingbourne ME10 . . . . . **36** F4
Buxton Cl
 Chatham ME5 . . . . **32** D1
 Loose ME15 . . . . **97** A8

Buxton Rd CT12............ 29 B2
BYBROOK 139 D5
Bybrook CT21............. 176 D3
Bybrook Ct TN24.......... 139 C4
Bybrook Field CT20........ 177 E3
Bybrook Rd TN24......... 139 C5
Bybrook Way TN20........ 177 E4
Bychurch Pl 7 ME15...... 75 A3
Byllan Rd CT17........... 148 E3
Byron Ave CT9.............7 J1
Byron Cl CT1............. 88 C7
Byron Cres CT16......... 149 B4
Byron Prim Sch ME7 ..... 10 C3
Byron Rd
  Gillingham ME7.......... 10 C3
  Maidstone ME14......... 75 B7
Bysing Wood Cotts ME13. 39 F1
Bysing Wood Prim Sch
  ME13.................. 62 A8
Bysing Wood Rd ME13 ... 62 A8
Bythorne Ct ME8......... 12 B1

C

Cabin The TN24............ 139 D7
Cade Rd TN23............ 156 B7
Cades Orch ME13.......... 61 E3
Cadnam Cl CT2........... 66 E3
Caernarvon Rd CT11...... 74 F1
Caernarvon Gdns CT10... 30 B5
Caesar Ave TN23......... 155 F4
Caesar's Way CT19....... 177 E7
Calais Hill CT2........... 66 E6
CALCOTT................. 45 E2
Calcraft Mews 6 CT1..... 67 B2
Calcutta Ho 3 ME15...... 97 E5
Caldecote Cl ME8......... 12 B1
Caldecot La TN29........ 201 D2
Caldecott Foundation Sch
  TN25.................. 158 B4
Calder Rd ME14........... 74 E7
Caldew Ave ME8.......... 11 C1
Caldew Gr ME10.......... 37 A3
Caledonian Ct ME8........ 33 E8
Caledon Terr CT1......... 88 A7
Calehill Cl ME14......... 75 C6
Calgary Cres CT19....... 178 E8
California Row CT3....... 90 E6
Callams Cl ME8........... 33 D6
Calland TN25............ 158 E5
Callaways La ME9........ 35 B6
Calleywell La TN25....... 173 A7
Callis Court Rd CT10..... 29 F6
Callis Grange Inf Sch
  CT10.................. 29 F7
Callisto Cl ME16......... 74 D3
Callis Way ME8........... 33 D5
Calverden Rd CT12....... 29 A1
CAMBER................. 203 A1
Camber Bourne Rd
  TN25.................. 172 C6
Camborne Manor 2 ME7. 10 C6
Cambourne Ave CT8...... 27 D8
Cambrai Ct CT1........... 67 D1
Cambridge Ave CT13...... 95 B7
Cambridge Cl CT7......... 27 B7
Cambridge Cres ME15.... 97 D7
Cambridge Gdns CT20.... 178 D5
Cambridge La ME9........ 60 C8
Cambridge Mews CT14.. 117 D3
Cambridge Rd
  Canterbury CT1......... 87 F6
  Deal CT14............. 117 D3
  Dover CT17............ 166 D7
  Faversham ME13....... 62 B6
  Gillingham ME8......... 33 C6
  Rochester ME2.......... 9 A8
  Sittingbourne ME10..... 37 B3
Cambridge Terr
  1 Chatham ME4..........9 F4
  13 Dover CT17......... 166 E7
  13 Folkestone CT20.... 178 E5
  Margate CT9............ 8 B1
Cambridge Way
  Canterbury CT1......... 87 F6
  5 Maidstone ME15..... 97 D7
Camden Cl ME5........... 32 B5
Camden Cres CT16....... 166 E7
Camden Rd
  Broadstairs CT10....... 29 E7
  Gillingham ME7......... 10 D7
  Ramsgate CT12......... 52 E6
Camden Sq 10 CT11...... 52 E7
Camden St ME14......... 75 A5
Camden Terr TN24....... 139 E1
Camellia Cl
  Gillingham ME8......... 33 D7
  2 Margate CT9........ 28 B8
Cameron Cl ME5.......... 32 B8
Cameron Ct CT17........ 166 A6
Cameron Ho CT14....... 117 C1
Camomile Dr ME14....... 75 F5
Campbell Cl CT6......... 23 C3
Campbell Rd
  Deal CT14............. 117 D4
  Hawkinge CT18........ 163 A5
  Maidstone ME15....... 75 A3
Camperdown Manor 5
  ME7.................. 10 A6
Campion Cl ME5.......... 31 E3
Campleshon Rd ME8...... 33 D5
Campus Way ME8......... 33 A8
Camp Way ME15......... 97 C6
Canada Cl CT19.......... 177 C6
Canada Mews CT14...... 117 C3
Canada Rd CT14........ 117 D3
Canada Terr 3 ME14... 75 A7

Canadian Ave ME7....... 10 F4
Canal Rd ME2.............9 C7
Canberra Gdns ME10.... 36 C4
Candlers Way CT4...... 108 F8
Canning St ME14........ 75 A6
Cannonbury Rd CT11.... 52 D6
Cannongate Ave CT21... 176 D3
Cannongate Cl CT21.... 176 D3
Cannongate Gdns CT21.. 176 E3
Cannongate Rd CT21.... 176 D3
Cannon Rd CT11......... 52 D7
Cannon St
  Deal CT14............ 117 C7
  Dover CT16........... 166 D8
  Lydd TN29............ 205 C6
  New Romney TN28..... 202 B7
Canon Appleton Ct CT1 .. 87 F7
Canon Cl ME1.............9 B2
Canon Gn CT3............ 91 A7
Canons Gate Rd CT16... 166 E8
Canon Woods Way TN24. 139 F6
CANTERBURY............. 87 C7
Canterbury Cathedral ★
  CT1.................. 88 A8
Canterbury Cathedral
  Archives ★ 15 CT1..... 88 A8
Canterbury Centre The
  (Mus) ★ CT1.......... 66 F1
Canterbury Christ Church
  Univ (Augustine House
  Campus) 11 CT1....... 87 F7
Canterbury Christ Church
  Univ (Broadstairs Campus)
  1 CT10.............. 29 C4
Canterbury Christ Church
  Univ (Hall Place Enterprise
  Ctre) CT2.............. 66 B1
Canterbury Christ Church
  Univ (Medway Campus)
  ME4.................. 10 B8
Canterbury Christ Church
  Univ (North Holmes
  Campus) CT1.......... 88 B8
Canterbury City Ret Pk
  CT1.................. 67 D4
Canterbury Cl
  Broadstairs CT10....... 29 D5
  2 Folkestone CT19.... 178 E6
Canterbury Coll CT3..... 113 A5
Canterbury Ct TN24..... 139 D2
Canterbury East Sta CT1. 87 F7
Canterbury Environmental
  Education Ctr CT2...... 67 B3
Canterbury High Sch The
  CT2.................. 87 D8
Canterbury Hill CT2...... 66 E5
Canterbury Ho 2 CT1.... 87 F8
Canterbury Ind Pk CT3... 69 A8
Canterbury La
  Canterbury CT1......... 88 A8
  Gillingham ME8, ME9.... 12 C1
Canterbury Pilgrims Hospl
  The ★ 23 CT1......... 87 F8
Canterbury Rd
  Ashford, Kennington
    TN24................ 139 E5
  Ashford TN24.......... 156 E6
  Barham ME9........... 129 C5
  Boughton Aluph TN25.. 123 C5
  Boughton Street ME13.. 63 D4
  Brabourne Lees TN25.. 158 F6
  Brabourne TN25....... 159 C8
  Challock TN25, TN27... 104 C1
  Chilham CT4........... 85 F1
  Denton CT4........... 129 A1
  Dunkirk ME13.......... 64 C3
  Elham CT4............ 144 E3
  Etchinghill CT18....... 161 D4
  Faversham ME13....... 62 E5
  Folkestone CT19....... 178 D7
  Folkestone, Foord CT19.. 178 E6
  Hawkinge CT18, CT19, CT15,
    CT4................ 163 B4
  Herne Bay CT6......... 23 A3
  Herne CT3, CT6........ 45 E5
  Littlebourne CT3....... 89 C8
  Lydden CT15.......... 147 C1
  Lyminge CT18......... 161 C7
  Sarre CT7............ 48 C7
  Sittingbourne ME10..... 37 B3
  Whitstable CT5......... 43 D8
  Wingham CT3.......... 91 A7
Canterbury Rd Birchington
  CT7.................. 27 B5
Canterbury Road Birchington
  CT7.................. 27 B5
Canterbury Road E CT11,
  CT12................. 52 A6
Canterbury Road Margate
  CT9.................. 7 G1
Canterbury Road Prim Sch
  ME10................. 7 D1
Canterbury Road W CT12. 51 D7
Canterbury Road Westgate
  CT8, CT9.............. 27 E8
Canterbury St CT9....... 7 I2
Canterbury St ME10..... 10 C1
Canterbury Steiner Sch
  CT4.................. 108 E7
Canterbury Tales The ★ 24
  CT1.................. 87 F8
Canterbury West Sta CT2. 66 F1
Canute Rd
  Birchington CT7....... 26 D7
  Deal CT14............ 95 C1
  Faversham ME13....... 62 C6
Canute Wlk CT14......... 95 D1
Capel Cl
  Ashford TN23.......... 138 F1

Capel Cl continued
  Broadstairs CT10.........8 F1
  Gillingham ME8......... 33 D4
Capel Court Pk CT18.... 164 D2
Capell Cl ME17.......... 96 C3
CAPEL-LE-FERNE......... 164 B2
Capel-le-Ferne Prim Sch
  CT18................. 164 C3
Capel Rd
  Bromley Green TN26... 171 B4
  Faversham ME13....... 62 B7
  Petham CT4........... 108 F3
  Sittingbourne ME10..... 36 E2
Capel St CT18.......... 164 B3
Capetown Ho 1 ME15... 97 F5
Capstan Row CT14...... 117 D7
CAPSTONE.............. 32 E7
Capstone Farm Ctry Pk ★
  ME7.................. 32 D5
Capstone Rd
  Chatham ME5........... 10 C1
  Gillingham ME7......... 32 F6
Captains Ct CT21....... 176 C1
Cardinal Cl ME12.........4 D7
Cardine Cl ME10......... 36 E7
Carey Cl TN28.......... 202 B6
Carey Ho 5 CT1......... 87 F7
Caring La ME14, ME17.... 76 E1
Caring Rd ME15, ME17... 76 C1
Carisbrooke Dr ME16.... 74 D4
Carlsden Cl CT17....... 149 A3
Carlton Ave
  Broadstairs CT10....... 30 A5
  Gillingham ME7......... 10 E4
  Ramsgate CT12......... 52 D6
  Sheerness ME12......... 1 C1
Carlton Cres ME5........ 32 D8
Carlton Gdns ME15...... 97 B8
Carlton Hill CT6......... 22 C4
Carlton Leas CT20...... 178 C4
Carlton Mans CT9......... 8 A3
Carlton Rd
  Ashford TN23.......... 139 A2
  Kingsdown CT14....... 134 C6
  Whitstable CT5......... 43 D2
Carlton Rise CT8........ 27 C8
Carlton Road E CT8...... 27 D8
Carlton Road W CT8..... 27 D8
Carman's Cl ME15, ME17. 96 F3
Carmel Cl CT4.......... 86 B2
Carmel Ct 2 CT7....... 26 F8
Carn Brae CT9...........7 J2
Carnoustie CT5......... 44 E8
Caroland Cl TN25....... 158 D5
Caroline Cl CT5......... 43 B6
Caroline Cres
  Broadstairs CT10....... 29 E6
  Maidstone ME16....... 74 D7
Caroline Sq CT9..........7 J3
Carpeaux Cl ME4........ 10 A4
Carpenters Cl ME1........9 E2
Carpinus Cl ME5........ 32 B1
Carriage Ho ME13....... 83 D5
Carriage Mews CT2...... 66 F1
Carrie Ho 3 ME16...... 74 E5
Carrington Cl ME7....... 10 F6
Carroway's Pl CT9........7 J2
Carter Cl CT3.......... 163 A5
Carter La TN29......... 191 D2
Carter's Rd CT20....... 177 F5
Carter's Wood TN26.... 183 B7
Carton Cl ME1.......... 9 D2
Cartwright Cl 1 CT2.... 71 C2
Cartwright & Kelsey Prim
  Sch CT3.............. 71 C2
Carver Dr ME9.......... 58 E6
Carvoran Way ME8....... 33 C5
Caslocke St 2 ME13.... 62 C7
Cassino Rd CT1......... 67 B2
Cassino Sq CT15....... 149 E2
Castalla Cotts CT14..... 117 D3
Castleacres Ind Pk ME10. 37 B6
Castle Ave
  Broadstairs CT10....... 30 B6
  Dover CT16........... 149 D1
  Hythe CT21........... 176 B3
  Rochester ME1......... 9 C4
Castle Bay CT20........ 177 F3
Castle Cl
  4 Folkestone CT20.... 177 F3
  Lympne CT21.......... 174 F2
Castle Com Coll CT14... 117 C4
Castle Cotts CT13...... 72 E5
Castle Cres CT21....... 176 C1
Castle Dene ME14...... 74 F8
Castle Dr CT16......... 148 F7
Castle Glen 9 CT20.... 177 F3
Castle Hill
  Folkestone CT19, CT18. 178 A8
  Rochester ME1......... 9 C6
  Thurnham ME14........ 55 D1
Castle Hill Ave CT20.... 178 C4
Castle Hill CP Sch CT19. 178 E7
Castle Hill Ct ME1....... 9 C6
Castle Hill Rd 4 CT16.. 166 E8
Castle Ho CT5......... 20 F3
Castlemaine Ave ME7... 10 F6
Castle Mayne Ave CT7... 27 F3
Castlemere Ave ME11..... 3 B5
Castle Mews CT14..... 117 A4
Castlemount Ct CT16... 166 E8
Castlemount Rd CT16... 149 D1
Castle Rd
  Chatham ME4.......... 10 B2
  Folkestone CT20...... 177 F3
  Hythe CT21........... 176 B4
  Maidstone ME16....... 74 D7
  Sittingbourne ME10..... 37 B5

Castle Rd continued
  Whitstable CT5........ 20 F2
Castle Road Bsns Prec
  ME10................. 37 B6
Castle Road Tech Ctr
  ME10................. 37 B6
Castle Rough La ME10... 14 F1
Castle Row CT1......... 87 F7
Castle St
  6 Ashford TN23..... 139 B2
  Canterbury CT1......... 87 F8
  Dover CT16........... 166 E8
  Queenborough ME11.... 3 A5
Castle View Bsns Ctr ME1. 9 C6
Castleview Ct CT17.... 149 B1
Castle View Mews ME1... 9 C6
Castle View Rd ME2...... 9 A7
Castle Wlk CT14........ 95 D1
Cathedral View CT2..... 67 A2
Catherine Cl 2 ME16.. 74 A3
Catherine St ME1....... 9 D3
Catherine Way CT10.... 30 A6
Catkin Cl ME5.......... 31 F1
Catsole Hill CT3........ 91 D2
Catterick Rd ME5....... 32 D2
Cattle Market CT13..... 72 F1
Catt's Hill TN30....... 189 E3
Catt's Wood CT4....... 109 F4
Cauldham Cl CT18...... 164 B1
Cauldham La CT18..... 164 B3
Caulkers Ho 7 ME4.... 10 B2
Causeway The
  Canterbury CT1......... 66 F1
  Sandwich CT13........ 72 D2
Cavalry Ct
  Deal CT14............ 117 D3
  Folkestone CT20...... 177 D5
Cave Hill ME15......... 74 F1
Cave La CT3.......... 91 D3
Cavell Sq CT14........ 117 A3
Cavell Way ME10........ 36 D5
Cavenagh Rd CT15..... 151 B6
Cavendish Ave ME7.... 10 E6
Cavendish Ct CT6..... 23 A5
Cavendish Pl 2 CT11.. 52 E6
Cavendish Rd
  Herne Bay CT6........ 23 A5
  Rochester ME1......... 9 D3
Cavendish St CT11..... 52 E6
Cavendish Way ME15... 76 B3
Caversham Cl ME8...... 11 F1
Cavour Rd
  Faversham ME13....... 62 C7
  Sheerness ME12......... 1 D2
Caxton Ho TN24....... 139 C3
Caxton Rd CT9......... 28 C8
Cayser Dr ME17........ 99 C3
Cazeneuve St ME1....... 9 C5
Cecil Ave
  Gillingham ME8........ 11 A2
  Rochester ME2.......... 9 B8
  Sheerness ME12......... 1 C1
Cecil Ct
  Ashford TN24......... 139 B3
  Herne Bay CT6........ 23 A4
Cecilia Gr CT10......... 29 F6
Cecilia Rd CT11........ 52 E8
Cecil Pk CT6.......... 23 A4
Cecil Rd
  Kingsdown CT14...... 134 D7
  Rochester ME1......... 9 C3
Cecil Sq CT9...........7 I2
Cecil St CT9............7 I2
Cedar Cl
  Ashford TN23......... 138 E3
  Birchington CT8....... 27 B7
  Broadstairs CT10....... 29 F7
  Margate CT9........... 8 B1
  Sittingbourne ME10..... 37 B2
Cedar Cres TN29....... 194 F3
Cedar Ct
  Folkestone CT20...... 177 E5
  Maidstone ME14....... 75 B5
  11 Tenterden TN30... 179 B4
Cedar Gdns ME9....... 56 E8
Cedar Gr ME7.......... 33 A5
Cedar Ho ME12......... 1 C2
Cedar Rd CT2.......... 68 A4
Cedars PRU ME16...... 74 D4
Cedars Sch The ME1..... 9 C3
Cedars The
  Barrowhill TN25...... 174 D8
  5 Sittingbourne ME10. 37 C5
Cedar Terr ME13........ 62 A4
Cedarview CT2......... 66 C1
Cedarwood Ho ME15.... 96 B6
Cedric Rd CT5.......... 7 C1
Ceil Villas CT14....... 94 B4
Celak St TN25......... 173 A6
Celestine Cl ME5....... 32 A1
CELLARHILL............ 38 C1
Celt Cl ME10.......... 36 F8
Celtic Rd CT14........ 117 A2
Cemetery La TN24...... 139 C4
Centenary Cl TN27..... 120 C8
Centenary Gdns CT13... 93 A2
Central Ave
  Chatham ME4.......... 10 B8
  Herne Bay CT6........ 22 D4
  Sittingbourne ME10..... 36 F4
  Woodstock ME9....... 58 D6
Central Bsns Pk ME2.....9 C7
Central Par
  Herne Bay CT6........ 22 E5
  Rochester ME1......... 9 D2
Central Park Gdns ME4...9 E2
Central Park Stad ME10. 102 C6

Central Pk CT12........ 49 D6
Central Rd
  Ramsgate CT11....... 52 D8
  Rochester ME2.......... 9 A7
Central Service Rd CT16 166 H8
Central Theatre The ★ 10
  ME4................. 9 F4
Centre 2000
  Maidstone ME16....... 74 C8
  8 Sittingbourne ME10. 37 A4
Centre Ct ME2...........9 E7
Centre Rd CT17........ 166 C6
Centre The
  Margate CT9...........7 I2
  Ramsgate CT12........ 29 A1
Centurion Cl ME8....... 10 F1
Centurion Wlk TN23.... 156 B4
Century Ct ME1......... 9 C5
Century Rd
  Faversham ME13....... 62 E7
  Gillingham ME8........ 33 D8
Century Wlk CT14...... 117 C6
Ceres Cl ME10......... 37 C5
Chada Ave ME7......... 10 E3
Chaffe's La ME9........ 12 E3
Chaffes Terr ME9....... 12 E2
Chaffinch Cl ME5....... 32 A7
Chaffinch Dr TN23..... 156 C3
Chaffinch Lodge 5
  CT16................ 149 B2
Chafy Cres CT2........ 67 F5
Chain Gate ME17....... 118 A8
Chain The 6 CT13..... 73 A1
Chalcroft Rd CT20..... 177 E4
Chalfont Dr
  Gillingham ME8........ 33 D6
  Herne Bay CT6........ 23 D7
Chalk Ave TN30........ 167 B2
Chalk Cl CT19......... 178 A7
Chalkenden Ave ME8.... 11 A2
Chalkers Way ME4...... 11 B4
Chalk Hill CT11, CT12... 51 F6
Chalk Hill Rd CT14.... 134 C5
Chalkpit Hill CT4....... 89 D3
Chalk Pit Hill
  Chatham ME4.......... 10 A3
  Staple CT3........... 92 B5
Chalk Pit La CT13, CT3.. 92 C5
Chalk Rd ME11.......... 3 A5
CHALKSOLE............ 147 C4
CHALKSOLE GREEN..... 147 C3
Chalksole Green La
  CT15................ 147 B2
CHALKWELL............ 36 E4
Chalkwell Ct CT17..... 166 A7
Chalkwell Rd ME10..... 36 D5
Chalky Bank Rd ME8.... 11 F2
Chalky Rd ME9......... 56 C6
Challenger Cl ME10..... 36 E7
CHALLOCK............. 105 B1
Challock Ct CT9.........8 F1
Challock Prim Sch TN25. 105 B1
Challock Wlk CT14..... 75 C6
Chalmers Way ME8..... 11 A4
Chamberlain Ave ME16.. 74 C2
Chamberlain Cl ME8.... 33 B5
Chamberlain Dr CT6.... 22 B4
Chamberlain Rd
  Chatham ME4.......... 10 B2
  Dover CT17........... 166 B8
CHAMBERS' GREEN...... 136 C4
Chambers Wharf La ME13 62 E8
Chancel Ct CT2......... 66 D1
Chance Mdw CT15..... 149 E6
Chancery La ME15...... 75 B3
Chanctonbury Chase CT5. 43 A6
Chandlers Wharf ME1.....9 B5
Chandos Rd 17 CT10.. 30 B4
Chandos Sq 16 CT10.. 30 B4
Chandos Terr CT12.... 52 E7
Channel Cl CT19....... 178 F7
Channel Lea CT14..... 117 C1
Channel Rd CT9....... 29 A6
CHANNEL TUNNEL
  TERMINAL........... 177 B8
Channel View 21 CT19. 178 E5
Channel View Ct 19 CT11. 52 F7
Channel View Rd CT17.. 166 C5
Channel Watch TN28... 202 E4
Channon Rd TN24..... 206 E7
Chantry Ct 15 CT1.... 66 F1
Chantry Hall CT1...... 87 F7
Chantry Pk CT7........ 48 D7
Chapel Cl CT18........ 161 D3
Chapel Cotts ME17.... 98 F5
Chapel Hill
  Eythorne CT15....... 131 C7
  Margate CT9.......... 29 A6
Chapel Hill Cl CT9.... 28 F7
Chapel La
  Blean CT2............ 66 A7
  Boyden Gate CT3..... 47 C8
  Bredhurst ME7....... 33 A2
  Broad Oak CT2....... 67 D7
  18 Dover CT16...... 166 D7
  East Studdal CT15... 132 C6
  Egerton Forstal TN27. 118 B2
  Gillingham ME7....... 33 A4
  Maidstone ME14...... 76 A5
  Newchurch TN29..... 185 C4
  Rhodes Minnis CT4... 144 B4
  Ripple CT14.......... 133 D8
  Staple CT3........... 92 B4
  St Margaret's at Cliffe
    CT15.............. 150 F6

Chapel La continued
Sturry CT2 .... 67 F5
Chapel Mews 2 TN23 .. 139 C2
Chapel Pl
16 Dover CT17 .... 166 D7
Ramsgate CT11 .... 52 D7
Chapel Place La CT11 .. 52 D7
Chapel Rd
Dymchurch TN29 ...... 195 C7
Ram Lane TN26 .... 120 F1
Ramsgate CT11 .... 52 C7
Tilmanstone CT14 .... 115 A3
Whitfield CT16 .... 149 A8
Chapel Row
Herne CT6 .... 46 A8
Kingsnorth TN23 ..... 156 A3
Lydd TN29 .... 205 C6
Ram Lane TN26 ...... 120 F2
Chapel St
Deal CT14 .... 117 D6
Faversham ME13 ...... 62 D6
Herne Bay CT6 .... 23 A5
Hythe CT21 .... 176 B2
Minster (Sheppey) ME12 .. 4 D6
Sheerness ME12 ...... 1 B2
Chapel The
Chartham CT4 .... 86 F1
Maidstone ME16 ..... 74 B3
Chaplains Wlk CT4 .... 86 E1
Chapman Ave ME15 .... 97 E8
Chapman Fields CT12 .. 51 D5
Chapman Ho CT14 ..... 117 B3
Chapmans Cl TN25 .... 105 C2
Chapmans Hill CT13 .. 93 B5
Chappell Way ME10 .... 36 E6
CHARING 120 D8
Charing CE Prim Sch
TN27 .... 120 C8
Charing Cl CT12 ...... 52 C8
Charing Cres CT8 ..... 27 D7
CHARING HEATH 119 C6
Charing Heath Rd
Charing Heath TN27 ... 119 F8
Charing TN27 .... 120 A6
CHARING HILL 103 D1
Charing Hill TN27 .... 103 E1
Charing Rd ME13 ..... 11 B3
Charing Sta TN27 .... 120 B7
Charlbury Cl ME16 .... 74 C3
Charlecote Ct ME8 .... 33 D8
Charles Cobb Cl TN29 .. 195 D8
Charles Cres CT19 .... 177 E7
Charles Ct CT8 .... 27 F8
Charles Dickens Sch The
CT10 .... 29 E4
Charles Drayson Ct ME13 .. 62 E7
Charlesford Ave ME17 .. 99 D3
Charles Ho CT14 ..... 117 B3
Charles Lister Ct CT17 .. 149 B1
Charles St
Deal CT14 .... 117 B4
Ramsgate CT11 ...... 52 E8
Charles St
Chatham ME4 .... 9 E3
Herne Bay CT6 ...... 23 A5
Maidstone ME16 .... 74 E3
Rochester ME2 ...... 9 A7
Sheerness ME12 ..... 1 B3
Charleston Ct CT10 ... 30 B3
Charlesworth Dr CT7 .. 27 B7
Charlock Cl ME16 ..... 74 D8
Charlock Dr ME12 ..... 4 A4
Charlotte Cl ME5 ..... 32 B6
Charlotte Ct 4 CT11 .. 52 E6
Charlotte Dr ME8 ..... 11 C1
Charlotte Pl 2 CT9 .... 7 J1
Charlotte Sq 8 CT9 .... 7 J2
Charlotte St
13 Broadstairs CT10 ... 30 B4
Folkestone CT20 ..... 178 E5
Sittingbourne ME10 ... 36 E5
Charlton Ave CT16 .... 149 C1
Charlton CE Prim Sch
CT16 .... 149 C1
Charlton Cl
Ashford TN24 .... 157 A8
Ramsgate CT12 ..... 29 B2
Charlton Ctr 3 CT17 .. 166 C8
Charlton Gn CT16 .... 149 C1
Charlton La CT4 ...... 111 C1
Charlton Manor ME7 .. 10 B5
Charlton Sh Ctr **3** CT16 .. 166 C8
Charltons The ME13 .. 63 F4
Charminster TN23 .... 155 E6
Charnwood CT5 .... 21 D1
Charnwood Rd CT6 .... 23 B1
Charollais Cl CT2 ..... 67 A2
Chartam Terr CT11 .... 52 D5
Chart Cnr ME13 ...... 62 B7
Chart Cnr ME17 ...... 98 B1
Charter Ho 11 CT16 .. 166 E7
Charter St
Chatham ME4 .... 9 F2
Gillingham ME7 ...... 10 C7
Chartfield Sch CT8 .... 27 F8
Chart Gunpowder Mill*
ME13 .... 62 B7
CHARTHAM 86 E2
CHARTHAM DOWNS .. 86 D1
Chartham Downs Rd
CT4 .... 109 C2
CHARTHAM HATCH ... 86 D6
Chartham Prim Sch CT4 .. 86 C2
Chartham Sta CT4 .... 86 D3

Chart Hill Rd ME17 ... 98 B1
Chart Pl ME8 .... 33 C3
Chart Rd
Ashford, Godinton Park
TN23 .... 138 D2
Ashford, Great Chart TN23 138 D1
Ashford, Stanhope TN23 .. 155 D6
Folkestone CT19 ..... 177 F6
Chart Road Ind Est TN23 139 D3
CHART SUTTON 98 B1
Chart Sutton Bsns Est
ME17 .... 98 B2
Chartway St ME17 .... 99 C1
CHARTWAY STREET ... 99 C1
Chartwell Ave CT6 .... 23 D4
Chartwell Ct
Chatham ME4 .... 9 E4
Maidstone ME15 .... 75 B3
Chartwell Dr ME16 .... 74 B4
Chartwell Gr ME10 .... 36 C3
Chase The
Chatham ME4 .... 9 D2
Gillingham ME8 ...... 11 A2
Ramsgate CT11 ..... 29 F1
St Margaret's at Cliffe
CT15 .... 133 F1
Whitstable CT5 ...... 43 C8
Chater Cl
Ashford TN23 .... 155 C8
Deal CT14 .... 117 C4
CHATHAM 9 E5
Chatham Ct CT11 .... 52 D8
Chatham Gr ME4 ..... 9 F1
Chatham Gram Sch for Boys
ME4 .... 31 F8
Chatham Gram Sch for Girls
ME5 .... 10 C2
Chatham Hill ME4 .... 10 B3
Chatham House Gram Sch
CT11 .... 52 E7
Chatham Pl CT11 ..... 52 E7
Chatham Rd
Kit's Coty ME20 ..... 53 D6
Maidstone ME14 .... 53 E1
Sandling ME14 ...... 53 E4
Tenterden TN30 ..... 179 A6
Whitstable CT5 ..... 44 C8
Woodchurch TN26 ... 169 A3
Chatham Ski Ctr ME7 .. 32 E6
Chatham South Sch ME4 . 31 F8
Chatham St CT11 ..... 52 E7
Chatham Sta ME4 .... 9 E4
Chatsworth Dr ME10 .. 36 B5
Chatsworth Rd 10 ME7 .. 10 C6
Chattenden Ct ME14 .. 75 B6
Chatwell Ct ME7 ..... 10 C5
Chaucer Ave CT5 ..... 21 B1
Chaucer Bsns Pk
Whitstable CT5 ..... 21 B1
5 Whitstable CT5 .... 43 C6
Chaucer Cl
Canterbury CT1 ..... 88 C7
18 Maidstone ME15 ... 97 E7
Rochester ME2 ..... 9 E8
Chaucer Coll CT2 .... 66 D3
Chaucer Cres CT16 ... 149 B3
Chaucer Ct 1 CT1 .... 88 B7
Chaucer Hospl The CT4 .. 88 A4
Chaucer Mews CT2 ... 65 E1
Chaucer Rd
Broadstairs CT10 ... 30 A3
Canterbury CT1 ..... 67 C1
Elvington CT15 ...... 114 B2
Gillingham ME7 ..... 10 D3
Sittingbourne ME10 .. 36 D3
Chaucer Tech Sch CT1 .. 88 C7
Chaucer Wood Ct CT1 .. 67 B1
Cheddar CT14 .... 139 B4
CHEESEMAN'S GREEN .. 156 F2
Cheeseman's Green La TN23/
TN25 .... 156 E1
Cheesmans Cl CT12 .. 50 C5
Cheffins Ho ME7 ..... 10 E7
Chegwell Dr ME5 ..... 32 B4
Chegworth Gdns ME10 .. 36 E1
Chegworth La ME17 .. 100 A6
Chegworth Rd ME17 .. 99 F5
Chelmar Rd ME7 ..... 10 B4
Chelmsford Ho ME15 .. 97 E6
Chelsea Ct CT21 ..... 176 C1
Chelsea Rd CT1 ...... 67 C4
Chelsfield Ho ME16 .. 74 D5
Cheltenham Cl ME15 .. 97 F6
Cheney Cl ME8 ...... 33 D5
Cheney Hill ME9 ..... 59 A5
Cheney Rd ME13 .... 62 F7
Chennels The TN26 .. 167 E7
Chepstow Ho 3 ME15 .. 97 F6
Chequer La CT3 ...... 71 D2
Chequers Cl ME5 .... 54 A8
Chequers Hill CT4 .... 109 C2
Chequers Pk TN25 ... 123 E1
Chequers Rd ME12 .... 4 E6
Chequers Sh Ctr ME15 .. 75 A4
Chequer's Terr ME12 .. 5 A5
Chequertree TN25 ... 172 B2
Cherbourg Cres ME5 .. 31 F7
CHERITON 177 D6
Cheriton Appartments
CT19 .... 177 F6
Cheriton Ave CT12 ... 52 B8
Cheriton Court Rd CT20 .. 177 C6
Cheriton Gdns CT20 .. 178 C4
Cheriton High St TN19 .. 177 D6
Cheriton Intc CT19 ... 177 C7
Cheriton Pl
Deal CT14 .... 117 D4
Folkestone CT20 ..... 178 D4
Cheriton Prim Sch CT20 177 C6
Cheriton Rd
Deal CT14 .... 117 C4

Cheriton Rd continued
Folkestone CT19, CT20 . 178 B5
Folkestone, Morehall CT19 177 F6
Gillingham ME8 ...... 33 D8
Cheriton Way ME16 ... 74 C7
Cheriton Wood Ho CT19 177 D7
Cherries The ME16 ... 74 A2
Cherry Amber Cl ME8 .. 33 F8
Cherry Ave CT2 ...... 66 D2
Cherrybrook Rd CT20 .. 177 D6
Cherry Cl
Lenham ME17 ...... 101 C5
Sittingbourne ME10 .. 36 D6
Cherry Ct
Ashford TN23 .... 139 B1
Broadstairs CT10 ... 29 E7
Folkestone CT19 .... 178 A6
Cherry Dr CT2 .... 66 D2
Cherry Fields ME10 .. 36 A5
Cherry Garden Ave CT19 178 A4
Cherry Garden Cres
TN25 .... 123 F2
Cherrygarden La CT15,
CT3 .... 113 E7
Cherry Garden La
Ash CT3 .... 71 E1
Folkestone CT19 .... 177 F7
Wye TN25 .... 123 F2
Cherry Garden Rd CT2 .. 66 D2
Cherry Gdns
Ashford TN23 .... 156 A5
Broadstairs CT10 ... 29 C3
Elham CT4 .... 144 F5
Herne Bay CT6 ...... 22 F4
Littlebourne-on-Sea TN28 .. 202 D6
Teynham ME9 .... 38 C2
Cherry Glebe TN25 ... 157 E3
Cherry Gr CT15 ...... 114 B2
Cherry Hill Ct ME9 ... 35 B6
Cherry La CT14 ...... 116 D3
Cherry Orch
Littlebourne CT3 .... 68 F1
Old Wives Lees CT4 .. 85 C2
Cherry Orchard La TN25 . 172 E4
CHERRY ORCHARD ... 74 B4
Cherry Orchard Mews
CT3 .... 68 F1
Cherry Orchard Way
ME16 .... 74 B3
Cherry Tree Ave CT16 . 149 C1
Cherry Tree Cl
Teynham ME9 .... 38 D2
West Minst ME12 .... 3 A8
Cherry Tree Dr ME13 .. 39 F3
Cherry Tree Gdns CT12 .. 29 B3
Cherry Tree Rd
Charing Heath TN27 .. 119 E7
Gillingham ME8 ..... 33 F8
Cherry View ME17 .... 97 B3
Cherry Waye CT15 ... 131 D7
Cherrywood Rise TN25 . 138 F4
Cherville La CT3 ..... 90 C7
Chervilles ME16 ..... 74 A2
Chesham Dr ME8 ..... 33 E6
Cheshire Rd
Maidstone ME15 .... 97 E7
Maidstone, Willington ME15 75 E2
CHESLEY 35 A3
Chessenden La TN27 .. 135 A1
Chester Ave TN26 .... 153 D5
Chester Rd
Gillingham ME7 ..... 10 D2
Westgate on Sea CT8 .. 27 F8
CHESTFIELD 21 E1
Chestfield Cl ME8 .... 11 E2
Chestfield Rd CT5 .... 44 C7
Chestfield & Swalecliffe Sta
CT5 .... 21 D2
Chestnut Ave
Blean CT2 .... 66 A7
Chatham ME5 .... 31 F3
Chestnut Cl
Ashford TN23 .... 138 E3
Chartham CT4 ...... 86 F1
Hythe CT21 .... 187 E8
Tenterden TN30 ..... 167 C1
Whitfield CT16 ...... 149 A8
Chestnut Ct ME13 .... 64 A3
Chestnut Dr
Broadstairs CT10 ... 29 D4
Coxheath ME17 ..... 96 B3
Herne Bay CT6 ...... 22 D3
Kingswood ME17 .... 99 D2
Sturry CT2 .... 68 A7
Worth CT14 .... 94 A4
Chestnut Ho 5 ME16 .. 74 A3
Chestnut La TN23 .... 156 C4
Chestnut Rd CT17 .... 166 B7
Chestnut St ME9 ..... 35 E4
Chestnuts The
Brabourne Lees TN25 .. 158 D5
Sellindge TN25 ...... 159 D1
CHESTNUT STREET ... 35 E4
Chestnut Terr CT21 .. 176 A1
Chestnut Wood La ME9 .. 35 E3
Chetney View ME9 .... 14 D4
Chevalier Rd CT17 ... 166 A7
Chevening Cl ME5 .... 32 B5
Cheviot Ct CT10 ..... 30 B5
Cheviot Gdns ME15 .. 76 A1
Cheviot Way TN24 ... 139 C4
Cheyne Cl ME10 ..... 36 F8
Cheyne Mid Sch ME12 ..... 1 E2
Cheyne Rd ME12 ..... 5 D3
Chicago Ave ME7 .... 10 F5

Chichester Cl
Ashford TN23 .... 139 B1
Gillingham ME8 ..... 34 A8
Chichester Rd
Folkestone CT20 .... 177 E6
Ramsgate CT12 ..... 29 B1
Chichester Wlk 2 CT12 .. 29 B1
Chickfield Gdns 4 ME5 .. 10 C2
Chiddingfold Cl ME12 .. 4 D6
Chiddingstone Cl ME15 .. 97 F6
Childgate Rd CT5 .... 42 F2
Childscroft Rd ME8 .. 11 F2
CHILHAM 107 C7
Chilham Ave CT8 ..... 27 D7
Chilham Cl
Chatham ME4 .... 9 E3
West Minst ME12 ..... 3 B8
Chilham Ho 1 ME15 .. 97 E8
Chilham Rd
Folkestone CT19 .... 177 E6
Gillingham ME8 ..... 11 A3
Maidstone ME16 .... 74 C7
Chilham St Mary's CE Prim
Sch CT4 .... 107 B8
Chilham Sta CT4 ..... 107 D8
CHILLENDEN 113 F8
Chillenden Windmill*
CT3 .... 91 F1
Chillington St ME14 .. 74 F6
CHILMINGTON GREEN .. 155 C5
Chilston Rd ME17 .... 101 D5
Chiltern Cl ME15 ..... 75 F1
Chiltern End TN24 ... 139 B3
CHILTON 52 A6
Chilton Ave
Sittingbourne ME10 .. 37 A3
Temple Ewell CT16 .. 148 C4
Chilton Ct
14 Folkestone CT20 ... 178 E6
Gillingham ME8 ..... 11 E1
Chilton Field CT3 .... 71 D2
Chilton Gdns CT3 .... 71 D2
Chilton La CT11 ..... 52 A6
Chilton Pl CT3 ...... 71 D2
Chilton Prim Sch CT11 .. 52 A6
Chilton Sq CT3 ...... 71 D2
Chilton Way CT17 ... 148 D3
Chimes The
Ashford TN24 .... 139 C3
Maidstone ME14 .... 76 A5
Rochester ME1 ..... 9 C5
Chineham Way CT1 ... 87 F6
Chippendale Cl ME5 .. 31 F1
Chippendayle Dr ME17 .. 100 D6
Chippie's Way CT13 .. 72 F1
Chipstead Cl ME16 ... 74 D6
Chipstead Rd ME8 ... 33 D4
Chislehurst Cl ME15 .. 97 F6
CHISLET 47 D5
Chislet CE Prim Sch CT3 . 47 C5
Chislet Cl CT3 ...... 47 A1
Chislet Ct CT6 ...... 22 C5
CHISLET FORSTAL ... 47 B5
Chislet Park Cotts CT3 .. 46 F1
Chislet Park Farm Cotts
CT3 .... 46 F2
Chislett Cl TN25 ..... 159 E2
Chislet Wlk ME8 ..... 33 D5
Chisnall Rd CT17 .... 148 E4
Chittenden's La TN29 .. 193 E5
CHITTY 47 D5
Chitty La CT3 .... 47 B6
Christ Church CE High Sch
TN23 .... 155 F5
Christ Church CE Jun Sch
CT11 .... 52 C6
Christ Church CE Prim Sch
CT20 .... 178 C5
Christchurch Ct
3 Chatham ME5 ..... 10 C2
1 Dover CT17 .... 166 D7
Christchurch Ho 11 ME15 . 97 E5
Christchurch Rd TN23 .. 156 B8
Christ Church Rd CT20 .. 178 C4
Christchurch Way CT16 . 149 B3
Christen Way ME15, ME17 . 97 F3
Christian Ct 3 ME2 ... 9 C8
Christie Cl ME5 ..... 32 B6
Christmas St ME7 .... 10 E7
Christopher Bushell Way
TN24 .... 139 E4
Christopher's Row ME9 . 60 A3
Chrysler Ave CT10 ... 22 B4
Church App TN28 .... 202 A6
Church Cl TN25 ...... 157 E3
Church Cliff CT14 .... 134 D6
Church Cotts
Rodmersham ME9 ... 59 D8
Tenterden TN30 ..... 167 C5
Church Court Gr CT10 . 29 E6
Church Cres ME17 ... 100 F6
Church Ct CT18 ..... 161 C6
Churchfarm Mews CT15 . 133 A1
Church Farm Rd ME9 .. 12 E3
Church Farm Way CT13 . 93 B6
Church Field CT3 .... 160 B1
Churchfield Pl CT9 .... 7 I2
Churchfields
Broadstairs CT10 ... 29 F7
Margate CT9 .... 7 J1
Churchfields Terr ME1 .. 9 B8
Churchfield Way TN25 . 123 E2
Church Gn
Hollingbourne ME17 .. 77 E3
Rochester ME2 ..... 9 C8
Church Haven CT14 .. 133 F5
Church Hill
Bethersden TN26 .... 153 D5

Church Hill continued
Boughton Street ME13 .. 64 A5
Canterbury CT2 ..... 66 C1
Charing Heath ME17,
TN27 .... 119 C2
Chatham ME5 .... 10 C2
Chilham CT4 .... 107 B8
Doddington ME9 .... 80 F8
Eythorne CT15 ..... 131 C8
Hawkinge CT18 ..... 163 D4
High Halden TN26 ... 167 E7
Hythe CT21 .... 176 C2
Kingsnorth TN23 .... 156 B3
Loose ME17 .... 97 C1
Ramsgate CT11 ..... 52 E7
Shepherdswell CT15 . 130 D4
Stockbury ME9 ..... 56 F7
Stone in Oxney TN30 . 189 F3
Sutton CT15 .... 133 A7
Temple Ewell CT16 .. 148 D5
Church Ho CT14 ..... 117 C7
CHURCH HOUGHAM .. 165 B5
Church Hts CT21 .... 176 C2
Churchill Ave
Chatham ME5 .... 32 A7
Deal CT14 .... 117 C7
Folkestone CT19 .... 178 C8
Herne Bay CT6 ...... 23 D4
Churchill Cl
Bridge CT4 .... 88 F1
Folkestone CT19 .... 178 D8
St Margaret's at Cliffe
CT15 .... 150 F5
Churchill Cotts ME17 .. 98 F6
Churchill Ct
Hythe CT21 .... 176 B1
1 Ramsgate CT11 ... 52 D7
Churchill Ho
Bridge CT4 .... 88 F1
2 Folkestone CT20 .. 177 F5
Maidstone ME16 .... 74 B2
Sittingbourne ME10 .. 37 C4
Teynham ME9 .... 38 C3
Churchill Rd
Canterbury CT1 ..... 88 C6
Dover CT17 .... 166 A6
Minster (Sheppey) ME12 .. 4 D6
Churchill Sch The CT18 . 163 A4
Churchill St 7 CT16 .. 149 C1
Churchill Way ME13 .. 40 B1
Churchill Wlk CT18 ... 162 F4
Church La
Adisham CT3 .... 90 D1
Aldington TN25 ..... 173 D7
Barham CT4 .... 111 F1
Boughton Aluph TN25 . 123 B4
Boyden Gate CT3 .... 47 C7
Brenzett TN29 ...... 191 F5
Canterbury CT1 ..... 87 F8
20 Canterbury, Northgate
CT1 .... 67 A1
Challock TN25 ...... 122 B8
Chartham CT4 ...... 86 D3
Chatham ME4 .... 9 F6
Church Hougham CT15 . 165 B5
Deal CT14 .... 117 B6
Harrietsham ME17 ... 100 E6
Hothfield TN26 ..... 137 F6
Iden TN31 .... 197 B4
Kingsnorth TN23 .... 156 B3
Kingston CT4 .... 111 D3
Lower Hardres CT4 .. 88 B2
Lydden CT15 .... 147 E8
Maidstone, Bearsted ME14 76 C4
Newington ME9 ..... 35 B6
New Romney TN28 .. 202 B5
Peasmarsh TN31 .... 196 C1
Petham CT4 .... 109 C3
Ringwould CT14 .... 133 F5
Ripple CT14 .... 116 D1
Selling ME13 .... 84 B6
Shadoxhurst TN26 .. 170 A7
Stockbury ME9 ..... 56 E8
Stourmouth CT3 .... 48 C2
Stowting TN25 ..... 160 A6
Sturry CT2 .... 67 F5
Waltham CT4 .... 125 F5
Westbere CT2 ...... 68 C7
West Langdon CT15 .. 132 D3
Whitstable CT5 ..... 43 A6
Womenswold CT4 ... 112 D2
Churchlands ME14 ... 75 B5
Churchlands Ho TN28 . 202 B6
Churchlands The TN28 . 202 B6
Church Marshes Ctry Pk*
ME10 .... 37 A7
Church Mdws CT14 .. 117 A6
Church Mews
Gillingham ME8 ..... 33 F8
Iwade ME9 .... 14 E4
Church Path
Deal CT14 .... 117 B5
Gillingham ME7 ..... 10 E6
Great Mongeham CT14 . 116 D3
Church Rd
Ashford, Aylesford Green
TN24 .... 157 A7
Ashford, Kennington TN24 . 139 E6
Ashford TN23 ...... 139 C2
Ashford, Willesborough
TN24 .... 157 A8
1 Broadstairs CT10 .. 30 B4
Burmarsh TN29 .... 185 E4
Charing TN27 ...... 103 D2
Chart Sutton ME17 .. 98 C1
Coldred CT15 .... 131 A3
Dover CT17 .... 166 A7
Eastchurch ME12 .... 5 D2

Chu–Con 217

Church Rd continued
Eastling ME13 82 B2
Faversham ME13 62 D7
Faversham, Oare ME13 40 B3
Faversham, The Brents ME13 62 D8
Folkestone CT20 177 C6
Harrietsham ME17 100 E6
Hoath CT3 46 E5
Hucking ME17 56 E1
Hythe CT21 176 C2
Kenardington TN26 182 A5
Littlebourne CT3 90 A8
Lydd TN29 205 C6
Lyminge CT18 161 C7
Maidstone ME15 97 F7
Maidstone, Tovil ME15 74 E2
Margate CT9 7 J1
Mersham TN25 157 E3
Molash CT4 105 F5
New Romney TN28 202 A6
Northbourne, Betteshanger CT14 115 C6
Northbourne CT14 116 A5
Ramsgate CT11 52 E7
Sevington TN24 157 B6
Sittingbourne ME9 37 E5
Sittingbourne, Murston ME10 37 B5
Smeeth TN25 158 C4
Stalisfield Green ME13 103 F5
Tenterden TN30 179 A7
Church Road Bsns Ctr ME10 37 B6
Church St (St Pauls) 7 CT1 88 A8
Church Sq
2 Broadstairs CT10 30 B4
Lenham ME17 101 D5
Church St
Broadstairs CT10 29 E6
Canterbury CT2 66 E1
Chatham ME4 10 A4
Deal CT14 117 B1
Dover CT16 166 D7
Eastry CT13 93 C2
Faversham ME13 62 D8
Folkestone CT20 178 D4
Gillingham ME7 10 E6
Maidstone, Boughton Monchelsea ME17 97 B2
Maidstone, Loose ME15 96 F5
Maidstone ME14 75 A4
Maidstone, Tovil ME15 74 E2
Margate CT9 7 J1
Minster (Thanet) CT12 50 C5
Nonington CT15 113 C5
Rochester ME1 9 D4
Rodmersham ME9 59 C8
7 Sandwich CT13 73 A1
3 Sandwich, The Butts CT13 72 F1
5 Sittingbourne ME10 36 E4
Sittingbourne ME10 36 E5
Whitstable CT5 20 F1
Woodnesborough CT13 93 B6
Wye TN25 123 E2
CHURCH STREET 20 F1
Church Terr
Chatham ME5 10 C2
Minster (Sheppey) ME12 4 C7
Church View
Aldington TN25 173 A6
Herne Bay CT6 23 C4
Newchurch TN29 184 E3
Worth CT14 94 B5
Church Way CT5 21 D3
CHURCH WHITFIELD 149 B8
Church Whitfield Rd CT16 149 B8
Church Wlk CT4 144 F4
Church Wood Cl CT2 66 B2
Churchwood Dr CT5 21 D1
Church Yard Pas 10 TN23 139 B2
Church Yd 4 TN23 139 C2
Chute Cl ME8 33 D4
Cinder Path CT10 30 A4
Cinnabar Cl ME5 32 A1
Cinnabar Dr ME10 36 C6
Cinnamon Gr ME16 74 A3
Cinque Ports Ave CT21 176 B1
Cinque Ports Rd TN28 202 C5
Circular Rd
Dover CT16 150 B1
Finglesham CT14 116 B7
Circus The CT6 22 E4
Citadel Cres CT17 166 B6
Citadel Hts CT17 166 B6
Citadel Rd CT17 166 B6
Citadel The (Immigration Removal Ctr) CT17 166 B5
Citroen Cl CT6 22 B4
City Bsns Pk CT1 67 C3
City Garden The 3 CT1 88 A8
City View CT2 87 C8
City Way ME1 9 D2
Claire Ct
Birchington CT7 26 F7
Broadstairs CT10 30 B5
Claire Ho 4 ME16 74 E5
Clandon Rd ME5 32 D2
Clanwilliam Rd CT14 117 D5
CLAPHAM HILL 43 D5
Clapham Hill CT5 43 D5
CLAP HILL 172 F7
Clapper Hill CT4 126 B3
Clare Dr CT6 22 C2
Claremont Cl CT14 134 C6
Claremont Gdns CT11 52 C7
Claremont Pl CT1 87 F7
Claremont Rd
Deal CT14 117 B5
Folkestone CT20 178 C5
Kingsdown CT14 134 C6
Maidstone ME14 75 B5
Claremont St CT6 22 C4
Claremont Terr CT13 93 D7
Claremont Way 2 ME4 9 F3
Clarence Ave
Margate CT9 8 D2
Rochester ME1 9 C4
Clarence Ct ME14 75 E4
Clarence Gdns ME12 6 E3
Clarence Pl
Deal CT14 117 D7
Dover CT17 166 D5
Clarence Rd
Capel-le-Ferne CT18 164 B2
Chatham ME4 10 B2
Deal CT14 117 D3
Herne Bay CT6 22 D5
Ramsgate CT11 52 C6
Clarence Row ME12 1 C2
Clarence St
Folkestone CT20 178 D5
Herne Bay CT6 22 E5
CLARENDON 166 B6
Clarendon Cl
Maidstone ME14 76 A4
Sittingbourne ME10 36 F1
Clarendon Gdns 7 CT11 52 D6
Clarendon House Gram Sch 15 CT11 52 E6
Clarendon Mews
1 Broadstairs CT10 30 A4
New Romney TN28 202 C8
Clarendon Pl
Dover CT17 166 C7
Maidstone ME14 75 A4
Clarendon Rd
Aylesham CT3 112 F5
Broadstairs CT10 30 A4
Dover CT17 166 C7
Margate CT9 8 A2
Clarendon St
Dover CT17 166 C7
Herne Bay CT6 22 C4
Clare Rd CT5 20 E2
Claridge Ct ME7 32 F4
Claridge Mews CT21 176 C2
Clarke Cres TN24 139 F4
Clarke's Cl CT14 116 F4
Clarklands TN29 184 E3
Clark Rd TN28 202 E4
Claudius Gr TN23 155 F5
Clavell Cl ME8 33 E4
Claxfield Cotts ME9 38 A2
Claxfield Rd ME9 60 A8
Claygate
Ashford TN23 155 F5
Eyhorne Street ME17 77 D2
Maidstone ME15 75 D1
Clearmount Way CT3 47 A1
Clearmount Dr TN27 120 C8
Clearmount Pk TN27 120 D8
Cleave Rd ME7 10 E3
Cleaver La CT11 52 E7
Clematis Ave ME8 33 B5
Clement Cl
Canterbury CT1 67 B1
Sittingbourne ME10 36 E8
Clement Ct ME16 74 D5
Clementine Cl CT6 23 D4
Clement's Rd CT12 29 C2
Clerke Dr ME10 37 A8
Clermont Cl ME7 33 A4
Clevedon Ct TN25 105 B2
Cleveland Cl CT16 149 B3
Cleveland Ct CT9 8 A3
Cleveland Ho ME16 74 B2
Cleveland Rd ME7 10 D6
Cleveley Lo CT11 29 E2
Cleven Lodge CT7 48 D6
Cleves Way TN23 155 E8
Clewer Lo CT5 20 F2
Clewson Rise ME14 75 B8
Cliff Ave CT6 23 C5
Cliff Cl CT21 176 D3
Cliff Dr
Herne Bay CT6 22 C4
Warden ME12 6 E4
Cliffe Ave CT9 7 F1
Cliffe Ho
Folkestone CT20 178 A3
St Margaret's at Cliffe CT15 150 F6
Cliffe Rd
Deal CT14 134 D6
Rochester ME2 9 B8
Cliffestone Ct CT20 178 B5
Cliff Field CT8 27 C8
Cliff Gdns ME12 4 E7
Cliff Hill ME17 97 D4
Cliff Hill Rd ME17 97 C4
Clifford Gdns CT14 117 B2
Clifford Ho 6 ME14 75 B4
Clifford Rd CT5 43 F8
Clifford Way ME15 74 E2
Cliff Prom CT10 30 C7
Cliff Rd
Birchington CT7 26 F8
Broadstairs CT10 30 B7
Dover CT15, CT16 150 C1
Folkestone CT20 178 A3
Hythe CT21 176 E3
Cliff Rd continued
Whitstable CT5 20 F3
Cliff Sea Gr CT6 22 C4
CLIFFS END 51 D6
Cliffs End Gr CT12 51 D5
Cliffs End Rd CT12 51 E5
Cliffside Dr CT10 30 A1
Cliff St CT11 52 E6
Cliff Terr CT9 7 J3
Clifftown Gdns CT6 22 B4
Cliff View Gdns
Leysdown-on-Sea ME12 6 D1
Warden ME12 6 E4
Cliff View Rd CT12 51 D6
Clifton Cl ME14 75 B5
Clifton Cres CT20 178 B3
Clifton Gdns
Canterbury CT2 66 D2
Folkestone CT20 178 C4
Margate CT9 7 J3
Whitstable CT5 43 D8
Clifton Lawn CT11 52 D5
Clifton Mans 7 CT20 178 C4
Clifton Pl CT9 8 A3
Clifton Rd
Folkestone CT20 178 C4
Gillingham ME7 10 C7
Margate CT9 8 A2
Ramsgate CT11 52 B8
Whitstable CT5 20 D1
Clifton St CT9 7 J3
CLIFTONVILLE 8 D2
Cliftonville Ave
Margate CT9 8 A2
Ramsgate CT12 29 B1
Cliftonville Ct
Margate, Cliftonville CT9 8 B3
Margate CT9 8 A3
Cliftonville Prim Sch CT9 8 C2
Clim Down CT14 134 D6
Clinton Cl ME17 96 B3
Clints La CT4 129 D4
Clipper Cl ME2 9 E7
Clipper Ct ME2 9 E7
Clive Ct CT9 8 B2
Cliveden Cl ME16 74 D7
Clive Dennis Ct TN24 139 E1
Clive Rd
Cliffs End CT12 51 D6
Margate CT9 29 A5
Rochester ME1 9 C3
Sittingbourne ME10 36 B5
Clockhouse TN23 138 F1
Clockhouse Pk TN25 105 C2
Clock House Rise ME17 96 C2
Clock Tower★ CT9 7 J3
Clocktower Par CT2 66 A6
Cloisterham Rd ME1 31 D7
Cloisters The
18 Canterbury CT1 66 F1
Lenham ME17 101 C5
Ramsgate CT11 52 D5
8 Sittingbourne ME10 36 E4
Whitstable CT5 20 F2
Clopton Ct ME8 33 D8
Close The
Ashford TN23 155 F7
Bridge CT4 88 F1
Canterbury CT1 87 D6
Canterbury, Hales Place CT2 66 F4
Canterbury, St Dunstan's CT2 66 C3
Faversham ME13 62 C6
Folkestone CT19 178 E8
Hythe CT21 176 B4
Lydden CT15 147 F8
Rochester ME1 9 C4
Wye TN25 123 E2
Cloudberry Cl ME16 74 D6
Cloudesley Cl ME1 9 B1
Clouston Cl CT18 163 B5
Clovelly TN28 202 E6
Clovelly Dr ME12 4 B8
Clovelly Rd CT5 43 D7
Clover Bank View ME5 32 B6
Clover Cl ME12 4 A5
Clover Ct ME10 37 B5
Clover Lay ME8 12 B2
Cloverlay Ind Pk ME8 12 C1
Clover Rise CT5 21 B1
Clover St 3 ME4 9 F4
Clover Terr 4 ME15 97 D8
Clowes Ct CT2 66 C4
Clubb's La TN29 199 D7
Cluny Rd ME13 62 F7
Clyde St
1 Canterbury CT1 67 A1
Sheerness ME12 1 E2
Clynton Way TN23 156 A7
Coach Dr TN26 138 A7
Coach House Mews The CT15 131 D5
Coach Rd
Charing Heath TN27 119 A6
Densole CT18 162 F8
Egerton ME17, TN27 118 E6
Coach Yd The ME16 74 B3
Coalpit La ME9 80 A6
Coast Dr
Greatstone-on-Sea TN28 202 E3
Lydd-on-Sea TN29 209 D8
St Mary's Bay TN29 194 F2
Coastguard Alley CT5 20 C1
Coastguard Cotts
Birchington CT7 26 D8
Conyer ME9 38 E6
Dover CT16 166 G8
Herne Bay CT6 21 F4
Coastguard Cotts continued
4 Hythe CT21 176 B1
Kingsdown CT14 134 D4
Leysdown-on-Sea ME12 19 E4
Lydd-on-Sea TN29 209 D5
Minster (Sheppey) ME12 5 C5
23 Ramsgate, East Cliff CT11 52 F7
Ramsgate, Pegwell CT11 52 A5
Sandwich CT13 95 A8
Coastguard Cotts The ME12 1 I1
Coastguard Hos ME12 6 C5
Coast Rd TN28 202 F7
Coats Ave ME12 3 A8
Cobay Cl CT21 176 D2
Cobb Ct CT9 7 I3
Cobblers Bridge Rd CT6 22 D3
Cobblestones ME7 32 F5
Cobbs Hill CT4 85 C2
Cobbs Mews 3 CT20 178 C4
Cobbs Pl CT9 7 I3
Cobbs Wood Ind Est TN23 138 F2
Cobb Wlk ME13 62 B8
Cobden Pl 17 CT1 67 A1
Cobden Rd
4 Chatham ME4 10 B2
Hythe CT21 176 B1
Cobdown Gr ME8 12 A2
Cobfield ME17 98 A1
Cobham Ave ME10 36 E1
Cobham Chase ME13 62 B8
Cobham Cl
Canterbury CT1 88 C6
Maidstone ME16 74 E4
Cobham Rise ME7 10 F5
Cobsden Cl TN29 195 A4
Cobsden Rd TN29 195 A4
Cobtree Cl ME5 32 C8
Cobtree Rd ME17 96 C3
Cobtree Wharf ME20 53 C2
Cobweb Cnr CT2 66 B4
Cockering Rd
Canterbury CT1, CT4 87 B4
Chartham CT4 86 E2
Cock La
Elham CT4 144 F4
Hamstreet TN26 183 A7
Cockreed La TN28 202 B7
Cock St ME17 97 D2
COCK STREET 97 D2
Codrington Rd CT11 52 D7
Cogans Terr CT1 87 E6
Coggan Ho 7 CT1 87 F7
Colburn Rd CT10 30 A2
Colchester Cl ME5 32 A7
Coldblow CT14 117 A1
Coldblow La
Hucking ME14 56 A2
Woodchurch TN26 169 D4
Coldbridge La TN27 118 B5
COLD HARBOUR
Lenham 102 F6
Sittingbourne 35 F7
Cold Harbour CT1 67 A2
Coldharbour La
Bridge CT4, CT3 111 D7
Forstal ME20 53 A1
Hucking ME14, ME9 56 B1
Old Romney TN29 200 C5
Peasmarsh TN31 196 E3
Sittingbourne ME10 14 F1
Sittingbourne ME10 15 A1
Wye TN25 124 B2
Cold Harbour La ME9 35 F6
Cold Harbour Rd ME13 103 A7
COLDRED 131 A3
Coldred Hill CT15 130 F1
Coldred Rd
Coldred CT15 131 B5
Maidstone ME15 97 F4
Shepherdswell CT15 130 E3
COLDRED STREET 131 A2
Coldswood Rd CT12 28 F2
Colegate Dr ME14 76 C4
Colegates Cl ME13 40 B2
Colegates Ct ME13 40 B2
Colegates Rd ME13 40 A2
Coleman Cres CT12 29 C1
Coleman Dr ME10 14 F1
Colemans Cl TN29 205 D7
Coleman's Stairs Rd CT7 27 A8
Coleman's Yd 3 CT11 52 E6
Cole Rd ME13 62 E7
Coleridge Gdns CT3 112 F6
Colesdane ME17 100 E8
Coleshall Cl ME15 97 F6
Coleshall Cotts ME9 14 D3
Cole Terr ME17 101 C4
Colette Cl CT10 8 G2
Coleville Cres TN28 206 E7
Colewood Rd CT5 21 E3
Colfe Way ME10 37 A8
Colin's Way CT21 177 A3
Collard Cl CT6 23 A4
Collard Ho CT1 88 C8
Collard Pl CT18 163 A5
Collard Rd TN24 157 A8
Collards Cl CT12 49 D7
Collards La CT4 144 E3
Collar Makers Gn CT3 71 F1
College Ave
Gillingham ME7 10 B4
Maidstone ME15 74 F3
College Cotts ME16 74 F3
College Ct
6 Ashford TN23 139 C2
College Ct continued
Canterbury CT1 67 B1
6 Maidstone ME15 75 A3
College Gdns CT8 27 E8
College Rd
Canterbury CT1 67 B1
Chatham ME4 10 A7
Deal CT14 117 D8
Maidstone ME15 74 F2
Margate CT9 8 A1
Ramsgate CT11 29 E1
Sittingbourne ME10 36 D3
College Row CT17 166 B7
College Sq 2 CT9 7 J2
College Square Sh Ctr CT9 7 J2
College Way CT3 91 A7
College Wlk
4 Maidstone ME15 75 A3
3 Margate CT9 7 J2
College Yd ME1 9 C6
Collett Cl TN25 142 D8
Collet Wlk ME8 33 D4
Collie Dr TN23 155 E5
Collingbourne TN23 155 E6
Collings Wlk ME8 33 D4
Collington Terr ME15 97 E4
Collingwood Cl
Broadstairs CT10 29 E4
Westgate on Sea CT8 27 D7
Collingwood Ct
Folkestone CT20 177 E5
7 Ramsgate CT11 52 D7
Collingwood Ind Est ME17 98 E2
Collingwood Rd
Kit's Coty ME20 53 C7
St Margaret's at Cliffe CT15 150 F8
Whitstable CT5 20 C1
Collingwood Rise CT20 177 E5
Collingwood Wlk ME10 36 B5
Collins Rd
Herne Bay CT6 22 C2
New Romney TN28 202 C5
Collison Pl TN30 179 D7
Collis St ME2 9 A8
Colman Ho 4 ME14 75 A4
Colombo Sq CT12 29 A1
Colonel's La ME13 64 A3
Colonel Stephens Rly Mus★ TN30 179 A8
Colonel Stephens Way TN30 167 B2
Colorado Cl CT16 149 B3
Colson Dr ME9 14 E3
Colton Cres CT16 149 B4
Coltsfoot Dr ME14 75 F4
Columbia Ave CT5 43 B7
Columbine Cl 4 CT5 43 C6
Columbus Ave CT12 27 D1
Com Coll Whitstable CT5 43 F8
Command Rd ME14 74 F8
Commercial Rd ME2 9 B7
Commissioners Ct ME4 9 F6
Commissioner's Rd ME2 9 C8
Commodore Ct CT21 176 C1
Commodore Rd ME14 75 C5
Common La CT17 148 E3
Common Rd ME5 31 B1
Common The ME1 9 C6
Common Way TN26 138 A7
Commonwealth Cl ME10 37 B3
Compass Cl ME1 9 C1
Compass Ctr ME4 10 A8
Compton Cl ME5 32 D2
Concord Ave ME5 31 E5
Condor Cl ME12 6 E3
Conduit Ho The★ CT1 67 B1
Conduit St ME13 62 D8
Coney Mews ME4 10 A1
Conference Wlk CT1 88 C8
Conifer Ct CT8 7 D1
Conifer Dr ME5 32 D1
Conifers The
Deal CT14 117 A2
Shepherdswell CT15 130 F2
Coniston Ave CT11 52 A7
Coniston Cl ME7 11 A6
Coniston Dr CT3 112 F6
Coniston Ho ME15 97 E7
Coniston Rd CT19 178 B7
Conker Cl TN23 156 C3
Connaught Cl ME15 97 F4
Connaught Gdns 9 CT9 7 J1
Connaught Mews 2 ME4 10 C2
Connaught Pk★ CT16 149 D1
Connaught Rd
Chatham ME4 10 C2
Dover CT16 149 D1
Folkestone CT20 178 D5
Gillingham ME7 10 D5
Margate CT9 7 J1
Sittingbourne ME10 36 E3
Conqueror Dr ME7 11 A6
Conquest Ind Est ME2 9 A5
Conrad Ave CT1 67 C3
Conrad Cl ME8 33 D4
Consort Cl ME14 75 B5
Constable Rd CT7 27 A8
Constable's Rd CT16 166 E8
Constancia Ct CT20 178 C5
Constantine Rd TN23 155 F5
Constitution Hill 8 ME5 10 B3
Constitution Rd ME5 10 B2
Consul Cl CT6 22 B4

Continental App CT9 . . . . 28 F6
Convent Cl CT15 . . . . 151 B6
Conventina Ho 3 CT11 . . . 52 D7
Convent Rd CT10 . . . . 8 G1
Convent Wlk CT11 . . . . 52 B5
Conway Cl
 Birchington CT7 . . . . 26 E7
 Hythe CT21 . . . . 176 B4
Conway Hall 16 ME7 . . . . 10 A6
Conway Mews ME7 . . . . 10 A6
Conway Rd ME16 . . . . 74 C6
CONYER 38 F5
Conyer Rd ME9 . . . . 38 F4
Conyers Wlk ME8 . . . . 33 D4
Conyngham Cl CT12 . . . . 29 B2
Conyngham La CT4 . . . . 89 A2
Conyngham Rd
 Herne Bay CT6 . . . . 23 D5
 Minster (Thanet) CT12 . . . . . 50 C5
Cooden Cl ME8 . . . . 12 A2
Cook Cl ME5 . . . . 32 C6
Cookham Hill ME1 . . . . 9 A2
Cookham Wood Rd ME1 . . 31 B8
Cooks La ME10 . . . . 36 F6
Cook's Lea CT13 . . . . 93 B2
Cooks Wharf ME1 . . . . 9 E4
Cooling Cl ME14 . . . . 75 C6
COOLINGE 177 F4
Coolinge La CT20 . . . . 177 F4
Coolinge Rd CT20 . . . . 178 D5
COOMBE 92 F8
Coombe Cl
 Chatham ME5 . . . . 32 B3
 Dover CT17 . . . . 149 A1
Coombe Ct CT17 . . . . 149 A1
Coombe Dr
 Shepherdswell CT15 . . . . . . 130 E5
 Sittingbourne ME10 . . . . 37 C4
Coombe Gr TN26 . . . . 120 F2
Coombe La
 Ash CT13, CT3 . . . . 92 E8
 Tenterden TN30 . . . . 179 A1
Coombe Lands TN30 . . . . . 188 D4
Coombe Rd
 Crabble CT17 . . . . 148 F1
 Dover CT15, CT17 . . . . 165 E8
 Folkestone CT19 . . . . 177 F6
 Maidstone ME15 . . . . 74 F2
Coombe Valley Rd CT17 . 149 A1
Coombe Way CT18 . . . . 163 C4
Coombe Wlk CT5 . . . . 43 A2
Coombe Wood La CT18 . 163 C4
Cooper Rd ME5 . . . . 32 B3
Cooper's Hill CT6 . . . . 22 F5
Coopers La CT1 . . . . 87 E7
Cooper's La TN25 . . . . 158 F2
COOPER STREET 72 B4
Cooper Street Drove CT3 . 72 B4
Cooting La CT3 . . . . 112 D8
Cooting Rd CT3 . . . . 112 E4
Copenhagen Rd ME7 . . . . . . 10 C4
Copinger Cl CT2 . . . . 67 A4
Copland ME12 . . . . 4 C6
Copperfield ME12 . . . . 5 F5
Copperfield Cl
 Ashford TN24 . . . . 139 C6
 Kingswood ME17 . . . . 99 D2
Copperfield Ct CT10 . . . . 30 B5
Copperfield Dr ME17 . . . . . . 98 E4
Copperfield Ho 6 ME4 . . . . . 9 F4
Copperfield Rd ME1 . . . . 9 C2
Copperfields TN29 . . . . 205 B6
Copperfields The ME1 . . . . . . 9 B4
Coppergate
 Canterbury CT2 . . . . 66 F2
 Gillingham ME7 . . . . 32 F5
Copperhouse La ME7 . . . . . . 11 B6
Copperhurst Dr ME7 . . . . . . 33 B3
Copperpenny Dr ME7 . . . . . . 33 B3
Copper Tree Ct ME15 . . . . . . 97 A5
Copper Tree Wlk ME5 . . . . . 32 C1
Copperwood TN24 . . . . 139 C4
Coppice Ct ME7 . . . . 33 B4
Coppice Rd ME5 . . . . 32 C2
Coppice The
 Hythe CT21 . . . . 176 B4
 Sturry CT2 . . . . 67 F6
Coppice View ME14 . . . . 75 E6
COPPINS' CORNER 120 A6
Coppins La ME9 . . . . 36 B2
Coppin St CT14 . . . . 117 D6
Coppock Cl 1 CT12 . . . . 29 B1
Copse Cl ME1 . . . . 9 E1
Copse The TN23 . . . . 138 D3
Copsewood Way ME15 . . . 76 A3
COP STREET 71 E4
Cop Street Rd CT3 . . . . 71 D3
Copt Cl CT2 . . . . 67 F7
Copthall Gdns 13 CT20 . . 178 D5
Coral Pk ME14 . . . . 75 B5
Coral Rd ME12 . . . . 4 B5
Corben Cl ME16 . . . . 74 B6
Cordelia Cres ME1 . . . . 9 A2
Cordingham Rd CT5 . . . . 43 A6
Cordova Ct CT20 . . . . 178 B4
Corianda Dr 14 ME16 . . . . . 74 A3
Corkwell St ME4 . . . . 9 E3
Cormorant Rd ME9 . . . . 14 E3
Cormorant Way CT6 . . . . 23 F4
Cornbrook Rd CT21 . . . . . . 187 D8
Cornelis Dr CT12 . . . . 50 B5
Corner Cotts TN26 . . . . 182 A6
Corner Field TN23 . . . . 156 B5
Cornes Cl TN24 . . . . 140 A1
Cornflower Cl ME14 . . . . 75 E4

Cornford Rd CT7 . . . . 27 A7
Cornforth Dr ME9 . . . . 58 E6
Corniche The CT20 . . . . 177 C3
Cornwall Ave CT11 . . . . 52 F8
Cornwall Cl ME15 . . . . 97 E7
Cornwall Gdns
 Canterbury CT1 . . . . 88 D7
 Margate CT9 . . . . 8 B3
Cornwall Ho
 Deal CT14 . . . . 117 A5
 5 Dover CT17 . . . . 166 D7
Cornwallis Ave
 Aylesham CT3 . . . . 112 F6
 Chatham ME4 . . . . 9 E1
 Folkestone CT19 . . . . 178 B6
 Gillingham ME8 . . . . 11 A4
 Herne Bay CT6 . . . . 23 C3
Cornwallis Circ CT5 . . . . . . 20 D1
Cornwallis Cl
 Ashford TN24 . . . . 157 B7
 Folkestone CT19 . . . . 178 B6
Cornwallis Cotts ME17 . . . 96 E2
Cornwallis Gdns CT10 . . . . 30 A6
Cornwallis Rd ME8 . . . . 74 D4
Cornwallis Rdbt ME8 . . . . . 11 A4
Cornwallis Sch ME15 . . . . . 96 F2
Cornwall Rd
 Deal CT14 . . . . 117 C3
 Gillingham ME7 . . . . 10 E1
 Herne Bay CT6 . . . . 22 B2
 Rochester ME1 . . . . 9 C3
Coronation Cl CT10 . . . . 29 E7
Coronation Cotts CT19 . . 177 D6
Coronation Cres
 Margate CT9 . . . . 28 B8
 Queenborough ME11 . . . . 2 F1
Coronation Dr
 Ashford TN23 . . . . 138 C1
 Leysdown-on-Sea ME12 . . . . 6 D2
Coronation Flats 5 ME4 . . 9 F3
Coronation Rd
 Chatham ME5 . . . . 10 C2
 Ramsgate CT11 . . . . 52 D6
 Sheerness ME12 . . . . 1 E1
Coronation Sq TN29 . . . . . 205 D6
Corone Cl CT19 . . . . 178 A7
Corporation Rd ME7 . . . . . . 10 D7
Corporation St ME1 . . . . 9 C6
Corral Cl ME5 . . . . 10 D2
Corrall Almshouses 5
 ME15 . . . . 75 A3
Corrance Gn ME15 . . . . 97 A8
Corsican Wlk CT6 . . . . 23 C3
Cortanore ME10 . . . . 36 E2
Cortland Cl ME10 . . . . 36 E6
Cortland Mews ME10 . . . . . 36 E6
Corunna Cl CT21 . . . . 176 A2
Corunna Pl CT15 . . . . 149 E3
Corylus Dr CT5 . . . . 43 A7
Cory's Rd ME1 . . . . 9 D6
Cossack St ME1 . . . . 9 D3
Cossington Rd
 Canterbury CT1 . . . . 88 A7
 Chatham ME5 . . . . 32 B1
Cosway Cotts TN25 . . . . . . 172 C1
Cotswold Cl TN24 . . . . 139 B4
Cotswold Gdns ME15 . . . . . 76 A2
Cottage Ind Est ME20 . . . . 53 B2
Cottage Rd
 Chatham ME4 . . . . 9 F6
 Ramsgate CT11 . . . . 52 E6
Cottage Row CT13 . . . . 72 F1
Cottall Ave ME4 . . . . 9 F2
Cottington Rd CT12 . . . . 51 B5
Cotton Hill Ho TN26 . . . . . 183 A7
Cotton Hill Wlk TN26 . . . . 183 A7
Cotton Rd CT1 . . . . 87 E7
Coulman St ME7 . . . . 10 D5
Coulson Gr CT14 . . . . 116 A5
Coulter Rd
 Ashford TN23 . . . . 155 D5
 Herne Bay CT6 . . . . 22 B2
Coulters Cl ME14 . . . . 75 D5
Coultrip Cl ME12 . . . . 5 B5
Council Cotts ME15 . . . . 96 A4
Countess Mountbatten Ct
 CT8 . . . . 27 E8
Country's Field TN29 . . . . . 195 C8
Country Ways ME17 . . . . . . 102 D3
County Rd ME14 . . . . 75 A5
County Sq 8 TN23 . . . . 139 B2
County Square Sh Ctr 16
 TN25 . . . . 139 B2
COURT-AT-STREET 174 A4
Court Cotts
 St Nicholas at Wade CT7 . . . 25 E2
 Wingham CT3 . . . . 91 A7
Court Dr ME16 . . . . 74 D4
Courtenay Ho ME13 . . . . . . 64 C3
Courtenay Rd
 Boughton Street CT2,
  ME13 . . . . 64 C5
 Deal CT14 . . . . 117 C8
 Maidstone ME15 . . . . 74 F2
Courteney Rd ME8 . . . . 33 B8
Courten Rd CT12 . . . . 64 F6
Courtfield Ave ME5 . . . . 32 B3
Court Flats CT3 . . . . 91 A7
Court Hall ME11 . . . . 2 F4
Court Hill CT3 . . . . 68 E2
Court Hill Ho CT16 . . . . 148 E4
Court La
 Detling ME14 . . . . 55 C5
 Preston CT3 . . . . 70 B6
Courtland Ave CT16 . . . . . . 149 A6
Courtland Dr CT16 . . . . 148 E4
Courtlands
 Deal CT14 . . . . 134 D6

Courtlands continued
 Herne Bay CT6 . . . . 23 B3
Courtlands Cl CT12 . . . . 51 E5
Courtlands Way CT8 . . . . 7 D1
Court Lodge CT14 . . . . 117 B6
Court Lodge Cotts ME15 . . 96 A7
Court Lodge Rd
 Appledore TN26 . . . . 190 C7
 Gillingham ME7 . . . . 10 F6
Court Mdw ME8 . . . . 11 B2
Court Mdws CT3 . . . . 89 F8
Court Mount CT7 . . . . 27 A6
Court Pl 5 CT20 . . . . 178 C4
Court Rd
 Burham ME1 . . . . 53 A8
 Deal CT14 . . . . 117 B1
 Sittingbourne ME10 . . . . 36 F7
 St Nicholas at Wade CT7 . . . 25 E2
Court St CT13 . . . . 62 D7
Courts The CT9 . . . . 7 E1
Court Tree Dr ME12 . . . . 5 B5
Court Wurtin TN23 . . . . 156 A7
Courtyard The TN24 . . . . . . 156 F6
Courtyard The CT3 . . . . 92 A6
Coventon La CT14 . . . . 94 A5
Coventry Gdns CT6 . . . . 23 E5
Coverdale Ave ME5 . . . . 97 D6
Coverdale Cl ME5 . . . . 32 B7
Covert TN23 . . . . 138 E1
Covert Rd CT3 . . . . 112 E4
Covert The ME5 . . . . 32 B1
Covet La CT4 . . . . 111 C2
Cowbeck Cl ME8 . . . . 33 D6
Cowden Rd ME14 . . . . 75 C5
Cowdray Rd CT14 . . . . 117 A3
Cowdray Sq CT14 . . . . 117 A3
Cowdrey Cl
 Ashford TN24 . . . . 157 A7
 Maidstone ME14 . . . . 74 B2
 Rochester ME1 . . . . 9 B2
Cowdrey Pl CT14 . . . . 88 B6
Cowgate Hill CT17 . . . . 166 D7
Cowgate La CT18 . . . . 163 C5
Cow La
 Canterbury CT1 . . . . 87 D7
 Dover CT17 . . . . 166 A7
Cowley Rise CT9 . . . . 29 C8
Cowper Cl CT5 . . . . 21 D3
Cowper Rd
 Crabble CT17 . . . . 148 E3
 Deal CT14 . . . . 117 C5
 Gillingham ME7 . . . . 10 D3
 Margate CT9 . . . . 7 J1
 Sittingbourne ME10 . . . . 37 B4
Cowstead Cl ME9 . . . . 34 D3
Cowstead Rd ME9 . . . . 34 D2
Cox Dr CT18 . . . . 163 A5
Coxes Ave CT12 . . . . 29 B3
Coxes La CT12 . . . . 29 B3
Coxett Hill ME13 . . . . 61 D5
Cox Gdns ME8 . . . . 11 A2
COXHEATH 96 C2
Coxheath Prim Sch ME17 . 96 C3
Coxhill CT15 . . . . 130 C3
Coxhill Cres CT17 . . . . 148 D3
Coxhill Gdns CT17 . . . . 148 D3
Coxland Cotts TN26 . . . . . . 181 B1
Cox St ME14 . . . . 55 E6
Cozenton Cl ME8 . . . . 11 E1
CRABBLE 148 F2
Crabble Ave CT17 . . . . 149 A2
Crabble Corn Mill ★
 CT17 . . . . 148 F3
Crabble Hill CT16, CT17 . . 149 A2
Crabble La CT17 . . . . 148 E2
Crabble Mdws CT17 . . . . . . 149 A2
Crabble Rd CT17 . . . . 149 A3
Crabtree La ME17 . . . . 119 B8
Crabtree Rd ME8 . . . . 33 D8
Crabtree Rdbt ME14 . . . . . . 53 E2
Craddock Dr 8 CT1 . . . . 67 B1
Craddock Ho CT1 . . . . 67 B1
Craddock Rd CT1 . . . . 67 B1
Craddock Way ME8 . . . . 33 D5
Cradle Bridge Dr TN24 . . 139 F2
Cradles Rd ME9 . . . . 34 C2
Crafford St CT16 . . . . 149 D1
Cragie Wlk ME8 . . . . 33 E4
Craig Ho ME1 . . . . 9 E1
Craighton Ho 2 CT16 . . . . 166 E7
Crampton Ct CT10 . . . . 30 A4
Crampton Tower Mus ★ 7
 CT10 . . . . 30 A4
Cranborne Ave ME15 . . . . . 75 C1
Cranborne Wlk CT2 . . . . 66 E3
Cranbourne Ave ME15 . . . . 97 B8
Cranbourne Cl CT11 . . . . . . 52 F8
Cranbrook Cl
 Gillingham ME8 . . . . 11 C3
 Maidstone ME15 . . . . 97 F7
 Margate CT9 . . . . 8 E1
Cranbrook Rd ME10 . . . . . . 36 D1
Cranbrooks TN25 . . . . 157 D4
Cranford Cl ME8 . . . . 11 D1
Cranleigh Cl CT5 . . . . 43 E8
Cranleigh Dr CT16 . . . . 149 B7
Cranleigh Gdns
 Chatham ME4 . . . . 9 D3
 Maidstone ME16 . . . . 74 C7
 Whitstable CT5 . . . . 43 E8
Cranmer Cl CT4 . . . . 89 B4
Cranmer Ct ME15 . . . . 97 B8
Cranmere Ct ME2 . . . . 9 C8
Cranmer Ho 6 CT2 . . . . 66 E1
Cranswick Cotts CT14 . . . 133 C8
Craufurd Gn CT20 . . . . 177 D5

Craven Cl CT9 . . . . 28 C8
Crawford Gdns CT9 . . . . 8 B2
Crawford Rd CT10 . . . . 29 F5
Crayford Cl ME14 . . . . 75 C6
Craythorne TN30 . . . . 179 B8
Craythorne Cl
 Hythe CT21 . . . . 177 B4
 New Romney TN28 . . . . 202 B8
Craythorne Ho TN30 . . . . . 179 B8
Craythorne La TN30 . . . . . . 179 B8
Creighton Flats 2 CT13 . . 72 F1
Creine Mill Lane N CT1 . . 87 E8
Cremer Cl CT4 . . . . 86 C2
Cremer Pl ME13 . . . . 62 A8
Cremers Rd ME10 . . . . 37 B5
Crescent Ho
 Margate CT9 . . . . 8 A2
 Ramsgate CT12 . . . . 52 C7
 Rochester ME2 . . . . 9 C7
Crescent Rd
 Birchington CT7 . . . . 27 A7
 Broadstairs CT10 . . . . 30 C8
 Faversham ME13 . . . . 62 D7
 Margate CT9 . . . . 7 H2
 Ramsgate CT11 . . . . 52 D7
Crescent St 1 ME10 . . . . . . 36 F4
Crescent The
 Aylesham CT15 . . . . 113 A3
 Boughton Street ME13 . . . . 64 A3
 Canterbury CT2 . . . . 66 F4
 Chartham CT4 . . . . 86 D1
 Chatham CT4 . . . . 86 D1
 Eythorne CT15 . . . . 131 C7
 Folkestone CT20 . . . . 177 E3
 Halfway Houses ME12 . . . . . . 3 E6
 Lower Halstow ME9 . . . . 13 C3
 Maidstone ME14 . . . . 74 F8
 Sandwich CT13 . . . . 93 E6
 Sheerness ME12 . . . . 1 D2
 Sheerness ME12 . . . . 1 H1
 Sittingbourne ME10 . . . . 15 A1
 St Margaret's at Cliffe
  CT15 . . . . 151 A5
 Teynham ME9 . . . . 38 D3
Crescent Way ME5 . . . . 31 D5
Cressey Ct 7 ME4 . . . . 9 E4
Cressfield TN23 . . . . 138 F1
Cress Way ME13 . . . . 62 A7
Cresta Cl CT6 . . . . 21 F4
Crest Rd ME8 . . . . 9 C1
Crestway ME5 . . . . 32 B8
Crete Road E CT18, CT19 . 163 D1
Crete Road W CT18 . . . . . . 163 B1
Creteway Cl CT19 . . . . 178 E8
Creve Coeur Cl ME14 . . . . . 76 A5
Crevequer Chambers 1
 ME8 . . . . 11 F1
Cricketers Cl
 Harrietsham ME17 . . . . 100 C6
 Hawkinge CT18 . . . . 163 B6
 Sittingbourne ME10 . . . . 36 F8
Crimond Ave TN29 . . . . 187 A4
Criol Rd TN26 . . . . 155 A2
Cripple Hill TN26 . . . . 152 D1
Cripple St ME15 . . . . 97 A7
Cripps Cl CT5 . . . . 112 E5
Cripps' La CT15 . . . . 150 F6
Crisfield Ct TN30 . . . . 167 B2
Crismill La ME14 . . . . 76 F4
Crispe Cl ME8 . . . . 33 D4
Crispe Park Cl CT7 . . . . 27 B7
Crispe Rd CT7 . . . . 27 A3
Crispin Cl ME13 . . . . 62 D8
Crispin Ct ME17 . . . . 96 C3
Crittenden Bglws ME15 . . . 96 A4
Crittenden Cotts ME15 . . . 96 A4
Crocken Hill Rd TN27 . . . . 118 C2
Crockham La ME13 . . . . 64 B6
Crockham Rd ME13 . . . . 64 C6
Crockshard Hill CT3 . . . . . . 91 B4
Crockshard La CT3 . . . . 91 B4
Crocus Dr ME9/ME10 . . . . . 36 F2
Croft Cl ME5 . . . . 32 C1
Crofters Cl CT21 . . . . 187 E8
Crofters The ME8 . . . . 33 F7
Croft Gdns ME17 . . . . 101 D4
Croft La CT20 . . . . 177 F5
Crofton Cl TN24 . . . . 139 C6
Crofton Rd CT8 . . . . 27 E7
Croft Rd TN24 . . . . 139 D2
Croft's Pl 8 CT10 . . . . 30 B4
Croft The TN30 . . . . 179 B7
Croftwood TN23 . . . . 155 D6
Croidene Ct ME12 . . . . 4 A6
Crombie Cl CT18 . . . . 163 B5
Cromer Rd
 Rochester ME2 . . . . 9 E6
 Sittingbourne ME9, ME10 . . 58 F8
Crompton Gdns ME15 . . . . . 75 B3
Cromwell Park Pl CT20 . . 177 D4
Cromwell Rd
 Canterbury CT1 . . . . 88 A4
 Maidstone ME15 . . . . 74 B5
 West Minst ME11 . . . . 2 F7
 Whitstable CT5 . . . . 20 E1
Cromwell Terr ME4 . . . . 10 A3
Crooked South Rd CT14 . 133 C2
Crookenden Pl CT4 . . . . 128 F8
Crook's Court La CT15 . . . 164 F4
Croombridge Dr ME7 . . . . . 10 F6
Crosier Cl ME9 . . . . 12 E3
Crosley Rd ME7 . . . . 10 D3
Cross Dr ME17 . . . . 99 B1
Cross Keys ME14 . . . . 76 C4
Cross La
 7 Faversham ME13 . . . . 62 D7
 Sittingbourne ME10 . . . . 36 E6
 Throwley Forstal ME13 . . . 104 C7

Crossley Ave CT6 . . . . 21 F4
Cross Rd
 Birchington CT7 . . . . 27 B8
 Deal CT14 . . . . 117 A2
Cross St
 2 Canterbury CT2 . . . . 66 E1
 Chatham ME4 . . . . 10 A4
 Gillingham ME7 . . . . 10 C6
 Herne Bay CT6 . . . . 22 D3
 Maidstone ME14 . . . . 75 A6
 Rochester ME2 . . . . 9 B8
Cross Stile TN23 . . . . 155 F8
Cross The CT13 . . . . 93 B2
Crossway ME5 . . . . 31 E6
Cross Way ME1 . . . . 9 C3
Crossways
 Canterbury CT2 . . . . 66 F4
 Chart Sutton ME17 . . . . 98 B1
 Sittingbourne ME10 . . . . 36 F1
Crossways Ave CT9 . . . . 29 A5
Crossways Cl TN29 . . . . . . 186 E2
Crouch Cotts ME13 . . . . 84 E8
Crouch Hill Ct ME9 . . . . 13 C3
Crouch La ME13 . . . . 84 E8
Crowbridge Link TN24 . . 156 F7
Crowbridge Rd TN24 . . . . 156 F6
Crow Cnr
 Brabourne TN25 . . . . 141 E1
 Rochester ME1 . . . . 9 C5
Crow Hill CT10 . . . . 30 B5
Crow Hill Rd CT9 . . . . 28 B8
Crow La ME1 . . . . 9 C5
Crown Ct CT14 . . . . 117 D6
Crownfield Rd TN23 . . . . . 155 F8
Crownfields ME14 . . . . 75 F4
Crown Gdns CT2 . . . . 66 E1
Crown Hill Rd CT6 . . . . 22 C4
Crown Ho ME1 . . . . 9 B4
Crown La CT4 . . . . 126 E3
Crown Quay La 5 ME10 . . 37 A4
Crown Rd ME10 . . . . 36 E6
Crown St ME7 . . . . 10 D6
Crows Camp Rd CT4 . . . . . 111 A5
Croydon Cl ME5 . . . . 32 C4
Cruise Liner Terminals
 CT17 . . . . 166 E5
CRUNDALE 124 D7
Crundale 2 ME4 . . . . 75 A5
Crundale Cl TN23 . . . . 155 F6
Crundale Rd ME8 . . . . 11 C3
Crundale Way CT9 . . . . 8 E1
Crusader Cl ME8 . . . . 33 B8
Cryalls Bsns Est ME10 . . . 36 C4
Cryalls La ME10, ME9 . . . . 36 C3
Cryol Rd TN23 . . . . 156 A7
Crystal Bsns Ctr CT13 . . . 73 B2
**Ctr for European Agri-
 Environmental Studies**
 TN25 . . . . 124 A1
Cubitt Ho CT19 . . . . 178 D6
Cuckolds Cnr
 Chillenden CT3 . . . . 114 A7
 Snargate TN29 . . . . 191 E7
Cuckold's Cnr TN26 . . . . . 168 B7
Cuckoo La
 Ashford, Singleton TN23 . . 155 E7
 Ashford TN23 . . . . 155 D6
 Postling CT21 . . . . 160 F2
Cuckoowood Ave ME14 . . . 53 F1
Cudham Cl ME14 . . . . 75 C6
Cudham Gdns CT9 . . . . 8 E2
Cudworth Rd TN24 . . . . 156 E7
Cullens Hill CT4 . . . . 144 F4
Cullet Dr ME11 . . . . 3 A3
Culling's Hill CT4 . . . . 144 F4
CULMERS 41 E1
Culmers Terr ME13 . . . . 63 E8
Culpeper Cl
 Hollingbourne ME17 . . . . . . 77 E2
 Rochester ME2 . . . . 9 E6
Culpepper Cl CT2 . . . . 67 A4
Culpepper Rd
 Coxheath ME17 . . . . 96 B3
 Gillingham ME8 . . . . 33 D4
Culter Field TN23 . . . . 155 E8
Culver's La TN29 . . . . 205 D5
Cumberland Ave
 Broadstairs CT10 . . . . 30 A5
 Canterbury CT1 . . . . 88 D7
 Maidstone ME15 . . . . 97 D8
Cumberland Dr ME9 . . . . . . 13 C3
Cumberland Rd
 Chatham ME4, ME7 . . . . 10 B7
 Gillingham ME7 . . . . 10 C7
 Margate CT9 . . . . 8 B3
 1 Ramsgate CT11 . . . . 52 D6
Cundishall Cl CT5 . . . . 43 C8
Cunningham Cres
 Birchington CT7 . . . . 26 E7
 Chatham ME5 . . . . 32 A8
Cunningham Ho ME1 . . . . 9 B4
Curlew Ave ME9 . . . . 13 B3
Curlew Cl CT6 . . . . 23 C2
Curlew Pl CT18 . . . . 163 A3
Curlinge Ct CT11 . . . . 52 A6
Curteis Rd TN30 . . . . 167 B1
Curtis La CT4 . . . . 126 D2
Curtis Rd TN24 . . . . 156 E7
Curtis Way
 1 Faversham ME13 . . . . 62 C7
 Rochester ME1 . . . . 31 D7
Curtis Wood Park Rd CT6 . 46 A7
Curtis Wood Pk Rd CT6 . . 45 F7
Curtis Wood Rd CT6 . . . . . . 45 F7
Curzon Cl CT14 . . . . 117 C3
Curzon Ho 5 CT11 . . . . 52 D6
Curzon Rd
 Chatham ME4 . . . . 9 F3

Curzon Rd *continued*
Dover CT17 166 B8
Maidstone ME14 75 A6
Cushings Wlk 13 CT5 20 D2
Cushman Rd CT1 87 E7
Cutbush Almshouses
3 Maidstone ME14 75 A4
1 Maidstone ME15 75 A3
Cutbush Cl ME17 100 D6
Cutbush & Corrall Ct 1
ME14 75 B4
Cutbush Ho 2 ME15 75 A3
Cuthbert Rd CT8 27 E8
Cut The 17 ME4/ME7 10 A6
Cuttings The CT12 52 C8
Cuxton Cl 11 ME15 97 F5
Cuxton Rd
Maidstone ME15 97 F5
Rochester ME2 9 A7
Cygnet Rd ME5 32 C2
Cygnet Way TN23 138 F1
Cylinder Rd CT21 176 B4
Cypress Ave TN23 138 E2
Cypress Cl CT5 43 C7
Cypress Ct ME7 10 F6
Cypress Gr CT15 114 B2
Cyprus Ct ME13 62 E7
Cyprus Rd ME13 62 E7

D

D2 Trad Est ME10 37 B6
Daglish Cl TN28 202 B6
Dagmar Rd ME4 10 B2
Daigor La CT12 28 D1
Daimler Ave CT6 22 B3
Dajen Bsns Pk ME4 10 C1
Dalby Rd CT9 8 A3
Dalby Sq CT9 8 A3
Daleacres Cvn Pk CT21 186 E7
Dale Ct ME5 32 A2
Dale Rd ME1 9 C3
Dale St ME4 9 E2
Dale Wlk TN24 139 C7
Dalewood ME10 37 A2
Dallas-Brett Cres CT19 178 E8
Dallinger Rd 1 CT7 26 F8
Dalmatia Ct CT17 149 A1
Dalmeny Ave CT9 8 D1
Dalmeny Terr CT21 176 A1
Dalton Ct 7 CT11 52 E7
Dalton St ME7 10 C6
Dame Janet Com Jun Sch
CT12 29 B2
Dame Janet Inf Sch CT12 29 B2
Damerham Cl CT2 66 E3
Damiem Cl ME4 10 A2
DANAWAY 35 C3
Danaway Cotts ME9 35 C3
Dan Dr ME13 62 A8
Dane Cl
Chatham ME5 32 C2
Hartlip ME9 34 D6
Danecourt Com Sch ME8 11 A2
Dane Court Gdns CT10 29 D5
Dane Court Gram Sch
CT10 29 E4
Dane Court Rd CT10 29 C6
Dane Cres CT11 52 E8
Dane Ct
Coxheath ME17 96 C2
Tilmanstone CT14 114 F4
Danedale Ave ME12 4 F6
Dane End Rd CT8 27 D8
Danefield Ct ME14 76 B4
Dane Gdns CT9 29 B8
Dane Hill CT9 7 J3
Dane Hill Gr CT9 7 J2
Dane Hill Row CT9 7 J2
Dane Ho CT14 117 D8
Danehurst CT8 7 C1
Dane John Ct 3 CT1 87 F7
Dane John Gdns★ CT16 87 F7
Dane John Mews 1 CT1 87 F7
Dane La ME9 34 D6
Danemore TN30 179 B8
Dane Mount CT9 29 C8
Dane Park Rd
Margate CT9 7 J2
Ramsgate CT11 52 E8
Dane Park Villas CT9 8 A2
Dane Pk ME15 96 C6
Dane Rd
Birchington CT7 26 D7
Margate CT9 8 A2
Ramsgate CT11 52 E8
Dane Rise CT9 29 C8
Danes Ct CT16 149 D2
Danes Dr ME12 6 D2
Danes Hill ME7 11 A6
Danes Mead ME10 14 F1
Danesmead Terr CT9 7 J2
DANE STREET 106 F6
Dane Valley Rd CT10, CT9 29 C8
Daniel Ho 5 ME16 74 E5
Daniels Ct CT5 20 C1
DANIEL'S WATER 154 D7
Danley Mid Sch ME12 3 E7
Danley Rd ME12 3 E7
Danson Way ME8 11 D2
Danton La CT18 162 C1
Darby Pl CT20 178 D5
Darby Rd CT20 178 D5
Darcy Sq TN28 202 E5
Darenth Cl CT6 23 B3
Darenth Rise ME5 32 B3
DARGATE 64 E7
Dargate Cl ME16 74 D7
Dargate Rd
Dargate CT2, ME13 64 F7
Yorkletts CT5 43 A3
Dargets Rd ME5 32 A3
Dark Hill ME13 62 C8
DARLAND 32 E8
Darland Ave ME7 10 E1
Darlinghurst Rd CT19 177 E7
Darlington Dr ME12 4 A6
Darlington St CT20 178 D5
Darnley Cl
Broadstairs CT10 29 F3
Folkestone CT20 177 F4
Darnley Rd ME2 9 A6
Darracott Cl CT14 117 B5
Darrell Cl CT6 22 C3
Darren Gdns CT10 29 F2
Darwin Coll CT2 66 E5
Darwin Ct ME1 9 D5
Darwin Rd
Birchington CT7 26 F8
Canterbury CT2 66 E5
Daryngton Ave CT7 26 C7
Davenport Ave ME7 10 E7
Davey Ct ME1 9 C5
David Ave CT9 8 D2
Davids Cl CT10 30 B3
Davidson Rd CT2 66 D1
Davie Cl ME12 3 B8
Davie Ct ME12 3 B8
DAVINGTON 62 A8
Davington Hill ME13 62 C8
Davington Prim Sch
ME13 62 C8
Davis Ave CT14 117 A4
Dawbourne TN30 167 B3
Dawes Rd CT2, ME13 64 C4
Dawes St ME7 10 C5
Dawn Rise ME12 5 F6
Dawson Ct 7 ME7 10 A6
Dawson Rd CT19 178 D6
Dawson's Row ME13 62 A6
Day Ho 2 ME14 75 B4
Daytona Way CT6 22 A4
Dayton Rd ME13 83 C3
Deacon Ind Est ME20 53 A2
Deacon Trad Ctr ME2 9 A6
DEAL 117 E6
Deal Castle★ CT14 117 D5
Deal Castle Rd CT14 117 D5
Deal Ent Ctr CT14 117 C7
Deal Ho ME15 97 E8
Deal Maritime & Local
History Mus★ 12 CT14 117 D6
Deal Parochial CE Prim Sch
CT14 117 C3
Deal Rd
Northbourne CT14 116 A4
Sandwich CT13, CT14 93 F5
Deal Sta CT14 117 C6
Dean Croft CT6 23 B2
Dean Ct 13 CT1 67 A1
Deane Cl CT5 43 E7
Deane Ct 8 ME7 10 C6
Dean Hill CT4, TN25 126 B2
Dean Mead CT19 178 B7
Dean Rd ME10 36 E6
DEANS BOTTOM 57 C5
DEANS HILL 57 D6
Deans Hill Rd ME9 57 D5
Deans Mill Ct CT1 66 F1
Dean St ME15 96 C6
DEAN STREET 96 D7
Deansway Ave CT2 67 F7
Dean's Wlk TN23 155 F7
Deanwood Cl ME8 33 D6
Deanwood Dr ME8 33 E4
Deanwood Prim Education
Tech Sch ME8 33 D3
Deanwood Rd CT17 148 E2
Deborah Cl CT5 43 F7
De Burgh Hill CT17 149 C1
De Burgh St 2 CT17 166 C8
Deedes Cl CT21 176 C3
Deerhurst Gdns ME16 74 D4
Deerson La CT3 70 A4
Deerton St ME9 39 A2
DEERTON STREET 39 A2
Defiant Cl ME5 32 B6
Defoe Cl ME5 32 B6
Deham Ho ME10 36 D5
De Havilland Cl CT18 163 B4
De Havillands CT4 89 E3
Delacourt Cl CT12 51 D5
Delamark Rd ME12 1 D2
Delane Rd CT14 117 A5
De l'Angle Ho CT4 86 D3
De l'Angle Row CT4 86 D3
Delaware Cl CT2 67 F6
Delce Jun & Inf Schs ME1 9 D2
Delce Rd ME1 9 D4
Delfside CT13 94 A8
Delf St CT13 72 F1
Delmaney Cl CT10 30 B5
Delmar Cl CT5 21 D3
De Mere Cl ME8 33 D6
Demozay Cl CT18 163 A4
Denbigh Ave ME8 11 D1
Denbigh Cl ME10 36 E7
Denbigh Rd CT12 29 A1
Dence Cl CT6 23 B5
Dence Pk CT6 23 B4
Dencorra Way TN23 139 A1
Dene Farm Barns CT3 91 A4
Dene Farm La CT3 91 A4
Dene The
Bethersden TN26 153 D5
Dene The *continued*
Canterbury CT1 88 B5
Hythe CT21 176 C2
Dene Wlk CT9 28 F7
Dengemarsh Rd TN29 208 A7
Denham Cl TN29 187 B4
Denham Rd ME9 35 B7
Denmark Rd CT11 52 E8
Denmark St CT19 178 E6
Denne Cl CT2 67 F7
Denne Manor La CT4 106 C8
Dennes La TN29 205 C8
Dennes Mill Cl TN25 123 D2
Denness Rd TN23 156 B7
Denning Cl ME16 74 B4
Dennis Way CT19 177 E7
Dennis Wilcocks Cl ME9 35 B6
DENSOLE 163 A8
Densole La CT18 163 A8
Densole Way CT18 163 A8
Denstead Cotts CT4 86 B8
Denstead Ct CT2 66 C4
Denstead La CT4, ME13 86 C7
Denstead Oast CT4 86 B8
Denstead Wlk 11 ME15 97 F6
DENSTROUDE 65 C8
Denstroude La CT2 65 D8
Dental Cl ME10 36 A5
Dental St CT21 176 C2
Dent-de-Lion Ct CT9 28 A8
Dent-de-Lion Rd
Margate CT9 28 A8
Westgate on Sea CT8 7 C1
DENTON 129 B3
Denton Cl ME15 97 E8
Denton Gn ME8 11 B4
Denton Way CT9 8 C1
Derby Cl ME10 36 D6
Derby Rd
Gillingham ME5 10 E2
Maidstone ME15 97 C8
Dering Cl
Bridge CT4 88 F1
Pluckley TN27 136 C4
Dering Rd
Ashford TN24 139 D2
Bridge CT4 89 A1
Herne Bay CT6 22 F4
Derings The TN29 205 B6
Dering Terr TN27 136 C3
Deringwood Dr ME15 75 F1
DERRINGSTONE 128 E7
Derringstone Downs
CT4 128 F6
Derringstone Hill CT4 128 F6
Derringstone St CT4 128 F7
Derville Ho TN28 202 B6
Derville Rd TN29 206 E7
Derwent Ave CT11 52 A7
Derwent Ho 3 ME15 97 E7
Derwent Way
Aylesham CT3 112 F6
Gillingham ME8 33 D8
Desmond Cres ME13 63 A5
D'Este Rd CT11 52 F7
DETLING 55 B1
Detling Ave CT10 30 A1
Detling Cl
Gillingham ME8 11 C2
West Minst ME12 3 B7
Detling Hill ME14 55 B2
Devon Ave CT14 117 C3
Devon Cl
Chatham ME5 32 C7
Gillingham ME8 11 F1
Devon Ct CT12 29 B2
Devon Gdns CT7 26 F7
Devon Rd
Canterbury CT1 88 D8
Folkestone CT19 178 D5
Maidstone ME15 97 C8
Devonshire Gdns CT9 8 C3
Devonshire Rd
Dover CT17 166 B8
Gillingham ME7 10 D7
Devonshire Terr CT10 30 B5
Dew La TN31 196 A1
Dexter Cl TN25 139 C8
Deyley Way TN23 155 C8
Dhekelia Cl ME14 75 A7
Dial Cl ME7 10 F6
Dial Rd ME7 10 F6
Diamond Ct ME12 1 C1
Diamond Rd CT5 20 E2
Diana Gdns CT14 117 A5
Diana Rd ME4 10 A2
Dibdin Rd CT14 117 D7
Dickens Ave CT1 67 D2
Dickens Cl ME17 98 E4
Dickens Ct ME2 9 D8
Dickens House Mus★
CT10 30 B4
Dickens Rd
Broadstairs CT10 30 B5
Maidstone ME14 74 E8
Rochester ME1 9 C2
Dickens Wlk CT10 30 B4
Dickens World★ ME4 10 A8
Dickley La ME17 101 A6
Dickson Ct 7 ME10 37 B4
Dickson Rd CT17 166 C8
Dicksons Bourne TN25 172 F6
Dickson's Cnr CT13 95 A6
Dieu Stone La CT16 166 E8
Digby Rd CT20 177 E5
Dignals Cl ME8 11 F2
Dignash TN25 121 E2
Diligent Dr ME10 36 F7
Dilnot La CT7 27 B3
Diocesan & Payne Smith CE
Prim Sch 23 CT1 67 A1
Discovery Rd ME15 76 B2
Discovery Wlk CT1 88 C7
Disraeli Cl ME15 97 E5
Dixon Cl ME15 74 F2
Dixwell Cl ME8 33 D5
Dixwell Rd CT20 178 A4
Dobbie Cl ME10 36 E6
Dock Exit Rd CT16 166 F8
Dock Head Rd ME4 10 A8
Dock Rd ME4 9 F6
Dockside Outlet Ctr ME4 10 A8
Doctor's La CT15 165 B5
DODDINGTON 80 E7
Doddington Ct ME16 74 E5
Doddington Place Gdns★
ME9 81 A7
Doddington Rd ME8 11 D3
Dodd's La CT16 149 A3
Does Alley 4 ME10 36 F4
Doggerel Acre CT5 43 F7
Dog Kennel La CT18 161 B7
Dogwood Cl ME5 32 D1
Dola Ave CT14 117 B6
Dolphin Cl CT10 8 G3
Dolphin Dr ME8 33 E5
Dolphin Ho
1 Dover CT16 166 E7
Rochester ME1 9 E5
Dolphin La CT16 166 E7
Dolphin Pas 3 CT16 166 E7
Dolphin Pk ME10 37 B5
Dolphin Pl 5 CT16 166 E7
Dolphin Rd
Lydd TN29 205 C6
Sittingbourne ME10 37 B5
Dolphins Rd CT19 178 D7
Dolphin St
Deal CT14 117 D7
Herne Bay CT6 22 E5
Dombey Cl ME1 9 C3
Domneva Rd
Minster (Thanet) CT12 50 B6
Westgate on Sea CT8 27 D8
Donald Moor Ave ME9 38 C2
Donald Troup Ho ME1 9 C4
Doncaster Cl 7 ME15 97 F6
Donegal Rd CT1 88 C8
Donemowe Dr ME10 36 F8
Donet Cl ME8 33 C5
Dongola Rd ME2 9 B8
Donkey La
Adisham CT3 112 C8
Appledore Heath TN26 181 C2
Donkey St CT21, TN29 186 E5
DONKEY STREET 186 D5
Donnahay Rd CT12 29 C3
Donnithorne Ho CT6 22 E5
Dorcas Gdns CT10 30 A6
Doric Ct CT11 52 C5
Dorman Avenue N CT3 112 E6
Dorman Avenue S CT3 112 F5
Dornden Gdns ME5 32 B2
Dorne Cotts TN27 118 E6
Dorothy Dr CT12 29 C2
Dorrit Way ME1 9 D2
Dorset Cl CT5 43 B7
Dorset Ct
Deal CT14 117 D2
Ramsgate CT12 29 B2
Dorset Gdns
Birchington CT7 26 F7
Deal CT14 117 C2
Dorset Pl ME13 62 C7
Dorset Rd
Canterbury CT1 88 D7
West Minst ME12 3 A8
Dorset Road Ind Est ME12 3 A8
Dorset Sq ME8 11 D1
Dorset Way ME15 97 C8
Dossett Ct CT14 117 A2
Dotterel Cl ME5 32 D2
Doubleday Dr ME9 37 E2
Douglas Almshouses
ME17 101 D5
Douglas Ave
Hythe CT21 176 C2
Whitstable CT5 20 E1
Douglas Bglws CT15 132 E8
Douglas Cl CT10 29 E5
Douglas Rd
Deal CT14 117 A3
Dover CT17 166 B8
Herne Bay CT6 23 A4
Lenham ME17 101 D5
Maidstone ME16 74 E3
Douglas Terr CT14 117 D5
Dour Ho The 13 CT16 166 D8
Dour Mews 12 CT16 149 C1
Douro Cl CT1 67 D1
Douro Pl CT16 166 E7
Dour Side CT17 148 F3
Dour St CT16 166 D8
Doust Way ME1 9 D5
Dove Cl
Chatham ME5 32 B6
Hythe CT21 187 D8
Kingsnorth TN23 156 C3
Whitstable CT5 43 C7
Dovecote Ct CT4 107 B8
Dove Ct 6 CT11 52 E7
Dovedale CT7 27 B7
Dovedale Ct
Ashford TN24 139 B4
Birchington CT7 27 B7
Dove Lea Gdns CT17 148 E3
DOVER 166 F7
Dover Castle & Princess of
Wales Regiment Mus★
CT16 166 F8
Dover Coll CT17 166 C8
Dover Discovery Ctr★ 20
CT16 166 D7
Dover Gram Sch for Boys
CT17 166 A8
Dover Gram Sch for Girls
CT16 149 C1
Dover Hill CT19 178 F8
Dover Ho 2 ME15 97 E8
Dover L Ctr CT17 166 E8
Dover Mus★ CT16 166 D7
Dover Patrol Meml★
CT15 151 C7
Dover Pl TN23 139 C1
Dover Priory Sta CT17 166 C8
Dover Rd
Barham CT4 112 A1
Bishopsbourne CT4 111 D5
Dover CT15 149 E4
Folkestone CT19, CT20 178 E7
Ringwould CT14 134 A6
Sandwich CT13 93 F6
St Margaret's at Cliffe
CT15 150 D6
Tilmanstone CT13, CT14 115 B5
Woolage Green CT4 129 D6
Dover St
Canterbury CT1 88 A7
Maidstone ME16 74 C2
1 Sittingbourne ME10 36 E4
Dover Trade Ctr CT15 149 C6
Dover Transport Mus★
CT16 149 A5
Doves Cnr CT14 115 A4
Doves Croft ME9 58 C7
Dowell Mews CT14 117 C3
Dowle Cl TN29 201 A7
Down Barton Farm Cotts
CT7 25 D1
Down Barton Rd CT7 25 E1
Down Court Rd ME9 59 C1
Down Ct TN23 155 E5
Downer Ct ME1 31 E8
Downhill Cl CT16 148 D6
Downings The CT6 23 A2
Downland Ct TN24 139 B3
Downlands
Deal CT14 134 B8
Harrietsham ME17 100 F6
Downland Wlk ME5 32 A5
Downs Ave CT5 20 E1
Downs CE Prim Sch The
CT14 117 B2
Downs Cl
Charing TN27 120 C8
East Studdal CT15 132 D8
Hawkinge CT18 163 A4
Maidstone ME14 75 B8
Sittingbourne ME10 36 D2
Downside
Bekesbourne CT4 89 E3
Folkestone CT19 178 C7
Rochester ME2 9 A7
St Margaret's at Cliffe
CT15 151 A6
Downside Rd CT16 149 B7
Downs Pk CT6 23 A5
Downs Rd
Canterbury CT2 66 F4
Deal CT14 117 C3
East Studdal CT15 132 E8
Folkestone CT19 178 C7
Maidstone ME14 75 B8
Ramsgate CT11 52 B6
Downs The
Chartham CT4 86 E1
Chatham ME5 31 D1
Preston CT3 70 C6
Ramsgate CT11 52 D5
Downsview ME5 32 C8
Downs View Inf Sch
TN24 139 E7
Downs View Rd ME14 75 B8
Downs Way
Charing TN27 120 C8
Sellindge TN25 159 C1
Dragonfly Cl TN23 155 D8
Dragonfly Way CT18 163 B4
Dragoon Ho 9 CT1 67 A1
Drainless Rd CT13 93 A5
Drake Ave ME12 4 D5
Drake Ct 3 CT11 52 F8
Drake Rd TN24 157 B7
Drakes Cl ME9 12 E2
Drakes Lee TN28 202 E5
Drapers Almshouses CT9 29 A8
Drapers Ave CT9 28 F8
Drapers Cl CT9 29 A8
Drapers Mills Prim Sch
CT9 29 A8
Drapers Windmill★ CT9 8 A1
Drawbridge Cl ME15 97 E8
Dray's Field ME9 79 A7
Dreadnought Ave ME12 4 A6
Dresden Ct CT8 27 D8
Drewery Dr ME8 33 C5
Drew La CT14 117 C4
Drill La CT3 69 B1
Drive The
Broadstairs CT10 29 F6
Canterbury CT1 88 B6

Drive The *continued*
Deal CT14 117 C5
Whitstable CT5 44 D8
Drop Redoubt Fort★ CT17 166 D7
Drop Redoubt Rd CT17 166 D7
Drove Rd ME12 3 E6
Drovers Rdbt TN24 139 A4
Drove The
Fordwich CT2 68 A4
Monkton CT12 49 B6
Northbourne CT14 116 A5
Whitfield CT16 149 A8
Whitstable CT5 44 D8
Droveway Gdns CT15 151 A6
Droveway The CT15 151 B6
Druidstone Pk★ CT2 65 F7
Drum La TN23 139 B2
Drum Major Dr CT14 117 B3
Drury Rd TN30 167 B1
Drybeck Ave CT11 51 F7
Dryden Cl CT1 88 C7
Dryden Rd CT16 149 B3
Drywall Ind Est ME10 37 B6
Dublin Ho 16 ME15 97 E7
Duchess of Kent Dr ME5 32 B3
Duck La
Canterbury CT1 67 A1
Shadoxhurst TN26 169 F7
Duckpits Rd CT4 126 A6
Duck St CT4 144 F4
Duckworth Cl TN24 157 B7
Dudley Ave CT8 27 C8
Dudley Cl ME15 97 F5
Dudley Rd
Ashford TN24 139 E5
Folkestone CT19 178 E5
Duke of Clarence Trad Est The ME12 1 B3
Duke of York's Royal Military Sch CT15 149 F4
Dukes Mdw TN26 183 A7
Dukes Meadow Dr ME7 32 F6
Duke St
Deal CT14 117 D7
Margate CT9 7 I3
Dukes Wlk 7 ME15 75 A4
Dukeswood CT5 44 D6
Dully Rd
Lynsted ME9 59 E6
Sittingbourne ME9 37 E1
Dumbourne La TN30 179 D2
Dumergue Ave ME11 3 B5
DUMPTON 29 E2
Dumpton Gap Rd CT10 30 A2
Dumpton La CT11 29 E1
Dumpton Park Dr CT10, CT11 30 A2
Dumpton Park Rd CT11 52 E8
Dumpton Park Sta CT11 29 F1
Duncan Cl CT5 43 D7
Duncan Dr CT7 26 E8
Duncan Rd
Gillingham ME7 10 D5
Ramsgate CT11 52 D7
Whitstable CT5 43 D7
Dundonald Rd
11 Broadstairs CT10 30 B4
Ramsgate CT11 52 C7
Dunedin Cl ME10 36 C3
Dunedin Dr CT16 149 B3
Dunedin Ho 9 ME15 97 E5
Dunedin Rd CT12 29 A1
Dunera Dr ME14 75 A7
Dunes Rd TN28 202 D3
Dunes The CT13 95 A7
DUNGATE 59 B3
DUNGENESS 209 F2
Dungeness National Nature Reserve★ TN29 209 B4
Dungeness Nature Reserve★ TN29 208 F5
Dungeness Rd TN29 209 A7
Dungeness Sta★ TN29 209 D2
Dunkeld Ho 6 ME15 97 E7
Dunkery Rise TN24 139 B4
DUNKIRK 64 D3
Dunkirk Cl TN29 195 B7
Dunkirk Dr ME5 31 F6
DUNKIRK END 195 B7
Dunkirk Road N ME13 64 B2
Dunkirk Road S ME13 64 B1
Dunkirk Sq CT15 149 F3
Dunlin Ct TN29 195 A3
Dunnett Rd CT19 177 E6
Dunning's La ME1 9 C4
Dunnings The ME16 74 A2
Dunnock Rd TN25 139 B7
DUNN STREET
Gillingham 55 A8
Westwell 121 E5
Dunn Street Rd ME7 55 A8
Dunoon Ct CT11 29 F1
Dunstall Cl TN29 195 A5
Dunstall Gdns TN29 195 A5
Dunstall La TN29 195 A5
Dunstan Ave CT8 27 D7
Dunstan Ho CT14 117 D8
Dunster Terr 3 ME15 97 E8
Durban Cl CT12 29 A2
Durban Cres CT16 149 C4
Durban Ho 7 ME15 97 E5
Durban Rd CT9 8 A1
Durham Cl
Canterbury CT1 87 F6
Durham Cl *continued*
9 Dover CT17 166 D7
Maidstone ME15 75 E1
Durham Hill CT17 166 D7
Durham Rd ME8 33 C7
Durling Ct ME8 12 A1
DURLOCK 92 B8
Durlock CT12 50 C5
Durlock Ave CT11 52 B5
Durlock Rd CT3 92 B7
Durlocks The CT19 178 E5
Durnford Cl CT2 66 E2
Durovernum Ct CT1 88 A7
DURRANT GREEN 167 B6
Durrell Gdns ME5 10 C1
Duval Dr ME1 31 E8
Duvard's Pl ME9 35 F1
Dyke Rd CT19 178 E5
DYMCHURCH 195 C7
Dymchurch Ho 1 CT1 88 B8
Dymchurch Martello Tower★ TN29 195 C7
Dymchurch Prim Sch TN29 195 C8
Dymchurch Rd
Hythe CT21, TN29 187 C6
St Mary's Bay TN29, TN28 195 A5
Dymchurch Sta★ TN29 195 B7
Dyngley Cl ME10 36 E6

E

EACH END 72 B1
Eadred Way ME10 15 A1
Eagle Cotts 8 CT11 52 D7
Eagle Hill CT11 52 D7
Eagles Cl ME10 37 C4
Ealham Cl
Ashford TN24 157 A8
Canterbury CT4 88 B5
Ealing Cl ME5 32 C4
Earl Cl ME5 32 B4
Earls Ave TN24 139 F1
Earl's Ave CT20 178 B4
Earlsfield TN25 173 A6
Earlsfield Rd CT21 176 D2
Earlsmead Cres CT12 51 C5
Earl St ME14 74 F4
Earlsworth Ct TN24 156 E6
Earlsworth Rd TN24 156 D6
Easole Hts CT15 113 D5
Easole St CT15 113 D5
East Blean Woods (Nature Reserve)★ CT3, CT6 46 B6
East Borough Prim Sch ME14 75 B5
Eastbridge Rd TN29 195 B8
Eastbrook Pl CT16 166 E8
EASTCHURCH 5 E3
Eastchurch CE Prim Sch ME12 5 E3
Eastchurch Rd
Margate CT9 8 E3
Minster (Sheppey) ME12 5 B5
East Cliff
Dover CT16 166 F8
Folkestone CT19 178 E5
Eastcliffe Hts 7 CT20 178 E5
East Cliff Gdns 22 CT19 178 E5
East Cliff Par CT6 23 A5
East Cliff Pas 23 CT19 178 E5
East Cliff & Warren Ctry Pk★ CT18 164 D1
Eastcourt Gn ME8 11 B4
Eastcourt La
Gillingham, Lower Twydal ME7, ME8 11 C5
Gillingham ME8 11 B3
East Court Sch CT11 52 G7
East Cross TN30 179 B7
East Ct 4 ME15 75 A1
East End Rd ME4, ME7 10 D8
Eastern Arm N CT16 166 H8
Eastern Arm S CT16 166 H8
Eastern Ave
Ashford TN23 139 A2
Halfway Houses ME12 3 D6
Queenborough ME11 3 B4
Eastern Espl
Broadstairs CT10 30 B5
Margate CT9 8 B3
Eastern Gdns TN24 156 E8
Eastern Rd
Gillingham ME7 10 F6
Leysdown-on-Sea ME12 6 G2
Lydd TN29 205 D7
Eastern Service Rd CT16 166 H8
EAST FARLEIGH 96 B7
East Farleigh Prim Sch ME15 96 B6
East Farleigh Sta ME16 96 B8
Eastfield Ho ME16 74 B2
Eastfield Rd 1 CT7 27 A7
Eastfields CT19 178 D6
Eastgate ME1 9 C5
Eastgate Cl CT6 23 B3
Eastgate Ct ME1 9 C5
Eastgate Rd TN30 179 C8
Eastgate Terr ME1 9 C5
East Gn ME10 15 A1
East Hall La ME10 37 C5
East Hill
Ashford TN24 139 C2
Tenterden TN30 179 B8
East Kent Coll CT11 52 D5
East Kent Ret Pk CT10 29 B4
East Kent Rly★ CT15 131 A7
East La ME12 1 B2
EAST LANGDON 133 A1
East Langdon Rd
Guston CT15 149 F7
Martin Mill CT15 133 B2
EASTLING 81 F6
Eastling Cl ME8 11 D3
Eastling Prim Sch ME13 81 F5
Eastling Rd
Eastling ME13 81 F7
Painters Forstal ME13 61 D2
East Lodge Rd TN23 138 F3
Eastmead Ave TN23 156 C8
Eastmead Trad Est TN23 156 C8
East Mountain La TN24 139 F7
East Norman Rd CT16 149 E1
East Northdown Cl CT9 8 E1
Easton's Cnr TN25 172 F4
East Park Rd ME20 74 A8
East Quay CT5 20 D3
East Ramp CT16 166 G8
East Rd
Chatham ME4 10 A7
Folkestone CT20 177 D4
Sandwich CT13 73 A8
East Row ME1 9 C5
EASTRY 93 A2
Eastry CE Prim Sch CT13 93 B2
Eastry Cl
Ashford TN23 156 A6
Maidstone ME16 74 C7
Eastry Ct CT3 112 F5
Eastry Mews CT13 93 B2
Eastry Pk CT13 93 C1
East Service Rd TN29 209 C2
East St
Ashford TN23 139 B2
Canterbury CT1 67 C3
Chatham ME4 10 A3
Dover CT17 166 C8
Faversham ME13 62 D7
Folkestone CT19 178 E5
Gillingham ME7 10 D6
Harrietsham ME17 100 E5
Herne Bay CT6 23 A5
Hythe CT21 176 D2
Sittingbourne ME10 37 A4
East Stour Ct TN24 139 D1
EAST STOURMOUTH 48 E1
East Stour Prim Sch TN24 156 D6
East Stour Way TN24 156 D6
EAST STREET 72 A2
EAST STUDDAL 132 D7
East Tank Farm Rd TN29 209 C2
East View
Brookland TN29 199 D8
Hersden CT3 46 F1
East Weald Dr TN30 167 B1
Eastwell 5 TN30 179 A7
Eastwell Barn Mews TN30 179 A8
Eastwell Cl
Maidstone ME14 75 C5
Shadoxhurst TN26 155 B1
Eastwell Mdws TN30 179 A8
Eastwell Terr TN25 122 E3
Eastwood Cotts ME9 38 E6
Eastwood Rd ME10 36 D5
East Wootton Cotts CT4 109 A4
Eaton Hill CT9 7 I2
EATON LANDS 176 C3
Eaton Rd
Dover CT17 166 B7
Margate CT9 7 I1
Eaves Ct ME10 37 B5
Eaves Rd CT17 166 A7
Ebbsfleet La CT12 51 A3
Ebony Cotts TN30 189 A6
Ebony Wlk ME16 74 B3
ECCLES 53 A6
Eccleston Rd ME15 74 F2
Echo Cl ME15 97 F6
Echo Ho ME10 37 B3
Echo Wlk ME12 4 D6
Eckford Cl CT18 162 F4
Eclipse Dr ME10 36 E8
Eddie Willet Rd CT6 22 B3
EDDINGTON 22 F3
Eddington Cl ME15 97 B6
Eddington La CT6 22 F3
Eddington Way CT6 22 E3
Edelin Rd ME14 76 A5
Eden Ave ME5 32 A7
Edenbridge Dr ME12 3 B8
Edenbridge Ho 2 CT1 88 B8
Edenfield CT7 27 B7
Eden Ho TN23 156 C8
Eden Rd CT5 43 A7
EDEN VILLAGE 36 F1
Edgar Cl CT5 21 D3
Edgar Ho CT14 117 B3
Edgar Rd
Canterbury CT1 67 B1
Dover CT17 149 B1
Margate CT9 8 A3
Minster (Thanet) CT12 50 B6
Edge End Rd CT10 29 F4
Edgehill Cl CT20 177 D4
Edger Pl 8 ME15 75 A4
Edinburgh Ho
Deal CT14 117 A5
7 Dover CT17 166 D7
Edinburgh Pl 7 CT20 178 B3
Edinburgh Rd
Ashford TN24 139 B2
Chatham ME4 10 C2
Gillingham ME7 10 D5
Edinburgh Rd *continued*
Margate CT9 28 B8
Edinburgh Sq ME15 97 C7
Edinburgh Wlk 5 CT9 28 B8
Edisbury Wlk ME8 33 D5
Edith Rd
Faversham ME13 62 C6
Ramsgate CT11 52 C6
Westgate on Sea CT8 7 D1
Edmanson Ave CT9 7 E1
Edmund Cl ME16 74 A3
Edmund St CT3 91 A8
Edna Rd ME14 74 F8
Edred Rd CT17 166 B8
Edward Ct ME5 10 C1
Edward Dr
Birchington CT7 27 B7
Sittingbourne ME10 14 F1
Edward Rd
Canterbury CT1 88 A8
Folkestone CT19 178 D6
Kingsdown CT14 134 C6
Queenborough ME11 3 B5
Edwards Cl ME8 33 C5
Edwards Rd CT16 166 D8
Edward St
Chatham ME4 10 A3
Rochester ME2 9 B7
Sheerness ME12 1 B3
Edward Terr 9 CT20 178 E6
Edward Vinson Dr ME13 62 E7
Edwina Ave ME12 4 A7
Edwin Rd ME8 33 C8
Edwins Pl ME9 35 C7
Edyngham Cl ME10 37 A8
Effingham Cres CT17 166 D8
Effingham St
Dover CT17 166 D8
Ramsgate CT11 52 E6
Egbert Rd
Birchington CT7 26 D8
Faversham ME13 62 C6
Minster (Thanet) CT12 50 B6
Westgate on Sea CT8 7 C1
EGERTON 118 F4
Egerton CE Prim Sch TN27 118 F3
Egerton Dr CT9 8 E2
EGERTON FORSTAL 118 D1
Egerton House Rd TN27 118 E4
Egerton Rd
Charing Heath TN27 119 C7
Maidstone ME14 74 E7
Pluckley TN27 119 B1
Temple Ewell CT16 148 E5
Eggarton La CT4 107 C2
Eggringe TN23 138 E1
Egremont Rd ME15 75 F2
Eider Cl CT6 22 D2
Eighteen Acre La TN29 200 D8
Elder Cl ME17 99 D2
Elder Ct ME8 33 B6
Elders The CT3 68 F1
Eldon Gr CT11 52 D6
Eldon Pl 4 CT10 30 B4
Eldon St ME4 10 A4
Eleanor Ct ME8 33 C3
Eleanor Dr ME10 36 E8
Elfrida Cl CT9 29 C8
Elgar Bretts Ct 10 CT1 87 F7
Elgar Pl CT11 52 D7
ELHAM 144 F5
Elham CE Prim Sch CT4 144 F4
Elham Cl
Gillingham ME8 11 B3
Margate CT9 8 C1
Elham Rd CT1 87 E6
Elham Valley Railway Mus★ CT18 177 A8
Elham Valley Vineyard★ CT4 128 D4
Elham Way CT10 30 A2
Eling Ct ME15 97 A8
Eliot Coll CT2 66 E4
Elizabethan Ct TN27 120 C7
Elizabeth Carter Ave CT14 116 F4
Elizabeth Ct
Broadstairs CT10 30 B6
Canterbury CT1 88 B6
Chatham ME5 32 A7
Gillingham ME8 11 C1
Herne Bay CT6 22 F5
Elizabeth Dr CT18 164 B2
Elizabeth Gdns 3 CT21 176 B1
Elizabeth Ho
Maidstone ME14 75 A6
Rochester ME1 9 C4
Elizabeth Kemp Ct 1 CT12 29 C1
Elizabeth Rd CT11 52 F6
Elizabeth St CT17 166 D6
Elizabeth Way CT6 23 B3
Ellen Ave CT11 29 E2
Ellen Cl TN27 120 B7
Ellen Ct CT3 89 F8
Ellenden Ct CT2 66 C4
Ellen's Hill CT14 116 E3
Ellen's Pl ME9 35 C6
Ellens Rd CT14 116 F2
Ellenswood Cl ME15 76 A1
Ellesmere Mews TN28 202 C8
Ellingham Ind Ctr TN23 156 A5
Ellingham Leas ME15 97 C7
Ellingham Way TN23 156 A5
Ellington Ave CT9 28 B8
Ellington Inf Sch CT11 52 C7
Ellington Pl CT11 52 C7
Ellington Rd CT11 52 D7
Ellington Sch for Girls CT12 29 D2
Elliot Cl CT1 67 C3
Elliot Ct CT6 23 C4
Elliots Pl ME13 62 D7
Elliott Park Sch ME12 4 A7
Ellis Dr TN28 202 C8
Ellis Ho 7 ME14 75 B4
Ellison Cl CT5 21 C1
Ellison Ct ME13 62 E6
Ellisons Wlk CT1 88 C8
Ellison Way ME8 12 A2
Ellis Rd CT5 21 A3
Ellis Way CT6 23 C2
Elm Ave ME4 9 E1
Elm Cl TN27 118 F3
Elm Cotts TN25 122 E3
Elm Court Ind Est ME7 32 E3
Elm Ct CT8 27 E8
Elmfield
Gillingham ME8 11 A3
Tenterden TN30 179 B8
Elmfield Ct
Coxheath ME17 96 C3
Tenterden TN30 179 B8
Elm Fields TN29 201 A6
Elm Gdns CT21 176 E2
Elm Gr
Maidstone ME15 75 B3
Manston CT12 28 D1
Sittingbourne ME10 37 B4
Westgate on Sea CT8 27 E8
Elm Ho 11 CT21 176 B2
Elmhurst Cl TN25 138 F4
Elmhurst Gdns ME4 9 E3
Elm La ME12 4 E5
Elmleigh Rd CT3 90 A8
Elmley Ind Est ME11 3 A2
Elmley Marshes Nature Reserve★ ME12 15 F4
Elmley Rd ME12 4 D3
Elmley Way CT9 28 F6
Elm Park Gdns CT17 165 F7
Elm Pl TN23 155 F7
Elm Rd
Aylesham CT3 112 E5
7 Folkestone CT19 178 E6
Gillingham ME7 10 E6
St Mary's Bay TN29 194 F3
Elms Ave CT11 52 D6
Elms Hill CT15 165 D6
Elmsmead TN31 197 B4
ELMSTEAD 142 F6
Elmstead Pl 12 CT20 178 E5
Elms The
Hersden CT3 46 E1
Teynham ME9 39 A2
ELMSTONE 70 E5
Elmstone Cl ME16 74 B2
Elmstone Gdns CT9 8 E2
Elmstone Hole Rd ME17 100 D1
Elmstone La ME16 74 B2
Elmstone Rd
Gillingham ME8 33 D7
Ramsgate CT11 52 D7
ELMS VALE 166 A7
Elms Vale Rd CT15, CT17 165 E7
Elmton La CT15 114 C1
Elmtree TN26 181 C1
Elm Tree Ave ME9 14 D4
Elm Tree Dr ME1 9 A2
Elmway ME12 5 F6
Elmwood Ave CT10 30 A8
Elmwood Cl CT10 30 A7
Elm Wood Cl CT5 21 C2
Elm Wood Way CT5 21 C2
Elswick Sq TN25 139 B2
Elventon Cl CT19 177 E7
Elverland La ME13, ME9 61 B2
ELVINGTON
Eythorne 114 C1
Hawkinge 162 E2
Elvington Cl ME16 74 D5
Elvington La CT18 162 E2
Elwick La 13 TN23 139 B2
Elwick Rd TN23 139 B2
Ely Cl ME8 11 E2
Embassy Cl ME7 10 F1
Emelina Way CT5 43 B6
Emerald Cl ME1 31 D7
Emerald Cres ME10 36 C6
Emerald View ME12 6 E4
Emily Rd ME5 32 B6
Emmerson Gdns CT5 21 D3
Emperor Way TN23 155 F4
Empire Terr CT9 28 E8
Empress Gdns ME12 6 D4
Emsworth Gr ME14 75 D6
Enbrook Rd CT20 177 E4
Enbrook Valley CT20 177 E5
Encombe CT20 177 D3
Endeavour Foyer The 8 ME4 10 B2
Enfield Rd CT14 117 D7
Engineers Ct 1 TN23 139 B2
English Martyrs RC Prim Sch 5 ME2 9 B8
Ennerdale ME13 62 E6
Ennerdale Gdns CT3 112 F6
Ennerdale Ho ME15 97 E7
Enterprise Bsns Est ME2 9 E7
Enterprise Cl ME2 9 D8
Enterprise Ctr TN24 156 E7
Enterprise Ctr The ME5 54 C8
Enterprise Rd
Maidstone ME15 75 A1
Margate CT9 29 A6

Enterprise Way CT9 29 A6
Enticott Cl CT5 21 A1
Epaul La ME1 9 C6
Eppe Cl 2 ME2 9 B8
Epping Cl CT6 23 B2
Epple Bay Ave CT7 27 B8
Epple Bay Rd CT7 27 A8
Epple Rd CT7 27 B8
Epps Rd ME10 36 E3
Epsom Cl ME15 97 F6
Eric Rd CT17 149 B2
Erith Cl ME14 75 A8
Erith St CT17 149 B1
Ernest Dr ME16 74 B5
Ernest Rd ME4 10 A3
Ernwell Rd CT19 178 D6
ERRIOTTWOOD 59 F3
Ersham Rd CT1 88 A7
Eshet Cl TN23 156 A7
Eskdale Ave CT11 52 A7
Esmonde Dr CT12 27 F2
Esmonde Ho 15 ME7 10 A6
Esplanade
Dover CT17 166 D6
Rochester ME1 9 B5
Westgate on Sea CT8 7 C1
Essella Pk TN24 139 E1
Essella Rd TN24 139 E1
Essentially Hops★ CT4 89 D3
Essetford Rd TN23 156 A7
Essex Ave CT6 22 B4
Essex Gdns CT7 26 F6
Essex Rd
Canterbury CT1 88 D7
Maidstone ME15 97 E6
Westgate on Sea CT8 27 F8
Essex St CT5 43 D8
Estelle Cl ME1 31 D7
Esther Ct ME10 36 E8
Estuary Cl CT5 21 E2
Estuary Rd ME12 1 C1
Estuary Reach ME4 9 F6
Etchden Rd TN26 154 A8
ETCHINGHILL 161 C3
Ethelbert Cres CT9 8 A3
Ethelbert Gdns CT9 7 J3
Ethelbert Rd
Birchington CT7 26 D8
Canterbury CT1 88 B6
Deal CT14 95 C1
Dover CT17 166 C8
Faversham ME13 62 C6
Folkestone CT19 178 D7
Margate CT9 7 J3
Ramsgate CT11 52 D6
Rochester ME1 9 C4
Ethelbert Road Inf Sch
ME13 62 C6
Ethelbert Sq CT8 7 C1
Ethelbert Terr
Margate CT9 8 A3
Westgate on Sea CT8 7 C1
Ethelburga Dr CT18 161 B7
Ethel-Maud Ct ME7 10 D7
Ethel Rd CT10 29 F5
Ethelred Ct ME13 62 C6
Ethelred Rd CT8 7 C1
Eton Cl ME5 31 F4
Ettrick Terr CT21 176 B2
Eureka Leisure Pk TN24 139 B5
Eurogate Bsns Pk TN24 139 B5
Eurolink Bsns Pk ME10 37 B5
Eurolink E ME10 37 C5
Eurolink N ME10 37 C7
Eurolink Way ME10 36 F4
Evans Rd TN24 157 A7
Eva Rd ME7 10 D3
Evelings Alley 18 CT5 20 D2
Evelyn Cl ME2 9 C8
Evelyn Ct CT21 177 A2
Evelyn Ho
9 Folkestone CT20 178 D5
5 Rochester ME2 9 C8
Evelyn Rd ME16 74 E3
Evenhill Rd CT3 89 E8
Everard Way ME13 62 B8
Everglades The ME7 32 F6
Evergreen Cl
Gillingham ME7 33 A5
Iwade ME9 14 D4
Evergreen Way TN23 138 E3
Everist Ct CT18 161 C6
Eversleigh Rise CT5 43 F7
Eversley Cl ME16 74 C6
Eversley Coll CT20 177 F4
Eversley Rd CT21 177 B3
Eversley Way CT20 177 F5
Evington Pottery★ TN25 142 D7
Evison Cl CT16 149 B2
Evorg Ho 6 ME4 10 B2
Ewart Rd ME4 9 E1
Ewe & Lamb Mews TN30 188 E3
EWELL MINNIS 147 E3
Exchange St CT14 117 D7
Exchange The CT5 20 E3
Exeter Cl CT19 177 D6
Exeter Wlk ME1 31 C7
Exmoor Rise TN24 139 B4
Exmouth Rd ME7 10 C7
EXTED 144 E5
Exton Cl ME5 32 C2
Exton Gdns ME14 75 F5
Eye The ME4 9 F5
Eyhorne St ME17 77 D2
EYHORNE STREET 77 C2
Eylesden Ct ME14 76 C4
Eynsford Cl CT9 8 F2
Eynsford Rd ME16 74 D7
Eythorn Court Barn
CT15 131 B7
EYTHORNE 131 C8
Eythorne Cl TN24 139 D5
Eythorne Elvington Prim Sch
CT15 131 C8
EYTHORNE GREEN 131 D7
Eythorne Rd CT15 130 E6
Eythorne Sta★ CT15 131 C8

F

Faggs Wood Forest Wlks★
TN26 170 D2
Fagus Cl ME5 32 B1
Fairacre CT10 29 E4
Fairacres Cl CT6 23 C4
FAIRBOURNE HEATH 100 B1
Fairbourne Heath Cotts
ME17 100 B1
Fairbourne La ME17 100 C4
Fairfax Bsns Ctr ME15 97 F4
Fairfax Cl
Folkestone CT20 177 D5
Gillingham ME8 33 D5
Fairfax Dr CT6 23 F5
Fairfax Ho ME15 97 F5
FAIRFIELD 29 E4
Fairfield
Deal CT14 116 F6
Elham CT4 144 F5
Fairfield Cl TN28 202 B7
Fairfield Pk CT10 29 E4
Fairfield Rd
Broadstairs CT10 29 E4
Minster (Thanet) CT12 50 B7
New Romney TN28 202 B7
Ramsgate CT11 29 E2
Fairfield Terr TN26 183 A7
Fairhurst Dr ME15 96 B4
Fairings The TN30 179 B8
Fairlawn CT5 21 D1
Fairlawn Rd CT12 29 B3
Fairlead Rd ME1 9 D1
Fairleas ME10 37 B2
Fairlight Ave CT12 52 B8
Fairlight Cotts 8 ME13 62 C7
Fairlight Glen Sch CT6 22 F5
Fairlight Rd CT21 176 A3
Fairmeadow ME14 74 F4
Fairoaks CT6 23 B3
Fairservice Cl ME10 37 C5
Fair St CT10 29 E4
Fairview CT21 175 A3
Fairview Ave ME8 33 B5
Fairview Cl CT9 8 A2
Fairview Com Prim Sch
ME8 33 C5
Fairview Cotts
Maidstone ME15 96 F5
Wormshill ME9 79 C7
Fairview Dr TN24 156 D6
Fairview Gdns
Deal CT14 117 A2
Sturry CT2 68 A6
Fairview Ind Pk TN26 183 D7
Fairview Rd
Elvington CT15 114 B1
Sittingbourne ME10 37 A3
Fairway CT13 95 A7
Fairway Ave CT19 178 A7
Fairway Cl
Rochester ME1 9 C1
St Mary's Bay TN29 194 F3
Fairway Cres CT5 43 A7
Fairways The ME13 62 A6
Fairway The
Deal CT14 117 C8
Herne Bay CT6 22 D2
Hythe CT21 176 C1
Littlestone-on-Sea TN28 202 D6
Rochester ME1 9 C1
Sittingbourne ME10 36 E1
St Mary's Bay TN29 195 A5
Fairwood Ind Est TN23 139 A1
Fairwood Ind Pk TN23 138 F2
Falcon Cl CT6 45 F7
Falcon Ct ME10 37 A2
Falcon Gdns ME12 4 D7
Falcon Ho 3 ME10 37 A4
Falcon Way TN23 155 E7
Falkland Pl ME5 31 E1
Fallowfield
Chatham ME5 32 B8
Sittingbourne ME10 37 A2
Fallowfield Cl ME14 75 E4
Fanconi Rd ME5 32 B3
Fancy Row ME14 76 C5
Fane Way ME8 33 D4
Fan The CT16 166 H8
Fant La ME16 74 B2
Faraday Ho ME1 9 D5
Faraday Rd ME14 75 C7
Fareham Wlk 10 ME15 97 F6
Farington Cl ME16 74 B4
Farleigh Ct ME16 74 A2
Farleigh Hill ME15 74 E1
Farleigh Hill Ret Pk ME15 74 E1
Farleigh La ME16 74 A1
Farleigh Rd CT2 67 A3
Farleigh Trad Est ME15 74 E1
Farley Cl
Chatham ME5 32 D2
Shadoxhurst TN26 155 A1
Farley Rd CT9 28 F7
Farleys Way TN31 196 B2
Farm Cl TN23 155 E7
Farm Cres ME10 37 A2
Farmer Cl
Hythe CT21 176 D3
Leeds ME17 99 A6
Farm Gdns TN31 196 C2
Farmhouse Cl CT4 128 F7
Farm House Cl CT5 43 F8
Farming World at Nash
Court★ ME13 63 D4
Farm La CT14 116 F6
Farm Rd
Chatham ME5 31 E3
Hamstreet TN26 183 A7
Farnborough Cl ME16 74 C2
Farncombe Way CT16 149 B7
Farne Cl ME15 97 A6
Farnham Cl ME8 12 B1
Farningham Cl ME14 75 C6
Farraday Cl ME1 31 D8
Farrar Rd CT7 27 A6
Farrers Wlk TN23 156 B4
Farrier Cl
Ashford TN23 138 F5
Maidstone ME14 75 E5
Farriers Ct ME8 34 C8
Farrier St CT14 117 D7
Farrow Ct TN23 156 A6
Farthing Cnr ME9 33 E3
FARTHING COMMON 160 D5
FARTHINGLOE 165 F5
Farthingloe Cotts CT15 165 F5
Farthingloe Ct CT17 166 A6
Farthingloe Rd CT17 166 A6
Farthings Cotts ME14 53 F1
Farthings Ct CT2 66 C4
Fauchon's Cl ME14 75 F3
Fauchon's La ME14 75 F4
Faulkners La CT2 66 A1
Faussett Hill CT4 109 E7
Faustina Dr TN23 155 F4
FAVERSHAM 62 A5
Faversham Cottage Hospl
ME13 62 C7
Faversham Ind Est ME13 62 F7
Faversham Miniature Rly★
ME13 62 B4
Faversham Rd
Boughton Lees TN24,
TN25 122 E5
Challock ME13, TN27 104 C3
Charing TN27 103 E1
Lewson Street ME13, ME9 61 B5
Pested TN25, ME13 105 B4
Whitstable CT5 42 C6
Wichling ME17, ME9 80 B4
Woodside Green ME17 101 E7
Faversham Reach ME13 62 D8
Faversham Sta ME13 62 D6
Faversham Stone Chapel★
ME13 61 E7
Favourite Rd CT5 43 B6
Fawley Cl ME14 74 E7
Fay Cl ME1 9 B3
Featherbed La
Iwade ME9 14 E2
Selling ME13 84 A7
Featherby Cotts ME7 10 F6
Featherby Inf Sch ME8 11 A3
Featherby Jun Sch ME8 11 A3
Featherby Rd ME8 11 A3
Felborough Cl CT4 107 C8
FELDERLAND 93 F4
Felderland Cl
Maidstone ME17 97 E5
Sandwich CT14 93 F5
Felderland Dr ME17 97 E5
Felderland La CT14 93 E4
Felderland Rd ME17 97 E5
Feldspar Cl
Chatham ME5 32 A1
Sittingbourne ME10 36 D6
Fellows Cl ME8 33 B6
Fennel Cl ME16 74 B3
Fennell Cl ME1 9 B3
Fenner Cl CT20 177 E4
Fenoulhet Way CT6 23 A5
Fenton Ct CT14 117 B6
Ferdi Lethert Ho TN24 139 E5
Ferguson Cl CT21 176 F2
Ferguson Rd TN29 207 F6
Ferguson Way CT21 176 A1
Fernbank Cl ME5 31 F2
Fern Bank Cres CT19 178 D6
Fern Cl
Hawkinge CT18 163 C6
Whitstable CT5 21 C1
Fern Ct
Broadstairs CT10 30 B5
Dover CT16 149 D1
Ferndale Cl ME12 3 D6
Ferndale Ct CT7 27 A6
Ferndale Rd ME7 10 E5
Ferndown CT7 26 D8
Ferndown Cl ME7 33 A5
Ferne La CT15 147 D3
Ferne Way CT20 177 E6
Fernfield CT18 163 C6
Fernfield La CT18 163 C7
Fernhill Rd ME16 74 A2
Fernlea Ave CT6 22 E4
FERNLEIGH 36 C2
Fernleigh Cl ME13 64 B3
Fernley Ct 11 CT20 178 D5
Fern Wlk ME10 37 C5
Ferrier Cl ME8 33 E4
Ferry Rd
Iwade ME9 14 E4
Queenborough ME11, ME12 3 D1
Ferry View ME11 2 F3
Fiddling La TN25 159 E6
Field Ave CT1 67 D3
Field Cl ME5 31 E6
Field End TN24 140 A1
Field End Pl ME13 64 A3
Fielder Cl 1 ME10 37 C5
Fielding St ME13 62 C7
Fieldings The ME10 36 E2
Field Mill Rd TN27 119 B5
Field View
Kingsnorth TN23 156 B4
Whitstable CT5 43 B7
Fieldview Cl ME12 3 C6
Field Way CT2 67 F5
Fieldworks Rd ME7 10 A7
Fiesta Wlk CT1 88 C7
Fife Rd CT6 22 B3
Fifth Ave CT9 8 B3
Fig Tree Rd CT10 29 F7
Fig Tree Wlk CT15 131 C7
Fiji Terr ME14 75 A7
Filer Rd ME12 3 E7
Filmer Rd CT4 88 F1
Finch Cl ME13 62 D6
Finch Ct ME14 74 E7
Finches The
Sittingbourne ME10 36 F3
St Nicholas at Wade CT7 25 E2
Finch Gr CT21 187 D8
Finch Mews CT14 117 C4
Findlay Cl ME8 33 D6
Findlay Ct 9 CT21 176 B2
FINGLESHAM 116 B8
Finglesham Ct ME15 97 C8
Finglesham Farm Barns
CT14 116 A8
Finlay Cl ME13 62 B7
Finn Farm Ct TN23 156 D1
Finn Farm Rd TN23 156 C2
Finsbury Ct CT11 52 E8
Finsbury Rd CT11 52 E8
Fintonagh Dr ME14 75 B6
Finwell Rd ME8 12 A2
Firbank Gdns CT9 28 D7
Firbanks CT5 43 F8
Fir Ct TN24 139 F1
Fire Opal Way 6 ME10 36 D6
Firethorn Cl ME7 10 E6
Firmin Ave ME17 97 D5
Firs Cl CT19 177 D7
Firs La CT19 177 D7
Firs Rd CT4 112 F1
First Ave
Broadstairs CT10 8 F2
Chatham ME4 10 C2
Eastchurch ME12 5 E5
Gillingham ME7 10 E3
Margate CT9 8 B3
Rushenden ME11 2 F3
Sheerness ME12 1 D1
Firs The
Deal CT14 117 C8
Hersden CT3 46 E1
First La ME17 76 E2
FIR TOLL 136 C6
Firtree Cl CT2 66 B3
Fir Tree Cl CT11 52 C6
Fir Tree Gr
Bredhurst ME7 33 B1
Chatham ME5 32 D1
Fir Tree Hill CT13 93 B6
Fisher Cl CT21 176 D1
Fishermans Ctyd CT14 117 D3
Fisherman's Wharf 9
CT13 73 A1
Fisher Rd
Canterbury CT2 66 D1
Chatham ME5 32 B7
Fishers TN28 202 E5
Fisher St
Maidstone ME14 75 A6
Sandwich CT13 73 A1
Fisher Street Rd ME13 83 E2
Fish Market CT19 178 E5
Fishmarket Rd TN31 197 B1
Fishmonger's La 8 CT16 166 E7
Fitzgerald Ave CT6 22 C4
Fitzgilbert Cl ME7 11 A5
Fitzmary Ave CT9 7 E1
Fitzroy Ave
Broadstairs CT10 8 G2
Margate CT9 8 B1
Ramsgate CT12 29 B2
Fitzroy Rd CT5 20 F2
Fitzthorold Ho ME7 10 E7
Fitzwalter Ct 1 CT16 149 B3
Fitzwalters Mdw CT3 91 D2
Fitzwilliam Rd ME14 75 F5
Five Acre Wood Sch
ME15 97 B7
Five Bells La 5 ME1 9 D4
Five Vents La TN29 201 B8
Fiveways 6 CT17 166 C8
Five Ways Ct ME4 10 A4
Fiveways Rise CT14 116 F5
FIVE WENTS 98 D2
Flagstaff Ct 1 CT1 88 A7
Flamingo Cl ME5 32 A7
Flamingo Dr CT6 22 E3
Flanders Cl ME10 14 F1
Flanders Field TN25 157 E4
Flax Court La CT15 131 C7
Flaxman Ct 13 ME7 10 A6
Flaxman Dr ME16 74 C6
Flaxpond Rd TN23 155 F7
FLEEDEN 154 E7
Fleet Ave ME12 1 C1
Fleet Rd
Rochester ME1 9 D1
St Margaret's at Cliffe
CT15 134 A1
Fleets La CT2 66 D7
Fleet Villas TN24 139 D7
Fleetwood Ave CT6 22 D4
Fleetwood Cl ME12 4 B6
Fleming Rd CT13, CT3 92 D6
FLEMINGS 92 D6
Fleming Way CT19 178 E8
Fletcher Rd CT5 21 B1
Fletchers Way CT14 117 A5
Flete Rd CT9 28 D5
Fleur de Lis Heritage Ctr★ 17
ME13 62 D7
Flimwell TN23 155 D6
Flint Cl ME10 36 E8
Flint Cotts CT7 26 F6
Flint Gn ME5 32 C3
Flint Gr CT10 29 E5
Flint Ho CT9 7 J3
Flint La
Lenham ME17 79 C1
Woodside Green ME17 101 C8
Flodden Rd CT14 116 F3
Flood Hatch ME15 74 D2
Flood La ME13 62 C8
Flood St TN25 157 D2
Flora Rd CT11 52 E8
Florence Ave CT5 43 B7
Florence Cotts CT11 52 D6
Florence Ct CT9 8 B3
Florence Rd
Maidstone ME16 74 E3
3 Ramsgate CT11 52 D6
Florence St 3 ME2 9 B8
Florida Cl CT16 149 B3
Florin Dr ME1 9 B4
Flower Rise ME14 74 F7
Flume End ME15 74 D2
Flying Horse La 6 CT16 166 E7
Foads Hill CT12 51 D6
Foads La CT12 51 D5
Focal Point Rd CT16 148 F4
Fodbury Ct CT8 7 C1
Foley Cl TN24 157 A7
Foley St ME14 75 A5
FOLKESTONE 178 F4
Folkestone Acad CT19 178 B7
Folkestone Central CT19 178 C5
Folkestone Ent Ctr CT19 177 F8
Folkestone Martello Tower★
CT19 178 G6
Folkestone Race Course
CT21 175 A6
Folkestone Rd
Brookland TN31 198 B3
Church Hougham CT15 165 D4
Dover CT17, CT15 166 B7
Folkestone Sch for Girls The
CT20 177 F4
Folkestone Sports & Ski Ctr
CT19 178 B6
Folkestone West Sta
CT20 177 F5
Folkstone Ho 4 ME15 97 F6
Folkestone, St Martins CE
Prim Sch CT18 177 B5
Folks Wood Way CT21 175 A4
Folly Rd CT20 178 E6
FOLLY TOWN 141 F7
Fonblanque Rd ME12 1 D2
Fontana ME5 32 A3
Fontwell Cl ME15 97 F6
FOORD 178 D6
Foord Almshouses ME1 9 B3
Foord Rd ME17 101 D5
Foord Road N CT19, CT20 178 D5
Foord Road S 14 CT20 178 D5
Foord St ME1 9 D4
Forbes Rd ME13 62 C6
FORD 46 E8
Ford Cl
Bridge CT4 88 F1
Herne Bay CT6 22 A4
Fordcombe Cl ME15 97 F7
Ford Hill CT3, CT6 46 E8
Fordingbridge Cl ME16 74 B5
Fordoun Rd CT10 29 F5
Ford Way TN23 138 F1
FORDWICH 68 A4
Fordwich Cl ME16 74 B7
Fordwich Gn ME8 11 C3
Fordwich Gr CT10 29 E7
Fordwich Pl CT13 93 F8
Fordwich Rd CT2 67 F4
Ford Wlk CT5 43 A3
Foreland Ave
Folkestone CT19 178 F6
Margate CT9 8 D1
Foreland Ct
Birchington CT7 26 D8
Ramsgate CT11 52 D5
St Margaret's at Cliffe
CT15 151 A5
Foreland Hts CT10 30 B7
Foreland Park Ho CT10 30 B7
Foreland Rd CT15 151 A4
Foreland Sch The CT10 30 A6
Forelands Sq CT14 117 B3
Foreland The CT1 88 B5
Foreness Cl CT10 8 G3
Forestall Mdw TN23 156 B4
Forest Ave TN25 138 E4

Forest Cotts TN25....... 105 C2
Forestdale Rd ME5....... 54 A8
Forest Dr ME5....... 31 F2
Foresters Cl ME5....... 31 F2
Foresters Way CT20..... 178 D5
Forest Hill ME15....... 74 F1
Forestry Cotts CT4....... 125 B7
Forge Cl
Eythorne CT15.......... 131 C7
Sellindge TN25.......... 159 D1
Sturry CT2.......... 67 F5
Forge Cotts
Boyden Gate CT3.......... 47 C8
Broadstairs CT10.......... 30 B5
Faversham ME13.......... 63 D8
Forgefield TN26....... 153 D5
Forge Field CT15....... 164 E5
Forgefields CT6....... 46 B8
Forge Hill
Aldington TN25....... 173 A5
Bethersden TN26....... 153 E5
Forge Ho
Canterbury CT1.......... 87 E6
Ickham CT3.......... 69 C1
Forge La
Ashford TN23.......... 139 B2
Boxley ME14.......... 54 C2
Boyden Gate CT3.......... 47 C8
Bredhurst ME7.......... 33 A1
East Farleigh ME15....... 96 C7
Egerton Forstal TN27....... 118 C1
Gillingham ME7.......... 10 E7
Leeds ME17.......... 98 F7
Maidstone ME14.......... 76 C4
Ramsgate CT11.......... 52 C7
Sutton CT15.......... 133 A6
Upchurch ME9.......... 12 F3
Whitfield CT16.......... 149 A8
Whitstable CT5.......... 43 D8
Forge Mdw
Harrietsham ME17....... 100 D6
Stone in Oxney TN30....... 190 A4
Forge Meads TN30....... 188 E3
Forge Path CT16....... 149 A8
Forge Rd ME10....... 36 E6
Forrens The 14 CT1....... 67 A1
Forrester Cl CT1....... 67 C2
Forson Cl TN30....... 179 B8
FORSTAL....... 53 B2
Forstal Cotts
Forstal ME20.......... 53 B2
Lenham Heath ME17....... 102 A1
Forstal La ME17....... 96 D4
Forstal Rd
Egerton Forstal TN27....... 118 C1
Forstal ME20.......... 53 C2
Woolage Village CT4....... 112 E1
Forstal The
Lenham Heath ME17....... 102 A1
Preston CT3.......... 70 B6
Wye TN25.......... 123 E2
Forsters ME17....... 98 E4
Forsyth Ct 7 ME7....... 10 C7
Fort Amherst* ME4....... 9 F5
Fort Burgoyne (Casemated Barracks) CT15....... 149 E2
Fort Burgoyne Rd CT16....... 149 E1
Fort Cl TN29....... 206 E6
Fort Cotts CT10....... 30 B4
Fort Cres CT9....... 7 J3
Fort Hill CT9....... 7 I3
Fort Lower Prom CT9....... 7 J3
Fort Luton* ME4....... 10 A1
Fort Paragon CT9....... 7 J3
Fort Pitt Gram Sch ME4....... 9 E4
Fort Pitt Hill ME1, ME4....... 9 E4
Fort Pitt St ME4....... 9 E3
Fort Prom CT9....... 7 J3
Fort Rd
Broadstairs CT10.......... 30 B4
Hythe CT21.......... 176 A2
Margate CT9.......... 7 I3
Fort St ME1....... 9 D4
Fortuna Ct CT11....... 52 D7
Forty Acres Hill ME12....... 4 C4
Forty Acres Rd CT2....... 66 E2
Forum Sh Ctr The 9 ME10....... 36 F4
Forum The 2 ME10....... 36 F4
Forum Way TN23....... 155 E5
Forward Way ME1....... 31 C6
FOSTALL....... 64 A7
Fostall Gn TN23....... 155 F7
Fostall Rd ME13....... 40 C1
Foster Cl CT19....... 177 E7
Foster Clarke Dr ME17....... 97 D5
Foster Clark Est ME15....... 75 B2
Foster Rd TN24....... 157 A6
Foster's Ave CT10....... 29 E7
Foster's Ct CT13....... 94 A7
Foster St ME15....... 75 A3
Foster Way CT14....... 117 B5
Fostington Way ME5....... 31 F1
Fougeres Way TN24....... 139 A4
Foulds Cl ME8....... 33 B5
Foundry Wharf ME1....... 9 E4
Fountain Inn Ct CT9....... 7 I3
Fountain La
Maidstone ME16.......... 74 A2
Sheerness ME12.......... 1 B2
Fountains Cl TN24....... 140 A1
Fountain St
2 Sittingbourne ME10....... 36 E4
3 Whitstable CT5....... 20 D2
Fouracre Cotts ME9....... 34 E6
Four Horseshoes Pk ME13.......... 41 D1
Four Oaks ME13....... 61 E8
Fourth Ave
Eastchurch ME12.......... 5 F5
Gillingham ME7.......... 10 E4
Four Turnings CT3....... 70 B3
Four Wents
Langley Heath ME17....... 98 E3
Maidstone ME17....... 97 F2
Fowey Cl ME5....... 32 C5
Fowler Cl ME8....... 33 C3
Fowlmead Ctry Pk* CT14....... 116 E8
Foxborough Cl CT13....... 93 B6
Foxborough Hill CT13....... 93 B5
Foxborough La CT12....... 50 C6
Foxburrow Cl ME8....... 33 D5
Fox Cl CT18....... 161 B7
Foxden Dr ME15....... 75 F1
Foxdene Ct CT5....... 42 F6
Foxdene Rd CT5....... 42 F6
Foxdown Cl CT2....... 66 E2
Foxglove Cres ME5....... 31 E4
Foxglove Gn TN24....... 139 F2
Foxglove Rd TN24....... 139 E1
Foxglove Rise ME14....... 74 E7
Foxgrove ME10....... 36 E7
Foxgrove Rd CT5....... 21 A1
Fox Hill ME10, ME9....... 37 D3
Fox Holt Rd CT15....... 146 B2
Foxhunter Pk The CT12....... 49 D6
Foxley Rd ME11....... 3 A5
Fox's Cross CT5....... 43 B4
Fox's Cross Hill CT5....... 43 A3
Fox's Cross Rd CT5....... 43 C3
Fox St ME7....... 10 C6
Fox Way CT4....... 128 F8
Foxwood Specl Sch CT21....... 176 F3
Frampton Rd CT21....... 176 A2
France Rd CT16....... 149 A5
Frances Gdns CT11....... 52 F8
Francis Cl CT12....... 51 D5
Francis Dr ME5....... 32 A2
Francis La ME15....... 97 F5
Francis Rd
Ashford TN23.......... 156 B8
Broadstairs CT10.......... 30 B7
Frankapps Cl ME9....... 35 B6
Frank Edinger Cl TN24....... 139 D4
Franklin Dr ME14....... 75 D4
Franklin Rd ME7....... 10 D5
Franklins Cotts ME15....... 96 C5
Franklyn Ho CT2....... 67 F5
Franklyn Rd CT2....... 87 C8
Franks Ct ME8....... 11 B2
Frank Walters Bsns Pk The CT10....... 29 D3
Freathy La TN25....... 139 C8
Freda Cl CT10....... 29 F1
Frederick Rd
Deal CT14.......... 117 A3
Gillingham ME7.......... 10 C4
Frederick St ME10....... 36 E4
Freedown The CT15....... 151 A7
Freeman Ct 3 ME10....... 36 E4
Freeman Gdns ME4....... 9 F2
Freeman's Cl CT5....... 43 A6
Freeman's Rd CT12....... 50 B6
Freeman Way ME15....... 97 E7
Freemen's Way CT14....... 117 B3
Freesia Cl ME7....... 10 F6
Fremantle Rd CT20....... 177 E5
Fremlins Rd ME14....... 76 C4
Fremlin Walk Sh Ctr ME14....... 74 F4
Frencham Cl CT2....... 67 A4
French's Row ME9....... 38 D2
Frensham Cl ME10....... 37 B4
Frensham Wlk ME5....... 31 F1
Freshfield La CT21....... 176 B4
Freshland Rd ME16....... 74 B4
Freshlands CT6....... 23 E5
Freshwater Cl CT6....... 22 B3
Freshwater Rd ME5....... 32 B7
Friars Ave ME5....... 31 F2
Friars Cl CT5....... 21 A1
Friars The CT1....... 66 F1
Friars Way CT16....... 149 A3
Friary Pl 3 ME2....... 9 B7
Friary Prec ME2....... 9 B7
Friary Way CT2....... 66 D2
Frid Cnr TN26....... 153 E7
Friendly Cl CT9....... 8 D1
Friends Ave CT9....... 29 D8
Friesian Way TN24....... 139 C8
FRINDSBURY....... 9 C8
Frindsbury Rd ME2....... 9 B8
Frinstead Wlk ME16....... 74 B7
FRINSTED....... 79 C7
Frinsted Cl ME8....... 11 C3
Frinsted Rd ME9....... 58 E2
Friston Way ME1....... 31 D8
Frith Bsns Pk TN25....... 172 B6
Frith Rd
Aldington Frith TN25....... 172 C6
Dover CT16.......... 149 C1
Frithwood Cl ME15....... 75 F1
Frittenden Cl TN23....... 155 E6
Frobisher Cl ME10....... 36 E7
Frobisher Ct 2 CT11....... 52 F8
Frobisher Gdns ME1....... 9 C2
Frog Farm Cotts ME9....... 13 A4
FROGHAM....... 113 C2
FROGHOLT....... 176 F7
Frog La CT4....... 111 C6
Frogmore Wlk ME17....... 101 C5
Frognal Cl ME9....... 38 B2
Frognal Gdns ME9....... 38 C2
Frognal La ME9....... 38 B2
Front Brents ME13....... 62 D8
Front Rd TN26....... 169 A1
Front St CT14....... 133 F5
Front The CT15....... 151 A4
Frost Cres ME5....... 32 A7
Frostland La TN26, TN29....... 184 C1
Froyle Cl ME16....... 74 C6
Fruiterer's Cl ME9....... 59 B7
Fulbert Dr ME14....... 75 F5
Fulbert Rd CT16....... 149 B5
Fulham Ave CT9....... 28 C7
Fullers Cl ME14....... 76 A4
Fullers Yd CT9....... 7 J2
Fulmar Ct TN29....... 194 F3
Fulmar Mews CT18....... 163 A3
Fulmar Way CT6....... 23 F4
Fulsam Pl CT9....... 7 H1
Fulston Manor Sch ME10....... 36 F2
Fulston Pl ME10....... 37 A3
Furfield Chase ME15....... 97 E4
Furfield Cl ME17....... 97 E5
FURFIELD PARK....... 97 D4
Furley Park Prim Sch TN23....... 156 C2
Furrell's Rd ME1....... 9 D5
FURTHER QUARTER....... 152 C3
Furze Hill Cres ME12....... 3 E6
Fusilier Ave CT20....... 177 B5
Fyndon Ho CT1....... 88 C7

G

Gabriel's Hill ME15....... 75 A4
Gadby Rd ME10....... 36 C5
Gadsby La TN26....... 152 F3
Gads Hill ME7....... 10 F6
Gagetown Terr 1 ME14....... 74 F7
Gainsboro Rd 4 CT7....... 26 F8
Gainsborough Ave 1 CT9....... 29 C8
Gainsborough Cl
Folkestone CT19....... 178 A7
Gillingham ME8.......... 33 D6
Sittingbourne ME10....... 36 B5
Gainsborough Dr
Herne Bay CT6.......... 23 E5
Maidstone ME16.......... 74 B4
Gainsborough Ho ME1....... 9 D5
Galena Cl
Chatham ME5.......... 32 A1
Sittingbourne ME10....... 36 C6
Gallants La ME15....... 96 A2
Galleon Cl ME1....... 31 C8
Galley Dr ME9....... 58 E6
Galliard St CT13....... 94 A8
Galloway Dr TN25....... 139 C8
Galloways Rd TN29....... 205 C5
Gallow's Cnr CT21....... 176 A2
Gallwey Ave CT7....... 26 E7
Galway Rd ME12....... 1 D1
Gammon's Farm La TN29....... 185 B3
Gammons Yd 6 CT2....... 66 F1
Gandy's La ME17....... 97 C2
Gange Mews 3 ME13....... 62 D7
Gann Rd CT5....... 20 F2
Gaol La 13 CT16....... 166 D7
Gap The
Blean CT2.......... 66 A7
Canterbury CT1.......... 88 B5
Garden Cl
Maidstone ME15.......... 97 E7
Rough Common CT2....... 66 A2
Garden Cotts CT3....... 91 A7
Gardeners Pl CT4....... 86 F1
Garden Hall The TN25....... 124 A1
Garden of England Pk (Mobile Home Pk) ME17....... 100 B7
Garden Pl TN24....... 139 E6
Garden Rd CT19....... 178 D6
Garden St ME7....... 10 A6
Gardens The
Coxheath ME17.......... 96 C3
Ivychurch TN29.......... 192 F4
Gardiner's Hill TN31....... 197 B6
Gardiner St ME7....... 10 C6
Gardner Cl CT18....... 162 F3
Gardners Cl CT3....... 71 E1
Garfield Pl 4 ME13....... 62 D7
Garfield Rd
Gillingham ME7.......... 10 D6
Margate CT9.......... 7 H2
GARLINGE....... 28 A8
GARLINGE GREEN....... 108 E5
Garlinge Green Rd CT4....... 108 E6
Garlinge Prim Sch CT9....... 28 B8
Garrard Ave CT9....... 28 B8
Garrington Cl ME14....... 75 C6
Garrison Rd ME12....... 1 B3
Garton Way TN23....... 155 C7
Gascoyne Cl ME15....... 76 B2
Gas House Rd ME1....... 9 C6
Gaskin Rd ME13....... 62 E7
Gas La ME13....... 63 F3
Gas Rd
Sittingbourne ME10....... 36 F5
Sittingbourne, Murston ME10....... 37 B6
Gas St CT1....... 87 F7
Gasworks La TN23....... 139 B2
Gatcombe Cl
Chatham ME5.......... 32 A5
Maidstone ME16.......... 74 B5
Gateacre Rd CT5....... 43 A6
Gatefield La 9 ME13....... 62 D7
Gatekeeper Chase ME8....... 33 F8
Gate La CT4....... 144 A4
Gate Quays CT9....... 7 I2
Gateway Ct 21 CT11....... 52 F7
Gateway The CT16....... 166 E7
Gatland La ME16....... 74 B2
Gault Cl ME15....... 76 A2
Gaunt's Cl CT14....... 117 A4
Gayhurst Cl ME8....... 33 D6
Gayhurst Dr ME10....... 36 C5
Gazedown TN29....... 194 F3
Gaze Hill Ave ME10....... 37 A3
Gazen Salts Nature Reserve* CT13....... 72 F2
Gean Cl ME5....... 54 A8
Geddes Cl CT18....... 162 F3
Genesta Ave CT5....... 43 B7
Genesta Cl ME10....... 36 E7
Geneva Ave ME8....... 11 A2
Gentian Cl
4 Chatham ME5....... 31 E4
Maidstone ME14.......... 75 E5
Geoffrey Ct CT7....... 27 A7
George Alley CT14....... 117 D6
George Cooper Ho 11 CT20....... 178 C4
George Gurr Cres CT19....... 178 D8
George Hill Rd CT10, CT9....... 8 E1
George La
Boughton Street ME13....... 63 F3
Folkestone CT20.......... 178 D4
Leeds ME17.......... 99 B7
New Romney TN28....... 202 B7
Rochester ME1.......... 9 C6
George Marsham Ho ME15.......... 96 F3
George Parris Ct ME12....... 4 C6
George Pk CT9....... 7 F1
George Roche Rd CT1....... 88 A6
George's Ave CT5....... 43 A7
George St
Ashford TN23.......... 139 B1
Deal CT14.......... 117 D7
Dover CT17.......... 149 C1
Maidstone ME15.......... 75 A3
Ramsgate CT11.......... 52 E7
Sittingbourne ME10....... 37 B4
George Stone Ho 25 CT20.......... 178 E5
George Summers Cl ME2....... 9 E8
George V Ave CT9....... 28 C8
George Warren Ct 1 CT9....... 7 J1
George Williams Way TN24.......... 139 E5
George Wood Cl TN29....... 205 C6
Georgian Cl ME11....... 3 A3
Georgian Dr ME17....... 96 D3
Georgian Way ME8....... 33 C4
Gerald Ave ME4....... 9 F2
Geraldine Rd CT19....... 177 F6
Gerald Palmby Ct CT14....... 117 C7
Gerlac Ho TN24....... 139 C5
Gerrard Ave ME1....... 31 E8
Gerrards Dr ME10....... 36 F2
Gibbons Rd ME10....... 36 B5
Gibraltar Ave ME7....... 10 B7
Gibraltar Hill ME4....... 9 F4
Gibraltar La
Hawkinge CT18.......... 163 A2
Maidstone ME14.......... 74 F8
Gibraltar Sq CT15....... 149 E3
GIBRALTER....... 162 F3
Gibson St ME10....... 36 E4
Gidd's Pond Cotts ME14....... 75 E6
Giddyhorn La ME16....... 74 C5
Gifford Cl ME8....... 11 C3
Gigger's Green Rd TN25....... 185 C7
Gilbert Cl ME7....... 33 A5
Gilbert Pl 9 CT20....... 177 E3
Gilbert Rd
4 Ashford TN24....... 139 B2
Ramsgate CT11.......... 52 D8
Gilbert Terr 2 ME14....... 74 F7
Gilbert Way CT1....... 87 E6
Gilchrist Ave CT6....... 22 C2
Giles Gdns CT9....... 28 F8
Giles La CT2....... 66 D4
Giles-Young Ct 7 ME10....... 36 E5
Gilford Rd CT14....... 117 D5
Gilham Gr CT14....... 117 B4
Gillett Rd TN29....... 205 D7
GILLINGHAM....... 10 D3
Gillingham Gate ME7....... 10 C8
Gillingham Gate Rd ME7....... 10 C8
Gillingham Gn ME7....... 10 E6
Gillingham Rd ME7....... 10 D5
Gillingham Sta ME7....... 10 D5
Gill La
Aldington Frith TN25....... 172 A8
Ruckinge TN26.......... 171 C2
Gillman Cl CT18....... 162 F4
Gillon Mews 9 CT1....... 67 B2
Gills Terr ME8....... 12 C3
Ginsbury Cl ME2....... 9 E6
Giraud Dr ME13....... 62 B8
Glack Rd CT14....... 116 F4
Glade The
Chatham ME5.......... 32 A2
Deal CT14.......... 116 F6
Gladstone Ct CT10....... 29 F4
Gladstone Dr ME10....... 37 C4
Gladstone Rd
Ashford TN24.......... 156 E7
Broadstairs CT10.......... 29 F4
Chatham ME4.......... 9 E2
Deal CT14.......... 117 C4
Folkestone CT19.......... 178 E6
Gladstone Rd continued
Maidstone ME14.......... 75 A6
Margate CT9.......... 7 I1
Whitstable CT5.......... 20 D2
Gladwyn Cl ME8....... 33 D4
Glamis Cl ME5....... 32 A5
Glanville Rd
Gillingham ME7.......... 10 D5
Rochester ME2.......... 9 A8
Glasgow Ho 8 ME15....... 97 E7
Glayton Gdns ME5....... 31 F4
Gleaming Wood Dr ME5....... 54 D8
Gleaners Cl ME14....... 75 E4
Gleanings Mews ME1....... 9 C5
Glebe Cl
Smarden TN27.......... 135 B2
St Margaret's at Cliffe CT15.......... 150 F6
Glebe Cotts ME13....... 81 E7
Glebe Ct CT12....... 50 B5
Glebe Gdns
Lenham ME17.......... 101 E5
6 Margate CT9....... 28 B8
Glebe La
Maidstone ME16.......... 74 A1
Sittingbourne ME10....... 37 B2
Glebeland TN27....... 118 F4
Glebelands
Alkham CT15.......... 147 D1
Ash CT3.......... 71 C2
Mersham TN25.......... 157 E4
Glebe Rd
Gillingham ME7.......... 10 E3
Margate CT9.......... 28 B8
Glebe The TN27....... 120 D7
Glebe Way
Ashford TN24.......... 139 D6
Whitstable CT5.......... 43 D8
Glemsford Cotts CT2....... 65 E1
Glen Ave CT6....... 23 C5
Glenavon Ho CT10....... 30 B7
Glenbervie Dr CT6....... 23 E5
Glenbrook Cl CT6....... 23 D5
Glenbrook Gr ME10....... 36 E7
Glencoe Jun Sch ME4....... 10 A2
Glencoe Rd
Chatham ME4.......... 10 A2
Margate CT9.......... 8 A1
Glendale 1 CT20....... 178 E4
Glendale Rd ME12....... 4 B7
Gleneagles Ct ME5....... 31 F2
Gleneagles Dr ME15....... 75 A1
Glenfield Rd CT16....... 149 B3
Glen Gr CT17....... 166 B7
Glen Iris Ave CT2....... 66 C2
Glen Iris Cl CT2....... 66 C2
Glenmore Ctr ME10....... 37 C6
Glen Rd CT14....... 134 C6
Glenside CT5....... 44 A8
Glenside Ave CT1....... 67 B2
Glen The
Minster (Sheppey) ME12....... 4 B7
Shepherdswell CT15....... 130 D5
Upstreet CT3.......... 47 D3
Glen Wlk CT5....... 43 A3
Glenwood TN30....... 167 B3
Glenwood Cl
Chatham ME5.......... 10 C1
Gillingham ME7.......... 33 A7
Maidstone ME16.......... 74 C5
Tenterden TN30.......... 167 B3
Glenwood Dr ME12....... 4 C6
Glistening Glade ME8....... 33 E6
Globe La ME4....... 9 F5
Gloster Cl CT18....... 163 B3
Gloster Ropewalk CT17....... 166 C5
Gloster Way CT17....... 166 C5
Gloucester Ave
Broadstairs CT10.......... 29 F3
Margate CT9.......... 8 D2
Gloucester Cl ME8....... 34 A8
Gloucester Mews TN28....... 202 C8
Gloucester Pl 17 CT20....... 178 D5
Gloucester Rd
Maidstone ME15.......... 97 D8
Whitstable CT5.......... 20 F2
Glover Cl ME10....... 14 F1
Glover Rd TN24....... 139 E1
Glovers Cres ME10....... 36 F3
Glovers Mill ME4....... 9 D3
Glynne Cl ME8....... 33 D6
Goad Ave ME5....... 32 B3
GOAT LEES....... 139 C8
Goat Lees La TN25....... 139 D8
Gobery Hill CT3....... 70 B1
Godden Rd CT2....... 67 A4
Godden Way ME8....... 11 A4
Goddings Dr ME1....... 9 A3
Goddington La ME17....... 100 B6
Goddington Rd ME2....... 9 B8
Godfrey Gdns CT4....... 86 F1
Godfrey Ho CT5....... 43 E8
Godfreys Cotts ME13....... 105 C8
Godfrey's Grave ME13....... 64 B7
Godfrey Wlk TN23....... 156 B8
GODINGTON PARK....... 138 E2
Godinton House & Gdns* TN23....... 138 C4
Godinton La TN23, TN26....... 138 D5
Godinton Prim Sch TN23....... 138 D3
Godinton Rd TN23....... 139 A2
Godinton Way TN23....... 139 A2
Godinton Way Ind Est TN23....... 139 B2
GODMERSHAM....... 107 A2
Godwin Bglws CT9....... 8 B3

Godwin Cl
Deal CT14 117 A3
Sittingbourne ME10 14 F1
Godwin Cotts CT9 8 A3
Godwin Rd
Canterbury CT1 87 C6
Dover CT16 166 F8
Margate CT9 8 A3
Godwyne Cl CT16 166 D8
Godwyne Ct CT16 149 D1
Godwyne Rd CT16 149 D1
Godwyn Gdns CT20 178 A4
Godwyn Rd
Deal CT14 117 C8
Folkestone CT20 178 A4
Gogway CT4 126 B5
Goldcrest Wlk CT5 43 B6
Golden Acre La CT8 27 D7
Golden Cl CT8 27 D7
Golden Hill CT5 43 F6
Golden Sq
New Romney TN28 202 A6
Tenterden TN30 179 B8
Golden St CT14 117 D7
Golden Wood Cl ME5 54 D8
Goldfinch Cl
Faversham ME13 40 C1
Herne Bay CT6 23 C2
Gold Hill TN25 121 D4
Golding Cl ME1 9 E1
Goldings The ME8 33 C8
Goldsmith Ct TN30 167 B1
Goldsmith Rd ME8 33 E5
Goldstone Dro CT3 71 E7
Goldstone Wlk ME5 32 A1
Goldthorne Cl ME14 75 C5
Goldups La CT4 84 C1
Goldups Lane Cotts CT4 84 C1
Goldwell Cl TN25 173 A6
Goldwell Hos TN25 173 A6
Goldwell La
Aldington TN25 173 B7
Great Chart TN23, TN26 154 F8
Goldwyn Com Specl Sch TN23 138 B4
Golf Ct CT14 95 C1
Golf Rd CT14 117 C8
Golf Road Pl CT14 117 C8
GOLGOTHA 130 F6
Gooch Cl ME16 74 D8
Goodall Cl ME8 33 E5
Goodban Sq CT3 71 D1
Goodcheap La TN25 140 D2
Goodfellow Way [3] CT16 166 D8
Good Hope CT14 116 F4
Good Intent Cotts TN27 119 A5
GOODNESTONE
Faversham 63 D7
Wingham 91 D2
Goodnestone CE Prim Sch CT3 91 C2
Goodnestone Hill CT3 91 D2
Goodnestone Park Gdns★ CT3 91 C1
Goodnestone Rd
Sittingbourne ME10 37 B4
Wingham CT3 91 B5
Good Shepherd Prim Sch The ME4 9 E1
Goodwin Ave CT5 21 E2
Goodwin Ct CT9 8 D3
Goodwin Dr ME14 75 B8
Goodwin Pk CT9 29 A5
Goodwin Rd
Ramsgate CT11 52 B5
St Margaret's at Cliffe CT15 151 A4
Goodwood Cl ME15 97 F6
Goose Cl ME5 32 A7
Goose Farm CT2 67 D7
Goosefields ME13 41 E1
Gordon Ave ME11 3 A4
Gordon Cl
Ashford TN24 139 D2
Sittingbourne ME10 37 C4
Gordon Cotts ME9 58 B6
Gordon Ct ME17 96 E3
Gordon Gr CT8 7 C1
Gordon Inf Sch ME2 9 A8
Gordon Jun Sch ME2 9 A8
Gordon Rd
Canterbury CT1 87 F7
Chatham, Luton ME4 10 B2
Chatham ME4 10 A7
Dover CT16 149 A5
Faversham ME13 62 E8
Folkestone CT20 177 D6
Gillingham ME7 10 E5
Herne Bay CT6 22 F4
Margate CT9 8 A3
Margate, Westwood CT9 29 A5
Ramsgate CT11 52 D8
Rochester ME2 9 A8
Whitstable CT5 43 D8
Gordon Sq
Birchington CT7 26 F7
Faversham ME13 62 E7
Gordon Terr
Lydd TN29 205 C5
Rochester ME1 9 C4
GORE 93 B3
Gore Cl CT13 93 B3
Gore Cotts ME9 12 E1
Gore Court Rd
Maidstone ME15 97 F5
Sittingbourne ME10 36 E2
Gore Ct TN24 139 C3
Gore End Cl CT7 26 F7
Gore Farm CT13 93 B3
Gore La CT13 93 B2
Gorely Ho [14] CT17 166 D7
Gore Mews [3] CT1 67 B2
Gore Rd
Eastry CT13 93 B3
Silver Street ME9 57 F5
Gore Street Farm Cotts CT12 49 A7
Gore Terr CT13 93 B3
Goretop La CT14 94 C6
Gorham Dr ME15 76 A1
Gorrell Rd CT5 20 E1
Gorse Ave ME5 31 F5
Gorse La CT6 23 C2
Gorse Mead TN23 155 F8
Gorse Rd ME10 37 C5
Gorst St ME7 10 C5
Goschen Rd CT17 166 B8
Gosfield Rd CT6 23 A4
Goshawk Ho [1] ME10 37 A4
GOSMERE 83 E7
Gosmere Farm Barns
Doddington ME13 80 E7
Sheldwich ME13 83 E7
Gosselin St CT5 43 E8
Goss Hall La CT3 72 A2
Goteley Mere TN24 139 C7
Gothic Cl CT14 117 B1
Gothic Cotts TN26 121 A1
Goudhurst Cl
Canterbury CT2 67 A4
Maidstone ME16 74 E4
Goudhurst Rd ME8 11 B3
Gough Rd CT20 177 E3
Gould Rd ME5 32 B3
Gower Ho ME14 75 A6
Grace Ave ME16 74 D6
Grace Ct [16] CT20 178 D5
Grace Hill CT20 178 D5
Grace Mdw CT16 149 A7
Grace Rd ME12 1 B1
Grace Sch [22] CT20 178 D5
Grace Wlk CT14 117 A5
Grafton Ave ME1 31 E8
Grafton Rd
Broadstairs CT10 29 F8
Sittingbourne ME10 36 F4
Grafton Rise CT6 22 C4
Graham Cl ME4 9 F6
Grainey Field ME9 34 E4
Grain Rd ME8 33 C3
Grampian Way ME15 76 A1
Grampion Cl TN24 139 C4
Grams Rd CT14 134 C8
Granada Ho [8] ME15 75 A4
Granada St [9] ME15 75 A4
Granary Cl
Gillingham ME8 11 F1
Maidstone ME14 75 E5
Granary Court Rd TN25 159 A4
Granary Pl CT5 43 D8
Grand Ct
[6] Folkestone CT20 178 B3
[7] Gillingham ME7 10 C6
Littlestone-on-Sea TN28 202 E5
Grand Dr CT6 22 C4
Grand Mans CT10 30 B3
Grand Par TN28 202 E5
Grand Pavilion CT5 20 F3
Grand The★ CT20 178 B3
GRANGE 11 B6
Grange Cres TN30 167 A3
Grange Ct
[1] Folkestone CT20 178 C4
[9] Ramsgate CT11 52 C6
Grange Hill ME5 10 B3
Grange Ho ME16 74 A2
Grange La ME14 54 A1
Grange Rd
Broadstairs CT10 29 F6
Deal CT14 117 B5
Folkestone CT19 177 E6
Gillingham ME7 11 A6
Herne Bay CT6 23 C4
Hythe CT21 176 B4
Ramsgate CT11 52 C6
Rochester ME2 9 B7
Grange Rdbt ME7 11 A6
Grange The
Ramsgate CT11 52 C7
Shepherdswell CT15 130 D5
Whitstable CT5 43 A6
Grange Way
Broadstairs CT10 29 F2
Rochester ME1 9 C3
Grant Cl CT10 29 E6
Grant Dr ME15 97 D6
Grantham Ave CT14 117 A5
Grantley Cl TN23 156 A8
Grant's Cotts ME17 101 B5
Granville Ave
Broadstairs CT10 30 B3
Ramsgate CT12 29 B1
Granville Cl ME13 62 C7
Granville Ct
Deal CT14 117 C2
Maidstone ME14 75 A6
Granville Dr CT6 22 B2
Granville Farm Mews [24] CT11 52 F7
Granville Ho [18] CT11 52 F7
Granville Marina [20] CT11 52 F7
Granville Par CT20 177 E3
Granville Pl
Folkestone CT20 177 F3
Sheerness ME12 1 D2
Granville Rd
Broadstairs CT10 30 B3
Deal CT14 117 C2
Gillingham ME7 10 E5
Kingsdown CT14 134 D3
Maidstone ME14 75 A6
Sheerness ME12 1 D2
St Margaret's at Cliffe CT15 151 B6
Granville Road E CT20 177 F3
Granville St
Deal CT14 117 D5
Dover CT16 149 C1
Granville The CT15 151 B6
Granville Theatre★ [25] CT11 52 F7
Grapple Rd ME14 75 A7
Grasmere Ave CT11 52 A7
Grasmere Gdns CT19 178 B7
Grasmere Pk CT5 44 B8
Grasmere Rd
Ashford TN24 139 C6
Whitstable CT5 44 B8
Grasmere Way CT3 112 F6
Grasslands
Ashford TN23 155 D7
Langley Heath ME17 98 E4
Grassmere TN29 194 E3
Grassy Glade ME7 33 B6
GRAVEL CASTLE 129 A8
Gravel Castle Rd CT4 129 A8
Gravel Hill ME13 103 C8
Gravel La CT15 165 A4
Gravelly Bottom Rd ME17 99 B2
Gravelly Field TN23 155 C8
Gravelly Fields TN23 155 C8
Gravel Wlk
[3] Ashford TN23 139 B3
Rochester ME1 9 D5
GRAVENEY 41 E2
Graveney Prim Sch ME13 41 E1
Graveney Rd
Faversham ME13 62 F7
Maidstone ME15 97 F7
Gray Cl CT18 163 C5
Graylen Cl CT14 117 C7
Graylings Ct ME10 36 C2
Graylings The ME1 9 B3
Grayshott Cl ME10 36 F3
Graystone Rd CT5 21 A2
Grays Way CT1 87 B6
Great Basin Rd ME12 1 B3
Great Burton Ho TN24 139 E5
GREAT CHART 138 C1
Great Chart Prim Sch TN23 155 D8
Great Conduit St CT21 176 C2
Great Easthall Way ME10 37 D4
Great Fishers TN23 155 C7
Great Ivy Mill Cotts ME15 96 F7
Great Lines ME7 10 B5
GREAT MONGEHAM 116 C3
Great Oaks Small Sch CT12 51 B2
Great South Ave ME4 10 A1
GREAT STONAR 73 B4
GREATSTONE-ON-SEA 202 E1
Greatstone Prim Sch TN28 202 D2
Great Stour Pl [3] CT2 66 F1
Grebe Apartments [15] ME15 97 E5
Grebe Cl CT18 163 A4
Grebe Cres CT21 187 C8
Grecian St ME14 75 A6
Greenacre CT4 111 D3
Greenacre Cl ME5 32 A5
Greenacre Dr CT14 117 C1
Greenacres CT14 95 B4
Green Acres CT15 131 D7
Greenacre Sch ME5 31 F5
Green Acres Cl CT6 23 B3
Greenbank
Ashford TN24 139 D6
Chatham ME5 32 B8
Green Bank Cl ME7 33 A5
Greenbanks CT18 161 C6
Greenborough Cl ME15 97 E6
Green Cl
Hawkinge CT18 163 B4
Rochester ME1 9 D2
Green Cloth Mews [2] CT1 67 B2
Greencroft TN23 155 E6
Green Ct
Bridge CT4 89 A1
Folkestone CT19 178 E7
Green Dell CT2 66 F4
Greenfield Cl ME20 53 A6
Greenfield Cotts
Boxley ME14 54 C3
[9] Canterbury CT1 87 F7
Greenfield Rd
Folkestone CT19 178 E7
Gillingham ME7 10 D6
Ramsgate CT12 29 C2
Greenfields
Maidstone ME15 97 E8
Sellindge TN25 159 E2
Greenfields Com Prim Sch ME15 97 E8
Green Fields La TN23 155 C7
Greenfinches ME7 32 F6
Green Gates CT16 149 A8
Green Hedges TN30 179 B8
GREENHILL 22 D2
Green Hill ME15 76 B1
Greenhill Bridge Rd CT6 22 D3
Greenhill Cl CT12 50 B7
Greenhill Gdns
Herne Bay CT6 22 D3
Minster (Thanet) CT12 50 B7
Greenhill La TN27 135 F7
Green Hill La ME17 100 D1
Greenhill Rd CT6 22 C2
Green Hills CT4 128 D8
Greenhithe [3] ME15 75 A3
Greenhouse La CT2 66 E2
Green La
Alkham CT15 147 D3
Ashford TN23 155 E5
Bethersden TN26 153 A2
Broadstairs CT10 29 E5
Capel-le-Ferne CT18 164 B3
Challock TN25 105 A2
Deal CT14 117 B1
Dover CT16 149 B3
Eythorne CT15 131 D7
Folkestone CT19 178 E7
Goodnestone CT3 92 B3
High Halden TN26 152 F3
Hythe CT21 176 A2
Langley Heath ME17 98 E3
Maidstone ME17 97 C3
Margate CT9 29 E8
Old Wives Lees CT4 85 C2
Platt's Heath ME17 100 F2
Rhodes Minnis CT4, CT18 143 E2
Rodmersham ME9 59 B7
Smarden TN27 135 A1
St Margaret's at Cliffe CT15 133 F1
Temple Ewell CT16 148 E6
Whitfield CT16 148 E7
Whitstable CT5 43 D8
Green Lane Ave CT21 176 A2
Green Lane Cotts ME17 98 E3
Greenleas [1] CT20 178 B3
Green Leas CT5 21 D1
Green Lees ME13 61 E2
Greenlees Cl ME10 36 B5
Greenly Way TN28 202 C6
Green Mdws
Dymchurch TN29 186 D2
Eythorne CT15 131 D7
Green Park Com Prim Sch (Lower) CT16 149 B4
Green Park Com Prim Sch (Upper) CT16 149 C4
Green Porch Cl ME10 36 F7
Green Rd
Birchington CT7 26 F8
Stalisfield Green ME13 103 C6
Greensand Rd ME15 76 A2
Greensand Ridge ME17 99 E2
Green Sands ME5 54 C8
Green's Cotts ME15 96 A4
Greenshanks ME9 14 E3
Greenside
High Halden TN26 167 E7
Maidstone ME15 75 B3
Greenside Ho CT9 7 F1
Greensole La CT12 28 E1
Green St ME7 10 C5
Green The
Blean CT2 66 A6
Burmarsh TN29 186 C4
Chartham CT4 86 D3
East Farleigh ME15 96 B7
Harbledown CT2 65 E1
Hythe CT21 176 B4
Littlebourne CT3 89 F7
Lower Halstow ME9 13 B3
Lydd TN29 205 B5
Manston CT12 28 D1
Sheerness ME12 1 I1
Warehorne TN26 182 D6
Woodchurch TN26 169 A2
Woolage Village CT4 112 E1
Wye TN25 123 E2
Greenvale Gdns ME8 11 B2
Greenvale Inf Sch ME4 10 A2
Greenview Wlk ME8 11 A4
Greenway
Chatham ME5 31 D6
Faversham ME13 62 B8
Green Way
Lydd TN29 205 C5
Maidstone ME16 74 B3
Greenway Court Farm Cotts ME17 78 A1
Greenway Court Rd ME17 78 A1
Greenway La ME17 100 A7
Greenways
Lower Halstow ME9 13 B3
Maidstone ME14 75 F5
Sittingbourne ME10 37 B3
Greenwich Cl
Chatham ME5 32 B4
Maidstone ME16 74 D4
GREET 80 D3
Gregory Cl
Gillingham ME8 33 E4
Sittingbourne ME10 37 A8
Gregory Ct TN25 123 E2
Grenadier Cl
Gillingham ME8 12 B2
Maidstone ME15 75 F2
Grenadier Way TN23 155 C8
Grenham Bay Ave CT7 26 E8
Grenham Rd CT7 26 F8
Grenville Gdns CT7 26 E8
Grenville Way CT10 29 E4
Gresham Ave CT9 7 E1
Gresham Cl [3] ME8 11 F1
Gresham Rd ME17 96 D3
Greville Ho CT17 166 C7
Greville Homes CT13 93 B2
Greyfriars Cl ME16 74 D5
Grey Friars Cotts [8] CT1 87 F8
Greyfriars Ct CT10 8 F1
Greyhound Chase TN23 155 D7
Greystones Rd
Cliffs End CT12 51 D5
Maidstone ME15 76 A2
Grey Wethers ME14 53 E4
Grey Willow Gdns TN23 155 D8
Grice Cl CT18 162 F3
Grieveson Ho ME4 10 A4
Griffin Cotts TN26 181 C2
Griffin's Cnr TN25 140 E7
Griffin St CT14 117 D7
Grimshill Ct CT2 66 C4
Grimshill Rd CT5 43 E8
Grimston Ave CT20 178 B4
Grimston Gdns CT20 178 B4
Grimthorpe Ave CT5 43 C7
Grinsell Hill CT12 50 E6
Grisbrook Farm Cl TN29 205 D6
Grisbrook Rd TN29 205 D6
Grizedale Cl ME1 31 D8
Groombridge Sq [13] ME15 97 F6
Groom Way ME17 101 E6
Grosvenor Ave ME4 9 E3
Grosvenor Cotts CT7 27 B3
Grosvenor Gdns CT9 7 I1
Grosvenor Hill CT9 7 I2
Grosvenor Ho [5] ME15 97 F5
Grosvenor Pl CT9 7 I2
Grosvenor Rd
Ashford TN24 139 D7
Broadstairs CT10 30 A4
Gillingham ME7 11 A1
Ramsgate CT11 52 C7
Whitstable CT5 43 D7
Grotto Gdns [6] CT9 7 J2
Grotto Hill CT9 7 J2
Grotto Rd [5] CT9 7 J2
GROVE 69 F8
Grove Ave ME12 6 G2
Grove Bridge TN25 174 D8
Grove Cl ME13 62 A6
Grove Cotts TN30 179 B6
Grove Court Farm ME13 64 A3
Grove Ct [4] ME2 9 B7
Grove Dairy Farm ME9 36 A6
GROVE END 58 C7
Grove Ferry Hill CT3 47 E3
Grove Ferry Rd CT3 48 A2
Grove Gdns CT9 7 G1
GROVE GREEN 75 E5
Grove Green La ME14 75 E5
Grove Green Rd ME14 75 F5
GROVE HILL 69 D6
Grove Ho TN27 136 C3
Grovehurst Ave ME10 14 F1
Grovehurst Rd ME10, ME9 14 E2
Grove La
Brookland TN29 191 D3
Iden TN31 197 C4
Grovelands ME17 101 E5
Grove Park Ave ME10 36 B5
Grove Park CP Sch ME10 36 B6
Grove Pl ME13 62 A6
Grove Rd
Chatham ME4 10 B2
Deal CT14 117 D3
Folkestone CT20 178 E6
Gillingham ME7 11 A6
Maidstone ME15 97 C7
Preston CT3 70 B8
Ramsgate CT11 52 D6
Rochester ME2 9 B8
Selling ME13 84 B4
Staple CT3 91 F6
Wickhambreaux CT3 69 D6
Grove Road Cotts
Wickhambreaux CT3 69 C2
Wickhambreaux, Frognall CT3 69 C3
Grove Terr CT1 87 E7
Grove The
Ashford TN24 139 E6
Barham CT4 128 F8
Deal CT14 117 C6
Dover CT16 149 C1
Herne Bay CT6 22 C2
Maidstone ME14 76 A3
Westgate on Sea CT8 27 F8
Groveway ME12 6 F2
Grove Way CT3 70 C7
Grovewood Ct ME14 75 E4
Grovewood Dr ME14 75 E4
Grummock Ave CT11 52 B7
Grundy's Hill [13] CT11 52 E6
Guardian Ct ME8 11 C1
Guernsey Way TN24 139 C7
Guestling Mill Ct [1] CT13 72 F1
Guildcount La [5] CT13 72 F1
Guildford Ave CT8 27 E8
Guildford Lawn [1] CT11 52 E6
Guildford Rd CT1 87 F6
Guildhall Ct [10] CT20 178 D5
Guildhall Mus★
Queenborough ME11 2 F5
Rochester ME1 9 C6
Guildhall St
[4] Canterbury CT1 87 F8
[18] Folkestone CT20 178 D5
Guildhall Street N CT19, CT20 178 D5
Guilford Ave CT16 149 A8

Guilford Ct CT14 117 D2
Guilford Ho CT13 95 A7
Guilford Rd CT13 94 E8
GUILTON 71 C1
Guilton CT3 71 B1
Guldeford La TN29, TN31 198 F3
Guldeford Lane Cnr TN31 198 D2
Gulland Ho 4 ME14 75 B4
Gullands ME17 98 E4
Gundulph Rd ME1 9 E4
Gundulph Sq ME1 9 C6
Gun La ME2 9 B7
Gun Lane Bsns Est 5 ME2 9 B7
Gunnis Cl ME8 33 D4
Gun Tower Mews ME1 9 B4
Gurling Rd CT15 133 F1
GUSHMERE 84 C7
GUSTON 149 E6
Guston CE Prim Sch CT15 149 E3
Guston Rd
East Langdon CT15 150 A8
Maidstone ME14 75 C6
Guthrie Gdns CT17 148 E3
Guy Cl CT10 30 A7
Gwyn Rd CT12 29 C2
Gypsy Cnr CT5 44 D3

H

Hackfield TN23 138 F1
Hackington Cl CT2 66 E4
Hackington Pl CT2 66 F2
Hackington Rd CT2 66 E7
Hackington Terr CT2 66 F2
HACKLINGE 94 C1
Hacklinge Hill CT14 94 B2
Hackney Rd ME16 74 C2
Haddon Dene Sch CT10 29 F4
Hadleigh Ct ME7 33 A3
Hadleigh Gdns CT6 23 B5
Hadley Gdns ME17 77 E2
Hadlow Coll CT1 88 B8
Hadlow Dr CT9 8 E2
Hadlow Rd ME14 75 C5
Hadrian Gdns TN23 155 F5
Haffenden Mdw TN27 120 C8
HAFFENDEN QUARTER 152 A7
Haffenden Rd TN30 167 B1
Haig Ave
Chatham, Luton ME4 10 A2
Chatham ME1 9 D1
Gillingham ME7 10 E4
HAINE 28 F2
Haine Ind Est CT12 28 F1
Haine Rd CT12, CT10 28 F2
Halden Cl ME15 97 F6
HALE
Birchington 26 B4
Chatham 32 D8
Hales Cl TN30 179 B8
Hales Ct TN30 179 B8
Hales Dr CT2 66 F3
HALES PLACE 67 A3
Hales Rd ME10 36 D1
Haleys Pl ME1 53 A8
Halfmile Ride CT9 28 E6
Halford Cl CT6 23 B2
Halfpenny Cl ME16 74 A2
HALFWAY HOUSES 3 E7
Halfway Houses Prim Sch ME12 3 D6
Halfway Rd ME12 3 D8
HALFWAY STREET 130 D4
Halifax Cl ME5 32 B6
Hall Ave TN24 156 F6
Hall by the Sea Rd CT9 7 H2
Hall Cl ME10 36 E6
Hall Cres CT14 116 F5
Hallcroft Ct CT11 52 C7
Hallett Wlk 10 CT1 67 B2
Halliday Ct CT21 176 A2
Halliday Dr CT14 117 D3
Hall Rd ME5 32 C3
Hallsfield Rd ME5 31 D2
Hallwood Cl ME8 33 D5
Hallwood Ho ME5 32 C2
Halstatt Rd CT14 117 A3
Halstead Cl CT2 67 B4
Halstead Gdns CT9 8 F3
Halstead Wlk ME16 74 C7
Halstow Cl ME15 97 B6
Halstow Way TN23 155 F8
Halt The
Elham CT4 144 F4
Whitstable CT5 44 A7
HAM 93 F2
Hambledon Ct ME16 74 B3
Hambrook Cl CT4 107 B8
Hambrook La CT4 107 C8
Hambrook Wlk ME10 36 F8
Hamele The CT2 67 F5
Hamelin Rd ME7 32 F8
Ham Farm Cotts CT14 93 F2
HAM GREEN
Upchurch 12 F6
Wittersham 188 C1
Hamill Terr CT1 67 B2
Hamilton Cl
Littlestone-on-Sea TN28 202 E5
Ramsgate CT12 29 B1
Hamilton Cres ME10 36 C3
Hamilton Ct
Chatham ME5 10 C1
Rochester ME1 9 B4
Hamilton Ho
Coxheath ME17 96 C3
Maidstone ME15 97 F5
Hamilton Rd
Ashford TN24 156 D6
Deal CT14 117 C4
Dover CT17 166 B8
Gillingham ME7 10 D7
Lydd TN29 205 C6
Whitstable CT5 20 D1
Ham La
Gillingham ME7 32 E3
Lenham ME17 101 C5
HAMLET OF SHELLNESS 19 E5
HAMMILL 92 E3
Ham Mill La TN26, TN29 183 A2
Hammond Cl CT15 113 E5
Hammond's Cnr TN29 201 E6
Hammond's Rd CT20 177 E5
Hamond Hill 6 ME4 9 E4
Hampden La TN23 156 A7
Hampden Mews TN23 156 A7
Hampden Rd TN23 156 A6
Hampshire Cl ME5 32 C7
Hampshire Dr ME15 97 C8
Hampshire Rd CT1 88 D7
Hampshires The ME17 100 C6
Hampson Way ME14 76 A4
HAMPTON 22 B5
Hampton Cl
Chatham ME5 32 A5
Herne Bay CT6 22 A3
Hampton Gdns CT6 22 A3
Hampton La TN25 141 C3
Hampton Pier Ave CT6 22 B4
Hampton Prim Sch CT6 22 C4
Hampton Rd ME14 75 C6
Hampton Vale CT21 177 B4
Ham Rd ME13 40 C1
Ham St Woods National Nature Reserve* TN26 171 B2
Ham Shades La CT5 21 A1
HAMSTREET 183 B7
Hamstreet Prim Sch TN26 182 F8
Hamstreet Rd
Bromley Green TN26 170 E5
Hamstreet TN26 183 C7
Ham Street Sta TN26 183 A8
Hamwick Gn ME5 32 C1
Hancocks Field CT14 117 A5
Hangman's La CT14 133 F5
Hannah Cl ME4 10 A3
Hanover Cl
Ashford TN23 138 F2
Deal CT14 117 D2
Margate CT9 8 E2
Sittingbourne ME10 36 E2
Hanover Ct
Broadstairs CT10 29 F4
Faversham ME13 62 B8
Hythe CT21 176 C1
Maidstone ME14 75 B5
Hanover Dr ME8 33 C4
Hanover Ho 6 CT20 178 C4
Hanover Pl CT2 66 F2
Hanover Rd ME17 96 C3
Hanover Sq CT6 22 F5
Hanover St CT6 22 F5
Hanscomb Ho CT2 66 E2
Hanslett's La ME13 61 D3
Hanson Dr ME15 96 F3
Hanway ME8 11 A2
HARBLEDOWN 87 B8
Harbledown Gdns CT9 8 E3
Harbledown Ho ME16 74 B2
Harbledown Manor ME8 11 B3
Harbledown Pk CT2 66 C1
Harbour Approach Rd CT20 178 E4
HARBOURLAND 75 B8
Harbourland Cl ME14 75 B8
Harbourne La TN26, TN30 167 E5
Harbour Par CT11 52 E6
Harbour Point CT19 178 F5
Harbour Sch CT15 165 E7
Harbour St
Broadstairs CT10 30 B4
Folkestone CT20 178 E5
Ramsgate CT11 52 E6
Whitstable CT5 20 D2
Harbour Twrs 16 CT11 52 E6
Harbour View Rd CT17 166 B8
Harbour Way CT20 178 E5
Harcourt Dr
Canterbury CT2 66 D2
Herne Bay CT6 22 B5
Harcourt Gdns ME8 33 E4
Harcourt Prim Sch CT19 177 E7
Harcourt Rd CT19 177 F7
Harden Rd TN29 205 D7
Harden's View TN26 182 D6
Hardinge Cl ME8 33 D4
Hardinge Rd TN24 139 C3
Hardres Court Rd CT4 110 A3
Hardres Rd CT11 52 E8
Hardres St CT11 52 E7
Hardstown ME4 10 A4
Hardwicke Ho TN27 120 B7
Hardwicke Rd CT17 166 B6
Hardwick Ho ME15 97 E8
Hardwick Rd CT20 178 A4
Hardy Cl
Ashford TN24 157 A7
Canterbury CT2 66 C1
Hardy Cl *continued*
Chatham ME5 32 B6
Hardy Lodge ME1 9 B4
Hardy Rd
Greatstone-on-Sea TN28 202 D3
St Margaret's at Cliffe CT15 150 E8
Hardy St ME14 75 A6
Harebell Cl
3 Chatham ME5 31 F4
Maidstone ME14 75 E5
Minster (Sheppey) ME12 4 A4
Harebrook CT11 29 F1
Haredale Cl ME1 31 D7
Hare St 2 ME4 10 B3
Harkness Ct 6 ME10 37 B4
Harkness Dr CT2 66 E2
Harlequin Cl CT6 22 E2
Harling Cl ME17 97 D5
Harman Ave CT21 174 F3
Harman Ct ME5 32 B3
HARMAN'S CORNER 36 B2
Harmers Way TN27 118 F3
Harmony Cl ME10 36 D3
Harmsworth Gdns CT10 30 A5
Harnet St 6 CT13 72 F1
Harold Ave
Gillingham ME7 10 E4
Westgate on Sea CT8 27 E8
Harold Ct ME13 62 C6
Harold Rd
Birchington CT7 26 E8
Deal CT14 117 D8
Margate CT9 8 B3
Sittingbourne ME10 37 B4
Harold's Rd CT16 166 E8
Harold St
Dover CT16 166 D8
Queenborough ME11 3 A4
Harper Rd TN23 155 F8
Harp Farm Rd ME14 54 C6
Harple La ME14 54 F1
Harps Ave ME12 4 C6
Harpswood ME17 77 F1
Harpswood La CT21 176 A4
Harptree Dr ME5 31 F5
Harrier Dr ME10 37 A2
Harrietsham Sta ME17 100 D6
Harriet Dr ME1 9 B3
Harriets Cnr CT5 43 B5
HARRIETSHAM 100 D5
Harrietsham CE Prim Sch ME17 100 C6
Harrietsham Ho 13 ME16 74 A3
Harringe La CT21, TN25 174 A6
Harriot Cl CT19 178 B7
Harris Gdns ME10 37 C5
Harrison Ct 4 ME8 11 F1
Harrison Dr ME17 100 E6
Harrison Rd 4 CT11 52 D6
Harrison Terr ME13 40 A2
Harris Pl ME15 74 E1
Harris Rd ME12 1 D2
Harris's Alley CT3 91 A7
Harrow Ct
Chatham ME5 32 C4
Stockbury ME9 56 D8
Harrow Dene CT10 29 E6
Harrow Rd ME7 32 F6
Harrow Way
Ashford TN23 155 E5
Maidstone ME14 75 E5
Harry Pay Cl TN24 139 D4
Harrys Rd ME9 38 D3
Harry Wells Rd CT6 22 B3
Hart Cl CT18 163 A4
Hart Hill TN27 103 A2
Hartington St ME4 10 A3
Hartley Cl ME15 97 F6
Hartley Mews ME8 11 B3
HARTLIP 34 E5
Hartlip Cl ME12 3 B7
Hartlip Endowed CE Prim Sch ME9 34 D5
Hartlip Hill ME9 34 F7
Hartnup St ME16 74 C2
Hartpiece Cl ME8 11 F2
Hartridge Farm ME15 96 A7
Harts Cotts TN26 183 A8
Hartsdown L Ctr CT9 7 H1
Hartsdown Rd CT9 28 D8
Hartsdown Tech Coll CT9 28 D8
Harts La 6 CT5 20 D2
Hart St ME16 74 F3
Hart Street Commercial Ctr ME16 74 F3
Harty Ave ME8 33 B3
Harty Ferry Cotts ME13 40 C5
Harty Ferry Rd ME12 18 E4
Harty Ferry View CT5 43 C6
Harty Terr ME12 5 A5
Harvest Ct CT6 23 C2
Harvesters Cl ME8 33 E7
Harvesters Way ME14 75 D4
Harvest La CT4 126 E5
Harvest Way
Ashford TN23 155 D7
Hawkinge CT18 163 B4
Harvey Ave CT14 117 C3
Harvey Ct CT19 178 A6
Harvey Dr
Sittingbourne ME10 37 A2
Whitstable CT5 21 B1
Harvey Gram Sch The CT19 178 A6
Harvey Pl
21 Folkestone CT20 178 D5
9 Folkestone CT20 178 E5
Harvey Rd
Ashford TN24 139 F1
Gillingham ME8 33 E8
Harvey St CT20 178 E5
Harville Rd TN25 123 C2
Harwich St CT5 43 D8
Harwick Dr TN28 202 C8
Harwood Ho TN25 123 E1
Harwood Rd ME8 12 B1
Hasborough Rd CT19 178 F6
Haskard Cl CT18 162 F4
Haslemere Trad & Ind Est ME15 97 F5
Haslewood Cl TN27 135 B2
Hassall Reach CT1 87 B6
Hassell St TN25 124 F2
HASSELL STREET 125 A2
Hasted Rd ME9 35 B7
Hasteds ME17 77 D2
Haste Hill Cl ME17 97 B3
Haste Hill Rd ME17 97 B3
HASTINGLEIGH 142 B6
Hastings Ave CT9 8 A1
Hastings Pl CT13 93 F8
Hastings Rd ME15 75 B3
Hatch La CT4 86 C5
Hatch Rd ME17 101 C5
Hatch St 3 ME13 62 C7
Hatfield Rd
Margate CT9 7 G2
Ramsgate CT11 52 D7
Rochester ME2 9 A8
Hathaway Ct
Gillingham ME8 33 D8
Rochester ME1 9 B5
Hatherall Rd ME14 75 B6
Hatherley Ct CT9 8 A3
Hatton Rd ME5 32 C3
Havant Wlk 8 ME15 97 F6
Havelock Pl CT3 71 E1
Havelock Rd CT14 117 C3
Havelock St CT1 67 A1
Haven Cl ME1 9 C2
Haven Dr
Hawkinge CT18 163 A4
Herne Bay CT6 23 F6
Haven The
Ashford TN23 155 F5
Brenzett TN29 192 A3
Hythe CT21 187 C8
Haventhorpe TN24 139 C3
Havisham Cl ME1 9 D2
Havock La 1 ME14 74 F4
Hawbeck Rd ME8 33 C3
Hawe Cl CT2 67 A4
Hawe Farm Way CT6 23 B2
Hawe La CT2 68 A7
Hawes Ave CT11 52 B7
Hawk Cl CT5 43 C7
Hawkesbury St CT17 166 D5
Hawkhurst Cl CT7 27 B8
Hawkhurst Rd ME8 11 B3
Hawkhurst Way CT10 30 A2
HAWKINGE 163 C5
Hawkinge Prim Sch CT18 163 B4
Hawkins Cl
Chatham ME7 10 A6
Sittingbourne ME10 36 E7
Hawkins Rd CT19 177 D6
HAWKSDOWN 134 B8
Hawksdown CT14 134 B8
Hawksdown Rd CT14 134 C8
Hawks Hill La ME9 58 C4
Hawkshill Rd CT14 134 D8
Hawk's La CT1 87 F8
Hawks Rd CT6 22 B2
Hawks Way TN23 155 E7
Hawkwood ME16 74 B5
Hawkwood Cl ME1 9 D5
Hawley Ct ME16 74 E4
Hawley Sq CT9 7 J2
Hawley St CT9 7 I2
Hawser Rd ME1 9 C1
Hawthorn TN26 190 D8
Hawthorn Ave
Canterbury CT2 67 A2
West Minst ME12 3 A8
Hawthorn Cl
Aylesham CT3 112 E4
Crabble CT17 148 E2
Hythe CT21 187 E8
Ramsgate CT11 29 E1
St Mary's Bay TN29 194 F3
Hawthorn Cnr
Herne Bay CT6 24 A3
Old Romney TN29 200 E3
HAWTHORN CORNER 24 A3
Hawthorne Ave ME8 11 C2
Hawthorne Cl CT15 131 D7
Hawthorne Ho 4 ME16 74 A3
Hawthorn Ho
5 Chatham ME5 31 F5
10 Sittingbourne ME10 36 E4
Hawthorn Rd
Kingsnorth TN23 156 B4
Sittingbourne ME10 36 E4
Hawthorns ME5 31 F1
Hawthorns The
Broadstairs CT10 29 C4
Chatham ME5 31 F6
Haydon Cl ME16 74 B4
Hayes Alley 17 CT5 20 D2
Hayes La ME9 56 F6
Hayfields ME5 32 D2
Haygate Ho ME1 9 C4
Hay Hill CT13, CT14 93 D2
Hay Ho CT21 176 B2
Hay La CT14 93 F2
Hayle Mill Cotts ME15 96 F8
Hayle Mill Rd ME15 96 F8
Hayle Rd ME15 75 A3
Haymakers La TN23 155 D8
Haymen St ME4 9 E3
Haynes Ho 3 ME14 75 B4
Hayrick Cl ME14 75 E5
Haysel ME10 37 A2
Hayton Rd TN25 160 A2
Haywain Cl
Ashford TN23 155 E5
Maidstone ME14 75 F4
Hayward Ave ME2 9 B8
Hayward Cl
Ashford TN24 157 A8
Deal CT14 117 A4
Hayward's Cl TN28 202 B6
Hayward's Hill ME13 82 C4
Hayward's Ho ME1 9 C6
Hazebrouck Rd ME13 62 A7
Hazel Ave ME16 74 C5
Hazel Cl CT15 131 C7
Hazel Ct
Birchington CT7 26 D8
Hersden CT3 68 D8
Hazeldown Cl CT17 148 E2
Hazel Gr
Chatham ME5 32 B8
Sheerness ME12 1 H1
Hazel Hts TN25 138 E5
Hazels The ME8 33 B5
HAZEL STREET 57 A3
Hazel Street Rd ME9 57 A4
Hazel Wlk CT10 29 C4
Hazelwood Dr ME16 74 B4
Hazelwood Mdw CT13 93 F7
Hazlemere Dr
Gillingham ME7 11 A5
Herne Bay CT6 23 D5
Hazlemere Rd CT5 43 A7
Hazling Dane CT15 130 F5
Hazlitt Dr ME16 74 D5
Hazlitt Pl ME15 97 B8
Headcorn Dr CT2 67 B4
Headcorn Gdns CT9 8 E2
Headcorn Rd
Gillingham ME8 11 B4
Platt's Heath ME17 100 F1
Head Hill ME13 63 D7
Head Hill Rd ME13 63 D8
Headingley Rd ME16 74 B6
Head Race The ME15 74 D2
Heard Way ME10 37 B5
Hearne Cl ME10 37 B5
Hearne Cl 3 ME10 37 C5
Heart in Hand Cnr CT3 23 F2
Heart in Hand Rd CT6 23 F2
HEARTS DELIGHT 36 B1
Hearts Delight ME9 36 B1
Heart's Delight La CT3 70 B3
Hearts Delight Rd ME9 36 B1
Heartwood Dr TN23 138 E3
Heath Cl CT2 67 F7
Heath Ct CT15 150 F6
Heather Cl
Chatham ME5 31 F4
Margate CT9 28 C8
Sittingbourne ME10 37 A3
Heather Dr
Maidstone ME15 75 B2
Tenterden TN30 167 B3
Heatherwood Cl ME17 99 E2
Heath Farm Sch TN27 119 C7
Heathfield ME17 98 E4
Heathfield Ave
Dover CT16 149 B2
Maidstone ME14 75 C7
Heathfield Bglws ME17 102 B1
Heathfield Cl
Chatham ME5 32 B7
Maidstone ME14 75 B7
Heathfield Rd
Ashford TN24 139 C3
Maidstone ME14 75 C7
Heathfield Way CT4 128 F8
Heath Gr ME16 74 A2
Heath Ho CT3 46 E5
Heathorn St ME14 75 B5
Heath Rd
Coxheath ME17 96 C3
Langley Heath ME17 98 E4
Maidstone, Cock Street ME17 97 C2
Heathside TN26 181 C1
Heathside Ave ME17 96 C4
Heath The
Appledore Heath TN26 181 C1
Whitstable CT5 21 B1
Heath Villas TN26 181 C2
Heathwood Dr CT11 29 E1
Heaton Rd CT1 87 F6
Hedgend Ind Est CT7 25 F3
Hedgerows TN23 155 D7
Hedgerow The ME14 75 E5
Hedgers Way TN23 155 D5
Hedges The ME14 75 A7
Hedley St ME14 75 A5
Heeley Cl ME9 58 E6
Heel La CT2 67 C8
Heel Rd ME13 104 B7
Heights Terr CT17 166 C6
Heights The CT5 43 C6
Helding Cl CT6 23 B2
Helena Ave CT9 28 E8
Helena Corniche CT20 177 C3
Helena Rd CT18 164 C2
Helena Villas CT21 177 B3

Hel–Hon 225

Helen Thompson Cl ME9 14 E4
Hellyar Ct ME1 9 C4
Helmdon Cl CT12 29 C2
Helvellyn Ave CT11 52 B7
HEMPSTEAD 33 A5
Hempstead Inf Sch ME7 33 A5
Hempstead Jun Sch ME7 33 A5
Hempstead La ME9 37 E3
Hempstead Rd ME7, ME8 33 A5
Hempstead Valley Dr
ME7 33 A4
Hempstead Valley Sh Ctr
ME7 33 A3
Hempsted St 11 TN23 139 B2
Hempton Hill TN25 160 C5
HEMSTED 160 D8
Henbane Cl ME14 75 E5
Hengist Ave CT9 8 B1
Hengist Rd
Birchington CT7 26 C7
Deal CT14 117 D7
Westgate on Sea CT8 27 D8
Henley Bsns Pk ME2 9 D7
Henley Cl
Chatham ME5 32 A6
Gillingham ME8 33 D8
Henley Fields
Maidstone ME14 75 E6
Tenterden TN30 167 B2
Henley Mdws TN30 167 A2
Henley View TN30 167 B2
Henniker Cl CT16 149 A5
Henry Ct CT1 87 F7
Henry St
Chatham ME4 10 B3
Gillingham ME8 12 A1
Henwood TN24 139 D3
Henwood Bsns Ctr TN24 139 D2
Henwood Ind Est TN24 139 D3
Herbert Dane Ct 10 ME13 62 D7
Herbert Rd
Ashford TN24 156 D6
Chatham ME4 10 A3
Gillingham ME8 33 E8
Ramsgate CT11 52 C6
Herbert St CT17 149 B1
Herdson Rd CT20 178 A5
Hereford Cl
Ashford TN24 139 C7
Gillingham ME8 11 D2
Hereford Gdns CT7 26 F6
Hereford Rd ME15 97 D7
Hereson Rd CT11 52 F8
Hereson Sch The CT10 30 A3
Hereward Ave CT7 26 E8
Heritage Cl CT5 43 A6
Heritage Ct 18 CT1 87 F8
Heritage Dr ME7 10 F1
Heritage Gdns CT16 166 E8
Heritage Rd
Chatham ME5 32 A6
Folkestone CT20 177 D6
Herlun Way ME7 11 A6
Herman Terr ME4 10 A3
Hermitage Cl CT21 176 B2
Hermitage La
Boxley ME14 54 F2
Detling ME14 55 B4
HERNE 46 B8
Herne Ave CT6 23 A4
HERNE BAY 22 E6
Herne Bay High Sch CT6 22 D3
Herne Bay Inf Sch CT6 22 F4
Herne Bay Jun Sch CT6 22 F4
Herne Bay Mus Ctr★ CT6 22 F5
Herne Bay Mus & Gall★
CT6 22 F5
Herne Bay Rd
Sturry CT3 45 E2
Whitstable CT5 21 C3
Herne Bay Sta CT6 22 E3
Herne Bay West Ind Est
CT6 22 C3
Herne CE Jun Sch CT6 46 A8
HERNE COMMON 45 F6
Herne Ct CT19 177 C6
Herne Dr CT6 22 C2
Herne Inf Sch CT6 46 B8
Herne Rd ME8 11 C2
Herne St CT6 46 A8
Herneville Gdns CT6 23 B4
Herne Windmill★ CT6 23 B2
HERNHILL 64 B6
Hernhill CE Prim Sch
ME13 64 B6
Hero Ho ME12 1 C2
Heron Apartments 3
ME15 97 F5
Heron Bsns Ctr TN24 139 D3
Heron Cl ME9 13 B3
HERONDEN 92 E1
Heronden Rd
Eastry CT13 92 F1
Maidstone ME15 97 F4
Heronden View CT13 93 A2
Heron Dr ME12 4 B5
Heron Forestall Ave
CT18 163 B4
Heron Ho TN23 138 F1
Heron Lodge 6 CT16 149 B2
Heron's Brook TN25 140 E6
Herons Cl CT4 107 C8
Herons Park - Lydd Int
Raceway TN29 205 C3
Herons Swimming Pool
CT6 22 F5
Heron's Way CT21 187 D8
Heron Way ME5 32 B7
Heron Wlk TN23 155 E8
Hero Wlk ME1 31 C7
Herschell Rd CT7 26 F8
Herschell Road E CT14 117 C3
Herschell Road W CT14 117 C3
Herschell Sq CT14 117 C3
HERSDEN 46 F1
Hersden Com Prim Sch
CT3 46 E1
Hertford Ct CT1 88 C8
Hertford Ho
Herne Bay CT6 23 A5
17 Ramsgate CT11 52 E6
Hertford Pl CT11 52 E6
Hertford Rd CT9 29 C8
Hertford St CT11 52 E6
Herts Cres ME15 96 F3
Hestia Way TN23 155 E5
Hever Cl ME15 97 F6
Hever Gdns ME16 74 E3
Hever Mews ME1 9 C3
Hever Pl
Canterbury CT2 67 A3
Sittingbourne ME10 36 D3
Hewitt Cl
Gillingham ME7 10 F6
Maidstone ME16 74 D7
Hewitt Rd 1 CT16 166 D8
Hewitts Pl TN24 139 F1
Hextable Cl
Ashford TN23 155 F6
Maidstone ME16 74 D7
Heyford Cl CT18 163 B4
Hibernia St 6 CT11 52 E6
HICKMANS GREEN 64 A2
Hickory Dell ME7 33 A5
HICKS FORSTAL 46 A4
Hicks Forstal Rd CT3 46 B5
Higgins' La ME4 9 F5
Higham Cl ME15 74 E2
Higham La CT4 111 B8
Higham View ME14 53 E4
High Bank ME1 9 D2
High Banks ME15 96 F5
Highbury Gdns CT12 29 B3
Highbury La TN30 179 A7
Highbury Wlk CT12 29 B2
Highcroft Gn ME15 97 F4
High Dewar Rd ME8 34 A8
High Elms ME8 11 E1
Highfield Cl
Gillingham ME8 33 D7
Hythe CT21 176 A4
Ramsgate CT12 29 B3
Rough Common CT2 66 B3
Highfield Ct
Herne Bay CT6 22 E4
5 Margate CT9 8 B2
Ramsgate CT12 29 B2
Highfield Gdns CT9 7 H1
Highfield Ind Est CT19 178 F6
Highfield La TN24, TN25 157 C6
Highfield Rd
Ashford TN24 157 A8
Gillingham ME8 33 D7
Halfway Houses ME12 3 E6
Ramsgate CT12 29 B3
Highfields Ave CT6 23 D4
Highfields View CT6 23 C4
Highgate Rd CT5 21 B1
Highgrove Rd ME5 32 A5
HIGH HALDEN 167 D7
High Halden CE Prim Sch
TN26 167 E7
High Knocke TN29 195 B6
Highland Cl CT20 177 F4
Highland Rd
Chartham CT4 86 D1
Maidstone ME15 97 E6
Highlands Cres TN29 195 A4
Highlands Glade CT12 28 E1
High Mdw CT17 149 C1
High Minnis CT4 143 F8
High Oak Hill ME9 35 D8
Highpoint TN24 139 D3
Highpoint Bsns Village
TN25 139 D3
Highridge
Gillingham ME7 10 F1
Hythe CT21 177 A3
High Ridge TN23 155 C7
Highridge Cl ME14 75 F5
High St The TN27 120 C7
High Snoad Wood TN25 105 A1
High St
Ashford TN23 139 C2
Bridge CT4 89 A1
Broadstairs CT10 30 A4
Broadstairs, St Peter's CT10 29 E5
Brookland TN29 199 E8
Canterbury CT1 87 F8
Chatham, Brompton ME7 10 A6
Chatham ME4 10 A4
Deal CT14 117 D6
Dover CT16 166 C8
Dymchurch TN29 195 C8
Eastchurch ME12 5 D3
Eastry CT13 93 B2
Elham CT4 144 F5
Fordwich CT2 68 A4
Forstal ME20 53 A3
Gillingham ME7 10 C5
Gillingham, Rainham ME8 33 F8
Herne Bay CT6 22 F5
Hythe CT21 176 C2
Lenham ME17 101 D5
Littlebourne CT3 89 F7
Lydd TN29 205 C6
High St *continued*
Lyminge CT18 161 C6
Maidstone ME14 74 F4
Manston CT12 51 D8
Margate CT9 7 I2
Margate, Garlinge CT9 28 B7
Minster (Sheppey) ME12 4 D6
Minster (Thanet) CT12 50 C6
Newington ME9 35 C6
New Romney TN28 202 B6
Queenborough ME11 2 F5
Ramsgate CT11 52 E7
Rochester ME1 9 C6
Rochester, Strood ME2 9 B7
Sandwich CT13 73 A1
Sheerness, Blue Town ME12 1 B3
Sheerness ME12 1 D2
Sittingbourne ME10 36 F4
Sittingbourne, Milton Regis
ME10 36 E6
St Margaret's at Cliffe
CT15 150 F6
Sturry CT2 67 F5
Temple Ewell CT16 148 D5
Tenterden TN30 179 A7
Whitstable CT5 20 D2
Wingham CT3 91 A8
Wye TN25 123 E2
HIGHSTEAD 24 A1
HIGHSTED 58 F7
Highsted Gram Sch ME10 36 F2
Highsted Rd ME9, ME10 36 F1
HIGHSTREET 42 F2
Highstreet Rd
Waterham ME13 42 D2
Yorkletts CT5, ME13 42 E2
High Street St Gregory's 8
CT1 67 A1
High Street St Lawrence
CT11 52 B7
High Trees Cl TN24 157 A8
High View Ave CT6 22 B5
Highview Cl
Boughton Street ME13 64 B3
Loose ME15 97 A8
Highview Dr ME5 31 D5
Highview Rd ME12 4 C7
Highview Sch CT19 178 D6
Highworth Gram Sch for
Girls TN24 139 A3
Hilary Cl CT6 23 C4
Hilda Rd
Chatham ME4 10 A3
Halfway Houses ME12 3 D6
Hildenborough Cres
ME16 74 C7
Hildersham Cl CT10 29 E5
Hilderstone Coll 2 CT20 29 F5
Hillary Rd ME14 75 A7
Hill Ave CT15 130 E5
HILLBOROUGH 24 A4
Hillborough Bsns Pk CT6 23 F4
Hillborough Dr CT6 23 F5
Hillborough Gr ME5 32 A3
Hillborough Rd CT6 23 B5
Hill Brow
Maidstone ME14 76 A5
Sittingbourne ME10 36 D2
Hillbrow Ave
Herne Bay CT6 23 B2
Sturry CT2 67 F7
Hillbrow La TN23 138 F1
Hillbrow Rd
Ashford TN23 139 A1
Ramsgate CT11 52 D8
Hill Chase ME5 31 E3
Hill Cres
Aylesham CT3 112 E5
Lenham ME17 101 D5
Hillcrest TN23 155 B8
Hillcrest Cl TN24 139 E6
Hillcrest Gdns
Deal CT14 117 A2
Ramsgate CT11 52 B6
Hillcrest Rd
Chatham ME4 9 F2
Hythe CT21 176 B3
Kingsdown CT14 134 D4
Littlebourne CT3 89 E8
Hillcroft Rd CT6 23 B3
Hill Ct TN27 103 E1
Hillden Shaw ME15 97 A8
Hill Dr CT13 93 B3
Hiller Cl CT10 30 A6
Hillfield Villas TN26 167 F8
HILL GREEN 34 C1
Hill Green Rd ME9 56 D8
Hill House Dr CT12 50 C7
Hill La CT18 162 B1
Hillman Ave CT6 22 A4
Hill Rd
Burham ME5 31 A3
Folkestone CT19 178 E8
Folkestone, Foord CT19 178 E7
Rochester ME1 9 A2
Hill Rise TN25 138 E5
Hillside
1 Folkestone CT20 177 E3
Rochester ME1 9 A2
Hillside Ave
Canterbury CT2 66 C2
Rochester ME2 9 B8
Rushenden ME11 2 F3
Hillside Cotts CT3 70 A1
Hillside Ct
Hythe CT21 176 C2
2 Rochester ME2 9 A7
Hillside Ind Est CT20 177 E4
Hillside Rd
Chatham ME4 10 A4
Dover CT17 149 A2
Minster (Sheppey) ME12 4 B7
Stalisfield Green ME13 103 E6
Whitstable CT5 21 A1
Hillside St CT21 176 C2
Hillstone Ct 5 CT16 166 E8
HILL STREET 142 F8
Hill Terr ME4 9 F3
Hill The
Charing TN27 120 D8
Littlebourne CT3 89 F8
Hilltop CT5 43 D7
Hill Top Cotts ME17 96 E2
Hilltop Ho CT2 66 C3
Hilltop Rd ME12 4 A5
Hill Top Rd CT6 23 B5
Hill View
Ashford TN24 139 C3
Margate CT9 28 D7
Hill View Ct CT4 111 E2
Hillview Rd
Canterbury CT2 66 C2
Whitstable CT5 43 D8
Hill View Terr CT18 161 D3
Hill View Way ME5 31 E5
Hillyfield Rd TN23 156 A8
Hillyfields Rise TN23 139 A1
Hilton Bsns Ctr TN23 156 B6
Hilton Cl ME13 62 D6
Hilton Dr ME10 36 B6
Hilton Rd TN23 138 F2
Hinchliffe Way CT9 29 D8
Hind Cl TN29 195 C8
Hinde Cl ME10 36 F7
Hinde Ho ME10 36 E6
Hines Terr ME5 10 C1
Hinton Cres ME7 33 A6
HINXHILL 140 D1
Hinxhill Rd TN24, TN25 140 D1
Hirst Cl CT16 149 B4
Historic Dockyard The★
ME4 10 A8
Hither Field TN27 120 C7
HOADEN 70 F4
Hoades Wood Rd CT2 68 A7
Hoad Rd CT15, CT18 146 A2
Hoads Wood Gdns TN25 138 E6
HOATH 46 F5
Hoath Cl ME8 33 B7
Hoath Farm The CT3 88 F7
Hoath La ME8 33 B7
Hoath Prim Sch CT3 46 E5
Hoath Rd CT3 46 C3
Hoath Way ME7, ME8 33 B5
Hobart Cres CT16 149 C3
Hobart Gdns ME10 36 C4
Hobart Rd CT12 29 A1
Hockeredge Gdns CT8 27 F8
Hockers Cl ME14 76 A8
Hockers La ME14 76 A8
HOCKLEY 82 C3
Hodge's Gap CT9 8 C3
Hodgson Rd CT5 42 F7
Hogarth Cl CT6 23 E5
Hogarth Ho ME11 2 F5
Hogbarn La ME17 79 A3
Hogben Cl CT18 161 B7
HOGBEN'S HILL 84 A6
Hogben's Hill ME13 84 A6
Hogbrook Hill La CT15 164 D8
Hogg La CT4 109 E2
Hog Gn CT4 144 F4
Hog Hill ME14 76 B5
Hogpound Cnr TN30 189 B6
Holbeam Rd ME13 82 A1
Holborn La ME4 9 F5
Holbourn Cl CT6 46 B8
Holbrook Dr CT12 29 B1
Holcombe Rd
Chatham ME4 9 F2
Rochester ME1 9 C3
Holdenhurst TN23 155 E6
Holder Cl ME5 32 C6
Holding St ME8 11 F1
Holiday Sq CT9 7 I3
Holland Cl
Broadstairs CT10 8 G2
Sheerness ME12 1 C1
Holland Ho ME1 9 D5
Holland Rd
Chatham ME5 31 E4
Maidstone ME14 75 B5
Hollands Ave CT19 178 F7
Hollicondane Rd CT11 52 E8
HOLLINGBOURNE 77 E2
Hollingbourne Hill ME17 77 F4
Hollingbourne Prim Sch
ME17 77 E2
Hollingbourne Rd ME8 11 C2
Hollingbourne Sta ME17 77 C3
Hollington Pl TN24 139 B3
Hollingworth Ct ME14 75 C3
Hollingworth Rd ME15 97 F5
Hollow La
Canterbury CT1 87 E5
Hartlip ME9 34 E5
Hollowmede CT1 87 E6
Hollow Rd CT3 47 B6
Hollow St CT3 47 C5
HOLLOW STREET 47 C4
Hollow Wood Rd CT17 165 E8
Hollybank Hill ME10 36 D4
Hollybush Cnr CT4 90 A3
HOLLYBUSHES 80 A8
Hollybush La CT3 69 A4
Holly Cl
Broadstairs CT10 29 C4
Chatham ME5 32 C8
Eastry CT13 93 B2
Folkestone CT19 178 E7
Gillingham ME7 10 E6
Hythe CT21 176 D3
Holly Dr ME12 4 B4
Holly Farm Rd ME15 98 C6
Holly Gdns
Maidstone ME14 75 B7
Margate CT9 8 C2
Holly Hill Rd ME13 64 D5
Holly La CT9 8 C2
Holly Mdws TN23 138 D3
Holly Rd
Ramsgate CT11 52 E8
St Mary's Bay TN29 194 F4
Holly Tree Cl ME17 99 E2
Holman Mews CT1 88 A7
Holme Oak Cl CT1 87 F6
Holmes Ct 5 CT1 88 B8
Holmesdale Cl ME15 96 F3
Holmesdale Terr 14
CT20 178 D4
Holmestone Rd CT17 148 E1
Holmes Way CT12 29 A3
Holmlea Cl TN24 139 E1
Holm Mill La ME17 100 B6
Holm Oak Gdns CT10 29 F4
Holmoaks
Gillingham ME8 11 E2
Maidstone ME14 75 C5
Holmscroft Rd CT6 23 D5
Holmside ME7 10 E3
Holmside Ave ME12 3 D6
Holmwood Rd TN23 155 E7
Holness Rd CT3 71 D2
Holt Cl TN23 155 C8
Holters Mews 13 CT1 88 A8
Holters Mill CT2 66 F2
Holton Cl CT7 27 A6
Holt St CT15 113 C4
Holtwood Cl ME8 33 D6
Holtye Cres ME15 75 B2
Holy Family RC Prim Sch The
ME15 97 F4
Holyrood Dr ME12 4 A5
Holy Trinity & St Johns CE
Prim Sch 14 CT9 7 J2
Holywell Ave CT19 178 D8
Holywell Ho CT19 178 D8
Holywell La ME9 12 F2
Holywell Prim Sch ME9 12 F3
Homebirch Ho 6 CT7 26 F8
Home Farm Cotts CT14 115 E6
Homefern Ho CT9 7 I3
Homefield Ave CT14 117 B6
Homefield Dr ME8 12 B2
Homefield Row CT14 117 B6
Homefleet Ho 13 CT11 52 F7
Homelands Cl TN25 159 D1
Homeleigh Rd CT12 29 B3
Homepeak Ho 12 CT21 176 B2
Homepine Ho 8 CT20 178 C4
Homersham CT1 87 D6
Homeside Farm CT4 126 F6
Homespire Ho 18 CT1 67 A1
Homestall Ct CT2 66 C4
Homestall La ME13 63 B5
Homestall Rd ME9 60 D3
Homestead TN23 155 D8
Homestead Cl 7 CT9 7 J1
Homestead Ct CT14 117 A4
Homestead La CT15 132 C7
Homestead View ME9 36 B2
Homestead Village CT11 52 C5
Homevale Ho 3 CT20 177 E3
Homeview 3 ME10 37 B4
Homeview Terr 2 ME10 37 B4
Homewood Ave ME10 36 D3
Homewood Rd
Sturry CT2 68 A6
Tenterden TN30 167 B1
Homewood Sch TN30 167 B1
Honduras Terr 8 ME14 75 A7
Hone St ME2 9 B8
Honesty Cl ME9/ME10 36 F1
Honeyball Wlk ME9 38 C2
Honey Bee Glade ME8 33 E6
Honey Cl ME7 33 A5
Honeycrock Hill ME9 56 F8
Honeyfield TN23 138 E1
HONEY HILL 65 E8
Honey Hill CT2, CT5 65 F8
Honey La ME15 98 B6
Honeypot Cl ME2 9 B8
Honeysuckle Cl
3 Chatham ME5 31 E4
Gillingham ME7 32 F4
Margate CT9 28 C8
Honeysuckle Ct ME10 37 B5
Honeysuckle Rd CT11 52 F8
Honeysuckle Way CT6 23 D2
Honeywood Cl
Canterbury CT1 67 B2
Dover CT16 149 A6
Lympne CT21 175 A4
Honeywood Ho CT16 149 A6
Honeywood Parkway
CT16 149 B5
Honeywood Rd CT16 149 A5
Honfleur Rd CT13 93 F8
Honner Cl CT18 162 F3
Honywood Rd ME17 101 C4

HOO 49 F6
Hoo Farm CT12 49 F6
Hook Cl
Chatham ME5 31 E5
Folkestone CT20 177 F5
Hook La
Brookland TN29 199 C6
Charing TN27 120 A7
Harrietsham ME17 100 C6
Hookstead TN26 167 C7
Hook Wall TN29 199 E5
Hoopers La CT6 23 D3
Hooper's Pl ME1 9 C4
Hooper's Rd ME1 9 C4
Hope La
New Romney TN28 202 A8
St Mary in the Marsh TN29 193 F2
Hope Rd CT14 117 D5
Hopes Gr TN26 167 D7
Hope's La CT12 29 C3
Hope St
Chatham ME4 10 A3
Maidstone ME14 74 F6
Sheerness ME12 1 C2
Hope View Sch CT4 107 D8
Hope Villas CT1 87 D6
Hopeville Ave CT10 29 E6
Hope Way ME12 1 C2
Hopewell Bsns Ctr ME5 32 C8
Hopewell Dr ME5 32 C8
Hop Garden Way CT1 87 E6
Hop Gdn TN26 181 C1
Hoppers Way TN23 155 D8
Hopsons Pl ME12 4 C5
Horatio Pl ME1 9 B4
Hornash La TN26 170 D8
Hornbeam Ave ME5 32 B2
Hornbeam Cl TN23 138 F3
Hornbeam Prim Sch
CT14 116 F4
Hornbrook La TN26 181 C7
Horne's Place Chapel★
TN26 181 D2
Hornet Cl CT10 29 D3
Horn Hill ME9 58 E2
Horn St CT19, CT20, CT21 177 B4
HORN STREET 177 B4
Horsa Rd
Birchington CT7 26 D7
Deal CT14 117 D8
Horsebridge Rd CT5 20 D2
HORSELEES 64 A2
Horselees Rd ME13 64 A2
Horseshoe Cl
Gillingham ME7 32 F5
Maidstone ME14 75 E5
Horseshoes La ME17 98 E4
Horse Wash La ME1 9 C6
Horsford Wlk ME13 62 A8
Horsham Hill ME9 12 E4
Horsham La ME8, ME9 12 D3
Horshams The CT6 23 D5
Horsley Cl CT18 163 B4
Horsley Rd ME1 9 B4
Horsted Ave ME4 9 E1
Horsted Inf Sch ME4 31 D5
Horsted Jun Sch ME5 31 D5
Horsted Ret Pk ME5 31 D5
Horsted Way ME1 31 D7
HORTON 86 F3
Horton Cotts CT4 86 E4
Horton Downs ME15 75 F1
Horton Gdns CT4 86 E4
Horwood Cl ME1 31 B8
Hoser Gdns CT7 27 A7
Hospital Hill CT20, CT21 177 C3
Hospital La
Canterbury CT1 87 F8
3 Chatham ME1 9 E4
Hospital Meadow Cotts
CT3 91 D2
Hospital Rd ME17 99 E8
Hotel Rd
Gillingham ME8 11 A2
St Margaret's at Cliffe
CT15 151 B6
HOTHFIELD 138 A7
Hothfield Common Nature
Reserve★ TN26 137 F8
Hothfield Rd ME8 11 F1
Hougham Court La CT15 165 A3
Houghton Ave ME7 33 B3
HOUGHTON GREEN 197 D2
Houghton Green La
TN31 197 C2
Houghton Ho CT19 178 C5
Houghton La TN31 197 C3
Housefield TN24 139 F2
Housefield Rd ME13 104 C6
House Mdw TN23 155 C7
Hovenden Cl CT2 67 A4
Howard Ave
Rochester ME1 9 D3
Sittingbourne ME10 36 D6
Howard Cl ME12 4 C7
Howard Dr ME16 74 B5
Howard Rd CT10 30 A3
Howard Sch The ME8 33 D8
Howbury Wlk ME8 33 D4
Howfield La CT4 86 E5
Howland Mews CT1 87 E6
Howletts Oast CT4 89 C5
Howletts Wild Animal Pk★
CT4 89 D6
Hoxton Cl TN23 155 D8
Hoystings Cl The CT1 88 A7
Hubbards Cotts ME8 12 C2
Hubbards Hill ME17 102 B6
Hubbard's La ME15 97 A3
Hubble Dr ME15 97 E7
Hubert Way CT10 29 E6
HUCKING 56 E1
Huckleberry Cl ME5 32 B3
Hudson Cl
7 Dover CT16 149 B3
Gillingham ME8 11 C1
Sturry CT2 67 F6
Hudson Rd CT1 67 B2
Hugh Pl 5 ME13 62 D7
Hugh Price Cl ME10 37 C5
Hugin Ave CT10 29 E7
Hulkes La ME1 9 E4
Hull Pl CT14 116 F6
Hull Rd TN29 206 E6
Humber Ave CT6 21 F4
Hume Ct CT21 176 D1
Humphrey Terr CT18 162 F4
Hundreds Cl CT8 27 D7
Hunger Hatch La TN27 119 F4
Hunstanton Cl ME8 33 E3
Hunt Cl CT18 163 A4
Hunter Ave TN24 156 E8
Hunter Cl TN24 156 E8
Hunter Rd TN24 139 E1
Hunters Bank CT4 144 F4
Hunters Chase
Herne Bay CT6 23 C2
Whitstable CT5 43 E7
Hunters Ct 5 ME7 10 C7
Huntersfield Cl ME5 32 C1
HUNTERS FORSTAL 23 C1
Hunters Forstal Rd CT6 23 C2
Hunters Way
Gillingham ME7 10 E1
Sheldwich ME13 83 C5
Hunters Way W ME5 10 E1
Hunters Wlk CT14 117 B6
Huntingdon Wlk 2 ME15 97 E7
Hunting Gate CT7 26 F8
Huntington Rd ME17 96 B3
Hunton Gdns CT2 67 A4
Hunton Hill ME15 96 A2
Huntsfield Ind Est CT20 177 D4
Huntsman La ME14 75 B4
Huntsmans Cl ME1 9 E1
Huntsman's Cnr ME4 31 E8
Huntswood TN23 138 E1
Hurst Cl ME5 31 E6
Hurstford La TN26, TN27 120 C2
Hurst Gr CT12 29 C1
Hurst Hill ME5 31 E2
Hurstings The ME15 74 D2
Hurst La
Capel-le-Ferne CT18 164 B4
Charing Heath TN27 119 E6
Sittingbourne ME10 14 F1
Hurst Pl ME8 33 F8
Hurst Rd TN24 139 C7
Hurstwood ME5 31 E4
Hurstwood Rd
Bredhurst ME7 33 B1
Warren Street ME13 102 E8
Hussar Ho ME1 9 C3
Hustlings Dr ME12 5 B5
Hutchings Cl 2 ME10 37 C5
Hutsford Cl ME8 33 D5
Huxley Ct 3 ME1 9 D4
Hybrid Cl ME1 9 D1
Hyde Ct CT17 166 C7
Hyde Pl CT3 112 F5
Hyde Rd ME16 74 D6
Hyde The CT4 86 B2
Hylands Cotts TN26 169 A2
HYTHE 176 D1
Hythe Bay CE Prim Sch
CT21 176 B1
Hythe Cl CT20 177 F5
Hythe House Sch ME12 3 E7
Hythe Pl CT13 94 A8
Hythe Rd
Ashford TN24 139 E1
Dymchurch TN29 186 E1
Lympne CT21 175 D4
Sittingbourne ME10 36 D5
Smeeth TN25, TN24 158 C3
Hythe St Leonard's CE Jun
Sch CT21 176 B2
Hythe Sta★ CT21 176 A2
Hyton Dr CT14 117 B6

I

Ian's Wlk CT21 177 A3
Ibis Cl CT5 43 B6
Ice Bowl The★ ME8 11 A1
ICKHAM 69 C1
Ickham Court Farm CT3 69 C1
IDEN 197 B4
Iden La TN27 119 B4
Iden Rd TN31 197 B3
Idenwood Cl ME8 33 D6
Iffin La
Canterbury CT1 87 E4
Canterbury CT4 87 E2
Ifield Cl ME15 97 F7
Ilex Rd CT19 177 F6
Illustrious Cl ME5 32 A6
Imbert Cl TN28 202 C6
Imperial Ave ME12 4 D7
Imperial Coll London (Wye
Campus) TN25 123 E2
Imperial Dr ME12 6 E4
Imperial Rd ME7 10 C3
Imperial Way TN23 155 C8
Impton La ME5 32 A1
Ince Rd CT2 67 F7
Ingle Cl CT7 27 B7
Ingleden Cl ME10 36 F8
Ingleden Park Rd TN30 167 C1
Ingle Rd ME4 9 F2
Ingles La 8 CT20 178 D5
Ingles Mews 4 CT20 178 C4
Ingles Rd CT20 178 C4
Ingoldsby Rd
Birchington CT7 26 E7
Canterbury CT1 87 D6
Folkestone CT19 178 E7
Ingram Cl CT18 162 F3
Ingram Rd ME7 10 E6
Inner Lines ME7 10 A6
Institute Rd
Chatham ME4 10 A4
Faversham ME13 62 D7
Intelligence Wlk TN25 138 F4
Inverary Ct CT11 29 E1
Inverness Ho 7 ME15 97 E7
Inverness Terr CT10 30 A3
Invicta Ct ME10 36 F7
Invicta Gram Sch for Girls
ME14 75 C4
Invicta Ho
Canterbury CT1 87 F7
Margate CT9 8 C1
Invicta Rd
Folkestone CT19 178 D7
Lydd TN29 207 I6
Margate CT9 29 B8
Sheerness ME12 1 D2
Whitstable CT5 43 F8
Invicta Villas ME14 76 C4
Inward Car Lanes CT16 166 G8
Inward Freight Lanes
CT16 166 G8
Iona Cl ME5 32 D1
Iona Rd ME15 97 A7
Irchester St 11 CT11 52 F7
Ireland Ct TN24 139 D2
Irene Astor Ct 7 CT20 178 D5
Iris Cl ME5 54 A8
Iron Bar La 4 CT1 88 A8
Ironside Cl ME5 32 A8
Irvine Dr CT9 29 C8
Irvine Mews 6 CT9 29 C8
Isis Cl CT21 175 A3
Island Rd
Upstreet CT3, CT7 47 D2
Westbere CT2, CT3 68 C7
Island Wall CT5 20 C1
ISP Sch The 12 ME10 36 E4
Italianate Greenhouse★
CT11 30 A1
Ito Way ME8 11 A3
Ivanhoe Rd
Herne Bay CT6 23 A4
Westgate on Sea CT8 7 C1
Ivans Field ME17 98 B1
Ivens Way ME17 100 D6
Iversgate Cl ME8 11 F2
Ivory Cl ME13 40 A1
IVYCHURCH 192 E3
Ivychurch Gdns CT9 8 E2
Ivychurch Rd TN29 192 B3
Ivy Cl
Etchinghill CT18 161 D3
Kingswood ME17 99 D2
Ivy Cottage Hill CT12 50 E7
Ivy Cotts TN23 155 C8
Ivy Ct CT2 66 E6
Ivy House Rd CT5 20 F1
Ivy La CT1 88 A8
Ivy Mews ME17 99 E2
Ivy Pl
Canterbury CT1 87 E7
Deal CT14 117 D7
Rochester ME1 9 A2
Ivyside CT8 7 C1
Ivy St ME8 33 F8
Ivy Way CT19 178 E7
IWADE 14 D4
Iwade Prim Sch ME9 14 D4

J

Jaarlen Rd TN29 205 B6
Jacinth Dr ME10 36 C6
Jacklin Cl ME5 31 F2
Jackson Ave ME1 31 E8
Jackson Cl ME8 11 C1
Jackson Rd CT1 87 E7
Jacksons Stables CT8 7 D1
Jacob Cl CT9 28 E7
Jacobs Ho ME12 1 D2
Jacobs Oak TN24 156 D6
Jacob Yd 8 ME13 62 D7
Jade Cl ME10 36 C7
Jaffa Ct 1 CT5 43 D8
Jamaica Terr ME14 75 A7
James Allchin Gdns
TN24 139 F4
James Cl
Ash CT3 71 D2
Lyminge CT18 161 C7
James Ct
Folkestone CT20 178 A4
2 Margate CT9 8 B2
James Hall Gdns CT14 117 C3
James Haney Dr TN24 139 F5
James Morris Ct 3
CT20 177 F3
James St
Ashford TN23 139 A2
5 Chatham ME4 9 F4
Folkestone CT19 178 D6
Gillingham ME7 10 C6
Maidstone ME14 75 A5
8 Ramsgate CT11 52 D6
Rochester ME1 9 C4
Sheerness ME12 1 E2
James Whatman Way
ME14 74 F5
Japonica Cl ME5 32 C2
Jardines Ct 9 CT11 52 D7
Jarman's Field TN25 123 F2
Jarrett Ho 10 CT20 178 C4
Jarrett's Ct 1 ME10 37 B4
Jarvis Dr TN24 157 A7
Jarvis Pl TN30 167 B3
Jarvist Pl CT14 134 D6
Jasmine Cl
Chartham CT4 86 E1
2 Chatham ME5 31 F4
Jasper Ave ME1 9 D2
Javelin Ent Pk TN25 139 E3
Javelin Way TN24 139 E3
Jayne Wlk CT5 43 B6
Jefferson Cl TN23 138 F1
Jefferson Dr ME8 11 C1
Jefferson Rd ME12 1 E2
Jefferstone Gdns TN29 194 E4
Jefferstone La TN29 194 E4
Jeffery St ME7 10 C6
Jeffrey St ME14 75 A5
Jellicoe Cl TN24 157 A7
Jemmett Rd TN23 156 A8
Jenkins' Dale ME4 9 F3
Jenkins Dr ME15 97 E5
Jenner Rd ME1 9 C4
Jenner's Way TN29 194 F3
Jennifer Gdns CT9 29 C8
Jersey Cl TN24 139 C8
Jersey La CT4 109 C6
Jersey Rd ME2 9 A8
Jesmond St 3 CT19 178 D6
Jesse's Hill CT4 111 B1
Jessica Mews
2 Canterbury CT1 67 B1
Sittingbourne ME10 36 E7
Jesson Cl TN29 195 A4
Jesson Court Cvn Pk
TN29 194 F4
Jesuit Cl CT2 67 A4
Jesus Hospl CT1 67 A1
Jetty Rd
Sheerness ME12 1 B3
Warden ME12 6 E4
Jewry La CT1 87 F8
Jeyes Rd ME7 10 C4
Jezreels Rd ME7 10 D3
Jillian Way TN23 155 E7
Jiniwin Rd ME1 31 D7
Jo-Ann's Ct 5 CT10 30 A4
Johannesburg Ho 2
ME15 97 F5
Johannesburg Rd CT16 149 C4
John Anderson Ct 11
ME13 62 D7
John Badger Cl TN24 139 E5
John Bowley Ho CT19 177 F6
John Dutton Way TN24 139 E4
John Graham Ct CT1 88 A6
John Hall Cl ME13 40 B2
John Nash Cl ME9 60 B8
John Newington Cl TN24 139 F5
John's Gn CT13 93 E6
Johnson Ave ME7 10 C7
Johnson Cl TN24 157 A7
Johnson Ct ME13 40 B1
Johnson Ho ME10 36 D4
Johnson Rd ME10 36 D4
Johnson's Cnr TN26 183 A4
Johnson Way ME12 4 A7
John St
Broadstairs CT10 30 B4
Maidstone ME14 75 A6
Rochester ME1 9 C4
John Tapping Cl CT14 117 B1
John Wesley CE/Methodist
Prim Sch The TN23 155 D7
John Wilson Bsns Pk CT5 21 B1
Joiners Ct ME4 10 B2
Jointon Rd CT20 178 B4
Jordan Cl ME15 97 E5
Joseph Conrad Dr TN25 172 F4
Joseph Conrad Ho CT2 66 D1
Joseph Wilson Ind Est
CT5 44 A7
Joss Gap Rd CT10 8 H1
Joyes Cl
Folkestone CT19 178 E7
Whitfield CT16 149 B7
Joyes Rd
Folkestone CT19 178 E7
Whitfield CT16 149 B7
Joy La CT5 43 B8
Joy Lane Prim Sch CT5 43 C7
Joy Wood ME17 97 D5
Jubilee Cl CT21 187 D8
Jubilee Cotts
Staple CT3 92 B6
Throwley ME13 82 D1
Worth CT14 94 B4
Jubilee Cres ME11 2 F5
Jubilee Ct
19 Broadstairs CT10 30 B4
17 Ramsgate CT11 52 F7
Whitstable CT5 21 A3
Jubilee Dr CT14 117 D3
Jubilee Field TN30 188 E4
Jubilee Fields ME8 12 D2
Jubilee Ho CT20 178 B4
Jubilee Rd
Littlebourne CT3 89 F8
Sandwich CT13 93 F8
Worth CT14 94 B4
Jubilee St ME10 36 E5
Jubilee Terr ME7 10 C6
Jubilee Way
Dover CT15, CT16 150 A2
Faversham ME13 62 E6
Judd Rd ME13 62 A7
Judkins Cl ME5 32 C6
Julian Ct CT19 178 B5
Julian Rd CT19 178 B6
Julie Cl CT10 30 A7
Julien Pl TN24 157 A8
Julie Rose Athletic Stadium
TN24 139 F4
Junction Rd
Gillingham ME7 10 D4
Herne Bay CT6 22 C2
Junior Kings Sch CT2 67 E5
Juniper Cl
Ashford TN23 138 E2
Canterbury CT1 88 A6
Chatham ME5 32 A4
Maidstone ME16 74 B6
Whitstable CT5 20 F1
Jupiter La TN23 155 E5
JURY'S GAP 203 D1
Jury's Gap Coastguard Cotts
TN31 203 E1
Jury's Gap Rd TN29 205 A5

K

Kain Ct 6 CT12 29 B1
Kake St CT4 125 E7
Katherine Ct ME5 32 B2
KEARSNEY 148 D3
Kearsney Abbey★ CT16 148 D4
Kearsney Ave CT16 148 E4
Kearsney Ct CT16 148 D4
Kearsney Sta CT16 148 D4
Keat Farm Cl CT6 23 F5
Keating Cl ME1 9 A3
Keddow's Cl CT21 187 D8
Kedleston Rd CT16 149 C5
Keefe Cl ME5 31 D1
Keel Ct ME2 9 D8
Keeley Mews ME7 10 E3
Keeper's Hill CT4 89 D2
Keith Ave CT12 52 A8
Kellaway Rd ME5 32 A2
Kelly Dr ME7 10 C7
Kelly Ho ME1 31 C7
Kelvedon Rd CT14 117 C2
Kemp Alley 2 CT5 20 D1
Kemp Cl ME5 31 E4
KEMPE'S CORNER 123 A2
Kempes Pl TN25 123 E2
Kemp Rd CT5 21 C2
Kempton Cl ME5 32 C2
Kemsdale Rd ME13 63 F6
Kemsing Gdns CT2 67 B4
KEMSLEY 14 E1
Kemsley Down Sta★
ME10 15 C1
Kemsley Prim Sch ME10 14 F1
Kemsley Sta ME10 14 E1
KEMSLEY STREET 33 C2
Kemsley Street Rd ME7 33 C1
KENARDINGTON 182 A6
Kenardington Rd TN26 181 E3
Kenbrook TN24 139 C7
Kendal Cl CT11 52 B6
Kendall Pl 1 ME15 97 D8
Kendal Mdw CT5 21 E1
Kendal Rise CT10 30 A5
Kendal Way ME8 33 D8
Kendon Bsns Pk ME2 9 D8
Kenfield Rd CT4 109 A6
Kengate Ind Est CT21 175 F1
Kenilworth Cl CT15 151 A6
Kenilworth Ct ME10 36 C5
Kenilworth Dr ME8 33 D6
Kenilworth Gdns ME8 33 D7
Kenilworth Ho ME16 74 B2
Kennedy Cl ME13 62 D8
Kennedy Dr CT14 117 B2
Kennedy Ho 8 CT11 52 F7
Kennel Barn Rd ME9 57 C5
Kennel Hill CT15 131 E6
Kennelling Rd ME13,
TN27 103 D5
Kennels The CT15 131 E6
Kennett Dr CT14 117 A2
Kennett La TN25 175 B8
Kennett Lane Cotts
TN25 175 B8
KENNINGTON 139 E6
Kennington CE Jun Sch
TN24 139 E7
Kennington Cl
Gillingham ME8 11 B4
Maidstone ME15 97 F7
KENNINGTON LEES 139 D7
Kennington Pl TN24 139 D7
Kennington Rd TN24 140 A1
Kensington Ho ME16 74 A2
Kensington Rd CT1 67 C4
Kent Ave
Ashford TN24 139 B3
Canterbury CT1 88 D8
Maidstone ME15 75 C1

Kent Ave continued
Minster (Sheppey) ME12 4 B6
Sittingbourne ME10 36 D3
Kent Battle of Britain Mus★ CT18 162 F4
Kent & Canterbury Hospl CT1 88 A5
Kent Cl ME1 31 C8
Kent College Canterbury CT2 66 C3
Kent College Canterbury Inf & Jun Sch CT2 66 A1
Kent & East Sussex Rly★ TN30 179 A8
Kent Gdns CT7 26 F7
Kent Ho
[4] Broadstairs CT10 30 A4
Folkestone CT20 178 B4
Kent International Airport CT12 28 B1
Kentish Ct [8] ME16 74 E4
Kent Life★ ME14 53 D1
Kent Masonic Liby & Mus★ [23] CT1 66 F1
Kent Masonic Mus★ CT1 66 F1
Kentmere Ave CT11 51 F7
Kent Music Sch [21] CT1 66 F1
Kenton Gdns CT12 50 B6
Kent Pl CT11 52 F6
Kent Rd
Folkestone CT19 177 E7
Margate CT9 29 B8
Sheerness ME12 1 C1
Kent Science Pk ME9 58 D6
Kent Showground ME14 55 C3
Kent St CT5 43 D8
Kentstone Ct ME4 10 A4
Kent Terr
Gillingham ME8 12 C2
Ramsgate CT11 52 F6
Kent View Dr ME12 5 D1
Kenward Rd ME16 74 C5
Kenwood Ave ME5 32 A4
Kenya Terr [7] ME14 75 A7
Kenyon Wlk ME8 33 B3
Kerry Hill Way ME14 74 E6
Kerton Rd TN29 209 D7
Keston Ct ME8 11 A2
Kestrel Cl
Kingsnorth TN23 156 C3
Sittingbourne ME10 37 A2
Kestrel Ct
[4] Sittingbourne ME10 37 A4
Whitstable CT5 21 A3
Kestrel Ho ME7 10 B6
Kestrel Rd ME5 32 C2
Keswick Ave ME10 37 C3
Keswick Ct ME7 11 A5
Keswick Dr ME16 74 B5
Kettle Dr CT18 163 B5
Kettle Hill ME13 81 F4
Kettle Hill Rd
Eastling ME13 81 F5
Throwley ME13 82 A4
Kevin Dr CT11 52 B6
Kewlands ME14 75 C6
KEYCOL 35 E6
Keycol Hill ME9 35 F5
Keyes Ave ME4 9 F2
Keyes Cl CT16 149 A5
Keyes Pl CT19 178 E7
Keynes Coll CT2 66 D4
Key St ME10 36 A5
Keys The CT18 163 C5
KEY STREET 36 A5
Keyworth Mews [7] CT1 67 B2
Khartoum Rd ME7 10 A6
Khartoum Sq CT16 149 A6
Khyber Rd ME4, ME7 10 B7
Kilbride Ct CT11 29 F1
Kilburn Ho [6] ME14 75 A5
Kilnbridge Cl ME15 96 B7
Kilnbridge Wks ME15 96 B7
Kiln Cl
Challock TN25 105 B1
Sittingbourne ME10 37 A3
Kiln Cnr CT21 176 B4
Kilndown Cl
Ashford TN23 155 E6
Maidstone ME16 74 C7
Kilndown Gdns
Canterbury CT2 67 A4
Margate CT9 8 E2
Kiln Field TN30 179 C7
Kiln La TN26 153 F5
Kimberley Cl CT16 149 C3
Kimberley Cnr CT10 29 F8
Kimberley Ct CT8 7 C1
Kimberley Gr CT5 42 F6
Kimberley Rd
Gillingham ME7 10 D3
Ramsgate CT12 29 A1
Kimberley Way TN24 156 C7
Kimberly Terr CT18 161 C7
King Arthur Ct ME10 36 E3
King Arthur Rd CT12 51 D7
King Charles Ct CT14 117 D2
King Edward Ave
Broadstairs CT10 30 A4
Herne Bay CT6 23 B4
King Edward Ct CT6 23 B4
King Edward Rd
Birchington CT7 27 A5
Chatham ME4 9 F2
Deal CT14 117 D8
Gillingham ME7 10 F6
Maidstone ME15 74 F2
[1] Ramsgate CT11 52 C6

King Edward Rd continued
Rochester ME1 9 C5
King Edward St CT5 20 D1
King Ethelbert Sch CT7 27 C7
Kingfisher Apartments [13] ME15 97 E5
Kingfisher Ave CT21 187 D8
Kingfisher Bsns Pk TN24 139 D3
Kingfisher Cl
Ashford TN24 157 A7
Iwade ME9 14 E4
Margate CT9 28 B8
Whitstable CT5 43 C7
Kingfisher Ct
Herne Bay CT6 22 D3
[11] Maidstone ME15 75 B4
Kingfisher Dr ME5 32 C7
Kingfisher Gdns CT21 187 C8
Kingfisher Ho TN23 138 F1
Kingfisher Mdw ME16 74 F3
Kingfisher Prim Sch ME5 32 B7
Kingfisher Wlk CT10 29 F5
King George Rd ME5 31 E4
King George Villas CT14 94 B3
King George V Meml Houses ME8 11 C2
King Lear's Way CT17 166 B5
Kingly Way CT17 166 A7
Kings Acre ME15 76 A1
King's Ave
Ashford TN23 139 A2
Birchington CT7 26 D7
Broadstairs CT10 30 B6
Ramsgate CT12 29 B1
Rochester ME1 9 C3
Sandwich CT13 95 A8
Whitstable CT5 20 E1
King's Bastion ME7 10 A5
Kingsbridge Ct [11] CT20 178 E5
Kingsbrook Pk CT1 67 A2
Kings Chase TN24 140 A2
King's Cl CT14 134 D6
Kings Cotts ME17 98 F6
Kings Ct CT14 117 D3
Kingsdale Ct ME5 10 C1
KINGSDOWN
Deal 134 D5
Lynsted 59 E4
Kingsdown Cl
Gillingham ME7 33 B4
Maidstone ME16 74 E4
Kingsdown Cotts ME9 59 E4
Kingsdown Hill CT14 134 D4
KINGSDOWN PARK 20 F3
Kingsdown Pk CT5 20 F2
Kingsdown Rd
Kingsdown CT14 134 D7
Lynsted ME9 59 D4
St Margaret's at Cliffe CT15 151 A7
Kingsdown & Ringwould CE Prim Sch CT14 134 C5
Kingsfield Rd CT6 23 B2
Kingsford Cl TN25 157 E4
Kingsford Ct CT17 149 B1
Kingsford St TN25 157 D5
KINGSGATE 8 G1
Kingsgate Ave CT10 8 F1
Kingsgate Bay Rd CT10 8 H2
Kingsgate Castle CT10 8 H2
Kingsgate Cl ME16 74 C4
Kingsgate Coll CT10 30 A8
Kingsgate La TN30 188 C5
Kings Hall The★ CT6 23 A5
KINGSLAND 136 C8
Kingsland Gdns CT14 134 B8
Kingsland Hollow TN29 195 A4
Kingsland La
Egerton Forstal TN27 118 E1
Westwell TN25 121 F1
Kingsley Rd
Maidstone ME15 75 A3
Whitstable CT5 43 E8
Kingsmarsh La TN29 201 C5
Kings Mdw TN24 139 E7
Kingsmead
Folkestone CT19 178 B8
Westgate on Sea CT8 7 C1
Kingsmead L Ctr CT2 67 A2
Kingsmead Prim Sch [22] CT1 67 A1
Kingsmead Rd CT1, CT2 67 A2
Kings Mews
[7] Canterbury CT1 67 A1
Margate CT9 7 J3
Kings Mill Cl ME10 36 E5
KINGSNORTH 156 A4
Kingsnorth CE Prim Sch TN23 156 B3
Kingsnorth Ct [2] CT20 178 B5
Kingsnorth Gdns CT20 178 C5
Kingsnorth Ind Est TN23 156 B6
Kingsnorth Rd
Ashford TN23 156 A6
Faversham ME13 62 C6
Gillingham ME8 11 C4
Kings Oak Mews ME5 31 F4
King's Orch ME1 9 C5
Kings Par [7] TN24 139 B2
King's Pk CT1 67 B1
King's Pl [5] CT11 52 E6
Kings Prep Sch ME1 9 C5
Kings Prospect TN24 156 E6
Kings Rd
Aylesham CT3 112 F6
Dover CT17 166 A7
Folkestone CT20 177 D6

Kings Rd continued
Minster (Sheppey) ME12 4 D7
Ramsgate CT11 52 D8
King's Rd
Birchington CT7 27 A6
Chatham ME5 10 D1
Faversham ME13 62 C7
Herne Bay CT6 22 F5
Kings Reach ME15 97 D8
Kings Ropewalk CT17 166 B5
Kings Row
[1] Maidstone ME15 75 A1
Rochester ME1 9 B4
King's Sch ME1 9 C5
King's Sch Canterbury The CT1 67 A1
King's Sch Recn Ctr The CT1 66 F2
Kings Sch The [16] CT1 88 A8
King St
Brookland TN29 191 D2
Canterbury CT1 66 F1
Chatham ME4 10 A4
Deal CT14 117 D6
Deal, Walmer CT14 117 D3
Dover CT16 166 D7
Fordwich CT2 68 A4
Gillingham ME7 10 C6
Maidstone ME14 75 A4
Margate CT9 7 J2
Ramsgate CT11 52 E7
Rochester ME1 9 C4
Sandwich CT13 73 A1
Sheerness ME12 1 B2
Sittingbourne ME10 36 E5
KINGSTON 111 D3
Kingston Ave CT9 28 C7
Kingston Cl
Crabble CT17 148 F3
Herne Bay CT6 23 F5
Ramsgate CT12 29 B2
Kingston Cres ME5 32 C4
Kingston Dr ME15 97 A8
Kingston Ct [3] CT20 178 B5
Kingsway
Chatham ME5 10 D1
Dymchurch TN29 186 E2
Gillingham ME7 10 E1
Kingswear Gdns ME2 9 C7
Kings Wlk ME14 75 B5
KINGSWOOD 99 E3
Kingswood Ave ME4 9 F2
Kingswood Cl TN24 139 D5
King's Wood Forest Wlks★ TN25 105 F1
Kingswood Ho [12] ME16 74 A3
Kingswood Prim Sch ME17 99 E2
Kingswood Rd
Gillingham ME7 10 D6
Kit's Coty ME20 53 D8
Kingswood Villas CT17 149 A2
King William Rd [6] ME7 10 C7
Kinross Cl ME5 32 B7
Kinson Way CT16 149 A5
Kipling Rd TN23 139 B2
Kipping Cl CT18 163 A4
Kirby's Hts [8] CT2 66 F1
Kirby's La CT2 66 F1
Kirkdale ME15 96 F5
Kirkdale Cl ME5 32 D1
Kirkdale Cotts ME15 96 F5
Kirkdale Rd ME15 96 F6
Kirk Gdns CT14 117 B2
Kirkstone Ave CT11 51 F7
Kirk View TN23 155 C8
Kirkwood Ave TN26 169 A1
Kirton Cl CT18 162 F4
Kitchener Ave ME4 10 A1
Kitchener Cl CT4 128 F8
Kitchener Rd
Dover CT17 166 A7
Rochester ME2 9 A8
Kitchener Sq CT19 178 E8
Kite Farm CT5 21 D3
Kitewell La TN29 205 D8
Kither Rd TN23 156 A7
Kit Hill ME13 84 D8
Kit Hill Ave ME5 31 E3
Kitsbridge La TN26 183 F5
KIT'S COTY 53 C7
Kit's Coty Ho★ ME20 53 C6
Kittiwake Cl CT6 23 F5
Klondyke Ind Est ME11 2 F4
Knatchbull Way TN25 158 E5
Knavesacre Ct ME8 33 D5
KNAVE'S ASH 46 C5
Knell La CT3 71 C3
Knight Ave
Canterbury CT2 87 D8
Gillingham ME7 10 D7
Knight Rd ME2 9 A6
Knightrider Ct ME15 75 A3
Knightrider St
Maidstone ME15 75 A3
Sandwich CT13 73 A1
Knights Alley [20] CT5 20 D2
Knight's Ave CT10 30 B6
Knights Ct
Dover CT17 149 B1
Sittingbourne ME10 36 E3
Knightsfield Rd ME10 36 D7
Knights Park Ind Est ME2 9 A6
Knight's Rd CT16 166 E8
Knights Templars CT17 166 C6
Knights Way CT16 149 A3
Knock Hill TN30 190 A2
Knockholt Rd CT9 8 F3

Knockhurst Ct TN30 167 C1
Knock Rd TN23 156 A7
Knockwood Rd TN30 167 C1
Knold Pk CT9 28 E8
Knole Rd ME5 32 C3
Knole The ME13 62 B7
Knoll Ct CT20 178 C4
Knoll Hill TN25 173 C3
Knoll La TN23 155 E7
Knoll Pl CT14 117 C2
Knoll The CT15 151 A6
Knoll Way ME12 6 D4
Knott Cres TN24 157 A7
Knott Ct ME14 74 F6
Knotts La CT15 150 F6
Knott's La [19] CT1 67 A1
Knotts Sq [1] TN23 139 C2
Knowle Rd ME14 75 B6
Knowler Way CT6 23 C5
KNOWLTON 114 C7
Knowlton Gdns ME16 74 B2
Knowlton Wlk [1] CT1 67 B1
Kohima Pl CT15 149 F2
Kyetop Wlk ME8 33 D6

L

La Belle Alliance Sq [9] CT11 52 E7
Laburnum Ave CT13 93 F8
Laburnum Cl CT16 148 E4
Laburnum Gr ME12 1 I1
Laburnum Ho ME12 1 C2
Laburnum La CT2 68 B7
Laburnum Pl ME10 36 E4
Labworth Cl ME12 3 E6
Lacey Cl ME17 98 E4
Lachlan Way [2] CT20 177 F3
Lackenden Cotts CT3 89 D6
Lacock Gdns
Loose ME15 97 A8
Maidstone ME15 75 A1
Lacton Oast TN24 157 B8
Lacton Way TN24 157 A8
Lacy Cl ME16 74 D7
Ladbrooke Ho [7] ME14 75 A5
Ladds Cnr ME7 11 B5
LADE 206 E6
Lade Fort Cotts TN29 206 E6
Lade Fort Cres TN29 206 E6
Ladies Wlk CT21 176 C1
Ladyfields
Chatham ME5 32 D2
Herne Bay CT6 23 D2
Ladyfields Cl ME9 35 F5
Lady Garne Rd CT15 164 F5
Lady Joanna Thornhill (Endowed) Prim Sch TN25 123 E2
Lady Shaw [18] ME15 97 E5
Ladysmith Gr CT5 42 F6
Ladywell [7] CT16 166 D8
Ladywell Ho [2] CT16 166 D8
Ladywood Rd CT2 67 F7
Lady Wootton's Gn [6] CT1 88 A8
La Galamina TN28 206 E8
Lagos Ave CT12 29 A1
Lakelands
Harrietsham ME17 100 E6
Loose ME15 97 A7
Lakemead TN23 155 E8
Laker Ho ME14 75 A6
Laker Rd ME1 31 C6
Lakeside TN23 155 E8
Lakeside Gdns TN26 120 F1
Lakeside Pk ME2 9 E7
Lakesview International Bsns Pk CT3 47 A1
Lakewood Dr ME8 33 C6
Laking Ave CT10 30 B7
Laleham Gap Sch CT10 30 B2
Laleham Gdns CT9 8 B2
Laleham Rd CT9 8 B1
Laleham Sch CT9 8 B1
Laleham Wlk CT9 8 B1
Lambard Ho [8] ME14 75 A5
Lambden Rd TN27 136 C6
Lamberhurst Farm ME13 42 F1
Lamberhurst Gn ME8 11 B3
Lamberhurst Rd ME16 74 B7
Lamberhurst Way CT9 8 F3
Lambert Ho CT14 117 B3
Lambes Ct ME8 33 D5
Lambeth Cl ME5 32 B4
Lambeth Rd CT1 67 C4
Lambourne Pl ME8 12 A2
Lambourne Rd ME15 75 F2
Lambourne Wlk CT1 88 C8
Lambourn Way ME5 32 C2
Lambsfrith Gr ME7 33 B3
Lamb's Wlk CT5 43 C6
Lambton Rd CT17 149 A1
Laming Rd CT7 27 B6
Lammas Dr ME10 36 E6
Lammas Gate ME13 62 D8
Lamplighters Cl ME7 32 F5
Lancashire Rd ME15 97 E7
Lancaster Ave CT18 164 C2
Lancaster Cl
Hamstreet TN26 183 A8
Ramsgate CT12 29 B1
Lancaster Ct ME8 33 C7
Lancaster Gdns
Birchington CT7 26 F6
Herne Bay CT6 23 D5

Lancaster Ho
Deal CT14 117 A5
[3] Dover CT17 166 D7
Lancaster Rd
Canterbury CT1 87 F6
Dover CT17 166 D7
Lancaster The CT10 30 B3
Lancaster Way TN23 138 F4
Lance Cl ME10 36 F8
Lancelot Cl CT14 117 A3
Lancer Ho ME1 9 C3
Lancet La ME15 97 A6
Lanchester Cl CT6 22 A3
Landbury Wlk TN23 138 F4
Landon Rd CT6 23 C4
Landor Ct ME7 33 A3
Landrail Rd ME9 13 B3
Landway The ME14 76 A4
Lane End CT6 22 D5
Lanes The CT12 50 D6
Lane's Wlk CT5 20 E2
Lane The CT15 149 F6
Lanfranc Gdns CT2 66 C1
Lanfranc Ho [5] CT1 67 A1
Lanfranc Rd CT14 117 C8
Lang Ct CT5 21 C3
Langdale TN23 155 E8
Langdale Ave CT11 52 A7
Langdale Cl ME8 11 D1
Langdale Rise ME16 74 C5
Langdon Ave CT3 71 F1
Langdon Cl CT15 150 F5
Langdon Cross CT15 150 C7
Langdon Prim Sch CT15 133 A1
Langdon Rd
Folkestone CT19 177 D7
Rochester ME1 9 C4
Langham Cl CT9 7 F1
Langham Gr ME16 74 C4
Langholm Rd TN23 156 A7
Langhorne Gdns [9] CT20 178 C4
LANGLEY 98 C4
Langley Gdns CT9 8 E3
LANGLEY HEATH 98 F4
Langley Ho [11] ME16 74 A3
Langley Rd ME10 36 F7
Langney Dr TN23 155 E6
Langport Rd TN28 202 C6
Langton Cl ME14 75 C5
Langton Cotts CT3 70 B5
Langton La CT4 88 A4
Langton Way ME15 74 F2
Lankester Parker Rd ME1 31 C6
Lansdowne Ave ME15 97 C6
Lansdowne Ct [9] ME4 9 F4
Lansdowne Prim Sch ME10 37 C3
Lansdowne Rd ME4 9 E2
Lansdown Rd
Canterbury CT1 88 A7
Sittingbourne ME10 37 C4
Lanthorne Rd CT10 30 A6
La Providence ME1 9 C5
Lapwing Cl
Hawkinge CT18 163 A3
Minster (Sheppey) ME12 4 B5
Lapwing Dr
Ashford TN23 156 D3
Lower Halstow ME9 13 B3
Larch Cl
Broadstairs CT10 29 D4
Hersden CT3 68 E8
Larchcroft ME5 32 A4
Larches The
Faversham ME13 62 A8
Whitstable CT5 43 C8
Larch Rd CT15 114 B1
Larch Terr ME12 3 A8
Larch Wlk TN24 139 C6
Larch Wood Cl ME5 32 D1
Larkey View CT4 86 E1
Larkfield Ave
Gillingham ME7 10 E4
Sittingbourne ME10 36 E6
Larking Dr ME16 74 D7
Larkscliff Ct CT7 26 D8
Larksfield Rd ME13 40 C1
Larkspur Rd ME5 31 E4
La Rocco TN28 206 E8
Lascelles Rd CT17 166 A6
Laser Quay ME2 9 D6
La Tausco TN28 206 D8
Latchgate CT20 177 C3
La-Tene CT14 117 B2
Lathe Barn★ TN29 186 D5
Latimer Cl CT6 22 B2
Latimer Pl [4] ME7 10 C7
Launder Way ME15 74 E2
Laundry Rd CT12 50 D7
Laura Pl ME1 9 A2
Laura Villas CT6 22 E5
Laureate Cl CT9 8 B2
Laurel Ave TN29 194 F4
Laurel Cl CT20 177 E6
Laurel Gr ME17 99 D2
Laurel Ho ME12 1 C2
Laurel Rd ME7 10 C7
Laurels The ME16 74 C2
Laurel Way CT4 86 E1
Laurel Wlk ME8 33 E6
Laurensfield CT12 50 C7
Laureston Pl CT16 166 E8
Laurice Ct [6] CT11 52 C6
Laurie Gray Ave ME5 31 D1

Lauriston Cl CT11 52 A5
Lauriston Mount CT10 30 A5
Lausanne Rd CT9 7 J2
Lausanne Terr 11 CT9 7 J2
Lavenda Cl ME7 33 A4
Lavender Cl
1 Chatham ME5 31 E4
Margate CT9 28 C8
Whitstable CT5 21 C2
Lavender Ct ME10 37 A3
Lavender Ho 3 ME15 97 D8
Lavender La CT12 51 C5
Lavender Mews 19 CT1 87 F8
Laverstoke Rd ME16 74 C8
Law Cl CT2 87 C8
Lawley Cl CT12 29 C1
Lawn Cl ME4 10 B2
Lawn Rd
Broadstairs CT10 30 A4
Deal CT14 117 C1
Lawns The 15 CT11 52 F7
Lawn Villas CT11 52 E6
Lawrence Cl
Folkestone CT19 177 F6
Loose ME15 97 A7
Lawrence Ct CT19 178 E6
Lawrence Gdns CT6 23 C4
Lawrence St ME7 10 C5
Laws La TN25 172 D7
Lawson Cl CT4 86 D2
Laxey The ME15 74 E1
Laxton Cl ME15 75 F3
Laxton Dr ME17 98 A1
Laxton Way
Canterbury CT1 88 C7
Faversham ME13 62 E5
Sittingbourne ME10 36 D6
Whitstable CT5 21 C1
Layfield Cotts ME9 14 D1
Layfield Rd ME7 10 F7
Lay La CT3 71 D2
Laylam Cl CT10 29 D5
Lazarus Hart Havens of Rest
The 4 CT11 52 F8
Leach Ho ME13 64 A3
Lea Cl CT21 176 B4
Leacon Cotts TN27 120 E4
Leacon Cotts The TN27 120 E4
Leacon Rd TN23 138 F2
Lea Ct ME4 9 E1
LEADINGCROSS GREEN 101 C3
Leafield TN25 159 D1
Leafy Glade ME8 33 B6
Leafy La ME16 74 E5
Leahurst Ct CT16 148 E4
Leake Ho 2 ME1 9 C1
Leamington Dr ME16 74 B4
Leander Cl CT14 117 A3
Leander Rd ME1 31 C7
Learoyd Rd TN28 202 C6
Leas Gn CT10 29 D4
Leaside Cotts CT21 176 B3
Leas Lift The★ CT20 178 D4
Leas Rd CT14 117 B4
Leas The
Faversham ME13 62 B8
Folkestone CT20 178 C4
Kingsdown CT14 134 D3
Minster (Sheppey) ME12 4 C8
Sheerness ME12 1 I1
Whitstable CT5 21 D1
Leatt Cl CT10 29 F4
LEAVELAND 83 B1
Leaveland Cl TN23 155 F6
Leaveland Cotts ME13 83 B2
Leda Cotts TN25 120 F3
Leech Ct ME1 9 D5
LEEDS 99 A7
Leeds & Broomfield CE Prim
Sch ME17 99 A7
Leeds Castle★ ME17 99 D7
Leeds Rd ME17 98 E3
Leeds Sq ME8 11 B3
Lee Ho CT14 117 C1
Leelands Ho CT14 117 B1
Lees Cl The TN25 158 D5
Lees Court Rd ME13 83 C5
Lees Rd
Ashford TN24 140 A1
Brabourne Lees TN25 158 E6
Lees Terr CT4 85 C2
Lees The CT6 23 C5
Leeswood TN24 140 B1
Leet Cl
Gillingham ME7 10 E6
Minster (Sheppey) ME12 5 B5
Leeward Rd ME1 9 C1
Leggett's La 10 CT5 20 D2
Leicester Ave CT9 8 C2
Leicester Ct CT9 8 D3
Leicester Gdns ME12 6 E3
Leicester Rd ME15 97 D7
Leigh Ave ME15 97 B6
Leigh Ct ME12 3 F5
LEIGH GREEN 179 F6
Leigh Green Ind Est
TN30 179 E6
Leigh Rd CT12 28 F1
Leighton Ct 3 CT16 149 C1
Leighton Rd CT16 149 C1
Leighville Dr CT6 22 D4
Leitch Row ME7 10 A7
Leivers Rd CT14 117 A3
Lenacre Ave CT16 148 F7
Lenacre La CT16 148 F8
Lenacre St TN25 122 B2
Lendrim Cl 11 ME7 10 A6
Lenfield Ave ME14 75 B4
Length The CT7 25 F2
LENHAM 101 D5
Lenham Cl CT10 30 A2
Lenham Ct 10 ME15 75 B4
LENHAM FORSTAL 102 B1
Lenham Forstal Rd
ME17 119 B8
Lenham Gdns CT9 28 B8
LENHAM HEATH 119 B8
Lenham Heath Rd ME17 101 C2
Lenham Ho ME17 101 E5
Lenham Prim Sch ME17 101 C5
Lenham Rd ME17 100 C1
Lenham Sta ME17 101 C4
Lenham Way ME8 11 A3
Lenmead ME17 100 C6
Lennard Ct 4 CT20 178 E5
Lennard Rd CT20 178 E5
Lenside Dr ME15 76 A2
Len Valley Wlk ME15 75 F1
Leona Ct 8 CT9 8 B2
Leonard Cl ME16 74 B6
Leonard Rd
7 Chatham ME4 10 B3
Greatstone-on-Sea TN28 206 E7
Leonard's Ave CT11 29 E1
Leonie Ct CT6 22 D4
Leopold Rd
2 Chatham ME4 10 A3
Ramsgate CT11 52 E8
Leopold St CT11 52 E6
Le Roux Cl CT18 162 F4
Lerryn Gdns CT10 29 F8
Lesley Ave CT1 88 A6
Lesley Chalk Ho 7 TN23 139 C2
Lesley Pl ME16 74 E5
Leslie Ave CT9 28 B8
Leslie Cres TN30 167 B2
Leslie Rd
Birchington CT7 27 A8
Gillingham ME7 10 D7
Leslie Smith Dr ME13 62 C7
Les Spickett Cl ME13 62 E6
Lested La ME17 98 B1
Lester Rd ME4 10 A3
Letchworth Ave ME4 9 F1
Leviathan Way ME4 10 A8
Lewd La TN27 135 A3
Lewis Ave ME8 11 B2
Lewis Cl ME13 62 A7
Lewis Court Dr ME17 97 C3
Lewis Cres CT9 8 B3
Lewis Ct TN23 155 F7
Lewisham Rd CT17 148 E3
Lewis Rd CT16 162 F3
LEWSON STREET 60 E7
Lewson Street Rd ME9 60 E8
Leybourne Cl ME5 32 A2
Leybourne Dr CT9 28 B8
Leybourn Rd CT10 30 B2
Leyburne Rd CT16 166 D8
Leycroft Cl CT2 66 E3
LEYSDOWN-ON-SEA 6 H2
Leysdown Rd
Eastchurch ME12 5 E3
Leysdown-on-Sea ME12 6 C1
Leysdown View 1 CT5 43 C6
Leys The CT12 28 D1
Leyton Ave ME7 10 E1
Library Rd CT2 66 D4
Libya Terr 6 ME14 75 A7
Lichfield Ave CT1 88 B6
Lichfield Cl ME8 11 D2
Lichfield Ho 12 ME15 97 E7
LIDSING 32 F1
Lidsing Rd ME14 54 E6
Liege Cl ME10 14 F1
Lighthouse Rd CT15 151 A5
Lilac Ct TN23 138 E3
Lilac Rd ME2 4 B5
Lilk Hill ME14 76 C3
Lillian Rd CT11 52 F8
LILYVALE 158 F4
Lilyvale Cotts TN25 158 F4
Lilyvale Rd TN25 158 F4
Lime Cl
Ashford TN23 138 F3
Chartham CT4 86 E1
Lime Ct ME8 33 C3
Lime Gr
Halfway Houses ME12 3 D5
Sittingbourne ME10 37 A4
Limehouse Ct ME10 37 D5
Lime Kiln Rd CT1 87 F6
Limekiln Rdbt CT17 166 D6
Limekiln St CT17 166 D5
Lime Kiln Wharf ME11 3 A5
Limepits Cross ME9 35 F3
Limes Cl TN30 179 C8
Limes Pl 15 ME13 62 D7
Limes Rd
Dover CT16 149 C1
Folkestone CT19 177 F6
Limes The
Ashford TN23 156 A5
Lenham ME17 101 D5
Old Romney TN29 201 A7
Limetree Cl ME5 32 B8
Limetree Terr ME17 101 E6
Lime Villas CT4 144 F5
Linces The CT16 149 B4
Lincoln Ave CT1 88 B7
Lincoln Cl CT5 21 D3
Lincoln Gdns CT7 26 F7
Lincoln Rd ME15 97 D8
Lincol n Rd ME7 10 D7
Lindale Flats CT14 117 C2
Linden Ave
Broadstairs CT10 30 B5
Herne Bay CT6 22 E4
Whitstable CT5 20 F1
Linden Chase CT2 66 E1
Linden Cl
Sittingbourne ME10 36 D3
Westgate on Sea CT8 27 E7
Linden Cres CT19 178 D6
Linden Dr
Elham CT4 144 F5
West Minst ME12 3 A7
Linden Gr CT2 66 E1
Linden Grove Prim Sch
TN23 155 F6
Linden Ho 5 ME5 31 F4
Linden Rd
Ashford TN24 139 D1
Chartham CT4 86 E1
Coxheath ME17 96 C4
Gillingham ME7 10 E5
Westgate on Sea CT8 27 F8
Lindens CT21 176 D2
Lindens The TN30 167 B1
Lindenthorpe Rd CT10 30 A6
Lindfield Cotts ME13 62 A6
Lindisfarne Gdns ME16 74 E3
Lindridge Cl CT6 46 A8
Lineacre Cl ME8 33 D6
Linen Ct CT1 87 F8
Lines Terr ME4 10 A4
Linington Rd CT7 27 A6
Link Hill La TN27 118 D3
Link La CT1 88 A8
Link Rd
Broadstairs CT10 29 F7
Tyler Hill CT2 66 E6
Links Cl CT6 23 A3
Links Cres TN29 195 A4
Links Ct CT14 95 C1
Linksfield Ct CT8 27 D7
Linksfield Rd CT8 27 D7
Links Rd CT14 117 C8
Links The ME5 32 B8
Linksway CT19 178 B8
Links Way TN28 202 D6
Linksway Cl CT19 178 B8
Link The TN23 155 E7
Linkway ME9 14 D4
Linley Rd CT10 29 E7
Linnet Ave CT5 43 B6
LINTON 96 F1
Linton Gore ME17 96 D3
Linton Park Sch ME17 97 A2
Linton Rd ME15 96 F4
Lionard Ho 3 CT2 66 E1
Lion Ct CT14 117 C5
Lion Field ME13 62 B7
Lion's Rd TN28 202 A6
Lion Yd
Faversham ME13 62 A6
3 Sittingbourne ME10 36 F4
Liphook Way ME16 74 C8
Lisa Ct CT5 21 A2
Lismore Cl ME15 97 A7
Lismore Rd
Herne Bay CT6 23 D5
Whitstable CT5 44 B8
Liss Rd CT13 93 A1
Lister Cl
Deal CT14 117 C5
Dover CT17 149 B1
Lister Ho CT9 29 A8
Lister Rd CT9 29 A8
Lister Way CT20 177 F3
Listmas Rd ME4 10 B3
List Mdws CT3 89 F8
List The CT3 69 C2
Listways Cotts CT3 113 B6
Little Acorns Sch TN30 167 A5
Little Acres TN25 171 E7
Little Ave CT14 116 F3
LITTLE BETTESHANGER 115 E5
LITTLEBOURNE 89 E8
Littlebourne Ave ME8 11 B4
Littlebourne CE Prim Sch
CT3 89 F8
Littlebourne Rd
Canterbury CT1, CT3 88 E8
Maidstone ME14 75 C6
Littlebrook Cl TN23 139 A3
Little Brook Rd TN23 139 A3
Little Buckland Ave ME16 74 D6
Little Charles St CT6 22 F5
LITTLE CHART 120 A1
LITTLE CHART
FORSTAL 137 C8
Little Chequers TN25 123 E2
Little Copse Cl CT4 86 E1
Little Ct ME16 74 D2
Littlefield Rd ME8 12 B2
Little Glovers ME10 36 F3
Little Hempen TN23 155 D8
Little Hill TN30 167 B2
LITTLE HOUSES 118 D2
Little John Ave ME5 31 F2
Little Kit's Coty Ho★
ME20 53 C5
Little Knoll TN23 155 F8
Little Mdw CT2 65 E1
Littlemead CT19 178 A7
LITTLE MONGEHAM 116 A2
Little Orch ME17 96 D3
Little Paddocks CT5 44 D7
Little Robhurst TN26 167 D8
Littlestone Ct TN28 202 E5
Littlestone Ho TN28 202 E5
LITTLESTONE-ON-SEA 202 F5
Littlestone Rd TN28 202 D6
Little Stone Stile Cotts
ME13 84 F4
Little Switzerland CT19 178 G8
Little Walton CT13 93 C3
Little York Mdws ME7 11 C4
Liverpool Lawn 18 CT11 52 E6
Liverpool Rd CT14 117 D2
LIVERTON STREET 100 F1
Livingstone Bldgs ME7 10 D5
Livingstone Circ ME7 10 D5
Livingstone Cl TN29 187 B4
Livingstone Rd
Broadstairs CT10 29 E6
Gillingham ME7 10 E5
Livingstone Wlk 6 ME15 97 F5
Lloyd Ct CT14 117 D7
Lloyd Dr ME10 15 A1
Lloyd Rd CT10 30 A5
Lloyds Gn TN30 188 D4
Loading Bay App CT13 73 A8
Loaland Bsns Ctr ME2 9 D8
Lobelia Cl ME7 10 E6
Locarno Ave ME8 11 A2
Lockham Farm Ave ME17 97 D5
Lockholt Cl TN23 138 E3
Lockington Gr ME1 9 C5
Lock La ME14 53 D1
Lockmeadow Entertainment
Ctr ME16 74 F3
Locksley Cl ME5 31 E2
Lock St ME7 10 C5
Lockswood ME16 74 D7
Loddington La ME17 97 A1
Loder Cl ME17 101 B5
Lodge Field Rd CT5 21 D1
LODGE LEES 128 F4
Lodge Rd ME14 75 D5
Lodge Wood Dr TN25 138 E5
Lomas Rd ME10, ME9 37 D4
Lombard St CT9 7 I3
Lombardy Cl ME7 33 A6
Lombardy Dr ME14 75 C5
LONDON BEACH 167 B5
Londonderry Ho 15 ME15 97 E7
London Pl 24 CT20 178 E5
London Rd
Canterbury CT2 66 D1
Deal CT14 117 B5
Dover CT16, CT17 149 B1
Dunkirk ME13 64 E2
Faversham ME13 62 B6
Gillingham ME8 11 C1
Hartlip ME8, ME9 34 D7
Hythe CT21 175 F3
Maidstone ME16 74 C6
Newington ME9 35 A6
Ramsgate CT11 52 B6
Rochester ME2 9 A7
Sittingbourne ME10 36 C4
Temple Ewell CT15, CT16 148 B6
Teynham ME9 38 C1
London Road Ret Pk
ME16 74 E5
London Road (River) CT16,
CT17 148 F4
London Road Temple Ewell
CT16 148 D5
London Road Trad Est
ME10 36 D4
London St CT20 178 E5
Lone Barn Rd ME17 102 B8
Lonefield TN26 155 B1
Longacre CT5 21 D1
Long Acre CT7 27 E5
Long Acre Cl CT2 66 E2
Longacre Rd TN23 155 D7
Longage Hill CT18, CT4 144 A1
Long Barrow The TN24 156 E6
Long Beech TN23 138 E1
Longbridge TN24 140 B1
Longbridge Terr CT21 175 F1
Long Catlis Rd ME8 33 D4
Longdown Ho ME5 31 F6
Long Dr CT13 93 C2
Longfellow Rd ME7 10 C3
Longfield TN30 179 A6
Longfield Cl CT5 21 D2
Longfield Ct CT5 21 D2
Longfield Pl ME15 97 C8
Longfield Rd CT17 166 B7
Longfields Dr ME14 76 A5
Longford Cl ME8 34 A8
Longford Ct ME8 34 A8
Longford Terr 9 CT20 178 D4
Longford Way 10 CT20 178 D4
Longham Copse ME15 75 F1
Long Hill CT4 85 C1
Longhill Ave ME5 10 B3
Longhurst Dr ME5 31 F2
Long La CT15 130 D7
Long Length TN23 155 D4
Longley Rd
Gillingham ME8 11 F1
Rochester ME1 9 C4
Long Market 2 CT1 88 A8
Long Mdw CT12 49 D6
Longmead Cl CT6 22 C3
Long Meadow Way CT2 67 A4
Longmete Rd CT3 70 C5
Longmore Dr ME12 5 C1
Longparish Cl ME15 97 F6
Longport CT1 88 B8
Long Reach Cl CT5 43 C6
Longridge ME10 37 B2
Long Rock CT5 21 D3
Long Row TN25 157 D2
Long's Acre TN25 123 E1
Longsfield TN25 173 A6
Long Shaw Cl ME17 97 D4
Longshaw Rd ME15 97 F5
Longtail Rise CT6 22 E2
Longtye Dr CT5 44 C7
Long Wlk TN23 138 E4
Longwood ME5 32 B1
Lonsdale Ave CT9 8 C3
Lonsdale Ct CT16 149 D1
Lonsdale Dr
Gillingham ME8 33 E7
Herne Bay CT6 22 B5
Sittingbourne ME10 36 C5
Lookers La CT21 176 B3
Loop Court Mews 9 CT13 72 F1
Loop St CT13 72 F1
LOOSE 96 F4
Loose Down Rd ME13 104 F7
LOOSE HILL 96 F5
Loose Inf & Jun Schs
ME15 97 A6
Loose Rd ME15 97 A7
Lord Cornwallis Ct CT19 178 C8
Lord Romney's Hill ME14 75 F3
Lords Cl ME9 37 E2
Lords Cotts ME13 83 C4
LORDS WOOD 32 C1
Lords Wood Cl ME5 32 B2
Lordswood Ind Est ME5 54 C8
Lordswood Inf & Jun Sch
ME5 32 B3
Lords Wood La ME5 32 B3
Lordswood L Ctr ME5 32 C3
Lord Warden Ave CT14 117 D2
Lord Warden Ho CT17 166 D5
Lord Warden Sq CT17 166 D5
Lorenden Park★ ME13 61 F3
Lorenden Prep Sch ME13 61 E3
Lorien Flats TN24 139 D7
Lorimar Ct ME10 36 C7
Lorina Rd CT12 52 C8
Lorne Cotts CT14 117 C7
Lorne Rd
Dover CT16, CT17 149 B2
Ramsgate CT11 52 C6
Lorraine Ct 1 CT19 178 E6
Loudon Ct TN23 138 E3
Loudon Path TN23 138 E3
Loudon Way TN23 138 E3
Loughborough Ct 2 CT11 52 E7
Louisville Ave ME7 10 D4
Lourdes Cl TN25 159 D1
Love La
Adisham CT3 90 F2
12 Canterbury CT1 88 A8
Faversham ME13 62 F6
Margate CT9 7 I3
Minster (Sheppey) ME12 4 D7
Rochester ME1 9 C5
Lovelace Cl ME8 33 D4
Lovelace Ct TN26 153 C5
Lovell Rd
Minster (Sheppey) ME12 4 A5
Rough Common CT2 66 B3
Love Street Cl CT6 22 C2
Lower Bannister Cotts
ME9 36 B2
Lower Blackhouse Hill
CT21 176 D3
Lower Bloors La ME8 11 E3
Lower Boxley Rd 10 ME14 75 A5
Lower Bridge St CT1 88 A8
Lower Buttermere Cl ME7 11 A5
Lower Chantry La CT1 88 A8
LOWER COX STREET 55 D6
Lower Denmark Rd
TN23 156 C8
Lower Ensden Rd CT4 85 D4
LOWER EYTHORNE 131 B8
Lower Fant Rd ME16 74 D2
Lower Featherby Rd ME7 11 B5
LOWER GOLDSTONE 71 F7
Lower Gore La CT13 93 B3
LOWER HALSTOW 13 C3
Lower Halstow Prim Sch
ME9 13 B2
LOWER HARDRES 110 A6
LOWER HARTLIP 34 E4
Lower Hartlip Rd ME9 34 E5
LOWER HEPPINGTON 109 F8
LOWER HERNE 22 F1
Lower Herne Rd CT6 45 E8
LOWER ISLAND 20 C1
Lower Lees Rd CT4 85 D2
Lower Mill La CT14 117 C5
LOWER NEWLANDS 39 A2
Lower Northdown Ave CT9 8 B2
Lower Norton La ME9 39 A1
Lower Queens Rd TN24 139 C3
LOWER RAINHAM 11 F3
Lower Rainham Rd
Gillingham, Lower Rainham
ME8 12 A3
Gillingham ME7 11 D5
Lower Rd
Eastchurch ME12 5 B3
East Farleigh ME15 96 B7
Faversham ME13 61 C8
Maidstone ME15 75 B3
Minster (Sheppey) ME12 3 E4
River CT17 148 E3
Staple CT3 92 B6
Stone in Oxney TN30 189 D5
Temple Ewell CT16 148 D5
Teynham, Lower Newlands ME9,
ME13 38 E2

Lower Rd *continued*
Teynham ME9. . . . . 38 B3
Woodchurch TN26 . . . . . . 169 B1
Lower Road E CT16 . . . . . . 166 H8
Lower Road W CT16 . . . . 166 G8
Lower Rowling Cotts CT3. 92 B2
Lower Sandgate Rd
CT20. . . . . 178 B3
Lower Sands TN29 . . . . . 186 E2
Lower Santon La CT3 . . 70 D7
Lower St
Eastry CT13 . . . . 93 B1
Leeds ME17 . . . . 99 A7
Tilmanstone CT13 . . . . . . 115 A2
Lower Stone St ME15. . . . 75 A3
Lower Tovil ME15. . . . . . . 74 E2
LOWER TWYDALL 11 C5
Lower Twydall La ME7,
ME8. . . . . 11 C4
Lower Vicarage Rd
TN24 . . . . 139 D7
Lower Wall Rd
Burmarsh ME9 . . . . 186 D8
Dymchurch CT21 . . . . . . 187 A7
LOWER WALMER 117 C4
Lower Warren Rd ME20 . . 53 E6
Lower Woodlands Rd
ME7 . . . . 11 A6
Lowfield Rd ME12 . . . . 3 E6
Lowslip Hill CT15 . . . . . . 165 A5
Lowther Rd CT17 . . . . . . 166 B8
Loxwood CT14 . . . . 149 B7
Lubbock Cl ME15 . . . . 97 E5
Lubbock Wlk ME8. . . . . . . 33 D5
Lucerne Ct CT5. . . . . 42 F6
Lucerne Dr CT5. . . . . 42 F6
Lucerne La CT15 . . . . 133 C2
Lucerne St ME14 . . . . 75 A5
Lucilla Ave TN23 . . . . 155 F4
Luckhurst Gdns CT9. . . . . . .8 E3
Luckhurst Rd
Ashford TN24 . . . . 157 A7
Crabble CT2 . . . . 148 E3
Luckley Ho TN25 . . . . . . 123 E2
Lucknow Cl CT15 . . . . . . 149 F3
Lucy Ave CT19 . . . . 178 B7
Lucy's Hill CT21. . . . . 176 B2
Luddenham Cl
Ashford TN23 . . . . 155 F6
Maidstone ME14 . . . . 75 C6
Luddenham Prim Sch
ME13. . . . . 39 E1
Ludgate Rd ME9 . . . . 59 F5
Lukes Cl CT17 . . . . 149 B1
Lukin Ho CT21 . . . . 175 F1
Lullingstone Cl ME7. . . . . 33 B3
Lullingstone Ct 14 CT7 . . 87 F8
Lullingstone Rd ME16 . . . 74 C7
Lumsden Terr 8 ME4. . . . . .9 E4
Lushington Rd ME14 . . . . 74 E7
LUTON 10 B2
Luton Ave CT10 . . . . 29 F3
Luton Ct CT10 . . . . 29 F3
Luton High St ME5 . . . . . . 10 C2
Luton Inf Sch ME5 . . . . . . 10 C2
Luton Jun Sch ME4 . . . . . 10 C2
Luton Rd
Chatham ME4, ME5 . . . . . 10 B2
Faversham ME13. . . . . 62 E7
Lyall Way ME8 . . . . 33 E4
Lychfield Dr ME2 . . . . 9 A8
Lydbrook Cl ME10. . . . . . . 36 D4
LYDD 205 D6
LYDD CAMP 205 B5
LYDDEN
Broadstairs 28 E4
Dover 147 E8
Lydden Hill CT15 . . . . . . 130 C1
Lydden Hill Race Circuit
CT4. . . . . 129 F3
Lydden Prim Sch CT15 . . 147 F8
Lydden Temple Ewell
National Nature Reserve★
CT15. . . . . 148 B7
Lydd (London Ashford)
Airport TN29 . . . . 206 A7
LYDD-ON-SEA 209 D7
Lydd Prim Sch TN29 . . . . 205 C6
Lydd Rd
Chatham ME5. . . . . 32 B5
New Romney TN28, TN29. 201 F6
Lydd Town Crossing
TN29. . . . . 205 D8
Lydd Town Mus★ TN29 . . 205 C6
Lydia Rd CT17 . . . . 117 A2
Lydos Cl TN29 . . . . 206 E5
Lyeat Ct CT2. . . . . 66 C4
Lyell Cl 5 CT7 . . . . 26 F8
Lyell Rd CT7 . . . . 26 F8
Lyle Cl ME2. . . . . 9 B8
Lyle Ct ME16. . . . . 74 C5
LYMBRIDGE GREEN 143 B4
LYMINGE 161 B6
Lyminge CE Prim Sch
CT18 . . . . 161 C7
Lyminge Cl ME8 . . . . 11 C5
Lyminge Way CT9 . . . . 8 C1
Lymington Ct ME15 . . . . . 97 F4
Lymington Rd CT8 . . . . . . 27 E7
LYMPNE 175 A2
Lympne Castle★ CT21. . . 174 F2
Lympne CE Prim Sch
CT21. . . . . 175 A3
Lympne Hill CT21 . . . . . . 175 A2
Lympne Ind Est CT21. . . 174 E3
Lynacre CT2. . . . . 66 C1
Lyn Ct CT20. . . . . 178 A5

Lyndhurst Ave
Gillingham ME8 . . . . 33 C7
Margate CT9 . . . . 8 B2
Lyndhurst Cl CT2 . . . . 66 E3
Lyndhurst Gr ME10 . . . . . 36 E2
Lyndhurst Rd
Broadstairs CT10. . . . . . . 30 A6
Crabble CT17 . . . . 148 E2
Dymchurch TN29 . . . . . . 195 C8
Maidstone ME15 . . . . 97 C8
Ramsgate CT11 . . . . 52 F7
Lyndon Way CT18 . . . . . . 161 C7
Lyngate Ct CT9 . . . . 8 D2
Lynley Cl ME15. . . . . 97 D6
Lynmouth Dr ME12. . . . . . . 4 C7
LYNSORE BOTTOM 127 D8
Lynstead Ho ME16 . . . . . . 74 A1
LYNSTED 60 A6
Lynsted Cl TN23 . . . . 155 F6
Lynsted La ME9 . . . . 60 B7
Lynsted & Norton Prim Sch
ME9. . . . . 60 A7
Lynsted Rd
Gillingham ME8 . . . . 11 B3
Halfway Houses ME12. . . . 3 E7
Lynton Court Mans CT9 . .8 B3
Lynton Dr ME5. . . . . 32 B3
Lynton Pl CT4. . . . . 89 A1
Lynton Rd CT17 . . . . 176 C1
Lynwood CT19 . . . . 178 C7
Lysander Cl
Broadstairs CT10. . . . . . . 29 C3
Littlebourne CT4 . . . . 89 E4
Lysander Wlk CT18 . . . . . 163 A4
Lytham Ave CT6 . . . . 22 D1

M

Mabledon Ave TN24 . . . . . 139 D1
Mabledon Cl TN28 . . . . . . 202 B6
McAlpine Cres ME15 . . . . . 96 F3
McCarthy Ave CT2 . . . . . . 67 F7
McClean Wlk ME12. . . . . . 17 C8
McCudden Row 8 ME7 . . 10 A6
MacDonald Par CT5. . . . . 43 A6
MacDonald Rd
Dover CT17 . . . . 149 A1
Gillingham ME7 . . . . 10 D6
Mace Ind Est TN24 . . . . . 139 C3
Mace La TN24 . . . . 139 C2
Mace Terr TN26. . . . . 155 A1
Mackenders Cl ME20. . . . 53 A6
Mackenders Gn ME20. . . 53 A6
Mackenders La ME20. . . . 53 A6
McKenzie Ct ME14 . . . . . . 74 F5
Mackenzie Dr CT20 . . . . 177 E5
McKenzie Rd ME5. . . . . . . 32 A3
Mackeson Ct 8 CT21 . . . 176 B2
McKinlay Ct CT7 . . . . 26 D8
MACKLANDS. 12 A2
Macklands Ho ME8. . . . . . 12 A2
Macklands Way ME8 . . . . . 12 A2
Madden Ave ME5 . . . . 31 E5
Madeira Ct CT20 . . . . 178 B3
Madeira Rd
Littlestone-on-Sea TN28 . . 202 E6
Margate CT9 . . . . 8 A2
Madeira Wlk CT11 . . . . . . 52 E6
Madginford Cl ME15 . . . . . 76 A2
Madginford Park Inf Sch
ME15. . . . . 76 A2
Madginford Park Jun Sch
ME15. . . . . 76 A2
Madginford Rd ME15 . . . . 75 F2
Madhuran Ct ME2. . . . . 9 A7
Madras Ho 2 ME15 . . . . . 97 E8
Mafeking Rd ME5. . . . . . . 31 F3
Magazine Rd TN24 . . . . . 139 B3
Magdala Rd
Broadstairs CT10. . . . . . . 29 E6
Dover CT17 . . . . 149 B1
Magdalen Cl ME7 . . . . 33 A4
Magdalen Ct
Broadstairs CT10. . . . . . . 30 A6
Canterbury CT1 . . . . 88 B7
Magness Rd CT14 . . . . . . 117 A2
Magnolia Ave
Gillingham ME8 . . . . 33 B5
Margate CT9 . . . . 8 D2
Magnolia Dr CT4. . . . . 86 E1
Magnolia Ho 3 ME16 . . . 74 A3
Magnolia Rise CT3 . . . . . . 23 D2
Magpie Ct ME12 . . . . 4 A6
Magpie Hall Rd
Chatham ME4. . . . . 10 A2
Stubb's Cross TN26 . . . . . 155 E2
Magpie La
Rhodes Minnis CT4 . . . . . 144 B3
Yelsted ME9, ME14 . . . . . 33 F1
Magpie Lodge 4 CT16 . . 149 B2
Magwitch Cl ME1. . . . . .9 B4
Maida Rd ME4 . . . . 10 B2
Maiden La CT1. . . . . 87 D6
MAIDSTONE 75 C3
Maidstone Barracks Sta
ME16. . . . . 74 E5
Maidstone East Sta ME14. 74 F5
Maidstone Gram Sch
ME15. . . . . 75 B2
Maidstone Gram Sch for
Girls ME16. . . . . 74 E5
Maidstone Hospl ME16. . . 74 A4
Maidstone L Ctr ME15. . . 75 C2
Maidstone Mus & Gallery★
1 ME14. . . . . 74 F5
Maidstone Rd
Bredhurst ME7, ME8. . . . . 33 B2

Maidstone Rd *continued*
Charing TN25, TN26, TN27 120 D6
Chatham ME7. . . . . .9 F2
Chatham, Walderslade ME5. 31 D4
Danaway ME9 . . . . 35 D4
Five Wents ME17. . . . . . . 98 E2
Gillingham ME8 . . . . 33 C6
Lenham ME17 . . . . 101 D5
Potters Corner TN25,
TN26. . . . . 138 D7
Rochester ME1 . . . . 9 C3
Maidstone West Sta ME16 74 F4
Mailyns The ME8. . . . . 33 D7
Maine Cl CT16 . . . . 149 B3
Main Gate Rd ME4 . . . . . . .9 F7
Main Rd
Queenborough ME11, ME12 . 3 B5
Sellindge TN25. . . . . 159 C1
Sheerness ME12 . . . . 1 B3
Main St
Iden TN31 . . . . 197 B4
Peasmarsh TN31 . . . . . . 196 B2
Maison Des Fleurs ME16 . 74 C2
Maison Dieu★
17 Dover CT11 . . . . 166 D8
Faversham ME13 . . . . 62 A6
Maison Dieu Pl 4 CT16 . 166 D8
Maison Dieu Rd CT16 . . . 166 D8
Maitland Ct ME13. . . . . . . 40 B1
Majestic Par CT20. . . . . . 178 C4
Major Cl CT5 . . . . 43 B6
Makenade Ave ME13. . . . . 62 E6
Malcolm Sargent Rd
TN23 . . . . 156 B5
Malden Dr ME14 . . . . 75 A8
Malham Dr CT9 . . . . 8 A1
Mallard Apartments 14
ME15 . . . . 97 E5
Mallard Cl CT5 . . . . 22 E2
Mallard Cres ME9 . . . . 14 D4
Mallard Ct ME12 . . . . 4 A6
Mallards TN24 . . . . 156 D7
Mallards Way ME15 . . . . . 76 A1
Mallings Dr ME14 . . . . 76 C4
Mallings La ME14 . . . . 76 C4
Malling Terr ME16 . . . . . . 74 C4
Mallory Cl CT12. . . . . 29 C2
Mallows The ME14 . . . . . . 74 E7
Mallow Way 1 ME5. . . . . . 31 D4
Mall The ME15 . . . . 62 C6
Malmains Rd CT17 . . . . . 166 A6
Malmedy Ct CT14 . . . . . . 117 A1
Malta Ave ME5. . . . . 32 A7
Malta Ho 17 CT1 . . . . 67 B2
Malta Terr 5 ME4 . . . . . . 75 A7
Malthouse Cl ME17. . . . . 101 D5
Malthouse Cotts
Boughton Lees TN25 . . . . 122 F4
New Romney TN28. . . . . . 202 A6
Malthouse Hill
10 Hythe CT21 . . . . 176 B2
Maidstone ME15 . . . . 96 F4
Malthouse La
Hamstreet TN26. . . . . . . 170 D1
Peasmarsh TN31 . . . . . . 196 D2
Malt House La TN30. . . . . 179 A7
Malthouse Rd CT17 . . . . . 66 F2
Malthouses The
Birchington CT7. . . . . 26 F7
Brabourne TN25. . . . . . . 159 B8
Malthouse The ME16 . . . . 96 A8
Maltings Bsns Pk The
TN31 . . . . 196 C2
Maltings Hall The CT11. . 52 D7
Maltings The
7 Canterbury, St Dunstan's
CT2 . . . . 67 A2
10 Canterbury, St Martin's
CT1. . . . . 88 A8
Deal CT14 . . . . 134 B8
Faversham ME13 . . . . 62 D8
Gillingham ME8 . . . . 34 A8
Littlebourne CT3 . . . . 89 F7
Loose ME17 . . . . 97 B4
Maidstone, Grove Green
ME14. . . . . 75 E5
Peasmarsh TN31 . . . . . . 196 C2
MALTMAN'S HILL 135 F3
Malt Mews ME1. . . . . 9 C5
Malus Cl ME5. . . . . 32 B1
Malvern Mdw CT16. . . . . 148 E5
Malvern Pk CT6. . . . . 23 D4
Malvern Rd
Ashford TN24. . . . . 139 B4
Dover CT17 . . . . 166 C7
Gillingham ME7 . . . . 10 E3
Temple Ewell CT16 . . . . . 148 E5
Mamignot Cl ME14. . . . . . 76 A5
Manchester CT ME5 . . . . . 32 C6
Manciple Cl CT2 . . . . 87 C8
Mandarin La CT6. . . . . 22 C2
Mandeville Ct 1 ME14 . . . 75 A5
Mandeville Rd CT2. . . . . . 66 E2
Mangers La CT16 . . . . . . 149 A2
Mangers Pl CT16. . . . . . . 149 A3
Mangravet Ave ME15. . . . 97 C7
Manktelow Ct CT10 . . . . . 29 F2
Manley Cl CT16 . . . . 149 A7
Manley Ho CT16 . . . . 149 A7
Mannering Ct CT17. . . . . 148 F3
Mannock Ho 6 ME1. . . . . 67 B1
Manns Hill CT4 . . . . 127 A6
Manor Ave CT14 . . . . 117 B4
Manor Cl
Canterbury CT1 . . . . 87 C5
Deal CT14 . . . . 117 A4
Herne Bay CT6. . . . . 23 F6
Maidstone ME14 . . . . 76 B3

Manor Cl *continued*
Rushenden ME11. . . . . 3 A3
Manor Cotts
Hernhill ME13 . . . . 64 B6
Langley ME17 . . . . 98 C5
Manor Ct
Canterbury CT1 . . . . 87 F7
Gillingham ME7 . . . . 11 C4
Maidstone ME14 . . . . 76 B3
Manor Dr CT7 . . . . 26 F6
Manor Farm Cl CT21 . . . . 175 A4
Manorfield
Ashford TN23 . . . . 155 E8
Elham CT4 . . . . 144 A3
Manor Gdns
Chatham ME5. . . . . 31 F4
Whitfield CT16. . . . . 149 A8
Manor Gr ME10 . . . . 36 D3
Manor Ho 14 ME7 . . . . 10 A6
Manor Ho The
Canterbury CT2 . . . . 66 F2
5 Folkestone CT20 . . . . . 178 B3
Sarre CT7 . . . . 48 D6
Manor House Dr
Ashford TN23 . . . . 156 D3
Maidstone ME16 . . . . 74 D3
Manor La ME1 . . . . 9 A2
Manor Lea Rd CT7 . . . . . . 25 F1
Manor Leaze TN25 . . . . . . 158 F5
Manor Mews
Chatham ME4. . . . . .9 F4
Ringwould CT14. . . . . . . 133 F5
Manor Pound La TN25. . . 158 F7
Manor Rd
3 Broadstairs CT10. . . . . 30 A4
Chatham ME4. . . . . .9 F4
Deal CT14 . . . . 117 A4
Dover CT17 . . . . 166 A6
Folkestone CT20 . . . . 178 C4
Herne Bay CT6. . . . . 23 F6
Lydd TN29 . . . . 205 C6
Milstead ME9. . . . . 58 F2
Rushenden ME11. . . . . 3 A3
St Nicholas at Wade CT7. . 25 F1
Whitstable CT5 . . . . 21 A2
Manor Rise
Dover CT17 . . . . 166 A6
Maidstone ME14 . . . . 76 B3
Manor St ME7 . . . . 10 A6
Manor Way
Ashford TN23 . . . . 138 F4
Leysdown-on-Sea ME12. . . 6 H2
Warden ME12 . . . . 6 D6
Manse Field TN25 . . . . . . 158 E5
Mansel Dr ME1 . . . . .9 A2
Mansell La CT15 . . . . 146 B4
Mansfield Dr ME8 . . . . 14 D3
Mansfield Wlk ME16 . . . . . 74 C7
Mansion Gdns CT16 . . . . 149 A4
Mansion Row ME7 . . . . . . 10 A6
Mansion St CT9. . . . . .7 I3
Mansions The CT10 . . . . . 29 E4
MANSTON 28 E1
Manston Court Cotts
CT12. . . . . 28 C2
Manston Court Rd CT12,
CT9 . . . . 28 D3
Manston Pk CT12 . . . . 27 D2
Manston Rd
Acol CT7, CT7 . . . . 27 D4
Margate CT12, CT9 . . . . . 28 C4
Ramsgate CT11, CT12 . . . 52 A8
Mansum Ct CT7. . . . . 25 F2
Mantles Hill CT14. . . . . . . 116 D1
Manwood Almshouse CT2 66 F3
Manwood Ave CT2 . . . . . . 66 F3
Manwood Cl ME8 . . . . 36 F2
Manwood Rd CT13 . . . . . . 94 A8
Maple Ave
Gillingham ME7 . . . . 10 E6
Maidstone ME16 . . . . 74 C6
Maple Cl
Ashford TN23 . . . . 138 E3
Broadstairs CT10. . . . . . . 8 E1
Rough Common CT2 . . . . . 66 B3
Maple Ct
Hersden CT3 . . . . 68 E8
Rodmersham ME9 . . . . . . 59 A7
Maple Dr
Hawkinge CT18 . . . . 163 C5
St Mary's Bay TN29 . . . . 194 C5
Maplefields CT18 . . . . 163 C5
Maple Gdns CT3 . . . . 68 E8
Maplesden Noakes Sch
ME16. . . . . 74 E6
Maple St ME12. . . . . 1 D1
Maples The
Broadstairs CT10. . . . . . . 29 D4
Minster (Sheppey) ME12. . . 4 B6
Maplins Cl 5 ME8 . . . . . . 11 F1
Mara Ct ME4. . . . . .9 F5
Marathon Paddock ME7. . 10 D4
Marble Cl ME7 . . . . 10 F6
Marc Brunel Way ME4. . . . 10 A7
Marconi Way ME1. . . . . . . 31 D7
Marcroft CT10 . . . . 30 B7
Mardale Par ME8. . . . . 12 A1
Marden Ave CT12 . . . . 52 B8
Mardol Rd TN24 . . . . 139 C5
Maresfield Cl CT16. . . . . . 149 B2
Margaret Cl CT6 . . . . 22 F4
Margaret St 10 CT20 . . . . 178 E5
MARGATE 7 H2
Margate Cl ME7. . . . . 10 E6
Margate Gate CT7. . . . . . . 27 C4
Margate Language Ctr 13
CT9. . . . . .7 J2

Margate Local History Mus★
CT9. . . . . .7 I3
Margate Rd
Herne Bay, Broomfield
CT6. . . . . 23 D2
Herne Bay CT6. . . . . 23 C3
Ramsgate CT10, CT12, CT11 29 F3
Margate Sta CT9. . . . . 7 H2
Marian Ave ME12 . . . . 4 A7
Marigold Dr ME10. . . . . . . 36 F1
Marigold Way ME16 . . . . . 74 A3
Marilyn Cres CT7 . . . . 27 B7
Marina Ct
Deal CT14 . . . . 117 D8
Hythe CT21 . . . . 176 C1
Marina Dr ME12. . . . . 4 A7
Marina Espl CT11 . . . . 52 F7
Marina Rd CT11. . . . . 52 F7
Marina The CT14. . . . . 117 D8
Marine Ave TN29 . . . . 186 F3
Marine Cres
7 Folkestone CT20. . . . . 178 D4
Whitstable CT5 . . . . 21 B3
Marine Ct
15 Dover CT16 . . . . 166 E7
Whitstable CT5 . . . . 20 F3
Marine Dr
Broadstairs CT10. . . . . . . 8 G3
Margate CT9 . . . . 7 I2
Marine Gap CT5 . . . . 20 C1
Marine Gdns CT9 . . . . 7 I2
Marine Ho CT5. . . . . 20 F3
Marine Hts CT8 . . . . 7 D1
Marine Par
Dover CT16 . . . . 166 E7
Folkestone CT20 . . . . 178 E4
Hythe CT21 . . . . 176 C1
Littlestone-on-Sea TN28 . . 202 E5
Sheerness ME12 . . . . 1 F2
Whitstable CT5 . . . . 21 A3
Marine Parade Mews 5
CT20. . . . . 178 E4
Marine Point CT20 . . . . . . 178 A3
Marine Rd CT14 . . . . 117 D4
Mariners Ct 2 CT5. . . . . . 43 D8
Mariners Lea CT10 . . . . . . 29 D4
Mariners Lee CT5 . . . . 20 E3
Mariners The ME1 . . . . .9 B4
Mariners View ME7 . . . . . . 10 F7
Marine Terr
Folkestone CT20 . . . . 178 E4
Margate CT9 . . . . 7 H2
Whitstable CT5 . . . . 20 C1
MARINE TOWN. 1 F2
Marine Walk St CT21. . . . 176 C2
Marion Cl ME5. . . . . 32 A2
Marion Cres ME15 . . . . . . 97 B8
Maritime Ave CT6. . . . . . . 23 C4
Maritime Cl ME2. . . . . 9 D8
Maritime Est ME2. . . . . 9 D8
Maritime Pl CT14 . . . . 117 D7
Maritime Way ME4 . . . . . . 10 A8
Marjan Cl CT17 . . . . 149 A1
Marjoram Dr ME9 . . . . 36 E2
Mark Ave CT11 . . . . 52 B5
Market Bldgs 4 ME14. . . . 74 F4
Market Colonnade 3
ME14 . . . . 74 F4
Market Hill CT21 . . . . 176 C2
Market La 12 TN23 . . . . . 139 B2
Market Pl
Aylesham CT3 . . . . 112 F5
Charing TN27 . . . . 120 C7
1 Faversham ME13 . . . . . 62 D7
20 Folkestone CT20. . . . . 178 D5
Margate CT9 . . . . 7 I3
Market Sq 12 CT16, CT17. 166 D7
Market St
Deal CT14 . . . . 117 D6
Faversham ME13 . . . . 62 D7
Herne Bay CT6. . . . . 22 F5
2 Maidstone ME14 . . . . . 74 F4
Margate CT9 . . . . 7 I3
Sandwich CT13 . . . . 73 A1
Market View CT3 . . . . 112 F5
Market Way CT2 . . . . 67 C2
Markland Rd CT17 . . . . . . 165 F7
Mark St ME4. . . . . 10 A2
Marlborough Cl
Broadstairs CT10. . . . . . . 29 E3
Littlestone-on-Sea TN28 . . 202 D6
Marlborough Ct
Folkestone CT20 . . . . 178 B4
Hythe CT21 . . . . 176 D1
Marlborough Ho
4 Gillingham ME8 . . . . . . 33 F8
Margate CT9 . . . . 8 C3
Marlborough Rd
Deal CT14 . . . . 117 A2
Dover CT17 . . . . 165 F7
Gillingham ME7 . . . . 10 B5
Margate CT9 . . . . 7 I1
6 Ramsgate CT11 . . . . . 52 D6
Marlborough Road Ind Est
CT14. . . . . 117 A3
Marlborough St CT5 . . . . . 43 D5
Marlborough Way TN24 . . 139 C5
Marler Rd CT19 . . . . 177 E6
MARLEY
Barham 111 B1
Deal 116 A8
Marley Ct CT2 . . . . 66 C4
Marley La
Chislet CT3 . . . . 47 A5
Finglesham CT14 . . . . . . 116 A8

Marley La continued
Kingston CT4 . . . . 111 B1
Marley Rd ME17 . . . . 100 F6
Marley Way ME1 . . . . 9 C2
Marlow Cl CT5 . . . . 21 B1
Marlow Copse ME5 . . . . 31 F1
Marlowe Arc 11 CT1 . . . . . . 87 F8
Marlowe Ave CT1 . . . . 87 F8
Marlowe Ct 12 CT1 . . . . 87 F8
Marlowe Rd
Ashford TN23 . . . . 139 B2
Dover CT16 . . . . 149 B3
Margate CT9 . . . . 29 C8
Marlow Ho CT7 . . . . 27 B7
Marlow Mdws CT2 . . . . 67 F5
MARLPIT 97 E2
Marlpit Cotts ME17 . . . . 97 E2
Marmion Way TN23 . . . . . 155 C8
Marquis Dr ME7 . . . . 33 B3
Marr Cl ME12 . . . . 3 F7
Marrians View 1 ME5 . . . . 10 C2
Marrose Ave CT12 . . . . 29 B3
Marrowbone Hill ME12 . . . . . 5 B5
Marsh Acad The TN28 . . . 202 B7
Marshall Cres
Broadstairs CT10 . . . . 29 E4
Rushenden ME11 . . . . .2 F3
Marshall Rd ME8 . . . . 33 C8
Marshalls Land TN30 . . . . 167 A3
Marshall St CT19 . . . . 178 E7
Marsham Cres ME17 . . . . . . 98 B1
Marsham St ME14 . . . . 75 A4
MARSHBOROUGH 93 B7
Marshborough Rd CT13 . . . 93 B7
Marsh Cres TN28 . . . . 202 B6
Marsh Farm Rd CT12 . . . . . 50 B4
Marsh La
Deal CT14 . . . . 117 A7
Teynham Street ME9 . . . . . 39 A4
Marshlands TN29 . . . . 195 B7
Marshlands Cl TN29 . . . . . 195 B7
Marsh Rd TN26 . . . . 183 F6
Marsh Rise ME10 . . . . 15 A1
MARSHSIDE 24 D1
Marsh St ME2 . . . . 9 B7
Marsh View
Hythe CT21 . . . . 187 C8
Sheerness ME12 . . . . 1 H1
Marshwood Cl CT1 . . . . 67 C3
Marstan Cl ME9 . . . . 12 E2
Marston Cl ME5 . . . . 31 E3
Marston Dr ME14 . . . . 75 C5
Marston Wlk ME5 . . . . 31 E3
Martello Cotts CT21 . . . . . 187 E8
Martello Dr CT21 . . . . 175 F1
Martello Ind Ctr CT19 . . . 178 F6
Martello Rd
Folkestone CT20 . . . . 178 E6
Folkestone, Sandgate
CT20 . . . . 177 E3
Martello Terr 1 CT20 . . . 177 F3
Marten Cl ME9 . . . . 178 B5
Martha Cl CT19 . . . . 178 E7
MARTIN 133 B3
Martin Ct
Gillingham ME7 . . . . 33 A3
Sittingbourne ME10 . . . . . 14 F1
Martindale Cl CT1 . . . . 88 A7
Martin Dale Cres CT15 . . . 133 C2
Martindown Rd CT5 . . . . . . 43 C7
Martin Ho TN25 . . . . 123 E2
MARTIN MILL 133 C2
Martin Mill Sta CT15 . . . . 133 C2
Martin Rd ME2 . . . . 9 B8
Martins Cl TN30 . . . . 179 C4
Martin's Cl CT12 . . . . 29 C2
Martins The TN26 . . . . 168 A8
Martin's Way CT21 . . . . . . 187 D8
MARTYR'S FIELD 87 F7
Martyrs' Field Rd CT1 . . . . 87 F7
Mary Ct ME4 . . . . 10 A2
Mary Green Wlk 5 CT1 . . 67 B2
Mary Hougham Almshouses
CT14 . . . . 117 D7
Maryland Ct
Gillingham ME8 . . . . 33 E5
Hythe CT21 . . . . 176 D3
Maryland Gr CT1 . . . . 88 C6
Mary Rd CT14 . . . . 117 A3
Masons Rd CT17 . . . . 149 B1
Mason's Rise CT10 . . . . 30 A5
Matfield Cres ME14 . . . . . . 75 C5
Matilda Cl ME8 . . . . 33 B8
Matthews Cl CT14 . . . . 117 C6
Matthew's Pl 9 CT16 . . . 149 C1
Matthews Rd CT6 . . . . 22 C2
Mattison Pl ME9 . . . . 78 F7
Matts Hill Rd ME9 . . . . 33 E2
Maugham Ct CT5 . . . . 43 D8
Maundene Prim Sch ME5 . 32 B5
Maunders Cl ME5 . . . . 32 C8
Maunsell Pl TN24 . . . . 156 D7
Maurice Ct CT9 . . . . 8 B3
Maxine Gdns CT10 . . . . 29 F5
Maxted Cl CT6 . . . . 23 C4
MAXTED STREET 143 B6
MAXTON 166 A6
Maxton Cl
Dover CT17 . . . . 166 A6
Maidstone ME14 . . . . 75 F5
Maxton Cl CT17 . . . . 166 A6
Maxton Rd CT17 . . . . 166 A6
Maxwell Dr ME16 . . . . 74 B6
Maxwell Pl CT14 . . . . 117 C4
Maxwell Rd ME7 . . . . 10 A6

Maybrook Ind Est CT1 . . . . 67 D4
Maydowns Rd CT5 . . . . 21 D2
Mayers Rd CT14 . . . . 117 A1
Mayfair 2 ME2 . . . . 9 C8
Mayfair Ave ME15 . . . . 97 A8
Mayfield Ave CT16 . . . . . . 149 C2
Mayfield Cl
Chatham ME5 . . . . 32 A1
Gillingham ME8 . . . . 11 E2
Mayfield Cl 3 CT16 . . . . . 149 B2
Mayfield Gdns CT16 . . . . . 149 C2
Mayfield Rd
Herne Bay CT6 . . . . 23 A3
Lyminge CT18 . . . . 161 C6
Whitfield CT16 . . . . 149 A7
Mayflower Ho ME1 . . . . 9 B4
Mayfly Dr CT18 . . . . 163 A4
Mayford Rd ME5 . . . . 32 D2
Mayforth Gdns CT11 . . . . . 52 B6
Mayhew Ct TN23 . . . . 156 A8
Maylam Gdns ME10 . . . . . . 36 B4
May Lodge CT14 . . . . 117 C6
Maymills Cotts CT13 . . . . . 93 B2
Maynard Ave CT9 . . . . 28 B8
Maynard Pl ME5 . . . . 10 D2
Maynard Rd CT1 . . . . 87 E7
Maypits TN23 . . . . 155 F8
Mayor's Pl 10 TN30 . . . . . 179 A7
MAYPOLE 46 F6
Maypole Cl CT18 . . . . 163 B6
Maypole La CT3 . . . . 46 E6
Maypole Rd CT3 . . . . 46 E6
May Rd
Gillingham ME7 . . . . 10 C4
Rochester ME1 . . . . 9 C3
Mays Rd 8 CT11 . . . . 52 C6
May St CT6 . . . . 23 F4
Maystreet Cross CT6 . . . . . 23 F3
May Terr ME7 . . . . 10 A7
Mayton La CT2 . . . . 45 C1
Maytree Cotts CT14 . . . . . 133 D8
Mayville Rd CT10 . . . . 29 E6
Mayweed Ave ME5 . . . . 31 E4
Meade The CT18 . . . . 162 F4
Meadow Bank ME1 . . . . 61 F2
Meadow Gn ME5 . . . . 32 C3
Meadowbank Rd ME4 . . . . . 10 A4
Meadowbrook CT20 . . . . . . 177 E4
Meadowbrook Cl TN24 . . . 139 D6
Meadow Brook Ct CT20 . . 177 E4
Meadowbrook Rd TN24 . . . 139 D6
Meadow Cl
Bridge CT4 . . . . 89 A1
Chatham ME5 . . . . 31 F5
Chilham CT4 . . . . 107 E8
Hawkinge CT18 . . . . 163 B6
Herne Bay CT6 . . . . 23 C4
Iwade ME9 . . . . 14 D4
Meadow Cotts
East Studdal CT15 . . . . . . 132 D8
Goodnestone CT3 . . . . . . 92 A2
Meadow Ct
Margate CT9 . . . . 29 B8
Westenhanger CT21 . . . . 175 B6
Meadowdown ME14 . . . . . . 75 E4
Meadowdown Cl ME7 . . . . . 33 A4
Meadow Dr CT5 . . . . 44 D8
Meadowfield Sch ME10 . . . 37 C3
Meadow Gr TN25 . . . . 174 D8
Meadow Hill Cotts CT15 . . 147 D1
Meadow Ho ME9 . . . . 36 B2
Meadow Rd
Ashford TN23 . . . . 139 A4
Canterbury CT2 . . . . 66 C2
Margate CT9 . . . . 7 F1
Sturry CT2 . . . . 67 F6
Meadow Rise ME9 . . . . 14 D4
Meadows The
Herne Bay CT6 . . . . 23 D2
3 Maidstone ME15 . . . . . . 74 E2
New Romney TN28 . . . . . 202 C6
Sittingbourne ME10 . . . . . 36 F2
Wittersham TN30 . . . . . . 188 D4
Meadowsweet Ho TN23 . . 138 F1
Meadow View
Hothfield TN26 . . . . 138 A6
Lydd TN29 . . . . 205 D7
Monkton CT12 . . . . 49 D6
Meadow View Ind Est
TN26 . . . . 183 C7
Meadow View Rd
Maidstone ME17 . . . . 97 B3
Shepherdswell CT15 . . . . 130 E5
Meadow Way
Eythorne CT15 . . . . 131 C8
Hythe CT21 . . . . 187 D8
Meadow Wlk
Maidstone ME15 . . . . 75 B3
Whitstable CT5 . . . . 43 C6
Mead Rd
Ashford TN24 . . . . 156 E7
Folkestone CT19 . . . . . . 178 D6
Meads Ave The ME10 . . . . . 36 D7
Meadside Wlk ME5 . . . . 31 F6
Meads Way TN29 . . . . 194 E3
Meadway CT17 . . . . 148 E3
Mead Way CT2 . . . . 66 E1
Mead Wlk TN23 . . . . 155 E8
Medina Ave CT5 . . . . 43 B7
Medlar Cl ME9 . . . . 58 A6
Medlar Gr ME7 . . . . 33 A4
Medlars The ME14 . . . . 75 D6
Medway City Est ME2 . . . . . 9 D4
Medway Com Coll ME4 . . . . 10 A1
Medway Ent Ctr ME2 . . . . . . 9 D8
Medway Gdns ME4 . . . . 9 F7

Medway Ho 7 ME14 . . . . . 74 F4
Medway Hts 5 ME4 . . . . 9 E4
Medway Maritime Hospl
ME7 . . . . 10 B4
Medway Rd
Gillingham ME7 . . . . 10 C7
Sheerness ME12 . . . . 1 C1
Medway St
Chatham ME4 . . . . 9 F5
Maidstone ME14 . . . . 74 F4
Medway Trad Est ME16 . . . 74 F2
Medway Villas ME15 . . . . . . 96 B7
Meehan Rd TN28 . . . . 202 E4
Meehan Road S TN28 . . . . 202 E3
Meeres Court La ME10 . . . . 37 C5
Meeson's Cl ME13 . . . . 81 E6
Meeting Ct CT9 . . . . 7 I3
Meeting House La 2 ME4 . . 9 F4
Meeting St CT11 . . . . 52 E7
Megan Cl TN29 . . . . 205 D7
Megby Cl ME8 . . . . 33 D6
Meggett La CT15 . . . . 164 C7
Megone Ct CT18 . . . . 163 A4
Meirs Court Rd ME8 . . . . . . 33 E6
Melbourne Ave
Dover CT16 . . . . 149 C4
Ramsgate CT12 . . . . 29 B1
Melbourne Rd ME4 . . . . 10 A3
Melbury Mews TN28 . . . . . 202 C8
Melford Dr ME16 . . . . 74 C4
Mellanby Cl CT7 . . . . 27 A6
Mellor Row ME10 . . . . 14 F1
Melody Cl
Gillingham ME8 . . . . 33 C4
Warden ME12 . . . . 6 E4
Melon La TN26, TN29 . . . . 193 B6
Melrose Cl ME15 . . . . 97 A7
Melsetter Cl CT7 . . . . 27 B7
Melville Ct ME4 . . . . 9 F6
Melville Lea CT13 . . . . 93 C7
Melville Rd ME15 . . . . 75 A3
Memel Pl 12 CT11 . . . . 52 D6
Mendfield St 5 ME13 . . . . 62 C7
Mendip TN24 . . . . 139 B4
Mendip Rise TN24 . . . . 139 B4
Menin Rd ME10 . . . . 14 F1
Mentmore Ho CT12 . . . . . . 29 C3
Mentmore Rd CT12 . . . . . . 29 C3
Menzies Ave CT14 . . . . 117 B1
Menzies Ct ME12 . . . . 4 A5
Menzies Rd CT16 . . . . 149 A5
Mercer Ct ME5 . . . . 31 E1
Mercer Dr ME17 . . . . 100 F6
Mercer Way ME17 . . . . 98 B1
Mercery La 5 CT1 . . . . 87 F8
Merchant Store The 7
CT2 . . . . 66 F1
Merchants Way CT2 . . . . . . 87 C8
Mercury Cl ME1 . . . . 9 A3
Meredale Ind Prim Sch
ME8 . . . . 12 A1
Meredith Cl ME17 . . . . 98 F7
Mere Gate CT9 . . . . 7 I1
MERESBOROUGH 34 A5
Meresborough Cotts ME8 . 33 F5
Meresborough La ME8,
ME9 . . . . 34 B5
Meresborough Rd ME8 . . . . 34 A7
Mereworth Cl ME8 . . . . 11 A3
Meriden Wlk CT18 . . . . . . 161 D3
Meridian Ct
Ashford TN23 . . . . 155 E7
Maidstone ME16 . . . . 74 E4
Meridian Pk ME2 . . . . 9 E6
Merino Way TN23 . . . . 155 E5
Merivale Gr ME5 . . . . 32 B4
Merleburgh Dr ME10 . . . . . 36 F8
Merlin Cl ME10 . . . . 37 A3
Merlin Ho
Chatham ME4 . . . . 10 B8
2 Sittingbourne ME10 . . . . 37 A4
Merlin Way
Ashford TN23 . . . . 155 E7
Gillingham ME7 . . . . 10 D5
Mermaid Cl ME5 . . . . 32 A6
Merritt Rd TN28 . . . . 202 E2
Merrivale Hts CT10 . . . . . . 30 A2
MERRYMAN'S HILL 4 C8
Merrywood Gr CT6 . . . . 23 C2
MERSHAM 157 E4
Mersham Prim Sch
TN25 . . . . 157 E3
Merton Cl ME5 . . . . 32 C5
Merton La CT4 . . . . 87 F4
Merton Rd ME15 . . . . 75 F2
Meryl Gdns CT14 . . . . 117 C1
Metcalfe Mews 1 CT1 . . . . 67 B2
Meteor Ave CT5 . . . . 43 B7
Meteor Cl ME10 . . . . 36 E8
Metropole Ct 2 CT20 . . . . 178 B3
Metropole Road E CT20 . . 178 B3
Metropole Road W CT20 . . 178 B3
Metropole The 3 CT20 . . . 178 B3
Meverall Ave CT12 . . . . 51 E5
Mews The
1 Maidstone ME16 . . . . . . 74 E5
Sittingbourne ME10 . . . . . 36 F2
Meyrick Rd ME12 . . . . 1 D2
Micawber Cl ME5 . . . . 32 A1
Michael Ave CT11 . . . . 52 G8
Michelle Gdns CT9 . . . . 28 A8
Micketts Gdns ME10 . . . . . 36 B4
Mickleburgh Ave CT6 . . . . . 23 B4
Mickleburgh Hill CT6 . . . . . 23 B4
Middelburg Ho CT19 . . . . . 177 D6
Middelburg Sq CT20 . . . . . 178 D4
Middle Cl TN23 . . . . 138 C1
MIDDLE DEAL 117 C5

Middle Deal Rd CT14 . . . . . 117 B5
Middlefields ME8 . . . . 34 A8
Middle Mead TN19 . . . . . . 178 B7
MIDDLE QUARTER 152 D1
Middle Row
3 Ashford TN23 . . . . 139 C2
2 Faversham ME13 . . . . . 62 D7
Middlesex Rd ME15 . . . . . . 97 D7
Middle St
Ashford TN23 . . . . 139 B2
4 Chatham ME7 . . . . 10 A6
Deal CT14 . . . . 117 D6
Middleton Cl ME8 . . . . 33 E4
Middleton Cotts TN25 . . . 122 E3
Middleton Ct 9 ME6 . . . . . . 10 E4
Middletune Ave ME10 . . . . 36 E7
Middle Wall CT5 . . . . 20 D2
Middle Way ME10 . . . . 37 B3
Midhurst CT15 ME15 . . . . . 75 A3
MidKent Coll (Chatham
Maritime) ME4 . . . . 10 B8
MidKent Coll (City Way Ctr)
ME1 . . . . 9 E4
MidKent Coll (Horsted Ctr)
ME5 . . . . 31 E6
MidKent Coll (Oakwood Park
Ctr) ME16 . . . . 74 C2
Mid Kent Sh Ctr The
ME16 . . . . 74 C7
Midley Cl ME16 . . . . 74 C7
Midsummer Hill TN24 . . . . 139 D6
Mierscourt Cl ME8 . . . . 34 A8
Miers Court Prim Sch
ME8 . . . . 33 F7
Mierscourt Rd ME8 . . . . 33 E6
Mikyle Ct CT1 . . . . 88 A6
Milbourne Gr ME10 . . . . . . 36 E7
Milburn Rd ME7 . . . . 10 C7
Mildred Cotts CT19 . . . . . . 177 F7
Mile Rd CT12 . . . . 48 F6
Miles Ct CT5 . . . . 91 A8
Miles Pl ME1 . . . . 9 D3
Milestone Cl CT19 . . . . 178 A7
Milestone Rd CT14 . . . . . . 117 B5
Miles Way CT7 . . . . 26 F7
MILE TOWN 1 C1
Mile Town Ind Est ME12 . . . 1 B1
Milford Cl ME16 . . . . 74 D5
Military Rd
Canterbury CT1 . . . . 67 A1
Chatham ME4 . . . . 9 F5
2 Dover CT17 . . . . 166 D7
Folkestone CT20 . . . . . . 177 E4
Houghton Green TN31 . . 197 E3
Hythe CT21 . . . . 176 B2
Ramsgate CT11 . . . . 52 E6
Stone in Oxney TN26,
TN30 . . . . 190 B4
Millais Rd CT16 . . . . 149 C1
MILLBANK 46 F7
Mill Bank TN29 . . . . 205 B6
Mill Bank Cotts CT13 . . . . . 93 A3
Millbank La TN29 . . . . 200 E7
Millbank Rd TN23 . . . . 155 F5
Mill Bay CT20 . . . . 178 E5
Millbrook CT21 . . . . 176 D2
Millbrook Cl ME15 . . . . 74 F1
Millbrook Mdw TN23 . . . . 138 E1
Mill Cl
Crabble CT17 . . . . 148 F2
Lenham ME17 . . . . 101 C4
Sandwich CT13 . . . . 72 E2
Wickhambreaux CT3 . . . . 69 C2
Mill Cotts
Queenborough ME11 . . . . . 3 A5
Ramsgate CT11 . . . . 52 D6
Worth CT14 . . . . 94 A4
Mill Court Cl CT6 . . . . 23 B2
Mill Ct
Ashford TN24 . . . . 139 D2
Sittingbourne ME10 . . . . . 37 A3
Milldale Cl CT14 . . . . 117 B4
Millenium Terr CT1 . . . . . . 87 C6
Millennium Way
Broadstairs CT10 . . . . 29 C4
Sheerness ME12 . . . . 1 C2
Millen Rd ME10 . . . . 36 E5
Millen's Row ME13 . . . . . . 83 B3
Miller Ave CT2 . . . . 87 D8
Miller Cl
Ashford TN24 . . . . 139 D2
Deal CT14 . . . . 117 C8
Sittingbourne ME10 . . . . . 37 A8
Wingham CT3 . . . . 91 B7
Miller Cotts TN24 . . . . 139 D2
Miller Ct ME12 . . . . 4 A5
Millers Ct
5 Ramsgate CT12 . . . . . . 29 B1
Whitstable CT5 . . . . 43 D7
Millers La CT12 . . . . 49 C7
Millers Wharf 1 ME15 . . . 74 E2
Millers Yd CT1 . . . . 87 E7
Millfield
Ashford TN23 . . . . 155 D8
Folkestone CT20 . . . . . . 178 D5
Hawkinge CT18 . . . . 163 C5
High Halden TN26 . . . . . 167 D7
Sittingbourne ME10 . . . . . 37 A3
St Margaret's at Cliffe
CT15 . . . . 150 F7
Mill Field
Ash CT3 . . . . 71 E1
Broadstairs CT10 . . . . 29 F5
Millfield Cl CT18 . . . . 163 B5
Millfield Manor CT5 . . . . . . 20 E1
Millfield Rd
Faversham ME13 . . . . 62 E7
Ramsgate CT12 . . . . 29 B3

Millfields
Chatham ME5 . . . . 32 D5
Shepherdswell CT15 . . . . 130 E4
Mill Fields Rd CT21 . . . . . . 175 F2
Mill Gn CT13 . . . . 93 A2
Mill Hamlet CT3 . . . . 69 C2
MILL HILL 117 A3
Mill Hill CT14 . . . . 117 A3
Mill Ho CT17 . . . . 148 F3
Mill La
Ashford TN24 . . . . 140 A1
Birchington CT7 . . . . 26 F6
Bonnington TN25 . . . . . . 172 E5
Bridge CT4 . . . . 88 F1
Canterbury CT1 . . . . 66 F1
Canterbury, Harbledown
CT2 . . . . 87 C8
Chatham, Bluebell Hill ME5 . 31 D1
Chatham, Luton ME5 . . . . 10 C1
Chilham CT4 . . . . 107 D7
Coxheath ME17 . . . . 96 D4
10 Dover CT16 . . . . 166 E7
Eastry CT13 . . . . 93 B2
Hartlip ME9 . . . . 34 E6
Hawkinge CT18 . . . . 163 B5
Herne Bay CT6 . . . . 23 B2
Lydd TN29 . . . . 205 D7
Lynsted ME9 . . . . 60 C5
Maidstone ME14 . . . . 74 F6
Margate CT9 . . . . 7 I2
Newchurch TN29 . . . . . . 184 F3
Nonington CT15 . . . . 113 F4
Northbourne CT14 . . . . . 115 F4
Preston CT3 . . . . 70 D6
Shepherdswell CT15 . . . . 130 F5
Smarden TN27 . . . . 135 A2
Stelling Minnis CT4 . . . . . 126 F2
Tenterden TN30 . . . . 167 B1
Whitfield CT16 . . . . 149 A8
Worth CT14 . . . . 94 A4
Mill Lane Cotts CT14 . . . . . 116 A4
Millmead Ave CT9 . . . . 8 D1
Millmead Gdns CT9 . . . . 8 D1
Millmead Rd CT9 . . . . 8 C1
Mill Mews CT14 . . . . 117 B4
Mill Pl ME13 . . . . 62 D8
Millpond Cl ME2 . . . . 9 B8
Mill Race CT17 . . . . 148 F3
Mill Rd
Bethersden TN26 . . . . . . 153 E5
Bramling CT3 . . . . 90 E6
Deal CT14 . . . . 117 C4
Dymchurch TN29 . . . . . . 195 B7
Gillingham ME7 . . . . 10 C6
Hoath CT3 . . . . 46 F5
Hythe CT21 . . . . 176 D2
Lydd TN29 . . . . 205 D7
Rochester ME2 . . . . 9 B8
Staple CT3 . . . . 92 B5
Sturry CT2 . . . . 67 F5
Mill Row CT7 . . . . 26 F6
Mills Cl ME12 . . . . 3 F6
Mill St
Maidstone, Loose ME15 . . 96 F5
Maidstone ME15 . . . . 74 F4
Sittingbourne ME10 . . . . . 36 E5
Temple Ewell CT16 . . . . 148 D5
Mills Terr ME4 . . . . 10 A3
Millstock Terr 2 ME15 . . . 74 E2
Millstream Cl
Faversham ME13 . . . . 62 C7
Whitstable CT5 . . . . 20 E1
Millstream Cotts CT5 . . . . . 43 E8
Millstream Gn TN24 . . . . . 156 F7
Millstrood Rd CT5 . . . . 43 E8
Mill Terr
Bridge CT4 . . . . 88 F1
Chartham CT4 . . . . 86 D3
Mill View
Ashford TN24 . . . . 156 F8
Woodchurch TN26 . . . . . 169 A3
Mill View Rd CT6 . . . . 23 A1
Mill Wall Pl CT13 . . . . 94 A8
Mill Way ME10 . . . . 36 F6
Mill Wlk ME16 . . . . 74 A3
Millwood Ct 4 ME4 . . . . 9 F4
Millyard Way CT15 . . . . . . 114 D1
Milner Cl CT15 . . . . 114 B1
Milner Cres CT3 . . . . 112 E5
Milne Rd TN24 . . . . 156 F8
Milner La CT2 . . . . 67 F5
Milner Rd
Elvington CT15 . . . . 114 B1
Gillingham ME7 . . . . 10 D7
Whitstable CT5 . . . . 43 A6
Milners ME17 . . . . 98 F6
MILSTEAD 58 E2
Milstead Cl
Maidstone ME14 . . . . 75 C5
West Minst ME12 . . . . 3 B7
Milstead & Frinstead CE
Prim Sch ME9 . . . . 58 E1
Milsted Rd ME8 . . . . 11 C3
Milton Ave CT9 . . . . 7 J1
Milton Cl
Canterbury CT1 . . . . 88 C6
Dover CT16 . . . . 149 B4
Milton Court Prim Sch
ME10 . . . . 36 E6
Milton Rd
Ashford TN23 . . . . 139 B2
Canterbury CT1 . . . . 88 A6
Dover CT16 . . . . 149 B4
Gillingham ME7 . . . . 10 C3
Sittingbourne ME10 . . . . . 36 E4
MILTON REGIS 36 C6
Milton Regis Halt★ ME10 . 37 A6
Milton Sq 4 CT9 . . . . 7 J1

Milton St ME16 74 C2
Mincers Cl ME5 32 C2
Miners Way
  Aylesham CT3 113 A5
  Hersden CT3 47 A1
Minerva Ave CT16 149 C2
Minerva Ho 4 CT11 52 D7
Minerva Rd ME2 9 A8
Minnis Field CT4 126 E2
Minnis Gn CT4 126 E2
Minnis La CT15, CT17 148 C2
Minnis Rd CT7 26 E7
Minnis Terr CT17 149 A2
Minnis Way CT14 94 B5
MINSTER
  Sheppey 4 B7
  Thanet 50 A6
Minster Abbey★
  Minster (Sheppey) ME12 4 D6
  Minster (Thanet) CT12 50 C5
Minster CE Prim Sch
  CT12 50 B5
Minster Cl CT10 30 A2
Minster Coll ME12 3 F6
Minster Dr
  Herne Bay CT6 22 D4
  Minster (Sheppey) ME12 4 B8
Minster Gatehouse Mus★
  ME12 4 D6
Minster Lodge 4 CT11 52 C6
Minster Rd
  Acol CT12, CT7 27 C2
  Faversham ME13 62 E7
  Gillingham ME8 11 C3
  Minster (Sheppey) ME12 4 B6
  Ramsgate CT11 52 B5
  Westgate on Sea CT8 27 F7
Minster Sheppey Prim Sch
  ME12 4 C7
Minster Sta CT12 50 C5
Mintching Wood La ME9 58 F2
Minter Ave CT18 162 F7
Minter Cl CT18 162 F7
Minterne Ave ME10 36 D2
Minterne Jun Sch ME10 36 D2
Minters Ind Est CT14 117 B6
Mint The CT2 66 C1
Miranda Ct ME12 1 C1
Misling La CT4 143 C7
Missenden Ct 6 CT20 178 D5
Mitcham Rd TN29 195 C8
Mitchell Ave
  Chatham ME4 9 F2
  Hawkinge CT18 163 B5
Mitchell Cl ME17 101 C5
Mitchell St CT19 177 D6
Mitre Rd ME1 9 B4
Mittell Ct TN29 205 B6
Moat Farm Cl CT19 178 C7
Moat Farm Rd CT19 178 C7
Moatfield Mdw TN23 156 B4
Moat Ho
  Canterbury CT1 87 F7
  Charing TN27 120 C7
Moat La
  Ash CT3 71 E1
  Fordwich CT2 68 A3
  Rough Common CT2 66 B4
Moat Pk TN27 120 C6
Moat Sole CT13 72 F1
Moat The TN27 120 C7
Moat Way ME11 3 A5
MOCKBEGGAR 39 B1
Mockett Ct 4 ME10 36 E4
Mockett Dr CT10 29 F7
Mock La TN23 155 B6
MOLASH 105 F4
Molehill Cnr CT5 44 D8
Molehill Copse Prim Sch
  ME15 97 D7
Molehill Rd
  Herne Bay CT6 22 A1
  Whitstable CT5, CT6 44 E8
Molineux Rd CT12 50 B6
Molland Cl CT3 71 C2
Molland La
  Ash, Guilton CT3 71 C2
  Ash, Paramour Street CT3 71 D6
Molland Lea CT3 71 C2
Molloy Rd TN26 155 B1
Monarch Cl ME5 32 A6
Monarch Dr ME10 14 F1
Monastery Ave CT16 149 E1
Monastery St CT1 88 A8
Monckton's Ave ME14 74 F7
Monckton's Dr ME14 74 E7
Monckton's La ME14 74 F7
Moncrif Cl ME14 76 B4
Mongeham Church Cl
  CT14 116 D3
Mongeham Rd CT14 116 E3
Mongeham View CT14 116 E4
Monica Cl ME13 84 E6
Monins Rd
  Dover CT17 166 B7
  Iwade ME9 14 D3
Monkdown ME15 76 A1
Monkery La TN25, TN27 104 D2
Monks Cl
  Canterbury CT2 67 A2
  Faversham ME13 62 B8
Monks Hill Cotts TN26 182 E6
Monkshill Rd ME13 42 B2
Monks Way CT16 149 A3
Monk's Way CT13 72 F3
Monks Wlk TN27 120 C7
MONKTON 49 D7
Monkton CE Prim Sch
  CT12 49 D7
Monkton Cl 2 TN23 155 F6
Monkton Court La CT15 131 D7
Monkton Ct CT5 44 D8
Monkton Gdns CT9 8 E3
Monkton Manor CT12 49 C7
Monkton Nature Reserve★
  CT12 49 C8
Monkton Pl CT11 52 D7
Monkton Rd CT12 50 A6
Monkton Rdbt CT12 49 D8
Monkton St CT12 49 D7
Monkwood Cl ME1 31 B8
Monmouth Cl ME8 11 D2
Mons Ct ME10 14 F1
Montacue Ct CT20 178 B4
Montague Ct ME12 1 C1
Montague Rd CT11 52 E8
Montague St CT6 22 D5
Montefiore Ave
  Broadstairs CT10 30 A1
  Ramsgate CT11 29 F1
Montefiore Cotts CT11 52 F8
Montfort Cl
  Ashford TN23 155 F7
  Canterbury CT2 67 A4
Montfort Rd
  Chatham ME5 31 F2
  Rochester ME2 9 A8
Montgomery Ave ME5 32 A7
Montgomery Rd ME7 10 C3
Montgomery Way CT19 178 E8
Montpelier Ave CT5 43 D6
Montpelier Bsns Pk
  TN23 138 F1
Montpelier Gate ME16 74 B5
Montreal Cl 8 CT16 149 B3
Montrose Ave ME5 10 E2
Monument Way TN24 156 F5
Moonfleet Cl ME10 15 A1
Moon Hill CT15 130 E4
MOON'S GREEN 188 A3
Moonstone Dr ME5 32 B2
Moonstone Sq 1 ME10 36 D6
Moore Cl TN29 192 A3
Moore St ME2 9 A8
Moorfield CT2 66 F4
Mooring Rd ME1 9 D1
Moorings The ME9 38 E6
Moor La
  Ivychurch TN29 192 D4
  Woodchurch TN26 180 E6
Moorland Rd CT15 130 E4
Moor Park Cl ME8 34 A8
Moor St ME8 34 B8
MOORSTOCK 159 C2
Moorstock La TN25 159 C2
MOOR STREET 34 B7
Moorwell Dr CT15 130 D5
Moray Ave CT7 26 F8
Mordaunt Ave CT8 27 E8
Morden St ME1 9 C4
MOREHALL 177 F6
Morehall Ave CT19 177 F6
Morehall Prim Sch CT19 177 F6
Morella Wlk ME17 101 C5
Morello Cl ME9 38 C2
Moreton Ct CT14 117 C2
Moreton Terr TN26 155 A1
Morgan Kirby's Gdn ME13 83 D5
Morgan Rd ME2 9 A8
Morris Ave CT6 21 F4
Morris Cl ME17 97 D5
Morris Court Cl ME9 37 D2
Morrison Rd CT20 178 E6
Morry La ME17 99 D1
Mortimer Cl TN23 156 B7
Mortimer Rd CT16 166 F8
Mortimer St CT6 22 F5
Morton Cl ME15 97 D6
Mossbank ME5 32 A3
Moss End Mews CT11 29 E2
Mossy Glade ME8 33 E6
Mostyn Rd ME14 75 C4
Mote Ave ME15 75 B3
Mote Hall Villas ME14 76 C4
Mote Pk ME15 75 D2
Mote Rd ME15 75 A3
Motney Hill Rd ME8 12 A4
Motorway Ind Est ME20 53 C2
Mouat Ct ME5 32 A3
Mountain St CT4 107 B6
MOUNTAIN STREET 107 B6
Mountbatten Ave ME5 32 A7
Mountbatten Ho CT14 117 D3
Mountbatten Way TN25 158 E6
Mount Castle La ME17 101 F1
Mount Charles Wlk CT4 88 F1
Mount Dr ME14 76 B4
Mount Ephraim Gdns★
  ME13 64 A4
Mount Field
  Faversham ME13 62 B6
  Queenborough ME11 3 A5
Mountfield Mews CT8 27 D7
Mountfield Rd TN28 202 C6
Mountfield Way CT8 27 D6
Mount Green Ave CT12 51 D5
Mount La
  Hartlip ME9 34 D4
  Maidstone ME14 76 B4
Mount Lodge ME1 9 B2
Mount Pleasant
  Aldington TN25 173 A6
  Blean CT2 66 A6
  Chatham ME5 10 B3
  Faversham ME13 40 B2
Mount Pleasant *continued*
  Forstal ME20 53 A3
  Kingsdown CT14 134 D5
  Minster (Thanet) CT12 50 C8
  Tenterden TN30 179 C8
Mount Pleasant Cl CT18 161 C7
Mount Pleasant Dr ME14 76 A5
Mount Pleasant Rd 4
  CT20 178 D5
Mount Pleasant Terr
  ME17 100 E2
Mount Rd
  Canterbury CT1 88 C6
  Chatham ME4 9 F3
  Dover CT17 166 A6
  Rochester ME1 9 B2
Mounts Cl CT14 117 A5
Mountsfield Cl ME16 74 D5
Mount St CT21 176 C2
Mounts View TN23 138 F4
Mountview ME9 36 B2
Mount View ME13 62 A5
Mount View Ct 3 ME4 9 F3
Mount View Rd CT6 23 A2
Moyes Cl CT12 51 D5
Moyle Cl ME8 33 D4
Mozart Ct ME4 9 E3
Muddy Bush Cnr CT3 90 F2
Muddy La ME10 37 B2
Mudie Cl CT18 163 A5
Muir Rd
  Maidstone ME15 75 A2
  Ramsgate CT11 52 F8
Mulberry Cl
  Gillingham ME7 33 A4
  Ramsgate CT11 52 F8
  St Mary's Bay TN29 194 F4
Mulberry Ct
  Canterbury CT1 87 F8
  Hythe CT21 176 D3
  Littlestone-on-Sea TN28 202 E5
  Maidstone ME14 75 B5
Mulberry Field CT13 72 F1
Mulberry Gdns TN30 179 B8
Mulberry Hill CT4 85 D1
Mulberry Rd
  Ashford TN23 138 D3
  Sittingbourne ME10 37 C5
Mummery Ct ME13 61 E2
MUNDAY BOIS 135 F8
Munday Bois Cotts TN27 135 F8
Munday Bois Rd TN27 118 E1
Mundella Prim Sch
  CT19 178 D6
Mungeam Ho ME1 9 C4
Munn's La ME9 34 E6
Munsgore La ME9 35 E3
Murrain Dr ME15 76 A1
Murray Rd ME2 9 C8
MURSTON 37 B5
Murston Inf Sch ME10 37 B4
Murston Jun Sch ME10 37 B5
Murston Rd ME10 37 B4
Murthwaite Ct ME12 4 A5
Murton Pl ME13 41 E1
Muscovy Rd TN25 139 C7
Muscovy Way CT6 22 E3
Musgrave Cl CT12 27 F2
Musgrave Rd ME10 36 F6
Musgrove TN23 156 A8
Musket La
  Eyhorne Street ME17 77 C2
  Leeds ME17 77 A2
Mus of Canterbury with
  Rupert Bear Mus★ 22
  CT1 87 F8
Mustards Rd ME12 6 D2
Mutrix Gdns CT9 7 E1
Mutrix Rd CT9 28 B8
Mutton La ME13 62 A6
Mymms Cl CT5 44 C8
Mynn Cres ME14 76 A4
Myrtle Cres ME5 31 F5
Myrtle Ct TN23 156 A3
Myrtle Gn TN23 138 D4
Myrtle Rd 5 CT19 178 E6
Mystole Ho CT4 108 B8
Mystole La CT4 108 C8

N

NACCOLT 140 E6
Nacholt Cl CT5 21 A2
NACKINGTON 88 A2
Nackington Ct 2 CT1 88 B6
Nackington Pk CT4 88 A4
Nackington Rd CT1, CT4 88 A3
Nagpur Ho 4 ME15 97 E5
Nag's Head La ME1 9 D4
Nailbourne Cl CT4 111 D3
Nailbourne Ct CT18 161 C7
Naildown Cl CT21 177 A3
Naildown Rd CT21 177 A3
Nairne Cl TN26 170 A8
Naldera CT10 30 C7
Namur Pl CT15 149 F3
NAPCHESTER 132 C3
Napchester Rd CT16 149 A8
Napier Cl ME10 36 C4
Napier Ct ME14 74 F7
Napier Gdns CT21 176 C1
Napier Prim Sch ME7 10 D4
Napier Rd
  Broadstairs CT10 29 E6
  Dover CT16 149 B2
  Gillingham ME7 10 D4
Napleton Ct 7 CT11 52 C6
Napleton Rd
  Faversham ME13 62 C7
  Ramsgate CT11 52 C6
Napoleon Wlk ME17 101 C5
Napwood Cl ME8 33 D6
Nares Rd ME8 33 D4
Nargate Cl CT3 90 A8
Nargate St CT3 90 A8
Narrabeen Rd CT19 177 E6
Narrowbush La TN29 200 B7
Naseby Ave CT20 177 D5
NASH 70 F2
Nash Cl ME5 32 C2
Nash Court Gdns CT9 28 F8
Nash Court Rd CT9 28 F8
Nashenden Farm La ME1 31 A8
Nashenden La ME1 9 A2
Nash Gdns CT10 30 B4
Nash Hill CT18 161 D6
Nash La CT9 28 F7
Nash Rd
  Margate CT9, CT10 28 F7
  Wingham CT3 70 D2
Nasmyth Rd CT7 27 A8
Natal Rd
  Chatham ME4 10 A3
  Dover CT16 149 C4
Nativity Cl ME10 36 E4
Nat's La TN25 141 A5
Nautilus Cl ME12 4 A6
Nautilus Dr ME12 4 A6
Naval Terr ME12 1 B3
Naylands CT9 7 H1
Naylor's Cotts ME7 33 B1
Neale St ME4 9 F2
Neal's Place Rd CT2 66 C3
Neame Rd CT7 27 A7
NEAMES FORSTAL 84 D7
Neason Way
  Folkestone CT19 178 F6
  Folkestone CT20 178 F6
Neath Rd TN29 204 A2
Neatscourt Cotts ME12 3 C4
Nelson Ave ME12 4 D5
Nelson Cl
  Ashford TN24 157 B8
  West Minst ME12 3 A8
Nelson Cres CT11 52 E6
Nelson Ct
  Birchington CT7 26 E8
  Chatham ME5 10 C1
Nelson Gdns ME13 62 C6
Nelson Ho 8 ME15 97 F5
Nelson Mews TN28 202 E5
Nelson Park Rd CT15 150 E8
Nelson Pl CT10 30 B5
Nelson Rd
  Gillingham ME7 10 D4
  Whitstable CT5 20 D1
Nelson St
  Deal CT14 117 D7
  Faversham ME13 62 C6
Nelson Terr ME5 10 C1
Nelson Wlk ME10 36 B5
Neptune Bsns Pk ME2 9 E7
Neptune Cl ME2 9 E7
Neptune Terr ME12 1 E2
Neptune Way ME2 9 E6
Nesbit Rd TN29 194 F4
Ness Rd TN29 205 C6
Ness The CT1 88 B5
Nether Ave TN28 202 D6
NETHERCOURT 52 A7
Nethercourt Cir CT12 52 A6
Nethercourt Farm Rd
  CT11 52 B7
Nethercourt Gdns CT11 52 B6
Nethercourt Hill CT11 52 B6
Nethergong Hill CT3 47 D3
Netherhale Farm Rd CT7 26 B3
Nethersole Cl CT2 67 A4
Nethersole Rd CT4 112 F1
Netley Cl ME14 75 D6
Nettlefield TN24 139 E5
Nettlepole La TN27 119 D1
Neville Cl ME14 75 B8
Neville Ho CT14 117 D6
Neville Rd
  Chatham ME4 9 E2
  Herne Bay CT6 23 F4
Nevill Gdns CT14 117 B1
Newark Ct 1 ME2 9 B7
Newark Yd ME2 9 B7
NEWBARN 161 B4
New Barns Rd ME14 75 A8
New Beverley Ho CT2 66 F2
New Bridge 12 CT16 166 E7
Newbridge Ave ME10 36 E7
New Bridge Way TN29 194 E3
New Brompton Coll ME7 10 B4
NEWBURY 59 D4
Newbury Ave ME16 74 C6
Newbury Cl
  Birchington CT7 27 B6
  Dover CT17 165 F7
  Folkestone CT20 177 D5
Newcastle Hill 8 CT11 52 E7
NEWCHURCH 184 E3
Newchurch La TN26 193 A7
Newchurch Rd ME15 75 A1
Newcomen Rd ME12 1 D2
New Cotts
  Guston CT15 149 E6
  Harbledown CT2 65 E1
  Teynham ME9 38 A4
New Covenant Pl 4 ME1 9 D4
New Creek Rd ME13 62 E8
New Cross St CT9 7 I2
New Cut ME15 96 D7
New Cut Rd
  Chilham CT4, ME13 85 A3
  Harbledown ME13 65 A1
  Maidstone ME14 75 D5
New Delhi Ho 5 ME15 97 E5
New Dover Rd
  Canterbury CT1, CT4 88 C6
  Capel-le-Ferne CT18 164 C2
Newenden Cl
  Ashford TN23 155 F6
  Maidstone ME14 75 D6
New Forest La CT4 85 B3
New Gardens Rd ME9 38 C2
Newgate Gap CT9 8 A3
Newgate Lower Prom CT9 8 A3
Newgate Prom CT9 8 A3
New Haine Rd CT12 29 A3
New Hall Cl TN29 195 C8
New House Cl CT1 87 E4
Newhouse Cnr CT3 48 D1
Newhouse Farm Cotts
  ME13 83 E7
Newhouse La ME13 83 D7
New House La CT4 87 C2
Newing Cl CT3 89 E8
NEWINGREEN 175 A5
NEWINGTON
  Folkestone 177 A8
  Ramsgate 29 B1
  Sittingbourne 35 A6
Newington CE Prim Sch
  ME9 35 B7
Newington Com Prim Sch
  CT12 52 A8
Newington Ct 7 CT12 29 B1
Newington Ent Ctr ME9 35 C8
Newington Ind Est ME9 34 F6
Newington Rd
  Peene CT18 177 A8
  Ramsgate CT12, CT11 29 B1
Newington Sta ME9 35 B6
Newington Wlk ME14 75 C6
New Inn Cotts ME15 96 C7
New Kempes Ho TN25 123 E2
New La TN29 205 C6
NEWLAND GREEN 135 D8
Newland Green La TN27 135 D8
Newland Rd ME12 2 F7
Newlands
  Ashford TN23 155 D6
  St Mary's Bay TN29 194 F3
  Whitfield CT16 149 B6
Newlands Ave ME10 36 B5
Newlands Dr CT14 134 B8
Newlands Farm Cotts
  ME13 104 C4
Newlands Ho CT11 29 E2
Newlands La CT12 29 D2
Newlands Prim Sch CT11 29 E1
Newlands Rd
  Charing TN27 119 F5
  Ramsgate CT12 29 D1
New Lincoln Ho CT19 178 D8
New Line Learning Academy
  ME15 97 B6
Newlyn Ct 1 ME14 75 A4
Newlyn's Mdw CT15 147 D1
Newman Ct 6 CT21 176 B1
Newman Dr ME10 37 A8
Newman Rd CT3 112 E5
Newmans Cl
  Broadstairs CT10 30 A6
  7 Hythe CT21 176 B1
NEWNHAM 81 C7
Newnham Cl ME8 11 C2
Newnham La ME9, ME13 81 D7
Newnham St ME4 10 B3
Newport Ct CT1 88 B6
New Rd
  Chatham ME4 9 F4
  Egerton TN27 118 F3
  Egerton TN27 119 A2
  Elham CT4 144 F4
  Eythorne CT15 131 C7
  Harbledown CT2 65 D3
  Herne CT2, CT6 45 C4
  Hythe CT21 176 B1
  Hythe, Saltwood CT21 176 B4
  Langley ME17 98 C5
  Minster (Sheppey) ME12 4 C6
  Rochester ME1 9 D4
  Rough Common CT2 66 B3
  Sheerness ME12 1 B1
New Rectory La TN23 156 B4
New Rents 5 TN23 139 B2
New Road Ave ME4 9 E4
New Road Cotts CT6 45 E5
New Road Hill TN25 172 F4
New Road Ind Est ME12 1 B1
New Road Prim Sch 4
  ME4 10 A3
NEW ROMNEY 202 A5
New Romney Pl CT13 93 F8
New Romney Sta★ TN28 202 C6
New Ruttington La CT1 67 A1
New St
  Ash CT3 71 E1
  Ashford TN24 139 B2
  Canterbury CT1 87 E7
  Canterbury, St Dunstan's
  CT2 66 E1
  Chatham ME4 9 E3
  Deal CT14 117 D7
  12 Dover CT16, CT17 166 D8

New St *continued*
Folkestone CT20 178 D5
Herne Bay CT6 22 F5
Lydd TN29 205 C6
Margate CT9 7 I2
Sandwich CT13 94 A8
Sheerness ME12 1 C1
[2] Whitstable CT5 20 D2
New Strs ME4 9 F6
Newton Cl
Chatham ME5 32 C2
[1] Maidstone ME16 74 E3
Newton Rd
Faversham ME13 62 D7
Whitstable CT5 21 B2
NEW TOWN 156 D7
New Town Gn TN24 156 D8
Newtown Rd TN23, TN24 156 D7
New Town St
Canterbury CT1 67 B2
Chartham CT4 86 C5
New Villas ME15 96 C7
Nicholas Cl ME16 74 A3
Nicholas Dr CT12 51 D5
Nicholas Rd TN24 139 B6
Nicholls Ave CT10 29 F2
Nicklaus Dr ME5 31 F3
Nickleby Cl ME1 9 C2
Nickle Cotts CT4 86 A4
Nickley Wood Rd TN26 170 C6
Nightingale Ave
Hythe CT21 187 D8
Whitstable CT5 43 B6
Nightingale Cl
Ashford TN24 157 B7
Chartham CT4 86 C6
Gillingham ME8 33 E6
Nightingale La CT15 113 C2
Nightingale Pl CT9 8 A2
Nightingale Rd
Dover CT16 149 C2
Faversham ME13 62 C7
Herne CT6 45 F7
Nightingales The CT9 28 F8
Nile Rd ME7 10 C4
Nine Acres TN24 139 C5
Nine Ash La ME13 63 D3
Ninn La TN23 138 B2
Niwrim Way ME12 1 H1
Nixon Ave CT12 29 C1
Noah's Ark Rd CT17 166 A8
Noah's Ark Terr CT17 166 B8
Noakes Mdw TN23 156 A8
Nobel Cl ME9 38 C2
Nobel Ct ME13 62 C7
Noble Ct CT9 28 A8
Noble Gdns CT9 28 A8
No Man's Orch Nature Reserve★ CT4 86 D7
No Name St [3] CT13 73 A1
NONINGTON 113 D5
Nonington CE Prim Sch CT15 113 C5
Nonington Ct CT15 113 E5
Nonsuch Cl CT1 88 C8
Nore Cl
Gillingham ME7 10 E1
Sheerness ME12 1 D1
Noreen Ave ME12 4 A6
Norfolk Cl
Chatham ME5 32 C3
Gillingham ME8 11 D2
Norfolk Dr TN23 139 A2
Norfolk Rd
Canterbury CT1 87 E6
Maidstone ME15 97 C8
Margate CT9 8 B3
Margate, Lydden CT9 28 D5
Norfolk Sq CT12 29 B2
Norfolk St [3] CT5 43 D8
Norman Castle★ CT1 87 F7
Norman Cl
Gillingham ME8 33 B5
Maidstone ME14 75 B6
Norman Rd
Ashford TN23, TN24 156 B7
Broadstairs CT10 29 F6
Canterbury CT1 88 A7
Faversham ME13 62 C7
Ramsgate CT11 52 B6
St Margaret's at Cliffe CT15 151 B6
Warden ME12 6 A6
Westgate on Sea CT8 7 D1
Whitstable CT5 43 E8
Norman St [8] CT17 166 D8
Norman Tailyour Ho CT14 117 D5
Norreys Rd ME8 33 E7
Norrie Rd CT7 27 A6
Norrington Mead [3] CT19 178 A7
Norrington Rd ME15 97 B6
North Aux Boiler House Rd TN29 209 C2
North Ave CT11 52 D6
North Barrack Rd CT14 117 D4
North Borough Jun Sch ME14 75 A6
NORTHBOURNE 116 A4
Northbourne Ave CT17 166 B8
Northbourne CE Prim Sch CT14 115 F5
Northbourne Park Pre Prep Sch CT14 115 D6
Northbourne Park Sch CT14 115 C6
Northbourne Rd
East Studdal CT15 115 E1
Gillingham ME8 11 B4
Great Mongeham CT14 116 C4
Northbourne Way CT9 8 E2
Northbrooke TN24 139 C3
Northbrooke La TN24 139 C3
North Camber Way CT16 150 B1
North Cl CT20 177 D4
Northcliffe Gdns CT10 30 A7
North Close Bsns Ctr CT20 177 D4
North Contractor's Rd TN29 209 B3
Northcote Rd
Deal CT14 117 D5
Kingsdown CT14 134 D4
Rochester ME2 9 A7
North Court Cl CT3 91 A8
North Court La CT14 115 A4
North Court Rd CT3 91 A8
North Cres ME17 96 D4
North Ct CT14 117 C7
North Ct [2] ME15 75 A1
North Ct CT12 29 B2
North Dane Way ME5 32 C4
NORTHDOWN 8 D1
Northdown
Ashford TN24 139 C4
Doddington ME9 80 F7
Stockbury ME9 56 D8
Northdown Ave CT9 8 B2
Northdown Bsns Pk ME17 101 F6
Northdown Cl
Lenham ME17 101 F6
Maidstone ME14 75 B7
Northdown Hill CT10, CT9 29 D7
Northdown Park Rd CT9 8 C1
Northdown Prim Sch CT9 8 C1
Northdown Rd
Broadstairs CT10 29 E6
Margate CT9 8 B2
Northdowns Cl CT15 132 B6
North Downs Cl CT4 85 C2
Northdown Trad Est CT10 29 E7
North Down View ME17 100 F6
Northdown Way CT9 8 C1
North Eastling Rd ME13 81 F8
NORTH ELHAM 145 A6
Northern By-Pass TN27 120 C8
North Exit Rd CT16 166 H8
Northfleet Cl ME14 75 C5
North Foreland Ave CT10 30 B7
North Foreland Hill CT10 30 B8
North Foreland Rd CT10 30 B7
NORTHGATE 67 A1
Northgate
Canterbury CT1 67 A1
Rochester ME1 9 C6
North Holmes Rd CT1 88 B8
North La
Canterbury CT2 66 F1
Faversham ME13 62 C8
[7] Folkestone CT20 177 E3
Selling ME13 84 F8
North Lea CT14 117 C7
Northleigh Cl ME15 97 A6
North Lockside Rd ME4 10 D8
NORTH LYMINGE 161 C7
North Lyminge La CT18 161 C7
North Military Rd CT17 166 C7
North Pends TN24 139 E5
Northpoint Bsns Est ME2 9 D8
North Pondside Rd ME4 10 A8
North Quay ME9 38 E6
North Quay ME13 40 D1
North Rd
Chatham, Brompton ME4, ME7 10 A7
Chatham ME4 10 B8
Cliffs End CT13 51 A1
Deal CT14 134 D6
Dover CT17 166 C8
Folkestone CT20 177 D4
Hythe CT21 176 B2
Queenborough ME11 2 F5
Sandwich CT13 95 A7
North Return Rd CT16 166 G8
North Road W CT21 176 A3
North Sch The TN24 139 D1
North Side Three Rd ME4 10 C8
North St
Ashford TN23 139 C2
Deal CT14 117 D7
Dover CT17 166 B7
Folkestone CT19 178 E5
Herne Bay CT6 23 A5
New Romney TN28 202 A6
Rochester ME2 9 B7
Sheldwich ME13 83 C8
Sittingbourne ME10 36 F7
Warmlake ME17 98 E1
NORTH STONAR 73 B6
NORTH STREET 62 C1
Northumberland Ave
Ashford TN24 139 D5
Gillingham ME8 11 E1
Margate CT9 8 C2
Northumberland Ct
Maidstone ME15 97 D7
Margate CT9 8 C3
Northumberland Rd ME15 97 D8
North View
Hersden CT3 46 F1
Maidstone ME15 75 B1
North View Cotts ME15 96 C7
Northwall Ct CT14 117 C7
Northwall Mews CT14 117 C7
Northwall Rd CT14 117 B8
North Way
Finglesham CT14 116 A7
Maidstone ME14 75 B7
NORTHWOOD 29 C3
Northwood Dr ME10 36 F1
Northwood Rd
Broadstairs, Ramsgate CT10, CT12 29 C3
Whitstable CT5 20 F2
NORTON ASH 60 F8
Norton Ave CT6 46 A8
Norton Dr CT12 50 B6
Norton Gr ME5 31 E3
Norton Knatchbull Sch The TN24 139 E2
Norton La TN26 153 D5
Norton Rd
Five Wents ME17 98 D1
Lewson Street ME13, ME9 60 E5
Norview Rd CT5 43 B7
Norway Dro CT15 151 A8
Norway Terr [4] ME14 75 A7
Norwood Gdns TN23 139 B2
Norwood La TN29 193 E8
Norwood Rise ME12 4 C7
Norwood St TN23 139 B2
Norwood Walk E ME10 36 C5
Norwood Walk W ME10 36 B5
Notley St CT1 67 A1
Notley Terr [3] CT1 67 A1
Nottingham Ave ME15 97 D7
Nottingham Rd CT7 26 F5
Nouds La ME9 60 D6
Nouds Rd ME9 60 D7
Nunnery Fields CT1 88 A7
Nunnery Rd CT1 87 F7
Nursery Ave
Maidstone, Bearsted ME14 76 B3
Maidstone ME16 74 B6
Nursery Cl
Densole CT18 163 A7
Ramsgate CT11 52 C7
Sheerness ME12 1 E1
Whitstable CT5 21 A1
Nursery Fields
Acol CT7 27 B3
Hythe CT21 176 A2
Nursery Gdns CT10 8 E1
Nursery La
Densole CT18 163 A7
Sheldwich ME13 83 D5
Whitfield CT16 148 F7
Nurserylands CT6 22 F3
Nursery Rd ME8 33 D8
Nursery Wlk CT2 66 E2
Nutberry Cl ME9 38 D2
Nutfield Cl ME5 32 B8
Nutfields ME10 37 B3
Nutley Cl TN24 139 C3
Nutts Ave ME12 6 G2
Nutwood Cl ME14 75 E4

O

OAD STREET 35 E1
Oakapple Ho [10] ME16 74 A3
Oakapple La ME16 74 A3
Oak Ave
Eythorne CT15 131 D5
Gillingham ME7 10 E6
Minster (Sheppey) ME12 4 F6
Oak Bglws TN29 205 C6
Oak Cotts
Barrowhill TN25 174 D7
East Studdal CT15 132 E8
Selling ME13 84 D4
Oak Croft ME14 76 B4
Oakdale Rd CT6 23 A4
Oakdene Rd CT12 29 C1
Oak Dr
Boughton Street ME13 64 A3
Hawkinge CT18 163 B5
St Mary's Bay TN29 194 F3
Oakenpole TN23 138 E1
Oakfield Ct CT12 52 B8
Oakfield Rd TN24 139 D5
Oakfields ME10 36 C3
Oak Gr CT15 114 B2
Oak Hall Pass CT21 176 C2
Oakham Dr TN29 205 D7
Oak Hill CT13 93 B6
Oak Ho [6] ME5 31 F4
Oakhurst Cl ME5 31 F3
Oak La
Lydd TN29 205 B6
Minster (Sheppey) ME12 4 F7
Upchurch ME9 12 D2
Oakland Cl ME5 31 F3
Oakland Ct
Cliffs End CT12 51 C5
Herne Bay CT6 22 E5
Oaklands
Ashford TN23 138 F1
Loose ME15 97 A8
Mersham TN25 157 E4
Sturry CT2 68 B7
Oaklands Ave CT10 29 E5
Oaklands Inf & Jun Sch ME5 31 F4
Oaklands Way CT2 68 B7
Oakleigh Cl ME5 31 E2
Oakleigh Ho TN23 155 E8
Oakleigh La CT4 89 B5
Oakleys The CT15 130 D5
Oak Lodge Rd TN28 202 B7
Oak Rd ME10 37 C5
Oak Ridge TN26 183 F8
Oaks Ave CT6 22 D2
Oaks Bsns Village The ME5 32 C1
Oaks Dene ME5 31 F1
Oakside Rd CT3 112 E5
Oaks Inf Sch The ME10 36 D2
Oaks Pk CT2 66 B3
Oaks Rd
Folkestone CT20 177 D6
Tenterden TN30 179 B8
Oak St CT14 117 D6
Oaks The
Broadstairs CT10 29 F7
Hawkinge CT18 163 B3
Hersden CT3 46 F1
St Nicholas at Wade CT7 25 F2
Whitstable CT5 43 B6
Oaks View CT21 187 C8
Oak Tree Ave ME15 97 C7
Oak Tree Cl ME12 5 A5
Oak Tree Gr CT9 28 A8
Oaktree Ho ME10 37 B3
Oak Tree Rd TN23 155 F8
Oak Trees [19] ME15 97 E5
Oak Trees Com Sch ME15 97 C7
Oakum Ct ME4 10 B2
Oakvale Cl CT17 166 B7
Oak Wlk CT21 176 C2
Oakwood [2] CT9 29 C8
Oakwood Ct ME16 74 D3
Oakwood Dr CT5 21 A1
Oakwood Ind Est CT10 29 E6
Oakwood Park Gram Sch ME16 74 C3
Oakwood Rd
Maidstone ME16 74 D3
Sturry CT2 68 A7
Oakwood Sch CT19 178 E7
Oakwood Terr ME10 37 C4
Oakwood Villas CT11 29 E1
OARE 40 A3
Oare Gunpowder Works Ctry Pk★ ME13 40 A1
Oare Marshes Nature Reserve★ ME13 40 B6
Oare Rd ME13 40 C1
Oast Cotts
Dargate ME13 64 D8
Sheldwich ME13 83 C8
Wormshill ME9 79 C5
Oast Ct
Margate CT9 28 F8
Sittingbourne ME10 36 E2
Oast Ho CT4 85 C2
Oast Ho The
Canterbury CT3 88 F8
[3] Gillingham ME8 33 F8
Oasthouse Field TN29 192 F4
Oast La ME13 104 E6
Oast Mdw TN24 139 F1
Oast Paddock The CT3 92 A6
Oasts The ME14 76 C4
Oast The
Canterbury CT1 88 B6
Staple CT3 92 A6
Oastview ME8 34 A8
Oaten Hill CT1 88 A7
Oaten Hill Pl CT1 88 A7
Oaze The CT5 43 C6
Occupation Rd TN25 123 F2
Ocean Cl CT7 27 B8
Ocean View
Broadstairs CT10 30 A1
Herne Bay CT6 23 F6
Ocelot Ct [6] ME4 10 B3
Octavia Ct ME5 32 B3
Octavian Dr CT21 175 A3
Octavian Way TN23 155 E5
Odd Rise ME7 11 A5
Odiham Dr ME16 74 C7
Odo Rd CT17 166 C8
Officers' Rd ME4 10 B8
Officers Terr ME4 9 F7
Offley Cl CT9 8 C1
Ogilvy Ct CT10 29 E7
Okehampton Cl TN24 139 F7
Olantigh Ct CT7 27 A7
Olantigh Rd TN25, CT4 123 F3
Olave Rd CT9 8 B1
Old Ash Cl TN24 139 C5
Old Ashford Rd
Charing TN27 120 C7
Lenham ME17 101 E5
Old Badgins Rd ME13 83 B6
Old Bailey The ME17 100 E6
Old Bakery Cl TN29 194 F4
Old Bakery Mews ME13 63 F4
Old Bakery The ME12 3 F5
Old Barn Cl ME7 32 F6
Old Billet La ME12 5 C6
Old Boundary Rd CT8 7 D1
Old Bridge Rd CT5 20 E1
Old Carriageway The ME7 32 F4
Old Charlton Rd CT16 149 D2
Old Chatham Rd
Kit's Coty ME20 53 D6
Sandling ME14 53 F1
Oldchurch Ct [3] ME16 74 E3
Old Church Rd CT4 86 E1
Old Coachworks The [10] CT13 72 F1
Old Coal Yd The [7] CT5 20 D1
Old Coastgaurd Cotts TN29 209 D3
Old Corn Stores The ME14 76 C4
Old Court Hill CT15, CT3 113 C6
Old Crossing Rd [1] CT9 28 B8
Old Dairy Cl [4] CT11 52 F7
Old Dairy Yd CT12 52 C7
Old Diary Mews The ME12 3 D7
Old Dover Rd
Barham CT4 112 B1
[5] Canterbury CT1 88 B6
Capel-le-Ferne CT18 164 C1
Old Dr ME15 96 F6
Old Dungeness Lighthouse★ TN29 209 D2
Old Farm Cl CT5 43 C6
Old Farm Rd CT7 26 D7
Old Ferry Rd ME9 14 E7
Oldfield Cl
Gillingham ME8 33 D8
Maidstone ME15 75 E1
Old Flour Mill The CT17 149 B2
Old Fold CT5 44 C8
Old Folkestone Rd CT17 166 A4
Old Forge La ME9 56 F3
Old Garden Ct CT4 86 E1
Old Gate Rd ME13 62 B8
Old Green Rd
Broadstairs CT10 29 F7
Margate CT9 8 C1
Old Hall Dr CT12 51 C5
Old Halls The [8] CT5 20 D2
Old Ham La ME17 101 A4
Oldhawe Hill CT3, CT6 46 D7
Old High St The CT20 178 E5
Old Hockley Rd ME13 82 C2
Old Hook Rd ME12 4 F2
Old Hop Gdn The TN31 196 C2
Oldhouse La TN29 191 E1
Old House La ME9 34 E4
Old Kingsdown Cl CT10 29 E3
Old Lain ME17 100 F6
Old Lenham Rd ME9 80 C4
Old London Rd CT21 175 F2
Old Loose Cl ME15 96 F5
Old Loose Hill ME15 96 F4
Old Maidstone Rd ME9 35 F5
Old Mead CT19 178 A7
Old Mill La ME20 53 C3
Old Mill Mews CT19 177 F7
Old Mill Rd ME17 76 F1
Old Oast Bsns Ctr The ME20 53 A1
Old Orch TN23 155 D8
Old Orchard The ME8 34 A8
Old Palace Rd CT4 89 C3
Old Park Ave
Canterbury CT1 67 C2
Dover CT16 149 A3
Old Park Cl CT16 149 A4
Old Park Ct CT1 67 C2
Old Park Hill CT16 149 B4
Old Park Rd CT16 149 B2
Old Pattens La ME4 9 D2
Old Pk Hill CT15 149 A5
Old Police Sta The [4] CT5 20 D2
Old Pond Rd TN23 155 F8
Old Print Ho [4] CT16 166 E7
Old Printworks Cl [5] CT5 43 D8
Old Priory Sch The CT11 52 D6
Old Railway Works (Ind Est) TN24 156 D8
Old Rd
Chatham ME4 9 F4
Elham CT4 144 F4
Sarre CT7 48 C6
Old Rectory Cl
Hawkinge CT18 163 B4
Mersham TN25 157 E5
Old Rectory The TN25 122 E2
Old Roman Rd CT15 133 C1
OLD ROMNEY 201 B7
Old Ruttington La CT1 67 A1
Old Saltwood La CT21 176 B4
Old Saw Mill The TN26 153 E6
Old School Cl
Lenham ME17 101 D4
Sturry CT2 67 F6
Old School Ct
Egerton TN27 118 F3
Folkestone CT20 178 B4
Old School Gdns CT9 8 A1
Old School Mews CT4 86 C2
Old School Pl ME14 75 A5
Old School The TN24 156 D8
Old School Yd [2] CT10 29 E5
Old Sch The
Capel-le-Ferne CT18 164 C4
St Margaret's at Cliffe CT15 150 F7
Old Stables The CT11 52 C5
Oldstairs Rd CT14 134 D4
Old Surrenden Manor TN26 154 C5
Old Surrenden Manor Rd TN26 154 C5
Old Timber Yard E CT12 52 A8
Old Timber Yard Ind Est CT12 52 A7
Old Tovil Rd ME15 75 A2
Old Town Gaol Mus★ [18] CT17 166 D8
Old Trafford Cl ME16 74 B6
Old Tree La ME17 97 D3
Old Tree Rd CT3 47 B7
Old Valley Rd CT4 128 F7

Old Vicarage Gdn CT2 67 F6
Old Vicarage Gdns TN25 123 E2
Old Vicarage The CT13 93 C7
Old Walting St 21 CT1 87 F8
Old Way TN26 190 D7
OLD WIVES LEES 85 C3
Olive Gr 2 CT11 52 F7
Oliver Cl ME4 10 B2
Olivers Row ME14 76 C4
Oliver Twist Cl ME1 9 B4
Olivine Cl
Chatham ME5 54 A8
Sittingbourne ME10 36 C7
Olliffe Cl ME5 31 F2
Omer Ave CT9 8 C2
Onslow Rd ME1 9 D3
Ontario Way CT16 149 B3
Onyx Dr ME10 36 D6
Opal Gn ME5 32 B2
Opie Wlk CT18 162 F3
Orache Dr ME14 75 E5
Orange St CT1 87 F8
Orange Terr ME1 9 D5
Orbital Pk TN24 156 F6
Orbit Cl ME5 54 A8
Orchard Ave CT14 117 B5
Orchard Bank ME17 98 B1
Orchard Bsns Ctr ME16 74 C8
Orchard Cl
Canterbury CT2 66 F4
Coxheath ME17 96 C3
Langley Heath ME17 98 E4
Littlebourne CT3 89 F7
Mersham TN25 157 E3
Minster (Thanet) CT12 50 B7
Ramsgate CT12 29 B3
Whitfield CT16 148 F8
Whitstable CT5 20 F3
Wingham CT3 91 A7
Orchard Cotts
East Farleigh ME16 96 A8
Faversham ME13 62 E5
Orchard Ct
Ashford TN23 156 B8
Chillenden CT3 113 F8
Herne Bay CT6 22 F1
Orchard Dr
Crabble CT17 148 E3
Hythe CT21 176 B1
Littlestone-on-Sea TN28 202 E6
Maidstone ME14 75 E4
Newington ME9 35 A5
Wye TN25 123 F1
Orchard End CT11 52 A5
Orchard Field TN26 153 D4
Orchard Fields CT21 160 E2
Orchard Flats CT1 88 D7
Orchard Gdns CT9 28 A8
Orchard Gr
Minster (Sheppey) ME12 4 C6
Whitstable CT5 43 D8
Orchard Ho 9 ME13 62 C7
Orchard Hts TN23 138 F5
Orchard Ind Est ME15 97 F3
Orchard La
Ashford TN24 139 F6
Challock TN25 105 B2
Monkton CT7, CT12 49 A8
St Nicholas at Wade CT7 25 F1
Orchard Mews CT14 117 D5
Orchard Pk CT6 23 D4
Orchard Pl
Coxheath ME17 96 C3
Faversham ME13 62 D7
2 Maidstone ME16 74 E3
Sittingbourne ME10 37 A3
Orchard Rd
Eastry CT13 93 B3
Herne Bay CT6 22 F3
Margate CT9 28 A8
St Mary's Bay TN29 195 A5
Tenterden TN30 167 A3
Orchard Residences The
CT1 88 A5
Orchard Row CT6 23 A1
Orchard Sch The CT1 87 F6
Orchard St
Canterbury CT2 66 E1
Gillingham ME8 33 E8
Maidstone ME15 75 A3
Orchards The CT4 144 F4
Orchard The
Maidstone ME14 76 B4
Monkton CT12 49 D6
ORCHARD VALLEY 176 B3
Orchard Valley CT21 176 A2
Orchard View
Ash CT3 71 F1
Detling ME14 76 A8
Tenterden TN30 179 C8
Teynham ME9 38 C3
Orchard Villas
1 Chatham ME4 9 F3
Kearsney CT17 148 E4
Orchard Way
Eastchurch ME12 5 D1
Peasmarsh TN31 196 C1
Orchid Cl ME12 4 A4
Orchid Ct TN23 156 D2
Orchids The
Etchinghill CT18 161 D4
Mersham TN25 157 E4
Ordinance Way TN23 138 F4
Ordnance St ME4 9 E3
Ordnance Terr 9 ME4 9 E4
Orgarswick Ave TN29 195 C7
Orgarswick Way TN29 195 C7
Orient Pl CT2 66 F1
Orion Rd ME1 31 C7
Orion Way TN24 156 E8
Orlestone View TN26 182 F7
Orlestone Villas TN26 183 A8
Ormonde Ct CT21 176 C1
Ormonde Rd
11 Folkestone CT20 178 E6
Hythe CT21 176 C1
Ormsby Gn ME8 33 E3
Orpins Cl TN25 158 D6
Orr Cl CT18 162 F4
Osborne Gdns CT6 23 D4
Osborne Rd
Ashford TN24 156 F8
Gillingham ME7 10 C5
Kingsdown CT14 134 C6
Osborne Terr CT9 7 J1
Osbourn Ave CT8 27 E8
Osbourne Rd CT10 29 F4
Oscar Rd CT10 30 B4
Osier Field TN24 139 E7
Osier Rd ME9 38 E3
Osprey Ave ME5 10 E2
Osprey Cl CT5 43 C7
Osprey Ct
2 Dover CT16 149 B2
Hawkinge CT18 162 F3
Sittingbourne ME10 37 A3
OSPRINGE 62 B6
Ospringe CE Prim Sch
ME13 62 A6
Ospringe Pl ME13 62 B6
Ospringe Rd ME13 62 B7
Ospringe St ME13 62 A6
Ostend Ct ME10 14 F1
Ostlers La CT7 48 D6
Oswald Pl CT17 149 B2
Oswald Rd CT17 149 B2
OTHAM 98 B7
Otham Cl CT2 67 A4
OTHAM HOLE 98 D6
Otham La ME15 76 C2
Otham St
Maidstone ME15 76 C2
Otham ME15 98 B7
Ottawa Cres CT16 149 C3
Ottawa Way CT16 149 B3
Otterbourne Pl ME15 75 E1
Otterden Cl
Ashford TN23 155 F6
Ashford TN23 155 F6
Otterden Rd ME13 81 D3
OTTERHAM QUAY 12 C3
Otterham Quay La ME8 12 B2
Otteridge Rd ME14 76 A3
Otterpool La CT21, TN25 174 D4
OTTINGE 144 D1
Otway St
Chatham ME4 10 A3
Gillingham ME7 10 D6
Otway Terr 1 ME4 10 A3
OUT ELMSTEAD 111 F2
Out Elmstead La CT4 111 F2
Outfall Ave TN29 209 C2
Oval The TN29 186 D1
Overland La CT3 71 A3
OVERSLAND 84 F7
Overton Ho ME12 1 D2
Owen's Cl CT21 177 B3
Owens Court Cotts ME13 83 F8
Owen Sq CT14 117 B2
Owens Way ME7 11 A6
Owletts Cl ME15 97 D8
Owl's Hatch Rd CT6 22 C1
Oxenden Cnr CT3 23 F1
Oxenden Cres CT3 91 A8
Oxenden Park Dr CT6 22 E4
Oxenden Rd CT20 177 E4
Oxenden St CT6 22 E5
Oxenden Way CT4 128 F8
Oxen Lease TN23 155 E8
Oxenturn Rd TN25 140 E8
Oxford Cl 5 CT5 20 D1
Oxford Ct CT1 87 F7
Oxford Mans 6 CT5 20 D1
Oxford Rd
Canterbury CT1 87 F7
Gillingham ME7 10 D3
Maidstone ME15 97 D8
Oxford St
6 Margate CT9 7 J1
Whitstable CT5 20 D1
Oxford Terr CT20 178 D4
Ox La TN30 167 B2
Oxney Cl CT7 26 F7
Oxney Cotts TN30 190 A4
Oyster Cl
Herne Bay CT6 22 B3
Sittingbourne ME10 36 E6
Oyster Mews 4 CT5 20 D1
Ozengell Pl CT12 29 A2

P

Packer Pl ME5 32 A8
Packer's La 5 CT11 52 E7
Padbrook La CT3 70 D6
PADDLESWORTH 162 C4
PADDOCK 104 E1
Paddock Cl
Deal CT14 116 F5
Folkestone CT20 177 F5
Lydd TN29 205 B6
Paddock Rd
Ashford TN23 155 E7
2 Birchington CT7 27 A7
Paddocks The
Ashford TN23 138 C1
Broadstairs CT10 29 F7
Densole CT18 163 A8
Gillingham ME7 33 A5
Herne Bay CT6 23 F5
Margate CT9 8 C1
Paddock The
Canterbury CT1 88 B8
Chatham ME4 9 F4
Dover CT16 166 D8
Old Wives Lees CT4 85 C2
Woodchurch TN26 169 A1
Paddock View CT5 43 E7
Pad's Hill ME15 75 A4
Padsole La ME15 75 A4
Padstow Manor 1 ME7 10 C6
Padwell La TN23 155 C8
Paffard Cl CT2 67 F6
Paffard Ct CT2 67 F6
Page Pl CT19 178 D8
Page Rd CT18 162 F3
Paget Row ME7 10 C5
Paget St ME7 10 C5
Pagitt St ME4 9 E3
Paine Ave TN29 205 C6
Painesfield Cl TN29 186 C4
PAINTER'S FORSTAL 61 E3
Painter's Forstal Rd ME13 61 E3
Palace Ave ME15 75 A4
Palace Cl CT5 21 B2
Palace Cotts ME9 80 F8
Palace Ct
Gillingham ME5 10 D2
Hythe CT21 176 C2
Palace Ind Est ME15 97 F4
Palace St 16 CT1 67 A1
Palace Wood Prim Sch
ME16 74 C6
Pal Cres CT7 27 E5
Palmar Rd ME16 74 D6
Palmars Cross Hill CT2 66 A1
PALMARSH 187 D7
Palmarsh Ave CT21 187 D7
Palmarsh Cres CT21 187 D7
Palmarsh Prim Sch
CT21 187 D8
Palm Bay Ave CT9 8 D3
Palm Bay CP Sch CT9 8 D3
Palm Bay Gdns CT9 8 C3
Palmbeach Ave CT21 187 D8
Palm Ct CT8 7 C1
Palmer Cl CT6 46 B8
Palmer Cres CT9 29 C8
Palmer Rd CT3 91 A8
Palmerston Ave
Broadstairs CT10 30 B3
Deal CT14 117 C2
Palmerston Ct CT14 117 D2
Palmerston Rd
Chatham ME4 9 F1
Dover CT16 148 F4
Palmerston St 4 CT19 178 D6
Palmerston Wlk ME10 37 C4
PALMSTEAD 127 D5
Palm Tree Cl CT15 131 D7
Palm Tree Way CT18 161 B7
Palting Way CT20 178 B4
Pamela Ct ME7 10 D5
Pannell Dr CT18 162 F4
Panteny La ME9 37 E2
Pantheon Gdns TN23 155 F5
Panton Cl ME5 32 C4
Paper La TN24 156 F6
Papion Gr ME5 31 E2
Papworth Cl 1 CT19 178 A7
Parade CT1 87 F8
Parade Rd CT20 177 F3
Parade The
Ashford TN24 156 F5
Birchington CT7 26 D8
Eastry CT13 93 B2
Folkestone CT20 178 E5
Greatstone-on-Sea TN28,
TN29 206 E7
Margate CT9 7 I3
Sittingbourne ME10 36 F2
Paradise CT11 52 D7
Paradise Cotts ME9 34 E5
Paradise Row CT13 72 F1
Paragon CT11 52 E5
Paragon St CT11 52 D5
Paraker Way CT21 177 B4
PARAMOUR STREET 71 D7
Pardoner Cl CT2 87 C7
Pardoners Way CT16 149 A3
Parfitt Way CT16 149 B2
Parham Cl CT1 67 B2
Parham Ct CT1 67 B2
Parham Rd
Canterbury CT1 67 B2
Chatham ME4 9 F2
Paris Cnr TN26 153 F6
Parish Cl CT10 29 E6
Parish Rd
Chartham CT4 86 C3
Minster (Sheppey) ME12 4 A5
Park Ave
Birchington CT7 27 A6
Broadstairs CT10 29 E2
Deal CT14 117 C5
Dover CT16 149 D1
Gillingham ME7 10 D3
Leysdown-on-Sea ME12 6 G1
Maidstone ME17 96 E2
Maidstone, Penenden Heath
ME14 75 B6
Queenborough ME11 3 B4
Park Ave *continued*
Sittingbourne ME10 36 E1
Whitstable CT5 20 F3
Park Barn Rd ME17 99 C5
Park Chase CT10 29 E2
Park Cl
Hawkinge CT18 163 A4
Margate CT9 8 D1
Park Cotts
Preston CT3 70 B6
Ramsgate CT11 29 E2
Park Cres ME4 31 F8
Park Crescent Rd CT9 8 A1
Park Ct ME13 62 E7
Park Dr
Hothfield TN26 138 A6
Sittingbourne ME10 36 D1
Parker Cl
Gillingham ME8 33 E5
Hamstreet TN26 183 A7
Parker Pl CT18 163 C5
Park Farm Cl
Folkestone CT19 178 C8
Shadoxhurst TN26 155 A1
Tyler Hill CT2 66 E6
Park Farm Prim Sch
CT19 178 C6
Park Farm Rd CT19 178 C7
Park Farm Ret Pk CT19 178 B8
Parkfield Rd
Folkestone CT19 178 C6
Gillingham ME8 11 F1
Park Gate CT10 29 F2
Park Ho
Dover CT16 149 D1
Maidstone ME14 75 B6
Park La
Bethersden TN26 154 C8
Birchington CT7 27 A6
Bishopsbourne CT4 111 C5
Elham CT4 144 F5
Maidstone, Cock Stone
ME17 97 D2
Maidstone, Ringlestone
ME14 74 F7
Margate CT9 8 A2
Parkland Ct CT10 29 F6
Park Lea CT14 117 C5
Park Mall Sh Ctr 2
TN24 139 B2
Park Manor ME7 10 B5
Park Mews 6 CT16 166 D8
Park Par TN29 195 C7
Park Pl
Ashford, Beaver TN23 156 B7
Ashford, Willesborough
TN24 156 F8
Dover CT16 166 D8
Herne CT6 46 A8
Margate CT9 7 I1
Park Rd
Ashford TN24 139 D6
Birchington CT7 27 C7
Broadstairs CT10 30 B6
Dover CT16 149 B2
Faversham ME13 62 D7
Folkestone CT19 177 E6
Herne Bay CT6 22 F4
Hythe CT21 176 B1
Littlestone-on-Sea TN28 202 E5
Maidstone ME15 75 C1
Margate CT9 8 A2
Preston CT3 70 D7
Queenborough ME11 2 F5
Ramsgate CT11 52 C7
Sheerness ME12 1 E1
Sittingbourne ME10 36 E3
Temple Ewell CT16 148 D5
Westgate on Sea CT7 27 D6
Park Road N TN24 139 B3
PARK SIDE 146 D7
Park Side CT14 117 C5
Parkside Com Prim Sch
CT1 67 D2
Parkside Ct
Herne Bay CT6 22 F5
Ramsgate CT11 52 D7
Parkside Pl CT1 67 D3
Park St
Ashford TN24 139 C2
Deal CT14 117 D6
Dover CT16 166 D8
Lydd TN29 205 C6
Park Terr
Throwley ME13 82 D1
Woodnesborough CT13 93 D7
Park Vale TN24 139 D6
Park View
Folkestone CT19 178 E7
Margate CT9 8 A2
Peasmarsh TN31 196 B2
Sturry CT2 67 F6
Park View Cl CT3 91 D2
Park View Ct ME15 75 E1
Park View Rise CT15 113 D4
Park View Terr 2 TN30 179 A7
Park Villas ME14 75 E4
Park Way
Coxheath ME17 96 D3
Maidstone ME15 75 B1
Park Way Prim Sch ME15 75 B1
Parkway The CT7 27 B7
PARK WOOD
Gillingham 33 D4
Maidstone 97 E4
Parkwood TN31 197 B4
Parkwood Cl CT10 29 F2
Park Wood Cl TN23 156 B5
Park Wood Forest Wlks★
TN26 181 C4
Park Wood Gn ME8 33 D5
Park Wood Ind Est ME15 98 A4
Parkwood Inf Sch ME8 33 E5
Parkwood Jun Sch ME8 33 E5
Park Wood Par 13 ME15 97 F5
Park Wood Rd CT2 66 C4
Park Wood Sh Ctr ME8 33 D5
Park Wood Trad Est
ME15 98 A4
Parr Ave ME7 10 D6
Parrs Head Mews ME1 9 C6
Parsley Way ME16 74 A3
Parsonage Chase ME12 3 F5
Parsonage Cotts ME9 58 A5
Parsonage Farm ME13 82 F4
Parsonage Fields CT12 49 C7
Parsonage La
Rochester ME2 9 C8
Sittingbourne ME9 36 A8
Parsonage Oast CT12 49 C7
Parsonage Rd CT6 23 A3
Parsonage Stocks Rd
ME13 82 F5
Parsonage Villas CT15 165 C5
Parsons Way CT16 149 A3
Partridge Cl CT6 23 C3
Partridge La ME13 62 D7
Pasley Rd ME4, ME7 10 A7
Pasley Road E ME7 10 B7
Pasley Road N ME4 10 B7
Pasley Road W ME7 10 A7
Passmore Way ME15 74 E1
Pastime Cl ME10 36 E8
Pasture The
Ashford TN24 139 D6
Hawkinge CT18 163 B4
Patchways TN29 184 E3
Path Field Cotts CT15 164 E5
Pathway The 22 CT10 30 B4
Patricia Way CT10 29 D3
PATRIXBOURNE 89 B3
Patrixbourne Ave ME8 11 C2
Patrixbourne Rd CT4 89 B2
Pattens Gdns ME1 9 E2
Pattens La ME1, ME4 9 E1
Pattens Pl ME1 9 D2
Patterson Cl CT14 117 A4
Pattison Farm Cl TN25 172 F4
Paul's Pl 8 CT16 149 C1
Pavement The TN30 167 B3
Pavilion Cl CT14 117 C8
Pavilion Ct 4 CT20 178 E4
Pavilion Dr ME10 14 F1
Pavilion Mdw CT17 148 E4
Pavilion Rd CT19 178 D6
Pavings The ME17 77 C2
Paxton Ave CT18 162 F3
Payden St ME17 102 D8
PAYDEN STREET 80 B1
Payers Pk CT20 178 D5
Payne's La ME15 97 B7
Pay St CT18 162 F7
Payton Cl CT9 29 A7
Payton Mews 4 CT1 67 B1
Peacock Mews 7 ME16 74 E4
Peacock Pl ME13 84 A6
Peacock Rise ME5 32 A4
Peafield Wood Rd CT4 127 E4
Peak Dr CT13 93 B3
Pean Court Rd CT5 43 D3
Pean Hill CT5 43 D2
Pearmain Wlk CT1 88 C7
Pearman Cl ME8 12 A1
Pearson's Way CT10 29 E7
Pear Tree Alley 2 ME10 36 E5
Pear Tree Cl CT10 29 C4
Peartree Cotts ME8 34 B8
Pear Tree La
Dymchurch TN29 186 D1
Gillingham ME7 32 E7
Loose ME15 97 B6
Peartree Rd CT6 23 C3
Pear Tree Row ME17 98 B5
Pear Tree Wlk ME9 35 A5
PEASMARSH 196 A2
Peasmarsh CE Prim Sch
TN31 196 B1
Peckham Cl ME2 9 C8
Pedding Hill CT3 71 A1
Pedding La CT3 92 A8
PEDLINGE 175 D4
Peel Dr ME10 37 C4
Peelers Ct CT2 66 F1
Peel St ME14 75 A6
PEENE 177 B8
Peene Cotts CT18 162 B1
PEENING QUARTER 188 B6
PEGWELL 52 B5
Pegwell Ave CT11 52 A5
Pegwell Bay Ctry Pk★
CT12 51 C2
Pegwell Bay Nature
Reserve★ CT12 51 C3
Pegwell Cl CT11 52 A5
Pegwell Ct CT11 52 B5
Pegwell Rd CT11 52 B5
Pelham Gdns CT20 178 A4
Pelwood Rd TN31 203 A2
Pemberton Ct CT21 177 B3
Pemberton Rd TN24 139 D2
Pemberton Sq 4 ME2 9 C8
Pembroke ME4 10 B8
Pembroke Ave CT9 7 F1

Pembroke Ct
Chatham ME4 10 A4
Folkestone CT19 178 E6
1 Ramsgate CT11 52 E7
Pembroke Gdns ME8 33 E4
Pembroke Ho TN28 202 E5
Pembroke Mews TN28 202 C8
Pembroke Rd ME17 96 C3
Pembroke Rise ME4 10 A7
Pembury Ct 6 ME10 36 E4
Pembury Gdns ME16 74 D3
Pembury Pl TN25 138 F4
Pembury St ME10 36 E4
Pembury Way ME8 11 E2
Penbury CT14 117 C1
Pencester Ct 3 CT16 166 E8
Pencester Rd CT16 166 D8
Penderel Mews TN30 179 B8
Penenden Ct ME14 75 B7
PENENDEN HEATH 75 B7
Penenden Heath Rd ME14 75 C7
Penenden St ME14 75 A6
Penfield La ME9 59 A4
Penfold Cl
Chatham ME5 32 B7
Maidstone ME15 97 E5
Penfold Gdns
Maidstone ME15 97 E4
Shepherdswell CT15 130 E5
Penfold Hill ME17 99 B8
Penfold Rd CT19 178 F6
Penfold Way ME15 96 F6
Pengelly Pl CT2 66 F2
Penhurst Cl ME14 75 F5
Penlee Point TN24 139 D5
Pennant Rd ME1 31 C7
Penn Cl ME10 37 B2
Penn Hill TN23 155 E6
Pennine Way
Ashford TN24 139 B4
Maidstone ME15 76 A1
Pennington Cl CT2 68 C7
Penny Cress Gdns ME16 74 C3
Penny Cress Rd ME12 4 A4
PENNYPOT 175 E1
Pennypot Ind Est CT21 175 F1
Penny Pot La CT4 108 B4
Penrith Ct ME7 11 A5
Penrose Ct CT21 176 C1
Penryn Manor 4 ME7 10 C6
Pensand Ho CT21 176 D1
Penshurst Cl
Canterbury CT2 67 A3
Gillingham ME8 11 E2
Penshurst Gdns CT9 8 F2
Penshurst Rd CT11 52 F7
Penshurst Rise ME13 62 B8
Penstocks The ME15 74 D2
Pentagon Sh Ctr ME4 9 F4
Pent Vale Cl CT19 178 A6
Pent Valley Tech Coll CT19 177 F7
Pepys Ave ME12 1 C2
Pepy's Way ME2 9 A8
Percival Terr CT17 166 B7
Percy Ave CT10 8 F2
Percy Rd
Broadstairs CT10 29 F5
Margate CT9 8 A3
Ramsgate CT11 52 D8
Peregrine Cl CT21 187 D8
Peregrine Dr ME10 37 A2
Peri Ct CT1 87 E6
Peridot Ct ME15 97 E5
Perie Row 9 ME7 10 A6
Perimeter Rd CT16 166 G8
Periwinkle Cl ME10 36 E5
Periwinkle Ct 3 ME10 36 E5
Perkins Ave CT9 28 F8
Perries Mead CT19 178 B7
Perrot Way CT18 163 B5
PERRY 70 C3
Perryfield St ME14 74 F6
Perry La CT3 70 C3
Perry's Cl ME13 62 D8
Perry St
Chatham ME4 9 E3
Maidstone ME14 74 F6
PERRYWOOD 84 C4
Perth Gdns ME10 36 C4
Perth Way CT16 149 C3
PESTED 105 B4
Pested Bars Rd ME17 97 D5
Pested La TN25 105 C4
Petchell Mews 11 CT1 67 B2
Peter Candler Way TN24 139 E4
Peter St
Deal CT14 117 D7
Dover CT16 166 C8
Folkestone CT20 178 E5
Petfield Cl ME12 4 C6
PETHAM 109 B3
Petham Gn ME8 11 C2
Petham Prim Sch CT4 109 C3
Petlands ME17 97 D5
Petrel Cl CT6 23 F4
Petrel Way CT18 163 A3
PETT BOTTOM 110 B5
Pett Bottom Rd CT4 110 C5
Pettfield Hill Rd ME13 82 B1
Pett Hill CT4 88 F1
Pett La
Charing TN27 120 D7
Silver Street ME9 57 B7
Pettman Cl CT6 22 F3
Pettman Ct 5 CT10 29 E5
Pettmans Mews CT5 20 C2
Pett's Cres CT12 50 B5
Petts La CT3 91 A8
Pevensey Ct ME16 74 F4
Peverel Dr ME14 76 A5
Peverel Gn ME8 33 D4
Peverell Rd CT16 149 B4
Pewter Ct CT1 87 F7
Pfizer Monk's Wall Nature Reserve★ CT13 72 E3
Pharos Dr CT16 149 E1
Pheasant La ME15 97 B8
Pheasant Rd ME4 10 C2
Pheasants' Hall Rd CT4 110 F2
Philip Corby Cl CT9 8 B2
Philippa Ho CT19 178 F6
Phillippa Ct ME10 36 E8
Phillip Rd CT19 177 E6
Phillips Ct ME8 11 B2
Phillips Rd CT7 27 A6
Phoenix Com Prim Sch TN24 139 D5
Phoenix Ct 11 ME7 10 C6
Phoenix Ind Est ME2 9 D7
Phoenix Pk ME15 97 F4
Phoenix Rd ME5 32 B2
Piccadilly Apartments 4 ME5 10 B3
Pickelden La CT4 107 F8
Pickering St ME15 97 B6
Pickhill Oast TN30 179 B4
Pickneybush La TN29 194 A7
Pickwick Cres ME1 9 C3
Picton Rd CT11 52 C7
Pie Factory Rd CT15 113 E2
Pier Approach Rd ME7 10 D7
Pier Ave
Herne Bay CT6 22 E4
Whitstable CT5 21 A2
Pierpoint Rd CT5 43 D7
Pier Rd ME7 10 E7
Pierremont Ave CT10 30 A4
Pier Road Ind Est ME7 10 D7
Pier Sports Ctr The CT6 22 E5
Pier The CT16 148 F8
Pigeon La CT6 23 A2
Pigtail Cnr ME12 4 E6
Pike Cl CT19 178 A7
Pikefields ME8 11 C2
Pike Rd CT14, CT15 114 E4
Pike Rd Ind Est CT15 114 D1
Pilar Ct CT8 7 D1
Pilckem Cl CT1 67 D1
Pilgrims Cl ME17 79 A3
Pilgrims Ct TN27 120 C7
Pilgrims La
Chilham CT4 85 E1
Whitstable CT5 43 B4
Pilgrims Lakes ME17 100 E6
Pilgrim Spring CT19 178 D8
Pilgrims Rd CT1 88 C7
Pilgrims View ME14 53 E3
Pilgrims Way
Boughton Aluph TN25 123 A4
Boxley ME14 54 E3
Broad Street ME14, ME17 77 C6
Canterbury CT1 88 C7
Charing TN27 120 E8
Detling ME14 55 B1
Dover CT16 149 A3
Eccles ME20 53 B6
Hollingbourne ME17 77 F3
Lenham ME17 101 B7
Thurnham ME14 76 E8
Westwell TN25 121 D5
Pilgrims' Way TN25 159 E8
Pilgrims Way Prim Sch CT1 88 C7
Pilot Rd ME1 31 C8
Pilots Ave CT14 117 A4
Pilot's Farm Rd CT4 110 A4
Pimpernel Cl ME14 76 B4
Pimpernel Way ME5 31 E4
Pimp's Court Cotts ME15 96 E6
Pincus Ho ME10 36 D5
Pine Cotts ME14 74 E8
Pine Gr
Gillingham ME7 33 A5
Maidstone ME14 75 B6
PINEHAM 149 D8
Pineham Rd CT15 149 D6
Pine Ho
3 Chatham ME5 31 F5
5 Maidstone ME14 75 B4
Pine Lodge ME16 74 C3
Pine Lodge Ct CT14 117 B5
Pine Pl ME15 74 E1
Pines Calyx★ CT15 151 B5
Pines Garden The★ CT15 151 B5
Pineside Rd CT3 89 E8
Pines The
Broadstairs CT10 29 D4
Canterbury CT1 88 A6
Pine Tree Ave CT2 66 E2
Pinetree Cl CT5 20 F3
Pine Tree Cl CT7 27 B7
Pine Way CT19 177 D7
Pine Wlk CT6 23 E5
Pinewood Cl CT12 29 C1
Pinewood Dr ME5 54 D8
Pin Hill CT1 87 F7
Pinks Cnr CT12 50 D6
Pinners Hill CT15, CT3 113 C6
Pinners La CT15 113 C5
Pinnock Wall CT14 94 D5
Pintail Dr ME9 14 E3
Pintail Way CT6 23 C2
Pioneer Bsns Pk CT11 52 C8
Pioneer Rd CT16 149 A3
Pippin Ave CT4 111 B8
Pippin Cl
Ash CT3 71 E1
Coxheath ME17 96 B2
8 Sittingbourne ME10 36 D6
Pippin Croft ME7 33 A6
Pirbright Cl ME5 32 D2
Pitstock Rd ME9 59 B5
Pittlesden TN30 179 A7
Pittlesden Pl 1 TN30 179 A7
Pittock Ho CT14 117 B3
Pitt Rd
Chartway Street ME17 99 A2
Maidstone ME16 74 B1
Pivington La TN27 119 C2
Pivington Mill Ind Est TN27 119 C2
Pixwell La CT14 116 D3
Place La
Hartlip ME9 34 D4
Woodchurch TN26 169 B3
Place The CT4 112 F1
Plain Cotts CT20 178 A4
Plain Rd
Brabourne Lees TN25 158 F5
Folkestone CT20 178 B4
Plains Ave ME15 75 C1
Plains of Waterloo CT11 52 F7
Plaistow Sq ME14 75 C6
Plantation Cl TN26 138 A7
Plantation Ct ME9 14 E4
Plantation La ME14 76 A3
Plantation Rd
Faversham ME13 62 C7
Gillingham ME7 11 A6
Whitstable CT5 21 D2
Platters The ME8 33 C7
PLATT'S HEATH 100 E1
Platts Heath Prim Sch ME17 100 F2
Playdell Ct 12 CT20 178 D4
Playden La TN31 197 C3
Playhouse Theatre★ 15 CT5 20 D1
Playing Fields CT13 93 E7
Playstool Cl ME9 35 B6
Playstool Rd ME9 35 A6
Plaza Ct 7 ME10 37 A4
Pleasance Road Central TN29 209 D7
Pleasance Road N TN29 206 E5
Pleasant Row 10 ME7 10 A6
Pleasant Valley La ME15 96 B4
Pleasent Pl ME12 3 E6
Plenty Brook Dr CT6 22 F3
Plewis Ho ME7 10 E7
Pleydell Cres CT2 67 F7
Pleydell Gdns CT20 178 D4
Plimsoll Ave CT19 178 E8
Plomley Cl ME8 33 D4
Plough Cotts ME17 98 D2
Plough Ct CT6 23 D2
Plough Hill CT15 165 C4
Plough La CT5 21 D3
Ploughmans Way
Ashford TN23 155 D5
Chatham ME5 32 A1
Gillingham ME8 33 E6
Plough Rd ME12 5 C5
Plough Wents Rd ME17 98 B2
Plover Cl
Chatham ME5 32 D1
Herne Bay CT6 23 F5
Plover Rd
Hawkinge CT18 162 F3
Minster (Sheppey) ME12 4 A5
PLUCKLEY 136 D7
Pluckley CE Prim Sch TN27 136 D7
Pluckley Cl ME8 11 C3
Pluckley Gdns CT9 8 E2
Pluckley Rd
Bethersden TN26 153 D7
Charing TN27 120 B5
Hothfield TN26, TN27 137 B4
Smarden TN27 135 D2
Pluckley Sta TN27 136 C3
PLUCKLEY THORNE 136 B6
PLUCKS GUTTER 48 F3
Plumford Rd ME13 62 A2
Plumpton Wlk
5 Canterbury CT1 67 B1
9 Maidstone ME15 97 F6
Plumpudding La ME13 42 E1
Plumstone Rd CT7 26 F1
Plum Tree Gdns TN26 169 B1
Plumtree Gr ME7 33 A4
Plum Tree La ME9 56 B8
Plumtrees ME16 74 A2
Plurenden Manor Farm Cotts TN26 168 D7
Plurenden Rd TN26 168 E7
Poachers Cl ME5 32 C5
Poachers End CT3 24 B1
Pochard Cres CT6 23 E3
Podkin Wood ME5 53 F8
Poets Cnr CT9 7 J1
Poets Wlk CT14 117 C1
Poison Cross CT13 93 B4
Poldark Ct 22 CT11 52 F7
Poles The ME9 12 E4
Polhill Dr ME5 31 F2
Pollard Cl TN23 155 F8
Pollard Ct ME7 10 C5
Pollard Pl 3 CT5 43 C6
Polo Way CT5 21 D1
Pomfret Ho CT4 86 D1
Pomfret Rd CT4 86 D1
Pommeus La CT14 133 D7
Poncia Rd TN23 156 A7
Pond Cotts
Herne Bay CT6 23 D2
Sittingbourne ME10 58 D8
Pond Dr ME10 37 A2
Pond Farm Rd
Hucking ME17 56 D1
Oad Street ME9 35 F1
Pond Hill CT3 90 D1
Pond Hill Rd CT20 177 C5
Pond La
St Margaret's at Cliffe CT15 150 D7
Womenswold CT4, CT3 112 D3
Pondmore Way TN25 138 F4
Ponycart La CT4 126 E3
Poorhole La CT10 29 B5
Poot La ME9 12 E5
Pope House La TN30 167 B4
Popes La CT2 67 F7
Pope St
Godmersham CT4 107 E4
Maidstone ME16 74 C2
Popes Wood ME14 75 F6
Popjack Rd ME9 58 E6
Poplar Cl TN23 138 F3
Poplar Dr
Elvington CT15 114 B2
Herne Bay CT6 22 D2
Poplar Field TN30 188 D4
Poplar Gr ME16 74 C5
Poplar La TN29 205 D7
Poplar Rd
Broadstairs CT10 29 E6
Ramsgate CT11 52 D7
Wittersham TN30 188 D4
Poplar Row CT7 27 E5
Poplars TN26 182 A7
Poplars The
Ashford TN23 156 A7
Bethersden TN26 153 E5
Hersden CT3 46 F1
Poplar View ME13 63 E3
Poppy Cl
Gillingham ME7 10 E5
Maidstone ME16 74 D3
Poppy Cres ME12 4 A4
Poppyfield TN31 197 C1
Poppy Mead TN23 156 C2
Popsal La CT3 91 B6
Porchester Cl ME15 97 A6
Portal House Sch CT15 151 A6
Port Cl
Chatham ME5 32 B3
Maidstone ME14 76 A5
Portebello Ct CT14 117 D7
Porter Cl ME12 4 A6
Porter's La ME13 62 B2
Porters Wlk ME17 98 E4
Portery The CT14 117 D6
Portland Ave ME10 37 C4
Portland Cl
Ashford TN24 139 C7
Hythe CT21 176 B2
Portland Ct
3 Hythe CT21 176 B2
Ramsgate CT11 52 E7
Portland Rd
Gillingham ME7 10 E6
Hythe CT21 176 B2
Portland Sq CT1 88 B7
Portland St 1 ME4 10 B2
Portland Terr
Ripple CT14 133 D8
Sheerness ME12 1 D2
Portlight Pl CT5 43 A6
Port Lympne Wild Animal Pk★ CT21 174 D2
Portree Mews ME7 10 E3
Port Richborough Bsns Pk CT13 73 A7
Port Rise ME4 9 F3
Portsdown Cl ME16 74 B2
Portway CT5 43 C8
Post Barn Rd ME4 9 F2
Postley Ind Ctr ME15 75 A2
Postley Rd ME15 75 A1
POSTLING 160 F2
Postling TN23 138 E1
Postling Rd CT19 177 E7
Postling Wents CT21 175 F8
Postmill Dr ME15 74 F1
Post Office Row CT4 84 D1
Pot Kiln La TN26 152 E4
POTTEN STREET 25 D3
Potten Street Rd CT7 25 E3
Potteries The ME9 12 E3
Potters Cl TN24 138 E6
Potters Cnr TN24 138 E6
POTTERS CORNER 138 F6
POTTER'S FORSTAL 118 B2
Potter St CT13 73 A1
Pottery Cotts TN25 140 E5
Potyn Ho ME1 9 C4
Pouces Cotts CT12 27 F1
Poulders Gdns CT13 93 E8
Poulders Rd CT13 93 E8
Poulsen Ct 8 ME10 37 B4
Poulton Cl CT17 165 F8
Poulton Close Bsns Pk CT17 148 E1
Poulton La CT3 92 C8
Pound Ct TN23 156 A3
Pound Farm Cotts CT18 177 A7
Pound Ho TN23 156 B8
Poundhurst Rd TN26 171 C3
Pound La
Ashford TN23 155 F4
Brabourne Lees TN25 158 F5
Canterbury CT1 66 F1
Elham CT4 144 F4
Molash CT4 105 F4
Pound Way CT20 178 D4
Powell Cl ME20 53 A3
Powell Cotton Dr CT7 27 B6
Powell Cotton Mus★ CT7 27 B5
Powerhub Bsns Ctr ME16 74 F5
Power Station Rd ME12 3 E7
Pratling St ME20 53 C4
PRATLING STREET 53 C3
Precincts The CT1 88 A8
Premier Bsns Ctr ME4 10 C1
Premier Way ME10 14 F2
Prentis Cl ME10 36 C5
Prentis Quay ME10 36 F5
Prescott Cl CT15 149 E6
Prescott Ho TN28 202 A7
Prestedge Ave CT11 29 E2
PRESTON
Ash 70 B6
Faversham 62 D6
Preston Ave
Faversham ME13 62 E6
Gillingham ME7 10 E1
Preston Ct ME13 62 D6
Preston Gr ME13 62 D6
Preston Hall Gdns ME12 6 E4
Preston Hill CT3 70 B1
Preston La
Faversham ME13 62 D6
Preston CT3 70 B5
Preston Malt Ho ME13 62 D6
Preston Par CT5 42 F7
Preston Pk ME13 62 D6
Preston Prim Sch CT3 70 C6
Preston Rd
Manston CT12 28 E2
Stourmouth CT3 48 D1
Wingham CT3 70 B3
Preston St ME13 62 D7
Preston Way ME8 11 B2
Pretoria Ho 8 ME15 97 E5
Pretoria Rd
Canterbury CT1 88 B8
Chatham ME4 9 F2
Gillingham ME7 10 D3
Price's Ave
Margate CT9 8 B2
Ramsgate CT11 52 C6
Prices Ct 5 ME10 37 B4
Priest Ave CT2 87 C7
Priestdale Ct ME4 9 E3
Priestfield Rd ME7 10 E5
Priestfields ME1 9 B3
Priest Fields CT6 23 F5
Priestfield Stad (Gillingham FC) ME7 10 E5
Priest & Sow Cnr CT5 21 B3
Priest Wlk CT5 21 C3
Primrose Ave ME8 33 B5
Primrose Cl ME4 31 E7
Primrose Dr TN23 156 B4
Primrose Gr ME9 58 A6
Primrose Hill CT4 86 B7
Primrose Ho 10 ME15 97 E7
Primrose La ME9 58 A6
Primrose Pl CT17 149 B1
Primrose Rd CT17 149 A1
Primrose Way
Cliffs End CT12 51 C5
Whitstable CT5 21 C1
Prince Andrew Rd CT10 29 E7
Prince Arthur Rd ME7 10 B6
Prince Charles Ave
Chatham ME5 32 B4
Minster (Sheppey) ME12 4 C6
Sittingbourne ME10 37 C3
Prince Charles Rd CT10 29 E7
Prince of Wales Rdbt CT17 166 D6
Prince of Wales Residential Pk CT21 187 E8
Prince of Wales Terr CT14 117 D5
Princes Ave
Chatham ME5 32 B5
Minster (Sheppey) ME12 4 D7
Prince's Ave CT12 29 B1
Princes Cl CT7 26 D7
Princes Cres 10 CT9 7 J2
Princes Dr CT13 95 A8
Princes Gate 18 CT20 178 E5
Prince's Gdns CT9 8 C2
Princes Par CT21 176 E2
PRINCES PARK 32 B6
Princes Rd CT11 52 D8
Princess Anne Rd CT10 29 E7
Princess Cl CT5 21 C3
Princess Margaret Ave
Margate CT9 8 E2
Ramsgate CT12 29 A1
Princess Mary Ave ME4 10 B7
Princess Rd CT5 21 C3
Princess St CT19 178 E6
Princes St
Deal CT14 117 D7
11 Dover CT16 166 D7
Maidstone ME14 75 A5
Prince's St
Margate CT9 7 J2
9 Ramsgate CT11 52 E6
Rochester ME1 9 C4

Princes Terr CT21 175 F1
Princes Way
Canterbury CT2 66 E1
Detling ME14 55 A1
Prince's Wlk CT9 8 D3
Prince William Ct CT14 117 D7
Prinys Dr ME8 33 C4
Prioress Rd CT2 87 D8
Prioress Wlk CT16 149 A3
Prior Pl ME1 9 B1
Prior Rd TN28 206 E8
Prior's Lees 8 CT20 178 D4
Priory Cl
Broadstairs CT10 29 F3
East Farleigh ME15 96 B8
New Romney TN28 201 F6
Priory Ct
Gillingham ME8 11 A2
Leysdown-on-Sea ME12 6 G1
Rochester ME1 9 D5
Priory Ctyd CT11 52 D6
Priory Fields Sch CT17 166 B8
Priory Gate 4 ME14 75 A5
Priory Gate Rd CT17 166 C8
Priory Gdns
Canterbury CT1 88 A6
Folkestone CT20 178 D4
Priory Gr CT17 166 C8
Priory Hill CT17 166 C8
Priory Ho CT17 166 C7
Priory Inf Sch CT11 52 D7
Priory La
Herne Bay CT6 23 A3
Sellindge TN25 159 D3
Priory of St Jacob CT1 87 E6
Priory Pl ME13 40 C1
Priory Rd
Aldington Frith TN25 172 C4
Dover CT16, CT17 166 D8
Faversham ME13 62 C8
Gillingham ME8 11 A2
Maidstone ME15 75 A3
Ramsgate CT11 52 D6
Rochester ME2 9 A6
Priory Row ME13 62 C8
Priory St 10 CT16 166 D8
Priory Station Approach Rd
CT17 166 C7
Priory The TN29 205 C6
Priory Way TN30 179 C7
Pritchard Ct ME7 10 C3
Pritchard Dr CT18 163 A4
Probyn Mews CT18 162 F3
Proctor Wlk CT18 162 F4
Progress Est The ME15 98 A4
Promenade
Birchington CT7 26 F8
Deal CT14 117 D3
Promenade The ME12 6 G2
Prospect Ave 8 ME2 9 B8
Prospect Cl CT8 27 E7
Prospect Cotts
Boughton Lees TN25 122 E3
Harbledown CT2 65 E1
Shepherdswell CT15 130 D4
Prospect Ct 20 CT11 52 E6
Prospect Gdns CT12 50 B7
Prospect Hill CT6 23 A5
Prospect Mews CT21 176 C2
Prospect Pl
7 Broadstairs CT10 30 B4
Canterbury CT1 88 A7
Dover CT17 149 B1
Eastling ME13 81 E6
Hamstreet TN26 182 F7
Maidstone ME16 74 E3
St Nicholas at Wade CT7 25 E1
Prospect Rd
Birchington CT7 26 F7
Broadstairs CT10 30 B4
Folkestone CT20 177 D3
Hythe CT21 176 C2
Minster (Thanet) CT12 50 B6
Prospect Row
Chatham, Brompton ME7 10 A6
Chatham ME4 10 A3
Prospect Terr
Elham CT4 144 F4
21 Ramsgate CT11 52 E6
Prospect Way TN25 158 E5
Provender La ME13, ME9 61 A6
Provender Way ME14 75 E5
Providence St TN23 156 C8
Puckle La CT1 88 A6
Pudding La
Ash CT3 71 D1
Maidstone ME14 74 F4
Pudding Rd ME8 33 F8
Puffin Ct CT18 163 A3
Puffin Rd CT6 23 F4
Pullman Cl CT12 52 C8
Pump La
Gillingham ME7, ME8 11 D3
1 Margate CT9 7 J2
Purbeck Rd ME4 9 E2
Purchas Ct CT2 66 C4
Purchase La TN26 154 E8
Purr Wood CT4 107 B2
Purser Way ME7 10 C7
Puttney Dr ME10 37 A8
Pye Alley La CT5 43 C3
Pym Ho TN27 120 D7
Pympes Court Farm Ctr★
ME15 96 E6
Pynson's Ind Est CT10 29 D4
Pyott Mews 3 CT1 67 B1
Pyrus Cl ME5 54 A8
Pyson's Rd CT10, CT12 29 D3
Pyson's Road Ind Est
CT10 29 D3

Q

Quain Ct CT20 178 C4
Quantock Dr TN24 139 B4
Quantock Gdns CT12 29 B3
Quarries The ME17 97 C4
Quarrington La TN25 158 B8
Quarry Cotts TN30 189 C3
Quarry Rd
Hythe CT21 176 B3
Maidstone ME15 75 A2
Quarry Sq ME14 75 A5
Quarry View TN23 155 D7
Quarry Wlk CT21 177 A3
Quarry Wood TN25 173 A6
Quay Cotts ME9 38 E6
Quay Ct CT5 20 E2
Quay La
Faversham ME13 62 D8
Sandwich CT13 73 A1
Quayside ME4 10 B8
Quay The ME9 38 E6
Queen Anne Rd ME14 75 B4
Queen Bertha Rd CT11 52 C6
Queen Bertha's Ave CT7 27 C8
QUEENBOROUGH 3 A5
Queenborough Dr ME12 4 B7
Queenborough Fst Sch
ME11 3 B5
Queenborough Rd
Halfway Houses ME12 3 C6
Queenborough ME12 3 C4
Queenborough Sta ME11 3 A5
Queendown Ave ME8 33 D5
Queendown Rd CT7 28 A3
Queendown Warren Nature
Reserve★ ME9 34 B3
Queen Elizabeth Ave CT9 8 D1
Queen Elizabeth Rd
CT16 166 F8
Queen Elizabeth's Gram Sch
ME13 62 D8
Queen Elizabeth Sq ME15 97 D6
Queen Elizabeth the Queen
Mother Hospl CT9 28 F8
Queen Mother Ct CT14 117 D2
Queen Mother Ct The ME1 9 B4
Queens Ave
Canterbury CT2 66 E1
Dover CT17 166 A7
Folkestone CT20 177 B6
Herne Bay CT6 23 D5
Queen's Ave
Birchington CT7 26 D7
Broadstairs CT10 30 B6
Maidstone ME16 74 D5
Margate CT9 7 I1
Ramsgate CT12 29 B1
Queensbridge Dr CT6 22 C4
Queens Ct
Ashford TN24 139 C3
Gillingham ME8 34 A8
2 Hythe CT21 176 B1
Margate CT9 8 A3
Queen's Ct CT6 23 A4
Queensdown Rd CT14 134 D4
Queensgate ME16 74 D5
Queens Gate Rd CT11 52 C8
Queens Gdns
Broadstairs CT10 30 B3
Herne Bay CT6 22 F5
Queen's Gdns CT16, CT17 166 D8
Queens Ho ME16 74 B3
Queen's Lea CT15 164 E5
Queens Lodge CT9 8 B3
Queens Mews CT14 117 D6
Queens Par
12 Faversham ME13 62 D7
Margate CT9 8 A3
Queen's Prom CT9 8 B3
Queens Rd
Aylesham CT3 112 F5
Minster (Sheppey) ME12 4 D7
Whitstable CT5 21 A2
Queen's Rd
Ash CT3 71 D2
Ashford TN24 140 A1
Broadstairs CT10 30 B4
Chatham ME5 10 D1
Faversham ME13 62 B7
Gillingham ME7 10 C4
Littlestone-on-Sea TN28 202 D6
Lydd TN29 205 C6
Maidstone ME16 74 C4
Ramsgate CT11 52 F7
Westgate on Sea CT8 27 F8
Queen's Rise CT14 133 F5
Queen St
Ashford TN23 139 B2
Chatham ME4 10 A4
Deal CT14 117 D6
Dover CT16, CT17 166 D7
Folkestone CT20 178 E5
Herne Bay CT6 22 F5
Margate CT9 7 I2
Ramsgate CT11 52 E6
Rochester ME1 9 C4
Queens The CT14 117 D5
Queensway
Dymchurch TN29 186 E2
Lydd TN29 205 C6
Queens Way ME14 55 A1
Queen's Way ME12 3 A8
Queenswood Rd ME20 53 D7
Queen Victoria Meml Hospl
CT6 23 B4
Quern Rd CT14 117 A2
Querns Pl CT1 88 B8
Querns Rd CT1 88 C8
Quern The ME15 74 E1
Quested Rd CT19 177 E6
Quested Way ME17 100 C6
Quetta Rd CT12 28 F1
Quex Ct CT7 27 B6
Quex House & Gdns★
CT7 27 B5
Quex Rd CT8 27 F8
Quex View Rd CT7 27 A5
Quickstep Cl ME10 36 F8
Quickthorn Cres ME5 31 E5
Quince Orch TN26 183 A7
Quinion Cl ME5 54 A8
Quinnell St ME8 11 E1
Quinneys Pl CT5 21 D2
Quinton Rd ME10 36 C7

R

Rabbit Hole CT4 129 A7
Radcliffe Ct CT21 176 B2
RADFALL 44 C5
Radfall Cnr CT5 44 C6
Radfall Gate CT5 44 C6
Radfall Hill CT5 44 D5
Radfall Rd CT5 44 D4
Radfall Ride CT5 44 C5
RADFIELD 38 A2
Radleigh Gdns ME1 9 E1
Radley Cl CT10 30 A6
Radnor Bridge Rd CT19,
CT20 178 E5
Radnor Chambers 13
CT20 178 D4
Radnor Cl
Herne Bay CT6 23 B1
Maidstone ME14 74 E7
Radnor Cliff CT20 178 A3
Radnor Cliff Cres CT20 178 A3
Radnor Park Ave CT19 178 C6
Radnor Park Cres CT19 178 C5
Radnor Park Gdns CT19 178 C6
Radnor Park Ho CT19 178 C6
Radnor Park Rd CT19 178 C6
Radnor Park W CT19 178 B6
Radnor St 20 CT19 178 E5
RAF Manston Spitfire &
Hurricane Meml Mus★
CT12 28 A2
Raggatt Pl ME15 75 B2
Raglan Pl 10 CT10 30 B4
Ragstone Fields ME15 97 E4
Ragstone Hollow TN25 173 A6
Ragstone Rd ME15 76 A2
Railway Ave CT5 20 E1
Railway Cotts ME9 38 D3
Railway Hill CT4 128 E8
Railway Rd ME12 1 C2
Railway St
Chatham ME4 9 F4
Gillingham ME7 10 D6
Railway Street Ind Pk
ME7 10 D6
Railway Terr
Margate CT9 7 H1
Queenborough ME11 3 A5
RAINHAM 33 E8
Rainham Cl ME15 75 A1
Rainham Mark Gram Sch
ME8 11 D2
Rainham Rd ME5 10 C3
Rainham Sch for Girls
ME8 33 C8
Rainham Sh Ctr 2 ME8 11 F1
Rainham Sta ME8 11 F1
Raite Gn 5 ME10 36 D6
Raleigh Cl
Ashford TN24 157 A8
Chatham ME5 32 A6
Raleigh Ct 1 CT11 52 F8
Raleigh Way ME12 3 E6
Ramillies Cl ME5 32 A6
Ram La TN25, TN27 137 C8
RAM LANE 120 E2
Ramp A CT16 166 H8
Rampart Rd CT21 176 B2
Ramparts The CT13 94 A8
Ramp B CT16 166 H8
Ramp C CT16 166 G8
Ramp D CT16 166 G8
Rampion Cl ME14 75 E5
Ramsey Cl
Canterbury CT2 66 E1
Maidstone ME15 75 A2
Ramsey Ho
8 Canterbury CT1 87 F7
Deal CT14 117 C3
RAMSGATE 52 C4
Ramsgate Holy Trinity Prim
Sch CT10 30 A1
Ramsgate Maritime Mus★
CT12 52 E6
Ramsgate Rd
Broadstairs CT10 30 B4
Broadstairs, Dumpton CT10,
CT11 29 F2
Margate CT10, CT9 29 A6
Sandwich CT13 73 A7
Ramsgate Sports Ctr
CT11 52 D7
Ramsgate Sta CT12 52 C8
Ramstone Cl TN25 158 E5
Rancorn Rd CT9 7 G1
Randall Rd ME4 9 E1
Randalls Row ME15 96 F5
Randall St ME14 74 F6
Randle Way ME9 37 E2
Randolph Cl CT1 88 A7
Randolph Ct CT8 7 C1
Randolph Gdns TN24 139 E5
Randolph Ho
15 Folkestone CT20 178 E5
Gillingham ME7 10 C5
Randolph La TN31 197 B3
Randolph Rd
Dover CT17 149 B1
Gillingham ME7 10 C5
Randolph Sq CT9 7 J3
Ranelagh Gdns 1 CT10 29 E5
Ranelagh Gr CT10 29 E5
Ranelagh Rd
Deal CT14 117 D5
Sheerness ME12 1 D2
Range Rd
Eastchurch ME12 5 D1
Hythe CT21 176 B1
Range Road Ind Est
CT21 176 B1
Ransley Gn TN26 183 F8
Ransome Way CT7 26 F6
Rare Species Conservation
Area★ CT13 93 E6
Raspberry Hill La ME9 14 D6
RATLING 113 A8
Ratling Rd CT3 112 F7
Rattington St CT4 86 E2
Ravelin Ho ME12 1 D2
Ravenlea Rd CT20 178 A5
Ravensbourne Ave CT6 23 B3
Ravenscourt Rd
Deal CT14 117 C5
Rough Common CT2 66 B3
Ravens Dane Cl ME15 76 A1
Ravenswood Ave 7 ME2 9 B8
Rawdon Rd
Maidstone ME15 75 A3
Ramsgate CT11 52 C6
Rawling St ME9 58 F3
Rayham Rd CT5 44 A8
Rayleigh Cl ME16 74 D7
Rayleigh Ho 2 ME15 97 D8
Raymer Rd ME14 75 B8
Raymond Ave CT1 88 A6
Raymond Fuller Way
TN24 139 E4
Raymoor Ave TN29 195 A4
Rayner Hill Cotts ME17 102 C5
Rayners Hill ME17 102 C5
Raywood Office Complex
TN27 120 B4
Reach Cl CT15 150 F5
Reachfields CT21 176 A1
Reach Mdw CT15 151 A6
Reach Rd
Lympne CT21 174 D2
St Margaret's at Cliffe
CT15 150 F5
Reactor One Rd TN29 209 C2
Reactor Two Rd TN29 209 C2
Readers La TN31 196 F5
Reading Cl CT14 117 B1
Reading Ho 4 ME15 97 F5
Reading Rd CT17 165 F7
Reading St
Broadstairs CT10 29 F8
Tenterden TN30 180 C2
READING STREET
Broadstairs 29 F7
Tenterden 180 C2
Reading Street Rd CT10,
CT9 29 E8
Readscroft Rd ME8 33 D5
Realgar Ct 4 ME10 36 D6
Reams Way ME10 15 A1
Rebecca Ct 6 CT9 8 B2
Recca La CT15, CT18 146 A4
Recreation Cl ME14 75 B6
Recreation Ground Rd
TN30 179 B7
Recreation Way ME10 15 A1
Rectory Bglws TN26 169 F8
Rectory Cl TN26 169 A2
Rectory Gdns CT5 21 D2
Rectory Grange ME1 9 C2
Rectory La
Barham CT4 112 A2
Harrietsham ME17 100 E5
Hythe CT21 176 B5
Lyminge CT18 161 C6
Maidstone ME16 74 A1
Rectory Rd
Broadstairs CT10 30 B5
Deal CT14 116 F4
Sittingbourne ME10 37 B3
St Mary in the Marsh TN29 194 B4
Rectory Way TN24 139 C5
Rectory Wlk TN26 183 A7
RECULVER 24 C7
Reculver Ave CT7 26 E8
Reculver CE Prim Sch
CT6 24 A4
Reculver Cl CT6 23 F5
Reculver Ctry Pk★ CT6 24 B6
Reculver Dr CT6 23 E5
Reculver La CT6 24 B6
Reculver Rd CT6 23 D5
Reculvers Rd CT8 27 F7
Reculver Towers and Roman
Fort★ CT6 24 D7
Reculver Wlk ME15 97 F7
Redan Pl ME12 1 E2
Red Barn La CT15 147 E3
Redberry Rd TN23 156 B5
Red Brick Cotts ME13 85 A6
Redbridge Cl ME5 32 C4
Redbrook St TN26 168 D5
Redbrooks Way CT21 175 F2
Redcliffe La ME14 75 B7
Redcot La CT2 68 B7
Redfern Ave ME7 10 E5
Redhill Rd CT8 27 E8
Red Ho The TN28 202 E6
Redhouse Farm CT14 95 B1
Redhouse La CT4 109 D6
Redhouse Wall CT14 95 B1
Redington TN24 139 C3
Redlands Ct CT17 148 E4
Redland Shaw ME4 9 E1
Red Lion Ct 6 CT21 176 B2
Red Lion La 11 CT5 20 D2
Red Lion Sq 7 CT21 176 B2
Redmill Cl CT20 177 E5
Redoubt Way TN29 187 B4
Red Rd CT2 64 D5
Red Robin Cotts ME9 35 B6
Redruth Manor 3 ME7 10 C6
Redsells Cl ME15 76 A1
Redsull Ave CT14 117 A3
Red Tree Orch TN23 155 E7
Redvers Cotts CT16 148 E5
Redvers Rd ME4 10 A2
Redwing Cl CT18 163 A3
Redwing Rd ME5 32 B7
Redwood Cl
Canterbury CT2 66 E2
Chartham CT4 86 E1
Chatham ME5 32 B2
Redyear Cotts TN24 140 A1
Redyear Ct TN24 140 A1
Reece Adams Ho CT18 164 B1
Reed Ave CT1 67 D3
Reed Cres TN23 156 C3
Reedland Cres ME13 62 C8
Reedmace Cl TN23 155 D8
Reeds Cl CT6 23 C4
Reeves Alley 1 CT5 20 D1
Reeves Cl CT2 87 C8
Reeves Pas 7 ME13 62 C7
Reeves Way CT5 21 C2
Reeves Yd CT5 20 D2
Reform Rd ME4 10 B2
Regency Cl
Gillingham ME8 33 C3
Sheerness ME12 1 B3
Whitstable CT5 43 F7
Regency Ct ME10 36 D4
Regency Pl CT1 67 B2
Regency Sch of English
CT11 52 D5
Regency Villas CT4 129 C5
Regent Dr ME15 97 A8
Regent Rd ME7 10 C4
Regents Ct 14 TN23 139 B2
Regents Pl TN23 139 B2
Regent St CT5 20 D2
Regents Wlk CT6 23 D5
Reginald Rd ME16 74 E3
Regis Bsns Pk ME12 1 B1
Regis Cres ME10 36 F7
Regis Ind Est ME12 3 A8
Regis Manor Com Prim Sch
ME10 36 E7
Reinden Gr ME15 75 F1
Remston Mews 12 CT1 67 B2
Remus Cl TN23 155 F4
Renault Cl CT6 22 A4
Rendezvous St CT20 178 D5
Rendezvous The CT9 7 I3
Renown Rd ME5 32 C2
Rentain Rd CT4 86 D2
Repton Cl CT10 29 F6
Repton Manor Rd TN23 139 A3
Repton Way ME5 31 F4
Reservoir Ave TN29 209 D2
Reservoir Rd CT5 20 E2
Resolution Cl ME5 32 A6
Rest Harrow ME13 83 C5
Restharrow Rd ME14 75 E4
Retreat The
Birchington CT7 27 B8
Doddington ME9 80 D7
Ramsgate CT12 52 B8
Rettendon Dr ME10 36 F8
Revenge Rd ME5 54 C8
Reynolds Cl CT6 23 B4
Reynolds La CT3 24 D3
Rhee Wall TN26 190 D7
Rheims Ct CT2 66 D1
Rheims Way CT1, CT2 87 E8
Rhodaus Cl CT1 87 F7
Rhodaus Ho CT1 87 F7
Rhodaus Town CT1 87 F7
RHODE COMMON 85 A6
Rhodes Gdns CT10 30 A6
Rhodes Ho 5 ME5 10 C2
RHODES MINNIS 144 A3
Rhode St ME4 10 A4
Rhodewood Cl ME15 76 A1
Ribston Way TN23 155 B8
Richard Ct 7 CT9 8 B2
Richardson Way CT12 51 D5
Richard St
Chatham ME4 9 F4
Rochester ME1 9 C3
Richborough Rd CT8 27 F7

Richborough Roman Fort★ CT13 72 E5
Richborough Way TN23 155 E5
Richborough Rd CT13 72 E3
Richdore Rd CT4 125 C6
Richmond Ave CT9 8 B1
Richmond Cl ME5 32 B4
Richmond Ct CT16 149 D1
Richmond Dr
Herne Bay CT6 23 E5
New Romney TN28 202 C8
Sittingbourne ME10 36 E7
Richmond First Sch ME12 1 E2
Richmond Gdns CT2 66 C2
Richmond Ho 26 CT20 178 E5
Richmond Meech Dr TN24 139 E4
Richmond Rd
Gillingham ME7 10 C7
Ramsgate CT11 52 D6
Whitstable CT5 21 B1
Richmond St
Folkestone CT19 177 D6
Herne Bay CT6 22 F5
Sheerness ME12 1 E2
Richmond Way ME15 97 A8
Riddles Rd ME10, ME9 36 C3
Ridge Meadow Prim Sch ME5 31 F6
RIDGE ROW 145 E1
Ridge The TN24 139 E6
Ridgeway CT21 175 A3
Ridgeway Cliff CT6 22 C5
Ridgeway Rd CT6 46 A7
Ridgeway Terr TN25 158 C5
Ridgeway The
Boughton Street ME13 64 A3
Broadstairs CT10 29 F3
Chatham ME4 31 E7
Crabble CT17 148 E2
Gillingham ME7 10 C7
Margate CT9 8 B1
Smeeth TN25 158 B5
Whitstable CT5 21 B1
Ridgeway Wlk CT6 46 A7
Ridgway ME16 74 B2
Ridham Ave ME10 15 A1
Ridham Dock ME9 15 B6
Riding Hill TN24 139 C6
Ridings The
7 Canterbury CT1 67 B1
Margate CT9 8 F3
Whitstable CT5 21 D1
Ridlands CT1 88 A5
Ridley Cl CT6 46 A8
Ridley Rd ME1 9 B4
Rigden Rd TN23 156 B7
Rigden's Ct 6 ME10 36 E5
Rigshill Rd ME13 103 B6
Riley Ave CT6 21 F4
Rimpton Ct CT10 29 F7
Ringlemere La CT13 92 F6
RINGLESTONE
Harrietsham 78 F4
Maidstone 74 E7
Ringlestone Cres ME14 74 F8
Ringlestone Rd ME17 78 D4
Ringold Ave CT12 52 A8
Ringsloe Ct CT7 26 D8
Ringwood Cl
Canterbury CT2 66 E3
Gillingham ME8 33 D8
Ringwood Rd ME15 97 C8
RINGWOULD 133 F5
Ringwould Rd
Kingsdown CT14 134 B5
Ringwould CT14, CT15 133 D4
Ripley Rd TN24 157 A8
Ripon Cl ME8 11 D3
Ripper's Cross TN26 137 D4
RIPPLE 133 D8
Ripple Cross CT14 133 F6
Ripple Rd CT14 133 F7
Ripplevale Sch CT14 133 E8
Risborough La CT19, CT20 177 D5
Risborough Way CT20 177 E6
Risdon Cl CT2 67 F6
Rise The
Ashford TN23 155 E7
Borden ME9 36 B2
Chatham ME4 10 A7
Gillingham ME7 33 A3
Halfway Houses ME12 3 C5
Kingsdown CT14 134 D5
Rochester ME1 9 D3
St Margaret's at Cliffe CT15 151 B6
Rising Rd TN23 139 A1
RIVER 148 E3
River Bank Cl 8 ME15 75 B4
Riverbank Way TN24 156 D6
Riverbourne Ct 6 ME10 36 F4
River Cl ME15 96 A7
River Ct
Chartham CT4 86 D3
Crabble CT17 148 F2
River Dale CT17 148 F3
Riverdale Rd CT1 67 B2
River Dr CT17 148 F2
Riverhead Cl
Maidstone ME16 74 D6
Margate CT9 8 B1
Sittingbourne ME10 36 C3
River Mdw CT17 148 F3
Rivermead Sch ME7 10 E6
River Prim Sch CT17 148 E3
River Rd CT13 73 B4
Riversdale Rd
Ashford TN23 156 C8
Ramsgate CT12 29 B1
Riverside
Chartham CT4 86 C3
Crabble CT17 148 F3
Temple Ewell CT16 148 C5
Riverside Bsns Pk TN24 139 D2
Riverside Cl
Bridge CT4 89 A1
Kingsnorth TN23 156 A4
Riverside Ct 11 CT2 66 F1
Riverside Ctry Pk & Visitor Ctr★ ME7 11 D5
Riverside Ind Est CT21 175 B1
Riverside Mews CT4 89 A1
Riverside Pk ME16 96 A8
Riverside Prim Sch ME8 12 A1
Riverside Rd CT13 51 A1
Riverside Ret Pk CT1 87 D6
Rivers Rd ME9 38 D2
River St
6 Chatham ME7 10 A6
River CT17 148 E3
Rivers Wlk ME17 101 C5
Riverview TN23 138 E1
River View
Gillingham ME8 11 D3
Maidstone ME15 74 F2
Rushenden ME11 2 F3
Sturry CT2 67 F7
River View Cl 6 ME4 9 F3
Riviera Ct 6 CT20 177 E3
Riviera Rd CT20 178 A3
Riviera The CT20 177 F3
Roach St ME2 9 A7
Road of Remembrance CT20 178 D4
Robert Brundett Cl TN24 139 E5
Robert Napier Sch The ME7 10 E3
Roberts Cl ME10 36 D7
Roberts Rd
Gillingham ME8 33 E8
Greatstone-on-Sea TN28 202 E1
Whitstable CT5 42 F6
Robert St CT14 117 D7
Robeshaw ME9 58 E2
ROBHURST 168 C2
Robina Ct CT9 8 D3
Robin Ct
6 Rochester ME1 9 D4
Whitstable CT5 21 A3
Robin Ho 5 ME16 74 E4
Robin Hood La
Chatham ME5 31 D1
Lydd TN29 205 C5
Robin Hood Lane (Lower) ME5 31 F2
Robin Hood Lane (Upper) ME5 31 E1
Robin La TN29 205 C6
Robins Ave ME17 101 C5
Robins Cl ME17 101 C4
Robin's Cl CT21 187 C8
Robins Ct ME14 75 B7
Robson's Yd CT17 166 C8
Robus Cl CT18 161 C7
Robus Terr CT18 161 C7
Robyn Cotts TN26 167 E8
ROCHESTER 9 B6
Rochester Airport ME1, ME5 31 C6
Rochester Airport Ind Est ME1 31 C5
Rochester Ave
Canterbury CT1 88 B7
Rochester ME1 9 C4
Rochester Castle★ ME1 9 C6
Rochester Cath★ ME1 9 C6
Rochester Ct
Canterbury CT1 88 B6
Rochester ME2 9 E8
Rochester Gate ME1 9 D5
Rochester Gram Sch for Girls ME1 9 C2
Rochester Ho 1 ME15 97 D7
Rochester Ind Coll ME1 9 D4
Rochester Rd
Burham ME1 53 A8
Chatham ME1, ME5 31 C4
Pratling Street ME20 53 B4
Rochester St ME4 9 E3
Rochester Sta ME1 9 D5
Rock Ave ME7 10 C3
Rock Hill Rd TN27 118 E2
Rockingham Pl CT6 23 B2
Rock Rd
Maidstone ME14 75 A6
Sittingbourne ME10 36 E4
Rockstone Way CT12 29 A1
Rockwell Ct ME15 74 E1
Rocky Bourne Rd TN25 172 D5
Rocky Hill ME16 74 E4
Rocky Hill Terr 2 ME16 74 E4
Rodmer Cl ME12 4 C8
RODMERSHAM 59 C8
Rodmersham Gn ME9 59 B7
RODMERSHAM GREEN 59 B7
Rodmersham Prim Sch ME9 59 B7
Rodney St CT11 52 D6
Roebuck Bsns Pk ME17 100 D5
Roebuck Ho ME1 9 E5
Roebuck Rd
Faversham ME13 62 A7
Rochester ME1 9 C5
Roentgen Ho ME10 36 D5
Roethorne Gdns TN30 179 B8
Roffen Rd ME1 9 C2
Rogersmead 14 TN30 179 A7
Rokesley Rd CT16 149 B5
Rolfe La TN28 202 B7
Roll's Ave ME12 5 C1
Rolvenden Ave ME8 11 C3
Rolvenden Dr ME10 36 B5
Roly Eckhoff Ho CT16 149 B3
Roman Amphitheatre★ CT13 72 E4
Roman Cl
Chatham ME5 31 D1
Deal CT14 117 B6
Roman Hts ME14 75 C6
Roman Painted House★ CT17 166 D8
Roman Rd
Canterbury CT4 88 D4
Dover CT16 149 D2
East Studdal CT15 132 C5
Faversham ME13 62 C7
Ramsgate CT12 29 C2
Whitfield CT15 149 D8
Roman Sq ME10 36 F3
Roman Way
Elvington CT15 114 B2
Folkestone CT19 177 C6
Kingsnorth TN23 156 C4
Maidstone ME15 97 E4
St Margaret's at Cliffe CT15 150 F5
Romany Ct ME5 10 D1
Romany Rd ME8 11 C2
ROMDEN 135 C1
Romden Rd
Smarden, Haffenden Quarter TN27 152 B8
Smarden, Romden TN27 135 D1
Rome House Cnr TN28 202 A6
Rome Rd TN28 202 A6
Rome Terr ME4 9 F4
Romilly Gdns CT12 29 C2
Romney Ave CT20 177 F5
Romney Cl
4 Birchington CT7 27 A7
Maidstone ME14 76 A3
Romney Ct ME10 36 E5
Romney, Hythe & Dymchurch Rly★ CT21 176 A2
Romney Marsh Ho TN29 195 C7
Romney Marsh Rd TN23, TN24 156 B6
Romney Marsh Visitor Ctr★ TN28 194 D1
Romney Pl ME15 75 A4
Romney Point TN25 138 F4
Romney Rd
Ashford TN24 139 E1
Chatham ME5 32 B5
Hamstreet TN26 183 A7
New Romney TN29 201 E3
Romney Sands Sta★ TN28 206 E8
Romney Warren Ctry Pk★ TN28 194 D1
Romney Way CT21 175 F1
Romsey Cl TN24 140 A2
Romulus Gdns TN23 155 F4
Ronalds Ct 6 ME10 37 A4
Rookery Cl
Ashford TN24 139 D7
Bredgar ME9 58 A6
Rookery View ME9 14 D4
Rook La ME9 35 F6
Rookston Cnr CT3 48 D1
Rooks View ME9 35 E6
Roonagh Ct ME10 36 E2
Roosevelt Ave ME5 32 A8
Roosevelt Rd CT16 149 B3
Ropemakers Ct ME4 10 A1
Roper Cl
Canterbury CT2 66 E1
Gillingham ME8 33 C3
Roper Rd
Canterbury CT2 66 E1
Teynham ME9 38 D3
Rope Walk Mews CT13 93 F8
Rope Wlk ME4 9 F5
Rosamund Ct CT19 178 C6
ROSEACRE 76 A4
Roseacre Cl CT2 66 E1
Roseacre Ct CT9 8 E2
Roseacre Gdns ME14 76 A3
Roseacre Jun Sch ME14 76 A4
Roseacre La ME14 76 A4
Rose Acre Rd CT3 89 F7
Rosebery Ave
Herne Bay CT6 23 E5
Ramsgate CT11 29 F1
Rosebery Cl ME10 37 D4
Rosebery Rd
Chatham ME4 9 E2
Gillingham ME7 10 D7
Rose Cotts
Hythe CT21 176 B4
Lenham Heath ME17 119 B8
Ramsgate CT12 28 F2
Rose Ct ME17 96 D1
Rosedale Rd CT9 8 A1
Rose Farm La TN27 136 A5
Rose Gdns
Birchington CT7 26 F6
Eythorne CT15 131 D7
Rose Gdns continued
Herne Bay CT6 23 C4
Minster (Thanet) CT12 50 B6
Rose Hill
11 Ramsgate CT11 52 E6
Wittersham TN30 189 B5
Roseholme ME16 74 D2
Rose La
Bishopsbourne CT4 111 C6
Canterbury CT1 87 F8
Lenham Heath ME17 119 B8
Roselands CT14 117 C1
Roselands Gdns CT2 66 D2
Roselawn Gdns 3 CT9 28 B8
Roselea Ave CT6 22 F3
Roseleigh Ave ME16 74 C5
Roseleigh Rd ME10 36 D2
Rosemary Ave
Broadstairs CT10 30 A3
Halfway Houses ME12 3 D6
Rosemary Cl 4 ME5 31 F4
Rosemary Cnr TN29 199 D8
Rosemary Ct 1 ME1 9 D4
Rosemary Gdns
Broadstairs CT10 29 F2
Whitstable CT5 44 A8
Rosemary La 15 CT1 87 F8
Rosemary Rd ME15 76 A3
Rosemount Cl ME15 96 F4
Rose St
Rochester ME1 9 D3
Sheerness ME12 1 C2
Rose Street Sch ME12 1 C2
Rose Terr ME13 62 D5
Rosetower Ct CT10 29 F8
Rose Wlk CT18 163 A4
Rosewood Dr TN25 138 F4
Rosewood Way CT7 27 B7
Rose Yd ME14 75 A4
Rosiers Ct 1 CT2 66 E1
Rossendale Ct 10 CT20 178 E6
Rossendale Gdns 8 CT20 178 E6
Rossendale Rd CT20 178 E6
Rossetti Ct CT7 26 F7
Rossetti Rd CT7 26 F8
Ross Gdns CT2 66 B3
Rossland Rd CT12 52 A8
Rosslyn Gn ME16 74 B5
Ross St ME1 9 D4
Ross Way CT20 177 E5
Rotary Gdns ME7 10 F2
Rothbrook Dr TN24 139 C7
Rother Vale ME5 32 C3
Rothley Cl TN30 179 B8
Rothsay Ct CT11 29 F1
ROUGH COMMON 66 B3
Rough Common Rd CT2 66 B3
Roundel Cl ME9 38 D2
Roundel The ME10 36 F2
Roundwell ME14 76 D3
Round Wood Cl ME5 32 A1
Rover Rd ME5 32 B2
Rowan Cl
Ashford TN23 138 E2
Staple CT3 92 A6
Sturry CT2 67 F6
Rowan Ct
Ashford TN24 156 E8
Broadstairs CT10 30 A5
Rowan Ho
4 Chatham ME5 31 F5
7 Maidstone ME16 74 A3
Rowan Lea ME5 10 B1
Rowans The ME12 4 B7
Rowan Tree Pk CT5 43 B6
Rowan Wlk ME4 9 E3
Rowbrocke Cl ME8 33 D3
Rowe Cl CT9 28 F7
Rowena Rd CT8 7 C1
Rowetts Way ME12 5 D3
Rowland Ave ME7 10 E2
Rowland Cl
Gillingham ME7 10 E1
Maidstone ME16 74 E3
Rowland Cotts CT21 174 F3
Rowland Cres CT6 23 E5
Rowland Dr CT6 22 C2
ROWLING 92 A2
Rowling St TN25 171 E6
ROWLING STREET 171 E6
Row The
Ash CT3 71 E5
Chillenden CT3 113 F8
Elham CT4 144 F5
Ruckinge TN26 183 F8
Roxburgh Rd CT8 7 D1
Royal Ave CT5 43 C5
Royal Cl CT10 29 F4
Royal Cres
Margate CT9 7 H2
Ramsgate CT11 52 D5
Royal Ct CT5 21 A3
Royal Eagle Cl ME2 9 E7
Royal Engineers Mus★ ME7 10 B6
Royal Engineers' Rd ME14 74 F7
Royal Espl
Margate CT9 7 F1
Ramsgate CT11 52 C5
Royal Fountain Mews ME12 1 B2
Royal Harbour App CT11 52 C5
Royal Mews 16 CT11 52 F7
Royal Military Ave CT20 177 D5
Royal Military Canal (dis)★ CT21 176 D2
Royal Military Rd CT21 175 E1
Royal Mus & Free Liby★ 25 CT1 87 F8
Royal Navy Way 2 CT5 43 A6
Royal Par CT11 52 E6
Royal Rd
Ramsgate CT11 52 D6
Sheerness ME12 1 D2
Royal St George's Golf Links★ CT13 73 E2
Royal School for Deaf Children The CT9 7 J2
Royal Sovereign Ave ME4 10 B7
Royal Star Arc 5 ME14 74 F4
Royal Victoria Hospl CT19 178 C6
Royal Victoria Pl 5 CT16 166 D8
Royds Rd TN24 156 D6
Royston Gdns CT15 150 F6
Royston Rd ME15 76 A3
Roystons Cl ME8 11 F2
Royton Ave ME17 101 D5
Rubery Dro CT3 72 C6
Ruby Cl 2 ME10 36 D6
RUCKINGE 183 F8
Ruckinge Cnr TN26 183 F8
Ruckinge Rd TN26 183 A7
Rucking Way ME8 11 C3
Rudge Cl ME5 32 D2
Ruffets Wood TN23 156 C3
Rugby Cl
Broadstairs CT10 29 F5
Chatham ME5 31 F4
Rugby Gdns TN23 156 C8
Rugby Rd CT17 166 A6
Ruglys Way TN27 120 B7
Ruins Barn Rd ME10, ME9 58 D6
Rule Ct ME12 3 B8
Rumfields Rd CT10 29 D4
Rumstead La ME17, ME9 56 D4
Rumstead Rd ME9 56 E4
Rumwood Ct ME17 98 B5
Runcie Ho 6 CT1 87 F7
Runcie Pl CT2 66 D1
Runham La ME17 100 E3
Running Foxes La TN23 155 D7
Running Horse Rdbt The ME14 53 E1
Runnymede Gdns ME15 97 A8
Runnymede Mews ME13 62 C7
Rusham Rd CT3 70 C1
Rush Cl
Chatham ME5 32 A3
Dymchurch TN29 195 B6
RUSHENDEN 2 F3
Rushenden Ct ME11 2 F3
Rushenden Rd ME11 3 A4
Rushett La ME13 60 F4
Rushmead Cl CT2 66 D2
Rushmead Dr ME15 97 A7
Ruskins View CT6 23 A1
Russell Cl ME10 36 C3
Russell Ct ME4 10 B3
Russell Dr CT5 21 D3
Russell Pl ME13 40 B3
Russell Rd
1 Folkestone CT19 178 D6
Kit's Coty ME20 53 D7
Russells Ave ME8 34 A8
Russell St
Dover CT16 166 E7
Sheerness ME12 1 C2
Russet Ave ME13 62 E5
Russet Ct ME17 96 C3
Russets The
Maidstone ME16 74 B5
Whitstable CT5 21 D1
Russett Cl CT3 71 F1
Russett Rd CT1 88 C8
Rutherford Coll CT2 66 E4
Rutherford Rd TN24 139 B5
Ruth Ho 2 ME16 74 E5
Ruth St ME4 10 A2
Rutland Ave CT9 8 C2
Rutland Cl CT1 88 D7
Rutland Gdns
Birchington CT7 26 F7
Margate CT9 8 C2
Rutland Ho 3 CT9 8 B2
Rutland Pl ME8 33 C3
Rutland Rd CT16 149 B3
Rutland Sch of English CT9 7 G1
Rutland Way ME15 97 E8
Ryan Dr ME15 76 A2
Rycault Cl 4 ME16 74 E3
Rycaut Cl ME8 33 D3
Rydal Ave CT11 52 B7
Rydal Ho ME15 97 E7
Ryde Cl ME5 32 B8
Ryder's Ave CT8 27 D8
Ryde St CT2 66 E1
Rye Ct TN23 155 D7
RYE FOREIGN 196 E1
Ryegrass Cl ME5 32 C6
Rye Rd
Brookland TN29 199 D8
Peasmarsh TN31 196 E2
Wittersham TN30 189 A2
Rye Wlk CT6 23 C2
Ryland Ct 5 CT20 178 E5
Ryland Pl 6 CT20 178 E5
Rylands Rd TN24 139 D5
Rype Cl TN29 205 C5
Ryswick Mews TN28 202 C8

Sabre Ct ME7 . . . . 11 A1
Sackett's Gap CT9 . . . . 8 C3
Sacketts Hill CT10 . . . . . 29 C6
Sackville Cl TN26 . . . . . . 138 A7
Sackville Cres TN23 . . . . . 139 A2
Saddlers Cl ME14 . . . . 75 E5
Saddlers Hill CT3 . . . . 91 D2
Saddlers Mews
    Ramsgate CT12 . . . . 28 F1
    Whitstable CT5 . . . . 21 D1
Saddler's Wall La TN29 . . 191 B1
Saddlers Way TN23 . . . . . 156 B5
Saddleton Gr 6 CT5 . . . . . 43 D8
Saddleton Rd CT5 . . . . . . 43 D8
Sadlers Cl ME5 . . . . 31 D2
Saffron Cl ME16 . . . . 74 B3
Saffron's Pl 14 CT20 . . . 178 E5
Saffron Way
    1 Chatham ME5 . . . . 31 F5
    Sittingbourne ME10 . . . . . 36 F7
Sage Rd ME1 . . . . .9 B3
Sailfield Ct ME4 . . . . 9 F7
Sailmakers Ct 5 ME4 . . . . 10 B2
St Agnes Gdns ME12 . . . . . 1 D1
St Albans Cl ME7 . . . . 10 E7
St Alban's Rd CT3 . . . . 46 E1
St Alphege CE Inf Sch 13
    CT5 . . . . 20 D1
St Alphege Cl CT5 . . . . . . 43 B7
St Alphege La 17 CT1 . . . . 87 F8
St Alphege Rd 4 CT16 . . 149 C1
St Ambrose CE TN25 . . . 123 E2
St Andrews CT19 . . . . . . 178 E5
St Andrews Cl
    Canterbury CT1 . . . . 87 E7
    Folkestone CT19 . . . . . . 178 B7
    Herne Bay CT6 . . . . 23 A4
    Margate CT9 . . . . 28 F7
St Andrew's Cl
    Maidstone ME16 . . . . 74 A2
    Whitstable CT5 . . . . 43 E8
St Andrews Gdns CT17 . . 149 B2
St Andrew's Gdns CT15 . 130 E5
St Andrew's Lees CT13 . . 94 A8
St Andrews Pk ME16 . . . . 74 A3
St Andrews Rd
    Gillingham ME7 . . . . 10 D7
    Ramsgate CT11 . . . . 52 F8
St Andrew's Rd
    Deal CT14 . . . . 117 C6
    Littlestone-on-Sea TN28 . . 202 E6
    Maidstone ME16 . . . . 74 A2
St Andrews Sch ME1 . . . . .9 C4
St Andrews Way CT14 . . 115 A3
St Andrew Terr CT17 . . . 149 A2
St Angela's Jun Sch CT8 . 27 D7
St Annes Ct ME16 . . . . . . 74 E4
St Anne's Ct
    1 Dover CT16 . . . . 149 B2
    Herne Bay CT6 . . . . 22 E5
St Anne's Dr CT6 . . . . 22 D4
St Anne's Gdns CT9 . . . . . 28 F8
St Anne's Rd
    Ashford TN23 . . . . 155 F7
    Whitstable CT5 . . . . 20 F2
St Ann's Rd
    Dymchurch TN29 . . . . . . 195 B7
    Faversham ME13 . . . . 62 B7
St Anselms RC Sch CT1 . . 88 C5
St Anthonys Sch CT9 . . . . . 8 C1
St Anthony's Way CT9 . . . . 8 C1
St Augustine of Canterbury
    RC Prim Sch ME8 . . . . . 33 D3
St Augustine's* CT8 . . . . 27 E8
St Augustine's Abbey
    CT11 . . . . 52 D5
St Augustine's Abbey (rems
    of)* CT1 . . . . 88 A8
St Augustine's Ave CT9 . . 28 F8
St Augustines Bsns Pk
    CT5 . . . . 20 D1
St Augustines Cath Prim Sch
    CT21 . . . . 176 A3
St Augustine's Cres CT5 . 21 D3
St Augustines Ct CT6 . . . . 22 F2
St Augustine's Ct 3 CT1 . 88 B8
St Augustines Pk CT8 . . . 27 E8
St Augustine's Pk CT11 . . 52 C6
St Augustine's Rd
    Canterbury CT1 . . . . 88 B7
    Deal CT14 . . . . 116 F4
    Ramsgate CT11 . . . . 52 D5
St Augustine's Sch CT8 . . 27 E8
St Barnabas Cl
    Ashford TN23 . . . . 155 F7
    Gillingham ME7 . . . . 10 D3
    Maidstone ME16 . . . . 74 C8
St Bartholemews Cl 4
    CT17 . . . . 166 C8
St Bartholomew's Hospl
    ME1 . . . . .9 E4
St Bartholomew's Hospl
    CT13 . . . . 94 A7
St Bartholomew's La 4
    ME1 . . . . .9 E4
St Bartholomew's Terr 2
    ME1 . . . . .9 E4
St Bart's Cl 5 CT17 . . . 166 C8
St Bart's Rd CT13 . . . . . . 93 F8
St Benedict's Lawn CT1 . . 52 D5
St Benedicts Prim Sch
    ME5 . . . . 32 C2
St Benets Ct TN30 . . . . . 179 B8
St Benet's Rd CT8 . . . . . . 27 E7
St Benets Way TN30 . . . . 179 B8

St Catherines TN29 . . . . . 201 A7
St Catherines Ct
    Ramsgate CT11 . . . . 29 F1
    Rochester ME1 . . . . 9 D5
St Catherine's Dr ME13 . . 62 D6
St Catherine's Gr CT12 . . 28 D1
St Cecelia Ho CT14 . . . . . 117 B1
St Christopher Cl CT9 . . . 29 D4
St Christophers Gn CT10 . 29 F5
St Christophers Mews
    CT11 . . . . 52 D8
St Christophers Sch 7
    CT1 . . . . 88 B6
St Clare Rd CT14 . . . . . . 117 C1
St Clements 8 CT13 . . . . 73 A1
St Clements Cl ME12 . . . . . 6 D2
St Clements Ct
    Broadstairs CT10 . . . . 29 E6
    Folkestone CT20 . . . . . . 178 F5
    Ramsgate CT11 . . . . 52 D7
St Clement's Ct CT5 . . . . . 23 A3
St Clements Ho ME1 . . . . . 9 D5
St Clements Rd ME12 . . . . 6 E3
St Clement's Rd CT8 . . . . . 7 C1
St Cosmus Cl TN25 . . . . . 105 B1
St Crispin's Inf Sch CT8 . . 27 E7
St Crispin's Rd CT8 . . . . . . 27 E7
St Cuby CT10 . . . . 30 C7
St Davids Ave CT17 . . . . . 166 A5
St David's Cl
    Birchington CT7 . . . . 27 B8
    Whitstable CT5 . . . . 43 E8
St Davids Gate ME16 . . . . 74 A2
St Davids Rd 5 CT11 . . . . 52 F8
St David's Rd
    Deal CT14 . . . . 117 C6
    Ramsgate CT11 . . . . 29 F1
St Denys Rd CT18 . . . . . . 163 B5
ST DUNSTAN'S 66 D1
St Dunstan's Cl CT2 . . . . . 66 E1
St Dunstans Ct 4 CT2 . . . 66 E1
St Dunstan's Rd CT9 . . . . . 8 A2
St Dunstan's St CT2 . . . . . 66 E1
St Dunstan's Terr CT2 . . . 66 E1
St Eanswythes CE Prim Sch
    6 CT20 . . . . 178 E4
St Eanswythe Way 19
    CT20 . . . . 178 E4
St Edmund's Jun Sch CT2 66 C3
St Edmund's RC Sch
    CT16 . . . . 149 D2
St Edmunds Rd 20 CT1 . . 87 F8
St Edmund's Rd CT14 . . . 116 E4
St Edmund's Sch CT2 . . . . 66 C3
St Edmunds Way ME8 . . . 12 B1
St Edward's RC Prim Sch
    ME12 . . . . 1 C2
St Elisabeth Ho CT1 . . . . . 67 A1
St Ethelberts RC Prim Sch
    CT11 . . . . 52 F8
St Faith's at Ash Sch CT3. 71 C1
St Faiths Ct ME14 . . . . 76 B4
St Faith's La ME14 . . . . . . 76 B4
St Faith St ME14 . . . . 74 F4
St Francis Cl
    Deal CT14 . . . . 116 F4
    Maidstone ME14 . . . . 75 B7
    Margate CT9 . . . . 29 D8
St Francis Ct TN23 . . . . . 155 F7
St Francis' RC Prim Sch
    ME15 . . . . 74 C4
St Francis Rd CT19 . . . . . 177 F6
St Gabriel's Ct 12 CT20 . 178 E6
St Georges Ave ME12 . . . . 5 D2
St George's Ave
    Herne Bay CT6 . . . . 22 D4
    Sheerness ME12 . . . . 1 C1
St George's Bsns Ctr
    TN23 . . . . 138 F2
St Georges Bsns Pk ME10 37 B4
St Georges CE Foundation
    Sch CT10 . . . . 29 C5
St George's CE Prim Sch
    ME12 . . . . 4 E6
St George's Cl CT5 . . . . . . 43 E7
St Georges Cres CT17 . . 166 B5
St Georges Ct CT17 . . . . 149 A2
St George's Ct ME12 . . . . . 3 B8
St Georges La CT1 . . . . . . 88 A8
St George's Lees CT13 . . 94 A8
St George's Pas CT14 . . . 117 D6
St Georges Pl
    Sandwich CT13 . . . . 94 B8
    St Margaret's at Cliffe
        CT15 . . . . 150 F6
St George's Pl
    Canterbury CT1 . . . . 88 A8
    Hythe CT21 . . . . 187 D8
St Georges Rd CT11 . . . . . 52 F8
St George's Rd
    Broadstairs CT10 . . . . 30 A4
    Deal CT14 . . . . 117 D6
    Folkestone CT19 . . . . . . 177 F6
    Gillingham ME7 . . . . 10 C6
    Sandwich CT13 . . . . 94 A8
St George's Sq
    3 Ashford TN24 . . . . . . 139 B2
    Maidstone ME16 . . . . 74 E3
St Georges St CT1 . . . . . . 88 A8
St George's St CT1 . . . . . . 88 A8
St George's Terr CT6 . . . . 22 E5
St Giles Cl CT17 . . . . 166 B5
St Giles Rd CT17 . . . . . . 166 B5
St Giles Wlk CT17 . . . . . 166 B5
St Gregory's Cl CT14 . . . 116 F4
St Gregory's Rd CT1 . . . . 67 B1
St Gregorys RC Prim Sch
    CT9 . . . . 28 E8

St Gregory's Rd CT1 . . . . . 67 B1
St Helen's Rd ME12 . . . . . . 1 E1
St Helier's Cl ME16 . . . . . 74 B2
St Hilda Rd CT19 . . . . . . 177 E6
St Hilda's Rd CT21 . . . . . 176 B1
St Jacob's Pl CT1 . . . . 87 D6
St James Ave CT12 . . . . . . 52 C8
St James' Ave
    Broadstairs CT10 . . . . 29 E5
    Ramsgate CT11 . . . . 29 B1
St James Cl ME12 . . . . .6 E4
St James' Gdns CT16 . . . . 43 B8
St James Rd CT14 . . . . . . 134 D5
St James St CT16 . . . . . . 166 E7
St James's Terr CT7 . . . . . 27 B8
St Jean's Rd CT8 . . . . 27 E7
St John Fisher RC Sch (Main
    Site) ME4 . . . . .9 E3
St John Fisher RC Sch (Sixth
    Form Site) ME4 . . . . 9 F2
St Johns Ave CT12 . . . . . . 28 F1
St John's Ave
    Ramsgate CT12 . . . . 29 A1
    Sittingbourne ME10 . . . . . 37 B3
St John's CE Inf Sch ME4. 9 E3
St John's CE Prim Sch
    ME14 . . . . 75 E4
St John's Church Rd
    CT19 . . . . 178 C6
St John's Cl CT18 . . . . . . 163 A7
St John's Commandery (rems
    of)* CT15 . . . . 146 E4
St John's Cotts
    Bethersden TN26 . . . . . . 153 D5
    12 Sandwich CT13 . . . . . 72 F1
St Johns Cres CT2 . . . . . . 66 D6
St John's Ct TN25 . . . . . . 157 A6
St John's Hospl 6 CT1 . . 67 A1
St John's La
    Ashford TN23, TN24 . . . . 139 C2
    Canterbury CT1 . . . . 87 F8
St John's Pl CT1 . . . . 67 A1
St Johns Rd
    Elvington CT15 . . . . 114 B2
    Hythe CT21 . . . . 176 A3
St John's Rd
    Dover CT17 . . . . 166 C7
    Faversham ME13 . . . . 62 D7
    Gillingham ME7 . . . . 10 C3
    Margate CT9 . . . . .7 J2
    New Romney TN28 . . . . . 202 A6
    Whitstable CT5 . . . . 21 D3
St John's St
    Folkestone CT20 . . . . . . 178 D5
    7 Margate CT9 . . . . 7 J2
St Johns Way ME1 . . . . 9 A2
St John's Way CT18 . . . . 163 A4
St Joseph's RC Prim Sch
    Aylesham CT3 . . . . 113 A5
    1 Broadstairs CT10 . . . . . 29 F5
St Julien Ave CT1 . . . . 67 D1
St Katherine Rd ME12 . . . . 3 B7
St Laurence Ave ME16 . . . 74 C8
St Laurence CE Jun Sch
    CT11 . . . . 52 B8
St Laurence Cl ME9 . . . . . 37 D2
St Laurence Ct CT11 . . . . 52 C7
ST LAWRENCE 52 B8
St Lawrence Ave CT11 . . . 52 B5
St Lawrence Chase CT11 . 52 B6
St Lawrence Cl CT11 . . . . 88 B6
St Lawrence Coll CT11 . . . 52 D8
St Lawrence Coll Jun Sch
    CT11 . . . . 52 E8
St Lawrence Ct TN28 . . . 202 A6
St Lawrence Forstal 1 . . . 88 B6
St Lawrence Gd The (Kent
    Cty Cricket Club) 1 . . . . . 88 B6
St Lawrence Ind Est CT11 52 B6
St Lawrence Rd CT11 . . . . 88 B6
St Leonards Ave ME4 . . . . .9 F2
St Leonards Ct 1 CT21 . . 176 B1
St Leonards Mews 5
    CT21 . . . . 176 B1
St Leonards Rd
    Hythe CT21 . . . . 176 B1
    Maidstone ME16 . . . . 74 C8
St Leonard's Rd CT14 . . . 117 B4
St Louis Gr CT6 . . . . 22 C4
St Lukes Ave CT11 . . . . . . 52 E8
St Luke's Ave ME14 . . . . . 75 B5
St Lukes Cl CT5 . . . . 43 E7
St Luke's Cl CT8 . . . . 27 E8
St Lukes Ct
    Ashford TN23 . . . . 155 F7
    Maidstone ME14 . . . . 75 A6
St Luke's Rd
    Maidstone ME14 . . . . 75 B5
    Ramsgate CT11 . . . . 52 E8
St Luke's Wlk CT18 . . . . . 162 F4
St Magnus Cl CT7 . . . . . . 27 A8
St Magnus Ct CT7 . . . . . . 27 A8
St Malo Ct 2 CT20 . . . . . 178 C4
ST MARGARET'S AT
    CLIFFE 151 A6
St Margaret's at Cliffe Prim
    Sch CT15 . . . . 151 A6
St Margarets at Troy Town
    Prim Sch ME1 . . . . 9 C4
St Margaret's Banks ME1. . 9 D5
St Margarets Cl ME14 . . . 74 B2
St Margaret's Cl CT5 . . . . 43 A6
St Margaret's Ct CT20 . . 178 B5
St Margaret's Ct 6 ME8 . . 33 F5
St Margarets Dr
    Deal CT14 . . . . 134 B8

St Margarets Dr continued
    Gillingham ME8 . . . . 33 C5
St Margaret's Inf Sch ME8 33 E8
St Margaret's Jun Sch
    ME8 . . . . 33 E8
St Margaret's Mews ME1. . 9 C5
St Margarets Rd
    St Margaret's at Cliffe
        CT15 . . . . 134 A1
    Westgate on Sea CT7 . . . . 27 F3
St Margaret's Rd
    St Margaret's at Cliffe
        CT15 . . . . 151 A5
    Westgate on Sea CT8 . . . . 27 E7
St Margaret's St
    Canterbury CT1 . . . . 87 F8
    Rochester ME1 . . . . 9 C5
St Marks Cl CT5 . . . . 43 E8
St Mark's Ct CT20 . . . . . . 177 D5
St Marks Ho ME7 . . . . 10 C5
ST MARTIN'S 88 B8
St Martins Ave CT1 . . . . . 88 B8
St Martin's Church* CT1. 88 B8
St Martins Cl
    Canterbury CT1 . . . . 88 B8
    Newington ME9 . . . . 35 C7
St Martin's Cl
    Detling ME14 . . . . 55 A1
    Dover CT17 . . . . 166 B5
St Martins Ct 4 CT1 . . . . . 88 B8
St Martin's Hill CT1 . . . . . 88 C8
St Martins Ho CT17 . . . . 166 D5
St Martin's Hospl CT1. . . 88 D8
St Martin's Pl CT1 . . . . . . 88 B8
St Martins Rd
    Folkestone CT20 . . . . . . 177 D6
    New Romney TN28 . . . . . 202 B6
St Martin's Rd
    Canterbury CT1 . . . . 67 B1
    Deal CT14 . . . . 116 F4
    Dover CT15 . . . . 149 E4
St Martins Sch CT17 . . . . 166 A7
St Martin's Terr CT1 . . . . . 88 B8
St Mary Ct 13 ME13 . . . . 62 D7
ST MARY IN THE
    MARSH 194 B4
St Mary of Charity CE Prim
    Sch ME13 . . . . 62 D7
St Mary's Ave CT9 . . . . 8 D1
ST MARY'S BAY 195 A4
St Mary's Bay Sta* TN29 194 F4
St Mary's CE Prim Sch
    6 Dover CT16 . . . . 166 E8
    Folkestone CT19 . . . . . . 178 F6
St Mary's Church* CT6 . . 24 C7
St Marys Cl CT18 . . . . . . 161 D3
St Mary's Cl
    Eastry CT13 . . . . 93 C2
    Hamstreet TN26 . . . . 183 A8
    Nonington CT15 . . . . 113 C5
    Woodnesborough CT13 . . 93 B6
St Mary's Ct
    16 Canterbury CT1 . . . . . 87 F8
    Herne Bay CT6 . . . . 22 E4
St Mary's Dr CT18 . . . . . 161 D3
St Mary's Gdns
    Chatham ME4 . . . . 10 B7
    St Mary's Bay TN29 . . . . . 195 A5
    Upstreet CT3 . . . . 47 E3
St Marys Gn TN24 . . . . . 139 E7
St Mary's Gr
    Tilmanstone CT14 . . . . . . 115 A4
    Whitstable CT5 . . . . 42 F7
St Mary's Mdw CT3 . . . . . 91 A8
St Marys Mews TN24 . . . 156 F8
St Mary's Pl ME9 . . . . 35 C7
St Marys RC Prim Sch
    CT5 . . . . 20 F2
St Mary's RC Prim Sch
    Deal CT14 . . . . 116 F3
    Gillingham ME7 . . . . 10 D6
St Mary's Rd
    5 Broadstairs CT10 . . . . . 30 B4
    Deal CT14 . . . . 117 C1
    Elham CT4 . . . . 144 F4
    Faversham ME13 . . . . 62 D7
    Gillingham ME7 . . . . 10 C6
    Minster (Thanet) CT12. . . 50 B4
    Patrixbourne CT4. . . . . . . 89 B3
    Rochester ME2 . . . . 9 B7
    St Mary in the Marsh TN28,
        TN29 . . . . 194 C5
    West Hythe CT21 . . . . . . 175 B1
St Mary's Row ME12 . . . . . 4 A6
St Mary's St CT1 . . . . 87 F8
St Mary's Terr 2 CT20 . . 178 E5
St Mary's View ME9 . . . . . 35 C7
St Matthew's Cl ME9 . . . . 35 C7
St Matthews Dr ME1 . . . . . 9 A2
St Mawes CT8 . . . . 7 C1
St Michael & All Angels
    Church 117 C4
ST MICHAELS 167 B4
St Michael's Alley 14
    CT11 . . . . 52 E6
St Michaels Ave CT9 . . . . 29 D8
St Michael's CE Inf Sch
    ME16 . . . . 74 E3
St Michael's CE Jun Sch
    ME16 . . . . 74 E3
St Michael's CE Prim Sch
    Houghton Green TN31. . . 197 C2
    Tenterden TN30 . . . . 167 A3
St Michaels Cl
    Canterbury CT2 . . . . 66 A1
    Pratling Street ME20 . . . . 53 C3

St Michael's Cl
    Chatham ME4 . . . . 9 F3
    5 Sittingbourne ME10 . . 36 F4
St Michael's Ct
    8 Folkestone CT20 . . . . 178 E5
    6 Rochester ME2 . . . . . . 9 B8
St Michael's Pl CT1 . . . . . 87 F8
St Michael's RC Prim Sch 8
    ME4 . . . . .9 F3
St Michael's Rd
    Canterbury CT2 . . . . 66 E2
    Maidstone ME16 . . . . 74 D3
    Sittingbourne ME10 . . . . . 36 F4
St Michael's St CT20 . . . 178 E5
St Michael's Terr TN30 . . 167 A3
St Michael's Wlk CT18. . . 162 F4
St Mildred's Ave
    Birchington CT7 . . . . 26 E8
    Broadstairs CT10 . . . . 30 A4
    Ramsgate CT11 . . . . 52 B5
St Mildred's Cl 4 TN30. . 179 A7
St Mildreds Ct
    Canterbury CT1 . . . . 87 E8
    Deal CT14 . . . . 117 C1
    Westgate on Sea CT8 . . . . 7 D1
St Mildred's Gdns CT8 . . . 7 D1
St Mildreds Pl CT1 . . . . . . 87 E7
St Mildreds Prim Inf Sch 6
    CT10 . . . . 30 A4
St Mildred's Rd
    Margate CT9 . . . . 8 A2
    Minster (Thanet) CT12. . . 50 B5
    Ramsgate CT11 . . . . 52 C6
    Westgate on Sea CT8 . . . . 7 C1
St Monicas
    Deal CT14 . . . . 134 C6
    Dover CT17 . . . . 166 C7
St Monicas Rd CT14 . . . . 134 C6
ST NICHOLAS AT WADE . . 25 E1
St Nicholas at Wade CE Prim
    Sch CT7 . . . . 25 E2
St Nicholas CE Inf Sch
    ME2 . . . . .9 A7
St Nicholas CE Prim Sch
    TN28 . . . . 202 B7
St Nicholas Cl
    Deal CT14 . . . . 116 F4
    Sturry CT2 . . . . 67 F7
St Nicholas Cnr CT7 . . . . . 25 F1
St Nicholas Ho CT3 . . . . . 71 D2
St Nicholas Hospl CT2. . . 66 C1
St Nicholas Lodge CT10 . 29 F4
St Nicholas Rd
    Canterbury CT1 . . . . 87 D6
    Faversham ME13 . . . . 62 A7
    Hythe CT21 . . . . 176 A2
    Littlestone-on-Sea TN28 . 202 E6
St Nicholas Rdbt CT7. . . . 26 B2
St Nicholas Sch CT13 . . . 87 F6
St Nicholas Terr 1 CT21 176 B2
St Patrick's Cl
    Deal CT14 . . . . 117 C1
    Whitstable CT5 . . . . 43 E7
St Patricks Rd
    Dover CT17 . . . . 166 A4
    Ramsgate CT11 . . . . 52 F8
St Patrick's Rd CT14 . . . . 117 C6
St Patrick's Row ME9 . . . . 59 B7
St Paul's Ave ME13 . . . . . 62 A7
St Pauls Cres ME13 . . . . . 64 A3
St Paul's Ct CT20 . . . . . . 177 E4
St Pauls Inf Sch ME14 . . . 75 A7
St Pauls Rd ME13 . . . . . . 64 A3
St Paul's Rd CT9 . . . . 8 A3
St Paul's St ME10 . . . . . . 36 E5
St Pauls Terr CT1 . . . . 88 A8
St Paul's Way CT20 . . . . . 177 D4
St Peter in Thanet CE Jun
    Sch CT10 . . . . 29 F7
ST PETER'S 29 E5
St Peter's Bridge ME14. . . 74 F4
St Peters CE Prim Sch
    Folkestone CT19 . . . . . . 178 E5
    Forstal ME20 . . . . 53 A3
St Peter's Cl ME12 . . . . 3 D6
St Peters Cotts 5 CT5 . . . 20 D2
St Peter's Ct
    Broadstairs CT10 . . . . 29 F5
    Faversham ME13 . . . . 62 B7
St Peters Footpath 2 CT9 . 8 A1
St Peter's Footpath
    Margate CT9 . . . . 7 J1
    Margate, Drapers Mill CT9 . 29 A8
St Peter's Gr CT1 . . . . 87 B7
St Peters Inf Sch ME1 . . . . 9 C3
St Peter's La CT1 . . . . 66 F1
St Peters Meth Prim Sch
    CT2 . . . . 87 F8
St Peter's Park Rd CT10 . . 29 F5
St Peter's Path ME1 . . . . . . 9 D5
St Peters Pl ME9 . . . . 60 A6
St Peter's Pl CT1, CT2 . . . 87 F8
St Peter's RC Prim Sch
    ME10 . . . . 36 D2
St Peter's Rd
    Boughton Street ME13 . . . 64 A3
    Broadstairs CT10 . . . . 29 F5
    Margate CT10, CT9 . . . . . 29 A7
    Whitstable CT5 . . . . 20 D2
St Peter's Row TN26 . . . 153 D5
St Peters Sch of English 20
    CT1 . . . . 66 F1
St Peters St 19 CT1 . . . . . 66 F1

St Peter's St
Canterbury CT1, CT2 . . . . . . 87 F8
Maidstone ME16 . . . . 74 F4
Sandwich CT13 . . . . 73 A1
St Peter St ME1 . . . . 9 D4
St Peter's Way TN26 . . . . 170 A8
St Peters Wharf Ret Pk
ME16 . . . . 74 F4
St Philip Howard RC Prim
Sch CT6 . . . . 22 E5
St Philip's Ave ME15 . . . . . 75 B2
St Pierre Ct CT14 . . . . 117 D5
ST RADIGUND'S 149 A2
St Radigund's Ct CT17 . . . 149 A1
St Radigund's Pl CT1 . . . . . 67 A1
St Radigund's Rd CT17 . . . 149 A1
St Radigunds St CT1 . . . . . 66 F1
St Richards RC Prim Sch
CT16 . . . . 149 D1
St Richard's Rd CT14 . . . . 116 F3
St Richard's Wlk CT17 . . . 166 A4
St Ronan's Cl ME15 . . . . . . 97 C7
St Saviour's CE Jun Sch
CT8 . . . . 27 E8
St Saviours Cl CT19 . . . . . 178 D7
St Saviour's Cl ME13 . . . . . 62 E7
St Saviours Ct CT8 . . . . . . 27 E8
St Saviours Rd ME15 . . . . . 97 D6
St Simon of England RC Prim
Sch TN23 . . . . 156 A8
St Simon Stock RC Sch
ME16 . . . . 74 C4
ST STEPHEN'S 66 F2
St Stephen's Cl
Canterbury CT2 . . . . 66 F2
Newington ME9 . . . . 35 C7
St Stephen's Ct CT2 . . . . . . 66 F2
St Stephens Fields 5 CT2 66 F1
St Stephen's Fields CT2 . . 66 F1
St Stephen's Gn CT2 . . . . . . 66 F3
St Stephen's Hill CT2 . . . . . 66 E4
St Stephens Ho 1 CT2 . . . 66 F1
St Stephen's Inf & Jun Sch
CT2 . . . . 66 F3
St Stephen's Lodge CT2 . . . 66 F2
St Stephen's Manor CT10 . 30 B7
St Stephens Mews ME1 . . . 31 E8
St Stephen's Mews TN23 156 A6
St Stephens Pathway 4
CT2 . . . . 66 F1
St Stephen's Rd CT2 . . . . . . 66 F2
St Stephen's Sq ME15 . . . . 74 E2
St Stephen's Way CT20 . . 177 F4
St Stephen's Wlk TN23 . . . 155 F7
St Swithin's Rd CT5 . . . . . . 21 B3
St Teresas RC Prim Sch
TN24 . . . . 139 B4
St Theresas Cl TN24 . . . . . 139 B3
St Thomas' Cross TN26 . . . 170 E3
St Thomas Hill CT2 . . . . 66 D3
St Thomas More RC Prim
Sch ME5 . . . . 32 A5
St Thomas of Canterbury RC
Prim Sch ME8 . . . . 11 B2
St Thomas' RC Prim Sch 24
CT1 . . . . 67 A1
St Thomas's Hospl CT13 . . . 72 F1
St Vincent Rd CT15 . . . . . 150 F7
St Vincent's Cl
Littlebourne CT3 . . . . 68 F1
Whitstable CT5 . . . . 43 E7
St Welcume's Way ME17 100 E6
St William of Perth Prim Sch
ME1 . . . . 9 B2
St William's Way ME1 . . . . . 9 D2
St Winifred Rd CT19 . . . . 177 F6
Salbris Cl TN29 . . . . 195 D8
Salem St ME15 . . . . 75 A3
Salisbury Ave
Broadstairs CT10 . . . . 29 F2
Gillingham ME8 . . . . 33 D8
Ramsgate CT11 . . . . 52 F8
Salisbury Cl ME10 . . . . 37 C4
Salisbury Ho
Canterbury CT2 . . . . 66 D2
4 Maidstone ME15 . . . . . . 97 D7
Salisbury Rd
Canterbury CT2 . . . . 66 E2
Chatham ME4 . . . . 10 A3
Deal CT14 . . . . 117 B2
Dover CT16 . . . . 149 D1
Folkestone CT19 . . . . 177 E7
Herne Bay CT6 . . . . 23 C5
Kit's Coty ME20 . . . . 53 D7
Maidstone ME14 . . . . 75 A6
St Margaret's at Cliffe
CT15 . . . . 151 B6
Whitstable CT5 . . . . 43 D8
Sally Port ME7 . . . . 10 A6
Sally Port Gdns ME7 . . . . . 10 B6
Salmestone Grange★ CT9 28 E8
Salmestone Prim Sch CT9 28 E8
Salmestone Rd CT9 . . . . 28 F8
Salmestone Rise CT9 . . . . . 28 E8
Salmon Cres ME12 . . . . 3 F6
Salters La ME13 . . . . 62 D4
Salter's La TN29 . . . . 199 C8
Salthouse Cl TN29 . . . . . . 199 D8
Saltings The
Iwade ME9 . . . . 14 D4
Littlestone-on-Sea TN28 . . 202 E5
16 Whitstable CT5 . . . . 20 D2
Salt Marsh La 21 CT5 . . . . . 20 D2
Salt's Ave ME15 . . . . 96 F3
Salts Cl CT5 . . . . 20 D1
Salt's Dr CT10 . . . . 29 E5
Salts La ME15 . . . . 97 A4
SALTWOOD 176 C4
Saltwood CE Prim Sch
CT21 . . . . 176 B4
Saltwood Gdns CT9 . . . . 8 E2
Saltwood Rd ME15 . . . . 74 F1
Samara Cl ME5 . . . . 32 A1
Samian Cres CT19 . . . . . . 177 C6
Samphire Cl ME14 . . . . 75 E4
Samphire Ct CT16 . . . . . . 166 E8
Samphire Hoe Ctry Pk★
CT15 . . . . 165 E2
Samuel Ct CT9 . . . . 8 A3
Samuel Dr ME10 . . . . 15 A1
Samuel Mews TN29 . . . . . 205 D7
Samuels Twr ME4 . . . . 10 B4
Sancroft Ave CT2 . . . . 66 C1
Sanctuary Cl
Broadstairs CT10 . . . . 29 F2
Kearsney CT17 . . . . 148 D4
Sanctuary Rd ME8 . . . . 11 A3
Sanctuary The CT13 . . . . . . 95 A7
Sandalwood Dr CT7 . . . . . . 25 F1
Sandbach Ho CT9 . . . . 8 B3
Sandbanks Rd ME13 . . . . . . 41 C2
Sandbourne Dr ME14 . . . . . 53 F1
Sandcroft TN28 . . . . 202 F7
Sandcroft Way ME15 . . . . . 75 A2
Sand Ct ME12 . . . . 6 G2
Sand End CT5 . . . . 43 C6
Sanderling Rd CT6 . . . . 23 F5
Sanderling Way ME9 . . . . . 14 D5
Sanders Ct ME12 . . . . 4 A5
Sandford Rd ME10 . . . . 36 B5
SANDGATE 177 E3
Sandgate Ct ME8 . . . . 33 F4
Sandgate Espl CT20,
CT21 . . . . 177 D2
Sandgate High St CT20 . . 177 E3
Sandgate Hill CT20 . . . . . 178 A4
Sandgate Prim Sch CT20 177 F4
Sandgate Rd
Folkestone CT20 . . . . 178 C4
Folkestone CT20 . . . . 178 D4
Sandgates CT4 . . . . 143 E7
Sandhurst Cl
Canterbury CT2 . . . . 67 A4
Gillingham ME8 . . . . 11 C3
Sandhurst Rd CT9 . . . . 8 F2
Sandilands TN24 . . . . 139 E2
Sandle's Rd CT7 . . . . 26 F7
SANDLING 53 F1
Sandling Cl TN23 . . . . 155 F6
Sandling Ct ME14 . . . . 75 B7
Sandling La ME14 . . . . 75 A8
Sandling Park Woodland
Gdn★ TN25 . . . . 175 E6
Sandling Prim Sch ME14 . . 75 B8
Sandling Rd
Hythe CT21 . . . . 175 F6
Maidstone ME14 . . . . 74 F6
Maidstone, Ringlestone
ME14 . . . . 74 F7
Sandling Sta CT21 . . . . . . 175 F6
Sandown Cl CT14 . . . . 95 D1
Sandown Cotts
Margate CT9 . . . . 8 A3
Teynham ME9 . . . . 38 E1
Sandown Ct CT14 . . . . 117 C7
Sandown Dr
Gillingham ME8 . . . . 33 D7
Herne Bay CT6 . . . . 22 D4
Sandown Lees CT13 . . . . . . 94 D8
Sandown Pl CT14 . . . . 117 C7
Sandown Prim Sch CT14 117 C7
Sandown Rd
Deal CT14 . . . . 117 D8
Sandwich CT13 . . . . 94 B8
Sandpiper Ct 3 CT7 . . . . . . 26 F8
Sandpiper La ME9 . . . . 14 E3
Sandpiper Rd
Chatham ME5 . . . . 32 D2
Hawkinge CT18 . . . . 163 A3
Whitstable CT5 . . . . 43 B7
Sandpit Hill CT3 . . . . 47 C4
Sandra Ct 5 ME2 . . . . 9 B8
Sandringham Ho ME1 . . . . . 9 B4
Sandringham Rd ME8 . . . . . 33 E3
Sandstone Ct CT20 . . . . . 178 A3
Sandstone Dr ME10 . . . . . . 36 E8
Sandstone Rise ME5 . . . . . . 54 C8
SANDWAY 101 A3
Sandway Rd ME17 . . . . . . 100 F4
SANDWICH 73 B1
Sandwich Bay Bird Obsy★
CT13 . . . . 94 E7
Sandwich Cl CT20 . . . . . . 177 F5
Sandwich Guildhall Mus★
CT13 . . . . 72 F1
Sandwich Ind Est CT13 . . . 73 B1
Sandwich Inf Sch CT13 . . . 72 F1
Sandwich Jun Sch CT13 . . . 93 F7
Sandwich Rd
Ash CT3 . . . . 71 F1
Cliffs End CT12 . . . . 51 D4
Eastry CT13 . . . . 93 C3
Eythorne CT15 . . . . 131 C8
Nonington CT15, CT3 . . . . 113 F6
Sandwich CT13, CT14 . . . . . 93 D5
Whitfield CT15, CT16 . . . . 149 A7
Woodnesborough CT13 . . . . 93 D7
Sandwich Sta CT13 . . . . 94 A8
Sandwich Tech Sch CT13 . . 93 F6
Sandwood Rd
Ramsgate CT10 . . . . 29 F1
Sandwich CT13 . . . . 93 F8
Sandy Cnr TN26 . . . . 154 F5
Sandy Dell ME7 . . . . 33 A3
Sandyhurst La TN25 . . . . . 139 B8
Sandy La
Ashford TN24 . . . . 140 B1
Daniel's Water TN26 . . . . . 154 E6
Hythe CT20, CT21 . . . . 177 B3
Maidstone, Harbourland
ME14 . . . . 75 C8
Maidstone, Penenden Heath
ME14 . . . . 75 C7
Maidstone, Ware Street
ME14 . . . . 76 B5
Tenterden TN30 . . . . 179 B7
Sandy Mount ME14 . . . . 76 B5
Sandy Pl TN25 . . . . 158 D5
Sanger Cl CT9 . . . . 7 I1
Sangro Pl CT1 . . . . 67 D1
San Remo CT8 . . . . 7 C1
Sanspareil Ave ME12 . . . . . . 4 A6
Santon La CT3 . . . . 70 E8
Sappers Wlk ME7 . . . . 10 C5
Sapphire Cl ME10 . . . . 36 C7
Saracen Cl ME7 . . . . 11 A1
Saracen Fields ME5 . . . . . . 54 C8
Sarafand Ho ME1 . . . . 9 B4
Sarah Gdns CT9 . . . . 29 D8
Sark Cl TN29 . . . . 195 C8
SARRE 48 D7
Sarre Ct CT7 . . . . 48 D6
Sarre Pl CT13 . . . . 93 F8
Sarre Windmill★ CT7 . . . . 48 D7
Sarsen Hts ME5 . . . . 31 F1
Sassoon Cl CT18 . . . . 163 A4
Satis Ave ME10 . . . . 36 E7
SATMAR 164 D3
Satmar La CT15, CT18 . . . 164 E4
Satmore La CT18 . . . . 164 C4
Saunders La CT3 . . . . 71 F1
Saunders St
7 Chatham ME4 . . . . 9 F3
Gillingham ME7 . . . . 10 C6
Saunders Way TN31 . . . . . 203 A2
Savage Rd ME5 . . . . 32 B3
Savernake Dr CT6 . . . . 23 B2
Savoy The 8 CT11 . . . . 52 C6
Saw Lodge Field TN23 . . . 156 C4
Sawpit Rd ME9 . . . . 59 B2
Sawyers Ct ME4 . . . . 10 B2
Saxon Ave ME12 . . . . 4 B6
Saxon Cl CT21 . . . . 176 E2
Saxon Rd
Bridge CT4 . . . . 89 A1
Faversham ME13 . . . . 62 C7
Ramsgate CT11 . . . . 52 B6
Westgate on Sea CT8 . . . . . . 7 D1
Saxons Cl CT14 . . . . 117 C8
Saxons Dr ME14 . . . . 75 B7
Saxon Shore
Sittingbourne ME10 . . . . 15 A1
Whitstable CT5 . . . . 43 C8
Saxon St 9 CT17 . . . . 166 D8
Saxon Way Prim Sch ME7 10 E6
Saxon Wlk ME9 . . . . 14 D4
Saxton Rd TN29 . . . . 206 E5
Saxton St ME7 . . . . 10 C5
Sayer Rd TN27 . . . . 120 C8
Sayers La 6 TN30 . . . . 179 A7
Scaffold St TN29 . . . . 209 D2
Scanlons Bridge Rd
Folkestone CT21 . . . . 177 C2
Hythe CT21 . . . . 176 A2
Scarborough Dr ME12 . . . . . 4 C8
Scarlett Cl ME5 . . . . 32 C5
Sceales Dr CT12 . . . . 51 D6
Sceptre Way CT5 . . . . 43 B7
School Ave ME7 . . . . 10 E4
School Cl The CT8 . . . . 7 C1
School Hill CT4 . . . . 107 B8
School Ho ME10 . . . . 36 E3
School La
Bekesbourne CT4 . . . . 89 C4
Blean CT2 . . . . 66 A6
Borden ME9 . . . . 35 F4
Boughton Street ME13 . . . . 63 F3
Fordwich CT2 . . . . 68 A4
Goodnestone CT3 . . . . 91 D2
Herne Bay CT6 . . . . 23 B1
Hoath CT3 . . . . 46 E6
Ickham CT3 . . . . 90 C8
Iwade ME9 . . . . 14 C4
Lower Halstow ME9 . . . . 13 B2
Lower Hardres CT4 . . . . . . 110 B6
Maidstone ME15 . . . . 75 E1
Newington ME9 . . . . 35 B7
Peasmarsh TN31 . . . . 196 B2
Platt's Heath ME17 . . . . . . 100 F2
Ramsgate CT11 . . . . 52 E7
Sittingbourne ME9 . . . . 37 D2
Stalisfield Green ME13 . . . 103 D6
Staple CT3 . . . . 92 A6
Stourmouth CT3 . . . . 48 E2
Wingham CT3 . . . . 91 A7
School Mews ME9 . . . . 14 E4
School Path CT3 . . . . 89 F7
School Rd
Appledore Heath TN26 . . . 181 C1
Ash CT3 . . . . 71 C2
Bethersden TN26 . . . . 153 D4
Charing TN27 . . . . 120 C8
Densole CT18 . . . . 162 E7
Faversham ME13 . . . . 62 C6
Hothfield TN26 . . . . 138 A7
Hythe CT21 . . . . 176 B4
Sandwich CT13 . . . . 72 F1
Sittingbourne ME10 . . . . 37 B3
Tilmanstone CT14 . . . . 114 F4
School View ME9 . . . . 58 C8
Schrieber Mews ME7 . . . . . 10 D5
Scimitar Cl ME7 . . . . 11 A1
Scocles Cotts ME12 . . . . 4 C5
Scocles Rd ME12 . . . . 4 C5
Scoggers Hill ME13 . . . . . . 85 A7
Scoones Cl ME9 . . . . 37 E2
Scotby Ave ME5 . . . . 32 B4
Scotchmen Cl ME12 . . . . 3 E7
Scotland Comm CT16 . . . . 148 D4
Scot's La TN25 . . . . 159 F8
Scott Ave
Canterbury CT1 . . . . 87 E5
Gillingham ME8 . . . . 12 A1
Scotteswood Ave ME4 . . . . . 9 F2
Scotton St TN25 . . . . 123 F2
Scott St ME14 . . . . 74 F6
Scott's Terr ME4 . . . . 9 F3
Scragged Oak Rd
Detling ME14 . . . . 55 C5
Hucking ME17 . . . . 56 C1
Scrapsgate Rd ME12 . . . . 4 A7
Scraps Hill ME9 . . . . 37 F4
Scrubbs La ME16 . . . . 74 D4
Sea App ME12 . . . . 6 E4
Seabourne Cl TN29 . . . . . . 195 B6
Seabourne Way TN29 . . . . 195 B7
Seabrook CE Prim Sch
CT21 . . . . 177 B2
Seabrook Ct CT21 . . . . 177 B3
Seabrook Gdns CT21 . . . . 177 B2
Seabrook Gr CT21 . . . . . . 177 A2
Seabrook Rd CT21 . . . . . . 176 E2
Seabrook Vale CT21 . . . . . 177 B4
Seacroft Rd CT10 . . . . 30 A1
Seadown Cl CT21 . . . . 177 A4
Seafield Rd
Broadstairs CT10 . . . . 30 A4
Ramsgate CT11 . . . . 52 C6
Whitstable CT5 . . . . 21 B3
Seaford Ct ME1 . . . . 9 B5
Seagar Rd ME13 . . . . 40 B1
Seager Rd ME12 . . . . 1 F2
Seagrave Cres CT19 . . . . . 178 F6
Sealand Ct ME1 . . . . 9 B5
Seamark Cl CT12 . . . . 49 D7
Seamark Rd CT12, CT7 . . . . 26 E2
Sea Meadows Sch CT10 . . 29 E7
Seapoint Rd CT10 . . . . 30 B3
Sea Rd
Deal CT14 . . . . 134 D6
Hythe CT21 . . . . 177 A2
Westgate on Sea CT8 . . . . . . 7 C1
SEASALTER 43 A7
Seasalter Beach CT5 . . . . . 43 A7
Seasalter Cl ME12 . . . . 6 E4
Seasalter Cross CT5 . . . . . . 43 A6
Seasalter La CT5 . . . . 43 A5
Seasalter Rd ME13 . . . . 41 E3
Seascape 10 CT20 . . . . 177 E3
Seaside Ave ME12 . . . . 4 C8
Sea St
Herne Bay CT6 . . . . 22 C3
St Margaret's at Cliffe
CT15 . . . . 151 A6
Whitstable CT5 . . . . 20 D2
Seathorpe Ave ME12 . . . . . . 4 C8
Seaths Cnr CT3 . . . . 91 A7
SEATON 69 D2
Seaton Ave CT21 . . . . 176 B3
Seaton Cotts TN25 . . . . . . 122 E3
Seaton Rd
Gillingham ME7 . . . . 10 E3
Wickhambreaux CT3 . . . . . . 69 D2
Seaview Ave ME12 . . . . 6 H1
Sea View Ave CT7 . . . . 26 E8
Sea View Cl CT18 . . . . 164 B1
Seaview Cotts 6 CT10 . . . . 30 B4
Sea View Cotts ME9 . . . . . . 13 B3
Seaview Ct CT10 . . . . 30 B3
Sea View Gdns ME12 . . . . . . 6 E3
Seaview Ho CT19 . . . . 178 D8
Seaview Hts TN29 . . . . 195 C7
Sea View Hts CT7 . . . . 26 D8
Seaview Rd
Gillingham ME7 . . . . 10 C4
Greatstone-on-Sea TN28 . . 202 E1
Sea View Rd
Birchington CT7 . . . . 26 E8
Broadstairs CT10 . . . . 30 A6
Cliffs End CT12 . . . . 51 D6
Herne Bay CT6 . . . . 23 C5
St Margaret's at Cliffe
CT15 . . . . 150 F4
Sea View Sq CT6 . . . . 22 F5
Sea View Terr
Folkestone CT20 . . . . 177 D3
Margate CT9 . . . . 7 G2
Minster (Sheppey) ME12 . . . . 5 A5
Seaville Dr CT6 . . . . 23 E5
Sea Wall
Dymchurch TN29 . . . . 195 D8
Whitstable CT5 . . . . 20 D2
Seaway Cotts CT5 . . . . 20 C1
Seaway Cres TN29 . . . . 194 F4
Seaway Gdns TN29 . . . . . . 194 F4
Seaway Rd TN29 . . . . 195 A4
Second Ave
Broadstairs CT10 . . . . 8 G2
Chatham ME4 . . . . 10 C1
Eastchurch ME12 . . . . 5 F5
Gillingham ME7 . . . . 10 E3
Margate CT9 . . . . 8 B3
Rushenden ME11 . . . . 2 F3
Sheerness ME12 . . . . 1 C1
Secretan Rd ME1 . . . . 9 B1
Secret Gdns of Sandwich
The★ CT13 . . . . 73 A1
Sedge Cres ME5 . . . . 31 E4
Sedgemoor Ho ME1 . . . . 9 E5
Sedley Cl ME8 . . . . 33 C3
SEED 81 A6
Seeshill Cl CT5 . . . . 43 E8
Segrave Rd CT19 . . . . 178 F5
Selbey Cl CT6 . . . . 23 C4
Selborne Ho CT17 . . . . . . 166 C7
Selborne Rd CT9 . . . . 29 B8
Selbourne Rd ME7 . . . . 10 D7
Selbourne Terr CT17 . . . . 166 C7
Selbourne Wlk ME15 . . . . . 97 F6
Selby Ct ME9 . . . . 38 D2
Selby Rd ME15 . . . . 97 F4
Selkirk Rd CT16 . . . . 149 B3
SELLINDGE 159 D1
Sellindge Prim Sch
TN25 . . . . 159 C1
SELLING 84 C6
Selling CE Prim Sch ME13 84 B6
Selling Ct ME13 . . . . 84 C5
Sellinge Gn ME8 . . . . 11 C3
Selling Rd
Chilham CT4 . . . . 85 B3
Faversham ME13 . . . . 62 F3
Selling ME13 . . . . 84 E6
Selling St ME13 . . . . 84 B6
Selling Sta ME13 . . . . 84 E7
Selsea Ave CT6 . . . . 22 D4
SELSON 93 A3
Selstead Cl ME8 . . . . 11 C2
SELSTED 146 B5
Selsted CE Prim Sch
CT15 . . . . 146 C6
Selway Ct CT14 . . . . 117 B3
Selwood Cl ME12 . . . . 3 E6
Selwyn Ct CT10 . . . . 29 F5
Selwyn Dr CT10 . . . . 29 F5
Semaphore Rd CT7 . . . . 26 F8
Semple Cl CT12 . . . . 50 C7
Semple Gdns ME4 . . . . 9 E3
Senacre La ME15 . . . . 97 E6
Senacre Sq ME15 . . . . 97 F7
Senacre Wood Prim Sch
ME15 . . . . 97 F7
Sene Pk CT21 . . . . 176 D3
Senlac Cl CT11 . . . . 52 B6
Serene Ct 12 CT10 . . . . 30 B4
Serene Pl 9 CT10 . . . . 30 B4
Sessions House Sq ME14 . 74 F5
Setford Rd ME5 . . . . 32 C6
Setterfield Ho CT21 . . . . . 176 D2
Setterfield Rd CT9 . . . . 7 J1
Settington Ave ME5 . . . . . . 10 C1
Sevastopol Pl CT1 . . . . 67 D1
Sevenacre Rd ME13 . . . . . . 62 C8
Sevenscore CT12 . . . . 51 A5
Sevenscore Farm Cotts
CT12 . . . . 51 A5
Seven Stones Dr CT10 . . . . 30 A1
Severn Rd ME5 . . . . 32 C5
SEVINGTON 157 B6
Sevington La TN24 . . . . . . 157 A7
Sevington Pk ME15 . . . . 96 F6
Sewell Cl CT7 . . . . 27 A6
Sexburga Dr ME12 . . . . 4 B8
Sextant Pk ME2 . . . . 9 E6
Seymour Ave
Westgate on Sea CT9 . . . . . . 7 D1
Whitstable CT5 . . . . 20 E1
Seymour Cl CT6 . . . . 23 B1
Seymour Pl CT1 . . . . 87 E7
Seymour Rd
1 Chatham ME5 . . . . 10 B3
Gillingham ME8 . . . . 12 C1
St Margaret's at Cliffe
CT15 . . . . 150 F8
Seymour Villas 10 CT20 . . 177 F3
Shackleton Cl ME5 . . . . 32 B6
SHADOXHURST 170 A8
Shadoxhurst Rd TN26 . . . . 169 C7
Shaftesbury Ave CT19 . . . 177 E7
Shaftesbury Ct CT14 . . . . 117 D2
Shaftesbury Dr ME16 . . . . . 74 C4
Shaftesbury Rd
Canterbury CT2 . . . . 66 F3
Hersden CT3 . . . . 46 E1
Whitstable CT5 . . . . 20 D1
Shaftsbury St CT11 . . . . 52 F7
Shah Pl CT11 . . . . 52 D7
Shakespeare Ct CT17 . . . . 166 B7
Shakespeare Pas CT9 . . . . . 7 H2
Shakespeare Rd
Birchington CT7 . . . . 27 A8
Dover CT17 . . . . 166 B6
Gillingham ME7 . . . . 10 C3
Margate CT9 . . . . 7 J1
Sittingbourne ME10 . . . . 37 A4
Shakespeare Terr 12
CT20 . . . . 178 C4
Shalder Ho ME7 . . . . 10 D7
Shalfleet Cl 1 ME5 . . . . 32 A7
Shalloak Rd CT2 . . . . 67 D6
Shallows Rd CT10 . . . . 29 D6
Shalmsford Ct CT4 . . . . 86 C2
Shalmsford Rd CT4 . . . . 85 E2
Shalmsford St CT4 . . . . 86 B2
SHALMSFORD STREET 86 B1
Shamel Bsns Ctr ME2 . . . . . 9 C7
Shamley Rd ME5 . . . . 32 D2
Shamrock Ave CT5 . . . . 43 B7
Shanklin Cl ME5 . . . . 32 C8
Shapland Cl CT6 . . . . 23 C3
Share & Coulter Rd CT5 . . . 21 D1
Sharfleet Cres ME9 . . . . . . 14 D4
Sharon Cres ME5 . . . . 31 F4
Sharps Gn ME8 . . . . 11 D5
Sharsted Hill ME9 . . . . 81 C8
Sharsted Way
Gillingham ME7 . . . . 33 A3

Sharsted Way continued
Maidstone ME14 76 B5
SHATTERLING 70 E1
Shatterlocks Inf Sch 7
CT16 149 B2
Shaw Cl ME14 75 C7
Shaw Cross TN24 139 D5
Shawdon Ave CT13 95 A7
Shawstead Rd ME7, ME7 32 D5
Shaws Way ME1 9 C3
Sheal's Cres ME15 75 A2
Sheals Ct ME15 75 A2
Shearers Cl ME14 75 E4
Shearwater ME16 74 B5
Shearwater Ave CT5 43 C7
Shearwater Ct ME12 3 B8
Shearwater Ho TN29 195 A3
Shear Way TN29 186 C5
Shearway Bsns Pk CT19 177 F7
Shearway Rd CT19 177 F7
Sheen Ct CT9 7 I2
Sheep Ct La CT4 126 A3
Sheepfold La TN23 156 C4
SHEERNESS 1 D3
Sheerness Harbour Est
ME12 1 B3
Sheerness Heritage Ctr★
ME12 1 D2
Sheerness-on-Sea Sta
ME12 1 C2
Sheerness Swim Pool
ME12 1 C3
Sheerstone ME9 14 D4
SHEERWATER 70 F6
Sheerwater Rd CT3 70 F5
Sheerways ME13 62 A6
Sheet Glass Rd ME11 3 A3
Sheffield Gdns CT14 117 C4
Shelden Dr ME8 33 F8
Sheldon Bsns Ctr ME2 9 D8
Sheldon Cl CT3 113 A6
Shelduck Cl ME9 14 E4
SHELDWICH 83 C6
Sheldwich Cl
3 Ashford TN23 155 F6
Ashford TN23 156 A6
SHELDWICH LEES 83 C5
Sheldwich Prim Sch
ME13 83 C6
Shellbeach ME12 19 D6
Shelley Ave CT1 67 C2
Shelley Rd ME16 74 C2
Shelley Rise ME1 9 A3
Shell Grotto★ 15 CT9 7 J2
Shellness Rd ME12 19 D7
Shellons St CT20 178 D5
SHELVIN 129 C3
Shelvin La CT4 129 C3
Shenley Gr ME14 53 F2
Shepherd Cl TN23 155 E5
Shepherd Dr TN24 157 A8
Shepherd Neame Brewery★
16 ME13 62 D7
Shepherd's Close Rd CT4 89 E1
Shepherds Cl Rd CT4 89 E1
Shepherd's Cross CT15 132 B1
Shepherdsgate CT2 66 F1
Shepherds Gate ME7 32 F5
Shepherdsgate Dr CT6 46 A8
Shepherds Gate Dr ME14 75 E6
SHEPHERDS HILL 84 A4
Shepherds Way
Langley Heath ME17 98 E4
Whitstable CT5 44 C8
SHEPHERDSWELL OR
SIBERTSWOLD 130 E5
Shepherdswell Rd CT15 131 A7
Shepherds Well Sta★
CT15 130 D5
Shepherds Wlk
Hythe CT21 175 E1
Whitstable CT5 44 C8
Shepperton Cl ME5 32 C4
Sheppey Cl 3 CT7 27 A7
Sheppey Coll ME12 1 C3
Sheppey Community Hospl
ME12 4 A5
Sheppey Cotts ME12 1 E2
Sheppey Leisure Complex
The ME12 1 D3
Sheppey Little Theatre★
ME12 1 C2
Sheppey Rd ME15 97 A7
Sheppey St ME12 1 B2
Sheppey Terr ME12 4 F5
Sheppey View CT5 43 C6
Sheppey Way
Iwade ME9 14 F6
Queenborough ME12, ME9 3 D2
Sittingbourne ME9 36 B7
SHEPWAY 97 D8
Shepway TN24 139 E5
Shepway Cl CT19 178 D6
Shepway Cross CT21 175 B3
Shepway Ct ME15 97 C8
Sheraton Ct ME5 31 F1
Sherbourne Dr ME16 74 B2
Sheridale Bsns Ctr ME2 9 A6
Sheridan Cl
Chatham ME5 32 C7
Maidstone ME14 74 E8
Sheridan Ct ME1 9 A2
Sheridan Rd CT16 149 B3
Sheriff Dr ME5 32 A2
Sheringham Cl ME16 74 D7
Sheringham Ho 5 ME15 97 D8
Sherman Cl ME7 11 B1
Shernolds ME15 97 B7
Shernold Sch ME16 74 D5
Sheron Cl CT14 117 A5
Sherriffs Court La CT12 49 E6
Sherwood Ave ME5 32 A2
Sherwood Cl
Ashford TN24 139 D7
Faversham ME13 40 B1
Herne Bay CT6 23 C2
Whitstable CT5 43 C6
Sherwood Ct CT8 7 C1
Sherwood Dr CT5 43 C6
Sherwood Gdns CT11 29 E1
Sherwood Ho ME5 32 A3
Sherwood Rd CT7 26 F5
Shillingheld Cl ME14 75 F5
Shimmin Rd ME9 58 D5
Ship Cl TN29 195 C8
Ship La ME1 9 E4
SHIPLAND 136 D8
Shipland Hos TN27 136 D8
Shipley Ct ME14 75 A4
Shipley Mill CL TN23 156 C4
Shipman Ave CT2 87 C8
Shipmans Way CT16 149 A3
Ship St CT19 178 D6
Shipway Ho CT21 176 D1
Shipwrights Ave ME4 10 B2
Shipwrights Lee CT5 20 C2
Shipyard Area ME13 40 D1
Shire La ME13 103 C6
Shireway Cl CT19 178 A7
SHIRKOAK 169 A5
Shirkoak Pk TN26 169 A5
Shirley Ave
Chatham ME5 31 D5
Ramsgate CT11 29 E1
Shirley Ct ME15 97 E5
Shirley Way ME15 76 A3
Shoebury Terr ME12 5 A5
SHOLDEN 116 F5
Sholden Bank CT14 116 E4
Sholden CE Prim Sch
CT14 116 F5
Sholden New Rd CT14 116 F6
Shooters Chase ME9 14 D4
Shooters Hill CT15 131 C8
Shooter's Hill 5 CT17 149 C1
Shore Cl
Birchington CT7 26 D8
Herne Bay CT6 22 B3
Shorefields ME8 12 B2
Shoregate La ME9 12 F6
Shoreham La TN30 167 A3
Shoreham Wlk ME15 97 F7
Shorland Ct ME1 9 B5
Shorncliffe Cres CT20 177 E5
Shorncliffe Ind Est CT20 177 D4
Shorncliffe Rd CT20 177 F5
Short La
Alkham CT15 147 D1
Snargate TN29 191 D6
Shortlands Gn ME15 97 F5
Shortlands Rd ME10 37 B4
Short's Prospect ME12 17 C8
Short St
3 Chatham ME4 10 B3
Chillenden CT3 114 A8
5 Sandwich CT13 73 A1
Sheerness ME12 1 C2
Shorts Way ME1 9 A3
Shotfield Cl CT3 70 C6
Shottendane Rd CT9, CT8 28 C7
SHOTTENDEN 84 D1
Shottenden La CT4 106 A7
Shottenden Rd
Gillingham ME7 10 D7
Shottenden CT4, ME13 105 D8
Shrimpton Cl CT4 85 B3
Shropshire Terr 1 ME15 97 E7
Shrubbery The CT14 117 C1
Shrubcote TN30 179 C7
Shrub Hill Rd CT5 44 D7
Shrubsole Ave ME12 1 D1
Shrubsole Dr ME14 53 F3
Shuart La CT7 25 F4
Shunters Cl ME13 62 E6
Shurland Ave
Leysdown-on-Sea ME12 6 H1
Minster (Sheppey) ME12 4 B6
Sittingbourne ME10 36 F1
Shutler Rd CT10 30 B5
SHUTTLEFIELD 162 A6
Shuttlesfield La CT4 144 D1
Sibert's Cl CT15 130 F5
Sibertswold CE Prim Sch
CT15 130 E4
SIBERTSWOLD OR
SHEPHERDSWELL 130 E5
Sidings Cl ME13 62 E6
Sidings The
Dymchurch TN29 195 B7
Lyminge CT18 161 C7
Whitstable CT5 20 E2
Sidney Cooper Gall★ CT1 66 F1
Sidney Rd
Gillingham ME7 10 C7
Rochester ME1 9 A2
Sidney St
Folkestone CT19 178 E7
Maidstone ME16 74 C2
Signal Ct 6 ME8 11 F1
Silchester Ct ME14 75 C7
Silecroft Ct TN23 138 E1
Silvanus Ho 5 CT11 52 D7
Silver Ave CT7 27 B6
Silver Bank ME5 32 A6
Silverbirch Ct TN26 155 A1
Silver Birch Ct TN26 155 A1
Silver Birches
Chatham ME5 32 A3
Sheerness ME12 1 H1
Silver Birches Mobile Homes
Pk TN26 171 A4
Silver Birch Gr TN23 156 B4
Silverdale ME16 74 A2
Silverdale Ave ME12 4 A6
Silverdale Dr
Gillingham ME8 33 F7
Herne Bay CT6 23 D2
Silverdale Gr ME10 36 D3
Silverdale Rd CT11 52 A5
Silver Hill
Chatham ME4 9 F3
Rochester ME1 9 A2
Tenterden TN30 167 B1
Silver Hill Gdns
Ashford TN24 140 A1
4 Chatham ME4 9 F3
Silver Hill Rd TN24 140 A1
Silverlands Rd CT18 161 C7
Silverspot Cl ME8 33 F7
Silver St
Deal CT14 117 D7
Silver Street ME9 57 F5
Silvers The CT10 29 C4
SILVER STREET 57 F5
Silver Tree ME5 32 B1
Silverweed Rd ME5 31 F4
Simmonds La ME15 98 B6
Simmonds Rd CT1 87 E7
Simon Ave CT9 8 D2
Simone Weil Ave TN24 139 B4
Simon Langton Girls Gram
Sch CT1 88 C5
Simon Langton Gram Sch for
Boys CT4 88 A4
Simon's Ave TN23 155 F7
Simpson Rd ME10 36 C5
Sinclair Cl ME8 33 E5
Sindal Shaw Ho ME5 31 E4
Singapore Dr ME7 10 B5
Singer Ave CT6 22 B4
Singledge Ave CT16 148 F6
Singledge La CT15 131 C2
SINGLETON 155 E7
Singleton Cl CT12 50 B6
Singleton Ctr The TN23 155 D8
Singleton Hill TN23 155 D8
Singleton Rd TN23 138 C1
Sion Hill CT11 52 E6
Sion Pass 12 CT11 52 E6
Sir Evelyn Rd ME1 9 B1
Sir John Fogge Ave
TN23 138 F4
Sir John Hawkins Hospl
ME4 9 E4
Sir John Hawkins Way ME4 9 F4
Sir John Moore Ave
CT21 176 B2
Sir John Moore Ct 5
CT20 177 E3
Sir Joseph Williamson's
Mathematical Sch ME1 9 C1
Sir Roger Manwoods Sch
CT13 94 B8
Sir Thomas Longley Rd
ME2 9 E6
Siskin Cl
Ashford TN25 139 B7
Hawkinge CT18 162 F4
Sissinghurst Dr ME16 74 B4
SITTINGBOURNE 36 D8
Sittingbourne Com Coll
ME10 37 C2
Sittingbourne Ind Pk
ME10 36 F5
Sittingbourne & Kemsley
Light Rly★ ME10 37 A7
Sittingbourne Meml Hospl
ME10 36 F3
Sittingbourne Rd
Maidstone, Detling ME14 75 E8
Maidstone, Penenden Heath
ME14 75 B6
Sittingbourne Retail Pk
ME10 36 F5
Sittingbourne Sta★ ME10 36 F4
Sittingbourne Sta ME10 36 F4
Six Bells Pk TN26 169 A3
Six Fields Path TN30 179 A7
SIXMILE 143 D5
SKEETE 160 D7
Skeete Rd CT18 160 D7
Skene Cl ME8 12 A1
Skinner Rd TN29 205 C6
Skinner's Alley 3 CT5 20 D1
Skinners Cl ME20 53 A6
Skinner St
Chatham ME4 9 F3
Gillingham ME7 10 C5
Skinner Street Prim Sch 12
ME7 10 C6
Skinner's Way ME17 98 E4
Skye Cl ME15 97 A7
Skylark Way TN23 156 D3
SLADE 80 E1
Slade Cl ME5 32 B2
Slade Rd ME17 102 D8
Slades Cl CT5 44 C8
Slatin Rd ME2 9 B8
Sleigh Rd CT2 67 F6
Slicketts Hill ME4 10 A4
Slip La CT15 147 C2
Slipway Rd ME12 1 A3
Sloe La CT10, CT9 29 B6
Slough Rd ME9 59 A3
SLUTSHOLE 64 A5
SLY CORNER 181 F5
SMALL HYTHE 179 C1
Small Hythe Cl ME15 76 B2
Smallhythe Place (Mus)★
TN30 179 C1
Small Hythe Rd TN30 179 B4
SMARDEN 135 A1
Smarden Prim Sch TN27 135 A1
Smarden Rd TN27 136 B6
Smarden Wlk ME8 12 B1
Smarts Cotts ME14 76 C4
Smeed Cl 4 ME10 37 B4
Smeed-Dean Ctr The
ME10 37 A4
SMEETH 158 C4
Smeeth Prim Sch TN25 158 D5
Smith Rd ME5 32 B3
Smiths Orch ME9 57 F5
Smith St ME2 9 A6
Smithy Dr TN23 156 C4
Smugglers Leap Cvn Pk
CT12 50 C8
Smuggler's Way CT7 27 A8
Snakes Hill CT3 91 A5
SNARGATE 191 E6
Snargate La TN29 191 C5
Snargate St CT17 166 D7
Snelgrove Ho 14 CT16 166 D8
Snell Gdns CT6 22 B2
Snipe Cl TN25 139 C7
SNIPESHILL 37 D4
Snodhurst Ave ME5 31 E5
Snodhurst Ho 2 ME5 32 A7
Snowbell Rd TN23 156 B4
Snowdon Ave ME14 75 B5
Snowdon Cl ME5 32 B7
Snowdon Par ME14 75 C5
SNOWDOWN 113 A3
Snowdown Ct CT3 112 F5
Snowdown Sta CT15 113 B3
Snowdrop Cl CT19 178 C8
Snow Ho ME7 10 E7
Sobraon Way CT1 67 D1
Solar Ct CT12 52 C7
Solent Gdns ME5 32 B8
Soleshill Rd CT4 84 E1
SOLE STREET 125 B7
Sole Street Cotts CT4 125 B7
Solomon Ho CT14 117 B3
Solomon Rd ME8 12 A1
Solomons La ME13 62 D7
Solomons Rd ME4 9 F4
Somerfield Barn Ct
TN25 174 C8
Somerfield Cl ME16 74 D5
Somerfield Hospl The
ME16 74 E5
Somerfield La ME16 74 D4
Somerfield Rd ME16 74 D4
Somerset Cl
Chatham ME5 32 C8
Sittingbourne ME10 36 C4
Whitstable CT5 43 B7
Somerset Ct
2 Broadstairs CT10 30 A4
Deal CT14 117 B3
Ramsgate CT12 29 B2
Somerset Rd
Ashford TN24 139 B3
Canterbury CT1 88 D8
Deal CT14 117 C3
Folkestone CT19 177 E6
Maidstone ME15 97 C8
Somme Ct CT1 67 D1
Sommerville Cl ME13 62 E7
Somner Cl CT2 66 D1
Somner Wlk ME15 97 F4
Sondes Cl CT6 23 A2
Sondes Rd CT14 117 D5
Sonora Way ME10 36 C7
Sorrell Rd ME5 31 F4
Sotherton TN24 156 E7
Souberg Cl CT14 117 C8
SOUTH ALKHAM 164 B8
Southall Cl CT12 50 C7
SOUTH ASHFORD 156 A8
South Ave
Aylesham CT15 113 A3
Gillingham ME8 11 B2
Sittingbourne ME10 37 A3
South Avenue Jun & Inf Schs
ME10 37 A3
South Bank of the Swale
Nature Reserve★ ME13 41 A6
South Barham Rd CT4 128 E6
South Borough Prim Sch
ME15 75 A2
Southbourne TN23 155 E5
Southbourne Gr ME5 32 A4
Southbourne Rd CT19 178 E5
South Brooks Rd TN29 207 H6
South Bush La ME8 34 B6
South Camber Way CT16 150 B1
South Canterbury Rd CT1 88 A6
South Cl CT1 88 A8
South Cliff Par CT10 30 B1
South Court Dr CT3 91 A7
South Cres ME17 96 C4
South Ct
Deal CT14 117 D6
Ramsgate CT12 29 B2
Southdown Rd ME12 3 E6
South Eastern Rd
Ramsgate CT11 52 D7
Rochester ME2 9 C7
Southenay La TN25 159 C4
Southern Way CT19 178 E6
Southernwood Rise
CT20 177 F4
South Exit Rd CT16 166 G8
Southfields ME1 9 C3
South Foreland Lighthouse★
CT15 150 F3
Southgate Rd TN30 179 C7
South Goodwin Ct CT14 117 D8
SOUTH GREEN 57 A5
South Green La ME9 56 F6
Southill Rd ME4 9 F3
South Kent Coll (Asford
Campus) TN23 156 A8
South Kent Coll (Dover
Campus) 16 CT16 166 D8
South Kent Coll (Folkestone
Campus) CT20 178 B5
South Kent Coll (South
Ashford Campus) TN23 155 F6
South Lea TN23 156 A3
Southlees La ME9 56 F3
South Lodge CT5 20 E3
South Lodge Cl CT5 20 E3
Southmead Cl CT19 178 A6
South Military Rd CT17 166 C5
South Motto TN23 156 B5
South of England Rare
Breeds Ctr★ TN26 169 D1
Southover Ct 2 CT20 177 E3
South Park Bsns Village
ME15 75 A1
South Pondside Rd ME4 10 A8
South Quay ME13 40 D1
South Rd
Chatham, Brompton ME4,
ME7 10 A7
Chatham ME4 10 B7
Dover CT17 166 B8
Faversham ME13 62 C7
Herne Bay CT6 23 A5
Hythe CT21 176 D1
Kingsdown CT14 134 D5
Sandwich CT13 73 A8
Southsea Ave ME12 4 C8
Southsea Dr CT6 22 D4
South Side Three Rd ME4 10 C8
South St
Canterbury CT1 67 C2
Deal CT14 117 D6
3 Folkestone CT20 178 E4
Lydd TN29 205 C6
Queenborough ME11 2 F5
Selling ME13 84 F8
Whitstable CT5 44 A7
Southstone Ct CT21 176 C1
SOUTH STOUR 157 B1
South Stour Ave TN23 156 C8
SOUTH STREET
Selling 84 F8
Stockbury 56 C7
Whitstable 44 A7
Southstreet Crossing CT5 44 A7
South Street Rd ME9 56 C7
SOUTH TANKERTON 21 A1
South Turbine Hall Rd
TN29 209 C2
South View CT3 46 F1
Southview Gdns ME12 6 D2
South View Gdns ME12 1 D1
South View Rd CT5 43 D6
South Wall CT14 117 B7
Southwall Ind Est CT14 117 B7
Southwall Rd CT14 117 B6
SOUTH
WILLESBOROUGH 156 E6
Southwold Pl CT8 27 E7
Southwood Gdns CT11 52 B6
Southwood Hts CT11 52 C6
Southwood Rd
Ramsgate CT11 52 C6
Whitstable CT5 21 B2
Sovereign Bvd ME7, ME8 10 F2
Sovereigns The ME16 74 D4
Sowell St CT10 29 F5
Spade La ME9 34 C6
Spanton Cres CT21 176 A3
Sparrow Castle 3 CT9 7 J1
Sparrow Way CT3 47 A1
Spartan Rd TN23 155 C8
Speakman Ct 5 CT11 52 C6
Spearhead Rd ME14 74 F7
Spearpoint Cnr TN24 139 F5
Spectrum Bsns Ctr ME2 9 E8
Spectrum Bsns Est ME15 97 F4
Speedwell Ave ME5 31 F4
Speedwell Cl
Gillingham ME7 10 E5
Maidstone ME14 75 E5
Speedwell Rd CT5 43 B6
Speke Rd CT10 29 E6
Spekes Rd ME7 33 B6
Spelders Hill TN25 141 A5
Speldhurst Cl TN23 155 E5
Speldhurst Ct ME16 74 D4
Speldhurst Gdns CT9 8 F3
Spembley Ct ME4 9 E4
Spence Cl CT18 163 A4
Spencer Cl ME5 32 A5
Spencer Flats ME5 32 B8
Spencer Ho 3 CT20 177 F5
Spencer Rd CT7 27 A8
Spencer Sq CT11 52 D6
Spencer St 9 CT11 52 D6
Spencer Way ME15 97 E7
Spenlow Dr ME5 54 A8

Spenser Rd CT6 22 F4
Spicer Homes ME10 36 F2
Spicers Ct CT21 176 C1
Spicers Field CT6 23 D2
Spicer's Pl CT3 69 C2
Spiers The ME7 11 C5
Spillett Cl ME13 62 B6
Spillway The ME15 74 D2
Spindle Glade ME14 75 C5
Spindlewood Cl ME5 32 B3
Spindlewood End TN23 138 D4
Spinnaker Ct 4 ME1 9 C1
Spinnens Acre Jun Sch
ME5 32 C1
Spinney La CT3 112 E4
Spinney The
Ashford TN23 138 E3
Chatham ME5 32 B1
Crabble CT17 148 E2
Maidstone ME15 75 B2
Margate CT9 8 E1
Spire Alexandra Hospl
ME5 54 A8
Spire Ave CT5 44 A8
Spires Acad CT2 68 C8
Spire St Saviour's Hospl
CT21 176 F2
Spires The
Canterbury CT2 66 F2
Maidstone ME16 74 D4
Spitalfield La TN28 201 F6
Spitalfield Terr TN28 201 F6
Spitfire Cl ME5 32 B6
Spitfire Way CT18 163 B3
Splashes L Ctr ME8 11 D1
Split Ho CT17 149 A1
Split La CT4 127 A5
Spong Wood Nature
Reserve★ TN25 143 A8
Sportsfield ME14 75 B5
Spot La ME15 76 A2
Spratling La CT12 28 F1
Spratling St CT12 28 E1
Sprig The ME14 76 A4
Springett Way ME17 96 D3
Spring Farm TN29 192 D5
Springfarm Rd TN29 192 C5
Springfield Ave
Maidstone ME14 74 F7
Tenterden TN30 167 C2
Springfield Cl CT11 29 E2
Springfield Pass CT21 176 B2
Springfield Rd
Dover CT16 149 B2
Gillingham ME7 10 E6
Margate CT9 8 E3
Sittingbourne ME10 36 D5
Springfield Terr 7 ME4 9 F4
Springfield Way CT21 177 B3
Spring Grove Sch TN25 123 C2
Springhead Rd ME13 40 D1
Spring Ho CT21 176 C2
Spring Hollow TN29 195 A4
Spring La
Canterbury CT1 88 C7
Fordwich CT2 68 A4
Hythe CT21 177 A4
Springside Terr CT18 161 C6
Spring Terr 15 CT20 178 D5
Springvale
Gillingham ME8 33 C6
Iwade ME9 14 D4
Spring Vale ME16 74 E4
Spring Wlk CT5 43 C7
Springwood Cl
Ashford TN23 138 E3
1 Maidstone ME16 74 A3
Springwood Ct TN28 202 B6
Springwood Dr TN23 138 E3
Springwood Rd ME16 74 A3
Sprotlands Ave TN24 139 F1
Sprotshill Cl ME10 36 E6
Spurgeons Cotts ME17 96 E2
Spurway ME14 76 A4
Square Hill ME15 75 B4
Square Hill Rd ME15 75 B4
Square The
Birchington CT7 27 A7
Chilham CT4 107 B8
Lenham ME17 101 D5
Selling ME13 84 A6
Sittingbourne ME10 14 F1
Squeeze Gut Alley 14 CT5 20 D2
Squire Ave CT2 87 C8
Squires Ct ME12 5 E3
Squires Way CT16 149 A3
Squirrel La TN25 138 F5
Stable Cl ME5 32 C5
Stable Ct
Chilham CT4 107 B7
Faversham ME13 62 D6
Stablemead CT19 178 A7
Stace Cl TN30 179 C8
Staceys St ME14 74 F5
Stade St CT21 176 C1
Stade The CT19 178 E5
Stadium Way ME10 37 C6
Stadler Cl ME16 74 D7
Staffa Rd ME15 97 A7
Stafford Cl TN23 138 F2
Stafford House Sch of
English 2 CT1 88 A7
Staffordshire St 11 CT11 52 E7
Stafford St ME7 10 C5
Stag Rd ME5 32 B5
Stagshaw Cl ME15 75 A2
Staines Hill CT2 68 B7
Staines Pl CT10 30 B5
Stalham Bsns Ctr ME11 3 A3
Stalham Ct ME7 33 B4
Stalin Ave ME5 32 B8
STALISFIELD GREEN 103 D6
Stalisfield Rd
Charing TN27 103 E3
Stalisfield Green ME13,
TN27 103 C5
Throwley ME13 82 C6
Stamford Villas ME12 5 C2
Stampers The ME15 74 D2
Stanbury Cres CT19 178 F7
Stancomb Ave CT11 52 C5
Standard Ave CT6 22 A4
Standen Cl ME8 33 E4
Standen La CT18 163 E5
Staner Ct CT12 52 A8
Staner Hill CT12 51 F8
STANFORD 160 B1
Stanford Dr ME16 74 C3
Stangate Dr ME9 14 D4
STANHOPE 155 F6
Stanhope Ave ME10 37 A3
Stanhope Cl ME14 74 E7
Stanhope Rd
Ashford TN23 155 E6
Deal CT14 117 D6
Dover CT16 149 C2
Rochester ME2 9 A7
Stanhope Sq TN23 155 F6
Stanley Ave
Minster (Sheppey) ME12 4 D7
Queenborough ME11 3 A4
Stanley Cl TN29 187 B4
Stanley Gdns CT6 22 F3
Stanley Pl
Broadstairs CT10 30 A4
Ramsgate CT11 52 E7
Stanley Rd
Broadstairs CT10 30 A6
Chatham ME5 32 C6
Deal CT14 117 D5
Folkestone CT19 177 E6
Gillingham ME7 10 C6
Herne Bay CT6 22 F4
Margate CT9 8 A3
Ramsgate CT11 52 D8
Whitstable CT5 43 D7
Stanmore Ct CT1 88 B7
Stansfeld Ave CT18 163 A4
Stansted Cl ME16 74 D7
STAPLE 92 A5
Staple Cl ME10 36 E5
Staplehurst Ave CT10 30 A2
Staplehurst Gdns CT9 8 E2
Staplehurst Lodge Ind Est
ME10 36 D5
Staplehurst Rd
Gillingham ME8 11 B3
Sittingbourne ME10 36 D5
Staple Rd CT3 91 C6
Staplers Ct ME14 75 B8
Staple St ME13 63 F5
STAPLESTREET 64 A5
Staplestreet Rd ME13 64 A4
Star Hill ME1 9 D5
Star La
Folkestone CT19 177 D7
Gillingham ME7 33 A7
Margate CT9 29 A5
Starle Cl CT1 67 B1
Star Mill Ct ME5 10 D2
Star Mill La ME5 10 D2
Starnes Ct 5 ME14 75 A5
Star Rd TN24 139 D2
Starvation Cnr 1 CT5 20 D2
Starveacre La ME9 36 B1
STATENBOROUGH 93 C4
Station App
Adisham CT3 112 E8
Birchington CT7 26 F7
Maidstone ME16 74 F3
Martin Mill CT15 133 C2
Minster (Thanet) CT12 50 C5
New Romney TN28 202 C6
Station App Rd CT11 52 C8
Station Approach Rd
CT11 52 D8
Station Chine CT6 22 F5
Station Cotts ME13 84 E7
Station Dr CT14 117 A1
Station Hill Cotts ME15 96 A7
Station Mews
Elham CT4 144 F4
2 Ramsgate CT12 29 C1
3 Tenterden TN30 179 A7
Station Rd
Adisham CT3 90 E1
Ashford TN23 139 C2
Bekesbourne CT4 89 C4
Birchington CT7 27 A7
Bridge CT4 88 F2
Charing TN27 120 C7
Chartham CT4 86 D3
Deal CT14 117 B1
Dymchurch TN29 195 B7
East Farleigh ME15 96 A7
Faversham ME13 62 D6
Folkestone CT19 177 F5
Gillingham ME8 12 A2
Harrietsham ME17 100 D6
Herne Bay CT6 22 E4
Hythe CT21 176 D3
Lydd TN29 205 D7
Lyminge CT18 161 C6
Station Rd *continued*
Maidstone ME14 74 F5
Margate CT9 7 H2
Martin Mill CT15 133 D1
Minster (Thanet) CT12 50 C5
Newington ME9 35 B6
New Romney TN28 202 C6
Pluckley TN27 136 C5
Rochester ME2 9 C7
Shepherdswell CT15 130 D5
Smeeth TN25 158 B3
St Margaret's at Cliffe
CT15 150 E8
Tenterden TN30 179 A7
Teynham ME9 38 D2
Westgate on Sea CT8 7 D1
Whitstable CT5 20 E2
Station Road E CT1 87 F7
Station Road W CT2 66 F1
Station Row ME9 38 D3
Station St ME10 36 F4
Station Terr TN28 202 C6
Steddy Cl 4 TN23 155 F6
Stede Hill ME17 78 F3
Steed Cl CT6 46 B8
Steeds Cl TN23 156 A1
Steeds La TN23, TN26 156 B1
Steele St ME2 9 A8
Steerforth Cl ME1 9 C2
Stella Maris RC Prim Sch
CT19 178 C6
STELLING MINNIS 126 F2
Stelling Minnis CE Prim Sch
CT4 126 F6
Stelling Minnis Windmill &
Mus★ CT4 126 F2
Stembrook CT16 166 D8
Stembrook Ct 4 CT16 166 D7
Stempe Cl CT18 163 B3
Stephen Cl CT10 30 A4
Stephen Ct 2 CT20 178 D5
Stephens Cl
Faversham ME13 62 B8
Ramsgate CT11 52 C8
Stephen's Cl CT9 28 B7
Stephenson Rd CT2 66 F3
Steps Hill Rd ME9 56 D6
Step Style ME10 37 B2
Sterling Ave ME16 74 C5
Sterling Cl CT10 29 E5
Sterling Ct 12 CT1 66 F1
Sterling Rd
Queenborough ME11 3 A5
Sittingbourne ME10 36 D1
Sterry Gdns ME15 97 E7
Steven Cl ME4 10 A3
Stevens Cl TN27 118 F3
Stevens Cotts TN30 179 A7
Stevens Ho CT17 166 C8
Stevenson Cl ME15 74 F3
Stickfast La ME9 14 A1
STIFF STREET 57 E7
Stiles Cl
Folkestone CT19 178 A7
Minster (Sheppey) ME12 4 A6
Stirling Cl
Gillingham ME8 33 E4
Rochester ME1 9 A3
Stirling Way CT12 29 A2
Stirlng Rd TN24 156 D7
Stisted Way TN27 118 F3
STOCKBURY 56 E8
Stockbury Dr ME16 74 D7
Stockbury Gdns CT9 8 E2
Stockbury Hill Wood Nature
Reserve★ ME9 56 D6
Stockdale Gdns CT14 117 C4
Stockers Brow ME9 59 A7
STOCKER'S HEAD 103 F1
Stockers Hill ME9 59 A7
Stocker's Hill ME13 63 E4
Stockett La ME15 96 D6
Stockham Ct CT19 177 E7
Stock La TN25 158 A4
Stocks Mill Windmill★
TN30 189 A3
Stocks Rd TN30 188 F3
Stocks The ME13 83 C6
Stockton Cl ME14 75 B8
Stockwood Chase CT2 66 A2
Stoddart Rd CT19 177 E6
STODMARSH 69 B6
Stodmarsh National Nature
Reserve★ CT3 69 D8
Stodmarsh Rd CT3 68 C3
Stombers La CT18 163 C6
Stonar Cl
Ramsgate CT11 29 E1
Sandwich CT13 73 A1
Stonar Gdns CT13 73 A2
Stoneacre★ ME15 98 B7
Stoneacre Cl ME8 33 D5
Stoneacre Ct 7 ME15 75 A1
Stoneacre La ME15 98 B7
Stone Barn Ave CT7 27 A6
Stone Bay Sch CT10 30 B6
Stonebridge TN25 141 A5
Stonebridge Cotts TN23 156 B8
STONEBRIDGE GREEN 119 A4
Stonebridge Green Rd
TN27 118 F4
Stonebridge Rd CT2 67 A2
Stonebridge Way ME13 62 B7
Stone Cnr TN30 189 A6
STONE CROSS
Aldington Frith 171 F6
Sandwich 93 E7
Stonecross Lea ME5 10 C1
Stone Cross Lees CT13 93 F7
Stone Cross Rd TN25 171 E5
Stonedane Ct ME13 62 C8
Stonegate TN25 123 E2
Stone Gdns CT10 30 B5
Stone Gn TN30 189 F4
STONEHALL 147 F8
Stonehall Rd CT15 147 F8
Stoneheap Rd CT14, CT15 115 E1
STONE HILL 159 A2
Stone Hill TN25 159 A2
Stone Hill Rd TN27 118 F2
Stone Ho CT10 30 B7
Stone House Mews CT10 30 B7
STONE-IN-OXNEY 189 F4
Stone Rd CT10 30 B5
Stonerock Cl CT2 68 B7
Stone St
Faversham ME13 62 C7
Lympne CT21 175 A4
Stanford TN25 160 C3
Stelling Minnis CT4 126 D4
Westenhanger TN25, CT21 175 B6
Stonestile Farm Rd
TN27 103 A3
Stone Stile La CT4 84 D1
STONESTREET GREEN 173 A7
Stoneway Pk CT4 126 D7
Stoney Bank ME7 10 F1
Stoney Rd ME13 64 B3
Stony La ME1 31 C5
Stonyway La CT15 165 C5
Stopford Rd ME7 10 D4
Storehouse Wharf ME12 1 A3
Stores Rd TN29 209 C2
Storey Cres CT18 163 A5
Stour Cl
Ashford TN23 138 E1
Chartham CT4 86 D2
Stour Cres CT1 67 D3
Stour Ct
7 Canterbury CT1 87 F8
8 Sandwich CT13 72 F1
Stour Ctr TN24 139 C1
Stourfields TN24 139 D4
Stourmouth Rd CT3 70 C8
Stour Rd CT4 86 D2
Stour Retail Pk CT1 67 D3
Stourside Studios 13 CT1 66 F1
Stour St CT1 87 F8
Stour Valley Cl CT3 47 D3
Stour Valley Ind Est CT4 86 E4
Stourville 9 CT1 87 F8
Stowell Cl TN23 155 C8
STOWTING 160 A8
Stowting CE Prim Sch
TN25 160 B8
STOWTING COMMON 143 A4
Stowting Hill TN25 143 A1
Straight La TN29 191 F1
Strakers Hill
East Studdal CT15 132 D8
Tilmanstone CT15 115 C1
Strand Approach Rd ME7 10 E7
Strand L Pool & Pk ME7 10 F7
Strand Rdbt The ME7 10 E7
Strand St CT13 72 F1
Strand The CT14 117 D4
Stranger's Cl CT1 87 C6
Stranger's La CT1 87 C6
Strangford Pl CT6 23 B2
Strangford Rd CT5 20 F2
Strasbourg St CT9 29 A6
Stratford Ave ME8 33 D8
Stratford Dr ME15 97 D6
Stratford La 2 ME8 33 F8
Straw Mill Hill ME15 74 E1
Stream Wlk CT5 20 D2
Street E TN29 209 D2
Streete Court Rd CT8 27 F8
Streete Ct CT8 27 F8
STREET END 109 F7
Street End CT3 71 E1
Street End Rd ME5 10 B1
Streetfield CT6 46 B8
Streetfield Rd ME8 11 F1
Street The
Acol CT7 27 B3
Adisham CT3 112 C8
Appledore TN26 190 D8
Ash CT3 71 D1
Ashford, Great Chart TN23 138 C1
Ashford, Kennington TN24 139 E6
Ashford, Willesborough Lees
TN24 157 B8
Barham CT4 111 F1
Bethersden TN26 153 D5
Bishopsbourne CT4 111 C6
Borden ME9 36 B2
Bossingham CT4 127 A7
Boughton Street ME13 64 A3
Boxley ME14 54 C3
Brabourne TN25 159 C8
Bredgar ME9 58 A5
Bredhurst ME7 33 B1
Brook TN25 141 B6
Chilham CT4 107 B8
Deal CT14 116 F6
Denton CT4 129 B3
Detling ME14 55 A1
Doddington ME9 80 E7
East Langdon CT15 133 A1
Eastling ME13 81 E6
Egerton TN27 118 F3
Eythorne CT15 131 D7
Faversham ME13 40 B2
Finglesham CT14 116 B8
Godmersham CT4 107 B2
Street The *continued*
Goodnestone CT3 91 D2
Guston CT15 149 E6
Hamstreet TN26 183 A7
Hartlip ME9 34 D5
Hastingleigh TN25 142 B6
Hawkinge CT18 163 B5
Hothfield TN26 138 A6
Ickham CT3 69 C1
Iwade ME9 14 E4
Kingston CT4 111 D3
Lower Halstow ME9 13 B3
Lympne CT21 174 F2
Lynsted ME9 60 A6
Maidstone ME14 76 C4
Martin Mill CT15 133 B3
Mersham TN25 157 E4
Molash CT4 105 F4
Newnham ME9 81 C8
Nonington CT15 113 D1
Northbourne CT14 116 A5
Patrixbourne CT4 89 B3
Peene CT18 177 A7
Petham CT4 109 B3
Pluckley TN27 136 D7
Postling CT21 160 F2
Preston CT3 70 C6
Selling ME13 84 B6
Shadoxhurst TN26 170 A8
Sittingbourne ME9 37 E3
Smarden TN27 135 A1
Staple CT3 91 F6
St Nicholas at Wade CT7 25 F2
Stockbury ME9 56 E8
Stone in Oxney TN30 190 A5
Stourmouth CT3 48 E1
Upchurch ME9 12 F4
West Hougham CT15 164 F5
Wickhambreaux CT3 69 C2
Wittersham TN30 188 D3
Womenswold CT4 112 D2
Woodnesborough CT13 93 C7
Wormshill ME9 79 A7
Worth CT14 94 B5
Street W TN29 209 C2
Stretton Ct CT14 117 D5
Stringer Dr CT7 27 A6
Strode Cres ME12 1 D2
Strode Park Rd CT6 23 A2
Strond St CT17 166 D6
STROOD 9 A6
Strood Ret Pk ME2 9 B7
Strood Sta ME2 9 C7
Strouts Rd TN23 155 D7
Strover St ME7 10 C7
Stuart Cl ME14 75 C6
Stuart Ct
Canterbury CT1 88 A6
Dover CT17 166 C8
Stuart Ho CT14 117 A5
Stuart Rd
Folkestone CT19 178 E6
Gillingham ME7 10 D3
STUBB'S CROSS 155 C2
STUDDAL 132 C7
STUDD HILL 22 A4
Studds Cotts CT6 22 A3
Studfall Cl CT21 187 D8
Studio Cl TN24 139 E6
Stumble La TN23 156 B1
Stuppington Court Farm
CT1 87 E4
Stuppington La CT1 87 F5
Sturdee Ave ME7 10 E4
Sturdy Cl CT21 176 D2
Sturges Rd TN24 139 B3
Sturla Rd ME4 10 A3
Sturmer Cl CT1 88 C7
STURRY 67 E6
Sturry CE Prim Sch CT2 68 A7
Sturry Court Mews CT2 67 F5
Sturry Hill CT2 67 F6
Sturry Rd CT1, CT2 67 C3
Sturry Sta CT2 67 F5
Sturry Way ME8 11 C2
Style Cl ME8 33 E4
Styles La ME14 54 C3
Subdown Cotts TN25 159 C8
Sudbury Pl CT8 27 E7
Suffolk Ave
Gillingham ME8 11 F1
Westgate on Sea CT8 27 D7
Suffolk Ct 7 ME8 11 F1
Suffolk Dr TN23 139 A2
Suffolk Gdns CT17 165 F7
Suffolk Rd
Canterbury CT1 88 D8
Maidstone ME15 97 D8
Suffolk St CT5 43 D8
Sugarloaf Wlk CT19 178 D8
Sullivan Cl CT1 87 D6
Sultan Mews ME5 32 C2
Sultan Rd ME5 32 C2
Summer Cl
Hythe CT21 175 F2
Tenterden TN30 167 C1
Summer Ct
Canterbury CT2 66 C1
Whitstable CT5 21 C2
SUMMERFIELD 92 B4
Summerfield Ave CT5 20 F1
Summerfield Rd CT9 8 E2
Summerhill TN23 155 E6
Summer Hill CT2 66 C1
Summer Hill Pk TN24 157 C7
Summer La CT2 66 E6
Summer Leeze TN24 156 E8

Summer Leeze Gdns TN24 156 E8
Summer Rd CT7 25 E1
Summerson Cl ME1 9 C1
Summerville Ave ME12 4 A5
Sumpter Way ME13 61 F7
Sunbeam Ave CT6 21 F4
Sunderland Cl ME1 9 A3
Sunderland Dr ME8 34 A8
Sunderland Ho 3 ME7 10 C7
Sundew Gr CT11 52 E8
Sundridge Cl CT2 67 A4
Sundridge Dr ME5 32 A4
Sun La
  Hythe CT21 176 C2
  St Nicholas at Wade CT7 25 F2
Sunningdale Ave 4 CT19 178 A7
Sunningdale Cl ME8 33 D6
Sunningdale Ct ME15 75 B4
Sunningdale Dr ME8 33 D6
Sunningdale Wlk CT6 22 D1
Sunny Bank
  Eythorne CT15 131 B8
  Hythe CT21 175 F2
  Sittingbourne ME10 37 B5
Sunny Cnr CT17 166 B5
Sunnyfields Cl ME8 33 E8
Sunnyfields Dr ME12 3 C6
Sunnyhill Rd CT6 22 C4
Sunnymead CT2 66 D7
Sunnymead Ave ME7 10 E5
Sunnyside
  Doddington ME9 80 E7
  Littlestone-on-Sea TN28 202 D6
  Lydd TN29 205 B6
Sunnyside Ave ME12 4 A6
Sunnyside Cl CT14 116 D1
Sunnyside Cotts CT14 117 C6
Sunnyside Gdns CT13 93 E8
Sunnyside Rd
  Folkestone CT20 177 D3
  Whitstable CT5 43 D5
Sunray Ave CT5 43 B7
Sun Rise TN25 138 F5
Sunset Cl
  Eastchurch ME12 5 F6
  Whitstable CT5 43 C6
Sunshine Ct 1 ME8 33 F8
Sun St CT1 87 F8
Sunstone Dr ME10 36 C7
Sun Terr ME5 32 B4
Sun Valley Way CT15 131 C8
Superabbey Est ME20 53 B2
Surf Cres ME12 5 F6
Surrenden Rd CT19 177 F6
Surrey Cl 4 CT12 29 B1
Surrey Gdns CT7 26 F7
Surrey Rd
  Canterbury CT1 88 D7
  Maidstone ME15 97 D8
  Margate CT9 8 B3
Surtees Cl TN24 156 E6
Susan's Hill TN26 168 E3
Sussex Ave
  Ashford TN24 139 B3
  Canterbury CT1 88 D7
  Margate CT9 7 J1
Sussex Cl CT6 22 B4
Sussex Dr ME5 32 A4
Sussex Gdns
  Birchington CT7 26 F7
  Herne Bay CT6 22 B4
  Westgate on Sea CT8 7 D1
Sussex Mans CT8 7 D1
Sussex Rd
  5 Folkestone CT19 178 D6
  Maidstone ME15 97 D8
  New Romney TN28 202 A6
Sussex St CT11 52 E7
Sussex Wlk CT1 88 D7
Sutherland Cl CT21 176 A2
Sutherland Dr CT7 27 B6
Sutherland Gdns ME8 33 E6
Sutherland Ho CT21 176 C1
Sutherland Rd CT14 117 C6
SUTTON 133 A7
Sutton Baron Rd ME9 58 A8
Sutton Cl
  Folkestone CT19 178 A7
  Gillingham ME8 34 A8
Sutton Cotts ME13 84 C3
Sutton Hts ME15 97 F6
Sutton La
  Ringwould CT14 133 F5
  Ripple CT14 133 C8
Sutton Rd
  Hersden CT3 46 E1
  Langley ME17 98 C5
  Maidstone ME15 97 D6
Sutton Row CT14 117 B5
Sutton St ME14 76 D4
Suttons The TN31 203 A1
Swadelands Cl ME17 101 C5
Swadelands Sch ME17 101 C5
Swaffer Way TN23 155 C7
Swain Rd
  Gillingham ME8 33 B6
  Tenterden TN30 167 D3
Swakeley Wlk CT5 21 D3
Swale Ave
  Rushenden ME11 2 F3
  Sheerness ME12 1 C1
Swale Cl CT6 23 A3
SWALECLIFFE 21 E3
Swalecliffe Ave CT6 22 B4
Swalecliffe Com Prim Sch CT5 21 B2
Swalecliffe Court Dr CT5 21 D3
Swalecliffe Rd CT5 21 B2
Swale Ho ME11 2 F5
Swale National Nature Reserve★ ME12 19 E4
Swale Sta ME9 15 A7
Swale View ME13 64 B6
Swale Way
  Sittingbourne ME10 14 F2
  Sittingbourne ME10 37 D5
Swallow Ave CT5 43 B6
Swallow Cl CT9 28 C8
Swallow Ct CT6 45 F7
Swallowfield TN24 156 E7
Swallow Ho
  Dover CT17 166 A6
  4 Maidstone ME16 74 E4
Swallow Rise ME5 32 A5
Swallows L Ctr ME10 36 F3
Swallows The CT13 94 A8
Swamp Rd TN29 201 B4
Swan Apartments 12 ME15 97 E5
Swan Cl ME10 37 B4
Swan Cotts TN30 188 D3
Swanfield Rd CT5 43 D8
Swan Gn TN25 159 D1
Swan La TN25 159 E2
Swann Way CT18 163 A4
Swan St TN30 188 C3
Swanstree Ave ME10 37 B2
Swanton La
  Littlebourne CT3 68 D2
  Lydden CT15 147 C6
SWANTON STREET 57 F3
Swarling Hill Rd CT4 109 C7
Swaynes Way CT13 93 B2
Sweechbridge Rd CT6 23 F3
Sweechgate CT2 67 E7
Sweet Bay Cres TN23 138 D3
Sweet Briar Ct ME16 74 D5
Sweetbriar La CT15 114 B2
Sweetlove Pl CT3 91 A8
Sweyn Rd CT9 8 A3
Swift Cres ME5 32 C6
Swift Ho 6 ME16 74 E4
Swinburne Ave CT10 30 A3
Swinford Gdns CT9 29 C8
Swingate Cl ME5 32 B2
Swingate Inf Sch ME5 32 C1
SWINGFIELD MINNIS 146 B3
SWINGFIELD STREET 146 E4
Swiss Way CT19 178 F7
Switch House Ave TN29 209 C2
Sycamore Ave CT3 112 E5
Sycamore Cl
  Broadstairs CT10 29 C4
  Chartham CT4 86 F1
  Dymchurch TN29 195 C8
  Herne Bay CT6 23 C5
  Hythe CT21 175 E1
  Lydd TN29 205 D7
  Margate CT9 28 E7
Sycamore Cres ME16 74 C5
Sycamore Dr CT14 117 B4
Sycamore Gdns TN29 195 C8
Sycamore Grange CT11 29 F1
Sycamore La TN23 138 E4
Sycamores The CT3 68 E8
Sydcot Dr CT14 117 D8
Sydenham Rd CT14 117 D7
Sydenham St CT5 20 D2
Sydney Ave ME10 36 C4
Sydney Cooper Cl CT2 66 B2
Sydney Cooper Gallery★ 22 CT1 66 F1
Sydney Rd
  Chatham ME4 10 A3
  Deal CT14 117 A1
  Ramsgate CT11 52 F8
  Whitstable CT5 43 E8
Sydney St TN23 156 C8
Sylewood Cl ME1 31 B8
Sylvan Glade ME5 54 A8
Sylvan Rd ME8 33 C8
Symmonds Dr ME10 37 A6
Symons Ave ME4 10 A2
Syndale Pl 5 CT11 52 F7

T

Tabret Cl TN24 139 D6
Tadburn Gn ME5 32 B4
Taddington Wood La ME5 31 E2
Taddy Gdns CT9 29 C8
Tadley Ct
  Gillingham ME7 10 F6
  Rochester ME1 31 C8
Tadworth Rd TN24 139 D5
Taillour Cl ME10 36 F7
Tail Race The ME15 74 E2
Talavera Rd CT1 88 D8
Talbot Ave CT6 22 B3
Talbot Rd
  Maidstone ME16 74 C6
  Margate CT9 8 B2
Tall Trees Cl ME17 99 D2
Tally Ho Rd TN26 155 C2
Talmead Rd CT6 23 B3
Tamarind Cl ME7 33 A4
Tamarisk ME12 19 E5
Tame La CT21, TN29 185 F6
Tamley La TN25 142 B6
Tams Gdns ME12 4 D6
Tangier Cl CT15 149 E3
Tanglewood Cl ME8 33 C6
Tangmere Cl ME7 10 F5
Tanhouse La TN31 196 A2
Tanker Hill ME8 33 D6
TANKERTON 21 A3
Tankerton Cir CT5 20 F3
Tankerton Ct CT5 21 B3
Tankerton Hts CT5 20 E3
Tankerton Mews CT5 20 E3
Tankerton Rd CT5 20 F3
Tanners Cl CT21 176 B4
Tanner's Hill CT21 176 C3
Tanner's Hill Gdns CT21 176 C3
Tanners St ME13 62 C7
Tannery Ct 5 ME10 36 E5
Tannery La
  Ashford TN23 139 C2
  11 Sandwich CT13 72 F1
Tapleys Hill CT4 110 B5
Taplin Ct 5 CT7 27 A7
Target Bsns Ctr ME15 97 F4
Target Firs CT16 148 D5
Tariff Reform Cotts ME13 62 D5
Tar Pot La TN25, TN26 184 B6
Tarragon Rd ME16 74 B3
Tartane La TN29 195 C8
Taryes Ho 2 CT11 52 C6
Tasker Cl ME15 76 B3
Tassell's Wlk CT5 21 D3
Taswell Cl CT16 166 E8
Taswell Rd ME8 12 A1
Taswell St CT16 166 E8
Tatchell Dr TN27 120 C7
Tatler Cl ME5 32 D2
Tatsfield Cl ME8 11 A2
Tattershall Rd ME15 75 A1
Taunton Cl ME15 97 F6
Taverners Rd ME8 33 E7
Tavistock Cl
  Chatham ME5 31 F1
  Gillingham ME8 33 E7
  Sittingbourne ME10 36 D4
Tavistock Rd CT11 29 E1
Tay Cl ME5 32 B5
Taylers Yd TN25 123 E2
Taylor Cl ME17 100 D6
Taylor Rd
  Folkestone CT19 177 E6
  Lydd-on-Sea TN29 206 E6
  Minster (Thanet) CT12 50 B6
Taylors Cl TN29 194 F3
Taylors Hill CT4 107 B8
Taylors La TN29 194 F3
Taylor's La ME2 9 B7
Taymouth Ho 1 CT16 166 E8
Taywood Cl TN24 139 F1
Teal Cl CT18 162 F3
Teal Dr CT6 22 E2
Teal Way ME9 14 E3
Teasaucer Hill ME15 96 F8
Teasel Cl ME14 75 F4
Teasel Rd ME5 31 F4
Teddars Leas Rd CT18 161 E4
Tedder Ave ME5 32 A7
Teddington Cl CT1 67 B2
Teelin Cl TN29 195 A4
Telegraph Hill Ind Pk CT12 50 D7
Telegraph Rd CT14 117 B3
Telescope Alley ME12 1 E2
Telford Ct
  Folkestone CT19 178 E6
  Herne Bay CT6 22 C2
Telford Ho 1 ME14 75 A6
Telford St CT6 22 E5
Telham Ave CT12 52 B8
Temeraire Hts CT20 177 C3
Temeraire Manor 2 ME7 10 A6
Templar Ct
  9 Canterbury CT2 66 F1
  11 Dover CT17 149 C1
Templar Rd CT16 148 D5
Templar St CT17 166 C8
Temple Cl
  Ashford TN23 155 F5
  Temple Ewell CT16 148 D6
Temple Ct CT2 66 D1
TEMPLE EWELL 148 D6
Temple Ewell CE Prim Sch CT16 148 D5
Temple Gdns
  Rochester ME2 9 A6
  Sittingbourne ME10 37 B3
Templeman Liby CT2 66 E4
Temple Manor★ ME2 9 A6
Temple Mews 10 CT1 87 F8
Temple Rd CT2 66 D1
Temple Side CT16 148 D6
Temple Way CT14 94 A4
Ten Acre Way ME8 12 B1
Tennison Way ME15 97 D6
Tennyson Ave CT1 67 D3
Tennyson Gdns CT3 112 F6
Tennyson Ho CT1 67 D3
Tennyson Pl
  Canterbury CT1 67 D3
  Folkestone CT19 178 E7
Tennyson Rd
  Ashford TN23 156 A6
  Gillingham ME7 10 C3
Ten Perch Rd CT1 87 D6
TENTERDEN 179 C8
Tenterden CE Jun Sch TN30 179 B7
Tenterden & District Mus★ TN30 179 A7
Tenterden Dr CT2 67 A4
Tenterden Inf Sch TN30 179 B7
Tenterden L Ctr TN30 179 B7
Tenterden Rd
  Appledore Heath TN26 181 B1
  Chatham ME5 32 B5
Tenterden Station Est TN30 179 A8
Tenterden Town Sta★ TN30 179 A8
Tenterden Vineyard★ TN30 179 C1
Tenterden Way CT9 8 C1
Terance Butler Ave ME2 9 E8
Terence Cl ME4 10 A2
Terlingham La CT18 163 A2
Terminus Dr CT6 23 D5
Terminus Rd ME16 74 A2
Terminus Wlk 3 CT20 178 E5
Terrace Apartments The CT21 176 C1
Terrace Cotts CT4 127 A6
Terrace Rd
  Elvington CT15 114 B1
  Maidstone ME16 74 E3
  Sittingbourne ME10 37 B3
Terrace The
  Canterbury CT2 66 F3
  Chatham ME4 9 F7
  Faversham ME13 62 A7
  Pluckley TN26 120 A1
  Rochester ME1 9 C5
  Shepherdswell CT15 130 D5
Terry's La CT5 20 D2
TEYNHAM 38 C3
Teynham Cl CT9 8 F2
Teynham Dr CT5 20 F2
Teynham Gn ME8 11 A4
Teynham Parochial CE Prim Sch ME9 38 C2
Teynham Rd CT5 20 F2
Teynham St ME9 38 F4
Teynham Sta ME9 38 D3
TEYNHAM STREET 38 E4
Thames Ave
  Gillingham ME8 33 E8
  Sheerness ME12 1 C1
Thames Ct ME12 6 G2
Thames View Inf Sch ME8 11 D2
Thames View Jun Sch ME8 11 D2
Thanet Cl CT10 30 B5
Thanet Coll
  Broadstairs CT10 30 A3
  Margate CT9 7 I2
Thanet Ent Ctr CT10 29 D7
Thanet Gdns CT19 178 F6
Thanet Ho 7 ME15 97 F5
Thanet Place Gdns CT10 30 B6
Thanet Rd
  Broadstairs CT10 30 B4
  Gillingham ME8 33 C4
  Margate CT9 7 J2
  Ramsgate CT11 52 F7
  Westgate on Sea CT8 27 D8
Thanet Reach Bsns Pk CT10 29 C4
Thanet Stars Sch of Dance & Drama CT9 7 I1
Thanet Terr TN26 138 A6
Thanet View
  Eythorne CT15 131 B8
  St Nicholas at Wade CT7 25 F2
Thanet Way
  Boughton Street ME13 63 D6
  Herne Bay CT6 23 C3
  Whitstable CT5 21 C2
  Yorkletts CT5, ME13 42 E2
THANINGTON 87 B6
Thanington Court Farm CT1 87 C6
Thanington Rd CT1 87 C6
Thatchers The ME16 74 B5
Theatre Royal★ CT9 7 I1
Theatre Sq 7 TN30 179 A7
Theatre St CT21 176 C2
THE BRENTS 40 D1
The Cut ME4 9 F4
The Davenport Ctr CT12 52 A8
THE FORSTAL 157 D3
THE LEACON 182 D7
THE LEES 105 A1
The Marlowe Acad CT12 29 A2
Theodore Pl ME7 10 C5
THE QUARRIES 97 C4
THE QUARTER
  Headcorn 135 B5
  Tenterden 179 A4
Theresa Rd CT21 176 B1
THE STOCKS 189 A3
THE VALLEY 103 D8
Third Ave
  Chatham ME5 10 C1
  Eastchurch ME12 5 F6
  Gillingham ME7 10 F4
  Margate CT9 8 B3
Thirlemere Cl ME16 74 D8
Thirlmere TN24 139 D6
Thirlmere Ave CT11 52 A7
Thirlmere Cl ME7 11 A5
Thirlmere Gdns CT3 112 F6
Thirsk Ho 6 ME15 97 F6
Thistlebank ME5 32 A3
Thistledown
  Deal CT14 134 B8
  Maidstone ME14 75 F4
Thistledown Cl ME7 33 A4
Thistle Dr CT5 43 B6
Thistle Hill Way
  Minster (Sheppey) ME12 4 A4
Thistle Hill Way *continued*
  Minster (Sheppey) ME12 4 C5
Thistle Wlk ME10 37 B5
Thomas Aveling Sch The ME1 31 C8
Thomas Cl TN23 156 A6
Thomas Ct 9 ME10 37 B4
Thomas Rd
  Faversham ME13 62 D7
  Sittingbourne ME10 37 B4
Thomas Rider Way ME15 97 E4
Thomas Seth Bsns Pk ME11 3 A3
Thomas St ME1 9 C3
Thomas Way CT3 47 A1
Thompson Cl
  Deal CT14 134 B8
  Folkestone CT19 178 B7
  Gillingham ME8 34 A8
Thomson Rd TN25 139 B5
Thornbridge Rd CT14 117 B2
Thorn Cl ME5 31 D1
Thorndale Cl ME5 31 D4
Thornden Cl CT6 22 B2
Thornden Ct CT2 66 C4
Thornden Wood Rd
  Herne Bay CT6 22 B1
  Whitstable CT6 44 E4
Thorndike Cl ME4 31 F8
Thorndike Ho ME4 31 F8
Thorndike Rd TN29 186 C4
Thorne Hill CT12 51 A6
Thorne Rd CT12 50 B6
Thorn Est The TN27 136 B6
Thorneycroft Cl ME17 99 D2
Thorneycroft Rd ME13 103 D5
Thorn Gdns CT11 29 E1
Thornham Rd ME8 11 C3
Thornhill Pl ME14 75 A6
Thorn Hill Rd ME12 6 D4
Thornhurst CT6 23 D4
Thorn La CT4 126 C2
Thornlea TN23 138 E2
Thornton Cl TN24 140 A1
Thornton La CT13, CT14 114 E7
Thornton's La 9 CT16 166 E8
Thorn Wlk ME10 37 C5
Thorold Rd ME5 10 B3
Thorpe Wlk ME8 33 D3
Thrale Way ME8 33 E4
Thread La ME13 64 B4
Three Acres Site CT19 178 B8
Three King's Yd CT13 73 A1
Threshers Dr ME14 75 E5
THROWLEY 82 E4
Throwley Dr CT6 22 C4
THROWLEY FORSTAL 82 D1
Throwley Rd ME13 82 D5
Thrupp Paddock CT10 8 G1
Thrush Cl ME5 32 B7
Thruxted La CT4 86 B1
Thundersland Rd CT6 23 B4
Thurlow Ave CT6 23 C5
THURNHAM 76 D8
Thurnham CE Inf Sch ME14 76 A4
Thurnham La ME14 76 C7
Thurstone Ct ME14 74 F6
THURSTON PARK 20 E1
Thurston Pk CT5 20 E1
Thyme Wlk ME16 74 B3
Tiber Cl CT19 177 C6
Tichborne Cl ME16 74 C6
TICKENHURST 92 D1
TICKHAM 60 D6
Tickham La ME9 60 C5
Tickner's La TN29 192 B1
Tideway The ME1 31 C8
Tilbury Rd ME8 12 A2
Tilden Cl TN26 167 D7
Tilden Ct TN26 167 E7
Tilden Gill Rd TN30 179 C7
Tile Fields ME17 77 D2
Tile Fields Cl ME17 77 D2
Tile Ho The CT21 176 C2
Tile Kiln Hill CT2 66 B5
Tile Kiln La CT19 177 F7
Tile Kiln Rd TN24 139 C7
Tile Lodge Cotts TN27 119 E8
Tile Lodge Rd TN27 119 E8
Tillard Cl CT4 109 B3
Tillery La TN29 200 A8
TILMANSTONE 115 A3
Timberbank ME5 32 A6
Timber Tops ME5 54 D8
Timeball Tower Mus★ CT14 117 D5
Timperley Cl CT14 117 B6
Tina Gdns CT10 30 A6
Tinbridge Pk ME13 63 A5
Tinker's Alley ME4 9 F7
Tintagel Manor 6 ME7 10 C6
Tintern Rd ME16 74 D7
Titchfield Cl 5 ME15 97 F6
Titchfield Rd ME15 97 F6
Tithe Barn La TN23 155 D8
Tithe Yd ME17 101 D5
Tivoli Brooks CT9 7 I1
Tivoli Park Ave CT9 7 H1
Tivoli Rd CT9 28 E8
Tobruk Way ME5 31 F6
Toby Rd TN29 206 E6
Todd Cres ME10 37 A8
Toddington Cres ME5 31 D1
Toke Cl TN23 138 C1

Tolgate La ME2 9 B7
Tolgate Way ME14 53 E4
Tollemache Cl CT12 27 F2
Toll Gate CT14 117 A4
Tollgate Cl CT5 43 C8
Toll La TN27 120 E7
Tolputt Ct CT19 178 E6
Tolsford Cl
Etchinghill CT18 161 D3
Folkestone CT19 177 D6
Tomay Cotts CT6 24 A3
Tomlin Dr CT9 29 C8
Tonbridge Ct ME16 74 D3
Tonbridge Rd ME16 74 C3
Tonford La
Canterbury CT1 87 B6
Harbledown CT2 87 A7
TONGE CORNER 37 F7
Tonge Rd ME10 37 C4
TONG GREEN 82 B1
Tontine St CT20 178 E5
Tookey Rd TN28 202 B6
Topaz Dr ME10 36 C6
Top Rd TN30 189 E3
Tormore Mews CT14 117 A4
Tormore Pk CT14 117 A4
Toronto Cl 6 CT16 149 B3
Toronto Rd ME7 10 E4
Torrington Cotts CT12 50 D7
Torrington Rd TN23 156 C8
Tothill St CT12 50 C7
Tourmaline Dr ME10 36 C6
Tournay Cl TN23 155 F8
Tourney Cl CT21 174 F3
Tourney Rd TN29 205 C5
Tourtel Rd CT1 67 A1
Tovey Sq ME7 10 F6
TOVIL 74 E1
Tovil Gn ME15 74 E2
Tovil Green Bsns Pk
ME15 74 E1
Tovil Hill ME15 74 E2
Tovil Rd ME15 74 F2
Tovil Sch ME15 74 D2
Tower Bglws CT7 27 A8
Tower Ct 4 CT20 177 E3
Tower Est TN29 186 E2
Tower Gdns
Hythe CT21 176 C1
Maidstone ME14 76 B4
TOWER HAMLETS 166 B8
Tower Hamlets Rd CT17 166 C8
Tower Hamlets St 1
CT17 166 C8
Tower Hill
Dover CT17 166 C8
Whitstable CT5 20 E3
Tower La ME14 76 B4
Tower Par CT5 20 E3
Tower Rd CT5 20 E2
Towers Point ME1 9 B4
Towers Sch The TN24 139 D8
Tower St CT17 166 C8
Towers The TN27 103 E1
Towers View TN24 139 C7
Tower View CT4 86 F1
Tower Way 1 CT1 87 F8
Town Hill CT4 88 F2
Town La CT4 86 C6
TOWNLAND GREEN 169 A1
Townley St CT11 52 D6
Town Rd CT4 109 C5
Townsend Farm Rd CT15 150 F6
Townsend Terr CT17 166 B5
Townwall St CT16 166 E7
Town Wlk CT20 178 D4
Tracies The ME9 35 C6
Tradewinds CT5 43 B6
Trafalgar Dr CT14 117 D4
Trafalgar Par ME12 4 B6
Trafalgar Rd CT7 27 F3
Trafalgar St ME7 10 C5
Tram Rd The CT20 178 E5
Tramways ME5 10 C2
Transformer Ave TN29 209 C2
Transom Ho 3 ME1 9 C1
Trapfield Cl ME14 76 C4
Trapfield La ME14 76 C4
Trapham Rd ME16 74 D5
Travers Gdns ME9 57 F5
Travers Rd CT14 117 A5
Travertine Rd ME5 32 B1
Treasury View CT3 90 C8
Trefoil The ME9, ME13 60 E6
Trefor Jones Ct CT16 149 B2
Trelawn Cres ME5 32 B2
Trenley Dr CT3 67 F1
Trenton Cl ME16 74 B7
Trent Rd ME5 32 B5
Trevale Rd ME1 9 B1
Trevino Dr ME5 31 F2
Trevor Dr ME16 74 C5
Tribune Ct ME12 3 B8
Tribune Dr ME10 36 F6
Trident Cl ME2 9 E7
Triggs Cotts ME9 38 D2
Trigg's Row ME9 38 D2
Trilby Way CT5 43 B6
Trimworth Rd CT19 177 F6
Trinity Cres CT20 178 B4
Trinity Ct
Deal CT14 117 A4
Forstal ME20 53 A3
Margate CT9 7 J3
Trinity Gdns CT20 178 C4
Trinity Hill CT9 7 J3
Trinity Homes CT14 117 C1
Trinity Pl
Deal CT14 117 A4
Ramsgate CT11 52 F7
Trinity Rd
Ashford TN24 139 B7
Folkestone CT20 178 B4
Gillingham ME7 10 C6
Sheerness ME12 1 D2
Sittingbourne ME10 36 F7
Trinity Sch ME1 9 D4
Trinity Sq
Broadstairs CT10 29 F7
Margate CT9 7 J3
Trinity Trad Est ME10 36 F6
Trinity Way ME12 1 D2
Tristram Way CT16 149 B5
Tritton Cl TN24 139 F7
Tritton Fields TN24 139 F7
Tritton Gdns TN29 186 D1
Tritton La TN28 202 B6
Trona Ct 7 ME10 36 D6
Troodos Hill ME14 74 F8
Trotts Hall Gdns ME10 36 F3
Trotwood Cl ME5 54 A8
Trotwood Pl 14 CT10 30 B4
Troubridge Cl TN24 157 B7
Troughton Mews CT9 7 H1
Trove Ct 7 CT11 52 F7
Troy Mews ME1 9 C4
Troys Mead ME17 77 D2
TROY TOWN
Brook 141 B5
Rochester 9 C5
Troy Town La TN25 141 B5
Trueman Cl CT2 66 A7
Trumpet Ho TN23 156 B8
Trunley Way CT18 162 F3
Truro Cl ME8 11 D3
Truro Rd CT11 52 F7
Tudor Ave
Dymchurch TN29 186 D1
Maidstone ME14 75 B6
Tudor Byway TN24 139 D6
Tudor Cl CT7 27 B8
Tudor Ct
Canterbury CT2 66 C4
Whitstable CT5 21 A3
Tudor End TN24 139 D5
Tudor Farm Cl TN23 156 A3
Tudor Gr ME8 33 F8
Tudor Ho CT14 117 A5
Tudor Ho★ CT9 7 J3
Tudor Mews CT14 117 B4
Tudor Rd
Ashford TN24 139 D5
Canterbury CT1 87 E7
Folkestone CT19 177 D6
Tufa Cl ME5 32 B1
Tufton Rd
Ashford TN24 139 D2
Gillingham ME8 11 F1
Hothfield TN26 138 A7
Tufton St
Ashford TN23 139 B2
Maidstone ME14 75 A4
Tufton Wlk 9 TN23 139 B2
Tumbledown Hill TN25 121 F3
Tunbridge Way TN23 155 C8
Tunbury Ave ME5 31 F1
Tunbury Avenue S ME5 31 F1
Tunbury Prim Sch ME5 31 F1
Tunis Ct CT1 67 D1
Tunis Row CT10 30 B5
TUNSTALL 58 D8
Tunstall CE Prim Sch
ME9 58 C8
Tunstall Rd
Canterbury CT2 67 A4
Sittingbourne ME10, ME9 58 D8
Tupman Cl ME1 9 B4
Turbine Hall Ave TN29 209 C2
Turgis Cl ME17 98 E4
Turketel Rd CT20 178 A4
Turmine Ct ME12 4 A5
Turnagain La 3 CT1 87 F8
Turnden Gdns CT9 8 E2
Turner Cl
Ashford TN24 156 E7
Sittingbourne ME10 37 A7
Turner Ct
5 Folkestone CT20 177 F5
Margate CT9 8 A2
Turners Ave TN30 179 B8
Turners Cl ME12 1 D1
Turner St CT11 52 E7
Turnpike Cl CT21 176 A2
Turnpike Hill CT21 176 A3
Turnstone Cl ME9 14 E4
Turnstone Ct TN29 194 F3
Turnstone Rd ME5 32 C1
Turrets The
Deal CT14 117 C1
9 Sittingbourne ME10 37 A4
Tuscan Dr ME5 32 C1
TUTT HILL 121 A1
Tweed Terr CT21 176 A1
Twelve Acres TN24 156 F8
Twiss Ave CT21 176 D2
Twiss Gr CT21 176 D2
Twiss Rd CT21 176 D2
TWITHAM 91 E6
TWYDALL 11 B2
Twydall Ent Ctr ME8 11 C4
Twydall Gn ME8 11 B3
Twydall Inf Sch ME8 11 B2
Twydall Jun Sch ME8 11 B2
Twydall La ME8 11 B2
Twyford Cl ME8 12 A2
Twyford Ct ME14 75 D6
Twymans Mill ME13 62 C7
Twyne Cl CT2 68 A6
Twysden Ct TN25 123 E2
Tydeman Rd ME15 75 F2
Tydeman's Ave CT5 21 C1
Tye La CT18 163 A5
Tyland Barn Wildlife Park★
ME14 53 E3
Tyland La ME14 53 F3
Tyler Cl CT2 66 F3
Tyler Dr ME8 33 E4
TYLER HILL 66 E6
Tyler Hill Rd CT2 66 C6
Tyler Way CT5 21 E3
Tyndale Pk CT6 23 B5
Tyne Cl ME5 32 C5
Tyrwhitt-Drake Mus of
Carriages★ 9 ME15 75 A3
Tysoe Ct ME12 4 A5
Tyson Ave CT9 7 E1
Tyson Rd CT19 178 E7

U

Uden Rd TN29 187 B4
Uffington Ct CT3 91 A2
Ufton Cl ME15 75 E1
Ufton La ME10 36 E3
Ulcombe Gdns CT2 67 A3
Ulcombe Hill ME17 99 F1
Ulcombe Rd ME17 98 E3
Ulley Rd TN24 139 D7
Ullswater Gdns CT3 112 F6
Ullswater Ho 5 ME15 97 E7
Ulster Rd CT9 28 F8
Undercliff CT20 177 E3
Undercliffe Rd CT14 134 D5
UNDERDOWN 108 B8
Underdown Ave ME4 9 F1
Underdown La CT6 22 F2
Underdown Rd
Dover CT17 166 B7
Herne Bay CT6 22 F5
Underhill Cotts CT18 177 B8
Underhill Rd CT20 177 B5
Underwood CT18 163 C6
Underwood Cl
Ashford TN24 139 D6
Canterbury CT4 88 B5
Maidstone ME15 74 F2
Underwood Ct 1 CT1 88 B6
Unicorn Cotts CT4 89 B5
Unicumes La ME16 74 C2
Union Cres CT9 7 J2
Union Pk ME15 97 F4
Union Pl
4 Canterbury CT1 67 A1
Chatham ME4 10 A4
Union Rd
Bridge CT4 88 F1
Deal CT14 117 D6
Minster (Sheppey) ME12 4 C7
Ramsgate CT11 52 F8
Union Row CT9 7 J2
Union Sq 3 CT10 30 B4
Union St
Canterbury CT1 67 A1
Chatham ME4 10 A3
Dover CT17 166 D6
Faversham ME13 62 C7
Maidstone ME14 75 A5
12 Ramsgate CT11 52 E7
Rochester ME1 9 C5
Sheerness ME12 1 B2
Unity Ct ME12 1 E2
Unity Pl 3 CT11 52 F7
Unity St
Sheerness ME12 1 E2
Sittingbourne ME10 36 E3
Univ Centre Folkestone 23
CT20 178 D5
University Rd CT2 66 D3
Univ for the Creative Arts at
Canterbury CT1 88 B7
Univ for the Creative Arts at
Maidstone ME16 74 C3
Univ for the Creative Arts at
Rochester ME1 9 E4
Univ of Greenwich The
ME4 10 B8
Univ of Kent (Canterbury)
CT2 66 D4
Univ of Kent (Universities at
Medway Campus) ME4 10 B8
Unwin Cl ME20 53 A3
Upbury Way ME4 10 A4
UPCHURCH 12 F4
Upchurch Wlk CT9 8 E2
Updown Way CT4 86 F1
Uphill CT18 163 B4
Uplands CT2 66 F4
Uplands Way ME12 3 C5
Uplees Cotts ME13 39 F5
Uplees Rd ME13 40 A3
Upnor Ho ME15 97 E8
Upper Approach Rd CT10 30 A3
Upper Balcom Mews 5
CT9 29 C8
Upper Brents ME13 62 D8
Upper Bridge St
Canterbury CT1 88 A8
Wye TN25 123 F2
Upper Britton Pl ME7 10 B5
Upper Chantry La CT1 88 A7
Upper Corniche CT20 177 C3
Upper Dane Ct CT9 8 B1
Upper Dane Rd CT9 8 B1
UPPER DEAL 117 B4
Upper Denmark Rd
TN23 156 B8
Upper Dumpton Park Rd
CT11 52 E8
Upper East Rd ME4 10 B8
UPPER EYTHORNE 131 C7
Upper Fans La ME9 14 C4
UPPER FANT 74 D3
Upper Fant Rd ME16 74 D2
Upper Field Rd ME10 37 B5
Upper Free Down CT6 23 B2
UPPER GOLDSTONE 71 E5
Upper Gore La CT13 93 A2
Upper Gr CT9 7 J2
UPPER HARBLEDOWN 65 F1
Upper Hunton Hill ME15 96 A3
Upper Luton Rd ME5 10 C2
Upper Malthouse Hill
CT21 176 B2
Upper Maltings Pl CT7 26 F7
Upper Queens Rd TN24 139 B3
Upper Rd
Dover CT15, CT16 150 C2
Dover, Eastern Docks
CT16 166 G8
Maidstone ME15 75 B2
UPPER RODMERSHAM 59 C6
Upper St Ann's Rd ME13 62 B6
Upper St
Hollingbourne ME17 77 E3
Kingsdown CT14 134 D5
Leeds ME17 98 F5
Tilmanstone CT14 115 A3
Upper Stone St ME15 75 A3
Upper Strand St CT13 73 A1
Upper Tickham Cotts
ME9 60 D6
Upper Vicarage Rd
TN24 139 D7
UPPER WALMER 117 B1
UPSTREET 47 D3
Upstreet CT18 161 D3
UPTON 29 F4
Upton Cl CT19 178 A7
Upton Jun Sch CT10 29 F4
Upton Rd CT10 29 F5
UPTON WOOD 130 E2
Urquhart Cl ME5 32 A5
Ursuline Coll CT8 27 D8
Ursuline Dr CT8 27 D7

V

Valebrook Cl CT20 177 C5
Vale Cotts ME9 57 A8
Vale Ct 10 CT11 52 D6
Vale Dr ME5 31 E6
Valence Ho ME15 97 C7
Valenciennes Ho ME4 10 A4
Valenciennes Rd ME10 36 E3
Valentine Cl ME7 11 A1
Valentine Rd ME15 97 E7
Vale Pl CT11 52 D6
Vale Rd
Broadstairs CT10 29 F4
Maidstone ME15 96 E4
Ramsgate CT11 52 D6
Ripple CT14, CT15 133 B8
Whitstable CT5 43 D8
Valerian Cl ME5 31 E4
Vale Sq CT11 52 D6
Valestone Cl CT21 177 B4
Vale The CT10 30 A4
Valetta Way ME1 9 B4
Vale View Com Sch
CT17 166 B7
Vale View Rd
Aylesham CT3 112 E5
Dover CT17 166 B7
Valiant Rd ME5 32 C2
Valkyrie Ave CT5 43 C7
Vallance The ME9 60 A6
Valley Cotts
Alkham CT15 147 C1
Stalisfield Green ME13 103 D8
Valley Dr ME15 96 F6
Valley L Ctr CT19 177 F7
Valley Park Com Sch
ME14 75 C4
Valley Rd
Barham CT4 111 E2
Canterbury CT1 87 E6
Crabble CT17 148 E3
Folkestone CT20 177 E4
Gillingham ME7 10 E4
Margate CT9 28 E4
Valley Rise ME5 31 F1
Valley The ME17 96 D3
Valley View CT15 131 C8
Valley View Rd ME1 9 B1
Valley Wlk CT21 177 B3
Vancouver Dr ME8 11 C1
Vancouver Rd CT16 149 C3
Vange Cottage Mews ME1 9 B4
Vanguard Way ME2 9 E8
Vanity La ME17 96 D1
Vanity Rd ME12 6 F2
Varne Ct 6 CT20 177 F3
Varne Lodge 5 CT20 177 F3
Varne Mews TN28 202 E4
Varne Pl CT19 178 F5
Varne Rd CT19 178 F5
Vaughan Dr ME10 36 F8
Vauxhall Ave
Canterbury CT1 67 C3
Herne Bay CT6 22 A3
Vauxhall Cres CT1 67 C3
Vauxhall Industrial Rd
CT1 67 D4
Vauxhall Rd CT1, CT2 67 C4
Vectis Dr ME10 36 F8
Ventnor Cl ME5 32 C8
Ventnor La 12 CT9 7 J2
Venture Cl TN29 186 D1
Vere Rd CT10 30 A4
Vereth Rd 2 CT11 52 D6
Vernon Pl
Canterbury CT1 88 A7
Deal CT14 117 D8
Verwood Cl CT2 66 E2
Vespasian Way TN23 155 F4
Vesper Ct TN27 135 A1
Vestey Ct CT8 7 C1
Viaduct Cl CT12 52 C8
Viaduct Terr TN26 182 F7
Viaduct The CT17 166 D5
Viburnum Cl TN23 138 E2
Vicarage Cotts ME9 13 C3
Vicarage Cres 8 CT9 7 J1
Vicarage Ct ME9 35 B7
Vicarage Gdn CT12 49 C7
Vicarage Gdns CT3 91 A7
Vicarage Hill CT4 109 B4
Vicarage La
Ashford TN23 139 C2
Blean CT2 66 A6
Charing Heath TN27 119 C7
Deal CT14 116 F5
East Farleigh ME15 96 B6
Elham CT4 144 F4
Faversham ME13 62 A4
Lower Halstow ME9 13 C3
Nonington CT15 113 C5
4 Sandwich CT13 72 F1
Selling ME13 84 C6
St Margaret's at Cliffe
CT15 150 F6
Tilmanstone CT14 115 A3
Vicarage Pl CT9 7 J1
Vicarage Rd
Gillingham ME7 10 C5
Minster (Sheppey) ME12 4 D7
Rochester ME2 9 B8
Sittingbourne ME10 36 E6
Vicarage St
Broadstairs CT10 29 E5
Faversham ME13 62 D8
Vicary Way ME16 74 D5
Vickers Cl CT18 163 A4
Victor Ave CT9 8 D2
Victoria Ave
Broadstairs CT10 29 E8
Hythe CT21 176 B2
Margate CT9 8 B1
St Margaret's at Cliffe
CT15 151 B6
Westgate on Sea CT8 27 F8
Victoria Cl ME5 31 D2
Victoria Cres
Ashford TN23 139 B1
Dover CT16 166 D8
Victoria Ct
Hythe CT21 176 C1
6 Maidstone ME16 74 E3
Victoria Dr CT6 22 C5
Victoria Gr
12 Folkestone CT20 178 D5
Hythe CT21 177 B2
Victoria Ho 7 CT5 20 D2
Victoria Hospl CT14 117 B5
Victoria Mews
Deal CT14 117 C6
Westgate on Sea CT8 7 D1
Victoria Orch ME16 74 B3
Victoria Par
Broadstairs CT10 30 B4
Ramsgate CT11 52 F7
Victoria Park Mews 2
CT16 166 E8
Victoria Pk
Dover CT16 166 E8
Herne Bay CT6 23 A5
Victoria Pl
Faversham ME13 62 C7
Hythe CT21 176 B4
Victoria Rd
Ashford TN23 139 B1
Broadstairs CT10 29 E6
Canterbury CT1 87 E7
Capel-le-Ferne CT18 164 B2
Chatham, Kit Hill ME5 31 E3
Chatham, Luton ME4 10 B2
Deal CT14 117 D5
Folkestone CT19 178 C5
Hythe CT21 176 C1
Kingsdown CT14 134 C4
Littlestone-on-Sea TN28 202 E5
Margate CT9 7 J2
Margate, Lydden CT9 28 D4
Ramsgate CT11 52 F7
Sittingbourne ME10 36 D4
Victoria Road Ind Pk
TN23 139 B1
Victoria Road Prim Sch
TN23 139 B1
Victoria Road W TN28 202 E5
Victoria Row
Canterbury CT1 67 A1
Ramsgate CT11 52 C5
Victoria St
Dover CT17 149 B1

Victoria St *continued*
  Gillingham ME7 10 D6
  Maidstone ME16 74 E3
  New Romney TN28 202 A6
  Rochester ME1 9 D5
  Rochester, Strood ME2 9 B7
  Sheerness ME12 1 D1
  Whitstable CT5 20 D2
Victoria Terr
  Hythe CT21 177 B2
  Minster (Sheppey) ME12 5 A5
  Rochester ME1 9 A2
  Sittingbourne ME10 36 D4
Victoria Yd 21 CT1 67 A1
Victory Manor 1 ME7 10 A6
Victory Pk ME2 9 E7
Victory Rd CT15 133 F1
Victory St ME12 1 C2
Vidal Manor ME7 10 C5
Viewlands ME5 10 C3
Viewpoint ME14 75 C8
Vigo Terr ME9 38 C1
Viking Cl CT7 26 D8
Viking Ct
  Broadstairs CT10 30 B3
  Canterbury CT2 66 F2
  Margate CT9 8 A2
Viking Ship 'Hugin'★ CT12 51 E5
Village View ME5 10 C2
Village Way TN26 183 A7
Villas The CT3 47 A1
Villiers Ct CT17 166 C7
Villiers Ho CT10 30 B7
Villiers Rd CT1 67 D1
Vincent Cl
  Broadstairs CT10 29 C3
  Folkestone CT20 177 E5
Vincent Ct ME12 1 D1
Vincent Gdns ME12 1 D1
Vincent Pl TN24 139 F4
Vincent Rd
  Kit's Coty ME20 53 C7
  Margate CT9 28 C4
  Sittingbourne ME10 37 C3
Vine Cl CT11 29 E2
Vine End CT11 29 E2
Vine Lands TN29 205 B6
Vine Lo CT11 29 E2
Vineries The ME7 10 E5
Viners Cl ME10 36 F1
Vines La ME1 9 C5
Vineyard Cres ME8 12 B1
Viney's Gdns TN30 167 C1
Vinson Cl ME13 41 D1
Vinten Cl CT6 46 B8
Vinters Rd ME14 75 B4
Vinters Valley Nature Reserve★ ME14 75 D5
Vintners Way ME14 75 E4
Violet Ave CT12 29 C2
Violet Cl ME5 54 A8
Violet Ct ME10 36 F2
Violet Way TN23 156 C2
Virginia Rd
  Gillingham ME7 10 C7
  Whitstable CT5 44 A8
Vixen Cl ME5 32 C6
Vlissingen Dr CT14 117 C8
Volante Dr ME10 36 E7
Vulcan Cl
  Chatham ME5 32 B7
  Whitstable CT5 43 C7

W

Wacher Cl CT2 66 F2
Waddenhall Barns CT4 126 B5
Waddington Dr CT18 163 A4
Waddle Cnr TN30 189 D3
Wades Cl TN29 194 B4
Wadham Pl ME10 37 B2
Waghorn St ME4 10 B2
Wagoners Cl ME14 75 E4
Wain Ct ME12 4 A5
Wainwright Ct CT10 30 B6
Wainwright Pl TN24 156 D8
Wakefield Way CT21 176 B1
Wakefield Wlk CT21 176 D1
Wakehurst Cl ME17 96 B3
Wakeley Rd ME8 12 A1
Wakeleys Cotts ME8 34 B8
Wake Rd ME1 31 C8
Walcheren Cl CT14 117 C8
Walcot Pl CT6 23 B3
Walden Ct CT2 67 A3
Waldens The ME17 99 E2
Waldershare Ave CT13 95 A7
Waldershare Ho CT15 131 D5
Waldershare La CT15 132 E2
Waldershare Rd CT15 132 A5
WALDERSLADE 31 F1
WALDERSLADE BOTTOM 32 A2
Walderslade Ctr ME5 32 A3
Walderslade Girls Sch 7 ME5 31 F5
Walderslade Prim Sch ME5 32 A3
Walderslade Rd ME5 31 F6
Walderslade Village By-pass ME5 31 F3
Walderslade Woods ME5 31 E2
Waldron Dr ME15 96 F6
Waldron Rd CT10 30 B2
Walker La CT7 26 D8
Walk The ME17 99 E2
Wallace Mews CT19 178 D7
Wallace Rd ME1 31 E8
Wallace Way CT10 29 E4
Wallbridge La ME8 12 D3
WALL END 47 F4
Waller Rd TN28 206 E7
Wallers Rd ME13 62 A7
Wallis Ave ME15 97 E5
Wallis Ct CT6 23 F5
Wallis Oak Ave 12 ME15 97 F5
Wallis Rd TN24 139 D2
Wall Rd TN24 139 B3
Wall The ME10 36 E5
Wallwood Rd CT11 52 F8
WALMER 117 C2
Walmer Castle★ CT14 117 D1
Walmer Castle Rd CT14 117 C1
Walmer Ct 3 ME14 75 A5
Walmer Gdns
  Cliffs End CT12 51 D5
  Deal CT14 117 A2
  Sittingbourne ME10 36 D5
Walmer Rd CT5 43 E8
Walmer Science Coll CT14 117 B2
Walmer Sta CT14 117 A1
Walmer Way
  Deal CT14 117 A2
  1 Folkestone CT20 177 F5
WALMESTONE 70 D3
Walmsley Ho 4 CT19 178 E6
Walmsley Rd CT10 29 F5
Walner Gdns TN28 202 B7
Walner La TN28 202 B7
Walnut Cl
  Ashford TN24 139 D6
  Broadstairs CT10 29 F2
  Chatham ME5 32 B8
Walnut Mews CT7 26 F7
Walnut Ridge TN25 173 A6
Walnut Tree Ave ME15 97 A5
Walnut Tree Cl 6 CT7 27 A7
Walnut Tree Cotts ME13 84 E8
Walnut Tree Dr ME10 36 D4
Walnut Tree La
  Loose ME15 97 A5
  Westbere CT2 68 D7
Walpole Rd CT9 7 J3
Walsby Dr ME10 37 A8
Walsham Rd ME5 31 F1
Walshaw Ho 2 ME14 75 A6
Walsingham Cl ME8 33 D3
Walsingham Ho 3 ME14 75 A6
Walter Burke Way ME4 10 A8
WALTHAM 125 E6
Waltham Cl
  Ashford TN24 140 A2
  Margate CT9 8 E2
Waltham Rd
  Gillingham ME8 11 C3
  Petham CT4 109 B3
  Waltham CT4 108 F1
Walton Gdns CT19 178 D7
Walton Manor Cl CT19 178 D7
Walton Rd CT19 178 D6
Waltons The CT19 178 C8
WANDEN 135 B7
Wanden La TN27 135 C8
Wanstall Ct CT7 27 A7
Wantsum Cl CT6 23 F5
Wantsume Lees CT13 72 E2
Wantsum Mews 7 CT13 72 F1
Wantsum Way CT7 25 E3
Warblers Cl 3 ME2 9 A7
WARDEN 6 D4
Warden Bay Rd ME12 6 E3
Warden Cl ME16 74 C4
Warden Ct 10 CT17 149 C1
Warden House Mews CT14 117 A4
Warden House Prim Sch CT14 117 A5
Warden Point Way 2 CT5 43 C6
Warden Rd
  Rochester ME1 9 C2
  Warden ME12 6 B5
Warden Terr ME12 5 A6
Warden View Gdns ME12 6 D1
Warden Way ME12 6 B5
Wardour Cl CT10 30 B4
Wards Hill Rd ME12 4 C8
Wardwell La ME9 13 C1
WARE 71 B6
WAREHORNE 182 D6
Warehorne Rd TN26 183 A7
Ware St ME14 76 A5
WARE STREET 76 B5
Warlingham Cl ME8 12 A1
WARMLAKE 98 D1
Warmlake ME17 98 F1
Warmlake Bsns Est ME17 98 E1
Warmlake Rd ME17 98 C1
Warner St ME4 9 F3
Warnford Gdns ME15 97 A8
Warnford Pl ME15 97 A8
Warre Ave CT11 52 C5
Warren Cl
  Folkestone CT19 178 F6
  Sittingbourne ME10 37 B2
Warren Dr CT10 29 E5
Warren Dr The CT8 27 D7
Warren Hos TN27 119 E8
Warren Hts TN25 158 E5
Warren La
  Ashford TN24 139 A4
  Lydden CT15 147 D6
  Yelsted ME9 34 C3
Warren Lo CT1 87 B6
Warren Rd
  Folkestone CT19 178 F6
  Kit's Coty ME5 53 D7
  Littlestone-on-Sea TN28 202 D6
Warren Ret Pk TN24 139 B4
Warren St
  Stalisfield Green TN27 103 A3
  Warren Street ME17 102 D7
WARREN STREET 102 D7
Warren The
  Brabourne Lees TN25 158 E5
  Selling ME13 84 E7
  Whitstable CT5 43 C6
Warren View TN23 138 F4
Warren Way CT19 178 F6
Warren Wood Com Prim Sch ME1 31 C8
Warren Wood Rd ME1 31 C7
Warten Rd CT11 29 F1
Warwick Cres ME10 36 C5
Warwick Dr CT11 52 B5
Warwick Pl ME16 74 E3
Warwick Rd
  Ashford TN24 139 E5
  Canterbury CT1 88 C8
  Deal CT14 117 D2
  Margate CT9 8 B2
  Whitstable CT5 20 D2
Washford Farm Rd TN23 155 E5
Washington Cl 4 CT16 149 B3
Washington Ho ME15 97 E5
Washington La TN29 200 C6
Wass Dro CT3 71 B7
Watchester Ave CT11 52 C5
Watchester La CT12 50 B5
Watchmans Terr 6 ME5 10 C2
Waterbrook Ave TN24 157 A4
Watercress Ho TN23 138 F1
Watercress La
  Ashford TN23 155 F8
  Wingham CT3 90 F6
Waterditch La ME17, TN27 102 E5
Waterfall Rd TN26 138 B6
Water Farm CT4 144 F4
WATERHAM 42 C2
Waterham Rd ME13 42 C1
Water La
  Canterbury CT1 87 F8
  6 Faversham ME13 62 C7
  Harrietsham ME17 100 A5
  Kingswood ME17 99 F3
  Maidstone, Bearsted ME14 76 E6
  6 Maidstone ME15 75 A4
  Painters Forstal ME13 61 F4
  Sturry CT2 67 F5
Waterlock Cotts CT3 91 A7
Waterloo Cres CT16, CT17 166 E7
Waterloo Hill ME12 4 D6
Waterloo Mans 14 CT17 166 E7
Waterloo Pl 10 CT11 52 F7
Waterloo Rd
  Folkestone CT20 177 D5
  Gillingham ME7 10 C4
  Sittingbourne ME10 36 D5
  Whitstable CT5 20 D2
Waterloo St ME15 75 A3
Waterloo Terr ME12 5 A5
Waterlow Rd ME14 75 A6
Waterman Ho TN23 156 B8
Water Mdws CT2 67 F4
Watermead Cl TN23 155 F7
Watermeadow Cl ME7 32 F6
Watermill Cl
  Maidstone ME16 74 B5
  Rochester ME2 9 C8
Waters Edge ME15 74 F2
Watersend CT16 148 D5
Waterside
  Ashford TN24 139 F1
  8 Maidstone ME14 74 F4
Waterside Cl ME13 40 D1
Waterside Ct 5 CT21 176 B2
Waterside Ct ME2 9 E6
Waterside Dr CT8 7 D1
Waterside Gate ME16 74 F5
Waterside La ME7 10 F7
Waterside Terr TN23 138 C1
Waterside View ME12 6 E4
Watersmeet Cl ME15 75 A1
Waters Pl ME7 33 A6
Water St CT14 117 D7
Waterstone Pl ME13 62 A6
Waterworks Hill CT15 133 B3
Waterworks La CT15 133 B3
Watery La CT4 109 C5
Watkin Rd CT19 178 C6
Watling Ave ME5 10 D2
Watling Pl ME10 37 A3
Watling St
  Canterbury CT1 87 F8
  Gillingham ME7 10 D2
Watson Ave ME5 31 D5
Watsons Cl TN25 139 C8
Watsons Hill ME10 36 E5
Wattle Cnr TN30 189 D3
Watts' Ave ME1 9 C4
Watts Cotts TN24 139 D7
Watts' St ME4 9 E3
Watts Yd 13 CT13 72 F1
Wat Tyler Way ME15 75 A4
Wauchope Rd
  Whitstable CT5 42 F6
  1 Whitstable CT5 43 A6
Wave Crest CT5 20 C1
Waverley Ave ME12 4 B7
Waverley Cl
  Chatham ME5 32 D2
  Coxheath ME17 96 C3
Waverley Rd CT9 28 C8
WAY 50 E7
Wayborough Hill CT12 50 D7
Way Farm Cotts CT12 50 E7
WAYFIELD 32 A8
Wayfield Com Prim Sch ME5 32 A7
Wayfield Rd ME5 32 A7
Way Hill CT12 50 E7
Wayne Cl CT10 29 E5
Wayside TN30 167 B2
Wayside Ave TN30 167 B3
Wayside Flats TN30 167 B2
Weald Cl ME15 97 C6
Weald Ct
  Charing TN27 103 E1
  Sittingbourne ME10 36 D2
Wealden Ave TN30 167 B1
Wealden Ct 5 ME5 10 B3
Wealdhurst Pk CT10 29 D5
Weald The TN24 139 C3
Wear Bay Cres CT19 178 F6
Wear Bay Rd
  Folkestone CT19 178 F5
  Folkestone CT19 178 F7
Weatherall Cl ME13 64 B2
Weatherly Cl ME1 9 C4
Weatherly Dr CT10 29 F2
Weavering Cotts ME14 75 E3
Weavering St ME14 75 F4
WEAVERING STREET 75 F5
Weavers The ME16 74 B5
Weavers Way
  Ashford TN23 155 E7
  Dover CT16 149 A3
Webb Cl CT19 178 A7
Webster Rd ME8 11 F1
Webster Way CT18 163 B4
WEDDINGTON 71 E3
Weddington La CT3 71 E2
Wedgewood Cl ME16 74 B5
Wedgewood Dr ME5 32 A7
Weeds Wood Rd ME5 31 F4
Weekes Ct ME11 3 A5
Week St ME14 75 A4
Weigall Pl CT11 52 C7
Weighbridge Way CT16 166 H8
Welcombe Ct ME8 33 D8
Well Cl CT2 68 A6
Weller Ave ME1 9 D2
Wellesley Ave CT14 117 C3
Wellesley Cl
  Broadstairs CT10 29 E3
  Westgate on Sea CT8 27 E7
Wellesley Ct 13 CT11 52 E7
Wellesley Ho CT14 117 C1
Wellesley House Sch CT10 29 F3
Wellesley Rd
  Ashford TN23 139 C2
  Dover CT16 166 E7
  Margate CT9 8 B1
  Sheerness ME12 1 E2
  Westgate on Sea CT8 27 E7
Wellesley Terr CT13 94 A8
Wellesley Villas TN24 139 C3
Wellfield Rd CT20 178 A5
Wellington Cl CT8 7 C1
Wellington Cres CT11 52 F6
Wellington Ct CT14 117 D3
Wellington Gdns
  2 Dover CT16 149 B3
  Margate CT9 7 J3
Wellington Ho
  6 Maidstone ME15 97 E5
  Margate CT9 8 C3
Wellington Par
  Deal CT14 134 D7
  Kingsdown CT14 134 E6
Wellington Pl
  Folkestone CT20 177 D3
  Maidstone ME14 74 F6
Wellington Rd
  Deal CT14 117 D5
  Folkestone CT20 177 D5
  Gillingham ME7 10 C4
  Margate CT9 28 D4
  Sittingbourne ME10 36 B6
  Temple Ewell CT16 148 D5
  Westgate on Sea CT8 27 E7
Wellington St CT5 43 D5
Wellington Terr CT20 177 D3
Wellis Gdns CT9 7 G1
Well La
  Fordwich CT2, CT3 68 A3
  Painters Forstal ME13 61 B3
  St Margaret's at Cliffe CT15 150 F6
Well Rd
  Lyminge CT18 161 C6
  Maidstone ME14 75 A5
  Queenborough ME11 3 A5
  Rushenden ME11 2 F3
Wells Ave CT1 88 B7
Wells Cl
  New Romney TN28 202 C6
  Tenterden TN30 179 B8
Wells Ho ME10 37 B4
Wells Rd CT19 177 F6
Well St ME15, ME17 96 E4
Wells Way ME13 40 B1
Well Winch Rd ME10 36 D5
Welsdene Rd CT9 28 B8
Welson Rd CT20 178 A5
Wemmick Cl ME1 31 D7
Wemyss Ct 13 CT1 67 B2
Wemyss Ho 14 CT1 67 B2
Wemyss Way CT1 67 C1
Wenderton La CT3 70 A2
Wenham's La TN29 192 E2
Wents Wood ME14 75 F5
Wentworth Ave CT9 7 E1
Wentworth Cl CT18 161 C6
Wentworth Dr
  Gillingham ME8 33 E7
  Ramsgate CT12 29 A1
  Sittingbourne ME10 36 C5
Wentworth Gdns CT6 22 D2
Wentworth Ho ME10 36 C5
Wesley Sch Rd TN23 155 D7
Wesley Terr CT18 161 C7
West Beach CT5 20 C1
WESTBERE 68 C7
Westbere La CT2 68 B7
West Blean Wood Nature Reserve★ CT6 45 D5
West Borough Prim Sch ME16 74 B3
Westbourne TN23 155 D6
Westbourne Gdns CT20 178 B4
Westbourne St ME10 36 E4
WESTBROOK 7 E1
Westbrook Ave CT9 7 F1
Westbrook Cotts CT9 7 G1
Westbrooke Cl ME4 10 A2
Westbrook Gdns CT9 7 G1
Westbrook La CT6 22 B3
Westbrook Prom CT9 7 G2
Westbrook Rd CT9 7 G2
Westbury Cres CT17 166 B6
Westbury Hts CT17 166 B6
Westbury Rd
  Dover CT17 166 B6
  Westgate on Sea CT8 27 E8
West Cliff CT5 20 D1
West Cliff Arc 10 CT11 52 E6
West Cliff Ave CT10 30 B3
West Cliff Ct CT10 30 B3
Westcliff Dr ME12 4 D8
West Cliff Dr CT6 22 B4
WEST CLIFFE 150 D6
Westcliff Gdns CT9 7 F1
West Cliff Gdns
  Folkestone CT20 178 D4
  Herne Bay CT6 22 B4
Westcliff Ho 4 CT20 178 D4
West Cliff Prom CT11 52 C5
Westcliff Rd CT9 7 G1
West Cliff Rd
  Broadstairs CT10 30 B3
  Ramsgate CT11 52 D6
West Cliff Terr CT11 52 B5
Westcourt La CT15 130 C5
Westcourt Rd ME7 10 A6
West Ct 3 ME15 75 A1
Westdean Cl CT17 148 E2
West Dr ME5 31 D5
WEST DUMPTON 29 D2
West Dumpton La CT11 29 E1
WEST END
  Doddington 80 D7
  Herne Bay 45 B8
West End TN26 168 F3
West End Cotts ME9 80 D7
Westenhangar Castle★ CT21 175 A7
WESTENHANGER 175 B6
Westenhanger Sta TN25 175 B7
Westerham Cl
  Canterbury CT2 67 A4
  Gillingham ME8 11 B3
  Margate CT9 8 F1
Westerham Rd ME10 36 C3
Westerhill Rd ME17 96 C1
Westerhout Cl CT14 117 C8
Westerly Mews 5 CT2 66 E1
Western Ave
  Ashford TN23 139 A3
  Bridge CT4 89 A1
  Chatham ME4 10 A8
  Halfway Houses ME12 3 D6
  Herne Bay CT6 22 E4
Western Cl CT17 166 C6
Western Espl
  Broadstairs CT10 30 B2
  Herne Bay CT6 22 C5
Western Gdns TN24 156 E8
WESTERN HEIGHTS 166 C6
Western Heights Rdbt CT17 166 C5
Western Ho CT14 117 C7
Western Hts★ CT17 166 C6
Western Link ME13 62 A8
Western Rd
  Deal CT14 117 C7
  Maidstone ME16 74 C2
  Margate CT9 29 C8
Western Service Rd CT16 166 G8
Western Undercliff CT11 52 C5
Westfield CT2 66 A6
Westfield Bsns Ctr ME2 9 C7
Westfield Cotts ME9 13 A2
Westfield Gdns ME9 35 C3
Westfield La CT18 161 C3
Westfield Rd
  Birchington CT7 27 A7
  Margate CT9 28 C8
Westfields TN27 136 D8
WESTFIELD SOLE 54 C7

Westfield Sole Rd ME5, ME14 54 D8
Westgate Ave CT7 28 A4
Westgate Bay Ave CT8 7 C1
Westgate Cl CT2 66 C1
Westgate College for Deaf People CT9 7 J2
Westgate Court Ave CT2 66 D1
Westgate Ct [8] CT2 66 E1
Westgate Garden Flats CT2 87 E8
Westgate Gr CT2 66 F1
Westgate Hall Rd [14] CT1 66 F1
WESTGATE-ON-SEA 7 B2
WESTGATE ON SEA 27 E7
Westgate-on-Sea Sta CT8 27 E8
Westgate Rd ME13 62 E7
Westgate Terr CT5 20 E2
Westgate Tower Mus★ CT1 66 F1
West Gn ME10 14 F1
West Hill Rd CT6 22 C5
WEST HOUGHAM 164 F5
WEST HYTHE 175 B1
West Hythe Rd CT21 187 A8
West La
Sheerness ME12 1 B2
Sittingbourne ME10 37 A4
Westlands Ave ME10 36 B4
Westlands Rd CT6 22 C3
Westlands Sch The ME10 36 B4
Westland Way CT18 163 B3
West Lane Trad Est ME10 37 A4
WEST LANGDON 132 D3
West Lawn Gdns CT20 177 D3
West Lea CT14 117 C7
Westlea Ct CT20 178 A3
Westleigh Rd CT8 27 D8
WESTMARSH 71 B7
Westmarsh Cl ME15 97 F7
Westmarsh Dr CT9 8 E2
Westmarsh Dro CT3 71 A8
Westmeads Com Inf Sch [11] CT5 20 D1
Westmeads Rd CT5 20 E2
WEST MINSTER 3 A7
West Minster Prim Sch ME12 3 B8
Westminster Rd CT1 67 C4
Westminster Sq ME16 74 B4
Westminster Wlk CT12 29 C1
Westmoors TN23 155 E6
Westmoreland Dr ME9 13 C3
Westmorland Cl ME15 97 E7
Westmorland Gn ME15 97 E7
Westmorland Rd ME15 97 E7
West Motney Way ME8 12 A3
Westmount Ave ME4 9 F3
Westmount Ho [4] CT9 8 B2
West Norman Rd CT16 166 E8
Weston Rd ME2 9 A8
Westonville Ave CT9 7 F1
Westover Gdns CT10 29 E7
Westover Rd CT10 29 E6
West Par CT21 176 B1
West Park Ave CT9 8 D1
West Park Rd ME15 75 B2
West Pas ME12 1 B2
West Pl TN29 199 D8
West Ramp CT16 166 G8
West Rd
Chatham ME4 10 A7
Cliffs End CT13 51 A1
Folkestone CT20 177 C4
Westree Ct [7] ME16 74 E3
Westree Rd ME16 74 E3
West Ridge ME10 36 D3
West Side CT15 133 A1
Westside Apartments [10] CT2 66 F1
West St
Ashford TN23 139 B2
Deal CT14 117 D6
Dover CT17 166 C8
Faversham ME13 62 C7
Gillingham ME7 10 D6
Harrietsham ME17 100 C6
Hothfield TN26 137 F7
Lenham ME17 79 E1
New Romney TN28 202 A6
Queenborough ME11 2 F5
Sheerness ME12 1 B2
Sittingbourne ME10 36 E4
Woodside Green ME17 101 E8
WEST STOURMOUTH 48 D2
WEST STREET 101 E8
Eastry 93 F1
Lenham 79 E1
West Street Cotts CT14 94 A1
West Tank Farm Rd TN29 209 C2
West Terr CT20 178 D4
West View CT19 178 D8
West View Cl CT6 22 C2
Westway ME17 96 C3
WESTWELL 121 E3
Westwell Ct TN25 121 E3
Westwell La
Charing TN25, TN27 120 F5
Potters Corner TN24, TN25 138 E7
Westwell TN25, TN26 121 B4
WESTWELL LEACON 120 D4
West Wlk ME16 74 B3
WESTWOOD
Barham 127 E8
Broadstairs 29 B5
Westwood Ct ME13 62 E3
Westwood Ind Est CT9 29 A6
Westwood Pl ME13 62 D5
Westwood Rd
Broadstairs CT10 29 C4
Kingston CT4 110 F1
Loose ME15 97 A7
West Wood Rd ME9 56 B8
Westwood Ret Pk CT10 29 A5
Westwood Wlk ME9 35 B7
WETHAM GREEN 12 F5
Wetheral Dr ME5 32 B4
Wexford Pl ME15 97 D6
Weybridge Cl ME5 32 C4
Weyburn Dr CT12 29 A1
Wey Cl ME5 32 C5
Weyhill Cl ME14 75 C6
Weymouth Cl CT19 177 D7
Weymouth Rd CT19 177 D6
Weymouth Terr CT19 177 D7
Wey St TN26 183 D3
Wharfdale Sq ME15 74 E1
Wharfedale Rd CT9 8 A1
Wharf Rd
Gillingham ME7 10 C7
Maidstone ME15 74 E2
Sandwich CT13 73 B4
Wharton Gdns TN24 156 E8
Whatman Cl ME14 75 C6
Whatman Ho ME13 63 F4
Whatmer Cl CT2 68 A6
WHATSOLE STREET 142 F5
Wheatcroft Cl ME10 37 B4
Wheatcroft Gr ME8 33 F7
Wheatear Way ME5 32 B7
Wheatfields
Chatham ME5 32 D2
Maidstone ME14 75 D4
Wheatley Rd
Ramsgate CT12 29 C1
Whitstable CT5 20 E2
Wheatsheaf Cl
Boughton Street ME13 64 A3
Loose ME15 97 B8
Wheatsheafe La CT15 133 B2
Wheatsheaf Gdns ME12 1 C1
WHEELBARROW TOWN 143 F8
Wheeler St ME14 75 A5
Wheelers The ME8 33 B6
Wheelwrights The ME17 100 D6
Wheelwrights Way CT13 93 B2
Wheler Ct ME13 62 A7
Wheler Rd TN27 120 C8
Wherry Cl CT9 29 A5
Whewell Terr [1] CT20 178 E5
Whiffen's Ave ME4 9 F5
Whiffen's Ave W ME4 9 F5
Whigham Cl TN23 155 D7
Whimbrel Cl ME10 36 F8
Whimbrel Wlk ME5 32 C1
Whinfell Ave CT11 51 F7
Whinless Rd CT17 166 A8
Whiston Ave TN26 153 C4
Whitbourne Ct [4] CT5 43 D8
Whitby Rd CT20 177 D6
Whitchurch Cl ME16 74 E4
Whitcombe Cl ME5 32 C3
White Acre Dr CT14 134 B8
Whiteacre La CT4 125 E4
Whitebeam Cl TN23 138 D4
Whitebeam Dr ME17 96 B3
White Cl CT16 149 B5
White Cliffs [11] CT20 178 D4
White Cliffs Bsns Ctr CT16 149 A6
White Cliffs Bsns Pk CT16 149 B6
White Cliffs of Dover Visitor Ctr★ CT16 150 A1
White Cliffs Prim Coll for the Arts CT17 149 A1
Whitecliff Way CT19 178 F6
White Ct [8] CT20 177 E3
Whitefriars Mdw [15] CT13 72 F1
Whitefriars Way [14] CT13 72 F1
Whitegate Ct ME8 33 D5
WHITEHALL 29 C1
Whitehall
Brookland TN29 199 E8
Sandwich CT13 95 A7
Whitehall Bridge Rd CT2 87 E8
Whitehall Cl CT2 87 E8
Whitehall Dr ME17 99 D3
Whitehall Gdns CT2 66 E1
Whitehall Rd
Broad Street ME14 77 A6
Canterbury CT2 87 E8
Canterbury, Harbledown CT2 87 D7
Ramsgate CT12 29 C1
Sittingbourne ME10 36 E2
Whitehall Way TN25 159 D1
White Hart Mans CT9 7 I3
Whiteheads La ME14 76 B4
WHITEHILL 61 F3
White Hill
Boughton Aluph TN25 123 B6
Challock TN25 105 E1
Chilham CT4 85 E1
White Hill Cl CT4 110 A8
White Hill Rd ME9, ME14 33 D1
Whitehorse Hill ME5 10 B3
White Horse Hill CT18 163 C3
White Horse La
[6] Canterbury CT1 87 F8
Otham Hole ME15 98 A6
Rhodes Minnis CT4 144 A3
White Horse Wood Ctry Park★ ME14 55 D2
Whitehouse Cres ME1 53 A8
Whitehouse Dro CT13, CT3 72 D7
White House Farm Ct CT15 113 E5
Whitelocks Cl CT4 111 D3
White Marsh Ct CT5 20 E2
White Mill Rural Her Ctr★ CT13 72 E2
Whitenbrook CT21 177 A3
Whitenbrook Dell CT21 177 A3
Whiteness Gn CT10 8 F1
Whiteness Rd CT10 8 G1
Whitepost [12] CT5 20 D2
White Post ME17 78 B5
White Post Gdns CT3 71 E1
White Rd ME4 10 A2
White Rock Ct ME16 74 E3
White Rock Pl [5] ME16 74 E3
Whites Hill CT14 115 B2
Whitewall Ctr ME2 9 D8
Whitewall Rd ME2 9 D7
Whitewall Way ME2 9 D7
Whiteway Rd ME11, ME12 2 F6
White Willow Cl TN24 156 D6
White Wood Rd CT13 93 B1
Whitfeld Rd TN23 156 B8
WHITFIELD 149 A7
Whitfield Ave
Broadstairs CT10 29 E7
Dover CT16 149 B2
Whitfield Cotts TN23 156 B8
Whitfield Ct CT16 149 A6
Whitfield Hill
Dover CT16 148 F4
Temple Ewell CT16 148 E4
Whitfield Lodge CT16 149 A8
Whitfield Rdbt CT16 149 A6
Whitfield Sch & Aspen Prim Sch CT16 149 A7
Whitgift Ct CT2 66 D1
Whiting Cres ME13 62 A8
Whiting Ho TN29 205 C5
Whitmore St ME16 74 D2
WHITSTABLE 20 C3
Whitstable Jun Sch [12] CT5 20 D1
Whitstable Mus & Art Gallery★ [14] CT5 20 D1
Whitstable Rd
Canterbury CT2 66 D2
Faversham, Goodnestone ME13 63 B6
Faversham ME13 62 E7
Herne Bay CT5, CT6 22 B3
Rough Common CT2 66 B4
Whitstable & Seasalter Endowed CE Jun Sch [10] CT5 20 D1
Whitstable Sports Ctr CT5 43 F8
Whitstable Sta CT5 20 E1
Whitstable & Tankerton Hospl CT5 21 A2
Whittaker St ME4 10 A4
Whittington Terr CT15 130 D4
Whybornes Chase ME12 4 C7
Whyman Ave ME4 10 A1
Whytecliffs CT10 30 A2
WICHLING 80 C5
Wichling Cl CT2 67 A3
Wickenden Cres TN24 157 A8
Wicken Ho ME16 74 E4
Wicken La TN25, TN27 120 E6
Wickets The TN24 156 F7
Wicketts End
[9] Whitstable CT5 20 D1
Whitstable CT5 43 D8
Wickham Ave CT11 52 G8
WICKHAMBREAUX 69 B2
Wickhambreaux CE Prim Sch CT3 69 C2
Wickham Cl ME9 35 B6
Wickham Court La CT3 69 B3
Wickham La CT3 69 B1
Wickham Mill CT3 69 C2
Wickham Pl ME17 101 D5
Wickham Rd CT3 69 B2
Wickham St ME1 9 D3
Wickham Terr ME11 2 F5
Wick La CT4 129 E7
Widgeon Wlk CT18 163 B3
Widred Rd CT17 166 C8
Wierton La ME17 97 E1
Wife of Bath Hill CT2 87 C8
Wigeon Rd ME9 14 E3
WIGMORE 33 B4
Wigmore Cotts CT15 131 C8
Wigmore Glade ME8 33 B4
Wigmore La CT15 131 C8
Wigmore Rd ME8 33 B4
Wigmore Wood CT15 131 C8
Wigwam Paddocks CT7 27 A8
Wihtred Rd ME9 37 D2
Wilberforce Rd
Coxheath ME17 96 D3
Folkestone CT20 177 E3
Wilbrough Rd CT7 27 A7
Wilcox Cl CT3 112 D5
Wild Air CT7 26 F8
Wilderness Hill CT9 8 A2
Wildfell Cl ME5 54 C8
Wildish Rd ME13 62 A8
Wildman Cl ME8 33 D3
Wildwood Cl ME17 99 E2
Wildwood Glade ME7 33 B4
Wildwood Rd CT2 67 F6
Wildwood Wealden Forest Pk★ CT2, CT6 45 E4
Wiles Ave TN28 202 B6
Wiles Ho TN28 202 B6
Wilfred Rd CT11 52 C8
WILGATE GREEN 82 F6
Wilgate Green Rd ME13 82 F6
Wilkes Rd CT10 29 E4
Wilkie Rd CT7 27 A8
Wilkinson Dr CT14 117 D3
Wilks Cl ME8 12 B2
Will Adams Ct [9] ME7 10 C6
Will Adams Rdbt ME8 10 F2
Will Adams Way ME8 10 F1
Willement Rd ME13 62 B7
WILLESBOROUGH 156 F8
Willesborough Ct TN24 140 A2
Willesborough Ind Pk TN24 140 A1
Willesborough Inf & Jun Schs TN24 157 A8
WILLESBOROUGH LEES 140 B1
Willesborough Rd TN24 139 F4
Willesborough Windmill★ TN24 140 A1
Willetts Hill CT12 49 D7
William Ave
Folkestone CT19 178 B7
Margate CT9 29 C8
William Gibbs Ct [14] ME13 62 D7
William Harvey Hospl TN24 140 C1
William Judge Cl TN30 179 D7
William Muge Ho [15] CT16 166 D8
William Pitt Ave CT14 117 B6
William Pitt Cl CT21 176 D2
William Rd TN23 156 B8
William Rigby Dr ME12 3 E7
Williams Cl ME9 58 E5
Williamson Rd TN29 206 E5
William St
Faversham ME13 62 D7
Gillingham ME8 12 A1
Herne Bay CT6 22 F5
Sittingbourne ME10 36 E4
Whitstable CT5 20 D2
Willingdon TN23 155 E5
Willingdon Pl CT14 117 C1
Willingdon Rd CT16 149 A5
WILLINGTON 75 E1
Willington Gn ME15 97 E7
Willington St ME15 75 F2
Willis Ct ME12 3 F5
Willis Ho ME1 9 C4
Willop Cl TN29 186 F3
Willop Way TN29 186 F3
Willoughby Ct [13] CT1 87 F8
Willow Ave
Broadstairs CT10 29 D4
Faversham ME13 62 A7
Willow Bank TN24 140 A2
Willowbank Cl TN29 195 A4
Willowbank Ct [12] ME15 75 B4
Willow Bank Ind Est ME9 14 E6
Willowby Gdns ME8 33 E4
Willow Cl
Canterbury CT2 67 A2
Harrietsham ME17 100 D6
Hythe CT21 175 E1
Margate CT9 8 C2
Willow Ct
Broadstairs CT10 30 A5
Folkestone CT20 177 E4
Loose ME15 97 A6
Whitstable CT5 43 E8
Willow Dr
Hamstreet TN26 183 A7
St Mary's Bay TN29 194 F3
Willow Farm Way CT6 23 C2
Willow Ho
Ashford TN23 138 F1
[2] Chatham ME5 31 F5
[8] Maidstone ME16 74 A3
Sheerness ME12 1 C2
Sittingbourne ME10 37 B3
Willow Lodge CT19 178 D7
Willow Rd
Great Mongeham CT14 116 C3
Whitstable CT5 43 C5
Willow Rise ME15 75 F1
Willows Ct CT2 66 C4
Willows Prim Sch The CT6 23 B4
Willows The
Ashford TN24 139 D6
Gillingham ME8 11 E2
Newington ME9 35 B6
Sheerness ME12 1 I1
Sittingbourne ME10 14 F1
Willow Tree Cl
Ashford TN24 139 F1
Herne Bay CT6 23 D5
Willow Way
Maidstone ME15 75 B3
Margate CT9 28 C8
Whitstable CT5 44 C8
Willow Waye CT15 131 D7
Willowwood [20] ME15 97 E5
Wills La TN29 184 C4
Willson's Rd CT11 52 D6
Wilmecote Ct ME8 33 D8
Wilmington Way ME8 11 B2
Wilmott Pl CT13 93 B2
Wilson Ave
Deal CT14 116 F4
Rochester ME1 31 E7
Wilson Cl
Ashford TN24 140 A1
Maidstone ME15 97 E7
Wilsons La ME15 96 A5
Wiltie Ct CT19 178 C5
Wiltie Gdns CT19 178 C5
Wilton Cl CT14 117 C5
Wilton Rd
Folkestone CT19 178 B6
Ramsgate CT12 28 F1
Wilton Terr ME10 36 B5
Wiltshire Cl ME5 32 C8
Wiltshire Way [4] ME15 97 E8
Wimborne Pl CT12 52 B8
Wimbourne Dr ME8 33 D6
Winant Way CT16 149 B3
Winch Dr ME9 58 E6
Wincheap CT1 87 E7
Wincheap Gn [4] CT1 87 F7
Wincheap Ind Est CT1 87 D7
Wincheap Prim Sch CT1 87 E6
Winchelsea Ct CT17 166 C7
Winchelsea Rd
Chatham ME5 32 B5
Dover CT17 166 B7
Winchelsea St CT17 166 B7
Winchelsea Terr CT17 166 B7
Winchester Ave ME5 31 F4
Winchester Gdns CT1 88 A6
Winchester Ho [3] ME15 97 D7
Winchester Mews CT14 117 B3
Winchester Pl [9] ME14 75 A5
Winchester Way ME8 34 A8
Winch Rd ME9 58 D6
Windermere ME13 62 E6
Windermere Ave CT11 52 A7
Windermere Ct TN24 139 C4
Windermere Dr ME8 33 D7
Windermere Gdns CT3 112 F6
Windermere Gr ME10 36 D3
Windermere Ho [4] ME15 97 E7
Wind Hill TN27 119 E7
Wind Hill La TN27 119 E7
Winding Hill ME13 83 F6
Windmill Ave CT12 29 B3
Windmill Cl
Ashford TN24 140 A1
Bridge CT4 89 A1
Canterbury CT1 88 C8
Herne Bay CT6 23 A2
Windmill Ct ME17 97 B3
Windmill Hill ME17 100 B1
Windmill Hts ME14 76 B4
Windmill La ME13 40 B1
Windmill Manor ME7 10 C4
Windmill Par CT11 52 C6
Windmill Quay Rd ME12 4 E2
Windmill Rd
Canterbury CT1 88 C8
Gillingham ME7 10 C4
Herne Bay CT6 23 A2
Sittingbourne ME10 36 D6
Whitstable CT5 43 D7
Windmill Rise ME12 4 E6
Windmill Row ME17 98 D2
Windmill St CT21 176 B1
Windmill View CT9 29 A8
Windmill Wlk CT12 29 B1
Windsor Ave
Chatham ME4 9 F2
Margate CT9 8 B1
Windsor Cl
Broadstairs CT10 29 E5
Maidstone ME14 75 B6
Windsor Ct
Deal CT14 117 C2
Gillingham ME7 10 D5
Margate CT9 8 B1
Windsor Dr ME10 36 D2
Windsor Gdns
Herne Bay CT6 22 B3
Warden ME12 6 D4
Windsor Ho
Deal CT14 117 A5
[6] Dover CT17 166 D7
Whitstable CT5 20 D1
Windsor Mews
[9] Margate CT9 7 J2
New Romney TN28 202 C8
Windsor Rd
Canterbury CT1 87 C6
Cliffs End CT12 51 D7
Gillingham ME7 10 D5
Windward Rd ME1 9 C1
Windyridge ME7 10 E1
Winehouse La CT18 164 D3
Wineycock ME9 81 C8
Winford Mews ME1 9 A2
Wingate Ct [7] ME10 36 E4
Wingate Rd CT19 178 D7
WINGHAM 91 B7
Wingham Cl
Gillingham ME8 11 C3
Maidstone ME15 97 F7
WINGHAM GREEN 90 F7
Wingham Ind Est CT3 91 B6
Wingham Prim Sch CT3 91 A7
Wingham Rd CT3 90 D8
WINGHAM WELL 90 E6
Wingham Well La CT3 90 F5
Wingham Wildlife Pk★ CT3 70 C1
Wing Ho ME12 6 H1
WINGMORE 128 B2
Wing Rd ME12 6 H1

Wingrove Dr
Maidstone ME14 75 E5
Rochester ME2 9 C7
Wingrove Hill CT17 148 E2
Wings Cl CT10 30 B5
Winifred Ave CT12 29 C2
Winifred Rd ME15 75 F3
Winkle Cl CT6 22 B3
Winnipeg Cl CT16 149 C3
Win Pine Ho CT21 176 A1
Winstanley Cres CT11 52 D8
Winstanley Rd ME12 1 D2
Winston Cl CT1 88 C7
Winston Ct CT7 27 A8
Winston Gdns CT6 23 D4
Winston Ho 4 CT20 177 F5
Winterage La CT18 162 C7
WINTERBOURNE 85 A8
Winter Dr CT18 163 B5
Winter Gdns & Queens Hall CT9 7 J3
Winterstoke Cres CT11 52 G8
Winterstoke Way CT11 52 F8
Winton Way TN29 195 A5
Wirrals The ME5 32 A4
Wises La ME10, ME9 36 A4
Wish The TN26 181 F6
WISSENDEN 152 F7
Wissenden La
Bethersden TN26 153 B6
Smarden, Romden TN27 135 D1
Wisteria Ho 11 ME15 97 E7
WITHERSDANE 140 F8
Withersdane Cotts TN25 124 A2
Witley Wlk CT16 149 B7
WITTERSHAM 188 D3
Wittersham CE Prim Sch TN30 188 D2
Wittersham Cl ME5 32 B5
Wittersham La TN31 197 B5
Wittersham Rd
Iden TN31 197 B7
Stone in Oxney TN30 189 C3
Wittersham TN30 188 C5
Wivenhoe TN23 155 E5
Wivenhoe Cl ME8 12 A2
Wolfe Ct CT14 117 D3
Wolfe Rd ME16 74 B2
Wolf Ho ME4 10 B8
Wollaston Cl ME8 33 D3
Wollaston Rd CT14 117 D4
Wolseley Ave CT6 22 A4
Wolseley Pl 4 TN24 139 B3
Wolseley Terr TN29 205 C5
WOLVERTON 147 F2
Women's Land Army Mus The★ CT15 165 E5
WOMENSWOLD 112 D2
Wood Ave CT19 178 E7
Woodberry Dr ME10 37 C3
Woodberry Flats CT10 30 A3
Woodbridge Dr ME15 74 F1
Woodbrook TN27 120 D7
Woodbury La TN30 179 A7
Woodbury Rd ME5 31 F1
WOODCHURCH
Margate 27 F3
Tenterden 169 A2
Woodchurch CE Prim Sch TN26 169 A2
Woodchurch Cl ME5 32 B5
Woodchurch Cotts CT7 27 F4
Woodchurch Cres ME8 11 C2
Woodchurch Ho ME8 11 C2
Woodchurch Rd
Appledore Heath TN26 181 C4
Margate CT7, CT9 28 A5
Shadoxhurst TN26 155 A1
Tenterden TN30 179 D8
Westgate on Sea CT7 27 F3
Woodchurch Windmill★ TN26 169 A3
Woodcock Gdns CT18 163 A4
Woodcote CT5 21 D1
Wood Cottage La CT19 177 D7
Woodcourt Cl ME10 36 E2
Woodcut ME14 75 A8
Woodfield Ave CT19 177 E7
Woodfield Cl CT19 177 E7
Woodford Ave CT11, CT12 29 D1
Woodford Ct CT7 27 A7
Woodford Rd ME16 74 B2
Woodgate CT4 110 E3
Woodgate Cl ME13 62 C8
Woodgate Ct ME13 84 E7
Woodgate La ME9 35 C2
Woodgates Cl TN26 167 D7
Woodgrove Prim Sch ME10 36 D3
Woodhall Terr ME11 3 A5
Wood Hill CT2 66 E6
Woodhurst ME5 31 D4
Wood La TN23 156 D3
WOODLAND 160 F8
Woodland Ave
Aylesham CT3 112 E5
Birchington CT7 27 B6
Woodland Cl CT17 148 E2
Woodland Cotts CT18 161 B7
Woodland Dr ME12 4 B7
Woodland Rd
Herne Bay CT6 22 B2
Lyminge CT18 160 E8
Woodlands
Blean CT2 65 F7
Chatham ME5 32 A2
Coxheath ME17 96 B3
Hernhill ME13 64 C7
Woodlands Cl
Maidstone ME14 75 B7
Peasmarsh TN31 196 C2
Woodlands Ct ME5 31 F3
Woodlands Dr CT21 177 A4
Woodlands Prim Sch ME7 10 F4
Woodlands Rd
Adisham CT3 112 C8
Ashford TN24 139 F2
Gillingham ME7 10 F4
Sittingbourne ME10 37 B3
Woodlands Terr ME7 10 F3
Woodland View TN30 188 E4
Woodland Way
Broadstairs CT10 8 G1
Canterbury CT2 66 D4
Dymchurch TN29 187 A5
Maidstone ME14 75 B7
Woodnesborough CT13 93 C6
Woodlawn St CT5 20 D2
Woodlea TN24 139 C3
Woodman Ave CT5 21 E3
WOODNESBOROUGH 93 C6
Woodnesborough La CT13 93 B3
Woodnesborough Rd CT13 93 E7
Woodpecker Dr ME9 14 E4
Woodpecker Glade ME8 33 D6
Wood Rd CT21 176 B1
Woodrow Chase CT6 23 A1
Woodruff Cl ME8 12 D4
Woods Hill CT4 125 C5
Woodshole Cotts ME9 14 D1
Woodside
Ashford TN23 155 E6
Boughton Street ME13 64 B2
Gillingham ME8 33 C6
Woodside Ave CT4 86 D2
Woodside Cl CT16 148 E4
Woodside Cotts ME13 64 B2
Woodside Gdns ME10 36 D2
WOODSIDE GREEN 101 F8
Woodside Rd
Maidstone ME15 97 C7
Sturry CT2 67 F7
Woods Ley CT3 71 D2
Wood's Pl CT17 149 B2
Wood St
Chatham ME7 10 A6
Dover CT16 166 D8
Lynsted ME9 59 F8
Sheerness ME12 1 D2
WOODSTOCK 58 E6
Woodstock Rd
Deal CT14 117 C4
Rochester ME2 9 A7
Sittingbourne ME10 36 E1
Woodstock Way TN24 139 C6
Woodvale Ave CT5 44 C8
Wood View CT3 46 E5
Woodville Cl CT1 87 D6
Woodville Rd
Maidstone ME15 75 A2
Ramsgate CT12 29 C1
Wood Yd CT14 117 D6
WOOLAGE GREEN 129 F8
WOOLAGE VILLAGE 112 F1
Woolaston Cl ME15 74 F1
Woolbrook Cl ME8 12 B2
Woolcomber St CT16 166 E7
Wooldeys Rd ME8 11 F2
Woolett Rd ME10 36 C5
Woolf Coll CT2 66 E5
Woollets Cl CT6 22 C3
Woollett St ME14 75 A5
Woolley Rd ME15 97 F7
Woolmer Dr TN24 157 A7
Woolpack Hill TN25 158 D5
Woolreeds Rd TN23 156 A7
Woolwich Cl ME5 32 A7
WOOTON 129 C1
Wootton Cl CT4 109 A4
Wootton Dr CT4 109 A4
Wootton Gn ME8 11 D3
Wootton La CT15, CT4 146 C7
Wopsle Cl ME1 31 D7
Worcester Cl
Faversham ME13 62 E6
Minster (Sheppey) ME12 4 C6
Worcester Dr ME10 36 D6
Worcester Gr CT10 29 F6
Worcester La CT3 88 E7
Worcester Rd ME15 97 D7
Wordsworth Cl ME5 32 C7
Wordsworth Gdns CT3 112 F6
Wordsworth Rd ME14 75 B7
Workhouse La
Chartway Street ME17 99 A1
Coxheath ME15 96 C4
Workhouse Rd ME13 82 F1
World's End ME9 60 E7
Wormdale Hill ME9 35 B3
Wormdale Rd ME9 35 B4
WORMSHILL 79 A7
Worsfold Ct 5 ME15 75 A1
WORTEN 137 F3
WORTH 94 B4
Worthgate Pl 2 CT1 87 F7
Worthington St 11 CT16, CT17 166 D8
Worth La CT20 177 E3
Worth Prim Sch CT14 94 B5
Wotton Cl ME15 97 E5
Wotton Rd TN23 156 B6
Wotton Trad Est TN23 156 B6
Wraightsfield Ave TN29 195 D8
Wraik Hill CT5 43 C5
Wrangleden Cl ME15 97 E5
Wrangleden Rd ME15 97 E5
Wreight Ct ME13 40 B1
Wren Ind Est ME15 97 F4
Wren's Cross ME15 75 A3
Wrens Ct ME9 58 A8
Wrens Rd ME9 58 A7
Wrentham Ave CT6 22 B2
Wren Way ME5 32 B6
Wright Cl ME8 11 C2
Wrights Cl TN30 179 A8
Wright's Way ME12 17 C8
Wrotham Ave 20 CT10 30 B4
Wrotham Rd CT10 30 B4
Wyatt Ho 1 ME2 9 A7
Wyatt Pl ME2 9 A7
Wyatt St ME14 75 A4
Wych Elm Way CT21 187 E8
Wycherley Cres CT16 149 B4
WYE 123 F1
Wye Bsns Pk TN25 123 E3
Wye Gdns CT9 8 F2
Wye Gn CT6 22 F3
Wye National Nature Reserve★ TN25 141 D7
Wye Rd TN25 122 F3
Wye Sta TN25 123 D2
Wykeham Cl ME11 2 F3
Wykeham Cotts ME17 96 F2
Wykeham Gr ME17 99 A7
Wykeham Rd ME10 37 B4
Wykeham St ME2 9 B8
Wyke Manor Rd ME14 75 A4
Wyles Rd ME4 9 E2
Wyles St ME7 10 C7
Wyllie Ct ME10 36 E7
Wyndham Ave CT9 8 B2
Wyndham Rd
Chatham ME4 9 E2
Dover CT17 166 B8
Wynd The TN27 103 D1
Wyndy La TN25 138 F4
Wynn Ellis Ho CT5 20 E3
Wynn Rd CT5 21 A2
Wytchlings The ME17 99 D2
Wytherling Cl ME14 75 F5
Wyvern Cl ME10 36 E7
Wyvern Sch The TN23 138 E1
Wyvern Way TN24 139 E3
Wyvill Cl ME8 33 E5

Y

Yardhurst Gdns CT9 8 F3
Yardley Ho CT10 30 B7
Yard The
Barham CT4 111 F1
Chatham ME5 32 B3
Yarrow Cl CT10 30 A3
Yarrow Ct ME14 75 F5
Yarrow Dr ME12 4 A5
Yarrow Rd ME5 31 F4
Yates Cl TN31 203 A2
Yaugher La ME9 34 C3
Yeates Dr ME10 37 A8
Yellow Sands ME12 19 E5
YELSTED 34 A1
Yelsted La
Chatham ME14 54 D7
Yelsted ME9 34 A1
Yelsted Rd ME9 56 A7
Yeoman Ct ME14 76 B3
Yeoman Dr ME7 10 F1
Yeoman Gdns TN24 157 B8
Yeoman Ho ME1 9 D4
Yeoman La ME14 76 B4
Yeoman Pk ME15 76 A2
Yeomans Dr CT2 87 C8
Yeomans Sq TN23 155 D8
Yeoman Way ME15 76 A2
Yevele Cl ME11 3 A5
Yew Cl TN23 138 E2
Yew Hedges ME13 81 E4
Yew Tree Cl
Broadstairs CT10 29 D4
Chatham ME5 32 D1
Deal CT14 117 A4
Stanford TN25 160 B1
Yew Tree Cotts ME14 53 F1
Yewtree Cross CT18 161 C8
Yew Tree Farm CT3 114 A8
Yew Tree Gdns
Birchington CT7 27 A7
Fordwich CT2 68 A4
Yewtree Ho 2 ME1 9 D4
Yew Tree Mews CT14 117 A3
Yew Tree Pk ME17 102 F1
Yew Tree Pl ME7 33 B1
Yew Tree Rd TN29 194 F3
Yoakes La TN29 192 F1
Yoakley Sq CT9 28 F8
Yoke Cl ME2 9 B8
Yokosuka Way ME7 11 A7
York & Albany Cl CT14 117 B1
York Ave
18 Broadstairs CT10 30 B4
Chatham ME5 31 F3
Gillingham ME7 10 C4
York Cl CT6 22 D4
York Hill ME5 10 C2
York Ho 10 CT17 166 D7
YORKLETTS 42 F2
York Mews CT19 177 E7
York Rd
Ashford TN24 139 D5
Canterbury CT1 87 E7
Deal CT14 117 D4
Herne Bay CT6 22 D5
Maidstone ME15 75 C2
Rochester ME1 9 C3
York St
Broadstairs CT10 30 B4
Dover CT16, CT17 166 D7
Ramsgate CT11 52 E6
York Street Rdbt CT16, CT17 166 D7
York Terr CT7 27 B7
Young Cl CT14 117 B6
Young's Pl CT15 164 F5
Ypres Ct CT1 67 D1
Ypres Dr ME10 14 F1

Z

Zarena Ct 8 CT20 177 F3
Zealand Rd CT1 87 F6
Zetland Ave ME7 10 E2
Zillah Gdns ME8 33 C6
Zion Pl CT9 7 J3